THE PRINCIPLES AND PRACTICE
OF MANAGEMENT

THE PRINCIPLES
AND PRACTICE
OF MANAGEMENT

Edited by
E. F. L. BRECH
B.A., B.Sc.(Econ.), F.B.I.M.

Associate Authors
R. M. ALDRICH
M.I.P.M., A.M.B.I.M.

H. E. BETHAM
F.C.A.

A. W. FIELD
B.Sc., A.M.I.Mech.E., F.B.I.M.

R. G. LAGDEN
M.I.M.S.M.

LONGMANS

LONGMANS, GREEN AND CO LTD
48 Grosvenor Street, London W.1.

*Associated companies, branches and representatives
throughout the world*

Second edition © Longmans, Green and Co Ltd. 1963

FIRST PUBLISHED	1953
TENTH IMPRESSION	1961
SECOND EDITION	1963
SECOND IMPRESSION	1963

PRINTED AND BOUND IN GREAT BRITAIN BY
HAZELL WATSON AND VINEY LTD
AYLESBURY, BUCKS

PREFACE TO SECOND EDITION

HOWEVER unusual the initiation, this Preface starts deliberately with a plea to reviewers—even more than to student readers—to read it, because of its bearing on the arrangement of the book and the presentation of the content.

Consumer satisfaction reflected in continuing and growing sales at profit to the producers is an accepted criterion of business success the world over. To accomplish this while contributing constructively to social advancement through higher education is an added gilding to the success. No less is the attainment of this volume in the few years of its life since first publication.

Acceptance and success, however, impose their own obligations. To the extent that this volume has gained standing as the authoritative British textbook for the serious study of management—standing thus abroad as well as at home—there is the obligation to bring its content and quality to the higher standards that are required to match the advancing levels of contemporary practice. Such is the purpose of this revised second edition. The revision has been thorough-going, the amendment comprehensive: there are new contributing authors, new matter in line with current thought, new presentation where application has advanced. To claim with a subject as wide as modern management that no aspect has been overlooked would be presumptuous, but it can be claimed that, within the limits of practical presentation, the volume offers some instruction on most of the facets of the role of any successful manager.

In fact, the comprehensive range of the revision is the source of one serious misgiving—for the already considerable length of the first edition has been extended in the second! Unavoidably so, if the revision was to accomplish its purpose. It can, perhaps, be taken as an Editor's privilege to forestall the criticisms of the reviewers: here indeed is a legitimate occasion, for there will assuredly be dismay at this greater size of the volume. Only one basic answer is the justifying explanation—the importance of the subject and the necessity to ensure that those who are practising, or aspiring to practise, the profession of management have opportunity afforded to see their skills and their roles in the round. The alternative treatment is a series of specialist handbooks, an approach that would negative the very objective of this work. That suggestion was made for the first edition and it will be repeated for the second; perhaps advances in the understanding of management principles and practices will make it reasonable for the third! Such a state of development, however, has not yet been reached, and it has therefore been felt advisable to retain the integrated comprehensive presentation, despite the consequential bulk. There is a business aspect too: this single volume will cost less this way than the sum of its components separately issued! If the alternative were suggested as a reduction in scope and depth of treatment, perhaps the reviewers can exercise their minds on recommendations as to which items in the contents should be eliminated or reduced.

The basic approach of the first edition has been preserved in the sense of "delegation" to each contributing author, and of maintaining the broad framework of the accepted four divisions of management practice. As was said in the Preface to the first edition, no attempt has been made to present these specialist sections in any common form or style. Each is the work of an authority with high-level practical experience in his own field. To preserve the full benefit of this expert knowledge, each contribution has been left in its author's own language and presentation. Inevitably, there is a limited measure of overlap in detail, and here and there a little contradiction in practice. But co-ordination of thought from the outset of the work has prevented disagreement in principle. Perhaps the only weakness that springs from this independence of treatment is the irritation of slight differences in terminology. No apology is offered for this, or called for, even though some criticism of this has been expressed in the past. Management is a relatively new field of organised knowledge, and for some years to come divergencies in word as well as in practice will necessarily characterise its development. It can but be hoped that the continuing spread of serious management study and of professional standards will in time bring out the fusion of thought and terminology into a common language.

To obviate irritation, however, the amount of cross-reference between the Parts and Chapters has been held down to the essential minimum.

In framing the content of our various Chapters and Sections, we have aimed at presenting the latest known and proven principles and practices. This is, we hope, an up-to-date study of management which will stand the test of time. Its best value will be obtained, we feel, as an aid to organised studies, where the lecturer or tutor can further expound points of principle set out, or bring forward as illustrations other practices and methods, as well as circumstances in which different techniques appear to contradict our views. In other words, we lay no claim to exhaustive or exclusive treatment of the various aspects of management covered. By the same token, we feel we have avoided providing in a textbook a substitute for the lecturer's or the student's own thinking. Much of the extra length of this second edition stems from the desire to present a rounded treatment of subject-matter in terms of contemporary ideas; this is particularly true of the major addition in the form of Part Five where there is consideration not only of the newer aspects of general management practice, but also of the underlying philosophical thought which is beginning to characterise the outlook of the more advanced managers. Such an addition is essential at a period when many of the up-and-coming younger managers have a background of high academic attainment and are bringing to the practice of their profession an unwonted depth of thought.

To the older, established managers, too, we are sure this volume has an important contribution to offer—in the refreshment of knowledge, in the presentation of new approach, in the stimulus to improvement of long-accepted but now perhaps deficient methods, and in the advancement of objectives and standards. In this context the new edition pays a compliment to all managers, because it is based on the expectation that they will accept analytical thinking as a vital factor in professional management competence.

Because of the background of its authors, this study of management has necessarily been written in industrial terms, with its bias mainly to the manufacturing industries and the distributive activities directly associated with them. A good deal of the matter, however—in the realm of practice as well as of principle—is of relevance to such purely commercial fields as wholesale and retail trade or the management of financial institutions, to the nationalised industries, and even to many aspects of the local and central government machinery.

In the past decade one significant change has characterised the industrial and commercial scene of Britain, as of every other major country in the world, in the recognition of the importance of the high-level skills involved in the practice of successful management. It is too early yet to talk of widespread acceptance of a "profession", but the notion is seriously gaining ground. Already there is acceptance of manager roles and objectives reaching beyond the confines of the profit position of an individual business, and the horizon of a truly-established and seriously-followed profession of management begins already to loom within human vision. Excellent educational work by a number of national and international bodies has been lending impetus to this evolution, drawing substantial support from the serious interchanges of thought and experience among many practising managers from many different settings. With justifiable pride can Britain look back on her own contributions as one of the leading pioneers in this movement. For the Britons of the bygone age, when the pioneering was laborious and seemingly fruitless, there is consolation in the later rapid progress that their own earlier foundation made possible. That their Lordships in Upper House of Parliament could stage a full-scale debate on the "Responsibilities of Management" would have been unthinkable to our forebears of a generation ago: in the winter of 1960 the event seemed not remarkable, momentous though it was. This of itself is a measure of the progress of the role of the manager in the national economy. This is, too, the justification for this seriously-designed revision to form the Second Edition.

E. F. L. BRECH
Editor

CONTENTS

PART TWO

PRODUCTION

PART THREE

PERSONNEL

PART FOUR

CONTROL

FOLDING CHARTS

ACKNOWLEDGMENTS

WE are grateful to the following for permission to include copyright material:

The Advertising Association for Advertising Expenditure tables; Anglo-American Council on Productivity for an extract from the First Report of the Council; The Board of Trade for tables from their *Census of Distribution, 1957*; British Institute of Management for extracts from their Review, Vol. III (1936), from *Committees in Organization* by Urwick, *A Report on the Administrative and Executive Problems of the Transition from War to Peace—Personnel*, and for a Pre-Production Chart; British Standards Institution for an extract from the Report for 1932; the Director of the Centre for Inter-firm Comparison for extracts from its brochure the Controller of H.M. Stationery Office for extracts from *Report on the Census of Distribution and Other Services, 1957, Combining for Research*, the Urwick Committee Report on *Education for Management*, and *Department of Scientific and Industrial Research—Report of the Research Council for the Year 1959* (Cmnd 1049); Mrs. Samuel Crowther for an extract from *My Life and Work* by Henry Ford in collaboration with Samuel Crowther; Division of Research, Harvard University Graduate School of Business Administration, Boston, for an extract from *Management Controls in Industrial Research Organization* by R. N. Anthony; *The Economist* for an extract from *Business Note* from the issue of 3rd September 1960; Sir Arnold Hall for an extract from a paper given by him in a seminar at the London School of Economics; The Illuminating Engineering Society for a section of the Schedule of Recommended Values of Illumination from the I.E.S. *Code for the Lighting of Building Interiors*; Industrial Welfare Society for an extract from a pamphlet on Welfare and Personnel Services, and from a document of a Study Group on *The Cost of Personnel Department*; The Institute of Office Management for an extract from *Clerical Job Grading and Merit Rating*; The Institute of Personnel Management for material from two broadsheets: *Functions of Personnel Department* by G. R. Moxon, *Personnel Management in Relation to Factory Organization* by L. Urwick; The Institution of Production Engineers for *Operational Research* by Stafford Beer, condensed from his George Bray Memorial Lecture; Macmillan & Co. Ltd., St. Martin's Press, Inc. and The Macmillan Co. of Canada Ltd. for an extract from *Laboratory*

Administration by E. S. Hiscocks; Sir Isaac Pitman & Sons Ltd. for three quotations from *The Making of Scientific Management* Vol. I by L. Urwick & E. F. L. Brech, and The Tack Organization for material from a survey of sales representatives' remuneration.

We have been unable to trace the copyright owners in "Business—A Profession" by the late Louis D. Brandels, which appeared in the June 1960 number of *The Executive,* and would welcome any information which would enable us to do so.

MANAGEMENT IN PRINCIPLE

By E. F. L. BRECH

CONTENTS

MANAGEMENT IN PRINCIPLE

1. THE NATURE OF MANAGEMENT

WITH some critical insight into the affairs of the times, an American philosopher some years ago christened our epoch that of "the managerial revolution".[1] By his choice of label he meant to emphasise that, in contrast to the bygone period of "the industrial revolution", when the mainspring of economic progress lay in technological development, the contemporary era depended for its motive power on personal skills of leadership and commercial acumen—the ability of some men and women to impel economic progress by their direction and co-ordinating of other people's individual efforts in the business of living. Divine Providence did not leave him long enough on earth to see how accurately his appraisal would hold true, even in circumstances where once again the technological factor exerts a major force—for within a decade the world of industry and commerce has entered on to another transformation, with highly complex automatic equipment and intricate electronic instrumentation as the foundations.

Science and technology are today coming to their full fruition. Accumulated knowledge garnered by patient painstaking labours in the backrooms is now borne in triumph to the board room; hardly a business can continue its affairs without some reference to the scientific and the technological. But there is no reversion to a mechanistic dominance: the era remains correctly dubbed that of "managerial revolution"—for one thing above all else is receiving universal acclaim, that the harnessing of science and technical knowledge is a task for "management". Exactly what that term means is not always clear, and not always agreed. What is clear and agreed is that it does mean some form of personal command of a situation such that technological, commercial and human aspects are interwoven into successful progress. Within a generation the British industrial scene has in this respect indeed undergone a revolution. Twenty years ago opinion was all but unanimous in the view that managers are born, not made—those currently in office, of course, being obviously born destined by gift to the roles held. Concurrent was the view that management did not matter much

[1] James Burnham: *The Managerial Revolution* (U.S.A. Publication, 1941; Putnam, London, 1942; Penguin Special, 1945).

3

anyway: to be technically competent or commercially capable was all that mattered; some mysterious over-pervading force ensured successful outcome, whatever the standard of leadership. The current-day contrast is seen most starkly in the daily and Sunday press: column-inches by the score, heavily in-boxed and lettered, show enterprises large and small, too numerous to be counted, pleading with the younger generation to come forward and be paid handsomely for being *trained* in management. Managers, clearly, are made, not born! And throughout the year, conferences provide the continuous platform for the incessant crusade for more and better management. A national management institute can count its members in tens of thousands; the Universities can claim about half of their annual output poured into management careers; serious business leaders can recurrently discuss among themselves the ways and means of raising management standards. All this in the setting of an age when nuclear power, space-satellites and radiation technology are the characteristic features of progress. Truly an era of "managerial revolution", when the harvesting of the fruits of technical achievement is vitally dependent on the skills of management—*whatever these happen to be.*

Those last few words are more important than a passing quip, for they point to one of the major weaknesses in the contemporary scene. There has indeed been substantial advancement in management practice, and a vast extension in the range, scope and depth of management studies; yet, curiously, there seems to be still no accepted understanding of the nature of the management role or of the skill it entails—no authorised version, as it were, of management principles or of the essential themes in the gospel that is preached. This is not to imply that the nature of management is not of itself understood: on the contrary, a clear analysis has been available as long as the earlier edition of the present volume, and before. There is, however, no *accepted*, universally adopted definition in the sense in which the scientist knows that all his confrères accept the one meaning for the one particular term. Not that this matters seriously; the differences are superficial rather than substantial, and in the event most managers appear to be doing much the same things in practice, whatever their theoretical understanding of their role. The drawback in this situation lies in the obstacles it creates to the advancement of knowledge and the pursuit of systematic studies. Where every man can claim to be his own authority, orderly cognitive argument is difficult; and management is now in the stage of development when it can benefit materially from the analytical review of experience and the constructive interchange of rationally based ideas. Like any body of knowledge, it can draw progress from disciplined comparative study.

In this respect, management suffers from the drawback inherent in its own setting: it is an employment undertaken and a skill practised by many thousands of persons in many different industrial and commercial communities—as well as in many other fields—within organisations of widely differing character and size, with numerous differences of objective and varieties of personal com-position. It has evolved numerous techniques for more effective performance, yet these are "tools" for carrying out a skill of which the real character is still imperfectly recognised. That there should be many controversies about the relative importance of various aspects of management is but a natural consequence of such a situation. Among the many persons who are occupationally engaged in management, most have qualified earlier in their industrial or commercial careers in specialised technical or professional fields—as engineers, chemists, accountants, company secretaries, and the like. They have risen to higher executive positions through years spent in the specialised practice of their profession or technology. Hence they tend, naturally enough, to have a bias or inclination to see management from a certain standpoint, and often lack the capacity to see it as a whole.

Ready illustrations of this tendency come to the mind of anyone with first-hand knowledge of the affairs of industry or commerce. To the engineer, for instance, management is primarily a matter of the design of product and the design of tools, associated with the layout of production flows and the field that has come to be labelled "production engineering"; from these it is but a small step to questions of planning, rate-fixing, piece-rates, bonus systems and other techniques that link up the technical operations with the daily activities of the operatives. To the accountant, management looms largely as a matter of figures; he is interested in the statistical data that record progress, usually couched in money terms; his interest is accordingly centred on procedures which enable him to "control" expenditure and to identify the expenditure with its out-come, and which show themselves in summary form in Profit and Loss Statements and Annual Balance Sheets. Newer lines of thought are less concerned with the recording of past financial history, the comparison of this year's progress with last year's, than with routines for the "control" of current expenditure against appropriate pre-determined standards. If one turns to yet another branch of technical industry, to the chemist, management appears primarily as a matter of formulae and mixtures, the flow of semi-solids, liquids or gases through a series of plant in which given chemical changes are carried out, and in which the most important requirements are the control of temperatures and pressures, the control of ingredients and of the quality of the emerging mixtures; the chemical manager's processes are running right if the readings are in accordance with the best standards, and if the samples at various stages of process come up to the formulae set.

To pick out the technical bias of managers in a technical field is not to imply criticism of such executives themselves. They have been trained and developed in a given atmosphere: their whole background has been concentrated on aspects of their technology, and, in the absence of any guide as to what management is or means, one cannot rightly blame them if their rise into the higher executive levels finds them unable to depart from the customary technological or professional standards to which they have for so long been subject.

Within the present generation a great deal of attention has been given to the "human factor"—an interest arising out of the wartime need to secure a higher level of labour utilisation, emanating primarily from the shortage of man-power. Experience gained in these abnormal conditions taught industrial managers that the productivity of people at work is enhanced by improvements in the physical and social environment of their work and by the promotion of a sense of participation in its achievement—such participation being not only effective performance of the allotted job, but in addition a sense that their contribution is of importance to major objectives and to the well-being of the organisation. Developments in this more human aspect of management have in their turn given rise to yet another specialist bias, this time in the direction of the human being. They have led many persons, erroneously, to the view that the specialist personnel aspect of management should dominate all others, and a new professional field of "personnel management" has emerged to parallel the more factual approach of the engineer and the accountant.

The detached observer can see the true position, that each of these specialist aspects is but a part of management, that all have a contribution to make to the total. The true character of management must be seen as a process or skill compounded of several essential elements, many of which are steeped in the traditional technologies, and each of which has its own contribution to make to the effective working of that process as a whole.

2. THE BACKGROUND OF MANAGEMENT

Through the misfortunes of war, bad harvests and man-made dislocations of trade, men and women the world over have been recurrently made acutely aware of the nature and complexity of an economic system. The basis of that system today, no less than in the simpler days of inter-tribal barter, is the acquisition of goods by the exchange of other goods. The difference in the modern system lies in the fact that usually money serves as the medium of exchange, because the "commodities" offered on one side are in the intangible form of mental or manual work. A man sells his services for a wage or a salary or a dividend, and with the money received he buys his goods in the shop or market.

The progress of civilisation has turned the simple mechanism of exchange into the complex structure of the twentieth-century world-wide industrial and commercial system, with its innumerable manufacturing units of all sizes and kinds, and its legions of trading, transport and financial houses. This complex pattern of economic activities forms the background of management. Despite its complexity in action, it rests on a simple principle: *all economic activity is directed to a parallel twofold aim of supplying the goods and services that consumers need, and providing the means by which they can purchase those goods and services.*

In this principle lies, too, the basic *aim* of management.

Management finds its role in this system because there are different contributory factors to be combined in the effective conduct of economic and social activities. There are the land and buildings, and the materials, whether used in raw state direct from natural sources or as the outcome of synthetic processes; the plant and equipment, machine tools, or, in the case of distribution, ships, rolling-stock and motor vehicles. Such factors of production and distribution are not of themselves productive—they need the skill and effort of man. Throughout the entire range of economic affairs, the dominant feature is the work of the men and women employed—the human effort in part directed to the manipulative and operative tasks, and in part to the mental processes of designing, calculating, drafting, planning, corresponding, selling, deciding, managing. It is the pervasiveness of this human element that gives management its special character as a social process. However these human forces are employed, they need to be unified, co-ordinated, welded into a team effort and directed effectively towards a given purpose. In this lies the *role* of management.

Some emphasis needs to be placed on the duality of aim in the basic principle of economics—the exchange of goods and the maintenance of employment. The rise of a "capitalist system" in the eighteenth and nineteenth centuries, and the emergence of large-scale unemployment in the twentieth, have both tended to add weight to what might be called the "producer" aspect: the current popular interest in "full employment" is ample evidence of this. Yet the same people are, broadly speaking, both the producers and the consumers. The citizens of any community are "producers" when regarded as employers, managers, shareholders, or employees and workers; but they are "consumers" (of themselves and through their families) when they give their attention to spending their earnings.

Neglect of the "consumer" aspect lies at the root of much of the topsy-turvy popular economics of our times, a topic which is outside the scope of the present volume. Management cannot afford to neglect the consumer interests in the daily conduct of its job, because their failure may well result in the breakdown of the whole system.

The various forms of enterprise or institution which provide the settings within which management operates do not call for specific description in the present context. In any country at any time, circumstances determine what the pattern of the economic system is like. At one end of the scale is a highly centralised Government-controlled pattern, such as the Soviet Union. At the other end lies the "free enterprise" pattern of the United States. The position in Britain lies well between: we have our national concerns like the Coal Board and British Railways, and other public corporations set up under earlier auspices, like the Port of London Authority, or the British Broadcasting Corporation, but the vast majority of our economic activities are conducted by commercial undertakings: single owners, partnerships, companies. They are of great variety in structure and size, ranging from the one-man shop or market-stall to the mammoth manufacturing and trading concerns whose employees run into the six-figure categories.

The Co-operative Societies represent a different principle in ownership, but from the standpoint of the practice of management, their character is closely comparable with that of any commercial company.

In all these varied types of enterprise, the process of management arises and flows in much the same way. There is, first, the need for lines of direction—the determination of objectives or purposes, the laying down of broad policy as the foundation for the achievement of such objectives and the translation of the policy into the plans and programmes of operation. Secondly arises the need for means of decision in exercising direction over the operations: the provision of the data as the medium for the mature mental process of responsible judgment in formulating reliable plans (decisions) and in attaining effective and economical outcome from putting the plans into action. Next come the requirements for the initiation and execution of action—the methods and procedures for guiding and regulating the personnel of the organisation in the performance of their

tasks and for maintaining adequate co-ordination; coupled with
these, the techniques of supervision to ensure that performance is in
keeping with policy and plan. Finally, there is a need for methods
of assessing achievement and results, as well as costs of operation, to
ensure that tasks are being carried out at appropriate levels of quality
of work and with adequate effectiveness and economy. Underlying
each phase of the complex process is the human facet inherent in the
all-pervading personal contribution—by those who carry out the
mundane tasks as well as by those whose lot it is to govern. Whatever its setting as to type of industry, trade or service, or as to type
and size of unit, the responsibility of management is to attain the
fulfilment of a given purpose as a contribution to the wealth and
social living of the community. Peculiar features of setting or of
organisation will affect in some details the structure and working of
management, but not its basic responsibility or function. Mr. John
Mantle, with his tiny workshop for the making-up of women's dresses,
has no Board of Directors or elaborate books of account; he has no
hierarchy of organisation, no techniques of production control; his
personnel management is in his own daily contact with his few
workers. But his contribution to real wealth and the character of his
function as a chief executive are directly parallel to those of his
namesake, Sir Joseph Mantle, the Managing Director of the million-
pound Mantle Dressmaking Company, Ltd., employing over 2,000
persons, with elaborate schemes of organisation, of planning and of
control to ensure the steady maintenance of a large programme of
output, directed to its subsidiary retail shops.

   In their respective ways, the two Mantles have the same purpose
to fulfil and the same factors to develop; they are responsible for
attaining an objective, for providing a policy for decisions on
economic direction, for establishing an organisation (simple or complex) with plans and programmes for production and distribution,
planning of rooms, equipment, material supplies, and storage or
transport facilities, teams of operatives and staff appropriate to the
work to be done, motivation (leadership) of such teams, co-ordination of effort and outcome, financial provisions, means of assessing
results. Both, in other words, are managers.

3. WHAT IS MANAGEMENT?

   Putting it into broad general terms, "management" is concerned
with seeing that the job gets done, and done efficiently. Its tasks all
centre on decisions for planning and guiding the operations that are
going on in the enterprise. That this is not usually recognised so simply
and clearly is due to the fact that in most industrial and commercial
activities the "management" is overshadowed by other factors—

either the technicalities of operation or the demands of commercial achievement in the pursuit of expanding sales, or perhaps even the complications of the financial and other control routines. These latter may well be unavoidable accompaniments of modern business, but it is important to realise that they are in fact only the *tools* for the manager's job: they are not the job itself, nor do they really help to explain what that job is.

The true nature of management can be more easily seen by analysis from simple example; for instance, the building of half a dozen houses on a small site:

(1) Obviously, the first requirement is to know what houses are to be built, how they are to be laid out on the site, the type of materials to be used, the dimensions, the style and quality, the fittings, and so on. These items may be regarded as the general policy of the particular building operation, and are provided by the architect's plans and specifications. In addition, there is the question of how to go about the work on the site—where to start, which way to proceed, whether to build one house through and then start the next, or whether to complete each stage on all six at once, how long to take and how many men to use. This may be regarded as formulating the general programme of operations, and is fixed by the master-builder, in agreement with the architect.

(2) On this operation the establishment of the "authority" in charge of the job calls for little special arrangement: the master-builder takes control—or a General Foreman is put in charge. As the job is comparatively small, will this "manager" remain on the site full-time? If not, arrangements are made to appoint one of the Trade Foremen to stand in as "manager", probably always as a working Foreman. His responsibilities for decision need to be defined—his relations with the architect's visiting representative, the limits to his powers of independent decision, and so on. Above all, his position as acting over-all Foreman needs to be made clear to all tradesmen and labourers on the job; he may himself be a bricklayer or a carpenter, but what matters from the management standpoint is his position and responsibility as supervisor nominated to act in place of the boss.

(3) The allocation of major jobs to the men is largely determined by their own trade skills. But many general jobs will arise for which men will need to be detailed by the Foreman: perhaps unloading lorries, or helping in certain other operations when their own is partially completed or temporarily held up. Quite certainly, from time to time, a "human planning" or allocation of tasks will have to be carried out by the Foreman. The engagement of additional or general labour is another item that comes into consideration here.

(4) A good deal of preparatory work will be done before any opera-

faults or errors left uncorrected, and so on. He is exercising a detailed supervision of work, and a "control" of progress in accordance with the pre-set plan or programme. The time-factor has also to be taken into account, and the master-builder has a further concern with the progress of actual costs as compared with the planned estimates.

(9) Co-ordination of work is very largely secured by the existence of the plans, but there is still a daily task for the Foreman to undertake. Perhaps at one stage the bricklayers are getting too far ahead of other trades; perhaps the carpenters are dropping too far behind, and will shortly hold up the next operation. In a smaller way, the need for co-ordination will arise whenever a lorry arrives with supplies and has to be unloaded: the Foreman must decide which men to call off, where to put the materials, and so on.

(10) Finally, the master-builder and the General Foreman (as well as the workers) will be all the time acquiring experience of how management and supervision are successfully applied on a building site. In a highly organised contracting firm cards, charts and other records would be used to keep note of progress as measured against programme, and actual cost as against estimate, and this information would be used subsequently as the basis of management decisions in setting future programmes. In an informal way, every manager and supervisor is acquiring and "recording" in his own mind experience of the best ways of planning and doing this and that. On the building site, the Foreman's keenness in observing and "recording" (remembering) the good and bad incidents in planning and in actual progress will make a big contribution to his effectiveness as a supervisor. So this "recording" process may be regarded as the last essential feature of the whole management activity.

Looking back at these ten items, it will be noticed that only one of them (item 6) is the physical job of building the houses. The other nine are concerned with preparations, with review of progress, with judgment of economic values, with supervision and leadership of the working team and with co-ordination of men and jobs. In other words, these other nine are the "management and supervising" activities associated with that operation of house-building.

Is it possible to reduce these "managerial" tasks to any broad general classifications?

Items 1, 2, 3 and 4 have a strong element of planning. They are concerned with predetermining the lines of operations, the methods, the equipment, the allocation of tasks, and so on. Item 3, in addition, contributes particularly to co-ordination. Item 5 is primarily a process of inspiration, or "leadership", but also has a strong element of co-ordination in it, by integrating the activities of the working group

tions start on the site—ordering of materials, hire o:
and so on. As soon as building starts, the detailed
comes very important: how the equipment is to be u:
tion of scaffolding; the sequence of jobs; the layout of
on the site; where to unload supplies in relation to wl
be used; alterations to programme or planned metho(
weather difficulties or non-arrival of certain supplie
ment. However much of the planning is done in ad
fications are bound to occur, and so some continuou
activity will be called for. In a building operation, of
of the sequence of jobs is predetermined by the typ
house, but even here adjustments are bound to arise
stance.

(5) To start the job off does not call for any issue of "c
the military sense, but it is the General or Trade F
to issue instructions as the work gets under way, ai
the working pace on the job. This is essentially a h
is in part concerned with attendance and time-keepii
breaks and tea-making; but it is in much larger me;
of keeping harmony and team-spirit, and encouragi
to get on with the job with a sense of responsibility ai
In other words, it is the task of keeping up moral(
quential good performance of operations.

(6) The actual building operations proceed according t
dictates of the various trades, and in accordance wi
and plans. They are the activities around which "n
weaving its pattern of planning, co-ordination and

(7) At many points, some at the outset and some lat(
builder and his Foreman will be required to make
on various aspects of the project and the activity.
will have been made in relation to choice of mat
methods, determined by judgments on compara'
these will have been enshrined in the initial sp(
programmes. Yet others will arise as work progre
delivery of some materials may suggest changes
operations or in methods of working, or perhaps a
to the architect for an alteration of specification.
ment has to be exercised as a basis of decision, ai
too, exclusively at the level of the foremen when
at stake, for example a minor change in plan beca
of a trade gang due to sickness-absence.

(8) As the job proceeds, the General Foreman (as v
tect's man and the master-builder) will be keepin;
gress. He will be watching to see that all the work i
to plan and specification, that the correct materi;
quality of workmanship is as laid down, that cc
are followed, proper finishing touches given wh(

through the issue of commands, together with the constructive supervision of performance in quality and output. Items 8 and 10 are concerned with checking the performance, i.e. with "control" of the operations to ensure that progress is satisfactory and that the methods applied may be recommended for future use. Item 9 is entirely co-ordination. Item 7 is a special aspect of "control", in checking and deciding comparative values relative to possible changes of planning.

It would thus seem from this simple analysis that there are four broad classifications in this example of "management":

(1) Planning, i.e. determining the broad lines for carrying out the operations (the policy, the general programme, the overall plans, the costs, the organisation), preparing the appropriate methods for effective action (equipment, tools, material supplies, working instructions, techniques, working teams, etc.), and setting the targets of expected performance and outcome (profitability).

(2) Control, i.e. checking current performance against predetermined standards contained in the plans, with a view to ensuring adequate progress and satisfactory performance whether physical or financial; also contributing to decision in continuing or changing the plans, as well as "recording" the experience gained from the working of these plans as a guide to possible future operations.

(3) Co-ordination, i.e. balancing and keeping the team together, by ensuring a suitable allocation of working activities to the various members, and seeing that these are performed with due harmony among the members themselves.

(4) Motivation (or inspiring morale), i.e. getting the members of the teams to pull their weight effectively, to give their loyalty to the group, and to the task, to carry out properly the activities allocated, and generally to play an effective part in the purpose or task that the organisation has undertaken; with this general "inspiration" goes a process of supervision to ensure that the working teams are keeping to the plans and attaining an adequate level of effectiveness and economy of work. (This is the process popularly labelled "leadership".)

An important point to appreciate is that the building of the houses could *not be effectively or economically carried out without these "management" activities*. The building itself could proceed, but there would be waste of skilled men's time and effort through many trials and errors, waste of material through absence of planning, and numerous delays and difficulties through faulty allocation of jobs and lack of co-ordination. This is the purpose and function of the management activity, to enable the building operation to be carried through smoothly, effectively and economically. The last of these three purposes means that the resources used in the operations will have been so deployed, in the judgment of the manager or foreman, as to attain the best possible outcome with the least necessary usage. At the heart of the manager's activity will have lain the consideration and judgment of the *economic* factors that could promote decisions appropriate to attaining such results through the medium of the groups of people engaged on the operations.

Since it is the activities of people that are directed, co-ordinated and regulated by management, it is correctly called a *social* process. In this it requires a special skill, concerned with getting the co-operation of people and their unified response in the performance of the given tasks, within the bounds set by the economic requirements. Admittedly, the skill of management necessitates attention also to technical factors, whether relating to the products, to materials or to equipment; yet, whatever the technological setting, there is the social element pervading—the thinking-ahead and planning, so that the activities of the people employed can run smoothly and economically, and the understanding of human behaviour, so that morale can be kept at a high level to ensure continuous and effective co-operation. The essence of the manager's role lies specifically in this responsibility for planning, motivating, co-ordinating and regulating ("controlling" as here described). It falls to him to know what are the circumstances within which his enterprise or establishment or department is operating, what are the objectives, what the factors bearing on effective performance, what the relevant technological considerations and the commercial items to which he must pay regard; in the light of mature deliberation on all such facts and factors, it is his responsibility to *decide* what actions should ensue and in what directions. It is thus that he issues his commands to "motivate" his subordinate personnel in fulfilment of the known purposes. Thus clearly does he take responsibility for the outcome, which he can review in the "control data" showing performance against plan, cost against estimate, outcome against target, and so complete the cycle of the management process. It is this feature of the management role that justifies the popular label "executive" frequently given to it: for he carries as his delegated task the assumption of *responsibility for the decision which leads to effective execution* of a given policy directed to a given objective. If any short description were to be formed for management it would have essentially to be in terms of "responsibility for so deciding the planning and regulating of the activities of people associated in a common task that the correct outcome is effectively and economically attained".

The inclusion of "effective" and "economic" is a significant item in the essence of executive responsibility: as was indicated in the simple example above, the operation *could proceed without manage-ment*, but (except for the chance case of accidental good luck!) it would be likely then to proceed with waste of materials and man-power, loss of time, poor quality results—all adding up to excess costs and the misuse of resources. The purpose of adding management is clearly to obviate such losses and waste. Put another way, *the attainment of efficiency and economy of operations is inherent in the essence of the management process*; the assumption of the manager's role implies the acceptance of these generic objectives among or alongside the specific objectives that constitute the responsibilities of his position. They may not be, and in fact usually are not, separately identified nor consciously posited, but their significance is not thereby diminished. These generic objectives are what is summed up on the business scene in the expression "the maximisation of profitability".

This notion links back to the observations made earlier about the setting of industrial and commercial management within the economic system; and in that context it raises some deeply funda-mental issues. These will be only briefly touched on here, because they are more fully reviewed in the more pertinent context of Part Five. Any individual business based on the private enterprise formula is seen by its owners as concerned with a first objective of earning enough profit to maintain its capital and to reward the enterprise of the founders/owners. There is, however, *inevitably* a basic objective underlying the gaining of profits: the business makes and sells particular articles, or provides certain services against a charge. These articles or services contribute to the living, well-being or con-tentment of the community at home, or of other communities abroad. If they do not, then they will not be sold or used, and the business will go out of existence through bankruptcy. As long as an enter-prise intends to continue in active existence, it has to satisfy its customers, i.e. contribute something deemed worth-while to the community seen as consumers. By doing this successfully, the enter-prise stands to make a profit for the benefit of its owners. The situation is basically no different in the case of a Co operative Society: the distinguishing feature lies only in the fact that the "owners" who receive the resulting benefit are the customers (mem-bers) themselves taking it in the form of a bonus (dividend on purchases).

The other aspect of this argument follows on in the same context: no enterprise can "create" its own labour, its own materials, its own equipment; it has to obtain these things from the general pool of resources in the community, and it does so by "buying" them with wages, salaries, the purchase price of materials, machines, etc. Much of this buying is done with borrowed money (fixed and working capital), and for the use of that money it is customary to pay a compensation in interest or dividend. So the owners of the enterprise acquire the use of and control over certain resources, human and material, for a given purpose. If they use these wastefully, the whole community suffers, for the wasted resources could have been put to good advantage elsewhere.

To go further will lead but to labouring the point; the simple conclusion can be stated. Whatever its particular form in terms of ownership or control, an enterprise cannot escape basic responsibilities to the community in which it is set. Responsibility for the effective use of human and material resources; responsibility for the quality and value of the products or services it supplies. The better its performance in both these directions, the more worthy its contribution to the community, and therefore the better the claim of its owners to the profits of their enterprise.[1]

This, however, is the responsibility which the owners (if they are not themselves serving as managers) delegate to the managers whom they establish. The full scope of this management responsibility can now be seen to have several facets. It usually occurs within an *overall economic* setting, because the enterprise is an integral part of the economic system. It also occurs within a *specific technological* setting determined by the particular operations or processes that it is undertaking. It has a *wide social context* in the form of notional contributions to the well-being of a community. It has unavoidable *financial implications* by reason of the capital that it is using, borrowed from other sources; and this capital has to be maintained intact by replenishment from gross earnings. Because it is directed to the planning and regulation of the activities of people, it is a *social process*, in the sense of intimate concern with human factors and personal or group behaviour. It is essentially *a process of responsible judgment and decision*, calling for high skills; the higher the level of management in the hierarchy of an enterprise, the wider and more comprehensive do these skills have to become. Underlying all this is the basic simple notion that in every facet of its role management must be concerned with *efficiency and economy*—not in a ruthless, mechanistic way, for that would defeat its objects; but in the broad-based sense of ensuring the continuing success of high-quality product through high-quality performance, with minimum waste and cost, with the full maintenance of capital invested, with the overall

---

[1] These arguments are more fully pursued in Chapters II and VII of Part Five: see pages 860 and 991.

contentment of the people employed, with provision for growth and development, and with satisfactory reward to the owners of the enterprise. No mean task!

4. THE ELEMENTS OF MANAGEMENT

Turning analysis into lines of practical action, the management role can be summed up as an exercise in deliberative and decisive responsibility combining four essential elements—*planning, motivation, co-ordination, control.* In practice the elements are clothed in procedures and tasks and do not appear in so simple a form. How they appear is, of course, the substance of the following Parts and Chapters of this volume, sub-divided into the four major activities that have long been characteristic of industrial-commercial enterprises: Marketing, Production, Personnel, Control. (A fifth major activity characterises many businesses—Research and Development —and this is dealt with specifically in Part Five.) The elements of management are often not readily apparent when so presented, and confusions ensue because of difficulties in terminology as well as in concept: some of these are dealt with in a subsequent section. Yet, if the practices of management within any of these major divisions are analysed, the validity of the four elements can be confirmed, for all the management activities can be classified to one or other of them. The elements do not, of course, all occur in management practice in the same form: planning and control tend to be found mostly in the garb of techniques and procedures, often closely inter-related with each other. Motivation, on the other hand, lies largely in personal action and attitude on the part of the manager, but many "personnel techniques" are certainly a contributory part of this element in practice. How the elements can be matched with management action (keeping still to the four main divisions used for this volume) is amply illustrated by the following summary:

A. *Planning*

(i) The primary management responsibility arising under this element is the determination of *policy,* i.e. the laying down of the aims of the organisation and the general principles on the basis of which it will operate. This is required not only in a general sense, but also in relation to each of the major divisions. Without a known policy in respect of all its activities, an enterprise cannot function effectively, if at all. A well-defined policy relating to all aspects of an organisation can be of considerable value in promoting co-ordination and smooth working.

(ii) A second general responsibility under the element of planning is that of *organisation structure.*

(iii) *Production.*—Some of the management activities concerned with planning in the field of production are:

Link with marketing to ascertain forecast of sales requirements and so to establish a true (potential) programme of output.

Preparation of programme and breakdown into sections.

Technical layout of operations.

Analysis of operations for allocation of jobs and machines.

Materials specification.

Budget of material supplies; pre-purchasing; pre-allocation (linking up with "control" element).

Method and time study to determine operation times and rates.

Machine loading and production planning.

Inspection routines.

(iv) *Marketing.*—Some planning activities are:

Market research ("assessment of potentials").

Economic forecasting and marketing intelligence.

Layout of sales territories and budgets.

Preparation of sales campaign, including advertising.

Budget of stocks to be carried.

Transport programme.

(v) *Financial Management.*—The planning activities in this field are closely related to the "control" element and are best considered there. Special features are: the provision of capital, the maintenance of working capital; availability of cash (for wages and other short-term disbursements); profit projection.

(vi) *Personnel*

Planning of labour supply; requisitions.

Selection and placement; forecasts for promotion.

Training and job instruction.

Working hours, holidays, substitute man-power, etc.

Cloakroom accommodation, canteen facilities and other amenities.

Management development programme.

B. *Control*

"Planning" lays down the programme to be followed and the standards or budgets to be attained. "Control" watches to see that the programme and the standards or targets are adhered to, or brings to light the reasons why not. In some recent methods of management (especially "Budgetary Control" and "Higher Control") the two elements are actually combined in one procedure.

(i) The Board of Directors has a general oversight of all the activities of the organisation and looks to the General Manager to bring forward the *"control" information* that will enable progress and cost to be checked against the policy, programme and targets laid down. In this sense, top management frequently uses the field of financial activities for providing the means of "control", calling them "management information" which forms the basis of decision.

(ii) *Production.*—The usual management activities relating to observing the productive performance or the progress of output are:

Progress control (often called "production control").

Utilisation of man-power, machine-hours, fuel, power.

Materials or stores control (to foresee and prevent shortages and waste of material).

Balance of components, work in progress, etc.

Quality control (perhaps by statistical methods).

(iii) *Marketing.*—Stock control (quantities of goods in stock).

Sales progress control, broken down into territories, products, salesmen's quotas, or any other desirable subdivision.

Delivery control (to check for transport delays).

(iv) *Financial Management.*—Here the planning and control activities are interlinked. The whole management accountancy system of a business is a scheme of control, or recording and checking the expenditure, but certain aspects of it are more readily recognised as "tools" of management; for instance:

Labour cost control (perhaps on the basis of work study standards).

Materials cost control.

Sales expense control.

Overhead expense control.

Standard costing systems.

Budgetary control (by which a complete plan of financial needs in relation to every aspect of production, distribution and personnel is prepared in advance and used for planning purposes and for subsequent continuous checking).

Higher control (a specialised system of pre-planned expense control, on simpler lines than the "budget").

(v) *Personnel.*—All forms of record and report, employee-rating, merit-rating, management appraisal, and so on.

C..Co-ordination

This element in management does not always use special techniques, but is largely achieved by the active skill of the manager or supervisor himself, giving practical form to his personal attitude of constructive co-operation and sense of mutual responsibility. As already indicated, any form of planning scheme is a help to co-ordination. Committees can also be used for this purpose.

D. Motivation (Leadership)

This again is an element in which special techniques are not available, but in which the human skill of the manager and supervisor is called into play. The task is to fuse the varied individual human capacities and powers of the many people employed into a smoothly working team with high morale and high productivity. It is a task closely linked up with the element of co-ordination. It is an element in their responsibility of which managers and supervisors have hitherto too

P.P.M.—2*

frequently been ignorant and negligent. There is a great deal to be said as to how this task can be carried out, but in brief the major points may be summarised as follows:

Securing interest, by keeping people informed of proposed developments and of progress.

Maintaining loyalty, by fairness in allocation of work, rates of pay, discipline, etc.

Maintaining personal keenness by fostering a sense of participation.

Promoting group harmony, by joint consultation.

Preventing frustration, by providing a sympathetic outlet for grievances and grumbles.

Preserving impartiality, by ensuring co-operative discipline and fairness in judgment.

Encouragement of responsibility in the affairs of the organisation.

Before leaving the consideration of the elements of the management process, it may be useful to comment briefly on the thoughts of Henri Fayol,[1] who, more than half a century ago, as an experienced General Manager of a large technical undertaking, found that the analytical study of the management process could contribute to his own better performance. Working from a different angle of approach, Fayol deduced *five* elements in the management process—planning (=prévoir), organising, command, co-ordination, control. The parallel with the analysis given above is striking, bearing in mind the fact of different and independent approach.[2] The one difference lying in Fayol's second element (organising) may perhaps be due to his participation in a large-scale enterprise, where problems of hierarchy and of channels of delegation and communication loomed large. He was clearly—and rightly—impressed with the importance of "organisation structure", but he was misled into regarding this as a specifically different element. "Organising", in Fayol's intended sense of establishing the correct pattern of delegated responsibilities, with consequent inter-relationships and channels of co-operative communication, is an aspect of the element of "planning": instead of methods or equipment or operational activities, what is being planned is the pattern of management activities themselves and certain modes of communication among them. On this basis, Fayol's elements can be satisfactorily re-written in complete accord with the grouping described above:

---

[1] See the historical notes in Appendix I, pages 85–86.

[2] Some confusion may be caused occasionally by reason of Urwick's published reference to "Fayol's *six* elements". Urwick felt that the Fayol notion of "prévoir" could not be adequately portrayed in English except by splitting it into two elements of "forecasting" and "planning". It can, of course, be counter-argued that "planning" *necessarily* implies the gathering and scrutiny of essential data (i.e. forecasting).

planning	— to prepare the necessary information and interpret it into programmes; to establish appropriate organisation, layout, methods, instructions, etc., etc.; thus to provide the basis for decision leading to action.
command	— to initiate action by communicating decision, to keep it in progress, and to supervise performance, while ensuring a high level of co-operative participation as the outcome of good morale.
co-ordinate	— to keep all activities in balance and in suitable combination.
control	— to review results, to record as necessary, to judge performance and cost, and to feed back as the guide to planning and/or command (=decision).

The full cycle of the process is thus completed, showing the first and fourth elements as the "deliberative" ones (=responsibility for consideration and judgment), with the second and third as mainly the "decisive" ones (=responsibility for executive action and performance). The inter-relation of the elements can be illustratively summarised in the diagram on next page.

5. TERMINOLOGY

The absence of agreed or authoritative views as to the definition of management and its fundamental principles has meant that there is as yet no accepted terminology. Through the wider professional interest in the subject over recent years, there is, however, gradually evolving a common pattern of wording in regard to the day-to-day activities of management, for instance, within such fields as Production Planning or Production Control, Cost Control, Budgetary Control, Personnel Procedures, and so on. With the generic terms "Organisation", "Management" and "Administration", some shreds of confusion and controversy persist, but they are no longer the battle-ground which they represented some years ago.

"Management" is gaining ground over the other two as the general descriptive label, undoubtedly because throughout industry and commerce the title "manager" is widely accepted (with "executive" as a common alternative). The chief complication arises from the influence of the Government and Local Authority Departments, to whose work the title "Public Administration" has long been applied. In some of the larger commercial organisations and the nationalised industries the term "administration" has been imported to refer to some activities of the higher level of management centred at Head Offices; generally speaking, no analytical reason lies behind this, but it can often be traced to the whim of a particular individual, or possibly to a mistaken notion of prestige. The usage is sometimes ex-

THE *PLANNING—CONTROL* FEEDBACK CYCLE

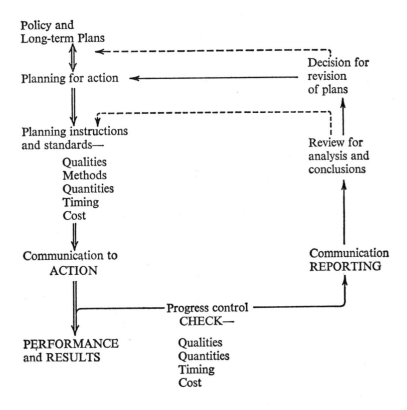

(Solid lines represent normally expected flow; broken lines represent periodic/possible alternative.)

The flow lines between the stages embody the human relations and actions (consultation, communication, motivation). Management judgment is exercised appropriately at all stages. The co-ordinated flow of the whole process in the cycle reinforces the unity of management action.

Note: The *planning-control cycle* is illustrated in terms of procedures in Fig. 83 of Part Four (see page 639).

FIG. 1.

tended by applying the descriptive term "administrative" to the offices or staffs that are engaged in the control activities; for instance, one sometimes find the name "Administrative Block" given to the office sections of the buildings of the large combines. References here and there in official reports, and in the title of the former Institute of Industrial Administration, have lent support to this use of "administration" in the industrial or commercial world. Even a brief conversation with the managers (or the self-styled administrators) themselves leads quickly to the conclusion that in their everyday thinking and talking, the label "management" is the one they apply to their own activities or responsibilities. There is a strong case for following this rather more natural trend of common opinion, i.e. for adopting "management" as the general title for the process as a whole. The creation within recent years of a British Institute of Management lends point to this argument.

Has, then, the word "administration" any part to play? In any sense that is synonymous with management the answer is "no". Equally, in any sense that suggests a superior process restricted to the upper executive structure, the answer had also best be "no". Popular usage does suggest that the main significance of "administration", wherever it is used, centres on the procedures which form the tools of management, i.e. the techniques or routines of planning and control. To this extent the term "administration" can be a useful label to apply to these aspects of the total process.[1]

In regard to the term "organisation" there does not today appear to be any difficulty: throughout the industrial and commercial world, and in far wider fields, including Government service, the label "organisation" is habitually used to refer to the structure of responsibilities and relationships allocated to the various executive and supervisory posts, i.e. "the Structure of Organisation". A few writers

[1] The question of terminology forms a major topic in a series of papers on "The Principles of Management and their Application", in the *British Management Review*, Vol. VII, No. 3. In the light of the progress that has been made in recent years in adoption of common wording, it is now difficult to appreciate the extent of the conflict that has bedevilled discussion in the past, or the amount of emotion generated therein. It seems incredible today that a serious-minded thinker and practitioner in management in the late 1940s could in all sincerity prepare to plead at the High Court for an injunction to withhold the publication of the new translation of Fayol—on the sole ground that the translator had rendered Fayol's French title *"Administration"* into English "Management". The translator, French by origin and early life but subsequently resident in England and a professional member of the Institute, felt that this English word exactly portrayed what Fayol intended, i.e. the whole process analysed above. But that was exactly what the objector held to be wrong: for him the process was known by the English label "administration". Had friends not dissuaded him from the action, literature might today be enriched by the legal proceedings devoted to resolving the tangle of the terminology of management.

have on occasions used "organisation" in a dynamic sense, thinking of it in much the same way as the process of management has here been described; this is now so unusual an approach that it can be regarded as eccentric, and set aside as unfortunate.

A further label is needed to designate the particular aspects of management that fall within the domain of the Board of Directors, i.e. the determination of objectives and policy and the exercise of overall control of the affairs of the enterprise. So far no single name has been agreed or is widely used for this purpose, although one school of thought used to call it "administration". As the persons on whom the responsibility rests are habitually known as Directors, it might be useful again to follow the trend of popular nomenclature add to deduce the label "direction".

A summary of the terms which are recommended as the most appropriate for general usage can therefore be set down as follows:

(1) *Management.*—A social process entailing responsibility for the effective and economical planning and regulation of the operations of an enterprise, in fulfilment of a given purpose or task, such responsibility involving:
>   (*a*) judgment and decision in determining plans and in using data to control performance and progress against plans: and
>   (*b*) the guidance, integration, motivation and supervision of the personnel composing the enterprise, and carrying out its operations.

(2) *Direction.*—That part of management which is concerned with the determination of objectives and policy and the checking of overall progress towards their fulfilment.

(3) *Organisation.*—That part of management which is concerned with the definition of the structure of:
>   (*a*) the responsibilities by means of which the activities of the enterprise are distributed among the (managerial, supervisory and specialist) personnel employed in its service; and
>   (*b*) the formal interrelations established among the personnel by virtue of such responsibilities.

(4) *Administration.*—That part of management which is concerned with the installation and carrying out of the procedures by which the programme is laid down and communicated, and the progress of activities is regulated and checked against plans.

Although not giving rise to conflicts, there are other aspects of terminology which cause confusions in discussions and some of these can be usefully reviewed in the present context. The first concerns the nature or essence of management itself. What is it? The purport of the present analysis argues that it is most exactly described as a "process", i.e. actively carried out by people along specific lines. It is, of course, a mental process, because factors of thought, judgment and decision are essential to its performance. It is *not* of itself a "technique", but it uses techniques as its tools or aids. As indicated above, it is a process with economic and social facets, and often occurs within a technological setting.

Competence in this process gives rise to a "skill", not in the sense of an in-born aptitude specifically separating some people from others. The skill has personal factors at its base, it is true, but a great part of it has to be developed and inculcated by serious effort and conscious learning. Nor is management a "hunch" in any sense at all —though there are a lot of people in management positions content to see it in this form: most of them imagine, of course, that *they* have the "hunch" to a high degree of excellence, and only the personnel serving under them know what this really means! The notion of "hunch" or "flair" frequently arises through a confusion with "business acumen", that is to say, an innate though rare capacity for swift evaluation of situations that can lead to commercial profit. It is found in many of the men who make comfortable livings out of buying and selling, even in the form of small-scale trading in street markets; it is found (and endorsed as more respectable) in the "big names" of property business, or of share dealing, or of financing take-overs. The skill here is a commercial acumen and not necessarily a management competence at all; in fact, some of these men could well prove to be poor managers in the customary sense of the term. There is, of course, an element of "entrepreneurial acumen" in any (higher) management responsibility—in the sense that the manager has to form a judgment and make a decision as a consequence of his personal interpretation of the situation he is dealing with; however much information is given to him to assist judgment, he has personally to reach a conclusion and decision, of greater or lesser significance, according to circumstances.

Science v. Art

Pertinent to this context is a passing reference to an age-long controversy framed in the wording—"Is management a science or an art?" The argument on this theme is seldom heard today in open terms, but vestiges of it abound in popular viewpoint. Some while back the argument raised passionate emotions, though without the disputants coming to any conclusion or any resolution of their divergences. To some extent the dispute raged over difference of approach, but to a much greater extent it was a confusion over terms rather than a serious conflict of opinion. Neither side troubled to make clear what they meant by the choice of respective label, "art" or "science". And neither went to the length of seriously analysing the true nature of the thing about which they were arguing: had they done this, much of the force of their alleged differences would have disappeared. Those defending management as an "art" meant by their claim that it had in it a very large element of personal skill, such that mere learning of techniques would not lead automatically to competence. So much of this skill was centred on human judgment and human considerations of co-operation and morale that any mechanistic approach could not achieve success. In serious analysis this could not, and would not, be denied. On the contrary, it would be re-emphasised. Does this criterion, however, constitute an "art"? What resemblance would it have to the skills of the painter or the musician? The analogy used by the advocates was that of the medical doctor—pointing to his understanding of the psychological and emotional factor in therapy and to the significance of "bedside manner" in his approach to the patient. All very true, and analogously relevant to the practice of management. Yet how does this constitute an "art", unless that label is being used in a very loose and general sense?

On the other side the advocates were more impressed with the significance of mature judgment as a factor in effective management. Without in any way denying the importance of "the human factor in management", this view fought shy of emotion because of the danger of its degeneration into "hunch" or uninformed and irrational decision; emphasis was laid on getting the relevant *facts* of a situation as the basis of deliberation and decision. Proceed, it was advocated, as the scientist does in his own realm: collect the facts and the data; study and analyse them as necessary; determine conclusions; check their validity; make the final decision; and again check its outcome. Such a "scientific method" approach has a cold mechanistic ring about it, but that was never the intention of the protagonists favouring "Scientific Management". Human aspects and situations were always among the facts to be studied and considered. Perhaps the choice of label was as inaccurate and as unfortunate as that on the other side of the controversy; it was chosen as a slogan during a campaign in America in the early 1900s, when no doubt it served a local purpose well. The passing of decades, however, fogged the significance of the label, and so later advocates came to speak of "the science of management". That a systematic body of knowledge underlies the competent practice of management hardly anyone today would deny; and much of that knowledge lies in various fields which are of themselves academic disciplines. The summation of such parts cannot constitute a new "science". What the advocates really mean is that competence in management necessitates both an adequate

MANAGEMENT IN PRINCIPLE 27

basis of knowledge and a mature systematic approach: they do not mean that management is on all fours with nuclear physics.

Thus from both sides the controversy disappears into the thin air of terminological inexactitude. Putting the essential parts of the two sides together, the true view of management emerges as a skilled process entailing human considerations, requiring maturity of judgment, a systematic approach, a wide range of knowledge. Add to this a foundation of ethical standards and one has all the makings of a profession: certainly *neither* a science *nor* an art, as these words are normally understood.

The Functional Role

In another direction entirely, another term which has caused a great deal of confusion over the years is "function", more as a label than in the adjectival form ("functional") descriptive of responsibilities and relationships. To unravel this tangle it will be necessary to make a brief historical review. The term began its management history with F. W. Taylor (see page 85 for chronological reference) in the form of his "functional foremen": the role of supervision he dissected into the various activities that were being carried out by the Section Foremen according to the pattern of management practices adopted by the American engineering concern in which Taylor was a manager. Many of these activities were concerned with planning procedures, and Taylor decided to establish specialist sections devoted to each item. In this way he came to an arrangement whereby the Department Superintendent had eight "foremen" to assist him in his supervisory role, to each being allocated a particular activity. He called them "functional" because he had given each his own special "function" to look after—using the term with no more than its normal meaning of "activity or task to perform".

Argument over the merits of the Taylor pattern brought the term into prominence, but confusion was allowed to grow apace from early times by reason of the unchecked emergence of two different usages of the term:

(a) In the United States, others followed Taylor in seeing "function" as a convenient label for the subdivisions of the management process on the basis of specific attention to each aspect. The term came into England with the same connotation. This is seen, for example, in the earlier editions of the Handbook of the Institute of Industrial Administration (1920s and 1930s) which referred to the membership being spread over "all functions of management": and these were listed as Production, Development, Purchasing, Distribution, Finance, Office, Personnel. There have been divergences of view as to which activities merit to be separated out, and varying lists have been produced over the years. Yet the basic notion remained—"function" referred to fields of activity wherein management was applied. By the same token, an organisation structure which provided a pattern of management delegation based on specialisation of activity has been customarily entitled "a functional organisation".

(b) Closer analytical study in Great Britain later gave rise to a more refined use of the term. It started from the arguments as to which activities merited separate identification as "functions", and was much interwoven with the earlier endeavours to get recognition for the serious study of management as a profession. Taking the widely accepted pattern of "four *functions* of management"— Production, Distribution (Marketing), Personnel, Control (Management Accounting)—to which nobody would object as a minimum, the thought developed that this was a misleading division. For it was not enough to expect of a production manager only a competence in production management; he needs wider skills in the management field, including a full understanding of the professional process of management itself with its four constituent elements. Within any manufacturing enterprise, the various activities of "production" will need to be planned and regulated, co-ordinated, their progress and outcome checked (controlled) against plans, their cost and expense similarly controlled; and the morale of the persons employed in those various activities supported by good human (personnel) management. In other words, *within the framework of those production activities* all four elements of the management process are being applied. Broadly summarised, these four elements fall into two categories—

(i) those concerned with the inter-related techniques of "planning" and "control", which also partly contribute to "co-ordination"; and

(ii) those directed to the "motivation" of high performance of the personnel engaged, coupled with balance and co-ordination of the human effort deployed.

These two categories are broadly what is meant by the content of the two functions labelled respectively "control" and "personnel". With appropriate characteristics they apply equally to activities which may be going on in the distribution (marketing) field: say, for example, the warehousing of finished products, their sale to customers through networks of regional salesmen, and the collection of payments from the customers. Thus these two elemental functions of "personnel" and "control" can be found identified with the management process *within* Production and *within* Distribution. The four commonly so-called "functions"—Production, Distribution (Marketing), Personnel, Control—are, therefore, of *different character*: the latter two necessarily occur within the former two. They cannot therefore, it was argued, be classified as the same thing. A more correct description would be to call Production and Marketing "fields of activity". Personnel and Control were the only two true "functions of management", occurring by their very nature within all fields of activity; the term "function" was required in this argument to be reserved for this designation. If a single word is needed as the description of the parts of an organisation which has its executive activities divided into the four traditional groups (Production, Distribution, Personnel, Control), the best choice would appear to be "divisions", i.e. "the four divisions of an organisation." It must, however, still be recognised that the latter two are different in character from the former: in the fact that the activities occurring within the latter two are in the nature of specialist delegation, that is to say, part of the essential elements of the management process is delegated on a specialist ancillary and advisory basis, but not including a delegation of the executive responsibility. Thus the term "functional" came to have a precise meaning which in popular usage widely superseded the earlier more general use.

The two usages have become current coin side by side, and the confusion is inevitable in any discussions, unless care is taken by the parties concerned to identify the way in which the label is being applied by them. Some further comments in this connection will be relevant in a later section dealing with organisation structure, for it is in that context that considerations of "functional" activities (in both senses) mostly arise. It is a pity that there are not as yet any agreed terms to designate the parts, sections and levels into which management is subdivided by delegation, because their absence so much hinders serious discussion in the exchange of experience and in the study of management. "Divisions" is appropriate for the major specialisations into which an organisation structure is patterned, and it is often used as a label, for example, Marketing Division, Manufacturing Division, and so on. "Levels" serves to indicate the relative ranking of positions with appropriate delegation of responsibility. What is really being sought is a set of terms or labels that will designate the "areas of decision" in the application of management: this is what the generic use of "functions" quoted above was intended to delineate—areas of decision such as forecasting, purchasing, marketing, manufacturing, selling, warehousing, office administration, and the like. Until more acceptable labels are determined, there is little else but to make do with what is already known, with deliberate precautions to avoid confusion.

In a later context reference will also be made to another label in which terminological tangles have long been common, namely, the notion of "staff"—in the sense of "staff officers" and "staff relationships".

Perhaps one more term may be usefully referred to here: the choice of "motivation" for one of the four elements of the management process. It is certainly an unfamiliar label in this context, and has been criticised as ugly—no doubt a valid criticism but not of specific significance! In the definition recorded above (see page 13), a final comment in parentheses indicates that this item is popularly referred to as "leadership". It corresponds also with what Fayol called "command". Either of these two terms might have been retained, but they each suffer from drawbacks. "Command" has too strong a connotation of unflinching, unquestioning discipline, and does not really admit the admixture of consultation and participation which are the concomitants of a democratic society. "Leadership" has the disadvantage of vagueness, because it is also used to describe an aptitude, a quality which some people maintain to be inborn, irrespective of its relevance to industrial management. This element in the management process is one to which the manager gives deliberate thought in promoting good response among his subordinates and in which he takes *positive* action. There is thus some advantage in choosing a description word which bears out these facets—and the notion of implanting "motive" to performance and co-operation has something to commend it. Even if the resulting word "motivation" is unwonted and ugly!

Turning briefly to the more specific aspects of management practice, it is fortunate to be able to say that terminology difficulties have been far less troublesome. They have indeed existed, but there has been far greater progress in attaining fairly widespread conformity in everyday usage. As referred to elsewhere in these pages, one of the main remaining fields where terminological divergencies are common is that of the titles used for executive positions. Seemingly simple and ordinary labels—such as Factory Manager, Production Manager, Marketing Manager, Sales Manager—can have widely and deeply differing connotations in different organisations. In consequence, there are sometimes corresponding divergencies in the usage of the terms covering the relevant activities: these will be seen and commented on as appropriate in the following Parts of this volume.

Broadly, however, unanimity is greater than difference, and the spread of serious management studies based on a commonly accepted literature will progressively reinforce the unanimity. Authoritative bodies have also in recent years assisted this progress by specific attempts at defining glossaries of terms recommended for use in management practice. Most notable among these are:

(a) *Glossary of Management Terms*—British Institute of Management (1954): brief trilingual summary of main terms.

(b) Federation Internationale de Documentation (1956); inventory of principal terms in three languages.

(c) *Terminology of Productivity*: Outlining summary of terms prepared by the European Organisation for Economic Co-operation (1950).

(d) *Specialist Terminology*:
   (i) British Standards Institution—*Glossary of Work Study* (1959).
   (ii) Institute of Cost and Works Accountants: *Terminology for Cost Accounting* (1952).

(e) "*Management Glossary*: *Principles and Practice of Productivity*." A comprehensive statement of definitions in the broad field indicated; published by the Office of Industrial Resources in the International Cooperation Administration, Washington, U.S.A.

A postscript is pertinent to this section with a reference to two terms having a wide currency in management discussions, though seldom precisely explained. These are the words "efficiency" and "effectiveness". Both will be found recurring frequently in this volume, because what they connote is basic to the management process in principle and practice. No distinction is drawn between them: both are used to convey the same idea of attaining an optimum performance or result with the minimum use of resources or at minimum cost. While many managers support this synonymous interpretation, there are some who prefer to draw a difference between the two terms. Inevitably, the distinction is slight and is a matter of nuance rather than of meaning: "effectiveness" is held to be the broader term in the sense just indicated without reference to any specific causes or circumstances; "efficiency" is then used to imply that there are mechanical or other physical factors involved. Whether there is justification in this view can be best left to individual judgment; it is not adopted in this study.

6. THE FOUNDATION OF MANAGEMENT—POLICY

Turning from background considerations as to the nature of the management process and the difficulties that have beset the serious study of it by reason of terminological confusions, it is appropriate next to give attention to major factors that will underlie the effective application of that process. In due course, an attempt will be made to determine certain "principles" upon which such effective practice can be based, but there are first two specific aspects that call for comment, namely, "policy" and "organisation structure". These two have a particular significance for management practice, and they may usefully be thought of as respectively the "foundation" and the "framework" of that practice. They are the subject of this and the following sections.

It is often overlooked that the activities, for the planning, guidance and co-ordination of which management is responsible, are directed to a given purpose or objective. In an earlier paragraph, the character of objectives found in the economic system was briefly examined: industrial and commercial enterprises in the last analysis exist in order to provide something directly or indirectly for the benefit of the citizen-consumer. Each enterprise individually has, as it were, a specific share in this general purpose, according to what has been determined for it by its founders, or their successors in the present-day body of governors or directors. Without such objective, it is difficult to see how management could be carried into effect, because it would have no goal or aim. A primary need in the practice of management is, therefore, to determine the objective and to define it in terms that all members of the enterprise can understand and appreciate. In practice this is seldom done overtly, though it may well be held to be implicit in the very nature of the activities of the enterprise. The weakness of leaving the objective unstressed lies in a danger of loss of perspective: managers and personnel employed may equally lose sight of the fact that they have a community of citizen-consumers to serve, directly or indirectly, in the guise of customers. They have, too, another inherent objective, namely, in the maintenance of their own employment. These two are mostly closely inter-related; to the extent to which customers can be retained because of the quality and efficiency with which they are continuously served, the vitality of the enterprise can be maintained and with it the durability of employment. Quality and efficiency thus become objectives in themselves, working to the benefit at once of the consumer and of the producer considered as employee. It was noted above, in the analysis of the management process, that efficiency of the operations managed is an *inherent* objective of that process. In practice much can be gained from making it an overt objective, rather than leaving it to be taken for granted—on the latter basis it is more likely to be overlooked.

Closely allied to the purpose of an enterprise are the principles on which it is to be conducted—what is commonly called "the policy". Responsibility for determining both the objective and the policy (they again are usually interrelated) rests first with those who have initiated the enterprise or who have made its existence possible by providing the necessary finance, without which an enterprise can be neither started nor continued. In the very small firms, the financial initiative may come from a single owner or two or three persons in partnership, whatever the legal form in which they establish the undertaking. These persons thus have responsibility for determining their objectives and policy, and of making these known to the personnel serving them. When large-scale activities are initiated, especially if sizeable plant and equipment are called for, the considerable financial resources required necessitate the formation of a company; and the legal formalities lead to the establishment of a Board of Directors to whom the providers of the capital (the shareholders) delegate their responsibility for determination of objectives and policy, and for overall control of performance and progress. In our own times we have become accustomed to industrial undertakings being initiated on a scale requiring so much invested finance (for example, atomic energy establishments) that the state itself has to be the supplier of capital, and a "national industry" is the form resulting: here an Authority or a Central Council takes the role of the Board of Directors, remaining answerable to the state through a Ministry and Parliament. Objectives and policy are thus formulated at "national levels".

One advantageous by-product of the legal form of the company lies in this very provision for a Board of Directors, for it identifies the group of men who, in a corporate sense, are responsible for "direction" (see page 24), i.e. for determining and making known objectives and policy, and then for so governing affairs that these are attained effectively. Even if all or some of the members of this Board of Directors should be full-time servants of the company in other capacities (for example, as managers or technical officers), they stand specifically identified in a corporate capacity for the formulation of policy and for overall control: that is their role and *raison d'être* as members of the Board of Directors. A clear line of demarcation can thus be drawn between the two sets of responsibilities, when they are so held: this position is further discussed later in the present section (see pages 40–41).

On the scale of the national corporations, while the Authority, Board or Council has a parallel corporate responsibility, its members are often engaged full-time in that "directorial" capacity and do not have the complication of holding subordinate responsibilities within the organisation.

Even in the somewhat dissimilar pattern of "co-operative trading", a central board or committee exercises the policy and overall control function, with certain delegations to locally established "General Management Committees". These in much the same way represent the providers of the finance, though here it is a notional representation in so far as the co-operative societies have accumulated funds earned from members' purchases. The immediate representation is of the "member" as such, but he is historically akin to the shareholder of a limited company.

In the setting of contemporary political and economic thinking, the idea that responsibility for the formulation of objectives and policy, and for overall control, rests as a matter of right with those who have provided the capital is often regarded as "reactionary", and associated with a system of "private capitalism". Yet it is a fact, not a notion; and it is just as true in the case of those undertakings for which the capital is provided by the State itself—the clearest example being the General Post Office. In the case of limited companies, it is, of course, ever more true that the shareholders do not exercise this responsibility; in many concerns they literally could not do so, because their number may run into hundreds or thousands—a meeting to determine policy would be akin to Trafalgar Square on bonfire night! Thus it is that the Board of Directors acquire, as it were by delegation and in their corporate capacity, the responsibility to formulate objectives and policy and to ensure their effective implementation. They render account of their stewardship (to the shareholders) in the Annual Accounts and by the Chairman's report at the Annual General Meeting.

In terms of "objectives", these thoughts on the centre of responsibility for policy underline a particular problem for the Board of Directors themselves to resolve—the problem of the balance of priority of objectives when each of those to be weighed has an inherent right to consideration. From the analytical considerations that have gone before, it will be clear that three legitimate objectives arise naturally within the responsibility of the ultimate authority:

1. to the community in the form of the citizen-consumers or the customers to be served;
2. to the personnel employed in terms of stability of employment as the counterpart of economic consumption;
3. to the shareholders who have made available the finance for conducting the enterprise.

All three have a *right* to be recognised and honoured; whether the rights are equal, or what is the order and proportion of priority can be an exercise in philosophy rather than a practical issue in management. On some aspects of this conundrum comment will be pertinent later in this volume.

The Nature of Policy

Policy can be briefly defined as the objective, the mode of thought and the body of principles underlying the activities of an organisation. In an industrial or commercial enterprise, it may be regarded as determining the share that the enterprise takes in the purposes of the economic system: the enterprise has been established—let it be repeated—in order to contribute something towards meeting the needs of consumers. For example, the objective and policy of the National Coal Board, and of all its constituent units right down to the pit, are centred on winning and distributing coal for the community. Similarly, in war or peace, a Royal Ordnance Factory exists as part of a central Ministry to supply the country's armed forces with the necessary weapons of war and war-like stores. These two national instances are, however, no different as to objective and policy from, for instance, an organisation such as the British Motor Corporation, or the smallest factory devoted to making, say, fractional horse-power motors on a small scale. Whatever the product on which the factory is engaged, its primary objective is to make adequate quantities of that product available for consumers at appropriate levels of quality, and at the best possible levels of price. The consumers may be either at home or abroad. In the case of concerns that are devoted to the manufacture of machine tools, baking plant or other forms of capital equipment, including basic industries like iron smelting or the making of steel billets, the objective is one or more stages removed from immediate service to the consumers: their task is to provide the equipment by means of which the modern industrial society obtains the wherewithal for its livelihood.

In the field of distribution, illustrations are just as readily found, ranging from the large Co-operative Store or the well-known Departmental Store on the one side, through various categories and sizes of retail establishment, down to the local one-man shop or the stall in the market-square. In each case the objective is to provide the means by which the goods which the consumer wants are put at his ready disposal. Or again, railway and road transport, the activities of the banks, the advances for house purchases from the Building Societies, the travel and theatre-ticket agencies, hotels and many other institutions, are there for the purpose of affording to citizens a variety of direct services that they need for the better enjoyment of living.

As noted above, the objectives of an organisation are seldom explicitly defined, largely because the capital structure of our industrial and commercial community has tended to focus attention on the earning of profits, and accordingly popular opinion has long tended to see the payment of dividends to shareholders as the primary objective. This is an inevitable consequence of the fact that the main criteria of effectiveness in a capitalist community are couched in terms of profit and loss figures. Directors and managers mostly overlook the morale value of stating clearly the objectives of their enterprise in relation to social or consumer needs. The war years taught valuable lessons as to the influence on worker and staff attitudes of a clear realisation of "working for the war effort" and of an appreciation of the way in which the equipment, product or service upon which they were engaged made its contribution to known national needs. That the lesson has not been entirely lost is evidenced by more recent endeavours to secure workers' interest in the export drive, by letting employees know the extent to which their work is devoted to the service of overseas consumers, and thereby to earning the foreign exchange with which essential imports for home needs may be purchased.

Clarification of objective is clearly the first element in policy.

In pursuit of the objective, policy is made up of two further elements:

(1) The first may be described as the ethical foundation of the enterprise. This in turn has two aspects (a) the one can be summarised as its standards of fair trading, i.e. the basic principles on which the enterprise proposes to conduct its relations with persons or firms outside itself; for instance, its customers, its dealers and the general public; (b) the other is fair standards of employment, i.e. the principles which the concern proposes to observe in regard to dealings with its employees.

(2) The second main element may be described as the organisational or operational foundation, concerned with the structure and conduct of the operations of the enterprise: this will also have two aspects: (a) the one relating to external operations, i.e. channels and methods of trading; (b) the other concerned with internal working, questions of equipment, methods of production, basic practices in personnel or control techniques, and so on.

It will be noted that in both elements of policy there is an "outside" and an "inside" aspect, dealing respectively with—(a) the relations of the organisation to the world outside, and (b) the people and methods making up the organisation itself. Thus a fully developed policy provides management with a basis for discharging effectively the economic and social responsibilities which devolve from its participation in the life of the community:

(a) To contribute to the economic needs of the community by the manufacture and supply of the products which it is set up to produce, or by carrying out the particular lines of trade or service that it is designed to provide.

(b) To contribute to the economic and social well-being of the community by improvements in the quality and volume of the products made available, and by reductions in the price at which they are available; in other fields, by improving the service that is being offered and lowering the cost without impairment of quality. It is by reductions in cost of existing products and services that a community makes advances in its standards of life, because, by having to spend less money on known or admitted needs, consumers have a margin to spend on the satisfaction of further wants, investment for savings purposes, or the pursuit of educational or recreational amenities.

(c) To improve the standards of employment by raising the level of working conditions and by enhancing personal and social satisfactions at work.

(d) To respect, or contribute to the advancement of, the local amenities of the particular community in which the enterprise is physically set.

(e) To provide for the continuing pursuit of efficiency in all activities and for the promotion of vitality in ensuring the future stability and progress of the enterprise, in maintaining its profitability and in the sound employment of the capital invested.

Formulation of its outlook and attitude in these social directions may be said to constitute the *general policy* of an organisation: such principles as it lays down will apply throughout its activities. In addition, a breakdown of policy will usually be required, especially in those aspects that are concerned with channels and methods of trading and production. In fact, once an organisation grows to even moderate size, its activities will need to some extent to be sectionalised, either by division into manufacture, selling, transport, etc., or by geographical divisions with subsidiary premises in other localities, or by the development of functional divisions in management. General policy will then need reformulating so as to set out the guiding lines for these different sectional aspects, to ensure adequate co-ordination of the various parts. Such sectional principles cannot be regarded as separate policies, but only as specialised or sectional expressions of the major general policy from which they all stem and to which they all relate.

The Formulation of Policy

The clear formulation of policy, in general and in sections, and its announcement within and without the organisation in a written declaration, can be of the highest importance in promoting the effectiveness of management. Policy is obviously the basis of the structure of organisation needed for carrying on the affairs of the enterprise: unless policy is clearly defined, it is not possible to frame an organisation, because it is not possible adequately to determine the appropriate executive responsibilities and relationships; nor can the appointed managers carry out these responsibilities with effectiveness and co-ordination. Perhaps more obviously, the clear formulation of policy underlies planning, whether in relation to the capital and equipment required, the premises, the channels of trade, the levels of employment, the purchase of materials, or many other more detailed aspects of the programme for getting the enterprise into operation and keeping its activities moving. It is also important to appreciate that policy has a considerable contribution to make to co-ordination, especially in the larger organisations, and to the maintenance of morale. Where policy is clearly defined, in its general and sectional aspects, the organisation is already a long way advanced towards ensuring that its managers will keep in step in the day-to-day discharge of their responsibilities.

The relevance of policy to morale is not often realised. Information as to objectives and policy is a known means of promoting and securing co-operation. In an organisation where managers keep all these things to themselves, and argue that workers or staff should get on with the job and "do as they are told", morale is often low: ignorance breeds indifference and suspicion, moods which manifestly hinder co-operation and will to work. Clear policy is an aid to information. It removes the sense of aimlessness, and promotes a sense of participation, besides inspiring in employees confidence in the soundness of management. They know what the company is trying to do; they know how plans are formulated for the attainment of the known ends; they are aware of the standards of trading and employment that have been laid down. They have in this knowledge a lead towards co-operation and the response of good effort in the performance of their own part of the total job. This is of particular importance to the managers and supervisors, for whom a clear understanding of the company's policy affords a firm basis for the daily practice of their responsibilities and the continuous promotion of sound employee relations.

Policy is also the basis on which the results of management can be assessed. The establishment of criteria of effectiveness and their use in assessing the achievements of the organisation is the other half of the responsibility of the Board of Directors, the higher level of management. It falls to them to ensure that the objectives of the enterprise are being attained and that the policies that have been laid down are being followed. They have then to ensure that all operations and activities are being carried out at an adequate level of effectiveness and economy: it is in this connection that the various types of control data and higher financial accounts come into play. At the lower levels of control, the function of such data is to ensure that plans are being followed and reasons for departures known, but in addition, the daily, weekly or monthly data are contributing to the overall periodic picture which will enable "top management", and the Board of Directors, to ensure that adequate standards of effectiveness and economy are being achieved and maintained throughout in the fulfilment of policy.

Policy must be clearly related to facts; in an industrial or commercial organisation this must mean that policy is based on forecasting, to ascertain market or production requirements and other fundamental factors of economic operation. Whether such forecasting is in the form of a systematic analysis based on techniques of market assessment, or whether it is a more formal review of economic conditions and expectations, is not of immediate moment in the present context. How the approach is made must largely be determined by the nature of the industry or trade, the type of product handled, and other specific circumstances of the company concerned. However attained, a factual basis is the first requirement in the formulation of policy, and in this direction important contributions can be made by the executives and functional specialists below the level of the Board of Directors. Responsibility for the formulation of policy necessarily and formally lies with the Board of Directors themselves, but this does not and should not preclude their obtaining substantial and valuable guidance from the members of the organisation below: in the first place these members' specialist knowledge can be the basis on which accurate and factual forecasts of markets and sales potentials are made. Their daily dealings with the problems of management afford them a more realistic appreciation of the circumstances in which trading has to be carried on—material supplies, machine capacity, man-power, and the many other factors that can so easily play havoc with even the best-sounding policy, if inadequately considered. They also have a closer view of the structure of management and so of the weaknesses and deficiencies that can be a bar to carrying a policy into effect. Apart from such positive contributions from the managers to the formulation of policy, there is another morale aspect here: if managers are to be expected to carry heavy responsibilities for the affairs of the organisation, they should rightly be consulted on and invited to contribute to the fundamentals of that organisation, i.e. its policy. They cannot be expected to show a high level of co-operation, or to secure it from their subordinates, if their own superiors adopt the "theirs not to reason why, theirs but to do or die" attitude in this all-important direction.

The Channels of Policy

In most cases, these contributions to policy from the members of the organisation will be co-ordinated by and focused through the Managing Director, as the one-half of this two-way channel of contact. If there is to be effective interpretation of policy into instructions for executive action, there must be a single source of reference.

This, in fact, is the purpose of the office of Managing Director: the individual holding it is at once a Director sharing in the corporate responsibility for determining objectives and policy, and the chief executive in command of the lines of management responsibility leading down to operations. He, in fact, is the first channel through which the process of management will flow. Equally, he is the final stage in the flow of contributions back from within the organisation, and thereby a focal point for consideration and consolidation. In organisations where some of the executives or specialists are also members of the Board, certain difficulties could arise from this situation unless there is clear understanding of the specific role of the Managing Director as the sole "chief executive" and thus the sole authoritative channel of interpretation and communication between the Board and the organisation below. To convey policy from the Board of Directors to the members of the executive structure is a task inherent in the role of the Managing Director, for his responsibility can be summed up as the combination of the first and last stages in management, i.e. interpreting policy into terms of operating instructions, and reporting back to the Board on the working of management. To him falls the responsibility for ensuring that in the first instance objectives and policy are known to all members of the organisation, and so to set the tone that will govern the level of morale through all subordinate ranks. In the smaller units, particularly in the case of the single owners, this first stage is inextricably intermingled with policy formulation: as his own boss, the single owner lays down the policy and interprets it all in the same breath. The same is largely true of the partnerships and the smaller companies, as well as of larger companies in which all the Directors also hold full-time executive appointments: the few men concerned at the top are at one time a Board of Directors sitting round a table in formal array, but for the greater part of their time they are individual managers, with the Managing Director as their chief. To draw the distinction between their two capacities is not always easy in thought and frequently very difficult in action. But in principle the distinction is there.

In larger organisations, the position of the Managing Director is usually clearer. The Board as such may contain a number of persons who carry executive responsibilities within the organisation, and in addition other persons whose services to the Company are restricted to the part-time duties required by attendance at Board Meetings. The Managing Director is specifically appointed and recognised as the executive head of the organisation, responsible to the Board for ensuring that policy is correctly interpreted and that there will ensue effective fulfilment of the policy so as to achieve the objectives. This is not for one moment to suggest that human frailties will not give rise to complications; for instance, any of the Directors also holding executive responsibilities for specific parts of the organisation may usurp the Managing Director's function and issue his own instructions which purport to be the sole interpretation of policy. Such bad practice, however, does not vitiate the principle: only the Managing Director carries responsibility to the Board for the interpretation of policy; he alone holds the dual role of Director-cum-executive. The other Directors must be seen as exercising *two distinct functions* or living two different roles: they share the corporate responsibility of Directors, as members of the Board, when sitting at Board Meetings; they return to their rather different position as executive subordinates to the Managing Director when they leave the Board Room to take up their responsibilities for specific parts of the organisation. The common habit of talking about "a Director in charge of", say, manufacturing or sales, involves a contradiction in terms.

In general discussion one frequently finds the "formulation of policy" spoken of as though it were a deliberate non-recurrent activity. That is, of course, in some respects true: at the outset of a business or at many stages of its development, the Board of Directors will make concrete and specific decisions which constitute the basic objectives and lines of working of the enterprise, i.e. its policy. These will, however, be variously modified and added to time and time again as the business proceeds; and so they should be. Policy, as the foundation of a vital process of commercial action, has itself to be kept alive and in tune with the action required, and thus the adjustment is a by-product of the serious review of performance and progress, in the light of new facts and changing circumstances. The important thing is that policy should not be vacillating, thereby producing an unstable foundation for executive action. This can be guarded against chiefly by the attitude of the Directors themselves, recognising the significance of this point and ensuring that all their considerations of policy adjustments and formulation is mature and thorough. Much is to be gained in this direction from "formalising" the Board's corporate actions in policy deliberation and decision; if Directors make it a practice to conduct their decisive policy deliberations within the formal framework of a Board meeting, with adequate explanatory documentation and record, experience has shown that a lot can be gained in the maturity with which policy is formulated. Naturally, more informal discussions and exchanges of view may well have preceded these final deliberations, but by this specific step the Board will have ensured that a definite policy decision has been taken. Moreover, the clear recording of that decision will also ensure that the decision is understood in the same way by all Directors and will make possible a reliable communication of it to the other members of the organisation. For most businesses it is no burden to go to these lengths whenever a Board has (major) policy considerations in hand: these do not normally arise as often as may be thought, and it could well be found that systematic treatment when such considerations do arise will not only reduce their recurrence, but—more important—obviate the necessity for the sorting out of trouble due to subsequent misunderstandings of policy.

For policy to exert its appropriate influence on the effectiveness of management below, it has to be "interpreted" or reflected in executive instructions. In the Managing Director's two-way role, this interpretation is also a continuous or recurrent process, carried out through his meetings and discussions with his subordinate managers, or partly through the issue to them of budgets and programmes. Some "interpretation" of policy occurs, too, in the form of his decisions on specific matters brought to him for consideration. It is an element in the skill of a Managing Director that he can make these decisions *ad hoc* in relation to the particular points while keeping true to the main pattern of policy laid down. Thus, the task of interpreting policy is one readily recurring among the daily activities of the chief executive.

Further interpretation of policy has also to take place at lower levels, especially in the larger organisations. The broad lines of "sectional" policy may have been laid down by the Board in formulating their general policy, or by the Managing Director in his major instructions. There will necessarily have to be some review and re-interpretation in the specialist terms appropriate to the various divisions of the enterprise: this is a natural item in the functional responsibilities of executives in charge of such divisons. In many instances this re-interpretation of policy at the lower levels merges into planning, and serves as the link between policy and programme of action. This is seen especially in the field of manufacturing: at the level of the Production or Factory Manager, policy is formulated in all the technical terms required for laying down the production plan or manufacturing programme. Similarly, in an enterprise which has adopted the techniques of budgetary control, policy is translated in financial terms into the form of approved expense budgets and related standards of performance.

These aspects of policy show how it is woven into the fabric of management and bring out clearly the important feature that policy must be flexible, capable of adaptation or re-interpretation in the light of changing circumstances. Yet, at the same time, it must be kept unified and consistent.

7. THE STRUCTURE OF MANAGEMENT—ORGANISATION

As policy is the basis of management in action, so organisation is its framework. It was defined earlier as the structure of the responsibilities allocated to the managerial, supervisory and specialist positions and of the (formal) relationships that arise in the discharge of those responsibilities. It was pointed out that it is now customary to use the term "organisation" only in this static sense, and clearly it is thus an aspect of planning—defining the managerial, supervisory and specialist responsibilities required in order to attain a certain objective and policy is, in principle, little different from the task of deciding what equipment is to be used, how it is to be laid out in the factory, or what materials are to be employed in manufacture.

The substance of an organisation structure is the descriptive definition of the responsibilities that are to be undertaken. A chart is *not* an organisation structure—it is no more than an illustration of the grouping of the responsibilities and of some of the authority relations that arise among those groups. Simply to draw lines from a chief executive to his subordinate executive colleagues, including diagonal lines to indicate functional or specialist relationships, may be a useful representation of certain facts in any given organisation, but it is only a pictorial presentation of specific relationships. Of itself it does not codify the responsibilities of the various executives or specialist posts concerned. This can be done only by clear definitions of the scope and breakdown of such responsibilities, with indication of the official to whom the executive in question is to be held responsible, who in turn is responsible to him, and the particular relations he needs to maintain with other executives not in his own direct sequence. The "relationships" are part of the planned pattern of the working of management, which is conducted from one section to another, not only through the senior to which these sections are attached, but by means of lateral or functional relations directly subsisting between the sections, enabling them to co-operate in the pursuit of the common task and in the fulfilment of the common policy. This is readily seen at work, for instance, within a manufacturing unit where there is a Planning Manager and a Factory Manager, both responsible to a senior production executive. The one has responsibilities, for instance, for laying down the manufacturing plans, the other has responsibilities for ensuring that the plans are carried out. Lateral relations exist between these two executives to ensure continuous co-ordination and co-operation in the mutually shared task of translating policy into an agreed output programme and seeing that the programme is fulfilled.

Similar illustrations can be drawn readily enough from the relations between, say, the Factory Manager and the Sales Manager within one organisation, or in the specialist relations between a Personnel Officer, responsible for recruitment, training, welfare and similar procedures, and a Factory Manager who carries full responsibility for the planning and attainment of production programmes. Schedules of responsibilities lay down in broad, general terms the field that these individual managers or specialists are called on to cover: illustrations of such schedules are set out in Appendix II.[1]

That the subject of organisation has for some time been of considerable interest is due to the many deficiencies or weaknesses that are characteristic of the structure of management in industry and commerce, leading invariably to inefficiency and high costs of operating, as well as to many personal experiences of conflict and confusion. It is astonishing how frequently the same deficiencies or weaknesses recur, and how often they are due to the absence of definitions of respective responsibility. There is, of course, the further difficulty of lack of agreed or authoritative principles of organisation structure from which a chief executive could draw guidance when he wants to set up a sound structure by defining the responsibilities and relationships of himself and his subordinates. He may, perhaps, have some help from contemporary literature, but he has still to rely largely on his own judgment. If starting with a new organisation, he is in a position to proceed analytically: to start with the formulation of management aims and policy; then to group for his own purposes the particular tasks that have to be undertaken; then deciding in broad outline the planning and control techniques; thus eventually arriving at groupings of responsibilities, duties and relations that will lead to a systematic structure.

When, however, trying to remodel an existing organisation, the problem is more complicated, because some regard must be paid to the present framework. In this case, the formulation of executive responsibilities can best be carried out with the active co-operation of the managers, supervisors and specialists themselves. Each can be asked to write down in broad outline the various tasks and activities for which he regards himself responsible, and the lines along which he proceeds to fulfil them. He can be asked to group these tasks under certain major headings, which have perhaps been broadly formulated in advance. Someone nominated as "Organisation Secretary" would collect these detailed documents, and after scrutiny take up with individuals concerned amplification or clarification of obscure points. Note should particularly be taken of items of duplication or omission that the

---

[1] The subject-matter of this section is comprehensively studied in a companion volume entitled *Organisation—The Framework of Management* (Longmans, Green & Co., London, 1957).

Organisation Secretary can recognise from his own more central standpoint. He would then proceed to analyse the completed documents, in order to obtain a comprehensive picture of how the total responsibilities of management are distributed, to ascertain how they contribute to the fulfilment of policy, and to mark out the instances of overlapping, duplication, deficiency or omission. The Chief Executive is then in a position to examine with his subordinates the "map" of the organisation territory as at present laid out, and to agree with them the ways in which certain fields or parts would be better regrouped, to ensure a higher degree of co-ordination, a better cover of management responsibility, a closer fulfilment of policy, a better distribution of load, or remedies to correct such deficiencies and gaps as have been revealed. The review would be rounded off by writing up the schedules along the lines illustrated in Appendix II.

The task thus set out may appear to be formidable and to lend support to the view that organisation is an aspect of management pertinent only to the larger units. Nothing, in fact, could be farther from the truth: even the smallest organisation can gain from knowing exactly how its management works. As soon as two or three managers and supervisors are brought into existence by growth from the very small stage, the need for demarcation of responsibilities becomes not only valuable, but essential to good management; and such demarcation is nothing else than the determination and definition of responsibilities and relationships, i.e. setting up an organisation structure.

Organisation Structures

It might be useful at this point to enter a warning against any search for "a typical organisation". There is, admittedly, a broad common pattern of organisation to be found in the average British companies. A Board of Directors represents the owners (shareholders) and carries a corporate responsibility for the objectives, the policy and the overall progress of the enterprise. Responsible to the Board is a chief executive (the Managing Director or General Manager) called on to translate policy into instructions for executive action, to initiate the whole process of management, and to answer to the Board for its effective operation throughout the enterprise. This responsibility is discharged by the processes of delegation, and is reported back to the Board through the medium of accounts, reports and statistics. Below the Managing Director come the hierarchy of senior, intermediate and junior managers, smaller or greater in number according to the size of the enterprise, and appropriately divided along varying lines according to the tasks to be undertaken, the prevailing needs and other factors. Some managers carry direct responsibility for the immediate operations of the enterprise; others hold appointments of specialist (functional) character. In either case the executives are sharing part of the total responsibility for the planning and regulation of the activities of the enterprise according to the particular division of function allotted to them. To enable these executives or managers to carry out their responsibilities effectively, they are assisted at the working level by "supervisors" whose responsibilities are less, if at all, concerned with planning, but mainly centre on the oversight of operations to ensure that plans are followed or departures from plan promptly reported to the responsible executive.

This rather characteristic general pattern is, however, only in a superficial sense "typical". The outward similarity of responsibilities at each major management level cloaks the very varied distribution or arrangement of them that will be found within even a small number of seemingly comparable organisations. It may broadly be said that there is no *general* pattern for the distribution of executive responsibilities: there would appear to be certain basic maxims of organisation structure commonly applicable, but with considerable differences in actual application. Paramount among these is the principle of the unity of management. Whatever the character, size or aims of an enterprise, the organisation structure represents from top to bottom the framework of a single process. Starting in "direction" and moving right down to the immediate supervision of the routine activities of making, distributing or recording, the whole scheme of management responsibilities is an integrated pattern, designed to carry out effectively the planning and regulation of these activities and to ensure that a given purpose is fulfilled at the optimum level of operating efficiency and cost. (An attempt to determine certain maxims or principles for the guidance of managers in this direction is considered in the following section.)

The fallacy of referring to a "typical" organisation is often paralleled in the error that there are "types" of organisation, the three most commonly referred to being labelled: (i) the line or military type; (ii) the line and staff; (iii) the functional. In the first, all responsibility is direct from subordinate to senior, and conversely; there are no specialist positions bringing to bear a subsidiary responsibility cutting crosswise into the up-and-down pattern. The second is described as a mixture of direct executive responsibilities with the specialist ancillary services, and is illustrated from widespread experience of everyday practice: the factory which has an executive in charge of production or manufacturing paralleled by a specialist (functional) personnel officer providing direct to the factory the numerous customary services. The third type is sometimes illustrated in the textbooks in chart form as a pattern of diagonal lines without up-and-down lines below the top level; its significance is said to be that each specialised activity has its own lines of responsibility for application reaching directly and specifically to the point of application. This is a conception difficult to understand in theory, and hardly capable of illustration from industrial practice; one may legitimately question whether, in the form in which it has been expounded, it has any validity at all.

From the descriptions of the practice of management that make up the later parts of this volume, it will be seen that, except in the very small enterprises, some form of specialist activity is nearly always present. This means that the pure (so-called) "line" type is seldom found, while the "line and staff" pattern, in simple or complex form, tends to be the commonplace one. The notion of "types" of organisation is thus one that serves little useful purpose, and from analytical consideration may be definitely written off as a somewhat pointless conception that has been allowed to go unchallenged. This is one of the situations referred to earlier in which difficulties can arise from inexactitude and consequential confusion in terminology. In a number of quarters the term "functional" is now commonly used as a descriptive of an organisation with exactly the same meaning as "line and staff"; and the phrase "a normal functional pattern" is becoming increasingly widespread as an alternative reference to the notion comprised in the "line and staff" structure.

The primary purpose of organisation structure is to afford an effective framework for the delegation of management responsibilities, and for the continuing co-ordination of such responsibilities though delegated. Note that the structure is only a *framework*; effective delegation and co-ordination are also determined by the attitudes of the holders of the delegation, and are assisted by the techniques which constitute the "tools" of management action. To be effective, delegation must ensure a genuine and specific transfer of responsibility for decision, i.e. of authority. This indeed is the significance of the "definition" of responsibilities and relationships by which the structure is constituted. *What* should be delegated and *to what extent* are the matters that have to be deliberated and determined specifically in each case concerned: that is what is meant by saying that a pattern of organisation needs to be "tailor-made", and hence that the search for a "typical structure" is vain. In broad outline, the substance delegated in the case of certain positions may well be similar from one enterprise to another; for example, the main responsibilities of a Factory Manager, or of a Personnel Officer, or of a Chief Accountant, may well be similar in a number of concerns.

This is, however, different from suggesting that a model definition of responsibilities should be drawn up for any of these positions. To determine the substance, extent and patterns of specific delegations is a matter of deliberation and judgment—an exercise in the "planning element" of the process of management, having regard to the facts of the situation concerned. One attempt has been made to arrive at an analytical principle to explain delegation, based on the economic theory of comparative costs.[1] A manager delegates responsibilities on the basis of reserving to himself those that he can perform *relatively* more effectively than the person(s) to whom he could delegate them. It is *not* on the basis that he himself can discharge these responsibilities better than the person(s) to whom he delegates, whereas he would discharge less well those that he delegates: he might in fact be able to discharge *both* kinds better or less well. The significant criterion (on the basis of the economic principle of comparative costs) is that, by delegating the particular responsibilities, he is able to reserve to himself and to perform adequately those that have the greater influence on effectiveness when retained in his own jurisdiction. Such an explanation is analytically sound, and can be found of practical value to a manager deciding what responsibilities to retain, and thus which others he is fully able to delegate.

The correct definition of responsibilities, as the medium of delegation, should ensure that there is effective transmission of authority adequately and commonly understood by all concerned. The pattern of delegation must mean that authority for decision, and responsibility for the outcome of the decision, is clearly made known and transmitted. Tools of management information assist the delegation: for example, an approved budget of expenditure correlates with the extent of decision delegated to the executive concerned, and the absence of variances in his actual results show the outcome of his application of the delegation. Authority to decide is thus seen effective in appropriate extent at various levels and in various sections of the organisation, for it clearly cannot belong only at the top. Continuous review of the performance and progress of operations, and of their cost, feeds back to the managers the facts upon which to exercise their judgment as the basis of ensuing decision—decision to keep things going as they are, or to make changes in plans or in the mode of their application. Delegation of authority, and of responsibility, supported by sound data for guidance, gives all levels of management the effective framework for co-ordinated executive decision and thus for effective performance.

[1] See Professor Sir Arnold Plant's paper on "Centralise or Decentralise?" in the collected volume of essays published under the title *Some Modern Business Problems* (Longmans, Green & Co., London, 1937).

Relationships in Organisation

In formulating an organisation structure, it has been indicated that "relationships" as well as responsibilities need to be defined; the explanatory label "formal" is usually added to mean that it is those relationships that are in fact enshrined with the pattern of responsibilities laid down. Other relationships also arise, namely, "informal" ones, which are the good (or bad!) personal working relations generated among the holders of the various positions. Both kinds are important for the effective practice of management—but the latter, the informal personal relations—are *not* a question of organisation structure. They are a reflection of personal attitudes and a matter of "management action" relevant to a later section of this study.

The formal relationships are those that the chief executive or the Board of Directors intend to see occurring as part of their design for the effective working of the organisation pattern. These are, therefore, enshrined in the definitions of responsibilities when correctly drawn up, and they fall into three broad categories, which can be conveniently described respectively as "direct", "lateral", "functional":

(1) *Direct (Executive) Relations.*—The relationship existing between a senior and his subordinates, and conversely. The senior may be a Managing Director or any other manager, and his subordinates the junior managers, supervisors and other grades down to the operative levels. The relations involved here are those of instruction on the senior's part and compliance by the subordinates. (This is not, of course, to suggest an authoritarian approach, as obviously the element of motivation requires a proper human flavour to the instructions and appropriate consultation with subordinates.) In principle, the relationship is that of "direct authority", in the customary sense in which a senior may give valid orders to subordinates within his jurisdiction: these relations are customarily described as "direct", and are readily illustrated from the position of a factory manager, chief accountant, supervisor and many other managerial or supervisory positions in industrial organisations *vis-à-vis* their immediate subordinates.

In the schedule of responsibilities, these *direct* relationships will be showing in two ways:

(*a*) at the head of any schedule there will occur the caption "responsible to", with indication of the superior position to which this one reports as a direct subordinate under authority;

(*b*) at the end of the schedule there will (may) be shown the subordinates (whether lower managers, supervisors, or rank and file) over whom this position has executive authority (command).

Some writings have in the past described these direct relationships as "line relations", borrowing an analogy from the notion of "line and staff" used to describe management activities themselves. This is an erroneous usage in terms of its origin in naval and military parlance: the term "line" specifically signifies *activities*, and by analogy it could be transferred to *responsibilities*; but not to the relations arising therefrom. In the context "line and staff", both terms refer to activities or responsibilities, or to the persons performing them.

(2) *Lateral Relations.*—The working relations between executives or supervisors at the same level of responsibility and holding parallel authority. In the exercise of management, two managers may both be responsible to a common senior for different sections of the activities of the enterprise; or they may be responsible to different seniors. The effective working of management calls for collaboration between them on points of mutual interest, without reference back to the common senior or to the respective seniors: the executive relationship thus set up between the two managers is described as "lateral" and it can be variously shown in the definitions of responsibilities, according to the pattern determined. For example, *it may be required* that one manager has to *consult* with another on a given matter *before* he takes a decision on this matter, even though the decision is one lying clearly to his jurisdiction; the definition would then begin with the wording "In consultation with . . . . ., responsible for determining and deciding . . . . .". Lateral relationships also exist in a more general sense—in the sense that every manager has an inherent responsibility for serving the enterprise as a whole as well as looking after his own part or section; and thus he has an obligation to display a co-operative attitude towards all colleagues. In this sense, formal lateral relations merge into the informal relations mentioned above.

(3) *Functional Relations.*—Those which arise in the case of a specialist position contributing a service to the managers and supervisors who compose the executive members of the organisation. The position and the service given arise primarily from specialised knowledge, i.e. within a certain field a body of knowledge and experience which is germane to the working and effectiveness of management in the organisation as a whole. (This notion was referred to above in connection with comments on confusions in terminology: see page 29.) Usually, it is only in the larger enterprises that such specialist services can be separated out into distinct positions, though the services themselves will arise in organisations of any size. The specialist (or "functional") officer has a responsibility for ensuring that the particular activities allocated to his jurisdiction are carried into effect throughout the organisation at a high level of effectiveness, a responsibility which has three aspects: the first is to assist in the formulation of the relevant sectional policy; the second is to advise his "line" colleagues and

subordinate members of the organisation on the working of management in that particular regard; the third is to be answerable to his immediate senior, usually the Managing Director, for the effective conduct of the particular specialised activities concerned, i.e. he is responsible for assisting the other managers and supervisors in carrying out those activities and for ensuring that their "line" instructions conform to the relevant specialist policy.

If a "functional" officer has subordinates or staff of his own, his relations with these persons are obviously of the "direct" type already described; similarly, his own relations with his immediate superior have the same character. But relations with other executives, supervisors and members of the organisation are of an indirect category, and are customarily labelled "functional". Illustrations can be drawn from the Personnel Manager or Officer responsible for ensuring that personnel policy is carried out by appropriate procedures and by an adequate standard of human relations at all levels of management and supervision; or from a Clerical Methods Manager, responsible for sanctioning routines and procedures, the design of forms, the purchase and the use of office equipment, etc., throughout the organisation.

Whereas these three categories of relationship arise widely and frequently in most organisations, a fourth kind is sometimes encountered which it will be pertinent to record here, namely:

(4) *Staff Relations.*—A distinct relationship arising from the appointment of a (personal) assistant to an executive. The arrangement is not often found in industry, and occurs mainly in the top levels of the organisation, e.g. a Personal Assistant to the Managing Director. His terms of reference may be of general or specific character, but the nature of responsibility is clearly defined as assisting the executive to whom he is allocated. The Personal Assistant is, strictly speaking, not an executive at all, and certainly of his own right carries no authority; he is best regarded as an extension of the personality of the executive he serves, either for general or for specific purposes according to the terms of reference. In such a capacity he clearly discharges his chief's responsibilities and equally clearly dispenses his authority; of himself he has no subordinates (except perhaps a secretary) and issues no instructions. Whatever he does within that organisation, he does on behalf of and with the authority of his chief. In consequence, it is only with his chief that he has any formal relations, and for these the label "staff relations" is used. No label can be applied to his relations with other parts of the organisation because *of himself he has none*; his activities and his daily contacts with the managers are part of the working of management within the organisation, but the character of his responsibility is such that he can have *no formal relations*, direct or functional, with other members of the organisation, apart from his chief.

P.P.M.—3*

Of these four types of relationships within an organisation the first and second are most frequently met. The "direct" contact of senior and subordinate arises in even the smallest working unit of a man and a boy, or a plumber and his mate, or the village shopkeeper and her girl. The "lateral" relationship can only emerge when there is more than one member in any one grade, for instance, two partners, both operating as principals, or two supervisors responsible to a Works Manager, each in charge of a separate department or section of the factory. The alternate Day Shift and Night Shift Managers of a department are related laterally—and many other illustrations can readily be quoted. "Functional" relationships develop as the unit begins to grow to larger size, though no numerical test can be laid down. Sometimes, the need for specialist service emerges early in growth, as is most commonly seen in regard to accounting and secretarial activities: even when still of quite small size, a manufacturing enterprise may need to engage specialist accountancy assistance, perhaps on a part-time basis in the person of a professional Secretary. The human problems of management are another field that often give rise to the need for expert assistance early in the growth of an enterprise, and the functional position of Personnel Officer is frequently brought into existence among the first of the specialist appointments below the Managing Director.

These groups of relationships give a meaning to an organisation chart and follow the layout of the chart. Direct relations are the verticals; lateral relations are the horizontals. Functional relations are customarily shown in dotted or broken form for distinction, and portrayed as diagonals from the specialist executive concerned directly to all other major points of relevant contact. In strict principle, however, they should be shown parallel to the horizontal and vertical lines. The distinction is illustrated in Plate 1: the dual portrayal there brings out the important point that, while in everyday practice a functional specialist will deal with subordinates of other executives on matters within his jurisdiction, in principle he is doing so with the concurrence of the immediate superior of such subordinates. In practice, this means that the functional specialist should keep that superior fully informed of instructions or decisions given to his subordinates.

Specialist (Functional) Responsibilities

In regard to his colleagues on the same executive level as himself, a specialist's functional *relations* are identical with lateral relations, but his *responsibility* is different. The particular features of a functional responsibility are:

(a) it originates in expert knowledge of a given field, and exists in order to provide specialist service to the "line" (operational) managers and supervisors;

(b) the functional specialist is always to be consulted before any decision is taken pertinent to his jurisdiction;

(c) he must ensure the attainment of the relevant sectional policy throughout those parts of the organisation where his jurisdiction extends;

(d) his decisions, rulings or instructions within the given field, and within the agreed policy, must be followed by the managers and supervisors, and cannot be gainsaid, overruled, or set aside except by his immediate senior executive;

(e) his responsibilities are mainly discharged by *other* executives and supervisors, and his "instructions" therefore pass through the direct and lateral channels of the organisation.

With the increasing attention given in recent years to practical consideration and discussion of organisation structure, it is perhaps unfortunate that the notion of "functional or specialist responsibilities and relationships" should have given rise to so much difficulty. As the foregoing comments indicate, the notion itself is simple and straightforward: it posits no more than that certain items in the process of management have been singled out for expert attention on the basis of an advisory and ancillary service to the managers who are carrying the main burden of executive operational responsibility. While some of the difficulties in practice have arisen because of lack of understanding of the notion or principle involved, by far the majority have arisen from three other sources:

(i) absence of definition of the responsibilities respectively allocated and therefore of the relationships required;

(ii) failure to honour the natural requirement of co-operative attitude;

(iii) unfortunate personal pre-occupation with (comparative) status, power or ambition.

No organisation approach can deal with the two last items, and the first has been adequately covered in these pages. Some difficulty in practice may perchance have come from confusions in terminology, as well as failure to understand, and it may be worth while to pursue these aspects a little further because of the widespread significance of the functional patterns in everyday management.

In all the difficulties and problems that arise in this context, the crux issue is always a variant of the one question—"Who has the authority to make the decisions and to issue the instructions embodying those decisions?" The parties to the difficulties are respectively the functional specialist(s) concerned and the executive manager(s) who use or apply those specialist activities. The question is thus translated into personal terms as: Does the specialist decide what is to be done and tell the executive to do it? Or does he *advise* the executive, leaving the latter free to decide for himself whether to accept that advice or not? In fact, of course, these two questions are not a correct antithesis; nor do they correctly express the true situation. They do, it is true, pose in a common and succinct form the almost perennial problem of "the line *versus* the staff", but this very succinctness is the cause of the persisting trouble. More explicit posing of the true factors involved, representing clearer understanding of the nature and significance of the "functional responsibilities" as an item in the overall process of management, would remove the problem by dint of mutual acceptance of a commonly shared role.

Functional responsibilities (the "staff") arise in specialisation of knowledge or services, as was explained above. So it falls naturally to the specialist concerned to determine the ways in which his part of the management process ought to be made effective in practice— what methods, procedures, operating instructions, and so on. Yet he is *not* the manager, and all his specialist services will be made effective within the jurisdiction of one or more executive managers; his services are in fact *their* tools, part of *their* exercise of manage-

---

The chart illustrates five functional relationships; in the organisation depicted there will, of course, be very many more.

The broken lines (– – –) show functional contacts between the Personnel Assistant and—

(1) The three Foremen of Component Manufacturing Sections (perhaps in regard to progress of apprentices or absence of some operatives);
(2) The Supervisor of the Accounts Department (perhaps in regard to recruitment of a new junior or a problem regarding one of the staff).

The dash-dot lines (–·–·–) show functional contacts between the Clerical Methods Manager and—

(3) The three Foremen of the Assembly Departments (perhaps in regard to Work Tickets or Stores Notes);
(4) The Supervisor of the Personnel Department Office (say, in regard to Record Cards);
(5) The Supervisor of the Sales Office (perhaps in regard to customer records or addressing of letters).

The two sets of broken and dash-dot lines show the functional relationships:

(a) Parallel to the horizontal and vertical relations, they represent the *formal* pattern of contact, i.e. the path along which *in principle* the contact flows;
(b) Diagonally they represent the *customary* direct contact between the parties concerned, though involving the functional specialist in a responsibility to keep the senior managers informed of the decisions or instructions given to their subordinates.

N.B. (i) The varying levels portrayed in this chart are for convenience of printing and not to be read as indicating status.
(ii) The omission of responsibility for "Buying" in the organisation illustrated is commented on in the text (see page 60).

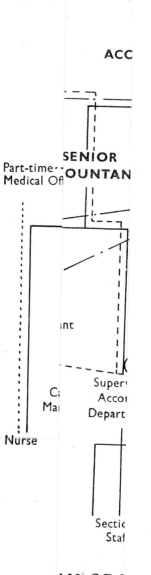

ACC

SENIOR

Part-time
Medical Of **OUNTAN**

int

Superv
Accou
Ca   Depart
Ma

Nurse

Sectio
Staf

AN ORC

ment responsibility. *Thus it is reasonable that these managers should be consulted before any such services or activities are applied among the people and operations under their jurisdiction.* This does not gainsay the specialist's expert knowledge, but it preserves the attitude of mutual co-operation; it enables the managers to develop and express confidence in the specialist, because there is explanation and consultation, followed by understanding and acceptance. If there should be genuine disagreement that cannot be resolved, the specialist is the expert authority, and he has no alternative but to report to the (common) superior for a decision binding to both parties.

All this, of course, is an exercise in good human relations, not in organisation structure.

In the case of the larger and very large enterprises or establishments, a particular difficulty emerges as a by-product of the size itself, because the functional specialist activities are carried out by members of "departments" often employing considerable numbers of personnel under the jurisdiction of a "head of department", who is the chief functional officer of the specialist activity concerned. This pattern, and the scale of the activity within the department, tends to mask the service or ancillary role which is the essential characteristic of the functional specialisation. The head of department himself can more easily appreciate this aspect of his position, in so far as much of his time and energy is devoted to advice and guidance given to his colleagues, the executive managers in the various operating departments—factories, sales offices, depots, etc. It must rest with him to ensure that his subordinates (the personnel within his department) also retain the correct appreciation of their role and character. This is particularly true in the case of those activities where the "work" of the department has, superficially, all the appearance of being a self-contained activity. A good example is the accounting and costing department: the daily routine tasks have all the appearance of a self-standing operation, which builds up to a pattern of financial information belonging to the Chief Accountant or Financial Controller, and used by him to "control" expenditure at top management or Board level. If the department is large, the senior accountants in charge can easily see themselves as "executives", responsible for the "management of routine operations". And so, of course, in that perspective they are; but for the department as such and, by implication, for all the members of it, the correct perspective is better seen in relation to the management process of the enterprise as a whole. In that context, their activity is directed solely to providing the data and instruments of the "control" element exercised by the various supervisors, department heads and managers—including those at the highest level linking with the Board of Directors. Thus, for example, cost data is the tool of control for the supervisors and managers of the manufacturing departments; sales statistics and turnover revenue data are the tools of control of the sales managers and supervisors; and so on. At the level of the Managing Director, the data is an overall control in the form of the periodic financial statements comparing the actual position with the budget forecasts. That the accounts and finance departments have large numbers of accountants and clerks does indeed involve various patterns of internal management in conducting their activities correctly and effectively, but *it does not alter the essentially functional role and relationship of these activities in the pattern of management conducted within the organisation overall.*

To round off these reflections on the functional principle in action, it may be useful to revert again to the problem of terminology, to the notion of "line and staff" commonly used as the alternative title for the combination of executive management and functional specialisation which has become the commonplace of most industrial and commercial organisations. It is the "staff" item in this label from which the terminology confusion stems, largely because this one word has now come to be used with two different connotations, which may not always be explicit from their context. The two usages are mostly found embedded in the one descriptive title "staff officer":

(*a*) In the sense explained above (page 51), this position would refer to an "assistant" accredited to a given executive of one kind or another, and authorised to take a range of decisions on his behalf. How far this authority extends is a matter of choice for the executive concerned, and one may assume that this has been (as it should be) clearly determined and indicated. In the common practice of industry, this position is largely exemplified by the so-called "Personal Assistant" with very limited scope of decision; but this is by no means inherent in the notion, and cases are not uncommon where a more senior and mature appointment is made, such that a large measure of responsibility and authority is exercised by such a staff officer. Here there is analogy with the "General Staff Officer" widely known and applied in the Armed Services, though the analogy cannot be pressed too far, because the industrial application is as yet relatively immature. Within the scope of the responsibilities carried by the superior, the "staff officer's" jurisdiction is general, a full reflection of his superior's authority (unless for special reasons some items are specifically withheld); his relations with other managers and members of the organisation are, as described above, non-existent, for he is but an extension of his superior and has no responsibilities or relationships in his own right. There is no question of "specialisation" or a functional responsibility arising in the case of the use of the term.

(*b*) In the second usage, the term "staff officer" is but an alternative label for the functional specialist in the sense that has now been fully described—a label clearly reflecting the specialist services supporting the "line" activities or responsibilities. This usage is most commonly encountered in informal discussion situations, rather than as a title, though it can occasionally be met in that way within the larger public corporations, such as the nationalised industries. This second usage is clearly very different in connotation from the former, and an attempt is sometimes made to provide some protection against confusion by describing this second form as "Specialist Staff Officer", in contradistinction to the "General Staff Officer" of the Armed Services.[1]

The Significance of Organisation

Reference was made earlier to the common view that organisation is one of the refinements of management, that the definition of responsibilities is all very well for the bigger and more ambitious enterprises, or those which like doing things with a sense of display. With the practical man, it is argued, there is no call for an organisation structure: he knows what his colleagues are doing, and they all get along quite well together by their mutual knowledge of each other and of the business as a whole. Experience has, unfortunately, proved this rather common view to be utterly erroneous, even in the case of quite small units. Again and again, difficulties in the operations or the management of a factory or a retail stores can be traced to weaknesses in organisation—either faults in the allocation of responsibilities and the determination of their relations or, more usually, to the absence of any real pattern of known responsibilities. Inevitably in such circumstances there occur overlapping, duplication of effort, and misunderstandings, and many important things are omitted because no one seems to be responsible for them.

Such casualness in regard to organisation springs from failure to appreciate its position as the framework of management: without a known and sound framework management cannot be effective. Organisation is closely related to policy, to planning, to control, to co-ordination and even to motivation. In the first place, as has already been said, the responsibilities that make up an organisation structure cannot be determined until policy is known, at least in outline. For the policy indicates what is going to be done, and in broad terms how: this alone makes it possible to draw up the proper framework for the necessary operations to achieve that policy. Con-

---

[1] To make this exposition complete, it needs also to be added that yet a third appearance of "Staff Officer" is very occasionally encountered; as a title within technical establishments (for example Research Laboratories), where it is used to designate the personnel officer concerned to provide the normal personnel management services for the technical staffs.

versely, of course, the existence of a stable and clear structure makes the dissemination and interpretation of policy easier, and enables its fulfilment to be more readily checked. The known distribution of responsibilities provides a foundation for more detailed planning of operations, methods, lines of working, equipment, routines and the like. Obviously it contributes enormously to co-ordination: the mere knowledge of who is doing what, and how the various responsibilities are interrelated, is in large measure a guarantee of co-ordination in the working of management. There is also a relevance to morale: much of the frustration that characterises so many of the executives and supervisors in Britain's industrial system springs from irritations due to lack of knowledge of their own and their colleagues' jurisdiction, from unfortunate experiences of wasted duplicated effort, or from a sense of despair due to lack of clarity as to limitations imposed on the exercise of responsibilities. The clear definition of responsibilities and relations contributes to better understanding which is reflected in a greater measure of self-responsibility, of co-operation, of will-to-work, of effectiveness in daily action, and so of productivity. This is not to argue that organisation structure alone can achieve efficiency; that could not be so, because it is only one aspect of the process of management. But it is in a special sense a fundamental aspect, because it is the framework without which the process cannot be carried out.

The main practical task in forming an organisation structure lies in this definition of responsibilities and the consequent inter-relationships—not on the basis of any standard form or pattern, but specifically designed to reflect the objectives, policy and intentions of "top management" and to co-ordinate with the procedures of planning and control that are being used. The design must seek to provide effective delegation of authority-plus-responsibility and so to create the framework for the full and effective exercise of the management initiative of the persons appointed to the positions— while preserving their overall co-ordination in common practice and purpose. This is not the context in which to pursue the detail of definition further: some brief illustrations are given in Appendix II following, but they can do little more than indicate the practical simplicity of defining responsibilities, once it is known what pattern is required.[1]

The point can be illustrated by reference to the chart in Plate 1 (facing page 54): the purpose of that chart is to illustrate certain

---

[1] This aspect forms the main subject-matter of the specialist publication referred to above under the title *Organisation—the Framework of Management*. See especially Chapters VI and VII for detailed consideration of the formation of an organisation structure.

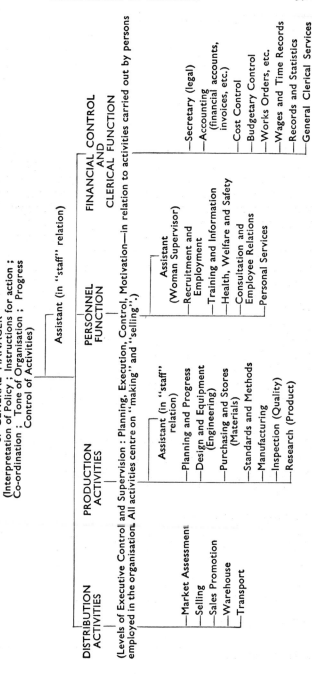

BOARD OF DIRECTORS
(Policy)

MANAGING DIRECTOR
or GENERAL MANAGER
(Interpretation of Policy ; Instructions for action ;
Co-ordination ; Tone of Organisation ; Progress
Control of Activities)

Assistant (in "staff" relation)

| DISTRIBUTION ACTIVITIES | PRODUCTION ACTIVITIES | PERSONNEL FUNCTION | FINANCIAL CONTROL AND CLERICAL FUNCTION |

(Levels of Executive Control and Supervision : Planning, Execution, Control, Motivation—in relation to activities carried out by persons employed in the organisation. All activities centre on "making" and "selling".)

DISTRIBUTION ACTIVITIES
—Market Assessment
—Selling
—Sales Promotion
—Warehouse
—Transport

PRODUCTION ACTIVITIES
—Assistant (in "staff" relation)
—Planning and Progress
—Design and Equipment (Engineering)
—Purchasing and Stores (Materials)
—Standards and Methods
—Manufacturing
—Inspection (Quality)
—Research (Product)

PERSONNEL FUNCTION
—Assistant (Woman Supervisor)
—Recruitment and Employment
—Training and Information
—Health, Welfare and Safety
—Consultation and Employee Relations
—Personal Services

FINANCIAL CONTROL AND CLERICAL FUNCTION
—Secretary (legal)
—Accounting (financial accounts, invoices, etc.)
—Cost Control
—Budgetary Control
—Works Orders, etc.
—Wages and Time Records
—Records and Statistics
—General Clerical Services

FIG. 2.—Chart of Organisation illustrating the Activities of Management.

relationships within the setting of a specific organisation. Like any organisation chart, it can do no more than display somewhat arbitrarily these inter-relationships in a summary form; it tells nothing about the substance of the responsibilities allocated, except what is read into it from one's own interpretations of the titles used, and these could well be widely different for different people with different backgrounds of experience. It will be accepted from common-sense readings of obvious labels that this chart relates to an engineering concern of some kind, probably manufacturing a range of light assemblies, and of medium-size in employment and turnover. It has many features which readers could—from their own personal standpoint of judgment—regard as "odd", and they might be tempted to condemn these as "wrong". There could, however, be no *justification for such condemnation based on the chart alone.* One special feature to mention is that the chart shows no Buyer or Purchasing Officer, though clearly someone must be responsible for this activity. All sorts of surmises are possible: perhaps the General Manager sees personally to purchasing as one of his own special responsibilities; or perhaps the Production Manager carries it; or perhaps the Planning Superintendent; cases have been known where this responsibility lies with the Chief Accountant. Suppose a position of Buyer is to be created, where should it figure on the chart? To whom should he be made responsible? There are persons to whom buying appeals as an activity of considerable commercial significance and who would without further reflection make the Buyer responsible to the General Manager, or perhaps even insist that he ought himself to be one of the directors. Much argument has been joined on this issue, but the problem need not be further pursued here: the one conclusion about which any definite stand can be taken is that *this illustrative chart affords absolutely no criteria at all for deciding where the position of Buyer should be inserted. That decision can be taken only after full consideration of relevant facts and circumstances, which a chart cannot possibly show.*[1]

The Personality Problem

A major problem that comes up in any consideration of forming an organisation structure is the question of "personalities". There has long been a controversy of "personalities *versus* organisation", a conflict of view as to whether an organisation should be formulated according to an analytical review of policies, facts, procedures, etc.,

---

[1] The responsibilities and activities of the Buyer are further dealt with in Chapter V of Part Two following (see pages 405–407). There is also a relevant comment in *Organisation—The Framework of Management*: see page 139 in Chapter VII.

without any reference to personalities, or whether the grouping of responsibilities should be built around the available personalities. The controversy is easily resolved, by the answer that neither argument is entirely true. In smaller units it is often inevitable that the distribution of responsibilities should conform to certain personality requirements, while in the larger unit, experience suggests that it is safer for the structure to be built up independently of persons. In neither case can it be safely said either that principle should be disregarded or that the personal element should be entirely neglected. The wise line of procedure would seem to involve treating organisation as a technical issue and adopting the following steps:

(1) Work from the known objective and policy of the enterprise.

(2) Define the responsibilities needed to secure fulfilment of the policy, and determine their appropriate groupings and relationships.

(3) Determine from these definitions specifications of the qualities, qualifications and experience required to discharge the responsibilities effectively, i.e. prepare specifications for the various executive, supervisory and specialist appointments.

(4) Select the persons to be appointed to the responsibilities in accordance with the specification; or, if it is decided to appoint someone not exactly conforming, set down the known objective reasons for the departure from the specification.

(5) Set the structure (responsibilities and relationships) to work according to the definitions, but if it is decided that certain departures should be countenanced, the known objective reasons for such departure should be set down; in every instance of departure it should be clear that basic principles are not being contravened.

(6) The test as to the soundness or otherwise of such departure will lie in whether or not harmonious and balanced working of management is attained throughout the organisation, so that management is in fact ensuring true efficiency of operations and a high level of morale in the working teams.

One special aspect of the personal factor in organisation structure is that of the span of responsibility or supervision of a manager over subordinate managers or supervisors. The point arises with most significance where the activities of the subordinate sections are interrelated in their current working. A widely accepted notion is that the number of such subordinates should be "limited to five or six", as though there were virtues in either figure. This notion originated from a Rumanian Management Consultant working in Paris in the early 1930s; he calculated the combinations of reciprocal interrelationships that must arise in the course of contacts between a superior and increasing numbers of subordinates. With five subordinates, the total of relationships ("direct and cross" as he called them) is 100; with six, the total increases to 222, and with seven to

490. This last figure he regarded as beyond the range of expected competence of the average individual executive. There is undoubtedly substance in the argument, and a clear conclusion can be derived that a definite limit is to be imposed on the span of responsibility (or "span of control" as it is popularly, but rather loosely, called). Personal make-up and the specific character of the responsibilities covered and circumstances concerned must, however, be taken into account. Some men, in certain circumstances, might easily be overburdened with only four subordinates, whereas here and there an individual may well be able to carry eight or nine persons reporting to him. This again is a matter on which considerable thought is to be exercised before a decision is taken, and a sound management appraisal will always counsel choosing the lower number of subordinates, at the executive or supervisory levels, rather than the higher one, if there should be any uncertainty in the decision.

Decentralisation

No commentary on aspects of organisation structure, however brief, can be complete without some reference to the problem of "centralisation v. decentralisation". Strictly speaking, this is not so much a "problem" as a notion around which a great deal of confusion and controversy has developed, much of it stemming from lack of precision in thought or in discussion. To review what is involved in this issue would virtually entail a recapitulation of all that has been said in foregoing pages, both about the process of management itself and about the purposes and means of delegating the responsibility that the process contains. For what can "decentralisation" mean other than a general or specific delegation of management responsibility? It is, in fact, confusion over words that mostly lies at the root of the controversy about the notion—confusion not only over the real significance of the term "decentralisation", but also over the nature of "operational" and "functional" responsibilities, with both of which it has to be associated. Without going deeply into the controversy, it may be useful to record here some observations to help in clarifying the subject. To begin with, a statement of what the terms can be held specifically to signify:

(a) "Decentralisation"—is best held to mean a state or pattern of organisation in which specific responsibilities have been "delegated": the implication of this is that "delegation" is the process and "decentralisation" the resultant embodiment of it.

(b) "Centralisation"—can only mean reserving responsibilities to given units or sections of a central headquarters, but such units not necessarily of themselves carrying top management authority.

It has been indicated above that the delegation or subdivision of management responsibility can be made on either of two bases:

(i) the whole of the process of command can be subdivided into the smaller self-contained units; or

(ii) the process of command can be subdivided in such a way that there is concentration of specialist responsibilities established to serve the units of direct command.

Naturally, the decentralised pattern reflects whichever basis has been used, the second being the one that gives rise to the combined pattern of "operational" and "functional" responsibilities. The distinction between these two in nature (already adequately stressed earlier) is the key to avoiding confusion in discussions of "centralisation v. decentralisation". Delegation of the "operational" responsibilities involves the decentralisation of the process of command itself; the managers of the decentralised sections are thus the users of the services provided by the specialist or functional sections. These latter are by their very nature *ancillary* to the operational sections—not implying any lesser importance, but specifically in character promoting the purposes of command, without in fact assuming any of that process of command *per se*. Management can be effective when decentralised only when full provision is made for the integration of the delegated responsibilities of both categories. Neglect in this respect is the cause of most of the difficulties of "decentralisation". In fact, one could go so far as to say that in the large-scale organisations there is often a deficiency in principle, because it is believed—erroneously—that the subdivided units of functional or specialist responsibility exist and function in their own right.

Turning now to the second term in the pair, taken literally "centralisation" would mean that *all* management decision is reserved to the one point of command: in this sense, it is not encountered in practice outside the one-man business. In a more common form, "centralisation" may be taken to mean that *responsibility for major management decision* is reserved to a group of (senior) executives at the headquarters. Once again, with an organisation of any size, this situation is unlikely to be met in practical existence to any large extent—some powers of major decision must lie at lower levels if the enterprise is not to be brought fairly soon to a standstill.[1] In common

---

[1] A case from personal experience was a trading business with a turnover of £1½ million, employing about 200 people, in which a single Managing Director decided pretty well everything. Something like 30 people from various levels went to him for decisions, and it was not uncommon for members of staff to be in the warehouses or offices still at 7 or 8 o'clock at night hoping to get in to see "the boss" for a decision on a relatively trivial matter. To draw the organisation chart of this business was well nigh impossible.

practice today, "centralisation" is understood to imply that major decision is reserved to (senior) executives at headquarters, and that, within a limited range (often not clearly specified or even known by the individuals concerned), day-to-day action is left for decision at the lower levels. Sometimes the term refers to the reservation of decision within functional or specialist responsibilities to headquarters departments: thus, for instance, in a manufacturing and trading concern, it may be arranged that all the accounting, cost accounting, and other control techniques are put into effect by a single system through all departments, with a Chief Accountant or Financial Controller responsible for the design and application of the system throughout. From the argument of foregoing pages it will be clear that such an arrangement is *not* correctly described as "centralisation"—unless responsibility for all *decisions* in respect of matters where financial and accounting aspects are pertinent is also reserved to this Financial Controller.

This whole discussion may be much assisted by recognising that "centralisation" and "decentralisation" are not clear-cut alternative states existing in ready-made form and applicable here or there, very much like taking one or other of alternative patent medicines. They go deeply into the process of management itself, and establishing the balance between them is part of the essential analytical task to be performed in determining an organisation structure. If there is any generalisation possible, it can be no more than advocating "centralisation" to be applied in regard to policy and procedures to ensure uniformity and balance of management action, whereas "decentralisation" should be the principle for management responsibility in executive action. Even this wide generalisation might well be found open to question.

As is so frequently the case with aspects of management practice, understanding and sound action can be attained readily if there is clarity of thought in terms of the underlying analytical principle, and nowhere is this more true than in the juxtaposition of "centralisation *v.* decentralisation".

8. PRINCIPLES OF MANAGEMENT

At many points in this Introduction, reference has been made to the absence of accepted authoritative principles of management. This has undoubtedly been one of the factors contributing to the persistence of weaknesses in industrial and commercial practice, chiefly because it has hampered the systematic study of the subject on a professional or systematic basis. It may at first sight seem strange, since management has been carried on so widely and for so long, that no common fundamentals should have been agreed. Four factors have contributed to this:

(a) Managers have been too exclusively concerned with practical problems, with much of their attention attracted to the technical or commercial factors rather than to the managerial; accordingly, they tend to be more concerned with detailed issues than with the principles that underlie such practice.

(b) There is a long-standing tradition that management is a special aptitude, which is to be found inborn in some individuals and missing from others. Industrial developments in more recent times have proved this view to be fallacious, but its persistence has hindered recognition of the underlying fundamental principles, common to management wherever it occurs and whoever is responsible for it.

(c) In most industrial countries, and particularly in Great Britain, economic progress was made mainly on technological foundations; that is to say, the improvement of machines and equipment, the development of better methods of transport, the improvement of materials, and so on; it is only in comparatively recent times that management has been identified as contributing specifically to industrial and commercial progress.

(d) The few writers or thinkers who have been attracted to the fundamental aspects of management, with a view to elucidating basic principles, have shown a marked tendency to approach their analytical task on a purely individual basis; they have not normally taken as their own starting-point the body of knowledge already existing as the result of contributions from earlier writers. In consequence, their writings have tended to conflict, or to lead to confusions, instead of building up a cumulative "knowledge" of management.

The possibility of defining principles of management has been the subject of a good deal of writing and discussion in past decades, in both Britain and the United States. In part this has come from increasing awareness of the extent to which observed weaknesses in management have common characteristics. It has also been fostered by the professional Management Consultants, whose whole activity is the diagnosis and remedy of management deficiencies. A number of the more expert professional Consultants have contributed to knowledge of the "laws" of management, and their efforts have been assisted by such professional bodies as the British Institute of Management, the Institute of Office Management, the Institution of Works Managers, and the corresponding societies in the United States.[1]

[1] Brief notes on the contributions from earlier writers on the subject are set out in Appendix I. A study of contemporary thought is to be found in the papers referred to earlier in the *British Management Review*, Vol. VII, No. 3.

Among the various suggestions put forward, there have been some that cannot rightly be called "principles" at all: they are rather methods for the better practice of management. A principle means a fundamental truth as the basis of reasoning, a primary element, a general law. It is commonly understood in this sense in the world of science or any other field of systematic knowledge: it must carry the same meaning in regard to management—the fundamental "principles" must mean the basic laws on which the practice of management is to be built up. They must necessarily be couched in general terms, because they have to be applicable within organisations of varying size and character. Moreover, they must be so formulated as *not* to include suggestions for *specific methods* by which they are to be implemented. The term "method" points always to a way in which principles are carried into effect: thus, any given *principle* of management *could* be carried into effect in different organisations by different methods. The value of principles of management in this fundamental sense lies in the foundation that they provide for its effective conduct, by marking out the essential features that must characterise the practice of management, irrespective of where it is occurring.

Principles of management could be deduced by *a priori* reasoning from the nature of the process of management itself, but a greater degree of acceptance is likely to be accorded to a body of principles drawn from practice, say, from a comparative study of observed strengths and weaknesses. This would necessitate a volume of first-hand research that has not so far been contemplated in this field.

A full set of principles must relate to the total process of management in action, and so to the essential elements which constitute it, i.e. the elements of planning and control, co-ordination and motivation. It has been noted above that one of the special aspects of planning is the determination of the responsibilities and relations that comprise the framework of management in action, i.e. the organisation structure; because of its particular importance in the working of management, separate "principles of organisation" should be identified. The following set of principles covering all these elements is put forward as an addition to existing knowledge: they have been deduced from analytical study of the practical working of management and checked by observation of strengths and deficiencies. They have also taken into account contributions from earlier writers on the subject, and are based on the definition and analysis set out in the foregoing sections.[1]

[1] A first approach to "principles of management" presented in a similar form is to be found in a paper published by the author in *British Management Review*, Vol. VII, No. 1.

A. Principles of Management (General)

1. In economic affairs, the primary purpose of the enterprise, and so of management's responsibility, is the provision of goods and services in accordance with the requirements of the consumer.

   N.B.—(i) This does not imply that the consumer requirements are to be the *sole* determinant of economic activity, without reference to other factors, such as the technical needs of production or design.

   (ii) In many enterprises the product handled is such as to contribute only indirectly to consumer needs: the ultimate purpose is still as stated, though one or more stages removed.

2. An essentially inter-related primary objective, inherent in the setting in the economic system, is the contribution to an overall effective level of employment at standards of earnings consistent with the socially accepted norms of "fair wages".

3. The interpretation of the purpose of an enterprise or organisation lies in the formulation of its policy. Sound policy, in relation both to overall purpose and to the activities of the various divisions or sections of the organisation, is the foundation of effective management.

4. The formulation of policy is the responsibility of the highest level of management; for instance, in a Limited Company, the responsibility of the Board of Directors acting on behalf of the owners (shareholders).

5. The formulation of policy, and the exercise of all aspects of management directed to achieving its fulfilment, must be based on adequate consideration of the relevant facts without and within the organisation.

6. The aim of management is, in achieving the purpose or task to which it is directed, to attain and maintain an optimum level of effectiveness and economy of operation in all the activities of the enterprise. Among the essential ways of attaining such effectiveness is the promotion of contentment and morale of the persons composing the organisation.

7. Management thus acquires a secondary social aim in the promotion of contentment and morale.

8. Because of its nature as a social (human) process, management responsibility must be carried into effect as a continuous and living activity on the part of the appointed manager(s), and cannot be replaced by techniques or systems designed for operation by subordinate personnel in the prolonged or recurrent absence of the manager(s).

9. Irrespective of the size of the organisation, or of the divisions into which its activities may in practice be divided, the process of management within that organisation is a unity, and its several parts or aspects must be recognised as related items in the one integral process.

10. The only reliable basis of approach to effective management in action is a systematic method based on: diagnosis of situation—ascertainment of facts—assessment and interpretation—decision and instruction—check results.

11. The criterion of management is to be sought in—(a) achievement of purpose; (b) the effectiveness of operations, measured usually in terms of productivity per man-hour employed or cost per unit of product produced or work performed; (c) the contentment of the members of the organisation. "Profits" may be a convenient index of the first two criteria.

B. Planning and Control

1. Ascertainment and assessment of all relevant facts, without and within the enterprise, are essential factors in sound planning and control.

   N.B.—(i) These two elements are *essentially* interrelated, control being the obverse of planning.

   (ii) Both are largely carried into effect by means of techniques or procedures, and form the "administrative" aspect of management. They provide "tools" of management, and so are always *means*, never *ends* in themselves.

   (iii) Apart from the techniques by which these elements are carried into effect, they are also to be reflected in the attitude of managers in discharging their responsibilities.

2. Two essential preliminary stages in the determination of plans are:
   (a) the formulation of policy, in general as well as in appropriate sectional terms;
   (b) the laying down of the responsibilities or tasks allocated to the various members of the group or enterprise, and of the (formal) interrelations consequently arising among them.

3. Sound planning and control require the determination and setting down of appropriate standards of performance in respect of the various activities or operations of the enterprise: these are to be determined by systematic analysis and assessment of the relevant facts.

4. The effectiveness and economy of activities or operations are controlled by a continuous comparison of actual achievements or results against these predetermined standards.

5. The selection of the personnel, equipment, materials, methods, processes, etc., to be used in carrying out the operations, should be based on a continuous review of all relevant factors, and determined on an analytical basis.

6. Effectiveness and economy of operations can be assisted by—specialisation, simplification and standardisation.

7. In striving for economy of operations, as the counterpart of effectiveness, it is important to keep a balance between long-term and short-term results or consequences.

8. In the application of techniques of planning and control, full regard must be paid to the human needs of members of the organisation: the techniques alone cannot secure effectiveness of operations, and neglect of human requirements inevitably militates against their successful application.

C. Organisation Structure

1. Organisation is an aspect of planning, concerned with the definition of:
   (a) the responsibilities of the (managerial, supervisory and specialist) personnel employed in the enterprise; and
   (b) the formal interrelations established by virtue of such responsibilities.
2. The structure of organisation of an enterprise is the framework for carrying out the responsibilities of management, for the delegation of such responsibilities, for the co-ordination of activities or operations, and for the motivation of members; the design of the structure must be directed to promoting the effective working, at all levels, of the four elements of management.
3. The responsibilities or activities of all (managerial, supervisory and specialist) members of an enterprise, or of all its main and subsidiary divisions or sections, should be clearly defined, preferably in writing: the definition should also specify the (formal) relations of each particular member or section to any others with which there is to be active contact.
4. When the size of the enterprise necessitates subdivision of responsibilities, the most useful broad division is into specific primary groups, determined by specialisation of function or operation.
5. When the increasing size or activity of an enterprise (or any other factors) threaten to impair the effectiveness of management through the overloading of members, appropriate provision is to be made for the delegation of responsibilities to lower levels in the direct line or to the specialist members; appropriate provision has then also to be made to ensure continuous effective co-ordination.
6. The definition of responsibilities and relationships forming an organisation structure should provide:
   (a) a single chief executive responsible to the policy-forming body for the effective conduct of all the operations of the enterprise;
   (b) adequate decentralisation of decision through the delegation of responsibility;
   (c) clear lines of responsibility linking the chief executive with the various points of decision or operation;
   (d) the span of responsibility or supervision of a superior limited to a reasonable number of (executive or supervisory) subordinates, if their activities are interrelated;
   (e) the integration of functional (specialist) sections in such a way as not to impair the clear lines of responsibility and command.

7. If responsibilities are properly defined, the delegation of responsibility, and its acceptance, automatically implies delegation of the corresponding authority to take decisions and to secure the carrying out of the appropriate activities. If limitations are intended to apply to any executive's responsibilities, they should be specifically mentioned in the definitions.

N.B.—When responsibilities are delegated, a superior is still to be held accountable for all the relevant activities of subordinates within his jurisdiction, whether he has issued specific instructions for such activities or not.

8. An organisation structure cannot be regarded as immutable; it must be flexible enough to admit of adjustment when required by changes in basic circumstances.

D. Co-ordination and Motivation

1. The aims of management, in the achievement of a given purpose or task through effective and economical activities or operations of persons associated in an enterprise or organisation, can be attained only if there is willing co-operation from and co-ordinated activity among those persons.

2. However sound the framework provided by the policy, plans and organisation structure of the enterprise, effective management implies a responsibility for deliberate and continuous co-ordination, and specific mechanisms to this end may be required.

3. The effectiveness of operations and the maintenance of co-operation among members of an organisation is in part determined by the personal and social contentment derived by them from their participation in the tasks of the enterprise.

N.B.—(i) A person employed in any organisation necessarily goes into that employment as a "total person", continuously subject to influences derived from temperament, background, domestic circumstances and many other factors external to the working situation.

(ii) It is now becoming increasingly recognised that inherent in management as a social process is a *direct* responsibility for the promotion of personal and social satisfactions of the persons under its jurisdiction; the attainment of such satisfactions in a "group situation" is one of the reasons for persons taking up employment.

4. Co-ordination of operations requires *balance* of activities as well as unification; it can be most effectively attained by direct continuous contact among the persons concerned, starting at an early stage of their activities, and proceeding with due regard to the relevant facts.

5. The issue of instructions (command) and the supervision of operations are among the channels through which the element of motivation is carried into effect.

6. Communications (instructions, etc.) should flow along the lines of

responsibility and relationship set out in the organisation structure.

7. Willing co-operation, through high morale (will to work) among members of an organisation, is promoted by:

   (a) keeping them informed of matters concerning the activities of the organisation;

   (b) consulting them in regard to its regulation and further development;

   (c) fostering in them a sense of self-responsibility for the performance of their tasks;

   (d) affording them opportunities for self-development, compatible with the purpose and interests of the organisation;

   (e) encouraging them to contribute to its effectiveness and development apart from the performance of their allotted tasks;

   (f) fostering their responsible participation in its management.

8. High morale is in part determined by the confidence and respect felt by subordinates for their superiors; outstanding among the factors promoting such confidence and respect is an unquestioned basis of fairness and objectivity in dealings with subordinates.

9. Members of an organisation cannot be expected to develop a spirit of willing co-operation in its purposes and tasks, unless they are able to anticipate reasonable security of tenure of their membership of that organisation.

10. Discipline means acceptance of the necessary rules or regulations of the enterprise, and is the natural concomitant of high morale: the need for special provisions for "the maintenance of discipline" is an indication that morale is not adequate.

11. Discipline, as a reflection of high morale, is best attained by fostering the sense of responsibility of subordinates—by enlisting their co-operation in the formulation of the code of regulations and by providing for independent review in cases of alleged grievance or dispute as to the application of that code.

12. However democratic its principles and structure, the level of morale of an organisation (its "tone") is largely a reflection of the human attitude and outlook of its chief executive.

9. THE THEORY OF MANAGEMENT

In the analytical review of the management process given in foregoing sections, emphasis has been directed to identifying and clarifying the four fundamental elements of which that process is composed —planning, motivation, co-ordination, control. These, it has been shown, are blended by the manager into a responsibility for the governance of given sets of operations, planning and regulating them towards an integrated, effective and economical accomplishment of the objectives which they are designed to serve. Such accomplishment is the *raison d'être* of the management process, and so of the manager's responsibility. In its everyday occurrence, however, this process is not itself readily visible, and in fact it is never at all seen as a whole. Manifestation occurs piecemeal—in individual actions by the managers exercising one or more of the elements in a specific situation; it is indeed this "invisibility" of management that makes the analytical study of it so difficult of acceptance by many of its practitioners. Moreover, the inner nature of the process is in everyday practice masked by the very actions and procedures through which it is carried into effect. This phenomenon will be readily apparent in the practical presentation that constitutes the following four Parts of this volume—where the management process is studied in the detail of its application within the main spheres of normal industrial and commercial activity.

The tasks, the actions, the procedures and attitudes that constitute the role of the manager seem mundane enough, but a great deal in the way of economic and social achievement depends on their sound fulfilment. In total they add up to the content of the "profession" of management—the body of knowledge, in terms of principle and of practice, which stands as the essential foundation of competence in action. If the notion of a "profession" is to be seriously accepted, so too must a corpus of principles, even if they are not yet adequately identified; and so, too, must a basic "theory" of management, however complex its enunciation.

To an industrial and commercial readership, the mention of "theory" is often anathema, because it connotes to them the antithesis of practical success. Yet, in this context, the notion of theory deserves closer examination. As a term used in industrial discussions, it frequently carries a derisive implication that the speaker regards himself as "a practical man" enjoying a measure of success from his practice, and that accordingly he has no time for what he chooses to regard as doctrines or vague ideas. He christens these "theories" because he is unable to relate them to any proof from his practice; he uses the term "theoretical" to imply that to him an idea may sound good, but he is not able at the moment to find any convincing counter-argument, nor does he want to admit the soundness of what is being offered. Frequently, too, this epithet masks ignorance, even if unwitting ignorance, and endorses instead a readiness to act "off the cuff".

Correctly interpreted, "theory" means a basic doctrine in which are enshrined the essential features underlying effective accomplishment; it is a thought process underlying action and deduced from a systematic study of previous action.

The main substance of the theory of management has already been set out in the earlier analysis which led on to the elucidation of the four essential elements, and its content was summarised in the definition given at page 24 above. This analysis and definition can now be re-formulated as a "theory", obviously without changing or adding to the essentials already deduced. Let it be recognised forthwith that *no practical purpose is served* by this re-formulation; it serves but to round off the consideration of management in principle, and perhaps to lend point to the argument that there is substance enough in the process of management to warrant its study at the level of an academic discipline.

The *theory of management* may be briefly posed by seeing it as a process of decision governing the actions of people, in allocating resources to the fulfilment of known objectives, and with optimum effect. All the essential features of the notion of management are contained in this statement of theory, as also are all the factors that contribute to successful management practice.

This claim is worth brief justification, in the following points:

(*a*) management is a *process* in the sense of a combined pattern of mental action and human behaviour; it is not *per se* an art, nor an inborn aptitude, nor a technique, nor a science;

(*b*) *decision* is of its essence, and this presupposes consideration and judgment preceding the decision, as well as facts and data from which to judge;

(*c*) the decision has to be carried into effect by other people who, for this purpose, may or may not have to be held under the jurisdiction of the manager; in either case he has to solicit or attain their effective co-operation, which implies an inherent social facet to the process, and a need for social skills;

(*d*) the objectives at any given times are determined, even though their determination may not be reached except through the judgment and decision which are the basis of the actions to accomplish them;

(*e*) the resources being used in the actions concerned could be used in alternative ways, the particular application being part of the basic decision—the criterion of judgment being the relative outcome from any given allocation of resources;

(*f*) the management process thus has *an essential economic character* in its primary concern for effective attainment of chosen or accepted objectives with optimum or minimum use of resources;

(*g*) the economic achievement can be ensured only by continuous review of the actions ensuing from the decisions, which means that the judgment and decision process is recurrent in the nature of a feedback circuit;

(*h*) to maintain this recurrent action and interaction is the crux of the responsibility inherent in the management process;

(*i*) basically, the management process is *future-oriented* by reason of its concern with planning what shall be done and how it will be done.

Clothing the theory in terms more akin to everyday happening, management is seen as a dual pattern of behaviour, the one aspect being the mental action of judgment/decision, and the other that of motivating people to co-operative participation carrying the decisions into effect. The economic and the social facets are thus inherently intertwined, even though at times their requirements may conflict: in a later chapter such conflict will be seen in the context of "change"— economic considerations often call for change as the inevitable concomitant of progress, in face of the deeply embedded natural human resistance to it. It is of the essence of management responsibility to apply mental and behaviour skills in such ways as to minimise this conflict, if not avoid it entirely—and certainly prevent it from hindering the attainment of progress. The theory of management fully supports the many-sided daily actions of the manager in practice: he considers his facts and his data to arrive at what he regards as the correct objective and decision; he may consult others in this regard, just as he will consult with them as to effective modes of action to carry the decision into action; he will communicate facts relevant to the decisions, and to the plans in which they are reflected, and will initiate action by command, motivating participating colleagues and members to high performance in fulfilment of the plans; he will have standards of test or judgment by which to review performance, thus ensuring effective control of operations relative to plans and to objectives. At every stage he will pay regard to co-ordination of effort, and his responsibility is made effective in the feedback circuit of planning and control, and made human or social by the medium of consultation and communication.

In the course of thus outlining the theory of management, incidental reference to the four elements has been obviously inevitable, but the correlation can be more specifically presented thus:

CONSTITUENT ELEMENTS	PHASES OF PROCESS
PLANNING	Information Judgment Decision
MOTIVATION & *CO-ORDINATION*	Consultation Communication Command
CONTROL	Record Review (Information)
Feedback to— *PLANNING*	Judgment Decision

Etc.

The theory of management requires that, whatever the specific objectives of an individual enterprise or company (that is to say, its policy within a given field of operations), the overriding and all-embracing responsibility is to secure effective and economical accomplishment of these operating objectives. In the terms used above, this means an endeavour to reach the best possible outcome from the operations with the minimum use of the resources devoted to them. These resources have been customarily summarised in the language of classical economics as the "factors of production", but they are more readily recognised in industrial language as a collection of physical and human properties—the premises in which the operations are housed, the plant and equipment used to carry them through, the manpower employed in a variety of occupations, whether of brain or of brawn, numerous materials of varied kinds major and minor, and fuel and power required for driving productive processes. All these physical resources become available to a business or industrial enterprise through the medium of the all-embracing financial resources covered by the term capital, which is used to exert command through purchase prices, through payment of wages and salaries, and through promise of interest and dividends. The resources, whether financial or physical, can be utilised in a variety of directions by any number of enterprises, any one of which can successfully bid for a share because it expects to make sufficiently effective use of them to earn back the purchase payments with an additional return in the shape of profit. This situation of *choice* between alternatives or among many possibilities is of the essence of the management role, otherwise there would not be decision; judgment and decision imply that there are at least two possible lines of action—even if these are no more than to act or not to act. The choice may well lie between present and future outcome, and in the case of future, between short-term and long-term. Since management decision is the basis of planning and of the initiation of action, there is an *essential interest in the future,* because little of the outcome can be immediate; in the industrial and commercial world the interest in the future is emphasised by the fact that manufacturing has to be undertaken largely in advance of demand, and marketing programmes formulated in anticipation of demand being stimulated.

The outcome that the enterprise will attain lies first and foremost in the quality and reliability of the product or service that it offers to its customers, associated with ready availability at required delivery times, and a price attractive enough to customers to hold a position in the market in competition with other suppliers. The successful enterprise will also offer as an outcome of its operations development effort leading to the improvement of its product or service, and the promise of maintaining or improving the earnings of its members. Through taxes, rates and other expenditures, it contributes to the fulfilment of social obligations, and, over and above all this, it seeks to earn a return on the investment for the benefit of those who have contributed the capital by means of which the shares of physical resources were acquired.

The Theory of "Management Information"

It is in this area of the utilisation and disposition of resources, and the assessment of the outcome from their application, that the judgment/decision aspect of the management process comes most into play. To accomplish this mental task soundly and reliably, the manager needs data—facts and figures, economic, physical and financial, providing a base from which to formulate plans, against which to exercise control of performance and progress. Such data is therefore commonly referred to loosely as "management information", and, if it is missing, decision can be determined only by hunch. It is in this respect that the notion of "scientific method" becomes relevant for the practice of management, namely, the sequential action of collating the relevant facts, considering and judging them, determining the conclusion to which that consideration leads, provisionally testing the conclusion, and finally issuing a firm decision in the light of the test. The latter becomes the plan, and when the performance data show departure from the intended programme, then the new facts are considered so as to give rise to the new decision or the revised plan. The feedback cycle is thus complete.

Because data is of the essence of this action and reaction, management information is commonly spoken of as the "tools" of the manager, yet these information "tools" are needed differently in different parts or levels of an organisation, and data procedures have to be appropriately worked out to meet specific requirements. Whether considered in theory or in terms of practice, management information is an essential feature of the management process, absorbed primarily in the elements of "planning" and "control", with secondary contribution in "co-ordination". In consequence, the procedures designed to give effect to the information must be interrelated with the pattern of delegation. The information is the means by which the manager exercises his judgment in forming his decisions: the scope and extent of these is determined by the responsibility (defined) delegated or allocated to his role, and are thus reflected by the divisions and levels of the organisation structure. Of any manager's decisions some or many will be routine, pertinent to the daily and weekly activities under his jurisdiction: if errors of judgment occur here, they can normally be corrected without heavy cost. Other decisions will refer to major action and will be *ad hoc* to situations of importance where errors of judgment could be capable of correction only at considerable cost. Sound principle would require that data availability should be appropriate to the significance of the decisions: where the costs of possible errors are high, more information is justified, even if it costs more to provide. Less information is justified where the error potential is insignificant. In terms of practice, statistical or mathematical techniques afford their true value to management in this respect, because they can facilitate the provision of minimum information pertinent to a given situation: e.g. sampling and probabilities instead of fully worked out figures. Very important in the theory of management information is the principle, that, for decision purposes, data is needed of *expected situations* more than of past or present: these latter are, in fact, pertinent only in so far as they foreshadow the expectation of the future. Management decision, being concerned with choices as the basis of future action (whether short or long-term), needs to be informed as to the possible outcomes of the alternatives being considered: data must provide not only the customary economic intelligence which is the background and setting for policy formulation and programme forecasting, but also some assessment or evaluation of the assumptions made in reaching the choice between the alternatives. Correctly, such data will be required more fully and with more accuracy or reliability, the more significant the decisions —presumably, the higher the level of the manager taking them or the greater the extent of his responsibilities.

Management information is, however, *not only specific* to each level or section of responsibility as delegated; it is pertinent, too, to the co-ordinated operation of the management process as a whole within a given organisation, especially in regard to the elements of "planning" and "control". (In a later Part of this volume, systems and procedures are described by which this basic requirement can be attained—for example, budgetary control in which the feed-back notion relates "actual" to "plan" and concentrates management's attention on the "variances" in respect of which decision is called for.)

The contemporary development of electronic computing equipment has emphasised the possibility of "making more information available to management". Desirable as this object may at first sound, it could in fact be a *disservice* to management, and the claims so widely made in these terms may well mask a failure to understand the true nature of management information. What management *needs* is no more than the data *necessary* to guide, assist and promote correct decisions leading to effective operations. No matter how detailed the data, they can never substitute the consideration and the decision of the manager. Automatic data processing can be recommended as a mechanism, if it can make correctly determined data available more quickly and presented more clearly, because then it can have two important consequences in management action: (i) it can reveal more promptly the variances of actual performance from targets set, thus enabling quicker remedial action to be taken by management and so prevent the loss or waste of resources; (ii) it can more quickly make known changes in circumstances which would render the original targets inappropriate, and thus can assist management to review and change the targets more appropriately to the change in circumstances. In both cases management is assisted in its basic task of securing optimum outcome from minimum application of resources—wherein lies the core of the theory of management in its economic aspect.

The Theory of "Social Responsibilities"

In the second aspect of the process—the human or social aspect— similar considerations arise, the essential features being the pattern of human relationships involved and the mode of their development through communication. It is of the essence of management (in theory or in practice) that there is a responsibility to command, at least in the sense of determining objectives and targets, formulating plans to attain them, and inviting thereto the co-operation of the participating members. This is an aspect where the theory is much clearer than the practice. Theory would take for granted as a fact that, if people choose to join in an enterprise or institution, engaging their services to its management in return for an agreed reward, they will co-operate in its purposes and seek to promote its good as well as their own. In theory, it could be enough to state that management has the responsibility to command, and its requirements will be fulfilled. This is *not*, however, to imply disregard for human considerations: on the contrary, theory recognises that effective operation and performance will come only from *willing* co-operation. Accordingly, the theory of management recognises the need for physical, environmental and psychological circumstances for its participating members such as to ensure full response to its motivation. (This has been recognised, as indicated earlier, in the very choice of the word "motivation".) Communication is a major medium for winning such co-operation—making known objectives, policies for action, targets, methods of operation, plans, attainments and progress, along with many matters that are more specifically of personal and social interest, with the intent of promoting the sense of participation that brings forth earnest and effective co-operation.

Translating this theoretical concept into practice involves many procedures, many problems of attitude, many difficulties of interpretation—which will be the subject of specific consideration later in the volume. These are all absorbed in the process of "supervision", "leadership", or "man management", and the important point in this context is that consideration of such human requirements germane to co-operation is recognised as an essential item in the theory of management. It arises from the very fact of the employment of men and women, which enjoins on management *per se* a social obligation; but it could be argued that human consideration arises equally from management's primary concern with effectiveness and economy of operation, for without securing full and earnest co-operation from its men and women employed, management could not attain high levels of efficiency. The two aspects should be combined, and they are so when the men and women employed recognise their own obligation to efficient working and their own contribution to the economy of their community.

In the light of aspects of management practice to be considered later in this volume, it is pertinent to ask at this juncture a question which can have far-reaching implications if answered in the affirmative: is it a correct conception of the theory of management to see entailed an *essential* obligation of responsibility to the community? Such an obligation would *per se* transcend the manager's initial accountability to the owners of the enterprise, and would enjoin on him an over-riding accountability to the community in which he is set. To some extent, obligations are imposed by statute or by Governmental requirement—for example, the stipulations of company law, safety statutes and similar legislation, regulations affecting weights and measures, or exchange controls, or the requirements of fair employment clauses. Local laws and restrictions have also to be observed, despite their burden or hindrance to a company's affairs.

There is, however, a deeper implication in the very statement of the objectives of the management process in theory, in the reference to optimum application of resources. To whom do these "resources" belong? In so far as they are physical materials purchased outright by a company through normal trading channels, it could be argued that ownership gives right of use at choice; yet even here there would have to be added "subject to any statutory or municipal stipulations affecting such materials or their use". Premises and plant frequently incur such restrictive stipulations, and there are many aspects of site or location in respect of which a company does not and cannot enjoy freedom of use or action at choice. When the "resources" are considered in terms of the time and attendance of men and women, all question of ownership disappears: as an employer a company is governed by many limitations inherent in the rights of man, in protective legislation, or in the social code of the community. Legally, the relationships subsisting between the employing company and the people working for it are governed by a code broadly subsumed under the description "law of master and servant", a designation clearly indicative of origin in an earlier epoch of our social history. However unchanged the legal pattern may remain, the spirit of the relationship and the mutual attitudes which surround it are, as we have just seen, greatly different: consultation and co-operation have become the keynotes, instead of discipline and obedience. The human "resources" are thus essentially subject to a social element of responsibility.

For different reasons, a comparable argument can be supported in theory in respect of physical resources. The first step in the argument links back to what was said in Section 2 above (see page 15) as to the primary objectives of an economic system. In itself this system is the now complicated mechanism by which the men and women of a community—whether considered as citizens of a given state or denizens of a world race—attain and maintain the means of livelihood. On both counts, as part-producers and as consumers, they are essentially linked into the maelstrom of economic activity by means of which they feed and drink, are clothed, sheltered, nurtured, educated, entertained, healed, and in the end buried! Accidents of historical development have given the economic system varied forms—here erected on a so-called principle of private enterprise, there on a formal corporate co-operative pattern, elsewhere in the form of state-owned trusts or commissariats. Nowhere do these forms maintain an immutable durability; nowhere are they exclusive and sacrosanct. They are the accidents of practice, but they reflect an essential purity of theory—the fundamental endeavour of man to earn his bread, and his wise recognition that this he can do better somehow or other in a co-operative form than by individual effort. On this reasoning, the physical resources that he uses—of land, of materials, or secondary equipment—are in basic theory the "property" of the community: at least in the sense that the first purpose of their disposition is the well-being of the community in which they are being developed or used.

The role of management is to promote effective and economical application of these resources; whatever the secondary purposes that may be interposed, the primary objective remains. Constitutional forms may have given over-riding rights of ownership and disposition of such resources to individuals, to companies, to governmental corporations, to national commissariats: but these cannot over-ride the primary objectives, for these are of fundamental existence in the nature of the economic endeavours of the human society. Management theory thus posits an essential social responsibility. That this is recognised as sound is seen in the practice of any nation when emergencies threaten its life or its livelihood. Whether in fear of invasion in 1940, or in economic crisis decades later, British management and the British populace accepted directives stringently negative to the requirements of private enterprise and the profit motive, and found it right that the needs of the nation should take priority over all else.

There is no call here to chase after the practical implications of this theoretical principle—save perhaps in one important aspect. Recognition of the principle lends point to seeing management as a "profession": for the pursuit of efficiency and economy is then seen as in the service of the community, a pre-requisite for professional status. Practical reflections of these basic notions will form the subject-matter of some of the chapters in Part Five below.

10. OUTLINE OF VOLUME

The following four Parts of this volume examine the principles of management applied in practice, through the description and illustration of certain proven methods and techniques. It is not practicable to give at every turn the particular circumstances that characterised the evolution or development of the method put forward, but as far as possible the techniques described are those which have been found capable of widespread and varied application. Yet, it would be a mistake to imagine that the techniques described can be applied without further analysis to any and every business. The purpose of the following Parts is to explain and illustrate how the process of management is carried into effect—and the reader should respond, if he wants to carry the techniques into practice, by analysing his own particular situation to see how each would be relevant, and how far the circumstances are sufficiently different to require some alteration in the treatment of the problem or the design of the techniques used. The easy accessibility of "systems" in recent years has sometimes been an obstacle to better management, mainly because it has led managers away from making a critical appraisal of their own situations and of the methods of management best suited to them.

Parts One and Two are devoted to management at work within the fields of marketing and manufacturing, the main branches of the economic system. In regard to marketing (Part One), the emphasis is deliberately placed on those aspects that more closely concern the manufacturing company with products to sell to customers; less attention, and in only a more incidental way, is given to wholesale and retail trade and to transport. These latter form separate fields of activity for which specific management techniques have been developed: the process and the elements of management there are similar, but it would take the present study too far out of balance between the Parts to have treated at length these specialist trading aspects.

Parts Three and Four are an examination of the two all-pervading aspects of management, as they are carried out within the fields of activity like marketing and manufacturing. The matter contained in them does not overlap with that of the preceding Parts, but should be studied alongside them. There is a danger in this method of presentation, in so far as it repeats the practice of industry in the separation of the aspects of the management process. The appointment of a specialist Personnel Officer or Financial Controller may often lead "line" executives to feel relieved of responsibility for human relations in their domain or for the effective control of operating costs: such a mistaken notion can just as easily arise if these functions are separately studied. The gain from specialist treatment, bringing more authoritative knowledge to bear, must not be offset by any suggestion that "Personnel" and "Control" are outside management or outside the responsibility of the managers in Production and Marketing.

In Part Five an endeavour is made to weave a co-ordinating pattern into the separate specialist studies, by examining some major aspects of management practice which have bearings on all the rest, and to review selected items of contemporary thought on the advancement of management competence.

AN OUTLINE HISTORY OF MANAGEMENT LITERATURE

EDITOR'S NOTE

THE following is a brief review of the contributions to the evolution of modern knowledge of the principles and practice of management. For readers who may be interested, a more detailed review is to be found in:

The Making of Scientific Management

Vol. I—*Thirteen Pioneers.*
Vol. II—*Management in British Industry.*
Vol. III—*The Hawthorne Investigations.*

By L. URWICK and E. F. L. BRECH

(Pitman, London, 1945–50)

*   *   *   *   *

While in the course of Britain's industrial revolution during the nineteenth century, a certain amount of attention was given to the development of management techniques, it was only in the later decades of the century that this subject became one of any width of interest. The technical periodicals and journals began from about the 1870s onwards here and there to carry articles on certain aspects of production management, and the analysis of costs, and gradually in the following ten or twenty years there emerged a category of recurrent topics which would today be classified as "management". An odd book or two had been published bearing on this subject prior to 1870, but it can rightly be said that the first volume to aspire to a title as an outstanding nineteenth-century contribution to the British literature of management was GARCKE and FELLS *Factory Accounting*, published in 1887. Here for the first time was the combination of the accountant and the engineer, representing the coordination of the two major aspects in management development at that period.

In 1894, F. G. BURTON began his occasional series of articles in *Engineering*, on the subject of engineers' estimates and cost accounts, two or three years later republishing some of them in the form of a small book. Just before the end of the century (1899), he brought out a full-length book of some merit: this was *The Commercial Management of Engineering Works*. Its character was more that of an accounting and office handbook than a textbook of management in the present-day sense, though it has two or three very interesting chapters on the managers' responsibilities. (Burton was Secretary and General Manager of the Milford Haven Shipbuilding and Engineering Company.) Between his two publications, however, Burton lost a good deal of his pride of place when in 1896 J. SLATER-LEWIS published his historic study entitled *The Commercial Organisation of Factories*. This was a new work by a General Manager, a highly qualified engineer, who had not previously written for the technical press. Here was a textbook of organisation and management in the best sense of the term, with many features that were astonishingly modern, decades ahead of their time—even an organisation chart, an illustration of the flow of documents, and interesting comments on the human aspects of management.

The next noteworthy contributor did not appear until 1908; this was a writer using the pseudonym "A General Manager" for a long series of articles on "Commercial Engineering". His identity was revealed as A. J. LIVERSEDGE in 1912, when the series appeared in book form. Its content was even more a commercial handbook than Burton's, largely consisting of market information.

Apart from the articles in the periodicals, presumably written for the growing middle-class readership employed in industry, even greater interest was beginning to be taken in management among the professional ranks of the technical societies, such as the Institution of Mechanical Engineers and one or two of the local Engineering Associations, notably in Manchester. In the annals of such bodies one or two names figure prominently, particularly after the turn of the century, as the main exponents of the "new" approach to management, and the first references to F. W. TAYLOR'S pioneer work (published in U.S.A. in 1895) began to appear.

No further textbook of any note, however, came on the market until 1914, when the first edition of *Factory Administration and Accounts* was brought out by ELBOURNE, assisted by two colleagues (HOME-MORTON and MAUGHLING), once again representing the combination of accountant and engineer. This book is a review of the best features of contemporary management practice, though with a significant degree of pioneer thinking in its presentation. It is perhaps a tribute to the foresight of its authors that the book long remained one of the classics of production management under the revised title *Factory Administration and Cost Accounts*. ELBOURNE'S other great work, *The Fundamentals of Industrial Administration*, first appeared in 1934, specifically prepared as an interpretation of the principles and practice of management for the benefit of students pursuing elementary courses for professional qualifications in that field.

Nineteen-fourteen was the year of another classic in early British management literature, *Engineers' Costs and Economical Workshop Production*, by DEMPSTER-SMITH and PICKWORTH. Whereas it probably attracted more contemporary attention, as being of stronger practical appeal, it did not have the seeds of prosperity within it, and disappeared with the passing of the years. It may be of interest to point out how frequently in the thirty years between 1885 and 1915 the subject-matter of articles and textbooks centred on estimates and costs—a theme reflected in the practice of management in the considerable contemporary

interest in premium bonus and similar incentive systems in the hands of
HALSEY, WEIR, ROWAN and others, following in the wake of Taylor.

While this general interest in management was emerging in Great
Britain in the fifty years after 1870, the American scene was witnessing
lively debate centring on the progress of *Scientific Management* under the
direction of F. W. TAYLOR and his associates. This little team of American
pioneers—of whom the best known were TAYLOR, GANTT and GILBRETH—
were more concerned with elaborating the techniques for the application
of systematic management than with writing up their findings in literature; they did, however, each produce two or three volumes, all of which
have lived down to our own times.[1] Taylor and his associates were,
broadly, concerned in the first place with diverting attention away from
the struggles over the division of the proceeds of industry, to the need for
a concerted effort to increase those proceeds for mutual benefit by better
planning and a better will-to-work, supported by incentive methods and
other forms of bonus technique. But much of their effort went into the
elaboration and advancement of techniques for the planning and control
of production, including such methods as time study, motion study, the
division and definition of responsibilities, planning charts, job tickets,
and many other of the features that are currently recognised as essential
to production control systems. They have perhaps come down through
the years more by their contributions in these directions than by their
more important fundamental contribution to the philosophy or principles
of management applied in human terms. In their own country they
gained, through accidental circumstances, a publicity that inevitably
entailed increasing public interest in the more easily understood and the
more pleasantly acceptable aspects of their work. In this country, the
publicity engendered serious suspicion in the minds of the leaders of
organised labour, and generated an emotional opposition that has
persisted even to our own day.

It would not be unfair to describe the first ten to fifteen years of the
twentieth century in Great Britain as a barren period in management
literature, even though the technical press and the journals of the societies frequently published articles and papers, many of them devoted to
the exposition of Taylor's teachings and methods. "Barren" is a fair
description, because of the superficial character of so much of this
writing, and because of its failure to secure any serious acceptance
among the industrial owners and managers. The outbreak of war in 1914
found British industry ignorant of contemporary advances in management thought and practice, save for such rare exceptions as Hans
Renold, Ltd., or the Cadbury organisation.[2]

Overlapping on the one side with Taylor, and on the other with the
First World War, was HENRI FAYOL, General Manager of a large French
mining and metallurgical concern. Almost at the close of a long executive career, Fayol took the opportunity of a paper to a Congress of a

---

[1] F. W. Taylor's main writings are available in collected form under the
title, *The Principles of Scientific Management* (Harper, New York).
[2] See *The Making of Scientific Management*, Vol. II, Chaps XI and XII.

Metallurgical Society in 1908 to review, as he saw them, the processes that went to make up his everyday practice as a chief executive; but it was some eight years later before this paper appeared in published form in the *Bulletin* of the Society, under the title, "Administration Industrielle et Générale", and another ten years before it appeared in English. The text was reproduced exactly as given in 1908, even to the extent of the note which foreshadowed additional sections to follow, intended to elaborate the author's basic conception of management as a process built up of the five elements: Planning, Organisation, Command, Co-ordination and Control. It is a matter of considerable regret that Fayol, despite his interest, did not see fit to complete the work or to add any further publication to his legacy in this field. It was only after his death in 1925 (then aged well over eighty) that his one and only paper on this subject secured wider recognition by its publication in book form, first in French and later translated into English.[1] The importance of Fayol's contribution lay in two features: the first was his systematic analysis of the process of management; the second, his firm advocacy of the principle that management *can, and should, be taught.* Both were revolutionary lines of thought in 1908, and still little accepted even in 1925. The seemingly unedited and unfinished state of Fayol's matter makes the real value of his analysis difficult to appreciate at first reading. Confusion is the reader's main reaction to the juxtaposition of overlapping "principles of administration" and "administrative duties". Yet in his simple deduction of the five elements of the process of management, he reached a conception that has stood the test of time, and has even been closely reproduced from an entirely different and independent analysis (cf. Introduction to this volume).

Throughout this first quarter of the century, MARY FOLLETT was gaining her experience of social and industrial problems, though she had not yet turned her attention at first hand to the principles and practice of management. It was not until 1924 that she gave her first paper to a Conference of the Bureau of Personnel Administration in the United States, and over the next four or five years she contributed the remarkable series of papers on the fundamentals of management, illustrated from practical events, that form such an outstanding addition to the literature of the subject. (*Dynamic Administration*: collected papers reproduced from the Bureau's Conferences.) Mary Follett, broadly, was less interested in the practice of management than in the extent to which the everyday incidents and problems reflected the presence or absence of sound principle. She was chiefly concerned to teach principles in simple language, amply illustrated from everyday events—not the mechanics of management, but its special human character, its nature as a social process, deeply embedded in the emotions of man and in the interrelations to which the everyday working of industry necessarily gives rise—at manager levels, at worker levels, and, of course, between the two. Bearing in mind she was speaking of America in the early 1920s, her thinking

[1] A new British edition, under the title *Industrial and General Management* appeared in 1948 (Pitman).

can be described as little less than revolutionary, and certainly a generation ahead of its time. There is no evidence that Mary Follett ever had
any contact with the persons who sponsored or conducted the Hawthorne Investigations, but the findings of those investigations, when they
appeared in their full form in the 1930s, were a striking testimony to the
soundness of her teaching. Again and again an incident described or a
conclusion drawn from the Hawthorne studies can be recognised as reflecting a principle or a fundamental tenet that Mary Follett had advanced from her own observations of the industrial situation.

In Great Britain the 1920s were marked by two or three publications
which have lived down to our own times as still having a value in the
study of their subject: O. SHELDON's *Philosophy of Management* (1924);
Factory Organisation, by NORTHCOTT, URWICK and WARDROPPER (1927);
URWICK's *Organising a Sales Office* (1928); POWELL'S *Payment by
Results* (1924). Perhaps, however, the really outstanding work of the
decade was one that has become lost to posterity because its contemporary sales did not justify keeping it in print. This was the DICTIONARY
OF INDUSTRIAL ADMINISTRATION, published by Pitman in 1927 as a collection of writings on the principles and practice of management by all
the known authorities of the day under the editorship of JOHN LEE. It is
a misfortune that this volume should have been born out of time, some
decades ahead of the day when its full value would have been appreciated.

During these years the interest in costing was beginning to spread
into its management aspects, and a few small publications were to be
found, a notable one being EMSLEY and LOXHAM: *Factory Costs* (1924),
now extant as *Factory Costing and Organisation*.

The corresponding period in the United States was considerably more
fruitful, probably because a larger industrial population provided the
publishers with the certainty of an adequate market. Again, many of the
books published then have come down to the present day in revised
editions, as, for instance, LAMBURGH's *Industrial Administration* (1923),
the two classics in the personnel field: TEAD & METCALF'S *Personnel Administration* (1920) and *Personnel Management*, by SCOTT, CLOTHIER
and OTHERS (1923). E. SCHELL'S *The Technique of Executive Control*
also dates from 1924. The climax of these series of comprehensive
studies was reached in America in 1931 in the first appearance of THE
HANDBOOK OF BUSINESS ADMINISTRATION followed by its more specific
companion THE (COST AND) PRODUCTION HANDBOOK (1934).

By this time, the subject of management had become, both in Britain
and in America, one of considerable contemporary interest, supported
by professional institutes; in the U.S.A., there was support as well by systematic studies at University level. The way was open for the great flow
of textbooks and treatises that make it so difficult for the historian to
pick and choose. Inevitably many of the studies were of a "bread-and-
butter" kind, concerned with the description and illustration of techniques for production management, for production control, for cost
control, for sales management and stores control, for personnel practices,

and the many other aspects of the day-to-day activities that go to make up the pattern of executive control in any medium or large-sized organisation. Inevitably also, many of such studies were short-lived, of passing interest only, because as practice developed, new techniques would be evolved and new textbooks called for. One can perhaps avoid the difficulty of selecting among this literature by refraining from specific mention, except to pay tribute to such pioneer British classics as T. H. BURNHAM'S *Engineering Economics,* ELBOURNE'S *Fundamentals of Industrial Administration,* and T. G. ROSE'S *Higher Control*—all dating from the 1930s.

Throughout these years there had been relatively little contribution to what might be termed the "theory" of management, i.e. the systematic study of the principles upon which the everyday practice of the executive process rested. Outstanding in this field was L. URWICK'S first major contribution to the literature of management, which appeared as a section of the *Dictionary* referred to above, under the title of "Principles of Direction and Control", a systematic scheme of the fundamentals of management, obviously the product of far-reaching and painstaking analytical thought, which even today has a valuable relevance to the study of the subject. (These "Principles" are available to present-day readers in a reproduction in ELBOURNE'S *Fundamentals.*) An equally useful American study was WEBSTER ROBINSON'S *Fundamentals of Business Administration,* first published in 1928. In 1931 came *Onward Industry* by MOONEY and REILLEY, an American classic in the study of organisation principles. This, not confining itself to industry, roamed over the whole field of organised human endeavour, in an attempt to find a common pattern of principles that would serve to prescribe a sound foundation for effective action. Subsequent editions appeared in 1939 and 1947 under the title *The Principles of Organisation* (with MOONEY now as sole author). Historically, this book in its earlier edition may be regarded as the first systematic study of organisation on scientific lines. Though concerned with the static aspects of the structure of organisation and the formal lines of relationship, it had inevitably to deal with many aspects of an organisation at work, and so many "dynamic" considerations came into the study: this gave rise to a short-lived fashion in the terminology of management—the use of "organisation" as the name for the total process as well as for the structure of responsibilities.

In 1933 came URWICK'S second book, *Management of To-morrow,* a combination of principle and practice, following largely on the lines of Mary Follett in the endeavour to discuss effective management in action in simple terms of everyday life in the factory and the office, but at the same time attempting to lay down the fundamental principles upon which such effective management must rest. It followed Mooney and Reilley in the use of the term "organisation" as the generic name, and brought out specifically for the first time the dual concept of the "dynamic" and "static" aspects. In spite of its limited issue, this book made a very important contribution to British literature and to the advancement of management thought: it was the equivalent in this country of its equally well-known contemporary in America, *Organisation Engineering*, by H. S. DENNISON (1931).

By the mid-1930's the possibility of a "science" of management was being canvassed, though by now the terminology tangle was already well to the fore. Many writers were using, not only the existing two terms "management" and "organisation", but beginning also to bring in the third member of the trilogy, "administration". This can be illustrated, for instance, by the joint Anglo-American publication (1937) of *Papers on the Science of Administration,* written and edited by GULICK and URWICK.

Apart from the two or three monumental works on the Hawthorne investigations, the last outstanding contribution to the literature of management before the outbreak of war in 1939 was CHESTER BARNARD'S *Functions of the Executive,* a penetrating analysis of the process of co-operation that is inherent in every aspect of management. Here the findings of the Hawthorne investigations were being used as an analytical instrument for examining the process of management, for the special purpose of throwing into relief its human or social character.

* * * * *

In the years that have passed since the end of the Second World War, the literature of management has swollen enormously in both Britain and the U.S.A., as well as in other countries. Serious study of the subject has been widely and vigorously extended, with the result that in almost every aspect there has grown up a numerous and comprehensive bibliography. The American contributions far outweigh all others, even all others combined; this is an easy situation to explain, in so far as the United States have so many long-established Colleges and University Departments where management studies figure as major items, and thus there exist substantial numbers of teaching and research staffs devoted to these subjects. The resulting literature is too considerable and extensive to permit of any sort of survey in short compass, as can be seen by reference to the catalogue or select lists of the Library of the British Institute of Management or other sources of bibliographical information. While it is invidious to select individual titles, leave may be presumed at least for the mention of a recent special study by the sociologist W. H. WHYTE called *The Organisation Man*: this presents perhaps the epitome of managerial development, reflecting the forecast of JAMES BURNHAM'S *Managerial Revolution*—for Whyte portrays and analyses, with almost frightening reality, the influences that the demands of large-scale management practice are exerting on the men and women of our day. A sociological and philosophical study, not a textbook, but of vital importance for every manager. Equally stimulating studies from a sociologist's hands, though with a more specific background of industrial investigation, have been the several books written by PETER DRUCKER (1948–59) stemming from his researches within the large American concern that was also the home of Mooney and Reilley (1931).

New publications in the British literature of management have also been numerous and have on the whole been of higher quality than those of previous decades. The war and immediate postwar years found interest centred largely in the fields of Personal Relations and Industrial Psychology, and a few references may serve to illustrate the trends. Books covering the human factor in management may be usefully represented by G. S. WALPOLE'S *Management and Men* (1944), W. C. PUCKEY'S *What is this Management?* (1944) and BROWN and RAPHAEL'S *Managers, Men and Morale* (1948). Or among those with a more specialised approach: C. H. NORTHCOTT'S *Personnel Management* (1945) and MAY SMITH'S *Introduction to Industrial Psychology* (1943). Techniques for production management have also figured in a variety of publications, illustrated by two such different works as WILLSMORE'S *Modern Production Control* (1946) and VERNON'S *Manual of Industrial Management and Maintenance* (1946). Similar studies have appeared in other fields, including those of Budgetary Control and the special applications devised by T. G. ROSE under the title *Higher Control*. During the later years of the war (1944–45), the BRITISH STANDARDS INSTITUTION brought out an interesting series of booklets on management methods called *Office Aids to the Factory*, and a similar contribution to the wider spreading of knowledge of management practice was made in 1947–48 by the MANAGEMENT LIBRARY in a series of *Letters to Foremen*.

An unusual study was GILLESPIE'S *Free Expression in Industry* (1948), an interesting and original plea for recognition of the morale factor in human relations by the inclusion in the structure of management of freely elected "morale leaders" parallel to the "technical" executives and supervisors. Other contributions came from Britain's oldest teaching establishment in the field of management: the Manchester College of Technology founded its Department of Industrial Administration in 1918, but its first systematic publications appeared in 1946 as *The Manchester Monographs on Higher Management*.

In the more fundamental field of management principles, additions to British literature have been sparse, the only outstanding publication being L. URWICK'S *Elements of Administration* (1943). A pioneer study was E. F. L. BRECH'S *Management: Its Nature and Significance* (1946–53), an attempt to analyse the process of management into its basic elements and so reach the basis for a "theory of management". An American author ALVIN BROWN published two works, similarly endeavouring to expound the essential factors in the structure of organisation, virtually in logical line of succession from MOONEY and REILLEY. These two books are *Organisation—A Formulation of Principle* (1945) and *The Organisation of Industry* (1947). A parallel study from a background of American public service administration (though more concerned with the executive processes of delegation and decision than with organisation structure) is SIMON'S *Administrative Behaviour* (1947). Another important American addition to literature in the more practical field is COPELAND and TOWL'S *The Board of Directors and Business Management* (1947), at that time the only study of its kind, systematically analysing the functions of the

Directors. Two British studies have in the interim complemented this work: *The Company Director* by ALFRED READ (1953) and *Company Direction* by J. W. SEYMOUR (1954), together providing a full review of the legal and functional responsibilities of directors in public and private companies. In the field of combined analytical and practical studies, a major pioneer work of recent years was the specialist though comprehensive volume *Organisation—The Framework of Management* by E. F. L. BRECH (1957).

British interest has also included other aspects of management practice, particularly where newer techniques are evolving: for example, in the realm of budgeting and financial control considerable impetus has been given by the Institutes of CHARTERED ACCOUNTANTS and of COST AND WORKS ACCOUNTANTS from their separate recognition of "management accounting" in the operating performance figures in the factory departments into an overall review of the commercial and financial position—the logical culmination of the development of earlier techniques in standard cost and "higher" control. Apart from specific reports by the two Institutes mentioned, there have been two or three special studies in this field, notably: the three volumes of *An Introduction to Cost Accountancy* by WARWICK DOBSON (1954), *Cost Control for Management* by EVANS HEMMING (1952), and *A Guide to Management Accounting* by BROAD and CARMICHAEL (1957). In the light of the emergence of electronic techniques in the control field, a special study for mention is *Electronic Digital Computers* by SANDFORD-SMITH (1957).

Throughout the postwar years, British studies of management practice have been assisted by numerous publications of the BRITISH INSTITUTE OF MANAGEMENT. The quarterly journal, *The British Management Review,* first appeared in the later 1930s, but was seriously interrupted by wartime difficulties and did not resume serious publication until 1946–47, continuing thereafter until merged into the monthly journal *The Manager* at a less serious level of treatment. Better known are the Institute's numerous pamphlets and booklets, in part reproducing Conference Papers on selected subjects, while others are specific studies of aspects of management practice. To supplement these aids to the practising manager interested to pursue serious professional development, the Institute has always maintained a reference and lending library service, plus a literature information service including monthly "abstracts" of British and foreign publications.

Within very recent years, literature from both American and British sources has included comprehensive reports of research projects directed to the deeper investigation of selected aspects of management, often sociological in character. A field of special interest in Britain has been that of selection, training and career patterns of managers: a major study published in 1955 was *Management Succession* by the ACTON SOCIETY TRUST, covering the policies and practices of the fifty-odd British firms employing over 10,000 persons. Two complementary studies were reported by COPEMAN in *Leaders of British Industry* (1957) and *Pay and Promotion for Executives* (1957).

With a more specific sociological background are reports published by or on behalf of some of the Universities which had sponsored research projects; for example:

(i) *Company Executive Development Schemes* (University of Manchester in association with the British Institute of Management, 1957): a comparative and analytical review of schemes for management succession as carried out by a sample of one hundred firms in north-west England.

(ii) *Technical Change and Industrial Relations* (University of Liverpool, under the direction of W. H. Scott, 1956): a study of the factors assisting and/or impeding the introduction of technological changes in a large steelworks.

(iii) *Management and Innovation* (University of Edinburgh, under the auspices of the Social Services Research Centre, 1960): a comparable study spread over a number of smaller firms, instead of being concentrated in one plant.

Another field of special interest in Great Britain, paralleling that in management succession, has been the experience of employing University Graduates in industrial and commercial positions on a large scale. This, virtually an unusual or unknown phenomenon before 1939, had by 1959 reached such a level that nearly half of all the Graduates leaving the Universities each year were entering industry or commerce as first employment. A first study of this development was made by P.E.P. (London) in 1954 and a full review was published under the title *Graduates in Industry* (Allen & Unwin, 1957). The subject was of sufficient popular interest to warrant the commercial publication of a *Directory of Opportunities for Graduates* (C. Labovitch: Cornmarket Press, 1957).

The literature of management has had many contributions made to it in recent years on an international scale, emanating particularly from the specialist departments and study groups of the European Productivity Agency. Under this stimulus, too, there has emerged a greater flow of studies and textbooks in European languages, many of them translations from the English or American sources. A truly international commercial venture, in a broader but related field of interest, is the series of Social Studies initiated by the North Holland Publishing Company of Amsterdam in 1957, most of the volumes published being of joint authorship, Dutch, English and American. Literature with an international character has been available for more than 25 years in the published volumes of the *Proceedings of the International Management Congress,* especially from the time of the Seventh Congress (1935) onwards. Originated in Prague in 1924, the Congress represents a forum of world-wide opinion in the field of industrial and commercial management and public administration. By the 1930s the Congress had settled into the rhythm of its three-yearly assemblies, held each time in a different country; the wartime interruption was made good with the resumption of the series at Stockholm in 1947. A considerable number of papers are prepared for each Congress under the auspices of the National Management Institutes of the many participating countries, the broad theme being determined by the International Committee on Scientific Management which is the sponsoring body. The volumes of Proceedings thus represent a collection of material on innumerable aspects of management principle and practice, prepared usually at the highest available level within the countries concerned. In more recent years (1958), this endeavour has been supplemented by a new body, the INTERNATIONAL ACADEMY OF MANAGEMENT, founded as a forum for the more distinguished contributors to the advancement of thought and practice; at the time of writing the Academy has produced no publications, but there is indication that it may become the focal point of high-level literature on an international scale comparable with anything in the academic world in other fields.

* * * * *

It would not indeed be untrue at the middle of the twentieth century to claim that the practice of management is supported by a body of thought and a volume of literature not far below that of other branches of human endeavour. That much of the literature is as yet superficial is an inevitable by-product of the early stage so far reached in the development of the management skills—the signs are many that improving and expanding practice is promoting depth of thought, and the deepening of treatment in literature will in due course be a natural corollary everywhere. The truth of this is already manifestly evident in the character of much of the literature emanating from American sources in recent years.

SCHEDULES OF RESPONSIBILITIES

THE following schedules, submitted as illustrations, are extracts drawn from various companies, in which full definitions of responsibilities had been laid down, though they have been remodelled here to conform to a common pattern of presentation. They may be used as guides for drawing up similar schedules, appropriate to the organisation concerned, but they should *not* be regarded as *models to be reproduced*, nor necessarily as suggestions for the content of responsibilities of corresponding executives in other organisations.

It is also relevant to point out that titles vary considerably: those used in the following illustrations are the ones adopted in the organisations concerned, and are *not* necessarily recommended as standards.

Title	*Code Reference*
Managing Director	LG/1
General Production Manager	LG/2
Factory Manager	LG/3
Work Study Supervisor	LG/4
Company Secretary	LG/5
Chief Accountant	LG/6
Clerical Methods Manager	LG/7
Personnel Officer	LG/8
Marketing Manager	LG/9
Sales Manager	LG/10

N.B.—Except in the cases of 6–7 and 9–10, these ten illustrations are NOT INTERRELATED.

The following schedules set down the main responsibilities in general terms, without attempting to specify duties or activities in detail. Some Directors prefer to follow the latter practice and this is a matter largely depending on individual preference. Definitions of responsibilities in the sense here illustrated provide an adequate basis for determining the scope of each position and for pointing to the interrelations. At the same time, they leave scope for initiative and a progressive outlook in interpretation. But they require vigilance to ensure continuous co-ordination and balance.

Sheet Ref.: LG/1
Date of Issue: May 1958.

Title: MANAGING DIRECTOR

Responsible to: Board of Directors.

Responsible for

1. Carrying into effect the policy laid down by the Board of Directors as set out in the Statement dated 12th September, 1957, and subsequent amendments as recorded in the Board Minutes.

2. Communication and interpretation of policy for the information and instruction of subordinate executives and, through them, of other members of the organisation.

3. Keeping the operations of the Company under constant review and presenting to the Board of Directors periodically accounts and statistics showing the progress and current position of the Company's affairs.

4. Maintaining definitions and structure of responsibilities of executive and supervisory positions in the organisation up to date with requirements.

5. Approving manufacturing, distributing and development plans submitted by the senior executives concerned.

6. Giving decisions and interpretations of policy in cases where a proposed course of action by an executive entails, for good reason, a departure from agreed policy.

7. Ensuring adequate arrangements to safeguard the continuity of supplies to customers.

8. Giving adequate attention to a continuous study, in association with the executives concerned, of the effectiveness of operation of all parts of the organisation. (In practice this responsibility will be carried out to a large extent by the customary periodical review of operating performance against budget standards.)

9. Determining and/or approving arrangements to ensure that adequate contact is maintained on the Company's behalf with Government Departments, and Technical, Trade and Research Associations, including those devoted to the advancement of management.

10. Ensuring adequate co-ordination of activities throughout the organisation.

11. Ensuring adequate facilities for the development of executive and supervisory staffs and the encouragement of management research.

Special Duties

1. To consider suggestions from subordinate executives in regard to the promotion of the Company's policy and organisation and to submit them objectively to the Board of Directors.

2. To review, from the standpoint of the Company as a whole, reports received from specialist executives in relation to their own field.

3. To ensure that all members of the executive and supervisory staff understand the nature and importance of budgetary control principles

and are familiar with the application of such principles to the activities carried out within their own jurisdiction.

4. To give adequate attention to promoting and maintaining a high level of morale among the executive and supervisory staffs, and throughout the organisation.

Limitations

1. Not authorised to incur capital expenditure in excess of £5,000 in any one financial year without the specific consent of the Board.

2. Not to dispose of the Company's properties or assets, other than stocks in trade of waste materials, without the consent of the Board.

Immediate Subordinates

Factory Manager.	Personnel Officer.
Sales Manager.	Research Engineer.
Chief Accountant.	Personal Assistant.

Committees—Ex officio member of all Committees set up in connection with the management of the Company's affairs. Empowered to appoint a subordinate to represent him on any such Committees, except those concerned with Finance and Technical Development.

Sheet Ref.: LG/2
Date of Issue: July 1957.

Title: GENERAL PRODUCTION MANAGER
Responsible to: Managing Director.

Responsible for

1. The formulation of production plans and programmes within the agreed policy, suitably designed to carry such policy into effect.

2. Co-ordination and control of all production activities.

3. Co-ordination of production plans and progress with sales programme.

4. Adequate supervision of production activities to ensure that progress is in conformity with plans: day-to-day responsibility for production activities rests with the local Factory Managers.

5. The maintenance of the Company's plant, machinery and tools in effective working condition; purchase of additional items as necessitated by production plans, and within budget limits.

6. Maintenance of the Company's premises and buildings, including adequate provision for renewals, redecorations, etc., as required to maintain the premises in good order.

7. Ensuring that local Factory Managers maintain factory services, power supplies, internal transport, etc., appropriate to requirements in accordance with production plans.

8. Co-ordination of the purchase and delivery of raw materials, tools etc., with progress of production.

9. Co-ordination of work in progress and stock levels at local factories with sales programmes and with current delivery position.

10. Establishment of suitable procedures for effective control and prevention of waste of materials, tools, etc., in local factory stores.

11. Ensuring provision for adequate research and technical development services in relation to the Company's products, materials and equipment, and also provision for adequate test of raw materials received, to ensure conformity with standards.

12. Ensuring that Managers and Supervisors within production divisions carry out personnel policy as advised by the Personnel Officer.

13. Continuous review of the Company's manufacturing operations in all aspects, to ensure the maintenance of a high level of effectiveness.

14. Continuous effective control over expenditure on account of manufacturing and development activities in accordance with budgets.

15. Ensuring that statutory and other legal records in respect of the Company's manufacturing activities are properly maintained and that internal records approved by the Managing Director are maintained.

16. Submitting to the Managing Director as required statistical and other reports in regard to manufacturing and development activities and expenses, and such other data as may be called for.

17. Attending, as representative of the Company, Trade Union or Joint Industrial Council negotiations dealing with matters of policy

affecting the Company's manufacturing activities or employment (as distinct from matters of routine procedure or local disputes).

18. Representing the Company at Trade Association or Technical Association meetings concerned with manufacturing or development.

Special Duties

1. Preparing for submission to the Managing Director at the appropriate time a budget indicating proposed manufacturing and development plans, designed to fit in with the Company's policy and Purchasing Budget in respect of plant, equipment, tools, materials, etc.

2. Determination of standards of manufacturing and development activity as a basis for continuous control over relative expenditure.

3. Collaboration with the Personnel Officer in determining wage rates and supplementary payments to concur with agreements reached within the Joint Industrial Council.

4. Collaboration with the Personnel Officer in regard to adequate provision for the training of supervisory staffs and skilled operatives.

Limitations

1. *Re* item 5 above: the General Production Manager is not authorised to incur expenditure on plant, etc., outside the agreed budgeted items without the specific consent of the Managing Director.

2. Direct responsibility for manufacturing operations is in the hands of the Factory Manager at each Works, unless for special reasons in times of emergency the General Production Manager decides otherwise.

Immediate Subordinates

Factory Managers, at North, South and East Works.
Planning Manager, at Head Office.
Chief Engineer, at Head Office.
Purchasing Agent, at Head Office.

Functional Contacts

Sales Manager, at Head Office.
Chief Accountant, at Head Office.
Cost Accountants, at North, South and East Works.
Group Personnel Officer, at Head Office.
Assistant Personnel Officers, at North, South and East Works.

Committees

1. *Ex officio* member of Group Works Council.
2. Company's representative on Joint Industrial Council.

Sheet Ref.: LG/3
Date of Issue: April 1956.

Title: FACTORY MANAGER

Responsible to: Managing Director.

Responsible for

1. Advising and assisting the Managing Director in determining the programme of production.
2. Planning and supervising all manufacturing activities for carrying out the programme of production when agreed.
3. Maintaining suitable procedures for the effective planning and control of production.
4. Maintaining quality standards of the Company's products.
5. Determining and maintaining scales of wage rates and piece-work prices in accordance with Agreements and local levels.
6. Maintaining in factory and subsidiary services adequate labour supply to ensure achievement of production programme.
7. Determining conditions and regulations of employment affecting all members of the factory personnel. For these and other matters concerned with personnel, the Factory Manager has a Personnel Officer as his immediate subordinate in an advisory capacity.
8. Promoting a high level of morale among members of the factory personnel in order to ensure a good standard of productivity.
9. The maintenance of discipline.
10. Conducting all contacts and negotiations with Trade Unions on the Company's behalf.
11. Maintaining equipment, plant and tools in effective condition.
12. The purchasing and storing of all raw materials for production.
13. Adhering to cost standards laid down.
14. Keeping contact with Development and Design Engineer in respect of quality standards, improvements, modifications, etc.

Limitations

Not entitled to purchase plant or materials in quantities in excess of £100 per month without the sanction of the Chief Accountant.

Immediate Subordinates

Personnel Officer.   Manufacturing Department Supervisors.
Buyer and Stores Keeper. Maintenance Engineer.
Chief Inspector.   Production Control Supervisor.

Functional Contacts

Chief Accountant, for financial matters and Cost Standards.
Sales Manager, for delivery, special orders and complaints.
Development and Design Engineer, for design and quality standards.

Committees—Members of Technical Development Committee and Chairman of Works Committee.

Sheet Ref.: LG/4
Date of Issue: June 1954.

Title: WORK STUDY SUPERVISOR

Responsible to: Works Manager.

Responsible for

1. Carrying out Work Studies of manufacturing and handling operations as instructed by the Works Manager and in collaboration with the responsible Foreman concerned.

2. Establishing accurate time standards and notifying these to interested parties in accordance with agreed procedures.

3. Determining appropriate time allowances in respect of operations carried out under non-standard conditions.

4. In collaboration with the Personnel Department, classifying operations into appropriate rate grades.

5. Determining and recommending to the Works Manager standard methods and equipment for all manufacturing and handling operations.

6. Determining and recommending to the Works Manager the correct sequence of operations and the appropriate personnel grades to be used.

7. Assisting the Works Manager in determining standards for material utilisation, reject percentages, etc.

8. Collaborating with the Office Manager in the determination and establishment of appropriate procedures to ensure the communication to all interested parties of time standards, job specifications, route cards, study sheets, work tickets, piece-work tickets, etc.

9. Co-ordination of work study activities with Production Control Office, Design Department and Drawing Office, Personnel Department, and Raw Material and Tools Stores.

Limitations

1. The Work Study Supervisor has no authority to issue or alter work standards without the approval of the Works Manager.

2. No authority to alter methods of operation without the approval of the Works Manager.

3. No authority to fix or quote rates of payment or piece-work prices.

4. Not to give any instructions or orders to operatives.

Immediate Subordinates—Work Study Staff.

Functional Contacts

Assistant Works Manager (Production Control Office).
Drawing Office Supervisor.   Toolroom Foreman.
Foremen of Manufacturing Departments.
Foremen of Inspection Department.
Personnel Officer.   Office Manager.

Committees—Co-opted member of Joint Production Committee.

Sheet Ref.: LG/5
Date of Issue: March 1957.

Title: COMPANY SECRETARY

Responsible to: Board of Directors.

N.B.—(a) The Secretary is also the Chief Accountant, and in this respect is responsible to the Managing Director according to the schedule set out on Sheet Ref. BC 2/1 (not shown here).

(b) In respect of the routine work of the Secretarial Department and the control of staff engaged in those activities, the Secretary has a functional responsibility to the Managing Director.

Responsible for

1. Fulfilment of the Company's legal responsibilities under the Companies Acts.

2. Preparation of agenda, minutes and other documents for regular and special meetings of the Board of Directors.

3. Attendance at Board Meetings.

4. Preparation of documents for Annual General or Extraordinary Meetings of shareholders and attendance thereat.

5. Dealing with the issue of shares and maintaining the statutory share registers and conducting appropriate activities connected with share transfers.

6. Ensuring that the Company's properties and interests are adequately insured and dealing with all insurance matters arising. (In matters connected with industrial insurance, or other aspects of National Insurance, this responsibility will be discharged in collaboration with the Personnel Officer.)

7. Custody and administration of the Company's property investments, patents and trade-marks.

8. Signing and sealing of agreements, leases and other official documents on the Company's behalf.

9. Advising the Managing Director in respect of legal matters pertinent to the Company's affairs, and conducting on behalf of the Board and/or Managing Director legal negotiations in connection therewith.

Limitations—None specified.   *Immediate Subordinates*—Nil.

Functional Contacts—With Personnel Officer in respect of Item 6

Committees—Nil.

Sheet Ref.: LG/6
Date of Issue: July 1958.

Title: CHIEF ACCOUNTANT

Responsible to

1. Managing Director in respect of all activities set out below.

2. The Chief Accountant also assists the Secretary by the supervision of the activities of the Staffs engaged on secretarial routines (share matters, etc.) and in this respect is responsible to the Secretary.[1]

Responsible for

1. Planning and control of all expenditure connected with fulfilment of Company's policy as interpreted by the Managing Director. Also for carrying out financial policy laid down by the Board.

2. Preparing and issuing budgets designed to express the Company's policy and to ensure the necessary control of operations.

3. Keeping adequate accounts and records covering all aspects of the Company's business transactions and preparing Annual Accounts for presentation to the Board and shareholders.

4. Keeping appropriate records and accounts designed to show the current position in respect of outside commitments and charges, and also designed to keep the Managing Director adequately informed in regard to the control of costs.

5. Preparing and issuing as agreed periodic statements to show the current operating and financial position in relation to the budget.

6. Drawing the Managing Director's attention to departure from policy, plans or budgets, or any other special features revealed by the periodic reports.

7. Passing all accounts for payment.

8. Receiving, banking and accounting for all moneys received, including foreign currency, bills of exchange and petty cash.

9. In collaboration with the Sales Manager ensuring adequate provision for collecting money due from customers.

10. Maintaining and issuing to managers concerned information for cost control of labour, material and overheads.

11. Preparing reports or statistics required by the Managing Director or for other executives as approved by the Managing Director.

12. Keeping statutory records regarding salaries and wages, and other internal records approved by the Managing Director.

13. Planning control and co-ordination of clerical methods throughout the organisation (in this responsibility the Chief Accountant is assisted by a Clerical Methods Manager: see Schedule LG/7).

[1] In this Company, the Secretary is a part-time professional appointment.

Special Duties

1. Collaborating with the Secretary in respect of secretarial routines (see note in opening item).

2. Collaborating with the Secretary in respect of statutory and other official records (see item 12 above).

3. Collaborating with the Personnel Officer in regard to salaries, engagement, employment and working conditions, and similar matters in respect of accounting and clerical staffs.

4. Advising the Managing Director on matters of taxation or other statutory financial matters on the Secretary's behalf.

5. Maintaining contacts on the Company's behalf with Government Departments or other organisations in respect of matters pertinent to the Company's finances, when so required by the Secretary.

6. Attendance at Board Meetings for routine matters of financial character, or when called for.

Limitations—None specified.

Immediate Subordinates

Assistant Accountant.
Cost Accountant.
Clerical Methods Manager.

Functional Contacts

All executives on financial matters.

All executives on matters concerned with cost control procedures or clerical methods, through the appropriate Assistant.

Personnel Officer concerning accounting and clerical staffs.

Committees—Available for attendance at Works Council when required.

Sheet Ref.: LG/7
Date of Issue: July 1958.

Title: CLERICAL METHODS MANAGER

Responsible to: Chief Accountant.

Responsible for

1. The planning of all clerical activities throughout the organisation, including methods of work, equipment, supplies and personnel required.

2. Sanctioning and/or refusing appointment of permanent or temporary clerical staff not in accordance with agreed budgets.

3. Authorising purchase of office machinery and equipment.

4. Provision and maintenance of records of office machinery and equipment.

5. Examination and approval of all proposals for forms, stationery, printing and other office supplies, to ensure that they conform to general policy and plans, and are such as to attain the desirable standards of simplification and economy.

6. Determination and sanctioning of office layout and use of accommodation available.

7. Determining office procedures and clerical methods and compiling a manual setting out details thereof.

8. Collaborating with the Personnel Officer in respect of records of accounting and clerical staff.

9. Installing and maintaining records of output, expense, etc., as necessary for the effective control of clerical operations and clerical costs.

10. Planning and supervision of central office services, namely, telephone and messenger services, inward and outgoing postal services, copy-typing pool.

11. In association with the Personnel Officer, ensuring the provision of office hygiene and the welfare of staffs.

Special Duties

1. The Clerical Methods Manager is entitled to undertake investigations or to call for a report on matters which he may consider to be departures from current policy or practice.

2. Before taking any decisions on findings of such investigations, he must report back to the Chief Accountant.

Limitations

1. While responsibility for the planning and requisitioning of additional members of clerical staff rests with the Clerical Methods Manager, the recruitment of such staff shall be handled by the Personnel Department and selected candidates submitted for approval to the Clerical Methods Manager.

2. Clerical methods, routines, forms, etc., relating to production planning and control shall be determined in collaboration with the Factory Manager.

3. Accounting routines can be determined only with the direct sanction of the Chief Accountant.

4. Clerical methods, routines and forms relating to Sales Office procedures shall be referred to the Sales Manager for approval.

Immediate Subordinates—Nil.

Functional Contacts—All executives and supervisors on matters pertinent to clerical methods, routines and documents.

Committees—Nil.

Sheet Ref.: LG/8
Date of Issue: September 1957.

Title: PERSONNEL OFFICER
Responsible to: Managing Director.

Responsible for

1. Advising and assisting the Managing Director in preparing the Company's personnel policy for formulation by the Board.

2. Ensuring that the Company's personnel policy is made known to all executives and supervisory staffs and to all employees of the Company.

3. Ensuring that the Company's personnel policy is effectively carried out throughout the organisation.

4. Developing and maintaining procedures for recruitment of personnel in accordance with the budgets and programmes laid down and in collaboration respectively with:

(*a*) Factory Personnel—the Works Manager and Manufacturing Department Supervisors.

(*b*) Office Personnel—the Chief Accountant.

(*c*) Sales Personnel—the Distribution Manager.

5. Developing and maintaining training facilities in accordance with the Company's policy and output programmes. To include arrangements for juveniles' attendance at local colleges.

6. Determining, for the approval of the Managing Director, the terms and conditions of employment for all personnel up to, but excluding, the senior executive level.

N.B.—"Senior executive level" means those members of the executive staff directly responsible to the Managing Director.

7. Defining, in collaboration with the Factory Manager and/or Chief Accountant, regulations and rules for the conduct of Factory and Office personnel while on the Company's premises.

N.B.—In accordance with the Company's policy, such regulations shall be worked out in consultation with representatives of the staffs concerned.

8. Carrying out on the Company's behalf all contacts with officials of the Ministry of Labour, including the Factories Inspectors.

9. Maintaining on the Company's behalf current relations with and handling all negotiations with Trade Unions, Employers' Associations, Educational Establishments, and other bodies concerning matters affecting employment in the Company's service.

N.B.—In the case of formal negotiations with Trade Unions, this responsibility is to be discharged in collaboration with the Factory Manager.

10. Providing appropriate secretarial services for the Company's Works Council and subsidiary committees.

11. Advising on and ensuring, in conjunction with the Factory Manager and Supervisors, the maintenance of adequate standards of working conditions, safety precautions, first-aid and factory welfare services.

12. Maintaining suitable records and statistics of employment. This responsibility will be carried out on the basis of collaboration with the Accounts and Office Methods Departments to ensure co-ordination with procedures in respect of wages, etc.

13. Interviewing and assisting employees in regard to personal difficulties and problems affecting ability and contentment in work.

14. The provision of canteen services within the financial limits laid down; executive control of Canteen Manageress and staff.

15. Providing adequate medical and health advisory services within the financial limits laid down by the Board. The Personnel Officer is the primary executive contact for the Medical Officer (part-time) and the executive responsible for Nursing and First-aid staffs.

16. Providing within the Personnel Department adequate current information regarding local and industrial wage rates and other matters pertinent to the fulfilment of the Company's policy, including statutory orders, regulations, etc., with a view to ensuring that such information is available to the Managing Director or other executives as and when required.

17. Ensuring the correct fulfilment of the Company's obligations with regard to employment, including Official Registers and Returns.

Special Duties

1. Advising the Managing Director on the formulation and development of personnel policy, in order to keep it up-to-date and in respect of special conditions arising, e.g. in times of emergency.

2. Assisting the Managing Director in the development of training schemes for executive and supervisory staffs and carrying such facilities into effect on the Managing Director's behalf.

3. Acting as an arbiter in cases of dismissal, to ensure that no employee is dismissed from the Company's services except on grounds that conform with the agreed personnel policy.

4. Negotiations: except in the event of a local dispute, or in the formal discussion of policy matters, the Personnel Officer will be the Company's representative in all Trade Union negotiations and contacts. In formal negotiations, the Factory Manager will serve with him.

5. To attend Trade Association meetings on the Company's behalf when questions of employment or personnel are under discussion.

6. To maintain in the Company's interests contacts with organisations and activities devoted to the development of personnel management.

Limitations

1. The Personnel Officer carries no absolute right to engage staff, whether for Factory or Office employment. In filling requisitions submitted by executives or supervisors, he will submit suitable candidate(s) for their acceptance.

2. He has no authority to determine rates of pay, salaries or wages without reference to—

(a) the senior executive concerned; or

(b) the Managing Director.

3. He has no authority to transfer or dismiss members of the Company's personnel without the approval of the senior executive concerned.

Immediate Subordinates

Personal Assistant (female staff).

Canteen Manageress.

Nursing Staff.

The Medical Officer (retained on a part-time basis for professional services).

Functional Contacts

All executives and supervisors regarding matters pertaining to employment and personnel.

Chief Accountant in respect of Personnel Department routines, records, etc.

Committees

1. *Ex officio* member of Works Council, normally serving as Honorary Secretary to the Council.

2. *Ex officio* member of any Sub-committees set up by the Council, including Canteen Committee.

3. Co-opted member of the Sports and Social Club Committee.

Sheet Ref.: LG/9
Date of Issue: January 1958.

Title: MARKETING MANAGER

N.B.—See Note at end of document LG/10.

Responsible to: Managing Director.

Responsible for

1. Within the interpretation of policy specified by the Managing Director, planning and carrying into effect appropriate activities for—
   (*a*) the assessment of markets and potential customer demand;
   (*b*) the sale of the Company's products;
   (*c*) the storing of finished products and dispatch to customers.

2. Preparation of sales budget showing anticipated sales and expenses in attaining them.

3. Keeping market conditions under continuous review in order to obtain the necessary information for the preparation of sales budgets and to assess the trend of actual and potential consumer demand.

4. Keeping price levels of the Company's products under continuous review in order to ensure that they are competitive and profitable.

5. Fixing prices for special qualities or orders on the basis of known costs and overhead margins.

6. Within the limits of the agreed policy, determining special conditions of sale in particular cases, e.g. appropriate discounts.

7. Keeping a continuous watch on acceptability of Company's products, and recommending research or investigation in respect of improvements in quality, new design or the correction of deficiencies.

8. Investigating serious or recurrent complaints from customers in respect of qualities, delivery or service, and passing forward to the Production Manager the findings of such enquiries.

9. Ensuring adequate control of distribution activities, so that costs are kept within the agreed budget levels.

10. In collaboration with the Personnel Officer, appointing appropriate staff for sales, clerical and warehouse purposes, and determining appropriate levels of remuneration and conditions of employment.

11. Undertaking appropriate activities for the developing of and promotion of sales of the Company's products.

12. Keeping contact with the Trade Association in respect of all matters concerned with prices and conditions of sale.

Special Duties

1. To submit to the Managing Director at six-monthly intervals a report of general economic conditions bearing on current and future sales of the Company's products.

2. To have available in the Marketing Department current information regarding qualities and prices of products sold by competitors.

3. To encourage from members of the Sales Staff contributions in respect of design or improvement of the Company's products.

4. To organise a yearly Conference of Sales Staff.

Limitations

1. No special market investigations involving a cost of more than £500 in any one financial year may be undertaken without the Managing Director's sanction.
2. No discounts outside the standard range may be granted without the Managing Director's sanction.

Immediate Subordinates

Sales Manager
Advertising Manager.
Assistant Sales Manager.

Functional Contacts

Factory Manager, re sales/production programme.
Chief Accountant, re financial matters and clerical methods.
Personnel Officer, in all matters regarding staff.

Committees

1. Member of Managing Director's Development Committee.
2. Chairman of Sales Conference.

Sheet Ref.: LG/10
Date of Issue: January 1958.

Title: SALES MANAGER
N.B.—See Note at end of this document.

Responsible to: Marketing Manager.

Responsible for

1. Planning and control of selling activities and associated warehouse and transport activities, in order to carry into effect the agreed sales budget.
2. Co-operation with Marketing Manager in determining sales budget.
3. Ensuring adequate control of the selling expense in accordance with agreed budget.
4. Maintaining adequate records of the Company's sales activities suitably analysed to show trends in conformity with budget and to reveal sources of excess costs.
5. Determining boundaries for sales territories within the United Kingdom.
6. The issue of instructions and information regarding conditions of sale to home salesmen and overseas agents.
7. Handling all contacts with overseas agents in respect of export sales.
8. The training of sales staff and supervision of all selling activities.
9. Maintaining adequate control of stocks in the main warehouse and in local warehouses in Northern and Western territories.

10. Considering and deciding on requests from salesmen or customers for special consideration in relation to qualities, prices, discounts or delivery.

11. Maintaining close contact with salesmen, and through them with customers, and making visits to customers at suitable intervals.

12. Taking up as a matter of urgency and dealing with complaints received from customers and passing report to Marketing Manager.

13. General supervision of Sales Office staffs and activities.

14. Ensuring the maintenance of adequate transport services within the budgeted costs.

Special Duties—None specified.   *Limitations*—None specified.

Immediate Subordinates

Warehouse Supervisor.
Transport Supervisor.
Salesmen.

Functional Contacts

Production Manager, in regard to customer complaints.
Chief Accountant, in respect of financial matters and clerical methods.
Personnel Officer, in regard to staff matters.

Committees—Attendance at Sales Conference.

NOTE.—The titles used in these last two schedules (LG/9 and LG/10) are unusual: the title "Sales Manager" is more frequently used for the senior post, carrying the wider responsibilities. The division of items between the two posts portrayed here may also be found a little unusual, being determined by specific circumstances in the organisation concerned.

*   *   *   *   *

A further set of responsibilities, in fuller detail and showing the considerable extent of interrelation within a given company, is contained in Chapter VII of Brech's *Organisation—the Framework of Management*.

CHAPTER I

MARKETING

THE provision of services to any community is not in most instances the direct concern of industry or commerce, but is catered for by local or national Government, and a study of services of this nature is not a part of this chapter.

However, many of the industrial and consumer products which are in constant and everyday use both in industry and in the home, in a developed country such as the United Kingdom, would never have come into general use had the provision of water, gas or electricity not been capable of matching, and perhaps leading, such industrial expansion as we have experienced.

In the drive to expand sales and markets in as yet undeveloped areas, consideration must be given to the levels of supply achieved by the main services. Exploiting national resources can and does give rise to related industrial development.

SCOPE AND DEFINITION

Emerson said: "If a man write a better book, preach a better sermon, or make a better mousetrap than his neighbour, though he build his house in the woods, the world will make a beaten path to his door."

This quotation may have been applicable in the nineteenth century, but it certainly is not capable of serious consideration in the highly developed marketing pattern of the second half of the twentieth century.

What is marketing? There are many definitions, but the definition which will be referred to consistently throughout this section is:

"Marketing is the process of determining consumer demand for a product or service, motivating its sale, and distributing it into ultimate consumption at a profit."

During the following chapters the various functions within the total marketing operation will be examined in broad detail, with each of the related functions being applied to that part of this definition of marketing.

The size of the company may dictate the number of executives employed in any one department within the company, but irrespective of size, this definition of marketing, and the consideration of the market which a manufacturer is to serve, will give rise to the same basic principles on which to operate.

The simplest form of marketing operation contains the same three basic elements as does the most complicated and detailed. For example, consider a village shoemaker who has his shop in the front part of his house and who makes the shoes, sells them, delivers them and collects the money all by himself. He is in close contact with his customers. If he misjudges consumer demand and makes his shoes too heavy, or the wrong style, etc., he very quickly learns about it. Furthermore, he is in a position to make changes to bring the product more in line with the demands of his customers. Not only is there the flow from production through to consumer of the product itself, and the return flow of money, but there is the vital flow of information about the customers' needs and desires.

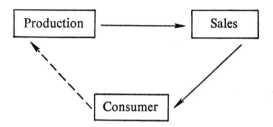

However, in most consumer goods (and, to varying degrees, industrial) marketing there will be no direct contact between sales and the ultimate consumer. In the United Kingdom, the ultimate consumer will reside in some 16,000,000 households. In dealing with mass consumer items of low unit cost, with perhaps a relatively low profit, it is not feasible economically to maintain this direct contact. Instead, there are retailers operating between the manufacturer and the consumer, providing a convenient place where the consumer can be brought into ready contact with the hundreds of items of grocery or chemist or electrical products which he or she requires.

Because there are some 600,000 retail shopping outlets in the United Kingdom, so there is the wholesaler or middleman who can serve the retailer with the variety and quantity of products received in bulk from the manufacturer.

Both these elements in the distributive link make an effective break between the *sales* department and the consumer, and this is the first difference between marketing as practised by the village shoemaker and marketing as practised by the majority of manufacturing companies.

The second important difference is that no longer is there any direct contact between the *production* department and the ultimate consumer, or even between the production department and the wholesaler and retailer. Why? Because the product is delivered by means of transport, either company-owned or contracted. So another available source of information about customer needs and attitudes has been severed.

If it is assumed that the *sales* department, through its efforts, has got the product into distribution at retail level, then we come to the next phase of our definition of marketing: distribution into *ultimate consumption*. Clearly, this is where *advertising* and *public relations* play their part. It is unlikely that the product will be the only one of its type on sale, and it is essential to take every possible action to increase the likelihood that when the consumer comes into a shop he or she will buy this particular product and not one produced by a competitor. It is better to recognise at the outset that the retailer is interested mainly in gross turnover and net profit. To get this he has to supply what his customer requires.

Public relations, through editorial columns and many other channels, all help in this objective—motivating the sale of the product. Sales promotion should complete the job that has been started by advertising and public relations, to ensure that the efforts of the production people in manufacturing, and the marketing people in selling and publicising the product, all combine together in moving the product the last three feet across the counter into the shopping basket and eventually to the home.

If the product is "bad" to the extent that it is not in keeping with what the consumer wants or needs, then unless this is realised promptly, the lack of communication between present-day marketing and the ultimate consumer can be fatal—financially. This is where *market research* comes in.

The fact that

—new ideas remain new for an increasingly short period of time,
—purchasing and user habits change,
—qualities, prices and methods of distribution vary,
—new products may need testing by the consumer before introduction into the market,
  advertising effectiveness can benefit from some form of measurement,
—distribution levels and share of market can be vital pieces of information,
—the market is a constantly changing combination of mixtures,

all involve market research, which, indeed, is the life-blood of many a large manufacturing concern. Market research does not have to be complicated. It may be carried out by one man; whatever its form it bridges the gap between the manufacturer and the consumer—the gap that is not present with the village shoemaker.

To refer back to the definition of marketing:

" . . . . the process of determining consumer demand for a product or service, motivating its sale, and distributing it into ultimate consumption at a profit."

The completion of the marketing process and the fulfilment of the whole company's efforts come with the ultimate three words ". . . at a profit."

Theodore Levitt[1] has claimed that the need which first produced the railways has not declined as both passenger and freight transport have continued to grow. The reason why the railways are in trouble is because that need has been filled by others; motor cars, transport vehicles, aeroplanes—it was not filled by the railway companies. The customers were gained by other companies because the railways thought of themselves as being in the "railway" business rather than in the "transport" business, and the reason why they defined their industry wrongly was because they were "railway" orientated and not "transport" orientated; they were "product" orientated instead of "customer" orientated. Mr. Levitt claimed four conditions which would ensure a history of bountiful expansion and undetected decay:

1. The belief that growth is assured by an expanding and more affluent population.
2. The belief that there is no competitive substitute for the industry's major product.
3. Too much faith in mass production and in the advantages of rapidly declining unit costs as output rises.
4. Preoccupation with a product that lends itself to carefully controlled scientific experimentation, improvement and manufacturing cost reduction.

Certainly an expanding population, providing new users who become increasingly affluent, is fine and is considerably better than a shrinking market. In itself, it is in no way sufficient to ensure a continuation of a company's growth.

Similarly, there is no guarantee against product obsolescence; if a company's own research does not make it obsolete then another's might or will. Mass production does generate greater pressure to sell the product, but mass production is the lure and not the means for achieving company growth of profit and leads to an emphasis on selling and not marketing which, being a more complex process, is perhaps easier to ignore or discount.

[1] A talk on "Marketing Myopia," printed in the *Harvard Business Review*, July/August 1960.

Selling focuses attention on sales, whereas marketing focuses on the needs of the buyer and the idea of producing a product which will satisfy the needs of the customer. What is offered for sale is determined not so much by the seller as by the buyer, and the seller takes his lead from the buyer in such a way that the product becomes a consequence of the marketing effort rather than selling the consequence of production effort. This is not to imply that mass production is out of place and that the benefits of highly-geared productive capacity are small. Of course this is not true, but mass production must grow from realistic assessment of a marketing need.

Harry Ford is often quoted for his statement that he "would give the customer a car in any colour he wanted, so long as it was black". Nevertheless, his real strength did lie in marketing even although this statement may have been a little hard to understand, as he decided that at a certain price (500 dollars) he could sell millions of cars. Having decided this, he fashioned a production system on which he could produce these cars. To quote Henry Ford's philosophy as expressed by himself:

"Our policy is to reduce the price, extend the operations and improve the article. You will notice that the reduction of price comes first. We have never considered any costs as fixed. Therefore we first reduce the price to the point where we believe more sales will result. Then we go ahead and try to make the prices. We do not bother about the costs. The new price forces the costs down. The most usual way is to take costs and then determine the price, and although that method may be scientific in the narrow sense it is not scientific in the broad sense, because what earthly use is it to know the cost if it tells you that you cannot manufacture at a price at which the article can be sold? But more to the point is the fact that, although one may calculate what a cost is, and of course all of our costs are carefully calculated, no one knows what a cost ought to be. One of the ways of discovering . . . is to name a price so low as to force everybody in the place to the highest point of efficiency. The low price makes everybody dig for profits. We make more discoveries concerning manufacturing and selling under this forced method than by any method of leisurely investigation."[1]

Seventy-five years ago no other form of transport could compete with the railways—who would have thought that aeroplanes weighing a hundred tons and more, flying at 40,000 feet, carrying one hundred or more passengers and travelling at 600 miles per hour, were possible? Yet they have made obsolete many of the benefits originally enjoyed by the railways. If the railway companies had thought of themselves as transportation companies and not railway

[1] Henry Ford, *My Life and Work* (Doubleday, Page & Company, New York, 1923), pages 146–7.

companies, then perhaps they themselves would have developed aeroplanes to meet the requirements of the customers they serve.

SETTING THE MARKETING POLICY

The vital factor in commerce is the amount of profit which will accrue from the total sales, and this again is dependent upon the gross profit taken on the goods and upon the expenses of distribution. In reverse, the price factor has an important bearing on sales and the expenses have a bearing on the efficiency of both production and selling methods. This suggests, therefore, that finance and financial control, production and sales are entirely interdependent, and no marketing programme can be either conceived or executed without the closest co-ordination between all three at the highest level, and a knowledge of the profit requirements properly understood and stated either as net return on capital employed, or as a gross or net percentage profit on net sales volume. The lack of this co-operation has been a major fault in many of the larger industries in the past, and it is only in recent years that executives have developed the technique of pooling their knowledge in committee or conference work to achieve harmony in planning. The same error does not usually apply to the smaller concerns because of the closer personal contact of those in executive posts, but such firms are often lacking in efficiency in other ways, their size limiting the selling organisation available to them.

Mr. R. Landers, former sales director of Lever Sales, said: "The operation of a company can be likened to a three-legged stool from which if you take away any one of the legs, the stool (or the company) collapses." The production department, the commercial or financial department and the marketing department can be so described.

As Remus Harris states in *Creativity and Marketing*:

"As a practical business function, marketing is the total procedure of creating customers efficiently."

Until a demand has been created and satisfied a market cannot exist at all and the profits of a company can result only from the efficient creation of and supply to customers. This, therefore, implies the establishment of the whole company on a marketing aspect—which in turn imparts to top management the responsibility for directing the company, and the personnel within the company, to the understanding that the eventual consumer is the ultimate being upon which the company will depend. For this policy to be successful and not merely a contrived statement, the senior management or leader of a company should have certain broad aims and abilities:

The will to succeed.

Creativity.

Flexibility.

The ability to operate within defined principles.

The art of leadership, consequent delegation of responsibility and development of personnel.

Good business judgment to which is allied the importance of timing.

An awareness of the general economic situation related to the particular industry, to the country and to the world as a whole.

Formulation of a commercial policy based on sound economic intelligence.

Direction and control of the marketing operation must always be on a flexible plan because of the many factors that are outside the influence of any one company and even of nationalised or state monopolies. It is essential to control the marketing policy at top management level by means of a committee consisting of production, finance and marketing heads under the direction of the managing director. To enable this committee or group to apply the dictates of successful marketing management, as much detailed information as is required must be available.

Similarly, marketing management requires the same analytical basis of approach to remove as much as is possible from the field of conjecture, "hunches" or inspired guesses, and to develop through scientific application the maximum results from the co-ordinated efforts of all sections within the company.

It is true that most problems become easier to resolve when set down in writing. The basis of the marketing policy for a company or for a principal brand should therefore be set out in carefully prepared plans. The basis for these marketing plans may be summarised as follows:

MARKETING PLANS

A. *Purpose*

1. Provide systematic approach to planning.
2. Eliminate confusion and misunderstanding among the many groups involved in the marketing function itself, advertising (agency and department), commercial, product development, public relations, research and sales.
3. Ensure as far as possible that all phases of the marketing operation are working to common goals with regard to individual products and the company as a whole.
4. Set forth the marketing group's recommendations to management in such a way that (*a*) they can be understood *quickly and easily*, and (*b*) that all information essential to an intelligent decision is readily available.

5. Provide a permanent record of the company's marketing planning, brand by brand, and the reasoning behind it.
6. Develop continuity of thought and effort from one year to the next.

B. *Structure*

1. *Marketing Strategy Statement*

   (a) *Objectives.*—Outline of the major goals which have been agreed upon for the period in question. These must be reasonable and capable of measurement or they will be meaningless.

   (b) *Strategy.*—How it is proposed to accomplish the goals which have been set. Description of major courses of action recommended. Must be concise, factual, specific.

   (c) *Reasons for recommendations.*—Brief explanation as to reasons for suggesting a given objective or point of strategy. The marketing strategy statement should be brief and direct. There is no room for unsubstantiated guesswork.

2. *Appropriation Recommendation*

   This document should be prepared in four parts, and should also be brief and factual:

   (a) *General summary statement.*—Short opening paragraph, giving total sterling appropriation recommended, sales estimates in units, expenditure per unit, resulting profit expressed as percentage of net sales, comparison with previous budget period on basis of total sterling expenditure, sales estimate and expenditure per unit.

   (b) *Itemised budget, by six months periods and total.*—Showing each major category of expense. Included in this should be brief descriptions of the nature of the effort recommended, e.g. sales organisation to call on specific outlets; national daily newspapers as the advertising medium. There should be provision for such items as departmental administration, share of line productions, research, etc.

   (c) *Comparison with previous period and explanation of differences.*—Taking each major category of expense from (b) above, show extent to which it is over or under previous period's budget, and explain major differences.

   (d) *Summary of major budget items versus previous period.*— Show major items in sterling and as a percentage of total.

3. *Copy Strategy Statement*

   The purpose of this is to set up for the advertising agency's creative people objectives which are in keeping with the overall marketing objectives. A further purpose is to avoid wasted creative time and effort by having the creative approach thought through *before* copy and layout work starts. It is a guide, not a definitive statement.

Structure

(a) *Major aims.*—Statement of creative objectives.

(b) *Product.*—Essential qualities or characteristics which should be reflected in the public's impression or image of the product.

(c) *Sales appeals.*—The most important points of superiority and appeal.

4. *Media Strategy Statement*

The purpose of this is to set up objectives for the media planning group which are in keeping with the overall marketing objectives.

Structure

(a) Statement of *media* objectives that defines: who must be reached, where, how frequently, creative requirements, etc.

(b) Strategy statement that explains how these objectives will be obtained within budget.

(c) Reasons for recommendation—brief explanation why.

5. *Sales Promotion Strategy*

Similar in purpose and form to the other strategy statements.

6. *Supporting Data*

This section will vary in size and complexity with the product and the size of the appropriation. Its purpose is to assemble in one place all the basic information needed to justify the various recommendations set forth in the marketing plan. It may contain, for example, such things as share of market and distribution charts, special sales drives, consumer attitude and usage research summaries, special reports on reach and frequency, distribution, pattern of proposed television schedule, pay-out plan for any schemes—such as couponing, package design, case packing, etc.

Such a plan for the marketing of a nationally advertised pickle might, therefore, be drawn up as follows:

Preface.—Marketing background (a summary to set the scene for the forthcoming recommendation).

Recommendations

1. Marketing strategy.
2. Appropriation recommendations.
3. Copy strategy.
4. Media strategy.
5. Sales promotion policy.

Appendix

1. Sales estimates.
2. Production problems.

3. Media plan.
4. Description of advertising.
5. The pickle market.
   (a) Types of pickle.
   (b) Brands, prices and trade terms.
   (c) Quantity discounts.
   (d) Case packing.
   (e) Distribution.
   (f) The market.
   (g) The consumer.
   (h) Consumer economics.
   (i) Competitive advertising.
   (j) Competitive merchandising.

To assist the main decisions that have to be taken in the formulation of a company's (marketing) policy, there are many outside sources of information which can be contacted to yield indications upon which the policy can be based. To quote some:

1. Board of Trade Returns.
2. Various Government White Papers.
3. Government Census of Distribution, 1957.
4. Cambridge Economic Intelligence Unit, which produces regular quarterly statistical data and production trends and price forecasts.
5. Various Research Organisations (as referred to in Chapter II).

ORGANISATION

Marketing management does not have to be complex. Its function does not, in fact, alter too much from company to company—whether it be a vast organisation employing thousands of people, or whether it be a smaller unit employing a few hundred. In the smaller company, the individual may play a greater part than in the larger company, but in both instances marketing management is a team operation and the sum total of the qualities of the persons in this group makes the team effective. Theoretically, it is feasible to believe that all members of the team may be equal, but the fact is that some are more "equal" than others. Because of these differences between people there has to be a difference in responsibilities and operation of the members of the marketing group.

The successful marketing organisation, therefore, must be directed properly. In order to achieve this direction each member of the marketing group should appreciate and understand fully the job for which he is responsible.

Fig. 3 shows the principal areas of responsibility for the main sections of the marketing group. Each of these sections is examined

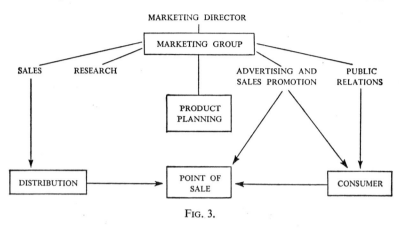

FIG. 3.

in more detail in the ensuing chapters, but it is as well to have an overall understanding of the responsibilities of these departments before proceeding with the more detailed examination.

1. Marketing Management

Through the marketing group meetings, the marketing executive (who will frequently be found bearing the title "marketing director") will ensure the participation of the members of his group—which will consist of the managers of the principal departments—in discussions affecting company marketing policy. These meetings must not be allowed to impart a stranglehold on day-to-day decisions, and individual managers should have their responsibilities and the level at which they can take decisions outlined to them.

2. Sales Department

In essence the sales department is responsible for distribution of the company's production through whatever channels may have been selected. This may involve the physical distribution of the goods as well as obtaining orders, but as this is more of a strictly functional operation there is a growing tendency to separate physical distribution, including stock control, warehousing, etc., from the sales department and to site this within the commercial responsibility.

3. Advertising/Public Relations

Both these departments have the prime responsibility of pre-selling the company's products to the consumer before a purchase is made.

4. *Product Management*

Many companies in both consumer and industrial marketing fields are developing brand or product managers, in whom is invested the responsibility for the planning and field operation of one or a group of products. Such a position may be sited in one of the departments or may be routed direct to the marketing director.

The product manager's prime responsibility is to increase the consumer sales of the product or group of products assigned to him and to ensure implementation of his company's policy. This he can achieve by co-ordinating all the various marketing and creative services at his disposal into a creative marketing plan. He must become the precursor of all that is contained within the plan.

At all times the product manager should act as a central source of information for the product, initiating developments on a continuous basis particularly as dictated by changing market conditions.

5. *Research*

Market or product research draws its information from channels of distribution, consumers and specific surveys, and relays its findings to the sales, advertising and public relations departments, as well as to management itself.

Proper communication is essential to sound organisation.

BUDGETING

On the assumption that the conditions of supply and demand operate normally, it is reasonable to base the whole structure of an industry or of a company upon the amount which it can sell. The sales forecasts, therefore, may be considered as the basis of industrial economy and may be the factor upon which all other activities depend. This applies equally to the village shoemaker or to the vast industrial concern. Logically, it will govern the amount of capital or plant which may be installed, the raw materials that will be required, the stocks and distribution to be achieved, the amount of promotional monies to be expended and, indeed, the size of the operation to be conducted. The first step, therefore, in any budgeting is the sales forecast.

Fortunately, it is seldom necessary to start sales forecasts, or indeed the whole operation of the planning of a commercial programme, from ground level, as most businesses will have some experience upon which to draw. However, whether developing a completely new industry, or progressing within one which is already established, the planning of a production programme based on the amount which can be sold is equally essential and will vary only by the margins of error dependent upon the normal fluctuations of business. These are reduced as far as possible by application of fundamental marketing principles by the management of the company —which demand sound judgment and detailed examination of pertinent factors and problems.

The task of financial and production planning and the preparation of the company budget will be made considerably easier by having available detailed marketing plans for the coming period. By the same token forward planning over, for instance, a five-year period can be related to capital and brand requirements only if realistic sales forecasts can be made. The matter of fact procedure which is applicable in the control of expenditure on a production unit allows for a more exact level of control than may be possible in marketing activities.

But establishing the sales forecasts does not remove the responsibility vested in the marketing director for maintaining low and economic marketing costs within budgeted figures. The upcharge of many consumer and industrial products, as between the cost at which the article is actually produced and that at which it is available to the consumer is such that it must dictate to a considerable extent the ultimate cost to the consumer. It is only necessary to consider the great number of people employed in the distribution of the products, in the shops and warehouses, in selling and advertising, in administration and in road and rail transport, to realise the expenditure which must be added to the cost of goods before they are sold to the consumer. This aspect becomes a greater significance in the marketing of products of high frequency sale through tens of thousands of retail outlets throughout the country.

When compiling marketing budgets it is necessary first to arrive at the total sales forecasts. To these can then be applied the total marketing expenses analysed in detail to the various departments. Marketing budgets will therefore include:

1. Total sales.
2. Total marketing expenses.
   (a) Selling expenses.
   (b) Delivery expenses.
3. Advertising and sales promotion.
4. Market research.
5. Public relations.

On a continuous basis it is possible to control the expenditure by means of monthly or quarterly analyses, depicting as much detail as may be possible or may be required by the company concerned. This will depend entirely on the use to which such details can be put. For example, a simple means of measuring sales results is as follows. Fig. 4 shows the quarterly sales results against budgeted figures. In this example it may be assumed that the marketing management appreciated the need for revision to marketing plans for the company or for the individual product to which this analysis may refer, so that the fourth quarter's sales were such that the total annual budget was achieved. Not all budgeting will be as accurate as this!

SALES

Quarter	Actual	Budget	Percentage of Budget Sales	Actual to Date	Budget to Date	Percentage of Budget Sales
Period	£	£		£	£	
Jan./Mar. .	1,100	1,000	110	1,100	1,000	110
Apr./June .	900	1,000	90	2,000	2,000	100
July/Sept. .	800	1,000	80	2,800	3,000	93
Oct./Dec. .	1,200	1,000	120	4,000	4,000	100
	4,000	4,000	100	4,000	4,000	100

FIG. 4.

A summary of expenditure can be shown in the same manner (Fig. 5), so that at any time during the period under consideration marketing and general management can relate performance to date to expenditure to date. A similar summary can also be arrived at for each of the other departments.

TOTAL MARKETING EXPENSE SUMMARY

Quarter	Actual	Budget	Percentage of Actual Sales	Percentage of Budget Sales	Actual to Date	Budget to Date	Percentage of Actual Sales	Percentage of Budget Sales
Period	£	£			£	£		
Jan./Mar. .	90	100	8	10	90	100	8	10
Apr./June .	90	100	10	10	180	200	9	10
July/Sept. .	120	100	15	10	300	300	11	10
Oct./Dec. .	100	100	8	10	400	400	10	10
	400	400	10	10	400	400	10	10

FIG. 5.

In total, the marketing budget may be outlined as follows:

SCHEDULES

SECTION I—INTRODUCTION

Foreword to Total Budget
No. 1. Net Sales Summary
No. 2. Total Marketing Expense Summary

SECTION II—SALES

"A" Consumer Sales	Foreword
Division	No. 3. Net Sales Summary
"B" Industrial	Foreword
Division	No. 4. Net Sales Summary
"C" Export	Foreword
Division	No. 5. Net Sales Summary
"D" Distribution	Foreword
Department	No. 6. Expense Summary
	No. 7. SELLING EXPENSE SUMMARY

SECTION III—ADVERTISING

No. 8. Consumer Products Total Budgets
No. 9. Industrial Products Total Budgets
No. 10. Export Products Total Budgets
No. 11. Comparison with 1959 and Sales Targets 1959/60

SECTION IV—MARKET RESEARCH

Foreword
No. 12. Expense Summary

SECTION V—PUBLIC RELATIONS

Foreword
No. 13. Expense Summary

SECTION VI—NEW PRODUCT DEVELOPMENT

Foreword
No. 14. Development Budget

SECTION VII—MARKETING RESERVE

No. 15. Reserve

CHAPTER II

MARKET RESEARCH

THE first limb of the definition of Marketing was that it was "the process of determining consumer demand for a product or service". It is to aid this process that market research comes in.

The appearance of market research as a new technique in the twentieth century is the result of the industrialisation of Western society in the nineteenth century. The industrial revolution saw the introduction of large-scale production methods and a hitherto unprecedented increase in population. Together these two factors made it possible for manufacturers to put cheap goods on the market in large quantities. The cheapness and the large quantities were of course related. The large quantities could be produced by reason of the increase in industrial inventions and manufacturing methods, and could be sold and consumed by reason of the increase in population and the increase in individual purchasing powers. The cheapness of the goods was made possible because the unit cost dropped when mass production became technically possible and mass consumption assured.

However, the industrialisation of our society brought problems as well as blessings for manufacturers. These stemmed from the ever increasing complexity of society which necessarily came in the wake of the industrial advance. In the earliest days there was less of a gap between the initial manufacturer and the ultimate consumer and fewer people in the nature of wholesalers, distributors and retailers through whose hands goods must pass before reaching their final goal. The manufacturer knew his customer at first hand and therefore not only did he know who he was, where he lived, what he did, but could make the goods according to the expressed wishes of each individual customer. Goods were not "ready-made"; they were "custom-tailored". Therefore no problem could arise that the manufacturer might not be making exactly what the customer required. With the increasing gap that more and more industrialisation brings between manufacturer and consumer, this problem becomes ever more acute. *Who is the customer and what is it he wants?* If the manufacturer guesses, uses intuition or backs a "hunch", he may find himself, should he be proved wrong in his estimate, with a whole line of mass-produced goods on his hands for which there is no market, and the cost of manufacture to him is therefore a total loss. How can he prevent, or cut down the risk of such a loss, which is not only an individual loss to him but a waste of economic resources of the country?

In the twentieth century market research has attempted to provide an answer. As always with definitions of subjects, a whole variety is available. A classic definition of the purpose of market research is: "To reduce the areas of uncertainty surrounding business decisions".

Market research gives information about the market in which a manufacturer is interested; this is its function, attempting to bridge the gap between manufacturer and consumer. Most market research is in relation to consumer goods, but its techniques can equally be applied to consumer services on the one hand (e.g. transport and household utilities) and on the other hand to capital or manufacturers' goods.

What market research does is first to set about collecting information about the market and the customers, and then analysing the findings. Broadly speaking, information about a market can be acquired in three ways: first by simple personal observation as to consumer habits and trends of consumer habits; secondly by the use of official publications and public data generally; and thirdly by carrying out sample surveys which are directed to the collection of new information to answer the requirements of specific manufacturers. It is obvious that these three categories show an ascending degree of sophistication and technique. The first is what every intelligent and forward-looking businessman should be expected to embark upon. It may be only a question of asking his wife what she feels about a particular product, situation or trend—although the suggestion that this will be anything other than an extremely doubtful and highly unreliable source of information would be a complete anathema to any research worker. The second is more complicated and requires what is normally called "desk research". A large variety of sources is available for the market researcher through public government statistics and trade information, while he also has available the internal data of the particular manufacturer for whom he is researching—in particular the sales figures of the company.

The third category starts where the second stops. Government statistics generally offer information which is by itself too general for the particular manufacturer's use. They have value in providing the general picture and showing how the product fits in with other markets, but they do not get down to the details with which manufacturers are concerned in relation to markets for products or services which compete with their own. Then it becomes necessary for the manufacturer to carry out sample surveys into the market.

It is this third type of inquiry to which most people are referring when they speak of "market research", and while the first type can be practised by any intelligent layman and the second without any specialised techniques, it is wise for the manufacturer to consider the employment of a specialist agent in the field where the third type is concerned. At the same time one should not forget the necessity and benefit of carrying out the other two varieties.

Some Sources of Information

(*a*) Information available inside a firm (e.g. sales data).
(*b*) Published information (e.g. Government statistics, published market surveys).
(*c*) Data available on request but not generally published (e.g. information from Government sources or trade organisations).
(*d*) New data collected by sample survey methods.

MAIN TYPES OF MARKET RESEARCH

It is appropriate to examine first the sample surveys which are the main preserve of market research and to consider what they can find out for the manufacturer.

The manufacturer must start by looking at the problem which faces him, and should outline the questions left unanswered by data already available. The first thing he must do is to define the market that he wishes to enter or has already entered. He must find out *who* are the actual buyers or potential buyers for his product or service. He must have an appreciation of the *size* of the market and whether it is growing, declining or a static market. This will give him some idea of the potential demand in the field in which he operates and is important, whether concerned with a new product or with one which the manufacturer has had on the market for some considerable time. He is also interested in the *character* of the potential and actual buyers of the product. Is it bought by the young, middle-aged or the old? By men or women or both, by rich or poor or by the middle-income group? He is also concerned with the *geographical* breakdown of the market. Is the product one which is bought in the towns or in the country, in the North or in the South? Furthermore, to what *uses* do the buyers put the product once bought?

Frequently a manufacturer is surprised by the difference between what he intended his product to be used for and what it is actually used for. The *market survey* aims to find the answer to these questions by going out and asking the consumers, or sometimes the retailers who sell to the consumers. To which particular question or questions it seeks the answers will depend on the terms of reference of each individual survey.

The market survey does not, of course, involve the questioning of all actual or potential customers for the product or service. In a mass market the expense and the time involved clearly make such a course quite impossible; therefore the form that such a survey takes is the interview of a sample of the relevant persons or households, such as teenagers or households in a specified part of the country, and obtaining from them answers to a questionnaire which has been organised in relation to the attitudes and other factors about which the enquiry is being made. The sample of persons interviewed may be selected in one of two ways, either at random or by means of quotas—these are commonly referred to as *random* samples or *quota* samples. They are two technical methods of selecting samples which require the specialised knowledge of the market researcher.

The "random" sample involves the haphazard and random selection of persons to be interviewed. "Quota" sampling involves the interviewing or questioning of a given number of persons within any particular part of the universe in accordance with the make-up of the total universe. To clarify this, if the country consisted of 20 million people: 5 million of whom earned £1,000 per year, 10 million earned £500 per year and 5 million earned £250 per year, then a survey of a town or part of this country using the "quota" sample method would involve persons to be interviewed on a ratio of 1 : 2 : 1 as above, irrespective of the numbers involved.

The "random" sample provides results that are completely reliable in a statistical sense within precisely defined statistical limitations. However, the quota sample is much less costly to operate and can provide results that are sufficiently accurate for most practical purposes. It is not necessary here to go into the technical problems of sampling theory and the decisions that have to be made as to the size of the sample, to weighting and selecting the sample.

After the sampling method has been decided, the design of the questionnaire becomes the most important aspect of the survey, for if it should be faulty it could easily lead to incorrect information from the persons interviewed and so give false and misleading results. Again, the framing of the questionnaire is a matter for the specialist. So too, the analysis and interpretation of the answers—which is the final stage in the survey—is a matter for the market researcher and not for the layman. This last fact is not always appreciated and it sometimes happens that after a survey has been made by market researchers, using the appropriate samples and questionnaire and tabulation data, the tabulated data is handed over to the company or manufacturer who has commissioned the survey, and it is left to him to carry out the analysis and the interpretation of the data presented. Yet this analysis and interpretation requires much the same specialised abilities as the earlier parts of the survey which are concerned with the collection of data. Most research agencies are willing, and indeed anxious, to carry research results to their natural conclusion in terms of the recommended course of action that should be followed.

This type of market survey which is carried out either once and for all or at irregular intervals, depending upon what information is required, is generally intended to solve a specific problem, and is not usually suitable for measuring the size of a market or measuring the competitive position in a market which is constantly changing. Repeated annually, the *ad hoc* survey can reveal secular trends but it will not show short-term fluctuations. For this purpose we must look to continuous regular surveys or panels which provide continuous study over a period of time. There are two main forms of panel survey, known as:

1. The Consumer Panel.
2. The Retail Audit.

These two methods of research are complementary and not alternative. While both indicate totals in sales and trends of the market, the Consumer Panel scores in the information it gives about the final consumer, while the Retail Audit scores in the information it gives about the pattern of distribution and the level of stocks in the shops.

The Consumer or Consumer-Purchasing Panel is a form of panel survey which estimates the final consumer behaviour, whether the whole household or a particular individual in the household. The panel consists of a permanent sample of consumers who, under agreement with the panel organisers, record their buying actions and hand over these records to the organisers at certain intervals. The vital thing is that the consumer on the panel must record his or her buying actions at the time he or she performs them. Persons are normally obtained for the panel through interviews in order to discover whether they or their households are appropriate for the sample, to ensure that it is representative of whatever social, economic or other group is being analysed. In the United Kingdom there is only one such panel of importance, organised by Attwood Statistics Ltd., consisting of 4,000 householders who make regular reports of their purchases of various brands of goods during the preceding week.

The Consumer Panel will give information, not only about the amount of purchases but about such characteristics of the buyers as their socio-economic class, geographical location, age, etc. The extent of the repetition of purchases of a particular brand by individuals can also be worked out from the data; a manufacturer launching a new product can find this particular information of great value. The main advantage of the Consumer Panel is that it gives a continuous record of the buying of the same persons, which the *ad hoc* survey cannot. Thus, by relating the continuity or lack of continuity of the persons' buying actions to factors such as changes in advertising, price, etc., the effect of these changes can be plotted. On the debit side is the expense of this method; also there are difficulties in relation to the members of the panel who may not co-operate, whose behaviour may be affected by long membership and who may, on the other hand, leave or be replaced at any time.

The Retail Audit gets information not from the consumer but from the retailer. It consists of a panel of shops which are checked regularly, and sales of various brands of goods are worked out. The most widely known inventory audit method of calculating sales by retailers is the "Nielsen Shop Audit", operated by the A. C. Nielsen Company which introduced this method some thirty years ago. In the United Kingdom, the Nielsen Company have several separate indices, such as one relating to food outlets, one to drug outlets, and one to confectionery outlets. It is always possible to extend these and produce an index relating to other goods and other fields. The main value of the Retail Audit is that it gives very accurate information to the manufacturer about his and competitive retail sales to the consumer, which he does not know from his own knowledge because his ex-factory sales in part or whole will be to wholesalers or retailers whose stocks may remain with them for a very considerable time, so that ex-factory sales only show up changes in demand in part, and at best after a considerable time lag. The shop audit not only gives total consumer sales, stock levels, trade purchases and distribution levels, but gives separate figures in the same way for various parts of the country—Nielsen divides the United Kingdom into certain optional combinations of Government Standard Regions including the Greater London Area—for various types and sizes of retail shops. The information on sales does not come from the retailer's memory. He is required to keep every invoice and also a record of any non-consumer trading. The actual auditing, i.e. counting of stock and analysis of invoices, credit notes, etc., is carried out by the Nielsen Company.

Product Testing

One type of *ad hoc* survey proves the attitudes of consumers to a product or to a particular problem, and will therefore give a manufacturer some concept of what the consumer wants in this particular field. This becomes particularly important when a manufacturer is developing a new product. Even if a manufacturer has a fixed idea for a new product, there will still be a great deal of scope in the establishing of its specific characteristics. The manufacturer may

BRAND 'A'

PACKAGES (ooo)

	CONSUMER SALES	– –
	RETAILER PURCHASES	——
	STOCKS	······

MONTH'S
SUPPLY
STOCKS

2.1	2.0	2.1	1.9	2.1	2.2	2.1	2.0	2.2	2.1	2.2	2.5	2.9	2.9	2.9	2.9
1206	1190	1214	1168	1314	1273	1263	1226	1366	1277	1395	1521	1653	1568	1682

1199 1195 1182 1203 1339 1368 1331 1330 1276 1249
1163 1191 1173 1203 1229 1181 1224 1222 1247 1203 1257 1236 1153 1083 1161
1158 1202 1157 935

	YEAR AGO															
% CHANGE	+10	+12	+2	+5	+12	+6	+5	+3	+5	+–	+2	+5	–6	–11	–7
MAX. SHOP DISTRIBUTION	87%	89	89	90	90	89	88	89	92	91	92	94	94	93	92
NET EFFECTIVE	86	86	87	87	88	86	87	87	89	88	91	92	92	90	89

2 MONTHS TO	JUL	SEP	NOV	JAN	MAR	MAY	JUL	SEP	NOV	JAN	MAR	MAY	JUL	SEP	NOV	JAN
	1958			1959						1960						'61

Fig. 6.

BRAND 'C'

PACKAGES (ooo)

	CONSUMER SALES	– – –
	RETAILER PURCHASES	——
	STOCKS	......

	I MAY 1958	I JUL	I SEP	I NOV	I JAN 1959	I MAR	I MAY	I JUL	I SEP	I NOV	I JAN 1960	I MAR	I MAY	I JUL	I SEP	I NOV	I JAN '61
MONTH'S SUPPLY	2.0	1.9	1.6	1.5	1.5	1.6	1.7	1.9	1.6	1.6	1.6	1.6	1.8	1.7	1.7	1.8	
STOCKS	376	453	474	413	377	373	374	396	432	390	412	396	421	452	419	413	435
	534	493	518	493	488	472	499	500	484	532	503	524	506	485	518	495	
	457	489	455	473	479	460	478	461	457	507	499	511	489	457	501	488	
YEAR AGO % CHANGE	–11	–5	–1	–3	–3	–9	+5	–6	–7	+3	+3	+11	+2	+5	+7	–2	
MAX. SHOP DISTRIBUTION	88%	89	89	89	90	89	90	90	90	90	91	91	92	90	90	91	
NET EFFECTIVE	84	85	86	84	84	87	84	87	86	86	85	88	87	87	87	88	

2 MONTHS TO

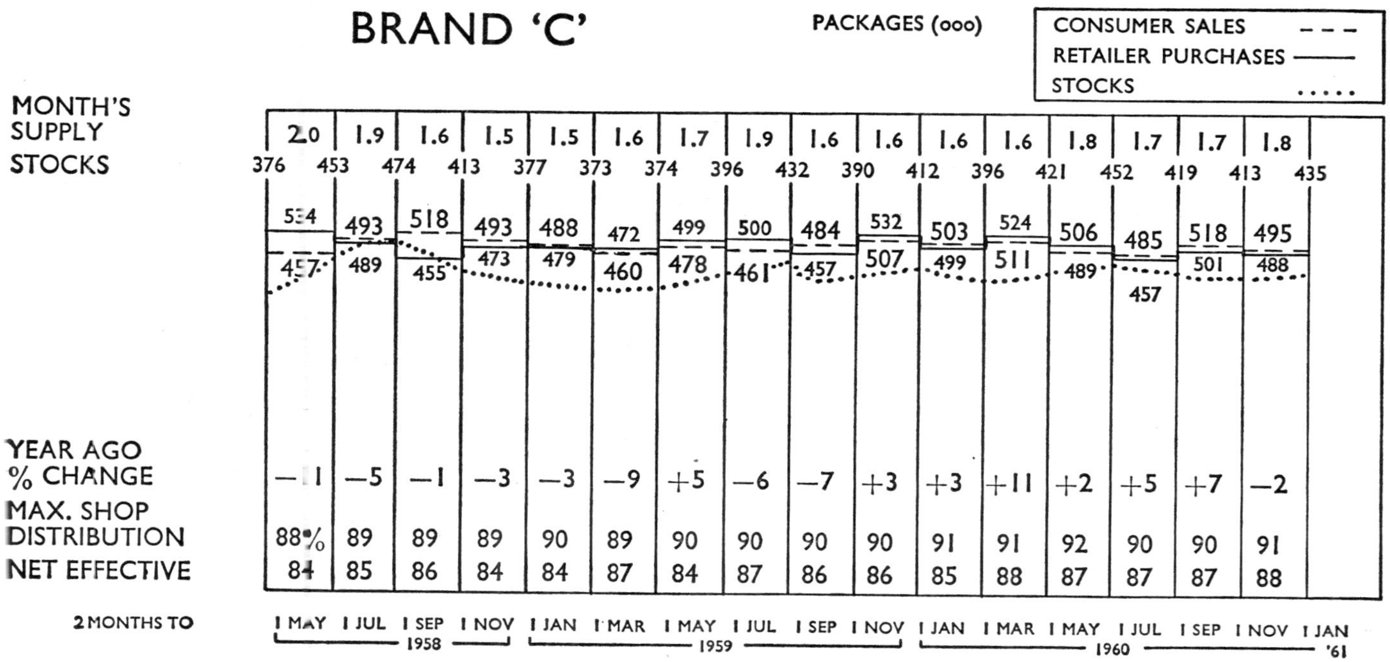

FIG. 7.

CONSUMER SALES
PRODUCT CLASS 'X'

PACKAGES (ooo)

Bi-monthly data

Period total	5086	5058	5332	5330	5151	5122	4798	4690	4680	4754
BRAND 'A'	23.2 / 1181	24.1 / 1224	22.9 / 1222	23.4 / 1247	23.4 / 1203	24.6 / 1257	25.7 / 1236	24.6 / 1153	23.2 / 1083	24.4 / 1161
BRAND 'A1'	4.2 / 213	4.3 / 216	3.6 / 192	3.6 / 189	3.6 / 185	3.6 / 182	3.4 / 162	3.3 / 155	3.3 / 156	2.7 / 128
BRAND 'B'	18.1 / 918	17.4 / 881	17.2 / 918	17.1 / 910	18.7 / 960	17.6 / 903	17.1 / 819	16.8 / 789	18.1 / 847	18.7 / 886
BRAND 'C'	9.4 / 478	9.1 / 461	9.1 / 484	9.5 / 507	9.7 / 503	10.0 / 511	10.2 / 489	10.3 / 485	11.1 / 518	10.4 / 495
BRAND 'D'	12.9 / 658	12.7 / 644	13.1 / 699	12.4 / 664	12.0 / 618	11.5 / 591	11.4 / 546	12.1 / 564	11.7 / 551	11.4 / 542
						0.4 / 22	1.2 / 59	1.6 / 77	1.6 / 73	
ALL OTHERS	32.2 / 1638	32.4 / 1642	34.1 / 1817	34.0 / 1813	32.6 / 1682	32.3 / 1656	31.0 / 1487	31.3 / 1466	31.0 / 1452	32.4 / 1542

2 MONTHS TO:

1 MAY	1 JUL	1 SEP	1 NOV	1 JAN	1 MAR	1 MAY	1 JUL	1 SEP	1 NOV	1 JAN
	—1959—						—1960—			'61

Annual data

Period total	20488	22824	27327	28944	30982	29195
	1955	1956	1957	1958	1959	12 MONTHS ENDED 1 NOV '60
BRAND 'A'	16.4% / 3354	20.4 / 4668	23.2 / 6340	25.3 / 7348	23.6 / 7306	24.2 / 7093
BRAND 'A1'		-5.7 / 1303			-3.9 / -1215	-3.4 / 869
BRAND 'B'	16.3 / 3350	14.1 / 3848	14.1 / 3848	18.2 / 5261	17.6 / 5458	17.8 / 5204
BRAND 'C'	—	14.2 / 3237	11.2 / 3066	10.2 / 2954	9.4 / 2893	10.3 / 3001
BRAND 'D'	22.3 / 4595	20.3 / 4624	17.2 / 4696	14.6 / 4228	12.6 / 3913	11.7 / 3412
ALL OTHERS	44.4 / 9089	39.4 / 8982	34.3 / 9377	31.7 / 9153	32.9 / 10197	32.6 / 9516

COPYRIGHT A. C. NIELSEN COMPANY LTD.

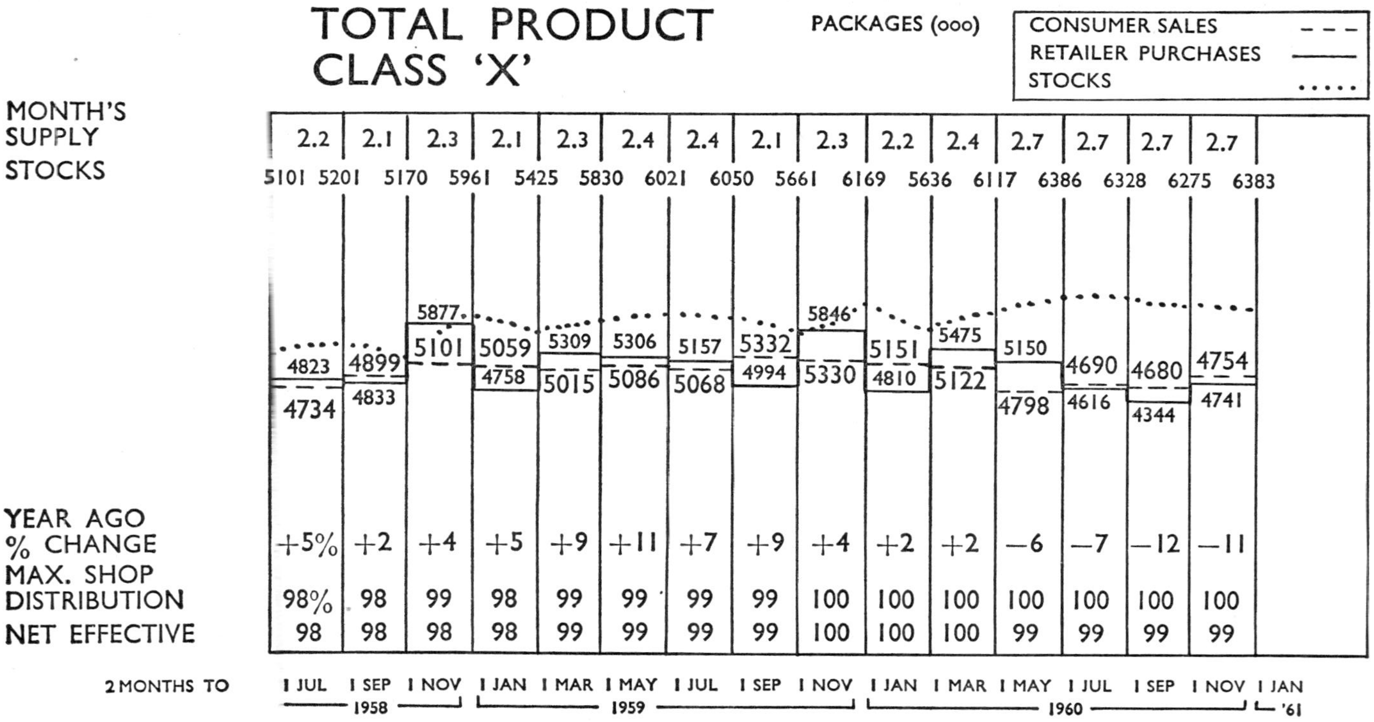

TOTAL PRODUCT
CLASS 'X'

PACKAGES (ooo)

CONSUMER SALES	– – –
RETAILER PURCHASES	———
STOCKS	······

MONTH'S SUPPLY

STOCKS	2.2	2.1	2.3	2.1	2.3	2.4	2.1	2.3	2.2	2.4	2.7	2.7	2.7	2.7	2.7
	5101 5201	5170	5961	5425	5830	6021	6050	5661	6169	5636	6117	6386	6328	6275	6383

CONSUMER SALES / RETAILER PURCHASES / STOCKS values:

4823 · 4899 · 5877 · 5101 · 5059 · 5309 · 5306 · 5157 · 5332 · 5846 · 5151 · 5475 · 5150 · 4690 · 4680 · 4754

4734 · 4833 · 4758 · 5015 · 5086 · 5068 · 4994 · 5330 · 4810 · 5122 · 4798 · 4616 · 4344 · 4741

	2 MONTHS TO														
YEAR AGO % CHANGE	+5%	+2	+4	+5	+9	+11	+7	+9	+4	+2	+2	−6	−7	−12	−11
MAX. SHOP DISTRIBUTION	98%	98	99	98	99	99	99	99	100	100	100	100	100	100	100
NET EFFECTIVE	98	98	98	98	99	99	99	99	100	100	99	99	99	99	99

I JUL I SEP I NOV I JAN I MAR I MAY I JUL I SEP I NOV I JAN I MAR I MAY I JUL I SEP I NOV I JAN

— 1958 — — 1959 — — 1960 — ⌐ '61

Fig. 9.

then ask the market researcher to find out from the group of customers to whom he plans to direct the product, exactly what product of this type they would be ready to buy and at what price. This study will give the manufacturer clear ideas on consumer preference and he may then go ahead and manufacture the product according to these specifications or preference. He may, however, be advised not to mass-produce a whole new line but only a few samples which he then may use—again with the assistance of market research—in what is generally known as a "product test."

This important form of research invites the consumer to try out the goods for a short period of time, rather than merely express an opinion without trial. This leads to the question of acceptance by the consumer at a practical stage, and is concerned with general acceptance and also with the influence of particular factors relating to acceptance, such as size, pack, continuance of use, etc. These acceptance tests vary, but basically they consist of going to a representative sample of prospective consumers with samples of the new product—either alone or comparatively with an established product in the same class. These tests are often called "blind" product tests because the new product, and any offered for comparison, are handed to the potential consumers without any identification other than a code letter or number. The purpose of the "blind" product test is to obtain an assessment of a product as such, divorced from other influences such as advertising and a particular brand's reputation.

Each participant of a comparative product test, for example, after he has had the two products for a sufficient time to try them out, is asked to express his preference for the one or the other. If the new product is preferred by the majority, it is reasonable for a manufacturer to go ahead with the product, while if the product is in a clear minority it may well be unwise to take the matter further. Preference for the new product will indicate possibilities for the manufacturer, but lack of acceptance may, by study of all the characteristics, show where improvements might be made to gain majority approval.

Research can be termed *qualitative* or *quantitative*—the latter where the sample of people interviewed is sufficiently large to distinguish reliably between and assign importance to the factors at work. When this is not so, the results are perhaps indicative only and no clear definition of issues is obtained; they are, therefore, qualitative only.

Discovering what people do is certainly fundamental, but equally important is to discover *why* they do it. What is the image the public have of the product and why is this so? In an endeavour to probe more deeply into the reasons for consumer behaviour and reactions, further techniques have been developed over the years to augment the more standard or established methods. *Motivational* research, which may involve a psychologist, more explicitly attempts to investigate the hidden reasons or motives which may not be quite the same as the rational explanations more readily offered in answer to the question "why?"

This very brief outline of some of the research methods available to a manufacturer in his market investigations is not intended to be comprehensive. Problems involved in product formulation, product testing and test-marketing bring into play many additional techniques. To these must be added research which deals with problems related to advertising, more appropriate to the next chapter. There are two main types of such research: media surveys which are designed to measure the audiences for advertising media, and are concerned with readership research, such as the Institute of Practitioners in Advertising survey on press publications and audience research on commercial television. Media surveys are generally continuous rather than *ad hoc*. Details of these are given later when dealing with the selection of media for advertisements. There is also the research which attempts to measure the efficiency of particular advertisements which have appeared, or will appear in these media. (See page 155 in Chapter III.)

SETTING THE BUDGET

With regard to the cost of market research and the amount of money which a manufacturer should devote to it, it is difficult to dogmatise in the abstract since, as always, circumstances alter cases. More market research may for example be required when a new product is being launched than at any other time during the product's subsequent life-cycle. The manufacturer is recommended to take the advice of his market research or advertising agency, or his own department, recognising that the amount of research expenditure is a management decision and should be based on the same principles as are stated in detail in the following Chapter under "Setting the Budget", and should be a properly related part of the marketing plan. In relation to the amount spent on advertising, which is now in the region of £400 million annually, the expenditure on market research is very small. In 1959 it is estimated that £4 million only was spent in this field—1 per cent. of the expenditure on advertising.

Planned market research is a product of this century, or more precisely of the last thirty years. Advertising agencies are largely responsible for its development, effecting its use in association with advertising campaigns as an extra service to clients. Today there are, additionally, market research organisations which are independent of advertising agencies, whilst the latter have developed in many cases marketing and market research groups of considerable consequence. At the same time, market research departments have developed within companies and businesses to provide a management and marketing service internally.

In 1947 the Market Research Society was established as a professional body with required codes of conduct and standards. By 1960 it had about 750 members and associates and the number is steadily increasing.

The manufacturer who is convinced of the need for research is faced with the problem of how to go about it. Since markets are continually changing it must be assumed that the need is recurrent so he should consider the following alternatives either singly or in combination:

1. Set up his own market research department within the company.
2. Carry out market research through his advertising agency.
3. Commission research through an independent market research organisation.

The first course will appeal to medium or large companies with a fairly considerable demand for market research, especially today where product development research is recognised as one of its major functions. Only the larger concerns can operate a fully self-contained department with fieldworkers and complete tabulating facilities, and keep the department busy all the time. Undoubtedly the manufacturer's own research department will have a greater knowledge of domestic problems, but may lack the opportunity of experiencing many different problems and the many different techniques with which the external research organisation normally deals. Often the best course is a compromise between the two, that is to say, a research department using outside facilities but employing on its own staff just those specialists (who may equally be technologists) who can define problems and interpret in practical terms. The research department within an organisation should be maintained largely independent of top-management in its approach to research problems, for without objectivity market research is likely to be futile.

Even when employing a research department within the organisation there are certain specialist items of research for which it is better to employ an outside organisation (for instance, A. C. Nielsen & Co. already referred to) if an analysis of distribution and sales at retail outlets is sought.

For the small company, and for the large company which is unwilling to go to the full development of its own operations department, there are now several important independent organisations which they can employ as specialists in market research. The *Directory of Market Research Associations* lists some 25 to 30 such organisations and is therefore a useful guide in the search for market research services. Any company which is liable to be using planned market research in any of the many forms it may take will be well advised to employ at least one properly trained expert to operate, control and advise on the selection and analysis of research.

In the application of market research to non-consumer fields, the same principles as have been outlined still hold good. Many industrial organisations through their trade association are in a fortunate position in assessing the total market and its growth potential.

In the paper industry, for example, research into and knowledge of technical requirements and advancements is considerable so that an assessment of future potential is made that much the easier and more reliable. The world-wide demand for paper and its related products is expected to double over a twenty-year period. The traditional source of much of the pulp from which paper is made— the coniferous softwoods—cannot be expected to meet this increased demand; other faster-growing trees and indeed other fibrous growths must be used. How will this affect the machinery on which paper is produced? What likely effects on the manufacture of packaging paper will there be from the developments in plastic, polyethylene, for example?

An industry which has a liberal availability of marketing information eases the sales problems, but it can never remove them. The fact that one manufacturer grows and develops is no reason for another to develop similarly at the same rate. The quality of the executives employed and their ability to use and interpret information at their disposal will certainly be the principal factor in deciding how any company or industry will grow. Faced with this information two management teams may take widely differing courses, the one better than the other.

ILLUSTRATION OF CONSUMER RESEARCH

A FIRM has produced a new variety of mixed pickle. In order to determine the marketing strategy for this product it wishes to know:

(a) The present state of the market for mixed pickles.

(i) Amongst housewives who purchase them for use at home.

(ii) Amongst men and women who order them when they are eating away from home.

(b) How its product compares with "X" the leading brand of pickles.

At a later date the firm may also carry out research to find a suitable name and package for its product and to determine which advertising platform it ought to adopt.

In order to carry out its current objectives the firm intends to undertake:

(1) A consumer survey amongst housewives ending with a recruiting question for a product test.

(2) A product test against "X".

(3) A consumer survey amongst men and women who eat mixed pickles away from home at least once a month.

The questionnaires for these surveys are shown in the following illustrative documents.

1. HOUSEWIVES CONSUMER SURVEY

AND

PRODUCT TEST CONTACT QUESTIONNAIRE

Questionnaire No..............   *Job No*.............

	Age of		
Name	H/w:	16–24	*Class:* AB
Address		25–34	C
....		35–44	D
....		45–54	
		55–64	
		65+	

Area: Have you a television set?   Yes
                                                                 No

                          IF "YES" do you sometimes   Yes
                          look at I.T.A. programmes?   No

142

Household Composition

Relationship to H/w.	Age	Sex M. F.	Tick head of household
H/w.			

Interviewer.................

Code No. ....

Supervisor ....

Date ....

Occupation of Head of Household

Type of work ....

Type of firm ....

Are you the person who does most of the cooking and shopping for yourself and your family (INTERVIEW ONLY RESPONDENTS ANSWERING "YES").

1. Do you ever buy any mixed pickles?   Yes
                                            No

IF PICKLES NOT BOUGHT CLOSE INTERVIEW.

2. When did you last buy any pickles?   Up to 1 week ago
                                            Over 1–2 weeks ago
                                            Over 2–3 weeks ago
                                            Over 3 weeks–1 month ago
                                            Over 1 month ago
                                            Can't remember.

IF PICKLES BOUGHT OVER 1 MONTH AGO OR "CAN'T REMEMBER" CLOSE INTERVIEW.

3. (a) What makes of pickles have you ever heard of?
   (b) SHOW LIST. Are there any other makes on this list that you have heard of?
   (c) Which makes have you tried?
   (d) Which make did you buy last?

HEARD OF:

(a) *Spontaneous* (b) *Prompted*[1] (c) *Tried* (d) *Last bought*

Baxters
Brands
Brother Bung
Burgess
Crosse & Blackwell
Chef
Epicure
Escoffier
Heinz
H.P.
Maconochies
Other

4. When you last bought mixed pickles:

   (a) At what shop did you buy them?

   Grocer (not Co-op.)
   Co-operative
   Greengrocers
   Dairy
   Chain store
   Department store
   General shop
   Other

   (b) How much did you buy?

   $\frac{1}{4}$ lb. or less
   More than $\frac{1}{4}$–$\frac{1}{2}$ lb.
   More than $\frac{1}{2}$ lb.
   More than 1 lb.
   D.K.

   (c) How much did you pay for them?

   Less than 1/-
   1/- to 1/5
   1/6 to 1/11
   2/- to 2/5
   2/6 to 3/-
   More than 3/-

5. (a) Does everyone in your family eat pickles?   Yes
                                                     No

   (b) IF "NO".
   Who does not eat them?

6. (a) At what meals do you serve them?

   FOR EACH MEAL ASK: (b) At what time is this?
                       (c) What did you last serve them
                           with at this meal?
                       (d) How many people were at the
                           meal?
                       (e) How much did you serve in all?

   [1] For prompting a card showing a list of brands is shown to the respondent.

7. | Meal | Time | Last served with | People | Served |
|------|------|------------------|--------|--------|
| .... | .... | .... | .... | .... |
| .... | .... | .... | .... | .... |
| .... | .... | .... | .... | .... |
| .... | .... | .... | .... | .... |
| .... | .... | .... | .... | .... |

8. We are asking a number of people to try some samples of pickles and let us know what they think of them. If you agree to take part in this test we would send you (quite free of course), a jar of one type of mixed pickles to try and a week later a jar of another type of mixed pickles. Then we would call back to find out what you thought of them. Would you like to take part in this test?

Yes
No

PRODUCT TEST RECALL QUESTIONNAIRE

Job No. ....

Name ....   Interviewer............................

Address ....   Code No. ....

....   Supervisor ....

....   Date   ....

1. (*a*) Have you tried both jars of pickles?   Yes
    No

IF "NO" CLOSE INTERVIEW.

(*b*) Which did you try first and which most recently?

62 first 84 most recently
84 ,,   62 ,,   ,,

(*c*) At how many meals did you serve............(one used first)?

(*d*) And............(one used second)?

Less than 2 meals
3 ,,
4 ,,
5 ,,
6 ,,
More than 6 ,,

IF ONE USED FOR LESS THAN 2 MEALS CLOSE INTERVIEW.

(e) How much of jar 62 did you use and jar 84?

        $\frac{1}{4}$ or less
        More than $\frac{1}{4}$–$\frac{1}{2}$
        More than $\frac{1}{2}$–$\frac{3}{4}$
        More than $\frac{3}{4}$–less than all
        All

(f) At what meals and what times of day did you serve jar 62 and jar 84?

62	84
19.	20. ....
....	....
....	....
....	....

2. What do you think was the main difference between the two jars?

62 was .... than 84

84 was .... than 62

ASK QUESTIONS 3–8 FOR JAR USED FIRST, THEN REPEAT FOR JAR USED SECOND.

Note: Code numbers 62 to 84 are used to identify the two samples which bear no other distinguishing marks.

3. How far up or down this scale would you rate jar......? (SHOW CARD A.)

4. Now I would like to take particular points one by one.
   Please look at this card and tell me which of these statements is nearest to your opinion of the sharpness of the pickles (SHOW CARD B).

> Much too sharp
> Rather too sharp
> About right
> Rather too mild
> Much too mild
> I don't really know

5. Now the size of the pieces? (SHOW CARD C.)

> Much too large
> Rather too large
> About right
> Rather too small
> Much too small
> I don't really know

6. Now the hardness or softness of the pieces? (SHOW CARD D.)

> Much too hard
> Rather too hard
> About right
> Rather too soft
> Much too soft
> I don't really know

7. Now the texture of the pieces? (SHOW CARD E.)

> Very good
> Good
> Fair
> Poor
> Very poor
> I don't really know

8. In general which of these statements comes nearest to your opinion of the flavour of the pickles? (SHOW CARD F.)

> Very good
> Good
> Fair
> Poor
> Very poor
> I don't really know

9. Now taking everything into account, which of the two jars did you prefer?

> No preference

10. (a) What is the reason for your choice? ....
....

(b) Any others ....

(c) Was there anything you particularly disliked about............ (the one preferred)?..

(d) Was the other one better in any way than the one you preferred?
....

(e) What did you dislike most about .... (the one not preferred)?
....

11. (a) Supposing you went into a shop and you saw the jar labelled.........
(one used first) on sale for 2/- and the one labelled .... (one used second) for 3/6 which would you buy?

> 62
> 84
> Other/D.K.

(b) Now supposing it was............ (the one used second) that cost 2/- and .... (the one used first) that cost 1/6 which would you buy?

> 62
> 84
> Other/D.K.

12. Did any members of your family prefer the other jar to the one you preferred?   Yes/No

IF "YES" which ones?   (Record by SEX and AGE.)

2. GENERAL CONSUMER SURVEY

PJN   *Questionnaire No*............   *Job No*............
(Cols.)

Name	Age: 16–24
Address	25–34
....	35–44
Town	45–54
Man	55–64
Woman at home	65+
Woman at work	T.V. set? Yes/No
Class: AB/C/D	Watch I.T.A. Yes/No

Marital status: Married   Occupation.....................................
                Single   (Of husband if married woman at home,
                Widowed   of father if single woman at home.)

We are carrying out a survey on the foods people eat.

1. Do you ever eat mixed pickles?   Yes

                                             No

IF "NO" CLOSE INTERVIEW.

SHOW CARD.

2. (a) At which of these places do you eat them?

                      Your home

                      Your canteen

                      Public house bars

                      Cafes and restaurants

(b) Do you eat them at any other places?.....................................

IF PICKLES EATEN ONLY AT HOME CLOSE INTERVIEW.

IF PICKLES EATEN AT MORE THAN ONE PLACE EXCLUDING RESPONDENT'S HOME ASK:

(c) Not counting your own home where do you eat mixed pickles most often? ....

3. How often do you have mixed pickles away from home?

                      More than 3 times a week

                      2–3 times a week

                      Once a week

                      More than once a fortnight

                      More than once a month

                      Less often than once a month

                      D.K.

IF PICKLES EATEN OUT LESS OFTEN THAN ONCE A MONTH CLOSE INTERVIEW.

FOR PLACE WHERE PICKLES EATEN AWAY FROM HOME MOST OFTEN.

4. Now I would like to ask you about eating pickles in ....?

(a) At what meals do you have them?

FOR EACH MEAL

    (b) What kind of food do you most often have them with at ....?

    (c) What brand of pickle do you usually have at this meal?

    (d) Are they already on the table or do you have to ask for them?

(a)	(b)	(c)	(d)
			On Table
Meals	*What eaten with*	*Brand*	*Yes*	*No*
Breakfast	....	....	
Mid-morning snack	....	....	
Mid-day meal	....	....	
Mid-afternoon snack	....	....	
Main evening meal	....	....	
Evening snack	....	....	
Other..................	....	....	

IF ONLY ONE BRAND MENTIONED.

(e) Do they serve any other brands at all?   Yes

No

IF "YES"

(f) What other brands?

(g) Do you ever have any .... (name other brands).
IF NOT. (h) Why not?

(f)	(g)		(h)
Other brands served	Ever eaten		IF NOT EATEN Why not?
	Yes	No	
....	....	....	....
....	....	....	....
....	....	....	....

5. How often do you eat at ....? (Place named in Q.4.)

CHAPTER III

ADVERTISING

THE definition of marketing with which this Part started had as its second limb the statement that it was the process of "motivating the sale" of a product or service. It is here that advertising comes in. Even if the manufacturer has established what the consumer wants and has gone ahead and produced it at his factories, he must still—as he will be distributing it physically to retail outlets and the like—inform the consumer at large of its existence. To do this the tool at hand is advertising. Thus advertising, properly regarded, is essentially a part of the organisation of the distribution of goods and services which in an advanced economy such as ours today tends to become of increasing importance.

As indicated in dealing with market research (Chapter II), markets must be found and created for an output of goods increasing in range number and variety. The contribution of advertising to our economic life is a vital and a highly beneficial part of the great revolution which is taking place in the marketing of consumer goods beginning about the end of the last century and still going on. Advertising must be considered in association with the development of branded merchandise and pre-packaging, which have completely transformed the business of marketing, both from suppliers' and consumers' points of view. Gains for the latter in ease of shopping, hygiene, quality control, standard weights and wide range of choice have been immeasurable. Retailing has been greatly simplified and a further simplification is now taking place with the rapid development of self-service.

Although it is true that a brand name may acquire some significance without advertising, advertising greatly accelerates the process of acceptance of brand-image and name. It is for this reason that advertising has come in the wake of the branding of goods, and accounts for the close inter-relation of branding and advertising.

Present-day Importance

The importance of advertising in national life is reflected in the fact that today about £400 million is spent annually on advertising. This represents over 2 per cent. of our national income, a level already reached 25 years ago, and, although the War brought it tumbling down, the percentage has been slowly climbing since 1945, as the following table shows, till it had just exceeded the prewar percentage.

UNITED KINGDOM ADVERTISING EXPENDITURE
RELATED TO NATIONAL INCOME

	National Income	Advertising Expenditure	Advertising Expenditure as Percentage of National Income
	£ million	£ million	
1938 . .	4,820	98	2·0
1946 . .	8,090	99	1·2
1950 . .	10,688	162	1·5
1954 . .	14,521	248	1·7
1958 . .	18,235	364	2·0
1959 . .	18,904	395	2·1

Source: *National Income and Expenditure Blue Book*, 1960.
Advertising Association.

Fig. 10.

If we take this country's advertising expenditure as a percentage of national income (i.e. 2·1 per cent. for 1959) and compare it with corresponding figures in other countries, we find that, although the United States of America is well ahead in this connection (2·9 per cent. in 1959), countries in Europe have lower percentages than this country. And it is indeed no accident that the higher a country's standard of living has risen, and the higher its industrialisation through which it has increased its living standards, the higher is that country's expenditure in advertising in relation to its national income. So, if this country is to achieve the prediction of doubling our standard of living in the next 25 years, we will need to increase not only our industrial output but our advertising.

The main problems facing the businessman in relation to advertising are four in number:

(1) Whether to advertise at all and, if this is decided in the affirmative:
(2) How much money to expend on advertising.
(3) Where to place advertisements.
(4) How to set about advertising.

SETTING THE BUDGET

It is right, therefore, to start with the proposition that if a manufacturer of goods, or a provider of services, has a sufficient volume of goods or amount of services to offer to make it necessary for him to develop a mass market, then advertising is essential for him. Essential, that is, if he is to dispose of his goods or services so as to make a profit, the end to which the whole process of marketing is directed. In the words of Lord Macaulay: "Advertising is to business what steam is to machinery—the great propelling power." By efficient distribution aided by advertising the manufacturer is constantly seeking to reduce his overall costs of production.

The manufacturer who has decided to advertise must next consider how much he will spend on advertising. This is a very difficult question, which is not capable of a simple answer applicable to all situations, businesses and products. What would be ideal is the possibility of calculating the amount of sales that would result from a stated amount of advertising expenditure. If this were possible, then the fixing of the advertising appropriation would be a simple matter of calculation and of cost accounting.

If sales rise after an advertising campaign this is not proof, with mathematical certainty, that advertising was the cause. Conversely, if sales fail to rise after an advertising campaign, neither is this proof that the advertising has been of no effect; perhaps without the advertising sales would have dropped. The reason for this lack of complete certainty is that sales of goods and services are affected by many other factors than advertising. However, this is no argument for refusing to advertise at all; advertising remains, and will always remain, in our present society, *one* of the causes of sales. Others are the price, the packaging, the efficiency of the sales force and, of course, the quality.

All this does not mean that advertising is a chancy and hit-and-miss affair. Indeed it is getting progressively less so, as advertisers and advertising agencies become more experienced, studying and measuring media, the habits of the consumers, the sizes of markets, and all the other factors which lend themselves to more or less precise measurement.

General considerations which should affect the amount of the advertising appropriation are:

1. Whether the product or service is new, established, or declining.

It is sometimes thought, naïvely, that only a new product or service needs to be advertised; but the great amount of advertising is not of new but of established products. This is because not only is the memory of the public short, but it is often exposed to advertising of competitive products. However, it is probably true to say that a new product will in its initial launch require a greater weight of advertising than one which is already established. At the other end of the scale, a declining product will generally require less advertising than either a new or an established one. What will be needed here is enough advertising to keep the sales at a sufficient level to obtain the last possible amount of profit from the product before it is finally taken off the production line.

2. What the type of article or service is.

Some products require a higher weight of advertising than others by their very nature. This is particularly true of articles of low unit cost, subject to frequent impulse purchases, such as cosmetics, toiletries and proprietary medicines. On the other hand, little advertising is needed for many articles of clothing, unbranded goods or basic raw materials required by industry.

3. What the manufacturer's competitors—or at least his principal competitors—are doing.

No advertising appropriation should be settled without taking into account the amount of competitive advertising which is appearing currently or expected in the future.

A word should be said about a frequent way of settling appropriations by taking an advertising/sales ratio (an "A/S ratio", as it is often called for convenience). This is a projection based on actual past sales of the previous year. To this figure is applied a given percentage which represents the advertising appropriation for the coming year. Although this has a certain merit in relation to keeping advertising expenditure in line with the profit/loss structure of the company, it can be dangerous since it represents too mechanistic an approach. The situation may be such that very heavy advertising is required, as with a new product, a new area of distribution, or to combat a difficult competitor who has sent his own appropriation soaring. Alternatively, to keep up to an established A/S ratio may in some years be a pure waste of money. Again it should be possible to modify an advertising appropriation in the course of the year in the light of sales and other developments—a weapon which is not always available on the production side. It may, therefore, be said that although an A/S ratio may be a yardstick from which to start, it should never be allowed to become the deciding factor dominating

An example of a typical Advertising Budget based on an Advertising/Sales Ratio

Sales quota in units:	150,000
Net sales value per unit:	£1 10s.
Net value of sales quota:	£225,000
Profit before advertising (%):	20%
Profit before advertising (actual):	£45,000
Advertising and Sales Promotion budget (actual):	£20,000
Advertising and Sales Promotion/Sales ratio:	8·9%
Expenditure per unit:	2s. 8d.
Estimated net profit:	£25,000
Net profit as percentage of net revenue:	11·1%

FIG. 11.

all else, because it is too mechanistic an approach and removes the fluidity which may prove very useful where all does not go as predicted when the appropriation was settled.

CHOOSING MEDIA

The selection of advertising media is the next problem of the advertiser. Will he use press, television, cinema, posters, transport, or a combination of some or, conceivably, all of them? In addition, will he use exhibitions, catalogues and leaflets? And what of window and other display material? This last is in reality a type of advertising, but it is more generally referred to as merchandising, or a branch of merchandising. About half the total United Kingdom advertising expenditure goes into the press, while television—although a new medium—is already taking over 15 per cent. of the total. Furthermore, unlike television advertising, the press percentage is taken up to a large extent by local advertising and classified advertising. These two media, press and television, are the main concern of advertisers, and other methods are rarely used on their own but as support for the front-line press and/or television advertising.

The following table shows the distribution of advertising between the various media. The figures for four years are shown in order to indicate the rapid growth of television:

	£ million			
	1956	1957	1958	1959
Press				
(*a*) *Space*				
(i) National and London evening news-papers	47½	51	54	63
(ii) Provincial newspapers	43	43	45	47
(iii) Magazines and periodicals	32	31	32	33
(iv) Trade and technical journals and other publications	23½	24½	27	27
(*b*) *Production Costs*	12½	13	14	15
Total press	158½	162½	172	185
Outdoor	26	25	24	26
Television	10½	27	48	60
Screen	5¼	5	4	4
Catalogues, leaflets, etc.	35	36	37	38
Window and interior display	22½	23	23	24
Exhibitions	11½	12	12	12
Free samples and gift schemes	12½	15	15	16
Miscellaneous (including radio)	6	6	6	6
Administration	21	22	23	24
Total	309	333½	364	395

Source: Advertising Association.
FIG. 12.

The extent to which television has grown is best shown by translating the above sterling figures into percentages.

	Percentage			
	1956	1957	1958	1959
Press				
(a) *Space*				
(i) National and London evening newspapers	15½	15	14½	16
(ii) Provincial newspapers	14	13	12½	12
(iii) Magazines and periodicals	10½	9½	9	8½
(iv) Trade and technical journals and other publications	17½	7½	7½	7
(b) *Production Costs*	4	4	4	4
Total press	51½	49	47½	47½
Outdoor	8	7½	6½	6½
Television	3½	8	13	15
Screen	2	1½	1	1
Catalogues, leaflets, etc.	11	10½	10	9½
Window and interior display	7	7	6½	6
Exhibitions	4	3½	3½	3
Free samples and gift schemes	4	4½	4	4
Miscellaneous (including radio)	2	2	1½	1½
Administration	7	6½	6½	6
Total	100	100	100	100

Source: Advertising Association.

FIG. 13.

Advertising requires much forward planning; space and time must be booked well in advance and ample time allowed in which to write and draw the advertisements. The selection of media has become a great art and the right choice of media can make all the difference between a successful and an unsuccessful campaign. This is true whether the advertising appropriation is big or small, although the smaller it is and the more selective the audience, the greater is the importance of choosing the right media.

The first thing to be done is to analyse the characteristics of the various media available. The selection of medium with the right characteristics is of vital importance to an advertiser. Some of the more important ones are these: [1]

(1) *The Type of People reached by the Medium.*

Some media are read, viewed or seen more by men than women or vice versa; more by young than old or vice versa; and, perhaps more important, different media are read, viewed or seen by

[1] These are only a few of the characteristics of a medium. If further detail is wanted, there is a very full analysis of media characteristics in Chapter II of J. W. Hobson's *The Selection of Advertising Media.*

different classes of people. The word "class" is generally dis-
approved today; nevertheless, it is still used in advertising and
market research to classify the population into five classes. They
are sometimes referred to as social-economic groups in an attempt
to avoid the ugly word "class". They are named after the first
five letters of the alphabet, thus:

Class	Description	Brief Definition
A	Well-to-do	Heads of households who are successful business or professional men, or senior civil servants, or have considerable private means.
B	Middle-class	Heads of households in younger age groups, will probably graduate later to Class A; those in older groups occupy the less senior positions in business and the professions, or the middle-grades of the Civil Service.
C	Lower middle	The families of the more highly-skilled workers, small tradespeople, and black-coated workers in the more important clerical grades.
D	Working class	The families of the great bulk of manual workers and of clerical workers in the less responsible positions.
E	Poor	Pensioners, widows with families, and those who, through periods of sickness or unemployment, or lack of opportunity, are unable to reach higher grades.

Thus advertising people are heard to talk of one medium as
being "distinctly A.B.", while another medium is said to cater
solidly for "C" class.

(2) The Geographical Coverage of the Medium

Many media are restricted to a part of the country, as are particular newspapers or television stations. It may be that the company's
particular product is more likely to be bought in the north than in
the south or in towns rather than the country. These factors are
obviously relevant in assessing the characteristics that a particular
medium must commend for the company to use it.

(3) The Physical Make-up of the Medium

Whether the medium is visual or oral, whether it moves, whether
it is in colour, are relevant to an advertiser because many products
can be more satisfactorily transmitted by one medium than another. Thus where food is concerned the use of colour helps

enormously to stimulate appetite appeal. On the other hand, if a product requires demonstration, television is obviously a more valuable method. In press advertising the question of whether a medium can offer large spaces will depend upon its size, and whether it can offer frequent repetition will depend upon the frequency with which it is published.

Having looked at the characteristics of the various media, the advertiser should examine their quantitative coverage. If he places an advertisement in a certain medium how many potential buyers of the product or service is he reaching?

At first there was little knowledge, either official or unofficial, of the circulation of newspapers and magazines. Publishers might make statements of their sales, but these were frequently not audited and often not reliable. Not until 1931, with the creation of the Audit Bureau of Circulation, was any advance made towards the provision of reliable figures of circulation. The circulations which were vouched for by the Bureau were only those which publishers calculated on the basis of copies actually sold to the final reader, a subtraction being made for copies being returned, either from wholesalers or retailer newsagents. However, many publishers did not submit their circulation figures to the Bureau, for reasons which were generally stated to be policy reasons. Moreover, mere circulation figures have the vital weakness that they do not indicate the number of persons who read the publication; therefore in time advertising people turned their attention from figures of circulation to figures of readership. Readership surveys began in the 1930s and readership measurement came to maturity with the *Hulton Readership Survey,* published annually for the ten years from 1947 to 1956. This survey has now been supplanted by the *National Readership Survey* which, since 1954, has been publishing quarterly or half-yearly readership figures. These services give information not only as to how far a particular publication has penetrated a particular group but also how far total readership of a publication lies in a particular group. Even readership figures are not the final answer to the quantitative assessment of media coverage because of the numerous possible definitions of the word "reader". A publication may be read fully or superficially, glanced at or digested. The *National Readership Survey,* realising the impossibility of defining where to draw the line, has taken all reading from the quick glance to the full perusal into its definition. Another refinement has appeared in so-called *Verified Readership Surveys,* where a reader is not counted as such if he cannot identify specific items in the publication which he claims he has read.

Furthermore, an advertisement may have a better chance of being seen or read in some publications than in others, and the search therefore has been taken one stage further towards the measurement, not of publication readership, but of advertisement readership with which, of course, the advertiser is primarily concerned. The *Survey of Advertisement Attention Values,* published by Hulton in 1949, is the best survey in this connection but is now very much out of date because newspapers and magazines have changed in size. The method used remains the standard practice, and a *Daily Mirror* Survey has brought some of the figures up to date for the national daily press.

More recently, since the advent of commercial television, similar attempts have been made on audience measurement in this field. A generally accepted method is the one which *Television Audience Measurement (T.A.M.)* provides. This consists of a mechanism which is attached to the television sets in a sample of households, which automatically records the times at which the set is switched on. After the sample returns have been grossed up, the resulting figure is an estimate of the number of sets in the country which have been switched on at any particular moment in time. This method is also capable of analysing the number, socio-economic group, age, sex, etc., of the persons viewing; this last depends upon the keeping of a diary by the householder with the television set on the panel. However, as will be seen, this estimate assumes that if a person is viewing television, that person will see the commercials which are on.

Also, attempts have been made to measure audiences in cinemas, of poster coverage and of the coverage of direct mail in this country. Results are less satisfactory, except in the case of cinemas, because the expenditure invested in these media has not been sufficient to merit large-scale research and the very nature of these media make it difficult to obtain a reliable assessment.

One final point that should be made is that there is no clear measurement of the amount purchased of the particular product by the readers of the particular publication or the audience of the television programme. A direct comparison of the readership and audience measurement can only be on the assumption that the more people reached, the larger potential volume of purchasers reached. Perhaps this further development of assessing media in terms of buyers for the advertiser's particular product will develop more in the future.

Having analysed media in this way, the next thing to do is to consider the principles to be followed in selecting the media. A short but full recipe for the good advertisement was put forward by the late Sir William Crawford, who required of advertising three things:

Concentration
Domination
Repetition

This is translated into a more detailed formula by J. W. Hobson into what he calls the three fundamental rules of an advertising plan: [1]

"1. Do not disperse your emphasis or your appropriation or your advertising design.

2. Be sure of being the biggest factor in your market at some point; be dominant with one appeal out of the many which your product and its competitors can advance; be dominant in some form of media if you cannot be dominant in all; be sure that some one factor emerges vigorously from your advertisement design.

3. Since advertisements have to create continuing habits if they are to reward the advertiser who invests in them, it is not enough to stop after a single impact, or jump about from one advertising objective to another, or from one product appeal to another, or from one set of media to another."

Hobson adds that, considering how simple and sensible these rules, are, it is surprising that people should so often fail to keep them.

"Concentration" is probably the most important, and to achieve it a sufficient weight of advertising must be achieved to impress the public who are the potential buyers of the product, and to impress them in a reasonably short space of time. Should the appeal be to a wide section of the public, as where a detergent or dentifrice is being marketed, this cannot be achieved on a national scale without spending sums of money which are completely beyond the purses of many manufacturers. Concentration has then to be achieved by advertising on an effective scale in one area only, until sales figures rise sufficiently to justify an extension to wider fields.

In such circumstances a selection is made of areas where sales of the product show promise, and public acceptance of the particular brands is encouraging. Before the advent of commercial television, the basis of such a campaign would perforce have been the local newspapers, possibly backed up by posters and displays in shops. Now, however, the area of the country covered by one of the commercial television companies, such as Southern Television or Tyne-Tees Television, can also be utilised for local campaigns.

HOW TO SET ABOUT ADVERTISING

Where a manufacturer advertises, one person should be given the responsibility for the overall advertising activities: in small com-

---

[1] From his useful book, *The Selection of Advertising Media* (Business Publications Ltd. 1955).

panies the sales manager often takes on this responsibility. If the size of the company warrants it, probably the best result will be attained by having a sales manager (or director) and an advertising manager (or possibly director) with a marketing director above both, the latter co-ordinating the whole of the marketing operation. However, the main decision facing the manufacturer who is setting about advertising is whether to do his own advertising or whether to employ an advertising agency and, if the latter, how to set about choosing his agency.

If one takes the total advertising in this country, it will be seen that approximately half of the advertising is placed through advertising agencies and this percentage has been increasing slightly since the end of the Second World War. A half may seem to be a small fraction for the agencies to deal with, but the total advertising figures include all local advertising and all classified advertising which accounts for a very large proportion and is not generally carried out, nor need be carried out, by advertising agencies. It is in national brand advertising which the advertising agencies command the field, and it is national brand advertising that most companies and manufacturers of products on a large scale require. For such advertising an agency is today vital, because by reason of their experience, their creative talent in inventing and executing advertisements and their knowledge of media, they can provide a service which it would be both too costly and too difficult for a manufacturer to develop for himself.

An advertising agency should be capable of seeing the manufacturer's marketing problems in their proper perspective; the marketing services which most advertising agencies have these days, in addition to the creative and artistic abilities of the agency, are available and of use to the manufacturer.

It should be remembered that the principal source of income to an agency stems from commission on space or airtime bought on behalf of advertisers. This commission—generally at the rate of 15 per cent. —can only be paid to a recognised advertising agency, not to an advertiser. Thus, it would not benefit an advertiser to book space direct; but by using an agency he obtains in effect, creative marketing and media-selection services for nothing.

A more difficult question is how to choose an advertising agency, or indeed, a number of agencies for in large companies with complex marketing arrangements it is not uncommon to employ a different advertising agency for different groups of products, which means that one agency is not overloaded with conflicting claims on its resources while there is at the same time a healthy rivalry for the best results.

This choice should be made carefully and deliberately, the manufacturer taking time and trouble to find out relevant information about the agency's suitability for the job. *The Advertisers' Annual* is a useful publication for obtaining a comprehensive list of the names of agencies and of the clients, products and services with which they each deal. This gives the potential employer of an agency an idea of the type of advertising, product and service that each particular agency is currently dealing with. It will be found that every agency has definite characteristics of its own—while some are good with fashion accounts, others will be at their best with technical advertising; some are well known for their handling of poster campaigns, while others are specialists in colour work. The *Advertisers' Annual* will also indicate the size of the agency and this may be important, because a big campaign usually requires the resources of a big agency. Other particularly important factors which should influence choice are the agency's reputation for creative talent, their record of successes with other clients, the calibre of persons to be assigned to the account and the extent of available marketing services.

Once a provisional selection of, say, two or three agencies has been made, the agencies selected will be willing to make a presentation to the potential client, giving information about themselves and their resources and practical *suggestions* as to the way they would approach the campaign. Once the agency has been appointed it is advisable to allow a fair amount of freedom in their plans and operations. There are obvious advantages in maintaining continuity of agency, since a campaign takes time to be planned, put into execution and have its desired effect; frequent changes of agency can play havoc with the success of campaigns. It is also usual to give the agency wide freedom in relation to methods of production of the advertisements, every one, however, being subject to approval at each stage of their preparation and final placing. Indeed it is important that a friendly working relationship should be built up between agency and client, for without this the best results are difficult to obtain. All relevant information about the company's background and policy, the products and methods of distribution, should be placed freely at the agency's disposal, together with the full details of the advertising budget. All this information the advertising agency should, of course, consider as strictly confidential.

CHAPTER IV

PUBLIC RELATIONS

THE process of "motivating the sale" of a product or service may also be achieved in a more indirect and subtle way than by advertising: this is by the use of what is generally known today as public relations. Public relations (or "P.R." as it is frequently referred to) is a sufficiently vague and comprehensive term to have been subjected to many widely differing definitions. The function of public relations is to promote the public understanding and acceptance of a company and of its products or services, the goal being to develop and maintain in the public mind a favourable image of the company and consequently promote the ultimate sale and usage of more of its products.

It is not, however, the purpose or indeed the ability of public relations to give a company a good reputation if it does not deserve one. Neatly, therefore, public relations might be described as "being good and getting credit for it". In America it is said that when Henry J. Kaiser, Jnr., was asked what were the P.R. policies of the Kaiser Industry Corporation—of which he was the public relations head—he handed the inquirer a card on which was printed: "Let your light so shine before men that they may see your good works. Matthew, Chapter 5, verse 16." These definitions may sound somewhat frivolous, but they do give a correct feeling of what public relations is about. On the other hand, for a more solid definition which indicates more what a company must do about public relations, that of Danny Griswold who in the *Public Relations News*—an American publication—defined public relations as: "The management function which evaluates public attitudes, identifies the policies and procedures of an individual or an organisation with the public interest, and executes a programme of action to earn public understanding and acceptance."

Public relations is a function of management: this cannot be overstressed. It is the top-level employment of the management function and colours, or should colour, every action which concerns a public or an attitude or an opinion about the company. It is not merely, as many people seem to think, a rather grand synonym for press relations. It is much more. Further reference will be made to this point, that newspaper publicity is only a part—and often a small part—of public relations, when dealing with the methods by which public relations should be pursued.

It may be asked why a company should concern itself with public opinion and what the public thinks of it, its products and services. It is only in this century that public opinion has become a major concern to the company. This is because public opinion, which has always been the final arbiter of the fates of great men and world leaders, has now necessarily turned its attention to the great corporations, groups and companies by which the world has come to be dominated in this century. The somewhat unwieldy pattern of private and public companies, generally with limited liability as a result of mid-nineteenth-century legislation, is one of the most significant features of today's social structure; the growth of these companies which stemmed from early industrialisation required greater and greater capital investment, and they have now taken the place of the single great man, at least in business affairs. The corporation has its responsibilities to that part of the public who are its shareholders and who provide it with the money to use as capital to carry on its business, and more recently has had to take on the role of the rich patron of earlier centuries, becoming philanthropist, benevolent employer and educator.

No longer is the company's only goal to make as much money as it can. Furthermore, public opinion has become important to the corporation because of the vast expansion of communication. The mass circulation of newspapers, the mass audiences for television, the speed of air travel, these have all combined to make it impossible for companies to hide their lights and their operations and to keep themselves to themselves. Their actions may now be revealed to mass populations in no time at all.

Present Position

The practice of public relations has advanced enormously since the end of the Second World War. The advance came first in the United States of America, where it has been said that public relations practitioners have grown more in numbers than any other management service group. In 1930 there were perhaps less than 1,000 persons engaged in public relations in the U.S.A., while today the estimate stands at 100,000. The majority of the 100,000 practitioners are in public relations departments of individual companies, while the rest form the public relations agencies giving advice and other services to client companies. As to expenditure on public relations, it is estimated that 2,000 million dollars will be spent by U.S.A. companies in 1960, and that by 1969 there will be an annual expenditure of 6,000 million dollars.

Not as much indeed is spent in this country, but the American figures have been quoted partly to show how huge public relations can loom in a modern industrial society, partly because it is commonly believed that, in promotional fields generally, the U.K. tends to follow American trends after a time lag. Also, there are no such clear figures and estimates of the numbers engaged and money expended in public relations in this country. It is a new business or profession and has had the same problems as did the advertising profession in gaining acceptance in the community. There is, however, an Institute of Public Relations whose members subscribe to the Institute code of conduct laid down for new practitioners in public relations. The code of ethics as produced by the Institute of Public Relations is as yet in embryonic form but will undoubtedly serve as a platform for future developments.

TECHNIQUES

On the first question of whether public relations should be employed, it is important to recognise which are the problems that public relations is capable of solving or helping to solve. Top management must know what problems public relations is capable of dealing with and, as has been said in a pungent article in the *Harvard Business Review*[1]:

"Too often management accepts the need for public relations before adequately appreciating what public relations does that is different and worth the price. Too often 'good public relations' is supported as a matter of policy while management proceeds to violate sound public relations practice at every turn."

A public relations problem is concerned with the viewpoints and attitudes, beliefs and actions of the public which impede the full and fruitful operations of a business company or other organisation. Public relations should be employed knowingly by every company concerned with the public. Publics differ. There is not only the general public but also the shareholders of the company, the employees of the company, the trade customers of the company, the press and every media through which public relations channels its activities, and the government. Each is interested in different things, and one great mistake made frequently in public relations is to forget this and to concentrate solely upon the general public which may be, for the particular problem, the least important of a company's publics. Probably the most important public a company has are its customers and its employees, but frequently they are not considered the responsibilities of public relations by top management.

[1] "New Perspective on Public Relations", by Thomas D. Yutzy and Simon Williams: May–June, 1955.

Consideration of Methods

The public relations practitioner, whether he be in an independent agency or in the particular company's public relations department, must first of all give guidance to the company in what it should do from a public relations standpoint. He must impart understanding to the management of the company, and give the management an accurate opinion of probable reaction to what is being planned. The next stage is to see that the actions of the company and the policy from which they spring are understood by all the groups of people whose opinion is important.

It is a fallacy to believe that simple publicity is the right road. This is a wrong concept of the public relations function; it is intrusive and can be dreadful. Such an approach reminds one of Arnold Bennett's remark about a young man trying to give a good impression: he said that the young man gave the impression of a young man trying to give a good impression. Public relations must use a wide variety of methods for the presentation of its material. Since it is concerned with relationships generally, it is wider than press publicity. Press publicity may result from public relations; it may not. A newspaper editor will not use material if it is of no news value. Thus a great deal will depend on the news value of the other items of news on a specific day. This makes timing important, and some sensational happening, if coinciding with the press release from the company, will cause it to lose its effect. Further, the probability of an editor publicising a release will be influenced by his view of the reliability of the information offered. On reliability, his judgment is generally based on the reputation of the source in this connection and to a lesser extent on the degree of personal contact with the company's public relations people over a period of time.

The main thing to remember is that a great weight of press clippings is no way to success in public relations. Not only may it have no effect, but it may sometimes engender a hostile attitude to the company while, on the other hand, one item published in the right place at the right time may achieve a great deal of benefit. The correct approach is to view all possible media as potential vehicles for public relations in its task of communication. Thus, for example, the trade and technical press may prove of greater value in a particular case than a series of articles in the general press. Because the readers of trade and technical journals tend to be both better informed and more influenced by factual information than the general public, all material should be very carefully prepared. Again, the public relations personnel often make valuable use of exhibitions and are often in charge of the planning and presentation of a company's exhibits on such occasions. So, too, they are normally responsible for the internal magazines of a company, and the House Organ is one of their best vehicles for spreading information to the right quarters. Since it is a periodical it can become known by regular repetition and operate to a schedule.

Also, public relations may extend to such educational media as local health authorities, schools, hospitals, technical colleges, women's associations—all valuable opinion-forming places by reason of their mantles of respectability and their impartiality. Television affords a comparatively new outlet for the public relations practitioner but is certainly a part of the function.

The use of media stresses the important difference between public relations and advertising. Whereas in advertising media space and time are bought, in public relations the emphasis is on "servicing" the media. What the public relations people, whether agency or internal department, should aim at is to get themselves accepted by the media owners as providers of reliable and interesting information. This distinction of communication, however, between buying and servicing the media should not cause one to underestimate the selling power of public relations. Many people feel that advertising is enough without public relations thrown in: that advertising expenditure is sufficiently costly without requiring further expense on public relations, particularly when the problem in hand is the increasing of sales of a product. It is often thought that advertising is concerned with the practical job of selling goods, whereas public relations deals only with the more rarified, head-in-the-clouds task of boosting the prestige of the company. Yet public relations may equally be concerned, though more indirectly, with the sales of the product as the advertising. The point is put well by Yutzy and Williams in their article referred to earlier:

> "The publicity functions that gradually were assumed by public relations just were not related consciously to sales . . . Until recently the predominant task of public relations has been to sell the virtues of the business enterprise itself, not its products. It is only with emergence of the social sciences in the past decade, revealing an almost frightening spectrum of variables affecting human behaviour and, more specifically, consumer motivation, that the objectives of both advertising and public relations have been associated with sales."

Furthermore, not only are advertising and public relations complementary methods of approaching and influencing the particular public, but the advertising may be powerless without the aid of public relations to effect a break-through in changing public attitudes. The writers add:

"One of the major identifying characteristics of a public relations problem, which is revealed most clearly when barriers to increased sales become the primary concern of management, is that the problem embraces deeply held opinions which block acceptance of the direct message of advertising. These opinions may result from ignorance, loss of confidence, fear or tradition; to be modified they may require the persistent diversified attack of public relations concurrently with other methods of sales appeal."

HOW TO SET ABOUT PUBLIC RELATIONS

The businessman who wishes to employ, actively, public relations for his company will want to know what is the best way to go about it. The choice here is similar to that presented to him when considering the use of market research. He may wish to adopt one or a combination of the following possibilities:

1. Set up a public relations department in his own company.
2. Engage the services of an outside public relations agency.
3. Engage the services of the public relations department of his advertising agency.

The first course does not restrict itself to the very large company only, mainly because public relations does not need a highly technical or large staff. One man, or woman, who has common sense, practical experience, ability, initiative, who can write, get on with people, will make a good public relations officer for a company. This will not constitute a public relations department, but such an appointment would be more than half way there, whereas for market research a whole field force and also technical experts on sampling techniques and statistics may be required for comparative results.

It is possible also to split the public relations work between a small department in the company and an outside public relations agency. This is made possible by the fact that, as shown earlier in this chapter, the practice of public relations consists first in the study and evaluation of public relations and the guiding of a company's policy based upon the interpretation of the public attitudes once probed and analysed; and secondly in executing a programme of action to earn public understanding and acceptance based upon the prior analysis and attitudes. It is thus possible to allocate the first portion of the programme, i.e. the evaluation and guidance, to the specialist public relations agency and to allocate the programme of action formulated thereon to the public relations department of the company.

Engaging the services of a public relations agency has the advantage of the employment of specialised talent in a field which, although not technical in the market research sense, requires an understanding of public relations. Such an understanding is not in this day and age one which the intelligent layman can justifiably boast. Further, access to the various kinds of media are of vital importance in the public relations field, and this is perhaps more likely to be available to an agency working full time in public relations which has the time and opportunity to build up contacts, than to a department of a particular company concerned with a particular problem.

The third course is for the company to engage the services of the public relations department of its advertising agency. This has the merit that because inevitably, where sales promotion is concerned, the work, techniques and methods of advertising and public relations interact throughout the whole campaign, it is generally useful to have a close tie-up between the persons working on the company's advertising and the persons working on its public relations. There may be disadvantages, depending on the problem of having a different and fresh approach to the advertising and the public relations. It must be remembered that, whereas the advertising is concerned with the direct approach and the "hard sell", public relations sends out its messages indirectly, using editors, newspapers, television programmes, producers, and the like to transmit the messages that they need to use. Also, public relations is concerned with many different viewpoints of many different publics, and thus requires a different approach to the "hard sell" of advertising a product or service.

The choice between these different methods can only be made in the light of the particular problems of the particular company. It might, however, be hazarded that a large and/or rapidly expanding company might be best advised to have a public relations department together with an outside press relations man to inject new thoughts, new ideas and approaches, and new media, and also an outside *top* level adviser on public relations. Each company and each problem is different.

Setting the Budget

Finally, there is the question of the cost. What the company should budget depends upon what the company's problems are and what the company wants out of its public relations. The businessman has to take the advice of the public relations practitioner, but this advice must make good sense. One has got to be persuaded of its use. There is as yet no fixed fee laid down for public relations; each agency has its own standard rates. As a guide, however, the *Public Relations Directory*, which was first published in 1960, suggests that:

> "The cost of a comprehensive campaign might average from £3,000 to £15,000 per annum, dependent upon circumstances."

The *Directory* also points out that there are certain rules which are applied in general practice for working out the fees. Estimates, according to the *Directory*, will generally be sub-divided between:

A fee which is inclusive of the advice, labour cost and overheads.
A budget for out-of-pocket expenses.
A budget for information media (e.g. printed material).

All advisory work is based upon the time which personnel require for the work and for the advice. Fees take into account, apart from a reasonable profit for the agency, the time of the personnel used and a retainer for the agency's services based on the fact that by reason of its confidential working for the company it is excluded from taking on other work for companies in the same field. If, in addition to giving advice, the public relations agency executes the programme of action, then the company will also pay a fee for the supervision of this work and for the amount of time involved in doing so.

The fees will vary with the size of the agency and the rate which it can command, and with whether the service to the particular company is confined to advice or is comprehensive in offering both advice and the execution of the programme advised. According to the *Public Relations Directory* the inclusive fee for a comprehensive service:

"is often calculated both in this country and in the U.S.A. by trebling the combined salary cost of all executive personnel used on any particular operation."

Next come the out-of-pocket expenses: they will include such items as expenditure on travel, entertainment, telephone calls, telegrams, press cutting service, special newspapers and magazines, subscriptions, stationery, stamps, radio or television monitoring, etc. As to the expenditure on informative media, this, the *Directory* points out, should be the client's direct responsibility, since a public relations agency cannot be expected to finance the whole outlay in the absence of interest on capital and a charge for handling. A detailed budget on media, however, cannot normally be recommended until a client's problems have been analysed and it is usually necessary, initially at least, to work on an *ad hoc* basis.

Fees are generally worked out on an annual basis, payable monthly, and are generally paid in arrears. This, of course, depends on the length of time involved, and many public relations agencies lay down a minimum period of one to three years for which they require a contract because of the long-term nature of the work. Time generally has to be allowed both for initial research into attitudes and for conditioning these attitudes once discovered, before a final public relations programme can be launched upon the public.

Whatever the intent, and however desirable a particular public relations campaign may sound, no public relations are justified if the eventual result is not to increase the sale of the company's products with which they are concerned.

Example of Public Relations

A brief impression of the function of public relations can be given by the following illustration.

A new glucose tablet was to be introduced to the market.

Glucose in powder form had been accepted as a strength-builder for invalids or those recovering from illness and for children. It was not regarded as a necessity for everyday life. Only a limited amount of money was available for this promotion and the manufacturer wished to obtain a wide sale among athletes and sportsmen as well as among those with more sedentary occupations who used their energy in other ways. Two things had to be established:

(a) Glucose was a good cure for fatigue, faintness and immediate hunger.

(b) Glucose was a good preventive for all the above and was therefore an immediate source of energy.

To assist in the initial launch of this product, public relations undertook to gain public notice for the glucose tablets on a public occasion where circumstances would be favourable to the objectives to be achieved.

(a) Glucose as a curative for fatigue, faintness and hunger was achieved by using the tablets strategically during the celebrations for the Coronation of Queen Elizabeth II. Permission was obtained from the British Red Cross and St. John Ambulance Brigade to supply all their stations set up along the route with cases of tablets. Free supplies of the tablets were sent, with the compliments of the manufacturer, to a number of well-known people who were to be present in the Abbey during the long ceremony. The supply of tablets to the Red Cross Stations was widely publicised through the press, and subsequent reports confirmed that the tablets were much used and stood up to the reputation which was being established for them.

(b) The second stage of establishing the "staying factor" of the tablets was carried out by staging a colourful "endurance" test requiring a man to ride on horseback non-stop from Plymouth to London, eating nothing but glucose tablets and drinking only water. This took thirty-nine hours and was covered by the press, radio, newsreel and Pathé Pictorial cameramen along the whole route. It was effective in two ways. It illustrated the power of the tablets in warding off fatigue and hunger; and it also showed them used in a "manly" context. From this the campaign widened to cover Wimbledon and other sporting activities where it became a normal matter for performers to take glucose tablets instead of sugar, and naturally obtained considerable press coverage. Glucose tablets became accepted by the public as an easy, harmless method of achieving an immediate "dose" of energy.

CHAPTER V

SALES MANAGEMENT

THE third limb of the definition of Marketing refers to: "distributing it (the product or service) into ultimate consumption. . . ."

Before any distribution can take place, a selling process has to be effected. It is the function of the sales department within a company, be it large or small, to effect this process. No product is truly sold until it has been consumed to the consumer's satisfaction. In the case of non-durable consumer items, such as ice-cream, this is readily apparent, but not so apparent with a car or packaging machine where presumably the "consumption" will take place over a long period of time. Here the aspects of after-sales service and of guarantee can be of considerable import.

All great countries have been founded upon a sound platform of commerce, the spearhead for which is the sales representative and the distribution team. Similarly, a successful company must have a reliable and effective selling organisation. Underlying any sales organisation is the need for recognition of the complex and varied characteristics in an individual. Personalities will play, in even the most sophisticated marketing situation an important part in the success of the sales organisation. Personalities are important in any aspect of management and in the function of departments within the company, but with the exception of the sales department such matters can usually be kept on an internal footing. The sales organisation is the living mouthpiece for the company which, to achieve its purpose must be extrovert in nature.

Sales management has to possess an imaginative centre—a concept based on a marketing idea. It has to have a spirit that will enable the sales team to translate the theory into practice. It must recognise the need to encourage the development of what may be a fairly simple thought into a creative selling idea.

For example: The term "wet-strength" and its use and value in a paper facial tissue had to be demonstrated to more than 16,000 chemists who were to be stockists and sellers of the new tissue which remained strong even when wet. This demonstration was carried out by the sales representative equipped with a small case containing: one jar full of water (with secure lid), three half-crowns tied with string into a single unit, samples of the new tissue, and plain "incognito" samples of "non-wet-strength" tissues which had been the established product hitherto. There was to be an introductory trade bonus valued as 7s. 6d. for the stockist, available on a given quantity of the new product ordered during the introductory period.

By using the jar of water to demonstrate the wet-strength of the new tissue, a visual demonstration against an existing standard was given. The three half-crowns placed in the tissues went straight through the non-wet-strength tissues; pulled out of the jar and replaced in a wet-strong tissue they remained hanging in the water from the side of the jar for the rest of the interview. Here was a practical demonstration of how a sneeze or nose-blow could be retained effectively in the tissue with the wet-strength. As the climax to the presentation, and just prior to obtaining an order, the representative took the tissue out of the jar, removed the 7s. 6d. from it and was able to refer to the fact that this was the additional profit to be made from placing an order during the introductory period. This was a simple but creative idea which produced tremendous results as it enabled the *theory* of the benefits of wet-strong tissue to be demonstrated *practically* to the stockists who were to sell the product to the eventual consumer.

To ensure a successful sales organisation, the company must look first at the direction and leadership that the sales director or sales manager is capable of imparting down the line. The size of the sales organisation, the extent to which it may include routine sales office procedure, must not be permitted to restrict the duties of the sales manager to the handling of routine matters. The sales manager has to organise his management function in such a way that he can personally lead and inspire his team to sell.

SALES MANAGER'S RESPONSIBILITIES

1. Relationship with:
   (a) Total marketing function.
   (b) Other departments within the marketing group.
2. Sales forecasts in relation to overall programme, e.g. finance and manufacturing capacity.
3. Operating within the budgeted expense figure to achieve a set quota.
4. Method and channels of distribution.
5. Merchandising at point of sale.
6. Sales office routine.
7. Territory planning and quota setting.
8. Control of sub-managers and sales representatives.
9. Selection of personnel.
10. Training and development of personnel.

11. Ensuring managers and sales representatives' understanding of company and sales policy, promotional and advertising ideas.
12. Securing and analysing market information.
13. Holding sales meetings as necessary.
14. Organising extraordinary sales operations and drives.
15. Controlling expenditure.
16. Maintaining an up-to-date awareness of improved sales techniques.

Many additional interpretations of the sales manager's functions can be mentioned that will be inherent in a good sales manager's make-up: [1]

He will feel the need to meet and talk with customers at all levels.

He will wish to participate in trade functions, to meet sales managers from other industries and companies to exchange ideas and views.

To appreciate the marketing policies of his company he will need an understanding of the effectiveness of the various advertising media and promotional aids.

He will have to evaluate and make recommendations on the relative return on expenditure of such items as:

(a) The need for providing sales representatives with a car.

(b) The level of sales representatives' expenses.

(c) Trade exhibitions.

(d) Mailing shots.

(e) Advice of call cards.

(f) Sales representatives' reports.

(g) The amount of delegation to local supervisors.

He must be able to receive and decline requests from his sales personnel and yet maintain their enthusiasm.

In all these matters it is possible to be completely analytical and perhaps to succeed. The sales manager is far more likely to succeed if in his dealings with his sales organisation he can be logical and firm and yet maintain warmth in his relationship with his inside and outside staff.

As an alternative to the employment of a full-time sales staff, a manufacturer can use the services of one or more sales agents to introduce and sell his goods. Organised selling agencies have developed quite substantially of recent years. They were a feature of the nineteenth century and have again come into vogue with the growing need for better representation current today. A manufacturer with a limited output cannot afford, or for some other reason, may not wish

---

[1] Another illustration of sales management responsibilities will be found in Schedules LG/9 and 10 of Appendix II to the Introduction (see page 94).

to provide the sales staff necessary to cover the country. It is economic policy to combine his selling with that of other manufacturers whose goods are sold to the same class of trade. A sales agent is therefore appointed who has a staff of sales representatives throughout the country carrying the goods of, say, a dozen manufacturers. Alternatively, a number of agents, each covering an area, are appointed separately. A third plan is to cover certain parts of the country, usually those in the vicinity of the factory, with the manufacturer's own sales representatives and appoint agents for the outlying areas.

The good agents make a definite contribution to the scheme of distribution. Their drawback to a manufacturer is that they are unable to give a high degree of concentration on his line.

SELECTION, TRAINING AND REMUNERATION OF PERSONNEL

It is important that certain fundamentals are established:

1. To obtain the right personnel the company must know:
   (a) What its sales representative is expected to achieve.
   (b) The degree of technical knowledge that is required.
   (c) The sources from which it can draw.
2. To conduct an interview to ensure that:
   (a) The company can assess the ability and fundamental attitude of mind of the candidate.
   (b) The candidate receives the right impression of the company.
3. To look ahead:
   Having selected its personnel, the company must then ensure proper training of its representatives both initially and on a continuing basis.
4. Remunerations to be geared to the job so that:
   (a) The representative in constant contact with other similarly employed persons remains reasonably satisfied with his present and potential earnings.
   (b) He is in a position to represent properly the company to the level that is expected.
   (c) He feels his efforts are appreciated as much as those of his colleagues in production or advertising, etc.

However effective and thorough may have been the planning behind the introduction of a product, its eventual success may depend upon the effectiveness of the company in its selection and training of sales personnel. Much of the responsibility for this will naturally lie with sales management and in their ability to conduct interviews with potential recruits. An equal degree of responsibility lies with the general management and their understanding and appreciation of the calibre of man required in their particular company.

The degree of technical knowledge possessed by a manufacturer's sales personnel will be dictated by the nature of the product to be sold. The sales representative involved in high-level negotiations on behalf of an industry, association or manufacturer may not possess the same technical ability or knowledge as certain of his colleagues, he must have an understanding of the product's or machine's basic performance. How else can he represent its claims properly?

Recruitment

The selection of personnel from universities, colleges and schools has reached a more advanced stage in the United States of America than it has in this country, but much progress has been made since 1945 and the industrial world and educational authorities are more concerned today with the placing of people in the right type of job when they have completed their studies than has ever before been experienced. Some manufacturers will not employ sales personnel from their competitors; some want only university graduates. There are few guiding principles that can be laid down, partly because no amount of paper study can replace the experience in selection and handling of men that can only be gained over a number of years, and also because the dictates of each job will differ according to the nature of the task.

The selection of promising men from within the company for recruitment into the field sales force carries with it the benefit of a knowledge of the company, its products and its operation. It helps to create a company image. The degree to which this is possible will be limited by the size of the company, but in any company irrespective of size some "inside" appointments are possible. This will have particular merit where technical products are concerned, calling for a high degree of speciality and knowledge.

Selection

Whether an applicant is interviewed individually or by a panel, where possible more than one interviewer should participate in the selection of sales personnel as this not only gives greater depth of judgment on the person but it will instil a greater feeling of confidence in the company by the applicant. The applicant will feel that this company is serious in its approach to people joining it and if selected will feel that he has gone through a worth-while "examination".

Training is a continuation of selection and the selection procedure should be planned with this in mind. Any selection procedure to be valid must be based on a precise knowledge of the job to be done.

Superficially this would appear simple. The truth is that each job is different and must be treated as such. The job specification is not something that can be carried in the interviewer's mind, it must be written down in considerable detail. A job specification should be written for each new appointment and should contain such details as territory, method of working, hours to be worked, written work required, types of customer to be called upon, remuneration, supervision available, any particular territory difficulties. From the job specification a profile of the man who will exactly fit the job is prepared. Here again this will be as detailed and precise as possible, realising that in all probability no such man exists. However, if one starts with perfection there is a greater possibility of getting near to it.

The next stage is to decide the outside limits of the profile which are acceptable. For instance, if the ideal man is 28, limits of 26 to 30 may be written in. Similarly, if an electrical engineer is ideal an applicant with a Higher National Certificate may be acceptable. This final profile is the basis of the selection routine. Many aspects of this profile can be dealt with in the application form which will be used to reject applicants where qualifications do not fall within the acceptable limits. Interviewers should mark the applicant on a selection form. Comparison between different interviews and recognising acceptable limits will enable a final selection to be made. Further, these marked forms revealing strengths and weaknesses can form the basis of the subsequent training programme.

Graphically, these stages can be shown thus:

Job Specification	Profile	Acceptable Limits	Selection				
A precise description of the job to be done	A precise description of the man to fit the job	Lower and upper limits of the profile	Outside Limit	Weak	Acceptable	Strong	Ideal

A judgment of the man's character may indicate the qualities, honesty, loyalty, determination, which are fundamental to success in selling. Clearly, also, the man must be properly dressed, clean, likeable, and so on, but any sales representative—whatever his technical qualifications should have certain *attitudes* of mind. In selecting a potential sales representative the interviewer has to judge whether the candidate does or will be able to possess these essential attributes:

(a) *Knowledge.* It is unrealistic to expect people without knowledge to perform any job satisfactorily, and recognising that this may come only from training, an impression could and should be obtained.

(*b*) *Belief.* If a salesman believes something and can express it, then he has the opportunity to impart to others; if he does not, then the sincerity of his approach will at some stage or other be questionable.

(*c*) *Skill.* Without the *skill* to translate the belief and the knowledge into a logical selling sequence the potential sales representative is unlikely to effect many sales.

The sales representative spends most of his time on his own and will be called upon to meet and sell to many different types of buyers. If he is to be a true representative of the company, then the company itself must know the sort of sales representative it requires. He cannot do his job adequately and to the best of his and his company's advantage if he has the opinion, rightly or wrongly, that he is there just to sell and to "leave the rest to somebody else". To represent the company properly he must feel he is part of that company and that his reports and suggestions do receive proper consideration and recognition. They may not be followed, but this does not mean he has to lose interest; a proper note of explanation from higher management can ensure his continuing loyalty and will foster the belief that his efforts and thoughts are of value.

In selecting a sales representative the company should decide how far it agrees with these policies before it sets out to get the man.

Training

"A good salesman is born, not made." How often this has been heard said! And how far short of the truth it falls!

There is, of course, some truth in it, as there is in most aphorisms, but the idea that one can give a good man a bag of samples, a price list and a territory to cover and let him go out and get on with it rarely applies any longer, if indeed it ever did. The degree of training or technical knowledge required will depend upon the industry in which the sales representative is selling. The sale of pre-packed nationally advertised consumer products in frequent use and having a quick flow through channels of distribution does not demand so high a technical knowledge of the product as does the sale of a raw material which will become a part of a manufactured article. Nevertheless, sales representatives in both industries will have to have a basic knowledge of their product, and although one may need a more detailed knowledge than the other, the sales representative who "does not know" the important qualities and obvious sales benefits of his product is unlikely to do more than a minimum amount of good in the distribution pattern in his company and, in fact, he may well be a hindrance rather than an asset.

By now many firms, large and small, are operating a form of sales training, in some cases a fully indoctrinating course run within the company; other companies making use of the variety of outside independent sales-training courses which cater for all aspects and levels of sales management. A convenient source of reference is the *Institute of Marketing and Sales Management.*

The proper training of a new sales representative is of such importance that a fuller examination is justified. Take for example a training timetable for a new representative joining a medium-sized manufacturing concern selling through the consumer or retail distributive channels. Before the new sales representative takes any direct responsibility on his own territory he should be exposed to the management and operating functions of the company.

Much time can be wasted during the first few weeks of a new appointment if too much is attempted. By exposing the new man to the actual field situation before proceeding into too great detail, the sales representative is able to obtain better understanding of the requirement of the job he is to undertake.

Suggested Timetable:

New sales representative-trainee joins "XYZ" company.

Previous experience: Four years in general office in an industrial concern.

One year as sales representative in a small wholesale company.

Age 24 years.

Educational standard: "O" Level.

Week 1.

Initial Introduction to the Company.

1st Day.		
	a.m.	Meeting with sales manager—outline week.
		Introduction to factory manager.
		Tour of factory.
		Laboratory and background to manufacturing process.

(See note (i).)

	p.m.	Manufacturing process.
2nd Day.		Manufacturing process.

3rd Day.		
	a.m.	Marketing.
		Advertising.
		Market research.
		Public relations.

	p.m.	Quality control . . . factory.

4th Day.   a.m.   Customer service, and logistical matters, such as despatch, credit, invoicing, sample and sales promotion material procedure.

          p.m.   Revision.

5th Day.   a.m.   Sales organisation and briefing for next four
          p.m.   weeks.

6th Day.   a.m.   Prepare essay on week's experience.
                                       (See note (ii).)

Note (i)

The importance of the factory manager personally making the arrangements cannot be too strongly emphasised if the maximum benefit is to be obtained from the few days spent in the factory by the sales representative. It should ensure the factory personnel attaching the necessary importance to the visit and will certainly give a degree of confidence to the new man, in that senior production personnel consider this time well spent. It will enable the factory manager to meet the company's sales representatives and will generally help to create a degree of co-operation and understanding between the two major arms of the company. Where possible, and if such a post is held, the sales training manager should also be present at regular intervals during the week's training.

Note (ii)

The new man will have seen many operations during this first week which will have been quite new to him. If he is to remember and make practical use of all he has seen and heard then he must take written notes. To place the notes in a tidy and natural sequence, starting with the incoming raw materials, through the manufacturing and processing operation, through the quality control functions to the final production and distribution of the product, calls for an early evaluation of his notes and the correlating of all these facts into a story or essay.

The essays should be read and commented upon by the factory manager and any of his technical staff he may nominate to check the routine content for him, and by the sales manager.

Week 2.
  1st Day   a.m.   Field sales manager . . . briefing.

          All   Working with established representative(s)
          week.   specially selected for training ability. Complete notes and short report for field sales manager.

Week 3.   Ditto.

Week 4.
    1st, 2nd   Ditto.
    and
    3rd Days.

    4th Day.   With field manager. The sales representative
                      should conduct sales interviews himself,
                      accompanied by the field manager. This will
                      enable the field manager to judge the degree of
                      training the representative has received before
                      he brings his own greater knowledge and
                      experience to bear.

    5th Day.   Field manager conducts interviews.
                      Representative to complete notes and report
                      for field manager.

Week 5.
    1st Day.   a.m.   Sales representative conducts sales interviews
                      accompanied by field manager.

               p.m.   Field manager gives final evaluation.

    2nd Day.   New representative goes into territory on his
                      own.

    3rd Day.   Ditto.

    4th Day.   New sales representative visited by field
                      manager.

    5th Day.   New sales representative visited by sales man-
                      ager (if possible).

After the first six to eight weeks a progress report should be
completed and, subject to the representative proving satisfactory, a
more detailed sales training course should be held at which from
four to twelve persons should be present. It is preferable for these
courses to be as widely varied in attendance as is possible, with sales
representatives from different parts of the country, and perhaps
personnel from other parts of the marketing group included.

The object and purpose of this final week's training is to indoc-
trinate the now receptive mind of the new man so that the experience
and knowledge he has gained during his initial sales training period
will be retained and acted upon instinctively in the field.

Suggested Final Week of Basic Training.

1st Day.   *The Company.*

    Subject :   1. Introduction.
                 Welcome to course.
            2. Company background and history.
            3. The industry.
            4. Marketing.
            5. Sales organisation.
            6. Market research.
            7. Advertising.
            8. Public relations.
    Summary : given by persons on the course.

2nd Day.   Subject :   1. Product knowledge.
            2. Tour of factory.

3rd Day.   *"Easy to Buy From."*

    Subject :   1. Introduction to salesmanship.
            2. Human relations.
                (*a*) The professional man.
                (*b*) The salesman.
                (*c*) Right mental attitude.
            3. Overcoming objections.
            4. Buyers and salesmen.
                (*a*) As others see us.
                (*b*) Some buyers we know.
            5. Selective selling.
            6. Planning your work.
            7. The "You" sales sequence.
    Summary : given by persons on course.
    FILM.   "Talkies".[1]

4th Day.   *Sales Technique.*

    Subject :   1. The approach.
            2. The presentation (the product).
            3. Closing the sale.
            4. Merchandising.
            5. Summary/assignment for Friday.
    "Talkies"   interspersed.

5th Day.   *Application.*

    Subject :   1. Sales presentation.
            2. 10–15 minutes sales interviews by
                members of the course, and evaluation.
            3. Course summary and discussions.

[1] One- or two-minute talks given either impromptu or prepared on any subject.

All the way through the course, the maximum care should be given to ensure that persons attending take part in what is going on and feel they are helping in it and not just at the receiving end of interminable lectures and pep-talks.

Refresher courses, area or national sales meetings, visits from senior personnel in other departments provide opportunities for continuous training.

Remuneration

The remuneration of sales personnel should where possible include some form of incentive. This need not be geared to the individual representative, as a group scheme may well be more satisfactory, especially in companies employing considerable numbers of representatives where the selling effort on the part of one man may be related to a sale by one of his colleagues, and may call for some larger grouping into a district or region.

The sales representative is entitled to think that what he is selling is profitable and excepting those cases where an individual representative is closely concerned with the budgeting of production, such as in the sale of pre-cast concrete, it is advisable to have an incentive scheme based on actual invoiced sales, and not on a percentage of the profit.

It is wise to consider at all times the merits and de-merits of various forms of remuneration and incentives. It is important to realise and seldom is fully understood, that the power of a disincentive often outweighs the power of any incentive.

When incentives are employed there is likely to be a corresponding disincentive. Activity after a competition declines, sales representatives with low performances lose enthusiasm when compared with high-performance sales representatives, winners are elated, losers are deflated.

The amount and manner of remuneration relevant to a sales force has much bearing on the sales manager's success or otherwise in selecting good sales representatives, in developing to the full their natural resources and potential, and in establishing a healthy and sympathetic relationship between the management and the man.

To achieve this objective, both general management and sales management will need a knowledge of:

(a) How other companies pay their sales representatives.

(b) Variations in the methods of remuneration, and which of these variations is most applicable to their sales team.

A recent survey of sales representatives' remuneration produced by the Tack Organisation has provided much valuable information on this subject.[1] Tack, in February 1960, summarised replies to questionnaires received from 593 companies. These companies varied in size from the very small to the very large, employing small, medium and large size sales forces—anything in fact from one to seven hundred sales representatives. As such, a total sample of 14,361 sales representatives' remunerations were examined.

Tack's purpose in conducting this survey was to achieve an over-all picture of the types of remuneration adopted by the 593 companies, selling to about 100 different trades, professions and industries, and also to provide examples of how the levels of remuneration have been established by product and industry.

The many pay systems used fell into the following general classifications:

1.	Salary only:	111 companies	(18·8%)
2.	Salary plus commissions:	249 companies	(42%)
3. (a)	Salary plus bonus (Individual incentive):	64 companies	(10·8%)
(b)	Salary plus bonus (Standard bonus):	51 companies	(8·6%)
(c)	Salary plus commission plus individual bonus:	64 companies	(10·8%)
(d)	Salary plus commission plus standard bonus:	21 companies	(3·5%)
4.	Commission only:	33 companies	(5·5%)

(a) *Definitions.*

(i) A bonus may be described as an award in addition to salary and commission paid, either on a general basis to all employees, or on a team or individual incentive basis. It is frequently paid quarterly, half-yearly or annually and is usually related to the company's general results over such a period.

(ii) A standard bonus is one made to all employees of a company, including the sales representatives

[1] These excerpts are reproduced with the kind permission of the Tack Organisation, to whom the author wishes to express warm appreciation. The full survey is set out in the brochure, *The Remuneration of Sales Personnel*, prepared and published by the Tack Organisation, Longmoore Street, London, S.W.1.

(*b*) *General Comments.*

   (i) The figures for companies using a *Salary Plus Commission* system of remuneration show a definite increase over the past six years.

   (ii) Many companies using a *Salary Only* system would like to include an incentive element but find it impossible or very difficult to do so.

   (iii) The percentage of companies paying *Commission Only* (5·5 per cent.) may be higher than expected but this figure includes agents who may sell for other companies as well.

Breakdown by systems

1. *Salaries Only* (18·8 *per cent. of sample*—111 *companies*)

   The following were some typical reasons given for using a *Salary Only* system of remuneration:

> "It is a fair system when a considerable amount of the sales representative's time may be spent on activities other than actual selling, i.e. attending exhibitions, arranging field demonstrations, making surveys, etc."
> "Ideal for the true technical representative whose effectiveness cannot be gauged by orders taken."
> "It is difficult to use any other system when sales suffer considerable seasonal fluctuations, i.e. sales of toys, seeds, calendars, etc."
> "Avoids friction between salesmen who feel that their territory has not the potential of that of their colleagues."
> "Allows more flexibility in moving representatives or reducing territories to increase sales force."

2. *Salary and Commission* (42 *per cent. of sample*—249 *companies*)

   The following were typical reasons given for using this form of remuneration:

> "It incorporates a reasonable basic income with incentive by way of commission to get the best out of the sales representative."
> "They must 'sell' to make a good living."
> "Salary provides security. Commission provides incentive."
> "When handling a range of products the commission element can be varied so that control through incentive can be exerted to move 'slow lines' or increase the rate of sale on those with a higher profitability."

3. *Bonus Payments*

   As mentioned, 200 companies within the 593 sample use bonus systems as follows:

(a) Salary plus Bonus
        (Individual incentive):   64 companies   (10·8%)
(b) Salary plus Bonus
        (Standard Bonus):   51 companies   (8·6%)
(c) Salary plus Commission
        Plus Individual Bonus: 64 companies   (10·8%)
(d) Salary plus Commission
        Plus Standard Bonus: 21 companies   (3·5%)

The following were typical reasons given for involving a bonus element in the remuneration structure:

> "A standard bonus to all employees within a company including the sales force, enhances the team spirit and makes each department interested in the activities of the other."
>
> "An individual bonus is an ideal award to the true technical representative whose value is known but cannot be related to sales returns."
>
> "Bonus, as opposed to commission, helps the man who takes over an unworked territory when initially his hard work may not show correspondingly big results."
>
> "Men like to have a lump sum at Christmas and holiday time."

As against these advantages, it was mentioned as a disadvantage that when a bonus is made annually, half-yearly or quarterly, the delayed reward is too far removed from the individual sale and has little or no day-to-day incentive value.

4. Commission Only (5·5 per cent. of sample—33 companies)

Within this group 10 companies employ full-time sales representatives and 23 employ agents who may sell for other companies as well.

Typical reasons given in favour of this form of remuneration:

> "A good way of building up a company as cost of the sales force is directly related to the value of the business attained."
>
> "This system attracts the very best men sure of their ability and ambitious to earn really big money."
>
> "For speciality selling it presents the sharpest edge of incentive to salesmen."

Agents.—Of the 23 companies employing *Commission Only* Agents, 10 are engaged in the clothing trade.

The following were typical reasons given for using this system of remuneration:

> "Payments against results enables a small company to expand and a large company to relate sales expenses to turnover."
>
> "This is the traditional form of remuneration in the clothing trade."

"Many agents already handling non-competitive but allied goods for other companies have useful ready-made 'connections'."

"It is the only way for a small company such as ours to achieve full national coverage."

As against these advantages, the chief disadvantages of employing men on an agency basis were given as:

"Difficulty of control."

"Lack of loyalty to any one company."

Competitions

Out of the total sample (593 companies) 144 operated some form of competition amongst their salesmen and, of these:

12 per cent. ran monthly competitions.
9 per cent. ran quarterly competitions.
29 per cent. ran annual competitions.
50 per cent. ran competitions at irregular intervals.

The most popular prizes appeared to be clothing for the sales representative or his family, and also gifts for the home.

N.B.—Where cash prizes are offered these money awards must be paid net, after appropriate tax deductions, unless the employer pays a gross sum, including tax, leaving the agreed net amount payable to the sales representative. Companies running monthly or quarterly competitions made the following typical comments:

"Competitions stimulate the sales representatives—our office staff are included in the team."

"They cost us £500 and are good value."

"They can be used for moving slow-selling lines."

"An excellent way of encouraging sales representatives to open new accounts."

"If properly organised they cannot fail—and the sales representatives will always respond."

Although a small number of companies who have experimented with competitions feel that they made little difference to the general selling effort, the overwhelming majority acclaimed their value.

Final Comment

From the general tone of the completed questionnaires it was obvious that most sales executives are very conscious of the great influence on their salesmen of the system of remuneration employed. More companies than ever before are keen to adopt fair pay systems which include incentives in one form or another. Although difficult to achieve in some cases, most companies try to evolve such a system of remuneration where "reward is commensurate with effort".

SALES OFFICE PROCEDURE

The importance of the Sales Office lies in the independent and detailed assessment of sales performance by means of recording all transactions and in issuing instructions impartially in accordance with the decisions of policy laid down by the sales manager.

The successful organisation of the sales office should remove from the field sales force—both representatives and sales management—as much of the routine procedure as is possible so that the maximum time may be spent on actual selling and training on the sales territory itself.

The office system and statistics play their part, but this part should be considered on its merits and should not be rated above its merits. Systems and statistics pass on an order and information but they do not of themselves produce results. Whatever can be done to ease the sales representative's task in his preparation of orders and reports should be done, and the importance of proper stationery cannot be over-stressed. If the sales representative has to record a five-digit reference number for an account or himself, then there are two more chances of an error than if he has to record a three-digit number. If the order could be pre-printed to contain the maximum amount of information, so that only the number of cases, or gross—or whatever the unit of measurement to be used—has to be added, together with the customer's name and other relevant information, then the possibility of error is again reduced.

Selling must come first, and this must still be the main occupation of those engaged on distribution.

The Sales Office cannot be based on a stereotyped plan; it must be built up to the needs of the business. It has certain basic functions which can be worked to but the methods must be adapted to individual requirements. On the other hand, some sales offices carry out duties which properly belong to the General Office, and there are many in which the actual bookkeeping is done.

Accountancy can hardly be said to come within the province of sales management, but if a choice must be made, it is better for the accountant to be responsible for the sales office than for accounting to come under the sales manager. There is, however, in most organisations, an easily defined line where accounting ends and sales records begin, which must be clearly understood by both to avoid duplication. While the sales office must draw many of its figures from the general office, the use to which such figures are put is essentially a matter for interpretation by those with a sales outlook.

Customer records, representatives territories and records are each a part of the routine function of the sales office, irrespective of which department within a company keeps these records and statistics.

All or part of the following principal functions will be carried out in the sales office, and where the function is not the particular responsibility of the sales office, there should still be a direct relation to the sales responsibility.

(a) Receipt of orders and their preparation—which will include checking.

(b) Recording of orders.

(c) Maintenance of customer records, representatives' records, statistics.

(d) Correspondence.

In recording sales, it is a matter of individual preference for each business to devise the information required.

The sales information required should first be scheduled, and when decided upon, a suitable record system should be made up to meet the requirements. The decisions will be:

1. Whether sales should be recorded in total sales, dozens, grosses, tons, units of packing or monetary values, or a combination of these.
2. The number of sections or classifications required, or will be required in the future.
3. The kind of accumulative or comparative totals which will be required over a period.
4. Whether it will be necessary to record invoices and payments.
5. What "flagging" will be required to show up important information at a glance. Its function being a reminder for action as and where required.

When these various alternatives are decided and scheduled, they should be correlated into a system and continue unaltered as long as possible.

Incoming Orders

Incoming orders will pass first through the sales office, or through the order department if it is a separate section. The grouping of all orders received, order-typing where necessary, credit control, despatching and invoicing may be the separate responsibility of a customer service or distribution section. In this event, correspondence with customers should be orientated with the sales outlook of the company and the manager of the section should be kept in close contact with sales policies and personnel.

The first process is a close scrutiny of the orders to see that all relevant information is written and correct, such as prices, discount and rating. Approval of credit can be made at this stage or later depending on whether this is the responsibility of the sales office or of the accounting section. It is usual to pass on orders immediately for invoicing and subsequent recording from the invoice, but this can be done from the orders either before or after invoicing depending on the number of orders involved.

Customer Records

The sales ledgers may provide all the information necessary to keep in touch with customers but, except in the smallest and simplest sales organisation, this is unlikely. It is, therefore, necessary to keep a record of customers and their purchases in the appropriate form. This can be provided by a simple card-index system, according to the frequency with which purchases occur and the number of customers involved.

The form in which the record is kept should be the subject of careful thought when planning such a record, as it is difficult to make alterations without loss of comparative figures at a later stage. The headings with the permanent information should be as detailed as possible. The buying information, address, names of executives or buyers, discount and terms, special preferences, etc., should be noted, and other information may be included which would be of use to other departments such as special delivery instructions. Credit facilities may also be shown.

Sales Records and Statistics

These should enable full representatives' sales results to be extracted as required. The compilation of regional or group statistics is also to be considered at this moment so that full statistical information is available for management analysis.

Movement of representatives to other territories or by promotion must not destroy the continuity of these records and a separate analysis of representatives' and territory results may be desirable. Alterations to territories brought about by increasing the numbers of representatives, or by replacement of an older more experienced man by a new representative, may also destroy the continuity of the records and must affect the decision on the keeping of the sales information, and the groupings under which this will be placed.

It is important to recognise the difference between a sales representative as an individual and his territory as a section of the business.

The division of company forecasts into regional or other groupings and into representatives' territories will enable a continuing or periodic assessment of the relevant performance against quota, budget or target figures.[1]

[1] See the text and illustration in Chapter 1 on page 120 and Fig. 4.

The availability of sales statistics is an essential requirement for the sales manager if he is to plan the development of his sales organisation and to study the facts and trends which are revealed by properly presented statistics. The actual decision as to how large a territory, how many accounts, can be looked after by one representative comes largely from experience, but much assistance can be gained from the proper representation and interpretation of statistics.

In assessing the extent of the territory in terms of the amount of business it should produce, many other factors are to be taken into account, the prosperity of the area, the number and size of multiple or big buyers, the local preference or otherwise for the particular commodity being sold, etc. It is therefore only possible to make a reasonable compromise between population figures and the known facts about the area to arrive at the best possible conclusions, which are reviewed from time to time in the light of development.

It is necessary to allocate a sales quota to each area and each sales representative. This is done in proportion to the assessment of the territory, and results in a figure for the territory which should appear against sales in all statistics as a plus or minus figure for discussion with the representatives. The success or otherwise of sales against quotas is a useful tool in the hands of a sales manager in promoting the efficiency of his outside staff. It can be used critically as occasion demands to censure the laggard, but its more important use is positive in stimulating effort by competition, with praise and reward to those who produce the best percentage increase in quotas.

A system of great help to sales administration and management is one in which the country is divided into small fixed territories, each of approximately the same population, and for which data such as population, number of houses, shops by type and such like is known. Apportioning a number of such territories to each representative provides a sales area which can always be adjusted to allow for increased sales representation without destroying basic records and the sales history. That is to say, sales figures are allocated to the small territory from which turnover for representatives, areas or sales regions may be obtained.

Journey Cycles

A journey cycle—the time taken by a sales representative in making his full round, and the order in which this can best be made —if recorded will permit not only a location of the sales representative but is convenient where statements or deliveries are allied to representatives' calls, and will enable a new man to pick up the routine in the event of replacement, sickness or holidays, etc.

Correspondence

All correspondence relating to customers and sales representatives should be directly related to the sales responsibility or to classify this more clearly, it should be sales orientated.

There are several reasons for this. In the sales representatives, it will cause confusion if they are receiving instructions and advice from several departments of the firm, and it would be embarrassing to the sales office not to know what the sales representatives are told. When such communications are passed through the sales office, there can be uniformity of approach and varying sets of instructions may be grouped together.

In the matter of more formal correspondence to representatives, advice on the stock position, statements, salaries, cheques, etc., the sales office should act as the collecting centre and forward daily to each representative in one envelope. It is usual to have a set of trays flagged with the sales representatives' names and as the various communications are received they are placed in the respective tray ready for posting.

There should be an emphasis on courtesy, friendliness and understanding in letters to customers, together with a clarity of expression, without which there is misunderstanding and friction. Most sales managers have experienced the difficulty of pacifying irate customers and sales representatives over letters written by office personnel who are not skilled in writing the right kind of letters.

Telephones

A pleasant and polite answer on the telephone can smooth away an irate customer's criticism of a company. A casual telephone operator merely increases the irritation.

AGENCIES

FORMATION OF AGENCY

THE relationship of principal and agent may arise:

1. *By Express Appointment.* No special formality is required except that an agent who is to execute a deed must have authority under seal.

2. *By Estoppel.* A person who has no authority at all may bind his principal if his principal so acts as to clothe him with the appearance of authority, as where a husband pays his wife's bills—whether for necessaries or luxuries.

3. *By Ratification.* This is equivalent to prior authorisation, and relates back to the date of the unauthorised act. But the following main essentials must be present:

   (*a*) The agent must have purported to act as agent. Thus an agent who forges his principal's signature does not profess to act as his agent, and there can be no ratification.

   (*b*) The principal must have been in existence and ascertainable when the contract was made. He need not have been named, but it must be possible to identify him. (Whether a person contracting for a non-existent principal incurs personal liability on the contract depends on the circumstances.)

   (*c*) There must be an act capable of ratification—a contract void from its inception, such as a contract *ultra vires* a company, or a contract on behalf of an alien enemy cannot be ratified, nor can an acceptance which is not unconditional.

4. *In Certain Cases of Necessity.* The courts are reluctant to extend agency of necessity, and it arises only:

   (*a*) Where a husband deserts his wife, actually or constructively, and she has no adequate means, when she has an irrevocable right to pledge his credit for necessaries as agent of necessity. (Adultery ends her authority.)

   (*b*) In certain cases when a person who is in possession of the goods of another is faced with an emergency in which it is impracticable to get the owner's instructions, e.g., a carrier in such a case may sell perishable goods, or a ship's master may pledge his cargo for the cost of repairs.

5. *By Presumption from Cohabitation.* The presumption arises from cohabitation rather than marriage; it is limited to necessaries

(note how they are defined) it is rebuttable by the husband. Unless there has been holding out, it is sufficient for him without notice to the tradesmen to forbid his wife to pledge his credit.

POSITION OF PRINCIPAL AND AGENT WITH REGARD TO THIRD PARTIES

The liability of the parties depends on their intention, but if no contrary intention appears the following general rules apply:

A. *If the Agent has Authority and names his Principal*

Generally the principal *alone* can sue or be sued on the contract. This rule may be excluded by express agreement, or by agreement implied from the terms of a written contract.

B. *If the Agent has Authority and discloses the Existence but not the Name of his Principal*

Again the general rule is that the agent can neither sue nor be sued, but a contrary intention is more easily inferred.

Special Cases. Whether the principal was named or not, the agent may be personally liable:

(1) If he signs in his own name a deed to which his principal is not named as a party. By section 123, Law of Property Act, 1925, the donee of a power of attorney may execute either in his own name or that of his principal.
(2) If he signs a negotiable instrument as a drawer or indorser in his own name, without adding words showing clearly that he is *signing* as agent—it is not enough to describe himself as *being* an agent. But if he purports to sign as *acceptor*, he cannot be liable unless in addition the bill is drawn on him.
(3) By Trade Usage, which applies unless inconsistent with the contract.

There was formerly a presumption that when an agent contracted for a foreign principal the agent alone could sue or be sued. This presumption no longer exists.

Where the Purported Agent is in fact the Principal. Here he can be sued and can himself sue provided:

(a) the supposed principal was not named; and
(b) the identity of the contracting party is not material.

C. *If the Agent has Authority but does not disclose the Existence of his Principal*

1. Here the agent himself may sue or be sued on the contract.
2. The undisclosed principal may also sue on the contract provided:

(a) that the agent's authority to act for him existed at the date of contract; and

(b) the terms of the contract are not incompatible with agency.

3. On discovering the principal, the third party can elect to sue him instead of the agent. There can be no *election* before he is discovered, but judgment against the agent, even before such discovery, bars further action against the principal, because the cause of action merges in the judgment.

D. *Effect of a Payment to the Agent*

1. Where the principal pays the agent the sum due to the third party, but the agent fails to pay the money to the third party, then:

(a) If the principal's existence was known to the third party, the principal remains liable to him, unless the principal has been misled by the third party's conduct into settling with the agent.

(b) If the principal's existence was *not* known to the third party, it has been held that a bona fide payment by the principal to the agent discharged the principal. But this authority is doubtful and perhaps the position is the same as in (a) above.

2. If the third party pays the agent, who fails to account to his principal, the third party is not discharged unless the agent had actual, implied, or ostensible authority from the principal to receive the money.

3. If an agent for the sale of goods owes a personal debt to the buyer, the buyer can only set off that debt against the principal if the principal led him to believe that the agent owned the goods and the debt accrued before the third party discovered otherwise.

UNAUTHORISED ACTS OF THE AGENT

A. *The Principal's Position*

1. Apart from ratification, the principal is bound only by authorised acts of his agent. But as regards the third party *"the apparent authority is the real authority"*—if the agent has ostensible authority to make the contract the principal is stopped from relying on any restriction on that authority which has not been communicated to the third party.

2. The common law rule has been extended in the case of mercantile agents by the Factors Act, 1889.

B. *The Agent's Position*

If the agent purports to act for a named principal when he had in fact no authority or exceeded his authority:

(1) If he knew he had no authority he is liable in damages in tort for deceit.

(2) Even if he acted innocently he is liable in damages contractually for breach of his "implied warranty of authority".

TERMINATION OF AGENCY

A. *Termination by Act of the Parties*

1. This occurs:

    (*a*) by mutual agreement; or

    (*b*) by the principal revoking the agent's authority.

2. Where there are contractual relationships between the principal and the agent analogous to those between master and servant, there is usually in implied term, as in other commercial contracts, that the employment shall be terminable by reasonable notice.

3. In other cases the principal may usually revoke the authority *at any time* before it has been exercised. But it is irrevocable:

    (*a*) When coupled with an interest, which is the case only if the authority was *created* to protect the agent's interest.

    (*b*) In certain cases relating to powers of attorney. (See L.P.A. 1925, ss. 126 and 127.)

4. If the principal has expressly agreed not to revoke the authority and he nevertheless revokes it, he is liable in damages for wrongful refusal to allow the agent to earn his commission.

5. An agreement not to revoke the authority and thereby prevent the agent earning his commission will not generally be *implied*. The moment when the commission itself becomes due depends on the wording of the contract. Note illustrations in relation to estate agents and how the court starts with the assumption that nothing is payable unless the property is sold and the price paid.

B. *Termination by Operation of Law*

This occurs:

1. On any event making the continuance of the agency unlawful, e.g. if the principal becomes an alien enemy.

2. On the principal's death, even if unknown to the agent. (But note L.P.A. 1925, s. 124, as to powers of attorney.)

3. On the agent's death.

4. On the principal's lunacy. But if the principal has held out the agent as having authority, it is presumed as regards the third party to continue until express notice of revocation is received by him.

5. On the principal committing an act of bankruptcy if he is adjudicated bankrupt on a petition presented within three months after the act.

RESTRICTIVE TRADE PRACTICES ACT, 1956

Under the normal rules of the law of contract no person can claim or enforce any rights from or against another person who has not actually contracted with him. So if A contracts with B to give some money to C, C cannot enforce A's promise against A since A contracted with B and not with C.

Section 25 of the Act (reproduced below) forms a statutory exception to this rule, since once a supplier has attached a price condition to goods sold by him he can in theory enforce the price condition against a retailer who sells below the stipulated price, even though that retailer is third or fourth in the commercial chain and had no direct dealings with the supplier, provided the defaulting retailer had "notice of the condition".

When does a retailer or other merchant have "notice" in the statutory sense? The latest authority on this question is Goodyear Tyre Co. v. Lancashire Batteries Ltd. (1958) in which the facts were as follows:

Goodyear were manufacturers who imposed price restrictions on the sale of their tyres. These restrictions, with others imposed by different manufacturers, were contained in a trade price list of some thirty pages. The British Motor Trade Association, acting as Goodyear's agents, sent circulars to many traders, including Lancashire Batteries Ltd., which called attention to Section 25 of the Restrictive Trade Practices Act, 1956, and gave notice that there were restrictions on the retail price and that details could be got from the respective manufacturers whose addresses were given. Lancashire Batteries, though they admitted the receipt of such a circular, sold Goodyear's tyres below the prescribed price. Goodyear sought an injunction.

Upjohn, J., making a fairly subtle distinction, held that "notice" in Section 25 meant "express notice of the actual terms". "The actual terms" were not specified in Goodyear's circular and the injunction was refused. The Court of Appeal, however, reversed Upjohn, J.'s decision and gave Goodyear their injunction. They ruled that "notice" in Section 25 does *not* mean express notice of the exact terms of the resale price conditions—express notice of their existence and where to find them is sufficient.

The Court of Appeal's ruling constitutes the law at present (1961), which is binding on any lower Court. But the ruling has been criti-

cised by academic lawyers and it would seem safest to specify the actual terms of the resale price conditions in any circular or the like issued in connection with goods sold by the supplier.

RESTRICTIVE TRADE PRACTICES ACT, 1956

"*Section 25.* Individual enforcement by legal proceedings of conditions as to resale prices.

"(1) Where goods are sold by a supplier subject to a condition as to the price at which those goods may be resold, either generally or by or to a specified class or person, that condition may, subject to the provisions of this section, be enforced by the supplier against any person not party to the sale who subsequently acquires the goods with notice of the condition as if he had been party thereto.

"(2) A condition shall not be enforceable by virtue of this section:

(*a*) in respect of the resale of any goods by a person who acquires those goods otherwise than for the purpose of resale in the course of business, or by any person who acquires them, whether immediately or not, from such a person;

(*b*) in respect of the resale of any goods pursuant to an order of any court, or by way of execution or distress, or by any person who acquires them, whether immediately or not, after such resale.

"(3) Nothing in this section shall be construed as enabling any person to enforce a condition imposed in pursuance of any restriction which is declared by an order of the Restrictive Practices Court for the time being in force under Part I of this Act to be contrary to the public interest.

"(4) Without prejudice to any other relief which may be granted in proceedings against any person in respect of a breach or apprehended breach of a condition which is enforceable against him by virtue of this section, the court may, if it thinks fit, upon proof that goods sold by the plaintiff have been resold by the defendant in breach of any such condition, grant an injunction restraining the defendant from reselling in breach of any such condition any goods already sold or thereafter to be sold by the plaintiff, whether of the same description as the goods proved to have been resold as aforesaid or of any other description."

Note: RE-SALE PRICE MAINTENANCE

"Perhaps most important of all, over the past five years, resale price maintenance has practically disappeared in the grocery trade. Though individual price maintenance is still legally enforceable, in fact competitive pressures applied by leading multiples have forced all manufacturers, except a handful, to abandon strict enforcement of price maintenance. This has enabled the more enterprising sections of the grocery trade to use 'pricing' of branded products as a competitive customer-getting device.

"Incidentally, the disappearance of resale price maintenance will result paradoxically in the disappearance of price cutting in the accepted sense, since there will be fewer and fewer known prices for the retailer to cut."

(Extract from *The Sales Director*, September 1961, commenting on contemporary trends.)

CHAPTER VI

CHANNELS OF DISTRIBUTION

IN the previous chapter the sales force is marshalled at the starting post, geared up and ready to go. To where are they going?

To call on the various channels of distribution through which their goods will be sold to the consumers, whether these be housewives in their homes or manufacturing concerns in their factories.

To ensure that the product is in full distribution and is available to the eventual consumer is, as has already been stated, one of the fundamental responsibilities of any sales department. Dependent upon whether the product is for ultimate consumption by the housewife, industry or in an overseas market, the channels of distribution will vary, but the same principles and problems will apply. It is necessary for the manufacturer's sales manager and sales staff to have a complete understanding of how *their* distributors operate, both for the purpose of determining the sales policy and its execution.

In deciding the channels of distribution required by a manufacturer or producer, it should be borne in mind that the nature of the goods themselves will largely determine the methods to be used. They are manufactured for and appeal to a specific market, either actual or potential. That market is either known or must be sought. There may be one customer or many.

The main channels of distribution can be considered under four main headings: —

TO THE CONSUMER

1. *Through Retail Stores*

Through one or a combination of three channels:

(i) wholesalers;
(ii) multiple stores;
(iii) retail stores.

2. *Direct to the Public*

This is a method of distribution usually reserved for highly specialised goods, and may entail a high percentage of door-to-door calls by sales representatives.

A well-developed aspect of this is selling by mail order, which may be direct to the public on a wide scale or used as a method of approach to traders offering the goods for resale. It is sometimes used in addition to other methods as a means of reaching potential customers more cheaply than by personal calls, and for its advertising value.

TO INDUSTRIAL USERS

Goods and materials used for the process of manufacture. Goods and services for industrial concerns. Special equipment, materials and machines for factory and office use. This type of product is usually sold direct to industrial concerns, and includes raw materials, accessories, tools and machinery, cleaning materials, office machinery, etc.

OVERSEAS

TO THE CONSUMER

The retail store is the final link in the chain of distribution for the bulk of consumer goods. Retail distribution is one of the main industries of the country and part of the national life. It is so complex and varied and performs so many functions, that it is difficult to grasp all the implications of the system by outlining its economic functions. For example, retail stores play a part in the social life of the country as a meeting-place for millions of women daily and exert considerable influence on their habits. As a direct result homes are better equipped, clothes are more attractive, cosmetics are more suitably applied. These stores offer advice on many subjects, from food to medicines, from the garden to the nursery, from the bathroom to the wardrobe. The success of retail trading does not depend entirely on strict economics. The element of service is often a factor of considerable importance and the differences between the cash-and-carry store and the service store can be very wide. The main function of the retail store is to provide a selection of goods easily accessible to the public as convenient to their homes as possible.

Retail shops are usually small units, each devoted to a particular group of products, and even the larger stores tend to retain the principle of dividing the store into departments, with the groups of products even more specialised than in the average smaller retail shop. The greater part of the retail system is planned in a well-organised and economic manner. The distribution of food and other staple products in regular demand is done at a low percentage of cost.

A major problem in the system is the considerable number of small shops with insufficient turnover and consequent need for high margins of profit. If the manufacturers provide a fixed margin of profit, sufficient to cover the less efficient shopkeeper, they are setting a standard of profit unnecessarily high for the modern, well-run shop. One may deplore the elimination of the "small man" in the retail trade, but he is not eliminated automatically, only when he ceases to trade efficiently and well.

The post-war years have seen the introduction of self-service stores and supermarkets, where the shopper can examine and select at his own leisure the products required. In the United States of America self-service stores and supermarkets handle 80 per cent. of the country's food and groceries turnover. In the United Kingdom, although not so marked as this, an increasing proportion of the food turnover is going through these, relatively few in number, types of outlet. By mid-1961 less than 5 per cent. of the number of grocery outlets (8,800 shops) operated on the self-service principle, but they handled more than 27 per cent. of the turnover.

Thence, to the operation of discount houses, where a customer serves herself from piles of merchandise simply laid out, with little attempt at any form of service or presentation, the bulk nature of the buying and the lack of service or fitments in the selling operation enabling the lowest possible price to be charged.

A study of the developments in retail distribution in the United States is an essential part of a United Kingdom sales manager's background. Many of the happenings in the United Kingdom during the late 1950s and early 1960s have been, and will continue to be, on similar patterns to those in the United States. In both countries retailing began essentially as a private brand business. Retailers would buy their products as merchandise in bulk form prior to breaking this down into smaller more economical weighed or measured units for their customers to take away. Few of the articles in grocers' stores bore a manufacturer's label—often the retailer would put his own label on the packages he would make up in his own backroom or store. As the availability of local or bulk merchandise became less, and as the growth of a national rather than a local attitude developed, so there came with it a demand for "reliable", constant products which would be the same today as yesterday. The shopkeeper found his time more and more taken up with shopkeeping and less time for the measuring, weighing and stamping on the price, involved with the buying of unbranded merchandise.

The national branded goods manufacturer emerged during these early days, around the turn of the century and up to the First World War; with their emergence the "retailer product" or "private" brand ceased to hold much importance. During the days of depression both in the United Kingdom and America in the twenties and thirties, when price was the foremost consideration, the "private brand" again emerged, undercutting in price and often in real value the products of the national manufacturers.

During the years of prosperity and development following the

Second World War, when the national manufacturers researched and developed new ideas and new products, the national brand again became the ready answer to which a retailer busily engaged in satisfying an increasing demand could turn. By means of its advertising, the national brand built up consumer demand that needed only the brand to be shown for it to sell. As more and more competition appeared in the retail distributive field, spearheaded by the development of the new and bigger stores—the supermarkets, the self-service stores—so a point was reached when new stores could no longer expect to draw new business from small long-established outlets, and the national-brand products again became subject to competition from the "private" brand.

Competition brought with it such schemes as trading stamps, "give-aways", loss-leaders and lower profits. As a private brand cannot be undercut in price by a competitor, many of the national chains passed to this form of merchandising in the belief that the higher percentage profit margin per unit sold—brought about by the lack of any need for advertising expenditure on the brand, or for research expenditure on new brands which would need to be undertaken by manufacturers if they were to remain important and expanding concerns—would halt the slide in profit figures. That this is not necessarily true is recognised by most authorities on grocery distribution, as the acceptance and preference for a national brand is deep-rooted in the average customer.

It is as well to study these matters, as in any consumer goods' marketing situation they may well have an important bearing on management decisions and good management decisions are based on an understanding of the problems to be solved.

Retail Stores

A *retail* outlet is a convenient place for the consumer to purchase household, personal and, indeed, all of the individual requirements for the person and the home. When a customer goes into a tobacconist's he expects to be able to choose the brand required, and the provision of a selection of brands from which he can make his choice is the retailer's *raison d'être*.

Only by putting his product into retail distribution can the manufacturer ensure distribution to the eventual consumer.

The independent retailer with, according to the Nielsen Indices, between one to four outlets (over five he becomes a multiple) can and does cater for local preference more easily than the national or multiple chain.

Multiple Stores

The multiple traders can be likened to a number of individual shops, each with the advantage of tapping the trade in its locality and the personal day-to-day contact of manager and staff with their customers, combined with the benefits of central organisation for buying, standardisation, of economy in administration and widespread goodwill.

The range of goods distributed in this way is fairly comprehensive but the main achievements have been in merchandise of everyday consumption or use, notably food, household goods, medicines and clothing.

Co-operative Stores

Co-operative trading plays a prominent part in the distribution of goods to the public, particularly food. The Co-operative movement consists of the Retail Societies scattered throughout the country and the Co-operative Wholesale Society with its counterpart in Scotland. The Retail Societies are many autonomous groups, ranging from a single shop in a small remote village to large organisations with hundreds of shops and their bakeries, dairies, delivery vans and central offices. The Co-operative Wholesale Society and the Scottish Co-operative Wholesale Society are producers and wholesalers for all the groups of Retail Societies—vast concerns with factories of many kinds, large warehouses, distribution systems and many other activities.

The mutual benefit system, where the customers own, govern and share the profits, applies to the Retail Societies and in turn through them to the Wholesale Societies. Their primary function, therefore, is retail trading, but they have extended so far beyond this field that this fact, together with their political and social activities—and over the passage of years, since the emergence of the Co-operative movement the political side of their character has become a disadvantage rather than an advantage—makes a marked division between them and normal retail businesses.

Chain Stores

The bazaar or chain store companies are fewer in number, but between them account for a great volume of business, particularly in the less expensive and small merchandise. They differ from the usual methods of selling in their self-selection system of selling openly from their counters and racks at low prices. Originally one-price or maximum prices, this policy has perforce been suspended, but it must be a low price limit to maintain the basic principle of such stores. The essential difference between the multiple outlet and the chain store is the diversification of the latter group although in recent years many multiples are themselves following a similar trend.

Department Stores

Department stores are few in number, but owing to the size of their operation they are usually important and certainly prestige factors in any manufacturer's distributive pattern. The department store includes in one building a large collection of shops, grouped into a company, which sets out to give a complete service to the consumer by serving her with the majority of her requirements. They differ from other types of retail stores by this concentration, in being able to draw their customers from a wide area and in not being dependent upon local trade. The origin of the department store rests primarily with the draper who expanded from the sale of materials for dressmaking and clothing into similar fabrics in furnishing, which in turn led to furniture of a general nature and then to the more specific items for the kitchen, bathroom, bedroom, garden, general household utensils, etc.

No plan for selling on any substantial scale to the public through retail stores can be complete without the co-operation of the multiple, departmental and Co-operative stores. The selling methods must be right, the goods strictly competitive in price and quality, and a service of prompt delivery assured before they are approached. In most cases it will be necessary to be sure of a public demand for the goods before such stores will buy them.

Buying is usually carried out centrally. It becomes necessary therefore to make plans which will satisfy the highly skilled professional buyers employed by these firms, and to do so in the face of the keenest competition on price, presentation and quality. Any weakness in these essentials will prejudice future relations with these traders and so should be eliminated beforehand.

A variation sometimes employed is for the manufacturer to open his own chain of retail stores for the distribution of his goods. The same end is achieved through "tied" stores. Tied stores (or public-houses in the case of a brewer) may be financed and partly controlled by the manufacturer primarily to distribute his goods to the exclusion of competitors, but may be privately managed. This system overcomes the difficulties of obtaining distribution through independent retailers, but gives added problems in other ways, such as retail organisation and selling. Apart from this, all other problems of marketing, advertising, etc. are similar.

The Wholesaler

The wholesalers perform a function not generally appreciated by the public and not always valued by commercial interests. The repeated slogans about "cutting out middlemen" and "direct from producer to consumer" are misleading and do not necessarily reduce the costs of distribution.

The wholesaler normally carries out his work of re-distribution in small quantities at a cost below that which would occur if any but the largest manufacturers were to do it direct. His travelling costs are lower because of the great number of lines he carries, his credit is better organised because he is in more intimate touch with his customers and his warehouse is laid out to assemble and deliver in his area.

The wholesaler buyers should be experienced men who keep their pulse on the selling side and alert for opportunities to develop the volume of sales. Large and rapid turnover is the keynote to growth and net profits in wholesaling.

Selling to Retail Stores

(a) *Through the Wholesalers*

To the manufacturers, the economy or otherwise of distributing through wholesalers is resolved by experience or can be calculated with some degree of certainty, according to the nature of the goods sold, the quantity of output, the extent of public demand and the margin of gross profit. There are many thousands of retail stores in each of the main trades (see Fig. 14).

They range from the larger stores with a brisk turnover to the remote "general store" in the smallest village. On a given line or range of goods, it is known or can easily be discovered what would be the margin of profit which the wholesaler would require to distribute such goods. Experience will tell that sales representatives can be employed to sell at a given percentage to various classes of traders and in a given volume. As soon as this becomes a greater percentage than the wholesaler's margin, plus the cost of selling to him, it no longer pays to go direct to the class of retailer he serves, but such trade should go through the wholesaler.

According to the Secretary of the Wholesale Grocers Federation the average net profit the British wholesale grocers were receiving in 1961 was 0·9 per cent. or $2\frac{1}{4}d$. in the £1 turnover. The gross profit is 6·9 per cent. These figures were arrived at following fifteen years of compiling average statistics from members of the Wholesale Grocers

RETAIL ESTABLISHMENTS BY KIND OF TRADE

Trade	Establishments (Numbers)		Turnover £'000	
1. *Grocers and Provision Dealers* .	149,109			2,042,269
2. *Other Food Retailers* . .	126,777			1,564,745
Dairymen		7,534	322,921	
Butchers		39,219	513,769	
Fishmongers, poulterers .		8,108	73,142	
Greengrocers, fruiterers (including those selling fish)		39,515	270,451	
Bread and flour confectioners		17,644	215,889	
Off licences . . .		8,802	112,656	
Other food shops . .		5,955	55,917	
3. *Confectioners, Tobacconists, Newsagents*	77,440			703,022
4. *Clothing and Footwear* . .	93,556			1,150,547
Boot and shoe shops . .		14,458	179,126	
Men's wear shops . .		14,906	245,136	
Women's wear, drapery and general clothing shops .		64,192	726,285	
5. *Household Goods* . . .	64,906			887,614
Furniture shops . . .		18,867	341,090	
Radio and/or electrical goods shops		12,037	233,824	
Cycle and perambulator shops (including cycle and radio shops)		7,332	61,273	
Ironmongers, hardware shops		24,050	188,935	
Gas showrooms . . .		1,363	29,727	
Electricity showrooms . .		1,257	32,765	
6. *Other non-food Retailers* . .	58,487			577,887
Booksellers, stationers . .		6,875	89,575	
Chemists, photographic dealers		18,129	269,845	
Jewellery, leather and sports goods shops . . .		17,220	134,586	
Other non-food shops . .		16,263	83,880	
7. *General Stores* . . .	3,713			872,233
Department stores . .		718	453,912	
Variety and other general stores		2,995	418,321	
TOTAL RETAIL TRADE .	573,988			7,798,317

Source: Board of Trade Census of Distribution, 1957.

FIG. 14.

Federation and confidence was expressed that the returns from 780 of 940 members gave a reasonably accurate indication of the true position.

It is important, however, to take some other considerations into account in deciding the extent to which a distribution through wholesalers is employed. It cannot be expected that they will put much sales effort behind the distribution of only one manufacturer's products. They will seldom distribute show-cards, leaflets or other advertising material to the retailer as the manufacturer's sales representatives would do.

For those companies who spend considerable sums of money on advertising and promoting their products to the consumer, to be in stock at a retail outlet may in itself be totally insufficient. In many of the low-unit cost items with a high-frequency sale, to be in stock but off display will retard considerably the possibilities of obtaining the maximum sale. Both manufacturers and distributors owe their existence to providing the consumer with the right product and both companies can help each other in doing this. The manufacturer has to appreciate that there are other products on the market similar to his own which the retailer must stock and show. To be successful over a long period of time, he must provide not only the sales promotion material at the point of sale which will sell his product alone, but he must recognise that he has to give the retailer an opportunity to benefit by featuring his particular range of products. The good merchandiser expects this, probably because his company believes in this philosophy.

(b) Direct

In the case of a normal widespread distribution, selling to retail stores should be considered in conjunction with distribution through wholesalers because only manufacturers with the largest sales organisations can hope to call on all retail stores direct. These larger firms, for example the great soap companies, achieve direct distribution to perhaps one hundred thousand or more shops through a staff of some hundreds of representatives, but only because they have so many lines in daily demand and so great a total turnover that even the small shop can order sufficient to justify a direct representative call. An assessment of sheer numbers of outlets in the field may not be a true guide as to the desirability of contacting the retailer direct, as in most trades—grocers, chemists, etc.—one-third of the outlets will do approximately three-quarters of the volume of business:

	Chemists			Grocers		
	Number of Shops	Per cent.	Percentage of Turnover	Number of Shops	Per cent.	Percentage of Turnover
Co-operatives .	1,034 ⎫	23·5	39·6	11,149	7·6	21·9
Multiples .	2,874 ⎭			17,367	11·8	24·2
Large Independent	2,981	17·9	25·3	9,456	6·5	15·4
Medium Independent	3,939	23·7	19·2	26,862	18·3	17·9
Small Independent	5,793	34·9	15·9	81,815	55·8	20·6
Total .	16,621			146,649		

Source: Nielsen.

Board of Trade 1957 Census.

Fig. 15.

Direct selling or calling on the larger retail stores with the subsequent routing of the orders taken, to a specific wholesaler can form an important part of the manufacturer's selling policy in order to ensure direct contact with the high-volume retail outlets. It is interesting to observe average gross profit margins in different categories of shops expressed as a percentage of their turnover. (See Fig. 16 on page 211.)

Mail Order

By distributing catalogues direct to the customer, mail order houses eliminate direct sales costings and can, under suitable circumstances, provide an alternative to distribution through retail outlets.

In America, where there is a very successful mail order business owing to the large rural population isolated from shopping districts, this method of selling has perhaps more to commend itself than in highly urbanised countries, but even in the United Kingdom a considerable volume of goods are sold through mail order and during recent years noticeable increases have been experienced in this trading method. It is perhaps true that much of this business is conducted by departmental stores as an additional means of distributing the wide variety of goods sold through their stores.

A disadvantage of mail order is the absence of personal contact with the product, although the design and layout of modern cata-

Non-Co-operatives	*Outlets*	*Percentage*
1. Grocers and Provision Dealers:	1–9	14·4
	10+	17·6
	All	15·4
2. Confectioners, Tobacconists, Newsagents:	1–9	14·6
	10+	17·7
	All	14·9
3. Ironmongers, Hardware shops:	1–9	26·0
	10+	34·9
	All	26·9
4. Booksellers, Stationers:	1–9	29·4
	10+	33·4
	All	30·6
5. Chemists, Photographic goods:	1–9	28·5
	10+	33·5
	All	30·4
6. Department Stores:	1–9	28·7
	10+	31·0
	All	29·2
7. Variety Chains: and Other General Stores:	1–9	34·2
	10+	31·6
	All	32·6
8. Co-operatives Generally (all business):	All	21·8

Source: 1957 Census of Distribution.

FIG. 16.

logues overcome this to an extent, combined with cost savings and convenience of selection. The instances where a manufacturer of advertised branded consumer goods relies solely on mail order distribution are virtually non-existent.

Group Trading

In 1954 from a total of 913 grocer wholesalers, three only operated voluntary groups which included a figure of 120 retail members. By early 1960 the number of wholesalers participating in group trading had grown to well over 100 and the number of retail members of these groups increased to 14,000.

As the retail members tended to be amongst the more progressive and high-volume outlets, the importance of their turnover in the grocery trade is probably double that of the percentage of the number of outlets. Group trading in the United Kingdom can be categorised under three main headings:

(a) Voluntary Group.
(b) Voluntary Chain.
(c) Retail Buying Association.

So far, these "groups" have been confined almost entirely to the grocery trade, although a few wholesale chemist concerns have made preferential terms available to retail members.

(a) Voluntary Groups

By mid-1961 some 8,500 retail grocers were members of the three principal voluntary groups. The voluntary groups consists of one wholesaler who offers to the retailer who associates himself with the group the benefits of group trading. Each retailer operates within a defined area which, normally speaking, will not overlap another. As with the voluntary chains, the groups have an identifying name and symbol and hold meetings with the retail members to discuss methods of operation, special terms, etc.

Instances of voluntary groups are:
The Alliance of Individual Grocers; operated by Peter Keevil and Sons Ltd. (who were the innovators of group trading in the United Kingdom).
Wavy Line Grocers Ltd.
D.B.C.—4 Star Group.

(b) Voluntary Chains

Over 150 wholesalers and upwards of 11,500 retail grocers are members of the five principal voluntary chains. The voluntary chain consists of the association of a number of wholesalers directed from one central office through which service to retail group members is planned and controlled. Each wholesaler and each retailer operates within a defined area and normally will not overlap another. The individual wholesaler is at liberty to continue his customary wholesale business with non-related retail outlets—as are voluntary group wholesalers—but the retail members of the voluntary chains will have an identifying name and symbol in addition to their customary trading title.

Instances of voluntary chains are:
V.G./VIVO
Spar
Centra
Mace

Both voluntary chains and groups offer to the wholesaler the benefit of being able to concentrate on the accounts of members and cut out others that may be uneconomic. The development of aggressive promotion tactics has stemmed from the original basic idea of lowering the cost of buying by rationalising distribution, that is by the retailer purchasing most of his requirements from one source, as opposed to the traditional purchase from a number of wholesalers or manufacturers, taking delivery on a more planned basis from one source and a simplification of accounting, etc. The retailer's time, previously spent on buying, can now be spent in more direct selling activities.

In both groups and chains retail members receive
—price advantages from bulk buying.
—support from press and television advertising.
—display material.
—advice on shop layout, and where pertinent, conversion to self-service.
—the opportunity to exchange ideas.
—participation in regular promotions of nationally advertised products.
—some voluntary groups and chains are prepared to lend money on favourable terms to retail members and help in providing trained staff to cover sickness and holidays.
—weekly deliveries on terms which would have been impossible on direct deliveries.

(c) Retail Buying Associations

Conditions of retail membership in voluntary groups and chains are rather more strict than in retail buying associations; the choice for the individual shopkeeper depending to an extent upon the value he sets on a greater independence.

About 15,000 retail grocers belong to some 250 *retail buying associations*, these associations consisting of a number of retailers who associate together for the common purpose of buying on bulk terms. Manufacturers are asked to supply goods either to a central warehouse or, where no warehousing facilities exist, by individual deliveries to members. Usually manufacturers will not deliver to individual members quantities below a certain specified minimum.

All these factors make group trading an extremely important part of the distribution system in the United Kingdom—a part which is likely to increase rather than decrease as competition develops, and with it also the need for aggressive buying and selling.

TO INDUSTRIAL USERS

Apart from the main structure of distribution of consumer goods, i.e. goods which are passed through channels of distribution to their ultimate consumers, there must be a secondary group where the goods or services are only a part of the complete chain, and where the sale is to a factory or other place where further process is necessary before being distributed to the final user. The range is wide and covers such raw materials of every kind which are the basic needs of the factory: iron, steel and other metals, wood, cotton and pulp, and all the many materials of manufacture. Such materials are sold on the exchanges, are sold direct from the mines, mills or forest, are handled by brokers and are dealt with by importers. This group also includes manufactured articles which are not complete in themselves but form part of the finished products: examples of this are component parts of aeroplanes or motor cars, plastic mouldings for television sets, etc.

Professional services are in a similar category, as these are for the use of industry as part of the process of manufacture and distribution.

In addition, there are many finished products required by industry for which a specialised type of selling is required: the machinery and plant, the transport vehicles, the office and canteen equipment and the buildings in which these things are housed.

There are many minor products which are necessary to the running of factory and office, all of which require a sales organisation to distribute. The list of such products is wide and varied, ranging from books and stationery to cleaning preparations and paint, from food supplies for the canteen to disinfectants. In this category, the bulk of the products are those already sold to the general public, but special packs and probably a special sales staff develop the sales to industrial users.

If, therefore, the main headings are considered in more detail, they would fall broadly into the following groups:

(a) Raw material.
(b) Manufactured articles for incorporation in other products.
(c) Professional services.
(d) Plant, machinery and transport.
(e) Sundry adjuncts.

Raw material

Buying and selling of the main groups of the basic raw materials of industry have reached the point of standardisation where the process is relatively simple. The majority of metals are dealt with through their appropriate exchanges, where a known quality can be purchased at a settled price. A similar position occurs in such materials as cotton, wool and grain. There are variations to meet particular needs, as, for example, the cotton exchange or its equivalent where a spinner may contract for the delivery of a specified grade on given dates to meet his future production programme.

Whether sold through organisations set up for the purpose, however, or direct from the producer to the factory, quality, price and service are main factors in effecting sales of raw materials. Subject to governmental restrictions, the market is open and readily accessible, the buyers are anxious to receive any product better and/or cheaper than they are at present using and are usually few in number, so that sales organisation on a large scale is rarely necessary. The problem is as much one of production as it is of selling, because the user of such material is buying on cold facts of quality and price, and these depend on production efficiency. On the research side the producer of raw materials has almost unlimited scope for the scientific development of his products, and on the cost side the works management can never cease to plan economy in production.

On the purely selling side, however, there is much to be done. The first essential is to develop sales personnel of the highest possible technical efficiency. The second is to classify fully and in great detail all the necessary information about potential buyers, what material they now use and in what quantities, how they could be approached and with what products, who are the key people in such firms and their background. Every kind of service must be given generously, and a team spirit built up between the two companies where the mutual interest is known and recognised on both sides.

The most productive development in this field of recent years has been the establishment of research teams by producers of raw material which are largely at the disposal of their customers. The wood pulp and paper industry, the steel industry, the chemical industry, the great oil-producing companies and the makers of light alloys, among others, have set up research laboratories of considerable size and efficiency for this purpose. The advice of such a team is invaluable to a progressive manufacturer, and in turn develops the market for raw material to the benefit of both concerns.

Manufactured Articles for incorporating in other Manufactured Goods

A similar set of circumstances occurs in this field, as such articles, even if manufactured, may be considered as the raw material of the finished product. Manufacturers of electrical equipment or television sets may buy their plastic mouldings from a specialist manufacturer; motor car and aeroplane manufacturers contract for a considerable number of component parts from outside sources and almost every manufacturer orders the necessary containers, bottles or cans from other firms.

Many of the industries supplying these "associated" articles have in themselves become exceedingly large organisations almost entirely devoted to supplying to other manufacturers. The makers of plastic containers and metal cans are but two manufacturers who, owing to the scale on which they produce, can offer a greater efficiency and economy than the individual manufacturer of a product could ever achieve. Standardisation and concentration of production enables a service, quality and price to be offered by the sales department responsible for distributing these articles to their users.

The development of pre-packed merchandise, and the increasing awareness of the importance of packaging as a means to generate sales volume for products which will be subjected to much competition on the retailers' shelves have led to rapid advances in all types of packaging. The manufacturer of consumer articles requires his product to be displayed or to be packed in a certain way. The packaging company through its sales organisation must be able to work with its customers, providing for their requirements and advising on the most suitable and economic way of meeting these requirements.

An example of this is found in the competitive toilet tissue market —where in less than ten years packaging has progressed from a simple paper band round a toilet roll to a fully wrapped multiple-roll pack in both paper and polythene. Banding, the first form of wrapping, was accomplished by hand—or sometimes by simple machinery which was originally designed for fixing labels on canned products, such as soups. Very close liaison between the packaging companies and paper manufacturers has been essential in the development of specialised converting equipment necessary for the present attractive and very much more hygienic packages for toilet tissue.

Professional Services and Operations

This group is wide and varied, and the details of the selling methods can only be worked out according to the individual problems. To many, the conduct of the service is, in itself, the selling medium required, such as in Banking. Others, such as Insurance Brokers, Consultants in Management and other aspects of business, Advertising Consultants and Agents, Commercial Art Studios and Industrial Designers, all require highly specialised and skilful selling methods peculiar to their particular approach.

The primary consideration of selling all such services is a sound appreciation of the object and purpose of the task to be performed, not from the point of view of those who create and carry out the service, but from that of a possible user. It is not sufficient for the salesman to believe wholeheartedly in the project, he must step into the shoes of the prospective customer to find out what will convince him of his need. In all selling of specialised services, it is important to know and understand the facts about the potential customer and his business. Skilled and well-paid men are essential. The provision of a social atmosphere and entertainment sometimes plays a part in overcoming barriers which may occur (perhaps through prejudice) and in promoting friendly co-operation so often necessary in achieving full satisfaction.

Machinery and Plant and Transport

This group requires specialised knowledge of the products to be sold and a wide general knowledge of the manufacturing processes or purposes for which they are to be used. It is essential that sales personnel should have a sufficient background of technical training and experience together with a keen interest in the customer's requirements. "Service" is of vital importance. A first-class organisation, allied to the sales department, should maintain the most alert watch over the installation and working of every item of plant and machinery to build up a reputation for "service"—sometimes as important as the products themselves.

Sundry Adjuncts

The range of smaller articles used by industry is very wide and conforms roughly to the needs of a household in that a factory, like a house, must be cleaned and painted, and the workers usually need food and clothing. As a rule, therefore, the manufacturers of smaller goods for household consumption can develop a trade with industrial users as an addition to their domestic business. Some firms, for instance overall manufacturers, may specialise in this type of business.

A manufacturer concerned in any form of industrial selling has to decide whether this can best be handled direct by the company or whether an agent specialising in the sale of related or allied materials can better serve his purpose.

The number of industrial outlets is considerable and varies widely from the very large company capable of buying in bulk quantities direct from the manufacturer, to the very small company which may well require only a small number of items which can be drawn from an agent or distributor in between himself and the manufacturer (see Fig. 16). This is, in the main, a straightforward selling problem, although it is usually necessary for the manufacturer to devote specialist salesmen and bulk packs to the operation. In general the buyers know what they want, and the firm which supplies the right article at the right price with efficient service can win a share of the business without undue elaboration of sales methods. The sales personnel selling to or through industry will need to possess a knowledge of the developments and techniques employed in the relevant industry in the same way that their counterpart in the selling of a consumer product through the retail distributive channels needs to be aware of the changing patterns of distribution and the likely needs of the eventual consumer.

PERSONNEL EMPLOYED IN U.K. INDUSTRY

	Personnel
(i) *Manufacturing Industries* Mining, Food, Chemical, Engineering, Electrical, Ship-building, Vehicles, Metal Goods, etc. . . .	8,790,000
(ii) *Civil Employment* Construction, Gas, Electricity, Water, Transport and Communications, Distributive Trades, Financial and Professional and Scientific Services, National and Local Government Services	14,630,000
	23,420,000
(*a*) *Schools* Number of Government-aided . . .	30,000
Number of Pupils	6,500,000
(*b*) *Hospitals* Approximate Number	3,000
Approximate Number of Patients . .	500,000

MANUFACTURING INDUSTRIES [1]

Total Establishments	61,958
Size of Establishment by Number of Employees	
11–99 employees	40,543
100–199 „	7,162
200–499 „	5,174
500 & over	2,633
Unknown	6,446

[1] Note: No records are available for establishments with less than 10 employees.

Source: Board of Trade Census of Production.

Figures as known at April, 1958.

Fig. 17.

OVERSEAS

In the post-war years exports and imports have been affected increasingly by governmental policies. Markets which have been developed over many years can be and are restricted overnight by the imposition of import tariffs, quotas or complete embargoes.

The development of hitherto undeveloped countries creates new markets for manufacturers of all types of products, whether they be capital goods or consumer durables. All of the skills in marketing and planning are needed to obtain and hold a share of export sales; the attitude that "we will give 'export' to 'Smith' to look after, as he has done a pretty good job for us over the years but isn't quite as good as he was" is fast dying.

Countries faced with balance of payments problems and the urgent need to increase their exports have acted fast to encourage industry to become export conscious. In the United Kingdom the establishment of the Board of Trade Export Services Department, and the setting up of the Export Credit Guarantee Department enabled manufacturers to start exporting at a reduced risk and with a greater knowledge of the markets to which they were trying to sell than was the case between the wars when the manufacturer had to rely largely upon his own sources of information and financial backing. The London Chamber of Commerce has made available to prospective exporters its considerable knowledge and experience on international happenings. Trade Commissioners in most trading centres throughout the world have become increasingly relied upon to provide vital information to the home manufacturer concerning conditions and requirements in any particular country or area.

The decisions which have to be faced still remain the concern of the individual manufacturer, however much help he may receive before he has to make his decisions.

Today it is possible to visit any part of the world in a relatively short space of time. Telegraphic communication is almost complete and it is possible that by the end of the 1960s a completely international operation will have become more widely accepted than was ever thought possible ten years previously.

The manufacturer is faced with the choice of setting up his own branch office and arranging shipment and storage of his products himself or of employing an agent or distributor in the overseas market to handle that end of his business whilst using a shipping agent to reserve him space on vessels destined for the overseas markets, or a combination of the two.

Agents or distributors may act either as sole importers re-distributing to the trade channels in their country, or as indentors for passing through direct orders from customers on which they receive commission. The rate of commission to be paid to an export agent can and does vary considerably. The names of companies interested in handling agencies, advice on suitable products required for overseas markets, advice on the best methods of packaging, etc., is available through the Board of Trade's offices throughout the country and from the Federation of British Industries in London, or the London Chamber of Commerce.

Special opportunities for British export trade development have been foreshadowed in recent years by the initiation of the "freer trade" movements in Europe: this is an area in which Britain has previously taken only limited trading interest, but the scope now is expected to be very considerable. The movement gained its major impetus from the formation of the "European Common Market" (officially styled the *European Economic Community* as created by the Treaty of Rome in 1953): this became effective in 1960 as a freer trade region embracing Belgium, France, Germany (West), Holland, Italy and Luxembourg, and the intention is eventually to develop into a full free trade community as an integral trading unit of over 160,000,000 people. As a consequence of this initiative, seven other European nations—including the United Kingdom—established a parallel form of co-ordinated trading known as the "European Free Trade Association" (commonly referred to as the "outer seven"). Late in 1961, the whole question of European trade development began to take on a new slant when Britain applied to join the "Common Market" grouping under the terms of the Treaty of Rome. That request being granted and the invitation being accepted, some of the other members of E.F.T.A. took a similar step, and the way was thus opened for most of the West European countries to become actively associated in an integrated free trading community.[1] From Britain's own point of view, participation in such a community could have very important consequences in the diversification and increase of export trading opportunities.

The growth of international advertising agencies, the extension of market research services and the total awareness of the need to expand overseas markets are all contributory factors in export marketing. Market research does not necessarily have to be an expensive item, but there will be instances where the full resources of an industry will be able to commission a far better and more comprehensive research than individual firms will be able to afford.

Local conditions will largely guide the decisions made as to whether stocks are to be held on consignment; the length of credit to

---

[1] The discussions determining these developments were still in an early stage at the time of going to press. (Editor.)

be given to the customer; the type of crating or packing required to ensure the arrival of goods at the end of their journey in sound condition. Banking houses can and do provide advice on the need for establishing *del credere* agents amongst the very many other services they perform for the potential exporter.

Obviously, if the selling has to be on a direct basis, with contact to the trade channels by the manufacturer's own sales representative, there must be an understanding of the language of the country and of the philosophies and background of the people themselves. Similarly, however good an agent may be, there is no comparable way to replace the impression gained by the personal visit. Many a good product has failed owing to incomplete awareness of these matters. The export manager has to have an understanding of his customers as does the home sales manager. To do this he must also familiarise himself with the competition he will face in his markets. He has to be able to advise management on the degree of risk the company will take in investing money in promotional programmes, as no company profits for long if investment is made only to find that during the years in which a return was planned availability to the market has been restricted and the rewards for development work done by them have been reaped by some other concern. It is therefore essential to have a competent export department, with a full knowledge of the sources of information, details on shipping, freights, duties, packing, landed costs, competition, market developments, advertising media and the suitability of the product for the market to which it is to be shipped.

Each country or group of countries should be considered as a market in itself and generalities may be misleading. If, however, the problem is studied as a whole, it gives a basis for a general procedure, always provided the fact is well understood that as the sales develop a more detailed study of each market will be necessary to obtain any substantial results.

The consideration of an export programme may be examined under three main headings:

Research and Planning.
Representation.
Home Organisation.

1. *Research and Planning*

The first essential is to consider the suitability of the products which are produced for the different markets of the world and if necessary to decide what are the adaptations or alterations in either the products themselves or their packaging. This entails an understanding and knowledge of the markets of the world or such markets as are considered suitable. Research on a wide scale is a big undertaking and may be very costly. Fortunately, it can be taken in stages over a period of time, or one section of the world may be taken first, followed by others as progress is made. Even a company with a substantial export business is well advised to make a detailed survey of its markets from time to time. With a company embarking on export sales for the first time it is highly desirable.

As referred to previously, the value of a personal visit is considerable. However, there are obviously many pitfalls for an inexperienced man visiting a country for a few weeks and making a decision based on such a short visit, and the importance of knowing whom to contact and where to go for information cannot be over-stressed. In most trading countries the commercial attachés at the various embassies can provide valuable help although they will be equipped to deal more with the general matters of a particular market and are less able to give a detailed examination of consumer demand for any particular product or service which must still be the responsibility of the manufacturer. They can and do provide a reliable source of general information.

The larger importers and distributors in the various countries of the world maintain offices or shipping agents in the United Kingdom. Their addresses can be obtained from the trade directories and it is generally useful to make contact with such firms, where a fund of information about their particular markets may be obtained. In London, for example, agents for importers to many lands have their offices, and themselves constitute a complete network of facilities to distribute to a large section of the world. Similarly, British Export Corporations in London, Liverpool and Glasgow will be in a position to transact business throughout the world.

Particular attention should be given to the services of the Board of Trade, together with the various periodical publications issued by subscription from various publishing houses. World conditions, levels of imports and exports, import licences, duties, currency arrangements, etc., are listed to form a complete record of the current position for day-to-day reference on these matters.

With these various methods available, the exporter can proceed to find out all relevant facts about the export of his goods to the various countries of the world.

The following headings will suggest the type of information useful in arriving at the plan for further procedure.

(a) Suitability of goods for the market, or adaptations necessary.
(b) Import licences, financial restrictions, quotas, law relating to the sale of the goods, labelling regulations.
(c) Shipping, freights, duties, packing.

(d) Final landed costs, cost of distribution, resultant consumer prices.

(e) Competition in price and quality to be found in each country.

(f) The desirability of assembly or packing abroad to facilitate import and shipping costs.

Having selected the markets for approach, the manufacturer can proceed by appointing agents or representatives and try to develop sales forthwith, or can embark on consumer research in the country or countries concerned before doing so. A good deal depends on the nature of the product. If the goods are to be established as an advertised proprietory, it is wise to make investigations before spending money on advertising and building up a brand name. If, however, it is a normal trading transaction, the difficulties can be learned while proceeding and methods adopted while feeling the way into the market.

2. Representation

The fact cannot be emphasised too strongly that selection of the agents or distributors to distribute throughout the markets abroad is of paramount importance. Where a firm can set up its own organisation and have direct representation, the selection of personnel is of equal importance. A firm distributing through agents or distributors, which is the usual practice, must take all possible steps to ensure that the man or company appointed to represent them is suitable in all respects.

The agent or distributor must of course attain to the necessary standard of integrity, and commercial standards in this respect vary considerably throughout the world. His other agencies must be agreeable to and if possible complementary to the manufacturer and must be connected with the right class of trade for distribution of the products. The following methods can be employed for this distribution of the manufacturer's products:

(a) By setting up an export unit and employing people with knowledge of markets and techniques. This may be done with or without overseas offices or subsidiary companies.

(b) Through a merchant house.

(c) Through an export agent.

(d) By appointment of an agent or agents overseas.

(e) By direct sales overseas employing a visiting salesman.

(f) By selling in London to offices or representatives of overseas firms.

(g) By direct mail.

These seven headings cover most of the possible methods but there are many combinations and variations.

Method (a). A complete export department. Clearly this is practicable only for a big organisation expecting to build up a very valuable export trade. Even if it is combined with the use of agents rather than overseas offices or subsidiaries, a comprehensive export department is expensive and it is a matter of simple arithmetic and accurate costing to judge whether it would be profitable.

Method (b). The Merchant. This is a particularly good means of enabling the smaller manufacturer to export, although it is used by many large corporations. Manufacturers with their own export sales organisation often sell through merchants for some lines and some markets because they find it economical. The special advantages for the small manufacturer are, briefly:

He is paid by the merchant in London in sterling and is not concerned about the credit-worthiness of overseas firms. The carrying of the financial risk and the covering of necessary credit is extremely valuable to many manufacturers.

He can get sound advice from a market expert—the merchant—on the suitability of his goods, on prices and on probable demand. The overseas selling is done for him.

He is relieved of anxiety about documentation, tariff questions and quotas, exchange regulations, shipping and insurance requirements. In fact the merchant takes most of the worry out of export for him.

Selling through a merchant does not mean that the ultimate price is higher. Selling and distributing abroad cost money anyway, and the merchant, who can spread his overheads over many lines, does the job economically. Merchants cannot sell if their prices are not strictly competitive.

Method (c). The Export Agent. This method is somewhat similar, except that the export agent is not responsible for payment, credit, etc. He will carry out the selling and probably the handling. In some cases merchant houses do business this way if both parties wish it.

Method (d). The Agent Overseas. A system widely used by many successful exporters—small and large. The main essential is to get a good agent, which requires care, and if possible personal contact. This is probably the most common method used by successful exporters and although some manufacturers may progress toward their own organisations in overseas countries, almost certainly in the earlier years during the development of their export business they will employ agents in the countries concerned.

An agent is usually paid by means of commission on f.o.b. (free on board) value of goods shipped during an agreed period of time. It is possible to make an agent a *del credere* agent, in which case he will also be responsible for the solvency of the buyers where shipment is effected direct to customers within his area of responsibility.

A good agent must remain a most important factor in the manufacturer's *distribution* arrangements for his products through an overseas market. The agent will advise the manufacturer about the need for holding stocks on a consignment basis, the right time for commencing an advertising campaign, the desirability or otherwise of shipping direct to customers as opposed to consigning all goods through the agent and, indeed, act as a part of the manufacturer's own business operation.

If a manufacturer wishes to export through an agent, he can still avoid some of the difficulties on the technical aspects of export—documents, insurances, packing, etc.—by using a reliable shipping and forwarding agent.

Method (e). Direct Sales. This method usually depends on having a principal or director with some knowledge of other countries who is keen to go out and sell. There are many cases where it is highly successful, particularly in the nearby European markets, but its application is more restricted than the preceding methods. Credit and finance have to be provided, and a smaller firm will again be wise to use a shipping and forwarding agent.

This method can sometimes be used in conjunction with a London confirming house. The overseas buyers—particularly stores and the like in some markets—place orders direct with the visiting salesman and then confirm them through a London house which is responsible to the manufacturer for payment.

Method (f). Selling in London. This is also of a rather limited application, but manufacturers of highly specialised lines often do a useful export trade by selling in London to visiting representatives or the London offices of overseas firms or their buying agents.

Method (g). Direct Mail. A method which is used successfully, but it requires very close and detailed knowledge of the necessary procedure.

3. *Home Organisation*

It is essential to have a competent export department at home to control efficiently the various functions necessary to ensure the smooth flow of export business. The main functions of this department are:

(a) *Export Office.* To deal with shipping documents, accounts export finance and currency.

(b) *Export Correspondence Section.* Where correspondence is handled by those who know the special requirements and if necessary the languages for the purpose.

(c) *Packing and Shipping Department.* For the physical handling of goods for export. An alternative is to employ a good shipping agent for the purpose.

(d) *Factory Representatives.* The full development of export markets calls for one or more travelling representatives on a full or part-time basis, to visit the agents and principal customers direct from the factory. It may be a director of the company, the export manager or a representative selected for the purpose.

(e) *Export Advertising Department.* Where advertising is conducted overseas, it may be dealt with by a special section, either of the advertising department or export department. Overseas advertising calls for separate treatment from home advertising, and unless it is devised specially for the nationals to whom it appeals, it will almost certainly miss the mark. This is not to deny the benefits of a common name or label which by its wide distribution assists its own sale. The advertising appeals may however, be very different in one country from another.

Sources of reference or information to aid exporters:
For the manufacturer entering into export for the first time, many potential pitfalls can be avoided if the trouble is taken to investigate specific procedures called for in many overseas markets. Some convenient sources of reference for guidance in this respect are as follows:
(a) London Chamber of Commerce, Cannon Street, London, E.C.4.
(b) Board of Trade—Export Credit Guarantees Department.
(c) Federation of British Industries, Tothill Street, London, S.W.1.
(d) Institute of Export, 14 Hallam Street, London, W.1.
(e) Trade Offices of Commonwealth Countries (various, mostly in London).
(f) Foreign Embassies (Commercial Section).

DELIVERIES

The operation of the delivery system may or may not be an integral part of the marketing operation. Irrespective of its siting within the company structure and over-riding all considerations of transport economy, the sales aspect of service to customers has to be considered. A system which permits undue delays in the delivery of the goods, although extremely economical, is a false economy as, in most instances, if the goods are not at the point of sale when the consumer requires them the sale is lost. Similarly, a system which enables delivery of the goods in anything but prime condition, with the resultant complaints, returns and dissatisfaction, will result in the same loss of sale. The despatch of goods is tied in with documentation which, in turn, gives rise to the invoices. However large the structure may be, the routine operation of the delivery system to be successful must be simple.

It is the responsibility of the despatch or delivery department to ensure that the products produced by the manufacturing sections of the company, translated into orders by the sales departments, are despatched and arrive in sound condition—at the right time in the right place.

System of Delivery

Rail or road? Very often the decision as to the method to be used for delivering the product to the customer will rest upon the type of transport available, rather than on the most desirable form of transport. Large-scale manufacture of machinery and equipment necessitates large-scale means of moving the output to its future site. Private contractors are available for this purpose and are widely used, particularly where a variety of shapes and sizes may need to be handled.

The movement of pulp for paper manufacture brings into play the use of waterways, as barges can and do take on considerable loads of this very heavy raw material and can provide an economical method of transport. Speed is not too essential. Where water facilities do not permit the use of barges, rail or heavy lorries come into service. The subsequent removal of the bulk reels of paper, especially made to specific measurements and often ordered in advance of requirement, to—for example—the publishers of newspapers or magazines on a company's own fleet of lorries enables a prompt supply of this raw material to be moved to the publisher at short notice. The manufacturer of bulk reels of paper has a more simple delivery task than does the manufacturer of a number of consumer items intended for distribution through retail or industrial channels, by reason of the fact that the number of outlets which have to be serviced are very much less than in the latter instances.

If a company is engaged in selling its products through grocery stores then it will probably be involved in a competitive situation which demands a quick delivery of its products following receipt of the order. Long-term contracts enable forward production planning and storage requirements. Maintenance of stocks based on sales estimates, with the errors in sales estimates which can and do emerge, are a constant source of concern to most consumer goods manufacturers—and this increases in complexity with the number of items on the manufacturer's price list.

In the aggregate, a very great quantity of material from raw material to finished products must be handled, stored or moved from place to place in the course of progress of consumer goods through the factory to the ultimate consumer. The skill and management of this movement can advance the smooth flow of industry and effect substantial economy in the total cost of distribution.

In the United Kingdom, with a high concentration of people in a relatively small area the problem of distance is not particularly great. Speed of delivery, ease of handling, size of stock, cost and the dictates of service required are problems which have to be solved, irrespective of the type of merchandise to be handled. What are the choices that are available?

Rail

It is possible to contract with the British Transport Commission for the storage of products at rail head depots. Into these depots the stocks may be despatched by road or rail, either direct from the factory or through a buffer stock control depot. Agreed freight rates which cover delivery to any part of the country at a basic charge per ton or unit are available.

Any delivery system outside the manufacturer's direct control must carry the hazard of being part of a shared system, and although it may represent the most economical means for the removal of goods, it may not measure up to the service required. Given a limited range of products which are relatively easy to handle and can be maintained at a full stock level, there is no reason why a workable system cannot be evolved, based on a delivery period of a given number of days. Deliveries to business centres will tend to be quicker than to outlying districts for obvious reasons, but this can be allowed for.

Road

If the manufacturer decides to make use of his own transport—either owned by him directly or contracted by him—then he must ensure that he has ample storage space available at points from which he can effect the required service to his customers. This will necessitate managers for the depots, and as with all well-run delivery arrangements, as simple an office function as is possible.

The timing of representatives' journeys to coincide with the delivery routes of the vehicles can be arranged. The functional planning for making up the loads to be delivered by any particular vehicle calls for personnel with experience of the roads, weights of traffic likely to be encountered in the course of delivery journeys, the time taken to load and off-load a vehicle, size of the average drop or shipment to be made, etc.

If a manufacturer controls its own transport fleet he has an opportunity to use the vehicle as a means of publicity. The contact the driver has with the shopkeeper may be the only contact apart from the sales representative that the customer has with the manufacturer and much good—or harm—can be effected, depending on the attitude of mind that is developed in the drivers.

Van-selling Delivery

Direct selling from a van employs the driver as both a salesman and a delivery man. Collection of cash necessitates a simple form of receipt and transfer of cash to the manufacturer. The driver can use a similar system to the one employed by manufacturers' sales representatives, except that it may be possible for the driver to hand in the money personally whereas the sales representative may have to bank it or forward it on to the manufacturer.

Warehousing

To establish the right stock level for the manufacturer's products must involve an understanding of the production capacity and flexibility as between one product and another, one size and another, etc. If, for example, goods are produced on average once every five weeks—then a minimum stock requirement will be seven weeks. This will allow for the routing of stocks from the factory to the depot and will provide a small margin to cater for the unexpected. Where the line is in constant production and is moved out of the depots at frequent intervals, then the stock level can be reduced accordingly. Ideally, a minimum stock level in this situation would be two to three weeks, with perhaps an average level of around four weeks.

The movement of stock on a "first in", "first out" basis concerns both marketing and general management and, as in the case of confectionery or tobacco, butter or meat, any product which is perishable will call for particular emphasis.

The principles of good warehousing would seem to apply equally to all types of products, the only important distinction being that special precautions must be taken where goods are perishable. Good stock control is important in any case, but a margin of error in control of perishables may result in a loss of goods which would not occur with non-perishable types.

It may serve the purpose of illustration if one system of storage is considered. An example would be a food manufacturing firm, making proprietary foods packed in cans, bottles or other containers with a wide distribution to wholesalers, multiples, co-operatives and retailers who have a variable turnover acording to seasons and with goods of variable keeping quality. Such an organisation has all the essentials of warehousing, stock-keeping, handling and transport.

Two types of storage would be provided and while they are to some extent interchangeable, it is as well to consider them as separate categories as far as possible to avoid confusion and overlapping.

(*a*) Raw materials and packing containers.

(*b*) Goods in continuous production and in seasonal production.

The warehousing and stock-keeping of raw material and containers is a matter of factory organisation and should be considered in the factory programme. If possible a separate storage should be provided. The raw material storage is best situated at the receiving end of the factory with the distribution storage at the despatch end.

The operation of the factory is in two phases. First there are lines in continuous production for those goods where the raw material is available at all times. Such production is tuned to the demand, and the finished products flow out of the factory. There must, however, be a certain proportion kept in stock in case of breakdown in the manufacturing or distribution systems. This stock is kept partly at the factory and partly at depots throughout the country.

The second phase of production is seasonal. Fruits and vegetables under contract to the factory are delivered in substantial quantities over short periods and the factory is keyed up to process and pack the resulting products. The finished products, however, are not sold immediately, but are stored—often for long periods—and provision must be made according to the particular circumstances of each product.

The exertion of stock control at every stage is a fruitful means of economy, and in the case under discussion would be of the "perpetual inventory" type, where all arrivals and withdrawals are recorded continuously and the stock position can be assessed at any time.

Selecting the Method

Accessibility of docks for export shipments, or aerodromes, distance from a railway siding or railhead, size of vehicle, rate of delivery, number of outlets, rate of deterioration of the product, cost of delivery, recognition of promotional value of company-owned vehicles, the benefits or disadvantages of running a company's own transport, all play a part in the selection of the method of transport to be employed in delivery of the goods. The essential purpose of a delivery system is to transport both raw materials and finished products between factories and distributive trades as is required by the selling situation.

Advice as to the best method to be used can be obtained from other firms in similar, but non-competitive, organisations, from direct approach to the British Transport Commission or from road haulage contractors.

BIBLIOGRAPHY

1. David W. Ewing: *Effective Marketing Action.* Harper, 1958
2. Dudley M. Phelps: *Planning the Product.* Irwin, 1947
3. John A. Howard: *Marketing Management: Analysis and Decision.* Irwin, 1957
4. Richard D. Crisp: *Marketing Research.* McGraw-Hill, 1957
5. N. A. H. Stacey and A. Wilson: *The Changing Pattern of Distribution.* Business Publications in association with Batsford, 1958
6. Louis Cheskin: *Why People Buy.* Business Publications, 1960
7. Remus A. Harris. *Creativity in Marketing.* American Marketing Foundation, Southampton (N.Y.), 1960
8. Harry Henry: *Motivation Research.* Crosby Lockwood, 1958
9. Loyd R. Coleman: *The Practice of Successful Advertising.* Rydge's (Australia), 1959
10. H. Lazo and A. Corbin: *Management in Marketing: Text and Cases.* McGraw-Hill, 1961
11. Institute of Marketing and Sales Management: *Manual of Sales Management.* Pitman, 1961
12. L. Hardy: *Marketing for Profit.* Longmans, Green, 1962.
13. Institute of Cost and Works Accountants: *An Introduction to Business Forecasting.* London, 1959
14. American Management Association: *Sales Forecasting* (Special Report No. 16). 1956
15. Elmer C. Bratt: *Business Forecasting.* McGraw-Hill, 1958
16. Booklets on Sales, Exports and other subjects. Published by London Chamber of Commerce

CHAPTER I

ACTIVITIES FORMING THE PRODUCTION DIVISION

THE MEANING OF PRODUCTION MANAGEMENT

PRODUCTION can be defined as the organised activity of transforming raw materials into finished products. In this sense raw materials can include anything from rough ore to an electric motor; the finished product of one industry is frequently the raw material of another. Production, therefore, includes all manufacturing and extractive industries.

Following the definition of management arrived at in the introductory chapters, Production Management then becomes the process of effectively planning and regulating the operations of that part of an enterprise which is responsible for the actual transformation of materials into finished products.

The physical features of production vary from industry to industry and are usually specific to each one, or even to particular companies. They can be seen and can be fairly easily appreciated in a tour of any particular factory. But the intangibles which go to build up effective management are not at all apparent and, as with expert performers in the arts or games, the more skilful the performance, the less apparent the effort; a well-run factory looks so easy to manage. In dealing with the management of production, therefore, less attention has been paid, in this part of the book, to the physical or material features than to the human factors, and to principles which are common to many, if not most, industries and companies. For this reason much of what is said has a wider application than to production in the narrow sense; it will be found to apply in many cases to the provision of services, such as transport.

It will be realised that principles by themselves are not enough, and that only experience and practice in applying them will give the aspiring manager that style, that apparently effortless success which is the hall-mark of skill. Adherence to sound principles is important —the man who adheres to them is less likely to run into difficulties of his own making than is the man who works by rule of thumb or instinct or takes refuge in expedients which, at best, are temporary. The road of compromise and expediency leads to muddle, if not chaos, particularly in production. This does not mean that identical problems must be solved in the same way, or that two businesses of exactly the same size, making exactly the same product, would be identical in structure and organisation. People differ and organisations reflect and are a compound of the personalities of which they are composed.

As explained in the Introduction, a job of management arises whenever a group of people are associated together in a common task. A group may be small, a mere half-dozen persons, or a large public company employing thousands, but whatever the size, someone must do the co-ordinating and regulating—the managing. In a small department of a factory, this someone may be called a charge-hand, in a larger department more likely a foreman, and the head of a company usually the managing director. In industry the title Manager, alone or qualified, is usually restricted to the head of a large division or department of a company, whilst Foreman, Over-looker, Charge-hand and such terms are used for the lower positions in the organisation structure. Whatever the title or size of group, the job is one of managing. In the following text, when it is intended to refer to any or all of these positions in a general sense, the term "manager" will be used.

One of the essentials in securing effective management is the separation of "planning" from "doing", both in organisation and in persons' minds. Work should be planned in advance and standardised as far as possible, so that those who supervise others, the managers and foremen, are free to fulfil their proper function of training and directing the doing and ensuring that operators conform to standard practices and methods. And in training and directing operators, managers must themselves plan ahead. Chapters II and III therefore deal with "planning" activities (Designing the Product and Production Administration) and Chapters IV, V and VI with "operating" activities (Supervision and Ancillary Services).

Activities Covered

In dealing with production, all those activities are covered which are concerned directly with the design and manufacture (process or production) of goods or materials. They are the activities which are generally understood to be done in the "works". Not every student manager will find his job, or the job he hopes to have, described in detail, but all normal activities carried on in the "works" are dealt with, as far as it is possible to do so in a book of this kind.

The following activities are covered:

(1) Designing the Product

This is done by the Technical Department which is concerned with specifying what is to be produced, and includes those activities usually associated with the Chief Engineer or Designer in a manufacturing company, or the Chief Chemist in a process factory. It includes the design of the Company's products, the preparation of drawings, specifications, formulæ, or other instructions to the Production Departments, experimental and development work, and the preparation of estimates and contracts for new enquiries or for orders from customers.

(2) Production Administration

This is dealt with in its specialised parts:

(a) *Production Engineering*—which is responsible for deciding and specifying how work is to be done and covers the investigation of methods, the preparation of process specifications, design of tools and equipment and the measurement of work and establishment of standard times.

(b) *Production Planning*—which decides and issues schedules for when work is to be done, and covers materials and stock records, preparation of long- and short-term manufacturing programmes, shop and machine loading and progress chasing.

(c) *Production Control*—which is a specific application of the control function, and is concerned with recording results and correcting for deviations from programmes and variations from standards. Strictly speaking, Inspection is a Control activity, but as it is seldom, if ever, under the authority of those responsible for Production Administration and is very much a specialised activity, it is dealt with separately.

(d) *Operational Research*—which provides Management with a quantitative basis for decisions through the ascertainment and measurement of facts, the probability of their accuracy or error, and the use of mathematical techniques and analogies for predicting results.

(3) Purchasing

The Purchasing Department is responsible for buying the materials required for production, and all other items and supplies not manufactured in the Company's own plant. It finds the supplier, negotiates prices and other conditions and places official orders. In some companies, particularly in process industries which have a very high material content of sales, it is a major activity often headed by a senior executive.

(4) Ancillary Services and Departments

This section deals with those Works departments which are

ancillary to production, i.e. they do not make any part of the product, but provide a service. They are dealt with under the following headings:

(a) Storekeeping.

(b) Inspection.

(c) Works Engineering—covering buildings and services, plant and tools and maintenance.

(5) Management in Production

This is concerned with the organisation and supervision of the actual doing, i.e. with people more than paper. It is general management on a smaller scale. The activities are considered under the following headings: inspiration and co-ordination and the integration of supervision and skill, selection and promotion, training, remuneration and incentives, performance, meetings and joint consultation.

INTEGRATION WITH MARKETING

Production is integrated with the marketing or distribution activity by the General Manager or other chief executive, through the coordination and reconciliation of the sales forecasts and programmes with production programmes. Production is not self-sufficient, but it can be looked upon as the middle links in the chain of activities, starting from the obtaining of an order or receiving an enquiry and ending with the dispatch to customer or sale over the counter. The production policy, forming part of the general company policy, must tally with the marketing policy. If the latter is to go for seasonal markets, production must be flexible enough to respond; if the policy is to keep production steady, stocks must be built up in preparation for the seasonal demand. Long-term production programmes must reflect long-term marketing or distribution plans, building up capacity of plant or sections of the works to meet changes in demand or emphasis in advertising. Technically too the policies must agree. Continual small modifications to design or product may prove disturbing to customers because of existing stocks; less frequent but more radical changes may be a better policy. Similarly, production must not place too much emphasis on quality with the consequent higher price if the sales policy is to go for a low-priced market where quality is not required.

There is often a tendency for sales and production staffs to be antagonistic. Certainly, ideal requirements for each do not always appear to coincide; to please the customer sometimes disrupts production. This antagonism is likely to develop in the very concerns where the production and sales divisions are well led by vigorous capable executives with a pride in their departments. The antagonism must be curbed and the departmental prides related to a co-ordinated whole. The biggest factor in bringing this about is the general sharing in the formation of policies. When the Board, who are primarily makers of policy, and the top management clearly define the wider purpose of the business, insisting that a primary purpose is to serve its customers well and to make a profit in doing so, and when the chief executives concerned share in formulating the secondary policies required to achieve this purpose, then there is likely to be unity of outlook, and production men will recognise that they have a duty to serve the sales departments and through them the customer.

It is not always possible to explain to operators at the desk, bench or machine exactly why certain instructions or actions are necessary (and indeed these can often look senseless or useless), but it is possible to explain policies and the reason for them. Instruction and actions can then be seen as a part or an expression of these policies whereupon the need for them will be understood; and understanding is the first essential to correct performance.

TYPES OF PRODUCTION

Production is a very wide term indeed, and it is not made much narrower through being qualified by the term "industrial". If it is assumed that all those persons engaged in the professions, central and local government service, and wholesale and retail distribution are not engaged in production, then according to the Ministry of Labour Gazette for March 1961, out of a total of 24,656,000 persons employed, 14,303,000, or 58 per cent. are engaged in production. A classification of all the types of production thus segregated can be divided into five main groups:

(1) Mines and Quarries, employing   .   .   .   845,000
(2) Agriculture and Fisheries, employing   .   .   967,800
(3) Building and Civil Engineering, employing   . 1,468,000
(4) Transport, Dock and Public Utilities, employing 2,050,000
(5) Manufacture, employing 9,066,000

Size and Diversity of Industry

Within each of these groups there are, broadly speaking, three types of production, or put in another way, production is carried on on three scales. They are: Job (usually small scale); Batch (usually medium scale); and Flow or Mass (usually large scale).

Job production is concerned with the manufacture of single products to a customer's individual requirements, i.e. "one-off". Each job or order stands alone and is unlikely to be repeated. No two jobs are exactly alike and long runs on a single product are uncommon.

Job production is carried on by a large proportion of the small manufacturing companies in Britain, and by many quite large companies. Because they are small and the proprietor so often discharges many or all of the executive functions of large companies, it is usually considered that small companies cannot use or have no need of all the "systems" and modern developments of scientific management, but the truth is that it is just in these small companies that the application of sound production management principles and the use of simple methods of production administration can effect so large an improvement in effectiveness.

Batch production operates in those companies where a batch or quantity of products or parts is made at a time, but where production on a part or product is not continuous. This occurs when there is a variety of products manufactured to stock and when orders are diverse, but for fairly large quantities and not for "one-offs". But perhaps the most common reason for batch production—and one which creates the complexities and many of the difficult problems of production administration—is the use of standard components in different products and models. This type of production is typical of industry, not only in Britain, but in most industrial countries, including the United States. It calls for general-purpose equipment, and machine tools, flexibility in organisation, and a high standard of skill at the foreman and executive level. Whilst the skill of all operators may not be as high as in factories on jobbing production, and tooling may not be so complex as on mass production, a high degree of skill is required in setting up tools and jobs and in deciding rapidly the most effective way to do a job. It is on this type of production in all industries that control is most difficult to secure and where badly designed and elaborate systems and paperwork can so easily clog the wheels and bog down production.

Flow or *mass production* is limited in general to the large-scale units, although continuous or flow operation is used, frequently and with advantage, for certain products or processes in factories mainly on batch production. In this type, products or parts of identical kind are in continuous production, going through exactly the same sequence of operations, and all processing units (machine, plant or operation) are always employed doing the same operation. Mass production has resulted in and depends on the development of the single-purpose type of machine. Frequently, only one product, and one or perhaps two or three models or grades only, are produced, and the production rate is high. Mass production reaches its most advanced stage in the large process industries like flour-milling and in factories making such standard articles as domestic refrigerators and vacuum cleaners. Factories operating on a mass-production scale are usually large, and employ thousands rather than hundreds. Many of the problems of management in this type of factory arise from the very size of the units and the consequent lack of contact between the higher management and operators, and the de-skilling of jobs, resulting in lack of interest in them.

These different types of production tend to give rise to rather different organisations, and with the usual management problems appearing more significant in one than another. In jobbing production a high proportion of skilled technical people are required, the sales organisation is usually relatively small and overheads are often low. Plant or production processes are varied and flexible but capital investment is small. Production planning is not usually a difficult problem, and management decisions are short term. Product cost is high.

On the other hand, mass production requires a highly organised marketing activity, accounting and commercial staff are large, and overheads high. Plant tends to be specialised and inflexible so that the emphasis in production is on maintaining a high and steady level of activity. Capital investment is high, and management decisions must be fairly long term. Unit cost is low.

Process production goes to the extreme in inflexibility and capital investment and consequently the emphasis is on very long-term decisions and a marketing organisation that can maintain a steady flow of orders.

Batch production is midway between the extremes and calls perhaps for the greatest flexibility of management and emphasis on production planning and production (or industrial) engineering. It also needs the most balanced organisation. Unit costs can be higher or lower than in the other types, and total profits per £ of capital employed or per employee likewise.

Automation has been used in the highly developed process industries, particularly in the chemical industry, for some time. It is now in use in mass-production plants and is being developed for smaller scale use. It is unlikely to lead to a reduction in the total number of people employed, any more than the industrial revolution did. In fact, the scarcity of persons available for production is forcing the development of automation. More higher skilled persons will be required and there will be fewer on direct production. The need to train and the lack of, skilled technical people is likely to retard the rate of application of automation and prevent a rapid "revolution".

The table in Fig. 18 illustrates this diversity of type and scale and gives examples of each type of production for each group of industries.

The development of a factory from job production to batch production occurs naturally, and as a rule creates no major problems. It is usually the logical result of a gradual increase in volume of turn-over, or of the application of standardisation of parts, as the business grows and its customers' needs become known. But it is the decision to apply mass-production methods that is fraught with danger and has proved so disastrous in many cases. The premature application of mass-production methods in the U.S.A. to the manufacture of domestic refrigerators, and of wireless sets in this country, are examples of the results to be expected. A factory laid out on mass-production lines is a single-purpose machine in itself, and a change in fashion, inventions and radical improvements in design may make it obsolete almost overnight. The loss of profit entailed by a shut-down for a changeover can be expensive, as even Ford found out. It is dangerous to set up a factory for mass production for a product still in its early commercial stages, or when it is subject to fashion or public taste, or if the market potentialities are not definitely known. The decision to do so therefore must be a deliberate one and taken only by the Board of Directors as a matter of high policy.

Industry	Type of Production		
	Job	Batch	Flow
Mines and Quarries	Quarries on special work for architecture	Normal mines	Oil wells
Agriculture and Fishing	Normal mixed farm	Special stock and poultry farm Large market gardens	Whaling, herring, kippering and salmon canning
Building and Civil Engineering	Bridges Individual houses	Housing estates Public works maintenance	Modern road surfacing
Manufacture	Special-purpose machines Prototype work	All manufactured articles and most engineering and consumption industries	Cars, vacuum cleaners, telephones, electric lamps and motors, sugar refining, flour milling, paper making
Transport	Furniture removal Plane chartered	All forms of transport	Public transport and special industries, e.g. milk

FIG. 18.

Size of Factory

In order finally to get in perspective the average or typical size of a manufacturing unit in Great Britain, analysis of the following most recent figures quoted in the Ministry of Labour Gazette in September 1959 reveals—for establishments employing more than ten people:

Just over half of the number of factories employ less than 100 persons but account for only 10 per cent. of the total number employed.

At the other end of the scale just over one third of the total number employed work in factories employing more than 1,000 each, although the number of factories is only 3 per cent. of the total.

Of the factories employing more than 100 persons each, 92 per cent. are in the groups 100–1,000 and employ 58 per cent. of those employed.

This latter group is most typical of British industry and is the size with which we are most concerned.

	Establishments		Employees	
	Number	Per Cent. of Total	Number	Per Cent. of Total
11–24 employees	14,874 ⎫	53	258 ⎫	10
25–49 ,,	14,625 ⎬		516 ⎭	
50–99 ,,	11,520	20	810	10
100–249 ,,	8,759 ⎫		1,351 ⎫	
250–499 ,,	3,293 ⎬	24	1,141 ⎬	46
500–999 ,,	1,524 ⎭		1,048 ⎭	
1,000–1,999 ,,	742 ⎫		1,021 ⎫	
2,000–4,999 ,,	328 ⎬	3	959 ⎬	34
5,000 or more ,,	74 ⎭		631 ⎭	
Total with 10 or more employees	55,739	100	7,735	100

FIG. 19.

ORGANISATION STRUCTURE

The importance to effective management of a sound organisation structure and of the understanding and application of its principles has been emphasised in the Introduction. In the present context it remains only to look briefly at the organisation structure needed for the Production Division. Frequently, this Division covers by far the largest number of persons and departments, and there is always the danger of having too many persons individually responsible to the head, i.e. the Works Manager, Production Manager, or whatever his title may be. This is a common fault: fifteen or even twenty people answerable directly to a Works Manager is no unusual situation and is a frequent cause of mediocrity, sluggishness and downright inefficiency in many of our factories today.

There are good reasons for thinking that the optimum size of a manufacturing unit is between 500 and 1,000 employees. In such a unit advantage can be taken of specialisation of activity and the use of production engineering and planning staff without losing the personal touch which comes from close contact between directors, executives and employees at all levels. This is recognised in the U.S.A. The productivity report on Welding made by the team which visited the United States in 1950, and published by the Anglo-American Council on Productivity, stated (page 55): "It is of interest that one major company had 125 separate works of which all but eleven employed fewer than 500 people. These smaller works were considered an advantage because they afforded a closer contact between employers and labour, which resulted in a better relationship between the two."

For a typical unit of any size between, say, 300 and 750 employees in the factory, the following diagram shows the basic structure for the Production Division, with suitable alternatives for the head of each department. (Titles of course are less important than definitions of responsibilities.)

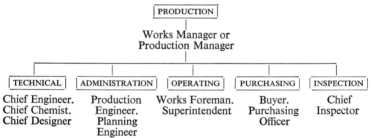

The technical activity is clearly a production activity, and is treated as such in this book. It is, therefore, shown in the diagram as responsible to the executive in charge of production. In some concerns, however, particularly where it is closely tied up with the sales division, the technical division is responsible directly to the Managing Director. In these cases Production Engineering and Planning may be separately responsible to the Works Manager. Or there may be two or three main operating divisions; for example, Processing, Packing and Storeroom in food manufacture, Printing and Binding in printing, Cutting, Making and Warehouse in clothing, and

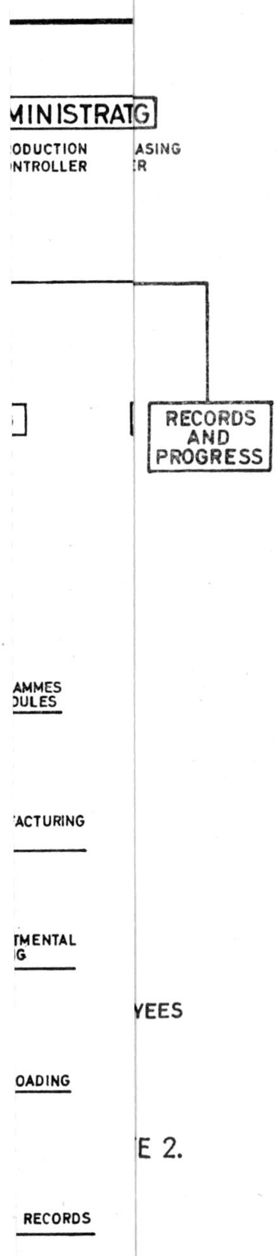

ODUCTION   ASING
NTROLLER   R

]   [RECORDS
                            AND
                            PROGRESS

AMMES
ULES

ACTURING

TMENTAL
G

YEES

OADING

E 2.

RECORDS

Machining and Assembly in engineering, each responsible to the Works Manager, without exceeding unduly the latter's span of control. On the other hand, if the technical activity is small and intimately bound up with works facilities, as is common in small jobbing businesses, it is often more satisfactory for one person to be responsible for the technical and administration activities. In a small factory of under 100 people, one person might be responsible for the technical, planning and inspection activities, the Works Manager himself directly supervising the several foremen or chargehands.

In the medium-sized factory employing 500–1,500 people, a more elaborate structure may be necessary. This may take the form shown in Plate 2. On this chart departments are shown in panels with activities listed below. In still larger organisations, each of the second-line departments may be further divided. In all cases, however, the general form would remain the same, and the line of responsibility shown should not be departed from except in unusual circumstances. In factories in which a Chemist is the technical executive, e.g. chemical processing and food factories, he is likely to be responsible for formulæ and methods, and not the Production Engineer. He may also be responsible for factory inspection and test.

It is sometimes maintained that the activities of Inspection and Test should be responsible to the Technical Manager and that Stores should be responsible to the Buyer. Whilst there are some arguments in favour of this, experience shows that there is an overriding reason why these departments should all be responsible to the "works" manager, i.e. someone directly responsible for the works departments. Persons in these departments spend all or most of their time on the factory floor and this is where they need to be supervised; absentee supervision from offices cannot be very effective.

Charts of this nature are insufficient by themselves; they can only indicate broad responsibilities and give a picture of the organisation as a whole. In order that each person in a supervisory position is quite clear about his detailed responsibilities and duties, definitions should be drawn up and handed to him by the senior executive. In addition, each person should be given a copy of the definitions for other supervisors in the form of a loose-leaf manual, including a copy of the organisation chart. Finally, it must be remembered that such organisation charts and definitions of duties soon get out of date; they should not be considered fixed and invariable for all time. As developments take place in Company policy, size or personnel, amendments may become necessary, and these should be put into effect in a clear and definite manner.

Illustrations of definitions of responsibilities have been set out in Appendix II to the Introduction. To assist those who are already engaged in the management of production and who have decided to tidy up their own organisation, an outline list is set out at the beginning of each section in the present Part.

PRODUCTION ADMINISTRATION

A word or two is required as an introduction to what is after all a relatively recent development of industrial organisation—the delegation to specialists of that function of Production Management concerned with forms and figures and forethought. Not that there has not always been a lot of figures and forethought required in business. But the setting up of a central department charged specifically with the task of doing all the planning and issuing of works orders and of keeping check on progress is relatively new. It is a development associated with the growth of scientific management, which had its birth at the end of last century, and with large and complex organisations.

Frederick Taylor, the "father of scientific management", back in the early days of this century, having set out to determine what precisely was a "fair day's work", discovered two things:

(1) that planning, work flow, material supply and other factors, which are the responsibility of management, affected output in addition to the effort of operators;
(2) that a tremendous amount of time and energy was wasted by skilled men in finding the best way to do a job or in doing it the wrong way, whereas the one best way could be determined scientifically and laid down in precise instructions for future repetition.

It is clear that although Taylor did not use the term "production administration" as a function of management, he recognised its content, and what is more, recognised its two parts, one connected with work flow or planning, and the other with methods.

Several common words have been pressed into service to describe the various activities of this branch of management, and most probably because it is not an exact science, but has developed in the solving of day-to-day problems, there is as yet no definition of their meaning. Terms such as planning, progress, production control, progress chasing, shop planner, progress clerk and so on have been used with different meanings, or to refer to different activities in different organisations and textbooks. The word "planning" is perhaps the most widely used. In some organisations it refers exclusively to the activities concerned with, and the department responsible for, determining the way in which a job is to be done, and the preparation of jigs and tools, operation times and so on. In others, particularly where there are few changes of method, and where new methods are not being continually studied, it is applied to the activity of preparing production programmes in relation to time, issuing shop schedules, and generally steering work through the shops. In other organisations the term is used for the whole process of production administration, including methods, programmes, shop orders and progress. There is indeed some justification for using the word "planning" for all the activities covered by Fayol's—"*prévoyance*". All forethought or work put into arranging beforehand how and when a job is to be done can be called planning, but with the need to specialise on the various activities of production administration, it is better in industry to be more specific and to use other terms for divisions of the activity. One of the earliest terms used, at least in England, for that activity of production administration dealing with programmes, particularly on the shop floor, was "progress". It has been widened from its use in describing the work of the assistant to the foreman who looked after the clerical work attached to programmes in the shop (as a progress clerk or progress chaser) to include all the activities associated with preparing production programmes. There are many variations of these terms, and of others in use, evidence that there is no clear idea of what is meant by production administration, nor what are its activities, duties and responsibilities. It may be thought that the technical characteristics of industry vary so widely that a common treatment of production administration, or a common terminology, is unlikely to be of any use.

Managers usually claim that their business is "different"—and with justification. No two businesses or organisations are exactly alike, any more than two persons are alike—and businesses are built up of persons. Nevertheless, not only the principles, but also the techniques of administration, and particularly of production administration, apply to all businesses. In this sense, businesses do not differ; production administration can be equally effective in them all, large or small, and whether they produce silk stockings or sewing machines, chemicals or cars. In order, therefore, that it can be discussed in relation to all industries, it is essential to define terms and to build up a commonly accepted use of such terms.

Definition of Terms

There are three distinct, though related and sometimes combined, activities concerned with getting production into stride and keeping check on its progress. They may be briefly described as follows:

(1) *Methods.*—Determining the most practical and economical way of doing a job, laying down standards for its performance, and designing the tools and equipment required. This can be best

described as *Production Engineering,* sometimes referred to as Industrial Engineering.

This term is valid whatever the industry; it is not specific to engineering, although the activities covered by Production Engineering have been developed rapidly and intensely in engineering. The study of methods and of the best way actually to do a job in a factory is an engineer's or requires an engineer's training and outlook. The product may be pottery or chocolates, or even farming, but in this age of mechanisation and the application of power, the plant for producing and the best way to use it is an engineering problem. It is therefore a production engineering problem. The fact that there is a professional Institution of Production Engineers gives added force to the term.

(2) *Programmes.*—Arranging for what work shall be produced, and when. It is the activity concerned with the clerical routines, pre-planning production, preparing schedules of work to be done, the issue of work orders and control of stocks of materials and components. Since the word "planning" is usually associated with this kind of activity, and is the most commonly used, the term *Production Planning* best describes it and will be used in this book.

(3) Checking up on performance against standards and programmes. This activity can best be described as *Production Control,* in line with the analysis of management activities (page 19). It must not be confused with its frequent use for the whole process of Production Administration. It is concerned with comparing actual results with standards which have been laid down by either of the two other activities and the statistics are prepared and used by them or by the Accountant. Action is ultimately taken by supervision, i.e. managers or foremen, as a result of any differences that are revealed.

The terminology position may now be summarised:

"Production Administration" consists of:

Production Engineering.—Methods, tools, standards of quantity and time, etc.

Production Planning.—Programmes, works orders, production schedules, shop loads, material stocks.

Production Control.—Recording results and performance, checking against programmes and standards, and pointing out corrective action required.

"Production Management" involves the use of these activities, coupled with the human task of supervising the actual execution of the work to be done, ensuring good morale and co-ordinating the team.

There is one further term, "tools", which requires explanation—having a special significance in engineering. The machines used for cutting and forming metal are called "machine tools", and tools handled or put into the machines just "tools". But tools are used in all industries—moulds in potteries, lasts in boot and shoe manufacture, trowels and hods in building, formes in printing and boxmaking, and so on. In this book, therefore, the word "tools" will be used to cover all such uses.

Systems and Dangers

It is necessary to sound a note of warning against believing many of the claims made by "systems", visible card records, movable bar or line charts, duplicating machines, and so on, in particular that they "control" production. They do nothing of the kind. Correctly designed, they make records rapidly available and present a mass of data in a simplified, easily comprehended form that can be grasped with a minimum of time or effort. They are tools of production administration, and as such can be very effective tools indeed; but like all other tools, they have to be used by workmen and cannot work of themselves. A few such tools effectively used are more successful than elaborate systems. There is a tendency to measure the effectiveness of "production control" systems by their complexity and by the amount of information that can be gathered from them. In this way small firms unwittingly cumber themselves with elaborate records and procedures and refinements of technique suitable only for the large-scale organisation—and even then of doubtful value. For this reason techniques and procedures described in Chapter III will be kept simple and sufficient to illustrate principles only.

It is important to remember that what is wanted in production administration work is a firm grasp of principles and the methods of setting about a problem, and that the actual methods adopted and forms used may have to be fitted to the particular case, modified and certainly simplified if possible, as experience is gained and conditions change.

Persons engaged in the administration of production must be aware of dangers like the following:

(1) Tendency to overrate the relative importance of production administration and to forget that it is only *part* of the total process of management—and never the most important. It appears increasingly important to persons who become wrapped up in it.

(2) Inclination to forget that production administration is a *tool* of management—and like all tools, must not be allowed to become rusty, but must be kept sharp (or up to date).

(3) Losing sight of the fact that production engineering, production planning and production control in action all bear on people and inevitably create reactions—good or bad.

(4) Failure to realise that production administration is a service to supervision and not an end in itself. It supplies information to production but must not dictate to supervision.

(5) The recurring temptation to make manufacture fit production control "systems", to compromise sound management principles for the sake of simpler production planning procedures, particularly when these have been in operation for some time. Systems must be flexible, adaptable and as simple as possible.

SUPERVISION

When designs have been prepared, and drawings, specifications, or formulæ issued, when methods of production and programmes have been worked out and the plant and tools provided, someone must still do the work or actually make the job. And when there are more than two or three persons jointly concerned with the doing, i.e. there is an organisation or a team, then someone must be responsible for generally overseeing the job, i.e. for supervision. If the team is larger than ten or a dozen, a full-time manager is needed, and we have management in action on a small scale. As the team or organisation gets larger, management becomes a bigger job, detailed supervision has to be delegated, and the title for persons performing the function changes, becoming Managing Director or General Manager at the highest level. Whatever the position in the organisation and whatever the title, this job of management involves supervision of people. Supervision is primarily and in the main a human problem—it is concerned with persons not forms. David Lilienthal, the man through whose leadership the great adventure in regional development in the U.S.A., the Tennessee Valley Authority, was so successful, said "making decisions from paper has a dehumanising effect, much of man's inhumanity to man is explained by it". And persons differ, they are not all cast in the same mould. It is a fundamental law of mechanics that every action has an equal and *opposite* reaction. But in the realm of management commands and actions of a supervisor must induce reactions in the *same direction* and not in an opposing one. The personnel activity has developed in industry to advise and assist management in dealing with human problems. But just as on production matters a manager is advised by the technical departments, planning, production engineers, chemists, inspectors and so on, but must remain responsible for ultimate action and what goes on in his department, so on personal problems he is responsible for their ultimate solution. There has been a tendency to look upon the person responsible for the Personnel Department as a Personnel *Manager* with authority to make decisions relating directly to problems of supervision in a department. This is a mistaken view of the personnel activity and a dangerous surrender of authority for a manager. A manager must always be responsible for all persons in his division of the organisation, and must therefore study the personnel or supervisory part of his job as keenly as he does the technical part—and the higher up the organisation structure he rises the more need there will be to deal with persons and situations instead of things. We have the technical knowledge today to raise productivity and with it our standard of life beyond all previous rates of increase; what is needed in addition is the ability to get people to work effectively and willingly together and as a co-ordinated enthusiastic team. The advice of the Personnel Officer should be sought whenever it might be helpful, but a manager must learn to deal with day-to-day problems himself. As in so many other cases, prevention is better than cure; it is better to prevent personnel problems by good management in day-to-day affairs.

The wider aspects of leadership, morale, welfare and what makes people willing to work are dealt with in Part Three. In Chapter VI of this Part we shall consider the problems to be faced by the manager in his own department. These will cover such topics as: inspiration and co-ordination; selection, training and promotion; remuneration and incentives; performance; meetings and joint consultation.

A special problem calling for mention here is that of status and titles. Between the Managing Director and the chargehand in a manufacturing company there are many management grades. In a company employing some 7,000 people, there were nine definite grades, and in a medium-size engineering firm employing 500–600 there were seven. In all grades management is, or should be, actively in action, although the degree of responsibility involved and the proportion of time spent on the two functions of management, control and supervision, vary. Generally speaking, in each division of an organisation the grade varies with the number of individuals for whom a person is ultimately responsible, but this is not true as between different divisions. The rank or status of a manager depends on factors other than responsibility for the performance of those under his charge; for example, technical knowledge or skill, responsibility for money, information and goodwill. A foreman in the works may have the same rank or status as the chief clerk in the general office or a section leader in the drawing office, though he may supervise many times more persons.

The proportion of time spent by managers on administrative work and on supervision varies with the grade, the chargehand spending almost all his time on actual supervision of persons and the Managing Director spending the greater portion of his time on administrative work. This can be illustrated as in Fig. 20. It is to be noted too that the amount of technical skill and managing ability required by a manager varies in the same way. A chargehand must himself be able to do all jobs for which he is responsible and his management ability need not be of a high order. The reverse is true of the Managing Director.

There is much heartache suffered by those of small mental stature on account of supposed or imagined lack of status or inadequacy of title. Those who worry about their status have none to worry about. Although by many much store is set on the title of foreman or man-

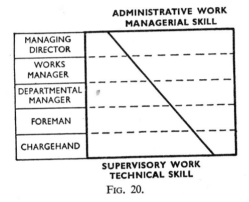

FIG. 20.

ager, it is not the title, but the duties that are covered by it, which are important. A person's value to a company and hence to the community, and therefore to some extent his status, is measured by his grade, which carries a certain remuneration and certain privileges. A chief chemist may be on the same grade as a works manager, and the chief inspector may be in the foreman's grade and remunerated accordingly. But a person's status to a large extent, like the respect he receives, is earned by him and extended to him by those around him, of their own free choice—it cannot be handed out by order or proclamation. To have earned respect and the status due to him is the hall-mark of a good manager.

CHAPTER II

DESIGNING THE PRODUCT—THE TECHNICAL DIVISION

RESPONSIBILITIES

BETWEEN the customer and the production departments there must be someone who interprets the customer's requirements and sets them out in a way which enables production to make exactly what the customer wants with the facilities available. The Sales Department may collect the information and make a first interpretation of requirements, but it must still be set out for the production departments in the form of working instructions. In engineering and similar factories these take the form of drawings with associated lists of parts, in others they consist of specifications, formulæ or recipes. Associated with this activity of specifying what is required, i.e. Design, is the problem of anticipating, or trying to do what will be required in the future and improving what is already produced—that is, Development. This latter is a broad term covering research, experiment, invention and development to full scale production.

These associated activities of design and development should normally constitute a department of the production division under the authority of a single individual, and can most appropriately be called the Technical Department. It must be recognised that the Technical Department is a vital link in the chain of production; it must not be thought of as a non-productive department. It is just as important therefore to study its effectiveness and plan its output as it is in the case of direct operations in the factory. The importance and extent of the activities of the department vary greatly. Many small firms manufacture articles or do work on parts entirely to customers' designs or specifications. Others, and often quite large firms, take up a patent or design or the manufacture of a standardised product and, resolutely refusing to consider orders for small variations, maintain a large production without any design department. In the case of the firms manufacturing to customers' orders, estimates and quotations must be prepared and submitted, and this is normally a job for the Technical Department; but when a firm manufactures standard products only, even this is not required, the Sales Department varying prices only in the form of discounts off price lists. Firms of the first type depend for success mainly on their production "know how" and efficiency, the latter need also marketing skill.

In between are the many firms in all industries which manufacture a range of products which either have to be modified for individual customers or continually improved to keep up with, if not ahead of, the market.

Since in business there is no standing still—stagnation is the first stage of decline—there must always be some development activity. In the firm manufacturing to customer's orders, such development activity is mainly concerned with production technique and facilities, and is most likely to be a responsibility of the Production Engineers. In all other firms there is, or should be, active and continuous development of the firm's products, and because of the need for a close liaison between design and development, these should be the responsibility of the same person. This person would normally be a member of the Technical Department.

The title of the head of the Technical Department varies more perhaps than that for any other activity. His job demands an intimate knowledge and experience of the processes and techniques of the particular industry and until recently his title usually indicated the old craft from which the industry developed (Head Brewer is still used in the brewing industry though he may be an industrial chemist).

Whatever the title given in individual cases, the following is typical of the responsibilities:

(1) Interpret the Company's policy in relation to design of its own products and interpret customers' requirements in relation to their enquiries and orders.

(2) Translate these designs and requirements into clear and adequate working drawings, specifications, or other instructions in a manner satisfactory to the Works Superintendent and issue to the production departments.

(3) Lay down and specify standards of quality and accuracy to maintain the Company's reputation and minimise production costs and to ensure standardisation and interchangeability as far as possible.

(4) Prepare estimates of the cost of producing a job to customers' requirements and send to Sales Department for transmission to customers, tenders covering cost and the margin of profit laid down from time to time by the Managing Director. Maintain such records as are necessary to enable this to be done quickly and accurately.

(5) Keep abreast of developments in the design, use and manufacture of the Company's products, and carry out development, research and experimental work to this end.

(6) Keep and store safely and tidily accurate file records of all drawings, specifications and calculations.

(7) Supervise work done and maintain discipline in the department. Ensure that all members of the department are adequately trained in their duties and particularly that juniors and apprentices receive a good technical and practical training.

(8) Adhere to the Company's personnel policy.

DESIGN

Factors Influencing Design

Customers' Exact Requirements

A satisfied customer is one of the best salesmen a firm can have; he is a perpetual recommendation. It is essential therefore for designers to find out exactly what the customer really requires. When the product is a shelf product sold ultimately to the public, it is mainly a market research job, although even then the designer has to seek information which the marketing staff and even the customer may not realise affects the design. In the large number of firms which supply equipment and intermediate products to other companies, it is usually left to the designer to ensure that he has all the information he requires. The salesman finds the markets and the customer and secures the order with a specification of requirements and conditions of service. But it is repeatedly found in practice that certain conditions and factors are taken for granted by the user and assumed by the designer, and when the product is put into service, it is found to be faulty in some respects and that the fault is in the design. The designer therefore must ensure that he has all the information.

A good way to meet this point is for designers to have by them a detailed and comprehensive questionnaire relating to the kind of products with which they deal. Whenever the designer tackles a new design, he should fill in the answers himself, seeking from either salesman or customer those which he cannot supply, or submit the whole questionnaire in the first place. An alternative is to submit a detailed statement of the design before final acceptance, but a customer is less likely to check this accurately than to give correct answers to specific questions.

A product need not be better than the market for which it is intended. At the same time, however good a design may be, it fails to satisfy the user if maintenance is difficult or troublesome or it is inconvenient in use. For example—motor-cars and factory equipment which are difficult to get at for service and repair, machines which are inconvenient for the operator, containers, bottles and cartons which are difficult to open or use, furniture which is comfortable but heavy to move and difficult to clean, detergents which are harsh on hands, cannot be considered well designed and do not sell easily. This means that designers must have a commercial outlook and should see their products in use in all kinds of conditions as often as possible.

Operator

One of the factors too often ignored, more particularly with designers of machines, is the convenience and comfort of the operator or user. With the development of production engineering and work study techniques, there has been much improvement in this respect in recent years, but one still meets plenty of glaring instances of this neglect. Power presses are seldom comfortable to operate, and it is quite common for the working position and operation of wrapping, packing and weighing machines to be unnecessarily tiring or to need a most unnatural stance. For example, tables or delivery chutes of machines cause operators to bend over, yet are so obstructed below that the operator cannot sit with knees bent and feet supported. How many sink units for the modern house have been designed with an eye to appearance, yet the user cannot stand with feet under the sink and must therefore work with the body off balance, with the consequent strain on back muscles. In other cases, operation handles require an unnatural stretch or action, or are hard to work.

Materials

It might be thought that all designers are aware that materials affect design. This is probably true, but it is worth emphasising that improvements and new materials are constantly being developed, and that there is a tendency always for busy designers to work in materials to which they are accustomed and of which they have had long experience and to neglect the newer ones. It means a continual reading of technical and scientific journals, close collaboration with the buyer—and an open mind. It is always worth while making suppliers aware of new requirements; there are always some who are ready to consider new uses and needs—they are the designers of another product.

Works Methods and Equipment

It is the general impression in most works departments that the designers have little idea of how a new product or part will be made—or could be made most economically. This is an indication of the lack of consideration given to the point by designers. Small modifications to designs can often result in considerable economies in production costs. This is a well-known fact to production engineers in engineering, but is often not realised in other industries. It can of course be overdone, and result in stereotyped design when improvement may be an asset. It is usual for engineering draughtsmen to spend some time in the works departments (it is ideal for them to go through every department), but it is by no means universal. There are so many processes in industry today that it is unusual for any one firm to employ a large proportion of them and impossible even then for technicians to have practical experience of them all. Chemists and other "designers" or technicians often have a scant knowledge of engineering or factory methods. Indeed, their profession is so specialised that it is difficult for them to gain such knowledge. It is important, therefore, to emphasise the need for the establishment of a routine or procedure which ensures that, where designers have not an intimate knowledge of production methods and technique in their own works, the works staff or production engineers have an opportunity of scrutinising designs or specifications before their form is finally determined.

It is essential for designers in the first place to understand and take into account the plant available and methods used, and to design with the method of production in mind. A common fault is to leave too much information to be supplied by too many people. There is a temptation always for the design or technical department to leave manufacturing and process details which become general practice in a works—"old Spanish customs"—to foremen, operators or inspectors. This is dangerous. All goes well as long as there are no staff changes, but when there are changes, often unexpected and due to death, sudden resignation, or need for expansion, the new people on the job take some time before they pick up the "know how", and mistakes occur. It is essential in specifications and on drawings to be specific and complete. For example, in process industries instructions like heat, soak, dry, etc., should be defined as to degree, and in engineering the limits in dimensions should *always* be stated on drawings and not be left to be remembered (or forgotten) in the production departments. All these factors can affect the quality of the product. Specifications and drawings therefore must be clearly, accurately and minutely defined.

Organisation of Department

The purpose of the Design or Technical Department is to prepare and issue instructions to the Works Department to enable them to manufacture. This is done with the aid of some or all of the following documents:

Specification.—A written description of the product (and its parts), process or formula.

Drawing.—This may be a pencil sketch, carbon copy, tracing or print (blue or white), showing the object, usually in three views (plan, elevation and end view) with dimensions. It should include all information required in manufacture, such as material, limits or dimensions, jigs and tools, etc.

Parts List.—A list of all parts of a product, with brief particulars of each.

Material Collation List.—A list of all material required, summarised.

Amendment Note.—A written statement of an amendment to either of the above.

Log of Design.—A classified record of designs or formulæ.

Register.—A record, indexed, of drawings, specifications and formulæ.

Specifications

Because technical people often have a poor command of language, specifications are sometimes not as clear as they should be. They should be written, bearing in mind that they are most likely to be used by persons having less knowledge of the subject than the writer. Short sentences should be used, the matter set out in headed paragraphs, and illustrated where it is difficult to explain adequately in words.

Drawings

A drawing should be an accurate pictorial specification of exactly what the object it represents must be. It must be accurate and complete. It is important, therefore, that drawings should be fully dimensioned, and that every dimension should be accurately defined. This means that the variation permitted for each dimension is stated, and this is done by stating the tolerance permitted. An explanation of tolerances, fits and limits is given later in Chapter Five, on page 456.[1] It is important to remember that a dimension has no real meaning unless the permissible variation from it is known. A statement should therefore be included on all drawings giving the general tolerance on all dimensions which are not individually limited. The following is a good example:

TOLERANCES ALLOWED

UNMACHINED SURFACES $\pm \frac{1}{16}$ IN.

MACHINED SURFACES AND CRS OF MACHINED

HOLES ± 0.015 IN. UNLESS OTHERWISE STATED

---

[1] See also B.S.S. 308, Part II, Engineering Drawing Office Practice, Dimensioning and Tolerancing (H.M. Stationery Office).

The principle of one part one drawing is now generally accepted for details and there is everything to be said for it. Drawings can be kept smaller—a great many parts can be satisfactorily reduced to a scale which enables 13 × 8-in. drawings to be used and, as this is a standard stationery size (foolscap), it simplifies filing. It also avoids the troubles and waste of time which occur in the works when several parts are shown on one drawing and more than one part is in production at the same time (a very frequent occurrence).

Parts Lists

Parts lists vary from very brief lists of parts, most of which are illustrated by drawings, to fairly lengthy and adequate descriptions of many of the parts listed. In practice a good deal of trouble is experienced with them because small items are omitted by oversight on the part of the person preparing the list. For this reason they should always be double checked. To avoid the lengthy and expensive job of writing them out on tracings and printings, they can be run off on duplicators, or other reproduction equipment.

Material Collation List

Since a parts list is prepared in a form to suit the works departments, if it is necessary either to purchase or allocate material for each order, then it is a great convenience to both the Stores Records and the Buyer to have a Material Collation List. This is a list of all material included on the parts list, material of the same kind and size being totalled and grouped and like materials being grouped together. It should be prepared by the Drawing Office and issued at the same time as the parts list.

Amendment and Revisions

It is always difficult to keep specifications, drawings and parts lists up to date, to ensure that all copies are corrected when alterations are made, and that no old copies are in use. Failure to do so can result in work being done incorrectly, with the consequent increase in costs. It is essential therefore to lay down a reliable procedure for dealing with the problem. Where it is impracticable to withdraw and reissue a corrected document, a standard Revision or Amendment Note should be issued by the originator of the document to be amended, and copies sent to *all* departments that receive the original document. It is unsafe, in practice, to issue copies only to the department which appears, at the time, to be affected. In normal circumstances certain departments may not need information which only concerns others; but unusual circumstances always arise, and it is then that all the information, including amendments, is required.

In the case of drawings, however careful the reissue of new drawings and the withdrawal of old ones, there are always wrong drawings left in existence. A simple and very safe method of issuing amended drawings is to differentiate between those which affect interchangeability and those which do not. For the former the drawing must be reissued with a new number of the part given a new number (if not the same as the drawing). When interchangeability is not affected, the number need not be charged (a suffix R1, R2, etc., to the original number, changed for each revision, is an added precaution). In both cases, if the original tracing is altered and not redrawn, a note of each amendment, numbered, should be made on the tracing.

Log or Record of Design

When there are many variations of design for various products continually being prepared, a log or record book should be kept, in which is entered every design, and against each, in headed columns, brief particulars of the various major parts of the design. It is surprising how often such a record is found to be of value to both the technical and production engineering staff and often to the sales staff too.

Sections and Specialisation

In line with the development of industry generally, designers and other technical men have become specialised, and in the larger firms the technical departments tend to be sectionalised, each section being headed by a senior man. Depending on whether there are many small designs or projects being dealt with at a time, or one large one, so sections either deal with all similar projects or all the same parts of each large project as it comes along. In either case, persons become highly specialised in their own class of work, and as this means that they become very familiar with and memorise all the details, which are never very easy to record and index, work is dealt with quickly, and the maximum use can be made of standardisation and previous experience. There is, however, an element of danger in such specialisation, not to be overlooked. When specialised knowledge, and a memory of unrecorded detail, are suddenly removed, as must happen from time to time, there can be a serious loss. For this reason it is important for the head of the department to keep in touch with all jobs and all divisions of work in the department, to examine and talk over with his staff all the new work coming into the department, and to insist that all vital information and data are adequately recorded.

A good deal of design work involves intricate and advanced mathematical calculations, and a special section is often set up to deal with them for the whole of the department. Such problems as the stresses in parts of machines, the strength of materials required and the quantities for large projects are dealt with in this section. The advantage of specialist skill has to be set off against the delay to which this arrangment almost inevitably gives rise, but in a large engineering drawing office, where it is impracticable for all draughtsmen to have the requisite knowledge, it is essential.

A much less certain case can be made out for the frequent arrangement of a separate section for checking all designs, or work produced in a technical department, before use. The aim, of course, is to ensure that all work is absolutely correct when issued to the works— faults found afterwards (or not found) are always expensive. Nevertheless, in practice the tendency is always for the designers to rely on this check. It promotes a better sense of responsibility and a higher standard if each man is responsible for his own work, arranging for such checking as may be necessary with his senior. Where 100 per cent. accuracy is vital, a final check is unavoidable.

In the same way parts lists, generally speaking, should be prepared by the man producing the design, since only he can be certain that everything is included. To avoid tracing parts lists for standard reference as is usual in engineering concerns, a tedious and expensive job, the modern duplicating machine should be used, the parts list being written in pencil directly on to the master sheet. Since the designers must in any case write out a list of parts somewhere, this overcomes the draughtsman's usual objection to the purely clerical or elementary work associated with the preparation of parts lists. Where, however, designs or projects incorporate standard designs or subassemblies, and material collation lists are also required, a special clerical section to deal with lists, compiling the material lists and gathering together copies of the standard subassemblies, can be effective and economical. Such a section should be responsible also for the issue of work from the department, ensuring that copies of originals and revisions are circulated correctly and superseded copies withdrawn.

Work Planning

The Design Department or Drawing Office is as much a production department as any in the works; it is in the direct line of manufacturing processes from receipt of an order to its dispatch. That its cost is usually included in overheads does not alter the fact and in some companies handling large projects the design and drawing time is included in the final price as a direct cost. It is just as important, therefore, to plan and measure work done in the Design Department as in a department of the works. To do this it is unnecessary to have time sheets or to clock on jobs, neither of which is popular or usual for office staff.

Since it is impossible to plan reliably without a measure of the time likely to be taken to do the work, let us first of all consider the problem of measurement. The usual reaction of designers and technical staff to any suggestion that their work should be measured is that it is impossible to say beforehand exactly how long it will take to think out a new design or solve an awkward designing problem. This may be so for completely novel designs never before attempted, but experience shows that in dealing with the normal run of work forming a company's regular production it is possible with practice to estimate the time normally taken within sufficient accuracy for it to be used for a measure of individual performance and for planning.

In a small office, the head of the department, and in a large one, the section leaders, should, when scanning each new job before allocating it to a designer or section, assess the standard time required for dealing with the job, i.e. the time which an average designer on that class of work in the department would take to deal with it, giving conscientious attention to it. Each job is allocated and the "standard time" for it recorded. As each job is completed and issued to the works, the designer (or group) is credited with the "standard" time on his weekly record. The total of the "standard" hours produced for the week, or other period, is compared with actual hours worked, and the weekly figure and cumulative total are recorded for each man and the department as a whole. Experience at estimating the "standard" time and in studying records of results enables the person doing so to become quite accurate. There is no need to use the times for any method of payment by results. If results and doubts about probable times are discussed fully with the person concerned, it has a beneficial effect on output. When such a scheme is first introduced, it will be found that the total standard hours produced in a period for each man and for the whole department is considerably less than the actual hours worked, but after a time, six months or so, performance improves (and estimates are made more accurately) and the standard hours agree quite closely with actual hours. Even if performance does not improve, the estimated time will at least adjust itself to actual time, so that planning can be accurate, but inevitably such a method of *measuring and examining* results has a beneficial effect on output.

Planning of work should then be dealt with in much the same way as it is dealt with for factory departments. Again in practice the most effective way is to show the length of standard time allowed each designer (or group) on a Gantt-type chart on a time base. A more flexible way is to mark the time along the edge of a card representing the job and place in pockets of a load board marked horizontally in weeks and months. In this way, not only can the load on each designer be seen and overloading avoided, but the date for completion of each job and new jobs coming in can be given and the effects on existing promises of dealing with urgent orders out of turn can be assessed. To ask a designer to drop a job to take up a more urgent one is inimical to concentration; to do so repeatedly is to invite small and large errors and too many of them. Planning can go a long way towards avoiding this.

Indexing and Filing

The correct filing and indexing of technical documents, specifications, formulæ and drawings is an important matter, but one often neglected. It is essential that there is no loss of time in finding them when they are required (and time so lost can be considerable), and that they are not damaged during storage or in the filing process. Moreover, it is even more essential that designers, whose time is valuable, can readily refer to data which has a bearing on a present problem when the filing number of the document containing it may not be known.

Dealing first with safety, it has been found that the most satisfactory method of filing all technical documents, except books, is a drawer-type metal filing cabinet. For maximum protection of documents, care in use, and most rapid reference, the suspended-type folder should be used, and in general the foolscap size is most satisfactory. The suspended folder method is also satisfactory for larger drawings if they are folded, although for very large drawings drawers are not suitable and cabinets opening from the top should be used. If drawings are standardised on commercial stationery sizes, e.g. foolscap (and this size is quite satisfactory for the majority of detail drawings), standard equipment can be used.

Protection against the hazard of fire should be given serious consideration; drawings, formulæ, specifications and the like are extremely valuable documents, and in most cases it would be physically impossible to replace or remake them unless another copy existed. It is advisable, therefore, either to store all such documents in genuinely fireproof equipment (much so-called fireproof equipment is only partially so) or to store one copy of the document some distance away from, and certainly in another building from, the master copy —or as a safeguard against a general conflagration to do both. An alternative to an exact copy is micro-film copies. These need special photographic equipment, but there are firms in most large towns who specialise in the service, and such copies have the great advantage of taking up very little space. Perhaps the most satisfactory way, if space is available. is to file the master copy (tracings of drawings) in a strong-room and have copies available in the department for reference purposes. This has the added advantage of preserving the master from damage and defacement in normal use.

In order to identify and file drawings and other documents, it is usual to give them an individual number. The simplest method, but one which has no other purpose than mere identification, is to number from one up, i.e. start at number one and number each successive document made or filed with the next unused number in a register. It is possible, however, to devise a system or code which ensures that the documents are filed in some sort of useful order and which facilitates memorising and identification. Such a code involves the separation of the items into groups or categories and their classification which makes a code useful and effective. In technical departments where the data, including specifications, abstracts from technical journals, etc., cover a very wide sphere, then the general classification used in public libraries in Britain can be used, and any public library will give detailed particulars or a demonstration. In general, however, the data or documents to be filed cover a limited field peculiar to the firm's activities or products. It is then necessary to build up a classification and code to suit this limited range. For specifications and formulæ dealing with processes, it will be found most useful either to classify according to names of processes, subdividing for subsidiary processes, or according to products. For drawings there are in general two alternative methods of approach, either to classify according to product or according to type of part. Where it is possible to use standardised parts in different products (and this should be encouraged), classifying should be according to part. Drawings of like parts are then filed together.

In order that items can be identified individually and in classes, they must be given symbols, and the symbols and the method of allocating them must satisfy the following requirements:

(1) Provide a logical classification.
(2) Result in a simple and flexible index.
(3) Allow of easy insertion of new classes.

Several forms of symbolisation have been suggested, but generally either alphabetical or numerical ones or a combination of both are found most satisfactory. The following example used in the aircraft industry in this country, taken from B.S. 1100 (page 19), illustrates a method suitable for a single product:

The number is VA521317 but each portion is thought of and spoken of independently, thus: V.A5.21.317.
The first portion V indicates the firm;
The second portion A5 indicates the aircraft type;

The third portion 21 indicates the subassembly;
The fourth portion 317 is the part number.

The part number may be modified to indicate for example the hand of parts, odd numbers being used for left-hand parts and even numbers reserved for right-hand parts.

Another example used an eight-figure code, all figures.

The number of the part is 61012314.
Figure six is the product category;
The second two figures 10 indicate the model;
The fourth and fifth two figures 12 indicate the tonnage in the code.
The last three figures 314 indicate the part number of the model 61012.

Perhaps the best method of all, providing maximum simplification and standardisation, is a decimal classification. For example, in a case where it is desired to file or store all like parts together, irrespective of the model for which they are used, in order to make reference to all such parts quick and complete, the class of part is coded in the first three figures, and the part number by figures following the decimal point, thus:

126·15 represents the 14th design of Part 26 in Group 1 of the firm's products.

If there are more than 99 parts to a group or product, three figures before the point must be used for parts and if the number of products or groups exceeds 9, the number before the point would become 5 figures e.g.: 1101·1, being the first design of part 1 of group or product 11.

Part numbers are allocated in a block to subassemblies. As drawings are filed in numerical order, all designs of the same part are filed together and all associated parts are filed adjacent to each other. From the Drawing Office point of view this is perhaps the most effective way of numbering drawings.

In practice, it is found that a symbol build-up of numbers only is most satisfactory; it can be extremely flexible within wide limits, and leads to less confusion on the telephone than one containing letters, many of which sound similar. Also to most people figures are easier to remember than letters.

Finally, it is good practice and generally accepted nowadays that part numbers and drawing numbers should be identical. This again simplifies identification and aids memorising frequently used parts and saves space and writing on documents. It certainly avoids errors and confusion in the works.

*   *Standardisation*

Standardisation to some extent has become commonplace. Indeed, it is taken for granted, in industry and everyday life. Many objects in common use, the telephone, motor-car, cycle, household articles (particularly electrical ones), boots and shoes, and even the ready-made suit, would not be so cheap as they are, were it not for the extensive, and intensive, use of standardisation. Yet a good deal more could be done to gain the advantages of standardisation both between different firms manufacturing the same product and within individual firms. And the benefits of standardisation begin, and its application for the most part must be worked out in the Design Department. More could be done between firms that make or use intermediate products, e.g. water and steam valves, household plumbing and fittings, books, bottles and similar articles, to ensure that overall sizes which make for interchangeability between one brand and another are standardised. And within a firm it is quite usual to find different draughtsmen designing similar parts for different products with only small differences, when an identical part would be quite satisfactory for both cases. Or again, materials are specified which have to be purchased specially when, with a little thought, a standard material or size in stock could be used.

The advantages of standardisation are:

To the producer:

(1) Bigger production batches and more continuous runs resulting in lower tooling and set-up costs.
(2) Possibility of breaking down operations, of increasing mechanisation and of using special-purpose high-production plant.
(3) Reduction in idle plant, tools and space.
(4) Reduction in stocks of materials, components and finished products.
(5) Reduction in overhead staff costs (drawing, design, planning and clerical).
(6) Less service and maintenance of products.
(7) Possibility of concentrating marketing effort and costs on smaller range.
(8) Generally, increased output and productivity and lower costs.

To the user:

(1) Lower prices.
(2) Interchangeability whatever the supplier.
(3) Improved stocks and supplies, service and maintenance.

It is as well, however, to remember that there are disadvantages, or rather, dangers in standardisation. If carried too far or adhered to too rigidly, it can sterilise design and make desirable or worth-while changes slow in adoption until too late (until, for example, a market is lost. Henry Ford nearly ruined his business by hanging on to his Model T just a shade too long). Standardisation is possible for most articles, the design or performance of which satisfies all normal requirements, e.g. bolts, pipes, roller chain, electric plugs and domestic irons. Complete standardisation is unwise for complex machines like lathes and electric motors, or to tie standardisation of dimensions to performance, when ultimate performance is not known. Furthermore, however desirable it may be to standardise and mass-produce certain articles, there is always a need for a special design for a special purpose. But the firm that adopts as its production policy mass production based on standardisation cannot economically deal with specials—in practice they do not mix—and it may well be that in this country with the accumulated skill and "know how" of generations, with a high level of craftsmanship reinforced by general education, the special product and not the mass-produced one will continue to be the normal, and indeed the most suitable for British manufacturing industries, for a long time to come.

The objects of standardisation are to facilitate the interchangeability of parts and to reduce costs by limiting variations of material, nomenclature, set-up, or process, as far as possible. It can be effectively used in the following wide variety of applications:

Nomenclature.—The sciences are built up on the application of defined terms. Similar precise definitions should be used in all technical work, and this applies particularly in the industrial Design and Technical Departments, and in the case of drawings, specifications and similar documents.

Dimensions.—Standardisation of dimensions and their definition by limiting the variation has become almost universal. By the use of such standards and tolerances and the rejection of parts whose dimensions do not conform to them, interchangeability of parts has become possible. Whitworth started the good work on screw threads, and today most articles and materials in general use, such as sheet metal, wire, rolled-steel sections, commercial stationery, boots and shoes, electric plugs and sockets are standardised as to certain vital dimensions. The method of specifying the desired accuracy of dimensions is dealt with in Chapter V under "Inspection", page 456 [1]

Quality.—Only by the standardisation of quality of raw material can a manufacturer ensure a reliable performance of his product, and without reliability there would neither be the safety nor the absence of trouble and inconvenience which we take so much for granted today. A standard quality is ensured by specifications laying down tests and performance.

[1] British Standards for Workshop Practice B.S. Handbook No. 2.

Tools.—This is a special case of quality, but is of special significance, because without standardisation of tools, interchangeability of parts and standard times and performance would be impossible, and on this depends all planning in factories. It also ensures accuracy of dimensions in such cases as drills for holes and taps and dies for screw threads.

Performances.—This again can be a special case of quality when applied to finished products. Standards for testing ensure that a product will do what it is designed or specified to do within prescribed limits. Standard times are a measure of performance for human operation (see page 302).

Processes.—There is always one best way, and in certain industries like the chemical industry, only one correct way, of doing a job. With standard materials and tools and specifications, methods can be standardised and a uniform product ensured.

Standardisation applied to industry in this country has been developed and organised by the British Standards Institution, which explores the need for, and issues British Standard Specifications in, the following four divisions: Engineering, Building, Chemical and Textile. In recent years the Institution has spread its activities to other industries, for example, clothing, and this widening interest can be expected to continue if the need is there. The activities of the Institution are briefly explained as follows:

"The Institution exists to assist British Industry by preparing British Standard Specifications, of which up to the present over 1,700 have been issued, exclusive of some 300 for Aircraft Materials and Component Parts issued in co-operation with the Air Ministry and with the Society of British Aircraft Constructors.

"The British Standards Specifications are based on what is best in present practice (and do not attempt to attain an ideal which might be too costly to adopt) providing a generally suitable standard of performance, quality, or dimension, and an equitable basis for tendering. They help to eliminate redundant qualities and sizes, and enable manufacturers to provide stock during slack periods and purchasers to obtain their requirements more rapidly. The Specifications are kept up to date; they do not interfere with individual initiation and invention, and they leave the producer as much freedom as possible in his methods of production. Wherever possible, the Specifications deal mainly with performance."

ESTIMATING AND CONTRACTS

Nature of the Activity

Estimating the total cost of a product or a job before manufacture is an activity which is carried on continuously only in those companies who manufacture to customers' special requirements. It is not a continuous activity in companies whose products are completely standard and made for shelf or warehouse stock. This means that it is not usually found in factories manufacturing articles which are eventually bought by the general public, like sewing machines, furniture, food, confectionery and ready-made clothing, but is limited, by and large, to firms making (or repairing) plant and equipment for other manufacturing companies and, of course, civil engineering and public works contracting. Standard products can be costed accurately and the selling price determined for repeat sales, this being varied only according to the quantities ordered or the type of customer and the service he renders to the ultimate consumer. This adjustment of prices is a Sales Department function. But when it is necessary to quote a prospective customer a price for supplying an article, machine, or plant before he is prepared to order (i.e. against an enquiry) some kind of an estimate of the ultimate costs has to be prepared. This can vary from an extraction from previous costs of the cost of each part or item to what may be called "guesstimating"—or intelligent guessing. When preliminary designs are not prepared in detail, the accuracy of the estimate depends on the skill with which the estimator interpolates from records of previous costs. Obviously, the more complete the records and the more effectively they are indexed, the more accurate will be the estimate. It is possible, of course, to estimate each detail, piece by piece, and to build up a complete estimate, but in practice this generally takes too long, and is too expensive, so that something between this and a pure guess is required.

The job of the estimator then is to arrive at as accurate a forecast as possible of the ultimate cost of a product or project before work on it commences or is authorised, and in the shortest time and at a minimum cost.

It is obvious that continually under-estimating will involve the risk of a loss on the year's trading and ultimate financial failure. It is not always realised that over-estimating can be equally serious. It not only loses individual orders, but, by thus limiting or reducing turnover, increases the burden of overheads and particularly of selling and estimating costs (since costs will be absorbed on unfruitful enquiries).

Methods and Practice

As the accurate determination of the correct price to be charged for a standard product is decided from a study of figures prepared by the Cost Department from actually recorded costs, or from a study of the market, we shall deal here only with estimating as it must be carried on in firms which have to quote for special orders.

Customers' Requirements

When dealing with an enquiry, the first and essential job is to find out exactly what the customer wants. This is not always as simple as might be thought. It is very easy for an estimator, experienced in his own firm's usual work and products, to make unwarranted assumptions. Also users of equipment may know what they want in general terms, but not be aware of the need to state certain working conditions or limiting factors. Furthermore, a customer may think he knows what he wants and ask for it, not knowing exactly what is available or what might be more satisfactory for his purpose.

It is very necessary therefore for the estimator to scrutinise the enquiry in detail and with the greatest care, looking for any gaps in the information and doubtful requirements. If in doubt, or if there is any information lacking, he must ask for confirmation before proceeding with the estimate. If there is not time to do this, the assumptions that are made should be noted and explained to the customer with the quotation for confirmation. If the estimator, from his knowledge of the trade or the customer, thinks that the customer really needs something different to fulfil the purpose he has in mind, then it should be suggested, even if it would mean a smaller order or no order at all. There is no sense in selling a customer something which he will later find he does not want, or which is inadequate; good advice given in this way establishes confidence and ensures future enquiries.

Certain standard information may always be required. For example, manufacturers of overhead travelling cranes always require to know, in addition to the weight to be lifted and the span across the track, the speed of lift required, the height, roof clearance, electric supply and atmospheric conditions (if in a foundry or chemical plant or similar situation). In such cases a standard data sheet should be printed, and either filled in by the estimator before beginning his estimate, or sent to the customer immediately on receipt of the enquiry for him to fill in and return. The latter course is advisable if only for confirmation.

Data

The basis of an estimator's work is the cost data. In order to do his job effectively he must have available records of costs, recorded and filed in such a way that they can be simply and rapidly referred to and used. The best method of filing will depend on the kind and extent of the data recorded, but the loose-leaf ring binder is very satisfactory in practice.

It is sometimes suggested that only elementary data is required.

such as for example the times to do operations, labour rates and the cost of materials as bought. These detail facts may be required in rare cases, but to build up estimates in such detail is expensive and usually unnecessary. What is wanted is costs of normal products or parts of them for each size or variation likely to occur, with some indication of extra costs incurred for additional special equipment. Standard costs (see Part Four) are a help with this problem, particularly when a detailed estimate is required.

If standard costs are not available, past costs of whole products (to take crane manufacturers, again, of whole crane) and of parts and normal materials (such as crabs, blocks, carriages, motors and girders) should be recorded. For the whole product and for major sub-assemblies the cost should be plotted on graph paper against the variable factor, horse-power, load, weight, or whatever it is. If there are several variable factors, it will be necessary to plot several graphs. It is not necessary to plot the cost of each value of the variable factor; four or five points will indicate the nature of the curve, which can then be drawn in for other values with sufficient accuracy. The values of costs can be plotted as detailed estimates are made, or better still, from previous actual costs. Gradually, a very comprehensive set of figures can be accumulated from which it is comparatively simple to find the cost for any set of factors, interpolating for values of a variable between those plotted.

Fig. 21 is an example (figures not actual) of the kind of graph referred to. In this case it is assumed that there would be a graph for

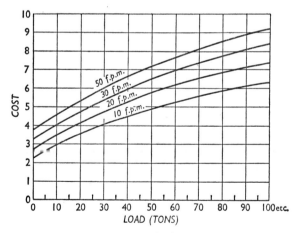

Notes.—Add 10 per cent. for variable speed.
Add £x for each 5 ft. lift above standard (15 ft.)

FIG. 21.—Cost Chart for Estimating.

each major subassembly and a set of curves for each type of each subassembly. The important thing is to find the variable factors against which the cost varies in a uniform manner; in the case of structural steelwork of a standard design it may be weight, for packing-cases superficial area, for electric motors horse-power, and so on.

In addition to such records of costs, it is necessary to have recorded information concerning limiting factors of the works plant capacity. The works will be able to handle production within a certain range without abnormal arrangements or equipment, but outside these limits, usually above a certain size or weight, it is impossible to produce, or special arrangements have to be made. For example, the kinds of limiting factors often overlooked, with disturbing results in the factory, are the maximum lifting capacity of cranes (and subassemblies or parts of special machines may be above this capacity), the size of machine tools, particularly the swing of lathes or the table of boring machines, the size of doorways or exits from erecting shops. It is essential to note all such capacities, and whenever an estimate is being considered for something outside previous experience, all unusual features must be examined for such snags.

Co-operation with Other Departments

It is most essential that, when a new type of job or one outside previous experience is being considered, special features should be referred to other departments interested, if there is the least doubt in the estimator's mind as to whether he has accurate information. The Production or Methods Engineers should be consulted whenever there is any question of tooling or special processes, and the Drawing Office if the design is unusual in any way. If tools and drawings are included as a direct charge in the estimate and it has not been possible to plot costs for reference purposes, these departments should be asked for their estimate. If this is normal procedure, a standard form can be used, relevant information being filled in by the estimator and sent to each department for completion and return. These departments should also be consulted on the delivery period to be quoted if special drawings, tools, or methods are required, unless the Planning Department are entirely responsible for progress through these departments as well as for production programmes.

A close liaison must also be maintained with the Sales Department and technical engineers or representatives. They are likely to be able to interpret a customer's real requirements when these are stated ambiguously in the enquiry, and can decide the best way to approach the customer if it is considered desirable to suggest an alternative or modified product. In many cases correspondence and contacts of this nature with the customer must go through the sales channels.

Delivery Dates

When new orders take their place immediately at the end of the queue or order book, there is usually no difficulty in deciding on what delivery to quote. The period is arrived at by dividing the total orders on hand measured in £ *s. d.* or some unit of volume by the works capacity per week in the same unit. This may be done for all products or each particular type according to whether each type is limited to the same rate of output or not. This measure can be in terms of value, volume, man-hours, or whatever unit is found to be sufficiently accurate; sales value is obviously the simplest and is often adequate, but it frequently does not accurately represent works capacity (or the varying proportion of bought-out parts or materials per pound of sales value and varying profit margins make it an inaccurate measure).

When, however, orders are booked for delivery at a definite time and some of the dates are beyond the period when all orders on the books could be completed at normal output rate, obviously some orders can be completed earlier. It is then not so easy to determine exactly when an order can be delivered, i.e. to know for what periods the works capacity is booked. The Planning Department will have this information, of course, and will have to be referred to if departmental detail programmes must be consulted. If, however, it is possible to allocate capacity in terms of a unit (value or some unit of volume), a simple production chart can be constructed. Production periods are marked off horizontally on a time scale. The capacity absorbed by orders already booked in each production period (week or month) is marked off vertically on the scale of unit of capacity. A line is drawn horizontally at the level of the capacity absorbed (with steps for planned increases or decreases). This should be corrected weekly or monthly and will show at a glance in what periods capacity is available and how much.

Whatever method is adopted, it is essential for all delivery promises to be made in line with the Planning Department programmes, or on a basis agreed by them and confirmed periodically.

Final Build-up of Estimate

The method of finally building up the estimate to include all charges, works overhead, administrative selling and profit margin, should be agreed upon with the accountant. Because the estimator cannot be expected to have the broad view of affairs and of sales policy in particular which is necessary in dealing with estimates, the estimator is sometimes only permitted to build up to the total works cost, or perhaps total cost, but not selling price, the final margin being added either by the Sales or General Manager. In many cases, however, the estimator compiles the final selling prices. When the appropriate overhead expenses and profit margin have been added (if not already included in the synthetic cost data) to make the selling price, it is advisable in any case for the final estimate or tender to be confirmed either by the Sales Manager or General Manager. To reduce the work on senior executives which this may involve, small tenders below a stated value can be sent to customers without reference, those above a high value referred to the General Manager and those in between to the Sales Manager. In practice, it is sometimes found necessary to vary the profit margin or the competitive strength of the price as a measure of selective selling. In times of depression and when orders at normal prices for any reason do not fill the works to capacity, it may be sound management to take work at little or no profit to help to carry the standing charges or overheads. On the other hand, because of inadequate plant, unwillingness to lock up a large part of works capacity, or for other commercial reasons, it may be desired to ward off certain orders unless an unusually high margin is considered to override such considerations. Only the General Manager is in a position to decide such matters.

An effective method of adjusting the selling price to attract or repel orders according to their material or labour content is to add different profit margins to each element of total cost, adding a higher percentage to that element which is in short supply. If, for example, an average profit margin on cost of 15 per cent. (13 per cent, on selling price) is required, material is on the average 70 per cent. and labour 30 per cent. of total direct cost, and it is desired to attract orders with a low rather than a high proportion of labour content, the following differential margins could be used:

Material	.	plus 11 per cent.
Labour	.	plus 25 per cent.
Overheads	.	plus 15 per cent.

This would yield 15·2 per cent. on total cost when material and labour are in the normal proportion, since:

11 per cent. of 70 per cent.	.	.	7·7 per cent.
25 per cent. of 30 per cent.	.	.	7·5 per cent.
			15·2 per cent.

But when the labour content is high, say 50 per cent. of direct cost, then the total margin would be:

11 per cent. of 50 per cent.	.	.	5·5 per cent.
25 per cent. of 50 per cent.	.	.	12·5 per cent.
			18·0 per cent.

which is higher than normal, and would tend to make such orders more uncompetitive. The total margin can be divided so as to attain the selection of orders desired.

Tenders

A tender or quotation is a written offer to do a certain amount of stated work or supply certain goods at a definite price and in accordance with stated conditions. Such a tender or quotation, when accepted by letter, note, or order, constitutes a contract in law. It is clearly set out and conditions clearly defined. Such conditions should be reasonable in character and stated in terms as precise and unambiguous as possible to avoid dispute and legal action. Simple English should be used as far as possible, and the long sentence with too many qualifying phrases avoided. It is not possible to cover here all the information, terms and conditions which at times have to be covered, but the following are the more generally used. Model forms of contract and tender can be obtained from most trade associations and professional institutions.

Specification.—The goods, work, or services to be supplied should be precisely stated by the use of a standard form of specification where possible. Outline drawings may have to be included if certain overall dimensions have to be adhered to. The specification must include limiting figures for performance and duty.

Price.—The net price must be stated and any discounts allowed. Terms of payment must also be stated; for large installations part payment on delivery or during erection may be required.

During times when costs are fluctuating (particularly rising) rapidly, as during and after the last war, the right is claimed to adjust prices to costs ruling at the time of dispatch. It is not a very commercially sound practice in normal times.

Delivery.—It should be made clear whether the delivery date is when it leaves the works or is delivered to customer.

Inspection.—The right or necessity for the customer to inspect may need to be specified.

Guarantee.—Any actual or implied guarantee should be most clearly defined. This question is a prolific source of dispute. The responsibility for equipment included, but bought from other manufacturers, should be made clear. Often the final supplier disclaims responsibility. Service for a limited period is sometimes included in the contract price; if so, the precise nature or limitation of such service should be defined.

Penalties for Non-fulfilment.—If any penalty for the non-fulfilment of any part of the contract is accepted, it should be most precisely defined, as dispute can easily arise and legal action follow any non-fulfilment under penalty.

Conditions Specified in Order.—Any conditions which have been stated or referred to by the customer in his enquiry or order must be specifically referred to in the tender; such conditions must be either accepted or repudiated.

RESEARCH AND DEVELOPMENT

A business cannot stand still: it must either develop or perish. There is no permanence or security in self-satisfaction. If a company for long remains satisfied with its products or productivity, it becomes moribund, and ultimately goes out of business or becomes absorbed by a more successful competitor. To flourish, a company must continually improve its products or services or develop new ones, and to do this it must not only be receptive to new ideas, it must continually search for and develop new materials, new methods and new products. This process of research and development is a specialised activity, it must be recognised as such and not just left to the spare-time activity of those who happen to be interested in it. Whilst some discoveries of value have been accidental, most have been the result of thorough and painstaking experimental work, and certainly the development of most new ideas to successful production has meant continuous and purposive application of time and ingenuity. Rule of thumb and trial and error can find the solution to development problems, but they are expensive and uncertain methods. Results are more reliable and less costly if development is organised scientifically. In those firms who do keep abreast of the times, development of some kind or another is always going on, but it is frequently not recognised as a definite or separate activity, nor is it consciously or continuously directed by anyone. Consequently, it is much less effective than it could be; progress is haphazard and results patchy. Moreover, experimental work that is carried out in the shops by foremen or operators on production does not get the concentrated attention it requires, is not likely to be scientifically carried out, and anyway interferes with the main activity of production.

This all means that development should be conceived of as a whole and should be the responsibility of a single individual in a concern who is (or is responsible to) the chief technical executive. It may be convenient to have experimental sections of the works responsible to the works executives, but the responsibility for development work as a whole, its conception, planning and results, should be the responsibility of the technical department. In fairly large firms, there is likely to be experimental work of one kind or another being carried on in several departments or divisions of the organisation, the design department experimenting with new products, the production engineers or toolroom developing new tools or machines, and production seeking for ways to improve processes. Each of these activities is development work, differing only in the matter of process, but not in the nature of the activity. On the other hand, all development work involves three stages:

First, research, either fundamental, seeking to find the fundamental laws of cause and effect and seeking knowledge for its own sake with little thought for what the results may be, or applied, finding ways of applying these laws to practical purposes.

Second, experimental and development work, in which the findings of research are developed and proved on a practical scale, on pilot plants or prototypes.

Third, the initiation of full-scale production and as a service to production.

If there is any need to divide up the activities of development work because of its scope or the size of the organisation, it is more correct to do so on the basis of these three stages, research, prototype or experimental, and process assistance, than to do so according to the type of work.

It is vital therefore that this important development activity should be controlled and staffed by men with good scientific training and experience; it is not only knowledge, but also the ability to comprehend the possibilities of new knowledge and to carry out scientific investigations that are essential. Development work properly coordinated in all its stages and imaginatively directed can then be of immense value to any company.

Obviously small companies are likely to find it impossible to conduct fundamental and original research work and must rely on bodies like the Universities, the Department of Scientific and Industrial Research and trade research associations and laboratories for such work. More support to and use of all these bodies could quite well be given by industrial firms, particularly the smaller ones who are unable to undertake research work on their own account. Some firms make arrangements for a University to do their research work for them, and others, particularly in areas where there is a local industry, are encouraging the technical colleges to help.[1] Whatever the assistance gained through these means in basic research, companies should carry out, or commission on their own behalf, development work aimed at improving their products or services and their tools and processes. In development work connected with a company's products, it is essential for the development engineers and chemists

---

[1] This subject is further considered in Chapter III of Part Five of this volume, where the services of the Department of Scientific and Industrial Research through the various trade and product associations are also described.

to work in close co-operation with the sales or marketing staff; indeed, most of the investigations which they will be called upon to make will arise from market research or investigations. Similarly, close co-operation and active collaboration with both production staff and production engineers are essential.

It is sometimes recommended that development and experimental work should be made to pay for itself in terms of yearly economies or profits. This is a mistake. It usually results, and inevitably must tend to do, in too careful a selection of the work undertaken and a reluctance to take a long view. This is understandable, since only the chief executive or the Directors are in possession of all the relevant facts to be able to take the long view and to assess the probable value of such work. Its actual value can rarely be accurately assessed in advance; it is seldom possible to calculate even the actual return on costs incurred. Nevertheless, such work can of course absorb too high a proportion of available resources, and this should be guarded against by budgeting of expenditure.

Finally, it should be remembered that employees in the production departments are always interested in development and the experimental department, and anything which can be done to encourage and satisfy this interest in the firm's products and affairs is sound management. The results, therefore, of research, experimental and development work which are applied in the factory or incorporated in the firm's products should be explained to all employees and particularly to those closely involved.

A word of warning is called for against the tendency for the Managing Director of a small firm, who is usually the proprietor as well, to be too actively associated with research. It is a common weakness where the proprietor has built up the business around his own technical knowledge or skill. But when the business is big enough to require the usual four or five senior executives, if a Managing Director continues to be actively interested in detail research, it inevitably results in his devoting too much time to the subject to the detriment of "general management". If the Managing Director has peculiar abilities or knowledge which make it advisable for him to direct technical and development work, the solution may be to appoint a staff assistant to relieve him of detail work, but to work under his immediate supervision, or to appoint a General Manager responsible to him for all other activities except technical. The danger must still be avoided of such work absorbing a disproportionate amount of the Managing Director's time.

CHAPTER III

PRODUCTION ADMINISTRATION

IT was shown in Chapter I that one activity of the administrative side of production is concerned with determining the most practicable and economical way to do all jobs. No longer is this left to the skilled and interested operator, proceeding by trial and error, successive operators making the same trials and the same errors to arrive at the same, or sometimes a different, result. As more machines, tools and equipment, some of them highly specialised, have been designed and become available, and new materials and processes developed, it has become increasingly a skilled technical job to keep abreast of developments and always to know the up-to-date or best way to do a job. It would be quite impossible today for the craftsman at the bench or machine to keep himself adequately informed and to do a job of producing as well. Skilled men are still required, but managers find under present-day conditions that these men need to be supported or supplemented by specialists, such as machine-setters, maintenance fitters or production engineers.

PRODUCTION ENGINEERING

The old type of foreman is apt to think that the appointment of a production engineer, process engineer, or chemist, reduces his usefulness, his value to the company, or his status. It does nothing of the kind, of course. It is true that, before the development of production engineering, and the use of chemists in the works as well as in the analytical laboratory, the Works Manager and his foreman supplied the production "know-how", and decided how a job should be done. But it is now recognised that the training and supervising of persons is a much more complex job than it once was, and to relieve a foreman of a large amount of administrative work makes a higher general performance possible and his job more valuable, not less. It is essential to separate planning from doing, administration from execution.

When a new material is developed or a new product designed, the method of production is obviously either known or worked out. But from then onwards all is change. Better methods of production are being discovered continually. Furthermore, in many factories, particularly those engaged in engineering, the detailed method of production for each part to be manufactured, the machines to be used and equipment required, is decided subsequent to design. The task of deciding the best method of production, of saying how a job shall be produced, and of finding new and better ways of doing so, should be the responsibility of a Methods or Production Engineering Department. In a company where the technical knowledge is supplied by chemists, production methods would be the responsibility of the works laboratory.

In deciding the most practical and economical way of doing a job, the production engineer or chemist must have regard for the costs of production, and therefore for the time to do the job. He must have some say also in new tools or equipment required. These are the three divisions into which the activities of the production or methods engineer usually fall—that is to say, method study, work measurement and tool or equipment design.

These three aspects all call for close collaboration with the Technical and Works departments. The design of jigs and tools might be thought to be a logical development of the Design or Drawing Office work and in some companies it is done in the Drawing Office. But it cannot be effectively developed without detailed study of methods and work being done in the factory, and, as will be shown later, this study forms the basis of standards for time, and hence for payment by results, production planning and costs. This study work calls for a specialised technique and training quite different from Drawing Office work. The outlook required is different too. It is more successful in practice, therefore, if it is recognised as a separate activity, and combined with the design of tools and equipment. To avoid it becoming too remote from or independent of the Drawing Office, Design Department or Technical Department, new drawings, designs or technical developments should always be referred to, and discussed with, the production engineers before final issue.

The development of production engineering as a special skill and the extensive use of specially designed tools and equipment have contributed largely to the very much greater output per man-hour in the U.S.A. than in this country. There is no doubt that it is through such development, adding horse-power to man-power, and taking out the manual effort from jobs, that the way lies to reduce man-hour requirements.

"The records of the United States and the United Kingdom have demonstrated that over a period of many years productivity in industry bears an important relationship to the amount of energy which is available per employee. In the U.S.A. the figure is approximately twice that in the U.K. This fact, in our opinion, accounts in large measure for the greater output per man-hour in many industries in the U.S."[1]

Because production engineers tend to get machine or gadget minded there is a danger that they will forget or neglect the human factor. Men should not be made into robots. The foremen may have something to say if the division of labour, for example, is carried too far, or if new methods are forced on them without consultation. Continued and close co-operation between the production engineers and works departments is absolutely essential.

Broadly, then, the function of the Production Engineering or Methods Department is to determine, in collaboration with the Design and Works Departments, the most effective, economical and suitable methods of production, to lay down standards for material and time, and to design special tools and equipment required. The following can be taken as typical of the responsibilities of the head of the department:

(1) Scientifically investigate processes and operations in order to:
    (a) Establish the correct way of carrying out processes and of performing operations.
    (b) Eliminate unnecessary and ineffectual operations.
    (c) Reduce operators' fatigue to a minimum.
(2) Obtain and if necessary prepare drawings for all jigs, tools and inspection equipment.
(3) Carry out studies to determine the amount of work involved in operations.
(4) Establish standard times which, when used as a wage incentive, will enable an average qualified operator, working well within his or her capacity, to earn at least the standard amount of bonus agreed between the operators and management, including an appropriate allowance for rest and fatigue.
(5) Collect, collate and file data relating to operation times to enable standard times to be rapidly and easily prepared.
(6) Investigate and report when required on all forms of excess cost.
(7) Establish and cultivate mutual confidence between the department's staff and supervisors and operators
(8) Adhere to the Company's personnel policy and see that subordinates do so.
(9) Train staff in the effective performance of their duties.
(10) Keep abreast of modern developments in manufacturing methods of all kinds, but particularly where related to the manufacture of the Company's products. In particular, recommend to the management the purchase of modern or improved designs of machines which will improve production, or reduce costs.

[1] *The First Report of the Anglo-American Council of Productivity.*

WORK STUDY

Man has always been interested in better or easier ways of doing things since he first thought of the wheel and cart to help him carry loads. The present industrial civilisation is the result of finding easier and quicker ways of doing work. Until a comparatively few years ago, however, man mainly concentrated on designing equipment and mechanism to save hard work. It is only in recent years that men, chiefly engineers, have studied the ways men do the jobs that men, and not machines, must do. F. W. Taylor, who established and popularised the scientific approach to this matter, began his studies into better methods of doing work in the Midvale Steel Works in the 1880s. Taylor was appointed, at an early age of twenty-four or so, chargehand of the lathe operators in the factory. He soon realised that the men were not giving an output that he knew was reasonable and easily attainable, and at first he had to use the disciplinary methods customary in those days (and for many years since). He discovered, however (and Taylor was a searcher for facts and reasons), that the difficulty and disagreements generally encountered lay in different ideas, rather abstract ideas, which everyone had of what constituted a "fair day's work". No one really did know in fact what did constitute a "fair day's work". He realised that if it were possible to find a way of measuring this abstract value in terms which had a basis in fact and could be understood, then most of the bitterness and mistrust would be eliminated. He determined to find a way, and adopted the scientific approach to the problem. He began a series of carefully controlled and recorded experiments on lathes, and started on his career of work study and scientific management.

"Taylor started with an individual worker at a lathe, started, as the trained research worker starts, to find out all about it, to observe what he was doing and leaving undone, to analyse and to measure every factor in his task which could be made susceptible to measurement. In short, he began to build up a 'science' of cutting metals on a lathe. Gradually he isolated the various elements and set to work to improve the factors which made for high performance, to eliminate causes of delay and interruption, to reduce the craft of the tradesman to precise and detailed written instructions."[1]

In addition to discovering exactly what the work content of a job in the lathe was, he discovered then that there were certain factors which affected total output. The method adopted by different operators for doing the same job varied—there was no one best way—and operators lost a good deal of time experimenting and trying out various ways themselves. In addition, planning of work and flow of

[1] *The Making of Scientific Management*, Vol. I, by Urwick and Brech, page 30.

material was uncertain, and caused a good deal of waste of time. Both these factors are management's problems; they are, in fact, the major part of management's administrative task.

It is a long time since Taylor made this approach to the study of the work content of a job and of factors affecting it, and today there can be no doubt that the scientific approach and the establishment of the one best way under correct conditions is essential to obtain a measure that is factual and will be accepted by the operators concerned of what constitutes a "fair day's work".

It is possible to say with reasonable accuracy exactly how many parts an automatic machine will produce per hour; the designer or machine setter can state precisely the rate of output of, e.g. a cigarette-making machine, an automatic machine producing screws, a printing machine, or an automatic loom on a given weave. But how many articles will be produced in a day or a week in a given factory; how many looms or automatic screw machines can an operator look after, and how many cigarettes can be made by hand per hour, chocolates wrapped, orders packed, or customers served in a Department Store? You will notice that the question is, how many *can*, not how many *are*. The answer to these questions can only be obtained with any degree of accuracy by studying the work being done, at the time it is done, the effort required, and the skill of the operators, and including in the study the conditions under which it is or may be done, and delays that may occur. It is not sufficient to take an average of past performance, to ask the operator or the foreman, or to take a spot check. That may tell us how many are being done, but it will not tell us how many can be done. Only *Work Study* can do that.

Furthermore, there are few methods of doing jobs which cannot be improved upon, however much they have been developed and however well they are being done today. New materials, new techniques, new equipment are being developed continually. Filling powder by scoop or chute was a slow as well as a dusty job until someone studying the dust problem remembered that fluids are filled by vacuum; insulation materials were cut by hand with scissors until someone studying how to increase production remembered how printers cut paper and cardboard to shape. Unexpected, and often substantial, improvements in output can frequently be obtained by objectively studying the way work is done with the aim of finding what is the best and quickest way to do it. It applies equally as well in the offices as in the works.

Gilbreth, the pioneer of motion study, who devoted the greater part of his career to the search for "the one best way to do work", was able quite early in his search to eliminate unnecessary movement and effort from bricklaying in the U.S.A., and obtained outputs, *without undue fatigue,* which skilled bricklayers in England consider impossible nearly fifty years later.

"Even in his very early days the results that Gilbreth achieved were remarkable. Thus, for instance, the work of bricklaying was so simplified that the eighteen motions formerly thought necessary to place a brick were reduced to four or five, and, indeed, in one case, to two. Those which remained were made as simple and effective as thorough study could make them. The final result was that Gilbreth's men, who had formerly worked to their limit to lay 1,000 bricks per day, were able, after a short period of instruction, to reach a daily output of 2,700."[1]

The daily approved output in England today is somewhere between 400 and 800!

Definitions of Terms Used

There has been a considerable lack of uniformity in terminology used in the field of work study and this has led to much misunderstanding. To avoid this it is necessary to define certain of the more frequently used terms. The following are definitions of terms as used and understood by authoritative workers in the field; they accord closely with the British Standard Glossary of Terms in Work Study (B.S. 3138:1959).

Work Study

Work Study is a tool or technique of management involving the analytical study of a job or operation for one or both of the following purposes:

(a) The determination of what exactly has to be done; what are the optimum conditions—methods, layout, batch size and equipment, and what cause of ineffective work can be removed.

(b) The measurement of the work content of the job for use in planning, costing, wage payment (incentive) and control.

Standard Time

The total time which would be taken to do a job or operation by an average qualified operator at a standard rate of working (i.e. standard performance), including allowances for fatigue and contingencies. This involves a definition of standard performance which is dealt with in detail later.

---

[1] *The Making of Scientific Management,* Vol. I, by Urwick and Brech, page 138.

Rating

A method of assessment (or numerical value of such assessment) of the observed actual rate of working or performance of an operator in relation to a concept of standard performance. It takes into account such factors as speed of movement, effort, dexterity and consistency.

Three different scales are in use: 60/80; 75/100; 100/133; the two numerical values representing what is commonly accepted in practice as equivalent to a "daywork" and a "piecework" level of performance respectively.

Job Evaluation

Methods of determining the relative worth of jobs on some scale usually by an analysis of the content of jobs under classified headings.

Merit Rating

Systematic and as far as possible objective, relative assessment of the behaviour, quality or value of employees by an analysis of classified characteristics, e.g. reliability, versatility, etc.

Method Study

Systematic observation, recording, analysis and critical examination of existing and proposed methods of doing work, the development of improved, easier and more effective methods, and the assessment of the effectiveness of revised methods, including layout, handling and flow.

Motion Study

Synonymous with Method Study—(though often used for detailed study of bodily movements in human effort).

Micromotion Study

More detailed study of finely divided elements of bodily movements in human effort based on an elaborate technique of analysis in terms of therbligs using ciné cameras, charts and counters.

Time Study

Systematic observation, recording and analysis of the times taken to do a specified job or operation or part of an operation, under specified conditions, at the same time assessing the rate of working or performance of the operator in order to establish the time necessary to do the work at a defined standard of performance.

Work Measurement

The application of techniques for establishing a standard time for a normally qualified operator to do a specific job at a defined standard of performance.

Rate Fixing

Rate fixing is a term used for the rather approximate or workshop method of setting a time or piece-rate for a job. It aims at setting a task or rate for a job as it is currently being performed with only an approximate allowance for ignorance to cover all factors likely to affect the actual time (including delays which should be prevented from occurring).

What is the Need for Work Study?

No one will deny the need to increase production per man-hour, now and always; only by so doing can we continually increase our standard of living. In order to do so, all wasteful, ineffective and unnecessary work or effort must be eliminated, and the only way to be sure of doing this is to study the work situation, establish the most practicable method, and standardise the method for future reference and training. Having established the work to be done and the way to do it, management must measure the amount of work involved. This measure is required for planning, and for control (see "Labour Cost Control", Part Four), and it can be used for payment by results. A measure which is a guess is no use for planning or control, a measure which is inaccurate is unfair to both operator and Company and leads to suspicion and distrust, and a measure which does not exclude ineffective work is uneconomic: to get an accurate measure requires scientific work study.

The effective use of Work Study can make very considerable savings in production costs. It is quite usual for output to be increased 25 per cent. or more when it is first applied, and for further increases to be repeatedly realised. By its use companies have avoided the considerable cost of new buildings and plant by increasing capacity of existing facilities and labour. It has made unexpected savings in companies already efficient and is equally effective in jobbing and batch production as in mass production, perhaps more so. Always the improvements and savings achieved much more than offset the trouble and cost incurred. Work Study as a permanent feature of enlightened management will go a long way to ensuring a continual increase in productivity.

This does not mean that economical production is impossible without Work Study or that any kind of diagnostic study is a cure-all for inefficiency. Nothing is more effective than high morale; and small units can be, and frequently are, more efficient, because they are more personal than big concerns, have a higher morale, and because all workers in them, from the manager down, feel a personal interest in their success. On the other hand, Work Study does *not* produce goods; it provides information and reveals inefficiency, but operators must still produce and management manage. The most modern tools and methods will not avail under poor management and low morale.

It will be noticed that we said Work Study *can* be used for payment by results. Payment by results is impossible without some kind of work measurement and unsatisfactory without accurate measurement, but the absence of piecework or other form of payment by results does not mean that work study is not required. If anything, it is then even more necessary. The mere measurement of production and work done, and publication of the results, has a beneficial effect on daywork shops, and anyway some form of planning and control is essential. It is always essential to improve and standardise methods and reduce ineffective and unnecessary work whatever the method of payment. But having obtained a reliable measurement of work, it might just as well be used for payment by results. Under good management a fair and equitable financial reward for work done is a powerful incentive to maintain a high output.

All too often times or rates for jobs are fixed by men appointed straight from the machine or bench, without any training and little knowledge of the subject and given the title of Ratefixer or Time Study Engineer. With some knowledge of the processes they go on to the job, make sure that it is being done correctly in their estimation, and proceed to record the time for doing the job a dozen or so times. An attempt is usually made to find an average operator (though none exists in this context) or a normally skilled one. A floor-to-floor time being found, an allowance (the same for all jobs and often too little) is made for fatigue and incidental delays, and a time or rate for the job fixed. This is not Work Study nor Time Study; it may be ratefixing. It usually gives rise to bargaining with operators so that a rate is first fixed which is known to be low, and when the operators claim a rate known to be high, a compromise somewhere near normal is accepted. This procedure misses altogether the real value of Work Study, which is the improvement of existing methods and the revelation of where and how management can reduce delays and unnecessary effort.

It is important to consider the operators' point of view and their reaction to Work Study; after all, they are the persons most affected, and without their co-operation, understanding and support it will not succeed as it should. There has been and still is a good deal of opposition to it, based mainly on the fear of consequent unemployment and the reputation gained by the early efforts of "efficiency experts" who rode roughshod over workers' feelings and over Unions, without the elementary courtesy of explaining fully to the persons most affected what it all meant and what was its purpose. The operator stands to gain appreciably from the sympathetic application of work study. In the first place, it reveals where unnecessary effort is being used and where operating conditions are unsatisfactory. It is also a measure of protection to operators on piecework or other method of payment by results, because, in obtaining a fair and accurate measure of the work to be done and laying down the method, conditions and standards to be maintained, it:

Ensures equality of reward for the same skill and effort, whatever the job.

Ensures that adequate time is allowed for relaxation and all personal needs.

Establishes a standard price or rate for a job which cannot then be cut.

Avoids delays and the consequent frustration and loss of earnings.

It is sometimes thought that the main or only object of Work Study is to increase output by making operators work harder, but this is not true. Actually, performance and output can be improved by:

Improving conditions, methods, tools, or layout.

Eliminating ineffective work and movement.

Ensuring better balance between operators, groups, or machines.

Better services (labouring, etc.).

Ensuring a steady flow of material and jobs to do (planning).

None of these items calls for more effort from the operator; they do call for a good deal more attention and effort from managements. It is along these lines that any substantial increase in output can be obtained.

There are two distinct, though inter-related phases of Work Study:

To determine the correct or most effective way of doing a job, i.e. Determination of Method, or more usually Method Study.

To establish the standard time for doing it, i.e. Work Measurement.

to which is usually, though not necessarily, added:

Evaluation of the standard time for wages purposes where the times are to be used for financial incentives.

METHOD STUDY

Method Study is the first stage of Work Study. It aims, by systematic observation and analysis of existing or proposed methods, to find the most practicable and most effective way of doing a job. It can be and has been successfully used not only for the improvement of industrial operations, but also for the design and layout of buildings, the operation of retail stores, and in offices and canteens. In industrial production it should always be used before a new design is put into production, and should be allowed to influence design, in the interests of economical production, as long as it does not conflict with the customers requirements or the essential performance of the product.

The department responsible for Method Study should not only be concerned with jobs, operations, and processes already in production, but also with new designs and new jobs before they are issued for production. Economical production or operation, the broad purpose of an industrial organisation, is influenced by all the following factors—Design, Material, Labour, Equipment, Methods and Quality Standards. Whilst a Work Study or Production Engineering Department may only be responsible for methods and probably equipment, it should certainly be allowed to offer comments and criticisms of all the other factors. All new designs, processes or operations should be vetted by this department, for it is at the drawing board or design stage that the greatest economies can often be made. Integration of ideas at this stage ensures that maximum advantage is taken of standardisation (page 266) and modern methods of manufacture.

The study of existing methods is undertaken in three broadly different circumstances:

To improve the present or establish the correct method for an existing job or process.

To improve methods generally.

To establish data from which process layouts and standard times can be pre-determined synthetically (see page 326).

This always involves the investigation of and improvement of existing methods.

When establishing the correct method for an existing job the amount of material and labour involved will obviously determine how detailed and intensive the study must be. In mass production or continuous processes, however small the part or operation, detailed study work is justified. The aim is to establish the most practical and economical method, to standardise this, and to install it, if necessary ensuring that someone is trained in its performance. It involves determining the standard time for the job.

In other cases a general study is made by department or by product in order to establish:

What operations are used from time to time, which are necessary, and the best method of doing them.

Machines, tools and equipment available or required, and their capacities and limitations.

Incidental operations and interferences, and their frequency.

What service work is required and who does or should do it.

The standard time for each operation and element of operations.

The scientific application of Method Study involves four stages:

Observation—diagnosis of situation, getting facts, and recording information.

Analysis—critical scrutiny of records, interpreting results and implications, and checking need for possible improvements of existing method.

Established Standards—methods, quality and procedures for maintaining them.

Install new methods and check against standards.

A number of techniques have been developed to facilitate both the recording and the later analysis of the information recorded. In addition to the following, which are in general use, cine-cameras are used for detailed motion study, and permanent recording of operations and motions.[1]

Symbols.—When recording a mass of information, it saves time and facilitates recognition if very frequently used terms are indicated by symbols. The following have been found to be most useful in practice:

○ Operation

➡ Transport

▽ Permanent Storage

▽ Temporary Storage

☐ Inspection

◑ Delay or Idle Time

Others can be used, but these are sufficient for most purposes.

Process Charts.—These show a sequence of events diagrammatically by means of symbols to help a person visualise a process or

---

[1] Examples and a more detailed description of analysis work are given by Ralph Barnes in his book *Motion and Time Study* (published by John Wiley & Sons, Inc., New York, Chapman & Hall, Ltd., London), and also in *Methods Time Measurement* by Maynard, Stegmorton and Schwab (published by McGraw-Hill).

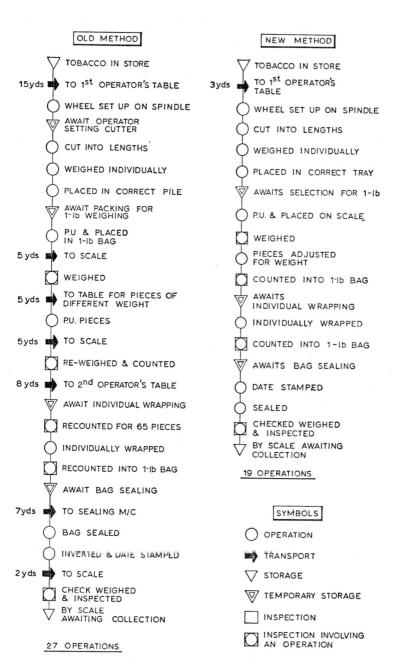

FIG. 22.—Material Process Chart. Cutting, weighing and packing tobacco.

291

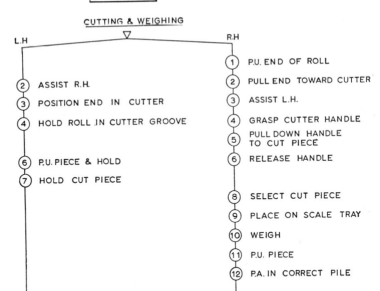

OLD METHOD

CUTTING & WEIGHING

L.H ▽ R.H

R.H
1. P.U. END OF ROLL
2. PULL END TOWARD CUTTER
3. ASSIST L.H.
4. GRASP CUTTER HANDLE
5. PULL DOWN HANDLE TO CUT PIECE
6. RELEASE HANDLE

8. SELECT CUT PIECE
9. PLACE ON SCALE TRAY
10. WEIGH
11. P.U. PIECE
12. P.A. IN CORRECT PILE

L.H
2. ASSIST R.H.
3. POSITION END IN CUTTER
4. HOLD ROLL IN CUTTER GROOVE

6. P.U. PIECE & HOLD
7. HOLD CUT PIECE

▽
12 OPERATIONS

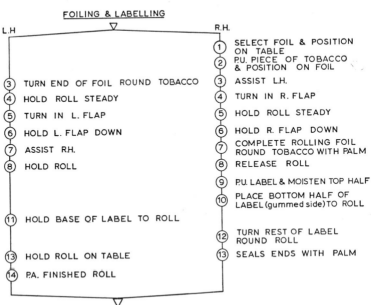

FOILING & LABELLING

L.H ▽ R.H.

R.H.
1. SELECT FOIL & POSITION ON TABLE
2. P.U. PIECE OF TOBACCO & POSITION ON FOIL
3. ASSIST L.H.
4. TURN IN R. FLAP
5. HOLD ROLL STEADY
6. HOLD R. FLAP DOWN
7. COMPLETE ROLLING FOIL ROUND TOBACCO WITH PALM
8. RELEASE ROLL
9. P.U. LABEL & MOISTEN TOP HALF
10. PLACE BOTTOM HALF OF LABEL (gummed side) TO ROLL

12. TURN REST OF LABEL ROUND ROLL
13. SEALS ENDS WITH PALM

L.H
3. TURN END OF FOIL ROUND TOBACCO
4. HOLD ROLL STEADY
5. TURN IN L. FLAP
6. HOLD L. FLAP DOWN
7. ASSIST R.H.
8. HOLD ROLL

11. HOLD BASE OF LABEL TO ROLL

13. HOLD ROLL ON TABLE
14. P.A. FINISHED ROLL

▽
14 OPERATIONS

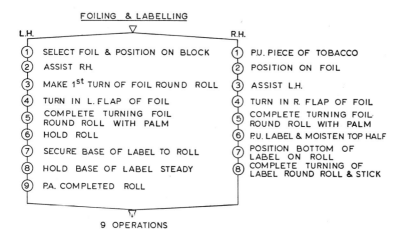

NEW METHOD

CUTTING & WEIGHING

L.H.   ▽   R.H.

                                        (1) P.U. END OF ROLL

(2) ASSIST R.H.   (2) POSITION IN CUTTER

(3) HOLD ROLL STEADY   (3) GRASP CUTTER HANDLE & CUT

(4) REMOVE WEIGHED PIECE   (4) P.U. CUT PIECE

(5) P.A. WEIGHED PIECE   (5) PLACE ON SCALE

▽

5 OPERATIONS

FOILING & LABELLING

L.H.   ▽   R.H.

(1) SELECT FOIL & POSITION ON BLOCK   (1) P.U. PIECE OF TOBACCO

(2) ASSIST R.H.   (2) POSITION ON FOIL

(3) MAKE 1st TURN OF FOIL ROUND ROLL   (3) ASSIST L.H.

(4) TURN IN L. FLAP OF FOIL   (4) TURN IN R. FLAP OF FOIL

(5) COMPLETE TURNING FOIL   (5) COMPLETE TURNING FOIL
      ROUND ROLL WITH PALM   ROUND ROLL WITH PALM

(6) HOLD ROLL   (6) P.U. LABEL & MOISTEN TOP HALF

(7) SECURE BASE OF LABEL TO ROLL   (7) POSITION BOTTOM OF
                                                LABEL ON ROLL

(8) HOLD BASE OF LABEL STEADY   (8) COMPLETE TURNING OF
                                                LABEL ROUND ROLL & STICK

(9) P.A. COMPLETED ROLL

▽

9 OPERATIONS

Fig. 23.—Operator Process Chart, cutting, weighing and packing tobacco.

293

operation as a means of examining it and improving it. They have the following advantages:

Information must be set down logically and systematically.
Faults become more obvious.
Enable the problem to be visualised, grasped and digested, particularly when explaining to or discussing with others.
Are cheap and quick to produce and involve no lengthy report.

Material Process Chart—records what happens to material. The symbols referred to above are used to indicate the sequence of the various processes which are involved. Times taken or distances travelled can be noted against each process.

Operator Process Chart—records what an operator does, showing the sequence and usually for each hand.

Examples of these two charts are illustrated in Figs. 22 and 23 for a fairly simple operation in the manufacture of tobacco. Analysis of the old method revealed:

Layout of tables, machine and bins of material was unsatisfactory.
Uneven work distribution between operations.
An unbalance of operator's hands, the left hand being largely inactive.
Unnecessary walking—unproductively.
The possibilities of reducing waste.

The new method, evolved from a study of these charts and the associated layout, resulted in an increased output of $33\frac{1}{3}$ per cent. Previously two girls in a team produced 30 lb. per day; with the new method, girls working independently (and therefore giving more flexibility) produced 20 lb. per day each.

String Diagrams (*Flow Charts*)—show the actual path of movement of operators, material or equipment. Coloured strings are stretched round pins stuck in a scale drawing of the layout at the place where operations occur. Different colours are used to indicate different persons, materials or equipment, and the length of the string is a measure, to scale, of the distance travelled. An example of this is given in Figs. 24 and 25 which show the old layout and the improved layout which resulted from a study of the string diagram. Previous to the study, £4,050 had been allocated for stockyard extensions with no annual savings in operation expected. In fact only £1,400 was spent in re-layout and new equipment (a saving of £2,650 in capital expenditure) and an increase in output of 20 per cent. was obtained. Distances travelled by material were reduced by 56 per cent., handling operations were reduced by 27 per cent. and man-hours were reduced by 20 per cent. on loading and 35 per cent. on unloading.

As well as using such charts, it is normally necessary to make detailed time studies of each operation in a job or in a department (see page 289). When data is being collected for pre-determined times a sufficient number of studies are made of all operations involved to yield a statistically adequate sample. These studies usually reveal faulty methods, equipment and layout, and improvements then need

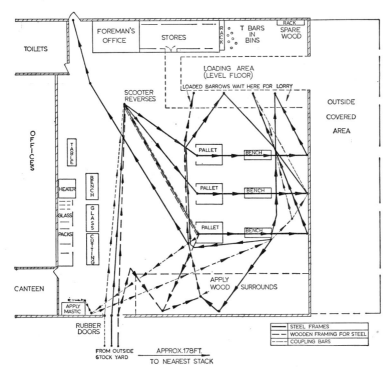

Fig. 24.—Illustration of typical string diagram Old Method.
Diagram shows paths of movement of steel frames,
wood surrounds and coupling bars.

to be devised before further studies are made. Thus method studies and time studies are complementary.

Process Specifications and Operation Layouts.—Having established by investigation and confirmed by trial runs which satisfy foremen and inspector the correct method or process, it is advisable to lay down the method in a specification, in as much detail as is necessary for the particular job. As well as the exact procedure to be followed, the specification should state clearly minimum standards of finish, tools and equipment to be used, service help to be supplied, and disposal of wastes, whenever there may be any ambiguity about these items. Standard specifications of this nature are a most vital and valuable product of work study. Not only do they form the exact definition of the amount of work covered by a price or time when piecework payment is in operation—and no piecework price or time should be fixed for a new job before some such specification has been prepared—but they become a standard reference in

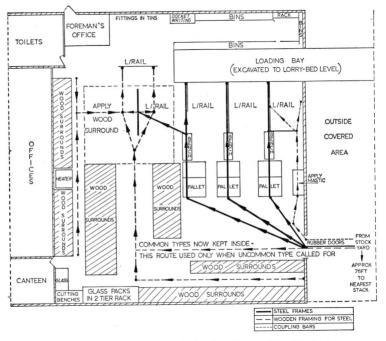

Fig. 25.—Illustration of typical string diagram New Method.

all cases of query or doubt at a later date. This becomes especially important when, at a later date, it is suddenly realised that standards of performance or quality of the product have changed, or piecework earnings have fallen or become inflated. In such cases it is usually found that practice has departed substantially from the original specification. Methods should either be brought back into line, or the specification (and piecework standard) modified. In either case it is quite clear to all concerned why modification is necessary. The

specifications in the form of Operation Layouts or Process Specifications provide the operator with his instructions and ensure that new

LAYOUT No.	OPERATION No.	OPERATION LAYOUT					PART	No.
1	2						Body	XXXX

DRG. No.	MATERIAL	BATCH QY	DEPT.	M/C OR GROUP	GRADE OF LABOUR	OPERATION		
1072/1	GM CSTG		CAPST	1	MF2	Bore, face & tap		

No.	OPERATION	STATION	TRAVEL	CUTS	FEED	R.P.M.	JIGS AND TOOLS
1	Chuck feed to stop & true	T1					3 jaw chuck & stop
2	Rough & finish face	RP	.64	2	H80 H120	750	H81
3	Rough bore for 1½"gas	T2	.75	1	A80	465	FS cutter
4	Finish ditto	T3	.87	1	H120	"	E91
5	Chamfer for tap	T4	.14	1	"	"	FS cutter
6	Tap 1½"	T5	.87			74	1½"taper gas tap NH STD

GAUGING PROCEDURE				
DETAIL	GAUGE	FREQU.		
1½"thrd	1½"taper gas M:	1/10	NOTE: Spigot in chuck to suit bore in 1st end to prevent crushing.	

PREPARED BY	DATE	AUTHORISED	TIME ALLOWED	
			SET-UP	PER 100
	30-8-45	30-8-45	2.00	5.85
		DATE	HOURS	HOURS

FIG. 26

operators on a job understand what they are required to do. Fig. 26
shows an Operation Layout, and the following is an example of a
Process Specification.

PROCESS SPECIFICATION

Welding Shop Operating—Profile Cutters

I. *Process*

This specification covers gas cutting in the Welding Department, procuring sheet metal (assisted by Service Operators), the disposal of all "off cuts" and scrap material, but not the disposal of waste and slag from the base of cutting machines.

II. *Operations*

1. Procure raw material sheet (assisted by service operator) from stock area and position on profile cutting machine stand.
2. Procure template or jig from template maker.
3. Position template in such a way that material is cut in the most economical manner.
4. Trace round template, or template tracing, using the oxygen pressures and feeds specified in table.
5. Where possible, remove all slag during machine cutting period.
6. "Firsts off" must be passed by the inspector before all production runs commence.
7. Change bottles of Propane gas.
8. Dress work on grinder, removing all burrs or slag where possible.
9. Book "on" and "off" job.

III. *Standard Times*

The standard time (or allowed time) covers all operations included in this specification.

When for any reason additional operations appear to be necessary, it must immediately be reported to the foreman. If it is found that they are necessary, either the standard time must be adjusted, or an allowance will be granted by the time-study engineer. Additional time not normally required is to be recorded as excess. No allowance will be made for additional time not reported.

Operators are to book off a job *immediately* it is completed, and on to the next job (or waiting time) at the same time. Waiting time must be booked to the appropriate cause.

First offs, after each set-up or reset, are to be submitted by setter for an inspection for approval before commencing production. Operators are not to book on to production until job has been passed for production.

When systematic Work Study is first undertaken in a department, even one apparently quite efficient, it is surprising how often weaknesses in planning, progress or servicing (particularly of tools and equipment) are revealed. Correcting only these is usually a source of increased productivity but calls for no harder work from operators. It does of course involve better staff work and an improvement in administrative methods and techniques (see pages 288–290).

More often, however, it is also found that a certain amount of re-layout is wanted and that much more use can be made of modern mechanical handling. In fact both layout and material handling are profitable subjects for work study; they are interdependent and a study of one involves the other.

Mechanical Handling

New handling equipment is continually being developed, and material handling is a particularly profitable field for economies.[1]

Handling material only adds cost to a product, it does not improve it nor add to its value. If it is performed manually it also involves fatigue of operators and is a source of accidents. It should, therefore, be reduced to a minimum. When it is realised that handling materials can in extreme cases amount to more than half of the cost of production, and that as much as 50 tons may have to be lifted, moved, or put down for every one ton of finished product, the possible savings are apparent. Furthermore, by keeping work on the move or eliminating handling operations, the total quality of material, therefore money, tied up in work in progress can be reduced and the productivity or capacity of a department can be improved very considerably from this alone—15 or 20 per cent. is not an unusual figure. In this connection it is much more important to eliminate picking up and putting down material than to speed its rate of moving.

Handling can be improved by taking advantage of the many mechanical handling devices now available, such as:

Stillage trucks and platforms (which keep work off the floor without a large number of trolleys having to be bought).

Fork-lift trucks (which serve the same purpose and in addition very much simplify and speed up stacking, storing, loading and unloading); when once installed these trucks are always used for more purposes than was originally foreseen.

Continuous overhead links conveyors (which use overhead space without taking up much, if any, floor space. They also keep on the move a large volume of work with little power or attention).

Spiral chutes (which in multifloor factories use gravity and avoid trucking and lifts).

Continuous finger tray elevator/lowerators, which serve the same purpose.

Special containers for all components of an assembly—for small screws and similar parts, or to facilitate emptying or transport.

Attachments for loading and unloading vehicles and decks.

[1] For detailed information on handling see *Material Handling,* by G. R. Imner (McGraw-Hill Publishing Co. Ltd.), and *Materials Handling in Industry,* Report of Anglo-American Council of Productivity.

It is generally recognised that it is possible to almost entirely eliminate handling, not only during, but also between, operations in the large mass-production factories, and that it is economic to do so even in England where the scale of production is much smaller than is possible in the United States. This latest development is termed automation. It is not revolutionary as is often claimed so much as evolutionary, being a logical development of the use of machines to do unskilled loading to machines and carrying between them, when quantity production makes investment in machines cheaper than employing labour.

The next stage at which to apply similar techniques, made possible by a combination of punched cards, electronics and magnetic tapes, appears to be the automatic control of machines (machine tools, looms, etc.), and the supply of materials to work stations, for even small batches. A record is made on a tape of the operations performed for the "first off". The tape then takes over control of the operations for the rest of the batch. This automatic control of machines may well have as great an impact on management and industrial relations as mechanical power did in the early days of the industrial revolution.

Reactions of Operators

The natural tendency and up to a point one of the objects of work study is to simplify work and operations. There are dangers in pressing it too far, however, dangers to the operator's outlook, and a risk of going beyond the point of minimum overall cost. Simplification of method or operation reduces the work content of a job, and therefore the operator's interest in that job. The emotional disturbance induced may be very real and entirely negative any reduction in effort achieved. It may be possible to counteract these effects by continually making the operators aware of, and interested in, the significance of the job—and this is management's responsibility. A remedy which can be effective and economical is to switch operators about, or to get them to do several or all the operations, however simplified, on a part or product. Over-simplification may also induce cramped or taut muscles; a variation of motions or a deliberate insertion of a fetching or waiting operation may prevent this.

One well-remembered case illustrates the danger of restricting output by over-simplification. An article was assembled from several components, some of which formed small sub-assemblies. There were many different types and sizes of the article. In order to get the benefits of simplification, assembly was arranged along two sides of a conveyor belt, each operator doing one operation. Work study revealed that because the times required for individual operations varied with the size and type of article, there were always some operators who did not have to work as fast as others. The conveyor belt was taken out, each operator supplied with an individual bench and a complete set of tools, and set to do the whole assembly, operation by operation for a batch. Output per operator was actually more than doubled—and the operators were undoubtedly more interested and contented.

Qualifications of Study Man

In Work Study the outlook and method of dealing with operators and foremen are important. A study man must preserve a completely open mind and start off with no assumptions. Nothing must be taken for granted. He must not only be observant, missing nothing, but also be critical, accepting nothing without query and confirmation. Normally he will accept the assurance and authority of the technical expert, but even then if still in doubt should insist on proof. At the same time he must be quite impartial in all issues and decisions and maintain a strict mental honesty in his own work. All improvements and modifications must be made through the foreman and operator, enlisting their unreserved interest and co-operation; such improvements must not be imposed as an order without the fullest opportunity for understanding and acceptance. To do this the study man must discuss his findings with both operator and foreman and invite their comments and suggestions. Old hands and skilled craftsmen do not, as a rule, believe that an outsider can suggest better ways of doing a job, or even be capable of knowing whether it is done correctly. They must be convinced that the ability to study work analytically is a craft as skilled as their own—and that "the looker-on sees most of the game"—if he is skilled in observation.

Study men should be trained by qualified persons. This is particularly so if their work is to include, as it most certainly should, measurement of work. So much of the technique has been proved, learnt and formalised into a science that it is wasteful and unnecessary for a person taking up the work to start at the beginning, and learn by trial and error as the original workers in the field had to do.

If it is necessary to train several persons at the same time and to undertake a general programme of study work in a factory, there is much to be said for engaging a first-class firm of management consultants. Not only can they train study men effectively, but they are more likely to be accepted by the employees of the firm concerned, and they can also train supervision and senior management in the most effective application and use of results and information.

MEASUREMENT OF WORK

The Need for a Standard of Measurement of Work

Sooner or later, and in one form or another, it becomes necessary to measure the performance of persons, to compare output per person or productivity. At the least, one wants to know how output or performance compares today with what it used to be; it is better still to compare it with what it could or should be. Ultimately this requires a measurement of work.

There is usually some difficulty about measuring the comparative performance of several departments in a company or different companies. If two factories are turning out the same product which is measured in tons or feet, then the overall cost per ton or per foot is a measure of performance which can be obtained readily and used for comparison. But how does one compare the costs or efficiency of two factories or departments making dissimilar products? Cost per ton or unit is no good. As between two different firms, only the percentage net profit is any measure, and that is affected by the type of market and selling costs which are not production costs. And between different departments in the same firm there would seem to be, at first sight, no measure of efficiency on a common and therefore comparable basis.

If, however, the amount of "effort" (or cost—material, labour and overhead services) which should have been used to make a given quantity of a product is known and also the amount actually used, then surely the correct amount as a proportion of the actual amount is a measure of performance or efficiency. The real value of output, in effort, hours or £ s. d., is the amount of cost which goes out of the factory or department in a useful form, i.e. it does not include all wastage and excess costs, avoidable, and of no benefit to customer or company. And input is the total of all effort and costs absorbed, including excess costs. What is required therefore to measure efficiency of production is:

(1) A measure of the amount of cost (material, labour and on-cost) which should be used per unit (the standard):

(2) A measure of the excess over standard.

Engineers have defined a unit for work done by machines; it is horse-power, and is the power expended when working at the rate of 550 foot-pounds per second (i.e. 550 lb. through 1 foot per second). No such precise definition of the amount of work which can be done by man, even an "average" man, is possible. Nevertheless, it is obvious that some measurement of the amount of work in a job, under known circumstances, is essential. Furthermore, quite apart from the question of total and relative costs, it is obviously necessary for a foreman to be able to judge objectively and fairly the relative performance of his operators and for higher management to be able to compare the performance of departments, in terms of effort and the utilisation of man-hours. It is even necessary for operators themselves to know the comparative results of their efforts; not always the most conscientious or most skilled operator makes the most effective use of his time. What is required again is a method of measuring work done in terms of a common and standard unit, a unit that does not depend on a foreman's opinion or the condition of equipment.

Again, it is essential to have some measure of the work content of a job in order to do any planning of production programmes. Those who have endeavoured to plan production with only the roughest of estimates of what work is involved, fully appreciate the impossibility of doing so satisfactorily.

Finally, the value as an incentive of payment by results, i.e. payment according to the work done or effort put in, is generally accepted. This raises again the problem of what is a fair day's work, and it has been shown earlier that one of the objects of work study is to obtain a standard measurement of the amount of work in a job. The old rate-fixing assessment was unsatisfactory, for it failed to take adequate account of the following factors:

The skill and experience of the operator.
The speed, effort and attention during the observed performance.
The strain on the operator and the specific fatigue involved.
The results of a critical analysis of each element of the operation.

An accurate unit of work must allow for all these factors; the first two are dealt with by a rating factor, the third by a relaxation allowance, and the fourth by work study.

There are four purposes for which some unit of measurement of the work content of a job is essential, they are:

Cost control.
Assessment and comparison of performance.
Production planning.
Payment for results.

In each case the results cannot be more accurate than the unit of measurement used. And as time is a factor common to all four purposes, it is obviously desirable to use a unit based on time, and this is done by expressing the work content of a job in terms of the time required to do it in "standard units".

Where the same article is being produced repeatedly, the work done is frequently calculated as "so many per hour", but this may be reversed to read "time to produce one or 100". If, then, the "time to produce" any article or to do any job of work is measured in terms of a common unit, we have a measurement of work which can be used for production control, planning, costing, payment, measurement of performance, comparisons and so on.

Units of Work

In measuring work in terms of time, it is to be remembered that there are three ways in which time may be spent when doing a job of work:

Effective.—Time spent effectively doing the job required.

Ineffective.—Time spent in doing things not essential to the task.

Relaxation.—Time spent in resting and other forms of relaxation to compensate for fatigue in order to be able to maintain a steady rate of effective work.

Any unit of work must include the first and third items but not the second. The unit used is defined as the amount of work performed in one minute at a standard rate of working, including time for relaxation. This unit involves a definition of a standard rate of working. A standard rate of working is taken to mean the normal or moderate rate which can be kept up without undue fatigue by an average qualified operator working well within his or her capacity. In industry this is roughly equivalent to normal "daywork" rate. Long investigation and study has revealed that in industrial conditions a person can put in such extra effort for continuous periods as will produce one-third more work, i.e. work at a rate one-third faster than at day-work rate.

At a standard rate of working a person can be said to produce 60 units of work in one hour, and this is taken as the basis for rating speed, effort, skill and attention during the time-study investigations, and is referred to as a "60 rating".

Rate of Working

Because the whole concept of work measurement in terms of "standard" units as applied to human effort depends on the ability of an observer to assess or "rate" an operator's performance or "rate of working", and because this assessment is used for wage payment purposes, the subject is slightly controversial. Not unnaturally those whose earnings are affected are suspicious of the validity of the claim that even trained observers can form an unbiased and consistent judgment of a person's rate of working. This is particularly so before the person whose work is to be measured has had any experience of the results. And Trades Union representatives, faced with conflicting statements by operators and management and being naturally sympathetic to their member's cause, can be expected to doubt the accuracy of times based on the assessment. Indeed the results of the old-fashioned "ratefixing" and of performance rating by untrained observers, has provided, in the past, some justification for these attitudes. But a tool is not to be condemned merely because it is dangerous in the hands of unskilled or careless users. Experience proves and it is now generally accepted, that persons adequately trained in performance rating can assess performance sufficiently accurately for all practical purposes. Experiments have proved that the assessment of properly trained and experienced observers are consistent within plus and minus 5 per cent. both between an observer's own ratings and between different observers.

But because inaccurate standards can be so misleading—and expensive—to management, can so annoy and destroy the confidence of employees and, between the two parties, can produce so much friction and trouble, it is supremely important that management should ensure that all persons appointed to use this tool are trained in its use by properly qualified persons.

Rate of working assumes some scale by which to measure rate. The early workers in this field chose as the basis for a scale, the two rates of working generally understood in industry, viz. at daywork and at piecework. They found, and experience since has proved, that piecework rate of working is about one-third faster than daywork rate of working. In a factory or department where there is no financial incentive for higher output, where morale is not depressed and supervision is reasonably good, i.e. where conditions are what one might term "just average", the normal average rate of working is at about a daywork rate. With some added urge, motivation or incentive, e.g. the acceptance of higher targets, better supervision, or financial interest in higher output, operators work faster or harder or more diligently. But how much depends on the individual, on conditions and on the incentive. The existing "daywork" rate would be known to the operators; the "piecework" rate would be problematical. For this reason "daywork" seems a reasonable basis from which to start and was used by the earlier investigators in the field of work measurement and by nearly all others since.

On this basis a standard rate of working (at Standard Performance) is taken to mean the normal or moderate rate which can be kept up without undue fatigue by an average qualified operator working well within his or her capacity and not responding to any incentive. Long experience has shown that in industrial conditions a normal person *can* put in such extra effort for continuous periods as will produce one-third more work, i.e. work at a rate one-third faster than at daywork rate. These two rates of working, one being one-third higher than the other, establish the scale for the measurement of rate of working. At standard rate a person is said to produce 60 units of work in an hour: at the higher rate which may be expected under "incentive" conditions, 80 units of work are produced and the scale of measurement is referred to as the 60/80 scale. In practice virtually all work observed is being performed at rates between something a little less than the 60 rate and about one-half more—90 (and very occasionally up to twice—120).

The *British Standard Glossary of Terms in Work Study (B.S.S. 3138: 1959)* recommends that the Standard Rating (for a Standard Performance) should refer to the higher level of performance (i.e. at "incentive" or "piecework" level). It is suggested that the lower (or "daywork") performance is "entirely artificial" and "can only be defined as three-quarters of the performance expected when an *incentive* scheme and *good* organisation are present". But incentive schemes are "artificial" and certainly vary tremendously in their design, quality and effectiveness, and *good* organisation is certainly relative and difficult to define with any exactness. Furthermore although the work study engineer will have no difficulty in understanding the 0/100 scale recommended in the B.S.S. and will find it slightly more simple to use, it is yet to be proved that it is easier for the operators to understand and accept—and it is the operators' understanding and goodwill that is so vital to management when dealing with work measurement.

Furthermore it is inherent in the B.S.I. definition of Standard Performance and Standard Rating (pages 21 and 22) that the Time Allowed for a job is issued at incentive or piecework performance and in practice this is likely to reduce the effectiveness of piecework as an incentive.

There are some who believe that piecework is out of date and that it creates more problems than it is worth. But as was said above, it is wrong to condemn a tool because it is used inexpertly or in wrong conditions. It may be inappropriate on the assembly line and in continuous-process factories, but for many years yet, the great majority of employees in works and offices will be engaged in more or less routine work where their output can be measured individually or in small groups. In these circumstances good managements can, and will, increasingly use the straight-piecework form of payment by results as a financial incentive (though not the only incentive). In piecework the "bonus" element or time saved is an important part of the incentive; it has a distinct motive power. An operator likes to be able to calculate his "bonus" easily (it is a common and valid criticism, by operators and Trade Unions, when this cannot be done). When an Allowed Time is issued at incentive (or piecework) performance as defined in the B.S.S., the difference between an operator's actual time and Standard will either *decrease* as he improves towards Standard or, if he improves beyond Standard, it is likely to be only by a small amount; in either case the incentive will be diluted. Furthermore for simplicity of calculation in the Wages Dept. an hourly rate appropriate to incentive earnings level (according to company policy) must be used and this will be different from the daywork rate. Not only is this an additional though small complication in the Wages Dept., but the daywork rate is the rate negotiated and agreed with the Trades Unions. To use a different rate for calculating wages will not only confuse operators but it may lead to misunderstandings and friction between different companies employing members of the same Union. In the engineering industry in particular it will make an already complicated wages structure still more confusing. From the overall management point of view, where piecework payment is to be used, the issue of Allowed Times at "dayrate" (or base rate) is recommended. (See page 325 for calculation of piecework.)

The manager or work study engineer who is reading this will have no difficulty in using or understanding either scale (or the 100/133 scale) or in translating from one to another. Therefore, as the 60/80 scale is, as yet, far and away the most commonly used, and examples and illustrations available have used this scale, it will be used in the following text (with references to the B.S.S. 0/100 scale where appropriate).

Although a rating scale, whether the 60/80 or the B.S.S. 0/100 or any other, cannot be defined or measured in absolute terms, it is possible to train persons to recognise and to rate levels of performance with sufficient accuracy and consistency for all practical purposes. As mentioned earlier, experience has shown that it is possible for the error in one observer's ratings and the error between observers to be consistently maintained at not more than 5 per cent. To maintain this accuracy and to guard against "drift" in their standard, which is essential if work measurement is to be of any real value, those rating performance must check their standard and their consistency frequently. Films which show operations at different levels of performance are now available for training and for proving.

The commonly used illustration of the concept of an acceptable incentive performance or a daywork performance is to imagine a person walking (a person of normal physique of course and not deformed or crippled in any way). If walking at 3 miles per hour over level ground, as one would when out for a stroll but not dawdling, is taken to be roughly equivalent to a 60 (or standard) rating, then a brisk speed, 4 miles an hour, at which one would walk when getting to a destination on time, is equivalent to an 80 rating,

P.P.M.—11*

and loitering, usually averaging 2 miles an hour, is equivalent to a 40 rating.

When practically no effort is involved, e.g. tying knots in thread or wrapping very light articles in paper, a rating of 90 coincides with the blur point, when it becomes practically impossible to distinguish with the eye the separate movements of fingers and hands.

When ratings as low as 30 or as high as 120 are recorded, the times to which they apply should be treated with suspicion and if possible ignored. Generally it is unnecessary to use times with ratings outside the limits of 50 and 100; there is usually something wrong if the rating is very low and it should be corrected.

Recognition of the skill factor is perhaps the most difficult. Long experience and close association with trained observers are essential before reliability can be acquired. The learner always tends to under-rate the highly skilled and overrate the unskilled operator, as he will at the beginning with speed and effort.

The standard rate of working assumes that a person, by taking the necessary rest or relaxation, is able to keep it up indefinitely over the normal working day. This means that the unit of work must include time for personal needs and relaxation. Experience and study have given us reliable information on the relaxation required under different conditions. It is a good deal more than is generally recognised, and may be as high as 50 per cent., or even 100 per cent. of working time in extreme cases, although when these figures are required it is obviously a case for improving conditions and reducing the effort and hence the fatigue involved.

Criticism is sometimes levelled at the use of relaxation allowances because so little is known about the subject. Certainly there is need for more information on industrial fatigue, but in practice the relaxation allowances given later have been found to give satis-factory results and in normal circumstances involve no serious errors. Very abnormal conditions should be improved if possible, and if not, special studies should be made to obtain data specific to those conditions.

In order that the measure of work shall apply to conditions in the shop where the work is being done, it is almost always necessary to add an allowance to cover incidental delays which do occur even in the best-run factories. These delays are least in continuous process work and on automatic machinery, but in general vary from $2\frac{1}{2}$ per cent. to 10 per cent. Only study on the shop floor can determine an appropriate and adequate figure. Morrow in his *Time Study and Motion Economy*, discusses in detail methods for finding the correct allowance required. (See page 319.)

Finally, one point must be made clear. It is not pretended that there is, as yet, an objective or absolute measure for "rate of working". The search goes on. W. D. Seymour[1] has pointed out that the perceptive factor may be more important than the spatial factor in determining increase in speed of operation or rate of working, and that one day it may be possible to measure the perceptive factor. In the meantime, however, the results of using the now conventional methods of measuring rate of working, by *properly trained observers*, justify their use. Margins of error are relatively small and skilled study men are alive to the possibilities of error.

Technique of Measurement—Tools

The tools required for making a time study are few, and unless micro-motion technique is to be employed, are quite simple. They are:

(1) *Pencil and Paper.*—Preferably a standard printed form or study sheet is used, designed to suit the kind of study and work being observed. On this sheet a complete record of operations and times is made for one or several complete cycles of operations.

(2) *Timepiece.*—A stop-watch is most convenient but is not essential. In some cases an ordinary pocket or wrist-watch is quite sufficient. In extreme cases, when the use of a stop-watch is for some reason objected to by the operators, it can be dispensed with and the technique of counting substituted.

(3) *Study Board.*—This is preferably of plywood, or other stiff material, and arranged with a clip to hold the study sheet, and a pocket or clip for the watch.

(4) *Ciné camera*, for micro-motion study work, with a timing device or a synchronous drive and counter on the camera.

A specially printed form should be used for recording a time study. A suitable form is shown in Fig. 28 (see page 314). On the reverse of the sheet an adequate description and details of the operation and notes should be recorded. Referring to Fig. 28, ratings are entered in the column headed R, the time at the end of each element in the column headed T, and later, the elapsed time calculated by deducting each time from the subsequent one, entered under E, as shown. As there is a column for running times, an ordinary watch can be used; if a fly-back stop-watch is preferred and always used, two columns only are required. Several types of stop-watch are in use, with the following variations: one hand, split hands, single knob or knob and slide for operating; minutes and seconds, minutes in decimals, or hours in decimals, calibration and so on. Either can be used and are equally effective when experience has been gained on the particular type and its operation has become completely auto-

[1] *Industrial Training for Manual Operators*—Pitman.

matic (in the same way that instantaneous operation of motor-car controls becomes automatic to a driver). It is claimed that the two-hand type (one hand can be stopped whilst the other continues) gives an observer more time to note the time. An observer, however, must be trained to note the time instantaneously, for it is essential when small elements are being timed, and studies involving such elements are frequently met with. The decimal division type (one revolution for one minute, reading to 0·01 minute) facilitates calculations from observed times.

For micro-motion study work special camera equipment incorporating a timing device is used. It requires expert observers to use and analyse its results, and because of the expense and the rather elaborate arrangements which have to be made, its use is generally limited to laboratory work, detail assembly and similar work in continuous production.

Techniques of Measurement—Rating

The actual elapsed time for an operation or job of work can be recorded accurately, since a watch is an accurate instrument of measurement. But this observed actual time must be converted to "standard" time, i.e. the time at a "standard rate" of working. As shown above, this is done by "rating" the observed time and "levelling" or converting the time to standard by multiplying by the observed "rating" and dividing by the standard rating (usually 60).

It will be obvious that the accuracy and effectiveness of work measurement depend on the reliability of the technique of rating. Rating is affected by the time-study engineer's

(1) Concept of standard performance.
(2) Ability to rate consistently the same performance at different occasions and by different operators.
(3) Ability to consistently detect and rate proportionate changes in performance (i.e. different ratings).
(4) Discrimination in selecting the "standard" time from several observed times.

To attain and maintain accuracy and consistency on all these counts, not only are training and experience essential but also the continuous, conscientious analysis and criticism of one's consistency of rating. One method of doing this has been developed by D. J. Desmond, M.Sc. (for his theory and detailed explanation see *Engineering* for October 20th, 1950).

In Desmond's method, actual observed times are plotted against the "Reciprate" (reciprocal of rating). When the times for several observations of an operation or element are so plotted a mean or average line can be drawn through them so that the scatter about this line is at a minimum. This is called the Study line. A similar line drawn from the origin through the points so that the scatter of the points about the line is a minimum is called the Operation line. The time corresponding to the point where the operation line intersects the 60 rating is the normal time for the operation. See Fig. 27 which illustrates the observed times plotted as above for the example of a study given in Figs. 28, 29 and 30 (pages 314 and foll.).

If the work content of the operation or element is constant and all observations are accurately rated, all points would lie on the operation line and both operation line and study line would coincide. If the study line does not coincide with the operation line it indicates an inability to appreciate accurately proportionate changes in rating. The "flatness" (or rating) is the amount by which the rate of slope of study line to slope of operation line is less than unity OA/OB. If studies so plotted always show a degree of flatness, the study engineer's estimate of standard time is incorrect as indicated by the intersection of the study line and operation line in relation to standard rating. The graph also shows at which ratings the study engineer is most in error. In practice the work content of an operation or element is seldom absolutely constant; it may vary with the quality of the material, with the tolerance or dimensions, or even with working conditions. For this reason, observed times when plotted, even if correctly rated, would not be exactly in a straight line. Nevertheless, such variations would only widen the scatter of points and a mean line drawn through them would still indicate the degree of flatness. Always bearing in mind the possible effects of variation in work content, studies regularly and periodically plotted in this way can provide a check on a study man's rating; the normal tendency to flatness can be detected and corrected, and inconsistency between studies and between observations minimised.

Techniques of Measurement—Making the Study

When making a work study it is usual to include observations of times taken, since, if the times are not wanted for measurement, they are required for analysis purpose. It is not possible here to describe in detail the exact procedure to be followed in all the various kinds of work met with in industry, but the following is a general outline of the procedure which is satisfactory in all but exceptional cases; it can be varied when particular problems are met with:

(1) Put the operator at ease.

It is obviously necessary to observe the work being done under normal circumstances; the circumstances are not normal unless an operator is working entirely at ease. It is therefore important to explain to the operator as much as is necessary of what is required of him, or of what is being done. For the first study in a department this is especially important, later on it is not so necessary. It

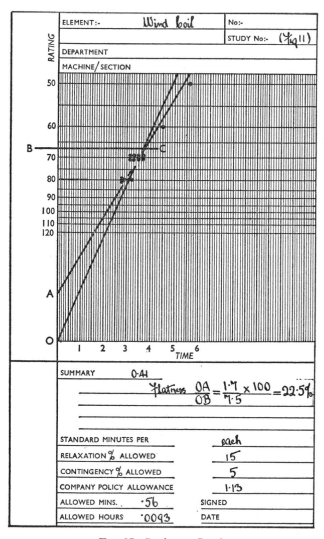

FIG. 27—Reciprate Graph

is essential to tell the operator that he is being studied and advisable for the study man to stand where he can be seen by the operator, and not behind his back. Nothing is more certain to put the operator on edge than to know he is being watched from behind. It is also advisable to ask the operator to carry on at his or her normal pace, neither speeding up nor slackening off, and making no especial efforts because an observer is present.

(2) Note all particulars of a job—brief description, conditions, inspection standards and so on. In machine-shop work it may be necessary to make a note of the machine, part number and even a description of the part. The nature and extent of the particulars will depend on the kind of study and the work being performed.

(3) List all operations in the sequence in which they are being performed. It may be necessary to run through the cycle two or three times in order to be quite sure that operations are being performed in the same sequence and none is omitted. It is at this stage, before any times are taken, that it may be found necessary to recommend immediate improvements in method, and this should be done if records taken would otherwise be wasted.

(4) Record the time taken and the rating for each operation as it is performed. An example of the records made is shown in Fig. 28. It is important to make a mental note of the rating for each element of time recorded during the time the element is being performed, and to record the rating before recording the time for the element. It is also important to be able to recognise accurately a break point between elements of operations so that each repetition of an element is strictly comparable. (This is absolutely vital when the records are to be used for synthetically built standard times.) It is this process of recording times and ratings that requires skilled training, and no records should be used until an observer is fully qualified and his records reliable.

In machine operations, elements of time which are entirely automatic or machine controlled are given an 80 rating; it is assumed that a machine maintains a "piecework" rate of working and yields the equivalent bonus on payment by results.

(5) Rating. The rating for each observed time must take account of the four factors—speed, attention, effort and skill. As compared with an element which is so simple as to require negligible skill, effort, or attention, e.g. folding letters or circulars, an operation which is performed in exactly the same time, but requires effort in addition, would be rated higher and so on. It requires concentrated and prolonged experience to enable an observer to take account of all factors and assess a correct rating almost instantaneously as is required for short elements of time.

(6) Record all time spent during the study and how it is spent, indicating any ineffective time. In order to be able to check that no time has been missed, it is advisable to make a note of when a study starts and when it ends. The continuous running method of recording time used in the illustration, instead of the method of noting the elapsed time by stopping the watch for each element, takes care of this point. It is important to record *all* ineffective

Fig. 28.—WORK STUDY SHEET

Element	R	T	E	R	T	E	R	T	E	R	T	E	R	T	E	R	T	E	R	T	E	R	T	E
Attach wire	80	·09	·09	80	·86	·08	80	4·00	·10	70	·70	·10	75	·60	·10	75	·43	·10	80	·20	·10	80	13·06	·08
Wind coil	80	·40	·31	70	2·42	·56	60	·32	·32	45	6·15	·45	80	·93	·33	80	·75	·32	70	·57	·37	60	·34	·28
Hammer coil	80	·49	·09	80	·46	·04	80	·41	·09	80	·24	·09	80	8·00	·07	80	·81	·06	80	·63	·06	80	·43	·09
Tie coil, 2 places	70	·80	·31	80	·80	·34	80	·70	·29	80	·52	·28	70	·35	·35	70	10·16	·35	70	12·00	·37	70	·77	·34
Half turn and cut	80	·89	·09	80	·89	·09	80	·81	·11	80	·61	·09	80	·45	·10	80	·21	·05	80	·10	·10	80	·87	·10
Hammer coil	80	·98	·09	70	3·00	·11	80	·90	·09	80	·69	·08	80	·54	·09	80	·29	·08	80	·16	·06	80	·95	·08
Tie coil, 2 places	80	1·38	·40	75	·40	·40	70	5·25	·35	75	7·08	·39	70	·95	·41	70	·75	·46	75	·55	·39	60	14·43	·48
Form, unload and reset	70	·78	·40	80	·90	·50	70	·60	·35	70	·50	·42	80	9·33	·38	80	11·10	·35	80	·98	·43	70	·87	·44
Attach wire	80	·96	·09	80	·66	·13	80	·50	·10	70	—	—	70	·32	·12	75	·22	·12	80	·98	·10			
Wind coil	80	·25	·29	70	·98	·32	70	·85	·35	40	·85	—	70	·65	·33	70	·57	·35	70	28·35	·37			
Hammer coil	80	15·30	·05	80	19·05	·07	80	·90	·05	80	·90	·05	80	·70	·05	80	·62	·05	80	·42	·07			
Tie coil, 2 places	80	·67	·37	75	·45	·40	70	21·30	·40	80	23·20	·30	75	25·05	·35	80	·97	·35	75	·75	·33			
Half turn and cut	80	·76	·09	80	—	—	80	·39	·09	80	·30	·09	80	·20	·15	80	27·07	·10	80	·83	·08			
Hammer coil	80	·86	·10	—	·58	·13	80	·46	·17	80	·39	·09	80	·29	·09	80	·14	·07	80	·92	·09			
Tie coil, 2 places	75	16·20	·34	—	20·00	·42	70	·79	·33	80	·72	·33	80	·63	·34	80	·50	·36	60	29·50	·58			
Form, unload and reset	60	·88	·68	70	·40	·40	75	22·14	·35	70	24·20	·48	70	26·10	·47	80	·88	·38	70	·85	·35			

Fig. 29.—WORK STUDY SHEET

Element	R	T	E	R	T	E	R	T	E
A. Wipe down, 20 strips	80	—	1·4	80	—	1·3	80	—	1·3
B. Feed strips, blank 7 and discard waste		(See below)							
C. Empty container	80	(140)	·25	80	(138)	·25	80	(142)	·3

B:—

R	T	E	R	T	E	R	T	E	R	T	E	R	T	E
80	·20	·20	85	·34	·20	90	·73	·22	90	·90	·18	80	·28	·24
90	·37	·17	85	·57	·23	90	·95	·22	100	7·07	·17	100	9·45	·17
90	·57	·20	80	·83	·26	90	5·15	·20	90	·25	·18			
80	·80	·23	90	3·03	·20	100	·33	·18	80	·49	·24			
85	1·00	·20	100	·20	·17	80	·55	·22	90	·74	·25			

FIG. 30.—WORK STUDY SHEET

Element	R	T	E	R	T	E	R	T	E	R	T	E	R	T	E	R	T	E	R	T	E	R	T	E
Load and start machine	80	·13	·13	60	3·49	·17	80	·78	·18	80	10·12	·17	—	13·44	·11	—	17·02	·29	80	21·02	·13	—	25·10	·21
Box up and lock	70	·35	·22	80	3·68	·19	90	·98	·20	—	·45	·33	80	·63	·19	80	·21	·19	80	22·75	·25	—	26·15	·80
Face inside	—	·68	·33	—	4·03	·35	—	7·33	·35	70	·70	·25	—	·95	·32	—	·57	·36	—	·88	·13	70	·35	·14
Form vee	90	·91	·23	—	·25	·22	—	·65	·11	80	·80	·20	—	14·21	·26	—	·79	·22	—	·96	·23	70	·32	·17
Box away	90	·98	·07	80	·32	·07	70	·76	—	80	·99	·19	80	·29	·08	90	·85	·06	80	23·44	·48	80	·40	·08
Index, turret and up	90	1·09	·11	80	·42	·10	—	8·49	·73	—	11·74	·75	80	·39	·10	80	·96	·11	70	·54	·10	80	·82	·42
Bore and turn, outside dia.	—	1·83	·74	90	5·20	·78	60	·63	·14	80	·95	·21	—	15·03	·74	—	18·13	·77	70	·62	·08	80	·93	·11
Turret back, index and up	80	2·01	·18	90	·36	·16	60	·68	·05	60	12·04	·09	80	·19	·16	80	·89	·16	80	·93	·31	80	27·11	·08
Centralise reamer	80	2·09	·08	80	·43	·07	—	9·09	·41	60	·47	·43	—	·44	·25	80	·96	·07	80	24·12	·19	90	·34	·23
Ream	—	·51	·42	80	·86	·43	60	·19	·10	70	·61	·14	90	·90	·46	—	19·39	·43	—	24·20	·08	80	·54	·20
Turret back and index	80	·64	·13	70	·96	·10	70	·26	·07	70	·70	·09	70	16·02	·12	90	·47	·08	—	—	—	90	27·61	·07
Tool box away	90	·68	·04	70	6·05	·09	80	·49	·23	80	13·00	·30	70	·18	·16	80	·54	·07	—	—	—	80	28·02	·41
Remove burr	80	·90	·22	70	·30	·25	80	·74	·25	80	·25	·25	80	·40	·22	80	·78	·24	—	—	—	—	—	—
Check (A)	60	3·23	·33	80	·52	·22	80	9·81	·07	80	13·33	·08	80	·66	·26	90	20·03	·25	—	—	—	—	—	—
Stop machine and unload	70	3·32	·09	—	6·60	·08	—	—	—	—	—	—	80	16·73	·07	85	20·10	·07	—	—	—	—	—	—
Check complete	—	—	—	—	—	—	—	—	—	—	—	—	—	—	—	—	—	—	—	—	—	—	—	—

Markers: **B** (break point), **C** (faulty rating), **D** (includes some ineffective time), **E** (work reset in chuck), **F** (overhead tool reset).

Commenced 10.22
Completed 10.50
Elapsed   28 mins. (which checks up)

Notes:
- **A** This operation should be done during next operation.
- **B** ? break point correct.
- **C** Faulty rating.
- **D** Includes some ineffective time.
- **E** Work reset in chuck (covered by contingency).
- **F** Overhead tool reset (covered by contingency).

time from whatever cause and however small—it may be required later during analysis. The observer must be quite clear as to what is ineffective time. Waiting time and inattention of the operator, talking, smoking and so on, are obvious, but wrong ways of doing an operation are not always so obvious, but may be just as ineffective.

(7) Record the times for a number of complete cycles. It is unsatisfactory to rely on one observation of a cycle of operations for a job. The number of complete cycles of an operation which need to be observed depends on the nature of the job and the information required from the study, and only experience of the particular circumstances can be any guide. With a trained study-man, the accuracy of the results of the levelled ratings for an element is not appreciably increased by taking more than nine or ten observations.

(8) Convert each recorded time into a standard time, and calculate and select the standard time for each operation. This is dealt with later under "Analysing and Working up the Study".

Thereafter, the procedure followed will depend on the use to be made of the information obtained. If a standard time is required for the job which is being studied, and it is considered the job is being done correctly, then the standard time is worked up immediately from the study. If it is thought that improvements can be made, the study is analysed to see whether improvements might be possible, and if any potential ones are revealed, arrangements are made with the foreman for them to be tried out, and further ones made until a satisfactory method is evolved. When improvements have been made, a check study should be made before the standard time is finally established for the job. If standard times are required for all operations, or elements of an operation, likely to be used in future jobs, as is frequently the case in batch production and general workshop practice as distinct from process work and mass production, then the times obtained for each operation must be tabulated and later analysed, selected and recorded for future use. The method of using such records for synthetic times is explained on page 326.

Examples of actual studies are given in Figs. 28, 29, 30, and they will be used for explaining how to work up a study. The description of elements and figures are in type; in actual use they would be written in, of course.

Fig. 28 is of an operation consisting entirely of manipulative elements: 16 cycles were recorded and, as so often happens, the observer, who was not very experienced at the time, missed three elements in cycle 11 and one in cycle 13. No ineffective time occurred during this study and the operator worked fairly consistently.

Fig. 29 is an operation consisting of three elements not performed as a cycle, the first preparing sufficient material for a short run, the second operating the machine at a speed entirely controlled by the operator, and the third emptying the container of completed work periodically.

Fig. 30 is an operation on a machine involving a cycle of operations, some purely manipulative and others (for which no ratings are entered) entirely controlled by the machine. In the first cycle the observer evidently made an error in reading the time at the break point between two operations, and these two readings would not be used. In the second cycle the rating for the last but one element is doubtful and would also not be used. In the fifth cycle the item marked D includes ineffective time due to the operator, and would not be used; similarly, the elements marked E and F in the sixth and seventh cycles would not be used, as they are not normal, and such occurrences would be covered by the contingency allowance. (They are noted, as the extent and frequency of occurrence of such contingencies may need to be assessed.) The observer has noted that the last but one element "check" could be done during a machining element. It will be noted that the total elapsed time checks that all time has been accounted for.

Working up the Study

Briefly stated, this consists of calculating the standard time for each element of an operation, making due allowance for relaxation and contingencies, and either—

(a) adding together the standard times of each element of the operation to find the total standard time for the operation; or
(b) recording the results for building up synthetic times of whole operations in the future.

There are, however, three distinct steps:

(1) For each element each observed time is converted to standard minutes and an average figure for all observations calculated or selected.
(2) This average figure is increased by an allowance for relaxation.
(3) The resulting figure is, if necessary, further increased by an allowance for contingencies. Usually this contingency allowance is added for the whole operation or job and not for each element.

Conversion to Standard.—To obtain the time at a *standard rate of working,* an actual observed time is multiplied by its rating and divided by standard rating (60 on 60/80 scale; 100 on B.S.S. 0/100 scale). Thus, if the actual time for an element is recorded as 0·6 minute, and the rating as 70, then the time at standard rate is:

$$\frac{0 \cdot 6 \times 70}{60} = 0 \cdot 7 \text{ std. mins.}$$

On the 0/100 scale and, say, a 90 rating, the time at standard rate is:

$$\frac{0 \cdot 6 \times 90}{100} = 0 \cdot 54 \text{ std. mins.}$$

This calculation is made for each recorded time of an element, and the average, minimum selected, or commonest time of the results is calculated or selected. Under normal circumstances the average, after rejecting doubtful or obviously incorrect times, is satisfactory, but if ratings are not dead accurate, the mean calculated time is better. In practice, calculating work is reduced by taking all recordings of the same rating together, or still further by averaging all times and all ratings. The former method is to be preferred in the early stages of training, and occasionally thereafter in order that the consistency of the observers' rating can be checked. For example, taking the second element, wind coil, in Fig. 27, the calculations would be set out thus:

Rating	Times	Total	At Std.	Std. for Element
50	·56	·56	·47	·47
60	·45	·45	·45	·45
70	·32, ·33, ·37, ·32, ·35, ·37, ·35, ·33	2·74	3·20	·40
80	·31, ·32, ·28, ·29, ·28	1·48	1·98	·39
	Total for 15 observations	5·23	6·10	

6·10 ÷ 15 is an average of ·407 standard min.
or approximately ·41 standard min.

The quicker though more approximate method is:

Total of all times 5·23 mins. for 15 observations
Average 0·348 min.

Ratings 1 at 50 =   50
1 at 60 =   60
8 at 70 =   560
5 at 80 =   400
———
1,070 for 15.
———

an average of 71·3

$$0 \cdot 35 \text{ min. at 71 rating} = 0 \cdot 35 \times \frac{71}{60}$$

$$= \cdot 414 \text{ std. min.}$$

or approximately ·41 min.

A study of the first method will show that the most nearly accurate time at standard would be ·40. Had all the ratings been dead accurate, there would be no discrepancy whichever way the average was calculated. It also shows the tendency in the early days of training for time-study men to overrate low effort or skill and to underrate high effort or skill. Working out each element as shown in the first method above brings this to light, and helps the study man to get his rating accurate. It is also possible to select the more nearly correct time. A still better way of maintaining accuracy and consistency of rating is to use the form shown in Fig. 27 for determining the standard time for operations or elements. It will be seen that the operation line in Fig. 28, cuts the standard rating (60) at a time ·41 min. which the above calculations gave.

Relaxation.—The time so calculated is the time which would be taken for that one element at a standard rate of working. But this rate cannot be kept up all day long without some break and allowance therefore has to be made for relaxation, i.e. to compensate for fatigue and the time required for personal needs. This is done by adding a percentage allowance to all elements. For example, if an allowance of 15 per cent. is appropriate, the time for the above element becomes:

$$0.41 + \frac{15}{100}$$
or $0.41 \times 1.15 = .472$ standard min.

When all elements of an operation are of the same type or involve the same effort, then the same relaxation allowance can be used for each different element, but in many cases certain elements of an operation require a higher relaxation allowance. For example, during an operation in a machine shop it might be necessary to lift a heavy casting of 50 lb. weight or more on to a machine, or in a warehouse to lift heavy parcels after packing on to a trolley or the floor, and the time for lifting would need to be increased by a far bigger relaxation allowance than for the other elements. Relaxation allowance therefore should be added to each element.

A good deal of thought and study has been given to the problem of industrial fatigue and the time required for relaxation to offset its effects and to enable a worker to maintain a steady output without permanent fatigue. In practice allowances between 10 per cent. and 20 per cent. are found to be satisfactory. In assessing relaxation there are five factors to consider:

(1) Whether the operation is sitting or standing.
(2) The weight of the thing moved, i.e. effort required.
(3) Concentration or attention required.
(4) Frequency of the cycle of operations.
(5) General conditions.

A basic allowance of 8 per cent. can be considered satisfactory in normal industrial conditions when the correct type of labour is doing the work sitting down and no physical effort, concentration, monotony, or trying conditions are involved. When the work has to be done standing up, then an extra 2 per cent. should be added, making 10 per cent. Obviously the heavier the article moved, whether it is tool or job, then the more the relaxation necessary to overcome fatigue. The following percentage additions have been found satisfactory in practice:

Lbs. Lifted	Percentage above 8 Male	Female
5	1	2
10	3	6
15	7	14
20	12	24
25	17	34
30	22	44
40	32	—
50	42	—

Above these maxima, lifting should have mechanical assistance.

For concentration or especial attention, 2—5 per cent. should be added. Jobs calling for the maximum amount under this heading are those like careful inspection of process work or engraving. Occasionally the whole operation is of very small duration, sometimes of the order of 10 seconds. In these cases an allowance of between 2 and 5 per cent. is made to provide relaxation from monotony.

In spite of the recognition by sound management that trying conditions of temperature, dust and so on are unwise, nevertheless they cannot always be avoided. For example: loading ovens and attending to vats can rarely be done mechanically. Allowance up to 10 per cent. (in extreme cases, even higher) is added in such cases.

The following table of percentages illustrates how total relaxation allowances are built up:

Job	Basic	Weight	Con-centration	Fre-quency	Con-ditions	Total
Wrapping (sitting) .	8	—	—	2	—	10
Assembly, M/c op-erating (standing)	10	—	2½	—	—	12½
Engraving (sitting) .	8	—	5	—	—	13
Attending to and filling a vat. .	10	2½	—	—	7½	20

Contingency Allowance.—When the total standard time for the whole operation has been calculated, it is usually necessary to add a contingency allowance. This entirely depends upon the conditions in the particular department, but if the figure would appear to be higher than 5 per cent., then there is obviously a large uncontrollable factor, and efforts should be made to improve the condition, since the incidence is likely to vary, and so therefore will the actual results and piecework earnings. In a machine shop, wear and tear of tools, and in a warehouse, queries with orders, are the kind of examples of contingencies which must be allowed for. Since they cannot be entirely prevented, it may be necessary to make prolonged studies in order to obtain a measure of the incidence of delays and a figure should never be used without some such study.

A statistical method of arriving at a correct allowance has been developed and is called Ratio Delay Activity Sampling. In this technique the proportion of total time available which a machine or operation is delayed, for known or determined causes, is assessed. It is based on statistical theory and if carried out properly is mathematically sound and accurate within known limits of error. Thus, it is possible by taking sufficient random observation over a limited period, and provided conditions do not change to calculate the percentage delay and the degree of error. The results can be used by management as a measure of effective machine time.

In this technique it is necessary to:

(*a*) decide in advance of the study the total number of time intervals (minutes, hours, etc.) for the study;
(*b*) consecutively number these intervals;
(*c*) determine by random sampling at which intervals observation will have to be made;
(*d*) record snap instantaneous observations at these intervals;
(*e*) calculate Ratio R of delay time for a cause (or all causes), and standard of error E thus:

$$R = \frac{d}{n} \quad \text{and} \quad E = \frac{d}{n^2}\left(1 - \frac{d}{n}\right).$$

where d is number of observations when machine or operation was delayed and n is total number of observations. Delays must be clearly defined and observable, observations must be taken over as long a period as is economical for the importance of the problem and the accuracy desired, and precautions must be taken to avoid operators who are being observed from behaving otherwise than normally because a study is being made.[1]

[1] A fuller discussion of this technique is given in *Work Sampling* by Hèiland and Richardson—McGraw-Hill.

Machine-controlled Elements.—Machining elements, that is elements or operations which are performed entirely automatically by a machine at a predetermined speed, are rated at an 80. This means, of course, that the machine is reckoned to be producing at exactly "piecework" speed. But the operator may only need to work for a portion of the machine cycle, and the standard time for the operator's work within the cycle may be less than the standard time for the cycle. The effective rating of the operation then cannot ever be as high as 80. For example, an operator working a machine producing an article, or completing an operation, in 3 minutes (or 20 per hour), and during this time having to do only 1·5 standard mins. of work, would be restricted to an effective rating of 1·5 × 20 = 30. The dilemma is whether to assess the work done as $3 \times \frac{80}{60} = 4$ std. mins. or 1·5.

In some cases it may be possible to arrange for the operator to look after more than one machine, in the above case it could be two, but even then the rating would only be 2 × 1·5 × 20 = 60. Where this is not possible, it is usual to credit the operation with compensating time of either all or some portion of the difference between the effective work and standard mins. at the 80 rating. If the machine time is a small part of the total operation, that is, there is considerably more work outside the machine cycle, then the operator does not have time to take any real relaxation during the machine cycle, and the whole of the difference should be credited as compensating time. But if the machine cycle is a large proportion of the total time, then only a proportion of the time is credited, depending on the amount of relaxation which can be taken during the machine cycle instead of at some other time. In any case, operators on payment by results expect to be able to be paid for the whole time, and, whenever possible, at a piecework rate if putting in a piecework effort. It is always advisable to record the amount of compensating time in a Standard Time in case it should later be found possible to utilise some of it; that there is any spare time may be disputed.

Typical Examples

The following is an example of how a Standard Time is calculated from a study using the study shown in Fig. 30.

Operation—Blanking size X main pole plates.

Element A.—Wipe down 20 strips (7 blanks per strip = 140 blanks)

Rating:—80   Time per strip:—1·4, 1·3, 1·3

$$\text{Average} = \frac{4 \cdot 0}{3} \times \frac{80}{60} = 1 \cdot 78 \text{ S.M.s.}$$

$$\text{Time} = \frac{1 \cdot 78 \text{ S.M.s.} + 12\frac{1}{2} \text{ per cent. relaxation}}{20 \times 7} = \cdot 014 \text{ per blank.}$$

Element B.—Feed strip, blank, and place waste on floor.

Rating	Time per Strip	Total Time at Std.
80	·20, ·23, ·23, ·26, ·24, ·27, ·22, ·22, ·25 ·24, ·19, ·26, ·28, ·24	4·45
85	·20, ·22, ·20, ·20, ·23	1·49
90	·17, ·20, ·17, ·20, ·20, ·19, ·19, ·22, ·22, ·20, ·20, ·20, ·18, ·18, ·25, ·21, ·18	5·10
95	·18, ·18, ·18	0·86
100	·17, ·18, ·17, ·18, ·17, ·17, ·18, ·17	2·31
	(48 observations)	14·21

$$\text{Time} = \frac{14 \cdot 21}{48} + 12\frac{1}{2} \text{ per cent. relaxation} = \cdot 336 \text{ per strip.}$$

$$\text{or } \frac{\cdot 336}{7} = \cdot 048 \text{ per blank.}$$

(NOTE.—The recorded time 0·14 (Fig. 29) at a 90 rating has been discarded as doubtful.)

Element C.—Empty container (every 20 strips).

Rating:—80   Time per 20 strips:—·25, ·25, ·30

$$\text{Average} = \frac{\cdot 80}{3} \times \frac{80}{60} = \cdot 354 \text{ S.M.s. for 140 blanks.}$$

$$\text{Time} = \frac{\cdot 354 + 15 \text{ per cent. relaxation}}{140} = \cdot 003 \text{ per blank.}$$

Total for operation = ·014 + ·048 + ·003 = ·065 per blank.
Add contingencies at 5 per cent. = ·0603 or 6·03 per 100 blanks.

STANDARD TIME = 6·83 per 100.

Payment by Results or Piece-rates

Having arrived at a time for measurement of the work content of a job, it is obviously convenient to use the unit, i.e. time, for piecework rate and calculations. In this case the Standard Time becomes the Allowed Time. That is, an operator is allowed this time in which to do the job, at daywork rate of wages. Many methods have been evolved and used in the past for paying the operator a bonus increment on his daywork earnings for saving time, i.e. doing the job in less time than standard. Some encourage high effort by paying at a higher rate when the job is done faster than at piecework rate, whilst others, like the Rowan, by paying for a proportion of the time saved endeavour to minimise the effects of variations due to inaccurate measurement.

Such systems are largely academic today, and it is generally accepted that straight piecework, i.e. payment pro rata with work done, is the only fair and satisfactory basis of payment. It is understood and accepted by operators and Trade Unions.

For straight piecework payment the operator is paid for doing the job in the Standard Time, however long it actually takes. Since operators like to think in terms of bonus earned above their flat rate, they are interested in the time saved, so that the total time they save on all jobs done in a week, expressed as a percentage of the time worked, is a measure of their performance commonly understood, and known, as the Percentage Bonus. For example, if an operator completes jobs for which, in total, 60 hours were allowed, by working at a steady piecework effort (an 80 rating), in 45 hours

$\left(60 \times \dfrac{60}{80}\right)$ then the time saved is 15 hours, and the bonus is—

$$\frac{15}{45} \times 100 = 33\tfrac{1}{3} \text{ per cent.}$$

The operator is paid for the whole of the 60 hours, but payment is usually shown thus (assuming for example that the hourly rate is 4s. per hour):

	£	s.	d.
Actual time, 45 hours =	9	0	0
Bonus time, 15 hours =	3	0	0
Total earnings	£12	0	0

This is obviously 60 hours at 4s. per hour.

If it is desired to pay per piece (the original derivation of "piecework") instead of for time allowed, then the Standard Time (time allowed) is multiplied by the rate per hour. For the example worked out above (page 323), the piece-rate would be:

$$\frac{6 \cdot 83 \text{ mins.}}{60} \times 4s. = 5 \cdot 5, \text{ or } 5\tfrac{1}{2}d. \text{ each.}$$

It is to be noted that the number of pieces to be finished per hour at dayrate is 60 divided by the Standard Time in minutes, and at piecework rate this figure is multiplied by $\dfrac{80}{60}$. For example, if the Standard Time is 5 minutes then:

Standard (or daywork) rate per hour $= \dfrac{60}{5} = 12$ pieces per hour

and piecework rate per hour $= \dfrac{60}{5} \times \dfrac{80}{60} = 16$ pieces per hour,

which is one-third faster.

Finally it occasionally happens that for good and sufficient reasons it is desired to pay more than one-third of the daywork (or basic) rate extra for a piecework effort. (The most straightforward way of paying more for a piecework effort is obviously to increase the basic rate, but the many agreements between employers and operators have been reasons for avoiding this.) If this should be so, then the Standard Time is first calculated (and clearly retained in calculations and records) and then increased in the desired ratio to obtain the Allowed Time. If, for example, it is decided to pay 50 per cent of the basic rate extra for a piecework effort (i.e. one-third more effort than daywork) then the Standard Time would be increased in the ratio $\dfrac{1 \cdot 50}{1 \cdot 33}$ or $\dfrac{90}{80}$.

Formulæ.—The above calculations can be reduced to the following formulæ, with certain convenient terms for common use:

(1) *Standard Minutes* (S.M.s) $=$ actual minutes $\times \dfrac{\text{rating}}{60}$.

(2) *Works Units* (W.U.s) $=$ S.M.s $+$ relaxation allowance

$$= \text{S.M.s} \times \left(1 + \frac{\text{relax. per cent.}}{100}\right).$$

(3) *Standard Time* (S.T.) $=$ W.U.s $+$ contingency allowance.

(4) If piecework effort is to be paid for by some bonus percentage B other than $33\frac{1}{3}$, then—

Allowed Time (A.T.) $=$ S.T. $\times \dfrac{1 \cdot B}{1 \cdot 33}$.

(5) Time to earn normal piecework (i.e. at 80 rating)

$$= \text{Allowed Time} \times \frac{60}{80} = \tfrac{3}{4} \text{ Allowed Time}.$$

(6) Output rate for normal piecework (i.e. at 80 rating)

$$= \frac{60 \text{ mins.}}{\text{Allowed Time in mins.}} \times \frac{80}{60} \text{ pieces per hour.}$$

$$= \frac{80}{\text{Allowed Time in mins.}} \text{ pieces per hour.}$$

Synthetic or Pre-determined Times

One valuable advantage of scientific work measurement over ordinary rate-fixing, in factories engaged on batch or jobbing production, i.e. where machines or operators are not continuously engaged on the same job, is that Standard Times can be established for operations or elements which are combined in different ways for different jobs. In such circumstances, quite a large staff of time-study men are required if every job is to be studied whilst it is running, but if basic data for each likely operation is first established, then a much smaller staff is adequate for preparing Standard Times.

From a large range of studies of all types of work and operations, and for all operators, Standard Times for each element are recorded. From a study of these, with rechecks when necessary, one Standard Time is selected as an average, or mean. Once the process or operations required are decided and laid down, the total Standard Time for a job can be built up by merely selecting and adding together the appropriate times for elements. To reduce clerical work, groups of elements which are frequently found in combination are summarised. Examples of this technique for machine operations are given in Figs. 31 and 32.

It is frequently found that the time varies with certain factors, such as weight, size, shape and accuracy. Time can be saved in determining the time for each variation, and a valuable check on results made, by finding the factor which controls the variation in time and plotting against this factor the standard times from a few studies along the range of variation. If the correct factor has been found, the results will lie approximately along a straight line or regular curve. If they do not, either the factor is wrong, the studies inaccurate, or there are unknown variations occurring during the studies. An example is given in Fig. 33. Such curves also form a valuable means of averaging results and of checking the accuracy of results. A curve (or straight line) drawn through plotted results indicates the mean result, and should be used for reading off standard times for values of the variable factor. Points which lie some way off the line are suspect, and should either be ignored or better still checked up.

BASIC TIMES FOR SYNTHETIC STANDARDS

MANIPULATIVE ELEMENTS—No. 4 HERBERT CAPSTAN LATHE

No.	Element	Selected Standard Time	Study Number							
			1	2	3	4	5	6	7	8
1	Start machine	·020	·019	·016	·015	·023	·010	·019	·016	—
2	Stop machine	·060	·068	·050	·050	·080	·063	·060	·056	—
	Pick up and load:									
3	A. Simple location	·150	·106	·073	·184	·176	·161	·153	·165	·133
4	B. Difficult location	·250	·365	·209	·291	·250	·327	·233	·223	·300
5	Load bar	·300	·380	·250	·123	·365	·300	·150	—	—
6	Feed bar to stop (including turret up)	·300	·364	·253	·460	·360	·154	·300	·232	·310
	True up:									
7	A. Bar work	·150	·140	·160	·175	·153	·195	·148	—	—
8	B. Chuck work	·300	·199	·324	·355	·330	·274	·225	·350	·320
	Unload and put down:									
	A. from chuck:									
9	(i) Light work, easy to remove or finish unimportant	·180	·162	·165	·185	·197	·129	·188	·171	·172
10	(ii) Heavy work, difficult to remove, or easily damaged	·260	·206	·308	·273	·219	·262	·290	·315	·358
11	B. from collet	·070	·059	·059	·069	·064	·100	·078	·056	·087
	Tighten down:									
12	A. Small effort	·140	·117	·147	·185	·111	·140	·190	·157	·137
13	B. Great effort	·300	·287	·277	·287	·300	·300	·295	·320	·410
14	Turret up	·070	·061	·066	·067	·062	·068	·065	·079	·096
15	Turret away to stop	·065	·058	·066	·062	·056	·064	·064	·056	·048
16	Turret away	·050	·070	·058	·050	·058	·057	·057	·040	·030
17	Index turret (away, index and up)	·095	·077	·108	·107	·094	·097	·088	·096	·089
18	Index front tool post	·095	·096	·096	·070	·084	·145	·083	·078	·080
19	Rear tool post up	·090	·073	·075	·086	·093	·084	·072	·081	·086
	Front tool post up									

FIG. 31.

GROUPS OF ELEMENTS FOR SYNTHETIC STANDARDS
NO. 4 HERBERT CAPSTAN LATHE

Constant Elements	S.M.s	S.M.s	S.M.s	S.M.s	S.M.s	S.M.s	S.M.s	S.M.s
Start machine . .	·020	·020	·020	·020	·020	·020	·020	·020
Stop machine . .	·060	·060	·060	·060	·060	·060	·060	·060
Pick up and load:								
A. Simple location	·150	·150	·150	·150	—	—	—	—
B. Difficult location	—	—	—	—	·250	·250	·250	·250
Tighten down:								
A. Small effort .	·140	·140	—	—	·140	·140	—	—
B. Great effort .	—	—	·300	·300	—	—	·300	·300
Unload and put down:								
A. Light work, easy to remove or finish unimportant .	·180	—	·180	—	·180	—	·180	—
B. Heavy work, difficult to remove or easily damaged .	—	·260	—	·260	—	·260	—	·260
Totals . .	·550	·630	·710	·790	·650	·730	·810	·890

Which can be summarised thus:

SUMMARY OF MANIPULATIVE ELEMENTS
NO. 4 HERBERT CAPSTAN LATHE

Constant Elements Depending on Type of Article	Light Work, easy to Remove or Finish Unimportant S.M.s	Heavy Work, difficult to remove or Easily Damaged S.M.s
Easy to locate, small effort to tighten .	·550	·630
Easy to locate, great effort to tighten .	·710	·790
Difficult to locate, small effort to tighten	·650	·730
Difficult to locate, great effort to tighten	·810	·890

FIG. 32.

Unfortunately this method is as yet little known or practised and those to whom it is new usually doubt whether it is practicable or even possible. The author, however, has found it completely successful, effective, and economical, and the method is included in the curriculum for training Work Study Engineers at the Department of Work Study and Staff Training of the Engineering Employers' Federation, Bristol, and is used by I.C.I.[1] and other large companies.

An even more fundamental approach to this method of predeter-

[1] "Development and Scope of Work Study", R. M. Currie, *Proceedings of I.M.E.*, 1954, Vol. 168, No. 25.

mining times has been made by several people, notably by Maynard, Stegmerton and Schwab (Method-Time Measurement) and Quick, Spear and Koelar (Work Factor System) in the U.S.A., and Lodge (Primary Motion Analysis) in England. They all divide operations into a limited number of fundamental manual motions for each of which a time has been established by extensive analysis of motion films and time studies, the time selected being determined by the nature of the motion and the conditions in which it is made. Hence the "correct time" for a manual job can be built up synthetically from an analysis of the fundamental motions involved in its performance. With suitable additions for relaxations and to meet com-

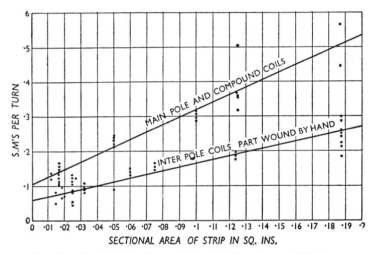

Fig. 33.—Standard time from studies plotted against variable factor.

pany policy in the matter of earnings, this time can be used for incentive standards. But it is for methods investigations and comparisons that these systems are likely to be most valuable, since they make it possible to build up a "best" method of time before a job or process is put into production, or as a standard with which to compare an existing method or time. In either case it calls for a good deal of skill not only in the use of these systems of predetermined times, but also in using information on, or knowledge of, the kind of operations or processes likely to be used.

Although the systems present the elemental data in a simple compact form, they must be applied by persons adequately trained in their use. In order to ensure that the systems will not get into disrepute through being used by incorrectly trained personnel, the training can only be obtained from recognised sources, and the time values are not otherwise available.

The use in a factory of standard times measured and established in another factory is not recommended. It is difficult for operators to accept their validity; in case of dispute there is no proof of their accuracy in the new conditions. Synthetic times developed in *the factory in which they are to be used* are likely to be more acceptable, no more expensive to establish, and the Work Study which is necessary yields valuable results in improving methods.

Special Cases

It frequently happens in process work that although the time for the process or reaction which has to take place is entirely controlled by the operator, there is an absolutely correct time. If the time is exceeded for any cause or reduced to increase output, then the resulting product is not up to standard. In such cases it is an easy matter to determine the Standard Time. But if it is desired to apply payment by results, payment obviously cannot be according to output. The solution is to pay full or piecework rate for standard output, and to decrease the rating, and therefore payment, as output falls below or rises higher than the standard figure.

It sometimes happens too that because operators think it is something inimical to their interests, they object to the use of a stop-watch, and their Trade Union organisation refuses to co-operate. Fortunately, this restrictive practice is dying, but its possibility must still be provided for. Correct time studies can still be made by counting the time interval. It is possible for a time-study engineer to train himself to count at the rate of 60 per minute with a small degree of error, no more than a second per minute either way. When using this method, it is necessary to break up an operation into short elements, because of the difficulty of counting as the count gets into high figures; it is preferable not to exceed 30 seconds. Generally, it is not possible to do long continuous studies, involving many short elements, by this method. It is very important to check the speed of counting regularly, preferably at least twice per day, and important too to check rating on other work, or with other study men. It is important to avoid external impressions, such as loud noises and visual interference. Periodic noises tend to confuse, and if the time interval is round about one second accurate counting becomes impossible. Providing these precautions are taken, quite satisfactory studies can be obtained.

TOOL AND EQUIPMENT DESIGN

It is impossible, in a book of this kind, to discuss in detail the technique and practice of tool design, usually referred to in engineering as Jig and Tool Design. Nevertheless, it is important for the student of production management to be aware of its importance, not only in engineering, but in all industries, and the part it can play. In England we have not been backward at inventing. Indeed, the Industrial Revolution started here, and the use of steam power for driving machinery was developed by Watt. But in this century we have tended to rest on our oars of tradition in the factories. We have lagged behind America in the use of horse-power and of specially designed equipment. As a result of the lead given by the mass-production automobile factories, we are rapidly taking up the slack in our engineering factories, but there is still much to be done and great scope for special equipment in the non-engineering and process factories.

One has only to go through the factories of well-known companies who make consumable goods such as Boots (pharmaceutical products), Cadburys (chocolates), The Metal Box Company (boxes), Lever Bros. (soap), and some of the shoe factories, to appreciate the use that can be made of conveyors, special machinery, gadgets and power.

In such factories cans are conveyed up and down buildings, and even along the ceiling; powder is filled by vacuum, like fluids, to avoid dust; articles are wrapped and packed automatically; conveyors are used to avoid persons lifting or carrying wherever possible, and most of the equipment is designed by the firms' own engineers. These engineers are equivalent to the jig and tool draughtsmen of the engineering industry, but whatever their title, the important thing is to recognise the need for such specialists, to employ capable men, and to make use of their abilities. The tendency usually is to make insufficient use of them, either because of a reluctance to make the capital expenditure on special plant they recommend, or because of resistance to change to new methods in the factory. Most of the productivity reports of the Specialist Teams from this country which visited the U.S.A. under the auspices of the Anglo-American Council on Productivity in the years 1950–52 give evidence of this.

Tool designers have two spheres of activity. First, the design of new tools, department layout and special machines for new programmes or models. This applies more especially in engineering, and has intensive application in the motor-car and aeroplane manufacturing industries. In this case the tool designers must be brought in at the design stage of the new product or model, the design of which can only be settled in relation to production methods. Tool design and tool making must be integrated with production programmes. This is a good reason why the production engineers should be closely connected with production planning.

Their second sphere is in designing improvements to present methods, and in this they must work closely with Work Study engineers. It is in this work that there is most scope in factories producing consumable goods. Work-holding devices, fixtures, special tools and departmental layout can be handled by a firm's own staff, but the design of special machinery usually has to be given to firms who specialise in this class of work.

In engineering factories the battle between special-purpose and general-purpose machines is not settled, and is never likely to be. It would appear that the British manufacturer generally must look for export business where quality and special skill are required, rather than mass production. This means more general-purpose machines, and the user, the tool designer and production engineer can help the machine manufacturer by taking their problems to him.

Tool designers and draughtsmen should develop a critical and inventive outlook, never being satisfied with past practice. There is a danger of their becoming stale, and to guard against this they should be given every facility and encouragement to visit other factories, and to invite designers into their own. Methods often have a common use in quite different industries and processes, and nothing but good can come of such interchange. For example, the sight of cardboard being cut in a printing factory gave an engineer the idea of how to cut insulation and conversely printers have used paint-spraying technique to prevent offset.

PRODUCTION PLANNING
Definition of Activities and Terms

The object of a production policy is to ensure that the products (or services) are supplied in the required volume, of the required quality, at the time required, and at a minimum cost. This demands effective and flexible production planning; effective in meeting all the requirements, and flexible to do so in spite of sometimes rapidly changing requirements or conditions. Delivery promises can be broken if assessments of capacity are wrong, and congestion, bottlenecks, idle time and other excess production costs can arise if all supplies (including information) are not forthcoming when they are required. Guesswork is not good enough and memory is an unreliable servant. In all but the smallest organisations a person cannot carry all the details of delivery dates, supplies and capacities in his head without making mistakes or neglecting something. Waiting for work, instructions, or tools, is one of the biggest contributory causes of high costs—or at least of costs being higher than they should be, i.e. excess costs. Well-thought-out schemes of production planning substitute facts for guesswork and reduce waiting time considerably. Orders must be delivered to time, and for economical production there must be a minimum of interruption to flow due to lack of work or information, and in order to maintain steady employment a balanced load of work must be maintained between departments. The objects of production planning, therefore, can be stated as:

(1) To relate orders and delivery promises or plans to capacities available or conversely to provide the capacity and production to meet agreed or accepted demand.
(2) To ensure that material and components are available when and where required.
(3) To produce a steady flow of work through all departments.
(4) To preserve a balance of work between the various departments.
(5) To preserve adequate manufacturing instructions to enable management and foremen to concentrate on supervision and production technique, and relieve them of detailed clerical work.
(6) To provide management with information to correct for possible delays and difficulties before they arise or become serious.

It is sometimes objected that production planning increases clerical staff and involves a large increase in paper-work. This is not usually true; it is more usual for there to be already a large amount of paper work, often on scrap pads and memo books, spread throughout the organisation. Simple and effective systems of planning merely replace this scrappy paper-work with well-designed forms, which ensure that the information required is recorded in a form most convenient to those who have to use it. A frequent objection, particularly from the old and experienced manager, to planning or departmental loading is that his business is different, and there are so many day-to-day alterations to suit customer or supplier that it just is not worth drawing up plans or programmes. Experience proves that good production planning inevitably reduces the frequency of change, and that in any case the existence of some plan reveals quickly the precise effect on production and promises already made which any new alteration will have. Too often factories flounder from one week to the next, attempting to meet the demands of pressing customers, nearly all of whom get their goods later than promised merely because too much has been promised.

It is necessary to be clear about the meaning and use of certain terms used rather loosely in connection with production planning in industry. Certain words which are in common use in normal speech and writing have a specific use in industry, and others are used with different meanings in different places. The meanings which will be attached to such words in this text, therefore, are set out below.

Production Planning.—The meaning and content of this term have been explained in Chapter I. It is used instead of the term Production Control, as defined in British Standards Booklet B.S. 1100, page 2, "the means by which a manufacturing plan is determined, information issued for its execution, and data collected and recorded, which will enable the plant to be controlled through all its stages".

Planning Department.—The department charged with the responsibility of planning production in the above sense.

Schedules.—Lists or charts setting out work to be produced in a period, or in order of priority or to stated dates. It is commonly used synonymously with programmes.

Capacity.—The amount of production which can be done in a period with the labour and facilities available in assumed conditions.

Loading.—The process of setting the amount of work to be done against the capacity available, for operator, machine, department or factory.

Stock Records.—The maintenance, usually by a system of records, of adequate stocks of materials and components to enable production to continue according to plans.

It will be obvious that the tools of the production planner are formed of figures and facts. For the tools to be effective the figures and facts must be accurate and available when required. It is understood that figures used by designers and accountants must be accurate, but not always recognised that they must be equally so for the planner. Too often the times for operations, or figures of output, are approximate within wide limits, and then there is surprise because plans do not turn out to be realistic.

The type of person employed on the work is also of importance. He must not only have a very good memory, but also must be logical and have an analytical type of mind—but not a single-track mind. That is, he must be able to take a wide view of his field of operations and take in and memorise many details and keep several major jobs or problems alive in his mind together. At the same time he must be resourceful (and not merely in finding excuses) but not easily flustered. Quite a specification! It certainly cannot be fulfilled successfully by a shop clerk who may happen to have a good memory of the firm's products but is without training or experience.

Executives in small factories of say less than 100 persons (and we have seen that there are more factories in Britain smaller than this than there are larger) need not be apprehensive that planning involves expensive "systems" and large clerical staffs. Planning is a mental process, the result of an attitude of mind, a determination to do things in an orderly way, and to do them in the light of facts and not of guesses. Simple records and schedules of weekly priorities with an accurate measure of capacity and demand can be as effective as the most elaborate systems.

The characteristics of effective planning are:

That it has a clearly defined objective in view.
It is simple and flexible.
Provides for and uses accurate records and data.
Establishes standards for measurement of results and progress.

Responsibilities

The following can be taken as an example of the responsibilities of the head of a Production Planning Department:

(1) Carry out the Company's manufacturing policy in relation to production programmes.
(2) Determine capacity of all manufacturing departments and prepare long- and short-term loads.
(3) Translate orders received from the Sales Department (via Design or Drawing Office) into orders on the Works Departments.
(4) Prepare schedules of production for all departments and issue them in such a form, and at such a time, as to enable the departments concerned to produce the work required at the right time.
(5) Maintain progress records to show actual against planned production, and take necessary action to correct deviations as far as possible.
(6) Advise the Sales Department when it becomes known that delivery promises cannot be maintained.
(7) Answer enquiries from customers as to the progress of their orders, remembering that good delivery and the honouring of delivery promises is an important part of the Company's reputation and manufacturing policy.
(8) Maintain accurate records of all material and component stocks and movements in and out of stores in such a way as to anticipate future requirements and always to have material available for production to customers' requirements.
(9) Requisition from the buyer materials and supplies required, giving the necessary information, including the time when goods are required, Prepare schedule of requirements for suppliers and integrate with the Company's production programmes, progressing as required.
(10) Train staff in the effective performance of their duties.
(11) Adhere to the Company's personnel policy and ensure that subordinates do so.
(12) Keep abreast of developments in modern production planning and technique.

A word is required on the inclusion of Stock Records under the Planner's authority. Both in text-books and in practice it is frequently put under the authority of either the storekeeper or buyer, on the misguided assumption that, because the storekeeper is responsible for actual stocks and the buyer for obtaining them, one or the other ought therefore to be responsible for records. The records are a tool and used mainly by the planners. The same records can be used once a year for stock valuation purposes, but their main purpose is to ensure that a proper production flow and balance between departments is facilitated by accurate stocks—and production flow and balance between departments is a Planning Department responsibility. It is fundamentally wrong for clerical work which can be done just as easily in an office, away from noise and under specialist supervision, to be done in a works department—and the stores is a works department. The buyer's job, on the other hand, is to buy and is concerned primarily with external agencies—he should not be responsible for level of stocks or accuracy of records.

Organisation of Department

The work of a Production Planning Department generally falls into three sections, dealing with three stages of the sequence of operations. They are:

(1) Compiling and recording facts.
(2) Developing plans.
(3) Putting plans into operation and controlling results.

In the first stage and section, information is gathered together, recorded and filed in a way which is suitable for use by planners, and so that reference to it is easy and rapid. The information is of three kinds, relating to:

> customers' orders and requirements;
> stocks of materials and components;
> plant available, capacities, operations and times.

Unless the organisation is of such a size that each kind of information is dealt with in a separate section, it is advisable for all of it to be handled by one section under the supervision of a person skilled in the work. Its organisation is mainly a problem of filing and entering-up figures or records from vouchers, i.e. transferring information and striking balances. It can usually be staffed with juniors, female, or relatively unskilled labour, but must be carefully supervised and checked by very reliable people. The absolute accuracy and double checking required in banks is not essential, but inaccuracies can be troublesome and costly.

The second stage and section comprises the vital part of planning. It is here that the effectiveness or indifference of results is ensured, and where the ability to scheme, think ahead and take all factors into account is so essential. It is a job mainly done on paper, juggling as it were with figures and charts. Sales budgets must be broken down into or integrated with long-term production plans, factory and departmental plans formulated, and weekly or daily or even hour-by-hour loads prepared. In small factories a few simple charts or schedules suffice, but in very large organisations a vast amount of detailed information, in the form of masses of figures, flows into the section, and must be rapidly and regularly collated and reissued for action. Extreme tidiness is essential, and if those concerned are not to be bogged down by a continuous stream of insistent enquiries demanding attention, much of the work must so be organised as to be dealt with in a routine manner by juniors.

The third stage consists of translating the plans into shop instructions and can be mainly of a clerical nature. In practice, however, it is at this stage that a certain amount of decentralisation is advisable, and the hour-by-hour machine or operation loading and the actual issue of jobs to operators is done either in or adjacent to the foreman's office, or in a shop office. Progress work, that is, checking performance against plans and reporting results (with recommendations for corrective action and requests for urgent actions) to foremen or other supervisors, which is really an aspect of control, is frequently carried out from the same office and even by the same persons.

These stages and the tools used are shown diagrammatically in the chart on the following page (Fig. 34).

The complexity of an organisation structure for production planning depends on the type of industry or manufacture rather than its scale. In mass-production and continuous-process manufacture, production planning consists of balancing the flow of materials (or components) from outside or component manufacturing departments, with consumption by the factory or assembly departments. Particularly is this so in the automobile or similar industries, where a good deal of preliminary work on materials is subcontracted, no large stock of materials is kept (or could be for the immense consumption rate) and a small interruption to production affects a large part of the factory and is very expensive. In those factories engaged on batch production of partly standardised products (by far the greater number in Great Britain), there is the added complexity of setting-up (time and cost), varying batch sizes, and the synchronisation of finishing dates for parts and sub-assemblies when batches vary so much. It is predominantly a question of continual adjustment in order to maintain balanced loads on departments and to correct for unforeseen delays. When the product is designed to customers' require-

PRODUCTION ADMINISTRATION SHOWING STAGES AND TOOLS USED

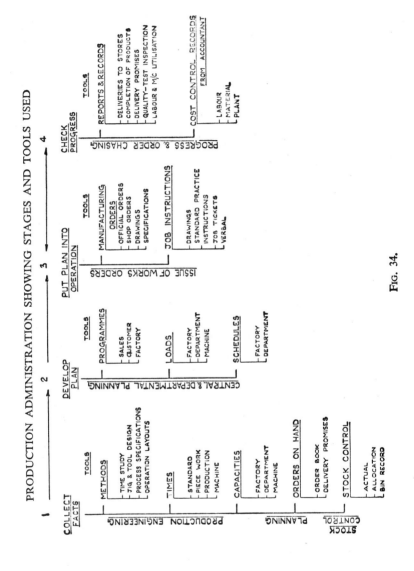

Fig. 34.

ments, the total process time is increased by the time required for design or preparation for each order, and consequently the period over which planning must extend is greater, making the problem more complex. Production planning is most complex when the product is mainly to customers' requirements, but is designed to incorporate many standard parts kept in stock. When the number of orders exceeds something like 50 per week, the amount of information to be handled becomes large and the department correspondingly so. Computers or programme-machines may then be an economical proposition.

Electronic computers have already made their impact on large organisations and groups of operating units. As they are made smaller and cheaper, they will be increasingly used by the smaller and more typical organisations. The kind of problem for which they are eminently suited occurs in a group of mills weaving cloth. The cloth is of different quality, weight, width, colour and design; the orders are for a different number of pieces, for one delivery or split deliveries, and for delivery at specified dates or to schedule; the looms differ, some being capable of weaving only plain and cheaper grades of cloth, others being versatile have a high capital value and should have the maximum time on the higher value material. Planning, therefore, is a complicated problem of determining the most profitable way of allocating production to available capacity. This is a problem which can be solved by "linear programming", involving a large number of equations and "unknowns", by an analogue computer; it can also be handled by a data-processing computer with the aid of punched cards. Similar problems have been solved in connection with minimising transport and depot costs and obtaining optimum results in oil refining.

Installing Production Planning

The question often asked by those who become aware that they must do something about the need for an effective planning scheme is: How long will it take to put in? As usual it all depends on the scheme, the job it has to do, and the limiting factors of the shortage of skilled staff, the continuity of sales programmes, market stability, and the delivery periods of stationery and special equipment. But unless all or most of these conditions are favourable, it is found in practice that it takes between one and two years to put in a complete scheme and to make it work effectively and permanently. The factor which most affects the time is the availability of skilled staff. But in whichever way it is tackled it takes time to get it running smoothly, and for everyone in the works, unaccustomed to "systems", to understand and support it. One cannot graft on something new and

P.P.M.—12*

expect immediate fruit. It is preferable first to prepare all process data and times, as these are seldom available in the form required. To plan on approximate data gives only approximate results—hit and miss—and the misses can be annoying, disturbing and discouraging to the works—but sometimes immediate results can be obtained with approximate figures and the Sales Department may be grateful for them.

Universality of Technique

The writer has had active experience of production planning in many industries, and has always found that the same principles, techniques and procedures are effective in each. Production planning is a universal activity, and the tools developed, systems, indices, forms, procedures, office machinery, and so on, are not peculiar to one industry. What follows in this section, therefore, can be taken to be of general application. Even though the illustrations relate to engineering, they serve their purpose by illustrating method and principle.[1]

Compiling and Recording the Facts

Production planning consists broadly of relating what is wanted to what is available, on a time basis. Obviously, this can only be done if all the facts are known—facts relating to what has to be produced and when, and facts relating to capacities and materials available. This in turn involves still more detailed facts of materials, stocks, plant, methods, labour, times, production, scrap, delays and amendments. To plan an operation like the erection of a bridge calls for the collection of all facts relating to that one operation only, but in a factory, production of one kind or another continues indefinitely, so that we have the added requirement that *all* the facts should *always* be available in a suitable form. One of the skills of production planning therefore is to be able to compile, record and index all the information required, so that it can be kept up to date, be speedily available and be readily and effectively used.

In the logical sequence of events, the orders from customers or sales requirements provide the first set of facts, but since we must consider a unit which is operating on a continuous basis, it will be more helpful if we consider first the permanent records which form

---

[1] A more detailed exposition of the practice of production planning is given in the booklets published originally by the British Standards Institution as B.S.S. 1100 but now obtainable from the British Institute of Management.
Part 1—*Principles of Production Control,*
Part 2—*Production Control—the Small Factory,*
Part 3—*Application of Production Control.*

the background as it were to all the planning operations. The first of these is Stock Records.

Stock Records

In a very few of the large mass-production units, materials flow straight into production within a day or two of receipt, but nothing like this is possible in the majority of factories. In most factories some materials or components must be kept in stock against a probable or a known future requirement, and it is therefore essential to know what stocks are available and when they need replenishing and when orders must be placed for further supplies. There are two rather different methods in use, one depending on a knowledge of the *actual* stock at any time, and the other on the amount of *free* stock, that is, the amount available and *not allocated* to or absorbed by future production. Which method to use depends on circumstances and the kind and extent of control required. The free stock method ensures that all future commitments are covered by orders, whereas the actual stock method only ensures that there is sufficient material in stock or on order to cover *normal* requirements with normal delivery periods from suppliers. It is difficult to be sure what will be normal, so that the actual stock method is dangerous and results often inaccurate owing to stocks becoming exhausted, when consumption is liable to fluctuate irregularly. For example, a stock equivalent to two months' normal demand of a material may be exhausted in two weeks if an unusual order absorbs an abnormal amount of this material; and it may not be possible to replace it in two weeks. The free stock method is almost essential in times of continually rising demand, but when production periods in the factory exceed the time for delivery of materials, excessive stocks may be created. Neither method prevents stocks running out if suppliers take longer than expected or promised to deliver the goods. Perhaps the simplest method of controlling actual stocks and one quite suitable where demand and delivery periods are steady, and actual quantity in stocks is only required to be known for annual stocktaking purposes (and is then counted), is to box or parcel the minimum stock quantity as described on page 428. When in similar circumstances a clerical record of actual stock is also required, the Bin Card record of stock movement and balance is satisfactory. Normally, however, conditions are not so stable and the job must be done clerically. The information which then has to be utilised or recorded is:

Amount required (for allocating).
Amount ordered (for allocating).
Amount used (for actual).

Amount received (for actual).

Balance.—free or actual.

Date and Job or Order No. (for reference).

Specification of material or part (for re-ordering).

Minimum stock (safety margin).

Re-order quantity (normal batch).

Unit value (for stock-taking purposes).

Because rapid reference is essential, it is usual to do all recording on visible edge cards, and much ingenuity has been used in their design and the equipment for housing them. There are numerous types from which to choose to suit varying uses and commodities, and three only are illustrated:

(1) For allocating future requirements from a free stock.

(2) For replacing stocks when actual stocks are reduced to a minimum figure and for recording orders placed.

(3) For allocating from a free stock and at the same time revealing actual stock.

Illustrations of suitable forms are given in Figs. 35, 36 and 37, with a few typical entries shown.

Allocating from Free Stock (Fig. 35)

This is the simplest form of record. The same columns and entries

Date/Job No.	Alloc.	Ordered	Free	Date/Job No.	Alloc.	Ordered	Free	Date/Job No.	Alloc.	Ordered	Free
			15								
14·2·48	4	–	11								
3·5·48	12	–	–1								
AB	–	40	39								
5·5·48	5	–	34								
6·5·48	1-Scrap (No 3)	–	33								

BATCH .... 40 ....   PATT No. ....

DESCRIPTION ....BUSH............   FRAME ....   PART No. ..../111.......

FIG. 35.

can be used for actual stocks, "issues" replacing "allocation" and "receipts" replacing "ordered", the "balance" being actual stock and not free. To open such a record the total present known requirements is deducted from the total stock available (ordered, in progress and in stock) and entered as an opening "free stock". An opening figure of 15 is shown in the illustration (from which subsequent entries can be followed). A new order is placed, or batch put into production, either when "free stock" is reduced to nil or a minimum reserve. The latter is only required if a very urgent order, using this part or material, is likely to absorb any existent stock and is likely to be required immediately or before other orders booked.

Replacing Actual Stocks (Fig. 36)

In this case further supplies are ordered or put into production when the actual quantity in stock falls to a predetermined minimum

RECEIPTS					ISSUES			
DATE	ORDER No.	QUANT.	REC?	OUTSTAND.	DATE	ORDER No.	QUANT.	STOCK
								14
					4·5·48	BP	4	10
10·5·48	AA	40		40				
16·5·48	AA		20	20				30
					20·5·48	BQ	3	27
24·5·48	AA		20					47

ORDER PT. 10   BATCH .40
DESCRIPTION   PART No. /111

FIG. 36.

(order point). This minimum quantity must be sufficient to supply normal issues from stock over the period normally taken to obtain replacement. The left-hand half of the record deals with the orders for replacement, the right-hand half with issues and actual stock balances.

Replacing Free Stock and Recording Actual (Fig. 37)

This record is a combination of allocation and actual stock records. It could be made comprehensive by adding a column for balance-on-order as in the second illustration. For all normal purposes it gives all the information required for maintenance of stocks; in the few instances when the balance on order is required, it can be found by totalling receipts and setting off against the quantity ordered. It needs greater care and skill from clerks than the first two illustrations, but when accurately maintained and checked periodically, the record of actual stock can be accepted for stock-taking purposes to avoid the annual physical check and the problems this involves. It will be

DATE	ORDER NO	ORDERED	FREE	ALLOC	REC?	STOCK	ISSUED	DATE	ORDER NO	ORDERED	FREE	ALLOC	REC?	STOCK	ISSUED
			4			14									
4-5-48	BP					10	4								
6-5-48	124		-1	5											
10-5-48	AA	40	39												
16-5-48	AA				20	30									
20-5-48	BQ					27	3								
22-5-48	125		32	7											
24-5-48	AA				20	47									

| DESCRIPTION | BATCH 40 | PART N° /111 |

FIG. 37.

noticed that the free stock and actual stock entries and records are independent of each other, and that actual stock at any time may be more or less than the free stock.

It may sometimes happen that there are a few items of stock which, because of their importance to production, require to be specially watched. The basic materials in certain process industries, like grains in flour milling, flour, sugar, etc., in food and confectionery, and linseed oil, solvents, etc., in paint, are important in this way, and the head of the Planning Department or the Works Manager himself may wish to have a visible record or wall chart of stocks of these items. A simple chart can be constructed as illustrated in Fig. 38. It is corrected daily or weekly by the Stock Records clerks. There are similar moving bar charts available from office equipment manufacturers which show three facts on each bar.

Records of Times and Capacities for Processes and Operations

The second type of basic data which must be compiled and made available is that which has to do with processes and operations carried on in the factory.

It is essential to have readily available the operations, plant required and production times for all products, parts and assemblies.

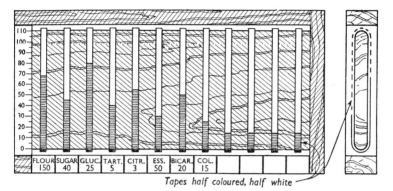

| FLOUR | SUGAR | GLUC. | TART. | CITR. | ESS. | BICAR. | COL. | | | | |
| 150 | 40 | 25 | 5 | 3 | 50 | 20 | 15 | | | | |

Tapes half coloured, half white

FIG. 38.—Movable Bar Chart.

This can be done in the form of a standard practice manual, or process book, or stock catalogue, but some kind of card filing is more convenient. In engineering and general manufacture, where there are many parts, many of which are standard, the information is best set out on Process Layouts or Master Route Cards. An example of such a process layout is given in the Appendix to this Chapter, Fig. 47, Operation Master (page 386).

In whatever way it is set out, the following information should be on one record:

Description and reference number of product or part.
Material and amount required for one unit.
Normal production quantity, i.e. production batch.
Operations or processes involved in manufacture.
Plant or machine and tools required for each operation.
Production time for each process or operation.

The production time is best expressed as the time allowed or standard time. To avoid a conversion to actual time for planning purposes, all charts and measures of capacity should be in terms of standard time. Thus, for a week of 45 actual hours, the available standard hours in a factory, where the normal bonus is $33\frac{1}{3}$ per cent., would be $45 \times 1\cdot33 = 60$ hours.

The Production Engineers will supply all of the above information (set out on Process Layouts, when these are used), deciding the normal production batch in collaboration with the Production Planning Department.

It is also necessary to have an accurate record of the plant and labour force available and their capacity. This may sound obvious to those in factories where a few continuous processes are in operation, but in the many factories on batch production with general-purpose plant and machines, it is often neglected, plant being taken out of commission because of breakdown and new plant or equipment installed without the Production Planning Department being informed. The Production Planning Department, therefore, should have a copy of the plant register, or at least a list of all plant, should be advised of all changes, and should keep the record up to date, it being the duty of either the foremen or Maintenance Department to inform them of changes. Similarly, either the foremen or Personnel Officer should inform them of changes in the labour force which will affect capacity.

Orders on Hand

Finally, the Production Planning Department must know what has to be produced, and therefore must know of all orders on hand and delivery promises made. This again can be a simple or elaborate job, depending on the type and number of orders. When customers are supplied from shelf stock, the Sales Department keep stock records of finished products and requisition (or order) on the Production Departments as free stock is absorbed. In other cases Production Planning are advised of the customer's actual order and requirements. In either case orders are recorded as received in the Production Planning Department, and marked off as completed. In most cases it will be found that the best way of doing this is on visible edge card records. The card must be designed to suit the kind of order and the information frequently required in connection with it, e.g. portion completed. Either one card can be used for one order (if there are always several items per order), or one line of the card for each order. The cards should be filed in some logical sequence, and it is of considerable help for reference purposes in the works and sales offices if it is arranged with the Sales Department for order numbers to be allocated to orders in the works in some code which designates the type of product. Orders are then filed in production groups and number sequence, providing a logical reference for planning purposes. It is important to log each order *immediately* it is received, to allocate a works order number immediately (if the sales order number is not used) and to cross off or enter the date immediately it is completed. Failure to do either of these things results in false computations of balance of work on hand and neglect to produce or over-production of orders.

Developing Plans
Long-term Plans or Budgets

Production plans must, of course, be based on sales demand. When there is no positive sales programme, plans can only be based on trends. Normally there are sales programmes both long term and short term, and broad or long-term production plans are developed from general conferences between all executives and the Managing Director when future sales programmes are discussed. In the case of the larger mass-production factories manufacturing consumption goods for the general public, such as cars and radios, proprietary foods, toilet preparations, etc., a definite sales programme is agreed upon, and this must be broken down by the Production Planning Department in a pre-production programme for the new product or sales push. When such a programme involves drawings, special tools, or plant, and detail manufacture or assembly, it should be set out in chart form on a time basis, so that the interrelated completion dates for each stage or part can be seen. Such a chart is shown in Fig. 39 taken from B.S.S. 1100, Part 3. Difficulties, due for example to lack of capacity to meet the programme, lack of equipment and need for special tooling, etc., are discussed by all concerned at the pre-production stage, and general agreement on all stages obtained before the programme is confirmed.

Usually no radical departure from previous demands is planned or expected. A more or less continuous flow of orders for the company's products or services is received, varying in volume from time to time. But it is still necessary for the Production Planning Department to take a fairly long forward view and to develop long-term programmes. In the first place, it is essential to know what is the total load on the factory represented by all orders on the books in order to know what delivery period can be promised to customers for manufacture to customer's order, or what finished stocks to carry when manufacturing to stock. It is also necessary to know whether this load will keep the departments or processes equally loaded. In this we encounter the problem which vexes all those interested in measuring overall output, planners, statisticians and economists—what measure of output to use in firms or industries manufacturing many different lines or products. A ton of cement is much the same wherever it is manufactured, but two yards of cloth may be very different in quality and in the amount of machine-hours and man-hours required for production, and two electric motors even of the same horse-power can be very different in design. The only accurate measure is machine-hours or man-hours, but the breakdown of every order into detailed man-hours for long-term planning is impractic-

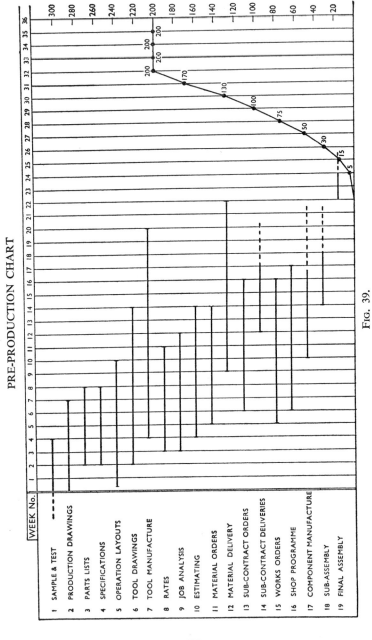

PRE-PRODUCTION CHART

| WEEK No. | 1 | 2 | 3 | 4 | 5 | 6 | 7 | 8 | 9 | 10 | 11 | 12 | 13 | 14 | 15 | 16 | 17 | 18 | 19 | 20 | 21 | 22 | 23 | 24 | 25 | 26 | 27 | 28 | 29 | 30 | 31 | 32 | 33 | 34 | 35 | 36 |

1 SAMPLE & TEST
2 PRODUCTION DRAWINGS
3 PARTS LISTS
4 SPECIFICATIONS
5 OPERATION LAYOUTS
6 TOOL DRAWINGS
7 TOOL MANUFACTURE
8 RATES
9 JOB ANALYSIS
10 ESTIMATING
11 MATERIAL ORDERS
12 MATERIAL DELIVERY
13 SUB-CONTRACT ORDERS
14 SUB-CONTRACT DELIVERIES
15 WORKS ORDERS
16 SHOP PROGRAMME
17 COMPONENT MANUFACTURE
18 SUB-ASSEMBLY
19 FINAL ASSEMBLY

FIG. 39.

348

able. It is frequently sufficient to use man- or machine-hours for the process or department common to all products or otherwise controlling (total) output. If a simple measure of volume is not possible, it will usually be found that value in £ s. d. is adequate, if the spread of kinds of product remains fairly steady and corrections are made for appreciable variations. The total load divided by the factory capacity per week (actual or budgeted) gives the time in weeks it would take to manufacture everything on order, and therefore the delivery period.

If there is only one or a few very similar products, and orders are executed in strict rotation, then little more information on future load is required. More often, however, there are many dissimilar products, each absorbing different amounts of each department's capacity, or orders are taken for delivery at a specified time, and not merely in rotation, and sometimes both conditions apply.

In either case, either orders must be taken for delivery according to capacity available, or capacity must be adjusted to suit orders received and delivery required, and in practice forward plans are made to reconcile these two alternatives. The problem resolves itself into a matter of setting off orders received against capacity, actual or budgeted. Taking first the case when orders are to be executed in rotation and not at a specified time, the period it would take to manufacture the total load (value, units, etc.) of orders on hand should be assessed periodically, weekly, or monthly. If the period varies, it must be decided either to adjust quoted delivery periods accordingly, adjust capacity, or (if the period is falling too rapidly) ask for more sales effort. When output measured in value, or volume, does not reflect capacity proportionately, and the only accurate measure is hours (man-hours or machine-hours), then it is necessary to divide the products made into categories of like kinds (if they do not fall naturally into definite categories) and, for each category, to select the most representative unit, taking into account demand and hours capacity absorbed. Orders are then recorded and assessed for capacity in terms of these representative units. Capacity can be checked departmentally in this way without a great amount of statistical work (see Fig. 40). Since for a given overall volume of production definite financial and production facilities are required, it is necessary to budget total volume and allocate this to the various categories. An example of the build-up of such a production budget using typical average units for each category of product manufactured is given in Fig. 41.

Having established such production budgets, or assessed the capacity required to meet the demand reflected in all orders on hand, the effect on plant and labour requirements and material supply

STANDARD HOURS OF LOAD

Product	Load in Equivalent Units	Department 1		Department 2		Department 3		Department 4		Department 5	
		Per Unit	Total	Per Unit	Total	Per Unit	Total	Per Unit	Total	Per Unit	Total
A	258	0·16	41·28	0·25	64·50	0·19	49·02	0·27	69·66	0·42	108·36
B	9	0·13	1·20	0·01	0·09	0·16	1·44	0·60	5·40	2·13	19·17
C	200	1·50	300·00	1·52	304·00	27·00	5,400·00	30·00	6,000·00	30·50	6,100·00
D	12	0·75	9·00	0·30	3·60	1·20	14·40	2·00	24·00	3·50	42·00
E	147	2·00	294·00	2·50	367·50	3·00	441·00	3·50	514·50	4·00	588·00
F	57	0·65	37·05	0·93	53·01	0·30	17·10	2·00	114·00	2·50	142·50
G	132	0·27	35·64	0·49	64·68	0·65	85·80	0·92	121·44	1·20	158·40
H	70	1·76	123·20	3·00	210·00	0·75	52·50	0·90	63·00	1·40	98·00
I	435	2·00	870·00	2·50	1,087·60	3·00	1,305·00	3·50	1,522·50	4·00	1,740·00
J	69	0·51	35·19	0·75	51·75	0·86	59·34	0·97	66·93	1·10	75·90
K	77	0·49	37·73	1·17	90·09	1·01	77·77	1·10	84·70	1·30	100·10
L	112	0·50	56·00	0·65	72·80	1·20	134·40	2·50	280·00	2·55	285·60
M	68	0·17	11·56	0·40	27·20	0·90	61·20	1·30	88·40	1·27	86·36
Total Std. Hrs.			1,851·85		2,396·72		7,698·97		8,954·53		9,544·39
Capacity			88		132		220		264		220
Weeks			21		18		35		34		43

Fig. 40.

(long-term contracts and minimum reserve stocks) must be assessed, and the information passed on to the appropriate department. Plant and labour requirements are not usually neglected, but the adjustment (particularly for a marked increase in output) of minimum stocks is also essential; it is frequently forgotten.

Factory Loads

In the case of orders which are quoted for delivery at a specified date or when it is necessary to build up a broad programme of the load on the works (or departments) represented by orders to be produced, it is necessary to log orders as they are accepted or put into the programme in the week (or period) concerned. This can be done either graphically or by merely listing orders on a sheet for each period. Perhaps the simplest is to record the value, in £ *s. d.* or other unit, of each order on a card in a visible edge system, one card for each week. If necessary, separate series of cards can be used for each department or process. A sliding coloured tab is slipped inside the visible edge of the card holder and is adjusted horizontally as each addition is made. The result at any time shows the load in each week, and, across all cards, the way the load varies. Alternatively, a wall chart can be used, being adjusted periodically. This can be done by small nails driven into a board in lines vertically to represent the scale of units, and horizontally in weeks. (The nails in effect being at the points of intersection of lines on a graph.) Coloured elastic is stretched round or through the nails to form a graph, separate colours representing budgeted and scheduled capacity. A similar result can be obtained by using squared paper blocking-in or crossing through squares as units of volume are absorbed or booked. Such charts show clearly where capacity is unabsorbed and available for new orders.

When the number of orders per week is small, it is possible to plan orders into a load board. An effective way of doing so is to originate a card or ticket for each order, and to draw a line along the top edge to a scale, equivalent to the number of hours or capacity absorbed by the order. These cards can then be slipped into horizontal pockets of a load board (see Fig. 42), behind each other and overlapping, with the load lines end to end, the board being marked with the same scale and divided into weeks. One pocket should be used for each unit of capacity (products, department, or group). In this way the load can be built up as far ahead as wished, it is readily visible, the completion date of existing or new orders can be seen, and it can be used for progress checking. The pockets can be made of metal or

SALES AND PRODUCTION BUDGET
BASED ON 30 PER CENT. INCREASE ON SALES FOR FINANCIAL YEAR

	Sales			Average Unit		Prelim. Budget Uniform Increase for all Categories		Final Budget Adjusted for Present Trends	
	Total Sales Value	No. of Units	Average Value	Unit taken as Std.	Est. Value of Av. Unit	Sales + 30%	Est. Prodn. in Units	Est. Total Sales	No. of Units at Av. Unit Value
Group 1: A	£ 51,786	45	£ 1,150	5-ton	£ 1,200	£ 67,400	56	£ 67,400	56
B	56,178	35	1,585	5-ton	1,600	73,000	46	73,000	46
C	15,201	89	171	2-ton	150	19,760	131	19,760	131
Total	123,115	—	—	—	—	160,160	—	160,160	—
Group 2: A	6,065	101	60	½-ton	77	7,880	102	11,470	149
B	17,458	132	132	2-ton	115	22,700	105	14,470	125
C	10,028	44	228	5-ton	175	13,040	75	18,542	106
Total	33,551	—	—	—	—	43,620	—	47,982	—
Group 3	23,287	—	—	—	—	30,250	—	30,250	—

			160 / 75	170 / 91	5-ton / 3-ton	150 / 90			
Group 4: A · · B · ·	28,519 6,964		— 	— 	— 	— 	37,020 8,870	247 98	34,500 11,390	223 126
Total ·	35,483		—	—	—	—	45,890	—	45,890	—
Group 5: A · · · B · C · D ·	17,285 6,105 3,580 3,780		906 211 h288 88	19 29 12·4 42	2-ton 2-ton 2-ton 1-ton	17 25 10 —	22,450 7,950 4,650 4,910	1,320 328 465 118	19,038 7,000 4,650 4,910	1,120 280 465 118
Total ·	30,980		—	—	—	—	40,190	—	36,826	—
Group 6 ·	9,242		—	—	—	—	12,000	—	12,000	—
Group 7 ·	7,371		—	—	—	—	9,580	—	9,580	—
Group 8 ·	23,150		—	—	—	—	30,030	—	30,030	—
TOTAL ·	£286,179		—	—	—	—	£371,720	—	£371,720	—

Fig. 41.

353

wood or even print paper stuck on to a board, the ends wrapped round the edges of the board, the scale being printed on the face of each pocket.

Departmental Loads—Long-term

Unless all orders received absorb the same proportion of capacity for each department and thus preserve a balanced load between departments, it is necessary to check regularly forward loads on departments in order to preserve balance. To do this the procedure

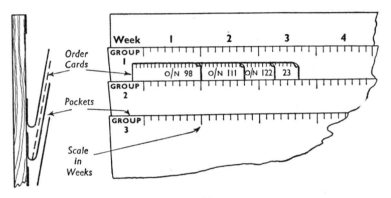

FIG. 42.

outlined above should be followed in a more detailed manner on a departmental basis. When output of the product is easily measured in terms of volume, this is not difficult, but when hours is the only measure because the individual jobs vary so much, the method of grouping into categories should be followed. All orders in hand should be analysed to find the number of units in each category. For each category the number is then multiplied by the hours required in each department and the figures for each department totalled and divided by capacity to find the load in weeks. Periodically (weekly or monthly) net differences in units for each category between orders received and despatched should be extended similarly and added (or subtracted) from previous loads. These periodic loads should be plotted to reveal any trend. An illustration of the assessment of capacity absorbed, calculated in this way, is given in Fig. 40. In such a case the loading in departments is obviously not balanced, and either orders must be increased to correct the underloading, or capacity in the overloaded departments must be expanded.

Departmental and Machine Loads—Short-term

Actual orders at some time have to be issued to the works for production.

In process and mass-production industries, where processes are in continuous operation on the same product (cement, steel, margarine, etc.), this amounts to little more than instructions for starting and stopping. When different grades of the same product are made, as in papermaking, or glass container manufacturing, an order of priority for each grade or kind must be determined. If each order takes its turn and there is no delivery period problem, no more need be done, but if it is required to know when orders will be completed, then the production scheduled must be measured and related to capacity. In most manufacturing industries a variety of different products, articles or components is manufactured in each department, and few departments, machines or operators make the same article continuously and permanently. It is then essential to issue instructions for production at the rate at which it can be completed. This means actually measuring the amount of work it is proposed to schedule for immediate production over a period. An approximate measure is no longer of any use, and if capacity and output cannot be measured accurately in some unit of volume, man-hours or machine-hours must be used. Thus we get what is commonly called *departmental or machine* loading. When instructions for production are issued in the form of a list of jobs or orders to be done in a period or in order of priority, such lists are usually termed *production schedules*.

It is at this stage that the planning problem becomes complicated and the technique needs most skill. The methods and techniques in use are many and varied, and indeed must be so to suit the widely different types and scales of production. In a book of this kind it is impossible to refer to them all. As, however, the principles underlying them all are the same and can be applied to all industries, a few illustrations will serve for an understanding of how the problem is tackled. Planning for batch production for a variety of machines or processes is about the most difficult, and will therefore be referred to in any specific illustrations.

At the loading stage of planning there are always opposing forces to be kept in equilibrium, the desire to meet customers with urgent demands and the undesirability of disturbing existing programmes; the need to keep inventories low, and the preference of the works for large batches, and so on. All such factors have to be remembered and allowed for when building up programmes or loads prior to issuing production schedules.

This detailed loading can either be made directly to machine or operator, or in two stages, first to department or groups, and then to individuals. If all machines are exactly the same and there is absolutely no difference in operator skill or aptitude, then loading immediately to machines or individuals is permissible. But where there are operator differences or idiosyncrasies it is far better not to lose the personal touch and to arrange for the production supervisor to have some or the last say in allocation of job. This can be arranged by first loading to department or group in the Production Planning Department, and then either the foreman or planning clerk in the department loading to individual or machine. The importance of this personal touch at the final stage of planning at the point of impact on the man or woman cannot be over-emphasised, and is too little appreciated. With Shakespeare,

> "We fortify in paper and in figures,
> Using the names of men instead of men,
> Like one that draws the model of a house
> Beyond his powers to build it",

dehumanising administration just where it most requires the personal touch. This accounts not a little for the indifference and even hostility to "systems" and to operators "leaving it to the planner", when a word or suggestion at the right time could do so much to help the job along.

The simplest form of scheduling—it is hardly "loading"—is by priority, keeping supervision informed at least several jobs ahead, and as far ahead as possible of the order of priority of each job. In its simplest form this is a written list. If a graphic or visual method is preferred, job tickets can be hung on hooks, one hook for each machine or operator, the next job always being uppermost.

A more comprehensive planning board consists of a series of four pockets for each machine and operator. The top two pockets each hold one job card, the lower two several. Into the top pocket is placed the job in production, in the second the next to be commenced, in the third jobs ready for production in order of priority, and in the fourth jobs waiting for material, tools, or completion of a previous operation.

Loading to capacity can be done by list, graphically or in a load board. If a list is used there should be three columns in which are entered respectively—job reference (name or number), capacity absorbed (hours, quantity, etc.), and the cumulative capacity.

Perhaps the most widely used graphic method is the Gantt chart. It suffers from the one defect that it is not easily modified, rubbing out and re-drawing lines being a time-absorbing occupation. When loads can be built up simply and are unlikely to be altered, the Gantt chart can be extremely useful and can be used to indicate progress. There are many variations, and illustrations are given in most books dealing with charts or production planning (e.g. see *Management's Handbook*, Ronald Press Co., New York); Fig. 43 is an illustration of a simple version showing the loading for two machines. The lines are drawn horizontally on paper specially printed, or on graph paper.

There are several methods of building a load board from materials likely to be available in any factory. They are usually made to take cards or strips of cardboard which are used to indicate the load. Perhaps the simplest is a board built-up of pockets as illustrated on page 354. To avoid preparing special cards, one of the cards used in

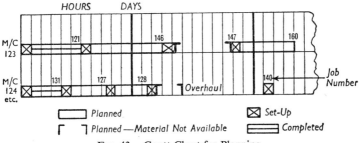

FIG. 43.—Gantt Chart for Planning.

connection with the issue of jobs, for example the job or time card, should be used, marking along the top edge a line representing the time required to do the job. It facilitates drawing the line to have a scale printed along the top as shown in the illustration of a Move Note in the Appendix to this chapter (Fig. 52). If the boards are large, the pockets can be made of metal, but for small ones they can be made of strips of strong paper when the scale can be printed on each strip, which is folded backwards and gummed to a backing board. A portable board can be made in this manner for charge-hands and foremen of small sections by using a piece of stiff cardboard as the backing board. There are of course several types of planning boards sold under proprietary names by office equipment suppliers.

Planning Problems

So much for the tools of loading; the technique can only be learnt by practice, but there are several precepts which are generally applicable. The first essential is to use an accurate measure. It cannot be too strongly emphasised that the accuracy of planning varies directly with the accuracy of the information and measurement of capacity and performance. However, much skill is used in loading, if the figures used are not accurate, departments will sometimes be overloaded and at other times short of work, resulting in overtime and idle capacity alternating violently, to the extreme annoyance of foremen and operators, and engendering a hostility to the planning engineers when co-operation is required. Furthermore, promises given to customers or the Sales Department are not kept, resulting in urgent action to retrieve the position, adding further disturbances in the shops and incurring excess costs due to "breaking down" jobs which are running to put in the urgent ones. In extreme cases the jobs superseded themselves become urgent, and eventually there are more urgent than normal jobs and planning becomes a continuous purge and a discredited instrument.

It is also important to allow for plant breakdown and maintenance and for absence of operators. For normal conditions this can best be done by loading to the normal standard hours produced per week as revealed in weekly Labour Control reports. This allows then for the average performance of operators. But over and above this the Planning Department must take steps to see that it is informed of any unusual breakdowns or absence likely seriously to affect plans, so that any necessary readjustments can be made. It is always advisable to schedule below capacity by a definite margin, which can then be filled up in the current period by urgent or rush orders.

In factories on batch production it will be found that a week is the optimum period for planning and shop loading purposes. Longer periods are apt to need too frequent revision, and a day is not long enough for collecting like batches together and for balancing up between machines or groups. Weekly schedules should be issued to departments long enough ahead for them to be given adequate consideration and preparation. The schedules themselves should be prepared far enough ahead by the planning engineers to enable their effect to be seen on work-in-progress and over- or underloading of certain machines in sections.

In factories on batch production of components for assembly into machines or units, the aim is to arrange for all components to be completed as nearly as possible together and in time for assembly to be completed by due date. For continuous assembly of one product or assembly of a special order, it is ideal to arrange for delivery of components to the job or to a work station or lay-by in the assembly shop at the rate required, or just in time, for assembly. In other cases components are delivered to a component stores, and if manufacture of components is not synchronised reasonably well with assembly, the stores will have to be larger than it need be. In assessing the production time for components (that is, the total time it takes to get them from the raw material stores to finished part stores), it is not sufficient to add up the time taken in each process or operation. In continuous-flow production, where conveyor assembly is in use, this may be nearly so, but in intermittent or batch production, where batch sizes differ, all parts do not need the same operations, and operator times vary, there must always be a float of work behind each machine or operator, and this fluctuates. In addition, some kind of inspection or checking and some transport are required after each operation, so that a job seldom moves to the next operation immediately the previous one is finished. This in-between operation time is frequently longer than the direct operation time. In any case, it must be allowed for and can only be found from experience. It will be found to vary with the component and normal time for a batch on any machine or section. The more effective the planning and subsequent control, the less is the work in progress between operations, the smaller the total production time, and the better the production flow.

There is of course a limit to the volume of figures and the number of factors which a normal staff can handle in a reasonable time with traditional methods. Electronic computers, however, make it possible to solve planning problems which involve a large number of factors and their application to such problems is now being developed. For example, a technique has been developed for using a computer for solving the kind of problem in which it is necessary to obtain the optimum conditions for operating a series of activities with a certain number of (linear) restrictions. Manufacture of different products, stocking of different items of commodities, physical properties of different components of a blend are examples of such "activities", and maximum plant capacity, maximum warehouse capacity, minimum cost of blend are respective "restrictions".

Example of Procedure

This example is once again taken from engineering, but the procedure is not restricted to it. It is in engineering that this detail planning technique has been most highly developed. Nevertheless, this procedure (and the documents illustrated in the appendix of this chapter) can be used, with suitable modifications, wherever batch production exists. It is an example of a procedure pruned to a minimum of "red tape" and paper work consistent with control and flexibility.

In order to illustrate the method of applying these planning techniques and to show how they hang together in practice, an actual example is described briefly below. The factory concerned manufactures products to delivery dates. The products all require an assembly stage and a variety of components, some of which are standard and others designed and manufactured for a particular order.

Copies of all works orders, which are identified by a number coded to indicate type of product, are sent to all departments concerned. The orders give the customer's name, a certain amount of technical data needed by the various departments, and state the delivery date promised. This date is in line with the general delivery period agreed with the Production Planning Department, and with the appearance of the sales load board (*Factory Loads*, page 351) kept up to date for the Sales Department by the Production Planning Department. The Production Engineers' and Production Planning copies go via the Drawing Office, who enter the date by which drawings will be ready after reference to their own planning board. The Planning Card used by the Production Planning Department is produced at the same time as the copies of the order and is attached to Production Planning copy.

As orders are received daily by the Production Planning Department they are recorded by the Records Section in the visible edge card record, one per line on cards filed in numerical order which automatically divides them into groups. Vertical columns of the card are used for indicating progress of main stages of the order. At the same time the number of units in each group on the order are added to the weekly list of orders received and dispatched, to be added to the cumulative total of units on order (dispatches are deducted).

The copies then go to the Forward Load section, where each order is scrutinised for special features which will affect planning and any notes of these are entered on the planning card. The measure of the capacity of the factory absorbed by the order is entered on the card and the card is filed into the appropriate week nearest the week indicated by the delivery date, according to existing load and budgeted capacity for each group of products. Each week is numbered, and the week number into which the card is filed is entered on the Order Record for cross-reference purposes. The week number is entered on the Production Engineers' copy of order to tell them (after allowing for normal production time) by when process information and tools will be required. The copy of the order is then filed.

The load (factory capacity and assembly capacity) is transferred periodically from the planning card file to a visible edge card index book, one card for each week, a coloured tab indicating the load. This reveals the distribution of load as far as orders are booked, and is used as a reference for scheduling, building of planning card load and keeping sales load board up to date.

As soon as the Production Engineers receive their copy of the order they examine it and any drawings attached, decide on the method of production of the whole and each part, and prepare process layouts, including standard times for each operation (calculated from synthetic data). All tools required are listed and any new ones noted for designing. The draft process layout is typed as a master, and is then available for use by Production Planning whenever they decide to initiate production. When tools have been designed, a tool manufacturing requisition is raised, giving the date the tools are required, and a process layout is prepared for these so that Production Planning will have documents for planning and control.

Each week, and at a date some 10 or 12 weeks ahead (time for the manufacture of components, assembly and test, and for planning routine) of the week to which it will apply, a provisional assembly schedule is prepared from orders in the Planning Card file. Slight adjustments may be made at this stage to allow for changes in capacity or urgency of orders, or other special circumstances. This provisional schedule is passed to the Stores Record section.

The Stores Record section takes the parts list for each order listed and allocates all materials and components on free-stock records, throwing up requisitions for new manufacturing orders or buying orders on which is stated the week number by when delivery must be made. Special parts are not allocated, but a requisition to manufacture is raised for them. The requisitions to manufacture are sent to the Document Printing section, who run off all works documents. These, in sets, are returned to the Component Planning section of the Production Planning Department, where they are filed under the week number first entered on the requisition for manufacture. This file, in week numbers, forms the provisional schedules for component manufacturing departments.

Final schedules for the assembly departments are prepared and issued one full week before the week to which they apply, and copies are given to Stores and Test. At this stage certain orders included on provisional schedules may have to be deleted because of non-delivery of special material, or delay in component manufacture. At some time it may be necessary to bring forward other orders to meet urgent demands for customers (after checking material and component position) or to balance the assembly capacity.

Final schedules for component manufacturing are built up by Component Planners at least two to four weeks earlier than the completion week to which they apply, using standard times on the production documents as a measure of load. This involves a good deal of juggling and skill to ensure that each section in each department is fully loaded, but not overloaded. Loading to machines and operations is done in the department.

When building up loads, consideration has to be given to the following factors:

Urgent orders.
Special parts or tools.
Availability of raw materials (suppliers may have to be chased).
Need for sub-contracting to cope with overloads.
Effect of change in demand on capacity of certain plant.
Excessive illness of operators, or breakdown of plant.
That maximum flexibility is provided for at each stage.

A department schedule is only made final just before it must be issued, and even then is just short of capacity for the department to allow for additions during the current week. This flexibility is of the utmost importance, especially in those factories on batch production and working to customers' orders. A production planning system which cannot respond quickly to urgent orders, changes in demand and difficulties with suppliers is not doing its job properly.

Putting Plans into Operation

Having decided when work shall be produced, authority must be given for it to commence and instructions given to get material on the move and actually to do the work. Methods for doing this vary from a copy of the customer's order to a detailed specification with part list and drawings and detailed manufacturing instructions, with all supporting documents for each part. Procedures are simplest at the opposite extremes of industrial organisation, i.e. in the small business with a working proprietor who can give verbal instructions and personal supervision, and in the continuous-flow mass-production factories where all work moves automatically through an established standard sequence of operations so that planning instructions are almost limited to starting the right amount of material at the first process. In between are the intermittent flow or batch production units, and it is in these that paper work becomes more complicated, and where consequently there is most need to find ways of reducing the work involved. Where personal supervision is adequate, there is no need to impose unnecessary or complicated systems. This is possible in small process units and in those factories where it has been possible to arrange for conveyors (either power or gravity) to control operators and the flow of work. In most cases, however, the managers, supervisors and operators must be provided with written instructions, and in their turn must render written records. It may appear a truism to say that paper work and systems must be simple in order to get all the information to all the departments requiring it promptly, accurately and regularly. But there are many executives who readily recognise this, yet only consider one form at a time and neglect to work out a co-ordinated system or procedure. Odd scraps of paper and memo books may be good enough for occasional use, but they are not effective vehicles for regular information and records. Specially printed forms should be designed for the purpose. The preparation and movement of forms should be considered as a co-ordinated whole just as production is. Foremen, storekeepers, checkers and all and sundry should not be allowed to start their own records and design their own forms without reference to a master plan and design, and it is advisable for one person to be made responsible for designing and authorising all new forms. The chief Production Planning executive should be competent to do so. Whereever possible, forms should be made to serve more than one purpose or record, and steps should be taken to ensure that they are promptly dealt with so that the last person to use a form is not unduly delayed. This means that design and layout of forms must be well thought out, providing for all the essential information and displaying it in a way that enables those who have to use particular information to recognise it quickly. For most purposes it will be found that forms are most effective when designed with headed panels for each item of information, the same information, such as Job No., appearing on all forms in the same place, heavy lines drawing attention to significant information. The Appendix to this Chapter contains good examples of well-designed forms. When forms are to be used on a typewriter, spacing of information or panels should suit typewritten spacing—on normal machines 10 per inch horizontally and 6 per inch vertically.

A manufacturing order is the executive authority to the works or department for production to commence. In the simplest cases this may be a copy of the customer's order on the firm, but in companies manufacturing proprietary lines to warehouse stock the works may never see a customer's order or know a customer's name. In most manufacturing units the order as received from the customer has to be translated into shop language with a good deal more information than is given by the customer. This is usually done by the Order Department or Contracts Department. Even when a customer's order is accompanied by a complete specification, there is usually much more technical information required in the way of formulæ, instructions or drawings, which have to be prepared. This is given on the documents described in Chapter 2, page 257. In most cases, of course from shoes to ships and toys to telephones, this involves instructions for the manufacture of individual components, and for their assembly. The manufacturing order for the whole product and the kind of information it gives varies widely according to the product and industry, and it would be of limited interest to describe a specific case, but in batch production at least, one component is very like another so far as arranging for its production is concerned. Material for it must be drawn from stores, it is subjected to one or more operations, delivered into a component or finished-part stores, and is subsequently reissued with others for assembly. It will be sufficient therefore if we understand the principles and procedure for putting previously prepared plans into operation as they apply to a component, knowing that they will apply to sub-assemblies and final assemblies by treating these as a unit.

Fig. 44 shows in the simplest form the order routine and documents used for production of a component. Information is required to authorise and record:

The movement of material from stores to a production point.
The identity of material as it is processed.
The preparation of machine and/or tools in readiness for work to be done.
Actual commencement of work, where and when.
The time allowed and actually taken to do the work.
Date when completed, and quantity good and scrapped.

In addition to the Production Engineers' and Production Planning Departments, this information is needed by some or all of the following departments:

The manufacturing department concerned—foreman or shop planner or progress clerk and time clerk.
The Inspector in the department.
Stores Department—material and finished.
Wages Department.
Accounts Department or Cost Office.

The following documents are required, at least:

Process Layout (Master Route Card or Operation Instruction) describing the method of production.—For each component.
Identity Label.—For each part.
Material Release Note (Requisition) for obtaining material.—For each part.
Job Card (Time Card)—describing and authorising operation.—One for each operation.
Planning Card (Move Note or Delivery Note)—for planning and progress information (the Job Card can sometimes be used).—One for each operation.
Cost Card—for calculating cost (standard or actual).—One for each part.

In many systems in operation more documents than this are in use, particularly for each operation, and whilst this may be justified in certain cases, the same results can usually be obtained with a smaller number. Certainly supervision must be better and the work and documents must be dealt with more quickly after operations are completed, but this is a strong argument in favour of the smaller number

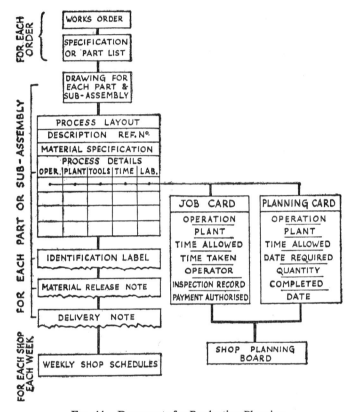

FIG. 44.—Documents for Production Planning.

of documents. In fact, it cannot be too strongly emphasised that paper work and the appearance of paper work must be kept to a minimum in an organisation—and on the shop floor especially. It is disliked by operators and foremen alike. As far as possible all writing and paper work of any kind should be done in offices by trained operators and not on the shop floor by operators at the machine or bench.

This is one of the two compelling reasons for the development and widespread use of pre-printed documents. The other is that they reduce to an absolute minimum the risk of errors due to transcription and recording of information. By pre-printed documents is meant production planning documents which are prepared, and bear, in printed or some variety of duplicated form, all information pertaining to a job or operation which is known before it is issued (e.g. job number, drawing number, tools required, etc.). There are two principal forms, one using a special carbon impression on chromo-surface (or ordinary) paper as a master, and the other using a stencil. Both have their advantages and adherents. In some cases they can make a substantial reduction in the amount of clerical work and labour required in the works.

Since generalities are not very helpful when studying planning in action, or devising procedures for the use of the documents involved, a specimen set of instructions and of all documents used is given as an Appendix to this Chapter (pages 385 et seq.). It covers the use of pre-printed documents, but these are not essential, and only the instructions dealing with the operation of pre-printing would be affected if hand-written documents were used; more information, of course, would have to be written in the shops. The instructions describe in detail how each document is used for authorising work to commence, recording work done and when, and the time taken and hence payment to be made. It is emphasised again that though this particular set of documents was obviously prepared for an engineering factory, the same documents of substantially the same design can be used in any factory making piece parts.

Documents for each part (or operation) should be sent to the department concerned with the weekly (or daily) schedule on which they are listed. A bundle of documents can, of course, constitute a schedule, but there is a risk of loss or misplacement which makes this inadvisable. Schedules should be sent to departments in time for the latter to make their own plans with ancillary departments, e.g. material and tool stores, so that everything is ready when the operator requires it.

Availability of Tools, etc.

The availability of tools, or their equivalent, formers, templates, etc., is frequently a problem in factories on job or batch production, particularly when these have to be manufactured specially for each order. When the tools have already been made previously, the problem is one of getting information to the tool stores in time for them to have the tools ready for when they are required by the operators. In this case it is advisable for the tool stores to be supplied with a daily or weekly schedule, or work sheet, as far in advance as it is necessary for them to prepare tools. If possible this should be limited to one day, and the schedule can then be given to the tool stores by the planning clerk in the shop concerned. The tool stores are then able to prepare the kit of tools, including drawings or other instructions, for each job, ready to be handed to the operator immediately it is asked for. When new tools have to be made for a job a suitable routine procedure must be worked out to ensure that tools are available when they are required. This procedure must be strictly adhered to in practice; there is often a tendency to allow such procedures, which involve ancillary departments like the toolroom, to go by default.

Although the procedure has been covered in the instructions given in the Appendix to this Chapter, it is a problem peculiar to itself, and the following additional notes might be helpful.

The Drawing Office or whatever the technical department is termed, must discuss tooling and special manufacturing methods with the Production Engineers during the design stage to enable special measures, or tools which will take an unusually long time to produce, to be dealt with. A copy of the works order or part list, with any drawings and other technical information, is sent to the Planning Engineers, who enter on it the date when tools must be ready and send it on to the Production Engineers. The latter prepare process and operation layouts, and decide what tools are required, sending a list of the tools, or the documents for each tool, whichever is more convenient to the Planning Engineers. The Production Engineers should then record all drawings which have to be prepared and the date by which they have to be completed, in order to enable tools to be prepared for when they are required. The Planning Engineers plan and schedule and progress the production of tools in the same way as they do production, including them on the normal production schedules when they are made or dealt with at all in production departments, to ensure that they receive the same attention as other work (they are one-offs, and production departments are very inclined to neglect one-offs and special work). If tool production is left entirely to the Toolroom and not controlled by the Planning Department, there are bound to be instances when tools are not ready when they are required, particularly when plans are revised, or jobs brought forward, as they must be at times.

Unless jobs are planned to individual machines by the Production Planning Department centrally, departmental schedules must be broken down into machine or operator loads in the department— foreman's office of shop planning office. The same technique is used as already explained for departmental planning (page 355), but more use is likely to be made of load boards. The one chosen will depend on the nature of the work and the complexity of operations. A board which helps to accumulate and reveal the load on a machine or operator, and when jobs are due to start and finish, is more useful. The Move Note (Fig. 52 in the Appendix to this Chapter) has been designed so that it can be used in this way.

PRODUCTION CONTROL

In this Chapter on Production Administration we have so far discussed preparing and establishing standards for operations and time plans for carrying them out. Supervision, that is managers and foremen, then take over the execution of the plans. But no matter how accurate the standards, or how perfect the plans, since human nature is fallible and not all the factors affecting production are under the control of management, there are in practice mistakes and failures to achieve plans and reach standards of performance.

To enable corrective action to be taken to limit and reduce the effect of these mistakes and failures and to prevent their recurrence, there must be some means of measuring deviations from plans and shortcomings in performance. This is an activity of *Control* discussed in detail in Part Four, of which Production Control is a specific case. There are five aspects of Production Control in which Production Management is interested:

(1) The control of variations from plans or programmes, commonly known in industry today as PROGRESS.

(2) The control of manufacturing costs by measurement and limitation of the excess costs of production referred to as COST CONTROL. In this part we are concerned with MATERIAL COST CONTROL and LABOUR COST CONTROL.

(3) The control of quality of the product. This has become a specialised activity, since it is a highly technical matter demanding a knowledge of the specific processes and skills in the particular industry. Control is maintained by inspectors and testers, and the activity is dealt with as an ancillary service in Chapter VI. It is significant that the modern application of inspection to quantity and process production has become known as QUALITY CONTROL.

(4) The control of MACHINE UTILISATION by drawing attention to the effective use of machines in terms of machine hours.

(5) AUTOMATIC CONTROL more generally called AUTOMATION. This includes control of continuous-flow production, centralised remote control and programme-machines or computers.

It is pertinent to point out here that there has emerged recently a science concerned with the nature of control in all its forms. It is termed "Cybernetics". Persons working in several branches of science, electronics, mathematics, economics, psychology, biology and others, have been studying complicated "systems" which exhibit a degree of feed-back of information and self-regulation and have found principles which appear to be common to all. The self-sensing and self-regulating circuits and systems in electronics are used for the automatic machine tool. Physiological control in the animal body involves a system of feed-back of information to the controlling organ, the brain. It is suggested that general theories that are being, or will be, developed in this new science will be of use to management, and the new science will help to take scientific management a great deal further along the road to making decisions on a quantitive instead of a subjective basis. It is already finding an answer to probblems in extremely complex situations which are generally beyond the scope of operational research (out of which the new science has grown), in industry at least.[1]

Progress

It will be recognised at once that controlling variations from production plans, or progressing, can be done only from a detailed knowledge of plans and results, and in any but the smallest organisations this means records of results. Since in practice it is usually found advisable, and is in fact recommended, to appoint special men as progress men or chasers, there is a danger that duplicate records are set up. The Planning Engineers must have records of results to keep their plans up to date and to adjust for them in future plans. If Planning and Progress are not integrated nor production planning documents and procedures designed to cater for both activities, each will have its own system of recording results. It is not unknown for the Planning Engineers to spend a good proportion of their time frantically adjusting their plans, *after* the progress men have made theirs! Planning schemes introduced by inexperienced persons have been held to scorn and failed on this account. It is particularly likely to happen when progress men have been operating before planning is installed or are appointed by or are responsible to foremen of departments.

In the first place, therefore, it is essential for progress to be a reponsibility of the Production Planning Department, and for the progress men to be under the authority of the head of this department. Secondly, all planning and production documents and procedures should be designed to incorporate records which the progress men will require. This has been done in the documents included in the Appendix to this Chapter. Thirdly, it is important to choose and train the right type of person. Because a progress man is likely to be frequently changing programmes or asking for urgent action, he must enlist the ready co-operation of supervisors. It is essential for

[1] This subject is dealt with at some length in Chapter IV of Part Five.

him to have a cheerful and friendly disposition, and yet be determined. If he is too assertive and overbearing, he will get little co-operation from supervisors; if he is too easy going, he will not get the results required. A retentive memory for detail is also essential and an extensive knowledge of the firm's products is advisable.

Progress can be organised in two ways:

(1) Each progress man responsible for a section or department.
(2) Each progress man responsible for one product or group of components.

In the larger units both methods may be seen in operation.

If it is laid down and clearly understood that a production schedule is an assignment which it is a foreman's duty to complete, then the former method is likely to be most satisfactory. Even then it may be found advisable to have one man responsible for the progress of customers' or urgent orders, throughout the factory, in addition to departmental progress men. What must be guarded against is a progress man building up so much authority that he wrecks planned schedules in his enthusiasm for short-term results.

The progress man's main "standards of reference" are the production schedules, weekly or daily, and lists of orders promised. It is one of the advantages of departmental production schedules that they are a department's assignment for completion by a given date. If work is crossed off as completed, work not completed, and, therefore, behind programme, can be immediately seen by the progress man. It is even better of course to know what jobs have been started late or are running behind programme. This means a record of when jobs started in addition to a record of when jobs are completed. It is not usually justified if most jobs do not last for longer than one day. In either case in factories or departments on batch production the best way of keeping an eye on whether jobs have started or finished *to time*, is by using a planning or load board, provided with a scale of time. Normally, however, sufficient control is obtained by checking jobs finished against the weekly or daily schedule, and it requires far less paper and clerical work.

Another aspect of progress work which is important is respect for delivery promises to customers. There is an unfortunate tendency in industry, more prevalent in a seller's market, to assume that a slight lateness on delivery promised is not very serious, and that to quote a better delivery than it is possible to maintain in order to get orders is good business. Both are bad business, bad for planning in the customer's factory and damaging to a firm's reputation, however good that might otherwise be. Broken promises should be looked upon like any other broken promises—it is just "not done". The incidence of broken promises is sufficiently important for a special report to be made weekly to the Works Manager. This should at least show the number of deliveries made overdue and its percentage of all deliveries. The incidence should be so small that the Works Manager should be able to see and deal either daily or weekly with a list of all orders promised and not delivered to time. Each order should be recorded at the time the promise is made, on a weekly (or daily) promise sheet. At the end of each week (or day) orders delivered should be crossed off, leaving broken promises. Prevention being better than cure, a duplicate of the promise sheet should be given to a progress man some time before the due date—time enough to check progress and take urging action if necessary.

It is important for tools to be completed on time, since tools not ready when required will throw production programmes out of gear. Therefore, tool orders must also be progressed, and the method recommended above for dealing with delivery promises by recording and throwing up deliveries due is effective, since it directs attention to jobs likely to be held up, in time for corrective action to be taken.

Shortage lists for raw material and components should be prepared regularly by the progress men for urgent action either by the buyer or component-producing departments. These can be collected from the stores or thrown up automatically by return of requisitions or material release notes. It is useful for stores, particularly component stores, to post up on a blackboard or wall chart all items out of stock. There are always some items or aspects of production which senior executives need to keep an eye on personally. Charts, wall boards, or special forms are useful for this purpose if—and only if—their number and the number of items on them are few, and the items which need attention "hit the eye". In process factories stocks of scarce materials may need especial attention, in others output of important products or the load on departments may need watching from time to time. Charts are most convenient for the purpose, lines being drawn vertically to a quantity scale for each item listed horizontally. In practice the weakness is that whilst a line can always be extended, it must be rubbed out to be shortened. A simple home-made board which provides adjustable lines is shown in Fig. 38 (page 345). If it is desired to keep an eye on the progress of a few important orders in a factory with a limited number of processes, as in printing, a chart can be used (as in Fig. 45); a circle or diagonal line can indicate that the process is required, and a tick or an opposite diagonal line that the process is completed. If a board is used, cardboard discs can be hung on hooks and removed as the process is completed. Dates written on the discs add a time element to the control.

Suppliers of office equipment can provide very ingenious adjust-

P.P.M.—13*

able visible charts or boards for progress work. Keen and impressionable planning and progress men sometimes see in them a cure-all for progress problems. It is assumed that they work. They do not: they are tools, and as such must be operated by people who must be trained to be skilful and reliable in their use. It is unwise to use visible boards when the number of items is large, hundreds or more,

ORDER	COMPS.	ENGRS.	PLATEN	WHARFE	MIEHLE	C. & C.	BIND.		
212 B. JONES	O		O				O		
215 SMITH & WELLS		O		O	O				
216 BRA. ENG.	O	O			O	O	O		

FIG. 45.—Order Progress Board.

as just as good results can be obtained by cards or paper and at less cost in labour or space. But, for a small number of items, they can be most effective.

Cost Control

Meeting the term Cost Control in this section dealing with production may cause the reader to pause and think—but this is an Accountant's job. True the Accountant is responsible for calculating and accounting for all costs, but only the person immediately responsible for actual expenditure can control the cost—and that means the man on the shop floor, the operator and the foreman. And for a supervisor to be in control of the costs for which he is responsible he must know what costs should be, and what they actually are, so that he can take action to reduce or entirely avoid differences, i.e. excess costs. A supervisor has neither the time nor the facilities to record and calculate his own costs, so that he must be provided with the information; that is, he must be provided with another administrative service, just as he is by the Planning and Progress Engineers on programmes and deviations from them for controlling production flow. For controlling costs the Accountant supplies the information in the form of Cost Control Reports showing:

For Material.—The cost of material used in excess of standard with an analysis of the causes of such excess.

For Labour.—The cost of labour used in excess of standard analysed in the same way as for material, the effective performance of each operator and department, and the total cost per unit of production.

The supply of these reports and their interpretation is a production administrative activity and, as such, is dealt with here.

It may be necessary first to distinguish clearly between the terms Cost Control and Costing, lest they should be confused or assumed to be synonymous.

Costing, as normally practised, is the computation of the total actual cost of a product or process *after* manufacture.

Cost Control, in the modern sense, is the control of all items of expenditure by regular and frequent comparison of actual expenditure with predetermined standards or budgets, so that undesirable trends away from standard can be detected and corrected at an early stage.

The former is historical, and whilst comparisons can be made between total cost and selling price of a product to reveal the profit (or loss), little can be done about any excess cost except to deduct it from any total profit for the period, since the cause of the excess is not known. Even if the cause can be found for any particular product or component, its incidence cannot easily be detected, so that little can be done about it. On the other hand, well-designed Cost Control techniques reveal the actual cause of *all excess costs* in some detail, their magnitude, and their trend, i.e. increasing or decreasing. They are revealed too, immediately after the event, so that foremen and all concerned are aware of cause and effect and can take immediate steps to improve unsatisfactory results. In this chapter we shall deal only with Direct Material and Direct Labour Costs. Overhead expenses, which are controlled by comparisons with budgets, is dealt with in Part Four. Suffice it to say here that supervisors must be presented with reports of actual expenditure, preferably compared with budget, regularly and immediately after the period to which they refer. Supervisors must be held accountable for all the expenses over which they have authority and control (e.g. loose tools, but not heating).

It has been explained earlier how the Production Engineers determine the correct material for use on a process or on a job, and the standard time for doing it. In practice, more material is used and more time spent over a period (e.g. a week) than the standard necessary for the total production for the period. The excess, of either labour or material, on any job usually has nothing to do with the job itself, but is due to such causes as careless operating and waiting for tools. What is wanted, therefore, to control these excesses is a record of them, not by job but by *cause*. And since the absolute cost of such excesses for a department is likely to increase with production, to get a true measure of performance it is necessary to know the relative cost and therefore to express the incidence of total excess costs as a percentage of total costs.

Finally, it will be appreciated that Cost Control figures must be presented to the persons who are responsible for the expenditure; that is, to the foreman or supervisor of the department. And to enable effective action to be taken, the reports must be rendered immediately after the end of the period to which they refer, e.g. by Tuesday of the following week. To be fully effective they must be broken down to sections of a department where this is appropriate. In order to avoid duplicating work and extra operations in the accounts or wages office, the preparation of these reports should be integrated with the preparation of the payroll and operating accounts.

Material Cost Control

Excess material cost is revealed either as scrap or as an excess withdrawal from stock compared with standard for the amount of finished product manufactured. The most effective way of controlling scrapped material is to prevent the disposal of such scrap by anyone except an authorised person, and then only to a stated receiving depot, e.g. stores, against a document, such as a scrap note stating the cause and signed by an inspector or foreman. The scrap notes can then be valued and summarised either daily or weekly in the form of a report showing the cost under each cause heading compared with previous average and budget. Since it is usually impossible to prevent all waste or scrap, it is not enough to record actual scrap and its value; it must be compared with some standard (previous average or best or a budget) so that differences on the wrong side are immediately apparent. A suitable form for this purpose is illustrated in Fig. 46. Other headings by cause can be used according to the type of product or process. For example, in a Foundry they would be:

Total Melt, Cupola, Risers, Moulding, Fettling, Total.

It is usual for the Accounts Department to provide an overall control as a check on whether all material is accounted for as good product or scrap. (In the absence of such a check, there is a tendency for scrap to be understated or "lost".) Such control is effected by comparison of standard amounts (as laid down in process layouts) with amounts actually used. It will relate to each material used and apply to each department or process. The difference should be accounted for by the scrap recorded; where it does not, steps should be taken to explain the discrepancy; it may reveal unsuspected waste.

When material is issued in bulk from stores or drawn on as required by operators in the department, and scrap, waste, or over-

QUARTER ENDING...

WEEK ENDING	TO EQUAL P.W. GUARANTEE			WAITING FOR JOB			WAITING FOR SET-UP			WAITING FOR TOOLS & DRG		
AVER. BT FWD												
1												
2												
3												
4												
5												
6												
7												
8												
9												
10												
11												
12												
13												
AVER. CAR. FWD.												

WEEK ENDING	POLICY			FAULTY MATERIAL			FAULTY EQUIPMENT			PLANT FAILURE			PLANNING		
AVER. BT FWD															
1															
2															
3															
4															
5															
6															
7															
8															
9															
10															
11															
12															
13															
AVER. CAR. FWD.															

MEMO

....DEPARTMENT

LA

ENT

FOREMAN		FOREMAN'S BONUS			
TOOL ATTEN	CESS	% ON TOTAL WAGES		BONUS	

EXCESS			
% OF TOTAL DIRECT	TRANSFERS		

DRAWING O						TOTAL	

MEMORAN	SIGNATURE

Plate 3

375

EXCESS MATERIAL COST

WEEK	TOTAL MATERIAL OR LABOUR		DUE TO OPERATOR		DUE TO MACHINE		FAULTY MATERIAL		OTHER CAUSES		TOTAL		REMARKS
	AMOUNT £ s d	%	AMOUNT £ s d	%	AMOUNT £ s d	%	AMOUNT £ s d	%	AMOUNT £ s d	%	AMOUNT £ s d	%	
BUDGET		100											
1													
2													
3													
4													
5													
6													
7													
8													
9													
10													
11													
12													
13													
TOTAL													

FIG. 46.

usage is not identified as such, as e.g. in industries using materials in sheets (press work) or reels (wire) or planks (casemaking), etc., it is impossible to issue only the correct amount for a job, and so to control usage in that way. A control can still be provided, however, by the Accounts Department rendering periodical reports showing the standard amount which should have been used for the products completed compared with actual bulk issues for the period. In any one period there will be slight differences due to variations in the amount of material in progress in the department, but over a period the difference should remain substantially constant (for a constant proportion of scrap) and a gradual improvement or deterioration will be revealed.

Labour Cost Control

Excess labour cost can arise from the following causes:

Waiting time paid to operators for periods when they are not able to work on jobs.
Low effectiveness where a guaranteed minimum rate is paid.
Premium payments, e.g. overtime, learning, etc.
Wrong grade of labour.
Unused capacity, i.e. low output for same indirect operators.
Excess piecework payment or excess time spent due to faulty material or faulty equipment.

Only excesses under the first heading are brought to the foreman's notice immediately and in detail, and only then when he personally signs or scrutinises each record of waiting time. Immersed as he is in the day-to-day problems of shop management, he cannot watch the incidence of each cause of excess cost, far less the total cost or its trend. It is necessary, therefore, to provide him with a weekly statement—his weekly operating statement as it were. Very detailed ones are often recommended, and daily reports are even used, but these involve the Wages Department (or some other Department) in a considerable amount of extra work and the foreman in an interpretation which is too detailed for him to give to it the necessary thought and attention. Of the several methods of presenting the essential information which the foreman must have, the form shown in Plate 3 is a good example. It is not suggested that this form covers all cases or includes all causes of excess costs or indices of performance that may be required, but it will serve as a basis for preparing a suitable form for any specific need, and it is one which with slight modifications only has been used in industry and proved most effective, giving the foreman the picture he requires of his labour costs and the necessary control.

The form covers a thirteen-week period, and is entered up weekly by the wages clerks, sent to the Works Manager, and thence to the foreman for information and action, and report back to the Works Manager if requested. It is returned to the Wages Office in time for the next week's entries to be made. The average figures for the previous quarter (or budget figures if preferred) are entered as the opening line, so that continuity is preserved, and, as each week's results are added, trends are revealed.

The top portion of the front of the form brings home to a foreman the total costs for which he is responsible and their make-up. It is an analysis of the payroll for the department rapidly summarised by the wages clerks from the different classes of time or job cards. The total excess costs are shown and expressed as a percentage of the relevant figure. The unmeasured labour cost, i.e. the amount paid on daywork, is shown, as this can be considered uncontrolled, and should be kept to a minimum. The difference between standard and actual wages is the total excess labour cost and is analysed by cause on the back of the form.

The standard for indirect wages is arrived at by agreeing on the number and therefore weekly cost of supervisors and labourers for a given number of operators. This number of operators can be expected to produce a normal number of standard hours per week. The total cost of supervision divided by the normal total standard hours gives a cost per standard hour for supervision, which, multiplied by the total standard hours recorded for the work, gives the standard cost for supervision for that week.

The bottom portion of the front of the form is used for remarks by wages clerks, Works Manager, or foreman, and for indices of performance. The total hours earned divided by total hours on standard (on piecework) is the *index of piecework performance*. A figure of 1·31 is equivalent to 31 per cent. bonus, of course. If work measurement is done correctly, as recommended earlier, this figure is a true measure of performance, and can be used for comparisons between departments. Dividing the earned hours to total clock hours (including daywork hours in both figures) gives the *overall effective performance* of the department.

The cost *per unit* is the total wages costs of the department divided by the total hours earned or tons produced or other unit of production, and shows the trend of the true effectiveness of the department. The cost per unit goes up if—

Piecework performance goes down.

Excess costs go up.

The total output goes down with the same supervision and other indirect wages cost.

Excess costs are analysed on the back of the form under two headings, those for which the foreman of the department can be held responsible, and those for which other members of the management team are responsible. The Works Manager may have to deal with the latter, but the foreman is expected to act on the former. The analysis of waiting time is picked up from the reason given on the time card record and the headings are self-explanatory; others can be used to suit circumstances. The item "To equal P.W. Guarantee" is the amount which has to be paid to pieceworkers over and above their piecework earnings when these are below the minimum guaranteed. Such operators were working below a satisfactory standard and well below normal. The cost of using a wrong grade of labour is picked up by the wages clerk from the job card when the grade of operator who does a job is different from that laid down by the Production Engineers and appearing in the standard data on the job card. It is ineffective use of labour by supervision. Excess cost due to faults in other departments is transferred out and vice versa.

In practice, when excess costs due to one or more causes are high or begin to rise, it is wise for the foreman to arrange to investigate personally over a limited period each incident recorded for these causes immediately it is reported. He is then able to find quickly the exact cause and to take effective remedial action. The report points to where such close attention is required, and it throws up the bad spots. To those unaccustomed to such reports, it is surprising how effective they are in drawing the attention of senior executives to increasing costs and deteriorating performance.

It is noted that in the example, provision is made for assessing a foreman's bonus, on the basis of his success in controlling excess costs in his department. The particular method used will depend on circumstances, but the report does reveal a measure which can be used in this way.

Machine Utilisation

At one time machine utilisation was considered to be more important than labour utilisation, idle machines more expensive than idle men. Although it is now realised that it may be wise to have a little spare capacity and machines available for operators thrown idle by breakdown on others, nevertheless it is still necessary to keep an eye on machine utilisation to ensure that there is no unnecessary idle productive capacity or capital. This is particularly true of automatic machines and plant, and plant in belt assembly or continuous production plant, where many delays on one machine may ultimately affect the whole plant.

Where, as in most cases, machines are attended or operated by individuals, the overall machine utilisation of a department can be calculated from operators' job cards by the wages office and included in the labour cost controls. Provision has been made for this on the form referred to above Plate 3. When this report, or other information, reveals that utilisation is unsatisfactory, it may be necessary to have a more detailed analysis for each machine. This is best done, as with excess labour cost, by recording the actual loss at source, that is, the delay or machine down time, at the time it occurs with a note of cause. The simplest method is to provide a daily log sheet for each machine, preferably fixed on a board or holder, on which the operator or attendant can enter the time machines stop or start, and the cause. The principal causes of machine delays are mechanical breakdowns, setting-up troubles and unsatisfactory material. The first can be reduced by an effective scheme of preventive maintenance (see page 447), the second by a great deal more attention to the training of setters and to design of tooling (particularly important in specialists and short-run production so common in Britain), and the last either by better inspection of incoming material, or by more attention to regularity of product from previous processes or operations.

Automatic Control or Automation

The four types of control described above all involve communication or "feed-back" of information to the originator of plans or instructions, who takes corrective action if this is judged to be necessary. The big step forward inherent in Automation is that instruments detect deviations or errors and make signals which cause the controlling agent automatically to take corrective action to maintain the machine or process on a desired course. Not only does this eliminate some or all operators and progress chasers or other human means of communication, but speed of response to signals and the accuracy of detection and of communication is infinitely greater. As the rather expensive and elaborate equipment is developed and simplified and becomes less expensive, it will find wider use. So far it has found its most obvious use in continuous-flow production, as, for example, the transfer-machine lines of the motor-car factories and in the chemical and oil industries, but it is being extended to small processes in general manufacturing and to individual general-purpose machines. In both cases higher machine utilisation and greater accuracy and reliability are obtained.

As a manifestation of Production Control, automation can be considered under four headings. The first two owe their development and success to the skill of the technologists, production engineers and plant designers, the others to the new science of electronics (which grew from the discovery of the thermionic valve).

(i) *Continuous-flow Production*

The large paper- and board-making machines are typical of the manually controlled plants which make a single product (though perhaps of varying quality or constituents) continuously. There are usually only a few operators and a few materials involved. Production planning is on a very long-term basis and is primarily concerned with ensuring a supply of materials and optimum length of runs.

Automatic control of continuous production is typified by the large chemical plants and oil refineries. Planning here is much more concerned with preventive maintenance, plant overhauls and service.

In engineering, automatic operation, though not control, has been developed in the transfer lines—so called because the article being machined (cylinder block, crankcase, etc.) is automatically transferred and transported from one machining station to the next along a line of machines linked by a conveyor. The machines, which are usually identical "unit" heads with different tool set-ups, are automatically moved into position for the machining operation and moved away again afterwards to allow the article to be transferred to the next station. An enormous amount of preliminary planning goes into establishing the tooling, machining operations and sequence and balance of operations for optimum output. Production planning is again primarily concerned with ensuring a regular supply of material (usually castings) and long-term decisions on periods of operation for balanced output of the whole manufacturing plant.

Continuously operating automatic plants can be classified thus:[1]

Relative Size

Large	Several operators to one plant. (For example: board-mill, chemicals, oil, electricity, etc.)
Small	One operator to one or more machines. (For example: cigarette-making, weaving, automatic lathes, etc.)

Product

Continuous	Materials flow through the plant; it is usually wasteful to stop and re-start the process. (For example: board-mill, chemicals, oil, electricity, many foodstuffs, paint, glass, etc.)

[1] *Automation and Skill*, by E. R. F. Crossman. No. 9 of Series.—*Problems of Progress in Industry*, D.S.I.R.

Separate Materials transported mechanically, the process can
articles   usually be stopped and re-started easily.
      (For example: transfer-lines for cylinder blocks
      and pistons, packing machines, printing presses,
      etc.)

Control

Manual   The operator directly controls the process and is re-
      sponsible for making all running adjustments.
      (For example: board-mill, older atomic energy
      plant, weaving, printing, etc.)

Automatic The operator sets desired running conditions and
      automatic devices ensure that they are maintained.
      (For example: new chemical and atomic energy
      plant, oil refineries, newer boilers, etc.)

Type of Process

Mechanical The process consists of mechanical actions such as
      cutting and shaping. The operator can easily visual-
      ise what is happening.
      (For example: transfer machines, final stage of
      glass-bulb making, packing, knitting, etc.)

Non-mechanical Chemical, physical or other processes where the
      operator cannot easily visualise what is happening.
      (For example; chemical, electricity, plastics, some
      foodstuffs, etc.)

(ii) *Centralised Remote Control*

Improvements in instruments, slave mechanisms and automatic communication techniques have made possible the control of industrial processes from a central position remote from the operations. Examples are to be found in steel making and manipulating (strip mills) and in transport. (An engine-driven ship at sea is perhaps the earliest example.) Here again production planning, as such, is primarily concerned with effective maintenance since a breakdown can be expensive or serious.

(iii) *Programmed Machines*

The Jacquard loom is perhaps the earliest example of a machine which automatically follows a pre-set programme. More recently electronics have been applied to the control of machine tools, particularly where complicated shapes have to be reproduced. In one system magnetic tape signals the machine table and head to move in accordance with a planned programme. To prepare the tape, information from the drawing is transferred in code to punched tape. This is fed into a digital electronic computer which translates the information into control signals on the magnetic tape. In another method co-ordinate dimensions are calculated from the drawing and punched into paper tape. This is fed into the machine control which calculates intermediate co-ordinates and transmits control signals to the machine table.

In a somewhat different application setting or positioning information is punched on to punched cards either from a preliminary set-up or direct from the drawing. The prepared card is then used for setting-up the machine (normally a skilled operation), an unskilled operator then loading and operating the machine.

Up till now, due to the high initial cost of equipment, there has not been a great deal of experience with this type of control, but indications are that benefits are derived not from savings in manpower but from accuracy and consistency of results and savings in total machine time. Because of the high capital cost they have been used mainly for large special-purpose machines but as computers and electronic control systems are simplified, reduced in size and price, it is likely that they will find their greatest use on the general-purpose machine and jobbing and batch production. By then computer programming will be an essential technique in production planning.

(iv) *Computers*

Electronic calculating and data-processing machines are not only required for automatic control of plant and processes. They are a form of automation in their own right, performing complicated "clerical" operations automatically, accurately and at fantastic speeds. More recently machines have been made which read words as well as coded messages and make limited decisions. They will only do this, of course, within the range of the information "fed" to them and if they are given precise instructions; they will not make qualitative judgments nor plan ahead.

Broadly speaking, there are two types of computers. The *digital* computer is the more flexible and finds the greatest use. By using electrical signals, storing, sorting and re-arranging them, it can carry out relatively simple calculations extremely rapidly. Consequently it can deal with a vast quantity of data in a very short time, completing calculations in a matter of minutes that would take an individual years to do by normal methods. The *analogue* computer finds its greatest use in research and design work since, by comparing electrical quantities it can solve complex mathematical problems. A mathematical "model" of the problem is built up and expressed in formulæ and linear or differential equations. The performance of a machine or system in dynamic conditions can be simulated by an electrical model incorporating elements representing variables which produce an infinite number of conditions. Thus the performance of a machine or system can be studied prior to building it. Since, in this sense, a works' organisation or a complex economic problem can be represented by a system, it should be possible to establish more precise plans and programmes for complicated situations than has been possible in the past.

What will be the impact of automation on Management? Will it make robots of us all, replacing supervision of men by supervision of machines? Automation is not a new function of management but it is a new tool or technique which is going to be increasingly used in the activities of design, research, planning, control and operation, i.e. in all the divisions of an organisation. Far from turning men into robots, it is likely to increase the demand for skilled and technical personnel, not only in the realm of middle management, but also on the factory floor where there will be more setters, "programmers" and planners and the proportion of indirect (overheads) to direct operators will continue to rise, as it has done for years. There is no evidence that the continuing trend towards more automatic control represented as automation will, of itself, cause more redundancy of labour than will quickly be absorbed by the continuing increase in demand for goods. The effect of more automation is to reduce the use of human labour for heavy, arduous and repetitive (and usually boring) jobs and to increase the number of jobs that are interesting or require more intelligence. To this extent it can and should reduce the strains and frustrations of industry.

PRINCIPLES

As in everyday life, so also in the particular activity of management, experience proves that as a basis for all conduct it is wise to adhere as closely as possible to sound fundamental principles. The more one departs from principles, the more necessity there is for hasty decisions and expedient action to meet awkward situations which ought not to have arisen. One cannot always be certain of where some decisions are likely to lead, but if they are made in accordance with proved principles, then they are certain to lead in the right direction and to satisfactory results in the long run. It is useful, therefore, to have a body of principles, if only of limited application, in this relatively new science of management.

From experience and the study of the operation of the administrative activities discussed in this chapter, the following principles emerge. They are *specific* applications of the *general* principles of planning and control given in the Introduction on page 68:

(1) Planning is a function of management to be distinguished from doing. In the structure of an organisation the two should be separated and those persons responsible for doing (executives and foremen) should be supported by administrative staff whose duty is to supply information on how and when work is to be done, standards of measurement, and reports on results compared with standards.

(2) There are three divisions of the administrative activities:
Production Engineering (concerned with methods and standards);
Production Planning (concerned with programmes or time plans);
Production Control (comparing results with standards and plans).
Each should be separately recognised, and its specialised techniques developed.

(3) To reduce human effort to a minimum and to increase output per man-hour, work must be studied scientifically.

(4) Work can be measured in a common unit and the work content of a job assessed. Standard Times expressed in a unit based on the rating of speed, effort, attention and skill, with a due allowance for relaxation, provide an accurate measure.

(5) Standards to be used as a basis for planning and control for the material and labour content of production can be established.

(6) The only satisfactory basis for payment by results is an accurate measure of the work content of a job.

(7) Production planning is impossible without reliable information; and accuracy of results (given constant performance by supervision and operators) varies directly with accuracy of information.

(8) The more the information which has to be transmitted, the less effective the results of planning are likely to be.

(9) As far as possible paper work must be done in offices by trained operators and not on the shop floor by operators at machine or bench.

(10) To be effective, planning must—
be simple, flexible and balanced; be based on accurate measurement, and provide means for measuring performance against plans.

(11) For production control to be effective, results must be compared with standards (of performance, cost or programme) in reports which reveal the extent and cause of any discrepancy. Such reports must be rendered promptly, and corrective action must be taken immediately.

PRODUCTION PLANNING DOCUMENTS

A. GENERAL DESCRIPTION

I. PURPOSE

THIS instruction describes a method of preparing and using Production Planning Documents which makes use of modern techniques and duplicating machines for preparing pre-printed documents for use in Planning, Production and Cost Accounting. The main purpose of pre-printed forms is to ensure that as much information as possible is entered on works production documents before they are issued to the works, and that such information, after careful check of original entries, is automatically transferred to all copies from a Master document. The method adopted has three important advantages; it prevents transcription errors, prepares all documents rapidly and economically, and reduces the amount of clerical work in the shops to a minimum.

II. DESCRIPTION OF FORMS

A Master Document is prepared for each component and each machine to be manufactured.

This Master is in two parts:

A. A Permanent Master (Fig. 47), on which is entered all permanent information relevant to production of the component or machine, including a summary of each operation in list form (i.e. process layout or master route card), and in the case of the technical design documents, design data required in the works.

B. A Variable Heading, on which is entered information relating to the particular order or batch to be manufactured.

The two portions married together form a complete Master Document for the particular batch.

C. Production Documents.—From the Component Master the following documents are prepared immediately an order is created:

1. *Material Release Note* (Figs. 48, 49)

Specifying type and quantity of material required for 100 units and for the batch. Only the total amount of material specified is "released" in the first instance, and more can only be obtained by presenting an Excess Material Requisition. After materials are issued it is returned to Planning, who adjust stock and progress records. It is then sent to Accounts, who debit and credit appropriate inventory accounts.

ORDER HEADING MASTER

CUSTOMER	QUANT.	DESCRIPTION	PART No.	JOB OR MACH. No.
Stock	40	Shaft·	140.2	342.B

DATE ISS.	MATERIAL RELEASE	SPECIAL INSTRUCTIONS	DATE DUE
10/8	40 Billets		Wk.35

LAYOUT ISS.	MATERIAL SPEC. & QUAN. PER	PATT. No.	DESCRIPTION	PART No.
1	M.152.9 2½"D 21.7/16"L		Shaft 70R A1	140.2

ROUTE

	1	2	3	4	5	6	7	8	9	10	11	12
DEPT.	9	9	9	9	9	9						
M/C OR GROUP	527	42	61	527	54	3A						

OPERATION MASTER

TYPE ON DOTTED LINE ONLY

OP. No.	DEPT.	MACH. OR GROUP	OPERATION	JIGS, TOOLS AND GAUGES	LABOUR GRADE O'HEAD REF.	TIME ALLOWED SET-UP	HOURS PER
1	9	527	Centre face turn		M7 C	.25	.5
2	9	42	Grind		M7 D	.2	.48
3	9	61	Key seat		M5 C	.2	.18
4	9	527	Screw		M6 C	.2	.16
5	9	54	Drill Peg Hole		M1 C	.05	.01
			(These times are purely imaginary)				

FIG. 47.

2. *Identity Label* (Fig. 50)

Used for identifying a batch and specifying each operation and the department where performed, i.e. the route. This label accompanies the work throughout all operations, and on it is recorded details of scrap and good work produced.

MATERIAL RELEASE NOTE — FABRICATIONS

CUSTOMER			QUANT.	DESCRIPTION	PART No.	JOB OR MACH. No.
			10	Bracket CE/OB/FV	120.25	350.B
DATE ISS.	MAT'L RELEASE		SPECIAL INSTRUCTIONS			DATE DUE
22/8	10 sets					Wk.50

REQUIRED BY	Layout Iss	FROM STORES		DRG. No.	DESCRIPTION		PART No.
	1	3 11	Sht 1 of 1	120.25	Bracket CE/OB/FV		120.25

STORES CONTROL	QUAN. PER PART	MATERIAL CODE No.	MATERIAL DESCRIPTION	Wt/Part	Total	QUAN. THIS BATCH	VALUE
	1	M190-4	18"x18" Temp 1	46 lbs			
	1	M190-3	14"x14" Temp 2	21			
	1	M190-1	$6\frac{1}{2}$"x18" Temp 3	8.9			
	2	M190-3	8"x$13\frac{1}{2}$" Temp 5	25.5			
	2	M190-1	$6\frac{1}{2}$"x$8\frac{1}{2}$" Temp 4	8	109.4		
	1	M181-76	1"x$2\frac{3}{4}$"x$4\frac{3}{4}$"	3.2			
	4	M181-11	$3\frac{1}{2}$"x3/16"x$1\frac{1}{8}$"	1			
	12	M181-8	$1\frac{3}{4}$"x3/16"x$\frac{5}{8}$"	2.2			
	2	M181-8	$1\frac{3}{4}$"x3/16"x$\frac{3}{4}$"	.4			
	4	M181-6	7/16"x5/16"x1"	1.34	8.14		
CUT		ISSUED	STORES SIG.			TOTAL COST	

FIG. 48.

MATERIAL RELEASE NOTE

CUSTOMER			QUAN	DESCRIPTION	PART No.	JOB OR MACH No.
			40	Shaft	140.2	342.B
REQUIRED BY	Date Iss.	MATERIAL RELEASE	SPECIAL INSTRUCTIONS			DATE DUE
	10/8	40 Billets				Wk.35
PROGRESS	Layout Iss.	MAT. SPEC. & QUAN. PER	PATT. No.	DESCRIPTION		PART No.
	1	Steel M 152.9 $2\frac{1}{8}$" dia 21.7/16" long		Shaft 70R A1		140.2
STORES CONTROL	STORES SIGN.	DATE ISSUED	WEIGHT cwts. qrs. lbs. ozs.	RATE		VALUE

FIG. 49.

3. *Job Card* (Fig. 51)

One for each operation as specified on the Master, giving the Time Allowed for the operation, and the Jigs, Tools and Gauges required.

On this is recorded the operator's name and check number and the number to be paid for. It is later used for wages computation.

IDENTITY LABEL						
CUSTOMER		QUAN. 40	DESCRIPTION Shaft	PART No. 140.2		JOB OR MACH. No. 342.E
DATE ISS. 10/8	MATL. RELEASE 40 Billets	SPECIAL INSTRUCTIONS				DATE DUE Wk. 35
LAYOUT IS. 1	MATL. SPEC. & AMOUNT' M.152.9 2⅜"D 21.7/16" L		PATT. No.	DESCRIPTION Shaft 70R A1		PART No. 140.2

¹ 9	² 9	³ 9	⁴ 9	⁵ 9	⁶ 3A	⁷	⁸	⁹	10	11	12
527	42	61	527	54							

FIG. 50.

CHECK No.	OPERATOR'S NAME		JOB CARD		WEEK ENDING	
Standard times marked thus * are provisional for special or small batches and are subject to re-study and revision for quantity production.	CUSTOMER Stock	QUAN. 40	DESCRIPTION Shaft	PART No. 140.2	JOB OR MACH. No. 342.B	
	DATE ISS. 10/8	MATL. RELEASE 40 Billets	SPECIAL INSTRUCTIONS		DATE DUE Wk. 35	

OP. No. 5	DEPT. 9	M/C or GRP. No. 54	OPERATION Drill peg hole	JIGS, TOOLS & GAUGES	LABOUR GRADE C	SET UP. .05	HRS. PER .01

TOTAL TO PAY FOR	PREVIOUSLY PAID FOR	PAY FOR THIS WEEK	PREVIOUS ACTUAL HOURS	Std. Hours at Base Rate			Standard Hours Earned on run
				Actual Hours at Nat. Bonus			Total Hours Earned
				TOTAL			

FIG. 51.

4. *Move Note* (Fig. 52)

One for each operation specified on the Master. On this is recorded the quantity passed forward, scrapped and to be rectified. It is returned to Planning Office when the operation is completed, where it is used for progress records.

5. *Delivery Note* (Fig. 53)

For the final operation only. On this is recorded the quantity finally delivered to Stores. The information is checked by Stores and entered on progress and stock records by Planning Office. It is then sent to Accounts, who debit and credit appropriate accounts.

6. *Progress Envelope* (Fig. 54)

In which all works' documents are kept until issued and after use, and on which is recorded the progress of the job (quantity and date) through the works.

MOVE NOTE	CUSTOMER Stock		QUANT. 40	DESCRIPTION Shaft		PART No. 140.2			JOB OR MACH No. 342.B	
SCHEDULE	Date Iss. 10/8	MATERIAL RELEASE 40 Billets	SPECIAL INSTRUCTIONS						DATE DUE WK 35	
PROGRESS	OP. No. 5	DEPT. 9	M/c or Group No. 54	OPERATION Drill peg hole		JIGS, TOOLS, GAUGES	LABOUR GRADE C	SET UP ·05	Hrs. Per 100/Ea. ·01	
STORES CONTROL D	CHECK No.	PASSED	No. SCRAP CAUSE		No. RECTIFY CAUSE			PAY FOR	INSPECT'R & DATE	
N										

FIG. 52.—*Note:* Layout of Move Note and Delivery Note should be identical alternative forms are shown in Figs. 52 and 53.

7. *Cost Card* (Fig. 55)

A facsimile of the complete Master, with additional columns for Cost Account purposes.

8. *Tool Requisition* (Fig. 56)

Advice of tools required and receipt for tools taken from Tool Stores.

From the Technical Specification Master the following documents are prepared:

9. *Official Order Record*

This is a complete copy of the Master, and includes all information, technical and commercial, relating to the order, i.e. Customer, Machines and Spares ordered, Prices, Delivery Instruction and Design Data.

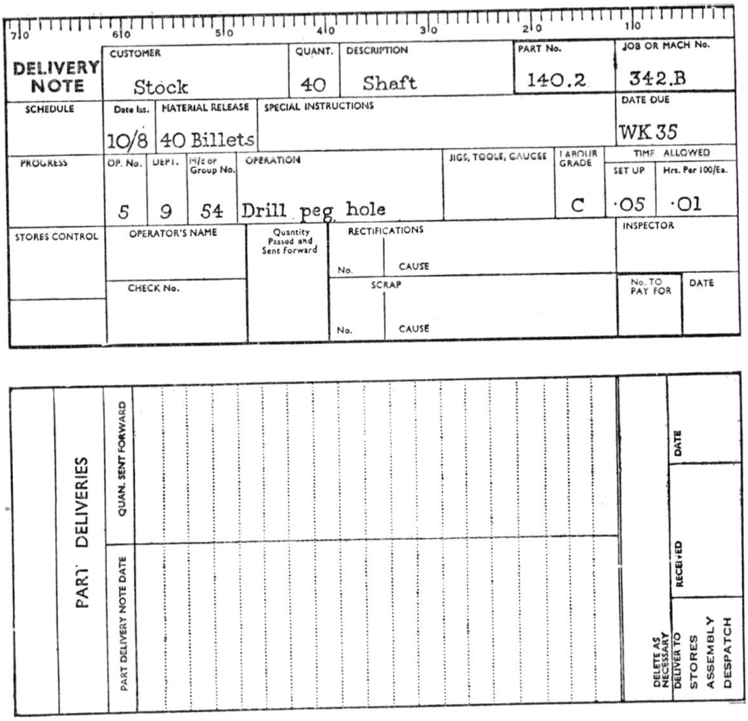

FIG. 53.

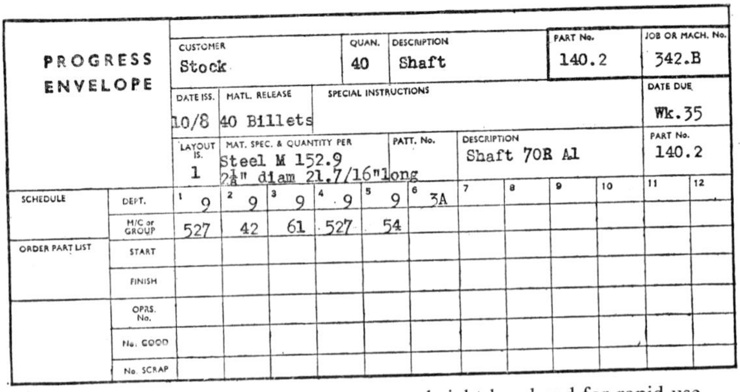

FIG. 54.—*Note:* Envelope open at top and right-hand end for rapid use.

COST CARD	CUSTOMER		QUANT.	DESCRIPTION		PART NO.		JOB OR MACH. NO.	MATERIAL · %		
	Stock		40	Shaft		140.2		342.B	LABOUR		
	DATE ISS.	MATERIAL RELEASE	SPECIAL INSTRUCTIONS					DATE DUE	A		
	10/8	40 Billets						Wk.35	B		
	LAYOUT ISS.	MATERIAL, SPEC. & QUAN. PER		PATT. NO.	DESCRIPTION			PART NO.	C		
	1	M.152.9 2½"D 21.7/16"L			Shaft 70R Al.			140.2	D		

ROUTE	DEPT.	9	2 9	3 9	4 9	5 9	6 3A	7	8	9	10	11	12	E
	M/C OR GROUP	527	42	61	527	54								TOTAL COST

OP. NO.	DEPT.	MACH. OR GROUP	OPERATION	JIGS, TOOLS AND GAUGES	LABOUR GRADE O'HEAD REF.	TIME ALLOWED SET-UP	TIME ALLOWED Hours Per	STD. RATE	LABOUR COST
1	9	527	Centre face turn		M7 C	.25	.5		
2	9	42	Grind		M7 C	.2	.48		
3	9	61	Key seat		M5 C	.2	.18		
4	9	527	Screw		M6 C	.2	.16		
5	9	54	Drill Peg Hole		M1 C	.05	.01		
			(These times are purely imaginary)						
								TOTAL	

FIG. 55.

10. Technical Specification

A complete copy, as in 9, but omitting price details.

11. Invoice Order

A copy of the commercial portion of the Master, including delivery details and prices of all items.

12. Dispatch Instructions

A copy of the commercial portion of the Master, omitting prices, but including data required for nameplates, etc.

13. Instruction Card

One for each assembly operation and for certain components. This card will give the operator all the technical data required at this operation.

14. *Planning Card*

One for each order. This will have only a brief description of the order as given at the head of the Master, but will have planning data added, and be used for building the Forward Master Load on the Works.

Part No.		Opn. No.	Clock No.	
Date Issued		Date Reqd.		
REMARKS :—				Total Tools Received
TOOL REQUISITION	Received Tools & Drwgs. to this Reference			
	Date	Signed		

FIG. 56.

B. PROCEDURE FOR USE OF DOCUMENTS FOR COMPONENT ORDERS

In the following procedure it is assumed that each person hands on a document to the person dealing with the next subsequent operation. The procedure is illustrated in the Flow Chart, Plate 4.

I. ORIGINATE ORDERS

A. STANDARD COMPONENTS

By *Standard* Components is meant those parts which are made against job numbers through a stock-control routine.

1. *Stock Record Clerk*

(*a*) Originate order when order point on stock of a component is broken by writing out a Requisition for Manufacture.

(*b*) Calculate quantity of material to be released (i.e. length of bar or number of castings, etc.), and enter on Requisition for Manufacture.

(*c*) Enter on Requisition for Manufacture the actual stock of castings or fabrications.

2. *Shop Schedules Clerk*

Receive Requisition for Manufacture from Stock Record Clerk, and scrutinise and amend batch quantity if circumstances call for this.

3. *Typist*

Type Component Order Heading Master from information on Requisition for Manufacture.

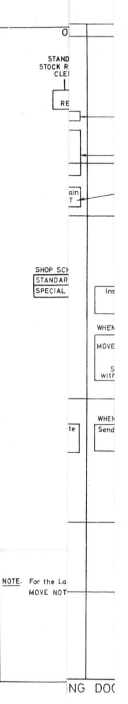

O

STAND
STOCK R
CLE

RE

ain
T

SHOP SCH
STANDAR
SPECIAL

Ins

WHEN

MOVE

S
with

te

WHEN

Send

4. *Duplicating Machine Operator*

(*a*) Take Operation Master for Component from file.

(*b*) Marry Order Heading Master and Operation Master, and run off documents on duplicating machine, thus:

> 1 Material Release Note. (For Fabrications two notes are usually required—one for Bar Stores and one for Plate Stores.)
> 1 Job Card for each operation.
> 1 Move Note for each operation.
> 1 Delivery Note (in lieu of Move Note for last operation).
> 1 Identity Label.
> 1 Progress Envelope.
> 1 Cost Card

The Cost Card is only necessary for the initial issue of a Master Operation Layout, and for Standard items is to be run off without Component Order Heading Master.

(*c*) Refile Master, and scrap Order Heading Master and Requisition for Manufacture.

5. *Shop Schedules Clerk*

(*a*) Receive Progress Envelopes containing all documents. Draw load line on all planning tickets and replace tickets in envelopes.

(*b*) File in the appropriate section of the "Standard" Waiting File under machine size sequence.

(*c*) Send Cost Card for new components to Cost Office.

B. SPECIAL COMPONENTS

By *Special* Components is meant those parts which are made only to special order numbers, and not to minimum and maximum stock requirements.

1. *Forward Load Planner*

(*a*) Scrutinise Order Parts List of machines on Assembly schedule for availability of material.

(*b*) For machines where material is not available, write out appropriate urge notes and pass to Buying Department.

(*c*) Where all material is available, raise Requisition for Manufacture for each special part on the Order Parts List.

(*d*) Obtain Operation Master copy and calculate quantity of material to be released, and enter on Requisition for Manufacture.

(*e*) Send Requisition for Manufacture to typist.

2. *Typist*

Type Component Order Master Heading from information on Requisition for Manufacture.

3. *Duplicating Machine Operator*

(*a*) Take Operation Master from file (or obtain from Production Engineers).

(*b*) Marry Order Heading Master and Operation Heading Master and run off documents as for Standard components.

(*c*) File Master, and scrap Order Heading Master and Requisition for Manufacture.

4. *Shop Schedules Clerk*

(*a*) Receive Progress Envelopes containing all documents. Draw load line on all planning tickets and replace tickets in envelopes.

(*b*) File in the appropriate section of the "Special" Waiting File under machine size sequence.

(*c*) Send Cost Card for components to Cost Office.

II. BUILD COMPONENT MANUFACTURING LOAD

1. *Shop Schedules Clerk*

(*a*) Each week, when departmental Assembly Schedules are built, scrutinise all jobs in both Standard and Special Component Waiting Files, and build up load on each department in priority order (i.e. according to date due on Heading). Write out draft schedules of loads.

(*b*) Should special circumstances warrant reduction of size of batch, arrange for duplicate documents for the second half of the batch.

2. *Typist*

Type departmental schedules from drafts.

3. *Forward Load Planner*

Record on Order Parts List week number of schedule for any special parts that have been scheduled.

III. ISSUE SCHEDULES

1. *Shop Schedules Clerk*

(*a*) Issue schedules to Shop Planners of department concerned one week ahead of the scheduled week.

(*b*) With the schedule, issue Move Notes and Job Cards to the department in which operations are performed, and send Material Release Notes and Identity Labels to the department in which the first operation is performed.

IV. MANUFACTURE

1. *Shop Planner*

(*a*) Build up load on planning board with Move Notes for each section.

(*b*) Send all Material Release Notes to Stores concerned, as requisition for raw material, and to enable Stores to prepare all the material in advance of requirements, stating day on which material will be required.

(*c*) On day previous to when job is to commence, send Identity Label to Stores marked with the machine number or operator to which the material is to be delivered, and the time by when it will be required.

(*d*) On day previous to when an operation is to commence, make out Tool Requisition and send to Tool Stores.

2. *Tool Stores*

On receipt of Tool Requisition put up kits of tools for job operation specified, and place Requisition with tools.

3. *Foreman or Chargehand*

As instruction for commencement of job, hand Move Note to operator.

4. *Operator*

(*a*) Take Move Note for new job and Identity Label for job finished to Time Clerk. Having been clocked on, retain Move Note for new job, and refix Identity Label to finished job.

(*b*) Present Move Note to Tool Stores for drawing, jigs, tools and gauges. (Retain Move Note.) Enter clock number on Tool Requisition and sign.

5. *Time Clerk*

(*a*) Clock the time on Job Cards of new job and job finished.

(*b*) Enter operator's name and department, with the week number, on the new Job Card, and place in current job tray.

6. *Inspector*

(*a*) After operator has completed job, make a final inspection, and make out Scrap Note for any scrap. If there is any faulty work which can be rectified, arrange for rectification, if possible, by the operator responsible.

(*b*) Enter on Move Note the quantity passed forward, the number to pay for, and, if any, the number scrapped. Date and sign Move Note.

(*c*) If batch must be passed forward before rectification, enter quantity to be rectified, and complete Move Note, and make out new Move Note and Job Card for this operation, and Identity Label, by hand. The foreman to arrange for completion of batch and any further documents, if required.

If operator is to be paid for any scrap or rectifications not sent forward (fault lying elsewhere), enter quantity to be paid for in panel of Move Note.

(*d*) Enter on Identity Label number of parts passed forward.

(*e*) Hand Move Note to Time Clerk.

(*f*) Sign Move Note each time a check inspection is made.

(*g*) For a final operation, on receipt of Delivery Note from Time Clerk, arrange for immediate transfer of batch to destination.

(*h*) If part deliveries are made from a batch, make out a part Delivery Note for any partial delivery with the part Delivery Note number.

7. *Time Clerk*

(*a*) When job is "clocked off", transfer Job Cards to "completed" tray.

(*b*) When Move Note is received from Inspector, transfer quantity to be paid for from Move Note to Job Card.

(*c*) Extend actual hours for job and enter on front of Job Card in panel immediately at right of "Actual hours at Nat. Bonus".

(*d*) At end of week write out new Job Cards when operator has to be paid for work done on a job not completed in that week.

(*e*) Enter on front of new Job Card the quantity previously paid for and actual hours for this quantity in panel "Previous Actual Hours".

(*f*) When completing a carried forward Job Card, deduct the quantity previously paid for, as shown on Move Note, to leave quantity to pay for on this card.

(*g*) Send Job Cards to Cost Office, and hand Move Notes to Shop Planner.

(*h*) For a Delivery Note of a final operation, mark off schedule and hand Delivery Note immediately to Inspection.

8. *Storekeeper*

(*a*) On receipt of Material Release Notes, prepare material, castings, or components, ready for issue.

(*b*) Enter on Material Release Note for raw materials the quantity (or weight) of material for batch to be issued.

(*c*) On receipt of Identity Label claiming the material, enter date issued, and sign Material Release Note. Send material to machine or operator indicated on Identity Label at, or before, time specified.

(*d*) Send all completed Material Release Notes to Planning Office once daily.

(*e*) On receipt of Finished Components from a manufacturing department, check description and quantity of goods with Identity Label and Delivery Note. Sign back of Delivery Note, with the date, and send to Planning Office. See that Identity Label is firmly fixed to special batches, and where necessary to standard batches.

9. *Progress Record Clerk (Planning Office)*

(*a*) On receipt of Move Notes, record completion of operation on Progress Envelope, File Move Notes in envelope.

(*b*) On receipt of Delivery Note for all components, mark off Office copy of Shop Schedule, and hand Delivery Note for Standard components to Stock Record Clerk.

(*c*) For Specials, in addition to marking off Final Operation on Progress Envelope, enter on Order Parts List that manufacture of component is complete. Send Delivery Note to Cost Office.

(*d*) File Progress Envelope in Orders Completed File.

(*e*) For weldings delivered to Casting Stores, mark Progress Envelope for Machine Shop batch "Weldings ready".

10. *Stock Record Clerk*

(*a*) On receipt of Material Release and Delivery Notes for Standard components, record receipts and issues on Stock Record Cards.

(*b*) Sign Material Release and Delivery Notes and send to Cost Office once daily.

C. PROCEDURE FOR USE OF DOCUMENTS FOR ASSEMBLY ORDERS

I. ORIGINATE ORDERS

1. *Forward Load Planner*

(*a*) At the time Requisitions for Manufacture are raised for special components (see item B. 1(*c*) on page 392), write out in pencil with carbon the Variable Heading for Assembly Master. See that any special instructions of general interest are included in the Variable Heading.

(*b*) At this stage, when there is more than one machine on an order, decide on the number of machines to be put through as a batch, and make out the Variable Heading for each batch quantity.

(*c*) Send Variable Heading to Duplicating Machine Operator.

2. *Duplicating Machine Operator*

(*a*) Take Operation Master for Assembly from file (or obtain from Production Engineers).

(*b*) Marry Order Heading and Operation Masters and run off documents as follows:

1 Move Note for each operation for each batch or machine.
1 Job Card for each operation (except Test) for each batch or machine.
1 Delivery Note in lieu of Move Note for Finishing and for Machine Painting Operation.
1 Identity Label for each machine.
1 Progress Envelope for each batch.
1 Cost Card for each order.

(*c*) Refile Master and Order Heading Master until advised that order is complete.

3. *Shop Schedules Clerk*

(*a*) Receive Progress Envelope containing all documents. Draw load line on all planning tickets and replace tickets in envelopes.

(*b*) File in Waiting File under machine number sequence.

(*c*) Send Cost Card to Cost Office.

II. BUILD ASSEMBLY LOAD

1. *Shop Schedules Clerk*

(*a*) Each week build up assembly load from load in Waiting File. Adjust, if necessary, to preserve as near as possible a uniform load through all Assembly sections.

(*b*) Write out draft schedules of load.

2. *Typist*

   (*a*) Type departmental schedules from drafts.

   (*b*) Record scheduled week number on Order Book Card Index.

III. ISSUE SCHEDULES

1. *Shop Schedules Clerk*

   (*a*) Issue schedules to Shop Planners of Department concerned one week ahead of the scheduled week.

   (*b*) With the schedule, issue Move Notes and Job Cards to the department in which operations are performed, and send Material Release to Assembly Notes and Identity Labels to the department in which the first operation is performed.

   (*c*) With the schedule, issue Job Instruction Cards.

IV. MANUFACTURE

1. *Shop Planner*

   (*a*) Build up load on planning board with Move Notes for each section.

   (*b*) Send Material Release to Assembly Notes to Stores concerned two days previous to when machine is to be built, to enable Stores to prepare material in advance.

   (*c*) In Assembly Shop, components for building will be put out on stillage platforms and parked by Stores inside Assembly Shop, identified by a handwritten tie-on label. Assembly Shop Labourer will collect and move platforms to Fitter.

2. *Foreman or Chargehand*

As instruction for commencement of job, hand Move Note to operator.

3. *Operator*

Take Move Note for new job and Identity Label for job finished to Time Clerk. Having been clocked on, retain Move Note for new job, and refix Identity Label to finished job.

4. *Time Clerk*

   (*a*) Clock the time on Job Cards of new job and job finished.

   (*b*) Enter operator's name and department, with the week number, on the new Job Card and place in current job tray.

5. *Inspector*

   (*a*) After operator has completed job, make a final inspection. If there is any faulty work which can be rectified, arrange for rectification, if possible, by the operator responsible.

(*b*) For Subassemblies, enter on Move Note the quantity passed forward, the number to pay for, and, if any, the number scrapped. Date and sign Move Note.

(*c*) For dealing with rectification in Detail Assembly, see paragraph B. IV. 6, page 395.

(*d*) Hand Move Note to Time Clerk.

6. Time Clerk

(*a*) When job is "clocked off", transfer Job Card to "completed" tray.

(*b*) When Move Note is received from Inspector, transfer quantity to be paid for from Move Note to Job Card.

(*c*) Extend actual hours for job, and enter on front of Job Card in panel immediately at right of "Actual Hours at Nat. Bonus".

(*d*) At end of week make out new Job Card for uncompleted jobs, and mark "Brought forward". On Job Card to be closed mark "Continued".

(*e*) Send completed Job Cards to Cost Office, and hand Move Notes to Shop Planner.

(*f*) For Delivery Note of a final operation mark off schedule and hand Delivery Note immediately to Inspection.

7. Storekeeper

(*a*) On receipt of Material Release to Assembly Notes, prepare material ready for issue.

(*b*) Mark off Part Lists for items issued. Send Part Lists to Cost Office when all materials on the order have been issued.

(*c*) Sign Material Release to Assembly Notes and send to Planning Office daily.

(*d*) Assembly Stores. Gather together all parts required, put up on stillage platform, write machine number on manilla label, tie on batch and park in Assembly Shop.

For Subassemblies follow same procedure, using trays and Identity Labels supplied.

8. Progress Record Clerk (Planning Office)

(*a*) On receipt of Move Notes, file in Progress Envelope, and mark off progress on envelope.

(*b*) On receipt of Delivery Note, mark off Order Book Card Index.

(*c*) When Delivery Note on last machine is received, transfer Progress Envelope to Orders Completed File.

9. Stock Records Clerk

(*a*) On receipt of Material Release to Assembly Notes, adjust records.

(*b*) Sign Material Release to Assembly Notes and send to Cost Office once daily.

D. PROCEDURE FOR USE OF ANCILLARY DOCUMENTS

I. GENERAL

A. The following ancillary documents are to be used in conjunction with the pre-printed documents, and are to be filled in by hand when required:

1. Excess Time Card.
2. Excess Material Requisition.
3. Stores Credit.
4. Waiting Time Card.
5. Scrap Note.

With the exception of the Stores Credit, these documents all record excess costs, i.e. money spent on either material or labour in excess of what need have been spent. It is vitally important, therefore, not only that they are accurately made out, but are authorised by a Foreman, so that the head of the department is aware of the excess costs in his department.

B. If either of the Material Documents, i.e. Stores Credit or Excess Material Requisition, or Scrap Note, are spoilt, they must not be thrown away, but must be marked across the face "cancelled", and sent forward with the other completed documents.

II. EXCESS TIME CARD (Fig. 57)

A. This is to be used whenever extra Standard Time is allowed on a job because of some unusual cause, i.e. when, because of some tem-

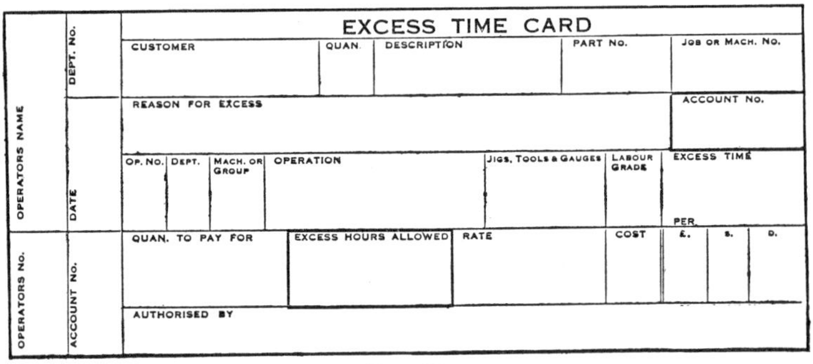
EXCESS TIME CARD
OPERATORS NAME
DEPT. NO.
DATE
OPERATORS NO.
ACCOUNT NO.
CUSTOMER
QUAN.
DESCRIPTION
PART NO.
JOB OR MACH. NO.
REASON FOR EXCESS
ACCOUNT NO.
OP. NO.
DEPT.
MACH. OR GROUP
OPERATION
JIGS, TOOLS & GAUGES
LABOUR GRADE
EXCESS TIME
PER
QUAN. TO PAY FOR
EXCESS HOURS ALLOWED
RATE
COST
£.
s.
D.
AUTHORISED BY

FIG. 57.

porary condition in the shop, more time will be required to do a job and the extra time can be assessed. It is not to be used when Standard Times are permanently adjusted.

B. It is only to be made out and authorised by a Work Study Engineer.

C. It is important to give the account number on which the excess cost is to be charged, and to state the exact reason for the excess, particularly showing the responsibility.

D. Excess Time Cards are to be attached to the Job Card to which they relate, and sent to the Wages Department.

III. EXCESS MATERIAL REQUISITION (Fig. 58)

A. This is to be used when an extra issue of material is required, because it will be impossible to finish the job with the amount of material available, due to scrap, loss, or shortage on original requisition.

B. Normally it will only be used when the amount of scrap is unknown, or material has been cut to waste.

C. Under "Reason for Demand" the exact details and the reason excess material is required must be shown.

	EXCESS MATERIAL REQUISITION	N⁰ 6		
	DATE	MATERIAL	PART	JOB OR MACHINE NO.	ACCOUNT NO.
PROGRESS	REASON FOR DEMAND			QUANTITY	RATE	VALUE
STORES CONTROL						
	ISSUED BY......................STORES					
					......FOREMAN
	DATE......................STOREKEEPER					

FIG. 58.

D. Excess material will only be issued against the signature of a Foreman or some higher authority.

E. The Material Requisition is to be forwarded to the Planning Office with Material Release Notes.

Note.—See Scrap Note for replacement of scrap.

IV. STORES CREDIT (Fig. 59)

A. This is to be used when, for any reason, job cancelled or material found to be surplus to requirements, material or components have to be returned to Stores.

	STORES CREDIT	N⁰ 6		
	DATE	MATERIAL	PART	PART NO.	JOB OR MACHINE NO.
PROGRESS	REASON FOR RETURN	RETURNED BY	QUANTITY	RATE	VALUE
STORES CONTROL						
	RECEIV D INTO......................STORES					
					......FOREMAN
	DATE......................STOREKEEPER					

FIG. 59.

B. It must be signed by the Foreman of the Department returning the materials or components.

C. Stores Credit Notes are to be forwarded to the Planning Department with Material Release Notes.

v. WAITING TIME CARD (Fig. 60)

A. This is to be used whenever an operator has to be paid for waiting time, i.e. the operator is prevented from, or delayed in, doing work.

B. It is to be made out in total by the Foreman or Chargehand, including the "time on" and "time off". Because an operator can, and might be tempted to, claim more waiting time than has actually occurred in order to artificially increase bonus earnings, it is most important that the exact time when waiting time commenced and finished shall be known and checked by the Supervisor responsible. It also gives the Supervisor the opportunity to investigate the cause, and to take steps to prevent its recurrence. It will be advisable for one card to be used for each incident. One card must never be used for waiting time on different account numbers.

C. The exact cause for the lost time must be stated, indicating the responsibility. When the responsibility is considered to belong to another department, and card should preferably be countersigned by the Fore-

		WAITING TIME CARD							
DEPT. No.		CAUSE				FOREMAN'S SIGNATURE			
OPERATORS NAME	WEEK ENDING								
		DAY	TIME ON	TIME OFF	TOTAL TIME	RATE	£.	s.	D.
OPERATORS No.	ACCOUNT No.								

FIG. 60.

man of the other department on the day the card is completed, in order that he can be made immediately aware of the lost time and excess cost, and take steps to prevent its recurrence.

D. Waiting Time Cards are to be handed in to the Time Clerk, who will confirm that all time in the day is accounted for.

vi. SCRAP NOTE (Fig. 61)

A. This is to be used to record components completely rejected as scrap.

B. It is to be made out by the Inspector rejecting the work, and the cause of the scrap must be clearly stated, and the account number indicating the responsibility entered, consulting the Foreman concerned if there is any doubt.

C. A Scrap Note is to be used for each job and operation, i.e. the scrap from several operations or different jobs *must not* be included on one Scrap Note.

D. Should it be necessary to replace the component scrapped, and therefore obtain further material, as may occasionally happen on the first operation of a special part, the material required may be drawn from the Stores by completing the bottom of the Scrap Note, and using the Note as a requisition instead of using an Excess Material Requisition. It is the Inspector's responsibility to find out whether it will be necessary to replace the material at this stage.

When replacement of scrap must be put through separately and cannot go with the original batch, the Scrap Note must not be used as a material requisition, but a new set of documents must be issued from

SCRAP NOTE					Nº	3101	
DATE	PART			PART No.	JOB OR M/C No.		ACCOUNT No.
DEPT.	CHECK No.	NAME		OPERATION AT WHICH SCRAPPED			
				No.	DESCRIPTION		
CAUSE OF SCRAP					No. SCRAPPED	COST	
						MAT.	
						LAB.	
RE-ISSUE OF MATERIAL AUTHORISED		INSPECTED BY				O'HD.	
			FOREMAN		INSPECTOR	TOTAL	
MATERIAL REQD.		AMOUNT		ISSUED		DATE	

FIG. 61.

the Planning Office. The Planning Office will decide whether to issue a replace order on receipt of a Scrap Note for which replace material has not been drawn. It will help the Planning Office, in the case of urgent jobs, if the Inspector refers the Scrap Note immediately to the Progress Engineer or Planning Office direct.

E. After summarising by Inspection Department, Scrap Notes are to be forwarded to the Planning Office, who will forward on to Cost Office.

CHAPTER IV

PURCHASING

RESPONSIBILITIES

THE Purchaser, or Buyer as he is alternatively called, is responsible for the largest single item in the trading account of most businesses, i.e. the material content of total cost. It is more than the cost of wages and salaries combined, more than administrative overheads, more than taxation. It can be quite a low percentage of Sales Value in service industries and for products for which sales and advertising costs are very high as with personal luxury articles, but can be as high as 70 per cent. in highly mechanised and process industries; generally it is around 40 to 45 per cent. and if the value of consumable stores, stationery and similar items normally reckoned as overheads, is included, the average figure for industry would be about 50 per cent. The Purchaser is not only responsible for signing orders for, and hence committing the company to pay for, this large amount of money, but by his skill and effectiveness he can reduce the amount or increase the value received for the outlay. Obviously therefore it is just as important that this activity of buying should be *effectively* performed as any other in an organisation; it ought not to be thought of lightly, nor staffed by persons without skill or training, nor its responsibilities be left loose and undefined. The word "effectively" is purposely used, because the measure of a Purchaser's value is not always the reduced prices at which he can obtain goods from time to time, but the success with which he can obtain satisfactory materials, find alternative better materials at an economic price, and at the same time obtain adequate continuous service from his suppliers. And continuous implies that a supplier is not forced out of business by unprofitable prices. The buyer should at all times maintain a high standard of commercial morality and honourable practice in the conduct of his business. Fortunately the professional body catering for buyers (The Purchasing Officers' Association) is doing a great deal to make "management" aware of its responsibilities in the matter and to raise the standard of training and of qualifications.

The person to whom the Buyer is responsible and the activities for which he is responsible vary more perhaps than for any other executive in industry. Problems of status as well as of organisation structure are involved. This is because the function of a Buyer is not properly understood or is not considered of great importance, or simply because the relative importance of materials in the total build-up of cost varies so much. In flour milling and sugar refining, for example, there is one primary material, it represents a very large proportion of total cost, and market fluctuations of its cost can have a big influence on profits. The Buyer may then be a first-line executive and even a director. Wood case making, printing and weaving are similar though not such extreme cases. But in most industries many diverse materials are used, prices remain relatively stable and large contracts for supplies are not frequent. In this more normal situation buying is a production activity following the designer and planner in the logical sequence of activities (though not necessarily lower in status). In a very small company it may be combined with other activities carried out for example by the Works Manager or Secretary, but in most companies it is a specialist activity requiring a sizeable staff which should be under the authority of a skilled Purchasing Officer who should be responsible to either the head of the production departments (Works or Production Manager) or, if there are a few but important primary materials, then perhaps to the Managing Director.

For what is a Buyer responsible? It is often claimed that the Buyer should be responsible for Stores records and even Stores Departments. It is argued that as the Buyer needs to keep records of requisitions, orders, part deliveries and such running contracts as there are, he can just as easily (and perhaps on the same document) keep records of stocks, and since he is responsible for obtaining materials, he should be the custodian until they are required for production. But in developing a sound organisation structure it is important to group like activities and skill together in order to take advantage of specialist skills, and a Buyer's skill is, or should be, as an interviewer, negotiator and interpreter of markets and his company's requirements (similar to but in the opposite sense to selling). Stores records are primarily a tool of those responsible for programmes (Production Planning); they more than anyone are most concerned with level of stocks, stock movements, allocations and replenishment, and in any case arrange for replenishment of finished and component stocks manufactured by their own company and must keep records for these. On the other hand the job of store-keeping is very much a works activity involving the active supervision of persons doing manual work on the shop floor, often well dispersed; it is not the kind of activity suitable for control from an office desk, the occupier of which must be available for interviewing suppliers' representatives for much of his day.

In the extractive and primary material industries (flour milling, etc.), there may be a case for the Buyer to maintain material records, but in normal manufacturing industry where (a) there is a wide variety of materials the demand for which varies with manufacturing programmes, and (b) store-keeping involves a good deal of dispersion and handling, then stores records should be a Planning activity (see page 336) and Storekeeping should be responsible to the Works Manager (see page 422). There may be instances where the persons who would normally be responsible for stores records or storekeeping are not capable of discharging this responsibility effectively, whereas the Buyer is a very capable person. In such cases the Buyer could no doubt absorb the responsibility of those activities, but such special cases should be recognised for what they are, expedients and as not adhering to the general principles of correct organisation structure.

The following can therefore be taken as defining the responsibilities of a Purchasing Officer or Buyer:

Responsibilities of Buyer

Responsible to :   Production Manager.
Responsible for :   Buying all materials and supplies.
Authority over :   Buying Department Staff.

Responsible for:

1. Buying all materials, supplies and equipment required by the Company, and to this end:
   (a) Study the commodity market and keep abreast of prices, price trends and deliveries.
   (b) Maintain up-to-date records (including catalogues and trade literature) of sources of supply of materials, services, products and equipment likely to be required by the company.
   (c) Adhere to the Company's Buying policy and interpret this policy to the staff under his authority.
2. Developing and maintaining an effective Buying service and to this end:
   (a) Interview suppliers' representatives, where advisable, in collaboration with an executive concerned.
   (b) Advise departments concerned of any changes in price, availability or delivery likely to affect normal routine buying or replacement of stocks.
   (c) Translate requisitions for supplies into orders or contracts on suppliers, ensuring that requisitions are duly authorised and within the limits laid down.
   (d) Issue enquiries to alternative suppliers, collating all quotations and accepting the most suitable, where necessary in consultation with or reference to the technical executive concerned.

(e) Progress and follow up orders and calls off contracts.

(f) Scrutinise and vouch for invoices received.

(g) Dispose of scrap, residues, surplus material and plant.

(h) Supervise and co-ordinate the work of those under his authority.

(i) Ensure the safety and good condition of records and equipment in the Department.

3. Developing and maintaining a high morale in the Buying Department, and to this end:

(a) Adhere to the Company's Personnel Policy; especially to ensure that members of his staff are doing the work most suited to their abilities and are provided with the opportunities of making the best and fullest use of their capabilities.

(b) Instruct, train and guide all under his authority in the exercise of their duties effectively and in accordance with the policies, plans and programmes laid down.

(c) Advise on the selection, appointment and promotion of all staff under his authority.

Co-operate with:	On:
Planning Engineers	Deliveries of materials and supplies, required for execution of orders received.
Production Engineers	Alternative methods of producing supplies required.
Design Office	Forward ordering in relation to Company's stated delivery dates. Specifications of materials and quotations for special equipment.
Works Engineer	Quotations for machine tools required. Quotations for plant required.
Estimating office	Price queries and delivery dates.
Accountant	Checking of invoices and passing for payment. Competitive prices of supplies.
Personnel Adviser	Staff absence, vacancies, general welfare and employment conditions.

Buying is very much a specialist activity. It calls for commercial acumen as well as a wide ranging knowledge of industries and materials. It is concerned with value for money as well as the technical suitability of materials bought and their arrival when required. Skill in the specialist activity can be taught, although buying is one of the occupations in industry where long experience in the job, in the particular industry or company, is especially valuable—buyers change their employer less than most executives. There are so many alternative suppliers of most materials and articles, all of whom claim by advertisement or direct approach that their product is the most suitable or the best, that only experience enables a Buyer to decide, without testing each time an order is placed, which firms he can rely on to supply what he must have. In fact the Buyer's m. responsibility is for buying materials and articles of the type and quality his colleagues (designers, plant engineers, office managers, etc.) require, in time for their needs, and at a price which secures for his company the best value for its money, choosing wisely from the many suppliers who tender their products. His colleagues state what they want and when (being the best judge), and the Buyer's job is to get it in time and at the best cost. His concern and experience is in commercial dealings and markets and to ensure a continuous, dependable and economical supply of the materials and articles his company needs.

The best value for money is not synonymous with low purchase price. It can be obtained in several ways:

1. By getting a better article at the same cost. In this case the company will only derive benefit for the better value to the extent that it can make use of the better quality article. A higher quality that cannot be taken advantage of has no higher intrinsic value.
2. By getting the same article at a lower cost. There is obviously better value here but a Buyer must be on his guard to see that future consignments do not fall off in quality; that he does in fact get the same article.
3. By paying a higher price for a much higher quality article. This can be justified and yield better value if, in the design or in use, full advantage can be taken of the added quality, e.g. by using less of the article or if it results in less labour, maintenance or more production.
4. By paying much less for a lower quality article where this lower quality is quite adequate for the purpose in view. This is a case of over-specification, a very useful and usually overlooked source of reduced costs. It is most likely to be revealed by work study, particularly applied to product design or formulation, but the Buyer should be on the look-out for cases where too high a quality, standard of accuracy or of finish is being asked for; his colleagues may not be aware of it.

In his frequent and wide ranging contacts with supplier industries, the Buyer is in a better position than his colleagues to know of alternative materials and products and of alternative methods of producing them. He is also in a position to get early information of new materials, processes and services. He has the responsibility of keeping abreast of these changes and of advising his colleagues of them.

Standardisation of design can result in a considerable reduction in the costs of production. This applies not only to the Buyer's own company, but to his suppliers too, and any standardisation should result in lower prices and better value.

Business conditions are never static. As the pressures of supply and demand vary, prices and the availability of commodities vary too. The swings, from conditions of scarcity to conditions of surplus capacity and back again, are made more violent than they would otherwise be, because so many Buyers do not pay due regard to market trends and plan ahead; they react only when the conditions have already changed considerably, adding force to the swing. As a result they get caught short of supplies or get over-stocked. It is a Buyer's responsibility to be acutely sensitive to the changes in market conditions and fully aware—so far as he can obtain the information from his colleagues—of his company's requirements into the future, so that, by forward planning, he can avoid the effects of short supply and high prices or of being left with too high stocks on a falling market. It calls for an ability to understand the implications of statistics of commercial and industrial activity and to co-operate with and advise his colleagues on the preparation of long-term plans and programmes. To this end he will need to keep certain records and charts himself and must ensure that he is supplied with the necessary information from his own company.

A Buyer has to build up dependable sources of supply; it is wasteful and unnecessary to send enquiries to *all* suppliers for every order. There must be mutual trust and fair dealing between buyer and supplier. This means that strictly ethical standards and methods are adopted by the Buyer, encouraging competition without taking unfair advantage of position or circumstances. The reception of customers' representatives should always be prompt, courteous and businesslike. It would be a good education and experience for a Buyer to become a salesman or representative for a time. It is fatally easy not to be interested in a new line, or a product competitive to one already giving satisfaction, and to miss opportunities of buying better or more economical materials through not being energetic enough to find out what is available. To tell a salesman that his price is high when it is low, to refer to imaginary competition, or otherwise to misrepresent directly or by implication in order to coax a lower price or an extra discount from a salesman induces instability into relations, is bound to lead to misrepresentation in return, and earns for the Company an unpleasant name. Such tactics belong to the past; they may succeed in isolated cases, but salesmen are quick to detect such methods and to use appropriate tactics themselves.

Fair dealing requires that advantage will not be taken of an obviously incorrect quotation which will mean a loss to the supplier. If a price which will not produce a profit is deliberately quoted, and known to be so, that is a different matter, but in general the Buyer expects the seller to make an adequate profit. How else can the supplier continue in business and to give service? A fair price which enables a manufacturer to make a reasonable profit and supply competitive goods and adequate service, including a margin for development, is essential in modern industry, and is as much a matter of interest to the Buyer as to the seller. Fair dealing also requires the Buyer to state clearly for what reason he has to turn down a quotation. This does not mean that he must disclose the competitive prices, but it is not fair to competitors to give inaccurate reasons for uncompetitive prices.

There must obviously be confidence and co-operation between buyer and seller, and in the long run a dependable supplier is a worthy partner to the Buyer. Such confidence and co-operation cannot be built up except on a basis of fair dealings.

POLICIES

A buying policy should be laid down clearly by the Board of Directors or by the Managing Director in line with company policy. It will be of course part of the production policy, or arise from it, and will be dictated by the kind of production programme adopted. For example, the programme may require much greater quantities at one time of the year than another, but the buying policy may be to take regular supplies over the whole year to suit the suppliers, and to take advantage of lower prices, stocking during the period of lower demand. It should not be left to the Buyer to operate as he thinks fit, with the risk of being reprimanded for what may be thought unwise use of discretion.

Three broad lines of policy are usual:

(1) *To buy on a Bargain Basis*
   This may be pursued in the case of staple commodities and for the major materials in process industries. It offers large profits on buying, with the consequence of large risks, and it is of a speculative nature. Speculation is an activity belonging to the Stock Exchange, and should not find its place in ordinary industrial activities. If it is pursued as a policy, it is usual for the buying to be under the control of a senior executive of the Company.

(2) *To buy on Contract*
   In this policy, contracts are given to suppliers for large amounts of future requirements, for a year, or for indefinite periods subject to review and cancellation with an appropriate period of notice. It has the advantage of avoiding the necessity for carrying stocks by the user and of giving a measure of stability to suppliers. It also gives the Buyer an assurance of continuity of supply and of ser-

vice. Under mass-production conditions, this latter feature is most important and the policy may be well justified.

(3) *To buy against Current Market Conditions*
This is the more usual policy, giving the Buyer a wide discretion. Orders are placed for the minimum quantity required for the replacement of stock to meet particular demands, and alternative quotations are obtained, either for each order, or occasionally as a check.

Frequently, in normal industrial conditions a combination of policies 2 and 3 are laid down, contracts being limited to certain major raw materials.

Sub-contracting

It is not unusual for a company to arrange for other firms to manufacture some part or parts of its own products or carry out some of the necessary manufacturing processes to its own design and specification. This was widely practised during the last war when large service and supply contracts had to be placed with a main contractor who sub-let or sub-contracted some of the work involved to smaller or more specialised manufacturers. The practice is widely used too in the motor-car industry where often as many as half of the components of a vehicle are produced by sub-contractors to the designing and assembling firm. It is also used in other industries, chiefly when a company's capacity to meet its customer's requirements is temporarily insufficient. In the latter case, cost is not always a decisive factor, but for a permanent arrangement it must be cheaper to sub-contract than to make. This can be so when advantage is taken of specialisation and of the lower overheads of small units. Small firms with specialised plant or techniques, e.g. gear-cutting, plastering, engraving, etc., can become highly skilled and efficient and their costs correspondingly low. Whether or not such sub-contracting is employed is a matter of policy, balancing the cost, lower or higher, against such factors as avoiding purchase of additional buildings and plant, effective control of quality and delivery, interruption of supply due to causes not under the company's own control (strikes, etc.). Sub-contracting is primarily a Buyer's responsibility though he may need the advice and assistance of Works departments for assessing the competence and capacity of the tendering companies. His main problem will be one of maintaining quality of product or servicing and maintaining regular and reliable delivery. He will also be involved in maintaining accurate records of contracts and deliveries; if these are not always up to date and accurate, considerable losses can accumulate. If sub-contracting becomes permanent and a large proportion of the company's supplies it is advisable to set up a special department, staffed with suitably qualified persons, under the Buyer, to deal with it.

Limiting Value of Order

It is usual for a limit to be placed on the individual value of any one order. This value may vary with the type of commodity. Orders above these limits are referred to a senior executive or the Managing Director for final authority. This may be necessary to fit in with financial policy when liquid capital is strained, or when the coincidence of several large orders in a period may strain the Company's arrangements for regular settlement of accounts.

Purchase of Capital Equipment

Purchase of capital equipment, additions to plant or buildings, or replacements thereto, should be dealt with in a special manner. Expenditure on such items does not arise as a matter of routine, and must in any case fit into any capital expenditure budgets or programme. It is, therefore, essential for all items above an agreed amount to be covered by a capital sanction authorised by the executive concerned. In a large concern it is advisable for certain executives only to be authorised to order capital equipment, and for the amount of capital expenditure per year and per period to be laid down for the executive concerned. In a period of expansion, it is possible without some such control, for a Company to undertake commitments for the purchase of plant which it cannot meet.

PROCEDURES

The type of order form and the procedure adopted for requisitioning and placing of orders vary widely. In all cases, however, it is strongly recommended that only the Buyer be authorised to place official orders on behalf of the firm. Works Engineers and Office Managers often contend that only they know what they require. This may be so, but the order should still go through the Buyer. Buying, and the associated records, are a specialised activity, and every use should be made of the specialised skill thus built up. In all cases, therefore, persons requiring materials should state their requirements to the Buyer on an official requisition. When the material or article must fulfil certain conditions, then the requisition must be accompanied by a specification. When the source of supply or the particular brand or maker of the article required is not stated, then it is the Buyer's responsibility to buy where he can. At other times it may be necessary for technical departments to obtain all this information first and to determine by test, or otherwise, what is most suitable.

When samples or quotations are required, then the requisition form should be used in the same way, stating that an enquiry or quotation only is required in the first place, and that these are to be submitted to the department originating the requisition, or not as stated.

Although the Buyer is not responsible for storekeeping or inspection, but is required to check and sign for the validity and accuracy of invoices rendered by suppliers, he should insist on a proper advice of goods received and of an adequate examination or inspection. Practice with regard to inspection of goods received varies, from a detailed inspection of all consignments (which can be very costly indeed), to a cursory examination of identification and quality. If suppliers have a thorough and adequate final inspection of their own production, it should only be necessary for a receiving firm to check that goods received are as specified on the order. The Buyer should select and train his suppliers so that he can rely on them to maintain his specified standards; by doing so he will enable the cost of inspection of incoming goods to be greatly reduced. However, some spot checking at least is desirable, as a protection against carelessness or error in the suppliers' organisation.

Order Forms

The layout of an order form suitable for normal requirements is shown in Fig. 62. All copies are made at one typing, and different colours are used to aid sorting and distribution.

The following example of standard practice instructions for the ordering of materials, supplies and outside services through the Buyer uses the minimum possible forms for adequate control, and can be taken as a basis from which to develop a satisfactory procedure for any particular company or set of conditions. For example, it may be necessary to obtain additional authority and signature for orders over certain amounts, or for certain materials, and central buying for associated or subsidiary companies would involve a modified routine.

(1) All materials, supplies, and services from outside contractors are to be ordered through the Buyer by sending to him a requisition setting out what is required.

(2) When the originating department wants to see quotations before placing an order, a requisition form is to be used marked plainly in capitals ENQUIRY. Quotations when received are referred to the department concerned. The Buyer may at other times refer quotations obtained at his own discretion to the executive concerned for advice on selection of the most suitable.

	Order No.
ALPHABETICAL FILING COPY	Order No.
ORIGINATOR'S COPY	Order No.
STORES COPY RECORD OF RECEIPTS & INSPECTION ON REVERSE	Order No.
NUMERICAL FILING COPY RECORD OF RECEIPTS & PROGRESS ON REVERSE	Order No.
ACKNOWLEDGEMENT TO BE RETURNED BY SUPPLIER	Order No.

PURCHASE ORDER

Reqn. No.	
A/C	

COMPANY'S NAME

Dept.

Telephone No.
REGent 0000   **AND**

Messrs.   **ADDRESS**   Date

Please supply,
in accordance with Conditions set out on back of this Order : —

Please quote our Order No on all advice notes and invoices

DELIVERY : —

ORDER NUMBER

For XYZ Ltd.

BUYER

FIG. 62.

(3) A capital sanction authorisation is to be obtained by the originating department for all purchases of a capital nature above £20.
(4) On receipt of a requisition, the Buyer translates the requisition into an order by typing out an official order set.
(5) An official order set comprises:
(a) Purchase Order (white) sent to supplier.
(b) Acknowledgment of Order (pink), being an exact copy sent to supplier for signature and return.
(c) Buyer's copy (white) for numerical filing.
(d) Stores copy (buff), with record of goods received and inspection report on reverse.
(e) Originator's copy (blue), sent to department originating the requisition.
(6) The Buyer:
(a) Sends first two copies to supplier.
(b) Sends third copy to Stores.
(c) Sends fourth copy to department originating requisition.
(d) Files own numerical copy in card index.
(e) Places alphabetical copy in unacknowledged file.
(f) Files requisition in box file in number sequence.
(7) Each day Buyer checks through unacknowledged file, and to firms who have not acknowledged within a week, writes an appropriate letter asking for acknowledgment and confirmation.

(8) As acknowledgment copies are received from suppliers, they are transferred to alphabetical file.

(9) When goods are received :

   (*a*) Stores arrange for inspection.

   (*b*) Inspection enter report on reverse side of Stores copy of order.

   (*c*) Stores copy of order is then sent to Buying Office, who transfer record to their copy, and take up any discrepancy, and report rejects to suppliers.

   (*d*) Buyer sends Stores copy of order, on same day, to stock control section of Planning Office, who transfer information to stock records.

   (*e*) For single or last consignments, Stores copy of order is returned to Buyer. For part consignments, Stores copy of order is returned to Stores.

(10) Invoices for goods received are submitted to Buyer for checking and authorisation.

(11) The following departments are authorised to use requisitions:

   Drawing Office—materials requiring long delivery periods.

   Stores Control—special materials and supplies.

   Stores—general consumable supplies and hardware.

   Production Engineers—plant, tools and equipment.

   Tool Stores—tool replacements.

   General Office—stationery.

   Pattern Shop—timber supplies and maintenance.

Records

It is essential for the Buyer to build up reliable records which will give him control of orders placed and comprehensive information regarding materials available and likely to be required, and standard and competitive prices. The extent of these records will depend upon the size of the firm, but the following records are the minimum which are required for effective control.

Copies of Orders

Two copies of the order should be filed, one filed under the Company's order number numerically, and the other under the supplier's name alphabetically. It is essential that one copy is available for very rapid reference. It is usual for the order to be known internally, and therefore the numerical copy is filed under its order number for rapid reference. Using the order set on the previous page, the length of the form is made $\frac{1}{2}$ inch shorter than a quarto-size sheet, i.e. $9\frac{1}{2} \times 8$ inches. The numerical copy is folded to within $\frac{1}{2}$ inch of the bottom, where the order number is repeated, making it 8×5 inches and suitable for inserting in a visible-edge cabinet, the quickest form of reference file. The top half of the back of the form, which is printed to receive delivery records, is uppermost after folding and filing in the cabinet. The alphabetical copy is filed in whatever way is found most convenient, and forms a cross index with the order file.

Record of Purchases

It is also necessary to keep a record of all purchases of each material or part. This is best done on a card file, with one card for each material or part. Each order placed should be entered with particulars of the supplier from whom ordered, the price and quantity. Suitable headings for such a card record are given at Fig. 63. It is

STANDARD PRICE		MATL.		CODE No.	
SUPPLIER	DESCRIPTION	PRICE	DATE	ORDER No.	QUANTITY

FIG. 63.

not necessary to keep a record of the value of purchases made for each supplier. This information can always be obtained, if required, from the Accounts Department.

Catalogues

A library of catalogues of suppliers of material and equipment likely to be used is invaluable, and should be kept in good condition, up to date and adequately indexed. Because of the varying size of catalogues, it often proves to be a difficult job, and it is frequently found that the simplest way is to use box files. Because many suppliers have a wide range of products, it is usually found impossible to file according to the kind of product or associated products, and one must rely on a straightforward numerical or alphabetical filing with a cross index. These indexes of catalogues can be broadened to include an index of suppliers of materials, whether catalogued or not. Although it may duplicate some of the information in trade directories, the latter can never be completely comprehensive.

Progress and Follow-up

It is as essential to progress orders on suppliers as it is to progress orders in the Company's works. Continuity of supplies can be as important as cost. Indeed, in mass production it is the essential prerequisite. Those connected with manufacturing industry in the period following the Second World War had frequent and bitter experience of this. Running out of stock of odd items, often quite small, resulted in products being held up in a half-finished or almost completed state for weeks on end. At such times very inflated prices were paid for supplies from alternative sources; output was more valuable than the increased cost incurred. Not only in mass-production factories is the delay serious, the restriction on turnover in any factory can be and has been quite large.

In difficult times, as in times of shortage, an outside progress man who visits suppliers personally and can get on personal terms with the man who matters, Works Manager or Planning Engineer, can be most effective. When much work is subcontracted it is almost essential, and advisable when there are running contracts that have to be co-ordinated with flow production programmes which are subject to acceleration or modification.

Progress can only be measured against a predetermined requirement, and the requirement in this case is the delivery date, which forms part of the contract to supply, accepted by the supplier when he accepts the order. In order that progress can be 100 per cent. effective, it is essential to know of every order not delivered to time. The simplest way of throwing up such orders is to keep the reverse of a Delivery Promise book, i.e. a Delivery Due book. Each order made out is entered in the Delivery Due book on the page for the day (or week) when delivery is due. Each day (or week) orders appearing as due should be checked with the order record, and if a delivery has not been received, follow-up action should be initiated.

Follow-up action will depend on circumstances, but usually starts with an "urge" letter or reminder. Such letters must not appear casual or merely routine, and for this reason must be as carefully compiled as any other letter. Although a standard form of letter can be used, it is better to have several forms (which can be selected to suit the circumstances or supplier), and individually typed letters are likely to command more attention than duplicated ones. Further promises given should be followed up with increasing pressure, and it is in difficult cases that the personal contact or outside progress man can be more effective.

SPECIFICATIONS AND CONTRACTS

It is essential for the Buyer to make absolutely clear to the supplier exactly what is required, the tests, if any, to be passed, and the conditions attached to an order, which, when accepted, becomes a contract in law. In order to state clearly what is required, Buyers are strongly recommended to use specifications, and wherever possible to use those published by the British Standards Institution, since they are likely to avoid special production—and hence higher prices. If there is not a British Standards Specification applicable, a specification should be obtained from or drawn up in collaboration with Designers, Technical Chief, or the Production Engineers. Such specifications can be made to cover general classes or particular goods, and do help to maintain uniform quality and avoid misunderstandings.

Conditions attached to the placing of an order and to which the supplier is to be held to comply should be drawn up in collaboration with the Technical departments and the Accountant and checked with the appropriate Trade Association which often have standard forms. The following can be taken as typical, although much more detailed and complex conditions are sometimes laid down:

Official Order.—No goods will be paid for unless an official order can be produced if required. Any specifications, drawings, patterns, etc., supplied by us with reference to this order remain our property.

Rejections.—Any article found to be defective, inferior in quality, or in excess of the quantity ordered, may be rejected and returned to you at your own risk and expense. A debit note will be sent informing you whether replacement is desired or not.

Suspension.—In the event of strikes, accidents, or other unforeseen contingencies, delivery may be suspended at our request.

Cancellation.—Undue delay in delivery or a continuation of defective supplies shall entitle us to cancel the order.

Advising.—An advice note quoting our order number must accompany the goods or be sent by post same day as goods are dispatched.

Invoicing.—An invoice must be sent on same day as goods are dispatched, and must quote our order number, failing which invoice may be returned.

Statements.—Monthly statements of account to be received by us not later than the 5th of the month following invoice date, otherwise payment may be deferred a month beyond the ordinary due date.

Terms.—Payment will be made during month following that in which goods are invoiced.

Liability for Injury or Damage.—This order is subject to the condition that in so far as it relates to erection or other work to be carried out on our premises or elsewhere to our instructions, you accept liability for and will indemnify us against all claims, costs or expenses arising in connection with such work, whether at common law or under statute, as a result of injury to or death of any person, or to loss of or damage to any property unless such claim arises solely as a result of neglect, default, or omission by ourselves or our servants.

Delivery.—To these works unless otherwise instructed. In case of overdue orders we shall be entitled to claim delivery by passenger train or other special transport at your expense.

Carriage.—All goods to be delivered carried paid unless otherwise arranged.

Empties.—No charge for any form of packing, including cases, barrels, etc., will be acknowledged except when expressly arranged, but every effort will be made to return such packages to you.

Just as a Buyer attaches conditions to his order, so also does a company usually attach conditions to its tender or quotation for the supply of goods. Some of these conditions may conflict with each other. As an order for the supply of goods is a contract in law, it is essential to resolve the conflict. The Buyer must either accept his supplier's conditions or obtain a written agreement to his own or to such modifications of the supplier's conditions as he requires. In particular, he should see that there is no clause in the conditions of sale, as sometimes occurs, which makes quite valueless any previously stated warranty or guarantee. It is also essential for an order to describe exactly what is being ordered or to ensure that the supplying firm's tender or quotation is exactly explicit. There are several ways in which the mention of some particular quality in goods may affect a contract for their sale, and confer on the Buyer rights for his protection or redress for errors. Words used in an order describing the goods becomes a condition of the contract and the Buyer should ensure that they correctly interpret his requirements. If a Buyer, in requesting an article from his supplier, uses certain words to describe it and the supplier offers one as so described, the words become a definite part of the contract and the Buyer may reject or recover damages accordingly. But a personal warranty given by a salesman does not make a term of contract. To avoid any later trouble, important properties or description of an article to be purchased should be written into the order or contract.

CHAPTER V

ANCILLARY SERVICES OR DEPARTMENTS

(Storekeeping. Works Engineering. Inspection)

STOREKEEPING

THE importance of storekeeping in modern industry is not always appreciated as it should be. Whilst the production departments are well equipped, the storekeepers are hidden away in cramped quarters, ill-equipped and with poor lighting conditions, and are generally underpaid in comparison with operators on production. It is not to be wondered at that loss of stock, wrong issues, unexpected running out of stock, and incorrect vouchers are a continual source of delay to production and of worry to production staff. To see the issue in its right perspective, it is only necessary to realise that the few persons in the Stores are responsible for and handle at one stage or another the whole of the material used by production. This may be worth 50 per cent. or more of the total sales value of production; the value of receipts and issues into and from Stores in a factory is greater than the total works cost, and at any time there is likely to be in stock material, components and finished products worth a quarter of the annual turnover—and yet frequently unskilled labourers are expected to be storekeepers. The truth is that storekeeping is more than a labouring job, and should be remunerated as such in order to attract and retain the necessary quality of personnel.

It may be said in answer that card indexes, stock control "systems" and goods bins de-skill the job. But card indexes are no substitutes for good storekeeping; they do not work of themselves, but must be used. A good storekeeper can have an amazingly comprehensive and detailed knowledge of a firm's products, which can be used by him rapidly and in a fraction of the time it takes to refer to an index or other record. Theirs is one of the few occupations in which a man's value to the company arises more from his experience with the company than from his technical or practical ability.

Persons should be selected for storekeeping who are tidy minded, and neat and tidy in their habits, and have a good memory. Tidiness can be taught, but whilst a person's memory can be improved, there are some who start with a big advantage by having a naturally good memory. It is essential also for a storekeeper to be good at figures or at least not to be bad at them. Whilst it may not be necessary for the ordinary storekeeper to enter up records, and it is in fact unwise for this to be necessary, he must be able to count and to count accurately without checking. It is surprising how often persons are selected for storekeeping who are constitutionally unable to concentrate sufficiently to count up to reasonably large numbers. Certainly far more care than is usually exercised should be taken in selecting persons who have either the right training or the right aptitude.

Kinds of Stores

Stores are places where material is kept and the kinds of stores fall into five broad classifications as follows:

Raw material.
Component or piece-part.
General supplies or indirect materials
Finished product or warehouse.
Tools.

To some extent the kind of stores influences organisation and activities, but, broadly speaking, the principles and methods of storekeeping, layout and records recommended in this section will be found generally applicable to all types.

Raw Material Stores

These are of two kinds, those dealing with bulk storage so frequent in the extractive and processing industries, and the ordinary kind of stores in which a range of raw materials is kept in bins or rooms. Stores for bulk storage are usually specially designed for their purpose, for example, silos for the storage of grain and bunkers for coal, and are in reality a stage in the manufacturing process and should be dealt with as such. Handling in these is a mechanical problem. In the case too of certain materials which are subject to excise duty, like tobacco, cocoa, tea, etc., there is the need for a "bonded" side of the stores under the close check and inspection of a representative of the Customs and Excise Department of the Government, from which material cannot be withdrawn until the appropriate duty has been paid or vouched for.

The layout and organisation of the ordinary kind of raw material store varies widely with the industry and size of factory, though principles are still generally applicable. In engineering, pig iron for the foundry, and rough castings and rolled-steel sections for the machine shops, are frequently stored outside, as they are unaffected by climatic conditions. In large factories a separate store for each material, or similar kind of material, is justified. In large food factories the main ingredients, colours and essences, and packing materials, are stored in separate stores; in textile factories the different types of fabric are kept separate; in printing, the paper, sundries and inks are kept in different stores. In large factories, each main shop may have its own raw-material stores supplied from the main stores.

In all cases it is advisable, and essential for smooth production flow, for the raw material stores to be at the input end of the factory. Unless production flow is arranged in the form of a U, this means that the raw material stores must be separate from the component and finished product stores.

Component Stores

Component stores, and here we are not concerned with process factories, are of four kinds:

(1) Standard stock used in a variety of assemblies or finished products—
    (a) Made on the premises.
    (b) Bought out.
(2) Made to order, or specials required only for one order or too frequently to justify carrying stocks—
    (a) Made on the premises.
    (b) Bought out.

These stores employ the majority of storekeepers in manufacturing industry, present the most diverse problems, and require the greatest skill and ingenuity to render first-class service. Layout invariably involves racks or bins, and adequate space is always a problem.

General Stores

For a variety of reasons it is often found advisable for all or most of the consumable (indirect or expense) materials, those which do not go directly into the product, to be stored on their own. Oils, greases, paint and rags are messy, and soon make a stores dirty and untidy. Furthermore, when the Component Stores is organised on a pre-selection and accumulation basis for assembly, it diverts the storekeeper's mind from his job to have to attend to individual wants for small supplies like files, emery cloth, wipers and so on.

Responsibilities

There are conflicting opinions and there is a good deal of loose thinking as to what a storekeeper's responsibilities should include and to whom he should be responsible. It is maintained by some that, in addition to looking after stores, he should keep all stock records and be responsible for ordering material. It is also maintained that the Head Storekeeper should be responsible to the Buyer, or to the Secretary, or to the Accountant, or to Production Control, or for sections of stores to be responsible to departmental foremen, and all these arrangements can be met with in practice. A storekeeper's job is to keep stocks, to receive and issue them, and in between to store them tidily in a minimum of space with the minimum of labour. It is a physical job. It is not his job to keep records: that is part of stock recording, which in turn is part of production planning. To function effectively, production planning must have up-to-date information of stocks, and must be able to refer to stock records immediately in building up production programmes. This cannot be done if the records are not in the Production Planning Office, and duplication should be avoided both on the score of cost and of accuracy.

As was made clear in Chapter III, the head of production planning is a specialist in the compilation and use of records; a storekeeper is not, but he must be a specialist in the physical handling and storing of materials. It is wrong therefore to ask a storekeeper to maintain records, or to expect it to be done as accurately in the works as it can in an office staffed with persons trained in the work. This does not mean that a storekeeper can forget all about stocks held; he can, by suitable technique, act as a back stop on the need for stock replacement or adjustment.

Since the storing of material is clearly a physical job, the Stores should be considered a works department, and storekeeping a works job, and the storekeeper therefore should be responsible to the Works Manager or Superintendent. As it is a specialist's job, all Stores should be under the supervision of one person, the Head Storekeeper (or alternative title). The foreman or head storekeeper is then able to co-ordinate the activities of the various stores and economise in labour. He is able to call on other sections of the stores when any one is suddenly overloaded, as frequently happens when large consignments of materials arrive, and in times of illness.

In view of the above, the following can be taken as the duties of a Head Storekeeper:

A. Generally to—

(1) Supervise the work of storekeepers, and to instruct and guide them in carrying out their duties, ensuring that they are effectively performed.
(2) Ensure cleanliness and tidiness in the Stores.
(3) Co-operate closely with the Buyer, Chief Planning Engineer, Inspection Department, and with production foremen generally.
(4) Adhere to the Company's personnel policy, and ensure that subordinates do so.

(5) Ensure that any records required are promptly and accurately made.

(6) Provide a prompt and efficient stores service to all departments.

B. Specifically to—

(1) Receive goods from outside suppliers, check-count and arrange for inspection of quality. Report to Buyer deviation from specification or order.

(2) Receive components produced in the works, and check-count.

(3) Store all material and components safely and tidily, and in a manner in which they are immediately available.

(4) Check actual stock of every item, preferably once every three months, but at least once every six months, and advise Stores Control of any corrections required.

(5) On receipt of appropriate release instructions, issue materials and components called for. Issue surplus to original requisitions only against Excess Material Requisition, and receive back materials in excess of requirements only against Material Returned to Stores Note.

(6) Record accurately—

(a) Receipt of all outside supplies on back copy of order arranging for inspection report on each consignment.

(b) Receipt of parts manufactured in works on Deliver to Stores Note.

(c) Issue of material on Material Release Note.

(d) Issue of finished parts on Parts List.

Storekeeping Methods

More "systems" have been sold to industry for storekeeping and stock control than for any other business activity. What are really offered are tools, and these are mostly to do with stock records already dealt with in Chapter III. In this section we are concerned with the use of such tools and with methods of actually storing the goods and materials.

The first fundamental principle of good storekeeping is the old maxim for good housekeeping, "a place for everything and everything in its place". To which should be added—"and know where it is!" Nowhere else in a factory is tidiness more important. Whether or not bins or shelves are used, materials and parts should be neatly arranged, and the whole stores should present an orderly appearance. If goods have to be stored on the floor, as they may be, it is essential to arrange them in bays with gangways and to keep them as tidy as if in bins.

Equipment and Layout

The equipment now available is so varied and most of it so well known that it is unnecessary to deal with it in detail here—a study of catalogues is a fruitful way of getting new ideas to meet specific problems. However, there are certain precepts, modern developments and pitfalls which should be generally known.

In the first place, it should be remembered that it is false economy not to have adequate space and adequate bins or racks (with a margin for growth). Since floor area is expensive, this means that the maximum use has to be made of height. When the goods to be stored stack easily and the quantities are large, equipment for stacking should be used. Stacking trucks with forks which can be raised by power, and wooden or steel platforms or pallets, answer the problem. When the goods do not stack, or the quantities are small, shelves or bins should be used, and again to economise in floor space these should be as high as possible. Bins up to 12 or even 15 feet high are quite satisfactory provided that light parts only are stored in the top half and that safe, convenient and easily moved steps can be provided. A modern design makes the maximum use of floor space by building the racks or bins in short self-contained sections, and erecting these on rollers which ride on rails let into the floor. Rows of

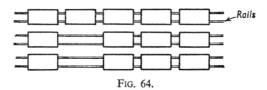

FIG. 64.

these sections are placed close together, and in each row there is one section missing, so that any section can be uncovered in any row as illustrated at Fig. 64.

Long bars or tube, or lengths of timber, should be stacked on end in racks which can be built up inexpensively of angle iron. Rods or stays are fixed to a horizontal back rail, so that they stand forward from the rails to act as divisions or compartments for the different sections of material. Very heavy bar must be stored horizontally for safety.

In general, metal racks or bins are preferable to wooden ones, they take up less space for the same load, and are more easily erected and adjusted afterwards. There are several manufacturers who supply standard equipment which is so made that it can be adjusted to suit the particular requirements of the stores.

Stores should be arranged so that goods are not received through the same entrance as that from which they are issued. Gangways should be sufficient to allow trolleys to pass and slopes or different levels should be avoided if at all possible. In Component Stores supplying an Assembly or Packing Department, the goods should be so stored that it is possible to work from one end of the store to the other, gradually accumulating components for an order or requisition in the sequence stated on the requisition. When a Store serves more than one department, each requiring substantially different materials or parts, the ideal layout is for the stores to be arranged past the end of each department and the goods to be stored as near as possibly adjacent to the department issuing them, thus:

Stores		
Dept. A	Dept. B	Dept. C

Classification

It is important that all materials and items stored should be identified by some simple, clear and logical system of classification. An effective system not only simplifies the storekeeper's job and identification throughout the organisation, but it also assures a minimum of duplication and variety. The introduction of such a system in a company using a large range of materials and components can lead to a quite amazing reduction both in variety and in total inventory cost.

For components which form part of the final product and which are made to a drawing, the method of classification must serve an over-riding purpose in the Drawing Office (see page 264). In general however, a system of classification to be effective must:

Provide rapid and accurate means of finding an item;
Reveal all items which are similar or can be used alternatively;
Ensure that items are automatically stored in their correct place;
Be flexible and provide for continuous additions.

A very satisfactory system is a code which uses numbers only to identify groups or classes of articles, the characteristics of classes being arranged so that identification proceeds from the general to the particular. An item is known by a number and all items have the same number of digits. The size of the code (number of digits) depends on the variety of items involved; in manufacturing industry it is found that a seven- or eight-figure code is adequate to include all materials, components, tools and plant.

The following two examples illustrate the technique:

Class	Code	Class	Code
Materials	1.......	Tools	4......
Copper	13......	Gauge	43.....
Strip	131.....	Caliper	435....
Covered	1312....	Stores	4357...
Stores (Elect.)	13124...	Size 6″	43576..
Size 1″ × ⅛″	1312407.		

Insulated copper strip 1″ × ⅛″ in
the Electrical Stores—1312407

A 6″ caliper-type gauge
in the Tool Stores—43576

It is advisable to commence classification as soon as possible and once established to insist that it is kept up to date. The results of the classification should of course be set out in a catalogue. In practice it is found that the logical form of the code greatly assists in memorising the numbers of items and reduces errors in identification, reference and storing.

Storing and Locating

There are broadly three alternative methods of storing a mixed variety of articles in a Store:

(1) When consignments are large or bulky, to carry the bulk stock in a reserved store and a small quantity of each article in the active store.

(2) To keep the whole stock of each article together, all articles of a like kind being stored together.

(3) As 2, but articles stored, irrespective of kind, in the order in which required in a normal list.

The second is usual and more satisfactory in practice. It makes for neatness and orderliness so vital in Stores, and storekeepers find it easier to memorise where everything is when articles of a like kind are stored together. Although there must be a record of where everything is, it would be obviously a very slow job if a storekeeper had to go to an index for many items. A person who knows where everything is is a treasure (and not such an uncommon one) and everything possible should be done to enable a storekeeper to become one.

A logical system of numbering items or parts is a further aid to memory, both for identity of a part and for location. If the part can be given a number according to its location in the Stores, it simplifies matters considerably for the storekeeper, but this is not recommended for general use. Almost invariably there are overriding demands from other departments for a system of code numbers which classifies parts or materials strictly according to kind and size, or to product or model and so on. (Methods of numbering which ensure minimum inventory, maximum flexibility, and avoid duplication, are described on page 264). A code of numbering for parts and materials which is built up according to kind and size is easier to remember than one built up according to location. However, it is essential to have in the Stores an index of location, and this should be based on a code built up logically. A simple code capable of unlimited expansion can be built up as illustrated at Fig. 65.

Number each bay or section of racks from 0 to 9 or 99.
Number each row of racks 0 to 9.
Number horizontal rows of bins or shelves in each rack 0 to 9.
Number vertical rows of bins in divisions or shelves in each rack 0 to 9.

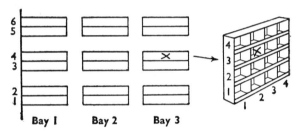

The bin marked X would be 3423.

FIG. 65.—Numbering of Stores Bins.

As stated earlier, recording of stock in the Stores is not in general recommended, and requisitioning for replacement of stocks is not normally therefore a storekeeper's duty. However, there are certain classes of material and articles which have a general-purpose use and which, in normal times, can be obtained at relatively short notice so that minimum stocks are small. Storekeepers can be made responsible for maintaining stocks of these without having to keep records. The minimum quantity for each item is first calculated and authorised. This is the quantity necessary to supply normal demand (with a margin of safety) through the period required for obtaining a further supply. This minimum quantity is then boxed, wrapped, or placed at the bottom of the bin and covered with a piece of cardboard, wood or sheet metal, and the remaining stock placed on top. When the loose stock has all been used, it indicates that the re-ordering point has been reached and a requisition is placed on the Buyer for further supplies. When new supplies are received, the minimum quantity is again boxed or covered. (This method can also be used as a danger signal on those items for which Stores Control are responsible for requisitioning.)

If it is found impracticable physically to identify the minimum stock or if for other reasons it is decided to keep a record of stock balances in the Stores, the bin stock card is the simplest method. This card is hung on the front of the bin to which it refers, and is entered up and the balance struck at the time stock is put in or taken out. This ensures promptness of records. The simplest design of card has rulings on one side for recording quantities received and issued, and on the reverse details of the item, its stock number, description, location, order quantity and minimum stock quantity. It can be originated by the Buyer and used as an advice of order placed and to be received. It is useful to print one side red, so that it can be turned this side uppermost when stocks are low as a visible reminder of the fact to the storekeepers.

To avoid the rush and additional work of stocktaking once a year at the financial year end, it is more satisfactory to arrange for what is termed perpetual inventory check. Providing each item in stock is checked and compared with the stock records, and the latter corrected if necessary at least once and preferably four times a year, the stock as recorded at the year end is usually acceptable for audit purposes. The simplest effective alternative methods for making this perpetual check are either for independent staff to be appointed to do nothing else but go round the Stores checking stock, or for the storekeepers to check so many items every day. The former, if more regular, is likely to be very monotonous for the staff concerned; the latter gives each storekeeper a vested interest in the accuracy of his stock. Either method is much more accurate than the usual annual stocktaking. In either case, to ensure that every item is checked with the required frequency, Stock Control should issue a daily list of items to be checked.

Receipts and Issue

A sound principle to observe in dealing with the receipt and issue of stores materials is that nothing is received and nothing issued without a written authority and signature for receipt. If this is not faithfully adhered to, it will be found too often in practice that verbal arrangements and memory are very unreliable. This means that a Goods Received Note or its equivalent must be made out by the Stores for all consignments received from outside suppliers, and an internal Delivery Note accompany all deliveries from works departments. All goods received from outside suppliers should be against an order from the Buyer, and the procedure can be used as outlined in the previous Chapter, "Purchasing" (see page 412). If a consignment is received which has not been authorised by a written order, as occasionally happens when senior executives give verbal orders and forget to confirm by official order, then a Goods Received Note should be written out immediately to notify Buyer, Stock Control and Accounts. Then if so desired and to keep records tidy, an official order set can be made out to cover the consignment.

It is important also to ensure that every consignment is checked and inspected, and it is preferable to do this independently of the supplier's Consignment Note—knowledge of what is stated on the Consignment Note is apt to lead to only cursory examination of the consignment, on the lazy assumption that what is stated must be correct. Inspection should be prompt, so that appropriate action can be taken without delay with the supplier, in case of discrepancy or fault. Goods received from internal departments will have been inspected, but count must be verified before signing the Delivery Note —the signature indicates responsibility for quantity and therefore records.

In order to link up planning procedures and to give the Stores an opportunity of preparing materials to be issued in advance of requirements and so avoid waiting time, requirements should be stated as far as possible, not on requisitions written by operators, but on Release Notes, issued by the Planning Office. Such notes are likely to be more legible and accurate, particularly if pre-printed. Also, since only the correct (standard) amount of material required will have been stated, more can only be obtained on presentation of another requisition or preferably an Excess Requisition, and thus there is provided an automatic check and record of excess usage, and therefore of excess cost.

If a list of materials or parts is required, a copy of the material or part list should be used, covered, if necessary, by a Material Release Note quoting the material or part list. Requisitions for long lists of parts, written out by works departments, always lead to inaccuracies. This copy of the material or part list is a Stores "tool", and therefore should be designed with this in mind, i.e. it should be set out in such a way as to minimise work in the Stores. Materials or parts which are stored together, e.g. nuts, bolts and small hardware, should be grouped together. Also if part issue of large batches are usual, provision should be made for this, with an extension margin for marking off each issue—the alternative is a separate list for each issue. The essential thing to bear in mind is to keep paper work in the works to a minimum—it is seldom expertly done outside an office properly equipped.

WORKS ENGINEERING

Buildings and Services

For production executives or those aspiring to such positions, information on the factors affecting the choice of site for a new factory or buildings is apt to be more than a little theoretical. It is given to few of us to have the opportunity of building a new factory from virgin ground—and being able to choose the ground. And even when it is decided to put up new buildings, their design is quite rightly the function of a specialist, the architect, who is, or should be, well aware of all the factors involved. Nevertheless, the production man must know of certain factors which vitally affect the production unit and the effectiveness of work done, and see to it that they are given due consideration when a new factory is built, or an existing one is extended—some of them are insufficiently understood by the technical specialist.

Choice of Site

A dominating factor affecting the choice of a site for a new factory is the availability of labour and its type or characteristics. The material factors, such as access to various means of transport; availability of services such as electricity, gas and water, drainage and foundation problems, can all be readily assessed by the technical experts, but the human factor is not so easy to assess. There has always been a tendency for industries to develop in certain towns or localities, as much because of local skill as for any other reason, e.g. needle manufacture at Redditch, chainmaking in the Black Country, and furniture-making at High Wycombe. There is more engineering skill and tradition in Birmingham than in Hereford, but there is more competition for it. Those who have tried to develop new industries in country districts or towns where the special skills which are required are not indigenous, have sometimes paid for the experience. Workers are not so mobile as one might expect, so that if local skill is not available, production methods must be de-skilled. It can and has succeeded in many cases, but the warning is that it is always more difficult, and takes longer, than is expected.

Another point to remember is that people do not like to travel far to work, so that there is likely to be more labour available in or near a residential area or housing estate than in a heavily industrialised area. It has been known for a firm to build a factory and then find it just cannot get labour at all.

Another factor often miscalculated is the room required for expansion—it will almost always be more than predicted. Adequate room for expansion is always a good investment.

Type of Building and Site Layout

The type of building and layout of site necessarily affect each other but both should be considered functionally, i.e. in relation to the work being done, and the best way to do it. In process factories, extraction and chemical industries, the buildings must be built round the processes. For example, in sugar refining and flour milling advantage is taken of gravity flow resulting in tall many-floored buildings. In the more normal type of factory, just as much attention should be given to production flow. This should be in one direction only.

The following is an outstanding modern example of how buildings can be designed round the process. The major factors which had to be taken into account in designing the new factory were:

A large number of items of packing materials, cartons, labels, etc.. had to be kept in stock, thus requiring a great deal of room.

An equally large number of items had to be kept in finished shelf stock, thus taking up even more room.

A small space required for process work, preferably on the ground floor.

Many different lines to be in production at the same time with relatively small runs.

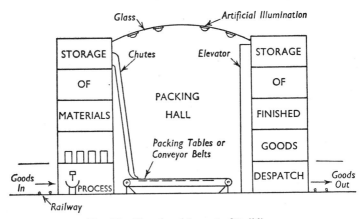

Fig. 66.—Functional Layout of Building.

The ultimate layout adopted is shown schematically in Fig. 66. The actual filling, wrapping, packing, boxing, etc., is performed on conveyor belts, of which there are many, each constituting a unit, running in parallel lines across the central part of the building. Packing materials are fed mostly by chute and delivered to stock floors by continuous elevators. The administrative departments form a block across one end of the building. This may appear a little un-orthodox, but a little study will reveal its many advantages and how functionally successful it is. Equally successful results can be obtained if trouble is taken to analyse the functional requirements of production in the same way.

Another example is given in Fig. 67. In this case there was in existence a traditional saw-tooth roof type of building which was too small for requirements; the roof was too low and the structure not strong enough to carry the size of cranes required for some of the activities and the site was restricted. In the solution adopted two end bays of the old building were removed, one of which was re-erected at the opposite end. An extension was built using the monitor roof type of construction which provided, economically, the height and span required and still enabled large cranes to be carried on the steel building structure. The form of structure used was in fact fitted round the layout which had emerged from detailed work study.

A factor which may have to be considered in industry more in the future than it ever has been in the past, particularly in very large concerns, is the size of the individual manufacturing units. Working groups are social groups, and play a dominating part in the building up of morale and of loyalty to either the Company's interests or to sectional interests. An employee is more likely to feel that he or she matters and to be loyal to the Company in a small unit than in a very large department or building. Research work is needed to throw light on the optimum size of units, but the point to remember with the design of buildings is that they can be too large from the human point of view.

The position of administrative and service buildings, the laboratory, drawing office, power-house, maintenance and repair department is always important, particularly in allowing for expansion. What can be the right position for the factory at one time may be quite wrong when the factory is extended.

Similarly, the position and size of canteens and parking conveniences for cycles, motor-cycles and cars must be given more consideration than used to be necessary. Canteens are an essential service in industry today, and a good deal of their undoubted value is offset if the buildings and conditions are very unsatisfactory, as they can be if of a make-shift nature. With the increasing distances which employees need to travel, and the consequent growing popularity of cycles and motor vehicles, adequate provision is required for parking. To many companies this problem is acute today; there is no need to invite the problem in the future.

The modern tendency in the design of buildings is for single-storey construction. From the Production Managers' point of view this

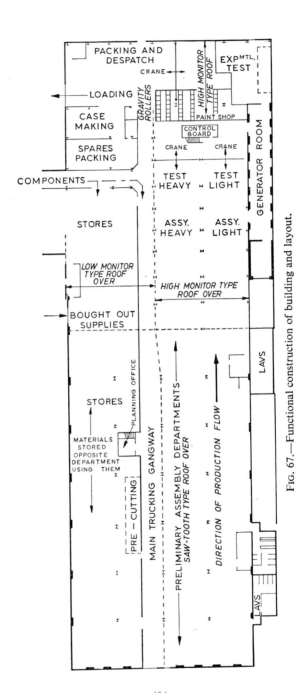

FIG. 67.—Functional construction of building and layout.

obviously has many advantages, giving greater scope for rearrangement and avoiding the transport delays inherent in multi-storied buildings. A single-storey building also is much easier to light and ventilate. When, because of the cost of floor area or restrictions of site, multi-storied buildings have to be used, windows should be as large as possible. The modern tendency is for the whole of the walls to be of glass by cantilevering the outside edge of the buildings from the main frame. Artificial lighting is expensive; the maximum possible window space avoids much of this expense. The expense is partially offset by the greater heat loss, but there is no way of compensating for the dull and depressing atmosphere of badly lighted shops, nor for continually working in artificial light. Respective advantages and disadvantages may be summarised as follows:

Single-storey

Rearrangement of production and departments easier than in multi-storey.

General supervision facilitated.

Good and uniform distribution of natural lighting.

Transport cheaper, quicker and easier.

Fire risks less than in multi-storey.

Window maintenance less (but roof maintenance more).

Heavy machinery can be installed anywhere.

Multi-storey

Departments are self-contained units and tend to better group feeling.

Factory more compact, and high-speed lifts are quicker than walking long distances.

Services (pipes and cables) shorter.

Gravity transport can be used for certain materials.

Less roof space and maintenance (gutters, covering, etc.).

Lavatory blocks more conveniently situated.

Good ventilation not so easily arranged.

Serious restriction on use of heavy machinery.

If there are strong reasons for having wide shops with a large floor area unobstructed, the lattice-girder type of construction can be used. These have been frequently used for aeroplane construction, where extremely wide shops with no roof supports at all are required; spans exceeding 100 feet have been built. For roofs which have to carry additional loads like cranes the Monitor type should be used.

Adequate artificial illumination, heating and ventilation are an essential prerequisite of effective production and accepted without reservation by modern managements. These aspects of factory services and working conditions are dealt with in Chapter V of Part Three. Keeping up good standards is a continuing responsibility of factory management; for example, the painting of factory buildings and workshops, like window cleaning, is frequently neglected. There is ample evidence of the psychological effects, beneficial and otherwise, of colour schemes and general appearance of the places in which people work. The colour scheme must be chosen with as much care as the materials of which the buildings are made—and emphatically should not be a drab brown. Whilst it is true that no colour scheme can be everyone's choice, there are some that will please most, and others that can only be described as depressing— a bright and cheerful one is a good investment. The Factories Act lays down that workshops must either be painted at least once every seven years, and washed every fourteen months, or lime-washed every fourteen months. It is today almost as cheap to put on a coloured distemper every year, and thus always to preserve a cheerful atmosphere, as only to wash down.

The following are other problems which may arise, and which should be given full consideration in advance, when planning new buildings:

If there are many piped services in multi-storey buildings, e.g. hydraulic power, gas, compressed air, in addition to the normal water and electric supply, the mains should as far as possible be taken up the building through a common shaft, like a lift shaft. This is a great convenience to the Maintenance Department.

Certain processes give off fumes or a great deal of heat. It may be advisable to site these so that they do not affect other departments. Effective extraction arrangements are necessary in any case.

High levels of vibration and noise can be minimised or insulated. It may be advisable to segregate departments in which vibration or noise cannot be avoided. The problem is accentuated if such are on upper stories.

When it is essential to divide a building into departments, standardised steel partitions, which can be ceiling height or lower as required, and can be solid half-glass or expanded metal, are most effective, and are easily moved when rearrangement makes this necessary. Brick walls are a great deterrent to schemes of rearrangement.

Layout

The one fundamental principle to which all good factory or departmental layouts must conform is that production generally must flow in one direction, and must never retrace its path in the opposite direction. Flow production reaches its ultimate perfection, of course, in the mass-production layouts on the conveyor belts in the automobile industry. But the same principle or unidirectional flow should be adhered to whatever the product or process. This applies to the factory as a whole, to units of it, to departments and to sections, although it cannot apply in detail in departments doing jobbing work. In continuous-process industries especially, such as food, chemicals, metallurgical, etc., the products usually pass through a fixed sequence of machines or operations; although there are exceptions, as in bulk processing, when some of the materials, having reached one stage, are fed back to an earlier stage. But in the fabricating industries, such a fixed sequence is not usually inherent in the manufacturing methods, and as the factory develops and methods

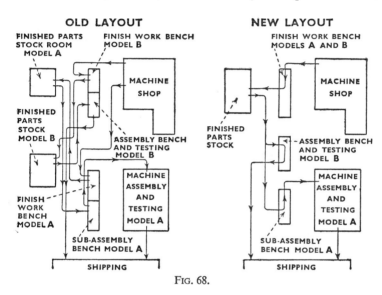

FIG. 68.

are altered, often the layout, like Topsy, just grows, and flow production is forgotten until reorganisation becomes essential.

An illustration of how a slight rearrangement of layout can greatly simplify production flow is shown at Fig. 68.

Types of Layout

There are two distinct types of layout common to all industries:

(1) Group layout, common in most jobbing factories. Machines or operators of a like type are grouped together, as for example in a machine shop where all centre lathes, all milling machines, all automatics, and so on, would be grouped together.

(2) Line layout, where machines or operators are arranged according to the sequence of operations. This is carried to its extreme in the automobile industries.

It is usually found that a combination of both types provides the best solution in normal manufacturing industries. Line layout is used when the number of a product or a component produced is sufficiently large to require certain machines or operators to be permanently engaged on that one product or component. The machines are permanently set up and arranged to produce that particular component as a line production unit, other components being dealt with on the batch system on group layout. There are certain advantages to be gained from line layout, even when used in this way for only some components, and it should be used whenever suitable. It reduces transport (and this is important for very large components), it reduces the overall production time and work in process between operations, and assures a more steady flow of products, since each machine tends to govern the flow of all the others. An example of how a department was relaid out on this basis, resulting in a considerable increase in production and reduction in cost, is shown in Plate 5 opposite.

On the other hand, the advantages of group layout should not be lost sight of, and it should always be used in preference to a layout that merely arises out of intermittent additions to machines to increase capacity. A group layout permits the supervision of each type of operation by a person who is, or becomes, a specialist. In jobbing or mixed production shops it does tend to ensure a tidier shop and better flow.

Problems of Layout

When the arrangement of a layout is being worked out on the drawing board, a great deal of time can be spent on redrawing the various possible arrangements. It will be found that cardboard templates cut to represent each machine, bench, or other equipment, are a great help. Before cutting out they are drawn in outline, showing principal features, to the same scale as that of the outline drawing of the building or department. If there are moving portions of a machine, e.g. traversing tables, these are shown at the fully extended and closed position, and operating levers and the position taken by the operator are indicated. These templates can then be moved about the drawings until the most satisfactory layout is found, when it is drawn in and dimensioned.

It is always difficult to visualise the relative positions of plant on the floors of multi-storey buildings. A very good model of the building can be made as follows. Stick on to plywood or perspex a plan of each floor, and cut out round the outline of the building. Assemble the plans in correct sequence on vertical steel bars about $\frac{1}{4}$ inch in diameter, separating each floor by distance-pieces long enough to enable the middle of the floor to be seen. This vertical distance will normally be more than would be correct for true to scale, but this

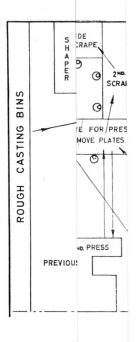

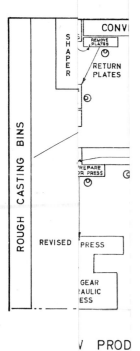

PROD

438]

does not in any way spoil the general effect nor the help the model can be in studying overall layout, transport and services. Coloured tapes can be used to indicate the path of various products, components, or services.

In factories where component or material stores and service departments, such as the toolroom in engineering factories, or the maintenance department in others, serve several production departments, it is always a problem to know where best to site them. The shape of the building may allow of no alternative, but when it is a single-storey rectangular building, so common in modern industry, a successful solution is to place the service departments along the outside walls, arranging the production departments at right angles to them across the shop. The sketch at Fig. 69 illustrates this for an engineering factory and shows how production is made to flow in one direction.

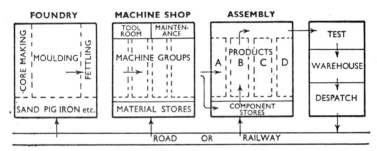

LAYOUT FOR SEPARATE SHOPS

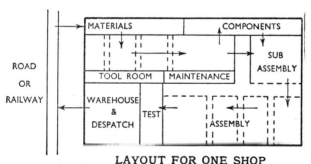

LAYOUT FOR ONE SHOP

FIG. 69.

An example of layout which emerged from detailed Work Study investigations is given in Fig. 67. It will be noted that the stores are sited the full length and parallel with the production shops, and that materials are stored opposite the department which uses them, reducing transport and facilitating communications. Although there are ten fairly self-contained departments dealing with sections of production, one way flow is provided. Limitations of site forced a change of direction at right angles from the Test department to the Packing and Despatch department where, in both departments, handling has to be done by crane. The change in direction was facilitated without involving a handling problem of "putting down" and "picking up" again unnecessarily, by arranging the intermediate operation of painting to be done on roller conveyors linking the two main departments.

At one time problems associated with countershafting made re-arrangements of layout as production developed and methods changed almost impossible, or at the least expensive. Individual motor drive provides the necessary flexibility (in addition to the important psychological benefits of an unobstructed view in the shop), and there is little excuse today for not rearranging for economical production.

Unfortunately, too little attention is paid by machine designers to the correct working height for operators at machines. The working height appears to result from constructional requirements of the machine instead of effective operating and minimum fatigue for operators. The Works Manager or Engineer of the factory using the machines, therefore, must watch this point and correct for it.

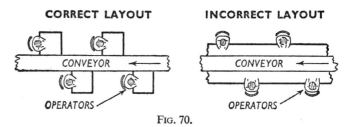

FIG. 70.

Machines should be elevated, or sunk, to make the operating height correct. This is essential if machines are to be linked up with conveyors—why should it not be for operators?

In planning a layout, a frequent fault is not to allow sufficient or any room for work stations, i.e. areas where work can be kept tidily in between operations. It is useful to have one for each machine group, and certainly one for each department, preferably at the incoming end. Such stations are a great help to progress men; they are easier to control than work left around sections or machines where it so easily gets mislaid or forgotten.

When arranging for work to be performed along conveyors, it is better to provide each operator with a small table at right angles to the conveyor and for the operator to sit facing the travel of the belt, than for the operators to sit along and facing the conveyor. The operators do not have so far to reach the belt and can more readily keep an eye on work travelling down the belt. This is illustrated in Fig. 70.

Plant and Equipment

The astonishing increases in production per man-hour obtained in many American factories (and some British ones) in the last few years are chiefly due to the use of horse-power for replacing man-power, putting machines to do the heavy work and men to do the designing, minding and maintaining. Among the conclusions that were common to almost all the reports of the Productivity Teams from Britain that visited the United States in the 1950's, the greater use of tooling and power for lifting and handling was given as a primary reason for the American superiority in output per man-hour. Also to quote Graham Hutton (*Future*, No. 2, November 1947): "Between 1924 and 1932, on the average, the annual output per worker employed in manufacturing industry in America was at least twice the volume turned out by a British worker in manufacturing industry. Today it is at least two and a half times the British figure"; and "between 1919 and 1939 American manufacturing industry as a whole used machinery of at least twice as much horse-power per employed worker as that used in British manufacturing industry; and today it is using machinery of at least two and a half times as much horse-power".

Evidently output is largely a matter of machinery and horse-power. If this is so, plant and tooling are likely to be more important than ever in the future. It is true that the larger scale of production possible in the U.S.A. with her huge home market makes elaborate tooling more economical than it can possibly be in Britain, yet much more can and will have to be done in the medium-size British factories if they are to flourish. Special assembly jigs and mechanical handling equipment (conveyors, fork-lift trucks, stillage trolleys and such like) as well as special-purpose machines can effect considerable improvements in productivity.

It is not always easy to decide on when to buy new machines or to replace old ones. Formulæ can be used, and several are given and discussed in *Engineering Economics*, Book II, by Burnham, and in the *Production Management Handbook*. In principle these set off the annual value of savings resulting from installation of the new machinery against the capital outlay and the profit the capital could earn in the business (or outside) if differently employed. Generally speaking, it is sound to err on the side of buying new plant; in the long run it pays to have modern plant. It is wise to reserve a substantial portion of annual profits for the express purpose of replacing old and buying new plant.

In general, there are two types of machines:

(1) Special-purpose—designed for a specific purpose for one article or product.
(2) General-purpose—capable of dealing with many sizes and types of work.

The special-purpose type of machine is common enough in process factories, and is much used in engineering factories on large-scale mass production. It usually enables a much higher output to be obtained than is possible on the equivalent general-purpose machine, and ensures absolute uniformity and standardisation of work turned out. It is high in capital cost, requires better toolroom service, is expensive in set-up and idle time, is soon made obsolete, and has a small secondhand value. On the other hand, the general-purpose machine is much more flexible (particularly important in times of slack trade), is cheaper to buy and maintain (spares are more likely to be available), and requires less special tooling. It may require higher skill on the part of the operators, but this is likely to be an advantage in the future.

In purchasing machines, the following points should be borne in mind:

If more than one machine of a given type and size are required, machines of the same capacity and output rate should be installed. This much simplifies machine loading, enabling Planning to load to a group instead of to individual machines.

Reliability is important—and valuable—particularly to Planning. Breakdowns not only involve maintenance costs and perhaps idle labour costs, but reduce turnover, a much more expensive matter.

Simplicity of set-up and of operating reduces idle time and human effort, expensive factors.

Automatic lubrication and totally enclosed features reduce maintenance and ensure continual operation. Too little attention is paid by designers to the need for protecting vital parts of a machine and enclosing as much of a machine as possible to protect it from dust and foreign matter. (If machines had aprons to the floor, operators could not use them for dumping rubbish underneath.)

Tools and Toolroom

It is in the engineering industry that the modern toolroom and its technique have been developed to their present high standard, partly because of the influence and enthusiasm of the youngest branch of engineering—Production Engineers. But all industries use tools, and most of them can learn quite a lot from the engineering industry of the advantages of tooling and of high-class toolroom service. In many industries the provision of small tool equipment is usually just one activity of the maintenance department, carpenter or even of the Works Manager, and no attempt is made to develop the rather specialised outlook and skill required. What follows therefore deals, so far as current practice is concerned, mainly with engineering shops, but managers in other industries are strongly urged to take a leaf out of the book of experience of the engineering industry and to devote time and attention to developing a first-class "toolroom" service wherever possible.

The production of tools (and in this context tools include jigs, gauges, patterns, templates, etc., and what applies to the toolroom applies to the pattern shop) has grown from an off-shoot of the machine shop or production departments to a highly skilled expensively equipped department. Its importance is greatest in those engineering factories engaged on high-quality production, or on large-quantity repetitive production.

Experience has shown that most of the filing and fitting together of parts during assembly can be avoided by the provision of well-designed jigs, fixtures and tools, for use during the machining or fabricating stages, to ensure absolute uniformity and interchangeability. Really high-quality work to fine limits can only be executed on a production basis with the aid of specially designed tools and holding fixtures. A dictum of all craftsmen is that it is as important to hold and secure the part or article being worked as to hold the tool correctly.

Because tools and jigs must be made to finer limits than the parts with which they are used, a toolroom or pattern shop must in general be equipped with high-grade and accurate machinery and tools, and staffed with highly skilled men. In very large factories it is true that manufacture of tools can with success be put on a production basis, many of the operations being simplified and de-skilled so that they can be produced on standard machines and by semi-skilled labour, but in the small and medium-size factories, which constitute a majority of engineering factories, the need for flexibility places the emphasis on all-round skill.

When beginning to develop a toolroom, it is a common mistake to underestimate both the capital cost of equipment that is ultimately required and justified, and the room required. Because it is not a production department in the narrow sense, there is a danger of squeezing it into unsatisfactory premises or denying it the space it requires to use effectively the valuable equipment with which it is provided. With the associated tool stores, one-tenth or more of the space taken up by the shop it serves may be required by the tool-room. The layout of the toolroom in relation to the tool stores is important too. Even in large factories, where the stores can have its own tool-repair section, it is advisable for the stores and toolroom to be adjacent. Tools that are returned to the stores should be examined without fail before they are put away, being reground, reset and repaired as necessary. It is usual for this to be done in the toolroom in a section set apart for the purpose, which should be under the authority of the toolroom foreman, and located immediately adjacent to the stores.

It is vitally important to integrate tool production with works manufacturing programmes. Failure to do so inevitably results in either jobs waiting while tools or jigs are rushed through, or manufacture commencing without them, with the consequent inaccuracy and increase in costs. If it is not possible to assign a completed date to a tool when its design is first decided upon, then the toolroom must be given the tool requirements for production schedules sufficiently far ahead to enable them to make the tools in time for requirements—and tools, gauges, or patterns, and so on, are not made in a day or two. Because of this need to integrate the work of the toolroom with production, it is advisable in engineering factories for the toolroom to be under the authority of the Works Manager or Works Superintendent. In non-engineering factories tool production, or its equivalent, is normally the responsibility of the Works Engineer.

Tool Stores

The organisation of tool issue, receipt and storage depends on the number of tools stored and handled, and the number of tools required per job. The simplest method, and one quite adequate for small tool stores in engineering and other factories, is the check system. The operator asks for the tool he requires, either by description or number, and in exchange for the tool hands in a metal disc on which is stamped his own name and number. This disc is hung or placed on the hook or space occupied by the tool. Normally an operator is only allowed a small number of discs, 5 usually being adequate. When, however, this results in too much waiting time at the stores serving hatch, or the jigs, tools, or gauges required for jobs are numerous and complex, other methods are adopted for tool issue. The production department notifies the toolroom a day or two ahead of jobs which will require tools (a copy of production schedules is often sufficient). The toolroom have an indexed record of the tools used for each job, and from this the storekeeper collects the set of tools in advance. Each tool number is entered on a Tool Receipt, which the operator requiring the tools signs before being allowed to take them away. From this receipt the operator's check number is transferred to the Tool Record Card, so that at all times there is a record of where every tool is. The Tool Receipt is cancelled when the tools are returned and the entry on the Tool Record is cancelled.

Maintenance

The need in all industries, manufacture, mines, docks, or transport for the efficient upkeep of buildings, plant and equipment is, one would think, too self-evident to need emphasising, yet its importance is not always realised. Most firms know the total cost of their maintenance staff, but few could say what is the excess cost of production due to plant failure and other production delays due to poor maintenance. It can be surprisingly high, up to 5 per cent. and even 10 per cent. of the total cost of direct labour, and with only 200 operators (male and female) on direct production at an average of say £10 per week, that is an excess cost of between £5,000 and £10,000 per annum! In certain types of industries, for example glass making, and similar process industries, with a high capital investment in plant, the maintenance department is nearly as important and has nearly as many employees as the production departments. In many companies in all industries, the controllable expenditure in overhead cost on buildings, plant and equipment, e.g. on repairs, renewals, services (heat, power), etc., may be equivalent to anything up to 25 per cent. of the cost of direct labour on production.

In large firms the maintenance department includes most of the skilled trades, each perhaps with its own department; a small firm is likely to need only one or two men in each of several trades, usually millwrights, electricians and carpenters. In medium-size firms, particularly those not engaged in skilled engineering, there are likely to be upwards of 10 or 20—and it may be found that each trade has its own foreman, each responsible to the Works Manager. This is wrong. Unless the skilled trades are also production departments, as happens in general engineering, all maintenance men should be in one department responsible to one person, who is in turn responsible to the Works Manager (or similar executive). Even in general engineering there is everything to be said for keeping maintenance apart from production and responsible to a maintenance foreman. Maintenance then is much more likely to be planned, and production executives, particularly the Works Manager, released from the disproportionate amount of time which breakdown problems absorb.

Responsibilities

What should such a maintenance foreman's responsibilities then be? The following can be taken as typical:

(1) Maintain all property, buildings, plant and machinery in good working order and ensure continuous supply of power, water, gas and air supplies and the efficient working of the sewage system.

(2) Periodically inspect and overhaul as necessary all such property, buildings, plant and machinery.

(3) Attend to breakdowns and other repair work promptly, so as to minimise to the utmost production delays or interferences with services.

(4) Supervise and control all personal work done in the section.

(5) Maintain discipline in the department.

(6) Adhere to the Company's personnel policy and ensure that subordinates do so.

(7) Establish and encourage among personnel in the department a spirit of service to production departments.

(8) Ensure that care is taken of tools and equipment used by the department.

(9) Ensure that operators make accurately any records required of them (e.g. time spent, work done).

(10) Continually watch all forms of excess costs (particularly waste of power) and reduce to a minimum.

In larger firms these duties would need to be shared by operators or sections in the following manner:

Millwrights or Mechanics Department.—Responsible for installation, upkeep and repair of all mechanical plant. It may have its own machine tools, and would be likely to include millwrights (who are skilled in moving and installing plant and machines), machinists, fitters, pipe-fitters and sheet-metal men. If the factory produces its own power, or steam, for process it will be responsible for the boilers and engines.

Electricians Department.—Responsible for electrical plant, motors, wiring, lighting, substation and switchboard, and if the factory produces its own power, the generating equipment.

Carpenters and Building Department.—Responsible for upkeep and repair, and small extensions of all buildings and furniture. It would include, besides carpenters, plumbers, bricklayers and painters.

When it is necessary to design special plant and machinery for the Company's own use, or to re-arrange plant frequently, a small Drawing Office is needed. In addition, there may be a small "outside" staff responsible for grounds, cleaning windows, lavatories and so on.

It is essential to have in the maintenance departments men who can work with little supervision and have a large amount of initiative, because by the very nature of the work they must at times work on their own, frequently outside normal working hours, and in conditions of emergency when just the right tackle or materials may not be available. It is necessary, too, to imbue the department with the idea of "service to production". Wage incentives for maintenance operators, which depend on overall effectiveness or performance of the departments they serve, are useful in this connection, though they cannot succeed if the attitude of prompt and ungrudging service is not always shown by the foreman and executives in the maintenance department.

Preventive Maintenance

The effectiveness of a maintenance department is indicated, not so much by the speed with which it does a repair, as by the way it keeps a plant running and free from any breakdowns and delays. It cannot of course be held responsible for neglect or misuse by operators; that is a major responsibility of supervision. But a well-devised scheme of preventive maintenance strictly adhered to is the soundest way of ensuring the minimum trouble from plant breakdowns. Such a scheme is based on the regular periodic inspection of every item of plant likely to give trouble, from boilers and large machines to steam traps and portable tools. It is often maintained that there is not time, or the staff is not available to carry out the necessary inspection; the truth is more often that the staff who should be doing preventive work are absorbed in "shutting the stable door". Once a system of routine inspection and of planned overhaul and repair has been running for some time, there is a net saving in time and labour.

(1) A plant inventory (if one does not exist) must be prepared, and, what is not usually included—the inventory details of parts of the equipment which are subject to wear, unexpected breakdown or neglect must be recorded. A suitable form for use in visible-edge binders as an inventory book is shown in Fig. 71.

(2) Determine the frequency of inspection and of lubrication or other service, if this is to be done at the same time, for each item of plant and machinery.

(3) Prepare inspection schedules in terms of location of plant and frequency of inspection.

(4) Assess standard times for the work. If in large works, routine maintenance work can be done on piecework.

(5) Prepare schedule of regular overhauls for equipment which needs them whatever its conditions, e.g. boilers.

It may not be possible at the start to define exactly all parts and points on a machine that require inspection, but as experience is gained, the information can be recorded. It is useful to prepare an inspection sheet or card for each item of plant, listing vertically each inspection point, with vertical columns in which the maintenance inspector can insert a mark as he inspects each point. He should enter on a report sheet only items which require attention, with comments. The reports should be scrutinised by the maintenance foreman for decisions, in consultation with production staff on when necessary work is to be done.

To prepare the inspection schedule the items of plant are set out in a time chart arranged with items vertically and each day (or week) of

Plant and Machinery Record (Mechanical)	LOCATION		DESCRIPTION		INSPECT	NUMBER	
	Maker and Description of Plant					MAKER'S NUMBER	

Supplier				FLOOR SPACE	WEIGHT	DATE DELIVERED	DATE IN OPERATION

Method of Holding Work	COOLANT	LUBRICANT	DRIVE		H.P.	AMPS	
			TYPE	SIZE OF PULLEY		NO LOAD	FULL LOAD

Capacity	ALTERATIONS	
	DATE	DETAILS

Accessories, Alterations or Remarks	Parts or Details for Routine Inspection

FRONT VIEW

REPAIRS			OVERHAULS		
DATE	DETAILS OF RUNNING REPAIRS	REPAIR ORDER No.	DATE	DETAILS OF MAJOR OVERHAULS	REPAIR ORDER No.

BACK VIEW

FIG. 71.

year horizontally. Plant should be grouped either departmentally or according to type, and the type of inspection or service indicated by symbols, as for example:

I Inspect.
○ Oil and grease.
△ Take up wear.
◇ Replace parts.
H Overhaul.

All inspections, etc., falling on each day (or week) can then be brought on to a daily (or weekly) tour or tours depending on the size of plant and number of maintenance inspectors required. The tours must be so arranged as to minimise walking time, take advantage of specialisation on certain types of plant if the quantity makes it possible, and to provide a certain amount of spare time for exceptional difficulties which may be encountered. It may be necessary, of course, to arrange for some of this work to be done outside normal production times. It is also important to attach to each tour, or to give to each inspector an exact definition of the duties to be covered.

Preventive maintenance cannot be said to be effectively under control unless, in addition to the routine inspection, there is also a record of breakdowns, which brings to the attention of management the frequency and causes of such breakdowns, and management do something about the evidence thus presented. Such records would need to classify breakdowns under the following headings, which show where the responsibility lies:

Faulty or insufficient maintenance.
Faulty design.
Faulty operator.
Unknown causes.

To collect and present the facts, the production supervision of the department or section in which the breakdown delaying production for an appreciable period, say a quarter of an hour, occurs, should record the breakdown on a Breakdown Report and send it to the Cost Office, via the Maintenance Engineer, giving the following information:

Plant affected.
Cause of breakdown.
Period of breakdown.
Loss of production.
Urgency.

The Maintenance Engineer should add his comments and ensure that the Report No. is quoted on the job cards of the men doing the repair, or alternatively record the hours and names of mechanics in the report. The Cost Office can then calculate the cost of the breakdown, and render a summary report to both Works Management and Maintenance Management showing the cost under responsibility, as illustrated at Fig. 72. Such a report brings home to those responsible, not only cost of repairing, but the value of the production lost, both are excess costs, reducing potentially available profit.

WEEKLY REPORT ON COST OF PLANT BREAKDOWNS

Department	RESPONSIBILITY AND COST									
	Maint.		Operator		Design		Unknown		Total	
	Prod. Loss	Repair Cost	Prod. Loss	Repair Cost	Prod. Loss	Repair Cost	Prod. Loss	Repair Cost	Prod. Loss	Repair Cost
Total										

FIG. 72.

In the very small firm an elaborate scheme of preventive maintenance is not required, and it is always more important to get a repair done than to record its cost. Excessive repair costs will be evident to manager or engineer. Nevertheless, preventive inspection should be practised, and it ensures that it will get the attention it requires if the person responsible is methodical, and this involves some simple form of inspection routine or schedule, perhaps one machine a day, which is rigidly adhered to.

INSPECTION

Need for Inspection

Inspection these days is taken for granted, but it is pertinent to ask why inspection is necessary. It is as nearly non-productive as any department or function in a factory can be, and to that extent can be considered an excess cost—and one of the aims of management is to reduce excess costs to a minimum. Then why inspection? One can still come across factories where there is no inspection department. In these it is usually found that either the foremen fulfil the function or else the employees are craftsmen skilled in their particular job, the works relatively small, and all employees, operators, supervision and administration distinctly above average. It is a human problem. The truth is that inspection is necessary because human beings are fallible and unless each person is a craftsman concerned only with producing a perfect article, bad work is likely to be passed off as good—particularly if there is anything to be gained by it. That is the reason, of course, why payment by results—quantity results—can tend to lower the quality standard. (Payment by results can include a factor for quality and entirely successful schemes on process work have been applied which pay a maximum bonus when standard quality and output is attained, bonus decreasing when output is higher and quality consequently lower.)

All this does not mean that a lot of inspection is essential. It does mean that it is, or the extent of its need is, primarily a management problem. The higher the morale, quality and type of work, and the better the management, the less the need for inspection (and the less there are of all other excess costs as well, of course). But human nature being what it is, some inspection is always necessary. It is necessary to maintain standards of quality and interchangeability of component. This latter has had the biggest influence on the growth of the inspection function. Interchangeability (that is, every repeat of a component being exactly identical, within narrowly prescribed limits, in size or vital dimensions) by eliminating all fitting and matching, reduces production time enormously. Without interchangeability the modern assembly-belt method would be impossible. Similarly, the repetition of process in say textiles or foodstuffs would be impossible without reliance on the quality of materials used, and this is only ensured by inspection during manufacture of the materials. And the make-up sections of the textile industry, as in the finishing sections of all industries, must depend on earlier processes for reliable standards of quality to avoid matching problems and to maintain production flow.

Aims and Objects of Inspection

But the aims and objects of an Inspection Department should be wider than merely to ensure interchangeability, important though it is. Its primary object of course is to control the Company's standard of workmanship and finish. This standard forms part of the Company's sales policy, and is interpreted in turn by the Managing Director, Works Manager and Chief Inspector. The quality of products and standard of finish should be as high as economically possible; that is, as high as costs and an adequate profit margin will allow. In practice this is a difficult matter, because there is inevitably a tug-of-war between the desire for high quality, strongly supported by the sales staff and designer, and greater output at less cost, the aim of the works departments. It is not made easier because quality is often impossible to specify precisely and is only arrived at empirically. Nevertheless, there is ample evidence that a high quality is the best form of advertising. It is especially true where reliability is more important than appearance or personal preference and for English manufacturers who do, or should, make for the quality market rather than for the cheap mass-production one.

In order to maintain these standards of quality and interchangeability, the first object of the Inspection Department in the works is to prevent faulty work from passing forward, either to next operation or to Stores; that is, to act as a kind of sieve or back stop. This is a negative kind of function. The inspection staff can and should have an equally valuable positive one not often appreciated: they should aim at preventing faulty work. From their observations of the nature and incidence of faults, inspectors should point out weaknesses, failings and faulty operation to production foremen, wherever possible suggesting where or how they may be prevented. The emphasis, of course, is on prevention. Tactful and intelligent inspectors working harmoniously with the production staff can do much to direct the latter's attention towards the prevention of faulty work and scrap.

In order that the inspection staff shall not be overridden by the production departments, the Chief Inspector should be independent of production, and responsible therefore either to the Chief Engineer or Chemist, or to the Works Manager (if he is also responsible for the technical and production administration departments). This is most important. It does not mean that in status the Chief Inspector is necessarily on the same level as the head of the Production or Technical Departments, but it does mean that he has direct access to an executive at that or a higher level who is not primarily concerned with output. Strictly speaking, he represents the customer for quality of the final product, and the assembly departments for the quality of products from component manufacturing departments. He must be quite free from undue influence. He must of course use his discretion, and to do this wisely in a company manufacturing to customer's order he must be in close contact with the Sales Department. Although an inspector has no responsibility for the quality of work *produced*, he is responsible for what is *accepted*, and in order to prevent waste production it may be customary to authorise inspectors to stop production which is continuing to fall below standard, insisting that the foreman responsible is immediately informed. Alternatively, there may be standing orders to those in charge of operating personnel, for production to be suspended if rejects have exceeded a given figure.

Responsibilities

The responsibilities of a Chief Inspector are normally to:

(1) Organise and supervise the work of inspectors, testers and viewers.

(2) Instruct and train staff in carrying out their duties and ensure that they are effectively performed.

(3) Adhere to the Company's personnel policy and ensure that subordinates do so.

(4) Give effect to the Company's policy relating to quality of products and standards of finish and performance.

(5) Inspect firsts-off and finished components and products, and carry out periodic check inspection during production. Report to operator and supervisor when processes or operations are not producing to standard. Reject work not up to standard.

(6) Carry out final running tests on finished products. Record results on official test sheets and pass for delivery only those up to the Company's standard. Refer back for rectification products not up to standard.

(7) Render reports on work inspected, recommending corrections to methods and equipment where such may be necessary to maintain standards of finish and performance or to increase productivity.

(8) Advise foremen on methods of gauging and inspection carried out by operators.

(9) Ensure that care is taken of tools, gauges and other equipment used in the Inspection Department.

(10) Inspect consignments received of bought out materials and parts when requested by Stores, and render a report to the Stores and Buying Department on quality and adherence to specification or order.

(11) Record work passed, rejected and to be rectified, arranging with the foreman for rectification when necessary.

(12) Count and vouch for work passed forward and to be paid for.

(13) Keep abreast of developments in methods of inspection and collaborate with the production departments in improvements to current practice.

These duties call for persons with special characteristics, developed spontaneously or else by training, in addition to skill in the technique of inspection. An inspector must, above all, be absolutely impartial at all times, and must always be able to make a decision which is unpleasant to workers who may be his friends. There can be no compromise with the facts and his judgment of them. This is much easier of course when the inspector is not responsible to the production staff, but he still has to live and work with his workmates, and some can be very unpleasant if they disagree with a decision, or if their wages are considerably affected by it. An inspector cannot afford to be persuaded against his judgment, nor to alter a decision against the facts; it is the kind of precedent of which operators always take advantage—and quality always suffers. Then too, sound judgment is called for, that is, the ability to review quickly the various facts and factors which affect the suitability or adequacy of a job in borderline cases. When there are dimensional limits, a decision is easy, but when the standard relates to finish or appearance, the standard must be carried in the mind yet not vary from day to day. Even in the case of dimensions, there can be a combination of borderline results which has to be set against the value of an expensive component scrapped or delay in delivery if it has to be remade. This is partly skill, but a person who is capable of sound judgment on any issue makes the more skilful inspector. Lastly, the kind of person who, as a rule, does not make a good inspector is the very fast skilled worker. Inspection work proves too slow for him and does not provide the opportunity for rapid rhythmic work and higher earnings for extra effort to satisfy his ambition.

If it is desired to pay inspectors on an incentive scheme, and this is often justified and can be successful when the kind of inspection is of a routine nature and not highly skilled, there must always be a second overriding check, quite independent of the first. The person making this second check must not be paid on an incentive scheme based on output. Associated with this check must be a severe penalty for any work passed which should not have been, e.g. loss of bonus for the whole of the week.

Types of Inspection

There are very nearly as many types of inspection as there are industries and jobs in them. In transport there are inspectors who check service as well as tickets, and wheel tappers who ensure safety, and in drawing offices there are frequently checkers who inspect all drawings before these are passed out. But in manufacturing industry, with which we are primarily concerned, inspection falls into the following categories:

1. Inspection of Raw Material

This involves chemical or microscopic tests for checking the ingredients or structure of a material, tests for hardness, durability and similar properties, and for moisture content, colour, or just appearance.

2. Inspection of Work in Process

This covers the whole range of factory inspection of parts and final assemblies, with all the skilled technique and accurate instruments for measuring to final limits on a production as distinct from a laboratory basis. Tests are made to determine either accuracy of form or dimension or degree of finish.

3. *Process Control*

Inspection of process conditions is required in chemical, food, paint and similar manufacture, heat treatment, drying and electrolysis, and other electrical treatment. When the correct conditions have been determined for production of a satisfactory material and uniform raw materials are ensured, tests which maintain these correct conditions automatically ensure correct products.

4. *Running Tests*

When the end product is a machine, it is usual to make running tests in conditions as similar as possible to those in which the machine will be working in service. Motor-cars have road tests; electric motors and generators, cranes and machinery designed to a customer's requirements are run on a test bed often in the presence of the customer or his representative, or tested on site before acceptance. When tests cannot exactly reproduce conditions (as for example with cars and electric motors), tests are carried out which exceed the severity of working conditions by a standard amount, so that uniformity of results is ensured. The amount by which conditions are more severe than normal is a factor of safety (or more strictly of ignorance, since it is an acknowledgment that occasionally conditions may be worse than normal by an amount not precisely known).

5. *Quality Control*

This is a statistical method of measuring deviation from standard quality by recording sample tests on a chart which immediately shows when work is being produced outside previously approved limits. It is applicable to all cases where limits can be worked to and is most suitable for continuous manufacture. This method was developed in engineering factories during the Second World War, but is now in general use, and has yielded startling savings not only in inspection costs, but also in scrapped material. It has the virtues of low cost and of early warning of a falling off in quality of production. The following is a summarised description of the method.[1]

> *Quality Control.*—This is a new procedure which has come into vogue during the past twenty years for the control of mass-produced articles by the application of the theory of probability to the results of examination of samples. A very important feature is that the examination is made close to the machine, and as soon as possible after the

[1] Extract from *Institution of Mechanical Engineers Proceedings*, 1947, Vol. 157, page 299, "Gauging and Metrology," by J. E. Sears. For an explanation of the application of statistical methods of control of quality, dimensions and standardisation see "Statistical Quality Control" by D. H. W. Allan published by Chapman and Hall.

articles are produced, so that the results serve to give a direct indication of tendencies in the production process, and enable corrective action to be taken before excessive errors arise, thereby avoiding unnecessary scrap. The method can be of very wide application, and is, of course, particularly useful in any case where test to destruction is required.

From the point of view of gauging between limits, two variants are possible. Control may be based either on the percentage of defectives found in samples (for which purpose provisional control limits should be set inside the ultimate work limits) or on recorded measurements of the individual parts in the samples. In either case there is a considerable saving in the number of gauges required; but for the second alternative, which is to be preferred, gauges of the indicating type are necessary.

It is claimed that the proper application of quality control can give as sure a result as 100 per cent. gauging, when due regard is had to the possibilities of human error due to fatigue in continuous operation of the latter.

Study of the data accumulated from the application of quality control should also afford information as to the performance of machine tools of the greatest value to designers in assessing tolerances for machined parts on a rational basis.

It is not perhaps sufficiently realised that, where defects are not very obvious, yet have to be detected, even 100 per cent. inspection is not reliable. Inspectors are human and suffer from fatigue, eye strain and monotony. Under such conditions what is thought to be 100 per cent. inspection, is often only 70 or 80 per cent. In these circumstances statistical sampling methods give as good, or better, results.

Limits

It will be realised, from what has already been said, that quality, accuracy and finish are relative; there is, in a practical manufacturing sense, no absolute measurement. To an engineer dead size means as accurate as he can measure with his micrometer, e.g. to a ten-thousandth part of an inch (0·0001"). In setting up any standard, therefore, it is not sufficient to state a single unit (of length, degree of heat, etc.), but to express the standard as a permissible variation between upper and lower limits, unless the accuracy obtainable with instruments normally in use is good enough, e.g. foot rule, or commercial scales for weight. When other than commercial accuracy is required, limits are essential, and the standard is specified as a unit with a variation "higher or lower" or "up or down" not to exceed given amounts. In engineering this is expressed thus: 2" plus or minus 0·005 inch, meaning a dimension of 2 inches plus or minus 5 thousandths, or between the limits of 2·005 inch and 1·995 inch.

In the British Standards and other standards of limits frequently used in industry, the following terms are used:

(a) *Limits*

Limits for a dimension or other unit of measurement are the two extreme permissible sizes (measurements) for that dimension (unit).

(b) *Tolerance*

The tolerance on a dimension (measurement) is the difference between the high and low limits of size for that dimension (measurement); it is the variation tolerated in the size of that dimension (measurement), to cover reasonable imperfection in workmanship. (In connection with the fit of a part into another, e.g. a shaft into a hole or bore, the following further terms are used:

(c) *Allowances*

The allowance is the prescribed difference between the high limit for a shaft and the low limit for a hole to provide a certain class of fit.

(d) *Fit*

The fit between two mating parts is the relationship existing between them with respect to the amount of play or interference which is present when they are assembled together. In general shop terms, a fit can vary between a "heavy drive" to a "coarse clearance", and British Standards lists fourteen such fits, including various classes of push and running fits.

A full, but simple, explanation of Limits and Fits for Engineering is given in B.S.S. 1916: Part I. A much more comprehensive analysis of standards, tolerances and fits, as used in engineering design and manufacture is given in *British Standards for Workshop Practice,* B.S.I. Handbook No. 2.

Organisation of Inspection

In order that the function of inspection shall not be negative only, it is essential to recognise that its task is to *control* the *quality* of production. Applying the principles of "control" set out on pages 68–69 above, there must be:

Standards of quality laid down.

Records of deviation from standards, i.e. records, not only of rejects, but also evidence of frequency and importance of rejects and where occurring.

Action to prevent recurrence as far as possible or to minimise frequency and to rectify if possible work rejected.

Standards should be laid down in writing in specifications or on drawings, and on the latter it is important to remember that a dimension has no meaning if not associated with a tolerance. It is essential that it is clearly understood in a shop, and stated on all drawings, that dimensions to which no tolerance is specifically given, i.e. open dimensions, are to be to a standard tolerance. In practice, dimensions relating to rough castings and other non-machined parts of a component are required to be to a tolerance of $\frac{1}{16}$ inch ($\pm \frac{1}{32}$ inch), and open dimensions of machined surfaces to a tolerance of twenty thousandths ($\pm$ 0·010 inch).

The actual organisation of the work of inspecting, recording and taking of corrective action must obviously vary very widely with the type of product, process and scale of manufacture. With armament and aeroplane manufacture, 100 per cent. inspection at all stages and operations is usually called for. In the manufacture of barrows, agricultural machinery, etc., a much less rigid inspection is required, and in the chemical process industries a different type of inspection altogether is required. The first and major factor affecting the organisation of the work is whether 100 per cent. inspection or only sampling is necessary. This is mainly an economic question, although as in the case of armament and aeroplane manufacture, absolute reliability is an overriding factor. The fact that 100 per cent. inspection results in a high proportion of inspectors ("non-producers") to operators, as high even as 1 in 3, and the fact that sample or check inspection which does reveal errors is usually sufficient to maintain a reasonably satisfactory standard, suggests that sample inspection is usually adequate, and in practice this is so. When, however, work which slips through sample checks creates serious assembly delays or expensive reactions from customers, then 100 per cent. inspection may justify its cost.

When sample inspection is adopted, it is essential for firsts-off a run or set-up to be inspected thoroughly. Thereafter, not only must samples be taken at a frequency to assure an adequate percentage check as indicated by experience, but there should also be random checks at irregular periods and of the batch. Although not foolproof, this usually reveals persistent faults and really bad work. The frequency of sample inspection must be laid down as part of the standard for each operator or process. A method of doing this for machining operation is illustrated on the specimen operation layout shown in Fig. 26. It remains then to decide on either centralised or floor inspection. In the former method all work from a department is sent to the Inspection Department or made to pass through an inspection crib before passing on to the next operation. In the latter method inspectors go on to the floor and inspect work at the machine or bench. Only a study of the conditions on the spot can reveal which of these methods will give the best or cheapest results. In considering which to adopt, the following advantages of each should be borne in mind:

Advantages of Centralised Inspection

> Easier and better supervision.
> Division of labour possible, permitting employment of less skilled labour.
> More thorough and less liable to interruption.
> Tidier shops, and therefore easier to control flow of work.
> More accurate checking for wage payment, and less chance of falsification.
> Easier to progress.
> Losses from lost or stolen work and hidden scrap at a minimum.

Advantages of Floor Inspection

> Far less handling. (In the case of very large components, transport to inspection crib is prohibitive.)
> Less delay due to time lag in Inspection Department.
> Less work in progress.
> Shorter production cycle time.
> Faults can often be rectified *immediately* and by operator *responsible.*
> Inspector can act as adviser to operator, with aim of *preventing* faulty work (particularly helpful with learners.)

It is not proposed to illustrate all the kind of records that should be made of the results of inspection, since these vary so widely, and obviously must be designed to suit the product and the organisation. As a help in the design of a Scrap Note, a very suitable form is illustrated in Fig. 61. Certain principles, however, must be adhered to if the amount of faulty work is to be controlled and steps taken to minimise what does occur. These are:

(1) Records must be rendered as soon after the event as possible and to the person first able to do something about it.

(2) To this end foreman should be supplied with a report item by item on the rejects in his department daily (or weekly or monthly). He should sign this and indicate action taken, and send on to the Works Manager (or other senior production executive). If he can scrutinise each scrap note, so much the better.

(3) The cost of scrap (material and labour) should be rendered to foremen on weekly cost control reports.

(4) Only inspectors should be allowed to reject or scrap any work, and scrap should not be received by Reclaiming or Stores Departments without a covering note signed by an inspector.

(5) Inspectors should be responsible for documents, arranging for the re-procession or rectification of faulty work, and ensuring that the need for so doing is brought to the attention of Production Planning.

P.P.M.—16

In a small firm, where personal contact between the higher management and the operator at the bench is both intimate and frequent, and operators consequently are more aware of the significance of their work and can be made more aware of the need for quality, few, if any, inspectors are required. Except for a final inspection of the completed product, it is likely to be more successful to put the onus of passing forward only good work on the operator. It cannot be done, however, if any slackness or slipshod work is allowed to pass unnoticed or uncorrected. There must be pride in maintaining a definite standard. By and large, workmen prefer to do good work and will do so if put on their honour and if the general standard is set by example.

CHAPTER VI

MANAGEMENT IN PRODUCTION

SUPERVISION—A HUMAN PROBLEM

PRODUCTION MANAGEMENT is concerned with getting things made or done. The *technical* function of this management is primarily concerned with material things, designs, processes and machines, the *administrative* function is concerned with facts and figures. The actual doing, execution of plans and supervision of the persons involved, is a *human* problem. It is concerned with people, who have emotions as well as abilities, rights as well as duties, free will as well as good will, and reactions that cannot be predicted with the accuracy of machine movements. It is a problem at least as old as civilisation; what makes it still so little understood apparently and so difficult to solve today is that conditions have changed, and changed rapidly in the comparative short industrial era. The manager's job—or the supervisor's—consists mainly of creating by word and action, by decision and example, by orders and organisation, an atmosphere within which people are motivated to work willingly, effectively, with continuous high effort; it is a job of *leadership*. Although a new type of leadership must permeate management from top to bottom (no section, department, works or organisation can be better than the man at the top), it is at the lower level of management, the level of "supervision" as it is commonly called, as exercised by the foreman, that serious lack of leadership causes most unrest and most reduces individual effectiveness. The foreman or supervisor, alone of the management hierarchy, is in constant daily touch with operators, and is most frequently giving direct orders and making personal decisions. Today he is often the weakest link in the chain of command.

The reasons and the difficulties are not far to seek. During the past few decades, the responsibilities of managers of all grades (including supervisors in this broad classification) have been steadily reduced or changed. Certainly their power "over" people has been reduced, even if their effective power is more. Specialists are now employed to do much of the work which, in the earlier days of the industrial era, occupied a foreman's time. Processes and methods are laid down by technicians and production engineers, the order of production is decided by planning clerks, piece rates are worked out by ratefixers, costs and performances calculated by accountants, and even engaging and discharging and Trade Union negotiations are largely performed by (though not the ultimate responsibility of) the Personnel Officer. Frequently, the foreman is not on or represented on Works Councils, Joint Production Committees, or other consultative bodies, and he is often obstructed by shop stewards. Furthermore, the effects of taxation have reduced the differential between his earnings and those of his skilled subordinates, reducing the incentives to acceptance of the supervisory role for all its status. Finally, foremen and other managers are often promoted from the ranks because of proficiency as operators and not for abilities as leaders of men and receive no training for the job of supervision or management. All this has a depressing effect on the standard of management as a whole.

One solution is to select supervisors and managers mainly for their abilities, even if latent, as leaders, and not only for their operating or technical skill, and then to train them specifically for the job of supervision. In addition to knowing something of the technical work being done by subordinates and associated specialists, the supervisory role consists of putting the right man in the right place, seeing that he is suitably rewarded for his efforts, giving him all the information he needs or should have, making decisions on the innumerable occasions which are not covered by standard practice, instructions and procedures, and continuously inspiring all his team to work willingly and well.

This is the point at which the role of the managers and of the supervisors becomes inextricably woven in with that of their specialist colleagues in the field of "personnel management"—a subject that is dealt with at length in the following Part.[1] The point will be stressed there that the Personnel Officer is an advisor and an assistant to all managers and supervisors: he can help them to be more effective in the performances of their human tasks, but he cannot—and certainly must not attempt to—take these tasks over. His role is essentially *ancillary*; to the managers and supervisors themselves must belong the role of *managing* the men and women at work. To consider what this entails, however, inevitably necessitates referring to a number of activities which are customarily thought of in the context of the "personnel function of management"; to go into such activities in this Chapter would, therefore, involve unavoidable overlap of subject and a great deal of duplication of text. Proper consideration of these activities is thus left over to Part Three, which should be read as an integral contribution to the con-

[1] See in particular Chapters I and II, pages 489–537.

sideration of the role of managers and supervisors in the management of production. It must suffice here to comment briefly on some selected aspects which more immediately arise within the purview of management and supervision in the factory.

Inspiration

Inspiring leadership in everyday work can have astonishing results in raising men's efforts much above the ordinary level. To attain this, managers must show by their enthusiasm and example that they have faith in the purpose of the job in hand and in the company's products or business, and are loyal to the company's policies, to their own seniors and to all their subordinates. It is not enough to show this on important occasions, it must be shown *always* in every small decision and action, in giving orders and receiving unpleasant ones, in reprimands and in commendation, in attempting the impossible and carrying out the routine jobs, in dealing with disputes and correcting or reporting grievances, in setting tasks and ensuring reward. To inspire his team and maintain a high morale, the manager must set himself a high standard and live up to it. Respect, like authority, cannot be handed out or ordered, it must be earned. Men on the shop floor have a pretty accurate assessment of their boss's character; they know him at least as well as he knows himself, and usually better. He has presumably been chosen for his superiority, and they therefore tend to set their own standard of behaviour by his.

Inspiration, then, is the essence of leadership. Loyalty is a principal ingredient—loyalty to subordinates, to management and to the purpose of the enterprise. Others are keenness, which is infectious; absolute honesty in all things, but especially in discussions; interest in and liking for people, resulting in personal sympathy and understanding; readiness to face awkward situations and to accept responsibility, but unwillingness to ask others to do anything one would not do oneself; an ability to make prompt and resolute decisions, however unpleasant; and finally a sense of humour.

Communication

The communication of information, ideas and decisions is a basic "tool" of supervision which is in constant use and must always be in good condition. It is perhaps true that what makes leaders inspiring and outstanding, in addition to that vital spark of enthusiasm and an unshakable faith, is the ability to convey ideas and information clearly, vividly and convincingly to others. How can employees understand and appreciate the purpose of their work if it is not explained to them? If facts are withheld or suppressed there is suspicion, where information is lacking there is rumour—which has a high rate of circulation. Secrecy separates people, common knowledge of a common purpose unites them. It is therefore essential for a supervisor to become proficient at communicating essential and accurate information and decisions; and the more effective in doing so he becomes, the more power with the people he will have—the more he will inspire.

The essential ingredients of information are, of course, facts. Many disputes and misunderstandings arise because *all* the *facts* of a case are not known to *all* the people concerned. Busy managers intent on their own job and immediate problems have difficulty in finding the time necessary to obtain all the facts bearing on their own work or that of their department, and to see that all essential facts are passed on.

This does not mean that the *manner* of passing on information is unimportant. In management we are dealing with persons who have feelings and emotions, and just because facts can be so cold and impersonal it is essential to present them with a certain amount of warmth and preferably in person. The spoken word is more effective (though less permanent) than the written, talks more effective than notices on the board, a word of encouragement often a stronger incentive than financial reward. A flash of humour is worth a good deal of legal argument and a ready sense of humour is an attractive and popular trait.[1]

Joint Consultation

A large part of a manager's time is necessarily spent in dealing with people, but little of it should be spent in actually giving instructions. For most of the time a manager should be passing on or receiving information as a result of which subordinates take action, if action is necessary. In doing so he should provide reasonable opportunity for the other persons to express their opinions, even if they have to be corrected or rejected. In this way all subordinates, and the rank and file, are made to feel that their opinions count for something and that "they matter". The larger an organisation becomes the more difficult it is to do this; information along the channels of communication, up and down, does not move very freely and decisions made high up may appear arbitrary. Resistance may be met with instead of ready co-operation. More formal means

[1] Two recently published books giving a great deal of useful advice and information which will help those wishing to improve their power of self-expression by the written word are *The Presentation of Technical Information*, by R. O. Kapp (Constable), and *Plain Words*, by Sir Ernest Gowers (published by H.M. Stationery Office).

of ensuring the flow of information becomes necessary and we have what is called "joint consultation . . ."

To the manager, joint consultation committees and other formal means of consultation are apt to appear unwieldy and time consuming, and to undermine his prestige and authority. They can do just this if the manager sits back and lets the committee do his work for him. But the manager must be continually alert to ensure that people turn first to their immediate superior for information or advice, and that information affecting people gets down to them from above quickly and sympathetically. Then this leaves the formal committee to deal with the inevitable grumbler and cases which go off the rails, usually due to personalities, and to act as a safety valve. How mechanisms of consultation can aid good management and supervision is discussed in Chapter II of Part Three.

Decision

Decision is another important element of leadership, and the nice balance between the impetuous, too hasty decision and a hesitating one or procrastination has to be cultivated. There are some people who find great difficulty in making up their minds and sticking to a decision. Highly skilled, technical persons and those trained in research often do not make successful managers for this reason; they have been so used to looking all around a question in every detail that they are unable to make a decision rapidly. Although it is essential to be able to make a decision, it must not be thought that it is possible to do so without a knowledge of the facts and without a good deal of thought. A manager must not always be forcing his ideas; he must be a good listener as well as a good talker, and above all must be able to get others to contribute their ideas and facts, and as far as possible, to share, or feel they share, in the decision. Sharing of decisions adheres to what Mary Follet called the "law of the situation".[1] When all the facts of a situation are found (the law discovered), all concerned, supervisors and operators, obey the law; there is not the same feeling as when obeying orders. Authority can still be exercised, but it is the authority of the facts of a situation.

Co-operation, Co-ordination and Integration

These are elements of the technique of organising action. Co-operation is really a state of mind that can exist only on a basis of knowledge and appreciation of a common purpose that is understood by all. Likewise, co-ordination needs all concerned to have all the information necessary at the time common effort is required. Integra-

[1] *Dynamic Administration,* page 58 (Metcalf & Urwick) (Management Publications Trust, 1945).

tion requires a pooling or gathering together of all the facts and ideas for the purpose of arriving at a best solution of a problem, one which is likely to be better than any one person's solution. In each case a sharing of information is required. In practice it means that there must be frequent meetings between those concerned; not necessarily large or formal meetings, but at least some opportunity to exchange views, ideas and facts. Under wise leaders this co-operation, co-ordination and integration ensures harmony, progress and effectiveness of the whole team. This is not a plea for formal meetings or committees; far from it. The atmosphere of committee rooms is apt to be deadening and sterile. But it does mean that the practice of bringing together those whose activities interlock is a good one and should take place at all levels. This again is a subject more fully discussed elsewhere in this volume: in Chapter VI of Part Five.

SELECTION AND DEVELOPMENT

Because selection and training schemes are matters in which the Personnel Officer advises and undertakes a good deal of the work, this does not mean that they are no longer the line executive's responsibility. Ultimately, the head of a department is responsible for the people he has working for him, he must retain the final right of decision about people added to his staff, retained or promoted. He has the duty of requesting and of considering the advice of the Personnel Officer, but he himself must make the final decision.

The skill of choosing subordinates is one which the young or newly promoted manager must learn, if he is to be successful. Many re-organisations would not have been necessary, and many unhappy organisations would not be so, had the executive at the head been skilled in the choice of men. Few persons remain what they are at

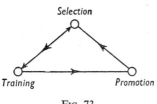

FIG. 73.

an early age. All are susceptible to training — particularly good and stimulating training. So this is equally important; and it makes for more stability and loyalty than introducing persons into an organisation from outside at a high level. To choose good material at an early age and then to train means that each promo-

tion is also a selection, so that Selection, Training and Promotion, vital elements in management, form as it were a triangle (Fig. 73).

Skill in selection of staff demands of executives that they shall be good listeners and better observers. Dominant men usually get "yes-men" round them. To learn of a man's abilities and potentialities one must draw him out and encourage expression of views and abilities;

this can only be done by giving him his head as far as possible. Although much-improved techniques have been developed to aid selection by interview and test, they are not sufficient by themselves, and personal evaluation, particularly of character and personality, has still to be relied on. Such evaluation should be continually practised if it is to be reliable. For it to be practised only in the case of important appointments and for the inevitable mistakes to be made is expensive and wasteful. But it can be practised without actual appointments being involved by studying the behaviour of people one meets and checking one's judgment later. It will be found, except in rare cases, that a conscious effort of evaluation has to be made, else the decision will be affected too much by emotional reactions and personal likes and dislikes.

REMUNERATION AND FINANCIAL INCENTIVES

Remuneration, salary or wages, is one of the provisions which go to make up a contract of service, written, verbal, or implied, and as such is a matter of legal importance. Although it is one of the duties of a Personnel Officer, where one is employed, to ensure that all legal conditions are complied with, every manager must make himself acquainted with such conditions lest by implication or otherwise he breaks the law or creates misunderstandings. Where there is no Personnel Officer, it is especially important for the chief executive to make sure that all foremen and other managers, and particularly newly appointed ones, understand the wage structure of their industry and conditions attached to it, including the formal mechanisms which may have been established by statute or by industrial Agreement.

"The labourer is worthy of his hire." The economic worth is the value in cash which the community places on a person's services. Ultimately, whether we like to think so or not, this means the scarcity value of services either individually or collectively. The higher collective value, of course, gave rise to Trade Unions and the use of strikes or organised absence. But there are other rewards for work (see Dorothy Sayers' booklet *Why Work?*). Recent authoritative surveys and individual investigations have revealed that financial reward is not the first, and is sometimes placed as low as the fifth, reason for remaining in a job. This may come as a shock to older foremen and those in mass-production industries, and gives point to what has already been said above about "inspiration". Nevertheless, a satisfactory level of earnings and method of wage payment is a basic necessity of a job, an essential requirement which must be satisfied before other factors begin to operate to engender the "will to work".

P.P.M.—16*

Kinds of Payment

Remuneration to employees takes two main forms:

Daywork or Time Rate.—Payment at a flat rate per hour, week or year, independent of the amount of work done or output achieved.

Payment by Results.—Payment which varies in some way according to work done or other measure of effort or results. Piecework is a form which is different from all other payment-by-results methods, in that payment varies directly with the amount produced at all levels of production.

Since most persons are inherently conscientious, it is probably thought by everyone, at some time or other, that a flat-rate weekly wage is an adequate incentive. But in cold, hard fact there are few of us who do not work harder for the stimulus of more reward for more effort. Hence it is that more and more employees in industry, hourly paid and staff, are being paid some proportion of their total earnings (even if annually) according to results. Provided that management is sound and is trusted and respected by operators, payment by results is effective as an incentive to higher output. Payment by results is not, however, a universal panacea. It goes only some way to meet one of the essential requirements of a job, the possibility of higher earnings for greater effort. It is a financial incentive, and as such is only one of many incentives. Financial incentives cannot be considered as an isolated factor affecting morale, or as producing predicted or invariable results depending only on the incentive, its type or power. But as part of the larger factor of financial reward or remuneration, they are a vital part of the personnel policy, which in turn is one aspect of the management policy, which in turn is an aspect of company policy.

Before going on to consider each form of payment in detail, it might be as well if we get the advantages and disadvantages of the two main forms into perspective. Broadly speaking, time rate involves the minimum of administrative and clerical work, but provides no financial incentive. Neither does it provide a measure of what labour cost should be, but only what it has been. It hides excess costs of low producers. Piecework provides the most direct financial incentive, and also, if properly applied, the most powerful incentive, but for maximum effectiveness it does involve adequate study and measurement of work done and clerical labour in calculating results. No one will deny that under certain circumstances there are adequate incentives to work well even with time-work payment. At the same time such circumstances are comparatively rare, and in industry it is generally found that output of all manual operators and most clerical workers is higher on some form of payment-by-results.

The disadvantages, or rather difficulties, of payment by results are, in addition to the extra clerical labour:

(1) By putting the emphasis on output, quality tends to suffer. (This is not inevitable and can be avoided by including quality in the "results" and by adequate supervision.)

(2) It can lead to disputes with operators over rates. (This is a function of the quality of supervision.)

(3) It requires careful and thorough preparation and measurement. (This is in reality an advantage, since it puts the emphasis where it is most required, i.e. on work study.)

(4) Methods other than direct piecework tend to confuse and be misunderstood and mistrusted by operators. This is particularly true of premium bonus methods (which share savings in cost between management and operator), and of so-called profit-sharing systems.

These disadvantages, or difficulties, should be read as signals for caution, not as reasons for not proceeding with some form of payment by results. There is no cheap or easy way to better results—all ways call for better management. Even where time rates or staff conditions are preferred to payment by results, it is necessary to measure results against standards either by department or by job, or both, for effective management control.

Prior to the introduction of any incentive scheme, it is essential to establish a sound wage-rate structure for all jobs and all grades of labour. It is advisable to do so whatever method of payment is used. This involves an analysis of all jobs, grading them, and fixing rates for all grades.

Job Evaluation

There is a strong case for the objective assessment of all jobs and operations carried on in industry in the country on a standard basis in order to establish once and for all the relative value of all jobs. For example, has mineworking a greater intrinsic value than skilled engineering say in the toolroom, and is the man at the coal face of more value than the shot firer, and the toolroom operator than the blast-furnace operator, bearing in mind responsibility, skill, risk, effort and so on? It should remove the cause of much argument and many disagreements and strikes if all jobs could be rated on a point system which would place them in correct relative position. Or would it? After all, the final arbiter of a person's value to the community must be what the community is prepared or forced, by scarcity, to pay for his services. An actor, or painter, or chief brewer, may earn far more than any such assessment would indicate. Nevertheless, in any one company, and certainly in one factory, it is possible to assess, in relation to all other employees in that concern, the scarcity value (due to long experience or local factors) of any job. Inequalities of reward are far more obvious in a small community like a factory and create as much dissatisfaction, no less damaging to morale because it is hidden, as in industry as a whole. For this reason an analysis and assessment of all jobs should be undertaken whenever possible or opportune. This job evaluation, as it is called, should most certainly be done before any form of payment by results is introduced or changed in a factory. In some industries certain occupations or grades are laid down by custom, agreement, or regulation, but even in these there are usually many jobs not defined or not covered by them, such as, for example, service labourers, semi-skilled operators, storekeepers, trolleymen and many others, which justify job evaluation.

Job evaluation is a method of giving a value to all jobs in an organisation according to certain characteristics of the jobs or required of the persons doing them. It is now generally recognised that there are four main groups of job characteristics:

1. Skill,
2. Effort,
3. Responsibility,
4. Working conditions;

and each group can be divided into sub-characteristics, effort for example consisting of mental and physical effort. All these major characteristics are present to some degree in all jobs, the degree varying from job to job. If the relative value of each group and each sub-characteristic is agreed upon at the start in terms of points or percentage, then each job can be assessed or rated for each characteristic and the total value of the job found. Such an evaluation will be as nearly objective as is possible, and, in any one company at least, jobs will be valued and rated strictly according to their relative importance to that company, and not as a result of bargaining or pressure. When the points values of jobs have been fixed, they can be given an hourly wage rate in relation to the minimum in the industry or company. In tackling such an analysis, there are four problems to settle:

(1) To determine the headings or characteristics for which each job shall be rated.
(2) To fix the maximum number of points to be given to each characteristic.
(3) To adopt a procedure which will ensure consistent rating.
(4) To set up a panel or team to do the actual analysis and rating.

Characteristics

The above four main headings can be further subdivided thus:

Skill	Responsibility	Effort	Conditions
Basic knowledge	Equipment	Physical effort	Surroundings
Experience	Material and product	—	—
Complexity	Safety of others	Mental effort	Hazard
Judgment	Supervision given	—	—

At this point one has to decide whether to go for still further subdivision, as obviously each of the above subdivisions can be qualified in many respects. However, to do so makes for considerable complexity, and consequently more time and effort to do the job, whereas the above divisions are adequate for most purposes and work well in practice. In a particular factory or organisation it may be found that one or two of the divisions only need be further divided.

Maximum Point Rating

With the particular organisation in mind and the kind of work carried on, a point rating is given to each main characteristic and allocated to each subdivision. Checks are then made with a number of well-defined jobs and the results reviewed critically. It may be found that some correction is called for. For example, they might be assessed first as Skill 40, Responsibility 30, Effort 20, Conditions 20. It may then be judged that Skill should have 45 points, allocated as to Basic Knowledge 15, Experience 10, Complexity 8, Judgment 12, and that in the particular factory Conditions are extremely good and safe, so that a rating of 12 points is adequate for this characteristic. Checks and rechecks are made until reasonable satisfaction is obtained. If there are certain jobs which have a rate established by agreements in the trade, these should be used as key checks (although it does not always follow that their established wage rate is correct).

Rating

When rating a job, it is absolutely essential that it is done objectively, and that all the persons on the rating panel use the same kind of scale for good, medium and poor. Where records are available, such as time for training or number of accidents due to specific causes, these should be used. Otherwise good, medium, poor and none can be thought of in terms of percentage and then applied to the maximum points. It is important that each member of the panel should make his assessment first and jot it down before comparing assessments to arrive at an agreed figure.

Panel

The panel should not be too large, but should consist of at least the Personnel Officer, Foreman of department concerned, possibly a representative of operators, and Works Manager or other senior executive. Being directly affected by the results, it is obviously more difficult for the operators' representative to be objective than for members of the management, and there is usually a tendency for them to rate higher. Nevertheless, if agreement between all members of the panel is always insisted on before fixing a rating, results are satisfactory, and it is elemental that those affected shall have a say in the assessments.

Wage Rates

In order to fix appropriate wage rates to each grade, it is usual to take as a basis the wages paid in the industry or company for the lowest and highest grades and to fix other wage rates pro rata. In certain circumstances it may be necessary to work within certain wage rates already established by agreement or by Wages Councils, and rates may have to be paid for certain jobs whatever the job grading value is assessed at. If maximum and minimum rates are already established, then the job grading results will enable a satisfactory scale of rates to be established for grades in between and beyond the limits. When existing rates must be incorporated these should be plotted against points rating for the appropriate job. A mean line then establishes rates for all ratings (a permissible difference plus or minus can be allowed for).

Daywork or Time Rate

This is simple enough to be generally understood. Payment is at a uniform rate for every hour worked up to a maximum number of hours in a day and a week, above which premiums are paid according to the industry and local agreements or arrangements. Premium payments are also usual for Sunday, holiday and night work. Until recently, staff employees were paid for a week whatever and whenever the hours worked, but with the diminishing difference between staff and works privileges, there is a tendency for staff to be paid for regular (as distinct from occasional) overtime.

Apart from premium payments for overtime, earnings of the operator on time rate are constant per hour or day. On the other hand, the labour cost to the employer increases for outputs below standard and decreases for outputs above standard. This means that the employer bears losses and retains savings with variations from standard output as shown in Fig. 74. This should be compared with the position under piecework as shown below.

Where output can be maintained at or near to standard, more or less independently of the operator's control, then daywork is satisfactory. This occurs on production assembly lines and where output

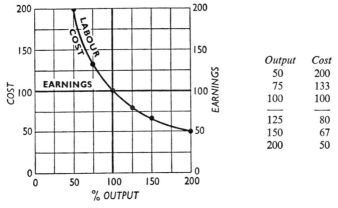

Output	Cost
50	200
75	133
100	100
125	80
150	67
200	50

Fig. 74.—Graph for Time-work Earnings and Cost.

is governed by the speed of machine or conveyor. In these cases, financial incentives, if required, should be tied to quality, overall output, or some other such factor.

Payment by Results

The various kinds of payment by results fall under three headings:

(1) *Piecework*—being payment at a constant rate of pay per unit of work produced correctly for all units whatever the number.

(2) *Premium Bonus Systems*—being methods of varying the rate of pay per unit or of sharing savings between Company and operator above or below a standard task.

(3) *Profit Sharing*—methods of distributing a portion of overall profits earned by the Company over a period (usually a year) to employees.

Piecework

Although piecework is perhaps the oldest form of payment by results (it was used in cotton spinning in Lancashire as early as 1876), it is still the most widely used, at least in England, no doubt because of its overriding advantages of simplicity and fairness. The most frequently raised objection to it, the fear of rate cutting, is not inherent in the method of payment, but arises from faulty measurement of work or rate fixing, which can occur however payment is made for work done.

Piecework can be paid on either a price per piece basis or on a time per piece basis. The result is the same in either case. For example, take the case of an operator, whose rate is 5s. per hour, doing a job for which the standard time at basic performance is found to be 4 hours, and actually taking 3 hours to do the job:

	On Time Basis	On Price Basis
(1) Piecework standard Time allowed Price	4 hrs.	$4 \times 5s. = 20s.$ each
(2) Total piecework earnings	$4 \times 5 = 20s.$	$10 \times 2 = 20s.$
(3) Bonus earnings	$20 - (3 \times 5) = 5s.$	$20 - (3 \times 5) = 5s.$
(4) Piecework bonus %	$\dfrac{4-3}{3} \times 100 = 33\frac{1}{3}\%$	$\dfrac{(10 \times 2)-(3 \times 5)}{3 \times 5.} \times 100 = 33\frac{1}{3}\%$
(5) Time in which job must be done to earn say 50% bonus (i.e. 1·5 × rate)	$\dfrac{4}{1\cdot 5} = 2\cdot66$ hrs.	$\dfrac{20}{1\cdot 5} \div 5 = 2\cdot66$ hrs.

From the company's point of view there is everything to be said for working on a time basis and in practice operators find it just as easy as the piece price basis.

The advantages of working on a time basis are:

1. It encourages respect for the value of time and as such is good management. In modern conditions one contracts to buy so much time. Workers always convert their prices to the time required to do the job.
2. Since work content of a job must first be measured in time before fixing rate, it is an added calculation to then convert to a price.
3. Wage rates may be changed without changing piecework times allowed, and a time allowed is the same whatever the hourly rate of the operator; piece price must be altered whenever basic wages rates are changed and for operators doing the same job on different rates of pay.
4. Work study, which is becoming increasingly important, is based on measurement of time taken, and effectiveness of work study depends upon records based on time.
5. Comparison between the true costs of production are not invalidated by wage changes. One hour of work today is equivalent to one hour of work in the past or future, so that whatever changes there are in the value of money or wage levels, comparisons of the effectiveness of production and other indices of productivity remain relevant and true for a long period. This is most important.
6. Piecework earnings based on time can be expressed and worked out by the workers simply as a percentage. Furthermore, when they

are based on the standard hour, the unit used in modern work study, the percentage bonus is the standard measurement of performance which can be used for comparing results between operators and department, between one period and another, and for the assessment of overall efficiencies for the payment of indirect operators.

7. Shop loading and programme planning, and the control of waiting time and other forms of excess costs, as well as the modern form of standard costing depends upon the accurate measurement of a job on a time basis.

The effect on earnings and on labour costs is shown in the diagram Fig. 74.

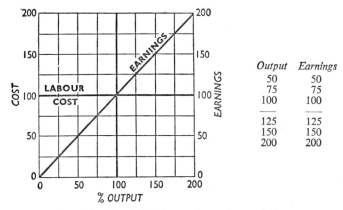

Output	Earnings
50	50
75	75
100	100
125	125
150	150
200	200

Fig. 75.—Graph for Piecework Earnings and Cost.

It will be seen that it has two most desirable features. Earnings of the operator increase pro rata with effort, a 50 per cent. increase in effort bringing a 50 per cent. increase in pay, and the *labour cost* to the Company is *constant*. (Total cost is reduced of course, due to greater absorption of overheads.)

In practice the principle of a guaranteed minimum earning modifies the result somewhat. Whilst earnings still increase above the minimum pro rata with effort, below the output equivalent to the minimum guaranteed earnings, pay is constant, but labour cost increases as in the time-rate diagram. In many industries this minimum is fixed at some level higher than day rate or standard, but why this should be so is difficult to see. A daywork rate should be paid for a daywork effort, and some other method found of paying an incentive to operators like labourers, for whom it is difficult to measure their output. The simplest and quite effective way is to pay such operators the same or some proportion of the percentage bonus earned by the department or group they serve or belong to. (They must not be paid *out of* the earnings of the piecework operators.)

It is usual for operators and management to think of piecework results in terms of "bonus", i.e. the earnings above standard. Its significance to the operator is obvious; to the management it is a most valuable measure of performance if work measurement has been done accurately. Referring to calculation above, it will be seen that the operator is paid 20s. for 3 hours' work and that this is equivalent to times wages (3 hours × hourly rate 5s. = 15s.) plus wages saved (1 hour at hourly rate, 5s.). This can be expressed as time wages (1 hour at hourly rate) plus wages saved (0·3 hours saved at hourly rate). That is to say, the operator is paid his hourly rate wages plus *all* wages saved, because he has done a job in less time than standard. This is the vital point and the reason why straight piecework is the only satisfactory method of payment by results for direct operators and the only one really acceptable to them because it does pay to operators *all* the savings made due to their efforts, is simple in operation and easily understood. It provides a positive and strong incentive at all levels (above any guaranteed minimum) and no other method is so satisfactory in practice. If it would seem that one of the other premium bonus schemes is required, there is strong reason to think that conditions are wrong somewhere and should be corrected rather than by-passed by inherently weak methods of payment.

At the time of writing there is a complication in some industries in Britain, particularly the large engineering industry, owing to piece-rates being calculated on a Base Rate which is less than the full day rate. For example, the base rate for a skilled fitter is 63s. per week (1s. 6d. per hour), but to this is added a "National Bonus" of 118s. 2d. (2s. 9¾d. per hour) making 181s. 2d. in all. Piecework earnings are calculated on the hourly base rate of 1s. 6d. only, the 2s. 9¾d. "National Bonus" being added for each hour worked. The effect on earnings and costs is shown in the diagram at Fig. 76 and in the figures in the table opposite.

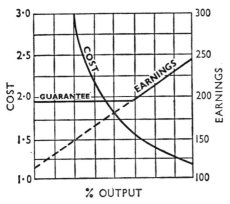

Fig. 76.—Graph for Piecework Earnings and Cost (Eng. Industry 1961).

Output	Earnings per Week		Cost
	Piecework	Total	
50	31·5	149·7	2·99
75	47·25	165·4	2·21
100	63·0	181·2	1·81
125	78·75	196·9	1·58
150	94·5	212·7	1·42
200	126·0	244·2	1·22

It will be seen that the earning graph is still a straight line, but it starts at a minimum figure (in practice the minimum guarantee is 14s. above the total day rate, i.e. 195s. 2d.) and the cost is not constant, but decreases with increasing effort.

Premium Bonus Systems

These were first introduced around the turn of the century, in the U.S.A. by Halsey, Taylor & Gantt, and in Britain by Rowan, the underlying thought being that employer and employee shared savings or profits resulting from outputs higher than standard. To operators on time rate this appeared "fair shares". As the mathematics of the idea were studied and understood, the proportion of the savings paid to the employee and the level taken as a basis for savings were varied to provide stronger or different incentives. In some schemes the proportion of savings going to employer and employee changed at different levels of output; in one, the Barth system, the proportion varied (geometrically) as output varied. In the original Bedaux system, which for calculation of savings was straight piecework, 25 per cent. of savings due to increased output was paid to supervisors in a department. It was this particular arrangement which proved so noxious to British workers, and so discredited the very sound methods of work measurement used by the Company from which the system took its name. The idea has since been completely dropped from all modern applications of premium bonus system.

The Rowan system, much used in Britain—before accurate methods of work measurement were well known—paid to operators, over and above a minimum day rate, the proportion of their base-rate wages represented by the ratio, time saved to time allowed. The effect of this was to cause earnings to rise rapidly immediately above standard output, but less rapidly the higher output became. Under this system it is impossible for an operator ever to exceed twice his base-rate earnings. It thus avoids high earnings due to loose rates, but has a low incentive to high effort.

In general, all premium bonus systems suffer from the marked disadvantage that they are difficult to understand by the operator and as such are suspect. The result is that whatever intrinsic incentive they may have is more than neutralised by the effect on general morale.[1]

Installation of Payment by Results Schemes

Payment by results does not automatically ensure worker satisfaction, higher output or less labour trouble. A scheme, however good in itself, will fail or cause friction and trouble if management is ineffective and its relations with labour are bad; under really effective management any scheme succeeds to a degree. For a scheme really to succeed, other conditions must exist:

Everything possible must have been done to improve and standardise methods of production, tooling, layout and organisation. Failing this all kinds of difficulties will arise, changes will have to be made which will give rise to argument and negotiation, and confidence will be shaken and be difficult to revive.

The scheme must be fair and this will depend most on the accuracy of measurement of work content. Inaccuracy of measurement leads to rewards which are not equitable between operators, fears of rate-cutting, and restriction of output. This will stifle many expected benefits from a financial incentive.

Calculations must be simple and results paid quickly. Complicated systems are looked on with much suspicion, and the longer the period between effort and payment the less the incentive.

It is also essential, however simple the scheme, to give a detailed explanation of it to everyone concerned, foremen as well as operators. The writer has found that the ability of operators in industry to grasp completely and understand the calculations and implications of the simplest and most direct schemes is unbelievably low. One is apt to forget that what looks simple to the initiated is a bit mysterious to people who left school long ago and are conditioned to their existing method of payment. And what appears mysterious is suspect. Furthermore, both foremen and representatives of the operators will understand quite clearly themselves, yet be quite unable to convey the facts to operators or to convince them of the fairness of a scheme.

For this reason it is essential to take trouble to ensure that all the main body of operators do understand what is involved and exactly how their efforts will be rewarded. It will require a great deal of patience. The first essential, of course, is an introductory meeting,

---

[1] Readers who are interested in such systems are recommended to Lytle's *Wage Incentive Methods* (Machinery Publishing Co.) for a detailed and penetrating analysis of premium bonus systems and of other incentive schemes.

either with all operators or their elected representatives, and an agreement on principles. This should be followed by smaller meetings of departments, sections and groups with explanations and illustrations in full. Finally, but most important, foremen and other managers must be completely "sold" on the scheme. It is to court certain trouble to put in any scheme against the wishes of or with the least doubts of the supervisors concerned. They must be 100 per cent. behind the scheme and show real enthusiasm for it. It helps considerably to give supervisors and a shop steward or other representative some training in the methods of work measurement used and methods of calculation and interpretation of results.

Before the scheme is finally installed there should be a trial period during which any changes in organisation or methods can be tried out, difficulties can be resolved and operators can see the possibilities of the scheme and its effects upon them.

Profit Sharing

The popularity of profit-sharing schemes ebbs and flows according to the general level of prosperity. They are popular with employees when there is profit to share, but become suspect and lose their savour when profits and therefore remuneration decline. Such schemes are more in the nature of sentimental attempts to meet the complaint of those who maintain that workers (as distinct from owners) do not get a fair share of increasing profits or prosperity, than deliberate financial incentives. Nevertheless, they are usually looked upon as forms of payment according to results—incentives to think of company prosperity and to work accordingly. As incentives to individual effort they fail in their purpose, and the mortality of such schemes is evidence that there is something unsound about them. There is no doubt that in certain circumstances particular forms of profit sharing can be effective, but success in a specific case is no guarantee, nor can it be expected to be, of success in other cases or in general. Such schemes are more likely to be effective or permanent in very small organisations where owner and employees work closely together, and business problems, as distinct from workshop problems, are apparent and can be understood and appreciated. They are likely to fail in general and in large concerns for two reasons:

They are based on false premises—in particular that profits can be shared but not risks.

As incentives they are too remote and lack power—reward is too remote from effort.

An arrangement which gives to persons a share in the profits of investment, without any sharing of risks is unbalanced and bound to be unsound. Profit-sharing schemes do not usually incorporate any sharing in losses; that is, there is no deduction from current or future earnings if the Company makes a loss or less than a normal profit. Employees' earnings are "guaranteed", but earnings of ordinary shareholders are not—profit is paid for the loan of capital and for the risk involved. Furthermore, in steady years most employees come to look upon their share of profits, whether paid monthly or yearly, as normal, and to adjust their standard of living accordingly. Frequently, the expected share out is actually mortgaged in advance. When the first lean year arrives, as it so frequently does, there is much disappointment, disillusion and bitterness. The slump in morale then appears to far outweigh the advantages, and in fact this is likely to be true.

As an incentive to individual effort, schemes of profit sharing, which depend on yearly results and on the actions of high executives who by single errors (like faulty buying of a major material, faulty decisions on sale policy, or bad design) can wipe out any efforts of the body of employees, have little direct effect. They are too remote from individual effort except to the few top executives, who can see the effects of their own individual actions. Operators on the bench cannot see the cumulative effect of their own individual efforts, indeed they are swamped or may be negatived by the efforts or lack of effort elsewhere.

One type of profit-sharing scheme which has attracted a certain amount of attention recently, goes some way to meet this last weakness, but it does not appear to have been tried in companies where the make-up of total cost as between labour and material may vary appreciably from year to year. In process and mass-production shelf-goods industries it may have some success. It is the scheme originated in America by the Nunn Bush Co. and its development, the Rucker Plan. A wages fund, out of which all employees are paid, is credited with a fixed percentage of gross sales, so that employees as a whole benefit by all of any increase in the productivity of their labour. They are guaranteed 52 weekly wage payments, and are paid on account until the final results of the year are known.

If it is thought that Company loyalty and co-operation should be engendered or bolstered by financial methods, then some form of co-partnership or purchase of shares in the Company may be successful, and there are several schemes now in operation (the Imperial Chemical Industries inaugurated a scheme of 1954 which sets a high standard). Certainly, for executives, senior and long-service employees, a stake in their company's assets should foster a feeling of joint ownership and responsibility.

PERFORMANCE

Measurement.—Most of us like to know how well we are doing. In industrial activity it is essential. A company must render an account at least once a year of its financial results. But the trading account is the result of the individual and collective actions of all employees from day to day in discharging their task, whatever it may be, and it is equally necessary for an account to be rendered of the results of their work, that is, of their performance. This is done for operators on piecework, since their output is measured. One of the very real advantages of measuring piecework on a time basis (page 474) is that the percentage bonus is a measure of performance which can be used for comparing individual and collective or departmental results.

Managers are responsible for the work, and hence the performance, individual and collective, of all employees under their authority. The total bonus percentage for a department is obviously one measure of departmental performance for which the foreman can be held responsible. But there are other performances, often not measured or not measured accurately. Perhaps the most important of these are: total overall costs per unit of production (for example, per standard hour), and excess costs (page 475). In some cases machine utilisation is equally important, as in transport and process industries. Although the quality of the product is usually checked if not controlled by the inspector, the production manager is responsible for results. All managers must see to it that they have accurate reports of all such measures of performance relating to their department and take energetic steps to improve performance continually.

Labour

The main source of information on the performance of labour is the weekly results of individual bonus percentages (or other record of results where piecework is not in operation), and the weekly Labour Cost Control report (see page 376) is used for this purpose. Weekly bonus results should be scrutinised regularly. Particularly good performances should be complimented: an ounce of appreciation is worth a ton of reprimand. Poor performances should be approached in a spirit of enquiry, and efforts made to find out whether there is anything which can be done to help the operator either by training or relieving (by advice or sympathy) the worries arising from personal situations outside the factory. The help of the Personnel Officer may be sought on occasion.

The Labour Cost Control report should be watched for signs of a falling off in performance, of rising cost per unit, and of rising percentage of excess costs. If the figures are normal or falling, no action is called for, but significant rises should be further investigated. In particular a continual rise in excess cost for one particular cause should be followed up, and may call for examination of each instance recorded for a week or two. This often reveals a trouble unsuspected or unnoticed.

In particular, chargehands of small sections should be trained to appreciate the significance of such records and to make their own investigations into means of improving performance or reducing excess costs. A bonus based on reductions in excess costs can be an incentive satisfactory to supervisor and company alike.

Machines

Machine utilisation for the department as a whole is revealed in the Labour Cost Control report, and this normally is an adequate index. If the results are unsatisfactory, or performance begins to fall, it may be necessary, until the cause is found, to arrange temporarily for a detailed record of down-time (idle machine time) on each or certain machines. Such detailed records should not be continued beyond their usefulness if they involve any clerical labour away from the machine or which affects an operator's output. At all times, records which are not used bring themselves and their originators into disrepute.

It is sometimes recommended that detailed records of maintenance and repair costs for each machine should be made. If such costs are heavy, it is necessary, but it is clerical work which can be avoided except when the comparative maintenance costs of similar machines are, or are likely to be, in question. If the difference is appreciable, a foreman knows without records; if there is doubt, detailed records must be kept for a period until costs are established.

Material or Product

The performance of finished machines or parts, or the quality of products, are other aspects of performance. It is often thought that this is the inspector's responsibility. It is not. Quality of product is the supervisor's (manager's or foreman's) responsibility; the inspector is really the representative of the customer (or Assembly Department or Sales Department), and is employed as a guardian of quality. The production supervisor must, in the end, produce a good-quality article, and it is for him therefore to get and use reports on the performance, or quality, of his product. As with labour, he must look for incidence of cause and follow up in an endeavour to cure the cause. Nor is it right to assume that there must always be some waste or scrap, or that a normal figure needs no further efforts to reduce it.

It is surprising to how low a figure scrap and faulty work can be reduced if the effort is made.

For process and continuous production work there is no better index of performance and guide to cause than the statistical method of quality control (referred to in Chapter V, page 455).

Productivity

A most important index of performance and one with which all managers are increasingly concerned, is output per man hour, usually referred to as productivity. Productivity, in the broader sense of course, is concerned with output per machine and per unit of capital employed, and it can be quite misleading to compare productivity in terms of output of labour only, between different factories or industries.[1] Since however labour is the largest item in the total cost of industry as a whole, only basic materials being extracted from the earth, obviously the effective use of it is of paramount importance. There is no common unit in which to measure output (unless the sales value of a company's product per man hour or man year be accepted and this ignores use of capital and therefore some other product of labour), and there is no universally used unit for input of labour. However, the "Standard hour" (or minute) now increasingly used in work study, can be sufficiently accurate to be acceptable as a common unit.

At least within an establishment where it is so used comparisons in productivity per standard hour can be made and should be quite reliable, particularly when comparing results past and present for the same production unit.

Control in Action

The manager of a production unit, Production Manager, Works Manager, Foreman, or whatever his status or title, must spend quite a large part of his time "controlling" the activities for which he is responsible, that is, checking performance against programme or standards and taking action to correct errors or undesirable trends. The higher a manager's position in the organisation, the more he will have to judge results from reports and other documents (such documents should therefore be designed to make deviations, shortages, excess costs, overdue items, etc., stand out from the mass of figures).

Cost control reports, presenting performance figures and analysing excess costs according to cause (described in detail on pages 375 and 376), should be used down to foremen level, the Production Manager

[1] See N.S. 38, *Higher Productivity in Manufacturing Industries* (published by International Labour Office, Geneva), for full discussion of this subject.

scrutinising them first, and discussing with his subordinates significant items, they in turn taking up in more detail with their assistants.

The Production Manager will examine other manufacturing expenditure by comparing with his Budget (see Part Four). He will have discussed this with his managers before it was agreed and will likewise discuss results with them when they are known, usually at monthly intervals. Time should not be wasted in going through every item, but thought should be given to items in excess about which something can be done. The Production Manager will also need to check, preferably weekly, output against the Planning Department's programme, and, if manufacturing to customer's delivery requirements, overdue deliveries. Failures here may involve re-arrangement of production facilities, overtime or extra shifts, or additional labour, and conferences with the managers concerned. He will also watch earnings not only as an index of performance but in order to forestall possible trouble. (Preventive action where labour relations are concerned, and especially involving earnings, is much easier than the usual lengthy and unhappy process of negotiation.) Reports on stock levels and items (purchased or finished) out-of-stock will need to be discussed with the Buyer, Storekeeper and possibly Planning Manager, and again production plans or purchasing programme may have to be adjusted with changes in material supply. Likewise, reports from the Personnel Department on absenteeism and turnover may indicate action, either in the organisation or in respect of labour recruitment.

There will be other control reports used by a particular company. The important thing is that the Production Manager should not just receive, read and file reports, but should at least frequently, if not regularly, discuss doubtful or unsatisfactory, as well as good, results with the persons responsible. In this way the reports are kept alive, and those responsible for results are concerned to do something about them. Production is under control.

GOOD MANAGEMENT

It could well be said that having pride in maintaining a standard is the hall-mark of good management. Before the standard can be maintained it must be set, and to know whether it is maintained performance must be measured. Where performance of a collection of people, an organisation, is involved, we are concerned in standards of behaviour, particularly by example. In all manifestations of management—one's own private affairs, a foreman managing a department or a manager running a large organisation—this need to set standards (aims, policies, targets, etc.) and to measure performance is inherent. The theme can be seen to run through this volume. Standards of design, quality, output, financial results and such like can be set down and measured quantitively. Although this cannot be done for such activities as general behaviour, motivation, co-ordination, consultation and co-operation, it is just as necessary to make a conscious and deliberate attempt to set a standard—a high standard. And this must be maintained—and it must be seen by all to be maintained by the manager.

Simply stated, the process of management involves the establishment of an aim or object, the setting of standards of performance (as high as practicable) revealing discrepancies and taking steps to correct such discrepancies and to improve performance. When this is carried out deliberately, continuously and successfully a manager can be said to be in control—and what is more the organisation will be in harmony and the captain will have "a happy ship".

BIBLIOGRAPHY

1. P. H. Miller: *The Practice of Engineering Estimating.* Oxford University Press, 1934
2. Anne G. Shaw: *Purpose and Practice of Motion Study.* Columbine Press, 1960
3. R. M. Currie: *Work Study.* Pitman for British Institute of Management, 1960
4. C. W. Lytle: *Job Evaluation Methods*: 2nd Edition. Ronald Press, New York, 1954
5. British Standards Institution: *Principles of Production Control, Production Control in the Small Factory, Application of Production Control* (B.S. 1100, Parts 1–3, 1943–1951). British Institute of Management.
6. W. D. Seymour: *Industrial Training for Manual Operations.* Pitman, 1954
7. F. Kay, Editor: *Purchasing.* Pitman, 1960.
8. H. G. Farquar: *Factory Stores Keeping: The Control and Storage of Materials.* McGraw-Hill, 1922
9. A. Battersby: *Guide to Stock Control.* Pitman for British Institute of Management (in press)
10. D. H. W. Allan: *Statistical Quality Control.* Reinhold, N.Y. (Chapman & Hall), 1959
11. Stafford Beer: *Cybernetics and Management.* English Universities Press, 1959
12. Department of Scientific Industrial Research: *Automation: a Report on the Technical Trends and their Impact on Management and Labour.* H.M. Stationery Office, 1956
13. G. Friedmann: *Industrial Society: the Emergence of the Human Problems of Automation.* Glencoe (Ill.), Free Press, 1955

CHAPTER I

THE PERSONNEL FUNCTIONS—THE NERVOUS SYSTEM OF THE ORGANISATION STRUCTURE

THE PERSONNEL FUNCTION

PERSONNEL management may be conveniently described as the part of the management process which is primarily concerned with the human constituents of an organisation. Its object is the maintenance of human relationships on a basis which, by consideration of the well-being of the individual, enables all those engaged in the undertaking to make their maximum personal contribution to the effective working of that undertaking. The first and very obvious implication is that it cannot possibly be something apart from or extraneous to the process of management as a whole, but is an essential element in its effectiveness, closely interrelated with that of management as a whole. Illustrations of this can only be too readily found from the annals of industry. Of what use is good personnel management when the organisation of production control is so weak that material or components do not consistently flow forward to the machining or assembly points, and accordingly prevent the operators in these shops from earning the incentive bonuses contained in the standard times? Or again, what can be the meaning of good personnel management in an organisation in which there is no stable policy, or in which no definitions of executive responsibilities are set up? To argue the reverse, viz. that no other function of management can be effective without good personnel management, is certainly correct, but it serves only to emphasise the point at issue—that the *personnel aspect or function is inherent in the process of management itself,* and in consequence is applied by all managers and supervisors throughout the organisation rather than by the Personnel Officer or his department.

Strictly speaking, the personnel function has two aspects: there is, in the first place, this responsibility attaching to all managers and supervisors for the way in which they manage their people and weld this human material into the team that carries out effectively the activities of the operating departments or sections. While this is primarily a matter of the exercise of leadership, it is also linked up with the carrying out of the established personnel policy and the smooth application of the procedures designed to secure the fulfilment of that policy. It necessarily entails on the part of the managers and supervisors an understanding of the principles of personnel management as well as close acquaintance with the personnel procedures and methods of the organisation itself. This first aspect is studied in its appropriate context later in this volume (see Chapter II of Part Five).

A "Service" Facility

The second aspect is the specialised responsibility which falls to the charge of the personnel specialist.[1] His task includes advising the company's Managing Director or General Manager, and through him the Board of Directors, on the formulation of personnel policy, and planning and supervising the procedures by which that policy is to be carried into effect. He is, as it were, the expert retained to deal with all policy, planning and methods concerning the management of people, parallel, for instance, to the engineering expert who has to deal with production policy, process layouts, engineering methods, tooling and the like, or to the chemist who is responsible for formulæ and quality standards. The Personnel Officer's responsibility entails in the main rendering a service to other managers, as well as advising them in the discharge of their own human responsibilities. He serves the other managers by many of the activities which are carried on within his own specialist department: the procedures of selecting and engaging, the records and returns, the statistics and study of absenteeism, the provision of canteen and medical services, and numerous other facilities. In the language of organisation theory, he holds a "functional responsibility" for all personnel matters.

The nearest analogy is in the human body. Personnel management is not the brain, the controller, nor only just a limb, a member, nor yet the bloodstream, the energising force. It is the nervous system. It is centred in the controlling unit of the brain, for personnel policy is a Board responsibility and is interpreted through the Managing Director. It is a two-way channel of information reaching out to every part of the body organisation: it is a live channel, not just a duct, and in some respects has automotive force. It is used in every action; if it atrophies, partial paralysis results; if it gets out of balance, there ensues instability, chaotic action, disequilibrium, which can be found in all stages of advancement, in close parallel with neurosis. But, above all this, it is inherent in the whole body and intimately associated with its every movement. The nervous system can never be thought of as an adjunct of the body—no more can personnel management be an extraneous or superimposed element

[1] See the text and footnote on page 494 for reference to the various titles used for personnel specialists.

on the structure of organisation. The personnel function lies embedded in the structure, is inherent in the dynamism of that structure, an integral part of the process of management itself.

THE AIMS OF PERSONNEL MANAGEMENT

Getting the Best out of Employees

The central purpose of the personnel function is the promotion of effectiveness of the people employed in the organisation in the performance of their allotted duties, by the substitution of co-operation in the common task in place of the suspicion and hostility which have so long been characteristic of relations between employers and employed. Put in simpler terms, this means getting the "best" out of the people by winning and maintaining their wholehearted collaboration. The personnel function does not exist for any such primary purpose as "making conditions easier" or "improving the lot of the worker": this is one of the *means*, though best regarded as one of the ordinary social responsibilities, of management. Personnel management must be among the means by which effectiveness and economy of operation are attained.

The Hawthorne Investigations

Among the research carried out, particularly in America, with a view to finding out what makes people give of their best, the most well-known programme was that carried out by the Western Electric Company of Chicago, popularly referred to as the Hawthorne experiment. This extended over many years, during which a systematic study was made of the behaviour and attitudes of groups of employees. The Company learned a great deal about the force of personal relations as a factor in management, and became aware of the influence that is exerted on the outlook and effectiveness of workers by the way in which authority over them is exercised or by the manner in which their services are appreciated or noticed.[1]

The major significant feature of the five and a half years of the Relay Assembly Room activities was the overall trend of output; the upward movement for something like three years and the following decline. One can forget for the moment the important variations within the general trend or the specific motivating forces at given stages and take only the broad curve. As to the final downward phase, we have the known evidence of one of the girls herself: "We lost our pride" was her own comment. For the earlier years the little team of workers had been the centre of interest for the whole factory, for its

---

[1] For a review of the whole programme, see *The Making of Scientific Management*, Vol. III, by L. Urwick and E. F. L. Brech (Pitman, London, 1948).

top executives, for a University Department, almost for a whole nation. "We mattered . . ." was the dominant emotion in the minds of those whose work lay in the glare of the limelight; and thus unfettered by regulative restrictions, and fostered by being consulted and expected to contribute to their own government, the subconscious power of contentment and achievement drove them to ever higher levels of physical effort and an upward streaming output curve. Even when physical working conditions were taken down to the lowest levels, output soared to unprecedented heights. "We mattered . . .", the impetus of interest and group loyalty devoted to a common purpose—not deliberate or conscious, but directed simply by unthwarted emotions harnessed in the service of the group.

Then came the turn. With the deepening of depression even an experiment in living human beings could not continue to absorb attention. Problems of output and markets began to claim more and more of the light, and as conditions worsened, the fear of unemployment—following in the wake of friends and colleagues—threw its ugly shadow ahead. Surely in these circumstances more earnings were essential to provide the standby for the threatening idleness. But the irrational emotion is stronger than the rational logic—output began to fall despite the financial incentives available. What was happening? "We were losing our pride—we were ceasing to matter."

An earlier investigation on different lines, but pointing in the same direction, was Matthewson's study of restriction of output among workers in a number of American factories. Some of his findings are almost unbelievable, and most of them are incomprehensible unless we have a belief in the influence of human emotions and feelings. All through the descriptions and analysis of the restriction of output by the spontaneous action of groups of workers, we are brought face to face with a new logic. What impels these workers to withhold their work and thus deliberately curtail their own earnings, building up elaborate precautions to attain the restriction—is not so much bitter individual experience, but a "belief" that management will cut down their rates, or a "feeling" that they will not be allowed to earn more than a given sum, or a "feeling" of improving their own security—when, in point of *fact*, they might be driving the organisation into bankruptcy. Once again the motivating force is found in emotional reactions, and lowered effectiveness is seen as a direct result of lack of good relations and consultations between management and employees.

These illustrations point right to the heart of the personnel function—the human being has powerful innate forces of an emotional kind; he has desires that are akin to the instinctive. These forces influence his behaviour both as an individual and as a member of the group.

They may be thwarted—and so make him a restricted collaborator, or even an unwitting saboteur. On the other hand, they can be harnessed, and thus weld him into a group as an active contributor, and so become an important element in achieving high morale. The task of personnel management lies just here—to harness, to weld, to foster human energies and emotions for the attainment of the purposes of the organisation, to the benefit of employees themselves, of the company, and—most important of all—of the community of which it forms a part.

THE PERSONNEL DEPARTMENT'S POSITION IN THE COMPANY STRUCTURE

In effect, the Personnel Manager's or Officer's task entails discharging a part of the responsibility of the chief executive himself. Put into other words, his is a "general management" function, and all his actions are really carried out on behalf of the General Manager. His position is simply an illustration of the ordinary principle of specialisation, the General Manager passing over to a suitably qualified person certain aspects of his own responsibility, in which expert knowledge and assistance are called for. As a consequence, it can be argued that a Personnel Manager's correct location in the organisation structure is that of "Personal Assistant to the Chief Executive", i.e. serving in "staff relation" to him. That he has both a functional responsibility to discharge in respect of the other sections of the organisation, and a direct responsibility in relation to the activities covered by his own Department, does not in any way detract from or interfere with this conception in principle, even though in practice it may be both customary and convenient to find the personnel specialist shown in an ordinary "line" executive position in the structure. This is likely to persist until such time as the principles of organisation are more fully appreciated throughout industry. Normally, the Personnel Officer must be responsible to the chief executive of the organisation. Nothing is to be read into this as regards personal status or salary: it is meant solely in terms of executive responsibility. There is, of course, a very strong case for the view that the personnel executive *ought* to be of the calibre to carry a place on the "top line".

No matter how small the company, whether employing twenty persons or two thousand, the managerial function of "personnel" must be performed. Employees have to be recruited and paid; they must have provision made for their food and drink; someone has to deal with their complaints; lavatories and cloakrooms have to be provided, and so on—the personnel work is there, even if frequently not in sufficient volume to require a full-time official. The point of growth at which it becomes necessary or desirable to appoint a full-time official cannot be laid down as a hard-and-fast rule. A number of employees of 400–500 is often quoted as a useful minimum, though in times of special employment difficulties firms with as few as 200 employees have found a specialist Personnel Officer invaluable, and numerous instances can be cited from among firms employing fewer than 150.

There is no set standard of personnel management. It varies from one works to another, or from one type of industry to another. Frequently it is practised more successfully in family concerns, where there is a long history of good individual relations than in the larger-scale organisation or nationalised concern, despite the existence in the latter of considerable formal attention to personnel activities and procedures. Variations in scope of activity are matched by variety of title: here it is "Employment Manager", there "Labour Superintendent", elsewhere "Labour Relations Manager", or "Welfare Officer". Yet, there may be little or no difference in the responsibilities carried out. Gradually the title of "Personnel Manager" or "Personnel Officer" has been gaining ground, and some degree of conformity is beginning to emerge in regard to the main lines of activity undertaken.[1]

The function of the Personnel Department is twofold—it is advisory and yet executive: *advisory* in the help that it gives to managers and supervisors in the daily discharge of their human responsibilities, and *executive* in the activities that it carries out and the services that it renders. As an illustration for a contribution to efficiency and for the benefit of employees, take the case of lighting in a manufacturing department. It is the Personnel Department's duty to ensure that conditions are of a certain standard, partly because the law requires it to be so, but more important because adequate lighting is an essential to effective work. Suppose in a certain company workers complain about the light, possibly to a member of the personnel staff while making a periodic visit to the factory. That official takes the point up with the departmental manager or foreman, tests are made to ascertain the quality of light, and perhaps the results do show a poor standard. The matter is for remedy—it may involve a complete overhaul of lighting in the department, or it may mean altering only one lamp. The action of the Personnel Department has been a service

---

[1] In the present text, the terms "Personnel Manager" and "Personnel Officer" will be used indiscriminately, with precisely the same significance. The other terms will not be used. The habitual reference in the MASCULINE gender is nothing more than a *matter of textual convenience*. It in no way suggests lack of appreciation of the excellent responsible personnel service rendered by many hundreds of women Personnel Officers up and down the country. Similarly, save where specifically called for otherwise, reference to the employee(s) is in the masculine form.

to the employees, and perhaps advisory to the electrical section in indicating the standard of illumination recommended for that particular job, leaving the electrical people to decide the means of attaining the standard and to give the instructions for the work to be carried out.

The responsibilities and status of the Personnel Officer will also vary from one firm to another, for they must depend largely on the circumstances of the organisation. But the general principle of reporting to the chief executive can always be preserved. In the following diagram the Works Manager, the Sales Manager and the Personnel Officer are all responsible to the General Manager, and all three have equal status. It is unlikely that the Personnel Manager's salary will be as high as those of the Works Manager or Sales Manager, but he has the same direct line of approach to the General Manager in the discharge of his responsibilities:

In another case, the status of the Personnel Officer is at the level of the Assistant Works Manager, but he still has direct access to the General Manager; in other words, the importance of his function is recognised, even though conditions require him to have a more junior status:

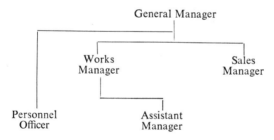

Dealing with other Managers

Questions of discipline and working conditions throw further light on the position of the Personnel Manager. The employee in a job is responsible to his chargehand, foreman or manager. Undoubtedly, were the Personnel Manager, during his walks round the factory or office departments, to observe anything wrong—such as unsafe conditions, time wasting, etc.—he would report it to the foreman or the manager of the particular section, and not try to give instructions or reprimand to the employee. A good Personnel Officer will at all times make the position so clear that there is never any doubt in the minds of his colleagues as to his intentions or any cause for doubt that he is endeavouring "to do their job" or "to undermine their authority". The Personnel Manager exercises "line" control only over the specialised activities which come within his direct jurisdiction: in a large organisation, such sections as those of the Employment Manager, the Canteen Manager, the Education Officer, the Safety Officer and Sports Secretary. The position of a full-time Medical Officer raises some difficulty, because of the medical profession's feeling that etiquette requires their direct report to the Managing Director, in regard to the medical service in the organisation, though a Personnel Manager would be responsible for the day-to-day routine and procedures connected with the medical services. This attitude is due to a failure to appreciate organisation principle—the Medical Department is part of the personnel activity, and the Medical Officer should be seen as a specialist consultant advising the Personnel Manager, and through him the Managing Director.

The arrangement of responsibility of the Personnel Manager and the status which he is given reflect a great deal on the way in which he can do his work. He must be able to deal with the other managers on a basis of a "Staff Officer", irrespective of his status in the company being inferior to those with whom he must discuss policy and give guidance on personnel matters. To do this successfully he needs to know that he has the complete sympathy and support of the Managing Director or the head of the concern, and, by his own personality and strength of leadership, be able to attain agreement with his colleagues on everyday problems. Whenever this is not so, he should always obtain "agreement to differ", he cannot allow friction to develop between a manager or foreman and himself or any member of his team. Similarly, there must be no feeling that he is condescending to give information or that he is withholding information to prop up his own importance. He must always be frank and make a strong point of keeping foremen or managers aware of negotiations or developments which may be going on in reference to members of their department. In his general day-to-day life, he must also be careful never to do things which are prohibited to other people by the code of rules or regulations.

A good Personnel Manager is generally popular with the employees in the factory and offices and with all whom he comes into contact. Cheap popularity can be obtained by propping up the bar in the local pub, but this type of "hail fellow, well met" popularity is not the kind which a Personnel Manager should seek. He should try to be scrupulously fair in his dealings with employees, ready and willing to give assistance to any member of his supervisory staff, sufficiently near to the ground to be able to talk to the man at the bench and the girl at her desk, about their problems in a way which inspires confidence and respect. He should have an inexhaustible fund of patience, and be prepared time after time to build his castles, see them smashed to pieces, and yet be ready to start all over again in another way. Above all, he needs to be completely impartial, and make it apparent in everything he does that he is unbiased. Decisions on any matter on which his advice is requested and in which it is his duty to intervene should be given only after an investigation of the facts and without fear and favour to either party.

Finally, the status of the Personnel Officer cannot be made by flowery language or extravagant claims of his importance; neither will he be able to function effectively unless he has the support of the chief executive on a policy which is genuinely seeking sound relationships with the employees, and accepted by all members of the management.

*   *   *

The following principles have been laid down by one authoritative writer as a guide to the place of the personnel executive in organisation:

1. Personnel management can never be completely isolated as a function. It is concerned with good industrial relations in the broadest sense. Consequently its results accrue in every contact between representatives of the management and their colleagues and subordinates. It cannot therefore be entirely "specialised". It should permeate every corner of the undertaking and every managerial action. On the other hand, there must be some specialisation if the undertaking is to remain up to date.
2. The determination of the personnel policy must therefore be a central function, the responsibility of the administrative authority (the Board), which looks to the chief executive to see that it is carried out.
3. The execution of that policy must also be a central function, since it penetrates every other function of the organisation. This is to say, if a specialised personnel manager is appointed, he should be responsible directly either to the administrative authority (the Board) or to the chief executive.
4. This does not imply that he need be equal in status to any other executive of second rank in the undertaking. The function is one with which the chief executive must concern himself personally to an exceptional degree (*vide* 6 below). If it is clear that the Personnel Manager speaks with his authority, the question of relative status is unimportant.

5. The Personnel Manager should be in direct "line" control of all units in the organisation specialising in various aspects of personnel work—employment, medical, welfare, etc.

6. There are, however, three aspects of personnel work—general relations between the undertaking and its employees, trade union negotiations and the development and promotion of higher executives—which are of such a character that they can only be handled effectively in the last resort by the chief executive directly. Where a Personnel Manager assists a chief executive in the preliminary stages of such matters, he should act in a "staff" capacity.

7. In order to secure uniformity of policy and integration of action in personnel questions between large production departments, branches, etc., and the Personnel Manager and the specialised personnel units, specialised personnel assistants should be appointed in such departments or branches. Such personnel assistants should be directly responsible to the manager concerned (a line relationship), but should be responsible to the Personnel Manager for training methods, etc. (a functional relationship).[1]

RESPONSIBILITIES OF THE PERSONNEL DEPARTMENT

One cannot closely define the activities of the Personnel Manager because of their variety and scope. One interesting summary is given in Fig. 77 opposite. How these activities are carried out in practice forms the matter of the remainder of this Part.

The smaller organisations often present interesting illustrations. Take the case of a factory employing 300 people, where the Personnel Officer is responsible for engaging both operating and clerical employees. With the assistance of a secretary or a junior clerk, he keeps all the records (using only a single card index); looks after the half-dozen apprentices, arranging with the local technical college their different courses; takes visitors round the plant when they come either by invitation of the Managing Director or Sales Department; in addition, he is responsible for seeing that no unauthorised person gets into the factory during the day-time, controls the commissionaire, issues clean overalls on Monday morning, makes up the pay cards, and finally, acts as the wages clerk on Friday night by helping the clerk in the Accounts Department to prepare and issue the pay packets. The number of applicants he would interview for employment would probably be very small, and the majority of his time could be devoted to doing these other tasks, while as long as morale remained good he would not be heavily occupied in dealing with terminations of employment.

[1] Extracted from "Personnel Management in Relation to Factory Organisation," by L. Urwick; published as a broadsheet of the Institute of Personnel Management.

FUNCTIONS OF A PERSONNEL DEPARTMENT[1]

Employment	Wages	Joint Consultation	Health and Safety	Welfare Employee Services	Education and Training
Liaison with Ministry of Labour and sources of supply.	Maintenance of Company's accepted wage structure.	Act as Negotiating Officer with Trade Unions.	Application of provisions of Factories Act.	Administration of Canteen Policy.	Training of new starters, apprentices, employees for transfer and promotion, instructors, supervisors.
Interview applicants, engagements, transfers, releases, dismissals.	Authorise changes in individual rates.	Knowledge of Conciliation and Arbitration procedure.	Contact with Factory Inspector.	Sick Club and Benevolent Schemes.	Encourage additional education through Day Continuation Schools, Attendance at Technical and Evening Institutes, Evening Classes, Lectures, Films, Dramatic, Musical and other societies.
Introduction of new starters to foremen.	Assessment and control of differential rates and special payments.	Maintain and improve machinery for Joint Consultations, i.e. Joint Production Committees and Works Committees, etc.	Works Medical Services.	Long-service Grants.	
Follow-up of new starters	Workroom and individual efficiencies.	Maintain and improve procedure for ventilating and dealing with workroom grievances.	Arrange (in co-operation with Medical Service): Medical Exam. of employees, Health Records, Supervision of hazardous jobs, Sick Visiting, Convalescence.	Pension and Superannuation Funds or Leave Grants.	Supervision and control of Notice Boards and Information Bulletins.
Maintenance of employee records.	Consultation with time study or outside consultants in respect of incentives.	Interpret and ensure understanding of Company personnel policy.	Fatigue studies and Rest pauses.	Granting of Loans.	Suggestion schemes.
Personnel statistics.	Authorisation of deductions from wages.	Advise and counsel junior staff and employees in collective dealing.	Accident Prevention and supervision of Safety Committees, Systematic Plant Inspection, Safety Education, Investigation of Accidents, Accident Statistics, etc.	Legal Aid.	Works Tours.
Employee interviews and consultations.		Act as Company representative in outside negotiations affecting personnel.	Administration of Workmen's Compensation.	Advice on individual problems.	Library.
Grading of employees.				Assist employees in Transport, Housing, Billeting, Shopping and other problems.	Works Magazine.
Hours of work and overtime.				Provision of social and recreational facilities.	
Legislation relating to employment.				Supervision of Committees, Red Cross, National Savings, Welfare of employees, etc.	
Attendance at appropriate Committees relating to employment.					

[1] Extracted from the broadsheet of the Institute of Personnel Management, by G. R. Moxon.

FIG. 77.

In contrast, take a large organisation with a number of factories spread throughout the country. Here we should expect to find a central Personnel Department controlled by a high-ranking executive, possibly serving as a member of the Board. His job would be the interpretation and maintenance of company policy, advising on the attitude the company should adopt in Trade Union negotiations, alterations in conditions, rates, bonus, and so on. He might have three or four Personnel Officers to deal with day-to-day activities and a large staff to look after routine matters, records and statistics, the operation of training schemes, supplemented by specialists for health, safety and first-aid. Each of the factories would have a responsible Personnel Manager on the site, with a close link with the central Personnel Department on matters of policy. In such an instance, the local Personnel Officer would probably be responsible for receiving requests for labour and supplying by promotion or engagement the people necessary to the production or service departments. It would be his job to contact the Employment Exchanges, advertise and take other necessary action to fill the vacancies, to interview applicants for employment and deal with people who wished to leave.

On the clerical side, most of the work may be covered by a Staff Manager; he or she would be responsible for engaging all clerical staff and would assist the Personnel Manager when appointments of a senior kind were being made. At set periods during the year the Staff Manager would prepare lists and, in conjunction with the departmental manager or section head, recommend to the appropriate Manager increases in pay or bonuses where they were paid. Separate records would be kept by the Staff Manager in regard to the clerical employees, and he would also be expected to examine the methods of work and to suggest improvements or economies whenever appropriate.

Interpreting the Company's Policy

Interpreting the company's employment policy is one of the major functions of the Personnel Manager. The company's policy is, of course, decided by the Board of Directors and sent through the Managing Director to all executives, managers and supervisors, for them to carry out. Some comply with the spirit of the policy, while others may become rigid and pedantic, interested more in the letter and in compliance with rules and regulations. This is particularly so where Trade Union consultation is newly accepted, and members of management have an "anti-union" attitude, which leads them to take the law into their own hands, completely ignoring the fact that the Board have entered into a local or national agreement with the Trade Unions. This is where the personnel specialist can exercise a valuable educational influence, and can also play a very big part in co-ordinating the executives' and supervisors' response to the Board's lead.

The company's personnel policy should be clearly defined and opportunity should be given for those whose responsibility it is to administer the policy to have their say in what shall or shall not be done, before the Board reaches a final decision. The Personnel Manager can also serve as a two-way channel of communication, so that employees too can have an opportunity of contributing to policy. In some organisations a Joint Consultative Committee serves this purpose in a more formal way. But it remains the task of the personnel specialist to ensure that whatever is decided by the company should always be made known throughout the works, either by public notices or through the managers and supervisors.

The value of a sound personnel policy cannot be over-estimated. It does not mean lavish expenditure, or spectacular welfare amenities. It means broad lines of guidance for managers and foremen, to encourage them to maintain standards of justice and supervision which will keep morale on a high level and so contribute to effectiveness of operation.

As an illustration of what a statement of personnel policy can include, the following schedule is reproduced: [1]

A. *Aims*

    (1) To enable the organisation to fulfil or carry out the main items which have been laid down as the desirable minima of general industrial employment policy.

    (2) To ensure that the employees of an organisation are fully informed on these main items of policy and to ensure co-operation in their attainment.

    (3) To provide within the organisation such conditions of employment and procedures as will enable all employees to develop a sincere sense of unity with the enterprise and to carry out their duties in the most willing and effective manner.

    (4) To provide the organisation continuously with adequate, competent and suitable personnel for all levels and types of occupations required.

B. *Principles*

    (1) To establish and maintain a Personnel Management function, responsible to the chief executive, and adequately financed for the fulfilment of its responsibilities.

        As a corollary, the broad lines of the Personnel Policy of the

---

[1] Extracted from a *Report on the Administrative and Executive Problems in the Transition from War to Peace* (Appendix I), published by the London Centre of the Institute of Industrial Administration, 1945 (now the British Institute of Management).

organisation should be defined by the Board of Directors on a parity of importance with other major aspects of policy.

(2) To guarantee to all employees a right of personal and confidential access to the personnel executive(s) or the executive acting in that capacity.

(3) To afford the greatest possible degree of stability in employment. This implies:

(a) Opportunity of permanent and continuous employment for competent employees.

(b) Adequate and objective methods of selection prior to engagement and of review during employment.

(c) The provision of appropriate training facilities (within or without the enterprise) to enable employees to secure the competence required—

(i) for effective performance of duties; and

(ii) for promotion when so selected.

(d) The filling of senior vacancies by up-grading and promotion so long as actually or potentially competent candidates are available.

(e) A guarantee against unfair dismissal.

(f) Adequate consideration of the influence of the employment on the organisation's policies and plans regarding production and distribution, so as to avoid employee displacement so far as is at all possible.

(4) To observe the recognised standards of Fair Wages. (This would not preclude the determination of standard Job Classifications and Base Rates or the operation of Output and other Bonus Schemes, provided they fall within the definition of Fair Wages.)

(5) To encourage fairness in the maintenance of discipline and to encourage employees to accept responsibility for discipline.

(6) To maintain a high level of working conditions, but regarding as a minimum the fulfilment—in letter and spirit—of the Factories Acts and other industrial Legislation and Regulations, with particular reference to adequate provision for the prevention of accidents, the rendering of first-aid, and the safeguarding and maintenance of health.

(7) To establish effective procedures for regular consultation between management and employees, in a genuine desire to keep employees fully informed of all matters bearing on their employment and to enable them to contribute to the effective management of the enterprise.

(8) To welcome and accord full freedom of association in membership of Trade Unions, but to accord equality of treatment to members and non-members alike.

(9) To assist employees in the development of social, educational and recreational amenities, and to encourage their collaboration with nationally or regionally established facilities; also to avoid the provision of amenities as an inducement to employment.

(10) To maintain these aims and principles of personnel policy without discrimination—though with the necessary differences of application—in respect of all types and grades of employees, using that term in its widest sense.

Negotiations

An important phase of the Personnel Manager's work is his participation in labour negotiations on behalf of his company. These may be of the informal kind at shop-floor level, involving discussions with a shop steward and a foreman, or of the more formal kind laid down in various Trade Union agreements. To some extent, of course, the greater part of the Personnel Manager's week is spent in discussions with individuals or groups of employees, but the more formal negotiations place on him a particularly important responsibility, which he carries on behalf of the chief executive.

The following case illustrates the significance of this responsibility:

In a London works, some 150 men were employed on a shift basis on production. The shop steward of the production departments and his deputy approached the foreman about an arrangement they would like to make during the Easter holiday. The suggestion was that instead of working on Monday, Tuesday, Wednesday and Thursday nights and finishing at 6 a.m. on Good Friday morning, the men should start work on the Sunday night, and thus be able to have as holiday from the end of the Wednesday night shift until the following Tuesday night, when they were due to return to work. The foreman, in discussing this with the stewards, said he could see no objection so far as he was concerned, and provided the four shifts were worked during the week it was immaterial to him on which nights the men came in. A few days later the Personnel Manager was approached by the head of the department, who repeated what had taken place between the foreman and men, and said that he was in agreement as, of course, it would mean they could clean down on the Thursday afternoon instead of having to employ an additional shift on the Friday for this purpose; he asked that the Personnel Manager should round off the matter with his shop stewards and give confirmation that the company had agreed.

A meeting was arranged, at which two stewards and two of the men from the shift were present. At the outset it was pointed out that this alteration was at their own specific request, and favourable consideration would be given to it in order that, firstly, the men might have the longer holiday, and secondly, as it would avoid some of the workers having to hang about on the Good Friday waiting for transport before they could get home. The Personnel Manager agreed to ascertain what other factors were involved before announcing the decision. He then found that in addition to the production workers, who received a fixed amount as a shift differential, there was an electrician, a fitter and a boilerman on the shift with varying ways of payment, so that three other unions would need to be consulted before agreement could be reached. The shop stewards of the various unions were then approached, but they immediately objected. Their first objection was that the negotiations had been conducted piecemeal, that they were parties to the Agreement covering shift work in the same way as were the production people, and had been ignored. Further, if work was started on the Sunday night, their National Agreement provided for payment at double time, whereas the production people could only claim time and a half in view of the Agreement in that industry; it was doubtful whether their District Organiser would agree to the fitter participating in this arrangement, particularly as the management had already accepted the offer of the production workers to do the additional shift without consulting them. The steward of the Electrical Union repeated the comments of his engineering colleagues. Suspicion was aroused in the minds of the maintenance workers that the negotiations which had taken place between the production workers and the management had been carried out in this way so as to "force" the maintenance people into accepting the time and a half instead of double time.

The matter was sorted out in due course—the night shift was worked, and everyone paid at their proper rate of overtime according to the agreed conditions, but not before there had been a good deal of high feeling generated.

The lesson to be learned from this example is to ensure that, before negotiations are entered into on any subject, enquiries are made so that everyone who could possibly be a party to the negotiations is represented from the start. A Personnel Manager alive to his job would take such precautions almost as a matter of course. Equal care needs to be taken to make sure that answers or decisions given in negotiations do not conflict with agreements or arrangements already entered into. Many so-called "local agreements" are in fact never written down, but have been accepted as valid by dint of long observance.

Representation on Committees

Very frequently—if not customarily—the Personnel Officer is a management representative on consultative committees functioning within the organisation. He has also often to sit on official or unofficial committees outside as company's representative. In other words, active membership of deliberating groups can be a substantial element in the Personnel Manager's daily work. He needs, therefore, to be broadly familiar with committee procedure, and to train himself to be a constructive participant in such gatherings.

FINANCIAL BUDGET FOR PERSONNEL DEPARTMENT

The principle of setting a financial budget for the personnel management function does not appear so far to have secured any widespread recognition; neither does there appear to have been any consistent action in the recording and control of the cost of a personnel department, and it is difficult to obtain any reliable evidence as to the general amount of money spent by companies on this function.

Some guide may be found from investigations made within recent years by the *Industrial Welfare Society* which produced the following overall summary from 49 firms submitting replies:

	Costs for Median Firm		Highest Percentage figure for any firm
	Per employee £ per annum	Percentage of total remuneration*	
Personnel Department salaries (incl. Welfare and Safety staff) . . .	£3 16 10	0·66	
Other direct costs . .	£1 12 8	0·28	
Total Personnel Department	£5 9 6	0·94	2·20
Medical Department salaries	£1 5 8	0·22	
Other direct costs . .	5 10	0·05	
Total Medical Department .	£1 11 6	0·27	0·74
Grand Totals . . .	£7 1 0	1·21	—

*The median total remuneration in the sample was £582 p.a., including all cash bonuses and holiday pay.

The firms submitting the data varied in size from 253 to 18,010 employees. The costs included in the summary covered normal "personnel administration" as well as Medical service, Safety section (even in those firms where it was not part of the Personnel Department), the Education and Training section (administration and clerical only), the Welfare service (excluding canteens, sports ground personnel and magazine editors). The full results may be seen in the

Industrial Welfare Society's pamphlet entitled *"the £ s. d. of Welfare in Industry."*

One important factor which needs to be borne in mind is that a number of the costs which are borne by the personnel management function would still be incurred and absorbed in the general costs of management or administration even if the Personnel Department did not exist. There is no sound reason why the activities of personnel management should not be costed and appropriate financial standards set, so that current expense can be controlled. Working on a budget basis, with need for specific permission to go outside the budget figure, would be one practical way.

No hard-and-fast rule can be laid down, and each individual concern would have to decide for itself a satisfactory financial level which would be justified by the contribution which personnel management makes to the effectiveness of management as a whole.

CHAPTER II

INDUSTRIAL RELATIONS

IT would not be untrue to say that "industrial relations" is but another term for "personnel management", the emphasis being placed on the aspect of employee relationships rather than on the executive policies and activities that are set up to foster good relations. Both are also closely allied to morale, which may be described as a readiness to co-operate warmly in the tasks and purposes of a given group or organisation. High morale makes for effective work and economical operation. High morale is a by-product of good industrial relations, which in turn are among the consequences of sound personnel management. In few British firms is there found a department specifically concerned with industrial relations as a distinct phase of personnel work. Special attention has, however, been given to this aspect by the Ministry of Labour where an Industrial Relations Department exists. This consists of a Headquarters Staff and a Staff of Conciliation Officers in each of the regions into which the country is divided. It is the duty of this staff to keep in close touch with all industrial developments. The main functions of the Industrial Relations Department are:

(1) Assistance in the formation and maintenance of joint voluntary machinery in industry.
(2) The prevention and settlement of trade disputes.
(3) Maintaining continuous touch with the state of relations between employers and workpeople.

The Headquarters Staff are also responsible for:

(4) The examination of all questions brought to the notice of the Government in regard to the relations between the employers and workpeople.
(5) The tendering of advice to Governmental Departments on industrial relations questions in general, and in respect of their responsibilities for wages and working conditions either on contracts or in respect of direct labour in their employment.

The normal methods by which the Ministry of Labour renders assistance in the prevention and settlement of industrial disputes are

507

based on the legislative authority of the Conciliation Act, 1896, and the Industrial Courts Acts, 1919, and may be summarised as:

(1) Conciliation.
(2) Arbitration.
(3) Investigation by formal enquiry.

MORALE AND CONSULTATION

Morale.—Management's responsibility for the promotion of morale is not a new development in industry. Even in the days of master craftsmen, the man had to be encouraged to give the highest value to his employer, by applying his knowledge and skill to the making of the article which the employer hoped to sell in order to pay wages and make his profit. At the time he was making the article he knew whom it was for, why he was making it, what sort of a job it would be used on, how much the master would charge, how much the material cost, and where it would come from. In all probability his work would be discussed at the local hostelry during the evening. Because he knew what he was doing, and why, and appreciated his significance in the chain of events, he could have a sense of pride and participation in his work—his morale was high. There is no fundamental difference today in dealing with morale—the atmosphere or spirit of an organisation; the happiness of its members; co-operation of one executive or one workman with another, and the indefinable "something" which impels the human being to work with a will or to do as *little* as possible in the available time—all is influenced by the outlook towards the job in hand and the general spirit of the workplace.

What are the factors which contribute towards a happy and successful organisation? The factors which the employee expects to be taken into consideration and on which he bases his value of the job in a factory or office? They are:

(a) Security.
(b) Good wages.
(c) Opportunity.
(d) Justice.
(e) Status.
(f) To know.
(g) Leadership.
(h) Getting the job done.
(i) Pride of product, etc.
(j) Suggestions schemes.
(k) Joint consultation.

(a) Security

One of the most important desires of an employee is to feel secure in his job, to know that at the end of each week he has a certain income, itself a foundation on which to build his future, and around which he can establish his home, the upbringing of his children and his social life. For centuries to come, industry will remember the devastation caused in the country in the 1930s; men who were unable to obtain work for years or who managed to do only a minimum of two or three days a week, the balance of time being what was known as "on the dole".

Many employees think it is better to have a steady job in an industry which is not likely to be seriously affected at times of trade depression than being able intermittently to earn very high wages for a shorter period. The prospects of full employment in this country in recent years have tended to lessen the desire for security in one particular firm, because of the opportunities which exist elsewhere, and owing to a shortage of labour, many more jobs are available than there are people to fill them in certain areas.

(b) Good Wages

The employee of today expects to be paid a wage, firstly, which is nationally agreed between his employer and the union; secondly, which will be sufficient to provide for his family at a reasonable level of subsistence, including entertainment and a modicum of savings. He does not necessarily work for the employer who pays the highest starting rate, but is much more concerned with the long-term prospect and opportunity for earning higher wages as a result of his own individual effort. *Good employers* emphasise the opportunity of bonus earnings based on sound incentive schemes. Good wages are an important contribution to a happy factory.

(c) Opportunity

A large percentage of employees never wish to do other than remain in their normal jobs, skilled in their trade; operatives often refuse promotion because of reluctance to undertake the additional responsibility. But there are others again for whom the opportunity of growth in responsibility and scope is an important stimulus, men whose morale is impaired if their chance of promotion is arbitrarily blocked. There is also a widespread social satisfaction felt when a fellow employee is promoted to a supervisory or managerial position. The wise employer will provide such opportunities for those who are able and willing to accept them.

The procedure of filling vacant posts is, of course, a matter closely bound up in the company's policy, and no strict ruling can be laid down. Differences in circumstances and conditions have to be taken into account; for instance, even in a company which normally promotes from within, at certain times it is conceivable that owing to expansion there are not available on the staff candidates adequately qualified for a given post, and in consequence an outsider, suitably skilled, would need to be engaged. The prospect of promotion only on length of service, on the basis of "waiting for dead men's shoes", is bad in any industrial undertaking. Even the most recent member of a department should be made to feel that the company is always on the lookout for eager and ambitious employees who are willing to move about from one job to another, and in the process to expand their knowledge as a prelude to improving their position.

(d) Justice

Justice in dealing with industrial conditions and discipline is now much more common than it was even a few years ago, largely due to the influence of the Trade Unions as well as a more enlightened outlook on the part of managers and employers. During the war years, the Essential Work Orders made it impossible to discharge or suspend an employee without good and valid reason. It was no longer possible to dismiss an employee without clearly defined reasons, adequate to stand examination before an Appeal Board, consisting of an independent chairman and a representative from a Trade Union and from an employers' organisation. This procedure did a great deal to get rid of arbitrary and ill-considered dismissals, and to promote a more tolerant attitude to alleged breaches of regulations or refusal to work to instructions.

The shortage of labour since then has always contributed to an improvement in the attitude of managers and a greater sense of justice in the control of factory and office discipline. The extent to which this more positive atmosphere contributes to the enhancement of morale and so to a better working spirit is widely recognised from practical experience gained in recent years.

(e) Status

The employee likes to feel that, in the eyes of his foreman and manager, he is regarded as having an important and responsible contribution to make to the work and progress of the organisation. He is also jealous of his skill, his craft, his status, or if in the ranks of supervision, of his responsibility. Recognition of this expectation can be a valuable factor to morale. The more important an employee can be made to feel, the better work he is likely to do.

(f) *To Know*

The communicating of information is one of the best ways of improving morale. Being "in the know" promotes co-operation, both because it gives the employee an understanding of what is going on, and because it encourages a sense of participation, of recognition.

(g) *Leadership*

In the Navy they use the expression "a happy ship" to denote a high level of morale in the ship's company. The "happy ship" is brought about in the first instance by the captain and his officers, who are all determined to make conditions on board pleasant and enjoyable, despite the handicaps of physical limitation and the trials and tribulations of battle. The captain of a ship is in a very similar position to that of a Managing Director or General Manager in an industrial undertaking. From him must come the example. His attitude will set the tone and his actions will be copied down to the lower levels of supervision. The way in which he deals with people will set the standard for relationships amongst individuals throughout the company. His sense of respect for the employees, the interest he takes in the individual's problems, his appearance at social functions or his friendly words while walking through the factory, afford a pattern which will rapidly improve the worker/employer relationships throughout the organisation. Some organisations are too vast for the Managing Director to be more than a figure-head, and in these the responsibility depends on the senior executives in charge of the operating units. The importance of the influence of the men at the top cannot be over-emphasised as a factor making for high— or low—morale. A large element in the skill of management at all levels is the capacity to get subordinates to give of their best in the team. Much of the capacity depends on personal attitude—the genuine willingness to develop in everyday contacts with subordinates the spirit of "informal consultation" will bring in its train the sense of "participation".

(h) *Getting the Job Done*

Planning may produce the machines, the materials and all the necessary tools—they may all be on the spot in their right places at the right time—but getting the best out of people in their day-to-day lives is not by any means so easy a job. The variety of factors which make a human being decide not to start work, or to go slow, or to refuse to work, are all due to influence of mind and emotion. If the lead from the mind produces a negative attitude, the work will not be done or will be done poorly.

One of the special fields of personnel management is to ascertain "what makes the worker like—or not like—to work" and to be in a position to advise other executives or supervisors on this all-important subject. One factor known to be of special significance is the attitude and outlook of the supervisor himself—the way in which he speaks to the men and women, his response when asked for information, assistance or advice, the impression he gives by his own everyday behaviour in the department, and the confidence he instils in the employees with whom he is associated. His influence probably contributes more than anything else to the attitude which the worker adopts towards his job and to the company in general.

Supervisors vary considerably, and it is impossible to lay down a formula which will produce the ideal. There are, however, common types frequently met in industry: the easy-going, happy-go-lucky individual who takes life very much as it comes, who never has cause to complain about the work, and has the knack of getting up a sense of enthusiasm in people; he criticises when necessary, in a friendly way, sometimes in a half-bantering, half-joking manner; yet while he disciplines his workers, they retain an affectionate regard for him— " 'Old so-and-so' is a jolly decent fellow to work for"! When things are difficult or production becomes more urgent, then usually he is able to ask for—and get—from each individual that extra little effort which collectively means so much. When it comes to a social function of any kind he can throw off his day-time responsibility and enjoy the fun and games with the rest. One cannot define what the peculiar "something" is that goes to make up this type of supervisor, but his presence in a factory is readily recognised.

The other common type stands in marked contrast—often a highly skilled technician and more knowledgeable than the one we have previously discussed, but the employees in his department avoid going to him on any personal matter: they prefer to seek the advice of the shop stewards or take some other line of approach. The happy atmosphere is missing, few smiles appear, and there is a tenseness about the department because the men and women are too acutely alive to a sense of "being supervised", expected to work on without regard to their personal problems and difficulties, and governed by a man whose main interest lies in the slide rule and the stop watch, and how much he can get out in how little time. To be caught missing from the machine or bench means a "ticking off", and even minor faults mean "the carpet" and a serious reprimand. Inevitably, employee turnover in such a department will be considerably higher, absence greater, and requests for transfers to other departments frequent whenever a pretext offers an opportunity. When that extra spurt is needed, there is nothing more to come, for the real enjoyment of work is missing. At social events, this same type of person is conspicuous by his absence, or if there, makes a hasty exit as soon as possible on some flimsy excuse, but mainly because he feels his position so important that he will jeopardise his dignity by remaining in so informal an atmosphere with men and women who are formally his subordinates.

What the supervisor is may seem at first to be a topic far removed from personnel management. So long as this function is thought of in terms of the records and activities of the Personnel Department, the relations may be difficult to grasp. When it is accepted as belonging equally to the managers and foremen, their influence on morale is among the most important factors in the human element of management—especially as it bears on getting the job done, and getting it done effectively and economically.

(i) Pride of Job, Product and Company

The importance of the human relationship factor brings in its train a danger, the danger of encouraging unnecessary sentiment and emotional mollycoddling. The foreman is not expected to go about flattering his people or "treating 'em soft". What is wanted is something more substantial, an attitude that reflects the policy of the company and suggests a readiness to make them full participants in its development. Fostering pride in his job is one of the most useful means, especially if backed up by the full information of a company's policy, plans, progress and problems. The supervisor can encourage his employees to be proud of their work, help them to see where they fit in the general scheme of things, what their part of the finished product is and what the final article itself is like. This is done in some companies by means of a display case, in which materials, components and finished products are set out in stages. A good deal can be done in this direction by suitable explanatory talks and demonstrations in the training courses for new employees, particularly if coupled with tours of various departments. A few firms have gone to the length of inviting employees' wives and families to see the factory.

Manufacturers of raw materials, sheet metal, and the like, may find it more difficult than in those companies where a finished article is placed on the market. A very successful way of demonstrating to the employees the final conclusion of their work is by having a number of completed products sent down for exhibition purposes from the firms who buy the company's goods, or alternatively to allow small groups of employees to visit other works or factories where the raw material is fabricated. Visits of this kind can, however, sometimes have unexpected repercussions.

In one company, where copper strip was finished to a very high specification, which included completely freeing it from scratches, burrs and blemishes and very elaborate packing arrangements, a party of workers visiting a customer firm where the strip was used found it treated no better than rough bar iron—stripped of its covering, thrown down, stood on and run over by trucks. The fine-limit specification obviously had no significance—worse than that, for the customer's insistence on supply in exact 20-foot lengths had no other consequence than being chopped up into 3-inch pieces by teams of young boys and girls! What happened at the strip factory when the visit was over can safely be left to the imagination!

An employee likes to feel that the firm for which he works is a good one. He likes, when talking to his friends and colleagues, to feel that his job is as good as or better than any elsewhere. Instilling this pride, however, must be based on reality and on a policy that gives substance and truth to it. One of its consequences will be a more positive attitude in the worker—he will avoid wasting material, make sure that the dripping tap is turned off, use up material which others might scrap, and return to the stores nails, screws and other small items at the completion of the job. Little things of this kind can mount up and make a useful contribution to the right side of the profit and loss account. The larger consequence will be reflected in productivity.

(j) Suggestions Schemes

This is another means by which a company can promote the morale of its employees. Frequently, in the daily performance of their job, they have bright ideas about the way in which things should or could be done. These ideas are often good ones, and if there is an opportunity for putting them forward, valuable improvements may result. But even more important is the emotional influence on the employees themselves: to them the scheme means first and foremost that the company is aware of them and interested in their contribution.

The usual way of conducting the scheme is through "Suggestions Boxes" installed in each department, with public announcements of awards for ideas which are original and are usable or adopted. Some firms leave the boxes permanently in position, repainting them in a different colour each month as a reminder and a stimulus to their use. Other firms, again, run the boxes, aided by a propaganda campaign, for a brief period every few months in the belief that familiarity or staleness will defeat the whole object of the scheme.

It is customary for a Suggestions Scheme to be supervised by a committee comprising five or six people representative of different parts of the organisation and competent to assess the ideas put forward and thus be able to recommend the award.

It is not often that we find Suggestions Schemes set up for office staffs, although in the modern office there are frequently numerous opportunities for economies in paper work and for the improvement of methods in routine clerical work. The re-drafting or re-routeing of a form might save considerable labour and time, and be worth an award comparable with those offered for factory ideas. The morale value of the scheme is, of course, also comparable.

A good deal of careful preparation must precede the establishment of one of these schemes, for the machinery has to work rapidly. Ideas will be killed if months elapse between their submission and their consideration. And the morale value will disappear if no answer at all is received by the suggester or if the scheme is conducted with an air of casualness and indifference. A badly run scheme may well damage morale.

JOINT CONSULTATION

Of all the schemes by which management seeks to bring its employees into responsible and full participation in the activities, the purposes of the enterprise, the process of "joint consultation" has attracted the greatest interest in industrial circles in recent years. Considerable impetus was given to this line of development by the special agreement in the engineering industry in 1942, supported officially by the Ministry of Supply as an employer. This agreement provided for the establishment of "Joint Production (Advisory and Consultative) Committees", representative of management and employees through the Trade Unions, for the mutual discussion of difficulties and problems and the improvement of methods of production and of productivity. The principle of such Committees was not, of course, new; it had a precedent in the Whitley Committee scheme, and had prototypes of a kind in the several "Works Councils" which, in the more far-sighted organisations, survived the retrogressive atmosphere of the 1920s and 1930s.

The purpose of any form of "joint consultation" is precisely what the title implies—a means of exchanging views and information, and of promoting communications among the various functions or sections or layers of the organisation. There is a growing weight of opinion now against the commonly accepted view of consultation as a joint action between "sides": many a spokesman has praised the "bringing together of the two sides" in a joint committee, without realising how negative is this approach. There are—or should be—no "sides" in an industrial organisation: there are differences of activity, of responsibility, of task, but all directed to the same purpose. What a joint committee bridges is this difference of function, not of interest or of aims. Without such a basis of honest principle and intention no scheme of joint consultation is of much practical use.

The representative committee form has been the most common pattern in British industry, even in those companies which had the consultative process in action for many years. The object is to provide a common understanding aimed at the betterment of relationships between worker and employer. Frequently in recent years there has developed a spate of committees, many of which have had similar functions but different names, often within one organisation. Wherever possible, it is advisable to have only one committee within an organisation, and its terms of reference should be sufficiently wide to deal with any matters arising. As already indicated, the importance is not in the committee itself, but in the sincerity behind the words "joint consultation". It is quite useless for a company to have twelve or twenty people sitting round a table once a month to deal with minor complaints when neither side is being frank or genuine with the other, where the committee is a farce, where workers put forward ridiculous and extravagant demands, and the management on the other side find equally ridiculous excuses for not meeting or for explaining away alleged deficiencies. Time is wasted, tempers frayed, frustration built up, and suspicion created which may take many years to eradicate. Where good intentions are only superficial, it does not take more than a few meetings for this to become apparent, and the continuance of the committee may then do far more harm than good.

Publicity alone will not make a successful committee, but it is an important element in its work; high value is to be attached to a proper channel by which information about the committee's work, progress and achievement is provided for the individual worker.

The question of how many committees should exist or what their functions are to be, is one which is rarely given sufficient consideration by top management. Frequently one finds five or six committees working in an organisation, totally unrelated to one another, sometimes having the same members sitting on each of the committees, discussing item by item the work which could be done quite easily in one full committee. There may, for example, be a Joint Production Committee, a Safety Committee, a Fire Committee and a Works Committee, with Subcommittees for Canteen and Social, and a Foremen's Committee. On all of these Committees, with the exception of the last, one would expect to find representatives of the employees, probably shop stewards representing the Trade Unions. There is hardly one item which could be put on the agenda of any of these Committees which cannot adequately be successfully dealt with by a single body with wider terms of reference centring on production.

Safety affects production; canteen arrangements affect production, insofar as they must be co-ordinated with the meal breaks for the employees. Fire precautions obviously affect production; and so on. Where circumstances require it, the single Works Council or Works Committee can be supplemented by *ad hoc* Subcommittees, set up to deal with these various matters in detail.

Subject-matters for discussion at Joint Consultation, while mainly restricted to matters which merely affect the particular concern, may, on occasions, have to pay regard to local questions of wider interest. This is particularly the case when a single industry or trade is predominant in the locality. Matters concerned with wages, piece-rates and bonuses are usually excluded from the scope of the Committees; these are usually considered more appropriate to direct negotiations, as in many instances National Agreements have to be considered in relation to the wage problems, and it is not always possible to find wage problems an agreeable subject for discussion by large groups of people, some of whom may have no knowledge whatever of the technicalities of the subject.

A summary of matters usually covered in joint committees may be listed as follows:

   (1) Absentees and lateness.
   (2) Accident prevention.
   (3) Avoidance of waste of time, labour and materials.
   (4) Canteens.
   (5) Holiday arrangements.
   (6) Issue and revision of works rules.
   (7) Distribution of working hours, breaks, time recording, etc.
   (8) Physical welfare questions—meals, drinking water, washing and cloakroom facilities, heating, safety, first-aid, etc.
   (9) Questions of discipline and conduct as between management and workpeople.
  (10) Terms of engagement for workpeople.
  (11) Training of apprentices, etc.
  (12) Library, lectures and social aspects of industry.
  (13) Suggestions and testing of method and organisation improvements.
  (14) Entertainments and sport.
  (15) Improving production.
  (16) Welfare fund, Sports Club funds, etc.
  (17) Grievances.
  (18) Canteens.

The whole object of joint consultation is to get rid of the division into "sides" within the factory, and to weld the workpeople and the management into a team. Exchange of information is therefore of great importance. Workpeople may give assistance on technical or mechanical matters in addition to ideas submitted through the Suggestions Scheme, and they can discuss with management likely reactions to proposals for new methods. Equally, from management's part there must be a readiness to impart information about

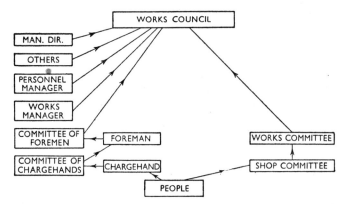

FIG. 78.—A Framework for Joint Consultation.

progress, plans, proposals for development and other factors that bear on the stability and security of employment and all the well-being of the concern.

Joint Consultation Committees vary in name, but are mostly similar in functions and certainly identical in purpose. It is of little avail to try to draw differences in scope or activity from differences in name. In general, however, the title "Works Council" or "Works Committee" refers to the bodies with a full range of terms of reference, while the "Joint Production Committees" pay more detailed attention to matters directly concerned with production. Some of the problems frequently are:

(a) Maximum utilisation of existing machinery.
(b) Upkeep of fixtures, jigs, tools and gauges.
(c) Improvement in methods of production.
(d) Efficient use of the maximum number of productive hours.
(e) Elimination of defective work and waste.
(f) Efficient use of material supplies.
(g) Efficient use of safety precautions and devices.

Just as the details of subject-matter brought up and the line of treatment taken in regard to them must vary according to local conditions, so, too, questions of constitution and operation of these consultative committees cannot be decided by hard-and-fast rules. Clearly, certain broad principles can be laid down, especially as such bodies are mostly elected from among employees of the various parts of the organisation. These constitutional points have been the centre of a good deal of controversy over the years—two of the most debated issues being the sizes of the management representation and the eligibility of employees who are not members of Trade Unions. Committees set up under the terms of an Agreement customarily have equal numbers of employee and manager representatives, the former being composed only of union members, though non-members participate in the elections. Though more progressive minds are inclined to feel that both these arrangements are unsound, the trend of common opinion today is along the "line of least resistance", and consequently opposed to the freedom that is offered by the more open-minded constitution. There are arguments for and against both points of view; one aspect that is frequently overlooked is this—that as matters covered by union negotiations are practically always excluded from the agenda of consultative committees, the case for restriction to union members means the arbitrary exclusion of the "independent" from independent representation.

As the basis for the constitution of joint committees, one study group with a good deal of experience of their working has laid down the following principles:[1]

1. *Structure*

The consultative mechanism should be composed of two parts, viz.:
(a) A Council or Committee composed of elected representatives of Management, Supervisory Staffs and Employees; and
(b) The ordinary mechanism for negotiations between representatives of Management and the Trade Unions.

2. *Terms of Reference*

(a) The Council or Committee should have as its terms of reference all matters affecting the employee during the continuance of his employment, except questions of wages where these are covered by Agreements and are dealt with by the organised negotiations referred to in item 1 (b) above.
Where special Committees are thought desirable for deliberation on specific issues, they should take the form of Subcommittees of the main Council or Committee, with the right to co-opt persons with special knowledge or experience of the issues under deliberation.
(b) For the second element, the terms of reference to be wages and conditions of employment in accordance with the national, regional or individual Agreements signed between representatives of the Employers and the Trade Unions.

[1] Extracted from the Institute of Industrial Administration Report already cited on page 501.

3. *Constitution of Council or Committee*

(*a*) Employee and Supervisory Staff representatives should be elected; those of Management should be nominated by the Chief Executive. The Personnel Executive should be an *ex-officio* member.

(*b*) All employees should have the right to vote for representation from the outset of their employment.

(*c*) Eligibility for election to membership of the Council or Committee should be restricted to employees with a minimum of twelve months' service in the enterprise, but there should be equal eligibility as between members and non-members of the Trade Unions.

(*d*) Representatives of the Supervisory Staffs should be elected by and from the Supervisory Staffs themselves, on the basis of appropriate qualifying conditions, which should not include the restriction of membership of a Trade Union.

(*e*) The establishment of the "constituencies" for representation purposes should provide for adequate representation of the technical and administrative (including clerical) staffs as distinct from the Supervisory and Management staffs.

(*f*) The Management representatives should be few in number, leaving the employee representatives with a clear majority. The Management representatives should be responsible Executives.

(*g*) All elected or nominated members of the Council or Committee should serve for a period of two years, with the proviso that there shall be an annual nomination or election of half the members in each category.

Supervisors' Committee

The idea that supervisors should have a Committee at which to discuss matters of general interest among themselves is rapidly gaining ground as a counterpart to employee consultation, because of the growing recognition of the importance of the foreman's function.

The foreman is management's representative, and in closer touch with the individual worker than anyone else; he has more opportunity of improving—or marring—relationships between the company and the worker, through the very nature of his day-to-day contacts within the working group. This is a principle which has received considerable emphasis in earlier pages. It is therefore equally important to provide a channel of communication between supervision and management, and to provide an opportunity for consultation among the supervisors themselves, recognising the extent to which they are isolated in their own job. This means of mutual discussion at their own level and from their own peculiar standpoint is in addition to their participation, through a supervisor representative serving on the main committees, in the general process of consultation. They are also brought more closely into touch with management, so that they can discuss common problems, suggest improvements, and advise on matters likely to affect company policy or industrial relationships, or production, technical development, etc. Information regarding costing, overheads, sales possibilities and problems can be brought to such a committee for discussion with great advantage. To have the foremen "in the know" on what the company want done is, of course, as important as telling the driver of the taxi where you want to go.

Shop Meetings

Some large firms have found useful the practice of holding a weekly meeting at which the Shop Stewards attend and bring forward all the difficulties or queries which have accumulated during the week. The Stewards keep their points for discussion until midday on Friday, anything arising after that (other than items of emergency) being dealt with by the following week's meeting. At noon on Friday, the list or agenda is handed to the manager by the convener or the senior shop steward in the department. Immediately after this, a typed agenda is posted on the notice board, so that the opportunity is given to all in the department to see the points which are being brought up for discussion on that day. The meeting starts at four o'clock; all the shop stewards in the department are present, including any who may be on shift work. The senior foreman and one other foreman and the manager of the department are also present. The items on the agenda vary considerably. A typical works agenda might be as follows:

(1) The reason for Smith's transfer from the large guillotine to the small one.
(2) Loss of earnings of an operator due to the late start of the Maintenance Department on the machine breakdown.
(3) The rate to be paid for a new job to be done in the department.
(4) The possibility of redundancy as the result of the mechanisation of the cold-rolling process.
(5) The number of sheets to be put through when rolling 14-gauge zinc.
(6) Investigation of the accident to a juvenile in the Press Shop.
(7) Lack of cakes on the tea trolley on Wednesday afternoon.

The Chairman of the meeting will be the Manager. Minutes will be made immediately after the meeting, and posted not later than lunchtime on Monday. Before the minutes are posted, they will be agreed with a shop steward in the department.

An occasional visitor (chiefly to emphasise the importance of the meetings) should be the Managing Director or the Director responsible for production in that department, or the Personnel Manager.

Joint Consultative Committee

Firms in which several trade unions are represented among the employees have to face a special problem in consultation, which can often be met only by the establishment of an *ad hoc* committee. The purpose of this is to bring together all the unions, so that a two-way channel of information is formed, and that matters may be discussed between the management and the union representatives in an organised way. It is usual for such a committee to be formed through the negotiation and acceptance of an Agreement, specifically determining the scope of the committee and incorporating detailed procedures to be adopted.

The items usually dealt with by such a committee are:

(1) Differentiation or variation from the basic union rates.
(2) Variation in the normal working conditions.
(3) General working conditions.

It is important to note the difference in dealing with a dispute within the works where a Joint Consultative Committee is in existence and the normal disputes procedure used in other cases. Where the Committee is in existence the matter cannot go to an outside organisation or to a Trade Union headquarters until it has been discussed within the works, and there is a "failure to agree" between the management and the employees. This type of committee has definite disadvantages for both employees and management. In the first place, many matters which might be the subject of a National Agreement or which have been laid down as a basis of discussion between the industries and the unions might be overruled by a Joint Consultative Committee, where members might act in ignorance of what was being done on the National or Industrial basis.

Another snag which arises frequently is that the shop stewards endeavour to negotiate matters with the management and register a "failure to agree", whereas if the item had to be taken direct to the union headquarters or division, advice could then be given to show that it was contrary to the desires of the Trade Union or had already been discussed and agreed at some other level. Thus a certain amount of time may be wasted on items which never need be discussed at all, or in any case delay carrying out the disputes procedure. Another disadvantage of the Joint Consultative Committee appears to be the antagonism which arises among non-union employees, who feel that the management are paying undue recognition to the unions as compared with the non-unionists in the organisation.

The terms of reference are set, but it is a little difficult, unless the meeting is in the hands of a strong Chairman, to avoid dealing with items which are not strictly the concern of the committee, without a certain amount of overlapping.

Joint Industrial Councils and Wages Councils

The Joint Industrial Councils were erected subsequent to recommendations made by the Whitley Committee (so called after its Chairman, the Rt. Hon. J. H. Whitley, M.P.). On approval of the Committee's recommendation by the Government the Ministry of Labour took very active steps to establish the Joint Industrial Councils, each council being particular to one industry. In the Civil Services, Local Government, etc., they are known as "Whitley Councils" but their functions are the same.

Under the recommendations of the Whitley Committee the J.I.C.s were to become the standard type of joint organisation and the recognised mechanism of consultation between employers and employed. The Councils were to have written constitutions and indeed the Ministry published a model: they had defined spheres of influence and functioned through national, regional and sectional councils. In the years between the Whitley Committee's report and the early 20s there was widespread enthusiasm for setting up these Joint Industrial Councils and at first they appeared to be ideal. Many of the J.I.C.s, however, did not attempt to fix wages and allowed this to be done by the older, well-established and traditional forms of collective bargaining. In this was contained the seed of their decay. The main spheres in which Joint Industrial Councils have succeeded are local government, public utilities, transport and those industries where employers are few and relatively large, where competition is not severe and there are traditions of relatively secure employment.

The J.I.C.s which have succeeded can be seen to have complied closely with the Whitley Committee's original recommendations that they should "consist of representatives of the associations of employers and workpeople meeting at regular and frequent intervals for the consideration of such matters as: ʻ

"1. The better utilisation of the practical knowledge and experience of the workpeople.
"2. Means for securing to the workpeople a greater share in, and responsibility for the determination and observation of the conditions under which their work is carried on.
"3. The settlement of the general principles governing the conditions of employment, including the methods of fixing, paying and readjusting wages, having regard to the need for securing to the workpeople a share in the increased prosperity of the industry.

"4. The establishment of regular methods of negotiation for issues arising between employers and workpeople, with a view both to the prevention of differences, and to their better adjustment when they appear.

"5. Means of ensuring to the workpeople the greatest possible security of earnings and employment, without undue restriction upon change of occupation or employer.

"6. Methods of fixing and adjusting earnings, piecework prices, etc., and of dealing with the many difficulties which arise with regard to the method and amount of payment apart from the fixing of general standard rates, which are already covered by paragraph (3).

"7. Technical education and training.

"8. Industrial research and the full utilization of its results.

"9. The provision of facilities for the full consideration and utilisation of inventions and improvements designed by workpeople, and for the adequate safeguarding of the rights of the designers of such improvements.

"10. Improvements of processes, machinery and organisation and appropriate questions relating to management and the examination of industrial experiments, with special reference to co-operation in carrying new ideas into effect and full consideration of the workpeople's point of view in relation to them.

"11. Proposed legislation affecting the industry."

In the main, the negotiating part of the J.I.C.s work attracts our attention here. Many of the constitutions provide that there shall be no stoppages of work, or lock-outs, till the dispute has been before the council—both sides are expected to conform with this provision as an "honourable obligation". When a dispute arises attempts have to be made to settle it locally. If this proves not to be possible the party who first gave formal notice of the existence of the dispute gives notice again to the joint secretaries of the National Joint Industrial Council. The secretaries appoint a Court of Arbitration with an independent Chairman. The Court is constituted equally of representatives from the employers and the workpeople, and if there is equal voting on considering a dispute the Chairman can give a ruling. The decisions of the J.I.C.s are binding in the same way as National Agreements made between (say) the Confederation of Shipbuilding and Engineering Unions and the Federation of Engineering Employers.

Side by side with the Joint Industrial Councils in their wages determining functions are the Wages Councils. These grew out of the Trade Boards which were formed, before the J.I.C.s, under the Trade Boards Act of 1909. The intention of the 1909 Act was to erect Trade Boards which would determine minimum wage standards in the officially recognised "sweated trades" (of tailoring, paper-box making, chain making and lace and net making by machinery). Their success provided them with a degree of attractiveness and by 1945 when they were all changed by the Wages Council Acts into Wages Councils there were fifty in existence. Now, however, a Wages Council does not fix or determine minimum wages, but makes recommendations to the Minister of Labour.

Wages Councils can be brought into existence by a variety of means. The Minister can bring one into existence on his own initiative if he considers circumstances warrant it; he can appoint a commission to enquire into the need for a Wages Council in any one industry and accept their recommendations.

The Minister will only bring a Wages Council into being (by means of a Wages Council Order) if he is satisfied that there exists in the trade or industry concerned no adequate machinery for fixing minimum wages. The only time, then, that a J.I.C. will make an application for the erection of a Wages Council for their own industry will be when it is obvious that there is or is very likely to be an inadequacy in the negotiating procedure and machinery previously employed. In this one respect the Wages Council might be regarded as the statutory counterpart of the J.I.C.

It was contained in the recommendations of the Whitley Committee that the Trade Boards should deal with the problem of collective bargaining if the J.I.C.s failed, but this position was not realised until the passing of the 1945 Act. The main spheres of work of the Wages Councils are in making recommendations to the Minister of Labour, for the fixing of minimum wage rates, and overtime premiums, and for regulating the lengths of the normal working week and of holidays. The Councils publish their recommendations and if the Minister accepts them they are given the force of law as a Wages Order under the Wages Council Act 1945. The Wages Council will be found in those industries with a history of poor labour relations and confused collective bargaining, but the existence of a Wages Council does not necessarily preclude the existence of a J.I.C. which might have other work to do. the Road Haulage Industry, for example, has both a Wages Council and a J.I.C.[1]

The subjects covered by such Councils are generally of the following order:

---

[1] A useful publication in this respect is the "*Directory of Employers' Associations, Trade Unions, Joint Organisations, etc.*" which is compiled by the Ministry of Labour. It shows the names, addresses of secretaries, and other information about these bodies and is published by H.M. Stationery Office, with periodic revisions.

(1) Securing the largest possible measure of joint action between employers and workpeople for the development of the industry as part of national life, and for the improvement of the conditions of all engaged in that particular industry.

(2) Wages, hours and working conditions of the industry as a whole to be taken into regular consideration.

(3) Measures for regularising employment and production also to be taken into consideration.

(4) The consideration for settlement between different parties and sections of the industry, of any existing machinery—and, with the object of securing the speedy settlement of difficulties, the establishment of machinery where it does not already exist.

(5) Collection of information and statistics on matters relating to the industry.

(6) Encouragement of design and processes study and also of research with the view to perfecting the industry's products.

(7) Provision of facilities for consideration of any improvement in machinery or method and utilisation of inventions, also adequate safeguarding of such improvements, and to secure that such improvement shall give to each party a share of the benefits arising therefrom.

(8) Publication of reports and enquiries into special problems of the industry, including the methods and comparative study of the organisation of the industry in this and other countries.

(9) Improvement of health conditions in the industry and, where necessary, special treatment for workers.

(10) Co-operation in all branches of the industry, for arranging education with the authorities and the supervision of entry into and training for the industry.

(11) Issue of authoritative statements to the Press upon matters of general interest to the community affecting the industry.

(12) Representation of opinions and needs of the industry to the Government, Government Departments and other authorities.

(13) Consideration of other matters which may be referred to by the Government or any Government Departments.

(14) Proposals for District Councils and Works Committees put forward in the Whitley Report, having regard in each case to any organisation which may be already in existence to be taken into consideration.

The following three functions have also been included in some of the constitutions:

(1) Consideration of measures for securing inclusion of all employees and employers in their respective associations.

(2) Arrangements for holding conferences and lectures on subjects of general interest to the industry.

(3) Co-operation in dealing with problems of common interest to the Joint Industrial Council and other industries.

DISCIPLINE

Discipline is essential in any undertaking where there is to be order instead of chaos. In industry it is essential to the attainment of the maximum productivity. The underlying philosophy of discipline is conceived in the proper thinking of the whole field of industrial relations. Its methods are profoundly influenced by the conditions of employment and by legislation, by the attitude of organised labour, and by the state of the productive processes at a given period. The modern conception of discipline is that it provides a pattern of acceptable behaviour and performance, as against the old-fashioned idea of chastisement or punishment for wrong-doing. There is now a more sincere attempt to arrive at the real cause of indiscipline, when dealing with irregularities of one kind and another. There is an evident trend that the power of the foreman to administer discipline without reference to anyone else is disappearing, and the imposing of any serious penalties now usually becomes the consideration of higher executives or even of a committee. It is, in other words, recognised that discipline obtained by fear is not a successful way of conducting affairs, and has a detrimental effect on the morale of the organisation.

The imposition of a penalty must be decided upon after careful examination of all the facts in an atmosphere where everyone is "cool, calm and collected".

The position of the Personnel Manager with regard to discipline should always be made clear. His service is advisory; he can assist in investigation and explain what is the right penalty to impose, but must never attempt to usurp the position of the foreman, Departmental Manager or other "line" executive, by taking away his responsibility for discipline. His own major task is to ensure that no reprimand or penalty is inflicted unless it is just, and that the decision arrived at is in accordance with the facts.

There is only one real way in which to provide a sound foundation for discipline; that is, to draw up a code of regulations and conditions agreed between representatives of employees and to supplement this by a recognised mechanism which provides for an employee to get a fair hearing when alleged wrongful acts are committed.

The following are typical examples of the cases that happen from day to day in a factory and with which a Personnel Manager might be called upon to deal:

(a) A telephone message was received in the Personnel Department from Mr. Smith, Manager of the Foundry, complaining of the persistent habit of an employee named Blank who rides his bicycle through the foundry yard every day and leaves it underneath the crane instead of in the shed provided. Smith asked for the employee's instant dismissal. The Personnel Manager immediately went along to see the Foundry Manager and to investigate the facts. After a while, they agreed to call in the employee's foreman, who would be able to confirm how many times the employee had been warned to keep his bicycle in the proper rack provided. The foreman stated that he had warned the employee once only and that unofficially about six weeks previously; he was, however, aware that Blank had continued the practice. It was then decided to interview Blank, and he was told that he could be accompanied by his shop steward if he belonged to a Trade Union (this step being taken in case it was subsequently decided to discharge the employee).

Smith, the Manager, left the interview in the hands of the Personnel Manager, who drew the employee's attention to the alleged breach of the Works Rules and asked if there was any explanation. Blank admitted the offence, but said he had not realised that this was a serious breach. When he was first employed with the Company, he went on, there had been no room in the cycle rack, so he left his cycle with some others in the shed. After about a week, his lamp and pump were stolen, he reported his loss to the Works Security Officer, but the articles were not returned, so he decided that as his bicycle was worth about £18 he would leave it where he could keep an eye on it. But this was the first time in two years that a complaint had been made about it. The Personnel Manager then pointed out that he was being pulled up, not because he left his bicycle under the crane, though this was admittedly wrong, but because he cycled through the foundry yard, which was against the rules. To this he replied that he usually arrived fifteen minutes before time in order to get things ready and have the machinery and equipment going by the time the shift would be starting work again. No notice had been posted in the department forbidding the riding of a bicycle through the yard, or he would not have done so.

Although a rule had been broken, there was no case for a penalty; it was doubtful whether he had ever been specifically told not to ride in the yard, and he had certainly had no real warning from the foreman that he was committing an offence. He was a most conscientious worker, and it was doubtful whether adequate cycle accommodation had been provided at that particular site.

It was unlikely that he would offend again, as the interview had brought home to him the existence and purpose of the ruling relative to cycling within the works and the proper storage of cycles.

It had also been established that accommodation for cycles was now insufficient, a matter clearly calling for attention by the management. The whole case had contributed to maintaining discipline in the department, and had enhanced the status of the Departmental Manager, foreman and Personnel Manager by the constructive way in which it had been handled.

(b) The Personnel Officer in a certain factory was asked by a Manager to take up a case of lateness. He had the employee's record traced back twelve months, and this investigation showed that the man had been most regular in his time-keeping up to a certain point, but had been thrown out of gear by some domestic trouble and had temporarily become a bad time-keeper. This was the first occasion he had been pulled up, so the Personnel Manager had no intention of dealing seriously with the matter, but gave a verbal warning, pointing out that home conditions had apparently now improved. If the man failed to respond, a more serious view would be taken.

(c) Another case was one of alleged slackness with which the foreman of the department was apparently able to make no headway. The Personnel Manager interviewed first the foreman and then the man, having obtained detailed evidence of what had not been done efficiently and how the employee was cited as being neglectful, careless, thoughtless and generally inattentive at his work. The man's attendance record was also obtained and a general opinion asked for from his Departmental Manager.

Armed with these facts, the Personnel Manager was able to send for the man and tell him quite pleasantly that reports had been received from his department that he was not giving satisfactory service, and perhaps he would like to talk the matter over. The foreman had complained that Blank was frequently missing from his job and spent a lot of time in the lavatory smoking. His lateness record was pretty bad, and generally speaking he gave the impression of being a man who was "fed up to the back teeth" with his job and would really like to pack up work altogether. The Personnel Manager put the last part over with a smile, and gave the employee the impression that whatever else had been said about him to his detriment, the Personnel Manager was still quite able to be sceptical, and, having engaged him when he first joined the firm, was prepared to listen to his story in a friendly way.

Blank then put up his side of the picture with a good deal of confidence: he was allowed to continue uninterrupted by questions. This enhanced the good impression that the Personnel Manager would listen to all he had to say—but he could be fairly sure that he couldn't get away with any bluff or soft soap! The Personnel Manager decided, as the other side of the story came out, that there were some genuine facts in this case that needed further consideration, and that it would not be wise to stage a straight talk from the foreman in his presence. Clearly, this man—a relatively new employee—had been the victim of circumstances, treated harshly in a previous job, and had not been properly run in his new department. A closer watch, and some help in the tricky bits of his job, would probably put him right. A friendly chat with the foreman brought to light that he had rather neglected Blank. . . . Three or four weeks later the foreman was the first to admit that he had got the makings of a good chap!

These cases throw some further light on the relationship of the personnel specialist to the "line" executives and supervisors, and illustrate the general principles outlined below. The Personnel Manager is seen operating as a "safety valve", the foreman accepts his position in the organisation (which foremen will gladly do when the personnel man is of good salt, knows his job and wins respect by his skill) and appreciates the practical value of being able to refer such matters to him. But the Personnel Manager does not pose as an arbiter; he prefers to see his role as more of a fact-finding one. So his first reaction is to get fuller details so that he can justify his position as an intelligent and informed onlooker. His second major contribution is to remove this highly emotional personal problem of discipline into a more detached atmosphere, and then his third task can be more effectively carried out—the careful interview of both parties, which will bring to the surface real causes which may be underlying the employee's bad behaviour, will afford an opportunity of any special mitigatory circumstances to be explained, and will bring home to the individual concerned the fact of his wrongdoing seen in proper perspective. Of course, there will be many cases when the man or woman is seriously at fault, and, maybe, recalcitrant; no other solution but removal will be of any use, as both Personnel Officer and foreman can see. But if there is a genuine human policy in the organisation and an appreciation of the high value of the asset represented by good morale, every endeavour will be made to avoid the solution of dismissal, which can rightly be regarded as a confession of failure or surrender.

At no point in this process of probing the human problems with which all disciplinary situations are fraught does the Personnel Officer remove or undermine the responsibility of the "line" manager or foreman. He is their trusted "assistant", and they have referred these cases to him because they know that he will investigate the issue thoroughly to their satisfaction, and that of the employee concerned —they realise, too, how important this latter respect is, and how easily any suspicion of unfairness or arbitrariness in matters of discipline can damage morale. The Personnel Officer does not make the decision as to the final solution; he discusses his finding with the manager or foreman, and recommends which line they should take. It is usually wiser for the foreman himself to communicate the decision to the employee, though frequently the supervisors may prefer to settle the matter with the employee in the presence of the Personnel Officer, especially if there has been any occasion for outspoken words earlier in the case.

The handling of discipline is a matter deeply embedded in the human responsibilities of management and supervision. It is one of the main factors in the practical skill of the manager or foreman, something to which their personal abilities and their training can both contribute, but the soundness of discipline in any organisation also depends largely on its personnel policy; where the process of consultation is well developed as a genuine element in the practice of management, discipline is nearly always better. It has been found of particular value for factory and office rules to be planned, not by the decision of management alone, but by joint deliberations among top management, supervisors and employees. Some firms have gone to the length of giving full responsibility for the maintenance of discipline to a representative panel which sits as a "court" or Appeals Tribunal to hear the more serious cases referred to it by the foreman or the Personnel Officer. The spirit underlying this development has been the belief that the more responsibility is given to people, the more positive is their response.

Without going further into details, this question of discipline may perhaps be summarised in the following principles, which were submitted to a conference of supervisors and endorsed by them.[1]

A. *Setting the Code*

  (1) Discipline means securing normally consistent behaviour in accordance with accepted rules. Discipline is essential to an ordered life, and especially to a democratic way of life. This means that it is essential to modern industrial administration, and we recognise this to be as true of the Socialist state as to any other political form.

  (2) Because of the inevitable group structure of industry, discipline is intimately bound up with relations within the organisation, and in consequence is affected by such factors as the background, social environment and emotional outlook of the employees concerned.

  (3) Because in essence discipline is the interpretation of a code, it is also closely tied up with personal feelings (sentiments, as they are called)—those non-logical emotional factors that determine so much of the behaviour of the average individual. In consequence, the effective application of discipline depends primarily on an understanding of the human being and of oneself in administering the code.

[1] Extracted from a paper on "The Administration of Discipline", given at a Conference organised by the Industrial Welfare Society, 1947, by E. F. L. Brech.

(4) Discipline is also closely connected with the policy and conditions of employment of the organisation concerned. The more broad-minded these are, the more stable and the easier is discipline likely to be.

(5) The code of discipline (including the section pertaining to it) must be decided in consultation with those who are to be under its jurisdiction or concerned in its application.

(6) The standards should be objectively the same for everyone. Where variations are obviously required for special categories owing to peculiarities of circumstances, these are to be admitted as based on objective grounds and so do not give rise to privileges.

(7) The code of discipline must be reasonable and simple, and not contain rules for the sake of rules.

(8) A good scheme of discipline entails the existence of a judicial machinery for appeals, preferably internal to the organisation concerned. In this connection it will be noted that a well-established Personnel Management function affords a useful contribution, though of a somewhat different character from that of an Appeals Tribunal.

B. *Carrying the Code into Effect*

(9) The maintenance of discipline is the core of the foreman's human responsibilities. He can achieve success only to the extent to which he regards his task as one involving constructive human principles in which the personal circumstances of the individual as well as the objective surrounding circumstances are taken into account.

(10) The maintenance of discipline is the responsibility of Managers and Supervisors by function. But in discharging this responsibility they should endeavour to share it as much as possible with the employees themselves, and thus encourage self-responsibility for discipline. Granted that a good code exists, it can surely be agreed that discipline is best where authority is least in evidence.

(11) In the last analysis, the effectiveness of discipline turns both on the soundness of the relations within the organisation and on the calibre and competence of the managers and supervisors, as well as on the ability of the latter to take a positive instead of a negative approach to their responsibilities in regard to discipline.

Misfits

It is inevitable that from time to time people will be placed in jobs which they do not like or for which they are not particularly suited. A variety of reasons may include these—environment, the dirty nature of the work, smell, lighting, the heat and, more regularly, incompatibility with the foreman or chargehand. The Personnel Manager must be prepared to deal with the problems as they arise and to give a sympathetic hearing in every case. Where there is any suggestion that the person is medically unfit for the job, the advice of a Medical Officer should be sought. The case of a man who is unhappy because of incompatibility of temperament needs particularly careful diagnosis by interview. Sometimes, after hearing separately the stories of the two parties, a joint interview may enable the difficulties to be smoothed out. But there will always be the cases where the difficulties of the "misfit" can be solved only by transfer to another department, or termination of the employment. Once again the most important aspect of the matter from the point of view of morale lies in the mere fact that the employee has had his case sympathetically reviewed.

An illustration of some of the difficulties was given by a recent event concerning two departments of a factory. In Department A the average wage was in the region of £10 per week, and in Department B between £11 and £14 per week. When certificates for light work had been given to certain employees in Department A by a doctor, they were transferred to tying up bundles of scrap in Department B: this meant a transfer from a hard and strenuous job to much easier and less important work—and at the same time being given another £3 a week in their wage packets for doing less! Many applications for transfer from Department A followed, appearing to be perfectly genuine and alleging the need for "light work". This placed a good deal of work on the Medical Department and the Manager before the real reason for the applications was realised.

When people were being directed to industry, there were many classes of employees deliberately refusing to settle down, doing their best to get the sack in the hope of transfer into another industry where the pay was higher and the work lighter. One young man was sent as a pipe-fitter to a large works in the "heavy industry" category. For fifteen years previously he had been engaged on the manufacture and assembly of bicycles. He was placed in the plumbing department as a pipe-fitter on maintenance work, but before two or three weeks had passed was doing everything he could, short of violence, to get the sack. The Personnel Manager saw him on many occasions, and finally transferred him to an entirely different job and department, having made it quite clear that the company were anxious he should settle down, and, by appealing to his better nature, got him to try again. This he did, and although he previously had a record for being late every day, refusing to work overtime, insolence and other misdemeanours, he proved before long to be one of the best employees in the company's service in his new job.

This type of change, however, is not made without considerable interest being taken by the Manager, the foreman, the chargehand and the Personnel Manager, who must all be prepared to see such human problems as a common task which they can successfully accomplish only by co-operation.

The Worker with a Personal Problem

When an employee has a grouse or a grumble, or is troubled by a personal worry, he is not concentrating on doing his work or producing the goods, and it is therefore a direct contribution to efficiency to make provision for such problems to be dealt with or for advisory assistance to be given to the workers. The worker's first line of approach is to the foreman, or to whomever may be his immediate boss; in a small company, this may be the owner himself.

Careful listening is the main requirement in such an interview. The reputation of management, and certainly the morale of many employees, may rest on the foreman, or the person who is dealing with the case. It is he who has to make the decision, to work out in his mind what is the right thing to do in the circumstances, what replies to give and how they will affect other things or other people. Sometimes the problem is beyond the foreman, and it is in circumstances like this, especially in the larger organisations, that the skill of the personnel specialist comes into its own. So the foreman or Manager makes an appointment for the employee to see the Personnel Manager, who, with his wider view of the organisation and special training in human problems, may be able to get to the heart of the difficulty immediately and take a decision on this issue. Or he may see that there is a genuine grievance here which can be solved only at a higher level, or which requires investigation on a wider basis.

Whatever the answer, it is essential that the foreman or supervisor be put in the know at once: nothing can be more annoying than to put forward a problem to the Personnel Department and then to find that the worker has the answer before the supervisor himself has been told. Normally, proper co-operation would mean that the opinion of the supervisor would be sought before a decision is arrived at, and the answer may be given in his presence. In the case of a more personal or domestic problem, of course, the Personnel Manager may deem it necessary to treat the matter as confidential, but he should tell the foreman so at once.

Absence and Lateness

These are only special aspects of discipline, and all that was said above in that connection applies here. From the standpoint of the manager or foreman, lost time means lost output and jobs not done; it also means lower utilisation of capacity and so increased costs of operation. There are three aspects of this problem to consider:

(a) The responsibility of the foreman or manager for dealing with the individual is part of his ordinary responsibility for the maintenance of discipline. To a very large extent the question here is the attitude of the foreman—whether he has a human skill which enables him to deal properly with offenders and yet keep up morale, or whether his negative and unsympathetic reprimands earn for him the disfavour of his workers. The good foreman tends to be less troubled by absence and lost time.

(b) The difficult cases, the persistent offenders, with whom the foreman finds himself beaten. Here reference to the Personnel Manager raises the enquiry to a plane of higher and more objective analysis, which can lead to the uncovering of important matters affecting that worker's attitude to his job.

(c) The records and procedures for keeping track of absence and lost time. These provide the data for the study of individual cases, as well as the analysis for assessing the position in the departments and factories. Figures of lost time, coupled with figures of personnel turnover, often provide an invaluable index to the state of morale in a department or a whole factory. (Further details on procedures are given in a later chapter.)

Levels of absence vary enormously from factory to factory, and from trade to trade, so that general comparisons serve very little purpose. But when the figure is going up to the 10 and 15 per cent. level, a serious situation is clearly revealed, unless there are specific emergencies such as an epidemic. Analysis of causes is very helpful. The main break should be into the two main categories—avoidable and unavoidable. Unavoidable absence is by far the easiest to deal with, as this is usually caused through ill-health and sickness certified by a doctor, and accidents will happen at work which are covered by First-Aid records, the information relating to the injury and possible length of absence being passed to the Personnel Manager and the Production Manager.

Avoidable absence can be subdivided into, say, domestic affairs, lassitude, lack of interest in the job, though there is also the one- or two-day sickness not certified, which may be genuine indisposition. The difficulty of knowing whether these cases are genuine or not is certainly great, and is a matter that the Personnel Manager should probe on behalf of the foreman. Careful interviewing may bring to light a sense of "fed-up-ness" in the individual, or definite low state of health (which can at once be referred to a doctor), or some domestic issue—at any rate, something which is not only impairing work when present, but also leading the employee to a remedy of spasmodic time off, so incurring a double loss of output.

The apathy of a man to his job must be very great if it is of such an intensity that it influences him to the extent that he stays away from work. Cases of this kind require a good deal of patient investigation; it must be found out whether there is something in connection with his job which he really dislikes; whether there is friction with the person in charge of him, or with whom he comes in contact. The Personnel Officer must quietly find out if his health is good and try to get information about his home. A man who is living apart from his wife, or having a domestic upheaval, may feel a lack of interest in everything he does, including his work; in tackling a subject of this kind, one needs to be very careful indeed, as a wrong impression is easily created, and instead of being able to help the man, one builds up a reputation of being a "busy-body". The quiet, frank, confidential talk with the Personnel Manager is the main line of diagnosis and remedy.

This situation is made more difficult when the company have a Sick Benefit Scheme; the only safeguard is the insistence on the production of a Medical Certificate as the basis for the claim for payment. A point worth mentioning here is that it is not a good thing to specify a week as the minimum absence in order to qualify for sick pay; this may lead to the situation where two or three days would be the absence if no sick pay was forthcoming, but the period develops into the week in order to qualify.

The gap between the black-coated worker and the man or woman on the factory floor is rapidly closing and all concerned must bring their influence to bear to make sure that, by the introduction of paid sick-pay schemes, manual workers play their part by not treating the sick pay as an additional holiday entitlement and making sure that they have the maximum from the company that they are able to draw.

Perhaps one important point of principle that emerges here is this, that these individual cases of human problems should rest in the hands of the experienced personnel specialist and should never be left to junior staff of the Personnel Department.

Domestic Affairs

This is a problem always met with, when, owing to the death of a relative or some illness, an employee is unable to come to work. These cases need to be dealt with very carefully. Firstly, make sure that the excuse is genuine, then see whether there is an opportunity for the company to help by any of their Welfare Schemes or by giving advice to the individual. A man who has a family of small children is put into a very difficult position when his wife is ill, and it may quite well be that it would take a day or so to obtain some domestic help or a relative who would look after the children. No one would expect a husband to leave home for work knowing that at home there is a family of young children, with a wife who is unable to get up. Even if the man did attend his work, he would be a most unusual person if he devotes his normal energy and gives his thought to the job in the way that he should.

There is only one thing that a person with domestic troubles can be expected to do, and this should be insisted upon throughout the Works Rules, namely, to see that a message is sent to the foreman or the manager of the department at starting time, so that the man's job is not left for an hour or two in the hope that he will turn up. This information will enable the foreman to see that the work goes on.

CHAPTER III

TRAINING, PROMOTION AND WITHDRAWALS

TRAINING POLICY AND PROGRAMMES

IN the form of apprenticeships often under written agreement, training has long been a recognised practice in industry. What is new in present-day arrangements is the development of systematic training for semi-skilled operations; this is, of course, of rather short-period duration, as against the years usually required for an apprenticeship to a skilled trade. Another feature that has accompanied recent training plans is the "introduction course", consisting of information about the firm, its policy and products, general layout, history and regulations. Visits to various departments are often included in the programme.

Contemporary interest in industrial training is based on the belief that the following advantages accrue:

    (a) More rapid development to full proficiency.
    (b) Increased production.
    (c) Improved quality of workmanship.
    (d) Less waste of material.
    (e) Better utilisation of machines.
    (f) Less damage to machines and tools.
    (g) Reduced unit costs and increased profit to the company.
    (h) Decreasing the amount of supervision.
    (i) Diminishing labour turnover.
    (j) Revealing special talents of employees.
    (k) Increasing the versatility of employees.
    (l) Improvement in employee morale.

Systematic instruction of new-comers in the activities of the firm and in the conditions which appertain to the whole range of its operation, from obtaining raw material at its source to the marketing of its products, will promote co-operation, as well as enhancing the individual's status when he can say to himself and to others—"I am a trained man". The co-ordination of methods is another important result, which can be particularly valuable where a similar operation occurs in different sections of the factory.

Once it is accepted that training is an asset to an organisation, it should be obvious that it needs to be based on a defined policy, and all schemes need to be properly planned and controlled. The idea has to be put across to all ranks of managers and supervisors, and regarded as a continuous process to be brought into operation when called for. The very large concern can have a training centre which is kept in unbroken session, but it is a mistake to think that systematic training has therefore no part in the organisation of the smaller unit.

It is equally important and applicable in the workshop employing 20 people, as in the mammoth factory where 10,000 are at work. Policy and effective plans are just as necessary, even though they are brought into use only now and again every few months. In the smaller concern, it will be the foreman's job to carry out the training or to allocate a skilled man to do the instruction according to the standards and methods laid down. Whatever the size of the unit, the content of training needs to be agreed by all who are likely to be responsible for it, it must be made quite clear what is to be taught, how it should be taught, and what degrees of accuracy are to be attained. How much can be achieved by systematic plans on these lines in even very small concerns was shown over many years through the special method of "Job Instruction Training" in the T.W.I. programme, by means of which foremen were taught just how to attain with their own new employees all the advantages of planned analytical instruction that could be acquired in a fully established training centre.

In the large organisation which carries out a full programme, the following training procedures are likely to be found:

(a) Introductory course (sometimes referred to by the American phrase "induction training").
(b) Training for semi-skilled work.
(c) Craft apprenticeship.
(d) Training for technical appointments.
(e) Training for clerical work.
(f) Education for juveniles.
(g) Students.
(h) Training for supervision.
(i) Training for management.

(a) *Introductory Course.*—This is the method of introducing new entrants to an organisation, with the object of gaining their confidence and promoting a high sense of co-operation. If the new employee is to become an effective member of the working force, he must be able to understand where he fits in, what the company does, how it serves the community, and how the employees get their information to or from the higher levels of the executives, what the rules and working conditions are, and a general picture of the activities of the organisation.

Procedures and methods would vary according to the age and

grade of the employees being introduced. With women employees, it is most valuable to let them spend a few days in an improvised training centre where they receive this general instruction, as well as preliminary instruction in the job. Sometimes, especially for machine operations, this can be extended to a week or ten days of systematic training, which gives the new-comers a much better sense of self-confidence and efficiency in using machines. When introduced into the machine shop, they have no fears of the machines or undue apprehension of the noise; concentration on the machine itself is easier, and settling down is also made easier through making friends with someone in the training centre—all of which help to develop participation in the social atmosphere of the workshop.

The introductory course need not be a lengthy procedure: it need not be done on the day that the employee starts work, although this is desirable. What must be ensured is that the employee, before he has been with the company many days, has been given information sufficient to hold his or her interest in the work he is about to do. In one large factory the range of information covered in the course is as follows:

1. *The Company and its Products.*—The history of the Company and its place in industry; the nature and uses of its products; the organisation of the Company and the functions of the main departments.

2. *The Management.*—The management structure of the Company; the names and functions of its principal officials, and others with whom the employee will be concerned in the course of his employment.

3. *Amenities and Employee Services.*—The location and facilities of the canteen, cloakroom, rest rooms, etc.; sickness benefit, pensions, benevolent, recreational and other employee services provided.

4. *Sources of Information.*—Where and from whom the employee can obtain information on such matters as wages, income tax, holidays, leave of absence; how he can obtain advice and assistance in connection with personal problems.

5. *Health, Hygiene and Accident Prevention.*—The health and safety practices necessary in the particular type of employment; the function and services of the medical department; the accident prevention organisation.

6. *Personnel Policy.*—"Standing Orders" and the reasons for them; wages policy; principles of discipline; the aims of, and existing machinery for joint consultation between management and employees; training, education, and promotion policy; employment opportunities; work of the Personnel Department.

7. *Working Routines and Procedures.*—Starting and stopping times; time recording system; meal breaks; the basis of payment of the wage or salary, how it is computed, where and when it is paid.

8. *The Employee's own Department.*—Introduction to the supervisor of the employee's own department, and to employee representatives and fellow workers; location of the department; work of the department in relation to other departments; the part played by the employee's job in the work of the department.

The question of whether all this information should be given at one time is a matter of opinion. Some feel that it is best to give it in small doses and to have the employee back again at various intervals over a period of about a month. There is a danger to be considered in this method, in so far that the average employee dislikes being what he calls "mucked about". Once he starts work producing nuts and bolts, he wants to get on with the job, and it is sometimes difficult to explain to him why he must pass through a course of general information—especially if he soon comes to feel that he knows all about it.

(b) *Training for Semi-skilled Work.*—That there is valuable advantage to the drawn from a policy and a systematic programme for the training of employees engaged on semi-skilled work was a lesson taught by the experiences of war. Traditionally, the semi-skilled job has always been learned—"picked up" would be a more accurate description—by a new employee from one already experienced. That the new-comer learned all the bad habits of the established operative, and that of an unnecessarily low tempo of work as well, was a feature which seemed not to attract attention; its significance in terms of costs had apparently never been appreciated. The traditional practice is, of course, still very widespread, probably even still the common practice.

It must be borne in mind that the range of occupations covered in the category "semi-skilled" is wide, and that the numbers of persons included are considerable, far in excess of those in the "skilled" trades. In some industries the line of demarcation is not easily fixed, whereas in others the existence of defined crafts and apprenticeships make the break-point quite clear. But if we take the general field of machine-minders, machine-operators on pre-set work, sewing machinists on straightforward garments, assemblers in a variety of components and products, gauges, many occupations in textile spinning and weaving, transport operatives and so on, it will be clear that the question of training for such employees is of no mean order, and that if each individual suffers a deficiency in development and proficiency of only 10–15 per cent. due to inadequate instruction, the loss of productivity to industry and of wealth to the community is nothing short of enormous!

As with most other aspects of employment, there have always been the few firms that have been fully alive to this point and have therefore long maintained systematic schemes of training for their semi-skilled employees, to parallel those for the craftsmen—even if the training required is only a matter of a few days' deliberate instruction by an older operative specially ear-marked for the purpose. Outstanding examples could be quoted of many well-known companies which maintain a training centre, using the most advanced methods based on the application of motion study.

The first serious move in the development of training for semi-skilled operatives was taken by the Ministry of Labour in the rapid extension of the Government Training Centres. The need arose chiefly through the introduction of women into industry in large numbers and in the demand for quick training in certain widely used engineering operations. Many of the jobs hitherto done by tradesmen were broken down into simpler stages, and by the use of jigs and fixtures, reduced to routine processes of semi-skilled character. This made possible short intensive training courses, composed of general instruction in the form of lectures, usually with illustrations and models, followed by gradual "coaching" on the job stage by stage in the quieter atmosphere of the centre, removed from the hurly-burly of a workshop. Later, the principle was adopted by many of the larger concerns, which established training centres of their own. In many of these, quite often recourse was had to the latest psychological knowledge on training methods, and the whole process of instructing semi-skilled workers made considerable strides forward.

The experience gained in the use of "element by element" training was sometimes applied to even skilled jobs, and it has certainly pointed the way to considerable possibilities of improvement in training methods.

The principle adopted is an extension both of motion study and of job analysis. By careful study of an operation, it is broken up into major parts, or phases or elements; quite often the breakdown of a job for time-study purposes affords a very useful analysis as the basis for training. In each element, a pattern of movement and action is then worked out. These, covering all the elements of the job, thus form an "operation specification" from the human point of view. The training consists of the two parts just referred to, i.e. the general knowledge of the operation—materials used, purpose, machine or tools, bench, special features, dangers and so on; plus specific instruction in performance. This latter part is taking one element in the early stages, so that the trainee gets ample opportunity of acquiring proficiency in each part without mental strain.

In the more complicated operations, the course of tuition in the general aspects of the job may also be given in graded stages.

The approach to training—often referred to as "part training"—

will be recognised as the core of the Job Instruction Training Programme in the T.W.I. Course for supervisors. One or two organisations specifically concerned with research and development in this field have experimented with an additional feature, the use of exercises designed to train the finger or hand muscles, and so to develop dexterities particularly required for various phases of the operation. When the operation specification is being prepared, the analysis is taken a stage further, and the particular dexterities involved are isolated. The special exercises are performed on "gadgets" which are so designed as to develop a particular pattern of muscular movement reproducing that required for the phase of the operation. Results are not yet available of adequate reliability to confirm or reject the worthwhileness of this development. There has apparently been a long controversy in the scientific psychological circles over the "Whole Method" versus the "Part Method"; that is to say, a controversy as to whether proficiency in training is greater when a job is taught in its entirety, or whether learning is facilitated by breaking the job into suitable parts and concentrating the training effort on each part separately. To some extent the controversy has of course been academic, because every job, apart from the very simple ones, has to be broken into some stages before it can be taught. The protagonists of the "Part Method" believe that such element of the operation should be treated separately as a training project, and the skill developed to a high level before the trainee progresses to another element; this raises integration problems, which in turn become part of the training process. The experimental attitude of many firms during the war years made possible practical demonstrations of this controversy; broadly, much of the evidence pointed to the superior value of the "Part Method", provided that the breakdown of the job is not carried too far and that adequate attention is given to the integration of the stages of training.

Another important principle drawn from war-time experience lay in the high value of a systematic approach to training, a view running counter to the long tradition of British industry that a skill is best acquired by gradual practice under the eye of a master craftsman. War time experience provided many demonstrations of even complicated skills being acquired in short intensive training courses set up on a systematic programme.

According to this programme the new recruit does not report on the job immediately on taking up employment, but spends one, two or three days in preliminary instruction, often in a specific Training Centre. There, apart from general information about the firm and its products, factory or office regulations and other such items of background information which will assist the employee in settling down, there is a brief training programme relating to the essential features of the technical operations. Where the skill is of high level, the programme is limited to the basic principles of the operation and further training is given under the supervision of the department foreman.

In most of these induction courses, training is assisted by pictorial or other aids—either photographs or diagrams illustrating the operations or the product, or charts, models, etc., that will assist in the better understanding of the nature and purpose of the operations being taught. Here and there films are used for training purposes, but only the really large organisations with extensive recruitment programmes can find this worth while. One particular device developed for war-time purposes (although it has subsequently disappeared from normal use) was the "Synchrophone", a combination of gramophone and still picture automatically interlinked; the gramophone record contained a simple lecture on, for instance, the operation of a machine tool, the picture frame is a large-scale presentation of the machine; as the lecture proceeds, special features of the machine are thrown into relief by automatic light signals wired within the frame and linked up with the words of the lecturer.

At first sight many of these schemes may sound as though they are of relevance only to the larger organisations. In the sense of establishing a Training Centre with continuous arrangements for induction courses, such as this, the comment may undoubtedly be true. But the principles upon which this approach to training has been built are of equal application in the smaller firms, and in a few cases in this country effective introduction and training schemes have been developed in even quite small organisations. The difficulty usually is that the senior executives of the small firms are not alive to the importance of training, and tend to hide behind their small size as an excuse for not taking any action. Admittedly in this case of small firms, the organisation of training is more difficult, because their needs are both smaller and less continuous; their recruitment programme may need nothing more than a few additional people here and there spaced out over the year.

Experience in the few cases where systematic training has been undertaken in small British firms underlines the importance of earmarking one person, perhaps a foreman, to be responsible for the planning and supervision of such training. An illustration from a small food manufacturer may be of interest. The significance of training was first realised in this firm when on a certain occasion the manager found himself faced with an official contract which necessitated the packing of certain supplies in steel-hooped wooden cases sent in by the purchaser. Hitherto, packing had been in cartons, and there now arose the need for nailing—a skill not customary for women. It might almost sound ridiculous to talk of "training" for so simple an operation. Fortunately, however, the supervisor of the department realised that if he allowed one or two of his women to damage their thumbs in the first half-hour of nailing, his chance of getting teams regularly to work would be materially decreased. He therefore decided to deal with the problem systematically, and organised a brief training course, based on breaking the job into its essential elements. Stage one was how to hold and wield a hammer, taking into consideration the fact that women in general have had little previous experience of this implement and that their natural tendency is for a wrong grip that would lose a good deal of the weight of the blow. The second stage was the positioning of boards and the holding of the nail whilst the first blow is struck, particular attention being given to hand and eye co-ordination, so as to hit the nail rather than the thumb! Stage three was concerned with guiding the nail by the direction of the hammer blow. These three stages were very easily trained on pieces of wood suitably marked out, so that by the time the trainees were transferred to nailing a case, they had acquired adequate skill to direct the nail into the $\frac{3}{8}$-in. thickness of the side-boards without protrusions. Similar further stages of training were devoted to the positioning of the hoop (using the hammer as a lever), the use of a steel punch for piercing the hoop, linking up again with the earlier element of driving in the nail to complete the operation.

The main feature about this operation illustration is its simplicity, but it does indicate the underlying principles of breaking the job into parts so that each one can separately be learned, and of planning the training of a well-defined programme. The foreman was able to train half a dozen women at a time, and needed to devote only about twenty minutes of his time in each two or three hours to explaining and practising the elements, leaving the team for the next thirty to forty minutes carrying out practical exercises. The half-day devoted to this scheme meant a considerable difference to the efficiency and the productivity of the nailers.

Another small firm was concerned with the manufacture of lenses, involving a rather tricky setting operation. It had been said that no one was ever "trained" for this job, but that the skill was acquired by a long period of gradual experience. Anything from twelve to eighteen months was regarded as quite common. The firm employed only thirty-five persons, of whom about ten were on the particular process. It was the probability of expanding markets after the war that led to consideration of training, and the General Manager decided to have the assistance of a Training Consultant. Careful analysis of the operation by the Consultant revealed that the job was very much more simple than was commonly supposed, and that by some modification in the approach to it, it was possible to lay down specific elements each open to instruction, in place of the "judgment" which had hitherto been regarded as the key to the skill. Working along "part training" lines, with the aid of one or two simple off-the-job exercises to develop particular finger dexterities, a training programme of three weeks' duration was devised, in which the whole of the skill was acquired at a comparable level of quality of output, supplemented by a further three-week period in which the trainee's quantity of output was raised virtually to the level of the skilled operative.

In the course of the analysis of the job, the Consultant raised a considerable number of technical questions, points on which the operating instructions were not clear, variations in quality specifications, and many other technical details which indicated that the designing and tooling of the operation were still far from satisfactory. The Manager was himself a technician of a high order, and confessed astonishment at the questions being asked on points of technical detail which suggested incomplete knowledge or development of the process. Before the training programme could be devised, these items had to be settled; the outcome of the whole review was, therefore, not only a considerable improvement in training, but also important modifications in the layout of the job in quality standards and in tools.

This incident is not an isolated case; frequently one of the by-products of systematic training built up on a part basis and thus necessitating a closer review of operations, machines and tools, has been technical improvement of a far-reaching character.

Over recent years a certain amount of attention has been attracted to training programmes worked out in one or two of the British hosiery manufacturing firms and which are likely to spread through the industry. Large numbers of female operatives are employed, and there has been the traditional policy of letting new-comers "pick up the job" from a neighbour. Some of the operations, however, involve rather special skills and learning periods, for these often stretch out over eighteen months or two years. This is too serious a drawback, and so the hosiery concerns have begun to pay more regard to training. Apart from getting their new recruits to a higher level of productivity quickly, one or two firms (large and small) have found that the assistance of organised training is a valuable publicity aid to recruitment. Results accruing from systematic programmes for the higher skilled operations have been little short of spectacular— for instance, training times for outerwear lockstitch machinists were reduced from eighteen months to fourteen weeks, and even then with a higher standard of workmanship than in the case of the traditional worker. The organisation of this programme provided a very good example of the part-training approach. Analysis of the operation of machining the various parts of say, a dress, revealed that the key to the skill lay in the control of the fabric as it ran under the needle, and that broadly five different patterns of handling were required to control the fabric at the different stages of making up the dress. Differences in fabric had also to be taken into account: knitted fabrics, for example, stretch easily, while some of the more open woven ones will easily fray. Hence one basic requirement in the programme was a series of exercises (especially devised away from the machine) for training in the handling of various fabrics—aligning edges, folding, turning in, guiding through a dummy machine for straight runs, corners and reverses. Following closely on this came the specific training in disposition of the fingers for the various types of seam (i.e. the five "patterns" of handling referred to above). This was devised in the form of some twelve to fifteen types of seam actually run up on the machine, using waste strips of fabric and assisted by a set of finished seams displayed on the wall. These seams were, of course, graded for difficulty. (Learners who had no previous contact with a sewing machine, or any who found certain stages particularly difficult, could be taught and practised on a specially devised machine which formed a chain stitch for easy removal and correction.) As each phase of the machining was mastered at an approved level of quality and speed, the trainee began to spend part of the day making up those parts of garments where such seams or machining were required. In this way, the trainee was never confronted by a whole garment or a difficult operation until the basic skill entailed had been mastered.

Later in the programme, special exercises were provided for fancy machining and for the finishing of the dress (which entailed special dexterity in knitted lines, because of the bulk and weight to be handled). Similarly, at appropriate intervals other special off-the-job exercises were included as necessary, and in the earlier phases the programme provided eye-muscle exercises to reduce the eye-strain from the concentration in learning. Throughout, pictorial aids, devices, etc., were carefully worked into the scheme.

Naturally such a programme is more easily carried out by the medium or large firms within a separate Training Centre, but the approach has been found just as valuable for smaller units, provided there is a forewoman or other person adequately trained in the method. Expense is very reasonable, and is easily off-set by the rapid climb of new recruits to proficiency.

Similar schemes have also been developed on the stocking and sock side of the industry, for the more difficult manual operations, such, for instance, as linking and seaming. They have proved more difficult to analyse, but two cases are known in which a systematic training course for linking (looping) has been developed with an improvement in training time almost as outstanding as that of the dress machinists. The difficulty in this case has arisen because of the more continuous nature of the operation, and the very fine and delicate dexterities involved in the finger work.

Brief reference is made in a later paragraph to training for clerical staffs, but it may be pertinent to observe here that the principles outlined above could be made of special value to the trainings of many of the operations in offices, particularly those involving the use of hand-operated mechanical equipment. Most work of this kind is directly concerned with the semi-skilled work in factories, and there is a big pioneer-field waiting to be explored in the application of "part-training" methods to the office.

(c) *Craft Apprenticeship.*—This is usually the title given to the apprenticeship of engineers and electricians, builders and the like, and consists of a period of training to be provided by the employer either with or without indentures. Some large firms provide practical training in model workshops, with their own school and gymnasium in the factory. Most training schemes are satisfied by the Higher National Certificates, but in a number of cases boys are encouraged to go farther and obtain their Degree in engineering or electrical work.

Another type of training is for the shop lad, and here the work would be done in the normal way with part-time day release, so that he can attend the local Technical College for courses. Juveniles should always be under good supervision and kept fully occupied, and it is important that someone who is genuinely interested in the boys' welfare should also be concerned. A useful method of obtaining interest is to get a skilled craftsman to take a boy under his wing or for the boy to adopt himself an "uncle", thus being able to discuss the many problems which arise from day to day in connection with his practical work.

The majority of our engineering shops are small ones, and the provision of adequate supervision when practical work is involved is one of the essentials with any scheme of craft training. Records should be kept of the amount of time the boy has spent on the different phases of work or machines, so that he can be transferred at regular intervals to the next stage of his training. At the end of his period of training he should receive a letter from the company confirming that he has satisfactorily completed his training and giving other information which might prove useful to a prospective employer at some later date.

(*d*) *Training for Technical Appointments.*—Some of the youths who have passed through their practical training are considered sufficiently bright to make it worth while for the management to have them trained in some other branch of the profession or trade. An electrical apprentice might be considered for training as a methods engineer or draughtsman, whilst a mechanical engineer might be considered for time-study work, designer, production engineering, planning, and so on. This may mean additional study in the new job or a period of practical training in the department to which he would be attached. Some companies insist that when an apprentice has completed his training he is attached for a period of one to three months to every department in the firm before finally deciding where he should be employed. The type of training necessary may differ according to the ideas of the particular company, but it is always a useful guide to discuss the youth's possibilities and prospects in conjunction with his parents and the Principal of the local Technical College. By this means a wider background to the problem and the various matters for consideration can be looked into.

It is the practice of some companies to engage for training young men who have come from the Universities or who have already reached a definite position in theoretical work together with a practical experience. It is an advantage, as a rule, to start young men in this position with a definite curriculum agreed upon, but without defining closely the final job which it is intended the company should give him. That depends to a large extent on the suitability of the individual, the flair which he may have for a particular type of work and many other factors which can be judged only as they arise. Trainees of this kind should be attached primarily to the head executive, who should make it clear that he has an interest in their well-being.

(*e*) *Training in Clerical Work.*—There seems to be a widespread popular view that anyone can be a clerk, that no particular skill or experience is required to deal with paper work, but those with knowledge of what really goes on in the offices are well aware of the extent to which good training can contribute to effective work. Moreover, sound training of clerical workers has proved of great value in providing experienced people capable of promotion to higher responsibilities. The maintaining of production records for storekeeping work may not, at first sight, appear to be important, until it is realised that the whole flow of output may depend on their accuracy; production lines could be held up if the information on the bin card or records were inaccurate—the record may point to adequate quantities of material in stock, but the bin is in fact empty! Practical training of this kind is a matter for individual firms, to teach the new employee methods for dealing with papers in that particular office. The amount of skill required for this purpose by the instructor is great, for not only does he need to be able to give a lucid explanation of the "whys and wherefores", but also be able to convince his "pupils" that the job is important and that it is being done in the best possible way.

Operators of machines (comptometers, typewriters and the like) can often be taught their work by the machine manufacturers, which has the big advantage that they are skilfully instructed in the special characteristics of the machines and will be trained to handle these expensive instruments with the necessary care. The training of typists is one of the jobs being given more prominence than any other today, owing to their shortage.

None of this special training, however, should be done without bearing in mind the practical aspects of what the person will be expected to do when trained: how futile, for instance, to insist on a girl reaching 140 words per minute at shorthand class only to be delegated to a person whose dictating speed never rises above 40!

(f) *Education of Juveniles.*—All juveniles should receive practical training on the job from the supervisor of his or her section in a similar way to new adult labour. In addition, it is considered that all juveniles need further education. Some will undertake evening classes on their own initiative, and should be released earlier in the afternoon to attend such classes. Some watch should, however, be kept on this, as attending evening school two or three times a week, after working all day, may prove detrimental to the vigour of young people and hence to their efficiency as workers. It is for this reason that many firms prefer to send their youngsters to school for one full day a week (or two half days).

The advantages of day-time education may be summarised thus:

(i) This continued education will become compulsory in due course; in the meantime, the benefit is spread to those juveniles who do not attend evening classes voluntarily.

(ii) Those who would normally attend would be able to go less often with consequent improvement in their health, vigour, industrial output and accuracy. Study during the day would produce much better results.

(iii) The scheme would be attractive to parents and boys and girls with ambition; therefore recruitment should be aided.

The obvious disadvantages are that the juveniles would always be away from their job on two half-days each week and would be paid for this time. However, it is considered that the fact that wages are paid during "school time" would be compensated later on by the increased usefulness of these juveniles.

(g) *Students.*—These would be specially selected and would have attained a minimum education level. They would be required to attend classes on two evenings a week in addition to two half-days. In this time (day and evening) their study would be directed towards an approved examination, normally taken at age 19–21. No hard-and-fast rule can be applied regarding time off, as this will vary according to the classes that are available locally, but it is recommended that two afternoons and not one whole day should be allocated to students who attend Technical College. Whenever possible, evening classes should be on the same day as the afternoon classes, and students could then have tea in the college canteen.

It is quite a good idea, when numbers justify it, to form a Students' Committee representing all types of students. The Personnel Officer and/or the Training Officer would be *ex-officio* members, but eventually the students should be able to manage their own meetings. The committee should have no executive power, all its recommendations and deliberations being passed on through the Personnel or Training Officer.

Students would need to be very carefully selected, and they should be interviewed by the head of the department concerned as well as the Personnel and Training Officers. School reports, too, would need to be reviewed, and each student given a test to ascertain his suitability for training. These facts and details of progress in training should be entered on the record card to save setting up a separate juvenile training card index. There should be every incentive to cause a boy or girl to wish to attend evening classes and to study for examinations. Preferential rates of pay might be considered, and any existing schemes of increments should take care of examinations passed.

Students should not be allowed to remain at one job or in one department, but should be moved about according to a prearranged scheme, which has been agreed by all concerned. Thus an engineering apprentice or student should spend some time in Stores, Fitting, Machine Shop, Assembly, Cost Office, Time Study, Sales Department and Personnel Department during his period of training.

Four types of student are suggested:

1. Technical Students

  (a) Students who have been employed in the Engineering, Electrical and Works Services Departments. Alternative names are Engineering Students or even Apprentices.

  (b) Age for acceptance about 15–18.

(c) A good general education would be required with a good grounding in mathematics and/or physics for intending engineers. Careful selection would be necessary, and a probationary period of from three to six months is suggested.

(d) The students would study for National Certificates in an appropriate branch of engineering, or would learn the theoretical side of their trade as craftsmen (e.g. carpenter) at the technical college.

2. Commerce Students

(a) Specially selected students who would be employed in the office or warehouse departments.

(b) Age for acceptance about 16 +.

(c) School-leaving Examination would be a prerequisite.

(d) Different examinations for these students are held, depending on their interests, ability and ultimate department in their firm.

3. General Students

(a) Besides these Technical, Commercial and Laboratory students, there may remain some juveniles who would like to study at evening classes (as well as at compulsory day-time classes). They might be employed in any department.

(b) Age for acceptance 16–18.

(c) Of good general education and adjudged capable of passing an examination in general higher education by the age of 19, science usually being one of the subjects studied.

4. Laboratory Staff

These would be mainly Chemists and Physicists, and would study for the B.Sc., preferably in Chemistry, Physics, Biology, or Pure Mathematics.

(h) *Training for Supervisors.*—Of all the aspects of industrial training that have claimed attention in recent years, the development of plans for the training of foremen have probably been both the centre of greatest interest and the line of most important advance. Some firms, of course, have maintained training schemes for supervisory staffs for many years, but these were among the exceptional rather than the common. As part of the earlier phases of the "management" movement, there were always one or two activities specifically devoted to foremen; for instance, the occasional week-end conferences organised by the Industrial Welfare Society and the two-year Certificate Course in Supervision sponsored by the Institute of Industrial Administration and covered by study courses at certain Technical Colleges (evening sessions). Broadly, however, real interest on any measurable scale did not emerge until 1940–41, when the impact of war-time expansion brought home to industry the deficiencies in the supervisory levels and the inadequate existing methods—mainly in terms of technical prowess—to make any real contribution to filling the gap.

Naturally enough, the first forward move was based on existing schemes; with the collaboration of the Institute of Industrial Administration, the Ministry of Labour evolved the three-month study course covering in concentrated form most of the matter of the pre-war two-year course. Colleges up and down the country co-operated, and very soon some thousands of foremen were able to get rudimentary basic instruction in the essentials of their supervisory tasks —principles and practice of production planning and control, the significance of cost control, the human aspects, personnel relations, the maintenance of discipline and so on.

Before long the "students" themselves began to show a measure of initiative; appreciation of their course led to recognition of how much farther they had still to go, and the particular need that they felt was for some means by which the general and basic instruction gained at the College course could be interpreted into dealing with their individual daily responsibilities and problems. In many parts of the country, nothing at all was ever done about it, but in some of the more thickly populated industrial areas, the scheme of "Supervisor Discussion Groups" was soon evolved. (The pioneer Group was formed in North-east London in the spring of 1942.) Their purpose was to provide an occasion for periodic informal meetings of foremen and similar staffs from a variety of firms in the locality, and for discussion of the practice of supervision on the basis of the principles learned in the course. These Groups are still flourishing and still making an important contribution to the strengthening of supervisors.

The next official development was the *Training Within Industry (T.W.I.) Programme for Supervisors.* With its origin in America, this scheme was adapted by the Ministry of Labour to British conditions and a service set up for its establishment in industrial organisations here. As the title implies, its central thesis is the principle that the greatest benefit for supervisors in training is drawn from a scheme that links up closely and immediately with their own everyday tasks.

Whether the *Training Within Industry Programme* has been an unmitigated success or not is open to question. Some firms have been enthusiastic in its praise, while others have felt that its pattern was somewhat stereotyped, and in consequence foremen have felt the training to be both artificial and superficial. To overcome this difficulty, one or two firms have experimented with internal group discussion methods. One of the leading Management Consultant firms has also done some pioneer work in this direction, using the small group technique and working to a scheme in which all the subject-matter which forms the basis of training is provided by the participating foremen themselves; thus the foremen can feel that they are actively sharing in a "review of management and supervision" rather than undergoing instruction. Experience is proving this approach to be of very great value, especially from the standpoint of the older foremen. The soundness of the group discussion technique as a constructive means of training has long been recognised, and in the case of its application to the development of foremen, there is the added benefit that the "matter" of the discussions is directly concerned with the daily tasks of those who are participating.

What should be the content of the supervisor training schemes? The answer must to some extent depend on the conditions prevailing in the firms concerned. For instance, in some industries the foreman necessarily has highly important technical functions which may deeply colour the pattern of his responsibilities. In many chemical and other process lines, problems of production planning and control do not arise at the foreman level, and little purpose is served by supervisors "devoting" more than general and superficial attention to studies of production and cost control. On the other hand, virtually every foreman will have human responsibilities, of wider or narrower scope, so that this field will need to figure in every programme. Broadly, the matter may be summarised in the generalisation that the requirements of any supervisory post are a combination of the following three factors: the arrangement, balance and emphasis being determined according to the particular circumstances of each post:

(1) Technical ability, covering both knowledge and skill.
(2) Personal qualities, centring round leadership and co-operation.
(3) Administrative ability, comprising mainly a knowledge and understanding of the significance of the organisation and control of production.

1. Technical Ability

From the nature of the responsibilities put upon the foreman or supervisor in a production department, it is clear that he must possess a minimum level of skill and knowledge of the processes under his jurisdiction. The more highly technical the processes, the greater the significance of this factor. But it still remains true that, whatever the process, no amount of technical ability is by itself sufficient for effective supervision.

2. Personal Qualities

The foreman or supervisor has to govern men and women in the performance of a task; he has to secure their effective co-operation in the common aim; he has to maintain law and order, settle disputes, meet complaints and grumbles. He has also to work in harmony with his counterpart in other sections, and with the management to which he is responsible. These personal qualities are usually summed up in the terms "leadership and co-operation", and are made up of varying combinations of many characteristics.

3. *Administrative Ability*

Supervision involves responsibility for interpreting "management" to operatives and for contributing to the control of production. The supervisor must therefore understand something about production and personnel management; and his effectiveness (if he is suitable on other grounds) can be increased only by the acquisition of a deeper knowledge of the administrative process; he is part of the executive scheme, and the more he understands what that scheme stands for, the more readily can he pull his weight in it.

It can be safely assumed that the training programme for supervisors will need, in most cases, to contain no items that are specifically devoted to the purely technical aspect of their responsibilities; that they will usually have acquired in the course of their service in the trade concerned. The training called for has to deal with the human and the administrative sides of their tasks, in general terms as well as in special relation to the methods of their own firm. Proficiency in these directions will require a twofold line of training: the acquisition of knowledge, plus some instruction or guidance in the daily application of that knowledge. This approach shows the value of the different phases of supervisor training referred to above—for instance, the Technical College course as a source of general knowledge, plus the internal group technique as a translation of that knowledge into practice. Broadly, the total content of this double training process may perhaps be summed up as follows:

(a) The acquisition of a certain body of knowledge: this will consist of:
   (1) General principles of production control and of methods which are frequently adopted in industry as a whole.
   (2) The specific methods of control used in the firm itself.
   (3) General knowledge of some of the specialised field of personnel management, as applied through the foreman.

(b) The growth in supervisory experience:

   (1) In the exercise of responsibility, leadership and co-operation.
   (2) In the use and application of control methods in so far as they form part of the foreman's or supervisor's function.

To a very large extent the first aspect will be very much the same in most firms, or at least in firms of comparable sizes. The variable element will be the study of the particular methods adopted in the firm concerned. In other words, there is a large part of the content of the training scheme under aspect (a) that could conform to a certain centrally established scheme; a complementary and very important part, however, will be peculiar to each firm itself, and will in particular include the second aspect of training.

In the main, the training under the second head will consist of what might be called "organised growth", consisting of systematic assistance in the acquisition and/or development of certain personal qualities—making up leadership and co-operation. Example, especially deliberate example from the supervisor's immediate chief, can play a very important part in this process, and ought certainly to have a place in the training scheme; for the rest, encouragement and guidance by group talks, discussions and conferences, or by across-the-table interviews, will form the most appropriate methods. The personal qualities to be inculcated should also include such items as the following, which are particularly important from the supervisor's point of view:

(a) Confidence in management and how to maintain it, especially in face of circumstances that give rise to doubts.
(b) Interest in the tasks of supervision.
(c) Ability to think objectively and constructively.
(d) Understanding of the value of self-analysis and constructive self-criticism.
(e) Ability to avoid worrying or being worried.
(f) Ability to apply job analysis and to realise the significance.

It is almost inevitable that much of the emphasis in training programmes for supervisors will be on the human aspects of their responsibilities. With most foremen already established, this will be the side of their task for which they have hitherto had little, if any, specific preparation. There are, undoubtedly, many foremen with the inherent skill of successful dealings with their fellow men: they need but little supplementary knowledge of the best practices of personnel management. But these gifted few stand in contrast to thousands who have no special flair, but who have adequate abilities and disposition to learn, and who thus need the special training that will enable them to copy the skill of those who are the "born leaders". Clearly, the question of selection of candidates for promotion is vitally linked up with this aspect of training. Nothing has been said here, so far, about the provision for training for potential supervisors, as distinct from those already in office: this, because the issue is one more relevant to selection than to training. The course of study and the subject-matter to be covered would be very similar in both cases, though of rather more generalised character in the case of the potential supervisors.

What are the qualities relevant to successful foremanship? Many lists have been drawn up and considerable controversy has taken place over them. Perhaps the sensible answer is that much will depend on the prevailing circumstances of the appointment, including the personalities to be contacted in the management structure in the course of discharging the supervisory responsibilities. In general terms, the following list has been drawn up as an open combination of desirable qualities for the average run of industrial foremanship appointments: [1]

(a) *Main*:
Self-control.
Fairmindedness.
Honesty and sincerity.
Tact.
Mental alertness.
Initiative.

(b) *Subsidiary:*
Sense of perspective.
Tenacity and courage.
Patience.
Courtesy.
Observation.

In the industrial world of today, no firm, large or small, can afford not to develop sound levels of supervision, which in effect means having a training policy and a plan of campaign for foremen. The plan should envisage preparatory training prior to appointment or in the early stages after taking over responsibility, as well as supplementary "refresher" sessions at later intervals. These could be in the form of the group discussions referred to above as organised within the medium-sized and larger organisations, or in the case of the smaller firms, these needs could be adequately met by active participation in the local Supervisor Discussion Groups which are to be found in many districts.

The planning of a supervisor training policy should be based on a clear aim—its purpose is to improve the effectiveness of supervisors in that capacity; it is NOT intended as a surreptitious means of push-

[1] This list was privately prepared. For a fuller review of the problem of selection, see *The New Foremanship*, by H. G. Burns Morton (Chapman & Hall), and occasional articles in the journals of the Institute of Personnel Management, the National Institute of Industrial Psychology and the Industrial Welfare Society.

ing them forward for promotion. Devising the programme to carry out the policy is likely, very quickly, to bring home to top management the need for two further fundamental principles. The one is the classification and definition of the responsibilities of the supervisors, especially in relation to "line" executives (e.g. Factory and Departmental Managers) and to service specialists. Experience with these programmes has almost invariably thrown into relief confusions over the distribution of responsibilities, and a good deal of difficulty can be avoided if the clarification takes place prior to the training, or at least as an early phase of the training programme itself. The second point calling for consideration is the status and conditions of service of the foremen. Their participation in the scheme emphasises the importance of their responsibility; it is highly important for the maintenance of their morale that the company's policy ensures that their conditions of service are of adequate standard in relation to other members of the staff.

(i) *Training for Managers.*—The earlier interest in training at the supervisor level has not only extended in scope, but has also led on to schemes for the training of managers. These raise large problems, involving matters both of organisation structure and of personal development, and the subject is more appropriately dealt with in Chapter VIII of Part Five below (page 1016) as part of the consideration of the profession of management.

*   *   *   *   *

The wording of the foregoing paragraphs appears to have been planned specifically in reference to manufacturing organisations. But everything that has been said has exactly the same application to supervisors in commercial organisations, or clerical departments. In an accounts section, for instance, the supervisor's "technical" field will be his or her knowledge of accountancy and the machines used. The "administrative" group refers again to the procedures or methods according to which the section works. The "human" facet is precisely as in the factory—save that the girls work with pen or typewriter and brain, instead of with hands and dexterity: it is doubtful whether even this distinction is valid or justified.

Training of supervisory staffs in clerical and commercial operations has been even worse neglected than on the industrial side, but is no less significant.

PROMOTION

A defined promotion policy should be the natural accompaniment of systematic selection, placement and training of employees. The underlying principle would be to fill all appointments from within whenever there is a suitable candidate qualified for promotion; in practice this means a regular procedure for advertising or notifying all vacancies to employees, and for ensuring that when foremen or managers have a job to fill, they think first of upgrading and not of looking for an outsider.

The Personnel Department—where one exists—would be one of the first to know that a vacancy for a chargehand, foreman or junior executive had occurred. Applications should be invited from suitably qualified employees who are interested, and the Personnel Manager should interview each one. He will need to be particularly careful to make objective assessments of the candidates, unbiased by partial knowledge from personal contacts. The interview should serve too to give applicants further knowledge about the appointment. Other relevant information would be the absence and lateness records of the past five years, together with a short report from the departments where he had previously worked.

Once the appointment has been made and the man or woman has been selected, they should be interviewed again and congratulated on their appointment, by both the Personnel and Works Managers. A letter setting out their new terms and conditions of employment and stating when this takes place should be given to the employee, and no interview of this kind should ever be completed without asking a question—"Is there anything else you would like to know about the job?" It is often wise to ask the Managing Director to have a few words with the man, or woman, just prior to his taking over the new appointment: this would do a great deal towards convincing the ordinary man that the Board of Directors and the executives are really interested in him.

Sometimes a promotion means sitting in a different part of the canteen, and this is where the Personnel Manager again should take care to see that he lunches with the new person and introduces him where necessary, so that he suffers no embarrassment.

WITHDRAWALS

1. Retirements

The Personnel Manager's part in dealing with the older employee reaching retiring age is the complement of his tasks in recruitment, training and promotion. Time was when the main problem in retirement lay in the financial position of the old people, but recent developments in National Insurance, supplemented by the much wider existence of contributory and savings clubs, have removed the greater part of this problem. Moreover, there is now greater readiness to stay at work to a later age, and far more opportunities of continuing in employment, in the interests of the country's economic progress.

From the company's standpoint, the more important aspect is morale value of the retirement; this turns on the Personnel Manager's attitude. Some reference will necessarily have been made to the impending termination during the preceding few months, but at the point of parting the Personnel Manager should arrange a special interview, with adequate time to make the employee feel that it is an important occasion. In the smaller firms, this pleasant task will naturally be taken over by the owner or chief director himself. The firm's policy may make this the occasion for a souvenir presentation. In any case it will be made clear to the retiring employee that the company is still interested in him, anxious to be kept in touch with him and always ready to help. All legal obligation to this employee may indeed have ceased, but there is no doubt that where a man has given a major portion of his working life to a firm, they have a moral duty to extend a considerate and helping hand to him—and they undoubtedly draw benefit from this contribution that such an attitude makes to the morale of all employees in the firm.

2. Terminations

For one reason or another, there will always be some employee whose service with the company comes to an end. For the Personnel Department a termination of employment involves a task with two distinct phases. There is the purely mechanical task of carrying out certain things to ensure that the departing employee is paid all money due, returns tools or equipment belonging to the company, gets back his Insurance card, and so on. But there is also the human side, the face-to-face contact with the employee concerned, and this should be an important personal responsibility of the Personnel Officer or his immediate functional deputy.

It is characteristic of the previous era that employees (then called "hands") were dismissed at an hour's or a day's notice without regard to the personal damage done to the individual by the shattering of security, to the morale of the factory or office, or to the fabric of society. The rising generation that does not know the industrial world of the days of heavy unemployment cannot readily appreciate the significance of the persisting cry for "security" or the almost unreasonable tenacity against even glaringly obvious redundancy.

The existence of a personnel policy usually means the inclusion of a guarantee against unfair dismissal, and the Personnel Manager is primarily responsible for seeing that the guarantee is upheld. Hence the importance of his personal task—in a case of dismissal to be sure of the facts, to know the employee's side, to make an objective appraisal to uphold the agreed decision, but to see to it also that the employee leaves with a sense of justice done rather than injustice suffered, and that his former mates do not bear a self-justified resentment.

The other side of the picture has a similar importance. The employee wishing to leave may be a genuine case—with reasons patently obvious. He may, however, bring forward a seemingly factual reason as the means of an underlying disgruntlement—perhaps unfair treatment, perhaps dissatisfaction with conditions or the progress, or perhaps the reflection of a sorry state of morale in the department.

It must be among the Personnel Officer's most important tasks to interview all employees wishing to terminate their service, not as a formality, but as an occasion for letting the individual make a contribution to his knowledge of the social relations of the organisation. From the employee whose termination is simply on factual grounds —getting married, removal from district, etc.—the Personnel Officer may get little but pleasant reminiscence. From those whose leaving reflects a sense of discontentment, this may become a valuable guide to weaknesses in organisation or supervision, or unsuspected grievances, and may perhaps disclose a chance of retaining the employee after all.

Wastage of employees can be a source of serious financial loss, and the Personnel Officer is making his most valuable contribution towards his real purpose in the organisation every time he avoids the termination of service of a good employee, especially if at the same time he is able to set in train correctives for adverse conditions hitherto unsuspected.

3. Redundancy

It happens in many companies that conclusions or cancellations of contract or other outside economic factors bring about a redundancy of operatives which looks like being longstanding. Where this takes place, it is usual for the last employees to come to be the first to leave, and this kind of clause will be found in many Trade Union Agreements. If the discharges are to be on a considerable scale, the detailed work needs to be carefully planned beforehand. In every case, the employees should be given either adequate notice or, alternatively, a week or two's pay in lieu of notice, so that they have the opportunity of seeking employment without being thrust on to public funds straightway. The Personnel Manager should plan to carry the Shop Stewards with him from the outset. The reasons for the redundancy should be carefully and fully explained. If there are to be several stages, this should be disclosed at the first meeting. Reference to the records or to specially prepared lists will enable, in each section or category, the principle of "last come, first go" to be observed. Where the lists are considerable, it is best to allow the Stewards a day or two to investigate the matter themselves; it will then be easy to find out how many cases are agreed and how many are queried. For those that are agreed, discharging machinery and a posting of notices can be arranged in the shop, and then individual notice given to each man. Whatever happens, the Personnel Manager should make sure that these notices are handed out in the department by himself, or by one of his representatives. They should not, in any case, be put into the pay packet, for wherever possible a full explanation should be given to each individual employee. The queries can be carefully scrutinised and finally agreed by the Personnel Officer and the Shop Stewards.

Apprentices and students under training are usually excluded by an Agreement which has been made either individually or by the Unions, and where the number of employees is reduced owing to redundancy they are kept on.

There will undoubtedly be the odd case which cannot be agreed, and this needs to be treated with a great deal of care, particularly if there is any suggestion that an employee is being unfairly treated. In such a case, it should be made clear that the person will be kept in the company's employ until such time as the matter is disposed of by negotiation, and this may, in fact, mean taking it either to a Joint Industrial Council in the industry or, alternatively, to notify the Ministry of Labour of the failure to agree and ask for an independent arbitrator to be appointed.

There is nothing that can injure a company so quickly as the apathetic attitude to a job which becomes apparent as soon as the word "redundancy" is whispered around. Men get restless and start looking around for other jobs, thinking the firm is going bankrupt; rumour follows rumour, and unless the Personnel Manager is alive to the situation, much damage can be done externally, as well as within the works.

A typical redundancy agreement is as follows:

REDUNDANCY

1. The Management shall keep the workers' representatives informed as to the volume of work available in the Works and shall consider any proposals put forward by them as to the utilisation of the labour force in relation to the work available.

2. On a reduction in the volume of work the Company shall discharge part-time and temporary workers before declaring a redundancy. For this purpose all workers shall be regarded as

temporary for 12 months following their date of engagement by the Company.

3. Redundancy shall apply departmentally and/or sectionally on the general principle of "last in—first out" in order of service. In determining between more than one employee on equal service, degree of skill and time-keeping will be taken into account.

4. Registered disabled persons shall not normally be discharged if to to do so would reduce the numbers of such employees below the statutory quota for the works.

5. Cases of special hardship shall receive individual consideration and shall be the subject of consultation with the workers' representatives.

6. Notwithstanding the above, the Company shall have the right to retain the services of any worker if, in their opinion, it is in the best interests of the Company and the employees generally to do so.

7. The Management shall provide facilities for the services of a local representative of the Ministry of Labour to be made available at the Works to assist workers declared redundant to obtain other employment. Apart from this, the responsibility for finding other employment lies with the individual worker with the assistance of the Ministry of Labour and not with the Company.

8. Workers declared redundant shall be given three weeks' warning of the Company's intention to give them one week's notice to terminate their employment. During such period of warning the worker will be free to terminate his service without notice and on leaving during such period receive one week's pay in addition to any other amounts then due to him.

9. Workers declared redundant may be allowed time off, with pay not exceeding a total of 5 hours, providing that the Management is satisfied that this time is genuinely required for the purpose of obtaining other employment.

10. Workers declared redundant who wish to have the opportunity of re-engagement by the Company, must, before leaving, notify the Personnel Manager accordingly. If a vacancy arises in the Works, the Company will notify such employees, if any, who were discharged as redundant within the previous six months and who are considered suitable for the vacancy in order that they may be given the opportunity of stating whether they wish to be considered for it. Any worker who is re-engaged during a period of six months following the date of his discharge as redundant will count his previous service and the period of absence for long service benefits subject to the provision of Clause 14 of the Agreement.

11. Nothing in this schedule shall affect the provisions of Clause 5 of this Agreement relating to the discharge of individual workers.

(*Extract from main Agreement on Conditions of Employment.*)

P.P.M.—19*

4. Disorderly Conduct

Under this heading the decision to discharge an employee is usually based on some definite evidence. It may be a breach of the works rules, a brawl or fight between two employees, the merits of which will need to be gone into very carefully by the Personnel Manager or sometimes by the Managing Director himself. In highly emotional cases, including drunkenness, it is wise never to make a decision on the day that the incident happens, but to wait until the next day. People who are giving an account of what has happened will give an entirely different story when they are cool, calm and collected, than they will when tempers are frayed.

5. The Unsatisfactory Worker

Some reference was made to this type of problem in an earlier section on morale. It may be that complaints drift into the Personnel Manager about an employee in such-and-such a department, until, finally, a definite request is received by the Personnel Manager to discharge the employee. The Personnel Manager usually handles this type of case with the foreman by seeing the man to explain that he has been unsatisfactory from a work point of view over a long period, that he has had several warnings and, despite these, no improvement has been shown, and finally it is felt that he must go. Where a man belongs to a union, he has the right to have his Shop Steward present if he wishes. Always try to discharge employees in a friendly way; there is no need to be hostile, abrupt or unkind. The Personnel Manager must, however, be very frank, and if the man being discharged protests that this, that or the other fact is incorrect, the person who made the allegations should be sent for immediately, and be required to repeat them in the presence of the employee. Hearing the facts on both sides, the Personnel Manager will have the final word, but it is much better to get agreement from the man that he has been unsatisfactory and that it is a logical thing for him to be discharged, as he has not improved.

The question of whether a discharged person should work out the notice is debatable. Most Personnel Managers think that an employee who is discharged—whether from factory or office—is best out of the gates as soon as it has been decided, and that he should be paid wages in lieu of notice rather than have him about the place, a misery to himself and everyone else, whilst he is serving his notice.

Finally, when it comes to the end, the man should be given a friendly hand-shake and wished good luck in whatever job he takes up. The fact that he has not been successful in one company is no criterion that he will not be an outstanding success in the next. He may well be helped to obtain a suitable job elsewhere, a matter in which the good Personnel Manager can really demonstrate his own skill.

CHAPTER IV

THE ACTIVITIES OF A PERSONNEL DEPARTMENT

THE PERSONNEL DEPARTMENT OFFICE

AMONG the functions of a Personnel Manager is that of supplying the factory and offices with recruits as required by the production or load of work, and of keeping up-to-date information about the personnel employed. This and many other activities necessitate the provision of suitable accommodation.

Where to place the department can be determined only by consideration of such factors as:

(1) Policy in regard to separate or central records.
(2) The location of the production departments.
(3) Location of main administrative offices.
(4) Access from the road.
(5) Availability to all employees.

The size of the staff required in the department must also be considered. Most factories have their Personnel Department near the works entrance, so that applicants for jobs and other visitors can be directed to the appropriate reception without getting lost in a maze of factory departments or without having to go through a number of offices, stores, etc. On the other hand, it is necessary to bear in mind that the Personnel Department must also be easily accessible to the employees, so that they are not discouraged from coming there with problems because it is situated in an out-of-the-way part of the factory, and involves a journey of several minutes. To arrive at a balance of these conflicting issues needs a careful review of all the relevant factors in each particular case.

Where the factory is a large one, with many big departments, it is advisable to have a separate small Personnel Office in each main department. This might also be an advantage where there are a number of storeys to the building, and time might be wasted by the employees leaving their jobs for a long time in order to visit the Personnel Department with their particular problem.

The layout of an ordinary Personnel Department needs to be given careful consideration, and a number of plans have been prepared for both simple and extensive departments. Wherever possible, the whole of the Personnel Department should be located together. This is particularly important where a Medical Section is concerned, as the amount of work which goes on between the two sections is considerable, and co-operation is made easier on many matters if they are situated in the same building, and can possibly use the same records, apart from the confidential professional information which the Medical Officer must keep himself in private custody.

SOURCES OF RECRUITMENT

It would depend on the size of the company whether the Personnel Department was split up into different sections. In a factory employing, say, about 500 people, it would be usual for the Personnel Manager himself to take on all new employees. The sources of supply are:

(a) Casual callers.
(b) Employees sent by the Ministry of Labour.
(c) Introductions from friends or relatives.
(d) Persons attracted by advertisements.

(a) In the first place, the *casual caller.* This is the person who, for some reason best known to himself, does not wish to go to the Employment Exchange in his search for work. Many men object to having to register with the Employment Exchange in order to get a job. Others feel that they can find employment for themselves, and in touring around for a job, do so, not with the particular object of taking the first job that they find vacant, but finding somewhere that suits their idea of a reasonable place in which to be employed. (The Personnel Officer, in dealing with these applicants, has to bear in mind any limitations on engagement which may be currently in force under Statutory Orders.)

(b) *Employees submitted by the Ministry of Labour.*—These are the normal cases of would-be employees sent for interview by the Employment Exchange, where details of every known vacancy in the locality are kept, filed in occupational order. When a worker calls at the Exchange for a job, he is interviewed, in the first instance, by the counter clerk and given a classification, and passed on to the Placement Officer, who, after a confidential chat, looks through the list of vacancies, firstly, in the home locality, and later in other jobs outside the radius of his own Exchange. Usually the applicant is given two or three jobs to go to before he is registered as unemployed, and an Introduction Card is issued by the Ministry, which is an introduction to the Personnel Department of the firm where the vacancy exists. The Ministry make a point of trying to place workers in the job which they want, or in the locality where they prefer to

Size of Firm	*Staff*	*Accommodation Required*
1.—Under 200[1]: Director, Manager or executive responsible, among other duties, for welfare and employment policy Secretary-assistant (qualified in first-aid) carrying out most of the routine work Clerk or clerical assistance (part-time) N.B.—*Much of the work may be deputed to the secretary-assistant, in which case she will need clerical help; otherwise, in the smaller firm, she may combine the duties of secretary and records clerk, or a part-time clerk may be employed on records.*		Executive's office Secretarial and records office Waiting and/or interview room First-aid room Small extra room for interviews or committees may be an advantage
2.—200–300: Executive responsible as in (1) *or* Personnel Officer Secretary-assistant Clerk N.B.—*The firm will not be large enough to justify the employment of a nurse, unless she has also certain welfare duties. Either the Personnel Officer or secretary-assistant should be qualified in first-aid.* *Whether a separate clerk will be required will depend on the scope of the work. As in (1), it should be possible to combine the secretarial and records work.*		Private office Secretarial and records office Waiting room Committee room (which can also be used for interviews) First-aid room (with screened rest couch or separate rest room) Store cupboard for protective clothing and first-aid supplies
3.—300–500: Personnel Officer Secretary-assistant Clerical assistance according to need N.B.—*In the firm of 300+, the appointment of a Personnel Officer should be made unless an executive can devote most of his time to the work. Secretary-assistant and clerical assistant now become essential. It may be worth considering the appointment of a nurse. Normally she would not have enough to keep her busy unless there were special hazards, a part-time medical service, sick visiting, etc., and unless she assisted the Personnel Officer in certain duties. Otherwise the arrangement should be as in (2).*		Accommodation as in (2), but separate rest room is necessary.

[1] It is deliberately assumed that progress has been made in the organisation of employment, welfare and health services in this size of firm. The small firm about to consider the whole subject should seek the assistance of the Industrial Welfare Society.

FIG. 79.—Extracted from a pamphlet

Size of Firm	*Staff*	*Accommodation Required*

4.—500–1,000: Personnel Officer
Assistant
Secretary
Records clerk and other clerical assistance according to the scope of the department
Nurse

N.B.—*One of the staff should be qualified in first-aid to assist the nurse when required or to take her place when she has to go out.*

Accommodation Required:
Private office
Office for assistant, secretary and records
Waiting room
Interview room
Committee room (*this can be used as additional waiting room or interview room*)

Surgery
Nurse's room
Waiting room (preferably divided for men and women)
Washrooms and w.c.'s for men and women
Rest room
Store for surgery supplies and protective clothing

4a.—500–1,000 (with part-time medical service): As above, with addition of part-time medical officer, and assistant to nurse (full or part-time according to scope of work in surgery)

As above, with addition of doctor's consulting room and separate waiting rooms for men and women

---

5.—1,000–3,000: Personnel Manager
Two or three assistants, with duties divided between them (e.g. employment, reinstatement, training, employee services)
Secretarial and clerical staff according to the scope of the work
Part-time Medical Officer
Nurse
Assistant nurse

N.B. (*a*)—*When clerical assistance is required in the surgery, the staff of the personnel office can usually assist. Additional nurses will be required if the firm works on shifts.*
(*b*)—*Firms in this category should consider the advisability of decentralising the work, i.e. placing certain services in the works proper instead of segregating them in the Personnel Department.*
(*c*)—*In this category, there might often be a good case for a full-time Medical Officer.*

Accommodation Required:
Private office
One or more offices for assistants
Secretarial and records office
Waiting room
Interview room
Conference room

Surgery (preferably divided into two for men and women)
Doctor's consulting room
Nurse's office
Waiting rooms for men and women
Washrooms and w.c. for men and women
Rest room divided for men and women
Store for surgery supplies
Store for protective clothing
Staff cloakroom

published by the Industrial Welfare Society.

work and they will circulate particulars to exchanges within a given area, or throughout the country.

Clerical workers or office staffs are usually dealt with through the same channels, but persons in technical or managerial grades are referred to the Appointments Departments. These are situated in different regions throughout the country, and specialise in finding employment for people with managerial or specialist qualifications or ex-officer grades from the Regular Armed Services. They are linked up by teleprinter, and a person registering at one can be assured that his particulars will be circulated should a vacancy exist in another area.

(c) *Introductions from Friends or Relatives already employed.—* Some companies pay a great deal of attention to these introductions, and from a morale point of view it is a channel that should be considered of great importance. The goodwill of the company has already been partly won before the employee starts work, by reason of his knowledge of conditions as gathered from his friends or relatives. He is therefore anxious to start. In some areas, particularly in many of the older industries, companies have for generations employed father and son, mother and daughter, in the same works, and applications for employment in the company are made when the children reach the age of twelve or thirteen. This often helps to weld employees together with the company, and one gets the impression of it being a "family concern". Priority, generally, should be given to introduction of relatives, but a danger here to be considered is the position when an old servant or employee asks for a vacancy to be found in respect of one of his relatives, and it is not possible to do this without increasing the agreed number of employees.

(d) *Persons attracted by Advertisements.—*The method of advertising varies according to the company's policy. Some firms prefer to place their own advertisements and give their name for interested applicants to know who they are. Others make a practice of never advertising their identity, but prefer to have a Box number; others an Advertising Agency—the advantages are that they are not bothered by people who have applied for a position and been considered unsuitable, whereas by the other method more people feel disposed to apply. The small service which should be given to all applicants for a job advertised in the Press is for the employer to take the trouble to acknowledge the application. To a person who has taken the trouble to sit down and write a letter applying for a job, it is most disheartening if, after watching the postman day after day, there is no reply to the letter he has written, whereas, for the sake of a stamp and a plain piece of paper and a plain envelope, the person may be told that his application was considered, but that his ex-

perience did not fill the qualifications desired, or that he was otherwise unsuitable. No name may even be mentioned, for the note may
be typed on a plain piece of paper without any reference to the name
of the employer.

Some companies make a practice, when inserting advertisements,
of saying that the job has already been offered to members of their
staff, and from this one presumes that a notice has been placed in the
works advertising the job without success. This is important, and is a
practice which the majority of people recommend to be followed, as it
does prevent people employed by the company from replying to an
advertisement inserted by their own employers—a situation which
sometimes has unfortunate after-effects for the applicant.

The shortage of technical labour being very great, companies
have found it necessary to do extensive advertising and this should
be handled by the company's publicity department so that they compete in size and coverage in the appropriate papers. Today advertising vacancies is highly specialised.

RECEPTION ON RECRUITMENT

Having attracted the prospective employee by advertisement or
introduction, we next need to see him and find out if he complies
with our requirements. He also needs to see us, to find out if we can
offer him the kind of employment he wants. The first impressions a
new employee receives when he enters the Personnel Department—
the way in which he is treated, the environment, cleanliness, lighting
and heating—are all most important. The personality of the receptionist and the friendliness of the greeting do much to impress the
man or woman with the attitude they are likely to meet as an
employee.

To make him comfortable in a physical manner is perhaps the
easiest, for one can provide a clean room with a comfortable chair,
and some reading matter in case—by accident—he has to wait to be
seen. In the interview room itself another important thing is to
avoid placing the candidate so that he faces the window or other
source of strong light. Interviewer and candidate should each be
able to see the other comfortably and clearly.

In a small company, the person acting as the receptionist is
probably a clerk or typist, and on her would fall the job of receiving
the applicant, getting from him what was required, or keeping him
interested for the brief waiting period which is often unavoidable. In
the large company, the receptionist would probably be a full-time
job. A good receptionist is of great value. The manner in which she
receives the new-comers to the company helps them to feel at home
whilst sitting in the waiting room. She should be able to sense the

mood of the individual and be able to converse intelligently, whether the applicant is looking for a junior clerical job or for a more senior appointment. The receptionist may often serve to receive all callers as well as those for the Personnel Department, an arrangement which often makes possible the employment in the capacity of a better-grade adequately trained girl.

Contrast this with the all-too-frequent procedure that one meets—

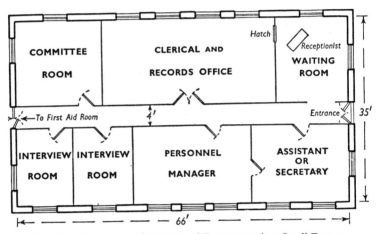

FIG. 80.—The Layout of a Personnel Department in a Small Factory.

a hard chair in a draughty corridor, to which one may be directed by a gruff, uniformed commissionaire, and there left to wait until someone decides at his convenience to see one.

Application Forms provide a useful basis for the employment interview, though opinion is divided as to whether they should be completed by the applicant in advance or by the interviewer from responses to questions put. To some extent the form needs to be related to the job, but information is a valuable guide to assessment. One would hardly think of asking for the schooling and academic qualifications, special training or professional organisations, in the case of applicants for routine labouring jobs. The information that is necessary in such cases consists of the name and address of the employee, his age, for whom he has worked in recent years, rates earned, whether he is suffering from dermatitis or any other similar industrial disease which may be influenced by the type of work being offered, reasons for leaving, military service and similar general points. On the other hand, some companies like to have very detailed information about all their employees—they want information about families (children and ages), past national service, medals and awards. References are also required by some employers, so that details are needed of names and addresses of past employers and information about the Department or Section in which the man or woman worked, so that they can easily be traced.

For junior or technically trained people, particulars of education are important, and it is also useful to know the type of college or the subjects studied and whether they are members of any professional organisations, have special interests or the like. Information should be as complete as possible, so that it is not necessary to bother the employee to answer questions once he has been engaged and has started work. Everything that is likely to be wanted should be obtained at the original interview.

The more common method of obtaining this information is by a question and answer at the interview; getting answers to questions is not always easy, and some Personnel Managers take the view that the subject is best dealt with by having a general talk with the individual about his past experiences and the type of job he would like. The first thing to do is to put the man or woman completely at ease, perhaps by a few minutes' conversation about general topics of the day, or whether they have had a good journey (if relevant). The serious business then begins more smoothly. One method is to ask the applicant to give a brief story of what he has done since leaving school. Quite probably much information is irrelevant, particularly if he has been at work several years. The details of previous employment, reasons for leaving, comments on health, obvious physical defects, and other such points of interest are noted. During the telling of the story, the applicant gains confidence and the interview becomes quite fruitful.

Completing the Application Form before the interview is held by many to be the better practice, though it has disadvantages, particularly when dealing with clerical or senior posts; some persons are rather sensitive and object to a person of a junior status, such as a receptionist, asking them for information which they regard as confidential. It can have a bad effect on the whole of the interview if the prospective employee has been "ruffled" before he gets to the Personnel Manager. In such cases, of course, the difficulty is often overcome by having written applications in advance (through the post) and interviews held by appointment.

Another disadvantage from the prior completion of the Form may be in this, that quite early in the interview either party may learn that there is no suitable job available or no basis for considering the candidate further.

Interviews differ according to the type of job which is vacant. Generally, these fall into three categories: unskilled or skilled labour; clerical; sales or supervisory staff. The interviewing of un-skilled labour is usually undertaken by the Personnel Manager for and on behalf of the Production Departments. The Personnel Mana-ger does the engaging, because it is more convenient or because there is an agreement between the Production and Personnel Managers that this is the best arrangement. In all cases, however, the foreman should be asked whether he would like to see the person, and fre-quently it is desirable that he should be present at the interview, or should have an interview with the applicant alone. It is important to note the underlying principle here, namely, that the foreman or manager of the department is responsible for the engagement and acceptance of the new employee, the Personnel Department acting in the capacity of agent.

By the time the foreman is called in to the interview, the Applica-tion Form should be completed and be available for his inspection, so that it is not necessary for the same questions to be gone all over again. The foreman can carry on the interview half-way through by explaining what has to be done in the department and the type of work which the prospective employee would do if employed.

There may be some differences in the routine for engaging clerical or office workers, but quite frequently in a large company the Section Leader or Departmental Manager would interview them, whereas in a small concern they are usually taken on by the Chief Accountant or someone acting for him. The terms of their engagement are set out by letter, which offers employment or confirms the arrangements reached verbally by the interview. The testing of shorthand-typists is usual, allowances being made for errors believed to be due to nervousness.

In the case of the Sales Staff, engagement is usually dealt with by the Sales Manager, the Personnel Manager serving as an assistant and a consultant. It is becoming more common for similar service to be given in the case of responsible technical staffs engaged for the Chief Engineer or Chemist. There are Personnel Managers whose acceptance has won such confidence that they play an *active* part in all appointments, even up to senior levels. In principle this is perfectly sound, and it is so far chiefly the limited experience and outlook of many Personnel Officers that has withheld their partici-pation in these wider responsibilities.

Contract of Employment

When an employee accepts a job, he does so in the belief that cer-tain conditions will be kept by the employer; namely, that he will be paid his appropriate rate of pay agreed at the interview and that certain other conditions will be maintained. The exchange of service or work in return for money constitutes the contract. The employee contracts to work for an employer for a given number of hours in return for consideration by way of wages. Contracts of employment are becoming more common in this country, and it is no longer unusual for an employee to be asked to sign a form agreeing to the terms and conditions on which he is engaged.

Contracts of employment are particularly used for senior officials. Such documents usually show the date on which work is to start, the rate of pay, the amount of notice to be given, the holidays granted and similar matters about the general affairs. The acceptance of the contract is proved by the person starting work. A form used in a small works is reproduced below:

TERMS OF EMPLOYMENT

Employment with the Company is subject to the following conditions:

1. Each employee is required to pass a standard medical examination by the Company's doctor upon engagement, and upon return to work after sickness.
2. Engagement and continuity of employment is subject to satisfactory references being obtained.
3. Employees are required to adhere to the regulations for employees of the Company as set out in the Works Handbook provided.
4. Employees must join the Life Assurance and Pension Scheme when eligible.
5. Employment may be terminated by 42 hours' notice on either side unless otherwise agreed in writing. Notice to be given by noon Friday.

RATE OF PAY AND WEEKLY DEDUCTIONS

Wages are based on a rate of   per 42 hours worked according to the Company's time clocks.

1. *Lateness.*—Time lost during the week will be deducted at the appropriate hourly rate.
2. *Absence.*—Absence for any cause other than sickness will not be paid for.
3. *Sick Pay.*—An ex-gratia payment in respect of sick pay may be made at the discretion of the Company.

Deductions from pay are made each week for the following:

INSURANCE   SPORTS CLUB   PENSIONS[1]

I have received a copy of the Works Handbook, and agree to the above terms of employment of the Company. I authorise, also, the deductions shown above to be made from my pay each week.

SIGNATURE.............................
WITNESS...........................   DATE.................

[1] Premiums will be deducted without further notice when employees become eligible.

A corresponding illustration for office staff is in the form of a letter which embodies the following points:

The terms and conditions of the appointment are as follows:

1. *Salary.*—The initial salary will be £   per week.
2. *Hours of Work.*—Mondays to Fridays, 9 a.m.–5 p.m.
3. *Date of Starting.*—Monday, ... Please bring with you Insurance Cards and Income Tax Form, and report to the Employment Department at 10 a.m.
4. *Termination of the Appointment.*—Will be subject to one clear week's notice by either side; such notice to be given by noon on Friday.
5. *Holidays.*—You will be entitled to two weeks' holiday annually, in addition to the usual Bank Holidays.
6. *References.*—The appointment and continuity of employment is subject to our obtaining a satisfactory reference from your previous employer and to your passing a standard medical examination by the Company's doctor.
7. *Pension Scheme.*—It is a condition of employment that employees, as soon as they become eligible, shall join the Pension and Life Assurance Scheme operated by the Company.[1]

We shall be glad to receive your letter confirming acceptance of the appointment, and this correspondence can then form the contract between us.

[1] Subject to the conditions of the National Scheme and contracting out.

The letter of appointment in some companies is becoming increasingly written by solicitors and lawyers, with the effect that it has ceased to be a friendly document between the two parties on the basis of the interview, and is becoming quite frightening to the applicant. In many instances it results in losing a good prospective employee.

SELECTION TESTS

There has been a good deal of loose talk regarding intelligence, aptitude and other formal tests applied in the selection of employees during the past years, and a tendency to overrate their significance. The novice in personnel management should regard such tests with some caution, and with an eye to the many other factors involved in the assessment of the individual. Authoritative bodies, such as the *National Institute of Industrial Psychology,* have made it clear that they do not regard intelligence or aptitude tests as the sole, or even most important, part of good selection; any such test should be taken as one of a number of points for consideration when deciding if an applicant is suitable for a particular job.

Selection comprises the whole process of assessing a candidate for a (more or less) specific job. It should start with the basic facts set out on an application form, and may include formal intelligence and aptitude tests. It must include an interview; this alone makes possible the interpretation of all the information and pointers about the individual, gathered from tests, application form and verbal questions. These, put together and rounded off, give a coherent and complete account of the individual, which, when related to the job in question, puts the decision as to suitability on reasonably firm ground.

It is not possible to measure mental ability directly, but with a well-validated intelligence test some indication is attained of the effect mental ability has had in enabling a person to acquire a certain knowledge or mental skill. Thus, if a large number of people of varying ages complete an approved test, from their scores it is possible to establish a fair average for age, and, on this basis, judgment of an individual's intelligence or special aptitude can be made with a reasonable chance of accuracy by a comparison of that person's performance with the performance of others. The average performance in fact becomes the yardstick by which the individual is measured. Tests vary considerably, especially in their suitability for different ages, or even for different educational backgrounds. Most include questions centring on vocabulary, arithmetic and reasoning processes, such as shape and space tests. Many Personnel Managers have been impressed by the experiments carried out during the war years, in which a good measure of accuracy was obtained in suiting certain people for jobs in the Armed Forces. The value of tests in these circumstances became widely recognised.

Obviously, the desirability of using formal tests for selection purposes must depend on the work to be undertaken; they are of little relevance to unskilled manual occupations, but may be of considerable significance for technical, skilled, operative or office occupations.

The design of tests is, of course, a task for the qualified psychologist. There is also a good case for their use in selection procedures to be avoided by the Personnel Manager unless he is able to call on the advice of an experienced psychologist in the choice and establishment of the tests to be used.[1]

EMPLOYEE RECORDS

The maintenance of information about the employees and the preparation of periodic reports and returns, summaries, changes and movements are among the best-known activities of any Personnel Department. It is, in fact, often said that too much attention is given

---

[1] No reference is made here to "temperament tests", because their application to industrial selection is still in an experimental stage.

to this aspect of the Department's responsibilities. In many instances, the allegation may indeed be true, but this should not be allowed to overshadow the real importance of the recording activities. Information—correct and reliable information—is a necessary basis for dealing with management problems, whether relating to individual cases or departmental matters. It is one of the essential functions of the Personnel Department to build up and maintain such information in up-to-date form. Similarly, the Department provides a service to other parts of the organisation in compiling periodic returns of employees engaged or leaving, lost time, apprentices in training and other matters of interest.

What information is recorded and what returns compiled must be determined by the needs of the organisation concerned—by the responsibilities of the Personnel Officer, reflecting the policy and aims of management. Some of the items of information that are likely to be required may be stated as follows:

(1) Personal data about individual employees prior to engagement. Source: Application Form.
(2) Any assessments made at engagement, including medical report.
(3) Employment history—transfers, promotions, wage and salary changes, etc.
(4) Absence and lost-time records.
(5) Weekly and monthly statements of engagements, losses and lost time. Analysis of terminations.
(6) Periodic returns of accidents and consequent lost time.
(7) Statements of strength, against planned requirements.

In addition, the work of the Personnel Department will necessitate the use of forms to carry out various procedures in a systematic way, for instance: requisitions of personnel wanted; advice of engagement; routine for termination.

Many methods and systems have been devised for carrying out these procedures, and no useful purpose would be served in the present context by outlining any one approach, to the exclusion of others. There is indeed a danger in suggesting anything like a "standard" form of records and procedures for a Personnel Department. Valuable guidance in designing or selecting systems may be had from publications of the *Industrial Welfare Society*, the *Institute of Personnel Management* and the *British Institute of Management*.

Certain fundamental points are of importance in devising a scheme:

(1) The first essential is to know clearly what activities within the Personnel Department are to be covered by the scheme, and what other departments or executives (if any) are to be brought into the procedures.

(2) Consultation with other interested parties in regard to planning the scheme will serve as a useful preliminary to its inauguration when ready. This will also ensure that the procedures are in line with the responsibilities and interrelations of the various parties concerned.

(3) Aim at simplicity in the design of all procedures and forms and records. Include only items for which there is a genuine need.

(4) Aim also at keeping the number and circulation of records and forms to the essential minimum. One copy of a notification form, for instance, can be made to circulate to two or three persons instead of each having a copy; its return to the Personnel Department will provide evidence that the necessary notifications have been made. (Many a Personnel Department has experienced the misfortune of earning the nickname of "paper-producing department".)

(5) There should be a unity in the conception of a scheme of routines and records, even though various ones are introduced from time to time. There is, in fact, great value in introducing new procedures gradually, but this ought not to mean that there are discrepancies or lack of interrelation between one procedure or record and another.

(6) Wherever possible the routines of a Personnel Office should be tied in with related activities carried on elsewhere, e.g. in a Wages Office, or in a Time Recording Section. This does not mean that the Personnel Department should have control of these activities: that must depend on circumstances. It is, however, a wasteful approach to duplicate work that is already being done elsewhere, or to draw up a procedure that does not tie in with a related routine carried on in another section.

(7) Avoid "bits and pieces" of records and forms. A single visible-index record, with appropriate markings and signals, is usually much more effective if well designed than a series of records and files for each employee. Another common error in this connection is the filing, or "hoarding", of papers for which there is really no permanent use.

WAGES

It could be argued that "wages" is a subject belonging to the personnel function; but it is also a significant element in costs, and so is of major concern to the "line" executives—the more so when wages schemes include payments by way of bonus on output. From the point of view of its position in the working of management, the question of wages needs to be considered from several aspects, which may be summarised as follows:

1. *Determining Basic Rates or Grades.*—This is a field for joint action by the Personnel Manager and the Factory Manager or Office Manager, or other appropriate "line" executive.

2. *Conformity with Agreements.*—This is an item on which the Personnel Manager is rightly to be regarded as the specialist, and the Managing Director would hold him responsible for ensuring that the Company does not go wrong under this heading. (Here the Personnel Manager's functional responsibility comes into play: if he cannot get a "line" executive to conform, he has the duty of reporting back, to secure remedial action at a higher level.)

3. *Conformity with Local Levels.*—Again an item for the Personnel Manager's special responsibility.

4. *Comparative Grading of Rates.*—This is really an aspect of the first item, and must be covered by the joint consideration of the Personnel Manager and "line" executives. The technique known as Job Evaluation or Base Rate Analysis is used in order to secure the correct comparative grading of jobs with the factory or the offices.

5. *Bonus Schemes.*—These depend upon output or some other criterion of performance and proficiency. They are closely linked up with the planning of production, and may be based on the same standards. Hence they are primarily the province of the "line" executives concerned, with the Personnel Manager holding a watching brief. (This aspect is fully dealt with in Chapter VI of Part Two.)

6. *Merit Rating Awards.*—These may be regarded as an individual counterpart of the foregoing items, and responsibility for them is distributed in the same way. The Personnel Manager may, however, play a bigger part in two ways: (i) as the person who carries out the mechanics of rating, and (ii) as the safeguard against any unintentional unfairness between one individual and another.

7. *Wage and Other Payments.*—This is solely a matter of the mechanics of the Wages Office. The Personnel Manager serves as the contact between employee and Wages Office in the event of queries, discrepancies, etc.

8. *Information to Employees.*—This is an aspect in which again the Personnel Manager exercises an advisory role. He must ensure that employees are properly informed of wage rates, bonus schemes, deductions, etc., at commencement with the firm or whenever changes are made. He must also assist Wages Office in securing an adequate presentation of weekly earnings and deductions on the pay-packet. Quite often, one of the Personnel Manager's most important tasks in this field is helping to make bonus schemes simple to present and easy for the employee to understand.

9. *Queries and Discrepancies.*—It is the Personnel Manager's primary responsibility to clear up doubts and difficulties raised by employees. Queries on wages, deductions, etc., are better directed to this department than to the Wages Office, and his staff should be trained in the sympathetic handling of such matters, especially in

dealing with the less educated persons who may find genuine difficulty in understanding the compilation of a weekly wage or the
correctness of income-tax deductions. The Personnel Department
should see this as one of their opportunities for promoting good
employee relations. (This does not mean that the Personnel Manager
and his staff have to acquire detailed knowledge of wage computations, income tax, etc.; they may themselves go to the Wages Office
for the explanation of a query and then "relay" it to the employee
concerned.)

10. *Holidays, Sickness Schemes, etc.*—Wage payments for periods
of non-working depend on the policy of the firm, and the only
practical problem arising is that of the mechanics of payment.

11. *Guaranteed Week.*—This may be seen as the modern form of
minimum wage legislation, supplementing a guaranteed minimum
base rate for the job with a guaranteed payment for so many hours'
attendance. It is, of course, the Personnel Manager's functional
responsibility to see that the guarantees are honoured.

Whatever may be the importance of other non-financial factors in
development of morale and contentment at work, there can be no
gainsaying the basic significance of wages or remuneration for work.
While most Personnel Managers will *not* subscribe to the view that
"the pay packet at the end of the week" is the only, or even the chief,
motive for work, they will equally recognise the primary economic
motive in work. Earnings are the means of livelihood; they must,
therefore, rank very high in importance to every employee. It is for
this reason that difficulties and disputes so often centre on wage
matters, even though the real causes of the high antagonistic feelings
revealed in a dispute may be in other aspects of manager-employee
relations. Wages questions are largely factual, so that there is no
excuse for their being a source of difficulty or confusion within a
single organisation. The Personnel Manager has here a field in which
to prove the importance and value of his own functional position.

JOB ANALYSIS AND SPECIFICATION

Job analysis and specification have been described as the scientific
study and statement of all the facts about a job which reveal its content and the modifying factors around it. This is a study that is of
considerable value to the beginner in personnel management. As a
basis there is needed a background knowledge of the structure of
organisation of the Company, the functions and relationships between the different departments, the processes of the firm's products
and what they are used for. The purpose of Job Analysis and Specification in relation to personnel management is for guidance in the

selection, engagement or transfer of employees, but they can also serve for the benefit of training schemes and the establishment of comparative wage scales.

Maine, in his *Job Analysis for Employment Purposes*, published in 1923, gave the following four reasons for introducing Job Analysis, which remain equally valid today:

(1) For improving working methods and processes.
(2) For protecting health and safety.
(3) As a basis for training employees.
(4) For employment purposes: (*a*) selection, transfer and promotion, and (*b*) the establishment of wage schedules and the adjustments and revisions.

The information given may be reproduced as a tabulated list or may be designed in a form. The details wanted are:

(1) The title of the job.
(2) The department in which the work is to be done.
(3) A description of the duties or work.
(4) The physical conditions of the job.
(5) The rate of pay, bonus or piecework.
(6) Any particular hazards, disadvantages or benefits.
(7) The length of training necessary.
(8) Opportunities for promotion.
(9) Personal qualifications required, including any special skills.

The application of job analysis and grading for the purposes of comparative rate-setting has been dealt with above in Chapter IV of Part Two.

MEDICAL DEPARTMENT

This specialist section of the personnel field is still relatively unusual, though increasing numbers of firms are coming to recognise the value of its contribution, and the loss of time from illness in the normal factory is considerable, rarely less than 10 per cent. One estimate has put it as at least 270 times as great as that due to strikes or industrial upsets. Numerous studies on fatigue, ill-health, and their effect on output, have been made by research bodies, with regard to both the physiological and the psychological aspects. Bodies such as the Industrial Health Research Board and the Tavistock Institute of Human Relations, have singled out such problems for investigation, and the latter organisation is prepared to advise firms as to ways of dealing with such problems. On the purely physical side there has already been a considerable extension of industrial medical services, which are becoming valuable assets in the pattern of industrial relations.

A Medical Officer attached to a factory, full-time or part-time, becomes the confidant of all employed, worker and management alike. The ethical doctor-patient relation must, at all times, be maintained, and everyone feel quite sure that information given to the Medical Officer at the factory will be as sacred as though given in the consulting room of the private practitioner. Frequently, when a Medical Officer starts at a factory in a full-time capacity, he has to be prepared for a number of setbacks—to be misunderstood, and to have prejudice against him. When employees are first told they must report to the Works Doctor, they often express resentment, refuse to be examined or to have anything whatever to do with the Medical Service. This is but a passing phase, for in a short time the surgery will be full of people who wish to see the doctor or nurse on all kinds of illnesses, domestic problems, and also those seeking advice on behalf of other members of their family. The patients, finding that they can obtain information and treatment within the works, rapidly become accustomed to the idea of seeing the Works Doctor on matters which they

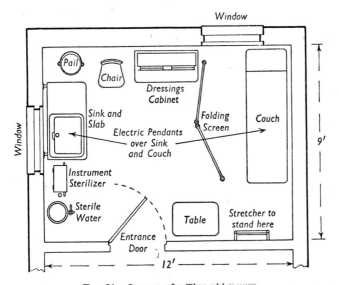

Fig. 81.—Layout of a First-aid Room.

would hesitate to take to their own practitioner. Frequently those who have objected in the strongest way are among the first to be converted.

The work of the Medical Department varies according to the size of the firm. Where only 100 or 200 employees are concerned, a Rest Room or Ambulance Room with facilities for treating minor injuries is all that is necessary, often with only part-time service from a specially trained employee in accordance with the 1961 Act covering First Aid. For the medium-size firm, State Registered Nurses with industrial guidance may be able to give adequate service under the professional guidance of a local doctor on a part-time basis. A doctor should be employed wherever possible, if only in an advisory capacity.

The work of a Medical Department will consist of:

(a) Assisting in fitting the individual into the most suitable job.
(b) Medical examination prior to engagement.
(c) Attending minor accidents and re-dressings.
(d) Giving advice on physical working conditions with special reference to the suitability of persons.
(e) General advice on the health of the employees.
(f) Encouraging accident prevention methods, by co-operation with the Safety Officer.
(g) Periodical examination of all juveniles.

In large factories where considerable numbers are employed, the Medical Department (or Clinic, as it is becoming more popularly known) covers services other than the first-aid, and many now include dentistry, ophthalmology, chiropody and electrotherapy.

Medical Examination before Engagement

Medical examination before employment should be the aim of all employers in industry. It reduces turnover by making sure that the people taken into the company's employ are physically suitable for the job, and creates contentment amongst the workers, because each employee knows himself able to do work which he is asked to do, and the heavy jobs do not fall on a few, the burden being equally shared. Some people occasionally object to being medically examined; when this happens, the Personnel Manager should make a point of explaining to the applicant that it is in his own interests, because the Medical Officer has the knowledge to see how the individual can undertake the work. Applicants for employment should always have an appointment made for them with the Medical Officer, so that waiting is avoided.

Medical Examination during Employment

Some companies insist on employees reporting back to the Medical Department if they have been away ill; this is a wise precaution, for there are a number of people who will return to work long before they are physically capable of renewing their normal job. Some try to return because of the money factor: having families to support, they are anxious to resume their normal earnings without delay. Others do it from the point of view of loyalty to the company, feeling that they are letting the firm down by being absent, if only for a few days. When an employee returns to work after being ill, he should not normally be allowed to start until he has seen a member of the medical staff. This is for two reasons: firstly, to ensure that the individual is physically able to do his normal job, and secondly, to protect other employees from possible lingering infection. A third subsidiary reason is to make possible the completion of the Medical History Record. Close liaison is always required here between the Personnel Department and the Medical Staff, and particularly if the illness has been severe and necessitates transfer to other work, maybe in a category where a lower level of pay is normally applicable. Where an employee is unfit for the job, he should be told so by the Works Medical Officer. It may be that the reason for unsuitability is one which the man would not wish to be made public, and the Personnel Department need only know that he is medically unfit for the work for which he was employed. A special problem for the Personnel Officer is created if there should happen to be no other suitable job immediately available.

Disabled Persons

Disabled persons should always be under the care of the Medical Officer and notice taken of the job on which they are engaged. A visit in the works to the man on his job is greatly appreciated, and on these occasions the Medical Officer should make sure that the work being done by a disabled person is within his limits.

CHAPTER V

PHYSICAL WORKING CONDITIONS

(Information. Recreation. Canteens. Amenities. Heating and Ventilation. Lighting. Legislation. Safety. Ergonomics)

INFORMATION

Booklets

THE practice of issuing a booklet to employees giving them information about the factory, working conditions, rules and other information is becoming increasingly popular.[1] The handbook is given to the employee on starting work; no charge is made and it remains his property. Sometimes supplementary booklets are issued to cover such subjects as Safety, Joint Consultation arrangements, Fire Precautions, Contributory Schemes and Pensions, etc. As a matter of principle any handbook of information for employees should always be prepared in conjunction with employee representatives and it is particularly important to have joint agreement on the conditions of employment and regulations, etc., which are published. Personnel Managers will know that, so far as Union members are concerned, it is not possible to alter works rules or impose new conditions of employment without prior consultation.

Notice Boards

A notice board is a useful method of distributing current information, for most employees find time to look at it either in the break period or at the end of the day. The practice of having separate notice boards for various items is not advisable. It is better to have in each Department one notice board which covers all information: it can be divided into sections—one for official notices or announcements from the company of interest to the employees in general, e.g. appointments of the Board, the financial results of the company, and similar general announcements; another for departmental notices, to include minutes of Committee and other meetings, shift lists, special instructions for dealing with the product, changes in

[1] The Institute of Personnel Management have published a broadsheet entitled "Preparing an Employees' Handbook", which deals in detail with the type of matter to be covered in such booklets.

hours or working conditions, or other items agreed at joint discussions. A Trade Union section should be placed at the disposal of the shop stewards in the department, who would be entitled to place any notice on that section which referred to the activities of the branch of which employees of the company were members. There would need to be some policy agreed with the shop stewards as to the type of notice which might or might not be placed on the board; for example, it would be undesirable for a notice to be posted in one company asking for pickets to be provided for another company, the employees of which were on strike. Similarly, political notices would be banned. A Sports Club section would be at the disposal of the Sports and Social Clubs, to cover announcements of dances, amateur dramatics and theatrical shows, and any other items of sporting or social interest to the company's employees.

Magazines

The practice of issuing a magazine or newspaper is also one that has been more widely developed in recent years. Quite simple leaflets are used in some firms, while large organisations with a big pay-roll that justifies the higher expenditure go in for an expensive booklet with many photographs, and printed on good paper with a stiff cover. The contents will be current information about the firm and its people, including topical items, family news, etc.; also sports results and club announcements. The more elaborate magazines, issued monthly or quarterly, have articles written by employees as well as special contributions, either dealing with problems particular to the industry and the work of departments in the company, or with wider contemporary events. Much thought and a great deal of detailed work are involved in producing a magazine of this kind, and it should never be started until the basic material for three or four editions is in hand or in sight.

The problem of whether to give these publications away or to sell them to employees is one which needs to be dealt with in each individual concern. There is no doubt that the majority of employees find them interesting and instructive, and where a factory consists of many departments, they can be of considerable educational value by descriptions of the work done in the various parts of the organisation, and by the news given about them.

A few firms adopt the practice of contracting with a publishing house who specialise in works magazines, to supply them with a given quantity of a general magazine in which the majority of the material is written by well-known writers, and two or three pages are specially inserted covering domestic matters pertaining to the company. The main advantage of this method is relative cheapness.

RECREATION

Sports Clubs

Sports Clubs attached to factories and commercial organisations seem to be more popular in the Midlands and the North of England than they are in the South. This is possibly due to the fact that in the Midlands and North, employees, generally speaking, live nearer to their work than in other areas. Many of the big London commercial houses, however, have had flourishing sports clubs for a good many years.

It is usual for the company to provide ground, or, where the numbers do not warrant this, to give financial assistance to facilitate a link-up with other sports organisations in the area. But the company should not seek to exercise control over the activities. Running expenses are met by voluntary subscriptions from employees who participate, supplemented by the proceeds of dances, musical and dramatic shows, socials and concerts—especially when the club premises carry a licence.

The usual constitution of a social club is in the form of a committee elected by members, i.e. interested employees, with the addition of one or two representatives of the company, often an Accountant and a Personnel Manager, to maintain liaison with the company, to provide secretarial service and to assist the club generally. The management and finances of the club should be in the hands of a strong Committee. Each section should prepare a budget, and expenditure above this amount must be subject to approval by the whole Committee. The accounts should be audited half-yearly and a statement made by the auditors. Any item covered by company payments should be included, so that members do not take them for granted.

The sectional interests—social, educational, different games and sports—can best be served by sub-committees which have a responsibility for planning, but which report back to the main Committee. An Annual General Meeting of members should be held and a report made of the activities and progress during the year.

In a small company it is usual for one of the employees to act as secretary and to do all the necessary work in connection with the club, receiving telephone calls and visitors with the permission of the management. But where a large number of employees are concerned, it has been known for the club to be looked after by a full-time secretary, whose wages and other administrative costs would be paid by the company, though perhaps with some arrangement for offsetting the club profits.

CANTEENS

Under the Statutory Rules and Orders No. 373, it is essential for canteens to be provided where the number of employees exceeds 250. The nature and extent of the accommodation will necessarily vary a great deal. This is a rather specialised field, and a Personnel Manager would be well advised not to rely entirely on his own knowledge and judgment. A body like the Industrial Welfare Society provides specialist information and assistance in this direction to its member-firms, and there are also professional firms of Catering Consultants or Contractors.

A canteen need not be elaborate; neither need great expense be incurred, and with very small firms a mess-room with tea facilities is often better than nothing.[1]

A few general points may be recorded as a matter of interest:

The Main Meal.—This may be the midday dinner or might quite well be breakfast or supper in the case of shift workers. The main meal is usually meat or fish and vegetables with a sweet. The amount of food and the way in which it is cooked are usually of greater importance to the working man than the way it is served. On the other hand, office workers seem to prefer a smaller meal served in pleasant surroundings.

Snacks.—Snacks, consisting of tea and cakes, sandwiches or rolls and butter, are sold by the canteen in the morning and afternoon breaks. In some factories tea trolleys are employed in order to take the food to the workers, who are able to eat it by their machines, whereas other managements find it more convenient for employees to go to the tea stations set up in the departments or to the main canteen.

Tea.—Tea is usually made in urns. Some of these, known as thermal urns, will keep tea hot for as long as eight hours. This is very helpful, particularly where it is necessary to make the tea in the canteen and to distribute it around the works if the area to be covered is great. Cleanliness in scalding out the urns after use is most important, and a frequent cause of complaint about the quality of the tea may be traced to the improper cleaning of the urn. Tea is one of the most profitable products of the canteen.

Cleanliness.—A Personnel Manager should always insist on cleanliness being a most important factor in the canteen. There should always be provision for the washing of hands by employees who are engaged in the serving or handling of food in any way. A

[1] The Official Factory Department Welfare Pamphlet No. 2, entitled "Mess Rooms and Canteens in Small Factories", will be found most helpful in giving details of the equipment and accommodation.

wash basin with hot and cold water should be in the centre of the kitchen and a good supply of soap and towels should be available. Epidemics can be passed on to a large number of people through contamination of food, and the drive by the Ministry of Health for cleanliness in catering establishments should be observed.

Outside Catering.—As catering is a specialised field, some companies have found it advantageous to place their catering in the hands of outside specialists. It is usual for the company itself to provide the premises and equipment, and for the caterer to provide the meals and service to the company's requirements, taking all profits. An advantage of this system is that the company is able to have a fixed amount set aside for catering, whereas in most instances when they do their own catering there is an indefinite loss, sometimes of a considerable amount.

Canteen Committees.—Canteen Committees representative of employees are usually a source of great help, particularly in dealing with the day-to-day problems and grumbles which arise. Committees of this kind need to be positive in their action, as well as being the safety-valve for complaints and the source of investigations. They should be advisory and not executive.

AMENITIES

Lavatories

Legal requirements with regard to lavatories both for men and women are defined in Section 46 of the Factories Act, which sets out the minimum standard. There are also local authority prescriptions to be taken into account. The field of factory hygiene is one now becoming recognised as a good mirror to reflect the attitude of management; the factory with a good policy and good executives wisely provides pleasant amenities, realising the value of their contribution of morale.

The amount of space devoted to this purpose and the cost entailed need not be great. Location and convenience of access are important, particularly bearing in mind means of avoiding congestion, the proximity of cloakrooms, etc. To some extent, so far as washing facilities are concerned, the nature of the work and the needs of the very dirty departments may affect planning.

In some organisations the provision of sanitary accommodation has been laid before a Works Committee for consideration.

Cloakrooms

Since a cloakroom is where the employee keeps outdoor clothing for the time he is at work, the most satisfactory method is to have a steel cabinet handy to where he is working. This, however, is not always practicable, although a bank of steel cabinets can often usefully be employed as a screen within the factory. Where general accommodation is being provided, the cloakroom should be a self-contained unit which can be locked up at a given time each morning and only opened at leaving-off time. This is probably the only way in which petty thieving or pilfering can be satisfactorily stopped. Some employers have numbered containers in cloakrooms, and have so arranged these that clock number and cabinet number tally. The manner in which the employees' clothes are to be kept depends to a certain extent on the amount of space available. *The Factory Department Welfare Pamphlet* on cloakrooms gives examples of clothing suspended from the ceiling or placed in containers. The more crude method of hanging hats and coats on pegs, which should be at least 18 inches apart, is still to be found in some works. The Factories Act requires that clothing is to be dried whilst the employee is at work, a point which is often overlooked; so the cloakroom needs to be heated—a point which raises but little trouble to add an additional radiator or two where steam is employed in the factory.

There should always be seats on which the employees can change their shoes; this does not mean anything more elaborate than a form or seat attached to a wall.

Whether a cloakroom attendant is employed full-time will depend on the number of people using the facilities. It is of great advantage, particularly where large numbers of women are employed, to have someone in charge of the lavatories and cloakrooms and available throughout the day. One aspect which needs to be carefully watched is to make sure that the cloakroom attendant does not usurp the duties of the medical staff by attempting to "doctor" female employees who may feel ill, instead of referring them to the nurse, from whom they could receive proper attention. This is a small point, but it is one which should be made abundantly clear to the cloakroom attendant at the time of her engagement.

The responsibility for lavatories and cloakrooms falls to the Personnel Manager, and it is a good plan to have the lavatory cleaners and attendants made directly responsible to him, to enable him to maintain high standards of cleanliness.

Complaints are sometimes heard from management that the employees do not appreciate decent lavatories and that they wilfully despoil them. This is not usually proved by facts, for where a high standard is provided and the shop stewards or other representatives of the men and women are asked to co-operate, they take a pride in keeping the lavatories and cloakrooms in the same condition as they would if they were at home.

HEATING AND VENTILATION

The importance of adequate ventilation has latterly been realised more than ever before, partly as an outcome of the blackout conditions which were enforced so rigidly during war-time, and partly because it has been widely realised that heating and ventilation are closely interrelated. One of the major problems in older factories has been "draughts", often giving rise to industrial unrest, poor morale and a sense of grievance in employees when nothing is done by management to relieve the unsatisfactory conditions. Lift shafts can be a particularly troublesome item in winter, as also are open doors where loading or unloading of vans or lorries has to be undertaken.

To ensure a comfortable and healthy working atmosphere, it is necessary to provide a definite circulation of air, warmed to a given temperature and evenly distributed throughout the factory. Fans drawing in cold air only may be worse than useless in severe weather conditions, and may easily exaggerate an already difficult situation. One method of introducing an adequate amount of air into a factory without causing draughts is by means of a fresh-air inlet fan, air-heating batteries controlled by modulating thermostats, and ranges of air distribution trunking fitted with draughtless air diffusers at regular intervals. With this system, the vitiated air from the factory can be extracted at high level, through ring-mounted exhaust fans, fitted in the walls or roofs. A plant of this type ensures an even temperature throughout. There is air movement over the entire factory, without cause of discomfort to the workers. Location of the plant above truss level ensures the saving of valuable floor space. The maintenance entailed on this equipment is small compared with a system made up of separate units.

Experience has proved it necessary to provide four changes of air per hour through the summer months and to make provision for recirculating during the winter a percentage of warmed air, as conditions allow. This may not prove suitable in all cases, particularly with work which involves hot processes; here it is better to have cold air under pressure a short distance above the employees' heads; or alternatively, on trunking with a swivelled funnel, so that it can be directed by the operator at his discretion.

It is perhaps of importance to emphasise that heating and ventilating is a specialist technological field about which the Personnel Officer should have general knowledge, but in which he should not lay claim to expert views unless he is qualified to do so by appropriate technical training,

LIGHTING

Many modern stations on London's Underground are noticeable to travellers because of intensity and colour of lighting, equivalent to daylight. The effect of good lighting in a factory is twofold: the benefit to output from clearer vision and the benefit to morale through the effect on the individual. Few conditions are more irritating than those associated with bad lighting, whether due to insufficient illumination or incorrect placing of the fittings.

The Factories Act provides certain minima, but these are low—too low for good and efficient working. As a guide to managers, the Illuminating Engineering Society has laid down certain standards as follows:

RECOMMENDED VALUES OF ILLUMINATION FOR SELECTED INDUSTRIAL OCCUPATIONS

(Extracted from the Code Published by the Illuminating Engineering Society)

	Lumens per sq. ft.
Assembly:	
Very small	100
Small	50
Ordinary	15
Large	7
Carpets:	
Weaving, designing, Jacquard card cutting, tapestry setting and beaming, mending, sewing and fringing . . .	20
Clothing Manufacture:	
Cutting, sewing, inspecting medium colours . . .	20
Pressing	10
Cotton Industry:	
Weaving, dark colours, fine counts	30
Light colours, fine counts	20
Grey cloth	10
Spinning, bale breaking. blowing, carding, combing, conditioning, twining, roving, slubbing, doubling (plain) .	7
Food Manufacturing and Preserving:	
Inspecting and grading	50
Refining, mixing, blending, cleaning, sweet making and confectionery	15
Bottling, canning, packing, flour-milling, bakehouses and cutting benches	15

Lumens per sq. ft.

Glass Works:
Fine inspection and glass cutting (cut glass) 50
Bevelling, decorations, etching, fine grinding and inspection   20
Cutting glass to size, glass-blowing machines, grinding,
  pressing and silvering 10
Furnace rooms and mixing 5

Hosiery:
Lockstitch and overlocking machines:
  Dark 30
  Light 15
Mending, examining and hand-finishing:
  Dark 50
  Light 20
Circular and flat knitting machines, universal winders, cut-
  ting out, folding and pressing 15
Linking or running on . . . . . . Special Lighting

Inspection (General):
Minute 200
Very small 100
Small 50
Fairly Small 20
Ordinary 15

Machine and Fitting Shops:
Very small bench and machine work, tool and die making,
  gauge inspection and precision grinding 100
Small bench and machine work, medium grinding, setting
  automatic machines 50
Fairly small bench and machine work, rough grinding . 20
Ordinary bench and machine work 15

Shoe and Boot Manufacturing:
Stitching, inspecting and sorting 20
Cutting, hand turning, lasting and welting, miscellaneous
  bench and machine work 15
Closing and clicking 30

Woodworking:
Fairly small bench and machine work, fine sanding and
  finishing 20
Cooperage, gluing, medium machine and bench work,
  planing, rough sanding, sizing, veneering and pattern-
  making 15
Sawmills 7

Woollen and Worsted Industry:
Perching 70
Burling and mending 50
Weaving fine worsteds 50

Lumens per
sq. ft.

Weaving medium worsteds and fine woollen . . . 30
Weaving heavy woollen 15
Warping, including balloon warping and warp dressing . 20
Spinning (mule and frame), winding, cropping, sorting
(including rag sorting and grinding), combing (coloured),
twisting (doubling) 15

Fluorescent lighting is now used extensively, and the wide area of light which this gives has made it most popular in factories. Great advances have been made in obtaining a pure white light or imitation daylight. The provision of light and the type of fittings and standards are usually the responsibility of the electrical department, but the Personnel Manager will be expected to express an opinion from the human standpoint and to deal with complaints which arise from poor lighting. Glare is often the cause of complaint, and is due to the effect of looking directly at a bright source of light, or at a direct reflection from a shiny surface. Vision is temporarily impaired, maybe not seriously, but with sufficient inconvenience to deflect attention from the job, and it is also a source of fatigue. Glare can usually be avoided quite easily by a change of working position.

For some types of close machine work it is usual to have what is known as local lighting, which is a low-voltage bulb fixed in such a position that it throws a light directly on to the machine. This has an important advantage, as it precludes any shadow being thrown on the work.

It need hardly be said that wherever daylight can be obtained, it should be provided in preference to artificial, however good. The cleaning of windows on a regular service basis will often provide additional daylight. Stacking boxes and goods against windows should be vigorously watched as a channel of serious loss of natural light.

The foregoing are points of general interest to the Personnel Officer or other manager. Lighting, again, is a special technical field in which the Personnel Officer should not pretend to be an expert— unless adequately qualified by appropriate technical training.

OFFICE CONDITIONS

All that has been considered in the past few sections are of relevance to working conditions for warehouses, shops and offices, as well as factory departments. Some of the special aspects applicable to office conditions are dealt with separately in Chapter V of Part Five below (page 961).

FACTORY LEGISLATION

The history of the legislation by Statute and by Orders, governing the conditions of work in factories, has long been a major item in the training of the Personnel Officer. One hundred and fifty years have provided the stage for that story, since the Health and Morals Acts of 1802, and for more than a century there has been a Factories Inspectorate to watch over the administration of the legislation. But the average Manager or Personnel Manager today is in a position where he is concerned with a level of conditions far above that prescribed: in other words, the Factories Acts are still of interest in detail primarily to those few employers—often in the smaller firms— who are unable to grasp the wisdom of high standards as an incentive to good work, and need the pressure and the threat of a penalty to conform even to the bare outline of officially prescribed minima.

The Personnel Officer needs to know his way about the Factories Act and the related legislation, including the Statutory Rules and Orders. To know these in detail is not an essential item in his competence, but he needs to know where to turn for this and that: it is no part of the function of the present volume to attempt to cover ground that is already well provided for in other publications, including the official *Guide to the Factories Acts* (H.M.S.O.).

A word on the position of the Factories Inspector may be in place. For most employers and managers, he or she has long ceased to be but the shadow of the law, something like an un-uniformed policeman. To their great credit, the Staff of the Factories Department have kept well abreast of new developments in the field of employment and personnel relations, and have been able to render valuable help both to Personnel Officers and to the many concerns which have not been able to develop their own personnel executive. Moreover, the department has gone to the length of establishing a specialist "Personnel Management Advisory Service" (since transferred to a parallel department) in order to be able to extend the scope of the assistance that they can render in the improvement of conditions and the betterment of employee morale.

The Annual Report of H.M. Chief Inspector of Factories has in recent years been not so much a vindication of the strong arm of the law as an annotated commentary on the progress of Britain's proficiency in the practice of personnel management.

OTHER LEGISLATION REGARDING EMPLOYMENT

The Truck Act was first passed in 1831, and was subsequently amended in 1887, 1896 and again in 1959. The object of the Act is to prevent an employer paying the wages of his workers in kind. That is to say, he must pay the employee the total amount of his wages, and cannot make deductions from them for food and tools or things of this kind. Another stipulation which is made by the Act is that the employee must be free to spend his money with whom he likes, and the employer cannot give directions to him as to where the wages are to be spent. The 1959 Act gave permission for the payment of wages by cheque on a basis of free and mutual agreement.

It should be understood, however, that certain deductions may be made, providing there is a contract in writing signed by the workman. The deductions to which he can lawfully agree are:

(a) Medicine or medical attention.

(b) Fuel.

(c) Materials, tools or implements if employed in mining.

(d) Provender to be consumed by a horse or other beast of burden used by the workman.

(e) Rent of a house let by the employer to the workman.

(f) Victuals dressed or prepared under the roof of the employer and there consumed by the workman.

Provision is made in the Act that the amount deducted for any of the above items must not exceed the real and true value of the goods, etc., supplied. Where it is a condition of employment that deductions may be made for the loss of tools or scrapped work and similar matters, the employer must keep posted in the workshop a copy of the notice. The employer must give particulars of the amount of fines or deductions and must be fair and reasonable. The employee is entitled to have details of the specific amounts deducted.

The whole question of the Truck Act has been under review for some years by official committees, and it is likely that thorough-going amending legislation will one day be enacted.

Disabled Persons Employment Act, 1944

The Disabled Persons Employment Act was passed in 1944, and provides that the Minister of Labour may instruct employers to take on a standard percentage of disabled persons. The standard percentage is now fixed at 3 per cent. under S.R.O. 1258. All employers are obliged to keep a register of disabled people in their employ, and a factory employing 1,000 people would have to find jobs for at least thirty who had registered as disabled persons.

Disablement does not necessarily mean the loss of a limb. All registered disabled persons carry with them a card showing that they have registered at the Ministry of Labour and are regarded as coming within the scope of the Act. It is important to note that an employer may not discharge a disabled person if by doing so he would bring the number of disabled persons employed below the standard percentage.

Reinstatement in Civil Employment Act, 1944

This Act provided that a person who had undergone a period of war service and who, on release from that service, desired to return to his pre-war civil employment, was entitled to reinstatement by his former employers subject to conditions and qualifications laid down in the Act. This Act will also apply to Reservists called to compulsory military service, and employers must give the same facilities of reinstatement whether an employee volunteered or was conscripted.

The Act provides for the employee to do certain things. He must apply for reinstatement on Form RE1 which he obtains from his demobilisation centre, or Employment Exchange. The application must be made within a period of four weeks of the end of his demobilisation leave, and he must be prepared to accept an alternative job if, due to circumstances beyond the control of the employer, there is no longer work available for him in his old job or occupation. Should the employer refuse to reinstate him or offer reinstatement in a position which is worse than previously held, the employee may refer his case to an Appeal Board, who have power to award either reinstatement or payment of compensation in lieu of reinstatement. The Reinstatement Committee have wide powers to exercise their discretion on the question of awarding compensation. Should either party be aggrieved at the decision given by the Reinstatement Committee, the case can then be referred to an umpire. His decision is final.

The effect of the Act applies to any class of employee called to National Service, and where necessary a person engaged may have to be discharged in order to provide a job for the returning ex-forces employee.

SAFETY AND SAFETY OFFICER

One of the most important functions of modern industrial management is that of maintaining safe working conditions within the undertaking, with a continuous effort to prevent accidents when and wherever possible. Accidents to employees are a serious drain on production, and consequently, like medical practice and treatment, "accident prevention" has made good progress. Enquiries into high accident rates reveal all-too-frequent physical or mechanical causes.

Accident prevention is the responsibility of management, and in a number of industrial undertakings this responsibility rests with the Personnel Department or Manager. In some, however, depending on the size of the undertaking and type of plant installed, the carrying out of this function is delegated to a specialist known as the Works Safety Officer or Accident Prevention Officer or Plant Safety Engineer.

Under the Building (Safety, Health & Welfare) Regulation, 1948, an employer employing more than fifty persons on building work is required to nominate a Safety Officer or "competent person". Thus, for the first time in industrial history, such person is given an official status, but in other industries it still remains the prerogative of the owner of the undertaking to decide how his accident prevention policy shall be put into effect and by whom. Opinion may differ as to the "line" of responsibility of such an officer, whether full-time or part-time. There is a good case to be made out for his being responsible to either the Personnel Manager or the Works Executive. The stronger argument is on the side of the latter—pinning on to the executive managers clear responsibility for safe working, with the specialist assistance provided. In the larger process plants, such as chemical works, steel works and so on, there is an equal case for "line" responsibility to the Chief Engineer, with functional liaison with the Personnel Manager.

The Safety Officer should be a man of qualities rather than qualifications; his efficiency and sincerity of purpose should be above question, and he should possess moral courage to a high degree, and so command respect of those with whom he comes into contact. He should be a good mixer. Technically, he must have had good experience of the industry in which he is employed, with an aptitude for approaching all his problems with a detached, impersonal and common-sense attitude.

The size of the undertaking and the nature of the process will determine whether he shall be a full-time Safety Officer or one who carries out safety work in conjunction with other responsibilities. Where there exists a well-developed Personnel Department, the need for a full-time safety specialist is often reduced.

Broadly, the functions of the Safety Officer may be described as the prevention of accidents by:

(a) Routine inspection of plant, buildings, gangways, materials, etc.
(b) Creating an active interest in safe working by means of propaganda.
(c) Training employees and advising members of the Supervisory Staff in methods of safe working.
(d) The supervision of works employees in respect of protective equipment and clothing, and compliance with works safety regulations.
(e) Advice, from the safety standpoint, on plant, layouts of shops, working methods, conditions, etc.
(f) Analysis of accidents and keeping historical (statistical) records.

Naturally, many of his activities have a direct relation to the requirements of the Factories Act (1959) and the Factory Orders, together with any special regulations for safety issued from time to time by the Minister; it is therefore highly important that he should have a comprehensive and up-to-date knowledge of them to a standard where he is in a position to advise management. Responsibility for compliance with legal requirements rests clearly on management, as the representative of the Board or the owner, and it cannot be passed on to, or usurped by, the Safety Officer.

The important obligation of maintaining good relations between a company and H.M. Factory Inspectorate should be a particular feature of the Safety Officer's duties by reason of his knowledge of the Acts, his specific industrial experience, as well as his intimate knowledge of the reasons for any accident that may occasion an investigation by H.M. District Inspector.

His association with the Personnel Department facilitates the routines attaching to his work, such as attending to Insurance Claims and making reports to H.M. District Inspector of Factories and the Ministry of National Insurance. This functional contact will also be of value in cases where legal proceedings ensue or where an accident gives rise to any strong feelings among employees. There is, too, a further advantage: the Safety Officer is, strictly speaking, a *technical* man whose particular qualifications lie in his knowledge of the plant and equipment and of the regulations. There is, however, a large *human* element, both in the cause of accidents and in the promotion of accident prevention: this is a fact on which the Personnel Officer is much better able to be the source of knowledge and advice. A safety scheme should never overlook the possibility of "accident-proneness" or other factors in the personal make-up of some individual employees who may sustain injury in circumstances which may have left other individuals unharmed. The investigation of any accident should always include—on the initiative of the Personnel Officer—reference to the purely human aspect.

In regard to the official requirement and procedures under factory and insurance legislation, the most desirable arrangement would appear to be:

(a) Primary responsibility vested in the Personnel Manager.

(b) Detailed work managed by the Safety Officer, where appointed.

(c) Liaison with factory and technical executives, as safety is part of their normal "human responsibilities".

In all aspects of his work, liaison with the Medical Department by the Safety Officer is all-important, for it is through the medium of "case" reports and records that he will get indication of accident trends, and the statistics so necessary in indicating the accident potential. He should make a daily visit to the clinic to study the

Minor Accident Log Sheets, abstracting from them such information as may be necessary for him to carry out investigations. Of course, he plays no part in the treatment of "cases".

The keeping of statistical records is important, especially in the form of graphs and charts, so that the appropriate steps are taken to investigate and correct any adverse trends at the earliest opportunity.

Liaison with the Surgery or Medical Department is an important factor in the human aspect of safety, to which reference was made above. The doctor or nurse may often be well placed to collaborate with the Safety Officer (and perhaps with the Personnel Officer himself) in the approach to the individual cases of recurrent accidents, having features which suggest that the cause lies in the human element instead of in the mechanical. In one engineering factory, recently, negligence in this direction allowed a young lad of sixteen and a half to persist on the same machine job without anyone bothering to make special enquiries, although he had attended at the clinic seventeen times in eight months for minor cuts and injuries!

The efficiency of a safety or accident prevention scheme depends on the co-operation of employees as well as on the skill of the Safety Officer. This is often a matter of training. Some companies incorporate training in safe working with their "Training within Industry" schemes; others use the discussion group method; but none of these methods can be more effective than informal talks to employees on the job, and instructive discussions with supervisors. A short informal talk to new entrants is useful to point out the specific hazards associated with the work upon which the employees are to be engaged, but not in a manner liable to give rise to fear, as this would defeat the object of the talk.

The investigation of accidents is an extremely important part of the Safety Officer's work. The investigation should be made as soon as possible after the occurrence, and should be approached with an open mind, free from any preconceived conceptions of a hypothetical nature. The plant should be examined for material evidence, and statements taken from witnesses and from the injured person, if possible. A conclusion should be arrived at only after careful consideration of the evidence in all its aspects, and great care should be taken to see that one does not become confused between the cause of the accident and the cause of the injury.

Unfortunately, many accidents and unsafe conditions arise in the general layout of the plant during the design stage in the Drawing Office—largely due to the "safety aspect" not being part of the draughtsman's outlook and to concentration on the engineering aspects in machine or plant design.

For these reasons, and providing the Safety Officer has the necessary experience and/or training, he should be given facilities for examining layouts in the initial stages, for the purpose of advising on any special measures he might consider should be taken to make the plant safe and, perhaps, to bring it into line with the requirements of the Factories Act. The "initial stage" means first of all in the Drawing Office, otherwise it may be too late to remedy an unsafe condition once drawings have been passed.

Routine inspection of gangways and sites will take up much of the Safety Officer's time. This should be carried out methodically and thoroughly, and, in the case of specific plant units or departments, it should always be carried out in the company of the person responsible for their running: this will avoid the impression that the Safety Officer is acting the part of a "snooper"—an outlook well calculated to destroy co-operation. The inspection should cover proper use of protective gear, operatives' attention to instructions, notices, faults in guarding, moving projections outside guards, lighting and general floor conditions in the immediate area. Operations that appear to be unsafe should be queried and constructive advice offered whenever possible. These routine inspections should always be made an opportunity of studying the working methods of employees in respect of machine operations, and particularly the handling of heavy goods.

The development of protective gear has been an encouraging feature in the present decade. Each industry has its own hazards, and these require the use of specific protective equipment, such as goggles, eye-shields, protective footwear, gloves, aprons, protective suits, respirators and breathing apparatus. In some industries, e.g. the chemical industry, the occupier or owner of the factory is by law required to supply protective equipment, and the employee himself has a legal obligation to wear it if there is risk of injury. Human beings are, however, often perverse about such matters, and many do their best to avoid wearing the equipment. These are the persons for whom the Safety Officer will always have to be on the alert.

Unless danger is immediate, the correction of employees found acting in this manner must, of course, always be left to the person responsible for their control.

From this brief review of the field of safety and accident prevention, it will be readily apparent that there is a call for special knowledge, a blending of human and technical. It is a channel through which the co-operation of supervisors and managers in the promotion of supervision of safety measures, or by the intermediary of a Safety Officer if one is appointed. The range of knowledge required is too wide to be within the scope of one individual, though length of service in one plant does enable the quick-minded man to acquire a good measure of valuable detail about its equipment and operation. The knowledge required, either in the Safety Officer himself, or in the combination of personnel and technical persons, say, sitting as an expert Safety Panel, may be summarised as follows:

(a) Full acquaintance with the site and plant of their own factory.

(b) General knowledge of electrical circuits and good "earthing".

(c) Elementary hydraulics and an understanding of the term "pressure".

(d) Elementary principles of engineering in so far as it relates to the particular industry.

(e) Outline of the production processes used.

(f) Factories Acts and special regulations.

(g) National Insurance requirements and official procedures.

(h) The human factors in accident causation.

(i) How to keep records and compile simple statistics.

When a Safety Officer is employed, either full-time or part-time, it is advisable for him to belong to an appropriate local organisation.

In many factories, it has been found valuable to make accident prevention one of the subjects of joint consultation, in order to encourage a high level of employee participation and responsibility. The large organisations may find it useful to have a series of Departmental Safety Committees, each undertaking the review of conditions in its own area, and following out many of the activities of the Safety Officer. On the other hand, even when a full-time man is employed in this capacity, the existence of an employee-management committee can do a great deal to promote safe working and to foster a sound conception of "prevention is better than cure".

These deliberations on the detailed working and requirements of the safety factor in production might easily give the impression that special provision is called for only in the larger organisations. This, however, is far from true. In most enterprises some danger arises; and it is the nature of the process, the layout of buildings, the character of the plant, and other such technical factors, rather than any matter of size, that brings the question of danger and safety into prominence. There may be, and often is, just as much call for "accident prevention" in the tiny concern as in the mammoth works. In the smaller unit, of course, no question of full-time service arises. Many a small firm has met this need and built upon it—built up an efficient "safety organisation" round the enthusiasm and interest of a foreman or other member of the staff. With the policy laid down and the necessary support and assistance given by the management, a foreman can learn a good deal about regulations, hazards, safety practices and so on, and be able to render invaluable service as an "honorary or part-time Safety Officer". All that has been said in the foregoing paragraphs then applies to him and his activities with equal validity.

ERGONOMICS

In many fields of management practice the past few decades have seen subjects rise to importance in public interest and then recede, sometimes leaving but few permanent relics. The human factor in management has been no exception, and latterly there has been a recrudescence of interest in this area recalling some of the pioneer work of half a century ago. Yet, with a more resounding title—for "ergonomics" is different more in name than in substance or approach from the early studies of the impact of nature and environment on men's capacity to work.

Ergonomics has been defined as "the scientific study of the relationship between man and his working environment". In America the emphasis has been laid more on the design of equipment and the term in use there, "human engineering", is more specifically "the design of human tasks, man/machine systems, and specific items of man-operated equipment for the most effective accomplishment of the job, including displays for presenting information to the human senses, controls for human operations, and complex man/machine systems". In practice ergonomics is a convenient grouping of relevant research (and research workers), in the independent disciplines of functional anatomy, applied human physiology and applied psychology.

It would be absurd to suggest that before the term ergonomics was coined, those engaged in the organisation of human work were unaware of the basic disciplines in these biological sciences. On the contrary, many of the principles involved may be classified as "common-sense" rather than as part of a scientific discipline. Some more sophisticated concepts have for many years formed a necessary part of the work-study approach to the analysis of human work.

Particular problems relating to military equipment during the Second World War provoked the interest of physiologists and psychologists in similar problems in industrial applications, and out of this has grown the present collection of data and experience. There is as yet comparatively little work available for examination which has arisen spontaneously from an industrial problem, and the emphasis, particularly in American literature, on military applications remains. In this country more emphasis has been placed on arriving at a basic theory, but this in itself may have affected the application of research findings in industry, since the form in which research results are available is not the best for assimilation into industrial practice.

The area of activity covered by the term ergonomics is clearly a very large one and since current research is necessarily involved in the less clearly understood areas of knowledge, it is impossible to treat the subject comprehensively in a brief survey.

What has been covered by systematic research under this designation may be illustrated in the following list of subject-headings from a privately prepared review:

A. THE APPLICATION OF THE RESEARCH TECHNIQUES OF FUNCTIONAL ANATOMY AND PHYSIOLOGY TO THE PHYSICAL PROBLEMS OF HUMAN WORK:
   1. The measurement of the dimensions of the human body.
   2. The limits of muscular forces.
   3. The practical application of anthropometric data.
   4. Energy expenditure and physical fatigue.

B. THE APPLICATION OF THE RESEARCH TECHNIQUES OF PSYCHOLOGY TO THE MENTAL PROBLEMS OF HUMAN WORK:
   1. The display of information.
   2. The analysis of perceptual elements in operator skill.
   3. The psychological aspects of fatigue.
   4. The use of psychological analysis of skill in operator training.
   5. Fault finding and diagnosis.
   6. The effect of age upon human skill.

C. ENVIRONMENTAL CONDITIONS:
   1. Lighting, heating and ventilating.
   2. Noise.
   3. The effect of cold on human performance.

Any distinction between "ergonomics" and "work study" must be an arbitrary one and one of degree. In no sense are they contradictory. The study of work must inevitably be concerned with the scientific study of the relationship between man and his environment. The difference in degree exists in the emphasis given to the word "scientific": research in this field in this country is conducted almost entirely by academic institutions primarily interested in the presentation of a scientifically respectable body of knowledge. The work study unit is mostly preoccupied with useable, if approximate, answers. The main concern must be that this apparent difference does not mean that what knowledge the scientist is accumulating, and which is useful, is being ignored by the practical man.

CHAPTER VI

EMPLOYEE SERVICES

MOST employees at some time or other have a problem which they want solved even though it is outside the scope of their employment. It may be advice on a legal matter, some question on a building society loan, how to get to a hospital, housing or accommodation difficulties, inadequate transport facilities, or some other general problem which affects them as individuals. A good personnel policy in a company provides an opportunity for dealing with these queries, sometimes in the employee's own time—for instance, during a break or dinner-hour. Assistance of this kind is known as "Employee Services", and is undoubtedly a great asset to a company in promoting goodwill and creating good morale. This is also one of the ways in which management discharges part of the "social responsibility" inherent in its role. Some of the common items arising are dealt with below.

ACCOMMODATION

A Personnel Manager will often be expected to find lodgings and accommodation for new employees, and frequently his assistance will be called upon when employees marry and wish to set up home. Without turning himself into a "local housing officer", he can often be of considerable help, either in an advisory capacity, or by keeping track of opportunities for accommodation that happen to come to his notice through local contacts. He is often also well placed to be in close touch with the official local Housing Authorities. It is easy to maintain in the department a register or record of the names of people in the locality who are willing to take a man or woman and to classify whether they are prepared to take a permanent lodger or merely willing to do it for a few nights. Usually after a matter of a few weeks, the new employee finds a home with one of his workmates or their relatives, and it is the exception to find that the worker remains at the same premises as those which are chosen for him. A plan which has been followed with some success is to insert a printed slip in all pay packets stating that the company is constantly being asked for lodgings, and if employees know of any addresses, would they let the Personnel Manager know. He should then make a practice of following up these addresses to ascertain details, especially the standard of comfort and cleanliness.

While the Personnel Officer will give every help to employees in this matter, he must avoid becoming implicated in responsibility for the rental or for the behaviour of the "lodger".

To some extent, the location of the works or factory will determine whether housing is an acute problem or not. To the average man with a family the importance of obtaining a suitable home cannot be over-emphasised. To many men with families the prospects of obtaining a house are more important than those offered by the job, and many a man has had to turn down a promising opening because of inability to secure suitable accommodation.

There are a number of schemes by which assistance can be given to employees, some of which are considered below.

(a) *Houses for Key Workers.*—Generally in the Development Areas, priority has been afforded in providing houses for key people through the local Councils. The cost of these houses is sometimes borne partly by the Government Department and partly by the occupier of the new factory.

New development factories under consideration would of course be planned by the Development Authority, having in mind the number of employees who would require to be housed at or near the factory site.

(b) *Small Dwellings Acquisition Act.*—This Act provided for houses to be purchased over a number of years (fifteen to twenty) at low rates of interest, where the house is required for the personal occupation of the owner. This is a very useful service, for it means that an employee is able to purchase a house for almost the same amount as he would be able to rent it. The amount of the loan in many approved cases is up to 95 per cent. of the total value of the property. Application for a loan in such cases should be made to the treasurer of the Local Authority.

(c) *The Company Tied Houses.*—Some industrial undertakings, particularly in coal-mining areas, erected houses for their employees when the mines were first opened and developed. The houses were let at nominal rents, some as low as 6*d*. a week. The accommodation was not good by present-day standards. Generally speaking, the houses were in rows and terraced, opening on to the street, with a back-yard of a few square yards of concrete or rubble. Many of these houses can be seen on the north-east coast and in Wales; some of course have fallen down, whilst others have been maintained in a good condition and are quite habitable. Employees living in these houses are able to work only for the particular firm which owns the houses. Should they decide to leave the employ of that company, they are legally bound to give up possession of the house, and this is incorporated in their contract of employment, either in writing or as a result of practice.

The company tied house has many advantages, and in recent years has been applied much more to executives and managers. It functions well, and has many points to its credit, although there are still a few people who would prefer to pay higher rent and not be under an obligation to their employers.

Where the company owns houses, it is usually the Personnel Department's job to collect the rents and to arrange details of tenancies, to keep a waiting list of people who are anxious to become tenants, and to regard the housing situation as one of the jobs to be looked after. A strong point in its favour is the good relationship which can be built up by the Personnel Department in their weekly rent collection visits with the wives and children and the personal interest which can be shown in the welfare of the employee.

(*d*) *Housing Schemes.*—Yet another way for a company to assist their employees in connection with housing is by the formation of a building society, financed by the company and receiving Government support or subsidy. In this case the employee becomes the lessor of the property, the owner for the time being is the company, and after a period of years the title in the property passes to the local council or some other body appointed by the Ministry concerned.

This is a particularly good scheme, and helpful when a new factory is being formed in an area where no houses exist to "let". It provides a great deal of flexibility in the design of the houses, and enables an estate to be laid out on rather better lines than would be possible were the cost to be fully borne by the company. The usual system in letting the houses of this kind is to allocate the first few to specially selected key people and the balance to be let on a necessity basis, those men with the most children or dependents getting first choice.

LEGAL AID

From time to time, employees have troubles which mean attendance at a police-court or county court, and when these problems arise the employee often comes to the Personnel Manager for assistance. Some large companies have legal members among the staff, and so expert advice can be had forthwith. Legal problems should be treated with great reserve, and a Personnel Manager should be cautious about attempting to give advice unaided.

Where an employee is involved in police-court proceedings, it is not unusual for the company or the man's Trade Union to provide a solicitor and for the costs to be repaid by the man at a later date, or alternatively treated as a works charge and given to the employee. Each case would, of course, need to be dealt with on its merits. A frequent problem which arises in this way is the possession of premises by a landlord, and often the threat of a County summons for possession of the rooms or premises in which a man lives can completely upset his normal work and cause absence, and it is well worth the few pounds which it will cost for the matter to be dealt with by the company's solicitor or someone specifically instructed to act on his behalf.

CONTRIBUTORY SCHEMES

With the coming of the National Health Act in 1948, a number of contributory schemes which were then in existence were dissolved. There are, however, still a number of funds to which employees contribute; the most common of these are the Sick Club, the Loan Club, the Christmas Club and the Clothing Club.

(*a*) *Sick Club*.—This is operated by a weekly payment, usually of 6*d*. per week from each member of the firm, occasionally collected through the Wages Department as a deduction. Payments of varying amounts are made to employees when they are absent owing to sickness: the amount may be £1 per week for the first six weeks, and 10*s*. per week for a further six weeks. Payment is usually made by the secretary of the Sick Club on production of a medical certificate. To obtain benefit, an employee must have been a contributor to the scheme for a given period, usually three months, and a medical certificate has to be produced each week that the employee claims payment. The first three or four days are not recognised, and the amount of sick pay in any one year is limited.

Accident pay, which is usually covered by the same Club, is sometimes on the same basis, and, in addition, a death benefit is payable.

It is not unusual for a company to be asked to make a grant on the formation of a Sick Club, and in some cases the members of the Accounts Department are asked by the workpeople to act as treasurer and auditor. Generally speaking, it is not desirable for the money to be paid into the company's accounts, for the reason that the employees often resent the company holding their money, and, of course, in the event of financial difficulties on the part of the company, the Sick Club money might be inadvertently commandeered.

(*b*) *Loan Club*.—Loan Clubs are usually operated departmentally. The man pays in to the collector whatever sum he wishes to save that week. There is no fixed limit, and he has the opportunity of withdrawing a given sum in a fixed time which he arranges with the secretary. If he fails to take a loan he has to pay a fine, and at the end of the year the accounts break even, or the contributions are returned with interest which has accumulated as a result of the fines paid by the non-borrowing members.

It is not often that the management are asked to handle the money in connection with such a Club. The money, collected by subscription each week, passes on to various members, who return it on given dates.

(c) *Christmas Club.*—A number of companies, in order to encourage thrift amongst their employees, offer, as an inducement, to pay interest on the money collected by the Christmas Club in any year. The usual procedure is to have sixpenny shares, with a maximum number which any one employee can hold. Payments start the first week in January and continue until the middle of December, including payments during the holiday weeks. It is not usual for anyone to be allowed to withdraw the Christmas Club contributions until the end of the year, and interest is paid at about 5 per cent. on the money saved, that is to say, 2s. 6d. on 50s.

The share-out of the Christmas Club money is made by special payment through the Wages Department, who are also responsible for the deductions from earnings throughout the year. Every endeavour should be made for the money to be paid out before the last Saturday before Christmas.

(d) *Clothing Club.*—Some firms provide overalls, others do not. There are a number of schemes for the provision of clothing to the worker on the job. One scheme, known as the Industrial Overall Scheme, provides for two sets of overalls each year on payment of a fixed sum each week. The same scheme also provides for the overalls to be cleaned, and this is a great help to the housewife.

Where overalls are provided and laundered free, employees rapidly get used to the idea of not purchasing their own overalls, and some become careless in the way in which they are looked after.

LOANS

The problem of lending money to employees is a difficult one, and at the same time one which requires to be dealt with with a good deal of flexibility. The budgeting of the working-man's household expenditure is generally so near the line that there is little left to put away for a rainy day, especially when so much is purchased on hire terms. When an emergency arises, the problem of finding a large sum of money is always one of great difficulty. Going to a pawnbroker and borrowing at a rate of interest sometimes solves the problem, but more often than not an approach is made to the employer with a view to obtaining a loan.

Loans generally fall into two categories. First, a "sub" or "a little on account". There is no reason why an employee should not be paid by way of a loan an amount which he has already earned, and which, by custom of trade, is held in hand until the next pay day.

Many employers are diffident about making arrangements for this facility, but there seems to be no reason for this obstacle being placed in the way of the working man. The usual procedure is for the man to apply to his foreman for two or three pounds as a "sub", and for the foreman to refer to the Personnel Department, who should readily accede to the man's request. There will, of course, always be the inveterate liar who will produce heartrending stories each week in order to obtain his money, but it is for the Personnel Manager to put an end to this type of borrowing as soon as he is satisfied that there is any suggestion of the man not being genuinely in need.

Secondly, there is the man who requires to borrow a sum of twenty to fifty pounds, perhaps as a deposit on a house or to purchase furniture when getting married, or for some other genuine reason. A loan in this case might be given after investigation of the facts by a responsible person employed in the company, and a proper statement setting out the amount of the loan and the basis on which it is to be repaid should be drawn up. The agreement should be stamped, and a copy of it handed to the employee at the same time as the authorisation is given for the amount which is to be deducted week by week until such time as it is repaid. Any question of a loan of a larger sum of money should always be regarded confidentially, but the manager of the department in which the man works would undoubtedly be asked for his views before a decision was made or a request granted.

TRANSPORT

The problem of getting employees to and from work affects only those factories which have to draw from a scattered area, or are isolated in rural surroundings. In the London area the travelling problem is probably more acute than anywhere else in the country, for it is not unusual for workers to travel from one side of the metropolis to the other, a journey which may take anything up to $1\frac{1}{2}$ hours morning and evening.

A Personnel Manager is expected to have a good knowledge of local transport conditions, to know the schedules of buses and trains around the starting and finishing times of the factory and to be able to deal with the problems which arise. A frequent complaint is the lateness and irregularity of the running of a bus. Sometimes the bus runs early, other times it is late, and thus causes an appreciable number of employees to be late for work. Of course, it is quite useless for a Personnel Manager to refer a complaint to a transport undertaking without being able to give factual information. The type of detail which the transport authority will want is the time at which the incident took place, the number of the bus, the number of people affected and the amount of time lost, also the cost of wages to the individuals where they are paid on a time-worked basis.

Usually transport officials are most helpful when properly approached, and will go to considerable lengths in order to ensure that the services for workpeople run smoothly, efficiently and on time. Where more people travel than the vehicle can cater for, additional services, particularly on short runs, can be provided by the local garage manager without reference to anyone else. On the other hand, if the number of people travelling to a given area becomes great, it is probable that the headquarters of the transport executive would arrange for a re-routeing or re-timing of transport to meet the demand.

Some factories operate their own transport, and in the Midlands districts buses leave for outlying places at given times, the driver remains on some light work in the factory until the end of the work period, and then takes the bus back to the city centre. Another system is for the employers to hire coaches, and for the employees to pay a normal fare, sometimes deducted from their earnings by special authorisation.

SUPERANNUATION

Apart from the National Insurance benefits through old-age pensions or those paid in the form of gratuities, pensions arrangements must be regarded as an integral part of the terms and conditions of employment. If a pensions scheme is to be satisfactory both for the employee and for the employer, and is to be actuarially solvent, the amount of pension accruing must be related to the amount of contributions paid during service with the employer. Modern pensions schemes usually relate the amount of contribution at any time to a scale of retirement laid down.

With the introduction of the National Insurance Act, 1959, the State developed a greater interest in pensions. This Act, with its provisions for graduated pension contributions, which are additional to flat rate National Insurance contributions, must be paid in respect of any employee (other than a National Insurance retirement pensioner) between ages 18 and 70 (65 for women), whose gross pay in employment exceeds £9 in any week, unless he is contracted out under a certificate obtained by his employer. It is this last proviso, viz. the provision for *contracting out,* as well as the discussion in 1960/61 on its advantages and disadvantages, that has tended to have an overall effect of increasing the impact and development of private occupational superannuation schemes. The main factors relevant to a "contracting out" decision are summarised in two main categories:

1. What a particular set of employees get out of it.
2. Other factors relating to the provision of a particular pensions scheme and the general attitude of the employer towards such schemes.

Under current conditions, the characteristics favouring "contracting out" may be listed as:

(a) Majority of employees above the marginal earnings bracket (say £12 to £13 per week for men or £10 10s. 0d. to £12 per week for women).
(b) Low labour turnover in the company's personnel.
(c) Provision of a contributory scheme.
(d) Benefits in excess of the maximum level of state graduated benefits.
(e) Desire to preserve contact with retired employees and further goodwill by securing a major part of retirement income.
(f) Lack of confidence that retirement benefits will not be left out of "politics".

It was recently reported that the development of private schemes was a success story for the 1959 Act, because one of its major objects —to preserve and encourage the best development of occupational pensions schemes—was well on the way to achievement. The latest figures show nearly four and a half million persons contracted out of the State Graduated Pensions Scheme, against the two and a half million estimated by the Government in 1958.

There are many types of occupational pension schemes, falling broadly into the categories of (a) non-contributory or (b) contributory, and covering unfunded schemes, privately administered funds, Group Life and Pensions Schemes, Endowment Assurance Schemes, Excepted Provident Funds. Generally speaking up to the Finance Act, 1956, privately administered pension funds were approved under Section 379 of the Finance Act, 1952, and insured schemes under Section 388 of the same Act. The chief points of difference between schemes currently approved under Section 379 and those currently approved under Section 388 may be broadly summarised as follows:

The Section 379 type of scheme covers privately administered funds and some deferred annuity schemes, all of which must be governed by trust deed and rules. The benefits payable during the lifetime of a member must be such as to be taxable. Interest income on the fund is free of tax, and both employers' and employees' contributions are allowed in full.

The Section 388 type of scheme covers endowment assurance schemes, some deferred annuity schemes and unfunded arrangements. A trust deed is not obligatory though sometimes used; the scheme, however, must have rules. The benefits payable during the lifetime of the member need not be such as to be wholly taxable, but at least three-quarters of the retirement benefit must be in taxable form. Interest income, if any, is taxable and, although employers' contributions are allowed in full, employees' contributions are allowed as life assurance premiums if the scheme is insured.

Local Authorities, Nationalised Industries and many industrial concerns set aside each year a contribution towards employees' pensions; the right to a pension often continues after the person terminates employment in the form of a paid-up pension, or, if transfer arrangements are available, a transfer value, both of which would include employers' contributions as well as any paid by the employee. Most modern pensions schemes allow for pensions in the case of ill-health and incapacity and there are several reasons from the employers' point of view why provision for early retirement should be incorporated. It is often provided that subject to production of evidence of satisfactory health a male member may elect to substitute for his pension a reduced pension which, after his death in retirement would continue to be paid to his widow for the rest of her life. Alternatively, on the death of a member in service and prior to normal pension age, a death benefit is paid to her of say one year's salary and in addition, the whole of the contributions paid by such member to date of death; while in other schemes the provision on death in service takes the form of a widow's pension ceasing usually on remarriage, extra allowances being given in the case of children under eighteen years of age.

It will be noted from the foregoing brief notes that the subject is one for expert advice. Before seeking such advice it is useful to have a basic understanding of the subject, and the book *"Pension Schemes and Retirement Benefits"* (by Gordon A. Hoskin, F.I.A.) is recommended for further study.

CHAPTER VII

TAKING A CASE TO ARBITRATION

In the majority of industries, rates of pay and certain basic conditions of employment are agreed between the headquarters of interested Trade Unions and the Association of Employers. Details are laid down in what are known as National Agreements, and their observance is one of the responsibilities of the Personnel Manager. These rates are known as "basic rates", and it is not unusual to find firms paying higher than these minimum figures. As a general rule, wage claims arise from disagreements between operatives and foremen on how much should be earned for a particular job; from such a humble beginning troubles can arise, which, if not settled within the works, become serious differences requiring settlement ultimately by "arbitration".

Within the framework of the Agreements, companies vary in the way in which they conduct negotiations with "organised labour". In the small firm, the manager or foreman, or the owner, would probably deal directly with the individual employee, taking a stand on what he can afford to pay in the way of "piecework" prices or bonus earnings, in relation to the profit he is making out of the sale of his products. By contrast, the large firm, employing some thousands of people spread in various factories all over the country, would have a central Personnel Department, the head of which would be responsible for negotiations arising out of the Agreements, as well as for participating in discussions in regard to modifications or the drawing up of new Agreements.

In the small firm, it is unlikely that there would be a Shop Steward: employees who are members of a Trade Union would accept employment only providing they were to receive the nationally agreed basic rate and other defined conditions as a minimum. In the event of any difficulty arising the District Organiser of the Union concerned would come in to help in solving the problem.

In many Agreements, the procedure in dealing with problems or disputes arising is laid down. Some Employers' Associations also insist on their members dealing along certain lines: in some cases, the matter must be referred to the Association, and negotiations from there on are taken out of the hands of the individual employer. He is called upon to give such evidence and data as the Association will require in conducting negotiations with the Unions according to the appropriate procedure.

In major matters of policy, it is not always the Personnel Manager who participates in the meetings as the company's sole representative. With the medium-sized concerns, that is, the majority of the factories in this country, negotiations are usually conducted by the Works Manager, the General Manager or the Managing Director, perhaps with the Personnel Manager in attendance. This is not necessarily a reflection on the latter's competence, but an admission of the part that the "line" executives play in employee relations. It also helps to arrive at earlier conclusions, because these executives are able to take binding decisions. There is nothing more aggravating to a group of employees or to an organiser of a Trade Union than to spend time and energy in putting forward a case and in full discussion of the pros and cons, only to find later in the meeting that the person present on behalf of the management has no authority to give a firm reply or take a conclusive decision—which means that the whole discussion must be repeated at another level. On the other hand, where a Personnel Manager has been established in an organisation, it is highly important that he should attend at all negotiations.

Until such time as the functional position of the Personnel Officer becomes really established, there is much to be said for negotiations being conducted by a top-line executive, who may be better acquainted with all the financial implications and better able to give a quick decision, provided he has the advice of the Personnel Manager on procedure and on what is being done elsewhere on similar problems. One advantage from this arrangement is that it keeps the Personnel Manager in a neutral position, serving as the source of expert knowledge and advice, but at the same time *au fait* with the details discussed: he avoids becoming suspect among the employees as having worked against them in connection with their application.

Broadly described, the procedure laid down for dealing with problems or disputes arising in the interpretation of Agreements is something like this:

The employee concerned raises a matter with his foreman, and if no satisfaction is obtained he calls in the Shop Steward. These two then go as a deputation to the Department Superintendent, the Personnel Manager, or the Works Manager, according to the arrangements laid down by the company itself. Failure to agree at this stage means that the matter is taken to the outside Organisers, either the Employers' Association or the Trade Union District Office. A defined "disputes procedure" applicable to the industry is then followed.

The sequence may be illustrated by the procedure applied in the heavy chemical industry, which is laid down as follows:

(*a*) Any question in dispute arising out of this Agreement between an employer and his employees should be dealt with in the first place by an employee or the Trade Union Shop Steward on his behalf, and by the appropriate representative of the Management.

(*b*) Failing a settlement within the works, the question should be discussed by a Trade Union Officer and by the appropriate representative of the management, who may avail themselves of the services of the Association of Chemical and Allied Employers.

(*c*) In the event of local agreement not being reached, the question should be referred for settlement to the appropriate Trade Union headquarters and to the Association of Chemical and Allied Employers.

(*d*) In the cases where the Trade Union headquarters and the Association of the Chemical and Allied Employers fail to arrive at a settlement, the difference is to be reported forthwith to the Joint Secretaries of the Joint Conference.

(*e*) If the Joint Industrial Council fails to settle a dispute, the aggrieved party should have recourse—

(1) To the Industrial Relations Department of the Ministry of Labour; and

(2) To arbitration, before giving the legal notice of cessation of work.

"Arbitration" will mean the formality of submitting the case for objective external investigation through the machinery established by the Terms and Conditions of Employment Act 1959. Recourse to this machinery will be made only when all the possibilities for settlement within the industry have been exhausted and use cannot be made of this form of Arbitration by workers whose remuneration or minimum remuneration is fixed by a wages council, by the Agricultural Wages Board, or by ministerial regulations. Nor does the procedure under the Act apply to workers covered by such Acts as the Civil Aviation Act 1949 and Television Act 1954, where there is already provision for settlement of remuneration questions by reference to the Industrial Court direct.

When a point of difference has arisen which the Joint Industrial Council cannot settle in its Court of Arbitration it is defined as a "claim" under the Act of 1959: a claim exists when a group, representative of workers or employers, seeks to establish whether or not terms and conditions of employment in a trade or industry with which they are themselves connected are being observed. Such a claim goes to the Industrial Court (*not* now to the *Industrial Disputes Tribunal*—which has ceased to exist) for decision, and when that decision is made it is legally binding. It must be noted that a claim can be reported by a representative body of workers but can only be reported on the employers' side by an organisation of employers and not by any one employer.

The Industrial Court is a permanent institution, but is not in any way subject to Government control. The assessors are appointed from panels comprising persons representing the industry and the Trade Unions. Whilst it is possible for the parties to be represented by counsel or solicitors, this practice is unusual. The rules of the Court are flexible and allow the President a good deal of scope in the way in which the evidence and the information are to be given. They are not given on oath, and the rules of procedure provide for both sides to be given a proper and full hearing, irrespective of the length of time taken. It is very rare for the Court to be unable to agree, but in such instances provision has been made, in the *Industrial Courts Act (1919)* for the matter to be referred to an umpire.

Alternatively, at the discretion of the Ministry, the matter could be dealt with under the conciliation procedure provided for in the *Conciliation Act of 1896*: this prescribes for the parties to meet under the chairmanship of an individual nominated by the Minister or agreed among the parties to act as conciliator. The decisions arrived at, however, are not legally binding, although in practice it has been customary for them to be accepted and acted upon.

A case taken to Arbitration usually has to follow certain recognised rules of procedure. There are instances where Arbitration is reached only after protracted negotiation through the earlier disputes procedure: several meetings may be prescribed at which the subject matter is discussed in the hope of reaching a decision. Arbitration is of necessity a final stage, resorted to only after all direct channels have failed. The amount of detail required in connection with a case going to Arbitration is considerable. Factual information of every kind has to be sought, for a case presented eventually to the Industrial Court is as serious as a High Court action. Personnel Managers realise that the point in dispute may be an extremely costly one: it may be a permanent addition to the company's wages bill as a result of the award.

As a matter of interest and because many managers and Personnel Managers have little opportunity of personal experience an hypothetical reference is set out in a narrative form.

CASE HISTORY OF A REFERENCE TO ARBITRATION

(Fictitious Characters)

The Personnel Manager of a company, Smith and Smith Limited, who belong to a trade association or federation, heard from a workman that at a branch meeting held recently it was unanimously decided to ask for another twopence per hour for all unskilled workers and fourpence per hour for all skilled and semi-skilled workers.

The same day, the branch secretary, who was also the convener of shop stewards in the factory, asked for an interview with the Personnel Manager, who, having granted the interview, had the claim put before him, and listened only to an outline of the bases of the claim. He then communicated the content of the claim to his Works Manager (the "line" management), and between them they agreed to call a meeting with the Works Manager in the chair, at which the detailed submissions of the Union in support of the claim would be put.

This was accordingly done and a very careful minute made of the meeting by the Personnel Manager. The Unions put their claim and the reasons supporting it, among which was an allegation that Smith and Smith's rates were poor, not only by comparison with local firms but by comparison also with the industry in which they were engaged. Having heard the reasons, the Works Manager, with no immediate information on hand to rebut the allegation of the stewards, adjourned the meeting to allow management to consider the claim. The Personnel Manager immediately initiated enquiries among neighbouring firms and industry at large to ascertain the rates of pay and current level of earnings of employees whose occupations and tasks corresponded as closely as possible with those of Smith and Smith Limited. He also took care to find out as much as possible about the size of the firm, the working conditions, and the kind of labour available to that firm, and whether any yearly bonuses, etc., were paid. Having elicited this information, it was collated into an easily-understood summary for the use of the Works Manager at the next meeting with the stewards.

At this meeting the Works Manager had before him the minutes of the previous meeting and the summary of information that the Personnel Manager had collected. He took each point that the Union had made and gave an answer to it. Some of these answers proved unsatisfactory to the Unions, who immediately sought to introduce such other matters as working conditions, bonus payments, etc., into the discussion, no previous mention having been made of these items. Nevertheless line management had been adequately briefed by the Personnel Department and the Works Manager was able to give a full and comprehensive reply. This consisted in the main of a statement to the effect that the management, having considered the submissions of the Unions, and by comparison with neighbouring firms and industry at large, considered that their employees were adequately compensated for the work they were called upon to perform. This reply proving unacceptable to the stewards, who stated that in their opinion the management's answer left the problem unresolved. They would take the answer back to their members but felt in any case that their members would "want to take it further". The meeting was then closed.

At a shop floor meeting later the stewards reported what was described as management's unconciliatory attitude and achieved the foregone conclusion of a vote in favour of "pursuing the claim to a satisfactory result". The stewards contacted their branch of the Union. Their full-time official at the branch gave the claim his blessing and wrote to the employers' association. In his letter he pointed out the "unfortunate circumstances" in which this claim had materialised, and pressed for an early date for a Local Conference to be held. In doing this he treated the second meeting, at which the Works Manager had given his reply, as the first stage in formal procedure. It would not have been impossible or unusual for a third meeting to have been held in the factory as a formal Works Conference: the outcome would probably have been similar to that of the second meeting and no useful purpose would normally have been served.

Such a Works Conference is necessary, however, after a stoppage. Despite the fact that most industries have a laid down procedure which must be exhausted before an official strike can be called, it is not unusual for the workers at any one factory to stage a stoppage to "demonstrate the strength of their intention to have their rightful claim conceded". Only after a return to normal working for a reasonable period should such a Works Conference be held.

But to return to our case, where the second domestic meeting has been accepted as the first stage in procedure. The full-time official at the Union's branch has written to the employer's association reporting a difference over a pay claim—"a failure to agree"—and asking for a date for a conference. The employers' association now start making arrangements by attempting to find mutually convenient dates for the meeting. The Union on their side start building a case, and the Personnel Manager must be ready to provide many, many details. In Local Conference the firm will have to put its position to a panel of employers, along with details of all its rates of pay, comparative statements, etc., in a form easily assimilated and readily understood.

In a claim dealing with wage rates, the Personnel Manager should now extend his enquiry among yet more firms. He should trace back the history of the rates and earnings on a normal week in his factory and compare them with other firms in the same industry, with the rates and earnings in manufacturing industry. He should compare the rise in earnings over, say, the past five years with the Cost of Living Index and the official average earnings figures published by the Ministry of Labour. All this information should be neatly documented and the correct conclusions drawn and stated for the employers' panel. It should be bound, together with all minutes of previous meetings, a clear and concise statement of the Union's claims and a preamble to the whole, dealing with the way the claim arose and on what bases the firm had rejected it. This documentation should be sent to the employers' association in advance of the conference so that the Chairman of the Conference is completely aware of the firm's position and contentions.

On the appointed date for the conference, the Personnel Manager and the Works Manager of Smith and Smith Limited attended at the offices of the employers' association before the Union official arrived. The Chairman of the Conference, having previously been briefed by the documentation, was in a position speedily to run through the case, clear up any points of doubt and decide on the procedure to be adopted in Conference.

In the actual Conference the panel of employers, the Personnel Manager and the Works Manager met the full-time officials of the Union and perhaps one or two stewards from the factory. The Union was asked to put its claim and the full-time official did this.

At this stage in procedure it is quite usual for further allegations to be introduced which had no part in the original discussions and for "evidence" to be offered of which no previous mention had been made. The case we are examining was no different and an adjournment was necessary for the Personnel Manager and the Works Manager to explain the situation to the panel. An opportunity was also taken to re-affirm to the panel that the company sincerely believed that their workpeople were adequately paid for the work they undertook, that the survey of rates and earnings the firm had produced proved their contention, and that they were accordingly not willing to accede to the Union's request for twopence per hour for unskilled and fourpence per hour for other workers.

The Conference was re-convened, the chairman rebutted the Union's original arguments in support of the claim, and dealt with the new evidence introduced at the Conference. He then informed the Union officials that, considering the strength of the company's argument, the employers' panel were "unable to recommend the firm to increase their rates". The Union officials expressed themselves concerned at the blow that had been dealt at good industrial relations and the way in which mutual trust had been dispelled: they asked for a further adjournment to consider the employers' answer.

After an interval the Union officials came once more into conference and said they had considered the company's attitude from the start of the claim, and the reply they had received at the Conference. This reply, they stated, was not acceptable and left them with no alternative but to fail to agree.

The chairman registered this, thanked the officials for their attendance and closed the Conference.

Throughout the whole of the Local Conference an independent shorthand-writer was present and the whole of the proceedings were recorded verbatim. They were subsequently printed and distributed to the company and the union by the employers' association. The chief concern of the Personnel Manager now became the formulation of policy in regard to the claim if the Union asked for it to be taken to the last stage of procedure. He was very busy after the Local Conference ensuring that all line management and all executives of the company were completely aware of the Union's arguments and the seriousness of the claim. He had the company payroll re-calculated on the basis of granting the Union's claim, to demonstrate the annual addition this would represent to the wages bill.

Meantime, the full-time district officials of the Union were reconsidering the claim. They forwarded the claim and their arguments to the Union's executives, who decided to press for it to go to the final stage of procedure—a Central Conference. At a Conference at this level it is the executive of the Unions who meet the officials of the Central Organisation of the Employers.

Finally the Personnel Manager was informed by his employers' association that the Unions had referred the claim to Central Conference. A date was stated and the attendance of representatives from the company required. The Personnel Manager sought meetings of his line management to ascertain the policy they wished to be pursued at the Conference. This done, he expanded and revised the documentation he had submitted to Local Conference and sent a copy to his employers' association. In an industry in which the procedure and the reference to an ultimate Conference is frequently invoked, the arrangements are almost standardised. It was such an industry to which Smith and Smith Limited belonged. Accordingly, references on disputes from many parts of the country were heard centrally over a number of days. A representative of the line management with sufficient status to speak authoritatively on the firm's policy accompanied the Personnel Manager to this Conference.

On the day before the Union executives were formally to put their claim a panel of employers, under a chairman, heard the firm's representatives. The Personnel Manager, being sufficiently experienced in procedure, put his company's case, stressing again that the firm believed they were paying a fair wage. He made reference to the way in which earnings on a normal week had, in his firm, risen at a rate which outstripped the rise in the Cost of Living Index. He referred to the ladder of promotion through the grades of worker that existed, and to the range of ability and merit rates that were open to a keen and conscientious worker. The contention that the workers of Smith and Smith were underpaid he refuted by reference to the survey he had undertaken with other firms, and pointed out that the fringe benefits his company provided were far in advance of their particular industry. Furthermore, he stated that to grant the increase claimed by the Union would so increase labour costs as to price the company's products out of the market and would force the company to consider, however reluctantly, the withdrawal of the costly fringe benefits.

On the following day the Conference proper opened. The Union executives made their case: the employers, after an adjournment, made a reply. The reply was in fact a faithful repetition of what the Personnel Manager had stated to be his company's position. The Union withdrew to consider the answer and on coming back to the Conference accepted the position the firm had stated, but drew attention to a number of anomalies they alleged to exist in the ranges of ability pay for certain grades of skilled men.

The chairman of the Conference drew the firm's attention to this, suggesting that it might be well to accept the present situation and agree to investigate the alleged anomalies back at the factory. The representative of line management concurred and the Conference was concluded.

Subsequently, in discussion at the factory, an investigation was made into the rates and ranges of pay for certain grades of skilled men. A re-arrangement of the scales which was not costly was made and this satisfied the men in the grades concerned. This settlement was reported by the Personnel Manager to the Employers' Association and by the Union to their executive. All discussions on this claim under procedure were then terminated.

It should be noted that in the unhappy event of agreement not having been reached in such an ultimate Conference the Unions do then, and only then, have the right to call an official strike.

THINGS A PERSONNEL MANAGER SHOULD KNOW

IN SOME DETAIL

THESE are matters which are his particular responsibility, and in which he would be regarded as the expert.

1. *Termination of Employment*
Time necessary to terminate the employment of a person paid by the hour, the week or the month.

2. *Wages Structure*
Within the industry, and rates paid by other firms doing similar work.

3. *Rates Paid*
Rates paid in other industries, particularly engineering, electrical, building trades, for his own company's maintenance workers. Rates for canteen workers and the rail and road haulage rates covering drivers and van-guards.

It is also advisable to know what staff rates are being paid by companies outside the industry. Everyone is in competition for staff—clerical, typing, office machine operators, administrative, professional and technical—and these grades have no relation to a particular industry.

4. *Agreements*
Details of procedure Agreements within his own company and any arrangements in the industry.

5. *Bonus Rates*
Make-up of bonus or piecework, how calculated and when paid.

6. *Wages*
The method of calculating wages, deducting lost time, rates for over-time payment and the extension of wages on a clock card or wages slip.

7. *Labour*
How to obtain labour through Employment Exchanges, Employment Agencies and Ministry of Labour Appointments Board.

Knowledge of advertising procedure and the construction of suitable advertising matter would also be an advantage.

8. *Labour Exchange Procedure*
What happens to a person when he visits the Employment Exchange and the procedure used there for coding by occupation. The resettling of ex-servicemen and the placing of disabled persons.

9. *Time Lost*
The monthly average of time lost for lateness and sickness for men and women employed in similar factories to his own.

10. *Notices*

Organise distribution of notices; responsibility for posting and removing (except those of the Trade Unions).

11. *Statutory Notices*

To know that Statutory Notices have to be posted within the works and to cover the following official registers to comply with the Factories Act:

> (*a*) Give details to Factory Inspector one month after occupation of any premises as a factory, giving details of nature of work and if mechanical power is used, etc.
>
> (*b*) Post at factory entrance abstracts of Factories Act, containing address of the Factories Inspector and the Examining Surgeon.

12. *Registers*

The keeping up-to-date of the following registers:

General Register.

Register for Young Persons.

Aliens Register.

Disabled Persons Register.

Register showing dates of whitewashing, cleaning, etc.

Register for reporting accidents and industrial disease.

IN GENERAL PRINCIPLE

There are many matters in the day-to-day life of a Personnel Manager, about which he will be asked and on which he should be able to give advice. His personal opinion on matters of this kind will, of course, carry great weight, and he will become the "Advice Bureau" for the employees in the factory.

1. *Superannuation and Life Assurance Schemes*

On behalf of his company, he should have a good general understanding of the principles of superannuation and life assurance, and a full grasp of the National Insurance schemes. In regard to the company's own policies and arrangements, he should be fully informed, or, at least, provided with documentation containing full explanations on this latter basis, he will need to know which member of the Secretary's Office (or Accountant's Departments) is to be consulted as the source of specific details in individual cases.

2. *Right of Search*

An employer is not entitled to search an employee, except in two circumstances. The first is where he has reason to believe that the employee has in his possession stolen property, and in the second, where the employee has agreed to be searched as one of the conditions of employment. The searching of individuals is a matter to be dealt with in a most careful way, and special arrangements should be made where women are employed, so that the searching is carried out by a matron or some other reliable woman employee.

3. *Job Analysis*

The Personnel Manager would be expected to know the methods by which a job is broken down and to have a general knowledge of all the jobs which have to be done in each department.

In addition to this, a knowledge of the following techniques is also advisable : —

Job Description—the necessity of completing a Job Description of vacancies as they arise as an aid to recruitment selection.

Follow-up Procedure—after one to three months to ascertain if new employee is satisfactory to supervision and also to ascertain if new employee is settling down happily in job and receiving adequate training from supervision. Any employment difficulties here.

Leaving Interviews—not only to determine why a person is leaving but to ascertain their opinion on the employment policies of the company, working conditions, attitude of supervision, promotion prospects, wage structure, etc., all of which may have an effect on the retention of good employees.

4. *Legislation Affecting Industry (S.R. & O.), etc.*

Information on these matters can nearly always be obtained from the Stationery Office, who will arrange to send on to employers copies of Orders which affect their industry.

5. *Moving Machinery Regulations*

Regulations regarding moving machinery, fire and lifting tackle, are dealt with in detail in the Factories Act. Constant reference to the Factories Act will need to be made as the points arise, but a copy of Redgrave and Others *"Factory, Truck and Shop Acts"* will be found invaluable.

6. *Training and Education Schemes*

Schemes which are available in other works, or at local Technical Schools, should be known in broad outline. Specific information on the training for a particular subject can be obtained by referring to the Principal of the local Technical College.

7. *Joint Consultation Committee*

The procedure and minutes should be carefully studied, and the methods of conducting a meeting on proper lines, the numbers needed to make a quorum and similar matters affecting committees should be studied. A good book on this subject is available from the Industrial Welfare Society and entitled "Works Committees".

8. *Works Outings*

The Personnel Manager will be expected to know how outdoor functions, such as Works Outings, Beanfeasts, Sports Days, etc., should be arranged, and he should make himself familiar with the organisation which is needed for this type of amenity, the towns which are able to cater for large numbers, the transport services required and available, and so on.

9. *Sports Club and Welfare Schemes*

These should be known in broad outline. Organising a Sick Club where none exists and the co-ordination of social events in which people at the company are interested. The Sports Secretary must be a man prepared to accept a lot of hard knocks, without ever receiving the bouquets.

10. *Works Magazines*

These need to be carefully planned, and a committee is usually appointed, as this tends to spread the number of contributors and the amount of copy available. Some companies believe this to be a matter for their Advertising Department. Suggestions from other firms can usually be obtained by asking for details from the Personnel Department. A useful guide on prices and the like is given by the Industrial Welfare Society.

11. *Labour Turnover*

Reduction of labour turnover is the aim of each Personnel Manager. Constant review of the Exit Book tends to lessen the number of people leaving. Labour turnover is unsatisfactory from every point of view.

12. *Court of Referees*

Procedure at Court of Referees should be understood, and the Personnel Manager should have a general knowledge as to how to prepare a case for presentation to such a body. Statements of the evidence to be given should always be obtained before the hearing, and witnesses need to be warned of the time at which they are to attend.

13. *National Insurance Act, 1946*

This Act should be considered and carefully read, so that it is possible to discuss matters which arise and on which information may be asked.

14. *National Insurance and Industrial Injuries Scheme*

This scheme has replaced the old Compensation Act, and an employee is no longer precluded from accepting money from his employers as sick pay, pending the settlement of his case by the National Insurance Office.

15. *Civilian Employment Act of 1944*

Reinstatement in Civilian Employment Act of 1944 makes it compulsory for an employer to take back into his service anyone conscripted into the services. Where an employee has been engaged to fill the vacancy caused by the call-up of the conscript, that person must be discharged in order to reinstate the original employee. Details of the Act should be studied.

16. *The Truck Acts 1891, 1940, 1959*

These make it clear that an employer may not deduct money without written authority. (These are now under official revision.)

17. *The Personnel Policy of the Company*

This has to be interpreted through the medium of the Personnel Manager, who should make it clear to all concerned of the capacity in which he is acting. The company's policy should be clearly stated and re-examined from time to time at meetings at which the Managing Director is present.

18. Accident Prevention

This is a specialised subject, and should be treated as such. The numerous references to the Factories Acts will need to be made. (Previous reference has been made in pages 598–603.)

19. Medical Department

The function of the Medical Department is to maintain and improve the health of the employees. Medical records should always be treated as confidential.

WHERE TO FIND

The Personnel Manager should know where to find information in books of reference, from technical bodies and other organisations from whom up-to-date and detailed knowledge of the particular problem can be obtained, and it is the duty of the Personnel Manager to see that he is quite familiar with its various aspects.

1. Clocking

Time Recording Systems vary a great deal. The usual type punches the card with a time stamp, and by this means a record is made on the clock card showing the attendance day by day. The ideal system is to have a master clock which controls all other clocking stations in the works. For the smaller unit the single clock is sufficient, and information about the various types offered can always be obtained from the clock manufacturers or by reference to such journals as the *Factory Manager, Industrial Welfare Society's Bulletin, The Manager*, etc.

2. Income-tax Allowances

Special allowances are granted to workmen in respect of tools and clothing. Details of these are not usually given in the Notes of Reference, but most books on income tax set out the details of allowances due in this respect. Alternatively, direct application could be made to the local Inspector of Taxes.

3. Fair Wage Resolution

It is usual for the Government, when placing a contract, to overstamp or overprint the documents with a special clause to ensure good working conditions and fair rates of pay. This is to ensure that labour employed for the contract enjoy conditions of a minimum guaranteed standard.

4. Ventilation and Seating Accommodation

In work-rooms, these two problems are dealt with by the Factories Act. Guidance can be obtained by reference to Part I, Section 4 (Ventilation) and Section 44 (Seating). The amendments of the Act in 1948 (Section 6) make it compulsory to provide seating accommodation for all classes of employees whenever practicable. This is a matter of fact which has to be established in each works. A knowledge of the law relating to employment and the various Orders which are issued from time to time are explained in the *Ministry of Labour Gazette* and commented upon in other journals. Reference to the Ministry of Labour should be made to clear up any doubtful points.

5. *Women's Problems*

Problems relating to women's work are discussed at meetings of the Industrial Welfare Society held in various parts of the country from time to time, and information relating to the particular problems on the employment of women is frequently given from this source. The Ministry of Labour Factories Inspectorate Department have a special section dealing with women's employment problems, and information can be obtained from the local office.

6. *Fatigue Problems*

Problems relating to fatigue are best handled in conjunction with the Medical Officer. Reference can be made to the Industrial Health Research Board, the National Institute of Industrial Psychology and the Institute of Personnel Management, who have available information from practical studies on this point.

7. *Mental Disorders*

These call for specialised treatment by a psychiatrist, who should be called in through the medium of the works doctor. Rehabilitation Centres, such as Roffey Park, Horsham, specialise in dealing with such disorders.

8. *Juveniles*

Juvenile employees present problems which are peculiar to adolescence. Co-operation with the Manager of the Juvenile Employment Bureau and the Headmasters or Headmistresses Department and the Ministry of Education can be very helpful.

9. *Cost of Living*

Problems on the cost of living are undertaken by the Government, who have research workers continually investigating. Comparisons are shown in the *Ministry of Labour Gazette* issued monthly, and a new basis for the cost of living came into operation in 1948. Details of the items which have a bearing on the cost of living are included.

10. *Telephone Numbers*

Telephone numbers of Trade Unions, Ministry of Labour, Factories Inspector, Police-station, Railway Station, Works Doctor and Fire Brigades, and those senior executives likely to be required outside working hours should be posted in the Gatekeeper's Office, and copies should be available at the Works Manager's Office, Medical Department and Personnel Department.

BIBLIOGRAPHY

1. C. H. Northcott: *Personnel Management: Principles and Practice.* Pitman, 4th Edition, 1960
2. May Smith: *Introduction to Industrial Psychology.* Cassell, 5th Edition, 1952
3. Elliott Jaques: *The Changing Culture of a Factory.* Tavistock Publications, 1951
4. H. Leavitt: *Managerial Psychology: An Introduction to Individuals, Pairs, and Groups in Organizations.* Chicago University Press, 1958
5. Allan O. Flanders and H. A. Clegg, Editors: *The System of Industrial Relations in Great Britain: Its History, Law and Institutions.* Basil Blackwell: Corrected Impression, 1956
6. G. Cyriax and R. Oakeshott: *The Bargainers: A Survey of Modern Trade Unionism.* Faber and Faber, 1960
7. D. J. Robertson: *Factory Wage Structures and National Agreements.* Cambridge University Press, 1960
8. Editors: R. T. Livingston and S. H. Milberg: *Human Relations in Research Management.* Columbia and Oxford University Press, 1957
9. Ministry of Labour and National Service: *Industrial Relations Handbook.* H.M.S.O., 1961
10. Ministry of Labour and National Service: *Directory of Employers' Associations, Trade Unions, Joint Organisation, etc.* H.M.S.O., 1960
11. J. M. Fraser: *A Handbook of Employee Interviewing.* MacDonald and Evans, 1954
12. K. Liepmann: *Apprenticeship.* Routledge & Kegan Paul, 1960
13. A. Redgrave: *Factories, Truck and Shops Acts.* Butterworth, 19th Edition, 1956, plus supplements to date
14. Ministry of Labour and National Service: *A Short Guide to the Factories Acts.* H.M.S.O., 1949, reprinted 1952
15. Various Broadsheets and Pamphlets: The Institute of Personnel Management. The Industrial Welfare Society. The National Institute of Industrial Psychology. The British Institute of Management
16. A. K. Rice: *Productivity and Social Organisation—The Ahmenabad Experiment: Technical Innovation, Work Organisation and Management.* Tavistock Publications, 1958
17. E. Moonman: *The Manager and The Organisation (A Study of Communication).* Tavistock Publications, 1961
18. R. F. Tredgold: *Human Relations in Modern Industry.* Duckworth, 1949

PART FOUR

CONTROL

By H. E. Betham

CONTENTS

CHAPTER I

THE NEED FOR CO-ORDINATED CONTROL

THE trends of development in industry and business during the past decade or so have been such as to place increasing emphasis on techniques of planning and control as "tools" of management, whether in marketing, in manufacturing, in the maintenance of equipment, or in the central administrative systems of a company. Manpower difficulties have heightened the trends; so, too, has the progress of automation in factory processes. The heavy expenditure necessary to instal and maintain this mechanisation and automation has increased the fixed charges which a company will have to cover, and this has made it doubly important for total sales and total production to be maintained at a consistently high level. As a result, companies have tended to "diversify" as well as to specialise, by making and selling various classes of goods, by putting eggs into more than one basket. By this means, it is hoped that even if demand follows a cyclical pattern, the peaks and troughs will not all occur at the same time.

Another factor which has led to a growth of interest in planning and control techniques available to management has been the contribution made by economists and industrial statisticians in helping to solve business problems. Economists have shown how it is possible to build up a reliable picture of future demand, both long and short term, based on a study of economic data. They have pioneered new ways of thinking about costs and values, and they have developed numerous techniques for helping management make the right decision in various circumstances.

Industrial statisticians have shown how mathematical techniques can be applied successfully to business problems. Trend analysis in the development of sales forecasts, linear programming techniques to help make the right choice in planning, sampling techniques to reduce the cost of control procedures are examples of some of these techniques.

In small or medium-sized firms, it is usually not possible to employ a number of specialists, and the managers will require to be skilled themselves in the application of these techniques to their own problems. Even if they employ consultants actually to instal procedures, conditions are always changing and they will need to know enough about the techniques to make appropriate alterations when necessary. In the larger firms it may be practicable to employ full-time specialists, but even here it is important for management to understand the principles involved. This knowledge is essential if the best use is to be made of the specialists—a lack of knowledge will mean an inability to take the right decision when points of difficulty are brought up for discussion.

A change that has occurred over the last decade or so is the growing emphasis on "planning" in association with "control". When budgetary control was first introduced some thirty years ago, it was usually taken for granted that the main emphasis was focused on the *control* aspect, on the comparison of actual results with budget, month by month, or week by week. Now there is a growing feeling that the main value of budgeting comes from the *preparation of the budgets* themselves. Top management is required, firstly, to set down systematically what its policies and plans for the year ahead will be, and, secondly, to co-ordinate and agree these proposals with all those managers who will be responsible for carrying them out. In other words, steps are being taken to plan efficiently well in advance of the operations themselves. Even with the most skilful budgeting, however, it can often be found that conditions alter so rapidly that policies and plans have to be changed from time to time, and the budgets soon become unrealistic. The need then is for a reassessment of the forward position rather than the throwing up of large variances from an out-of-date budget. Unfortunately, a complete re-assessment of all aspects of a business takes up a vast amount of management and staff time. It is for this reason that some firms are hoping to develop a *fully integrated system of management planning and control* based on automatic data processing systems. Once installed, these should make possible almost continuous review of the forward prospects and current trends, and assessment of their effect on the existing policies and plans, without taking up too much management time.

Some of the effects of the increasing complexity of business operations today are only gradually being appreciated. One aspect that is currently receiving attention is the urgent need to plan well ahead—in fact several years ahead. If the business is hoping to grow—and growth is almost a necessity for survival these days—additional productive capacity will be required from time to time. Since several years are usually required to plan and construct this additional capacity, the decision to make a start must be taken well in advance of actual requirements. To start too late may mean missing the boat, and being overtaken by one's competitors. To start too soon may mean crippling the firm by locking up large sums of money in buildings and plant that cannot yet be profitably employed. It is therefore vital to be able to make a reasonably accurate assessment of the trend of future demand.

Equally important is the need to estimate accurately in advance the management and specialist resources that will be required. Successful growth can only be achieved if fully trained manpower is available to manage and operate the new developments.

Another feature of modern business life is that managements need not only to understand planning and control techniques which can be applied in their own field, but they need to have a good working knowledge of the problems met with in related fields. This is due to the interlocking nature of so many aspects of business activities. To take a simple example, an architect used to consider that his main preoccupations were with the design of buildings and the supervision of their erection. Then with the growth of so many specialist services in a modern building, his role became more of a co-ordinator than a designer. In recent years, he has also had to be something of a costing expert, in order to be able to guide his clients in selecting from numerous alternatives.

In the same way, the chief executive of a business is becoming more and more a co-ordinator, and in order to be able to co-ordinate effectively, he must understand the principles that govern the working of the business in all its aspects. He also has to co-ordinate in terms of time, because he must make sure that long-term, annual and short-term plans all dovetail together. In practice this co-ordination will be achieved by the team of managers responsible for running the business, and the chief executive will be asked to give his approval. This means that if a manager is to pull his weight, he must also understand the policies, and the major problems which affect these interlocking activities, as well as in his own field of operations. He will, of course, need to understand the latter in rather more detail than his chief.

In practical terms this means that an operating manager must no longer confine his knowledge and experience to the various technical and specialised operations under his control. He must understand how the operating plans interlink; what effect a change in volume will have on unit operating costs; what effect the purchase of a new machine would have on overall profits, and so on. Accordingly, in this Part the emphasis of presentation will be laid on what may be called "Co-ordinated Control", in other words helping managers in their main problem of learning how to use the various planning and control procedures and how to co-ordinate them.

The next Chapter contains an outline of the general nature of *control*[1] and some of the principles which should be observed if control is to be effective. In later Chapters an outline of the more important control techniques—including *budgetary control*—is followed by detailed descriptions of the application of these techniques to various sides of the business. The Appendix contains a fully integrated worked example showing step by step how *budgetary control, profit planning, standard costing* and *marginal costing* techniques can be applied in a manufacturing business.

[1] In the interests of brevity, the single word "Control" is used in the following Chapters to describe this function of management. It should be interpreted as meaning "Co-ordinated Control" in its widest sense, i.e. including the various aspects of planning.

CHAPTER II

CONTROL—AN OVERALL SURVEY

A BUSINESS may be controlled by a sole proprietor, a partnership, the directors of a limited company or the officials of a nationalised undertaking. In each case, the general aim of the men in command can be considered as helping in the attainment of the overall objectives of the business. Thus the overall goals of a business will usually include prosperity, growth and continued life, whereas a human being must necessarily limit the time span of his aims and activities.

At any given point in time, the managers of a business are likely to find that their influence on the future success of the business is restricted by many factors which they can do very little to alter in the short term. The capacity and efficiency of the plant, the amount of working capital, the personal qualities and technical skills of the management and staff, the reputation of the company with the general public, the quality, range and variety of its products—these are all factors which if judged to be inadequate may take a number of years to put right.

On the other hand, there is one area of management activity vital to success, where shortcomings can be remedied much more quickly —and this is the function of control. Control cannot of itself ensure that a loss is turned into a profit or that a business continues to grow, but it is one of the most important factors which will contribute to these aims. Indeed, lack of care and attention in exercising control will soon put any business on the rocks. The reason why improvements in control can be introduced comparatively quickly is that control is a matter of organisation and techniques—and organisation can be changed at will. What takes time is deciding *how* to alter it, and subsequently getting people to accept the changes.

THE NATURE OF CONTROL

The true nature of *control* in business is frequently misunderstood. This is due partly to ambiguity as to the meaning of the word, and partly owing to the difficulty of getting a comprehensive picture of the way control operates. The word "control" is frequently associated with restrictions or restraints, whereas control in management has a positive meaning. It can be defined as "*Guiding and regulating*

*the activities of a business or any of its parts by means of manage-
ment judgment, decision and action for the purpose of attaining
agreed objectives".*[1]

In order to clarify the true nature of control in a business setting,
it is helpful to analyse the way control operates in other less complicated spheres of activity, and then to trace through points of
similarity. Such a comparison can be made with the example of a
man filling a bath, who wants to ensure that when the bath is full the
water is at the right temperature. His actions can be analysed as
follows:

> *Objectives.* He decides mentally on his "objectives", e.g. he wants
> a full bath, just comfortably hot.
> *Operating Plan.* In order to achieve these objectives, he decides
> on his "operating plan", e.g. turning the hot tap fully on and the cold
> tap half on.
> *Control Comparison.* After a suitable interval—say when the bath is
> one-third full—he tries out the temperature of the water. He finds it
> too hot, so has to decide on corrective action.
> *Corrective Action.* His decision is then to turn the cold tap full on
> also.

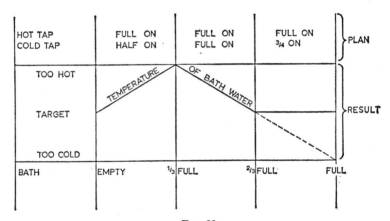

FIG. 82.

His subsequent action will be to repeat the test when the bath is
about two-thirds full. If he now finds that the water temperature is
just right, he knows that further corrective action is needed, otherwise the bath will be over-cooled when full. Accordingly he turns off
the cold tap one-quarter turn. A final test when the bath is nearly full
confirms that this decision was a correct one.

[1] This definition is in line with the one given analytically in the Introduction to this volume (see pages 13 and 18).

Thus, in a simple process of filling a bath, three separate cycles of control are necessary—each cycle consisting of: planning, comparing, deciding on corrective action. The interesting feature to emerge from this analogy is that corrective action is based either on a comparison of actual results already achieved with the corresponding expected results, or on a forward assessment of how the final results will compare with target if no further action is taken. (See diagram at Fig. 82.)

A comparison of this control procedure with the control function in a business setting reveals many similarities. There is the same need to decide on objectives and operating plans; to compare actual

THE CONTROL CYCLE

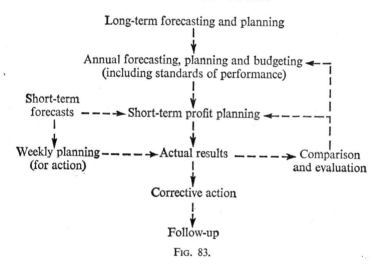

FIG. 83.

with target results; and to decide on corrective action by reference to actual or expected divergences. In fact, there are really just three major differences—the need in a business setting for:

(i) Long-term as well as short-term planning.
(ii) Consideration of the economic or financial aspects as well as the operational or physical aspects.
(iii) Control and co-ordination of the activities of the business as a whole as well as its individual parts.

The various stages of control (in order of time) can be expressed in diagram form (Fig. 83).

The first step in examining this control cycle in more detail is to review the nature of business objectives from the aspect of control.[1]

THE NATURE OF OBJECTIVES

Brief references have already been made to the nature of certain overall *objectives* in a business—prosperity, growth and continued life. It is true that these somewhat materialistic aims do not paint the whole picture, and in many instances the management of a business might consider that these are purely subsidiary goals. For example, the directors of an aircraft manufacturing company might consider that their primary aim was achievement—achievement in building the world's best aircraft. In another case, the overall objective might be to provide services giving maximum value for money to the general public, and so on. Nevertheless, however valid these objectives may be, they cannot be used as the starting point for control, because progress in attaining them must of necessity be a matter of opinion rather than fact. For control to operate effectively, it is essential to be able to measure progress towards specific targets in factual terms—and the objectives described in the introductory paragraphs of this Chapter comply with this condition.

Taking the above three objectives in order, the prosperity of a business can be measured in several ways. Leaving aside for the moment the nationalised industries, the general aim will be to earn a satisfactory annual profit, having regard to the expected return on the capital employed in the business. By *capital employed* is meant the total funds received from or belonging to shareholders and loan creditors, which will have been used either to acquire fixed assets or to provide the funds needed for working capital.

A get-rich-quick speculator operating entirely on his own will no doubt do all he can to *maximise* his profits and his ratio of profits to capital. He will be awake at night thinking of ways and means of increasing both. In the average business of today, however, it would be more accurate to state that the overall aim is to earn a *satisfactory* return. The directors or proprietors will decide what they consider to be a reasonable return, having regard to all the circumstances, and they will not worry unduly so long as this rate is actually achieved. Only in one respect will they be continually seeking to maximise profits—and that is in the maximisation of operating efficiency. Factors to be taken into account in assessing the target rate of return on capital will be the general level of interest ruling

---

[1] These comments reflect, in terms of the practical business situation, the analytical presentation of the "planning-control" cycle described and illustrated in the INTRODUCTION to this volume: see page 22 (and the diagram at Fig. 1) and pages 13, 17–18 and 68.

at the time, the economic climate, competitors' activities, and, in particular, the extent to which the company is expanding. This leads on to the consideration of the second basic objective—growth.

A young and expanding business will naturally consider that growth of turnover is the primary objective. All eyes will be on the trend of the total market, and on the share of the market which the business can secure and retain. It is true that profits are also important, because if sales were achieved only at a loss, working capital would soon be dissipated. Nevertheless, it is probable that the business will be content with a lower return than they would hope to secure in the future. Profits ploughed back now by way of improvements to product or plants, or profits "foregone" through reducing sales prices or increasing advertising expenditure, may be of critical importance in strengthening the hands of the management *vis-à-vis* the firm's competitors. The net result may therefore be an increase in immediate turnover, combined with an increase in profit of *future* years.

Over a period of years, the primary objectives of a business may change in emphasis. After a period of rapid expansion, the management may decide to consolidate the position won. The emphasis will then be on maximising profit through paying increasing attention to economy and efficiency. Later, when working capital has been replenished, the management may embark on a further period of expansion, with the emphasis on spending money to obtain more and more sales.

In view of the likelihood of this alternation of emphasis occurring from time to time, it is evident that one of the key points in any effective system of control is to ensure that everyone in the management team knows what the current policy is.

Coming now to the third objective of "continued life", it might be thought at first sight that so long as a business was prosperous and growing, this would automatically ensure continued life. However, it is always possible for a hitherto successful business to enter into a sudden decline, and there have been numerous examples of this during the last few decades. A major cause is lack of financial wisdom and control, caused perhaps by over-optimism leading to heavy purchases of materials or plant immediately prior to a severe slump in both activity and prices. Other causes are lack of care in providing for management succession, or inadequate planning ahead in the fields of research and development. These, however, are management rather than control problems, and in this Part we shall be concerned only with the financial control aspects.

All the remarks given above apply equally to a nationalised undertaking, except that instead of aiming at earning a profit, they would hope to earn a satisfactory "trading surplus". The earning of such a surplus would then strengthen their hands against competitive undertakings because it could be used to finance additional capital expenditure without incurring additional interest charges.

Having considered the general nature of overall objectives, the various stages of planning and control shown in Fig. 83 will now be looked at in more detail.

PLANNING TO ATTAIN OBJECTIVES

1. *Long-term Forecasting and Planning*

A decade or so ago, many firms considered they were being very progressive if they took the trouble to draw up plans for the year ahead. Today quite a number of firms are planning five years or more ahead. There are many reasons for this—some of the more obvious ones are the unavoidable time lag between deciding to build a new factory or factory extension and being able to operate it; the time needed to find and train suitable management staff; the need to obtain a long-term view of financial requirements; the time taken on research into a new product, and so on.

When long-term planning is first started, it is usual to concentrate first on the factors referred to above, viz. capital additions, manpower requirements, finance and research. It is soon realised that if these provisional plans are to have any meaning, it is essential to gear them into comprehensive plans covering the activities of the business as a whole. Consequently, all the functional sides of the business will be encouraged to develop their own long-term plans. When this long-term planning is first started, it is inevitable that there will be an air of unreality about it. No one can say whether a plan for a period of five years ahead will prove realistic or otherwise, and there is no previous experience to go on. The whole exercise makes much more sense by the time a whole cycle has been covered. By then, the plans drawn up five years beforehand, modified as necessary as the years have passed, can be compared with reality.

It is highly probable that the key to these long-term plans will be the forecasts of the total market demand in the industries concerned. Superimposed on these will be the estimates of what share of this market the management hope to acquire. Specialist help in building up these industry forecasts can frequently be obtained from official sources. In other instances it is possible to trace a relationship between facts already known and subsequent demand for goods by the general public. If such a link can be established, it provides a useful pointer to future sales.

Long-term planning can be considered as formalising what many firms are probably doing on an *ad hoc* basis, viz. looking ahead for new ideas and new products, and deciding how to make them. Because it becomes part of the established routine, it is less likely that suitable opportunities will be overlooked. The plan for, say, five years ahead will at first consist only of highlights, but as the years pass, more and more detail will be filled in, until eventually the plans become fully documented and become the detailed plan for the year ahead. Long-term planning is particularly important in those industries where it takes several years to provide additional productive capacity.

2. Annual Forecasting, Planning and Budgeting

While future long-term planning is being considered, management will be giving final approval to the plans for next year, the plans which were perhaps first considered on a provisional basis five years earlier.

It is probably true to say that the majority of firms in this country undertake some sort of annual "policy" planning, but there is a considerable variation in the extent to which operations are planned. Some firms are content merely to draw up a sales forecast and an estimate of profits, combined perhaps with a budget for capital expenditure and a forecast of cash movements. Planning of this sort has several uses. It enables a forecast to be given to shareholders of their expected income. It enables financial management to plan ahead. It also helps top management to make up their minds about the precise nature of the overall objectives, and to communicate their overall decisions to operating management. This is particularly important where there is a "conflict of interest" to be resolved, such as a choice between capturing an additional share of the market, or maximising profits for the year.

On the other hand the individual managers in the business cannot find out from overall operating plans of the kind described above what their own particular targets are. They merely know that the sum of all their efforts is a specified output, or sales turnover, and that the financial effect of their combined efforts will be the earning of a specified profit. Hence such plans cannot really be used as a basis for motivation of departmental management or personnel, or for subsequent control.

In order to overcome these drawbacks, an increasing number of firms are now supplementing the overall planning with detailed budgeting, covering both overall and departmental objectives, activities and resources. A budget has been defined as[1] "A financial and/or quantitative statement, prepared prior to a defined period

---

[1] *Terminology of Cost Accountancy*, published by the Institute of Cost and Works Accountants.

of time, of the policy to be pursued during that period, for the purpose of attaining a given objective".

In practical terms, the budget for a particular department will specify the quantity of output the department will be expected to produce during the year ahead, and the resources that management will need to produce this output, e.g., details of materials, man-hours, machine hours, power, steam, supervision and so on. To enable this departmental budget to be fitted into the overall picture, each of these resources will be costed out at the price or rates expected to be paid during the period.

It is important to note that the budget, even if subsequently broken down into months ("phasing" as it is called) is not intended to be carried out to the letter. It is merely the best possible estimate that can be made at the time of the policy that will be pursued during the forthcoming year or other budget period. As such, it serves several useful purposes over and above the normal benefits obtained from advance planning.

It provides a means of co-ordination of the activities of the business as a whole; it acts as a convenient means of communicating policy proposals and policy decisions and it provides a basis for subsequent control. Dealing with each of these in turn, co-ordination is possible because for a brief period while the budgets are being prepared, everyone is prepared to look ahead and put down on paper what they are planning to do. Then while there is still plenty of time, a reasonable balance can be achieved, i.e. between sales and production volumes, or between costs and profits. There will probably be no similar opportunity for complete co-ordination until budget time comes round again next year.

The whole exercise will of course be useless unless the budgets are soundly based. This means that full use will be made of forecasts of external conditions such as economic climate, total public demand, consumer preferences, price trends, wage rates, etc. In addition, wherever work study engineers have been able to arrive at suitable standards of performance for factory or distribution operations, these will be built into the budgets. In other cases reliance will have to be based on managers' own estimates.

Regarding the use of budgets for communicating policy proposals and policy decisions, there is in fact a two-way flow. Proposals usually start their life in the various departments which make up the scene of operations—at the coal face, to use a popular expression—and are then summarised, with the help of the accountants, as they pass up the management pyramid until they finally portray the overall effect of the detailed proposals. Top management may or may not make certain modifications in addition to the normal give and take necessary to achieve co-ordination; and the rubber-stamped proposals are then sent down the line again back to their originators. It is to be hoped that any significant amendments will be explained to those concerned, so that they have an opportunity to express agreement before the final decisions are taken. This will help to ensure that the budgets are attained. The way in which budgets are used as a basis for control is explained in Chapter III.

3. *Short-term Profit Planning*

Because so many factors have to be considered, the preparation of annual budgets usually has to be started several months before the year begins. As a result it may well happen that the budget is out of date by the time it comes into operation. In order not to destroy the link with long-term planning or to reduce the value of the annual budget as a control base, it is often advisable to keep the original budget unchanged and to deal with the changed situation by establishing short-term "profit plans", perhaps covering a period of three or four months. Thus the budget might have been drawn up on the assumption that selling prices would remain unchanged, but if the intensity of competition is suddenly stepped up, it may be necessary to make a drastic revision in policy—including a reduction in price and an increase in advertising. The effect of both these changes and of any revised ideas on future demand would be incorporated in the short-term profit plans.

In drawing up these short-term profit plans, one of the key factors to be taken into account is the *trend* of recent results, costs, etc. As illustrated in the example of filling a bath, the cumulative position to date may be in line with target, but the final result may be disappointing, unless some immediate action is taken. In order to highlight the way things are going, it may be useful to re-calculate from time to time the expected overall result for the year, basing such calculations on the sum of:

    (*a*) Results achieved to date—e.g. January to March.
    (*b*) Short-term profit plan for next three months—e.g. April to June.
    (*c*) Original budget figures for remainder of year (unless it would be more appropriate to project (*b*)).

4. *Weekly or Daily "Activity Planning"*

The plans which have been considered above—long term, annual and short term are aimed at establishing objectives and specifying policies to be pursued. They set the strategies and point out the routes to be followed. It is usually essential to supplement this planning with weekly or daily "activity planning". These plans will cover all the main activities—sales, production, maintenance, etc.

Since they are prepared for the purpose of getting the job done rather than weighing up the financial aspects, they will be expressed in physical terms and they will be far more detailed than the longer-term plans. They point out the tactics to be followed and show just how far along the road one is to travel each day. They will be based on an assessment of the current order and stock position, or on short-term forecasts of future demand, and on expected production capacity. These plans should of course be drawn up within the framework of the annual budgets or short-term profit plans. In this way, the policies agreed by top management will find expression in the more detailed plans lower down the line.

THE REGULATING FUNCTION OF CONTROL

Management, having agreed on long-term, annual and short-term plans, need to exercise the regulating function of control to ensure either that these plans are carried out or that they are appropriately modified where circumstances warrant it. In the last resort, where it becomes apparent that the original objectives cannot be attained during the period under review, then it is the job of the control function to point out the probable extent of the deficit at the earliest possible moment. The man looking forward to a hot bath does not want to wait until the bath is full before discovering that the hot water supply has run cold.

Assuming that the directors or proprietors of a business are dissatisfied with their existing methods of control and that they begin to seek advice on possible improvements, it is quite likely that they will be faced with a dilemma. They will find that there are a number of alternative methods, and a choice must be made as to the most suitable. Comments on some of the basic types of control are now given.

1. *Visual Control*

In earlier days, the head of a business might make a point of walking round on a tour of inspection each day. He would be relying on visual control for assurance that everything was going according to plan. Nowadays, there are two distinct types of visual control—supervision of operator performance by foremen and supervisors, and control of mechanised operations through frequent inspection of a control panel. In recent years, there has been a tendency in some quarters to suggest that top management ought to spend more time seeing what is happening on the shop floor or on the road, and less time looking at paper work. It may be that the best answer in such cases is to reorganise and streamline the paper work so as to improve its effectiveness for control purposes and to require less management time for its comprehension. This is one of the objects of the "Control by Exception" techniques, as explained below.

On the other hand, there have been many instances where the visual control exercised by foremen and supervisors has been strengthened by suitable control reports in which actual performance is evaluated and compared with a standard. Control by instrumentation is more usually concerned with technical or quality considerations, but there are numerous examples of control instruments being used primarily for cost reduction. Examples are meters recording usage of power or steam in production operations, and machines recording machine stopped time. The information obtained from these instruments will subsequently be recorded in control reports and compared with standards, so that they are really a part of the measurement process in "control by exception".

2. Control by Exception

The distinguishing features of this approach are frequent measurement and evaluation of actual progress, and comparison with the appropriate target figures. Management is called upon to make a decision on future action only if this comparison reveals an actual or expected divergence or "variance". This is the technique used by the man filling the bath, who used his hand as a measuring instrument. It is the technique employed in piloting an aircraft when flying by instrument rather than by eyesight.

In measuring progress towards operational or "growth" objectives, e.g. sales turnover or production output, comparison is made of results achieved to date with the planned results for the same period. On the other hand, when measuring progress towards the financial or economic objectives, e.g. trading profit for the period, control must be exercised both over the values earned (e.g. sales turnover or production output valued at predetermined unit costs) and over the costs incurred in achieving the sales or production outputs. This is necessary because profits cannot be attained directly in the same way that one can make a given quantity of finished products — they are the residue left over after all the costs of making and selling goods have been matched up with the corresponding revenue obtained from customers.

In practice, then, control by exception means comparing—(a) actual performance with expected performance, and (b) actual costs with target costs, in such a way that suitable corrective action can be taken if things go wrong. One of the first essentials is to break down the overall objectives into component parts, each part usually relating to a separate function or division of management. This procedure lends itself to delegation of authority and immediate responsibility. The head of each such function or division knows what his own particular objectives are, and he is given the means of checking up at frequent intervals to ensure that everything is going according to plan. Similarly, the overall control problem is simplified, because general management can look at a comparatively few grouped totals instead of at a mass of detail. They only need to delve into detail if one or more of the grouped results begin to get out of line with expectation, and the functional management concerned are unable to satisfy the central control that the position is being remedied.

Control by exception depends for its effectiveness upon a number of factors, for example:

(i) The validity of the target figures. Unless plans and control standards are soundly based, comparison with actual results may reveal little more than that the target figures were wrong.

(ii) Both targets and actual results must be linked with managerial responsibilities—otherwise it will be difficult to make corrective action effective.

(iii) Control reports must be issued sufficiently quickly and frequently to enable corrective action to be taken before it is too late. The general rule is that speed of presentation is more important than precise accuracy of detail.

3. Pre-control

Corrective action during a control period is sometimes impracticable, e.g. in the case of a firm unwilling to get rid of employees temporarily surplus to requirements. Where these circumstances are likely to arise, control action must be exercised during the budgeting stage rather than subsequently. For example, the best opportunity for making reductions in the cost of maintenance labour may be at the time the maintenance budget is agreed rather than later. In other words, it is easier to reduce costs if advance notice is given. Men can be switched to other work, or natural wastage can be used to effect reductions. Annual charges of all kinds must also be controlled before the commitments are entered into, because no subsequent control comparisons can lead to a reduction in these costs.

4. Control through Motivation

It is important to remember that no method of control will prove effective unless the firm's employees are motivated in some way to achieve good results. If management is slack and apparently uninterested in achievement, then the operatives and staff will soon follow suit and work at the slowest possible rate.

Motivation is usually encouraged if everyone in the management team has an opportunity of taking part in deciding on target levels, and of subsequently being supplied frequently and promptly with the appropriate control results. Any attempt by top management to impose targets without any prior discussions with those concerned may have the reverse effect, and result in everyone trying to prove that the targets were wrong. This is the reason why so many early examples of budgetary control came into disfavour—lack of attention to motivation.

5. *Control by* ad hoc *Decisions.*

However detailed the annual and short-term planning, examples will always occur of unplanned incidents calling for management decisions during the year. These will usually be projects of one kind or another, e.g. a sudden request to acquire some new equipment which was not foreseen at the time the annual budget was prepared. This is another instance where control must be exercised before the commitment is agreed to and the contract placed. Control is in essence a check that the project being suggested represents the best way of investing the necessary funds.

6. *Internal Controls to guard against Pilferage, Theft and Fraud.*

This is a specialised aspect of control upon which guidance can be obtained from those concerned with the audit of a firm's activities and transactions.

CORRECTIVE ACTION

It has already been shown that corrective action can be taken either when a divergence from plan has occurred, or when it looks as if a divergence will occur unless action is taken now. In order to establish the latter possibility, it is essential to report control results by successive periods as well as for the cumulative position to date. Only if this is done can trends be disclosed, and then projected to show estimated future positions. Corrective action may involve:

    (i) Operational action—
      e.g. getting rid of operatives whose performance is below standard.
    (ii) Financial action—
      e.g. increasing the selling prices of certain products.
    (iii) Modifications to future plans—
      e.g. bringing forward a sales promotional scheme, deciding to step up production of a profitable line of products, etc.

Follow-up

Managers who have initiated corrective action of one kind or another will usually wish to check whether their decisions have been implemented, and whether the action has had the desired effect.

There is a further aspect of "follow-up" to be considered—long-term improvements. Even if current performance is in line with budgets, management must be continually on the look-out for ways of effecting long-term improvements in productivity. If this is not done, a business may subsequently be at a disadvantage compared with competitors who have been more successful in this respect. In other words, for any given volume of saleable output, management should have their eyes firmly fixed on a downward trend over the years in the usage of resources, whether man-hours or machine time, materials or power consumption, management time or clerical effort.

Technical research, statistical analysis, operational research and work study all have a part to play in effecting such improvements.

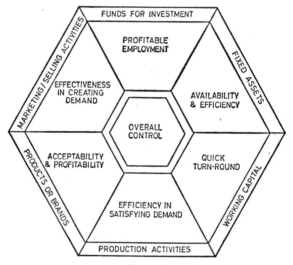

FIG. 84.

FUNCTIONAL CONTROL

Having considered some of the general aspects of managers' responsibilities for planning and control in the attainment of overall objectives, it is now necessary to examine the ways in which these overall objectives can be broken down according to function. It is not much use telling the manager of a factory department that the overall aim is to increase sales turnover and profits—he needs to have a much clearer guide to his immediate objectives if he is to operate efficiently.

The diagram given above (Fig. 84) shows how the day-to-day "line operations" of a business can be broken down into seven sections—each section having basically different aims. Research and development has been excluded because it is concerned more with long-term developments than with day-to-day operations.

Each of these aspects of control is reviewed in more detail in Chapters V to X.

1. Disposable Funds

Funds for investment in capital projects may come in the first place from shareholders or loan creditors, but in the case of a business that has been running for a number of years, these will already have been used in a number of ways. However, any business that is being run on profitable lines will automatically obtain each year further funds for allocation—to be used either in distribution as dividends, etc., or in strengthening the working capital, or in investment in "capital projects". These funds will come from the profits earned and the sums set aside for depreciation of fixed assets.

An important type of decision which top management have to take from time to time is the allocation of the total sum available between the different possibilities. It is probable that there will be conflicting views which have to be reconciled. Shareholders will certainly be hoping for increased dividends—and this may be an important consideration if additional finance is to be raised in the near future. Marketing management may be pressing for an increase in distribution facilities or in stock cover. Production management will be pressing the claims of new and improved plant and equipment.

Financial management will play a big part in helping to arrive at valid decisions, by evaluating the various alternative courses of action. Similarly, operating management will be concerned with the relative merit of various proposals for additions or improvements to fixed assets. Once again, various competing claims have to be evaluated and compared before a choice is made. Shall we extend the capacity of X department by buying additional equipment, or shall we replace the existing machines in Y department by improved models? Or shall we defer both these projects until next year when something much better may be available and meanwhile make improvements to the plant in Z department? These are typical questions, and in order to help answer them, various control techniques have been developed in assessing probable results, e.g. Pay-Back, Rate of Return, Discounted Cash Flow, etc. These techniques are described in Chapter IX.

2. Plant Management

As soon as project decisions have been made, and capital commitments are entered into, the nature of management control alters.

Control has to ensure that the work of construction, erection, installation or modification is being carried out as efficiently as possible. When the work has been completed, it becomes the responsibility of maintenance management to see that the plant is kept in an efficient state, and that it is available when required by operating management. This will mean carrying out *just sufficient* planned maintenance to ensure that breakdowns are not frequent. At the same time, the job of production management is to see that maximum use is made of the available plant. Idle plant means idle capital, while the "occupancy" and maintenance costs of this idle plant have to be met out of the profit margins earned on plant that is being worked. The overall effect of idle plant on return on capital can therefore be very unfavourable.

Techniques which help to ensure that the aims set out above are achieved include budgetary control (for capital expenditure and maintenance costs), together with mechanical or manual methods of recording and analysing machine utilisation.

3. Working Capital

Working capital is needed in any business because of the time lag between paying for materials and operating costs, and getting the money back again (together with added profit) from the customer. From the point of view of operating management, it can be regarded as: (*a*) stocks of raw materials, work in process and finished products; (*b*) "liquid" assets such as debtors and working cash balances. (If suppliers are in the habit of giving credit, then less "working cash" will be required than if they insist on immediate payment.) The overall aim of operating management in this area must be "quick turn-round". If stocks are kept low, and debtors are persuaded to pay promptly, the cycle of cash-stocks-debtors-cash will be completed more quickly. This has the double advantage of reducing the average capital employed (and so increasing the rate of return) and of releasing funds for other profitable activities.

Techniques which help in the control of working capital are described in Chapter VIII.

4. Production Activities

Under this heading are included all those activities directly concerned with the acquisition of raw materials and the conversion of those raw materials into finished products. Planning and control techniques of general use in this field include budgetary control and standard costing. Because it is possible to establish an exact relationship between input of resources and the resulting output, it is nearly always possible to keep a close check on performance against standard (or other target). Because of the repetitive nature of so many of the production activities, corrective action for the future can be based on a study of previous or current performance reports.

5. Marketing Activities

"Marketing" as distinct from "Production" covers the functions of (i) Marketing policy and services; (ii) Advertising; (iii) Selling; (iv) Distribution to customers. Except in the latter instance, there is no automatic relationship between "input" of marketing effort and "output" of sales to customers. The sales in any one week may, for example, be affected by a combination of the following factors: current advertising, the delayed effects of earlier advertising campaigns, current sales promotional schemes, price changes, competitors' activities, Government action, the general economic background. Small wonder that control techniques in this field do not as yet match the usefulness of those in the production field!

Budgetary control will help to show whether money spent is in line with plan, but can give little guide as to whether value for money has been obtained, except in the general sense of comparing actual with target profits. Much work is being done at the present time to develop analytical techniques which will provide management with more effective control.

6. Products or Brands

An aspect of marketing that has been developed in recent years is that of Product or Brand management. The brand manager's aim is to concentrate on everything that happens to a particular product or group of products, from the acquisition of raw materials to the despatch to the customer. He therefore cuts right across the boundaries of production and marketing management, and is particularly interested in product costs and profit margins. Cases have often come to light where the ascertainment of product costs on a precise basis has shown that a firm was unknowingly losing money on some products. The losses had been concealed because they were more than offset by profits on other lines.

Standard costing, marginal costing and profit-planning techniques have a particular application to this field.

7. Overall Control

Overall control is concerned with the job of co-ordinating all the above activities, and of holding the scales between conflicting interests. For example, a frequent cause of conflict is the differing requirements for effective working of production and marketing management. Production management like a steady volume of output throughout the year, with the minimum number of varieties. If demand expands, and they have to order new equipment, they will hope that sales can take the whole output of the new machines—they would particularly dislike very expensive new equipment under-utilised. On the other hand, marketing management require a wide range of products—they are always hoping that one or more of these will prove to be "winners". With new lines they prefer to go slowly at first, until they can assess public reaction. If sales are seasonal, they hope that production levels can be adjusted to suit—otherwise the excessive build-up of buffer stocks will handicap sales promotional activities and reduce average yield on capital.

A further vital task is the co-ordination of the operational activities with the profitability or financial aspects. It is pointless for production and marketing managements to be arguing about the weekly output of tinned carrots, if a recent movement in prices has made the whole operation unprofitable. What they should be deciding is what to can in place of the carrots—and this means assessing relative profitability.

Profits, however, are notoriously elusive, and even if there is no change in raw material prices, an overall profit can be turned into an overall deficit by the loss of an important customer. Accordingly, one of the primary aims of any system of control must be to ensure that there is adequate co-ordination of the operational and financial aspects of business activities.

ORGANISING FOR CO-ORDINATED CONTROL

In earlier days, the accountant's main role was looking after the cash balances, paying wages, getting in sums due by customers, preparing annual accounts, and calculating the amounts paid to shareholders by way of dividend, etc. Later, various specialist activities were developed, including taxation calculations and product costing. Costing was developed as a specialised technique in the years following World War I, and the ability to build up product costs—through detailed apportionments of all expenditure—became an essential feature of accounting life. This was because the prices paid for work under "Cost-plus" contracts were based on such costs, and mere estimates were unacceptable.

During the last few decades, accountants have concentrated their attention to an increasing extent on helping management in their job of planning and controlling activities. "Management accounting" is really a set of techniques which enable the operational framework of a business to be clothed in financial terms. And since money is the one common denominator, it enables management to look at the whole as well as at the parts, and to see whether planned objectives are being achieved. Financial accounts alone give no detailed guide to efficiency—they merely show overall results. On the other hand, operational data in quantitative terms can indicate efficiency in various sectors of the business, but unless linked to money, cannot show up the relative importance of each factor, or the overall effect on profitability.

It is logical for the accountant to perform this management accounting service, because many of the figures needed for control purposes will also be required in fulfilling the statutory obligations of a limited company, e.g. keeping proper books of account and preparing annual accounts. Reference has been made above to the "accountant". In practice, many firms will now divide up the responsibilities for financial management as follows:

Financial Controller

Budgeting   Financial   Cost
and Profit   Accountant   Accountant
Planning

Reference has been made earlier in this Chapter to the need to ensure co-ordination of the various aspects of management activities.

A way has to be found of ensuring that while marketing and production management are free to undertake their own operational planning, someone in the business can take an overall view. Such an overall view must take into account:

(a) Operational plans for each side of the business.
(b) Proposed stock levels (raw materials and finished goods).
(c) Expected profitability.
(d) Financial requirements.

It seems clear that although responsibility for *agreeing* the overall plans must rest with the Board (or equivalent), the responsibility for preparing and co-ordinating them must lie with the financial function. This can be achieved, as illustrated on the above diagram, by setting up a separate section of the financial controller's department to deal with budgeting and profit planning. Close links would be established with those sections of the business concerned with the day-to-day or week-to-week operational planning.

MANAGEMENT INFORMATION

A collective term used to define data supplied to the various functions and levels of management as an aid to the efficient planning, co-ordination and control of business operations and as a basis for making sound decisions. Management information can be distinguished from, but may overlap, data supplied for other purposes, such as:

(*a*) Data forming part of the normal administrative routines, e.g. payroll calculations, sales orders, amounts due from customers, etc., internal control procedures (i.e. as a check against clerical errors or fraud).

(*b*) Data required for statutory or other special purposes, e.g. accounting information and stock valuations, etc., required for preparing annual accounts, taxation computations, insurance purposes, etc.

Management information [1] may be divided into broad groups relating to:

(i) Future probabilities and expectations, policies and objectives, plans, projects and programmes.

(ii) Current results and performances.

(iii) Past results, performance reports and general background data.

(iv) Past, present and future in the form of trend reports, graphs or charts.

The appropriate data may be expressed in quantities or values and may be accompanied by oral or written information. The type and frequency of information required will naturally depend upon the particular management activity, but it is possible to set out certain general principles. One of these principles is related to the "pyramid of control". There are many instances of otherwise perfect systems of control falling into disrepute merely because too much detail found its way on to the managing director's desk. The general rule is that as information is passed up the management pyramid, so should *some* detail be omitted, and the control reports issued less frequently. Whereas the Board may get monthly summary reports (mainly in £.s.d.), the production manager will need weekly control sheets, giving quantities as well as value, while the foreman or supervisor may want daily reports of output, of performance, and of other key factors under his control. Since the purpose of these control reports is to stimulate corrective action, it is evident that promptness of presentation is of more importance than accuracy of detail. Many firms prefer to make use of four- or five-weekly reports, rather than adhering to the calendar month. Two four-weekly and one five-weekly period make up a quarter, and the fifth week can be so timed as to include public holidays or annual shutdowns.

Management information reports may be introduced for a par-

[1] The principles underlying the role of "data" as the basis of "management information" for decision in planning and control are discussed at length in the INTRODUCTION: see pages 77–78.

ticular purpose, but very frequently they continue to be produced long after this purpose has been served. It is therefore advisable to carry out a periodic review—say once every three years—of all management information reports, and to make recommendations for their rationalisation or improvement.

CHAPTER III

BUDGETARY CONTROL AND STANDARD COSTING

WHEN a group of managers meet together to discuss ways of improving the existing planning and control procedures, it is seldom possible to obtain a unanimous decision on a prescribed course of action. A similar difference in opinion is likely to occur when a group of accountants get together for the same purpose. One of the basic causes of the unfruitful discussions and confusion which can so often arise is neglect to distinguish between management's *responsibilities* for planning and control, and the various *techniques* which can be used as aids in carrying out these responsibilities.

As an example of the difference between these two aspects of control, a factory manager has a responsibility for planning ahead and for exercising control over factory performance and costs. In fulfilling these responsibilities he may be requested to draw up an annual budget, to give a forward estimate of manufacturing costs for each product, and to report from time to time how actual results compare with expectation. However, it may be left entirely to the factory manager to *choose* what methods, procedures and techniques he uses in carrying out these responsibilities. For example, he may decide to use flexible budgetary control and standard costing.

Again, marketing management have a *responsibility* for short-term Profit Planning, i.e. for planning in detail what products they propose to sell in what quantities and at what prices, in order to achieve the overall target profit for the period. To help them in carrying out these tasks, they can *choose* from a number of techniques which in recent years have come to be associated with profit planning—for example, marginal costing and break-even analysis.

This Chapter contains a description of some of these basic techniques—*budgetary control, standard costing* and *marginal costing.* Subsequent chapters explain in more detail how these techniques are applied in carrying out the various management responsibilities. Other techniques which are more concerned with particular functions of management—such as those used in measuring the profitability of projects—are also described in later chapters.

BUDGETARY CONTROL

Budgetary control techniques can be considered under three headings:

(a) Budgetary Planning.
(b) Budgetary Control.
(c) Flexible Budgetary Control.

Budgetary Planning—(Budgeting)

The first step in building up the series of budgets that are to cover the business as a whole is the preparation of the "output" budgets, covering sales and production, in quantities and value. Budgets will usually be based on forecasts. Whereas a forecast is the expression of an opinion, a budget is a reflection of management's *intentions*. For example, the sales budget may be based in the first instance on the sales forecast, but will probably include policy amendments of one kind or another, such as a decision to strengthen sales of certain products and suppress others. Again, if production capacity is limited, it may be impossible to meet the anticipated demand, and the sales budget may have to be based on the expected capacity to produce.

It cannot be emphasised too strongly that these output budgets are not "blue-prints for action"—they are indications of specific objectives which it is hoped to attain and of policies it is hoped to follow, having regard to expected external conditions. If external conditions change to a significant extent, objectives and policies may also be changed. Besides showing the anticipated levels of sales and production they also show the intended make-up of the total volume of business, perhaps spread over a wide number of product groups or restricted to a relatively few lines. Thus the budgets act as pointers to the policy of diversification or concentration, to putting eggs in several baskets or only one. In those businesses with marked seasonal fluctuations in the volume of sales, it is usual to break down the budgets over the various control periods in the year, at the same time giving effect to expected peaks and troughs. This is known as "phasing the budgets".

The next step in the budgeting process is the preparation of the "departmental" budgets which show what each section of the business is expected to contribute towards overall objectives by way of departmental output or services. The budgets will also indicate in quantitative terms the resources to be used in carrying out these functions together with the anticipated costs. These budgets should not be regarded as imposing fixed "limits" or "sanctions" on departmental activities. Like the output budgets, they are expressions of company policy, and they set out the intended methods, resources and costs applicable to the budgeted output. If it is subsequently found that actual output differs from expectation, then it is only reasonable that actual departmental activities and costs should also

P.P.M.—22*

differ from budget. The procedure (described below) which enables the budget figures to be adjusted to allow for this is known as "flexible budgeting".

It is important to make sure that departmental budgets correspond with departmental responsibilities. It is then possible for departmental managers either to prepare their own budgets, or at any rate to examine and agree them with the accountant or "budget officer" before they are finally approved by top management. This approach is not only more likely to arrive at a realistic result than one which depends on estimates prepared solely in the accountant's office, but in addition will provide greatly increased possibilities of control.

Raw materials used in the finished products may be entered on departmental budgets, but in a process industry where raw materials pass through a chain of operations it is often not possible to measure the flow of materials at intermediate points. In these cases the cost of raw materials required will usually be shown on a separate budget. Capital expenditure budgets will be prepared setting out the expected outgoings on additions to, and replacements of, fixed assets. Financial budgets will be prepared by the accountant showing expected movements in working capital.

The final step in budgeting is the assembly of the various detailed budgets into an integrated whole. When the various parts have been fitted together it becomes possible to calculate the budgeted overall profit and the budgeted "capital employed" figure at the end of the budget period. It is then possible to see whether the budgeted return on average capital employed is in line with long-term policy. If the detailed calculations show that the expected profit is below recent experience, or below the target which would be considered reasonable, recourse will then be had to "Profit Planning" procedures, in an attempt to increase the planned profits (see Chapter IV). The control aspect of budgeting is now described.

Budgetary Control (Comparison with Budgets)

It is unfortunate that the term "Budgetary Control" is very frequently considered by the layman to consist of a rigid system of control imposed on management, by which a manager is put on the carpet if he exceeds his budget. The very word "control" conjures up an idea of restraint in many people's minds. It is all too common to find instances where the budgeted sales, production or profit figures are regarded as fixed targets that must be achieved at all costs, regardless of the trend of general conditions. If sales are considered to be the primary target, then over-generous allowances may be granted in an attempt to boost sales. If profits are the key factor, then expenditure on research, development, maintenance, etc., may be cut back so as to reach the desired figure.

Budgetary control used properly should help in the attainment of the overall objectives of growth, combined with a satisfactory return on capital. If it is to be used successfully despite fluctuations in the level of demand and other external conditions, it is essential for the budgets to be capable of adjustment to these changed circumstances, and for certain guiding principles to be observed:

1. Budgets should be related to responsibilities, as described above.
2. Budgets must be prepared in sufficient detail, so that the precise nature of subsequent variances from budget can be determined. In particular, it is necessary to distinguish between the cost behaviour of each type of cost. "Pre-control" can only be carried out effectively if the budget is prepared in the same amount of detail that would be required for a periodic control report on which corrective action could be taken.
3. Deciding on the most suitable budget period is really a matter of compromise. The shorter the budget period, the easier it is to budget with reasonable accuracy. On the other hand, there are several reasons why a budget should cover, if possible, a period of a year. The preparation of a detailed budget takes a lot of management time and there would be a tendency for the work to be skimped if it had to be carried out more frequently than this. If the budgets are used as a basis for preparing standard product costs, frequent budget changes would necessitate frequent revision of these product costs, and thus minimise some of the advantages of standard costing. Again the control value of a budget is reduced if the period is too short—in the ultimate, actual results would always agree with the budget. A useful compromise can sometimes be achieved by budgeting in detail for six months ahead, in outline for a further half year, and repeating the procedure at the end of every six months.
4. For reasons similar to those given in 3 above, it is inadvisable to revise the budget unless external conditions have altered so much that a radical change in policy is indicated. Supplementary short-term planning will take care of minor fluctuations in conditions, and the question of budget revision would only arise if these plans got very much out of line with budget.

If it is discovered that a minor item has been accidentally omitted from the budgets, the usual procedure is to adjust the position by including the item in the periodic control reports as a budget allowance offset by a "revision variance". There is then no need to adjust the original budget or the standard costs.

5. Budgets will be shown wherever possible in quantitative as well

as in financial terms. This will facilitate use as a basis for shop floor and other controls in physical terms. It also makes it easier to establish the links with short-term production planning, etc.

Flexible Budgetary Control

The success or failure of a business in attaining its objectives can depend upon the combined effect of three separate factors:

(a) The effectiveness and efficiency with which operations or activities are carried out on the shop floor, in the field, or in the office.

(b) The influence of external factors wholly or mainly outside management's control.

(c) Management's skills in making valid decisions, in co-ordinating and communicating these and in exercising overall control.

The aim of *flexible budgetary control* is to show up separately the effect of the first two of these factors so far as is possible, so that corrective action can be guided in the right direction. One of the key points to be observed in flexible budgeting is an assessment of the "cost behaviour" of each element of cost, viz. whether it can be regarded as variable, semi-variable or fixed. Raw material costs are variable, because a 10 per cent. increase in volume will mean a 10 per cent. increase in the total cost of materials used. Maintenance costs may be "semi-variable", i.e. partly variable and partly fixed. Rent and rates are examples of fixed costs, because these costs will be unaffected by the sort of volume changes that are likely to occur within a year. In the long run, all costs can be considered variable, e.g. doubling the turnover over a period of several years will probably mean doubling both the size of the factory and the number of managers—but the purpose of flexible budgetary control is to stimulate efficiency in the short-term, and long-term considerations are immaterial.

When each item of cost in a manufacturing unit has been classified in the way described above, it becomes possible to work out what the costs *should be* for any given level of departmental activity. The "expected" cost is usually known as a budget "allowance" and comparison of this allowance with actual costs provides a valid basis for assessing performance. Thus in the case of direct labour, the budget allowance is calculated by reference to the actual output achieved and the standard labour cost per unit of output (the latter being derived from the standard times established for each product). A simple comparison of actual labour costs with the original budget figures would not provide an indication of efficiency, because of the probable difference between budgeted and actual volume of throughput.

Part of the difference between actual cost and the flexed budget allowance may be caused by variations in wage rates, and this "rate variance" would be isolated before arriving at the "efficiency variance". Similar procedures would be followed in determining the "price variance" and "usage variance" in the case of other directly variable costs such as raw materials. With semi-variable costs such as service labour, the budget allowance may be read off from a previously prepared schedule or chart which shows the agreed usage or cost at all possible levels of departmental activity.

Only in the case of relatively fixed costs such as management salaries, rent, rates, etc. would the comparison of actual costs be made with the original budget figures.

The procedures described above have shown how it is possible to distinguish between controllable factors (efficiency) and non-controllable factors (price or wage-rate variations). Fluctuations in the volume of demand provide another example of non-controllable factors—at least so far as production management is concerned. If sales suddenly drop off by 20 per cent., the factory manager may be asked to cut back his production by the same percentage. This means that 20 per cent. of his normal production capacity will be underutilised, with a corresponding wastage of fixed expenses associated with this capacity (supervision, maintenance, depreciation, occupancy costs, etc.) Under flexible budgetary control, this wastage of expenditure is shown up separately as a "volume variance".

Flexible budgetary control can be applied to those aspects of marketing and selling operations where the cost is dependent on the work done, e.g. in the case of salesmen's journeys, distribution costs, etc. It cannot, however, act as a guide to the *effectiveness* with which results are obtained from the expenditure of marketing effort.

PROFIT PLANNING TECHNIQUES

Reference has already been made to the short-term "Profit Planning" which marketing management will undertake to ensure that overall profit targets are attained. Exactly the same procedures may be followed during the process of arriving at agreed operating plans for the year. When the annual budgets are first assembled, it may be found that the budgeted profit is less than the figure considered desirable. Ways and means must then be considered for increasing the target profit.

When making decisions of the kind referred to above, management need to be in possession of certain basic types of information relating to the products under review. For example:

(a) What these products are likely to cost at budgeted levels of output.
(b) The average profit margin per unit of product at budgeted levels of sales.
(c) How unit costs and profit margins will alter if the volume of production or sales alters.

The principal costing techniques which have been developed to help in providing answers to the above questions are described below.

Detailed examples of the application of profit planning techniques, including the use of Break-Even analysis and Profit Planning charts are given in Chapter IV.

PRODUCT COSTING

The calculation of accurate product costs became a matter of importance during the last world war. Many firms which had been content to work with estimated costs as a basis for pricing out goods to customers, suddenly found that with war-time contracts they were required to prove what their products had actually cost, otherwise they did not get paid. As a result, cost accountants were in good demand, and many books and articles were published on the subject of cost apportionment and product costing. In the case of cost-plus contracts, every penny that could be apportioned to a product meant a corresponding increase in profit earned. When peacetime conditions were restored, cost accountants continued to supply product cost information to management on the same basis and, in many instances, still do so. One of the uses to which these product costs can be put is to work out each month what the total profit amounts to (by deduction from sales), in fact a sort of competition can develop between the financial and the cost accountants, to see who can produce the most accurate figure of total monthly profit in the shortest time!

From the point of view of marketing management, however, the costs do not really provide the information that is needed, despite the care which may have been taken with cost apportionments. One disadvantage is that these meticulously accurate figures are often not available until a month or so *after* the period to which they relate, whereas management would much rather have a less accurate but nevertheless reasonable estimate of the cost *before* the period started. Another drawback is the fact that these "historical" product costs tend to vary from month to month, partly on account of genuine cost increases such as those caused by wage rate or material price increases, and partly owing to fluctuations in the volume of sales.

For profit planning or price fixing purposes, what is required is an indication of the product cost that can be expected to apply throughout the year, if sales are maintained at around the average level. Where a firm sells a very large number of products, the clerical work involved in calculating out product costs each month becomes unwieldy, and some other method of costing would have to be introduced.

A method that has frequently been used is *cost estimating*. This has the advantage of providing information in advance, but it suffers from the disadvantage that it is difficult to prove whether individual estimates are accurate or otherwise. A periodic check is usually kept on estimates by subsequently multiplying out the quantities of each product manufactured by the estimated costs, and reconciling the total with the cost of manufacture found by normal accountancy methods. There is no proof, however, that compensating errors are not occurring.

Both historical and estimated product costs suffer from several further disadvantages. If external conditions should change after the product costs have been calculated, it is difficult to know to what extent the costs need amendment. If trading conditions become difficult, management may wish to cut prices to a level which will just cover variable costs and make some contribution to overheads. The product costs prepared as described above give no guide to the extent to which this is practicable. A further point is that no clue is given in either method of the extent to which the costs have been increased by avoidable wastage and inefficiency. As a result of these drawbacks increasing interest has been shown in recent years in the technique of "Standard Costing".

STANDARD COSTING

It is perhaps advisable to make clear that the term "Standard Costing" does not mean asking the branches and sections of a business to prepare their accounts and costs in a standard way—the term "Uniform Accounting (or Costing)" is reserved for this.

Standard costs are similar to *estimated costs,* in the sense that both are "predetermined" costs, i.e. determined before rather than after the period to which they relate. Unlike estimated costs, standard costs are built up brick by brick, as it were, from the various cost elements, and they are directly linked—as the name *standard* costing implies—with certain operational standards used for control purposes. These standards are those that relate to the volume of output, to the quantities of materials used and to the performance or efficiency with which operations and activities are carried out.

A further link between these standard product costs and the control of efficiency is established by converting these standards into £.s.d. by making use of budgeted rates of expenditure. The difference between estimated and standard product costs is shown in diagram form below (Fig. 85).

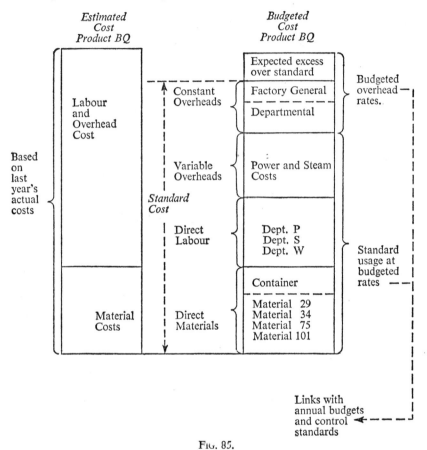

Fig. 85.

Thus standard costs indicate what products *should* cost if the budgeted levels of output are achieved, and operators work at standard performance.

Calculation of what the products *should* cost provides a better basis for comparing relative profitability than working out each month what the products *have* cost. So many incidental factors (such as a major plant breakdown, or a temporary falling off in demand) can affect actual costs for any one month that it would be necessary to take the average of several months before arriving at a

reliable and representative "actual" cost for comparative purposes—
by which time, of course, the knowledge is obtained far too late to
be of any practical value. In the same way a businessman who had
to make many rail journeys to a certain destination with a choice
of routes would be more likely to find out which was the quickest
route by studying the railway timetable than by travelling over each
route in turn and timing the separate journeys himself.

The calculation of a standard cost does not imply that these costs
will remain unchanged over a lengthy period. Quite apart from
changes in the price level, continuous efforts will be made to streamline and improve the methods of operating, with a view to improved
quality or lower costs. Every time a significant change of method
is made there will be a corresponding change in the standards. This
means that in a progressive business, with a good team of operators
consistently achieving "standard performances", the standard *cost*
of the products in real terms (i.e. excluding the effect of changing
values of money) should be progressively reduced.

Because standard costs are only prepared at infrequent intervals
—usually annually—the clerical costs involved in monthly calculations are avoided. This means that costs can be worked out for a
wider range of products than would otherwise be practicable. As the
costs do not fluctuate from month to month, there is no need to
average out.

Standard Costs for Control

In addition to their use for profit planning purposes, standard
costs can be used as a basis for control of actual results. For example, the "volume variance" referred to above can be calculated
by comparing total budget allowances (flexed) with the total standard costs of the output achieved (see Appendix).

Ideal or Attainable Standards?

When standard costs are being used for control, a policy decision
has first to be taken. Should the standard cost be set at such a level
that it would be attained only if maximum capacity is utilised,
organisation is perfect, and all operations and activities are carried
out at 100 per cent. efficiency? Or should it take into account the
knowledge that capacity will be only partially utilised, that some
breakdown and material losses will occur, and that operatives will
not be working at standard performance? In other words, should
the standards be "ideal" or "attainable"?

There are two schools of thought about this. One view is that the
standards ought to be set at an ideal level, because only if this is
done will the full extent of potential savings be seen. Another valid

reason for deciding on ideal standards is that, if variations caused by altered methods and fluctuating prices are excluded, the standard costs will remain unchanged over a period of years. They are therefore more suited for use as a base against which subsequent progress can be judged than if they are varied from year to year.

The other view is that "attainable" standards offer a much better incentive for improvement in operating efficiency than do "ideal" standards. This incentive is provided by the satisfaction gained in beating budget. As previously explained, there is nothing to stop "attainable" standard costs being gradually moved nearer to "ideal" costs, as year by year improvements in organisation and efficiency are achieved. The four-minute mile was not an "ideal" target as events have proved, but was an "attainable" performance which acted like a magnet for many years. Once achieved, a new attainable target has to be set and passed, and the long-term approach to the ideal performance—should such exist—tackled anew. Another advantage claimed by the exponents of attainable standards is that these automatically provide the information necessary for profit planning. With ideal standards, adjustments have to be made to bring them into line with reality.

On balance, attainable standards seem to be more widely used than ideal standards, probably because they are easier to introduce. Management are inclined to look askance at cost figures which are widely different from the current level of costs, despite the advantages obtainable from spotlighting the difference between the two sets of figures.

COST/VOLUME STUDIES

Reference has already been made to the desirability of knowing the effect on product costs and profit margins of changes in the level of output or sales. Standard costs relate to only one level of activity— the budgeted level. A method which works well enough where only one product is being made—or where different products are manufactured in separate sections of the factory—is to analyse the standard product cost into fixed and variable elements. This is illustrated in Fig. 86 opposite.

Standard costs can be analysed in this way, because the "bricks" from which they are built up are also used for control purposes— and for control it is essential to classify the cost behaviour of the item (fixed, variable or semi-variable). It will be noted that before arriving at the split between fixed and variable costs, the semi-variable costs must also be split into their fixed and variable elements. Certain costs, e.g. heating of factory and offices, cannot be considered as fixed costs because their incidence will be affected by external influences (such as the weather). These costs will not, however, be affected by changes in the volume of output so that they will be included with fixed costs when dividing up the total product cost.

Other costs such as clerical salaries are not necessarily "fixed"—a method study investigation may reveal that considerable savings can be made. Nevertheless, these costs are unlikely to vary if there is a sudden alteration in the level of sales or production, and they will have to be included in fixed costs for profit planning purposes. "Constant costs" would be a better term for them, emphasising that they are likely to remain unchanged unless management takes effective action where the need exists. The same thinking underlies the American practice of referring to fixed costs as "non-variable" costs.

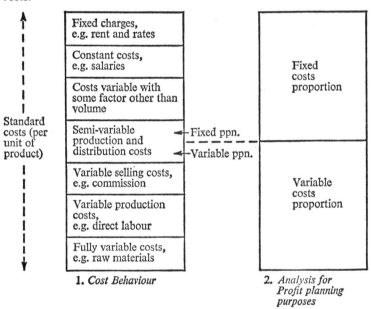

1. *Cost Behaviour*

2. *Analysis for Profit planning purposes*

FIG. 86.

With the completion of this analysis, it becomes possible to work out the effect on unit costs of probable changes in the volume of output and sales. Thus the "variable" costs (i.e. variable from a control point of view) will work out at the same cost per unit of product whether output falls or rises. On the other hand, the fixed cost element will alter in inverse ratio to the proposed volume of throughput. Thus a theoretical doubling of the budgeted output would not alter the variable cost element, but would halve the fixed cost element per unit and increase the profit margin correspondingly. In practice such a major variation would undoubtedly affect variable costs, e.g. by causing a substantial increase in overtime payments, but within the limits of all probable variations during the space of a year the conclusions drawn from a simple analysis into fixed and variable elements should be reasonably reliable. If a really major fluctuation is anticipated, then the standard product cost would have to be re-calculated.

Where several products are being manufactured in the same section of the factory, the position is not quite so straightforward. In-

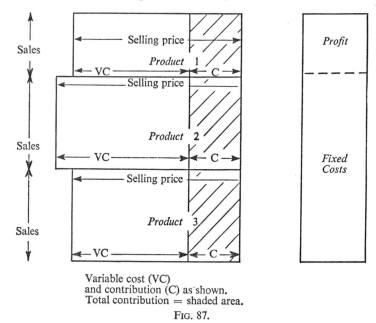

Variable cost (VC)
and contribution (C) as shown.
Total contribution = shaded area.

FIG. 87.

creasing or reducing the volume of output of any one product will alter the incidence of fixed costs on *all* the products being made in that part of the factory because the same total of fixed cost will be spread over a different total of output.

MARGINAL COSTING

The complexities caused in trying to work out the effect on standard product costs of proposed changes in product volumes has been a major factor in the development of new methods of costing. There is a growing body of opinion which favours the idea of including in standard costs only the variable or "marginal" cost elements. The fixed cost elements of the "full" standard costs are excluded and are considered separately as annual charges which have to be met out of the "contributions" obtained from the sale of products ("contribution" is equivalent to selling price less variable cost multiplied by quantities sold): see Fig. 87.

The diagram shows how three products, with different sales volumes, raw material costs and selling prices, contribute the same amount per unit (C) towards the total of profit and fixed costs. The total sum contributed by each product differs in each case because of the different sales volumes. In practice, the contribution per unit would also vary from product to product.

Once the contributions for all products have been calculated, the effect on total profits of proposed or probable changes in the volume of sales of any product can be readily determined: Increased (or decreased) sales (in units) × contribution per unit = increased (or decreased) overall profit. With this information, profit planners have a basis for working out the overall effect of increasing selling prices, of substituting one product for another, or of any other suggestions for raising profitability. In practice, they would also have to consider whether the changes in the volume of sales would be likely to affect the incidence of "fixed" costs.

Full Costs v. Marginal Costs

There is a sharp division of opinion between those who advocate the traditional approach—the allocation of all costs to products—and those who favour the newer or "marginal" approach of allocating only the variable costs.

There is universal agreement that variable costs (and the variable element of semi-variable costs) incurred directly on the product should be regarded as product costs. There is an increasing measure of agreement that costs of general administration should be regarded as block charges that have to be met out of the margin earned on products. There is considerable disagreement on the treatment of other fixed costs, such as departmental or factory overheads.

The protagonists of Marginal Costing take the view that it is illogical to include in product costs those charges that will be incurred regardless of the level of output. They suggest that these items are more properly regarded as costs of being in business, and as such should be charged off to the Profit and Loss Account for the period. They point out that in profit planning it is often required to know the effect on profits of increasing or decreasing the volume of business, or by how much it is permissible to reduce selling prices and still obtain a contribution towards fixed overheads. Marginal costs will provide this information, whereas "Full Costs" (i.e. product costs built up after full apportionment of the costs incurred) will not.

In reply, those who hold the more orthodox view point out that one of the objects of preparing product costs is to be able to compare one product with another. If the full costs properly chargeable to the product are not included, any such comparison would be misleading.

Another purpose of costing is to provide information against which to assess selling prices. Even if selling prices are fixed in the short term by reference to market conditions, in the long run the prices must be adjusted to cover the full costs involved and provide a margin over for profit. Not to know what the full costs are places an unnecessary handicap on the business. A further point is that by including the full costs in the standard costs used for control, the cost of under-utilised facilities is automatically brought to the attention of management through the segregation of "volume variances". Finally, it is conceded that management need to know for profit planning purposes what proportion of the total product cost is represented by variable costs, but this information can be supplied by dividing the full costs into two parts.

After considering the above views, one can only conclude that each case must be treated on its merits—there can be no general answer. The choice beween full and marginal costing can also influence the calculation of overall results, and this aspect is discussed in Chapter X.

"Direct Process" Costs

Marginal costing is of particular significance in helping management in short-term planning. A disadvantage already noted is that because marginal costing does not take into account fixed costs such as plant depreciation, it may give a misleading picture of long-term considerations.

An approach which seems to hold out promise as being a useful tool for long-range profit planning is to include in product costs all items which will tend to vary with the volume of output of that product over, say, a five-year period. Thus in a canning factory, a decision to treble the output of a certain product would mean doubling or trebling the canning lines, with a consequent increase in both variable costs and fixed costs such as supervision and depreciation. These costs, which approximate to the "direct costs" in a process industry, would accordingly be allocated to products. There would, however, be little or no increase in the general factory charges, and these would continue to be treated as "block" charges for the period.

If management have been used to looking at "fully allocated" standard costs and profit margins, it is important that they understand the need to look for relatively higher margins if either marginal costing or the compromise "direct process" costs are introduced. This is illustrated in the following example. The unit costs per ton are based on a budgeted output of 1,400 tons per annum.

	"Full" Cost	*"Marginal"* Cost	*Direct Process* Cost	*Fixed Costs (per annum)*
Selling price (per ton) .	£10	£10	£10	
Raw Materials	£2 10 0	£2 10 0	£2 10 0	
Add Departmental Charges				
Direct Labour . .	£1 0 0	£1 0 0	£1 0 0	
Power and Steam .	10 0	10 0	10 0	
Depreciation of Plant .	17 6		17 6	} £1,750
Supervision . .	7 6		7 6	
	£5 5 0	£4 0 0	£5 5 0	
Add Factory Charges:				
General Services . .	5 0			} £1,400
Fixed Charges . .	15 0			
Total product costs (per ton) . . .	£6 5 0	£4 0 0	£5 5 0	
Margin (per ton) . .	£3 15 0*	£6 0 0†	£4 15 0‡	
Administration Charges .				£2,250
			Total	£5,400

* Profit before administration charges.
† " Contribution " towards fixed costs and profits.
‡ " Contribution " towards fixed charges common to all products and profits

CHAPTER IV

PROFIT PLANNING AND BREAK-EVEN ANALYSIS

REFERENCE has been made in the previous Chapter to the Profit Planning carried out by marketing management, and to the costing techniques which are available to help in this planning. An example now follows showing how standard costing can be used to throw light on an unsatisfactory profit picture.

Example of Standard Costs for Profit Planning

The XYZ Company makes four products, in a factory consisting of four departments. The budgeted sales and costs of production for the year are as follows:

	Product	A	B	C	D	Total
Sales	(units)	5,000	4,000	10,000	2,000	
	(selling prices)	100s.	150s.	80s.	100s.	
	(sales value) (£)	25,000	30,000	40,000	10,000	£105,000
Raw Material Costs						
	(per unit of product)	50s.	80s.	40s.	50s.	
	(total cost) (£)	12,500	16,000	20,000	5,000	£53,500
Conversion Costs	(Departments 1, 2, 3, 4)					£31,500
Total Factory Cost						£85,000

Profit (before deducting general charges common to all products) £20,000

Less: Factory general services   £3,000
        Marketing costs   £6,500
        General administrative costs   £5,500

£15,000

Net Profit £5,000

The directors are not entirely satisfied with the proposed overall return of just under 5 per cent. on sales, and they decide to make a check on the profitability of each product.

Their calculations are as follows:

Product	A	B	C	D
Quantity (units)	5,000	4,000	10,000	2,000
Selling price	100s.	150s.	80s.	100s.
Less:				
Raw material cost . .	50s.	80s.	40s.	50s.
Conversion costs (averaged)* .	30s.	30s.	30s.	30s.
Margin†	20s.	40s.	10s.	20s.
Per cent. to selling price . .	20%	26⅔%	12½%	20%

* Conversion cost £31,500 divided by total output, 21,000.
† Margin available to cover general charges and profit.

The directors now consider that the reason why profits are not higher is the low margin obtained on product C. They accordingly decide to reduce production of C, and step up the production of the other products. Before taking this step, however, they decide to ask the accountant to check the figures. The accountant's first move is to discuss the whole problem with his colleague, the work study manager. They decide that the direct labour and power standards that have been worked out for each product for departmental cost control purposes will provide the necessary means of allocating the departmental costs for profitability purposes. They record the quantity of each product which it is proposed to pass through the departments concerned (each product passes through two or three departments) and then build up the budgeted costs in each department as follows:

	Standard Hours		Budgeted Cost	
	Per Unit	Total	Per Hour	Total
Dept. 1. Direct labour costs:				£
Product A 5,000 units . .	0·5	2,500	5s.	625
Product B 4,000 units . .	2·0	8,000	5s.	2,000
Product D 2,000 units . .	1·0	2,000	5s.	500
Total		12,500		3,125

Similar calculations would be carried out for other costs. These would then be summarised:

Dept. 1. *Total Conversion costs*

	Direct Labour £	Power and Steam £	Other Costs £	Total £
Product A 5,000 units	625			2,500
Product B 4,000 units	2,000	Completed as necessary		3,000
Product D 2,000 units	500			1,000
	£3,125			£6,500

The next stage would be to put together the departmental totals to arrive at the total costs. This is the normal procedure for arriving at the budgeted conversion cost, and it is assumed that the total agrees with the £31,500 already noted.

Product	A	B	C	D	Total
Output (units) . . .	5,000	4,000	10,000	2,000	21,000
Conversion Costs	£	£	£	£	£
Dept. 1 . . .	2,500	3,000		1,000	6,500
2 . . .	5,000		5,000		10,000
3 . . .		3,000	5,000	2,000	10,000
4 . . .		2,000		3,000	5,000
Total	7,500	8,000	10,000	6,000	31,500
Cost per unit . .	30s.	40s.	20s.	60s.	

The final stage is to substitute these "standard costs" of conversion for the average costs previously used by the directors.

Product	A	B	C	D	Total
Sales (units)	5,000	4,000	10,000	2,000	
Selling price	100s.	150s.	80s.	100s.	
Less: Raw material cost . .	50s.	80s.	40s.	50s.	
Standard conversion cost (as above) . . .	30s.	40s.	20s.	60s.	
Margin	20s.	30s.	20s.	(10s. loss)	
Per cent. to selling price . .	20%	20%	25%	−10%	
Previous figures: . . .	20s.	40s.	10s.	20s.	
	20%	26⅔%	12½%	20%	

It will be seen that the true position is very different from that previously envisaged. The company is actually making the highest percentage on product C (instead of the lowest), while it is making a loss (before allocating any part of the general charges) on product D. The directors would accordingly concentrate their attention on this product, and decide whether the loss can be turned into a profit, or whether it will be necessary to discontinue production. The decision would not be an easy one. To raise selling prices might result in a decrease in the volume of sales—already very low—which would more than offset the extra margin. A better solution might be to find some way of reducing operating costs, without lowering quality unduly.

Another possible solution—to stimulate sales by lowering selling prices—would first call for further investigation into the "cost" behaviour of the items included in the total conversion costs. In the case of product D, it may be found that the 60s. conversion cost is made up of 30s. variable costs (direct labour, power charges, supplies, etc.) and 30s. representing fixed charges (supervision, rentals or depreciation of expensive machinery, etc.). With this information, it is now possible to work out the effect of variations in the volume of sales:

Product D

Sales per annum (units) . .	2,000	4,000	6,000
Raw material costs (per unit) .	50s.	50s.	50s.
Variable conversion costs . .	30s.	30s.	30s.
Fixed conversion costs (£3,000) .	30s.	15s.	10s.
Total costs	110s.	95s.	90s.
Selling price	100s.	100s.	100s.

From this table it is seen that, if sales are trebled at 6,000 units per annum, there would be a margin of 10s. per unit. This would hardly allow for much reduction in selling prices in order to stimulate demand, and it would probably be necessary to find a way of reducing variable costs as well.

Summarising the conclusions drawn from this example:
(1) In addition to reviewing overall profitability, the profitability of each product should be reviewed.
(2) Standard data used for control of departmental costs can also be used in establishing standard product costs.
(3) In considering possible courses of action to improve profitability it is necessary to distinguish between fixed and variable costs.
(4) Information about product profitability is required well in advance of management decisions concerning pricing or marketing plans.

BREAK-EVEN ANALYSIS

The separation of costs into fixed and variable elements enables a calculation to be made of the "break-even" level of sales. At this level, the total revenue earned on sales would exactly equal the total of fixed and variable costs, so that the business would make neither profit nor loss. Once this break-even point has been established, management will know that a higher level of sales will result in a profit—since the fixed costs will not be affected—while for the same reason, any lower volume of sales will result in a loss.

A convenient way of showing this type of information is by drawing up a Break-Even chart. Alternative methods of doing this, based on the data set out in the example on page 673, are illustrated below (see Charts on pages 678, 679, 682 and 684, Figs. 88–89 and 92–93).

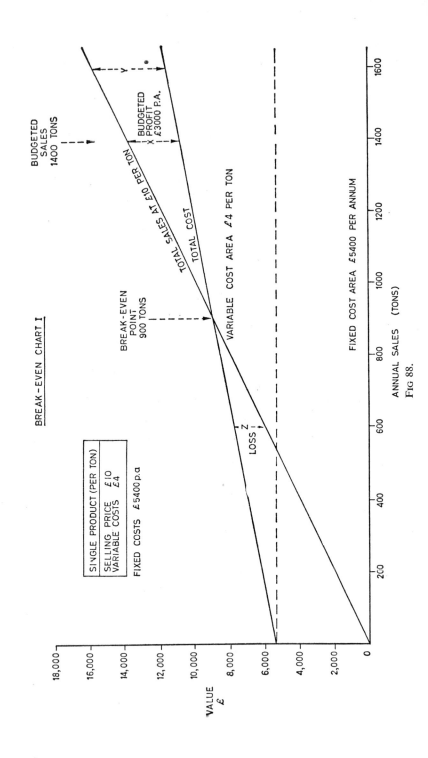

BREAK-EVEN CHART I

SINGLE PRODUCT (PER TON)	
SELLING PRICE	£10
VARIABLE COSTS	£4

FIXED COSTS £5400 p.a

BUDGETED SALES 1400 TONS

TOTAL SALES AT £10 PER TON

TOTAL COST

BREAK-EVEN POINT 900 TONS

BUDGETED PROFIT £3000 P.A.

VARIABLE COST AREA £4 PER TON

LOSS

FIXED COST AREA £5400 PER ANNUM

ANNUAL SALES (TONS)

FIG 88.

VALUE £

18,000
16,000
14,000
12,000
10,000
8,000
6,000
4,000
2,000
0

200   400   600   800   1000   1200   1400   1600

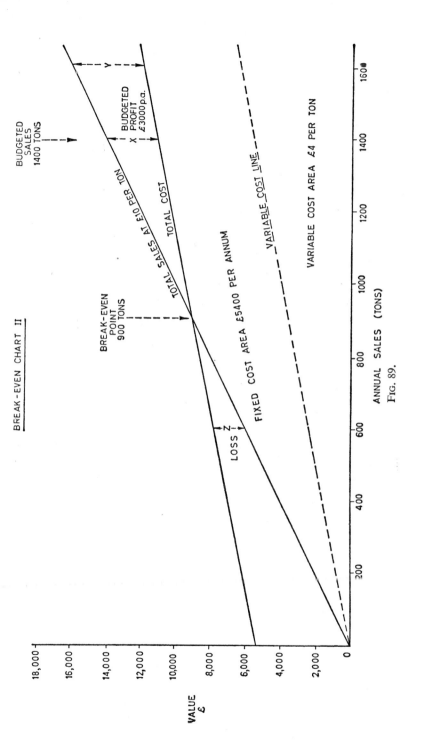

BREAK-EVEN CHART II

BUDGETED SALES 1400 TONS

BUDGETED PROFIT £3000 p.a.

TOTAL SALES AT £10 PER TON

TOTAL COST

BREAK-EVEN POINT 900 TONS

FIXED COST AREA £5400 PER ANNUM

VARIABLE COST LINE

VARIABLE COST AREA £4 PER TON

LOSS

Y

X

N

VALUE £

18,000
16,000
14,000
12,000
10,000
8,000
6,000
4,000
2,000
0

200   400   600   800   1000   1200   1400   1600

ANNUAL SALES (TONS)

FIG. 89.

Break-Even Chart I

The fixed charges are first inserted along the bottom of the chart. The variable cost at the budgeted output (1,400 tons) is then worked out (1,400 × £4 = £5,600) and this cost is measured out vertically along the 1,400 ton line, starting from the total fixed cost line. The point so obtained is then joined to the fixed cost line at zero tons (variable cost at zero tons = zero), and extended in the other direction to give the total cost line (fixed plus variable costs). Finally the sales value at 1,400 tons (£1,400) is inserted on the chart, and the total sales line ruled in, passing through this point and through the "zero–zero" point. The vertical distance between the total sales line and the total cost line at the budgeted sales level of 1,400 tons indicates the net profit (£3,000) which should be obtained if sales just reach this level. If sales should rise to 1,600 tons per annum, the indicated net profit (y) then obtainable is £4,200. On the other hand if sales should fall to the break-even point of 900 tons, the profit would fall to zero. Any further fall would involve the business in a loss—at only 600 tons, the chart shows that the loss (z) would be £1,800. All this information can of course be calculated from the table itself, but the chart may be preferred by those who like to see the position at a glance. It also provides a convenient basis for trying out alternative planning ideas.

Break-Even Chart II

Although the foregoing procedure is the one most usually described in text books, an alternative method of constructing the chart has certain advantages over the traditional method (see Fig. 89). The only difference between the two charts is the treatment of fixed and variable costs. In the second, the fixed costs have been superimposed upon the variable costs instead of vice versa.

The advantages claimed for drawing up the chart in this way are that it shows more clearly that at any given level of sales, variable costs are first covered, and then a contribution is made to overheads (i.e. fixed costs) and profit. Thus at the break-even point of 900 tons, the vertical distance between the sales and the variable cost lines is £5,400, exactly equal to the fixed costs. At a level of 600 tons, the "contribution" is only £3,600, thus failing to cover fixed costs by the amount equal to the net loss of £1,800 (z).

High and Low Break-Even Points

If the ratio of fixed costs to variable costs is high, a business is said to have a high break-even point, because a relatively small drop in turnover can turn a profit into a loss. Similarly, where fixed costs represent only a small proportion of the total, the business will have a low break-even point, because although a fall in turnover will lead to lower profits, the break-even point will not be reached until sales fall to much lower levels. This is illustrated in the two intermediate diagrams shown at Figs. 90–91.

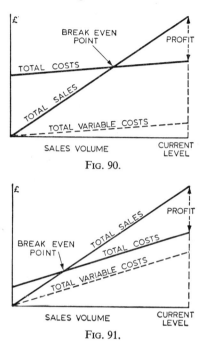

Fig. 90.

Fig. 91.

It must be emphasised that the straight line relationships shown in the above break-even charts would be unlikely to apply over a wide range of output levels. In practice, fixed costs would tend to rise if output rose appreciably, while the incidence of variable costs per unit might also increase as overtime working became more intensive. At the same time, increased sales might only be obtained at a lower price per unit, so that there would be a tendency for total sales and total cost lines to meet again at a second break-even point when output was pushed to uneconomic levels. However, for short-term planning purposes, it is probable that only small variations in output will occur, and in these circumstances, the simpler straight lines chart may suffice.

PROFIT PLANNING CHARTS

In those cases where management is using the marginal costing approach, and is accustomed to looking at "contribution" and fixed

PROFIT PLANNING CHART I

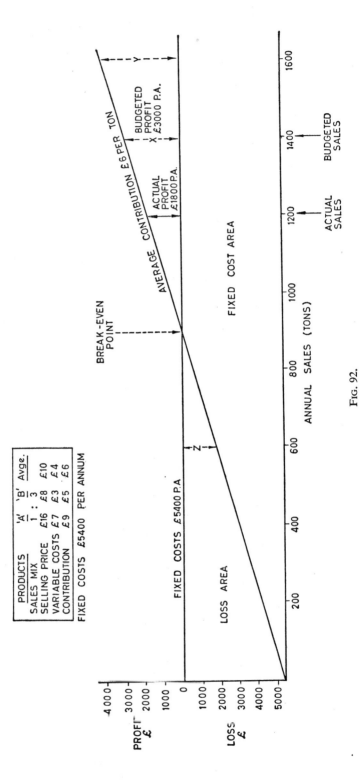

FIG. 92.

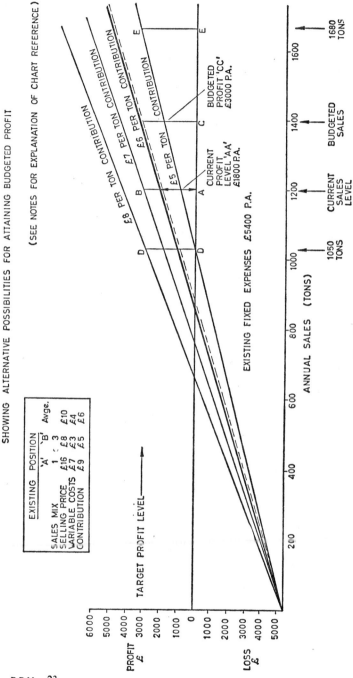

PROFIT PLANNING CHART II

SHOWING ALTERNATIVE POSSIBILITIES FOR ATTAINING BUDGETED PROFIT

(SEE NOTES FOR EXPLANATION OF CHART REFERENCE)

FIG. 93.

P.P.M.—23

costs rather than at sales and total costs, a further simplification is possible. In the Profit Planning charts, variable costs are omitted, and the contribution earned at varying levels of output is plotted against the fixed costs.

Profit Planning Chart I

The fixed cost line (Fig. 92) is first inserted as in the original chart (Fig. 88). The contribution line is then drawn in, passing through the zero–zero point and the break-even point. In order to simplify reading off profits and losses, the scale on the left is altered, so that the original fixed cost line becomes the £zero line. Profits or losses are then marked off in this scale, as shown. The profit or loss at any level of sales is read off by noting the vertical distance of the contribution line from the zero line (i.e. x, y or z as shown in the two earlier charts).

The main advantage of a chart of this nature, apart from its simplicity, is seen when variable costs—such as raw materials—fluctuate in price from week to week or month to month, and selling prices are adjusted accordingly. The aim would be to keep the "contribution" at a constant figure, but if this does vary, the new line can be easily plotted on the chart. Any change in the relationship between contribution and fixed costs can be quickly seen, as when an increase or decrease in the volume of sales is being considered.

In order to show how a profit planning chart can be used where more than one product is being sold, it will now be assumed that the above details of selling price, variable costs and contribution are in fact average figures for two products A and B, and that the actual details are as shown on the chart. It will also be assumed that the actual level of total sales is settling down at a rate of 1,200 tons per annum, compared with a budgeted figure of 1,400 tons. The chart shows that if the two products are being sold in the proportions shown, the annual rate of profit will be only £1,800 instead of the £3,000 expected.

Profit Planning Chart II

This shows (Fig. 93) how various alternative methods of restoring the actual level of profit to the target figure can be worked out, as an aid to management decision:

Eight possibilities for raising £1,800 p.a.
profit level to target figure of £3,000 p.a.

Chart
Reference

AB   (i) Reducing variable cost by £1 per ton, e.g. by improved efficiency or using cheaper materials.

AB   (ii) Reducing fixed cost by £1,200 p.a.

CC   (iii) Raising sales volume by 200 tons p.a. without incurring any net additional expense, e.g. by improved sales appeal, re-direction of marketing effort, or improved performance.

CC   (iv) Raising sales volume by 200 tons p.a. by achieving economies in operating costs and using the savings for additional advertising or "order-getting" activities.

DD   (v) Raising selling prices by £2 per ton and allowing for a sales drop of 150 tons p.a.

DD   (vi) Altering the sales mix to 3 tons of A to 1 ton of B, and allowing for sales drop of 150 tons p.a.

EE   (vii) Raising the volume of sales by 480 tons p.a. as the result of lowering selling prices by £1 per ton.

EE   (viii) Raising the volume of sales by 480 tons p.a. as the result of increasing the expenditure on advertising or "order-getting" activities by amount equivalent to £1 per ton on the increased tonnage.

CHAPTER V

FACTORY CONTROLS—PLANT MANAGEMENT

A REVIEW of control procedures associated with fixed assets is a logical starting point for a review of the business by functions. Land and buildings, plant and machinery, equipment and vehicles—once acquired, these assets will normally be held so long as they serve a useful purpose. This means that during the formulation of the annual policy plans for the business, detailed consideration must be given to these assets, and to the way in which it is proposed to use them during their working life.

It is true that land and buildings will usually retain or even increase their value over the years, but for various reasons, including access difficulties, it is seldom practicable to dispose of any portions that become surplus to immediate requirements. Plant, machinery and equipment, even if quite recently installed, would probably just fetch scrap value. It is only in the case of movable items of equipment such as fork-lift trucks, or vehicles for which there is a good second-hand market, that the question of re-sale can be seriously considered. Apart from these exceptions, and excluding those instances when a business is sold as a going concern, expenditure on a particular fixed asset must be regarded as irrecoverable once the contract to acquire or construct the asset has been signed. It is for this reason that the cost of such an item is often referred to as a "sunk cost". In these circumstances, the aim of management must be to ensure that maintenance and eventual replacement of existing assets are carried out as economically as possible, and that maximum use is made of the assets during their working life in carrying out profitable activities. In this way, the investment in fixed assets will be made to yield the maximum return.

This Chapter deals with the maintenance and replacement of existing fixed assets, and with the control of work in progress during the construction of additional fixed assets. It also describes the measurement of the use made of plant and machinery in terms of time and saleable output.[1] Control procedures which help manage-

[1] This Chapter and the following one need to be read in conjunction with Chapters III and V of Part Two, where the manufacturing and maintenance activities are considered from the standpoint of the physical aspects rather than the financial. The two aspects are, of course, closely inter-related: financial considerations are equally important to the Factory Managers and the Manufacturing Department Heads as to the Financial Controllers or Cost Accountants.

ment to evaluate the relative pros and cons of alternative ways of investing in fixed assets are described in Chapter IX.

PLANT AVAILABILITY AND UTILISATION

Where demand for a product is heavy, output may be limited only by the capacity of the factory to produce. In such circumstances every piece of plant and equipment will be operated to the maximum extent. This maximum, in the case of continuous operation, could be as high as 168 hours a week—but sooner or later a period of overhaul would be required, which would put the item of plant out of action for some time. Continuous working of this nature may be necessary in some industries due to the nature of the process. Thus a glass factory operates a furnace continuously for 168 hours a week for the best part of a year, but eventually the furnace has to be taken out of action and the walls re-lined, over a period of several weeks or months. In other industries plant may be operated 24 hours a day, but the necessary maintenance would be carried out at weekends. Thus in all cases where plant is being operated on a maximum basis, some reduction must be made from the theoretical maximum in arriving at the number of hours per week that would be available for actual production over a period. Where there is operating on a single or double shift basis, the theoretical maximum working corresponds to hours of attendance, but a reduction must be made for hours needed for maintenance. With overtime working outside the normal shift hours, the time available for production will be correspondingly increased. This "Machine Available Time", as it is appropriately called, is an important figure to determine in advance, because it provides the basis for calculating the plant capacity—in terms of potential output—in any period. It also indicates the planned division of the total machine time between production and maintenance. It is preferable to have this decided in advance, than left for discussion on an *ad hoc* basis each time the question of overhaul is considered:

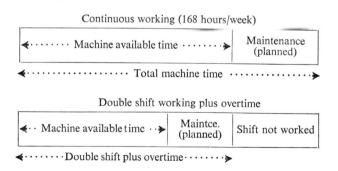

Continuous working (168 hours/week)

◀ · · · · · · · · Machine available time · · · · · · · ·▶   Maintenance (planned)

◀ · · · · · · · · · · · · · · · · · · Total machine time · · · · · · · · · · · · · ·▶

Double shift working plus overtime

◀ · · Machine available time · ·▶   Maintce. (planned)   Shift not worked

◀ · · · · · · · · Double shift plus overtime · · · · · · · ·▶

One of the purposes of calculating the "machine available time" is to provide a yardstick against which actual use of the plant can be compared. The object of this comparison is to spotlight unplanned stoppages, or excessive change-over time, etc. In order to distinguish between these factors and idle machine time caused by lack of orders, it is usual to deduct the latter from the machine available time before taking it as a base. It would also be necessary to make a deduction for any time during which it is planned to test the plant on experimental production:

◀ · · · · · · · · · · · · · · · · Double shift working · · · · · · · · · · · · · · · · ▶

◀ · · Machine available time · · ▶	Maintenance (planned)	No orders

In order to arrive at the time during which it is hoped the plant will be actually used for normal production, deductions must be made for four further kinds of planned stoppages ("ancillary time") —tea and meal breaks, cleaning, change-over, starting and stopping time. After making these deductions, the planned running time is arrived at—the time for which it will be planned to man up the machine and produce output:

◀ · · · · · · · · · · · · · · · · Double shift working · · · · · · · · · · · · · · · · ▶

Maximum running time	Ancillary time	Maintce. (planned)	No orders

◀ · · · · · · · · Machine available time · · · · · · · · ▶

Up to this point, the breakdown of the total machine time has been assumed to have been worked out in advance as a basis for calculating the expected production requirements. If the analysis is repeated for each item of plant in the factory, it is possible to calculate the total plant running hours, and from this to deduce the requirements for labour, power and steam, etc. However, before equating the planned running time and the required output, one further deduction must be made from the former. Experience shows that however carefully the work is planned, some unforeseen breakdowns or hold-ups will occur: for example, mechanical and electrical breakdowns, waiting time (waiting for materials, operators, supervisor, repairs, etc.). For planning purposes, it is usual to make an estimated allowance for these possible occurrences based on previous experience:

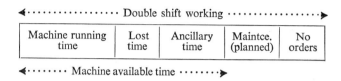

For control purposes, it is necessary to record the actual allocation of total time between the various items described above. It may be practicable to obtain a record of actual running time by automatic methods. The next step is to calculate the length of time the machine should have run, based on the actual output achieved. The standard machine performance in terms of output per minute or per hour of continuous running must be ascertained, and by applying these standards to the actual output, the standard or theoretical machine running time can be calculated. Any excess of actual over standard running time may be due to faulty production not included in the production count, to non-recording of stopped time, or to mechanical defects causing the rate of machine operation to slow down.

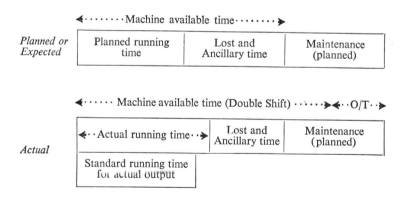

Control could be exercised by comparing actual running time with standard, actual lost time with expected, actual ancillary time with planned, and so on. However, owing to the possibility of the actual machine available time differing from the corresponding planned figure—e.g. due to a sudden influx of orders causing overtime to be worked—it is preferable to make use of control ratios.

Control ratios which have proved useful are:

(i) Machine availability $= \dfrac{\text{Machine available time}}{\text{Total machine time}} \times 100$

(ii) Machine utilisation $= \dfrac{\text{Actual running time}}{\text{Machine available time}} \times 100$

(iii) Machine efficiency $= \dfrac{\text{Standard running time}}{\text{Actual running time}} \times 100$

(iv) Machine effective utilisation $= \dfrac{\text{Standard running time}}{\text{Machine available time}} \times 100$

Comparison can then be made between the planned utilisation or efficiency index and the corresponding actual indices.

A continuous watch over these indices for each of the major plant items, combined with investigation of unfavourable trends or tendencies, should help to ensure that maximum use is made of the potential capacity of the plant. A worked example showing the calculation and use of these ratios is given in the Appendix.

Maximum Capacity to Produce

Reference has been made above to the utilisation of individual plant items in terms of time. One of the primary tasks of production management is to review the productive capacity of the plant as a whole in terms of volume, weight or unit quantities.

The first step in establishing a pattern of control is to determine the maximum output that *could* be obtained from the plant, assuming that demand for this output existed. Before this question can be answered, it is necessary to obtain a ruling on the number of shifts to be worked. The business may be in the habit of working single shift, plus overtime when necessary. Double shift working would only be contemplated if demand should justify it. In this case, the maximum capacity would probably be based on double shift working, since it is improbable that any higher rate of working would be practicable. Each case would have to be considered on its merits, and in some circumstances it might be reasonable to base the maximum on round-the-clock operations. Having decided on the number of shifts, the next step is to calculate the output that is theoretically possible during these hours. If a factory is divided into separate divisions or sections operating in parallel, each producing its own group of finished products, then it will be necessary to work out separate output figures for each section. If the factory is divided into a series or chain of processes or operations through which the raw materials or work in progress pass in turn before finally emerging as finished products, then it will be possible to establish a single output figure, expressing the overall capacity.

In the latter case, it will usually be found that each "link" of the chain has a different maximum capacity, and the overall capacity is limited by the "link" with the lowest potential throughput. The ascertainment of this potential bottleneck is of major importance from the point of view of plant design, as well as operational control. In control terms, the output of this section of the plant is referred to as the "key factor", since it sets the limit on the overall output. It will be appreciated that one of the objectives of the plant engineers will be to step up the potential output of the weakest link in the chain, in which case another link will automatically become the "key factor." It is unlikely that a whole series of operations will ever be completely in balance from an output point of view.

The desirability of establishing the "key factor" in a series of operations is particularly important when a number of different products are being manufactured in batches. If only one product is being produced, the maximum output can be clearly established as so many tons (or other units of quantity) per week. This figure would be obtained from technical data or systematic studies. If several different products are produced, and each product passes through the "key factor" process at a different rate per hour, then it is no longer possible to talk about a maximum tonnage unless the "product mix" is specified. This is illustrated in the following example:

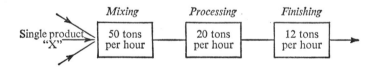

The figures shown relate to maximum capacities. The maximum capacity of the whole process is 12 tons per hour.

If a new product Y is then produced alternately with X, in equal quantities, and if this product has to pass through the finishing stage twice, then the maximum output of the plant is reduced to an average of 8 tons per hour (Product X 4 tons, Product Y 4 tons put through twice). On the other hand, if product Y has to pass through the processing stage twice, and only once through the finishing stage, the maximum output will remain unaltered at 12 tons per hour, since the capacity of the processing stage is more than adequate (6 tons X plus 12 tons Y = 18 tons per hour).

One of the objects of establishing the maximum capacity is to use this figure as a control base against which to compare actual throughputs. It would create obvious difficulties if one had to state that the maximum capacity was 8–12 tons according to circumstances, i.e. the product used. There are two ways in which it is possible to arrive at a common denominator for measuring the output of a machine-controlled operation—one is to make use of the notion "unit tons" and the other "standard machine hours". Thus in the first example above one could give factors of 1 and 2 to products X and Y respectively, and then describe the maximum output as 12 unit tons per hour. Assuming that the plant is capable of 70 "running hours" per week (see above) the maximum capacity could be expressed as 840 unit tons per week. Alternatively, this output could be described simply as "70 standard machine hours per week." This is a more straightforward way of describing total output where there is a large variety of different products. The above information would be accompanied by a list of "standard output rates per machine hour for each product" e.g. X 12 tons per hour, Y 6 tons per hour, etc.

Turning now to the case of a factory organised in parallel, it may happen that a section of the factory is allocated to the manufacture of a group of products by manual methods. It is possible that mechanical equipment is used to supplement these operations, but it will be assumed that the volume of output is determined primarily by the number of operators and the efficiency with which they work. In circumstances such as these, it is equally valuable to be able to calculate a maximum output figure for use as a control base, but rather more assumptions have to be made in establishing it than are necessary in the case of machine-controlled activities. In addition to deciding on shift hours, it is necessary to determine what number of operators should be taken as the practical maximum, and at what level of performance they can be expected to work. The former figure can be based on the maximum number of employees that have been employed in the past at any time, or that are likely to be employed in the immediate future. The latter point is dealt with by assuming that the operatives will be working at "Standard Performance" (see Part Two, Chapter III, page 306).

From this point onwards, the procedure is similar to that described above for machine-controlled operations: If only one product is being manufactured, the work study department will be asked to establish the standard times for the various operations, so that the maximum output can be established. Owing to the flexibility of labour a "key factor" will probably not be relevant. An example is given below (based on single shift working):

Maximum number of operators 20.

Attendance hours 45.

Hours available for work 40 hours/week.

Standard times per case of finished product:

Preparing: Product P 20 mins., Product Q 40 mins.

All products—Finishing 15 mins. Labelling and Packing 5 mins.

Totals: Product P 40 mins. Product Q 60 mins.

Calculation of maximum output per week (assuming operators work at standard performance):

Operator-hours available for work 800.

Output achievable: $800 \times \dfrac{60}{40} = 1{,}200$ cases of Product P

or 800 cases of Product Q,

or 600 of P, 400 of Q, etc.

In view of the variability of the product mix, the maximum output would be described as 800 standard hours (or 48,000 SM's) and both planned and actual output would be measured in the same terms.

Planned Utilisation of Capacity

When policy plans are being prepared at the beginning of each financial year, one of the key questions to be considered is the extent to which it is proposed to make use of available capacity. Those firms that are in the fortunate position of supplying products for which there is a large unsatisfied demand will, of course, aim at making use of maximum capacity. Other firms less favourably placed will have to decide what quantity of products they think they can sell in the forthcoming year, and then work out what this means in terms of productive capacity. The typical experience of a developing business is to be short of capacity in early years but as capacity is gradually expanded and demand levels off, a state of equilibrium is reached. At this stage, the management will probably aim to make use of 80–90 per cent. of their maximum capacity for most of the year, with a higher utilisation during peak periods.

This "capacity usage" ratio, as it is frequently termed, is an important figure to watch. If, when the operating plans have been prepared for a part of the factory, it is found that this index has dropped by some 10–20 per cent. compared with the previous year, it is a clear indication to management that the fixed charges associated with that part of the factory will have to be absorbed by a correspondingly lower volume of output. This is likely to have a harmful effect on profit margins unless selling prices can be increased, but in this case the effect may be to reduce the level of demand, and thus lead to a still lower utilisation of productive capacity. In other words a vicious circle is created.

Consideration of these factors emphasises the importance of close collaboration between the marketing and production sides of the business. If marketing management are put in the picture regarding the difficulties caused by under-utilisation of capacity, they may be stimulated to develop new products or make some other arrangements for utilising the spare capacity.

PLANT MAINTENANCE

One of the benefits obtained from keeping a detailed record of plant running time and plant stopped time is the information provided as to the incidence of maintenance and repair work. For example, the records may show that some machines, on which extensive planned maintenance work is carried out at regular intervals, never break down or require repair during the periods when they are being used for production. On the other hand, other items of plant on which very little advance maintenance is carried out may be breaking down at frequent intervals, necessitating the transfer of operators to other machines.

Consideration of these two extremes immediately raises the query as to how important it is to avoid breakdowns. It is only when this question is answered that it becomes possible to estimate how much planned maintenance work is required, or to attempt to exercise control over maintenance costs. An airline company provides an obvious example where breakdowns must be avoided at all costs—hence maintenance inspections and overhauls will be carried out at frequent and regular intervals, as prescribed by statutory regulations. Such a company cannot save money by reducing the frequency of maintenance attention, and any savings will come principally from increasing the efficiency with which the work is carried out. There is then a double benefit—any saving of time in carrying out the necessary maintenance jobs will not only cut down on maintenance costs, but it will also increase the time available for carrying profitable pay loads. On the other hand, a company making durable consumer products with plenty of spare capacity, may decide that planned maintenance should be reduced to a minimum, since a breakdown will involve no loss of production. Indeed, the only advantage obtained from overhauling plant before it actually breaks down may be that by so doing the total maintenance cost is less over a period, on the "stitch in time saves nine" principle. In the majority of instances, it is probable that a compromise between these two extremes is desirable.

Most businesses will normally be working somewhere near their maximum capacity, so that a serious breakdown will lead not only to a repair bill, but also to subsequent overtime working to make good the lost production. In some cases, where the maximum hours are already being worked, a breakdown will lead to loss of turnover and profits. If the breakdown is prolonged, there may be a loss of customers as well.

It is clear that the first essentials in drawing up the maintenance policy plans for the year are a knowledge of:

(a) the relationship between the frequency and extent of inspection and the frequency and extent of plant breakdowns;

(b) representative costs of inspections, overhauls, breakdowns, making good production lost through breakdown.

The basic difficulties which are inherent in trying to provide factual evidence for conclusions reached in this field are that data can only be built up over a lengthy period, and in the meanwhile general conditions may have changed. Despite the difficulties, it seems possible that future economies in the days of automation will come from studies such as these rather than from savings in direct labour or materials.

Maintenance Budgeting—Labour

Assuming that maintenance policy has been agreed for each major group of machinery or plant, the next step required in the control of maintenance costs is the preparation of a maintenance budget. In the past, maintenance costs have been regarded by accountants as an expense which requires budgeting in the same way as rent, or depreciation, i.e. the total cost must be assessed and included in the budget of general manufacturing costs and expenses. It is not unknown for this figure to be obtained by difference, i.e. by deducting all other items of expense (which can be estimated with reasonable accuracy), together with the hoped-for profit, from the anticipated sales figure and thus arriving at a balancing figure of maintenance and repairs which the engineer is advised must not be exceeded. Such a hit-and-miss method of arriving at an allowable overall cost of maintenance will probably understate the effort required and so will lead to either a complete disregard of the budget by the engineers, or alternatively if the budget is followed, a gradual deterioration in the efficiency of the plant.

The modern concept of a maintenance budget is a document which will set out in some detail the agreed maintenance policy for the year. Like all budgets, it does not pretend to be a "blue-print for action". The actual maintenance effort will depend on many factors which can only be resolved as the year progresses—the volume of production, the type of product being manufactured, the type of material being processed, the extent of overtime working, the incidence of breakdowns, etc.

Fortunately for engineering management, it is usually possible to provide some flexibility in planning the actual work load. Thus if an unexpectedly high number of emergency repairs have to be carried out in any week, planned overhauls due to be carried out then can be deferred until conditions become normal. If the maintenance staff looks like being unexpectedly slack, planned overhauls can be brought forward, or men allocated to stand-by capital work. In theory, the working of overtime when necessary should contribute to flexibility, but in practice overtime working is often regarded as a regular feature—however deplorable—for which work has to be found.

The net result of the above factors is that it is often quite a simple matter to budget for the total cost of the *engineering staff* during the forthcoming year. This total is found by projecting forwards the average number of men employed in the previous year, allowing for any planned increases or decreases, and multiplying the result by 52 times the average weekly pay (including overtime). In other words, owing to the importance attached nowadays to retaining skilled operators, it may be assumed that the total cost of engineering staff will remain relatively stable from week to week.

What is not so simple to budget—and this is where the real object of control lies—is the *work* which the men will do during the year. If control is slack, the work will be allowed to accumulate, until eventually a case is made out for working longer overtime hours, or taking on more staff. To be effective as a means of subsequent control, the maintenance budget must be built up from certain basic assumptions, which will be clearly specified. Then if subsequent events show that actual conditions differ from expectation, the necessary adjustments can be made when comparing actual costs with budget. This is very similar to the procedure that is followed when a budget is prepared for the production activities of a business. Labour costs are budgeted on the basis of achieving a specified volume of production—if the actual volume of production differs from budget, then a corresponding adjustment is made when comparing actual labour costs with budgeted costs. The only real difference is that, in the case of maintenance, it is much more difficult to find out to what extent the actual work load differs from that visualised when the budget was prepared.

In the absence of recognised procedures, the following principles can form the foundation for drawing up the maintenance budget in such a way that basic assumptions are made clear:

(i) Budget for the total number of man-hours that will be available for engineering work (proposed number of men × number of weeks × average hours worked per week).

(ii) Allocate this total time over the different categories of work which it is proposed to carry out, e.g.
   (a) periodic lubrication, cleaning, adjustments, change-overs, etc.;
   (b) planned inspections;
   (c) planned overhauls;
   (d) repairing breakdowns or defects reported by departments;
   (e) alterations and improvements;
   (f) capital projects.

(iii) List out the major items which it is expected will be carried out under headings (b), (c), also (e) and (f) so far as these are known. Insert the expected total times for each of these major items, and reconcile with the total time allocated. ("Plant history" cards on which details of maintenance hours booked on each item of plant over a number of years have been recorded will provide a valuable aid in arriving at these estimated times, although it must be remembered that they will not indicate whether previous experience was efficient or otherwise. The position can only be clarified if the work involved is studied systematically as described in Part Two.)

(iv) Specify the expected level of production on which the above calculations have been based, particularly as it affects the incidence of breakdowns (d).

(v) Evaluate the budget in terms of £.s.d. (see page 699 below).

Carrying out the above procedure will obviously entail a lot of work, but if it leads to a reduction in the cost of maintenance without reducing operating efficiency, it will be work worth doing.

A further important benefit obtained from budgeting maintenance activities in detail is the opportunity offered for co-ordination with production activities well in advance of actual requirements. At the same time, the budget will provide the accountant with a reliable basis for calculating maintenance costs for the forthcoming year for inclusion in product cost estimates required for profit planning purposes.

Maintenance Control—Labour

Owing to the irregular nature of the work carried out, the maintenance budget provides little help in controlling the work done on a week to week basis. As the year proceeds, however, it should be possible to compare actual cost with budgeted cost, and actual work carried out with budgeted work—assuming that actual work done is analysed in the same way as that suggested for drawing up the budget, and that comparison is made with the appropriate proportion of the budget, depending on the length of the period being compared.

It should be noted that if the firm employs planner-estimators to assess the time required on each major job before it is begun, information will be available to indicate the efficiency with which actual jobs are carried out. In the absence of such estimates, the actual time taken on such major jobs will be compared with the allowed time included in the budget. If the actual time is in excess of budget, it will be difficult to pinpoint the reasons for the excess.

As indicated in the preceding section, it is comparatively simple to budget for the total cost of the firm's engineering staff—covering both maintenance and capital work. If it is considered that economies are possible, then one of the most effective ways of achieving them may be simply to reduce the budgeted number of men by one or two each year, and to allow natural wastage to reduce the effective numbers on the pay roll in the same proportion. This procedure would be carried on for a year or so until a state of balance had been achieved. An increase in budget would only be permitted where a good case could be made out for an additional work load.

Summing up the ideas underlying the control of maintenance costs through detailed budgeting:

(a) The first step is to agree on maintenance policy—e.g. to decide to what extent planned inspections and planned overhauls should be undertaken, having regard to an agreed permissible frequency of plant breakdowns.

(b) Next, both budgets and actual maintenance data should be classified according to the type of job, e.g. routine maintenance, emergency repairs, planned maintenance, alterations or additions, etc.

(c) Statements should be attached to the budget giving details of the major jobs that are planned to be carried out during the year, or specifying basic assumptions made, e.g. an assumed frequency of breakdowns.

(d) Records should be kept of actual time spent on jobs during the year, and, if possible, these times should be compared with pre-determined estimates of time required. Comparison should be made with budget, after adjusting for differences in basic assumptions.

(e) Budgets and control statements will be prepared primarily in quantitative terms, but will also be evaluated in terms of £.s.d.

(f) The main benefits obtained from budgeting are in the opportunities afforded for long-term reduction of maintenance costs, for more effective co-ordination with production activities, and for providing a more accurate advance assessment of maintenance costs for profit planning purposes.

Maintenance Control—Spare Parts and Materials

Control of spare parts and materials used in maintenance and repair work is of necessity closely associated with the control of maintenance labour. Policy decisions will be taken concerning the frequency of planned inspections, and supplementary decisions made regarding the extent to which parts should be replaced before they are completely worn out. When the necessary policy decisions have been made, a maintenance materials budget can be built up, divided into the same categories as the maintenance labour budget. In order to avoid going into too much detail, it is usual to list separately the major items and to cover the smallest items by a percentage addition to the budgeted maintenance labour cost.

Plant History cards, on which a record is kept over a number of years of maintenance attention in the form of man-hours worked and jobs done, can also be made to indicate the usage of major items of materials or spare parts. These cards will then provide a useful aid to the preparation of maintenance material budgets. The cost of these major items will be evaluated as suggested below.

Control of actual usage of materials and spare parts can be carried out in several ways. In most instances it will be possible for engineering management to approve the details of items required before they are issued from stores. However, in order to guard against duplicated withdrawals from store, it will also be essential to record actual usage of all major items and to compare this usage with the corresponding items included in the maintenance budget—or against previously approved detailed estimates if such are prepared.

The Plant History cards already referred to are a useful aid to control. Certain plant items may require replacement at irregular intervals and it is essential to be able to look back over several years in order to check on frequency.

THE EVALUATION OF MAINTENANCE COSTS

From the previous comments, it will be realised that quantities—whether of man-hours or material items—form the basis of maintenance budgets and maintenance control. Only in the case of material items of low value is it necessary to control in terms of £.s.d.—and then only for the reason of avoiding unnecessary detail.

There are several reasons why it is preferable to control labour costs and major items of materials in quantitative terms in the first place. Basic records must of necessity be kept in these terms, so that unnecessary clerical work in evaluating these quantities is avoided. If comparison is made only in financial terms, and an excess cost is disclosed, no corrective action is possible until the underlying quantitative reasons for the excess have been uncovered. Furthermore, because the true incidence of maintenance can only be assessed over a lengthy period, it is essential to be able to make valid comparisons over a period of years. This comparison is vitiated if made in financial terms, owing to the effect of changing price levels. At the same time, in order to get a perspective view of operating costs as a whole, and to estimate the incidence of maintenance costs on product cost estimates and profit margins, it is necessary to evaluate *total* maintenance costs in terms of £.s.d. It may also be necessary to arrive at an *approximate* cost of *detailed* maintenance operations, in order to be able to consider the total cost of maintenance labour, materials and overheads for any job in relation to other factors.

Following these requirements, various short-cut methods have been established for evaluating maintenance budgets and actual costs. For example, it is usually adequate to use an average rate per hour for evaluating labour costs, based on the average earnings of the entire maintenance staff. If maintenance costs form a relatively high proportion of total costs, it may be advisable to distinguish between two or three categories of labour, but little purpose will be served in trying to be more exact. If overtime is accepted as a regular feature of maintenance working then the overtime premium can be included in arriving at the average rate. There is no point in spreading the premium over those jobs which happen to have been actually carried out during overtime periods. If overtime is only worked occasionally, then it may be better policy to use the normal rate for evaluating labour costs, and to throw up the cost of overtime premiums as a separate excess cost whenever it occurs.

With regard to maintenance materials, it is becoming standard practice not to charge out separately the cost of low-value items. As already described, the cost is apportioned to jobs on a suitable pro-rata basis, usually as a percentage on maintenance labour. A labour-saving method of pricing out materials of higher value is to decide on standard prices which will remain constant for several years. When a quantity of any given material is purchased, any variation between actual cost and standard cost is transferred to a price adjustment account. All issues of the material are then charged out to jobs at the standard price, and this procedure can make a considerable saving in clerical work. Any balance on the price adjustment account at the year end is included in general factory overheads, and dealt with accordingly.

The Allocation of Maintenance Costs

The analysis of maintenance costs by type of job, and by individual jobs, has already been considered. It is now necessary to consider the allocation of these costs to processes and products.

In many firms it is the practice to allocate all maintenance costs to production departments. Materials used and time worked for jobs carried out in any department would be charged out to that department at cost, plus a percentage addition (perhaps as high as 150–200 per cent.) to cover the overhead charges of the maintenance department. The theory behind this allocation is that the production manager is primarily responsible for maintenance costs, because maintenance is caused by use of the plant for production. It also seems to be considered that the production manager will help to improve maintenance efficiency, because he will resent being charged with an excessive cost for this service.

There is a growing body of opinion which considers that this procedure falls between two stools. The chief engineer cannot be expected to worry unduly about reducing costs, because the whole of the costs of the department and staff are charged out to other managers. The production managers are in no position to criticise the maintenance costs—in all probability if they make too much fuss they will have difficulty in getting any maintenance work done at all for them in future years—and even if the departmental maintenance costs do seem to be excessive, they can always blame the maintenance department. The position is in no way improved if production management is given an advance estimate of the expected cost of each major job. There is usually no alternative but to accept.

There seems much to be said for placing responsibility for maintenance costs fairly and squarely on the shoulders of the engineering management. The fragmentation caused by spreading these costs over numerous production departments is then avoided, and they can be looked at as a unified total, analysed by type of cost, and by type of machine. The balance between capital work and maintenance jobs can be more clearly seen, and the long-term trends more easily traced. The fact must be recognised, however, that production management can influence the extent of maintenance work, and this point can be taken care of by basing the maintenance budget on certain basic assumptions—as suggested above—and arranging to "flex" the budget if actual conditions differ from expectation.

The apportionment of maintenance costs to products for *costing* purposes—rather than for control purposes—can still be achieved independently during the budgeting stage, as illustrated in the example set out in the Appendix.

DEPRECIATION AND REPLACEMENT OF PLANT

The cost of an electric motor which forms part of a finished product is directly recovered when the product is sold, together with the appropriate proportion of profit. An electric motor attached to a piece of process machinery will be used for making many products, and it is clear that some means must be found for recovering the cost of the motor—and of the piece of machinery to which it is attached—during its *probable* life. It is of course quite impossible to know exactly how long any particular item of plant will last before it is discarded as being either worn out or obsolete, but a reasonable attempt has to be made to estimate this life, because it would be unwise to try and recover the whole cost of a major item of plant in say two or three years if its normal life was around ten years. There is every chance that competitors making the same product might have acquired the same kind of plant, and be prepared to spread the cost over the expected life of ten years, so that if the industry is working on narrow profit margins, they would be able to under-cut a firm which was trying to recover its plant costs too quickly.

The usual method adopted by accountants for carrying out the above procedure is to capitalise the cost of all plant acquisitions, including the initial cost, the cost of any additions, and of subsequent replacements of the whole of a piece of plant or machinery. These capitalised costs are then written off to revenue over a period of years by way of an annual "depreciation charge".

The cost of maintenance, alterations and modifications, and of partial replacements are usually charged direct to profits in the year in which the work is carried out. However, if alterations include a major improvement element, part of this cost may also be capitalised.

It will be realised that depreciation is not a cost in the same sense that rent or maintenance charges are. It is merely an accounting device for spreading the cost of an item over a number of years, and making sure that sufficient sums are retained in the business to replace each item of plant as it becomes due for replacement.

This is a point that needs careful watching in a business with a large amount of plant, due for replacement at around the same time. Assuming that annual profits of say £10,000 have been earned over a five-year period, and that no dividends have been paid out meanwhile, it might be thought that the cash balance (or equivalent investments) should have risen by about £50,000 over the five years. In fact, if the annual depreciation on the plant due for renewal at the end of the five years amounted to a further £10,000 per annum, then the cash funds should have risen by £100,000 over the five years due to the accumulation of both profits and depreciation provisions. If the position is not watched and fully understood, there is always the chance that the unexpected accumulation of cash may be diverted to other purposes—perhaps in the acquisition of another business—and then there is a serious shortage of funds when the plant has to be replaced. If such a position actually arose it would usually be possible to retain the various items of plant for a further period, probably at an increasingly high cost of maintenance. If this should happen at a time when major technological improvements were occurring in the industry, it might have a serious effect on the competitive position of the business.

In recent years an exactly similar position can arise for an entirely different reason—the continuous decline in the value of money. In the previous example, even if the management made a point of retaining the accumulated depreciation in the business in the form of realisable securities, they might easily find that the cost of the replacements amounted to £100,000 compared with the original cost of £50,000. This means that the whole of the accumulated profits as well as the accumulated depreciation will be needed to acquire the replacements, and the business is virtually back where it started, with all its laboriously earned profits wiped out. In practice, no business is likely to find itself quite so seriously placed, because normally only a small proportion of the total plant will fall to be replaced in any one year. The example serves, however, to illustrate the importance of making suitable provision for replacement of plant, over and above the normal depreciation provisions.

There are varying views on how this should be done. Some accountants take the view that assets should be included in the balance sheet at original cost, and that depreciation should be looked upon as writing off this cost over a period of years. Any further sums likely to be required in replacing the assets would then be met by means of a separate provision for this purpose to be included in the accounts. Other accountants and many economists would favour valuing the fixed assets at replacement cost each year, and calculating the depreciation by reference to this value. The argument behind this reasoning is that a business starts with certain fixed assets. As and when production operations are carried out, these assets gradually wear out, and the eventual replacement of the assets is brought a step nearer. It seems only logical to include in the production costs of any period an appropriate proportion of this replacement cost, and to regard the cost of the original asset as being irrelevant.

Quite a number of accountants, who would otherwise favour such a procedure, are deterred because of the practical difficulties of making an annual revaluation of these fixed assets. At least one large European group of companies does in fact carry out this revaluation, and has published articles describing how it is done. The Institute of Chartered Accountants in its recommendations to members adheres for the present to the traditional method, but has advised its members to encourage the carrying out of suitable experiments by companies wishing to make use of the replacement cost method.

Deciding on Replacement

One of the important policy decisions to be taken every year is concerned with the replacement of plant and machinery. It is probable that in many businesses there is no such thing as a replacement policy. Plant is retained as long as possible, or until repair costs become obviously uneconomic. When replacement can no longer be avoided, the only decision requiring consideration is what sort of replacement to buy.

In the U.S.A. detailed studies have been made in recent years regarding the problems surrounding the replacement of plant. Some of the conclusions reached by American companies are that it pays to have an active replacement policy—to decide what sum shall be allocated for replacement each year, and what plant shall be replaced. Having decided which particular items of plant should be replaced, the next question for decision is—would it pay to wait a year, two, three years, etc., before replacing it? In other words if the replacement is delayed for a short while, will there be an opportunity of acquiring a much improved version? (This is a problem familiar to all motorists who have wondered whether to change to a new model now or later.) If replacement is delayed, then other items can be considered for replacement this year, and so on.

In trying to make a choice among the numerous alternative courses of action, one important principle holds good. Costs which have already been incurred, i.e. the costs of the existing machines, are irrelevant. Accordingly it is quite immaterial whether an item of plant that is being considered for replacement has been fully depreciated or otherwise. All that need be taken into account are future costs that will be incurred with one alternative, compared with future costs to be incurred if the other alternative is chosen.

CAPITAL PROJECTS IN COURSE OF CONSTRUCTION
(WORK IN PROGRESS)

Assuming that a decision has been taken to replace a particular item of plant, or that a capital project of the type described in Chapter IX has been decided upon, control is necessary to ensure that the work is carried out as economically as possible, and that the authorised capital sum is not exceeded without good cause.

The control of capital expenditure is usually carried out in three stages. The first stage is the drawing up of an outline scheme, with a minimum of detail. The purpose is to obtain approval in principle.

If a new building is under consideration, the proposals would include the architect's sketch plans and an approximate estimate of cost. The next stage is reached when approval in principle has been given. A precise budget is drawn up accompanied by the necessary detailed plans (including the architect's working drawings for buildings) and showing the proposed methods of carrying out the work and the final estimate of cost. Specific approval for the budget is obtained at the appropriate management level. If the work involves more than one function, the budget will be broken down by responsibilities. The third and last stage is the comparison of actual costs with budget as the work proceeds. A precise comparison can of course only be made after the work has been completed, but little benefit will be obtained in learning at that stage the exact amount of any variation from the budgeted cost. It is equally useless to wait until the accumulated cost to date has reached the agreed limit, and then attempt to cut down the inevitable excess cost. There is only one way of achieving effective control during the course of construction, and that is to make a periodic re-assessment of the probable total cost, preferably just before a new commitment is about to be incurred.

This technique can be illustrated by taking as an example the erection of a house or other building by a series of sub-contracts, as in the following illustration:

A. Original estimate (approved in principle)   £
    1,500 sq. ft. at £3 per sq. ft. 4,500

B. Final estimate (specifically approved)
    Stage 1. Foundations and drainage 500
          2. Brickwork, carpenter 1,900
          3. Tiler 200
          4. Plumber and electrician 800
          5. Plasterer 300
          6. Fittings and finishes 1,100

                                £4,800

C. Progress Review

After completion of stage 2 the position is reviewed:

			£
Work completed Actual cost of Stage 1			550
Actual cost of Stage 2 (to date)	.	. 1,800	
Estimated cost of Stage 2 (to complete)	.	180	
			1,980
Work not yet started Contract placed for Stage 3. Tiler .	.	.	220
Estimated costs Stage 4. Plumber and			
Electrician .	.		800
Estimated costs Stage 5. Plasterer .	.		300
			3,850
Revised estimate for fittings and			
finishes (Stage 6)	.		1,200
			£5,050

The review shows that if latest estimates prove accurate, the final cost will exceed the agreed limit by £250. This information is known while there is still time to decide what shall be done—either to obtain approval to the higher figure, or to achieve economies totalling £250 by cutting down on stages 4 to 6.

Exactly the same procedure can be followed in reviewing the total expenditure to date and outstanding commitments for any kind of capital project.

CHAPTER VI

CONTROLS FOR PRODUCTION AND DEVELOPMENT ACTIVITIES

OUTPUT BUDGETS

WHEREAS the previous Chapter referred to the *provision* of productive capacity, this Chapter is to be concerned with the *use* of such capacity and with the control of production costs related thereto.[1] The first step is the consideration of the proposed *budgets of production* to be attained from the capacity provided. The level of production that is finally agreed with marketing management for inclusion in the annual policy plans is usually formalised in the *Production Budget*. This will indicate the proposed utilisation of capacity for each section of the factory, and will specify the anticipated volume of output—either in detail for each product or in total for each product group. The production budget serves several purposes. It forms part of the integrated policy plans for the year, and is thus an instrument of co-ordination. It acts as a means of communication to all levels of production management regarding the proposed work load for the forthcoming year. It is the starting point for working out what production resources will be required. Finally, it acts as a convenient base against which to assess actual performance during the year, i.e. performance in achieving the desired output targets.

Its usefulness in achieving the last two objectives is increased if the budget is "phased". A phased budget will show the expected level of output in each month or other short-term period, taking into account expected seasonal peaks and troughs. Phasing is usually carried out by superimposing on the budget the pattern of previous years' production experience. The sales budget will be similarly phased, and the two budgets will have to be fitted in with each other, after taking into account proposed stock build-ups or run-downs. Phasing is of course unnecessary where the variations that have occurred have followed a random pattern rather than showing any pronounced seasonal trend.

Short-term Production Planning

Those companies making durable goods that can be stored without fear of deterioration may be able to adhere rigidly to their production budget, particularly if it is phased to take into account ex-

[1] See the footnote at page 686.

pected seasonal variations. If actual sales should exceed expectation, then the excess demand can be met from buffer stocks built up in previous periods. If sales fall away, then the unwanted production can be stored until required. Only if there is a really major divergence from plan, or there is a serious difficulty in obtaining raw materials, etc., will it be necessary to depart from the original yearly or half-yearly plan. If either of these events should occur, a revised budget will be drawn up, and a re-assessment made of the company's position as a whole, including the effect on profit margins, selling prices, etc.

Other companies may find that it is impracticable to follow the budget precisely, and they may have to supplement the budget with short-term planning. Such companies would include those with limited storage facilities and those making perishable goods. Short-term plans would show both the proposed output, and the methods and resources needed to achieve it. The procedures are described in detail in Part Two (see Chapter III). The proposed output would be decided on after taking into account the original budget proposals, the up-to-date stock positions, orders on hand (if any), and the latest short-term forecast of current demand. As soon as the actual production for the day or week is known, comparison will be made with the short-term production plans, item by item. Any difference will be noted, and steps then taken to correct the position during the next period.

Comparison of Actual with Budgeted Output

Of equal importance is the comparison of actual with budgeted output. In some cases, as has already been noted, the budget is intended to be followed precisely, and a continuous check against budget is then of obvious importance. In other cases, where actual production is based on short-term plans, it is important to keep a check on the relationship with budget. If the level of actual production (and of the short-term plans) begins to vary to a significant extent from the budgeted level, then it may be necessary to re-assess the overall position, and to decide what corrective action can be taken. If this is not done, opportunities may be lost for retrieving an unfavourable profit trend.

The comparison of actual with budgeted output is often expressed as a percentage, usually known as the "Activity" ratio. The two indices "Capacity Usage" and "Activity" can be plotted in graphical form over a period of years, and provide a useful guide to long-term trends. The following example shows how these indices are calculated in the case of companies making use of phased budgets:

Quarter ended	Maximum Capacity (tons)	Budgeted Output (tons)	Capacity Usage (%)	Actual Output (tons)	Activity (%)	
					Plan	Actual
March .	1,200	1,200	100	1,100	120	110
June .	1,200	800	67	800	80	80
Sept. .	1,200	900	75	800	90	80
Dec. .	1,200	1,100	91	900	110	90
Total .	4,800	4,000	83	3,600	100	90

It will be seen that whereas the maximum capacity is 1,200 tons per quarter, the production budget is set at an average of 1,000 tons per quarter. This average budgeted output per quarter is taken as the base for working out both planned and actual activity. This method of calculating the activity index is helpful in arriving at the appropriate flexible budget allowance for semi-variable expenses (see pages 662–663). The indices will be worked out for departments and for sections of the factory.

As stated in the previous Chapter, where more than one product is being handled in the same department, the output must be measured in a suitable common denominator, such as unit tons, standard machine or labour hours.

BUDGETING OF PRODUCTION RESOURCES

Having reached agreement with marketing management on the proposed total volume of output, and on the tentative allocation of this output between individual products or groups of products, the next step is to work out from the production output budget the year's requirements for production resources that will actually be "used up" in achieving this output. These resources will include raw materials, packing materials, man-hours of direct and ancillary labour, steam, power and other utilities. In budgeting for these costs, the first step is to calculate the required quantities of each item, and the second step is to evaluate these quantities in terms of £.s.d. The third step is to specify how the usage and cost of each item can be expected to vary if the actual volume of production, or the actual "product-mix" differs from that laid down in the budget. The detailed procedures underlying these general principles are described under appropriate headings below.

The budget of production resources, like the budget of production output, serves several purposes. When the budget has been evaluated in terms of £.s.d. it can be integrated into a summary budget designed to show what total profits will be earned during the year. It can also be used as a basis for calculating out in advance the expected cost of individual products, and so lead to an advance assessment of expected profit margins, which should be capable of reconciliation with the total estimated profit.

The budget will provide advance warning to factory and departmental management of the resources required during the year. The value of this information will be increased if the budget is phased, and the budget broken down by "responsibility centres". This is also a pre-requisite for effective control.

The combined budget of production output and production resources acts as a co-ordinating link between profit planning and profitability review on the one hand, and operational or "activity" planning and control on the other. Since selling prices must usually be held stable over relatively long periods, profit plans must be drawn up well in advance, and must be based on certain assumptions regarding the volume of production and sales, and the costs of achieving them. These assumptions will be contained in the appropriate budgets. However, as the year progresses, it is likely that actual conditions and actual results will differ from those visualised when the budgets were prepared. Taking production costs as an example some raw materials may be costing more than was anticipated in the budget, others less; steam costs may have risen owing to an increase in the price of coal; labour performance may have varied from standard, or previous expectations; overtime working may have risen steeply. All these factors will naturally affect the unit costs of the various products being manufactured, but it would be extremely laborious to have to continually re-calculate the unit costs of all products to see whether profit margins were being impaired. This task is avoided by comparing actual costs with budgeted costs (after flexing the latter to take into account fluctuations in volume) by departments or "responsibility centres" rather than by products. This comparison can be made without difficulty, and it highlights the direction in which corrective action should be taken. If no such action is possible, then at least the cause of the excess cost will be known, which will help management to decide on their future policy.

Summing up the above remarks, the budget is broken down over products or product groups for the purpose of planning or reviewing profit margins. The same budget is broken down by departments and responsibilities for planning and control of departmental activities and costs. This common link enables variations from budget in either direction to be kept under control, without the need for recurrent cross-reference between the two functions of management. This two-way link can be shown diagrammatically opposite.

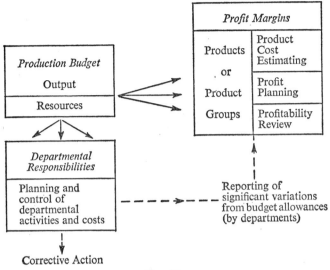

FIG. 94.

Some of the ways of dealing with these departmental "variances" are illustrated in the worked example given in the Appendix to this Part.

DIRECT MATERIALS

1. Budgeting for Direct Materials

Direct materials include raw materials forming part of the product, and containers or packing material that can be directly associated with individual products. Materials that are used in too small a quantity to be worth identifying with individual products, e.g. glue or string, are usually described as "Supplies" or "Indirect Materials" and are included in departmental or factory overheads.

In budgeting for direct material costs, it is necessary to consider separately the quantities, qualities, varieties and unit prices of the materials to be used. The first three of these factors will be provided by the technical specifications or formulae, which will usually set out the quantities, qualities and varieties of materials to be used in making a specified quantity of each finished product. The total quantities of each material necessary to produce the budgeted output can then be worked out by simple calculation.

The next task will be to decide on a suitable price to use in evaluating the budgeted usage. If forward contracts have been placed for the principal materials, these will provide the necessary prices. If materials are bought on a day-to-day or week-to-week basis, an attempt must be made to predict the average price that will have to be paid for each material over the budget period—usually six months or a year. The object is to arrive at representative prices which can be used as a foundation on which to build the policy of the company in terms of selling prices, profit margins, etc.

A difficulty sometimes experienced is that the product specification may be expressed in one measurement, e.g. length or volume, while the price may be expressed by reference to another measurement, e.g. weight. In this case it will be necessary to establish standard conversion factors from examination of previous results, or detailed studies.

2. *Choice of Materials*

Part of the function of Production Planning, as described in Part Two, is to make sure that suitable raw materials are on hand when required. Other functions are to see that the correct quantities are issued from store, and where there is a choice of materials, to see that the right choice is made. This is an aspect of material control that is receiving increasing attention, partly owing to the ever-growing number of materials becoming available. In many cases it is not just a question of substituting one raw material for another. There may be alternative combinations of raw materials, so arranged that whichever combination is selected, the requisite quality conditions will be satisfied.

When this sort of position arises, there are two ways of selecting the combination of materials that gives the lowest overall cost. One way is to sit down with a piece of paper and try out different combinations until one giving a lower cost than other selections seems a likely choice. (If there are many possible combinations, it may be impracticable to try out every alternative.) The other way is to make use of *Linear Programming,* a mathematical technique which can be used to select the combination with the lowest cost, as the result of systematic searching. (See Part Five, Chapter IV, page 932.)

3. *Control of Usage*

Unless adequate control is maintained over the usage of direct materials, avoidable losses can be incurred in several ways. One aspect of this control is to make sure that the agreed plan has in fact been followed, and that the correct materials have been used. There may be a tendency for operators to use excessive quantities of relatively expensive easily worked materials and to compensate for this by using too little of the relatively cheap difficult-to-work material.

Losses may occur at any stage during actual processing, through evaporation, seepage, spoilage, breakages, etc. Humidity may be an important factor during storage, and deterioration may occur if humidity is too great. On the other hand, if goods are sold by weight, losses will arise if the finished products contain less than their normal moisture content. Similar losses will occur if containers are over-filled, or if products are over-weight. (A textile firm selling cloth at a nominal weight per square yard can lose money if this weight is fractionally exceeded, since the yarn is bought by weight and the cloth is sold by the yard.)

For these reasons, a continuous check on the actual usage of materials compared with target is usually an important feature of factory control procedures. This control is particularly important when materials form a high proportion of the total cost.

Control of usage is established by:

(a) Measurement of the quantity of each material used.
(b) Counting or measuring the quantity or volume of output, by products, and multiplying by standard quantities of raw material per unit (from product formulae or specifications).
(c) Calculating the budgeted or standard usage of materials from (b), and comparing with actual usage. (Comments are given below of the procedure necessary when variations in formulae are permitted.)

Although it is usually possible to obtain an accurate count of completed production, it is frequently very difficult to measure the quantities of materials used—particularly in continuous-process industries. Where materials are being issued almost continuously, it may be possible to record approximate weight or volume by means of a measuring gauge, but the accuracy will seldom be good enough to provide data for control purposes. Another method is to measure the quantity of material in store at the end of every control period and to calculate the usage from the "deliveries into stock" figure, by adjusting for increases or decreases in stock. Here again it may be difficult to measure the stock sufficiently accurately to give suitably reliable figures for a short-term control. The only real solution in these difficult cases seems to be to make the comparison over a comparatively long period, and to select for the stocktaking date the time when stocks are low.

In the case of engineering and similar industries, the measurement of direct materials is usually a matter of accurate recording by the stores clerk. A useful procedure to facilitate pinpointing excess issues is to record the standard issue of materials or parts on one type or colour of form, and to record any additional issues on a different kind of form.

Another practical difficulty met with in trying to compare actual and theoretical usage of materials is the existence of work in progress at the end of the control period. There is no short cut—the work in progress must be measured, and its material content assessed. The best solution once again is to arrange whenever possible for work in progress to be at a minimum on the closing date of the control period.

If management is successful in obtaining an accurate count of production and work in progress and an accurate measurement of materials used, it is possible to compare actual with standard usage, and to assess the extent of any losses. Each business will know what percentage of overall process loss is considered reasonable, and only if actual losses start to exceed the accepted percentage will investigations be set on foot.

With batch production, it may be possible to measure out precisely the quantities of materials issued for each batch. In these circumstances systematic recording of surplus material returned to store or transferred to other jobs will be necessary, and it should then be possible to make a straightforward comparison of actual and theoretical usage as each batch is completed. In this way control can be exercised on a short-term basis without the complication caused by evaluation of raw material stocks or work in progress. Stocktaking will only be necessary at, say, quarterly or half-yearly intervals, when an overall reconciliation of material usage can be made as a check on the individual batch results.

4. The Price Factor

Variations in the prices at which raw materials are acquired can have a bigger effect on profit margins than variations in efficiency of use. Although this statement is generally true, it does not follow that management can do very much about it. Nevertheless, it emphasises the importance of keeping a close watch on the prices at which materials are actually purchased, or at which they could be purchased at current market rates. There can be no doubt that good buying can make an important contribution to the profitability of a business. It must be remembered, however, that competitors can be expected to have good buyers also. The object of control so far as material prices are concerned, is to ensure so far as possible that opportunities for profit obtained through good buying are not frittered away through faulty planning, or lack of knowledge about the effect on profits and profit margins of material price fluctuations. Faulty planning could mean requesting, when prices are high, a purchase of a large quantity of materials that could have been deferred until later in the year when prices were lower. Or it could mean failing to substitute a cheaper for a dearer material where various alternatives or combinations are permissible. Lack of knowledge of the effect of price variations could lead to failure to raise or lower selling prices in line with competitors, and thus result in a loss of turnover and/or profits.

5. *Pricing Material Issues*

Before continuing with the review of material control procedures, it is necessary to consider the complications caused by the length of time that materials are usually held in store. None of these complications would arise if materials were purchased on the day they were used. For example 40 lb. of a certain material may have been purchased in April at 24s. a lb. and 80 lb. in May at 27s. a lb. If 60 lb. of this material are withdrawn from stock during May, at what price should they·be charged to production? There are several alternative methods:

(a) *First in, first out ("F.I.F.O.")*

With this method, it is assumed that materials are issued to production in the order in which they are received:

	Price per lb.	Total Value
Issues: 40 lb. received during April . .	24s.	£48
20 lb. received during May . .	27s.	£27
60		£75
Stock on hand at end of month:		
60 lb. received during May . . .	27s.	£81

(b) *Average Price*

Here it is assumed that when a further quantity of material is put into store, it is not possible to distinguish between these materials and earlier deliveries. Hence it is necessary to calculate out a new average cost every time a new delivery is received, and to charge out issues to production at this figure:

	Price per lb.	Total Value
Stock at 1st May		
40 lb. received during April . .	24s.	£48
Receipts		
80 lb. received during May . .	27s.	£108
120 lb. received at average price .	26s.	£156
Issues: 60 lb. received at an average price of 26s.		£78
Stock on hand at end of month: 60 lb. valued at same price		£78

In the majority of cases, a choice is made between these two methods. Each has certain advantages and disadvantages. The "first in, first out" method is comparatively simple to operate if receipts into stock are made at reasonably long intervals. However, it is not so suitable for operation by mechanical means as the "average cost" method. Moreover, it tends to distort the comparison between one month and another if there has been a considerable fluctuation in prices and if stocks are held for some time. Thus material charged to production last month might just have exhausted a batch of material bought many months earlier at a relatively high price. This month's issues might have been acquired later in the year at a very much lower price. The averaging of receipts which forms the basis of the "average price" method has a smoothing effect in such instances. In practice, there are many variations on the way in which the average can be calculated.[1]

A more serious criticism of the first in, first out method—and to a lesser extent of the average price method—is that in periods of steadily rising prices, trading profits will tend to be overstated, with the reverse applying during deflationary periods. They will not be overstated on a strict accounting basis, but they will overstate the profit earned on *trading operations*, as distinct from profits earned through *rising values*. This comes about because the cost of materials used and charged against sales during the year will be consistently less than the cost that would be incurred if the materials were bought on the day the sales were made. Selling prices, however, will tend to be geared to current replacement costs of the materials concerned.

This situation is accentuated when a period of rapidly falling prices follows a period of rising prices. Profits may vanish as the result of the combined effect of lowered selling prices and the utilisation of material acquired in previous periods at much higher cost.

The two following methods of pricing out material issues have been designed to overcome some of these difficulties.

(c) *Last in, first out ("L.I.F.O.")*

This method assumes that the latest receipts into store are used first. Reverting to the previous example:

Issues:		Price per lb.	Total Value
60 lb. received during May . . .		27s.	£81
Stock on hand at end of month:			
40 lb. received during April . . .		24s.	£48
20 lb. received during May . . .		27s.	£27
60			£75

It will be seen that the cost of issues charged to production is higher under this method than under the two earlier methods (£75

[1] See *Terminology of Cost Accountancy*, p. 14 (published by the Institute of Cost and Works Accountants, London).

and £78 respectively). This method has many advocates, but it only seems to be used to any extent in the U.S.A. and certain other overseas countries. Its main advantage is that whereas it does not depart from an "actual cost" basis, it goes some way towards meeting the views put forward by the exponents of the "Replacement Price" method, which is considered next.

(d) *Replacement Price*

The idea behind this fourth method is that materials issued from store during the month, together with materials still held in store at the month end, should be valued at the replacement price then ruling. This is the nearest practicable approach to ensuring that materials are valued on the basis of prices ruling when the finished products are sold.

Adopting this method of valuation means that materials will no longer be charged to production on the basis of actual cost. They will be charged at a notional price, equivalent to the price that would have been paid had all the materials been bought during the period in which the goods are sold. The difference between actual and replacement cost will be transferred to a Reserve Account, and at the end of the year, the net balance will be transferred to Profit and Loss Account as a separate item. This difference will represent the net profit or loss *attributable to buying material in advance*.

In the above example, it may be supposed that the market price of the material rose to 28s. by the end of the month. The entries would then be as follows:

	Price per lb.	Total Value
Stock at 1st May b/f:		
40 lb. received during April @ 24s.	[1]27s.	£54
Receipts:		
80 lb. received during May	27s.	£108
120		£162
Issues:		
60 lb. valued at replacement cost	28s.	£84
Stock on hand at end of month:		
60 lb. valued on same basis	28s.	£84
		£168
Surplus on re-valuation, transferred to Reserve a/c		£6

[1] Replacement price current on 1st May.

(e) Standard Prices

It is now necessary to consider one other method of pricing out materials—"Standard Pricing".

Reference has already been made to the budgeting of material prices and material costs, against which actual prices and costs can be compared. In some industries, it is helpful to take this a stage further, and to actually price out materials at the agreed predetermined or "standard" price. The difference between the actual cost and the standard cost would be dealt with in exactly the same way as the differences under the Replacement Price method. The standard price can be introduced when the goods are taken into stock—in which case there will probably be a variance each time goods are purchased. Alternatively, the goods can be taken into stock at actual cost and valued at standard each time they are issued—in which case variances will only arise on issue. The choice of method may be influenced by the selected policy for valuing stocks for balance sheet purposes.

The method is particularly apt where the company manufactures products whose selling prices are held constant for a considerable period. When these selling prices are fixed, a view has to be taken concerning the average price which it is anticipated the firm will have to pay for materials. The management expect that actual purchases of materials will take place at prices which are slightly above or slightly below this predetermined price. They will take no action to alter selling prices unless the divergence from standard price becomes really substantial. To give them the necessary information to decide whether or not to leave prices as they are, it is more helpful to segregate these price "variances" than to charge the full actual cost of materials to production each month. If the latter course is followed, a lot of clerical work or detailed investigation will be needed to track down the reasons for fluctuations in material costs—and this could be entirely avoided by "skimming off" the price variances "at source".

In the above example, it will be presumed that the standard price had been set at 24s. a lb., and that the rise of 3s. in the price which had occurred during the month was regarded as a temporary fluctuation rather than a permanent rise. Entries will be as follows (assuming that receipts are entered at standard):

	Quantity	Standard Value		Variance	
May 1st Stock b/f . .	40 lb.	(24s.)	£48		
31st Receipts . .	80 lb.	(24s.)	£96	3s.	£12
31st Issues . .	60 lb.	(24s.)	£72		
31st Stock c/f . .	60 lb.	(24s.)	£72		

If it is decided to hold stocks at actual, and to "skim off" the variance when the material is issued, the variance on issue in the above example would be $60 \times 3s. = £9$. A further variance of £3 would arise when the balance of the May receipts (20 lb.) was issued.

The disadvantages of a standard pricing system are mainly the difficulties that arise if actual prices tend to diverge from standard prices to such an extent that the latter become unrealistic. When this happens it is usually advisable to alter the standard prices, and this will also mean adjusting the value of stocks held at the time of the price change. Standard pricing of materials is often used in conjunction with "standard costing" of products (see Chapter III).

(f) *Comparison of Methods*

To complete the review of the different methods of pricing out materials used in production, the five methods described above gave the following values for charging out the month's issues:

	Price per lb.
Standard price	24s.
First in, first out	25s.
Average price	26s.
Last in, first out	27s.
Replacement price	28s.

The variation in prices emphasises the importance of correct decisions on pricing methods.

MATERIAL COST CONTROL REPORTS

The purpose of a material cost control report is to provide management with information which pinpoints the reasons for actual cost differing from budgeted or expected cost. One aspect of this control—comparison of actual with standard usage—has been considered above, and in the material cost control report, the resulting usage variance is expressed in appropriate money values. Another aspect of control is to show up the effect on material costs of changes in material prices since the budgets were prepared. The usual way of doing this can be illustrated by considering one material (out of a number) used in the manufacture of a single product.

The first step is to calculate the standard usage, multiply this by the budgeted price, and so arrive at the expected or "standard" cost. This is compared with the actual cost to give the total variance. In order to break this down into its component parts, the "price variance" is established by multiplying the *actual* usage by the excess price. The "usage variance" is then found by multiplying excess usage by the *standard* (*budgeted*) price.[1]

E.g. Standard cost 25 gallons @ 24s. = £30
Actual cost 28 gallons @ 25s. = £35

£5

Analysed as:
Price variance 28 × 1s. = £1 8 0
Usage variance 3 × 24s. = £3 12 0

£5 0 0

If several different products are made from the same material, it may not be practicable to record the issue of materials separately for each product. In this case, the standard material usage for each product will be calculated separately, then accumulated, and finally compared with the total actual usage. This makes it possible to calculate the total *usage variance*, and the total *price variance* for each material. If during the course of operations the usuage variance shows a tendency to increase, steps might have to be taken to record issues of material for each product over a short period, in order to find out which one was getting out of line. The use of more than one material in a product does not of itself create any special difficulties; the standard usage for each material is calculated in the normal way. Complications can arise, however, where one material can be used as a substitute for another, thus in the following example, an alternative formula is used whenever the relative level of prices makes this an economical proposition.

Standard Formula					*Standard Price*	*Standard Cost*
2 lb. of A	.	.	.	.	. £5	£10
3 lb. of B	.	.	.	.	. £6	18
—						—
5						£28
—						—

Alternative Formula (to be used only if total cost based on current prices cheaper than cost of standard formula)

3 lb. of A	.	.	.	.	. £5	£15
2 lb. of C	.	.	.	.	. £7	£14
—						—
5						£29
—						—

[1] As an alternative the calculations can be as follows: price variance: *standard* usage multiplied by *excess* price; usage variance: *excess* usage multiplied by *actual* price.

Assuming that actual prices in week 23 are A £5, B £7, C £7 10s. comparison of these formulae gives the following result:

	Standard Formula	Alternative Formula
A	£10	£15
B	£21	
C		£15
	£31	£30

The alternative formula will accordingly be used and assuming that actual usage is the same as standard, there will be a net variance from standard per 5 lb. unit of £2 (£30 – £28), due to the combined effect of increased price and changed formula.

It may be more informative to management in cases of this nature to subdivide the net variance and show separately the favourable variance due to changing the formula, and the unfavourable variance due to the price increases:

In the above example this would give:

(a) Price variance (£31 — £28)	£3
Less (b) Formula Variance (£31 — £30) . . .	£1
	£2

Another type of variance which may be thrown up in some factories is a reflection of "degrading" of materials. If spoilage or breakage occurs, expensive materials may be returned for re-use, but because they have become mixed with cheaper materials, they can only be used as substitutes for such materials or as "fillers". No physical loss has occurred, only a loss in value and of effort already expended, which may frequently go unrecorded. It is often worthwhile carrying out a special investigation to find out the extent of such losses. If significant, it may be necessary to introduce routine control procedures which will disclose losses of this nature as a regular feature.

BUDGETING AND CONTROL OF LABOUR COSTS

In the previous Chapter examples were given of the calculation of maximum capacity in the case of (a) a machine-controlled process and (b) unrestricted manual work including manual operations in which mechanical equipment is used, but where the rate of output is determined by the performance of the operators rather than by the speed of the machines.

During the formulation of the annual operating plans, the task of production management is to decide on the extent to which this capacity will be used; and on the production resources which will be required to achieve the target output.

Production labour represents one of the most important of these resources, and for control purposes is usually considered under three headings—*direct, ancillary* and *indirect* labour.

Direct labour is the term given to describe labour that can be associated directly with the products being made. Direct labour is usually regarded as a variable cost for control purposes. In the case of unrestricted manual work there can be no doubt about this, because the output is entirely dependent on the number of operators allocated to the job, and the efficiency with which they work. In the case of machine-controlled work the variability may sometimes be questioned, partly because of the restriction imposed by the machine, and partly because of the lack of flexibility. Nevertheless there is usually scope for flexibility in the time worked on the job—if output rises, overtime will be worked—if output drops, operatives can be switched to other work for part of the day.

Arguments are sometimes put forward by management that labour should be treated as a fixed cost because the firm has decided not to discharge any men who are surplus to immediate requirements—either because they have agreed to a "no redundancy" policy, or because they wish to hold on to skilled operators who might be difficult to attract back again when conditions improve. Despite these reasons, it is probably better to treat the direct labour costs as variable, and to throw up where necessary the excess cost attributable to such a policy.

Ancillary labour is the term used to identify those operatives who are not working directly on the process, but who are nevertheless engaged on productive work. For example, in a textile weaving shed the loom operators would be classified as "direct labour" because they are working directly on the product being made. The attendants who clean down the looms in between weaving operations are a necessary part of the production effort, but they do not work directly on the products as the loom operators do. They would therefore be classified as "ancillary workers." By contrast, the time-keeper who records the attendance hours of the factory employees is only indirectly associated with the weaving shed or with any other productive process, and he would therefore be classified as *indirect labour*.

The key to the difference between the three types of labour is the extent to which the cost of labour can be directly allocated to products, process cost centres, or departments. *Direct labour* can be wholly allocated to a product or process cost centre. *Ancillary labour* can be wholly allocated to the department in which the products are made or the process is carried on. Indirect labour cannot be so allocated, and for costing purposes it would be necessary to spread the cost ("apportion" as distinct from "allocate") over the departments or products on some previously agreed basis.

The different classifications of labour are shown in the diagram below, Fig. 95, of a factory manufacturing one product W in a

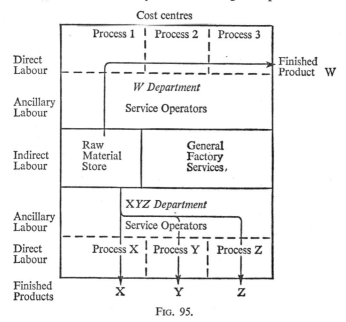

FIG. 95.

series of operations, and three products X, Y and Z by parallel operations.

Direct Labour

Having classified the total labour establishment into appropriate categories, the first step in building up the budgeted direct labour requirements for the year will be to examine the output budget, and to take particular note of the range or "swing" of output between the several peaks and troughs. This information will be provided by the phased budget described in previous pages. When the proposed level of output has been noted, it is possible to arrive at an approximate assessment of direct labour requirements by comparing budgeted output with last year's actual output, and then budgeting for a corresponding increase or decrease in the existing labour establishment. However such a procedure can only give a very approximate guide, and it has the great disadvantage of automatically perpetuating past inefficiencies without disclosing their extent. Also, if the firm makes a number of products and there is a considerable variation in the product mix from year to year, the estimate of requirements may be very wide of the mark.

There is only one satisfactory way of budgeting for precise labour requirements and establishing the basis for subsequent control, and that is by building up the labour budget from the output budget through the media of *labour standards* established for each product. There are two ways of arriving at these standards and each will be considered in turn—"managerial estimates" and "work study standards".

(a) Managerial Estimates

Although it is generally recognised that standards obtained through work measurement provide the most satisfactory basis for control, it frequently happens that management are anxious to introduce control over labour costs before the work study department has had time to establish these standards. This position often arises because work study men must spend time in studying the methods before they measure the time required for each job.

In these circumstances, departmental management will be asked to estimate the man-hours needed in each cost centre for each product. The estimates will usually be based on examination of previous production records. When the output budget is evaluated in terms of these standards, a reasonably accurate assessment of future requirements will be obtained, but once again the extent of "built-in" inefficiencies will not be known. The standards will represent average achievement over a working day after allowing for breakdowns and other causes of stopped work.

(b) Work Study Standards

These will be obtained from work study observations of each process. As explained in Part Two, the standards will specify the time required by a fully trained operator to carry out each operation, assuming that the operator is working under normal conditions and is "motivated" to work efficiently.[1] This motivation can arise from effective management control, or from the operation of a suitable incentive scheme. The standard times will include full allowances for relaxation time, tea breaks, etc., and for unavoidable waiting time due to the nature of the process. No allowance, however, will be made for unplanned waiting time such as that caused by breakdown, waiting for materials, etc.

It follows from the above that a good team of operators should be able to obtain the average level of output corresponding to the appropriate standards, providing that management and organisation are equally effective. If management control becomes weak and ineffec-

[1] See Part Two, Chapter III (pages 303 and following).

tive, if breakdowns and hold-ups become frequent, and if the rate of operator performance drops, all these factors will act to reduce the average level of output attained. The extent of the short fall in output —or what comes to the same thing, the excess time taken for the output actually achieved—can be measured precisely by comparison of actual with standard.

The example below of the two methods of using these standards, firstly for control, and secondly for budgeting purposes, is based on the situation outlined in the factory diagram above (Fig. 95).

Example of Direct Labour Control

Factory management are anxious to obtain better control over the labour costs of the four products they manufacture, because profit margins are dwindling, and marketing management is pressing for a reduction in costs per unit. The work study staff establish the following standard times for product W:[1]

Process 1—20 SMs.
Process 2—12 SMs.
Process 3—18 SMs.

In order to introduce a provisional form of control over product X, pending the establishment of measured standards, the departmental manager states that the overall rate of performance should be 2 tons per man-hour.

Production data for week 1 is:

W: 240 tons output. 250 hours worked in the three processes, plus 30 hours waiting time recorded.

X: 150 tons output. 80 hours worked in all.

Control data is worked out from the above, details as shown below. In this example, "hours" means "man-hours".

Product W

Output 240 tons. Total SMs per ton 50.

Output expressed in standard hours $= 240 \times \dfrac{50}{60} = 200$ hours.

This output in fact took 250 hours, so that the rate of performance was only $\dfrac{200}{250} \times 100$ per cent. of the standard expected from a good team of operators. $\dfrac{200}{250} \times 100$ per cent. $= 80$.

For convenience, this is referred to as an "80 performance", on the basis that standard performance (achieving the specified output in the standard time) is described as "100 performance".

[1] *SMs* is the accepted term for "Standard Minutes" as derived from measurement of work loads. The subject of "work measurement" is fully described and illustrated in Part Two, Chapter III.

One of the advantages of expressing the results achieved by operators in producing output as a "performance index" is that, regardless of the volume or variety of work undertaken, it is possible to compare these indices from week to week, and to draw conclusions from the comparisons.

The next step taken by management would probably be to calculate the performance separately for each of the three processes. This would indicate whether the poor overall performance was being caused by a bottleneck in one of the three cost centres. At the same time the reasons for the 30 hours' waiting time would be investigated to see whether this could be reduced in future. There would also be the possibility to be considered that unrecorded waiting time might have contributed to the poor performance figures. In some cases, particularly where incentive schemes are in operation, it may be possible to calculate separate indices for each operator.

Another useful index figure, which supplements the "operator performance index" described above, is the "overall performance" index. The two indices are similar, except that in the latter waiting time is included in the actual hours figure. Thus in the above example the "overall performance" index for product W is:

$$\frac{\text{Output in standard hours (200)}}{\text{Total time worked on production (280)}} \times 100.$$

This works out at 71, compared with the operator performance index 80. These two indices, plotted from week to week in chart form, give an extremely concise bird's-eye view of the overall efficiency of labour operations.

Product X

A simple calculation shows that 150 tons of actual output compares with a theoretical output of 160 tons (80 hours × 2). The weakness of this form of control is that no one can be certain whether the original estimate was optimistic.

Labour Control Reporting

It will be appreciated that the above control over direct labour operations has been obtained entirely in physical terms without introducing the money factor. Even overtime working can be dealt with in the same way, the premium rates being expressed as extra hours paid for over and above the attendance hours actually worked. In addition to calculating the performance indices just described, it is usual to report in a "Labour Cost Control Report" the details of standard hours, actual hours and the variance between the two.

There will be a separate report for each departmental manager, and a periodic summary for the factory manager. There are many advantages from controlling labour costs in this way. Control data is expressed in terms that everyone on the shop floor understands—hours of work. The underlying reasons for excess costs are clearly highlighted without having to be searched for, and much clerical work in turning recorded hours into money is avoided. Furthermore the trends from year to year can be followed without having to make adjustments for changes in wage rates.

On the other hand, the totals of the weekly labour control reports should be converted into £.s.d., in order to facilitate reconciliation with the weekly pay roll, and to allow for the incorporation of the control data in a departmental operating statement (see Appendix to this Part). Where there is a risk of highly paid operatives being allocated to jobs which are normally carried out by lower grades of labour, it may be necessary to record money values in the detailed labour controls. Again if wage rates have risen during the year, it will be necessary to show separately the excess cost attributable to this factor. In these circumstances the procedure will be similar to that described for the control of direct materials. The "labour wage rate variance" will first be obtained by multiplying total hours worked by the average increase in rates, and then the "efficiency variance" established by multiplying out actual and standard hours at the budgeted wage rates. Ancillary and Indirect Labour (see below) will also be included.

The accurate budgeting of labour costs will only be possible after some experience has been gained of comparing actual hours worked with the appropriate standards. The budget is supposed to indicate the costs which it is anticipated will be incurred if the policy of the company—as expressed in the annual operating plan—is carried out. It is in no sense a collection of cost targets that could only be attained if nothing ever went wrong. For this reason, it is not possible to arrive at the budgeted hours of labour merely by multiplying out the budgeted output by the appropriate work study standards. Some allowance must be included in the budget to recognise the fact that operator performance in recent experience has settled down at say 80 or 90. Again, if the budget is to be realistic, some allowance must be included to cover "reasonable" waiting time, again based on a study of past experience. When the budgeted hours have been determined, the budgeted cost would be calculated by evaluating the hours at the expected average wage rates payable during the budget period.

It must not be thought that the inclusion of these allowances weakens the effectiveness of the budget in helping to control costs.

The reverse is actually the case. Departmental management are usually relieved to find that they have not been set an impossible task in doing as well as, or improving on, budget. Once they become convinced of its value, they will often take the initiative themselves to find ways and means of reducing costs, through the progressive reduction from year to year of the allowances originally included for sub-standard performance or non-productive time.

The comparison of actual waiting time with budgeted waiting time is an example of the "principle of exception" to which reference has already been made. If waiting time were thrown up as an excess cost each week without any yardstick for comparison, management would be forced to review the figure each week, and decide whether or not it was excessive. If an "unfavourable variance" is shown on the statement only when the agreed allowance is exceeded, this is equivalent to the flashing of a warning light. When the light is not on, no management time need be given to it.

In the example of a factory labour control given above, only one product was shown passing through each process. It would be quite possible in some businesses for several products to pass through the same chain of operations in batches, or to pass through *some* of the processes. For example, product W1 might pass through processes, 1 and 3, W2 through 1, 2 and 3, while W3 might pass through 2 and 3, and so on. Under these conditions, it is usually impracticable—or unnecessary—to record the time actually worked on each product. The production record will, of course, give details of the quantities of each product passing through the process, and by multiplying up these quantities by the appropriate standard times, it is possible to calculate the total "standard hour equivalent" of the output. Actual hours worked, either including or excluding waiting time, are then compared with this total, and usually no attempt will be made to break down any excess over the products themselves. For example, waiting time may have occurred as the result of the foreman forgetting to order up the necessary containers for the product, or may be due to a machine breakdown. These costs are much better treated as departmental overheads than as specific charges to a particular product.

If it is found that poor performance is always obtained when a particular product is being worked on, then it is possible that the standard has been assessed at too low a figure. In this case it may be correct to allocate the estimated excess cost to the product until such time as the standard can be reviewed.

Overtime Control

Overtime working provides another example of an excess cost

which is usually better treated as a departmental overhead. It may be purely fortuitous that product X is made during overtime, while product Y is not. The control of overtime working is a complex matter that calls for considerable care. One of the purposes of preparing a phased budget is to enable both operating and control management to calculate in advance precisely how much overtime will have to be worked during peak periods. It sometimes comes as a considerable shock to management when the total overtime premium payable over the year is collected together as one figure, and included as such in the annual budget. Sometimes overtime is unavoidable, as when it forms part of an arrangement to provide continuous working. In other cases, it may be due to seasonal peaks in demand, or to pressures to finish contracts on time, or to the desire to make up weekly wages to an acceptable figure. There seems to be a good case for considering the two categories separately to enable management to concentrate on reducing the "avoidable" overtime.

The first opportunity open to management for reducing overtime is during the budgeting stage. They may decide it is possible to enrol part-time workers during the peak periods instead of working overtime. Or it may be preferable to work an extra shift for part of the year. The next opportunity is during the production planning stage. If systematic sales forecasting techniques are employed, it may be possible to predict with some accuracy the probable demand over the next few weeks or months. If storage space is available this will mean that production can be planned so as to smooth out the work load, and so avoid the overtime working that would have been unavoidable had planning been entirely on a day to day basis.

Control reports can show what overtime premium hours (or costs) have been incurred, but it is not so easy to arrive at a suitable yardstick for comparison. There is no difficulty in the case of regular unavoidable overtime—comparison will be with the budgeted figure. It is the intermittent overtime that causes the difficulty. For example, the budget may show that peak production during one month in the year will cause overtime working costing £1,300 in extra rates. Some managers will say this is equal to £25 a week, and suggest this figure be shown in the weekly labour control as the "allowance" for overtime premium. This hardly seems an effective treatment as it appears to encourage overtime working when it is not necessary, and to give a totally inadequate allowance when it is. The position is not improved by treating it as a fully variable cost, which it clearly is not. Another method sometimes suggested is to give the allowance included in the budget for the particular period shown. The difficulty here is that the peak period may come earlier or later than anticipated, or be split into several peaks. Again, the volume of actual demand may differ considerably from expectation.

In view of these difficulties, a recommended method is to build up in advance a schedule showing the authorised overtime premium hours for given levels of weekly or monthly production, based on a specified labour complement. Each time a labour control report is prepared, the appropriate overtime premium figure is read off from the schedule. No allowance will be given by this method for sudden pressures of work, and it will be assumed that the work load is evenly spread during the period. By this method any excess shown will represent a cost that could have been saved by careful planning. The schedule will provide the information needed for assessing the total overtime cost to be included in the annual budget. The procedure outlined above for reading off an allowance based on the actual level of output (as indicated by the "Activity" index) is an example of *Flexible Budgetary Control* as described in Chapter III above.

ANCILLARY AND INDIRECT LABOUR

The control of ancillary labour cannot normally be based on the measurement of the work load, since the duties carried out may be of an intermittent nature. The loom cleaner may spend a considerable part of his time waiting for looms to become ready for cleaning. Nevertheless it may be desirable to employ a number of such cleaners, because chance may decide that several looms become free at the same time, and it would be uneconomic to hold up fresh work while waiting for one man to deal with each loom in turn.

The usual method of achieving control is to decide on an agreed *allocation* of men—or of man-hours—at varying levels of output or activity. These allocations would be based on the recommendations of the work study department, and would be agreed by the departmental management. Next, they would be set out as a "Flexible Budget", in a similar way to that described for dealing with over-

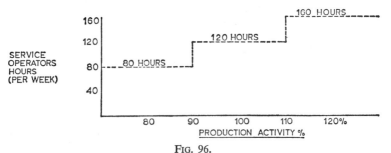

FIG. 96.

time premiums. Alternatively the information could be set out in graphical form—either in the form of a "stepped" line (Fig. 96): or as a straight line (Fig. 97): the straight line being so arranged that it bisects the stepped lines. The stepped chart shows that, if actual

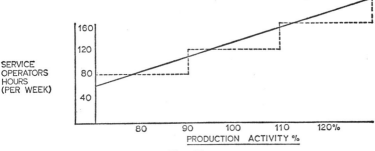

SERVICE
OPERATORS
HOURS
(PER WEEK)

PRODUCTION   ACTIVITY %

FIG. 97.

production is equal to the average budgeted level (taken as 100 per cent. activity), 3 service operators working a 40-hour week will be required. If production should rise by 10 per cent., an extra man will be needed, and if it falls to the same extent, only 2 men will be required. In the straight-line chart these variations are smoothed out. It might be thought that the stepped line would be more effective than the straight-line chart as a means of control, but this is not necessarily so. The reason for this is that if production in the above example fluctuates from week to week around one of the activity levels at which an extra man is needed and use is made of the stepped chart, the following position may be shown:

		Activity %	Service Operators' Hours		
			Allowed	Actual	Variance
Week 24	. .	88	80	85	5
25	. .	90	120	88	32
26	. .	87	80	80	—

whereas if the straight line graph is used, the sudden jump either way is avoided. The use of the latter implies that there may be some way of providing extra assistance short of providing an additional man, and this is usually true.

In some cases, the total allowable cost for ancillary labour can be broken down into a fixed and variable element, and shown either graphically (Fig. 98); or expressed as a formula. Thus in the above example, the total service operator hours allowed for any tonnage of output would be given by the formula: 80 plus (1·6 × tonnage) hours. In budgeting for ancillary labour use is made of these schedules or charts to establish the budgeted hours corresponding to budgeted output or activity. Both budgets and control statements will be converted into £.s.d. as described for direct labour.

Criticism is sometimes raised that the preparation of flexible bud-

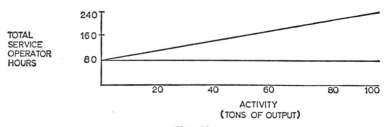

FIG. 98.

get charts takes up a lot of time each year. If many charts have to be prepared it is sometimes possible to make them last for a number of years by gearing them to the percentage utilisation of maximum capacity, rather than to the planned activity for the year.

Little need be said about the control of *indirect wages* because it will follow a similar pattern to that of ancillary labour, except for the fact that the allowed hours will be the same as the budgeted hours—in other words the cost is likely to remain constant regardless of fluctuations in the volume of output.

To conclude these comments on the control of labour costs, it is worth noting that the term "ancillary labour" is of particular value in process industries, which will normally be using "process costing" as distinct from "job costing". Under *process costing* all labour employed in a process department—including clerical workers—is treated as a "direct expense". The labour charged directly to processes in this way can then be split up into direct and ancillary labour, depending on the variability with output as already described.

In a jobbing firm, such as jobbing engineers or jobbing printers, such a distinction is unnecessary. *All* labour other than that working directly on the job in hand is treated as indirect labour, and is included in departmental or factory overheads.

POWER CONTROL

From time to time views are expressed that, when automation becomes more universally applied, management controls as we know them today will become unnecessary. All excess costs will then be eliminated because of the corrective action taken on the spot by automatic means. This may be a long way off, but many firms employ at least one semi-automatic procedure for preventing excess power costs being incurred, and perhaps this must be regarded as a step in the right direction. Reference is made here to the automatic warning bell that sounds the alarm if the demand for current during the previous ten minutes has exceeded the previously agreed limit. If, under a "maximum demand" clause, the surcharge on the whole of the current consumed during the month or quarter is to be avoided, instant action must be taken to reduce the load during the remainder of the thirty-minute control period.

The usual treatment of *power charges* for control purposes is to allocate to each production and service department a proportion of

	POWER CONTROL				Month......		
Cost per KW hr. ....d.	KW Hrs.			Cost			
	Std.	Act.	V'ce.	Allwd.	Act.	V'ce.	
Department A Department B Department C Lighting Mains Losses	Based on actual output						
Maximum demand charge Fixed charge							
Total cost	£						

FIG. 99.

the total cost, according to the metered or estimated usage. While it is perfectly logical to do this, it does have the effect of preventing the make-up of the total cost being seen, unless steps are taken to show the total position in a comprehensive report such as that shown above (Fig. 99).

Although control information would be shown in this way, it would still be possible to allocate the total cost to departments if desired. Alternatively, only the cost of the current actually consumed would be so allocated and the fixed charge, maximum demand charge, mains losses and lighting charges would be allocated to factory overheads.

The effective control of the power consumed means separate metering for each section of the factory taking current, or for those sections that are the principal users. It also means systematic reading of meters, say once a week, after the production activities have ceased, and the calculation of weekly usage. Metering should as far as possible coincide with departmental responsibilities. If this is not possible, it means that apportionments will have to be made, in order to arrive at the correct charge to be included in the departmental operating statements. The amount of interest displayed in power control reports by departmental management will be considerably reduced if a high percentage of the total cost is represented by arbitrary apportionments.

The next step would be to establish through technical studies the "standard usage" of power, under varying conditions and with different kinds of throughput. It may be found that the power consumption should vary in direct proportion to the tonnage of throughput—or to the length of time the plant was running. Alternatively, in such operations as grinding it may be found that the consumption will depend on the particular raw material being ground. Power used for lighting purposes would be compared with a fixed budget figure.

Experience has shown that, where the power costs in a business amount to a significant total, a control on these lines is well worth while. It might be thought perhaps that the introduction of such a control could have little effect on the quantity of current consumed, and that the clerical effort involved was therefore a waste of time. In practice, the introduction of such a scheme usually has the effect of increasing "cost consciousness". This leads to cutting down wastage of power, and to, more energetic reporting of defects that should be put right. Thus, in one example where power costs were brought under control, it was found that conveyor belts and motors were switched off when not in use, whereas previously they had been left running. Defects, such as slipping clutches, were immediately reported. All this was achieved because the control report was prepared in such a way as to show up cost variances by departmental responsibilities. A cost report which merely compared the total usage of power with the standard usage would be unlikely to have any effect on reducing waste, because no one manager would be able to trace the result of any action taken.

If the control is to be really effective, it is important to make sure that the standards really do reflect the power consumption that should have occurred in the particular circumstances. Otherwise variances thrown up on a control report may be due to different conditions, or different materials passing through the process, rather than being caused by inefficiency. The annual power budget, for inclusion with the budget of other factory expenses, would be built up from detailed consideration of the budgeted activities in each department, by applying the appropriate standards, and evaluating the total usage at the estimated rate per unit. Separate figures would then be included for maximum demand charges, fixed charges, mains losses, lighting, etc., based on managerial or technical estimates.

The "allowed" cost included in the specimen power control given above would be obtained by multiplying standard usage by budgeted rate. If the actual rate per unit differed from the budgeted rate, this would be included in the departmental variances, and the KWh figures would then give a better guide to comparative efficiency.

Steam Control

Although the main savings in steam consumption and steam production will come from technical studies, experience has shown that substantial further economies are possible if suitable cost control procedures are introduced.

For control purposes, the boiler plant producing steam is virtually treated as a separate business activity, whose object is to supply the needs of the producing departments in the most economical way. The costs of steam production are controlled by reference to the activity of the boiler plant, as indicated by the quantity of steam distributed. The cost of fuel consumed would usually be regarded as being directly variable with the weight of steam produced, while labour costs would tend to be constant. Standards for steam usage in the production departments would be established by technical studies.

The weight of steam produced can be obtained by measuring the weight of water evaporated, while the actual usage of steam can be measured by steam meters at the outlet points. There will inevitably be mains losses due to condensation and leakage, and it is usually advisable to throw up this figure as a separate item on the control report. This is better than apportioning it over the users of steam— it means firstly that the departments using steam will be charged with the exact quantities shown by the steam meters rather than with an inflated figure, and, secondly, it directs the attention of management more forcibly to the full cost of the lost steam.

The steam distributed to production departments will usually be charged out to them at a predetermined price per lb. of steam, so that if the actual output at the end of the period is less than anticipated, the boiler plant costs may not be fully recovered. This is the same problem that is faced by a factory supplying goods at a predetermined price when output falls off, and it is discussed in more detail in Chapter X.

In other instances, steam usage is charged out to production departments by the boiler plant at the end of each month or quarter at the actual cost per lb., so that if activity slackens off, the cost per lb. of steam will be correspondingly raised. This system avoids complications but it obscures the fact that part of the actual cost of the steam is due to under-utilisation of boiler capacity, and it upsets the long-term comparison of steam costs in the user departments. Considerable complications can occur where different qualities of steam are produced, or where power is generated as part of the steam-producing process. In the latter case, an equitable way has to be found for apportioning the cost of production to the two end-products; in fact there are several ways, depending on one's point of view, but each method gives a different set of unit costs.

CONTROL OF OTHER FACTORY ACTIVITIES

The control of other factory activities follows a similar pattern to procedures already described. Generally speaking, budgets will be prepared to show the expected activities in some detail, together with the anticipated cost. Variations in production output will normally have no effect on these activities, so that control will be effected by a straightforward comparison of actual costs with budgeted costs.

RESEARCH AND DEVELOPMENT

Many industrial firms find it necessary to spend considerable sums of money on *Research and Development*. Indeed, as competition at home and abroad increases in intensity, the importance of this function as a major contributory factor in attaining overall objectives of growth and profitability becomes increasingly emphasised as the years go by.[1] The first step to be taken in deciding how Research and Development costs can be controlled is to examine what sort of activities will usually be carried out, to consider whether these can be classified under broad general headings, and to note what kind of costs will be incurred. Although it is obvious that experience will vary considerably according to the particular industry, or, by reason of size and type of firm, it will usually be found that certain features of the work are the same in each instance—it is for this reason that it becomes possible to write about the *control* of research and development cost in a general sense. For example, it will usually be found that the activities carried out can be divided into the following categories:

(a) Improvements to existing products: Efforts may be made to improve the "sales-appeal" of the product through better appearance, texture, flavour, aroma, lasting qualities, effectiveness in operation, etc.

[1] From the standpoint of the management of the technical activities involved, this subject is considered at length in Chapter III of Part Five (see page 876).

(*b*) Reduction in cost of existing products: Activities may consist of finding cheaper but equally suitable raw materials, or devising cheaper methods of processing. In either case, the lower cost may lead to selling-price reductions, and an increased volume of sales.

(*c*) Creation of new products: Here the object is either to follow up suggestions made by marketing people regarding desirable new products, or to develop new products "out of the blue". (An example of the latter is the creation of selective weed-killers, which were discovered accidentally during research into plant fertilisers.)

(*d*) Fundamental, basic, or exploratory research: In many cases, research workers in industry find that there is a need to undertake work not specifically connected with products. It may be necessary to find out certain facts, or to establish patterns of behaviour, either with regard to raw materials, or to the conditions under which the products will be used. Finding the answers may then subsequently open the way to improvements in specific products, etc.

Consideration of the type of cost likely to be incurred in carrying out the above four groups of activities shows that in nearly all cases the bulk of the expenditure will consist of salaries and laboratory upkeep, and that a relatively small proportion of the total will be spent on materials and supplies. In other words, a major portion of the total will be "fixed" in the short-term, and only in the long-term will there be any significant variations in the levels of expenditure. There are, of course, laboratories where considerable amounts of expensive equipment have to be installed as essential to their work.

Looked at from a purely financial point of view, research and development costs can be covered by normal *budgetary control* procedures. A budget can be prepared, based on the existing or proposed numbers of personnel, the expected average salaries, and the expected outlay for equipment and supplies, and other expenses. Comparison of subsequent actual costs will show whether or not the budget is being adhered to, but, as indicated above, it is unlikely that variances will prove to be of any great significance in the short period, or even within one year.

However, if management are to exercise *effective* control over research and development costs, some means must be found of controlling the *work being carried out* as well as the total cost of the activity. In some respects, the problem is similar to that of the control of maintenance costs. Furthermore, since the work is nearly always non-repetitive in nature (unlike maintenance work), the whole emphasis is on "pre-control", rather than on post-mortems

FIG. 100 Research and Development Control 19...

A. Man-hours

Details of Project	31st March Budget Hours	31st March Actual Hours	30th June Budget Hours	30th June Actual Hours	30th Sept. Budget Hours	30th Sept. Actual Hours	31st Dec. Budget Hours	31st Dec. Actual Hours
Product Improvement								
Project 121	1,400							
Project 122	1,000							
	2,400		2,300		1,800		2,300	
Cost Reduction								
Project 35	800							
Project 37	300							
Project 49	100							
	1,200		1,200		900		1,000	
New Products								
Project 153	500		700		700		900	
Basic Research								
Project 74	600		800		600		800	
Total Man-hours (ex. holidays)	4,700		5,000		4,000		5,000	

Total Staff:
Budget = 10
Actual =

738

B. Costs

	31st March		30th June		30th Sept.		31st Dec.	
Total Staff:	*Budget*	*Actual*	*Budget*	*Actual*	*Budget*	*Actual*	*Budget*	*Actual*
Budget = 10 Actual =	£	£	£	£–	£	£	£	£
Total Salaries (inc. holidays)	4,500		4,500		5,000		5,000	
Other Costs								
Supplies	750		750		600		750	
Maintenance and equipment	500		500		500		500	
Heat and light	200		150		100		200	
Cleaning, etc.	150		150		120		150	
Management, admin., etc.	1,250		1,250		1,250		1,250	
Total Research and Development Costs	7,350		7,300		7,570		7,850	
Budget Revisions								
£								

Note: The figures inserted in the above control report are the budget figures agreed with the management of the Research and Development Department just prior to the year's commencement.

At the end of each quarter, details would be inserted of actual man-hours and costs, also details of projects for the following quarter, together with budget amendments if applicable.

of expenditure already incurred. Bearing these points in mind, a suggested method of exercising control over research and development activities is as follows:

1. Draw up long-term and annual budgets—showing total allocation of funds for research and development (in comparison with similar allocations for advertising and sales promotion, and with the expected overall profit).

2. Break down annual budget into short-term periods (e.g. quarterly) and give quantities and cost for each item (man-hours, total salaries, depreciation, etc.).

3. For the period immediately ahead (e.g. for the next three months), prepare schedule of projects to be undertaken, with list of priorities, and estimated man-hours to be spent on each project. For that part of the budget (e.g. the last nine months) for which it is not possible to foresee in any detail what projects will be undertaken, prepare estimates of total time to be spent on each of the four main groups of work.

4. Reconcile with total budget figures: See the example set out in the two tables in Fig. 100.

5. Without introducing elaborate records, obtain a reasonably reliable record of the time (and money) spent on each project each quarter, and of results achieved. At the end of each quarter, compare actual figures with budget figures, and look into reasons for significant variances (e.g. where times spent on any one project differs materially from plan).

6. Draw up detailed schedule of projects planned for the following quarter, having regard to the experience of previous quarter, and to expected future benefits.

7. Reconcile with budget totals for period, but where this is not possible, decide whether to amend or postpone one or more projects, or whether to press for a revision of the total budget figure.

CHAPTER VII

CONTROLS FOR MARKETING AND ADMINISTRATIVE ACTIVITIES

THE last two Chapters covering factory operations have been concerned in the main with physical activities. In the case of most of these activities there is a specific relationship between the input of resources and the resulting output. These "standard" ratios, which can be established by systematic studies, enable control to be exercised through the application of the "exception" principle. Management will expect the usage of most resources to vary in proportion to output, and attention can be directed to any exceptions from this rule. The position is different when one comes to consider the control of *marketing* and *selling* activities, because continuous and identical effort over a lengthy period may lead to widely differing results from month to month. The end-product of these activities is a decision on the part of the customer to purchase the company's products at the stated prices. There is also an important difference of framework in dealing with the control of the office and related activities which make up the *administrative* side of a business.

Although there is this difference of setting, there is no remarkable difference in the lines of approach. In the case of the factory, the logical starting point for a review of control procedures was seen to be the maximum capacity that existed, and from there the proposed utilisation of this capacity was considered, together with the expected output. The final stage was the planning and control of the various production activities to ensure that the expected output was actually achieved, and that the unit costs were kept as low as possible. With marketing and selling activities the first step is to consider the *maximum possible demand*, i.e. the total market that exists at the date of the review. The next step is to decide what percentage of this market it is hoped to secure during the coming year, and to specify what this will mean in terms of sales quantities and value. The final step is to plan and control the marketing and selling effort in such a way that *so far as possible* the expected sales are achieved, and the profit margins on the products sold kept as high as possible.[1]

In the case of both factory and marketing activities, separate consideration will from time to time be given to ways and means of increasing the maximum potential. The factory will do this by de-

[1] The subject of marketing and forecasting is more fully considered in Part One of this volume (Chapters I and V) from the standpoint of the Marketing and Sales Managers.

signing and building new plant. Marketing management will increase potential demand by designing new products, or finding new markets. Control procedures in each case must be specially designed to suit the particular purpose.

MARKET FORECASTS

The assessment of the *total market* for a range of products can be sometimes made comparatively simply; it is necessary to find a measurable factor that governs demand, and then decide what ratio should be taken to indicate annual usage. Thus the total market for radio valves could be assessed by finding out:

(a) How many new sets are sold in a year, and how many valves each set contains (average figures)?

(b) How many sets acquired in earlier years are in use at the present time, their estimated average life, and how many replacement valves are bought on average during this life?

Assuming that the answers to these questions are:

(a) 1,500,000 new sets, each containing 4 valves;

(b) 8,000,000 existing sets; 6 years average life; 3 valves;
the total annual sales of valves is seen to be:

6,000,000 valves in new sets (1,500,000 × 4);

4,000,000 valves in existing sets (8,000,000 × $\frac{3}{6}$):
giving a total annual market of 10,000,000 valves.

Calculations of this kind will give the total market likely to be experienced under *average* conditions. It is well known that total demand will not follow a steady pattern from year to year, except perhaps in the case of certain essential commodities like bread, soap, etc., for which there is normally no substitute, and for which demand is of a continuous nature. With other commodities, there will be a tendency for customers to defer making purchases when conditions are unfavourable, e.g. due to economic slumps, credit restrictions or increases in direct or indirect taxation. In many cases, these deferred purchases will all be placed when conditions have improved, thus accentuating the cyclical swing of demand.

The assessment of the total market for a particular year is thus partly a matter of calculation, and partly one of prediction. Prediction may be largely a matter of judgment, but it can frequently be based on published official forecasts of future conditions. Thus in the case of countries in tropical regions, official estimates will be made each year concerning the expected size and value of the native crops. These estimates are of great value to companies exporting goods to such countries, because the total market for their goods is likely to vary in direct proportion to the money put into circulation from the sale of crops.

A more precise estimate of the total market can be obtained through market research studies of existing demand, based on systematic sampling.

Share of Market

The assessment of the existing and future total market provides the starting point for the long-term and annual policy planning. The existing market share will be established by comparing the current rate of sales with the total market. The trend of the total market and the actual market share over the last few years will be plotted and studied, and the appropriate conclusions drawn from any unfavourable tendencies. Decisions must be taken whether to aim at an equal or an increased market share in the forthcoming year. Assuming that the management is content to retain its existing market share, and that the forecast for next year's total market is 10 per cent. up on the previous year due to improving trade conditions, this will mean the company will have to aim at a 10 per cent. increase in its own sales compared with the previous year.

At this point two other factors will have to be considered. Decisions must be taken on the extent of the marketing and selling effort needed to obtain these extra sales, and on the production and distribution capacity required to meet the increased demand. If competitors are not particularly active, it may be that the hoped-for additional business will be obtained without any increase in marketing activities, but it would obviously be unwise to count on this. Competition for the extra business may be severe, and if this is to be overcome, a more-than-proportionate increase in marketing effort may be needed.

The factory will probably be working already at somewhere near its economic maximum, and a request for an additional 10 per cent. production may mean overtime working, or making up the shortfall by buying the manufactured articles from third parties. Again, the proposed increased in the volume of business may mean acquiring additional outside storage space for raw materials or finished products, involving extra rent and handling charges.

The net effect of all the above factors is that, before a decision is reached regarding the budgeted share of the market—and the corresponding budgeted sales figure—it is necessary firstly to review the physical or operational aspects and limitations, and secondly to consider the profitability of any additional business. Physical limitations can be overcome, but there may be little point in doing this if the net result is an out-of-pocket loss on the additional business obtained. It may be better in the long run to hold back the extra marketing effort until extra productive capacity has been obtained.

These considerations emphasise the importance of preparing detailed sales forecasts and budgets, co-ordinating the latter with other budgets, and calculating in advance the expected profitability of the company's products; at the same time, in view of changing conditions and changing prices, it is evident that a close and continuous watch must be kept on the trend of actual results during the year. Each of these aspects of marketing and sales management is now considered in turn.

Annual Sales Forecasts

One way of arriving at a sales forecast has already been discussed —looking at the way the total market is likely to behave, and assessing the share of this market that it is hoped to obtain or retain.

Another way is to build up the total forecast from much more detailed forecasts applying either to sales areas or to individual products. These forecasts must obviously be developed within the business—it is not possible to look at a "total market" position for individual products, because no two manufacturers will make exactly the same product. There is always the possibility that the total market for a group of products may be declining, and yet a firm may sell one or two products within that group whose sales are rising progressively from year to year. It is necessary to look at the detailed position as well as the overall position. There is a close analogy here to the behaviour of the share markets. An individual share may continue to move for some years against the trend set by the shares of other companies in the same industrial group.

The usual method of building up a sales forecast by areas is to ask the various area managers to submit estimates of sales in their area for the forthcoming year or other budget periods. These area forecasts would be made on the assumption that no changes are made in existing marketing arrangements, either of product variety, prices, advertising and sales promotion activities, or of sales staff. If changes in any of these are actually planned, it will be better to make a separate adjustment for them later. In drawing up the forecasts, the area managers will discuss the current sales trends with branch managers and sales representatives. This discussion will include a detailed review of sales to the principal customers. It may be known that some of these are likely to be lost, while there may be prospects of others coming in. An advantage of building up an area forecast in this way is that it can be used later as a basis for comparison with actual area sales. Variations from target can then be associated directly with the management responsibilities concerned. When the area forecasts are complete, they are summarised and reconciled in total with the forecasts prepared in other ways. It may first be necessary to make adjustments in the case of areas in which previous estimates have proved to be either consistently optimistic or the reverse.

Sales forecasts by individual products will be built up in the first place by brand managers or their equivalents. These managers will have a special knowledge of developments affecting the products for which they are responsible—increased production, changes in design or price, etc. They are accordingly in a good position to decide whether there is likely to be any variation in the trend of recent sales of each product.

In the absence of any special developments, the sales forecast for each product or group of products will usually be determined by forward projection of recent trends. It will be assumed that if sales have risen by 5 per cent. during each of the last three years they will go on rising at this rate, if they have fallen by this amount they will go on falling, and so on. It should be noted that this forward projection of past results could not be expected to serve any useful purpose in the case of fashion goods. (Each year would have to be considered on its own merits.)

The above procedure may give useful results for a number of years—in fact for as long as the trend continues. Eventually the time will come when an upward trend will suddenly be reversed, whereas the forecasts were probably making provision for the usual increase. There is of course no sure way of knowing in advance when an established trend is about to be reversed. A man walking up an undulating mountain road on a foggy day cannot tell how near he is to the summit. He only knows that he has not reached the top because he is walking uphill for longer periods than he goes downhill. Eventually he finds that he is beginning to descend for longer periods than he rises, and he then knows that he is past the summit. In exactly the same way, business management can only be reasonably certain of a change of trend after the change has first been detected and then confirmed.

It is thus vitally important to be able to detect a change of trend immediately it has occurred, and as soon as confirmation is received, to take immediate corrective action. It is surprising how frequently a sudden reversal of the trend of sales is allowed to go unnoticed for many weeks, until the warehouses are overflowing with unsold stocks. It may be wishful thinking on the part of the management, who are hoping that each week will bring a recovery that never comes.

Sometimes the position is obscured by random fluctuations and seasonal peaks and troughs. In these circumstances several techniques can be used to smooth out the fluctuations, and thus to show the overall trend. The best known of these is the calculation and comparison of the "Moving Annual Total". The "Moving Annual Sales Total" is in fact the last twelve months' sales, no matter when the figure is compiled. Thus if the total is taken out during the month of September, the twelve months' total would cover the twelve months up to 31st August. Next month a new total would be calculated, this time the twelve months to 30th Sepember. Each new total is most easily obtained by adding in the latest month and dropping off the earliest month. Because the total always covers a year, the effects of random and seasonal factors are entirely eliminated. If the total is plotted each month in graphical form, the trend of sales can easily be seen.

Returning to the forecasting of next year's sales by areas and products, the various forecasts will be assembled and compared, and a compromise will be agreed upon if the totals differ. Suitable adjustments will then be made in respect of new developments, etc., as already described. Agreement having been reached with the calculations based on the estimated share of market, the agreed forecasts then become the basis for the Sales Budget.

SALES BUDGET

Sales forecasts will usually be expressed in quantities wherever this is practicable. When this is so, the *sales budget* will also be expressed in quantities as well as in financial terms. In other instances, both forecasts and budgets will be expressed only in financial terms. A merchandising business dealing in many thousands of articles would find it impracticable to consider budgeting in quantities, and budgets would be built up by product groups, in values.

The sales forecast represents an objective view on what is likely to happen so far as can be assessed. Various policy considerations may be superimposed on this forecast, e.g. a decision to suspend manufacture of certain products or to single out others for special attention—and when these have been incorporated, the sales budget will represent the official sales policy of the management. It will not be finally agreed, however, until it has been fully co-ordinated with the factory budgets, and until the profitability aspects have been considered (see Chapter IV).

In pricing out the sales budget quantities, use will normally be made of the current price lists, but if an increase is imminent, effect would be given to it. Where different terms are given to different classes of customers, e.g. according to the size of the annual turnover, it will be necessary to strike an average based on past experience.

Some companies find it difficult to make any detailed analysis of the sales budget by product groups beyond a period of say three to six months. It may then be necessary to work to a "provisional" sales budget for the year, giving broad totals only, and to prepare a detailed budget for the shorter period. Similar detailed budgets would be prepared at suitable intervals during the year. On the other hand, many companies are finding it essential to budget ahead for more than one year. One purpose of these long-term budgets is to give advance warning to the factories of the probable demand for the principal products in the near future. If they are to serve this purpose, it is evident they must be broken down in reasonable detail.

Sales budgets are not intended to indicate what must be achieved by the year end, come what may. They are an expression of the policy of the company with regard to sales, based on certain assumptions concerning customer demand, the state of competition and so on. If actual conditions should change during the year, then it is only logical for the policy to be revised as well. If sales budgets are to be effective as a basis for subsequent control, it is essential for them to be revised during the year if external conditions have changed to any material extent. On the other hand, too many changes would defeat the purposes for which the budgets are prepared. One of the primary purposes is the co-ordination of planned activities and profitability. Every time a sales budget is amended it means the alterations have to be followed through to see what the effect will be on their other factors. Production management will soon begin to complain if there are frequent changes of sales policy during the year.

A reasonable compromise must therefore be worked out, resulting in budgets being maintained unaltered for a reasonable length of time but not to such an extent that they become unrepresentative of current sales policy. Looked at from another point of view, the control obtained from comparison of actual sales with predetermined targets will be minimised if the targets are revised too frequently. Everyone can shoot arrows into bulls'-eyes if they stand sufficiently close.

Phasing of sales budgets will give the same kind of advantages as those applicable to the phasing of production budgets (see Chapter V). It will be easier to tell if the underlying trend of sales is altering if comparison of actual sales is made with a phased budget. The planning of marketing activities, sales journeys, etc., will also be achieved more effectively if the expected swing in sales demand is clearly set out in advance. Another benefit obtained from phasing applies to the planning of stock cover and storage facilities. The agreed aim may be to hold say four weeks cover at all times. If sales are subject to seasonal fluctuations, this will mean that production will have to be stepped up to meet both the increase in demand and the increase in stock cover. Arrangements will also have to be made to provide the additional storage space required immediately prior to peak periods. The phasing of sales and production budgets will provide the basic information required for these purposes. An example of a phased budget is set out below:

Month	Unphased Sales Budget	Seasonal Pattern[1]	Phased Sales Budget
	£		£
January	2,000	1/20	1,200
February	2,000	1/20	1,200
March	2,000	1/12	2,000
April	2,000	1/12	2,000
May	2,000	1/8	3,000
June	2,000	1/8	3,000
July	2,000	1/12	2,000
August	2,000	1/20	1,200
September . . .	2,000	1/20	1,200
October	2,000	1/20	1,200
November . . .	2,000	1/12	2,000
December . . .	2,000	1/6	4,000
	£24,000		£24,000

[1] Based on average sales pattern in previous years.

Short-term Sales Forecasts

As explained in Chapter V, some companies may be able to adhere to their quarterly or half-yearly production plans, as provided for in the production budget without having to make any short-term modifications. With other companies, it may be essential to estimate as precisely as possible the level of future demand on a week-to-week basis. This will apply particularly to firms making perishable goods or bulky articles with limited storage facilities. Some of these firms may be able to work to specific orders received from customers, but this would obviously not be possible with those who give an "off-the-shelf" service. It is these firms that need to supplement their phased budgets with up-to-the-minute short-term sales forecasts. An example of the procedures involved is given in Chapter VIII in connection with the control of finished goods stocks.

SALES CONTROL

Sales control—in the sense of comparison of actual with target sales—can be carried out in several ways. It is usually advisable to make use of all these methods at some stage of management control.

Comparison with Corresponding Period in Previous Year

This is a well-tried method of reporting sales data, usually showing the results for the current week or month, and the cumulative figures from the beginning of the year. The figures relating to product group totals will be of particular interest to the Board and the General Management of a company, because they will provide an indication as the year progresses of the report that will eventually be made to shareholders. Shareholders are, of course, not interested in achievement against budgets or other standards—they look more for a progressive increase from year to year in both sales and profit. In a smaller business the figures will be of equal interest to the sole proprietor or partners. Marketing management will naturally be interested in the same figures, but they will expect to be supplied with rather more detail—usually by individual products, and by territories (areas, regions, branches, etc.). In some cases they may decide it is worth while to keep analysed records of sales to principal customers, or by classes of customer, e.g. chemists, grocers, wholesalers, etc. These records would usually give an analysis by product groups.

The degree of detail provided will depend to a great extent on the ratio between the cost of providing such an analysis, and the average value of sales turnover for the units selected. Thus if the average customer spends £1,000 a month on the firm's products, such an analysis may be well worth while. If he only spends £10 a month, then an analysed sales record by customers would probably be uneconomic. *Total* sales by customers will be obtainable without difficulty from the sales ledger records. A useful compromise can often be made by deciding to rely on sampling techniques. By this means, a reasonably reliable analysis can be made with a minimum of clerical effort.

Comparison with Immediately Preceding Periods

The importance of detecting a change in trend as soon as possible has already been noted. Comparison with previous years either on an actual or cumulative basis will not necessarily provide sufficient indication, because the fluctuation that can occur in the previous year's figures may help to mask a change of trend this year. For this reason it is usually advisable to compare actual sales for the week or month with two or three immediately preceding periods as well as with the previous year's figures. A better way is to plot the key figures in chart form—this will show both the trend and the comparison with the previous year—and if desired, with budget—in a form that can be easily assimilated.

Comparison with Sales Budget

In the case of businesses that have to contend with seasonal peaks and troughs, the comparison with last week or last month suggested above may not disclose a change in trend. An increase sustained over two or three weeks may be merely representing the beginning of the peak season. It is usually true that a better guide to the underlying trend can be obtained by comparison with a phased budget. Such a budget incorporates all that is known about total sales expectation for the year, having regard to any new developments affecting this year but not previous years. It also incorporates past experience on seasonal fluctuations, by phasing the budget on the basis of this experience. Any major divergence from this budget is therefore likely to indicate some unforeseen trend or tendency concerning which it may be necessary to take action.

Comparison against budget is of particular value when used in the control of sales performance in each sales territory. The budgets will have been agreed in the first instance by regional management as being targets that should be attainable if there is no major change in external conditions. This results in their having a natural interest in the subsequent comparisons of actual sales with the budget they helped to prepare. Each salesman will either be supplied with figures showing the sales and target figures for his own district, or he will have an opportunity of examining these at regional offices. The total effect will be considerable "motivation" towards beating budgets, particularly if it is made clear that higher levels of management are very interested in the comparisons. Alternatively, where incentive schemes are preferred, the scheme can be based on such comparisons.

A further reason for comparing actual sales with budget is frequently overlooked. The whole structure of the company's operating policy for the year is usually expressed in the sales budget, which in turn is based on certain assumptions regarding external conditions. The first warning that some of these assumptions may prove incorrect is when actual sales begin to diverge from budget. The divergence *may* be due to slackness or inefficiency on the part of the sales staff, but it is just as likely that the divergence is caused by changing external conditions. Whatever the reason, a clear warning is given to management that policy and plans for the year call for review.

Sales Control Data

Reference has already been made to the desirability of preparing sales budgets in quantitative terms as well as in money values. The original records of actual sales to customers will usually indicate quantity, price and value—the exceptions being in the case of retail establishments, where it is possible that either no record is made at all or that only total value is recorded. The summarisation of the actual sales figures for inclusion in sales control reports will normally follow the method adopted for preparing the budget. Sometimes money values for product groups will be included in the budget and in control statements, the latter being supplemented by quantity records for sales of individual products.

Orders Received or Deliveries Invoiced?

A question which is sometimes difficult to answer is whether summarised control returns should be built up from sales orders received, or from deliveries invoiced to customers.

A summary of sales values, i.e. deliveries invoiced, is essential to the preparation of the periodic financial accounts, but the extent to which these sales figures are analysed either by product groups and products, or by areas and regions, is a matter of choice. Some such analyses will be essential if it is desired to compute profit margins earned by products or areas, etc.

The analysis of sales values by products may not be available, however, until a week or so after the end of the period to which they relate, and it is usually considered worth while finding a quicker way of establishing the trend of sales. In some cases the analysis of sales deliveries by quantities may be obtainable more quickly, and the same figures can then be used for stock control purposes and for the information of management. However, in the case of a company that accepts orders from customers, as distinct from a merchandising business that sells goods off the shelf for cash or credit, the earliest indication of sales trends by products is obtained from an analysis of orders received. Quite apart from the value which management place on an early indication of a change in trend, the efficient operation of a production planning system often depends upon early knowledge of actual demand.

In deciding whether to undertake the analysis of orders received as well as sales deliveries, the advantages of earlier knowledge will have to be weighed against the cost of the additional clerical effort.

Orders on Hand

In some businesses, particularly those in which production is based on orders in hand, it is vitally necessary to know what the unfulfilled orders on hand amount to. For example, a glass-making factory needs to keep a close watch on the outstanding order position, so as to be able to plan well in advance when to close down or start up a furnace. To start up a furnace and then find there was insufficient demand to keep it in continuous production over a reasonably long period would be a very costly procedure. In these circumstances it is usual to keep a running record of the balance of orders outstanding by posting to this record the daily or weekly total of orders received and deliveries made in satisfaction of orders—analysed in each case according to requirements. Provision must also be made for making deductions from the outstanding balance where orders are cancelled. Periodically, individual orders actually outstanding would be listed, and the totals agreed with the balances shown on a record as follows:

Unit = 100 sq. ft.   Record of orders outstanding.   30th June

Product	Orders b/f 23rd June	Orders for Week Ended 30th June	Orders Fulfilled (deliveries)	Cancel-lations	Orders c/f 30th June
PZ 1	105·2	28	24	—	109·2
2	27·6	—	7·60	3	17·0
etc.					

Sales Control Forms

Where some of the orders are for forward delivery, it will be advisable to analyse the balance according to months when delivery is due. Examples of other Sales Control Report forms are given in Figs. 101–106 (see pages 753–5).

RETAIL SALES

A manufacturing and marketing business can obtain the requisite sales statistics by analysing orders received, delivery notes or invoices sent to customers, according to particular requirements. A retail business selling to the public on a cash basis may not be so favourably placed. For example, in shops which sell groceries or other foodstuffs; hardware, and other general goods; and in all self-service shops and supermarkets, there is usually no time in which to write out a written record of the goods which the customer has selected. This means that no reliable analysis by products or product groups can be obtained at the time of sale.

Sometimes a broad analysis is possible by segregating the categories of goods sold—for example in a chemist's shop toilet preparations would be on one counter, drugs and medicines on another. Then by installing separate cash registers on each counter, a sectional sales total is theoretically possible. In practice, it may be found that little reliance can be placed upon this analysis, because

FIG. 101   Weekly Summary of Sales Orders

Unit of quantity ... Dozen Cans   W/E 17th March, 19 ..

Product	Orders Received			11 *weeks to date*		
	This Week	*Last Week*	*Previous Week*	*This Year*	*Budget*	*Last Year*
Product Group A A1 A2 A3, etc.						
Total						
Product Group B B1 B2, etc.						
Total						
Product Group C C1 C2, etc.						
Total						
Grand Total						

FIG. 102   Monthly Summary of Product Sales (deliveries)   June 19. . . .

Product	Sales (*deliveries*)			6 *months to date*		
	This Month	*Budget*	*Last Month*	*This Year*	*Budget*	*Last Year*
	Qty. £	Qty. £	Qty. £	Qty. £	Qty. £	Qty. £
Product Group A A1 A2 A3, etc.						
Total						
Product Group B B1 B2, etc.						
Total						
Product Group C C1 C2, etc.						
Total						
Grand Total £						

Note: An alternative is to summarise by 4-weekly periods.

FIG. 103   Monthly Summary of Area Sales (deliveries)   June 19. . . .

Areas	Sales (deliveries)			6 months to date		
	This Month	Budget	Last Month	This Year	Budget	Last Year
	Qty. £	Qty. £	Qty. £	Qty. £	Qty. £	Qty. £
Area N Region N1 N2, etc.						
Total						
Area SE Region SE1 SE2, etc.						
Total						
Area SW Region SW1 SW2, etc.						
Total						
Grand Total £						

FIG. 104   Monthly Sales Summary   June 19. . . .

Sales	Sales (deliveries)			6 months to date		
	This Month	Budget	Last Month	This Year	Budget	Last Year
	Qty. £	Qty. £	Qty. £	Qty. £	Qty. £	Qty. £
Product Group A Product Group B Product Group C						
Total						
Area N Area SE Area SW						
Total						
Previous years:						

FIG. 105   Monthly Sales Summary   Area N   31st March, 19. . . .

Region N1	January		February		March	
	Actual	Target	Actual	Target	Actual	Target
Salesman 1						
Salesman 2						
Salesman 3						
Salesman 4						

FIG. 106   Customer Statistics   Customer . . . .

Month	This Year				Last Year				Previous Years		
	Total	Product Groups			Total	Product Groups			Total	Total	Total
		A	B	C		A	B	C			
Jan.											
Feb.											
Mar.											
April											
May											
June											
July											
Aug.											
Sept.											
Oct.											
Nov.											
Dec.											
Total											

These statistics would usually be kept in £s.

some customers may insist on obtaining their total requirements at one counter.

Other methods may therefore have to be found to obtain a suitable breakdown of total cash sales. One method applicable to fixed price articles is to maintain accurate quantity records of articles sent to the shops, and to arrange for a weekly (or 4-weekly, etc.) stock check at each shop. By adjusting for differences in opening and closing stocks, the delivery figures for each article are converted into quantities sold. These totals are then multiplied out by the appropriate selling prices, and the total compared with the actual cash received total. Any differences will include losses through wastage, deterioration, breakages, pilferage and clerical errors.

Where the shop sells very many articles, the above method would be somewhat cumbersome. In these circumstances, where selling prices are fixed for reasonably long periods, it may be possible to use the "Selling Price Control" method. Under this procedure, all issues of goods to the shops are charged up at selling price. At the end of each control period, stocks are taken and also valued at selling prices. Reconciliation should then be possible with the total cash sales, and since deliveries to the shops can be analysed, the analysed cash sales can be obtained. This can be illustrated as follows:

		Period No. 37	W/E ....
Deliveries to shop	(at Selling Prices)		
Product Group	23	£505	
Product Group	31	£320	
Product Group	59	£875	

Stocks at S.P.		Opening	Closing
Product Group	23	£360	£620
Product Group	31	£310	£280
Product Group	59	£125	£520

Total Cash Sales	£1,050

Reconciliation	Total	Product Group		
		23	31	59
	£	£	£	£
Opening Stock	795	360	310	125
Deliveries	1,700	505	320	875
	2,495	865	630	1,000
Closing Stock	1,420	620	280	520
Theoretical Sales	£1,075	£245	£350	£480
Actual Sales	£1,050	?	?	?
Pro-rata analysis	£1,050	£239	£342	£469

Apart from the opportunity of analysis which this method gives, it is an extremely effective check against stock losses due to pilferage, errors, etc. The system would not be suitable where selling prices are frequently changed.

MARKETING, SELLING AND DISTRIBUTION COSTS

The sum of money which a company is prepared to spend on marketing and selling costs is usually decided by Board policy. The objective of marketing and selling management is then to use this money as effectively as possible by building up goodwill, stimulating demand and obtaining maximum sales turnover at agreed selling prices. In the case of distribution, the objective of management is to anticipate as accurately as possible where and when to send the firm's products, in what quantities and in what varieties. Having decided this, the next task is to send the goods to their ultimate destination and to store them as cheaply and effectively as possible until they are required.

When these two sets of objectives are considered from the point of view of cost control, it will be seen that there is a basic difference in outlook. Marketing and selling management are not necessarily trying to cut down expenditure—they are trying to make the sums they spend more effective in achieving turnover. Distribution management on the other hand can be considered as an extension of production management, i.e. moving the goods one stage nearer the customer. Like production management, their objective is to carry out prescribed tasks at the least cost.

Until comparatively recent times, it was thought that the only control possible with marketing and selling costs was to compare actual costs with a previously agreed budget figure. This comparison is, of course, an essential part of the overall financial and management control—a company would soon run into difficulties if it plunged into a heavy advertising campaign or increased its sales force in disregard of previously agreed plans. Orders might come pouring in, but the diminution in funds available to meet production requirements and the limits set by existing production capacity might prevent these orders being fulfilled.

Something more than comparison of actual with budget is needed, however, if management is to exercise effective control. The something extra is a check on the *effectiveness* of the marketing or selling effort. This means that an attempt has to be made to compare the "input", e.g. money spent on advertising, time spent by salesmen in calling on customers, etc., with the "output", e.g. sales orders received. There are many reasons why it is extremely difficult to make an effective comparison, and to draw worth-while conclusions. Nevertheless a considerable amount of research and investigation is being undertaken in this field at the present time, because the rewards for more effective control are very great.

Some of the factors which make it so difficult to draw logical conclusions from comparisons are the activities of competitors, changes in the economic background, unaccountable changes in public taste, the ratio of selling price to prices charged by competitors, complications caused by policy decisions of customers with multiple branches, etc., etc. Some of the techniques which are being used to throw light on these problems are mathematical or statistical. The usual aim is to try and hold constant some of the factors which can effect the end result, allow other factors to fluctuate, and then to observe what effect these fluctuations have had.

The more traditional techniques include performance and cost analyses, followed by analytical studies of physical operations. Cost analysis can play a part in determining the effectiveness of advertising. For example, comparative estimates can be made of the number of potential customers who will receive an advertising message, if a given advertising allocation is spent in various ways. On the other hand, this analysis will not show up the different *impacts* which the various methods of advertising will make on the public, nor will it provide any clue as to the *amount* of advertising that is economically justifiable. Management judgment, aided by market research and statistical analysis, provides the only answer to these problems.

With selling expenses, it is usually possible to build up worthwhile controls over performance and effectiveness. Many companies arrange for salesmen to keep a record of the number of calls they make in a week. It is usual to draw up a rota of sales journeys, arranged in such a way that the salesmen call on every customer once in every cycle. The performance of salesmen, in terms of calls, can then be found by comparing actual calls with plan.

This, however, is only part of the story, and further analysis is necessary to find out what proportion of calls resulted in orders from customers. This percentage can be compared with a target figure. The real effectiveness of the salesman can only be judged, however, if the *quantities* of each variety ordered by the customers are examined and compared with some sort of yardstick—usually the previously agreed sales budget.

These checks on salesmen's performance can at best be only a guide to their effectiveness. Conditions change so quickly that to achieve only 80 per cent. of target in the current period may represent a far better performance than 100 per cent. achievement in the last period. Fluctuation of one kind or another will tend to average out over a period, so that a better guide to a salesman's performance and capabilities will be attained by looking at the trends over a reasonable period of time.

Complaints are sometimes received from salesmen that certain journeys or areas are easier than others, and that a comparison of relative performance is therefore unfair. Or they may complain that the introduction of a new product has meant they have inadequate time in which to deal with orders for the other products. In cases of this nature, some companies have sent trained observers round with the salesmen, to find out what an average work load amounts to in terms of time. Studies are taken of the time needed for travelling, for talking to customers, for writing up reports, etc. When the total "standard times" for each journey have been established, comparison can be made with actual performance by salesmen, and the scope for economy and/or redistribution of the work load determined.

ADMINISTRATIVE EXPENSES

Administrative expenses, consisting of items such as salaries, rent, rates, stationery, etc., tend to remain at a constant level in the short term, and to be unaffected by changes in the volume of throughput. This means that normal budgetary control procedures are possible —a straightforward comparison of actual expenses with the original budget.

The fact that actual administrative costs are in line with budget does not however necessarily mean that administrative *operations* are being carried out effectively. If the budget had been prepared solely on the basis of projecting into the future previous actual expenses, any built-in inefficiency will remain hidden.

Significant cost savings can hence only be achieved by *ad hoc* studies of the factors involved—for example by a close study of the organisation structure to see whether this is out of balance or unwieldy, by work measurement in the office, by O & M studies, by improvements in data processing procedures, and so on. When studies of this kind have revealed what the target costs *should* be, the latter can be incorporated in the budget of administrative expenses. Any delay in implementing the recommendations will then be spotlighted when actual expenses are compared with the streamlined budget.

CHAPTER VIII

CONTROL OF WORKING CAPITAL AND DISPOSABLE FUNDS

HAVING examined some of the ways in which management can exercise control over the operations carried out in a manufacturing and marketing business, it is now opportune to consider the other side of the coin. In other words, to consider how the attainment of the desired return on capital employed is dependent on the control of capital resources as well as on the earning of profits.

Fixed assets such as plant and machinery have already been considered in Chapter V. The primary aim here is to obtain maximum availability and maximum utilisation at a minimum cost of maintenance. The same consideration would apply to capital invested in land and buildings. There is normally no question of finding an alternative use for the *money* once it has been sunk in acquiring fixed assets—since with the possible exception of motor vehicles, re-sale values would not justify a change of mind. On the other hand there may be a possibility of change of use of the *asset*—a building can be changed from a warehouse to an office—a piece of machinery can be altered to deal with a different range of products. Such alterations, however, will usually involve the spending of large sums of money, and as such come under the heading of a "project" to be considered on its own merits. Such projects are reviewed in the next Chapter.

Other assets such as stocks of all kinds, work in progress, debtors, realisable investments and cash come into a different category, because they either represent cash, or can be turned into cash within a comparatively short space of time. For this reason they are usually referred to as "Current Assets". From the point of view of control, they can be divided into two groups:

(a) Working assets needed for existing operations.
(b) Disposable Funds.

WORKING ASSETS AND WORKING CAPITAL

Working assets needed for existing operations include stocks of raw materials, work-in-process, stocks of finished products, amounts owing by customers and a "cash cushion". Confusion is sometimes caused because of the custom of describing working assets as "working capital". Working capital indicates the amount of shareholders' or proprietors' capital which must be set aside for working assets and is therefore the figure usually looked at from a financial control viewpoint. It does not represent the total value of these assets, because the latter are partly financed by suppliers, in the period of credit allowed for payment of the goods. This credit is equivalent to a permanent interest-free loan.

One of the characteristics of working capital or "circulating capital" as it is sometimes called, is that it is continually changing in form, although there may be no change in the total sum involved. Thus cash will be used to pay for raw materials, raw materials are converted into finished products, finished products when sold become amounts due from customers, and the latter are eventually converted back into cash. This is illustrated in the following example (which has been deliberately simplified by assuming that no profit is being earned).

A business decides to start immediate production of a new range of products by manual methods. £12,000 is allotted as working capital for this project, and pending later delivery of suitable plant, it is decided to sell the finished product at a price equivalent to the cost of production. On the day that this new production is about to start, the £12,000 has been allocated as follows:

Stocks of raw materials for 4 months' production . . .	£8,000
Cash in hand for 4 months' wages	£4,000
	£12,000

At the end of 2 months the position is as follows:

Stocks of raw materials for 2 months' production . . .	£4,000
Finished products stocks, 2 months' production (at cost) . .	£6,000
Cash in hand for 2 months' wages	£2,000
	£12,000

At the end of month 3, one further month's production has been made and one month's production sold at cost. The position is then:

Stocks of raw material for 1 month's production . . .	£2,000
Finished product stocks, 2 months (at cost)	£6,000
Amounts due from customers	£3,000
Cash in hand for 1 month's wages.	£1,000
	£12,000

At the end of month 4, a further month's production has been made and sold, and customers have paid up for their previous month's purchases. The position then is:

Stocks of raw materials	Nil
Finished product stocks, 2 months (at cost)	£6,000
Amounts due from customers	£3,000
Cash received from customers	£3,000
	£12,000

£2,000 out of the sum received from customers is then used to purchase further raw material stocks, and the final position is then the same as at the end of month 3:

Stocks of raw materials for 1 month's production . . .	£2,000
Finished product stocks, 2 months (at cost)	£6,000
Amounts due from customers	£3,000
Cash in hand for 1 month's wages.	£1,000
	£12,000

It will be seen that despite all these movements, the total working capital remains unchanged at £12,000.

If instead of paying for these new supplies, arrangements had been made with suppliers for 1 month's credit, working capital requirements would be reduced to £10,000, and £2,000 cash would be available for other purposes. The position could then be set out as follows:

Stocks of raw materials (not yet paid for) . .	£2,000
Finished product stocks	£6,000
Debtors	£3,000
Cash (working balance)	£1,000
	£12,000
Less Creditors for raw materials . . .	£2,000
Working Capital	£10,000
Cash available for other purposes . . .	£2,000

If creditors could be persuaded to give *three* months' credit, then the position would be:

Working capital	£6,000
Cash available for other purposes . . .	£6,000

and so on.

Several conclusions can be drawn from this example:

1. Taking advantage of the maximum period allowed by suppliers for payment of invoices will automatically help to reduce requirements for working capital. The only reason for not taking advantage of the maximum credit period would be if the business was not short of capital, and if favourable discount terms were offered by the suppliers.

2. It is clear that the longer a given sum of money takes to circulate as described above, the more working capital will be needed to finance operations meanwhile. Hence another way of reducing working capital requirements is to ensure that there is a quick "turn-round", i.e. getting cash back to cash in the shortest possible time. One way of achieving this is to cut down on the average stock cover held. If finished product stocks in the above example were cut from 2 months' to 1 month's cover, a further £3,000 would be released for other purposes. Another way is to keep a close watch on debtors' accounts, to make sure that overdue accounts are kept to a minimum.

3. In the above example there was in fact no "margin of safety". If the debtors had not paid up regularly or if sales had lagged, the business would have been short of working capital. A margin of safety, a cash cushion, is therefore necessary, but investigations should be made from time to time to make sure it is not excessive.

In normal circumstances a company will hope to earn a profit on each sale that it makes, and at the same time to recover in the selling price a suitable contribution towards depreciation of fixed assets. When trading conditions are difficult a company may sometimes have to cut its prices in order to retain business, but unless in the long term prices are higher than current outgoings, there will be no profit for shareholders and no funds being accumulated for the subsequent replacement of worn-out or obsolescent plant.

STOCK CONTROL

The planning and control of raw material stock is usually a joint responsibility of the buyer and the production manager. Finished goods stocks are frequently found to be no one's particular responsibility, probably because they in fact represent buffer stocks between the two main divisions of the business, production and marketing.

There is always a conflict of interest over the quantity of stocks which should be held, particularly where there is a seasonal peak. Production management would like to keep production at a steady level throughout the year, and let buffer stocks be used to even out the peaks and troughs in demand. Marketing management would like to keep adequate stocks of all products throughout the year, to ensure that no sales are lost through being out of stock. General management, seeking to obtain the maximum return on capital, is anxious that stocks shall be kept as low as possible throughout the year, even if sales are lost now and again.

A compromise arrangement is to plan for level production for a number of months, then to step up the output to a higher level, to be maintained until the peak demand is reached and finally to reduce production to the lowest possible level immediately prior to the slack season. Three changes in the level of production thus have to be planned for, but advance knowledge of requirements will help in attaining smooth change-over and stability for 3–4 months will help to improve efficiency. By this arrangement, stock cover can be held within certain well-defined limits throughout the year. It will certainly not fluctuate as much as it would if production were held level throughout the year.

If some arrangement of the kind described above is planned, then the expected demand in the period immediately ahead must be ascertained, either by summarising orders already received, or by forecasting the forward short-term demand. In forecasting on a short-term basis, phased budgets combined with analyses of current trends provide a very useful aid. Knowing the expected level of demand, and the actual stocks on hand at the end of the previous week, it is possible to calculate at what level production should be set over the forward period to keep stocks of finished goods within the planned limits.

Two things can upset these plans. Actual weekly sales can differ from expected demand, and actual weekly production can also differ from planned production. If one or both of these events occur, the actual stock of finished goods at the end of the week will differ from the planned stock level on that date—e.g. it may be 50 dozen cases over. At first sight, it might be thought that the remedy would be to reduce the planned production for the following week by this amount—50 dozen cases. Assuming that the whole of this excess stock comes about as a result of a fall in demand, it could be due either to the beginning of a downward trend, or it could be merely a random fluctuation, which will perhaps be more than made good in the following week. In the latter circumstances, to reduce the next week's production by 50 dozen cases would merely accentuate the difficulty of meeting an abnormally high weekly demand. On the other hand to make no reduction at all would lead to overstocking if a downward trend has developed.

The solution recommended is to "smooth out" the variance, by adjusting a fixed percentage of it each week—say 25 per cent. If demand recovers immediately, not much harm will have been done. If it goes on falling, a further 25 per cent. can be deducted next week, and a start will have been made in matching up the production level to the reduced level of demand. If substantial differences occur, then it will be advisable to re-plan the whole position on the basis of revised forecasts.

Stock control as just described calls for the regular provision of quantitative information. At the same time, information about stocks is also required in terms of value, usually for two reasons. Firstly, stock values are required periodically in order to be able to calculate the profits made during each period and prepare a Balance Sheet. Secondly, a value control is often maintained as a check against losses, pilferage, etc. Goods put into stock are valued either at cost, standard cost, or standard selling price. Goods taken out of stock for despatch to customers are priced out at the same value, and the control account balance correspondingly reduced. Periodically the actual stock on hand is listed, priced out at the appropriate value, totalled and agreed with the control account balance.

It is frequently found that the quantities and value records are maintained in parallel. It should usually be possible to make one basic record serve both purposes. Stock Control is discussed in more detail in Part Two, Chapter III (see pages 341–344).

(see pages 341–344)

CASH CONTROL

Responsibility for the control of cash is usually placed with financial management. Apart from the security aspect, control consists mainly in ensuring that adequate funds are available when required, and that surplus funds are not left lying idle. The key to control is accordingly the forecast made of future cash receipts and cash requirements. These forecasts are often made on a provisional basis for several years ahead, on an annual basis, and more precisely for shorter periods ahead. The information for these forecasts is obtained from operating budgets, budgeted balance sheets and discussions with management. When the annual cash forecast has been agreed, it will usually be known as the "cash budget", and incorporated in the summary budgets.

The short-term forecasts will be considered, and if at any time there is likely to be a shortage of funds, steps will have to be taken to adjust the position, either by postponing certain expenditure, or by borrowing the balance required. (The same procedure will have been carried out before agreeing the annual cash budget.) A daily or weekly check will be kept on the actual cash balance, and comparison made with the short-term plan. Explanations will be obtained for any major discrepancies.

The ordinary cash book does not provide a very good basis for forecasting cash requirements, or obtaining a view on current movements, because so many different types of cash transactions are mixed up and interspersed with each other. Neither does the Balance Sheet provide any real help—it merely shows by how much the cash balance has increased or decreased during the year. A statement showing the main movements of cash during the year can, however, be prepared by comparing the latest Balance Sheet with the preceding one. Such a statement is usually described as a "Source and Application of Funds" Statement. An example of such a statement is given in the worked example contained in the Appendix to this Part.

DISPOSABLE FUNDS

During the course of trading, profits and depreciation provisions will gradually accumulate, and the cash balance will show a corresponding increase. Part of this increase will be subsequently absorbed by taxation charges for the year, and part may be needed to finance additional working capital requirements. The balance will be available for allocation to other uses, in accordance with agreed policy decisions.

Some of the ways in which these available funds can be utilised, and some of the points which influence the policy decisions are considered below.

Replacement of Depreciated Assets

One of the purposes of charging depreciation provisions in the profit and loss account is to ensure that an adequate amount of revenue received is accumulated in the business to meet the eventual need to replace fixed assets such as buildings, plant and machinery. There is no necessity, however, for the funds obtained in this way actually to be used for replacement of the particular assets which have been depreciated, or in fact, for replacement of any assets. The Directors may decide not to replace all or part of the assets when they wear out, but to embark upon some new project, and to use the accumulated depreciation provisions for this purpose. Alternatively, the monies could be used to finance additional working capital requirements, but in this case the Directors would need to be satisfied that, as and when the assets being depreciated were due for renewal, some other way of raising the cash required for replacement would be available.

In periods of inflation it will be usual to find that the cost of replacing assets is considerably higher than the original cost of the item being replaced. If depreciation has been calculated by reference to the *original* cost of the asset—the usual procedure—then additional sums will have to be allocated out of profits, over and above the depreciation provisions, to meet the higher cost of replacement. If depreciation has been calculated each year on the basis of the estimated *replacement* cost of the asset, then the accumulated depreciation provision will probably still not cover the full cost of the replacement. This is made clear in the following example, which assumes 10 per cent. depreciation, and a 5 per cent. rise in values each year.

	Original Cost	Estimated Replacement Cost	Depreciation on Replacement Value (10% p.a.)
	£	£	£
Year 1 . .	1,000	1,000	100
Year 2 . .	1,000	1,050	105
Year 3 . .	1,000	1,102	110
Year 4 . .	1,000	1,157	116
Year 5 . .	1,000	1,215	121
Year 6 . .	1,000	1,276	128
Year 7 . .	1,000	1,340	134
Year 8 . .	1,000	1,407	141
Year 9 . .	1,000	1,477	148
Year 10 . .	1,000	1,551	155
			£1,258

Thus nearly £300 would have to be provided out of profits in addition to the depreciation provision. Alternatively, the shortfall could be made good each year by retrospective adjustments to the depreciation provisions. Factors to be taken into account before deciding to replace a particular asset are discussed in the next Chapter.

Dividends to Shareholders

(a) Maximum Distribution

The maximum sum that can be distributed to shareholders as dividend is determined by the amount of profit earned, as recorded in the official Balance Sheet and Profit and Loss Account. Under the provisions of the Companies Acts, it is illegal to distribute as dividend more than the profits earned. Shareholders' capital can only be repaid in certain prescribed circumstances, and then only if the regulations laid down by the Acts are followed. Various accounting procedures have been established over the years to ensure that profits are correctly stated. At one time the primary objective was to ensure that profits were not *overstated*. Since the passing of the 1948 Companies Act, however, auditors have to certify that the accounts as drawn up represent a true and fair view of the state of the company's affairs. Accordingly, accountants now have to ensure that profits are neither overstated nor understated. In carrying out these responsibilities, they need to be satisfied that depreciation rates are adequate, and that stocks on hand at balance sheet dates are correctly valued.

Accountants are not technical experts, and cannot be expected to make an assessment themselves of the depreciation rates required, or of the values of stocks on hand. They have to rely on technical opinions on these matters. On the other hand, they have established certain general principles to help them ensure that profits are correctly calculated. Two of the most widely accepted principles are *conservatism in assessment* of unrealised values, and *consistency of treatment* from year to year.

One of the rules adopted in the interests of conservatism is never to include a profit in the accounts until it is realised (except in special cases, such as apply to companies engaged on long-term contracts). An example of the application of this rule is that even if the market price of raw materials held at the Balance Sheet date had risen well over cost, the materials would still be valued at cost, and no profit would be taken until the finished articles had been made and sold. The best example of consistency from year to year is seen in the valuation of finished goods stocks and work in progress. Whatever method of valuing these stocks has been adopted in the past—i.e. at material cost, prime cost, factory cost, full cost, etc.—will be used in the future. If it is really desired to change the basis of valuation, then it would be necessary to recalculate the valuations made in earlier years, and to attach a suitable note to the accounts. It would also be essential to obtain the agreement of the Inland Revenue officials.

(b) Minimum Distributions

It has long been customary for well-managed companies to be conservative in their dividend distributions. By retaining profits in the business, money can be spent on additions or improvements that would otherwise not have been available. Also, it is easier to maintain a constant dividend record from year to year if profits are not distributed up to the hilt in the good years.

On the other hand, recent events have shown that to be too conservative in providing shareholders with income on their holdings may give rise to the possibility of take-over bids. The actual rate of dividend declared will depend upon these factors, as well as on purely financial considerations, e.g. the need to conserve funds for repayment of maturing long-term indebtedness.

Investment in New Projects

In deciding on suitable projects for the employment of funds not required for other purposes, the usual procedure is to consider a number of alternatives and to select the one most likely to yield the desired return on the capital expended. Some of the ways in which this can be done are described in the next Chapter. In some cases other considerations may apply. Capital expenditure may be incurred on new factory buildings in order to give better working conditions; on improved welfare facilities for the staff; or on new head offices, in order to collect together scattered staff and improve co-ordination. Many of the items of this nature are not strictly justified on a short-term profit-earning basis—it is really a matter of striking a reasonable compromise between the interests of shareholders and those of the management and staff.

In other cases funds are provided for facilities which it is *hoped* will contribute to long-term profits, but in respect of which it is quite impossible to make any precise estimate of the eventual benefit. Such projects would include the provision of research laboratories, management training centres, etc. Decisions regarding allocation of funds for these purposes are policy decisions, on which little or no guidance can be obtained from the application of control techniques.

CHAPTER IX

AD HOC DECISIONS AND PROJECT EVALUATION

MANY decisions made by management relate to repetitive activities. For example, decisions on the level of production, the number of salesmen required, the price at which goods are sold, have to be taken over and over again—these are the decisions covered by the usual budgeting and short-term planning procedures. On the other hand, decisions on the best way of increasing productive capacity, whether to replace a certain machine with a new model that has just become available, to open up a new market overseas, to mechanise a manual process—these relate to "once-for-all", or "*ad hoc*" problems that are unlikely to be repeated in precisely the same form. They can conveniently be described as *ad hoc* decisions.

With repetitive activities, it is the usual practice to examine the performance achieved and the costs incurred *after* the end of the period being reviewed. No examination of control data can affect what has already happened, but because it is known that the same operations or activities will be repeated, the information can be used to influence future performance and costs, through taking appropriate corrective action. One of the basic features of *ad hoc* decisions is that there are always alternative courses of action to be considered. They can be sub-divided as follows:

(*a*) Selecting from alternative courses of action, when no capital outlay is involved.

(*b*) The comparison and evaluation of alternative ways of investing capital funds, i.e. project decisions.

Each of these are considered in turn.

SELECTING A COURSE OF ACTION

Certain aspects of choosing from alternatives have been considered under the heading of Profit Planning in Chapter IV. The problems dealt with there were of the kind that occur with considerable frequency, and for this reason, regular control information would be provided, such as product costs and profit margins or contributions.

Other instances can occur where decisions are required for problems which arise only at infrequent intervals, and these will call for the working up of control data on an *ad hoc* basis. Typical examples of this kind of decision are: whether to manufacture or to buy-in a component needed in a finished product; whether to carry out certain engineering or maintenance work in the company's own workshops or to put the work out to contract.

The guiding principle to be observed in arriving at the decision is to include on the comparative statement prepared for the purpose only those values and costs that will be influenced by the decision. All past expenditures and all future costs which will continue to be incurred but which will be unaffected by the decision, must be ignored. Thus in arriving at the total cost of carrying out work in the company's workshops it would be wrong to include those general overheads—such as Head Office administrative charges—which would not vary whichever way the decision went.

The question often arises whether floor space should be included in the costs of alternative courses of action. This is a similar problem to the treatment of administration costs. If there is no alternative use for the space, then the cost should be excluded. If the space can be used for other profitable purposes, then the "opportunity cost" should be taken into account.

"Opportunity Costs"

By this title is meant the cost of a lost opportunity, rather than the actual cost incurred. For example, take the case of a firm owning two houses for use of its area management—a small house on the south coast and a larger house in a nearby market town. The smaller house costs £100 p.a. in rates and maintenance charges, the larger one £300 p.a. A decision is made to reduce overheads by using only the smaller house, and to let the other. Both houses are equally suitable for the company's purpose. It is subsequently realised that this was the wrong decision. In view of its situation the smaller house could have been let for £600 p.a. whereas the larger house was actually let for only £200 p.a. (tenants paying all charges in each case).

The "opportunity cost" of choosing to occupy the smaller house is:

Rent lost (£600 − £200)	£400
Less saving in maintenance charges etc. (£300 − £100)	£200
	£200 p.a.

The actual cost of the house occupied (£100 per annum) is irrelevant, and so is the comparison of annual charges without taking into account potential income.

The question of alternative uses for money crops up when decisions have to be taken whether to make or buy a particular article, or whether to rent or buy a building. The latter is a particularly complex problem. Factors to be reviewed include:

(a) The percentage of the cost obtainable on mortgage, and the interest payable.

(b) The amount of marginal capital needed to complete the purchase or erection of the building, and the alternative uses to which it could be put.

(c) The comparison of the "opportunity costs" of each alternative.

(d) The probable long-term trend of property values.

Utilisation of Alternative Capacity

Another example of an alternative choice problem can arise when the policy to be adopted in allocating production levels between two or more similar factories has to be decided. For example, in a manufacturing business the firm's sole product is made at Factory A and Factory B. For a number of years, the latter factory has produced 60 per cent. of the total output. The directors regularly keep an eye on the all-in costs at each factory, and for the current year, the planned utilisation and the estimated costs are as follows:

	Factory A	Factory B
Planned output per week	80 tons	120 tons
Cost per ton	£3 6s. 0d.	£3 12s. 0d.

It is quite possible that the directors may consider taking advantage of the cheaper "all-in" cost of Factory A by switching to it some of the tonnage produced at Factory B. In order to review the possibilities they call for a statement of *maximum* weekly capacity at each factory, which is found to be as follows:

Factory A   100 tons   *Factory B*   200 tons.

Accordingly, they may decide to make use of the maximum capacity at Factory A by switching 20 tons per week to it. The accountant then works out the new allocations and the new all-in costs as follows:

	Factory A	Factory B
Planned output per week	100 tons	100 tons
"All-in" cost per ton	£3 0s. 0d.	£4 0s. 0d.

It may be imagined that the directors are on the point of issuing the necessary instructions when it is suddenly realised that the new arrangement will actually *increase* total costs by £4 per week, instead of reducing them as had been hoped. This is confirmed by the accountant, who produces a statement showing the total costs broken down into fixed and variable elements. Under the original plan, the costs were:

	Factory A		Factory B
Fixed charges per week	£120		£240
Variable costs 80 @ 36s.	£144	120 @ 32s.	£192
	£264		£432

while under the revised plan, the costs are:

	Factory A		Factory B
Fixed charges per week	£120		£240
Variable costs 100 @ 36s.	£180	100 @ 32s.	£160
	£300		£400

Hence the net result of switching 20 tons from Factory B to Factory A is to increase total variable costs by £4 per week. The original comparison was misleading because of the differences in the percentage utilisation of maximum capacity in the two factories. If the cost of production had been worked out on the basis of 100 per cent. utilisation of capacity at each factory, Factory B at £2 16s. 0d. per ton would show a lower all-in cost than Factory A (£3 per ton).

The conclusions reached from this example are that "all-in" costs per unit can be misleading when it comes to choosing a course of action, and that the only real guide is provided by a comparison of variable costs applicable to each alternative. Furthermore, no meaningful conclusions can be drawn from an inter-factory comparison of unit costs unless they are both based on the same utilisation of maximum capacity.

PROJECT DECISIONS

Ad hoc decisions of the type considered above can usually be reversed if necessary, because there has been no investment of capital funds. With project decisions, however, there is rarely the same opportunity to correct mistakes. If the new factory proves to be much more costly to operate than was contemplated when it was at the drawing board stage, very little can be done about it. It is evident that the only cost information that is likely to be of any value in helping to arrive at a correct decision is a careful assessment of what *future* costs are likely to amount to, in the particular circumstances envisaged. (This provides another example of the growing emphasis placed nowadays on forward or "projected" information for control purposes. No amount of subsequent cost control can make good a faulty decision based on an inaccurate forward assessment of operating costs.)

Capital Projects

A project decision is frequently made on a provisional basis during the annual budgeting stage, leaving the precise details to be settled nearer the time of starting work on the project. It is helpful to those endeavouring to plan and control the cash resources of the business to receive advance information of such projects, and particularly helpful to be supplied with information about *all* contemplated capital expenditure at the time when annual budgets are being summarised and agreed. If this is not done, surplus cash balances may be allocated to other purposes, and then if a request is received for urgent capital expenditure, the need may arise to sell securities only recently acquired, or even to postpone other projects considered less urgent.

Where the business is largely decentralised, a useful way of encouraging local management to submit their plans for capital projects well in advance is to introduce differentials in the sanctions required. Thus local management may be authorised to carry out capital work up to £5,000 without reference to Head Office, but if the outline of the project is first included in the annual budget statement, the sanction would be increased to say £10,000.

Project decisions invariably mean choosing between alternatives. If no alternative is available, no decision will be required. This means that a comparison must be made between the pros and cons of each method. It is usually found that some of these pros and cons can be expressed in quantitative terms, others cannot. An example of this is seen when a decision has to be taken whether to increase productive capacity in anticipation of selling a new range of products. Estimates can be made of the additional income and the additional costs resulting from this action, but the decision may be influenced by other factors, e.g. whether it will be regarded by other manufacturers as an intrusion into their fields, and will thus lead to retaliatory action. In such circumstances, the method of approach is to make the best assessment possible of the effect of measurable factors, and for management then to make the decision in the light of all the known facts.

Replacement Decisions

The optional replacement of a piece of plant can be regarded as an investment of funds to be compared with other opportunities. If a certain capital sum is available, the question may arise whether it should be used to replace some of the existing out-moded plant by more up-to-date equipment and thus save on operating costs, or should it be used for building up additional capacity?

In this case the comparison will be between savings made on the one hand, and additional income on the other.

Confusion is sometimes caused over the question of depreciation charges on the asset which it is proposed to replace. It is sometimes thought that money will be saved by scrapping an existing machine on which there is a heavy annual depreciation charge, and by substituting a newer and cheaper machine, with a correspondingly lower annual depreciation cost. Unless a machine has a high re-sale value, which is unlikely, it is never possible to "save" on depreciation; the actual cost of the machine was incurred in the year in which it was installed, and it is only a convenient accountancy arrangement to spread this cost over the life of the machine. The real comparison in the above instance would be to see what return would be obtained over the expected life of the new machine by way of savings in "out-of-pocket" costs such as wages and power charges, etc.

Sometimes there is a reluctance to consider replacing a relatively new machine that has proved unsatisfactory in use because by so doing a heavy book loss would be incurred. This is analogous to the feelings of an investor who when faced with the need to realise capital decides to sell his most promising shares (which have risen and are likely to go on rising) rather than face a heavy loss by selling shares which have fallen well below the purchase price (and are likely to go on falling).

EVALUATION OF CAPITAL PROJECTS

The relative merits of alternative courses of action not involving the investment of capital sums can be demonstrated by a straightforward comparison of future revenue and future costs. If capital is to be expended on a project, some way must be found of comparing the benefits obtainable during the expected life of the project with this capital sum. This brings in the question of time. There are several methods which can be used for making the assessment, involving the calculation of:

(a) "Pay-back" Period.
(b) Rate of Return.
(c) Discounted Cash Flow.
(d) Present Value Comparisons.

"Pay-back" Period

In this method the additional income or expected savings per annum are compared with the net outlay, by dividing the latter by the former. Thus if savings of £1,500 per annum are obtained from an investment of £6,000, the *pay-back period* is four years. The normal way of making use of this method is to establish various criteria for different types of project, based on previous experience. If for example it is found that office machinery has an average life of five years—it then being replaced by newer equipment—it would be logical to expect the pay-back period to be well within this period, perhaps two or three years. Similarly if process machinery has an average life of ten years, it might be agreed that no new equipment will be bought unless the pay-back period is five years or less.

The method has many advantages. It is simple to calculate, easily understood, and provides a good working rule for including or excluding alternative proposals. Its principal disadvantage is that if several alternatives are being compared, and the expected periods during which income will be received (or savings made) are markedly different, these differences will not be taken into account. The differences may be important particularly where the sums involved are large, and in these circumstances it is advisable to make use of one of the more sophisticated techniques described below.

Rate of Return

Another way in which decisions on projects are made is to compare the *rate of return expected from the investment* with some predetermined target rate. If business management were in the habit of always seeking diligently the maximum return on capital, this comparison with a target figure would be unnecessary. The search would go on until management was satisfied that the most profitable opportunity had been found. In fact, what usually happens is that requests come up the line for developments of one kind or another. A factory manager wants to install a new type of plant that he has seen when on a visit abroad. A marketing manager wants to launch out on a new range of products, the general manager wants to buy up the shares of a potential rival, and so on. Some means must be found for deciding whether to accept or reject the various proposals, and, as suggested above, the usual procedure is to see whether the anticipated return is up to standard. If not, the sponsors of the proposal may be asked to reconsider it, to see whether the potential income can be increased to the desired extent. Even if this is not practicable, the project may still be accepted for special reasons, but this would be a question of policy. The general rule would be that the expected return must be equal to the prescribed target figure.

In fixing the standard, a company may have regard to its previous experience, to the average rate ruling in the particular industry (if this is known), or to the rates currently obtainable on stock-exchange securities. When the average rate of interest obtainable on government securities was 3 per cent., a company might have considered that a 10 per cent. return was extremely adequate. When the rate rises to 6 or 7 per cent. a 10 per cent. return would hardly seem an adequate reward for all the additional risks taken in carrying on a business, and the expected target might well be set at 20 per cent.

Under normal business conditions, there are four ways in which a return of say 6 per cent. per annum could be obtained from an investment of £1,000;

   (i) Investing the £1,000 in an asset that brings in a perpetual income of 6 per cent. An example would be the purchase of freehold ground rents, or of government securities.

  (ii) Investing the £1,000 in property or securities which, although yielding no income, increase in value over the years to give the desired return. (Savings certificates provide an example of this sort of investment.)

 (iii) Advancing £1,000 to a third party at 6 per cent. per annum on a secured loan, interest being paid annually and the loan being repayable at the end of a specified period.

 (iv) Sinking £1,000 in a project which yields an annual return of 10 per cent. for fifteen years, but has no residual value.

Although there is no difficulty in seeing that the rate of return is 6 per cent. in the case of (i) and (iii), it is by no means clear at first sight that the true return specified in (iv) is equivalent to 6 per cent. per annum. The majority of business projects come under this latter category, because they usually involve spending money on plant or equipment which will have no ultimate value, but which will bring additional income (or savings) during a specified period. It is therefore important to be quite clear on the way in which the true return is calculated. A manager who sat down to work out the true rate of return in the above example might work through the following stages:

  (a) Realising that the 10 per cent. apparent return is too high because no allowance is made for the depreciation of the capital invested in the project, his first step might be to deduct depreciation from the total revenue, and then recalculate the return :

Total earnings	£1,500
Less depreciation (equal to original cost)	£1,000
Total profit in 15 years	£500

equivalent to £33 6s. 8d. per annum. On the original investment of
£1,000 this works out at 3⅓ per cent. per annum. Further thought
would show him that this calculation does not measure the true return, because the gradual accumulation of the depreciation provisions—totalling £1,000 in 15 years—means that the capital at *risk*
is gradually reduced from £1,000 to nil. In other words, the investment in this project is on all fours with a loan by a Building
Society to be repaid by equal annual instalments covering capital
and interest, thus resulting in the progressive reduction in the
amount of capital outstanding. This leads on to the next step.

(b) Having established that the capital at risk gradually drops from
£1,000 to nil over the 15 years, it is reasonable to work out the
ratio of the net earnings calculated as in (a) above to the *average*
capital employed during this period. Taking a simple average,
this is equivalent to £$\frac{1000}{2}$ or £500. In other words, the average
rate of return now works out at 3⅓ × 2, or 6⅔ per cent. per annum
on the average capital employed.

In many instances, particularly where the sums involved are small,
this method may give reasonably reliable results. However, it must
be realised that the method gives only an approximation of the *true*
rate of return being earned, and where the rate of return is high, or
large sums are involved, it may be advisable to use one of the
methods described below.

Discounted Cash Flow

The true rate of return on the project described above is determined by *discounting the stream of annual earnings* at a rate such
that the accumulated present values of these payments will equal
the sum originally invested in the project. The present value of £100
due one year hence is £94 6s. 0d. if the discount rate is taken as 6
per cent., because £94 6s. 0d. invested for one year at 6 per cent.
would bring in £5 14s. 0d. in interest, and £94 6s. 0d.+£5 14s. 0d.
=£100. Similarly for year two, the present value is £89, and so on.
In a business situation, income is not received in annual instalments,
but can be considered being received in monthly instalments (most
customers would settle their accounts monthly). Accordingly it is
more correct to assume that the return on investment is received
monthly, and to work out present values on this basis. If interest is
received monthly, the present value of £100 received over year one
is £96 18s. 0d.—this can be proved by a detailed calculation of the
position at each month end.

The tabulation below of present values proves that the true rate of return obtained when £1,000 is invested in a project which yields £100 per cent. per annum for fifteen years is 6 per cent. per

Present values of £100 p.a. received by
monthly instalments over 15 years, discounted at 6 per cent. p.a.

Year	Present Value £	Year	Present Value £
		b/f	575
1	97	8	64
2	92	9	61
3	86	10	58
4	82	11	54
5	77	12	51
6	73	13	48
7	68	14	46
		15	43
c/f	575		£1,000*

* If the exact monthly figures were listed the total amount would be £998.

annum and not 6⅔ per cent. as arrived at by the average method. In actual practice it would not be necessary to work out the separate values for each year—it is possible to refer to interest tables which will give in one figure the present value of a stream of payments over a given period of years. This means that if one knows what capital sum is to be expended, and what annual revenue will be obtained over how many years, it is possible to read off from the tables the true rate of interest applicable without going through the detailed calculations shown above. Thus the present value of £100 per annum received by monthly instalments over 15 years amounts to £1,132 if interest is taken at 4 per cent., to £998 with interest at 6 per cent. and so on. Since £998 is approximately equal to the sum invested, this proves that the true rate of return is 6 per cent.

For those who find the concepts of discount rates and present values hard to understand, the position may be clarified by looking at it in another way. A Building Society advancing £1,000 *now* and collecting repayments of £100 per annum by monthly instalments over 15 years would be in exactly the same position as the sponsors of the project described above, i.e. they would be charging 6 per cent. interest on the balance of loan outstanding at monthly intervals throughout the fifteen years. The borrower, if he wished, could work out how much of each monthly instalment represented interest and capital respectively, and at the end of the fifteen years he should find that he has just repaid the outstanding capital sum. If he used the short cut "average return" method, he would arrive at the conclusion that he was paying $6\frac{2}{3}$ per cent. per annum in interest.

This is a general rule that the return shown by the average return method is always somewhat higher than the true rate of return. This difference can be quite appreciable with higher rates of return, e.g. if £5,000 is invested in a project bringing in £1,000 per annum for fourteen years, the average rate of return works out at

$$\frac{(14,000-5,000) \times 100}{5,000 \times 14 \times \frac{1}{2}} = 25.7\%$$

whereas the true rate of return, assuming that income is received in monthly instalments, works out at only 20 per cent.

A point to be borne in mind if the average return method is used for assessing new projects is that the overall return on the total fixed assets in an established stable company (after deducting depreciation) is likely to be much nearer to a true rate of return than would be the case with individual projects. For example, in such a business there is a tendency for new capital expenditure each year to be equal to the sums accumulated by way of depreciation. This means that if one ignores inflation the net book value of fixed assets remains relatively constant, and if the income earned is also constant, comparison of the two sets of figures gives the true rate of return. Hence if new projects are to maintain the overall level of profits, management must either calculate the true return in each case, or work to a somewhat higher percentage if they use the average return basis.

Discounted cash flow evaluations become more complex if the expected revenue varies from year to year, or if the total investment is spread over several years. In cases like this, it is usually necessary to work through the calculations on a trial-and-error basis. For example, suppose in the table given on page 779 the annual income had been as follows:

Years 1 & 2	Nil
3	£200
4 & 5	£150
6	£133
7–15	£100

The true rate of return would still be 6 per cent., but the only means of establishing this would be to try out several rates until the rate selected resulted in the total of the present values for years 1–15 equalling the original investment, as shown in the table opposite.

	Annual Income	7%	6½%	6%	5½%
Year 1	Nil				
2	Nil			—	
3	£200			172	
4	£150			123	
5	£150			115	
6	£133			97	
7	£100			68	
8	,,			64	
9	,,			61	
10	,,			58	
11	,,			54	
12	,,			51	
13	,,			48	
14	,,			46	
15	,,			43	
Total present values		£945	£972	£1,000	£1,030
		Too low		Equals investment	Too high

Present Value Comparisons

Another method of evaluating alternative projects is based on a modification of the discounted cash flow procedure. Under this method the first step is to assess the rate of interest at which additional capital could be raised. The income (or cost savings) which can be expected from each project is then discounted at this rate as described in method (c) above, and the *present values* so determined are compared with the outlay required. The project which shows the biggest relative excess of present value over proposed outlay is, other things being equal, the one to choose. In practice, projects may be financed out of retained profits, so that it will be necessary for the Board to decide on a suitable rate of return which can be taken as indicating the current "cost of capital".

Example:

Current cost of capital is agreed at 8%.

	Project 1 £	Project 2 £
Investment (the assets have no residual value)	800	800
Annual income (received by monthly instalments)	—	—
Year 1	300	200
2	400	200
3	300	300
4	200	400
5	100	200
Total income receivable	£1,300	£1,300

Present values are obtained from interest tables as follows:

	Project 1 £	Project 2 £
Year 1	288	192
2	355	177
3	247	247
4	152	305
5	70	141
	£1,112	£1,062

Since the total present value is well in excess of the capital outlay in each case, management would conclude that both projects are worth considering. Clearly Project 1 is more attractive as an investment proposition than Project 2, since with the same capital outlay the excess of present value over investment is £312 compared with £262. It has been possible to arrive at these conclusions without going through the process of trial-and-error associated with the previous example.

CHAPTER X

OVERALL CONTROL

THE previous Chapters have been concerned with controls applicable to production, marketing or financial managements. It is now necessary to look at control from a general management point of view, i.e. at overall control.

The first step in this direction is taken when the specific objectives for the year are set out in the form of policy plans and budgets. When these are put together as an integrated whole, it can be seen just how far along the road towards its long-term objectives the business is expected to move during the year. The next step is usually taken once a month, with the preparation of monthly operating statements, which measure the progress achieved towards operational and profit targets. As these statements are required for control purposes, speed of preparation is one of the essentials. Accordingly, methods have to be adopted which will permit a reasonably accurate result to be calculated in the shortest possible time. Cost of preparation is a further consideration. With normal accounting methods, it is possible to prepare an accurate profit statement at any time, provided that the management is prepared to suffer the dislocation and extra expense caused by stock-taking. For purposes of monthly reporting, it is usually advisable to rely on methods of profit calculation that do not need a physical stock check.

Once a year, or at interim Balance Sheet dates, a more accurate assessment is made of the progress achieved during the year. The official set of accounts, including Balance Sheet and Profit and Loss Accounts, are required by statute in the case of limited companies or partnerships. When audited, they are used for calculation of tax charges and the assessment of dividend possibilities. They are also used to support applications for further finance, either from shareholders or loan creditors. Even the sole trader usually finds it advisable to have a set of audited accounts.

The principal item of interest in these official accounts is of course the annual profit earned. If the management is to make effective use of the monthly operating controls, it is important to make sure that the cumulative profits shown can be reconciled with the profit shown in the annual accounts. There will always be reasons why the two sets of figures do not coincide. For example, management may consider it prudent to provide for possible losses on contracts in the annual accounts, whereas the monthly operating statements would normally only include losses as they arise. Another frequent cause of difference may be the methods adopted for stock valuation. For a recently introduced system of monthly accounts, stocks may be valued at full standard cost, while for annual accounts some other basis may be used in order to conform with the practice of previous years. So far as possible these differences in treatment should be avoided. Even if it is possible to explain the reasons for a difference between total annual profit and the cumulative total of the monthly profit figures, too large a difference will tend to reduce the interest taken in the monthly reports and will thus reduce their effectiveness.

The remainder of this Chapter contains comments on some of the points to be taken into account in measuring progress towards overall objectives.

MEASUREMENT OF OVERALL ACTIVITY

In many instances the volume of sales provides a useful basis for measuring the overall activity or "growth" of a business. Where a company manufactures a wide range of products it may not be possible to measure growth in terms of sales volume and it may be more appropriate to take the value of sales turnover as the basis. In this case, some means must be found of eliminating the effect of price changes before calculating the percentage increase. Sales volume or turnover is a useful basis for measuring growth because the figures are usually available, but a more effective measurement is obtained by calculating the "values added", i.e. the difference between raw material cost and net sales value. Suppose, for example, a company has the following sales position:

		This Year	Last Year	Change
Product A . .	Sales (in	1,000	1,100	−100
" B . .	dozens)	2,200	2,000	+200
		3,200	3,100	+100
	Per Dozen	£	£	£
Product A . .	40s.	2,000	2,200	−200
" B . .	20s.	2,200	2,000	+200
		£4,200	£4,200	—
	Per Dozen	£	£	£
'Value A . .	20s.	1,000	1,100	−100
Added' B . .	5s.	550	500	+50
		£1,550	£1,600	£−50

For the two products A and B, the sales prices are respectively 40s and 20s. per dozen as shown on the table; the corresponding materials prices are 20s. and 15s. respectively. Comparison of two years' sales is shown: there can be little doubt that the margin available for covering conversion costs and profit (the "added value") is of greater significance in assessing "growth" than either sales volume or sales turnover. In the example, this method alone shows that the trend of factory activity has in total been unfavourable.

MEASURING PROFITS AND STOCK

Methods

Although most managers do not need to know how to prepare accounts or profit statements, it is usually advisable for the different principles applying to the calculation of profits to be understood by all who hold managerial responsibility.

The general rule for calculating profit is to match up costs incurred with the revenue obtained when the goods are sold. If all goods are sold on the day they are made there is no problem—it is simply a question of comparing cost with revenue. If goods are held in stock for a month on average, then expenditure incurred this month has to be compared with revenue earned next month. The way this is done is to assess the value of *stocks of finished goods* on hand at the end of the month, and then to transfer this amount of expenditure from one month to the next. The same procedure is used in calculating annual profits—expenditure incurred this year on goods sold next year is transferred from one year to the next. The calculation of stock values is therefore an essential preliminary to the determination of profits for the period.

There are two ways of arriving at stock values for this purpose. One way is to make a physical count of the goods on hand and then to evaluate these quantities at their estimated cost to make. The other way is to keep a running record of the "standard value" of goods put into stock from the factory, and taken out of stock on sale. The balance of this account gives the standard value of stocks on hand at any time, without the necessity for a physical count.

In many instances, there may be a considerable volume of *work in process* at month ends, and exactly the same "carry-forward" adjustments are necessary as with finished goods stocks. The same two methods can be used for arriving at the values—a physical count of partly finished items, evaluated at appropriate rates, or a running record of work in process standard values. The latter is obtained by recording on the "in" side the standard cost of all work done on good production, and on the "out" side the standard value of finished production transferred to the finished stock account. It will be appreciated that the physical count method—which is used for financial accounting purposes—usually gives the most *accurate* assessment. There is always the danger that clerical errors may be made in the running record. On the other hand, the separation of actual costs into "standard costs" and "excess costs" provides information for control purposes, while the calculation of standard product costs gives an easy means of analysing total profits by products.

Assuming that it has been decided to prepare monthly profit and loss statements through the application of standard costing procedure, the statements required for measuring progress consist of:

    (i) annual operating budgets;
    (ii) standard costs for each product;
    (iii) monthly operating statements;

together with supporting schedules of control standards and detailed control reports. Alternative methods of preparation are illustrated by detailed examples set out in the Appendix.

Full or Marginal Costing?

In Chapter IV, the choice of full or marginal costs was looked at from the point of view of profit planning. A suggestion was made that standard product costs could be divided into fixed and variable portions, thus providing the same opportunities for calculating the effect of volume changes as with marginal costing. The inference of this is that, for profit planning purposes it is possible to combine the advantages of both methods. Product costs are, however, also used for calculating the profits made in each period, and for this purpose it is necessary to make a definite decision to use one method or the other. The decision is particularly important if there are significant changes in stock levels between one period and another. This is illustrated by showing the differing effect on monthly profits in the example below.

Example. A factory has a capacity of 1,000 tons a month and budgets for its operating costs. Variable manufacturing costs are £10 per ton and there are in addition fixed charges of £10,000 per month. Variable selling costs are £5 per ton, and fixed selling prices are £30 per ton. In month 1 it makes 1,000 tons and sells 800 tons, in month 2 it makes 800 tons and sells 1,000 tons. Actual costs are the same as budgeted costs.

The results before adjusting for stocks on hand are set out opposite:

	Month 1	Month 2
Sales (tons)	800 tons	1,000 tons
Sales value	£24,000	£30,000
Variable selling costs		
(£5 per ton)	£4,000	£5,000
Factory output (tons)	1,000 tons	800 tons
Factory costs		
Variable (£10 per ton) . . .	£10,000	£8,000
Fixed	£10,000	£10,000
Stock movements	+200 tons	−200 tons

If *marginal costs* are used, factory output costs £10 per ton. The value of the 200 tons put into stock during month 1 (and vice versa in month 2) is therefore £2,000. Profits are accordingly:

	Month 1		Month 2	
Sales less selling costs . .	(800 tons)	£20,000	(1,000 tons)	£25,000
Factory cost of sales				
(£10 per ton) . . .	£8,000		£10,000	
Factory costs (fixed) . .	£10,000		£10,000	
		£18,000		£20,000
Net Profit		£2,000		£5,000

The actual variable factory costs, after adjusting for the value of the stock increase or decrease, exactly equal the factory cost of sales:

	Month 1	Month 2
Factory costs (variable) actual	£10,000	£8,000
Stock adjustment . . .	−£2,000	+£2,000
Absorbed on sales (as above) .	£8,000	£10,000

The increase in profit of £3,000 in month 2 can be explained as an increase of tons sold (200) at contributory margin (£15 per ton).

If *full costs* are used, a decision must be made on the budgeted output. Assuming this is based on the month 1 level of output, the factory standard cost works out at £20 per ton (£20,000÷1,000). The value of the 200 tons put into stock during month 1 (and vice versa in month 2) is therefore £4,000. Profits are as follows:

	Month 1		Month 2	
Sales less selling costs .	(800	£20,000	(1,000 tons)	£25,000
Factory cost of sales (£20 per ton) .	tons)	£16,000		£20,000
(a) *Profit on sales*		£4,000		£5,000
Factory costs:				
Actual		£20,000		£18,000
Stock adjustment . . .		−£4,000		+£4,000
		£16,000		£22,000
Absorbed on sales (as above) .		£16,000		£20,000
(b) Under-absorbed (*volume variance*)		—		£2,000
Net Profit (a)−(b) . . .		£4,000		£3,000

The decrease in profits of £1,000 in month 2 can be explained:

Increased tonnage sold (200) at profit margin (£5 per ton)=£1,000.
Less under-absorbed fixed costs £2,000=net decrease of £1,000.

Thus, although there is no difference in the total profits when both months are taken together, the results shown in the separate periods are dependent on the method of costing used. At first sight the fact that the marginal costing approach shows that profits have risen in a month when sales have risen, whereas the "full" costing procedure shows the reverse, would appear to be a strong argument in favour of the former. Further consideration shows that the marginal cost method reflects the marketing result but takes no real account of what has happened in the factory regarding the utilisation of capacity. Those who support the "full" costing technique would say that the under-utilisation of 200 tons capacity in month 2 is a very real loss. The opportunity for making saleable goods was lost and can never be made good except at the expense of the output of future periods. It is therefore correct to show that the increase of £1,000 in the profit on sales has been more than lost as the result of the under-utilisation of capacity.

As stated in an earlier Chapter, no general rule can be laid down on this matter. It is a question partly of personal preference, and partly of designing a system to suit the particular circumstances. If the general management of the business is influenced mainly by marketing men or economists, then it is probable that marginal costing will be preferred. If, however, the influence comes mainly from the technical or financial sides of the business, then the chances are that the "full" standard costing procedures will be preferred.

Again, much will depend on whether the business is working anywhere near full capacity, or whether the business is able to set its own prices, or follow the lead set by competitors.

The different results obtained, depending on the method of treatment (i.e. full or marginal costs), are also illustrated in the worked example in the Appendix.

MEASURING RETURN ON CAPITAL EXPENDITURE

Assuming that profits earned on sales have been measured and compared with target, the final step is to see whether the expected return on capital has been achieved. Unless this check is made, it is always possible to attain any desired level of profit merely by pumping in more capital.

The problem of arriving at a satisfactory basis for valuing fixed assets is discussed later, but in the meanwhile it is assumed that capital employed is to be calculated from the Balance Sheet values.

Capital employed can be looked at from several points of view. For example, the ordinary shareholders of a company may originally have subscribed £30,000 as capital. As the result of a recent revaluation of fixed assets, and the retention of profits earned, the book value of their holdings may increase to, say, £50,000. This represents the money they would get if the company were liquidated and all assets realised their Balance Sheet values. (The market value of their shares is more likely to be assessed on a current earnings basis than on an asset break-up basis.)

From the point of view of overall management control, the value of ordinary shareholders' funds is irrelevant. As a general rule, assets obtained from debenture stockholders or loan creditors should be just as capable of earning profits as assets bought out of shareholders' funds. The only exception may be loan capital that is secured on a particular asset of the company. For example, a mortgage loan may be obtained for the construction of new administrative offices. Such a loan is secured on the building, and would not be obtainable at the same rate of interest if it were used for normal trading purposes. In these circumstances it may be preferable to exclude the loan from the total capital employed. With this possible exception, the capital employed figure used as a basis for assessing the overall return should be the total capital obtained from all sources. It will be equivalent to the total of fixed and net current assets shown on the other side of the statement.

It is sometimes suggested that *total current assets* rather than *net assets* should be included in the total capital figure, since all assets used in the business should earn income, regardless of whether they have been financed by permanent capital or by short-term creditors. A case can be made out for treatment either way. In working out the ratio of profits to capital employed, it is advisable to work on an average figure for the latter, rather than taking the year end amount.

Subsidiary Ratios

It is usually found helpful to break down the overall return into two subsidiary indices:

(i) Percentage of profit on sales.

(ii) Ratio of sales per annum to capital employed.

An overall return of 15 per cent. might be made up of a 5 per cent. profit on sales and a 3 : 1 ratio of annual sales to capital employed. If these two ratios are plotted over a period of years, they can act as pointers to management showing whether action needs to be taken to improve the overall ratio. In the above example if the overall ratio fell to 12 per cent., the analysis would show whether this decrease has been caused by lower profitability on sales, or to a lower ratio of sales to capital employed. It is often possible to break down these subsidiary ratios by product groups.

If a business is operating a system of budgetary control and standard costs, the rate of profit earned on sales will usually be kept under continuous control, but the ratio of sales to capital employed is frequently ignored. Thus a merchandising business dealing in three main groups of products might show the following results:

	Product Group		
	23	30	31
Annual Sales . .	£1,200,000	£1,000,000	£600,000
Trading profit . .	£24,000	£90,000	£60,000
Percentage to sales .	2%	9%	10%

At first sight, the management would perhaps take the view that product group 23 was not up to the profitability standard of the other product groups, and might consider replacing it with some other more profitable lines. However, further investigation reveals that the total capital employed of £2,040,000 can be split up over the three product groups as shown below. It is then seen that the ratio of sales to capital—the "capital turnover"—is very much higher in the case of product group 23 than with the other groups:

	Product Group		
	23	30	31
Capital employed .	£240,000	£1,000,000	£800,000
Ratio of sales to capital	5:1	1:1	0·75:1
Return on capital .	10%	9%	7½%

In fact, as the result of this high turnover ratio, product group 23 actually brings in a better overall return than the other groups.

Calculating the Value of Capital Employed

No particular difficulties arise with regard to working capital. As already suggested the values taken should be the average values during the year. These values would normally be the values taken for stock control purposes—there is no need to take account of adjustments made purely for year-end balance sheet purposes, e.g. writing down values because of raw material price fluctuations.

The position is different with regard to fixed assets. Owing to the length of time over which fixed assets are held, considerable difficulties arise in finding a suitable basis for valuation. This difficulty is accentuated in recent years, owing to the progressive decreases in the value of money, and the consequent gradual rise in the cost of fixed assets from year to year. The written down values in the balance sheet may not provide a suitable basis, since these are more a reflection of depreciation policy than of the current value of the plant.

In making a decision on the method to be adopted in valuing fixed assets for calculation of control ratios, it is important to reflect on the purposes for which the information is needed. Nothing can be done about the period that is past, but the information may be of use in influencing future operations. If a low capital turnover ratio and a low overall return are seen to apply to a particular group of products, it may be possible to effect improvements. Alternatively, if no such improvements seem feasible, it may be possible to switch the plant to other uses, or failing that to close down that section of the plant altogether. On the other hand, higher-than-average ratios would suggest to management the directions in which expansion should be planned.

The basis of all these decisions is comparison, comparison of one section of the plant with another, of one factory with another, or of one firm with others in the same industry. If comparisons are to be meaningful, it is essential for the basis of valuation to be consistent. If the comparisons are intended to be a guide to future action, the values used must be applicable to current conditions. Both these conditions are satisfied if fixed assets are valued at replacement cost if comparatively new, or at replacement cost subject to a suitable deduction for wear and tear (this is the normal basis for valuation for fire insurance purposes).

The principal drawback to this procedure is the difficulty in deciding on suitable replacement values and on suitable deductions for wear and tear. An alternative procedure which may give reasonably reliable figures during inflationary periods is to take the original cost (before deducting depreciation) as the assessment of present value. If the item is new, it will represent current values. If the item is say ten years old, the original cost may approximate to current replacement costs suitably reduced for wear and tear.

OTHER CONTROL RATIOS

Certain well-established ratios are used for testing the financial soundness of a business. These ratios include the following:

(a) Ratio of *current assets to current liabilities*. This ratio should always be higher than 1:1, and many firms aim at a ratio of 3:2, or even 2:1. Should the ratio ever approximate to 1:1, it is an indication that further sums may have to be obtained from shareholders, or from loan capital sources. Alternatively, fixed assets may have to be sold in order to restore the ability to meet liabilities as they fall due.

(*b*) The same ratio, but using *liquid assets* instead of current assets. Liquid assets include cash and items which can be expected to turn into cash shortly, such as amounts due from customers. Although stocks of raw materials and finished products are regarded as part of the firm's current assets, money may be locked up in them for a considerable time, particularly if customers' demand has suddenly dried up. It is well known that bankruptcies and liquidations frequently occur because firms have "over-traded". All available funds are put into stocks of goods, and then when demand falls off, no money is available to pay for current wages and expenses.

(*c*) The ratio of *debtors to sales turnover*. The exact ratio which would be considered reasonable would depend on the credit terms allowed.

CONCLUSION

As a final comment to this Chapter on the measurement of overall results, it may be pertinent to point out once again that recording and evaluating what has happened in the past only serves a useful purpose if it enables better decisions to be taken regarding future action. For this reason, it is essential to review at regular intervals the various information and control reports which are being issued to management at all levels and to make sure that altered circumstances since the date of the previous review have not reduced their effectiveness.

To conclude Part Four, worked examples of an integrated set of management information reports are provided in the Appendix. These reports of necessity relate to a particular situation, but the principles illustrated should be capable of application to other circumstances, and it is hoped that the examples will prove helpful to anyone faced with the problem of designing effective systems of management control in a manufacturing and marketing company.

WORKED EXAMPLES OF
MANAGEMENT INFORMATION REPORTS

CONTENTS

NOTE: *For convenience of reference between text and forms, the examples in the following pages are set out sideways.*

I. INTRODUCTION

The attached worked examples have been designed to illustrate some of the ways in which periodic management information reports can help management set and attain objectives. They show how work study or management standards can be used as a basis for profit planning or control; how flexible budgetary control and variance analysis will help management decide on appropriate corrective action; and how links can be established with the financial accounts. Finally, they show the alternative uses of "full" and "marginal" costing techniques.

The following statements may appear to some readers to be unduly complex at first sight: the detail has been developed in these examples in order to illustrate the several different complications that can arise, and how they can be dealt with.

HEBCO LTD.

LIST OF MANAGEMENT INFORMATION REPORTS ETC.

	Figure No.
Management Structure	A–1
Plan of Factory	A–2
Balance Sheet	A–3
Operating Standards	A–4
Budget Statements, etc., for half-year to 30th June:	
Sales and Production Budgets	A–5
Materials Budget	A–6
Production Departments Budgets	A–7
Plant Costs Budget (Maintenance and Depreciation)	A–8
Factory Operating—Summary—Budget	A–9
Standard Product Costs	A–10

II. THE BACKGROUND

HEBCO Ltd., a company with a share capital of £150,000, makes and sells three different kinds of products. The outline of its general management structure is shown below, together with the detailed structures of factory management. (Details of the other functions have been omitted to avoid making the example too complex.)

At 31st December, 19—, the total book value of the shareholders' stake in the business, i.e. the total value of "capital employed",[1] amounted to £253,743. Details of the make-up of this capital employed, and of the corresponding assets are set out in the Balance Sheet on Fig. A–3 (column headed "31st December").

In earlier years, the business had been earning profits which were equivalent to a 15 per cent. return (before tax) on the total value of the capital employed, but more recently the increasing competition at home and abroad has tended to depress selling prices, while at the same time various increases in costs have progressively reduced profit margins. As a result, the Board are finding it increasingly difficult to operate at a profit.

The Board decide that there is a reasonable chance of restoring the business to a profitable position, but that one of the first essentials will be to reorganise their management information and control procedures. Under the existing system, monthly reports are prepared showing the sales and production achieved and the profits earned, but no information is given on the reasons why results have fallen below expectations, or which pinpoints the responsibilities for excess costs. Also the information is usually received far too late to be of value in detecting trends or correcting faults.

A small team consisting of the accountant and the work study officer is accordingly set up and is charged with the task of introducing more effective control procedures.

After a short investigation, it is decided to introduce flexible budgetary control combined with standard costing and profit planning. Use would be made of work study standards wherever these were available. The budgetary or cost control procedures would include "accounting by responsibilities", and use would be made wherever possible of "management by exception".

The standard product costs built up by reference to product specifications, standards and budgets would be

---

[1] There are no loan creditors.

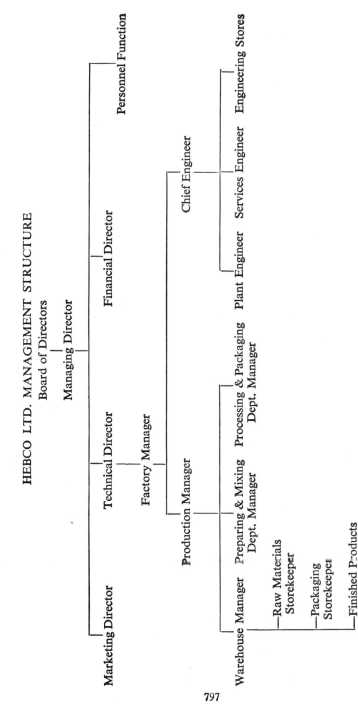

HEBCO LTD. MANAGEMENT STRUCTURE

Board of Directors

Managing Director

Marketing Director — Technical Director — Financial Director — Personnel Function

Factory Manager

Production Manager — Chief Engineer

Preparing & Mixing Dept. Manager — Processing & Packaging Dept. Manager — Plant Engineer — Services Engineer — Engineering Stores

Warehouse Manager
— Raw Materials Storekeeper
— Packaging Storekeeper
— Finished Products Storekeeper

Fig. A–1

797

divided into "fixed" and "variable" elements. Profit planning charts (derived from "break-even" charts) would be built up from the latter information, and used as a basis for helping management to select the most suitable line of approach for attaining profit targets.

The same budgets and standards would be used as the basis for periodic control reports. In view of the limited experience obtained so far in sales forecasting, it is decided to make a start by budgeting for the six months to 30th June. Subsequently, when greater experience has been gained of sales forecasting, long-term planning will be introduced covering a period of five years ahead, and detailed budgeting will be carried out annually.

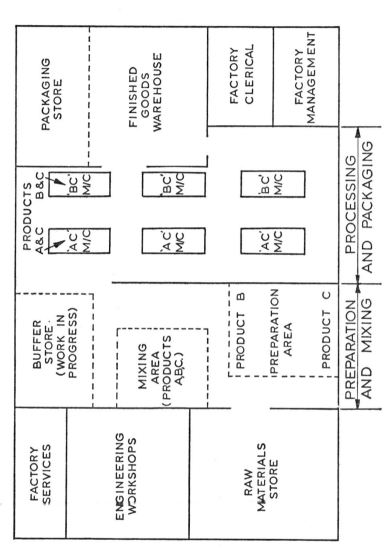

Fig. A-2.—Plan of HEBCO Factory.

The plan shows the following areas:

PACKAGING STORE

FINISHED GOODS WAREHOUSE

FACTORY CLERICAL

FACTORY MANAGEMENT

PRODUCTS A&C **B&C**

'AC' M/C | 'BC' M/C

'AC' M/C | 'BC' M/C

'AC' M/C | 'BC' M/C

BUFFER STORE (WORK IN PROGRESS)

MIXING AREA (PRODUCTS A,B,C.)

PRODUCT B

PREPARATION AREA

PRODUCT C

PROCESSING AND PACKAGING

PREPARATION AND MIXING

FACTORY SERVICES

ENGINEERING WORKSHOPS

RAW MATERIALS STORE

III. ESTABLISHING WORK FLOW AND OPERATING STANDARDS

Before starting to prepare the half-yearly budgets, a plan of the factory is obtained (Fig. A-2) and the path traced by each product (from raw materials intake to finished goods warehouse) established. The separate areas of responsibility, as indicated by the organisation structure, are marked on the plan.

Raw materials for each product, after withdrawal from store, are transferred to the Preparation and Mixing Department. In the case of products B and C some preparation (carried out manually) is necessary before mixing, but no preparation is necessary for product A. After mixing, the three products pass through the buffer store to the Processing and Packaging Department. The latter contains two kinds of machinery—three "AC" machines and three "BC" machines. The AC machines are considerably more costly to install and operate than the BC machines. Product A can only be processed on the BC machines, and product B on BC machines. Product C, however, can be processed on either type of machine according to availability, but will whenever possible be processed on BC machines, because of their lower cost.

Operating Standards (Fig. A-4)

Detailed studies of the various operations have been carried out in the past by the Work Study Department with the object of simplifying or improving operating methods. Further studies are now carried out to establish operating standards (in physical terms) for all variable costs and for the output of the AC and BC machines in the Processing and Packaging Department. These standards are set out in Fig. A-4, together with the budgeted rates applicable to the half-year to 30th June. The physical standards will normally remain unaltered unless there is a change of method, but the budgeted cost rates per unit are likely to be changed for each new budget period. Management estimates would be used as a temporary measure where work study standards were not yet available.

No "direct" labour standards have been shown for Mixing because the time taken for this task is small, and the mixing is carried out when required by one of the departmental supervisors.

Capital Employed

Capital Employed	31st Dec. £	28th Jan. Actual £	30th June Budget £
Share Capital	150,000	150,000	150,000
Capital Reserve	38,000	38,000	38,000
Revenue Reserves & Unappropriated Profit			
General Reserve	62,000	62,000	62,000
Unappropriated Profit at 1st January	3,743	3,743	3,743
Balance of Profit and Loss Account for period		(211)	*5,550
	65,743	65,532	71,293
	253,743	253,532	259,293

*Subject to provision for tax

Note on Depreciation
(i) Buildings fully depreciated
(ii) Plant and machinery being depreciated at 10% p.a.

Assets

Assets	31st Dec. £	28th Jan. Actual £	30th June Budget £
Land and Buildings			
At 1st January, at cost or valuation	100,000	100,000	100,000
Depreciation for period (see note)	(52,000)	(52,000)	(52,000)
	48,000	48,000	48,000
Plant and Machinery			
At 1st January, at cost or valuation	144,000	144,000	144,000
Additions for period, at cost		488	2,280
Depreciation at 1st January	(76,000)	(76,000)	(76,000)
Depreciation for period (see note)		(1,200)	(7,200)
	68,000	67,288	63,080
Trade Investments, at cost	22,000	22,000	22,000
Total Fixed Assets	138,000	137,288	133,080
Stocks.—Raw Materials	21,680	21,680	24,680
Work-in-process	2,250	1,830	} 12,650
Finished Products	16,800	16,100	
Engineering Stores	12,000	12,000	12,000
	52,730	51,610	49,330
Liquid Assets (Net)			
Sundry Debtors	67,200	} 64,634	} 76,883
Cash and Bank Balances	10,013		
Less: Sundry Creditors	(14,200)		
	63,013	64,634	76,883
Net Current Assets	115,743	116,244	126,213
	253,743	253,532	259,293

Fig. A-3

OPERATING STANDARDS

Materials	Budgeted Rates per unit	1st half-year Standard Usage (per ton of finished product)
Material No. 21	£10	0·5 tons (all products)
37	£18	0·5 ,, (prod. A) 0·25 ,, (,, B) Substitute for No. 37 (if cheaper)
38	£19	0·25 tons (prod. B) 0·5 ,, (,, C)
42	£6	
Packaging material	£1	1 case of 100 containers
Direct Labour		
Preparation (product B)	8/- per hour	9·0 Std. hours per ton
,, (,, C)	,, ,, ,,	6·0 ,, ,, ,,
Processing & Packaging Dept.		
AC M/c	,, ,, ,,	2·5 Std. hours per M/c hour
BC M/c	,, ,, ,,	1·66 ,, ,, ,, ,,
Power and Steam (Per M/c hour)	*Power*	*Steam*
Processing & Packaging Dept.		
AC M/c	180 kW. Hrs. @ 1d.	0·5 tons @ 20/-
BC M/c	90 ,, ,, ,,	0·33 ,, ,, ,,
Output Standards		
Processing & Packaging Dept.		
'AC' M/cs	Product A	3·33 M/c hours per ton
	,, C	2·0 ,, ,, ,, ,,
'BC' M/cs	Product B	4·0 ,, ,, ,, ,,
	,, C	2·0 ,, ,, ,, ,,

Fig. A-4

OPERATING BUDGETS

I. SALES

1st half-year

Period	Bud. S.P. per ton	1		2		3		4		5		6		Total	
Weeks		4 wks to 28 Jan.		4 wks to		5 wks to		4 wks to		4 wks to		5 wks to		26 weeks	
Product		Tons	£	Tons	£	Tons	£	Tons	£	Tons	£	Tons	£	Tons	£
A	£65	120	7,800											780	50,700
B	£50	100	5,000											640	32,000
C	£40	80	3,200											540	21,600
Total		300	16,000											1,960	104,300
Less Allowance			345												2,300
			£15,655												£102,000

II. PRODUCTION

Normal shift hours: 45 per week

Budgeted M/C running hours: 40 per week

Period	1		2		3		4		5		6		Total	
Weeks	4 wks to 28 Jan.		4 wks to		5 wks to		4 wks to		4 wks to		5 wks to		26 weeks	
6 Processing M/c	3 AC	3 BC	AC	BC	AC	BC	AC	BC	AC	BC	AC	BC	AC	BC
Product	Tons	Tons	Tons	Tons	Tons	Tons	Tons	Tons	Tons	Tons	Tons	Tons	Tons	Tons
A	120												720	
B	40	100											240	600
C		40												240
Total	160	140											960	840
	300 tons												1,800 tons	

Fig. A-5

803

Operating Budgets (Fig. A-5)

As the HEBCO profits are limited by capacity to sell rather than capacity to produce, the sales forecasts are the starting-point for the half-yearly budgets. The forecasts are prepared on the assumption that selling prices of the three products remain unchanged. In order to help in the planning of production and stock levels, the forecast sales are broken down into the six control periods of four or five weeks into which the half year is divided (see Fig. A-5).

Before these forecasts are finalised as the official sales budget, the corresponding production targets are set out for the same periods, after taking into account planned changes in the stock level. If no production difficulties arise, the sales budget will then be finalised, subject however to possible amendment later if budgeted profit margins are unsatisfactory. In the example, it is planned to reduce stocks of finished products by 160 tons during the half year, but for the first four-week period, both sales and production are budgeted at 300 tons.[1] In order to plan and balance the labour and machine loading, the allocation of the budgeted production to the two groups of processing machines is shown in the budget (based on output standards per Fig. A-4). This budgeted allocation will also assist in the computation of

the production costs for product C (which can be processed on either group of machines).

The Sales and Production budgets, when agreed, provide the foundation stones for building up the remaining budget statements.

Materials Budget (Fig. A-6)

The budgeted production of 1,800 tons of finished products will require a theoretical usage of 1,800 tons of raw materials, divided up as shown in the table of material requirements in Fig. A-6. The detailed figures are obtained by multiplying budgeted output by the material usage standards set out in Fig. A-4. Budgeted rates per ton are supplied by Buying Department, and the total cost obtained by extension.

No allowance is included in the standards for process losses, but from previous experience it is known that excess usage of materials usually amounts to under 5 per cent.

The budget statement contains a reference to material No. 38 which can be used as a substitute for No. 37 on a ton per ton basis. It will only be so used if the current replacement price of No. 38 should fall below that of No. 37—at the date the budget was prepared the price was £1 per ton higher.

[1] On the basis of 40 machine running hours per week.

MATERIALS BUDGET

1st half-year

Product Requirements	Budgeted Output Tons	Material Requirements				Packaging (cases)
		No. 21 Tons	No. 37 Tons	No. 38 Tons	No. 42 Tons	
A	720	360	360	substitute for No. 37 (same quantity)	150	⎰1,800 cases
B	600	300	150		240	⎱of containers
C	480	240				
	1,800	900	510		390	1,800
Unit costs		£10	£18	£19	£6	£1
Total costs	£22,320	9,000	9,180		2,340	1,800

Fig. A-6

PRODUCTION DEPARTMENTS—BUDGETS

I. DEPARTMENTAL CONVERSION COSTS

1st half-year

Control Basis	Conversion Costs (excl. Plant costs)	Total all Departments	Preparation & Mixing Dept.	Processing & Packaging Dept. Total	'AC' M/c	'BC' M/c
		£	£	£	£	£
Variable	Direct labour	8,112	3,312	4,800	2,880	1,920
Semi-v.	Ancillary labour	1,680	720	960	480	480
,,	Overtime premium	120	120			
,,	National insce., etc.	810	330	480	270	210
Variable	Power	3,240		3,240	2,160	1,080
,,	Steam	2,400		2,400	1,440	960
Semi-v.	Routine maintenance (lubrication, etc.)	1,200		1,200	690	510
,,	Cleaning	720	720			
Fixed	Supervision	1,638	318	1,320	720	600
	Total	£19,920	5,520	14,400	8,640	5,760

II. PLANT COSTS (PER SEPARATE BUDGET)

	Total all Departments	Preparation & Mixing	Processing Total	'AC' M/c	'BC' M/c
Maintenance overhauls, repairs, depn.	17,280		17,280	12,960	4,320

III. BUDGETED OUTPUT

	Total all Departments	Preparation & Mixing	Processing Total	'AC' M/c	'BC' M/c
Standard hours		8,280 (man hours)	(M/c hours)	2,880	2,880

IV. STANDARD COSTS (PER STANDARD HOUR)

	Total all Departments	Preparation & Mixing	Processing Total	'AC' M/c	'BC' M/c
Production activities		13s. 4d.		£3 0 0	£2 0 0
Plant costs		—		£4 10 0	£1 10 0

Fig. A-7

PLANT COSTS BUDGET
(PLANT MAINTENANCE AND DEPRECIATION)

1st half-year

| | Control Basis | Total | Labour | | Materials | Outside Contracts | Over-heads | Process & Packaging | | |
			Fitters	Elecn.				Total	'AC' M/cs	'BC' M/cs
Maintenance & Repairs										
Routine maintenance (lubrication, etc.)	SV	*1,200						} 10,080	} 8,160	} 1,920
Planned inspections	See note	2,520								
Planned overhauls	SV	4,800								
Emergency repairs		2,760								
Alterations & Improvements										
Capital Projects	See note	11,280 / *1,080 / *1,200								
*Less costs transferred		13,560 / 3,480								
Total—Mtce. overhauls & repair jobs		10,080						10,080		
Depreciation of Plant, etc.										
Depreciation at agreed rates	F	7,200						7,200	4,800	2,400
Total to be charged to Factory operating		£17,280						17,280	12,960	4,320

The allowed cost for planned inspections or planned overhauls is based on an assessment of the work actually done during the period. The same comment applies to alterations, improvements and capital projects.

* These three items add up to the sub-total of "costs transferred".

807

Fig. A-8

Production Departments—Budgets (Fig. A-7).

In the third part of this statement, the work load involved in converting raw materials to finished products is calculated from the budgeted output (Fig. A-5) and the appropriate output standards (Fig. A-4). The next step is to calculate out the costs of carrying out the work in the two departments, and the result is set out in the first section of the statement. The variable costs are calculated by reference to the usage standards given in Fig. A-4. Other costs are budgeted by reference to the expected level of activity during the half year, and in the light of recent experience. It is intended to make a more specific examination of the requirements for each of these items after more experience has been gained. Meanwhile it is agreed that for semi-variable costs (except overtime premium) each 10 per cent. change in activity will lead to a 5 per cent. change in the budgeted allowance, with pro-rata adjustments for smaller variations.

Overtime premium included in the Preparation and Mixing Department budget is recognition that overtime is authorised when departmental "activity" runs above 105 per cent. of average, and that there will be seasonal peaks and troughs during the half-year.

The total budgeted conversion cost of each department is divided by the budgeted

output (measured in standard hours of work) and the result expressed as a standard cost per standard hour.

For convenience, the total plant costs from Fig. A-8 are summarised here and also expressed as a standard cost per standard machine hour.

Budgeted Plant Costs (Fig. A-8)

Maintenance and repair costs are considered to be primarily the responsibility of the Chief Engineer, but the budgeted costs of planned inspections and planned overhauls are built up from detailed records and agreed in advance with production management. The budgeted allowance subsequently granted for these costs will be related to the work actually done during the period—if planned overhauls are postponed, the allowance will be similarly deferred.

Routine lubrication, cleaning, etc., is considered to be a direct charge to the production department concerned. Emergency (breakdown) repairs are budgeted by reference to previous experience, and are treated in the same way as the semi-variable departmental costs described above.

The budget includes the estimated cost of any alterations, improvements or capital work to be carried out by the maintenance staff or outside contractors during the period; the total cost of jobs to be done during the

FACTORY OPERATING—SUMMARY BUDGET

	£	£
Materials		
As per Materials budget		22,320
Conversion Costs		
(a) *Direct*		
Production activities—per Deptl. budgets	19,920	
Mtce. & Depr.—per Plant costs budget	17,280	
Total direct conversion costs		37,200
(b) *Indirect*		
General charges:		
Factory management	7,500	
Factory general services	4,200	
Factory clerical	3,180	
Total indirect conversion costs		14,880
(equiv. to 40% of direct costs)		
Total Factory Operating Costs		£74,400
Note: Expected variance at 5%		£3,720

1st half-year
Details of
Factory General Charges

	£	£
Management:		7,500
General Services:		4,200
Clerical:		3,180
		£14,880

Fig. A–9

STANDARD PRODUCT COSTS (PER TON)

	Budget rate per unit	'A' Qty.	'A' £ s. d.	'B' Qty.	'B' £ s. d.	'C' Qty.	'C' £ s. d.	Profit Planning Basis
Materials								
No. 21	per Ton £10	Tons 0·5	5 0 0	Tons 0·5	5 0 0	Tons 0·5	5 0 0	
37	£18	0·5	9 0 0	0·25	4 10 0	—	—	
38 (substitute for 37)	£19	—	—	—	—	—	—	
42	£6	—	—	0·25	1 10 0	0·5	3 0 0	
			14 0 0		11 0 0		8 0 0	
Packaging material			1 0 0		1 0 0		1 0 0	
Total Materials			15 0 0		12 0 0		9 0 0	Variable
Production Activities								
Preparation & Mixing	Per hour 13s. 4d.	Std. hours	—	Std. hours 9·0 man hrs.	6 0 0	Std. hours 6·0 man hrs.	4 0 0	
Processing & Packaging		'A' M/c: 3¼ M/c hrs. @ £3	10 0 0	'B' M/c: 4 M/c hrs. @ £2	8 0 0	'A' or 'B' M/c: 2 M/c hrs. @ £2 10 0	5 0 0	
			10 0 0		14 0 0		9 0 0	Variable
Plant Costs (Mtce. & Depreciation) Processing & Packaging		'A' M/c: 3¼ M/c hrs. @ £4 10 0	15 0 0	'B' M/c: 4 M/c hrs. @ £1 10 0	6 0 0	'A' or 'B' M/c: 2 M/c hrs. @ £3	6 0 0	Fixed
Total direct costs of conversion			25 0 0		20 0 0		15 0 0	
General Factory Charges 40% of total direct costs of conversion			10 0 0		8 0 0		6 0 0	Fixed
Total Standard Costs			£50 0 0		£40 0 0		£30 0 0	

PLUS 5% ALLOWANCE FOR EXPECTED VARIANCES

Fig. A 10

Based on
'Full' Standard Costs

← Period Budgets —— 1st half-year →

	Previous Half-year (Estimated Actual)			Budget for Half-year to 30th June			4 weeks to 28 Jan.	4 weeks to ….	5 weeks to
	Tons	Price	£	Tons	Price	£			
Sales delivered									
A				780	£65	50,700			
B				640	£50	32,000			
C				540	£40	21,600			
Total				1,960		104,300			

Less: Factory Cost of Sales

	Sales Allce.	Per ton	£
A	600	£50	39,000
B	800	£40	25,600
C	900	£30	16,200
Total	£2,300		£80,800

(83,100)

Gross Margin

	% of Sales	Per Ton	
A	21·9	£14 4 8	11,100
B	17·5	£8 15 0	5,600
C	20·9	£8 6 8	4,500
Total	20·3	£10 16 4	21,200

Less: Selling and Administration expenses   11,930

Net Trading Profit   £9,270

Expected Profit after allowing for 5% factory operating variances (£3,720)   £5,550

Equivalent to a return of 4·4% p.a. on the B/S value of Capital Employed

Fig. A–11

year is then analysed between labour, materials, overheads, etc., as shown on the table. A comparison of the total labour cost shown in the budget with the current weekly pay roll $\times 26$ will reveal whether or not there is scope for any reductions in staff.

The calculated depreciation costs (plant and machinery) are also included in the statement.

Factory Operating—Summary Budget (Fig. A-9)

This statement includes the budgeted indirect costs of conversion—those charges that cannot be identified with a specific operating department. They include management salaries, certain general services such as welfare, etc., and clerical costs. These are all regarded as costs unaffected in the short term by fluctuations in the volume of output, so that subsequent control will consist of a straightforward comparison with the original budget.

The budget total shows the total outgoings for which the factory manager will be responsible; the total of £74,000 is transferred to the budgeted Work-in-Process and Finished Goods Account on Fig. A-12. It is expected that actual costs will exceed budget by 5 per cent.

Standard Products Costs (Fig. A-10)

On this statement all the budgeted costs set out in Figs. A-6 to A-9 have been re-analysed by products instead of by management responsibilities, and have been shown as a "standard cost" per ton. Since the starting-point in each case is the same, e.g. standard quantities, standard times, budgeted unit prices, etc., a link is established between standard product costs and subsequent control statements. This link will avoid the necessity of frequent re-calculation of product costs.

For profit planning or pricing purposes, it is useful to know what part of the total product cost is variable with output and what part is represented by an apportionment of fixed costs.

Material costs are clearly variable, and General Factory Charges can be considered as fixed in the short term. The remaining items of cost are partly variable, partly fixed and HEBCO decide that a sufficiently accurate classification for product costing purposes can be obtained by regarding the costs of Production Activities as variable, and the "Plant Costs" (overhauls, repairs and depreciation) as fixed. For *control* purposes, however, it is necessary to look at the cost behaviour of each item separately, as indicated in departmental or plant costs budgets.

No allowance is included in the standard product costs for sub-standard performance, and a note at the bottom of the sheet gives a warning that when estimating future profits it must be anticipated that actual costs are likely to exceed standard by about 5 per cent.

BUDGETED

WORK-IN-PROCESS AND FINISHED GOODS ACCOUNT

(All Items Valued at Standard Factory Cost)

					1st half-year
			£	£	£
1 Jan.	Balance b/f:			2,250	
	Work-in-process				
	Finished Goods				
	A	150 tons	@ £50	7,500	
	B	120 ,,	,, £40	4,800	
	C	150 ,,	,, £30	4,500	
		420		16,800	19,050
30 June	Add: Value of work done during the half-year (per Factory operating summary budget)				74,400
					£93,450
30 June	Value of goods sold during half-year (per budgeted Profit & Loss statement)				80,800
30 June	Balance c/f:			2,250	
	Work-in-process				
	Finished Goods				
	A	90 tons	@ £50	4,500	
	B	80 ,,	,, £40	3,200	
	C	90 ,,	,, £30	2,700	
		260		10,400	12,650
					£93,450

Fig. A-12

813

Budgeted Sales and Profit Statement (Fig. A-11)

Because of the expected change in stock levels, it is not possible to arrive at the profit for the half-year by adding the budgeted factory costs (Fig. A-9) to the budgeted selling and administrative expenses and deducting the total from the budgeted net sales. The method adopted in Fig. A-11 is to arrive at the budgeted "Gross Margin" by deducting the standard cost of sales (budgeted sales volume multiplied by standard cost per ton) and the estimated sales allowances from the budgeted sales total. Further deductions are then made (as shown in Fig. A-11) resulting in an expected profit for the half-year of £5,550. This is equivalent to 4.4 per cent. per annum on the Balance Sheet value of capital employed, and the Directors decide that this is the most that can be expected under present circumstances. The gross margins on each of the three products are considered reasonable, and the whole set of budgets for the half-year is approved. Comparative figures are provided for the previous half-year's results, and space is left for inserting the four-weekly period budgets.

Budgeted Work-in-Process and Finished Goods Account (Fig. A-12)

This statement acts as a useful check on the arithmetical accuracy of the budget statements, and summarises the overall effect of the budget proposals on stock and work-in-process levels. The statement will reflect the Board policy for the period regarding variations in these levels.

Source and Application of Funds (Fig. A-13)

If HEBCO earns a profit equivalent to that included in the half-yearly budget, the liquid funds of the business will be increased by the same amount (£5,550); they will also be increased by the amount provided for depreciation (£7,200) and by the planned decrease of finished goods stocks (£6,400). On the other hand, the company consider that a further £3,000 will be needed to finance raw material stocks (owing to rising prices) and £2,280 is required for capital additions. The above factors are detailed in the statement of Source and Application of Funds (Fig. A-13) from which it will be seen that the net effect is an estimated rise of £13,870 in the net liquid funds during the period.

SOURCE AND APPLICATION OF FUNDS

1st half-year

	28th Jan.	30th June
	Actual	Budget
Net liquid assets 1st January		
Sundry debtors	67,200	67,200
Cash and bank balances	10,013	10,013
	77,213	77,213
Less creditors	14,200	14,200
	63,013	63,013
Increase in funds during period:		
Net trading profit (Loss)	(211)	5,550
Depreciation charged	1,200	7,200
Decrease in stocks—work-in-process	420	} 6,400
—finished goods	700	
	2,109	19,150
Less: Decrease in funds during period:		
Increase in raw material stocks	—	3,000
Capitalised additions to plant & machinery	488	2,280
	488	5,280
Net increase	1,621	13,870
Net liquid assets at end of period	£64,634	£76,883

Fig. A–13

815

As a separate exercise, the accountant of the company would prepare a budgeted statement of *cash and bank* receipts and payments to make sure that the balances held were sufficient to meet all probable needs. The statement would be on similar lines to that shown for liquid funds, but would take into account expected changes in debtors' and creditors' balances.

Balance Sheet (Fig. A-3)

This is set out in columnar form, with comparison between the estimated actual position at 31st December and the budgeted position at 30th June. The total value of capital employed is shown as being increased by £5,550—the expected profit for the half-year—while the assets side of the balance sheet shows the corresponding changes in fixed assets, stocks and net liquid assets respectively.

V. SHORT-TERM PROFIT PLANNING

Budgeting, whether carried out annually or half-yearly, is usually undertaken well before the start of the first control period: this is to give time for the necessary discussions, adjustments and final co-ordination and approval. As the starting-point for budgets is usually the sales forecast, this means that the latter document must be prepared several months in advance of the first control period.

The HEBCO sales forecast for the half-year to 30th June was prepared early in October, and during the following three months it became apparent that the forecast had been over-optimistic. The trend of sales during the latter part of the year pointed to the fact that tonnage sold during the half-year to 30th June would be about 10 per cent. below budget. Moreover it was probable that the "product mix" would also differ from budget.

The Directors came to the conclusion that in order to offset this decline in sales volume it would be necessary to increase selling prices of all products by £5 per ton. Before confirming this decision, they called for the Budgeted Sales and Profit Statement, with a view to assessing the effect of the above changes. It was thought that an increase of £5 per ton would not lead to any further decline in sales.

A scrutiny of the budgeted profit statement showed that it is not possible to assess the effect of volume or "product mix" changes without considerable re-calculation. In order to get over this difficulty, the accountant agreed to prepare a similar statement on marginal costing lines, showing the contribution of each product towards the fixed charges and profits for the period.

BUDGETED SALES AND PROFIT STATEMENT

Based on Marginal Costs

Period Budgets ——— 1st half-year

	Previous Half-year (Estimated Actual)					Budget for Half-year to 30th June			Period Budgets		
	Tons	Price	£			Tons	Price	£	4 weeks to 28th Jan.	4 weeks to	5 weeks to ....
Sales delivered A						780	£65	50,700			
B						640	£50	32,000			
C						540	£40	21,600			
Total						1,960		104,300			

	Sales Allce.	Marginal Cost of Sales Per ton	£	Price	£
Less					
A	600	£25	19,500	30,600	
B	800	£26	16,640	14,560	
C	900	£18	9,720	10,980	
Total	£2,300		£45,860		48,160

Gross Contribution	% of Sales	Per Ton			
A	60·3	£39	4	8	
B	45·5	£22	15	0	
C	50·9	£20	6	8	
Total	53·8	£28	12	10	56,140

	£
Less: Plant overhauls, repairs and depreciation	17,280
Factory general charges	14,880
Selling and admin. expenses	11,930
	44,900
Net Trading Profit	£12,050

Expected profit after allowing for 5% Factory operating variances (£3,720) £8,330

Equivalent to a return of 6·6% p.a. on the B/S value of capital employed.

Fig. A–14

817

Budgeted Sales and Profit Statement (Marginal Costs) (Fig. A-14)

If a comparison is made between Figs. A-11 and A-14, it will be seen that the main difference is the substitution of the "marginal" product costs for the "full" costs in arriving at the cost of sales. The marginal costs are calculated by adding together the variable elements of the standard product costs per ton given in Fig. A-10. The fixed factory costs which are thus excluded from the marginal product costs are deducted in Fig. A-14 as a block charge from the total contributions figure.

One other important difference needs to be noted. The budgeted profit for the half-year shown in Fig. A-14 is greater than that shown Fig. A-11 by £2,780. This difference comes about as the result of the planned decrease in finished product stocks during the half-year, and the exclusion of fixed costs from marginal costing stock valuations:

Decreases in stocks during the half-year to 30th June (budgeted)

			£
A	60 tons at fixed cost content £25 =	1,500
B	40 tons at fixed cost content £14 =	560
C	60 tons at fixed cost content £12 =	720
		2,780

If stocks during the following half-year should increase by the same quantities, the position would be reversed, and the profit shown by the marginal costing method would be £2,780 less than that shown by the other (see more detailed explanation on page 787).

On examination of Fig. A-14, the directors can see at a glance that the effect of a 10 per cent. decrease in sales will be to reduce contributions—and final profit—by 10 per cent. of £56,140 = £5,614. Armed with this knowledge, they can now revert to the "official" budgeted sales and profit statement and work out that the expected profit of £5,550 will in fact be converted into a loss of £64 unless steps are taken to improve profitability by increasing selling prices, etc. They can also establish the fact that an increase of £5 per ton on the anticipated volume of sales (10 per cent. below budget) should ensure that the final profit amounts to around £8,000 in the half-year—assuming that there is no change in product mix or other factors.

Consequently, the directors confirm the decision to increase selling prices by £5 per ton from 1st January.

Profit Planning Chart (Fig. A-15)

In order to keep the position under constant review, the accountant prepares a "Profit Planning" chart. The chart at Fig. A-15 relates to the four-week period to

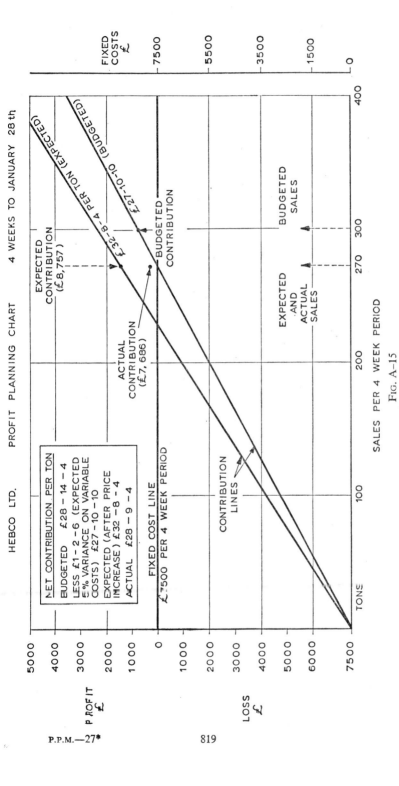

HEBCO LTD.   PROFIT PLANNING CHART   4 WEEKS TO JANUARY 28 th

NET CONTRIBUTION PER TON

BUDGETED   £28 – 14 – 4
LESS £1 – 2 – 6 (EXPECTED
5% VARIANCE ON VARIABLE
COSTS) £27 – 10 – 10
EXPECTED (AFTER PRICE
IMCREASE) £32 – 8 – 4
ACTUAL   £28 – 9 – 4

FIXED COST LINE
£7500 PER 4 WEEK PERIOD

CONTRIBUTION
LINES

EXPECTED
CONTRIBUTION
(£8,757)

£32–8–4 PER TON (EXPECTED)

£27–10–10 (BUDGETED)

ACTUAL
CONTRIBUTION
(£7,686)

BUDGETED
CONTRIBUTION

BUDGETED
SALES

EXPECTED
AND ACTUAL
SALES

SALES PER 4 WEEK PERIOD

FIG. A–15

FIXED COSTS £: 7500   5500   3500   1500   0

PROFIT £: 5000 4000 3000 2000 1000   0
LOSS £: 1000 2000 3000 4000 5000 6000 7500

TONS   100   200   270   300   400

P.P.M.—27*

819

28th January, and budgeted and "expected" contributions are plotted in relation to budgeted fixed costs. The data on the chart are drawn from the information set out in Fig. A-26. The vertical distance between the contribution line and the fixed cost line represents the expected profit or loss at varying levels of sales volume.

Actual sales for the four-week period to 28th January proved to be in line with the recent trend, and the total tonnage sold was 10 per cent. below budget.

	Total Sales	Tonnage Sales			% Sales Mix		
		A	B	C	A	B	C
Budgeted sales	300	120	100	80	40·0	33·3	26·7
Actual sales	270	80	120	70	29·6	44·4	26·0
Variance	−30	−40	+20	−10	−10·4	+11·1	−0·7

As will be seen from the details given above, there was a considerable variation in the sales mix—the percentage sales of product B increased mainly at the expense of the more profitable product A.

In order to avoid building up stocks of finished products, the volume of production was also cut back by 10 per cent. In actual fact stocks were reduced by 10 tons during the period, because 10 tons of work-in-process had to be scrapped as faulty, and this tonnage

The "expected" contribution line is the budgeted line amended for the price increase.

For reasons which will be explained later, the actual contribution for the four weeks to 28th January did not come anywhere near expectation. The contribution earned is marked on the chart with an "X".

VI. RESULTS FOR THE FOUR-WEEK PERIOD

Details are as follows:

Production	Total	A	B	C
Budgeted tonnage	300	120	100	80
Actual tonnage (good)	260	60	120	80
Actual tonnage (scrapped)	10			10

The actual results achieved and costs incurred are shown in the control reports for the four-week period listed below. Figures in brackets in these reports represent either deductions or "favourable variances".

Material Control (Fig. A-16)

In the Preparation and Mixing Department, 248 tons of raw materials were dealt with, and transferred to the Processing and Packaging Department; 30 tons of material for product A which had already been mixed in the previous period and included in work-in-process at

MATERIAL CONTROL REPORT

Output (Tons)	Material	Budget Cost per unit	Actual Cost Quantity (Tons)	Cost per Ton	Value £	Total Tons/£	Variances Price	Sundry	Usage	Standard Cost Quantity (Tons)	Value £
		Per Ton	Preparation and Mixing Dept.								
30 tons A	No. 21	£10	125	£12	1,500	5	250	Mix 50	50	120	1,200
120 ,, B	,, 37	£18	—	—	—		150			45	810
*90 ,, C	,, 38 (subst.)	£19	50	£22	1,100	5	(73)		90	75	450
	,, 42	£6	73	£5	365	(2)			(12)		
240 tons	Totals (tons)		248 tons			8 tons			128	240 tons	
	Totals (£)				£2,965	£505	327	50			£2,460
		£1 per case	Processing and Packaging Dept.								
†60 tons A	Packing materials			20/9d. per case	290		10	Rejects 70	20	260 cases	260
120 ,, B											
80 ,, C	Scrap (std. cost)		10 tons of 'C'	Per Ton £8	—						(80)
	Value of raw mtl. recovered		10 tons of 'C'	(£1)	(10)						
260 tons					280	100	10	70	20		£180
					£3,245	605	337	120	148		£2,640

(* Of which 10 tons subsequently rejected as faulty.)
(† Including 30 tons of raw material for product 'A' mixed in previous period and included in work-in-process at 1st January.)

Fig. A–16

821

1st January were transferred to the latter department from the buffer store. Ten tons of product C were spoilt during preparation or processing and had to be sold as scrap at £1 per ton.

In the material control report, the actual costs of materials used are compared with the standard cost—the latter being calculated by reference to actual output, usage standards, and budgeted material prices. Prices of all materials except No. 42 were higher than those included in the budget; No. 37 had risen to £23 per ton, so that No. 38 was used in substitution, having risen by £3 to £22 per ton. The extra cost of using 50 tons of the latter material at £22 instead of 50 tons of No. 37 at a budgeted price of £18 per ton is analysed as:

Price variance 50 × (£22 − £19) = £150
Mix   „   50 × (£19 − £18) = £50

The latter could be equally well described as "Formula substitution" variance.

The difference between the standard cost of the raw materials scrapped (valued at £8 per ton) and the scrap value received is written off as variance due to "Rejects".

Preparation and Mixing Department Operating Statement (Fig. A-17)

The direct labour in this department is engaged wholly on preparation of materials for products B and C. Different groups of operatives are required for each product, and separate cost centres are therefore established for Preparation B and C. Mixing the materials is carried out as necessary by a supervisor—the time involved is too small to make it worth while charging out separately. In order to assist in planning the labour loading, and in measuring the "activity ratio" of the department as a whole, the output tonnage figures are converted into standard hours of direct labour.

As actual throughput of B and C was in excess of budget, the standard hours equivalent is higher than budget, and the activity ratio works out at:

Department

$$\text{Preparation B } \frac{1,080}{900} \times 100 = 120$$

$$\text{Preparation C } \frac{540}{480} \times 100 = 112$$

$$\left.\right\} \; \frac{1,620}{1,380} \times 100 = 117$$

OPERATING STATEMENT

I. ACTIVITIES

ACTIVITY RATIO 117%

4 weeks to 28th January

Pro-duct	Output		Std. Man Hours per ton	Cost Centres	Man Hours				Control Ratios			Standard Costs		
	Budget Tons	Actual Tons			Actual Waiting Time	†Budget	†Stand	†Actual	Activity %	Operator Perfce. %	Overall Perfce. %	Per Hour	Budget Hours	Std. Hours
B	£ 100	120	9	Preparation 'B'	50	900	1,080	1,150	120	94	90	s. d. 13 4	£ 600	£ 720
C	80	*90	6	" 'C'	40	480	540	560	112	96	90	13 4	320	360
Total					90	1,380	1,620	1,710	117	95	90		920	1,080

II. COSTS AND VARIANCES

Control Basis	Original Budget	Allowed Cost		Actual Cost	Variances					
					Total	Labour	Services	Sundry	Faulty Work	Volume
	£	£		£	£	£	£	£	£	£
V	552	648	Direct labour (8/- per hour)	720		65				
S/V	120	130	Ancillary labour	138						
S/V	20	30	Overtime premium (direct labour)	15						
S/V	55	60	Nat. insce., etc.	60						
S/V	120	130	Cleaning	121			(9)			
F	53	53	Supervision	55				2		
	£920	1,051		£1,109	69	65	(9)	2	40	(29)

Standard Costs Absorbed

120 tons B @ £6 = 720
*80 tons C @ £4 = 320
£1,040

*10 tons of C rejected as faulty.   † Direct labour hours, excluding waiting time.

Fig. A-17

823

Overall performance ratios are calculated by comparing actual hours worked on production with the standard hour equivalent of the work done:

Department

Preparation B $\dfrac{1,080}{1,150} \times 100 = 94$ $\left.\begin{array}{l}\\\\\end{array}\right\}$ $\dfrac{1,620}{1,710} \times 100 = 95$

Preparation C $\dfrac{540}{560} \times 100 = 96$

The overall performance for the department after taking waiting time into account works out at 10 per cent. below "standard performance", i.e. at 90.

$$\frac{1,620}{1,800} \times 100 = 90$$

and the same result is shown in each cost centre.

The details set out in Figs. A-5 and A-7 showed that the total budgeted production for the 26 weeks amounted to 1,800 tons, while the cost of preparation and mixing for the same period was put at £5,520. In breaking down these figures to arrive at the budget for the four-week period to 28th January, it was decided to divide by $\frac{4}{24}$ths rather than $\frac{4}{26}$ths—this is because the half-year contained approximately two weeks of holiday shut-down. Actual salaries and other factory fixed charges for the half-year will be similarly apportioned when arriving at the amounts to be entered in the control statements. This procedure tends to spread the costs over the periods of actual production, and avoids producing a statement showing losses incurred while the factory is shut down for statutory or annual holidays. The same principle is adopted in spreading the cost of holiday pay over the periods of production.

The "allowed cost" for direct labour is calculated by reference to standard hours produced (1,620) and the budgeted rate of 8s. per hour. The allowances for semi-variable costs are obtained by flexing the original budget figure by one-half of (activity ratio less 100) per cent. The allowance for overtime premium is read off from a special schedule of allowances: e.g. at 117 per cent. activity = £30 per week. The actual overtime paid was less than this allowance, due partly to a temporary transfer of staff from the Processing Department.

Due to the increase in the level of activity, the standard cost of the work done (£1,080) is £29 greater than the allowed cost (£1,051). This difference is shown as a "favourable" volume variance, and arises because the fixed costs (and the fixed element of semi-variable costs) are unaffected by an increase in activity.

Cumulative 'Actuals' for 4 weeks to 28 Jan.

(Original budget Prepn. B 225 hrs. Prepn. C 120 hrs.)

	Cumulative				Week No:	4			3	2	1
					Week ending:	Jan. 28			Jan. 21	Jan. 14	Jan. 7
	Prep. B	Prep. C	Total			Prep. B	Prep. C	Total	Total	Total	Total
Control Indices (Actual)						Std. Hrs.	Std. Hrs.	Std. Hrs.	Std. Hrs.	Std. Hrs.	Std. Hrs.
Activity	120	115	117			113	121	116			
Operator Performance	94	96	95			85	97	89			
Overall Performance	90	90	90			85	81	83			
Actual work done on measured & estimated work (Std. hrs.)	S. Hrs.	S. Hrs.	S. Hrs.			Std. Hrs.	Std. Hrs.	Std. Hrs.	Std. Hrs.	Std. Hrs.	Std. Hrs.
	1,080	540	1,620			255	145	400			

Direct Labour

Cost Centre	Std. Hrs. per Ton	Tons		Cumulative Hours		Standard	Variance	Actual			
Preparation B	9·0	24·4				Hours	Hours	Hours	Hours	Hours	Hours
„ B	9·0	3·9									
„ C	6·0	24·2									

	Cumulative Hours	Standard	Variance	Actual			
Measured work	1,150	220	45	300			
Estimated work		35	5				
Measured work	560	145		150			
Sub-total	1,150	—	50	450			
Waiting time (direct labour) Prep. B — Prep. C 30	50		30	30			
	560 / 40	400	30				
Total attendance hours	600 / 1,800	400	80	480			
Overtime premium hours	37½ / 37½	—	—	—			
Total hours paid for	1,200 / 637½ / 1,837½	400	80	480			
	£	£	£	£	£	£	£
Cost of attendance hours	720	160	32	192			
Cost of overtime premium hours	15	—	—	—			
Total cost	£735	£160	£32	£192	£	£	£

Other Labour

	Allowed Hours	Actual Hours		Cumulative £	Allowed	Variance	Actual			
Ancillary labour	80	90		138	32	4	36	Actual	Actual	Actual
Cleaning	132	132		121	33	—	33			
Supervision				55	13	1	14			
Total cost				£314	£78	£5	£83	£	£	£

← Summary → | ← Width of this week's control sheet → | ← Previous weeks →

Note: The figures in the right-hand overlapping column of previous weeks' reports have been omitted; in practice they would be visible, and could be cross-added to give the four-weekly totals.

Fig. A-18

825

PROCESSING AND PACKAGING DEPARTMENT
OPERATING STATEMENT
I. ACTIVITIES

ACTIVITY RATIO 85%

4 weeks to 28th January

Product	Output (Budget Tons)	Output (Actual Tons)	Std. M/c Hrs. per Ton	No. of M/cs	Cost Centres	M/c Hrs Available	Running Hrs Budget	Running Hrs Stand	Running Hrs Actual	Activity %	Utilisation %	Eff'cy %	Effective Util'n %	Per M/c Hour	Budget Hours	Stand Hours	Direct Labour	Power	Steam
'A'	120	60	3¼														2·5 / 8/-	15/-	10/-
'C'	40	80	2	3	'AC' Machines	540	480	360	396	75	73	91	67	£3	1,440	1,080			
'B'	100	120	4														1·66 / 8/-	7/6	5/-
'C'	40	Nil	2	3	'BC' Machines	540	480	480	504	100	93·	95	89	£2	960	960			
Total	300	260								*85					2,400	2,040			

$$* \frac{£2,040}{£2,400} \times 100 = 85\%$$

II. COSTS AND VARIANCES

Control Basis	Orig. Budget Total	'A' M/c	'B' M/c	Allowed Cost		Actual Cost	Variances Total	Labour	Steam & Power	Sundry	Method	Volume	Standard Costs Absorbed
	£	£	£	£		£	£	£	£	£	£	£	£
V	800	480	320	680	Direct labour	720							60 tons of A @ £10 = £600
S/V	160	80	80	150	Ancillary labour	155		60					
S/V	—	—	—	—	Overtime premium	10							120 tons of B @ £8 = £960
S/V	80	45	35	75	Nat. insc., etc.	80							
V	540	360	180	450	Power	475			25				
V	400	240	160	340	Steam	320			(20)				80 tons of C @ £5 = £400
S/V	200	115	85	185	Routine maintenance (lubr., etc.)	190				·5			
F	220	120	100	220	Supervision	220							
	£2,400	1,440	960	2,100		£2,170	210	60	5	5	5	80	£1,960

PLANT MAINTENANCE AND DEPRECIATION COST REPORT

Plant Activity (per Fig. A—9)
'AC' M/cs 75%
'BC' M/cs 100%

4 weeks to 28th January

Original Budget	Allowed Cost		Actual Cost	Processing & Packaging 'AC' M/c	'BC' M/c	Method	Operating	Volume of Work	Volume of Output	Standard Costs
		Maintenance & Repairs	£							*Std. Hours*
200	185	*Routine maintenance (lubrication, cleaning, etc.)	190				5			'AC' M/cs 360 @ £4½ = £1,620
420	420	Planned inspection	440				20	250		'BC' M/cs 480 @ £1½ = £720
800	1,050	Planned overhauls	1,075	(Analysed			25			
460	430	Emergency repairs	420	as			(10)	(30)		£2,340
1,880	2,085	Sub-total	2,125	necessary)			40	220		
180	200	*Alterations & Improvements	218							*Absorbed*
200	250	*Capital projects	270							60 tons 'A' @ £15 = £900
2,260	2,535	*Less costs transferred	2,613				40	220		120 tons 'B' @ £6 = £720
580	635		678				(5)			
1,680	1,900	*Depreciation of Plant, etc.*	1,935				35	220		80 tons 'C' @ £6 = £480
1,200	1,200	Depreciation at agreed rates	1,200							£2,100
£2,880	£3,100		£3,135			240	35	220	540	

Total £1,035

£2,160 'AC' M/cs
£720 'BC' M/cs

Note: The above costs would also be analysed in more detail on supporting schedules, showing labour (by craft), materials, outside contracts and overheads, etc., and giving details of major jobs carried out.

* These three items add up to the sub-total of "costs transferred".

FIG. A—20

827

Owing to the subsequent rejection of 10 tons of product C, the standard costs absorbed in finished production are £40 lower than the standard cost of work done, and the difference, representing the departmental costs of preparing the 10 tons, is written off as a "Faulty Work" variance. Although included on the departmental operating statement, it does not follow that the Preparation Department was responsible for the rejection. A separate investigation would be necessary to determine this responsibility.

Preparation and Mixing Department—Weekly Labour Control Report (Fig. A-18)

This is an illustration of the more detailed weekly control sheets that would be circulated to departmental management. Similar weekly sheets would be prepared for the Processing and Packaging Department, giving details of machine, labour, power and steam costs.

Processing and Packaging Department Operating Statement (Fig. A-19)

Owing to the increased demand for product B, the BC machines have had to be allocated wholly to this product. Consequently the 80 tons of C have had to be made entirely on the more expensive AC machines, instead of being split 50:50 as visualised in the budget.

The excess cost of this switch (£80) is found by deducting the standard costs absorbed by the finished production (£1,960) from the standard cost of the work done (£2,040). It is shown on the statement as a "methods" variance.

The output of the BC machines, when converted into standard machine hours, is equal to the budgeted output (i.e. activity is 100 per cent.) but in the case of the AC machines, activity amounted to only 75 per cent. of the budget. The departmental activity (85 per cent.) is obtained from the comparison of standard costs of budgeted and standard hours.

$$\frac{2,040}{2,400} \times 100 = 85\%.$$

The other three sets of ratios are calculated as follows:

(i) Machine utilisation: $\dfrac{\text{Actual hours run}}{\text{Available hours}} \times 100$

(ii) Machine efficiency: $\dfrac{\text{Standard hours}}{\text{Actual hours run}} \times 100$

(iii) Effective utilisation: $\dfrac{\text{Standard hours}}{\text{Available hours}} \times 100.$

The calculation of the "original budget" figures for the four-week period, and the subsequent calculation

FACTORY OPERATING STATEMENT

Items in £ 4 weeks to 28th January

Original Budget		Actual Cost	Variances								Standard Costs	
			Total	Price	Mix	Re-jects	Operat-ing	Method	Vol. of Work	Vol. of Output	Absorbed	Factory Output
	Materials											
3,420	Preparation & Mixing	2,965		327	50		128					60 tons 'A' @ £50 p.t. = £3,000
300	Processing & Packaging	280		10		70	20					
3,720		3,245	605	337	50	70	148				2,640	
	Production Activities											
920 (Activity 117%)	Preparation & Mixing	1,109	69			40	58			(29)	1,040	
2,400 (85%)	Processing & Packaging	2,170	210				70	80		60	1,960	
3,320		3,279	279			40	128	80		31	3,000	120 tons 'B' @ £40 p.t. = £4,800
	Plant Costs											
1,680	Mtce. Overhauls & Repairs	1,935					35	240	220			
1,200	Depreciation	1,200					—					
2,880		3,135	1,035				35	240	220	540	2,100	
	*General Charges**											
1,250	Factory Management	1,310					60				60 tons 'A' @ £10	80 tons 'C' @ £30 p.t. = £2,400
700	Factory Services	680					(20)				120 tons 'B' @ £8	
530	Factory Clerical	572					42				80 tons 'C' @ £6	
2,480		2,562	522		110		82			330	2,040	
12,400		12,221	2,441	337	160	110	393	320	220	901	9,780	10,200

* These expenses would be detailed on supporting schedules.

FIG. A-21

of "allowed costs" follow similar lines to those described for the Preparation and Mixing Department. The volume variance (unfavourable) of £60 is a reflection of the under-utilisation of the AC machines, and is obtained by deducting standard cost of work done (£2,040) from the allowed cost (£2,100).

Plant Maintenance and Depreciation Cost Report (Fig. A-20)

Routine maintenance has already been considered in the departmental operating statements, and is included in the "costs transferred" deducted below. It is advisable to include the item on the maintenance report in the first place in order to review in perspective the whole cost of the engineering department. This is particularly necessary where men are switched from time to time between routine maintenance and the other maintenance jobs.

The allowed costs for planned inspections and planned overhauls are based on consideration of the work actually done during the period. An important overhaul originally planned for February was brought forward into January, so that the allowed cost is adjusted accordingly. The reduced allowance ($7\frac{1}{2}$ per cent.) for emergency repairs is due to the 15 per cent. decrease in the activity of the Processing and Packag-

ing Department. The calculation of these "allowed costs" enables the overall variances to be split between operating and volume of work variances.

Allowed costs for alterations, improvements and capital projects are also based on assessment of the work done.

The method variance of £240 is worked out in the same way as that shown on Fig. A-19—standard cost of standard machine hours in the Processing and Packaging Department, less the standard costs absorbed, and is a further reflection of the excess cost caused by processing 40 tons of C on the AC machines in place of the BC machines. The volume variance reflects the 25 per cent. under-utilisation of the AC machines—25 per cent. of £2,160 = £540.

Factory Operating Statement (Fig. A-21)

This statement summarises the statements already considered and includes the totals for factory management, factory services and factory clerical costs.

The standard cost of factory output (£10,200) is greater than the "standard costs absorbed" (£9,780) by £420, and this difference is due to the work in process at 1st January included in this period's factory output (see Fig. A-24).

SALES OPERATING STATEMENT

4 weeks to
28th January

Total Tons	Sales	Total £	A Tons / Prices	A £	B Tons / Prices	B £	C Tons / Prices	C £	Variance Total	Variance Mix	Variance Price	Variance Volume
300	Budgeted sales at budgeted mix and budgeted prices	£16,000	120 / £65	7,800	100 / £50	5,000	80 / £40	3,200				1,600
270	Actual sales at budgeted mix and budgeted prices	£14,400	108 / £65	7,020	90 / £50	4,500	72 / £40	2,880				
270	Actual sales at actual mix and budgeted prices	£14,000	80 / £65	5,200	120 / £50	6,000	70 / £40	2,800		400		
270	Actual sales at actual mix and actual prices*	£15,350	80 / £70	5,600	120 / £55	6,600	70 / £45	3,150			(1,350)	
									£650	400	(1,350)	1,600

	Sales Allowances Rebates, discounts, etc:	Total £	A Av. Rate	A £	B Av. Rate	B £	C Av. Rate	C £	Variance Total	Expense	Price	Volume
	On budgeted sales	£345	2%	156	2¼%	125	2%	64				
	On actual sales	£400	2¼%	140	2¼%	165	3%	95	£55	60	30	(35)

Original Budget	Selling & Admin Expenses Details would be listed here	Actual Cost			Variance			
£1,835		£1,820			(£15)			

* All prices increased by £5 per ton on 1st January.

FIG. A–22

831

The "volume of output" and "mix" variances are calculated as follows:

Volume of output

Budgeted tonnage	300	
Actual tonnage	260	

Under-absorption of $\dfrac{40}{300} \times £2,480 = £330.$

Mix

At budgeted mix, the 260 tons produced would have resulted in the following absorption of costs:

			£
A	104 tons @	£10 =	1,040
B	86⅔ tons @	£8 =	694
C	69⅓ tons @	£6 =	416
			2,150

compared with £2,040 actually absorbed, giving a mix variance of £110.

Sales Operating Statement (Fig. A-22)

Despite the increase of £5 per ton in selling prices, total sales values fell short of budgeted sales by £650, and this statement analyses this variance into its constituent parts. The sales mix variance of £400 reflects the effect on total sales values of selling a larger pro-

portion of the less expensive products. The second and third lines on the statement have been inserted merely to show how the variances are calculated.

Sales and Profit Statement (Fig. A-23)

This statement starts with the actual sales of the three products, and after deduction of actual sales allowances and the Factory Costs of Sales (at *standard*), arrives at the gross margin which would have been obtained if the factory had incurred no operating variances.

The actual operating variances (which relate to the actual *production* for the four-week period) are then transferred from the Factory Operating Statement and deducted to arrive at the Gross Profit of £1,609. Finally, Selling and Administrative expenses for the period (as detailed on Fig. A-22) are deducted, resulting in a net Trading Loss of £211 instead of the hoped for profit of £800.

An explanation for this disappointing result is provided by the detailed analysis included on the statement. The Factory Cost of Sales variances (volume and product mix) are obtained by following through the same procedure as that shown on Fig. A-22 for sales variances.

(Favourable variances shown in brackets)

	Previous Periods			Actual			Variances					Budget		
	4 weeks to......	4 weeks to......	5 weeks to......	Tons	Price	£	Volume	Product Mix	Prices	Ex-penses	Fact. Optg.	Tons	Price	£
Sales delivered A				80	£70	5,600						120	£65	7,800
B				120	£55	6,600						100	£50	5,000
C				70	£45	3,150						80	£40	3,200
Total				270		15,350	1,600	400	(1,350)			300		16,000
Less: Sales allowances					400		(35)		30	60			345	
Factory cost of sales (at standard)					10,900	11,300	(1,240)	(260)					12,400	12,745
Gross Margin A (% to Sales / Per Ton)				26.1	£18 5 0							21.1 (% to S.P.)	£13 14 0	
B				24.8	£13 12 6							17.5	£ 8 15 0	
C				30.3	£13 12 10							23.0	£ 9 4 0	
Total				26.4%	£15 0 0	4,050	325	140	(1,320)	60		20.3	£10 17 0	3,255
Less: Factory variances:														
Price					337				337					
Product or material mix					160			110						
Operating (inc. Method v'ce £320)					1,043						1,093			
Volume of output					901	2,441	901							
Gross Profit					1,609									3,255
Less: Selling and administration expenses					1,820					(15)				1,835
Net Trading Profit/(Loss)						£(211)	1,226	250	(983)	45	1,093			£1,420

£1,631

Less expected variances (5%)   620

£800

FIG. A–23

WORK-IN-PROCESS
(Valued on basis of Standard Costs)

28th January.......

Date		Total Value	Analysis			
			Materials	Production Activities	Plant Costs	Factory General
		£	£	£	£	£
1 Jan.	Balance b/f Work-in-process at 1st January	*2,250	1,250	800	200	—
28 Jan.	Add: Value of work done during the 4 weeks (as detailed in Factory Operating Statement)	9,780	2,640	3,000	2,100	2,040
		12,030	3,890	3,800	2,300	2,040
	Less: Value of completed production output transferred to finished goods warehouse during same period					
	60 tons of A	3,000	900	600	900	600
	120 tons of B	4,800	1,440	1,680	720	960
	80 tons of C	2,400	720	720	480	480
		10,200	3,060	3,000	2,100	2,040
	Balance c/f Value of work-in-process at 28th January	£1,830	830	800	200	—

* Including 30 tons of Product A at raw material content only (£420).

STOCK OF FINISHED PRODUCTS

28th January.......

Date		Products			Total Value	Analysis			
		A	B	C		Materials	Production Activities	Plant Costs	Factory General
		Tons	Tons	Tons	£	£	£	£	£
1 Jan.	Balance b/f Stock on hand at 1st January	150	120	150	16,800	5,040	4,530	3,870	3,360
28 Jan.	Add: Value of completed production output trans- ferred from factory during the 4 weeks	60	120	80	10,200	3,060	3,000	2,100	2,040
		210	240	230	27,000	8,100	7,530	5,970	5,400
	Less: Value of goods sold and despatched to customers during same period	80	120	70	10,900	3,270	3,110	2,340	2,180
	Balance c/f Value of stock on hand at 28th January	130	120	160	£16,100	4,830	4,420	3,630	3,220

Fig. A-24

Items in £

FACTORY OPERATING STATEMENT
(Using Standard Marginal Costs)

4 weeks to 28th January

Original Budget		Actual Cost	Variances								Standard Costs	
			Total	Price	Mix	Re-jects	Operating	Method	Vol. of Work	Vol. of Output	Departmental	Factory
	Materials											60 tons 'A' @ £25 = £1,500
3,420	Preparation & Mixing	2,965		327			128					120 tons 'B' @ £26 = £3,120
300	Processing & Packaging	280		10			20					80 tons 'C' @ £18 = £1,440
3,720		3,245	605	337	50	70	148				2,640	
	Production Activities											
920	Preparation & Mixing	1,109	69				58	80		(29)	1,040	
2,400	Processing & Packaging	2,170	210			40	70	80		60	1,960	
3,320		3,279	279			40	128	80		31	3,000	
7,040	Total Marginal Costs	6,524	884	337	50	110	276	80		31	5,640	6,060
	Plant Costs											
1,680	Maintenance Overhauls & Repairs	1,935	255				35		220		As	
1,200	Depreciation	1,200	—				—					
	General Charges										Budget	
1,250	Factory Management	1,310	60				60					
700	Factory Services	680	(20)				(20)					
530	Factory Clerical	572	42				42					
5,360		5,697	337				117				5,360	
12,400		12,221	1,221	337	50	110	393	80	220	31	11,000	

Fig. A–25

835

Work-in-Process and Stock of Finished Products (Fig. A-24)

These statements are built up by transferring the totals from the Factory Operating and the Profit and Loss statements for the period. If desired, the two accounts could be combined in one statement. The total values have been analysed by the various categories of costs, thus facilitating the use of the statement for other purposes, e.g. for calculating stock values on a marginal cost basis (see Fig. A-27) or for Balance Sheet purposes.

Source and Application of Funds (Fig. A-13)

Balance Sheet (Fig. A-3)

The figures at 28th January are inserted on these statements, and can be compared with either the 31st December position on the budgeted position at 30th June (see comments on budgeted statements).

Columns would be included to allow the subsequent monthly figures to be added to the statements.

VII. OPERATING STATEMENTS DRAWN UP ON MARGINAL COSTING

The Board of HEBCO Ltd. are undecided whether to continue with the above method of reporting monthly results or whether to adopt marginal costing—in which case only the standard variable costs are allocated to products.

They have already appreciated the advantages of the latter method for profit planning purposes and they decide to ask the accountant to prepare the results by both methods for a few months, so as to gain experience of the relative pros and cons.

Factory Operating Statement, using Standard Marginal Costs (Fig. A-25)

As already described, the costs of departmental "Pro-

duction Activities" are regarded as fully variable for product costing purposes, but for control purposes they contain an element of fixed costs. This gives rise to the small "volume of output" variance shown in Fig. A-25. The top half of the statement is in fact identical with that shown in Fig. A-21, except that the standard costs absorbed in production shown in the right-hand column are based on the marginal costs, i.e. the variable elements of the standard product costs given in Fig. A-10. The reason for the difference of £420 between departmental and factory standard costs absorbed has been explained in the notes to Fig. A-21.

In the lower half of the statement, Plant costs and Factory general charges are regarded as fixed costs and

Based on
'Marginal' Standard Costs

(Favourable variances shown in brackets)

4 weeks to
28th January

Revised Budget				Actual			Variances					Budget		
Tons	Price	£		Tons	Price	£	Volume	Sales Mix	Price	Ex-penses	Fact. Optg.	Tons	Price	£
			Sales delivered											
108	£70	7,560	A	80	£70	5,600						120	£65	7,800
90	£55	4,950	B	120	£55	6,600						100	£50	5,000
72	£45	3,240	C	70	£45	3,150						80	£40	3,200
270		15,750	Total	270		15,350	1,600	400	(1,350)			300		16,000
			Less: Sales allowances											
340			Factory cost of sales (marginal)	400			(35)					345		
6,336		6,676		6,380		6,780	(704)	44	30	60		7,040		7,385
Per Ton			**Gross**		*Per Ton*	£						*% to S.P.*	*Per Ton*	
43 11 6			**Contribution** A		£43 5 0	3,460						59.5	£38 14 0	
27 12 6			B		£27 12 6	3,315						45.5	£22 15 0	
26 1 6			C		£25 13 0	1,795						53.0	£21 4 0	
% to Sales														
61.8														
50.2														
57.0														
£33 11 10		9,074	Total	55.8%	£31 14 10	8,570	861	444	(1,320)	60		53.8%	£28 14 4	8,615
			Less: Factory variances (marginal costs)											
			Price		337				337		516			
(5%)		317	Operating (inc. method v'ce £80)		547	884	31							—
£32 8 4		8,757	**Net Contribution**		£28 9 4	7,686							£28 14 4	8,615
+5%			Less: Plant overhauls, repairs and											
		5,360	depreciation		3,135						255			2,880
		268	Factory general charges		2,562					(15)	82			2,480
		1,835	Selling and administration expenses		1,820									1,835
		7,463				7,517								7,195
		£1,294	**Net Trading Profit**			£169	892	444	(983)	45	853			£1,420

£1,251

Less expected
variances 5%

£620

£800

Fig. A–26

837

are compared directly with the original budget. Certain variances relating to these costs shown on Fig. A-21, viz. product mix £110, method £240 and volume of output £870 are not shown on the marginal costs statement, because these differences do not arise when the full cost is charged against profits as a block figure.

Sales and Profit Statement, using Marginal Standard Costs (Fig. A-26)

This statement follows the same form as that described in Fig. A-23, except that the marginal costing approach, as already described for the budgeted statement on Fig. A-14, has been used.

A difference of £380 between the results shown by the two methods is explained by the decrease in stocks of finished goods during the four weeks (see notes relating to Fig. A-14 on page 818).

$$
\begin{array}{lll}
 & & £ \\
A - 20 \text{ tons @ £25} = & -500 \\
C + 10 \text{ tons @ £12} = & +120 \\
\hline
 & & 380
\end{array}
$$

It should be noted that when making comparisons between products in Fig. A-26, product A has the highest ratio of gross contribution to sales, whereas in Fig. A-23, product C had the highest ratio of gross margin to sales. This reversal of order is explained by the fact that Plant costs (maintenance and depreciation) are much higher for product A than product C, and these costs have not been deducted before arriving at the gross contribution.

In the notes on Profit Planning (Section V), it has been shown that the marginal costing approach lends itself to working out the effect of changes in volume or product mix. Advantage has been taken of this fact by inserting in the left-hand column revised budget figures, reflecting both the increased selling prices and the reduced volume of total sales. The result gives the profit that could reasonably be expected under present conditions, and it is this figure that was plotted on the Profit Planning Chart (Fig. A-15).

This procedure often provides a quick way of arriving at the estimated profit for a period within a day or so of the end of the period, when perhaps only the total sales figure is known. In the case of HEBCO Ltd., the actual profit turned out to be very much lower than this amended budget figure, due to the combined effect of an unfavourable change in the product mix, higher raw material prices and sundry excess costs in factory operating. With practice, the accountant would be able to anticipate many of these factors, and so arrive at a reasonably accurate assessment of actual profits.

WORK-IN-PROCESS
(Valued on basis of Standard Marginal Costs)

Date		Total Value	Materials	Production Activities
		£	£	£
1 Jan.	Balance b/f	2,050	1,250	800
28 Jan.	Add: Value of work done during 4 weeks	5,640	2,640	3,000
28 Jan.	Less: Value of completed production during 4 weeks	7,690 6,060	3,890 3,060	3,800 3,000
28 Jan.	Balance c/f	1,630	830	800
	STOCK OF FINISHED PRODUCTS (Valued as above)			
1 Jan.	Balance b/f	£ 9,570	£ 5,040	£ 4,530
28 Jan.	Add: Value of completed production during 4 weeks	6,060	3,060	3,000
28 Jan.	Less: Value of goods sold and delivered during 4 weeks	15,630 6,380	8,100 3,270	7,530 3,110
28 Jan.	Balance c/f	9,250	4,830	4,420

Fig. A–27

This does not detract from the value of the actual results, since the latter can give the only true guide to the trend of events.

The actual results of the period are inserted on the Profit Planning Chart (Fig. A-15) as a guide for future planning.

Work-in-Process and Stock of Finished Products (Fig. A-27)

This is similar to Fig. A-24, except that stocks are valued at marginal cost.

VIII. CONCLUSION

The Board are satisfied that the system of budgeting, profit planning and reporting results introduced by the accountant and work study officer provides a greatly improved management tool for planning and control, and should help in the gradual attainment of higher profits.

With regard to the question of "full" versus "marginal" standard costs, the Technical Director is strongly in favour of the former, while the Marketing Director is equally strongly in favour of the latter.

A decision is accordingly deferred, but meanwhile the accountant is engaged on trying to devise a compromise procedure that will suit all members of the Board.

BIBLIOGRAPHY

1. Robert N. Anthony: *Management Accounting*. Irwin, Revised Edition, 1960
2. D. F. Evans-Hemming: *Flexible Budgetary Control and Standard Costs*. Macdonald & Evans, 1952
3. T. G. Rose: *Higher Control in Management*. Pitman, 6th Edition, 1957
4. Harold C. Edey: *Business Budgets and Accounts*. Hutchinson, 2nd Edition, 1960
5. Fred V. Gardner: *Profit Management and Control*. McGraw-Hill, 1955
6. John Y. D. Tse: *Profit Planning Through Volume-Cost Analysis*. Macmillan, N.Y., 1960
7. H. Bierman and S. Smidt: *The Capital Budgeting Decision*. Macmillan, N.Y., 1960
8. R. Warwick Dobson: *An Introduction to Cost Accounting*. Volume I. Gee & Co., Revised Edition, 1958
9. M. J. Moroney: *Facts from Figures*. Penguin Books, Revised Edition, 1956
10. Institute of Chartered Accountants: *Standard Costing*, 1956; *Terms used in Published Accounts of Limited Companies*, 1962
11. Institute of Cost and Works Accountants: *Report on Marginal Costing*, 1961; *Terminology of Cost Accountancy*, 1952; *Cost Reduction*, 1956
12. Association of Certified and Corporate Accountants: *Management Accounting*, 1954; *The Planning and Measurement of Profit*, 1957
13. O.E.E.C.: *Budgetary Control*, 1959; *Cost Reduction in Industry*, 1961
14. British Institute of Management: *Increasing Profits in the Smaller Business*, 1960; *Efficiency Comparisons within Large Organisations*, 1962
15. Harvard Business Review: Collections of reprinted articles—*Statistical Decision Series, Planning Series, Control Series, etc.*

PART V

MANAGEMENT IN PRACTICE

By E. F. L. Brech

CHAPTER I

MANAGEMENT ACTION

THE preceding four Parts have portrayed various aspects of the way in which management is seen in action in the setting of an average run of industrial enterprises, trying to make the best use of the techniques that recent contemporary development has evolved. The alternative approaches to several problems obviously make clear that no one firm could be found conforming closely to all of the many different activities portrayed in these Parts. But the principles of approach are common, and the four Parts do afford to managers a basis for a reliable and sound approach to pursuing effective performance of operations and continuity of progress. Developments in recent years have given rise to so many variations in technique that it is not easy to portray precisely how any one firm is likely to be putting its management process into practice, unless that is done in the form of a specific illustrative case-study. Yet these differences in technique are not of fundamental importance, for they are but the "tools" of the managers, and "tools" can be readily designed in different ways to apply in practice the same sound principle.

Techniques and tools frequently mask the reality of the management process, for they are more readily evident than are the mental actions of judgment, decision, co-operation and communication that underlie them, and which they are there to assist. As was repeatedly emphasised earlier in this study, the essence of the manager's role lies in this dual responsibility for judgment and decision directed to planning and regulating a given set of operations towards known objectives, and for securing the human performance and co-operation that will ensure the effective accomplishment of those objectives with satisfaction and contentment. The keynote of the responsibility lies in the combination of the two facets, "economic" and "social". On the one hand, the managers have to use limited and often costly resources to attain objectives at optimum levels of cost and profit—an essentially economic task, for which reliable data is an inescapable need. On the other hand, the managers have also to work amid various groups of persons to secure a full measure of co-operation with and through them, despite their differing relationships—some are direct subordinates of the managers in supervisory or in rank-and-file positions, some are their

own superiors, some are colleagues in comparable lateral positions
of responsibility, some are specialists from whom to draw advice or
service. Any one manager is more than a man in command of a
team of "workers" or other subordinates: he is a component member of a complex web of persons with responsibilities and tasks
closely interrelating with each other's. The application of techniques
in the process of planning and control interplays with this human
task, and the skill of the manager lies very much in how aptly he
can combine the two facets of his role. Their requirements are often
different, sometimes in conflict, but the manager is never in a position to assume that either one overrides the other. The notion of
interrelated planning and control could at times mislead the unwary
into overlooking the importance of the co-operation factor in successful management—a danger that is increased by the development
of mechanised and electronic apparatus which make the data of
planning and control more easily and more speedily available. Undue
concentration on the feed-back notion in management action—control figures pointing specifically to the decision required to apply the
correcting plan—could lead many a manager to a misconception of
the true nature of his role: the many and varied procedures and
techniques that are available to him must not suggest that management is but a matter of routine application of systems. The basic
social responsibility, a personal task of consideration and decision
in human terms as well as economic, stems from *the essence of
management responsibility for the guidance and planning of other
people's activities.* Within each element of the process the personal
attitude of the individual executive is an important part in attaining
effectiveness of operation. Herein lies part of the true skill of
management—in loose terms, the "art" that parallels the "science".
There is a good analogy in the craftsman: he needs basic knowledge
of the principles underlying his craft, of materials and tools, of
methods and lines of work, and so on; his training and skill make
possible the proper application of his craft that results in high-grade
work; well-designed and efficient tools make his task easier and his
work better, his quality and finish of a higher order; but they certainly do not replace his skill, nor can they. So too with management, the tools cannot be a substitute for the manager's personal task
of responsible consideration and decision, associated with co-operation and communication. It is when the "tools" take the place of the
manager that the process breaks down, to give place to the rule-of-
thumb "management" that had become so widespread a characteristic of a passing age of industry.

True management is a continuous, living process in which an
individual must take specific responsibility. It begins with an

examination and assessment of the relevant facts; with these properly appreciated, the broad plans can be formulated and then the more detailed programmes laid down, including provision for the necessary equipment, materials, and so on. The definition and allocation of tasks to the members of the organisation is a further stage in the planning, and, while the work and activities are proceeding, a further human responsibility for co-ordination and motivation arises. The management process completes its round in the supervision of activities and the checking of progress to ensure performance at an adequate standard of effectiveness, in accordance with plans. Underlying the whole process is the policy of the enterprise, the objectives and the principles that form the basis of its management.

In the general pattern of industrial or commercial organisation, management action is found in three broad levels: the Board of Directors, the Managing Director (chief executive), and the hierarchy of managers and supervisors.

(1) The responsibilities of the Board of Directors may be summed up as the formulation of policy and the overall control of the organisation. The major tasks arising are: the determination and statement of policy on general lines as well as the chief features of the sectional aspects; economic appraisal of policy, projects and programmes; the provision of adequate financial means; schemes of control by which the activities and progress of the enterprise are to be assessed; the appointment of the executive authority designated to manage the concern (the Managing Director); provision for the legal responsibilities towards the community (in respect of the legal requirements of Company Law, the custody of property, and so on); plans and motivation for the continuing development and vitality of the enterprise. From among its number the Board elects a Chairman to preside over its deliberations. This Chairman is not as such an executive official of the company, but the president of the Directors, who holds office only at their formal deliberations and those of the shareholders. Frequently, the same individual is both Chairman and Managing Director, but this should not mislead as to the true character of the Chairman's position.

(2) The Managing Director holds a dual office. As a member of the Board he shares the corporate responsibility of the other Directors, but his special position of chief executive he holds alone. It falls to him in this capacity to be the link between the Board and the rest of the organisation: to present the objectives and to interpret policy; to encourage participation in the formulation of policy; to ensure the continuing economic adjudication of activities; to issue the appropriate instructions that will set the organisation to work; and to maintain effective co-ordination and a high level of will-to-work. His responsibilities for morale are

especially important, because it is from him that the "tone" of the organisation is set—his attitude and outlook are likely to be reflected by the managers at lower levels, even down to the ranks of supervisors and operatives. Naturally enough, there will be certain differences in the detailed make-up of the responsibilities allocated to individual Managing Directors, but the character of such responsibilities will be broadly the same throughout.[1]

(3) Various managers and supervisors responsible to the Managing Director make up the rest of the organisation. This is where all the differences in the size and character of various enterprises will come into prominence. A small trading unit may have only a Managing Director and half a dozen junior assistants: the chief executive is really an owner-manager, whose business is clothed in company form as a matter of legal convenience. A small manufacturing company may have a Chief Engineer serving as a technical executive to assist the Managing Director on matters concerned with design, plant, tools and quality, while an Accountant looks after the financial aspects and assists in selling, at the same time supervising such clerical routines as are carried out; the Managing Director may himself look after the factory and all general aspects of production, with the assistance of a Senior Foreman. In the medium-sized and larger enterprises, whether in manufacturing or commerce, the total process of management is customarily split up among a hierarchy of managers and supervisors, who together form "the organisation". Their scope and character are necessarily varied: this is where the definitions of responsibilities come into play. According to the needs and circumstances of the enterprise, and in accordance with its objectives and policy, the total process of management under the Managing Director is divided into appropriate sections, groups or functional units, each with its responsibilities and relations determined as part of the whole. Each executive, specialist, or supervisory post, in other words, is specifically set up to play a given role in the total pattern of management. Some of the tasks may be temporary ones—for instance, work of special technical development directed to bringing out a new product; or looking after a subsidiary factory evacuated for security purposes; or the building up and running of an Export Sales Department, for subsequent merging into the general sales activities. In such cases, a temporary executive appointment may well be made, with specific responsibilities which will be terminated or modified or merged in due course, as required. Briefly, then, the organisation of any medium-sized or larger concern, whatever its field of economic activities, will consist of a complex of responsibilities and relations, determined by reference to the approved objectives and policy, and providing a framework within

[1] A comparative summary of the responsibilities of the Board of Directors and of the Managing Director is contained in Chapter VIII of *Organisation— the Framework of Management.*

which the total process of management (including supervision at the operating level) can be effectively carried out in appropriate co-ordination.

What these managers (and supervisors) do, how they spend their working hours, is the subject-matter of the preceding Parts of this study, and how the various aspects of activity fit into a coherent pattern is illustrated in Fig. 107 overleaf. The core of the tasks performed by all the managers lies in the definition of management itself—to take responsibility for the planning and guidance of the sections of activities entrusted to them and for the motivation and co-operation of the persons entrusted to their jurisdiction. The human element in this task is very much the same in most managerial and supervisory posts, whatever their field of activity. Some differences of degree can be found, as between, say, a manager and foreman : the latter has a more circumscribed human job in the guidance and supervision of men and women at the working level, and in promoting a high sense of morale among them. The manager's personnel responsibility, on the other hand, may be more remote, directed to the supervisors themselves, getting a good team spirit among them, encouraging them and helping them in their own direct motivation task, thus setting the human "tone" of the department or section as a whole. Among themselves, managers may again find differences of emphasis due to particular circumstances : in highly technical manufacturing operations, largely process-controlled, the human responsibility may be less prominent than the technical. Similarly, the character of the staff and work under the jurisdiction of, say, a Chief Accountant or a Retail Store Manager, may give rise to quite a different pattern of human relations and problems from that of the large-scale light engineering factory.

So far as the other facet of management is concerned, the techniques and procedures by the medium of which judgment and decision are attained exhibit more differences than similarities. These techniques, as the methods or "tools" for carrying the management process into effect, necessarily reflect the policy and organisation of the enterprise and must, therefore, be to some extent specific to an individual enterprise. For instance, routines for production control may be differently worked out in two factories that have much the same product and layout and work from the same fundamental principle of measured standard times. In this fact lies the weakness of the "systems" that are sometimes offered to managers by firms specialising in the sale of a given type of office equipment. Superficially, the "system" is widely applicable in a set way; but its application in that set way may cause serious weaknesses in the working of management in some organisations. The advances made

BOARD OF DIRECTORS
(Policy and Overall Control)

MANAGING DIRECTOR
or GENERAL MANAGER

(Interpretation of Policy; Instructions for Action; Organisation Structure;
Budgets; Co-ordination; Tone of Organisation; Progress Control of Activities and Performance)

————ASSISTANT (in "staff" relation)

(Levels of Executive Control and Supervision: Planning, Execution, Control, Motivation, Co-operation—in relation to activities carried out by
persons employed in the organisation. All activities centre on "making" and "selling")

RESEARCH AND DEVELOPMENT ACTIVITIES	MARKETING ACTIVITIES	PRODUCTION ACTIVITIES	PERSONNEL FUNCTION	CONTROL AND CLERICAL FUNCTION
—Fundamental Research	—Market Assessment	—Planning and Progress	—Recruitment and Employment	—Secretary (legal)
—Product/Process Development	—Commercial Programme	—Design and Equipment (engineering)	—Conditions of Service	—Accounting (financial accounts, invoices, etc.)
—Quality Standards	—Selling	—Purchasing and Stores (materials)	—Training and Information	—Cost and Budgetary Control
—Technical Data	—Sales Promotion and Advertising	—Methods and Standards	—Health, Welfare, Safety, Amenities	—Economic Assessments
—Plant Development	—Warehouse	—Manufacturing	—Consultation and Employee Relations	—Wages and Time Records
—Instrumentation	—Transport	—Inspection (Quality)	—Personal Services	—Records and Statistics
	—Economic Intelligence	—Maintenance	—Management Development	—General Clerical Services
		—Works Administration		

Fig. 107.—Chart of Organisation illustrating the Activities of Management.

in the study of management in recent years have led to the wide-spread use of common principles underlying techniques of control, though these will differ in detail application from factory to factory, or office to office.

The Unity of Management

The layout of the management activities forming the matter of the foregoing Parts of this study might easily give an impression of four separate fields of action without apparent unity. This is an inevitable, if unfortunate, consequence of the form of presentation that has to be adopted in order to do justice to the more expert knowledge underlying the various practices in each field. More unfortunate, however, is the fact that this apparent separation reflects the tendency, commonly met in everyday industrial life, to see and think of the practice of management itself in the same separate compartments. This tendency is found in its extreme form, of course, in the very large organisations which are actually set up on the basis of specialist divisions, in many instances having representation at Board level through a so-called "functional director". An almost natural corollary follows in the inclination of the specialist managers or officials to over-emphasise their own particular activity and to neglect their obligation to contribute co-operatively to the well-being of the organisation as a whole.

To obviate or prevent this separatism within an organisation is among the main tasks of a General Manager or other form of Chief Executive. To him falls the responsibility for ensuring that the basis and the framework of management (i.e. the policy and organisation of the enterprise), especially in the larger units, are determined with a clear recognition of the fundamental unity of the process of management itself. His own attitude must be characterised by a determination to preserve that unity. In this task the owner or manager of a small organisation has a big advantage; not only because in such a unit each man in the management structure customarily embraces tasks in more than one field, but also because the owner or chief executive is in a position to exercise closer unification through the smaller personal span that has to be covered. To some extent the smaller the size of the unit, the less the danger of separatism. There is, of course, a corresponding danger in these smaller units that the bias or the deficiency of a given individual at the top may lead to the over-emphasis of some aspects of management or the neglect of others, thus leaving an out-of-balance which is not corrected by a compensating specialist in the particular fields neglected.

How the unity of management may be effected in practice can be shown by two illustrations:

Take the case of a small firm, for instance, one manufacturing spectacle lenses, employing some 70 people all told. At its head there is a Managing Director, who is virtually the owner and is the technical brain behind product and processes. Because of the special requirements of the trade, his technical skill is of particular relevance to customers, and it is only natural therefore to find that he makes himself personally responsible for sales. In charge of the small factory he has established a Works Manager, a man who has been trained in this field and has grown up through the firm; latterly he has been devoting time to learning something about factory organisation and management. The scope of his responsibilities is, of course, limited, and some of his friends from larger enterprises might well mentally classify him as "a glorified foreman". He is entrusted with full executive responsibility for production activities and carries out his tasks with the aid of three foremen: one looks after the tools and equipment, polishing heads, moulds and rough-lens stores, with a small staff working under him; a second looks after the processing operations, which for convenience are divided into four sections, each headed by a skilled working chargehand; the third foreman has responsibility for quality standards, for the inspection of lenses at intermediate and finished stages, for opinions on flaws and faults; he also maintains the stock of finished lenses and attends to despatch to customers, assisted by two girls for the packing and paperwork. In the office, the Managing Director has a good-grade Secretary with a small staff, to whom are entrusted the keeping of books and accounts, the payment of wages, the maintenance of personnel and wage records, the issue of customer invoices, and the other processes that go to make up the routines of a General Office. Included in the responsibility of this "Secretary-cum-Office Manager" is the functional control of the two girls who, under the jurisdiction of the inspector, carry out the office routines in connection with stock records and despatch.

To the Works Manager himself fall, apart from the general oversight of the factory, the special tasks of planning and progress of production, the control of quality through the definition of standards and material specifications, and a general responsibility for the human aspects of management (the personnel function), even though he expects that the detailed contacts and activities will in the main be carried out by his three foremen.

Clearly the Managing Director is himself serving in three capacities—he is a General Manager, a Sales Manager and a Technical Director or Manager.

This small organisation is representative of many thousands in British industry; perhaps its structure is more clearly defined than is customarily the case. The important point at issue is that there is no activity set out in the foregoing Introduction and Parts that this little unit cannot carry into effect. Some of them, of course, may not be necessary in a formal way, the same purpose being attained by simpler means. Market research provides a useful instance: the Managing Director's personal contacts with the Prescription Houses (which are his wholesalers and his customers) enable him to keep track of new trends in customer demand, such as fashion in the shapes of frames and lenses. His participation in Trade Association discussions enables him to have advance information of possible lines of National Insurance development that may have a bearing on his sales and manufacturing programme. Or again, in the case of budgetary control, the simplicity of the range of products makes the analysis of expenses less important; but not for one moment could it be suggested that the control of operating costs and expenses is not just as necessary in this tiny unit as in one ten or a hundred times its size. The same is true in regard to the planning of production or the control of progress through the sequence of operations. Naturally, the basis on which these activities are set up and the procedures by which they are carried into effect would be very much more simple than has been suggested in the relative chapters of this study, but the principles there set out to underlie such activities will apply in just the same way, and to a very large extent it may be possible to apply, with minor modifications, even the detailed routines suggested, if they are found to be justified.

In the personnel field a similar line of argument again applies; in matters of selection and training, in discipline, in consultation (especially of the informal kind), the principles described apply without variation; the techniques adopted will be much simpler and much less formal. Recruitment and training are, in fact, good examples because the skills entailed in spectacle-lens grinding and polishing are intricate, calling for a quasi-craft development.

The unity of management is clearly emphasised by the personal control of the single Managing Director, and by the continuous personal contact between himself and the Works Manager on production matters, himself and the Secretary-cum-Office Manager on control details. It is interesting, perhaps, to conclude the illustration by pointing to a thought that has been frequently emphasised in the Introduction, namely, that it is the attitude of the chief executive that can make or mar both the unity and the efficiency of an organisation; this is no less true in this small unit than in the larger ones where it may be more obvious.

A Case on Larger Scale

The second illustration is drawn from a firm of considerably larger size, though again representative of the units which characterise certain industries. This is a garment manufacturing firm employing about 2,300 people. Its organisation structure is something like the pattern represented in Plate 1 in the Introduction (facing page 54), with obvious modifications of the division shown under the Design Engineer. This firm is of sufficient size to warrant having a full range of the activities described in the foregoing Parts. To portray the unity of management in action within such an organisation would mean little more than rewriting in specific form all that is set out in the foregoing 800 pages. The point can be made equally well in more concise form by selecting certain aspects for the purpose of illustration.

(1) The Managing Director (who uses the title "General Manager") maintains co-ordination, and therefore provides the first basis of unity in management, by four particular features:

(i) He has defined in writing the responsibilities of all his major and second-line executives, and a copy of the definitions has been issued to each of them. From the outset, therefore, they are clear as to who does what, and where their fields of responsibility begin and end. His own drafting of the schedules has ensured that there are no gaps and no duplication.

(ii) It is his practice to maintain daily individual contact with each of the top-line executives, and he has encouraged these in turn to follow the same practice with their own subordinates. In this way he and they keep a finger continuously on the pulses of the organisation, and are readily in a position to spot at the very earliest moment divergencies or deficiencies before they can become serious.

(iii) In addition, he adopts the practice of a fortnightly "Progress Meeting" of the senior executives, with the second-line men called in as pertinent. This meeting, while informal in character, follows a definite Agenda, and is intended primarily for the purpose of co-ordination. There are occasions when the hour or so devoted to it represents more a social gathering than a serious management meeting, because there is nothing calling for major attention: but none of those attending feel that such occasions are a waste of time, because of the considerable contribution that these regular contacts make to the unification of knowledge and thought on the affairs of the company.

(iv) Latterly, the Board have decided to introduce a budgetary control scheme and the details are now being worked out. When complete, all costs and expenditure will be controlled by pre-determined standards, and a further highly important contribution to the co-ordination of management in action will have been established.

(2) At a lower level, unity is illustrated by the attitude, for example, of the Production Manager in regard to the making-up sections of the factory and the maintenance of plant. Long before the budgetary control scheme had been mooted, the Production Manager had developed well-defined plans in respect of current and future output, and had gone to the trouble of establishing a Planning Office. Thus, one of the common weaknesses of the larger manufacturing organisations has been overcome by the integration of, for instance, the purchase of materials with the known forward making-up plans; by the co-ordination of engineering activities and maintenance requirements with pre-planned production operations; by the control of work in progress in relation to available man-hour and machine capacity. That this emphasis on co-ordination has made a serious contribution to the well-being of the manufacturing side of the organisation is evident from even a few minutes' conversation with the department heads and foremen.

(3) Further illustrations can be drawn from the company's activities along functional lines:

  (i) Plans have already been laid for determining the budgets on an annual and quarterly basis, with four-weekly statements. The basis of operation will be a regular meeting of the Sales Manager, the Production Manager and the Chief Accountant with the General Manager—of course, with adequate consultation of subordinates at a lower level who have particular knowledge and information that may be required in framing the budget.

  (ii) In regard to the records maintained within the jurisdiction of the Production Manager, for instance those of the Planning Office, there is close co-ordination with the requirements of the Accountant's Department, the more so now to meet the particular needs of the procedures for cost and budgetary controls. The introduction of a Clerical Methods Manager has been a useful means of co-ordinating the planning of procedures, to ensure that full advantage is obtained from such control schemes in relation to all the recording and communicating activities carried on throughout the organisation.

  (iii) The work of the Personnel Department is in turn tied in with all other activities. For instance, the absence records maintained in the Department are tied in with the time-recording and job-costing procedures carried out under the jurisdiction of the Accountant; in effect, the basic material for the Personnel Department's absence records is supplied from the Accountant's offices, leaving the Personnel Department to deal with their peculiar part of this activity, i.e. the contact with the individuals concerned, as distinct from the gathering of the information. Similarly, in regard to recruitment of new personnel, there is close co-ordination with the Production Manager; in the first place, the Personnel Officer's participation in the General Manager's Progress Meetings (see item (1) (iii) above) keeps him informed of forward plans, and accordingly all recruitment and training programmes are based on known or estimated future trends of output. The actual technique of recruitment is based on close co-ordination between the Personnel Department and the managers and foremen in the cutting and making-up sections, in order to ensure not only that all accepted candidates conform to the general standards required by the company's policy, but also that they fit in with the individual supervisor's own assessment of his needs and are not likely to give rise later to incompatabilities on a personal basis. The same co-ordination is found in action in regard to the upgrading of juniors and lower-paid operatives whenever better jobs become available, as well as in regard to transfers between Departments. Training required for most of the manufacturing and making-up departments is long; this forward view, co-ordinated with sales forecasts, has been an important factor in promoting efficient development in face of expanding trade.

In the early stages of the development of management within this organisation, it was the outlook and attitude of the General Manager himself that set the pace and determined the tone. But gradually as the organisation pattern became established, and as the various procedures were formulated, the growing sense of responsibility among the senior and lower executives prompted a ready response to the lead given in a wholehearted readiness to seek co-ordination as the natural corollary of everyday activities.

Unity of management practice can be appreciably assisted by soundly designed procedures of planning and control information. Data, whether in physical or financial terms, are essential media of effective management action. And *how* data are made available can materially affect the exercise of that action, for good or ill. The major contribution of contemporary practice in schemes of budget control and similar forms of management accounting lies in a two-fold characteristic: the one aspect is the possibility of aligning data for decision and control with the pattern of delegation of responsibility; the other is the design of the data procedures such as to ensure that the several specific elements form an integrated scheme unifying overall information at the top levels of management. Within such schemes any one departmental manager will receive daily, weekly, four-weekly, or other periodic figures portraying actual performance and expenditure against the targets, plans or budgets relevant to his own responsibility. He knows that he has made his own responsible contribution to formulating the targets and budgets (one aspect of decision), and that the "variances" thrown out in the statements are matters on which he is expected to decide and initiate the corrective action (i.e. control interrelated with decision). This may be in a change of plan rather than a remedial step in the existing situation, and in this case he has to ensure reference to other managers who may be concerned. Above all else, he knows that the periodic information relevant to his own departmental responsibility is an integral part of a full scheme of "management information" which reflects the policy of his company and parallels the structure of its organisation. With this knowledge, he can use these "tools" with the full assurance of objectivity and the conviction of integration with colleagues sharing the role of management with him.

Management action in this style releases high-level human endeavour from the constraint of conflict for the better pursuit of progress.

"MANAGEMENT SERVICES"

AMONG the remarkable features of progress in British industry and commerce in recent years has been the increasing development of "management aids", mostly involving specialist skills. Stemming from longer-standing traditional techniques like Work Study or Cost Accounting, these later developments largely reflect the impact of the scientific approach on the industrial scene, supported by increasing employment of men of higher mental calibre within the management teams. The combined scope of the traditional and new techniques is already quite considerable, but the substantial differences of purpose and method are sometimes not appreciated. In consequence, there has been some significant confusion in discussion as well as practical difficulties in organisation.

Latterly, the label "management services" has come into use in reference to one or more of these specialist activities, sometimes as the title of a department. The further spread of this fashion may well make the confusion serious, and it seems appropriate to initiate studies directed to clarifying the issues involved, so as to afford lines of guidance for practical application, especially in the larger companies and corporations. The activities concerned seem to fall into four categories which, while logically distinct, inevitably have a large measure of interrelationship. For purposes of the present context, these four may be labelled respectively: diagnostic, intelligence, control, development.

1. *Diagnostic*
   Activities directed primarily to collating, reviewing and assessing the facts of a situation in order to determine basic arrangements, to improve methods, to design systems, to measure work-loads, to formulate standards.
   For example—Work Study; Layout and Flow Studies (Handling); O & M (Systems Analysis); Operational Research; Organisation Structure Studies; Capacity Assessment.

2. *Intelligence*
   Activities directed to appraising economic and market conditions as the basis for the formulation of commercial and development policy, the determination and financial appraisal of plans and programmes and guidance for management decisions.
   For example—Economic Intelligence; Statistical Data; Interpretation of Market Research; Forecasting (long-term); Linear Programming; Capital Forecasts and Profit Projection; Similation Studies (Evaluation of Expectations).

3. *Control*

Data procedures or similar techniques which afford to management the means of assessing "actual" against plan or target, and therefore aiding decisions in regard to continuing/amending operations.

For example—Performance and Cost Control (Labour, Yield, Machine Utilisation, Fuel & Power); Budget Control and other Management Accounting; Operational Statistics; Data Processing.

4. *Development*

Activities directed to future orientation of operations and of management, with particular reference to vitality of progress.

For example—Scientific Research ("fundamental"); Technical Development (Process, Materials, Equipment); Methods (Control) Engineering; Product Formulation; Management Development; Management Advisory Services.

These various categories of activities go deeply into the whole practice of management. Their study, therefore, requires to start from clarity in understanding the nature and significance of the management process and of the techniques by which it is applied.

NOTE. It is *not* in any way suggested that the provision and management of these various activities should be or could be co-ordinated within one "department" or under one "top manager"

* * * * *

The above notes were prepared by the author for a seminar held under the auspices of the British Institute of Management in February 1961.

CHAPTER II

SOCIAL SKILLS AND RESPONSIBILITIES

IN examining the concept of the social elements inherent in the process of management, exerting influence both on the determination of its objectives and on the mode of its application, it is soon apparent that words are not helpful to analytical study. "Social" has renderings with wide difference of interpretation, even if basically they stem from management's essential concern with the activities and livelihood of people. Whatever the varieties of meaning attaching to the word, the concept has major significance for management action and calls for the manager's deliberate attention.

A brief recapitulation may serve to set the context. Management is of itself a social process directed to economic ends—social in the sense that its main task lies in planning, motivating, co-ordinating and regulating the activities of *people* who are, by the very fact of their membership of the organisation in which they are employed, associated in a common task concerned with the production and distribution of goods or the provision of specific services. This task is, however, in pursuit of the economic purpose of the livelihood and well-being of the people themselves, and of their community, and management thus has a *primary economic* aim. The social factor, albeit essential to the management process, represents a *secondary* aim. Strictly speaking, this social facet embraces three distinct connotations: the first is concerned directly with the people forming the team whose activities are being managed; the second relates to the impact of the enterprise on the communal setting (physical or human) within which it is carried out; the third refers back to a communal aspect of the economic objective as the basic purpose of the activity. Recognition of these several "social responsibilities" confronting the manager in the context of his everyday job has been gaining ground slowly but steadily in recent years. The notion is not new: it can be found in the thinking and attitude of an early pioneer like F. W. Taylor before the turn of the century; it can be seen overtly reflected in the choice of title of the British writer, Oliver Sheldon, in his *Philosophy of Management* twenty-five years later. What is perhaps new is that recognition of the notion should have *practical* repercussions in the attitude and activity of the manager himself— an aspect that will have reflections in further comment in later sections of this Part.

In reference to the people who are employed in, and therefore form part of the human make-up of, the organisation which is being managed—be it industrial company, commercial business, national or municipal undertaking, or any internal section of these—the phrase "the social aspects of management" has already become part of the contemporary industrial jargon, though to many writers it represents nothing more than an elaborate term for the "personnel function". Correctly interpreted, however, it has a deeper and fuller significance: management is neglecting its social purposes if it causes among its people frustrations, discontent, conflicts, an abiding sense of grievance, suspicion and the other negative mental states that bar the way to happiness and satisfaction in the enjoyment of association in a common task well performed. The negative attitude can and does arise in an *individual's* mind because of events or situations in which *he* has been personally involved with a supervisor or a manager; but it arises more powerfully and more deeply when the unfortunate situations have been experienced commonly by *a group of people*, for example the members of a section or a department under one supervisor. Teams and groups are formed in factories or offices for the better performance of the operations to be carried on, and their arrangement is often thought of as no more than a technical pattern. Such a view carries inherent dangers, for it overlooks the gregarious instinct that is a basic human characteristic. Men associate in groups of one kind or another from a largely instinctive motive; and their experience has reinforced the instinct—a fact well recognised in the adage "unity is strength". Protection is stronger when men and women have the bonds of association; self-interest of the individual is better promoted by unison with his fellows in the group. Apart from any technical requirements, the human facets of teams and sections need to be taken into account in management's plans and in the manager's behaviour towards his subordinates. By constructive and consultative leadership he can have the strength of the group to support him, just as he will have this strength to resist him, even defy him, if his attitudes are negative. In winning group support he contributes also more powerfully to personal satisfactions. That skilful fulfilment of this social obligation also has direct and indirect economic benefits is neither a valid nor a relevant objection to its inherently social character, though many a cynical voice has been heard in this sense. Within the management process in practice, the economic and the social are inextricably interwoven: by the promotion of satisfaction among employees, which means the achievement of social purposes, management is contributing to its own self-interest on the economic plane, for from high morale flows

efficiency of operation, high performance, economy of materials and
time, and low cost.

The Human Environment

Skilful pursuit of social responsibilities necessitates sound understanding of the human environment within which management is
applied, and the understanding can be effective only if it starts at
the top. The first manifestation has to occur at the level of policy,
in the attitude and outlook of the Board of Directors or other governing authority. In practical form this recognition occurs as "personnel
policy" and its main expression is the lead that is given to top
management and, through them, to the subsidiary levels of responsibility forming the organisation structure. The scope and content of
the policy are all the things that have been examined in the course
of Part Three above, and their reality is reflected in the measure of
sincerity that the higher ranks of management display in the formulation of any decisions that will have a bearing on the human tone
of the organisation they are controlling. More and more companies
have been discovering in recent years that—to put it realistically, if
crudely—good personnel or social policy pays, and they have made
serious and far-reaching endeavours genuinely to frame and apply
high standards. Some have publicly proclaimed their intention and
their standard, one going even to the length of using the label "Our
Faith" in an open statement in the national press.[1]

The implication of "profiting" from such an approach can be
taken by some readers as evidence of cynicism or bad faith: but do
such readers really require practical managers to be evangelical or
philanthropic in attitude? The managers have a realistic task to perform and important economic objectives to accomplish through the
medium of human co-operation. They have an obligation to take all
steps to make co-operation effective, and if contentment contributes
to this they will pursue it: does it impute bad faith because they
have their objectives in correct perspective? The manager is not *per
se* a "welfare officer" or "social worker"—his primary role is an
economic one, and his social obligation essentially secondary, in the
true philosophic sense of those terms. The important inescapable
requirement is that he must recognise the significance of the social
factor, and give it its due attention, in all sincerity to promote the
contentment and participation from which alone effective co-opera-

[1] See Chapter 6, "Human Relations in the Board Room", by E. F. L. Brech,
in *Human Relations and Modern Management*: edited by E. M. Hugh-Jones
(North Holland Company, Amsterdam, 1958). There is also an excellent
portrayal of an outstanding policy in this sense in Wilfred Brown's *Exploration in Management* (Heineman, London, 1960).

tion will stem. The policy is his foundation in this endeavour; the personnel practices are his support and aid in attaining it; the specialist personnel officer and staff are his advisors and aides, though recognising that the responsibility for implementing the policy rests primarily with the managers themselves and not with the specialists.

Top management attitude in the human facet can be reflected also in the attention given (or, more usually, talked about but not given) to realistic "management development". Of itself this is, of course, an aspect of personnel policy, one of major significance because it is the main medium for ensuring that the requisite understanding of human relations and co-operation is developed as part of the skill of the oncoming ranks of managers and that they have an adequate appreciation of how to make full use of the specialist personnel practices that are provided in the organisation as an expression of the policy and in support of its implementation. To this aspect further consideration will be given later in this Part.

To attain the requisite "human tone" of an organisation requires, however, more intimate human tasks than just the practice of personnel techniques: it means the blending into a contented co-operative team of many persons and groups of persons. For the better conduct of its activities an organisation is divided into sections, according to lines and flow of work, to stages of production, to specialist allocations of responsibility, or other such objective bases: such divisions or sections represent formal grouping of the persons and their activities—managers plus rank and file—all of which together make up the enterprise. In any organisations of more than a few people, however, there are other groupings that do not stem from physical or formal arrangements and that cannot be portrayed on a chart; these are flexible groupings, at various levels or even between levels. They arise among people who have some factor in common in their association at work, and they arise usually among small numbers. The basic cause may be a proximity of work, or participation in related tasks; it may arise from the origin of association—for instance, new recruits who start work on the same day in the same or adjoining departments; or again, it may spring from the fact that certain persons have come from the same home locality, and are now "strangers" in their place of work. Similar informal associations are often found, for example, among quality inspectors whose work is carried out in a given department though they themselves do not belong to that department, belonging instead to the common pool of inspection. This informal association may even arise from a sense of negative unity of purpose, as is seen from systematic resistance to new methods of work or from the extensive existence of restriction of output, which, while having no formal basis, is organised by an underlying mutual agreement. It has been found also that these informal groupings will be different for different purposes, among the same body of people. This pattern of relationship is part of the life-blood and of the nervous system of an organisation, but it cannot be reduced to principles, to routines or to formalities. It springs from the natural human tendency to association, from the need of the individual to feel the support of his fellows, and recognition of its existence must be an essential feature in the effective working of good management. The aim of the manager, in so far as he can exert influence, must be to "direct" the force of informal association to the well-being of the unit over which he is set and of the enterprise as a whole; thus, too, to the good of the people employed themselves. Success in this will be achieved only if morale is good, and morale will be good only where the human outlook of management is sound, based on sincerity of endeavour to promote genuine participation. The methods available to the manager are in this essentially human task few and simple; they are summed up in what may be called the social skills of communication and co-operation—informing, listening, consulting, promoting security, participation.

These skills are in the main the expression of an attitude of mind that recognises the essential contribution of people to the progress of the organisation and is reflected in a genuinely human tone in the daily working of management.[1]

Social Skills in Management

Nowhere is the test of social skill in management practice better in evidence than in the leadership of men through *change*. The all-too-natural human resistance to change has in some industries widely held up the adoption of new methods of production, which would substantially improve efficiency and the earnings of the men themselves. Management has no option here but to seek every means in its power to press ahead with the improvements. Obviously, it will use the social channels of information and consultation, but even if the modifications entail a certain interim measure of discontent and insecurity—even involving short-term pockets of unemployment and transfers to new jobs—the overriding economic need of the community for the assurance of its survival and the promotion of its progress must receive prior consideration.

The manager's economic role and objectives necessitate on his

[1] Some of the studies that have contributed to this line of thought are to be found in *The Making of Scientific Management*, Vol. III, *The Hawthorne Investigations*, by L. Urwick and E. F. L. Brech (Pitman, 1948). See also *Free Expression in Industry*, by J. J. Gillespie (Pilot Press, 1948), and *Exploration in Management*, by Wilfred Brown.

part an almost eternal vigilance for opportunities of improvement—in products, in materials, in equipment, in methods. At times, such improvements may call for *changes* in location, if the full benefit of technical development is to be attained or if the full advantage of economic opportunities is to be taken. At other times, the extent of the change called for is less dramatic, but none the less real, in its impact. It would, in fact, not be untrue to say that *change* is an inevitable corollary of progressive management and perhaps even its symbol. At the same time, *change* is basically anathema to man, for at heart he is essentially conservative; this can be seen as readily in the primitive societies as in the more sophisticated and established communities. If it seems at times that there are phases in human development when man is prepared to become more flexible in outlook and more progressive in attitude, this may well be found an accident of place or time or person. Can it be possible that the "non-conservative" persons are drawn to flock to the places where vigorous change is temporarily in process? Is this perhaps the explanation of the extent to which the United States has been prepared almost incessantly to countenance and accept change in the course of the past century? Is it possible, too, that after the passing of time, the innate conservatism may reassert itself and the resistance to change set in once again? In the older established industrial communities there is ample evidence that basically the human being does not welcome change and sometimes goes to considerable lengths to resist it.

Management has to fulfil its responsibility in attaining change in face of this strong inherent resistance among the members of the teams through whom alone the change can be made effective. It has to overcome the resistance, an attainment which it can reach only through a high degree of social skill: man has to be won to co-operate in the change, by the process of being adequately informed, adequately consulted, made to feel that change is something that he can understand, that will be to his benefit and that he can therefore welcome. Truly a mammoth task for any manager!

These social skills have been described by Elton Mayo as "the capacity to receive communications from others and to respond to the attitudes and ideas of others in such fashion as to promote congenial participation in a common task". These management has to apply in the course of normal everyday practice and through the medium of various other activities, many of which are not specifically personal in character, but technological or commercial. It is important, therefore, that these skills become habitual to the attitude and action of the managers, so that appropriate attention is given as a normal feature of behaviour to the human relations context within which management practice is carried out. The managers are often absorbed in their technological, commercial or administrative tasks and may by inclination tend to overlook the natural element of co-operation and motivation which must be part of their executive activity. True, such technological or commercial responsibilities are also an essential part of their task as managers, but these must not be seen as exclusive to the inherent social features. Only rarely, and mostly incidentally, does a social item of activity occur in isolation: for example, when a manager is dealing with an individual personal problem of discipline or poor work, or when he is appraising a member of the team, or perhaps resolving a conflict between two or more persons or groups. This phenomenon is often not appreciated, because of the broad tendency in recent years to over-compensate for previous neglect of the human relations factor in management; the compensation has too often been vague and superficial. What is required to make the social skills of the manager effective is that his management attitude and action should become permeated with an understanding of the human relations facet of his responsibility and of the extent to which his skills in these directions will either attain a high level of morale in the team working under his command or, alternatively, hinder effective co-operation and thereby impair good performance.

Most managers find themselves having to apply such skills at different levels and not only at the level of the rank and file. It is the latter which figure most prominently in literature and in discussions, but there are many managers for whom direct contact with the rank and file is limited and for whom the application of social skills relates to persons themselves established in the intermediate layers of the structure. This is especially true of managers in the higher echelons of the organisation: their influence on the human relations pattern, as far as the rank and file are concerned, is one of attitude and direction, to reflect the sound intentions that are enshrined in policy and ensure that these are made effective below. Their own contact in the human relations field is usually with other managers, supervisors or various grades of specialist officials. The human factor and the need for social skills are none the less important in this area, and as great a degree of appreciation is called for as is required for those directly in command of operations. From some points of view, the application of social skills at these intervening levels, calls for higher competence, because more complex situations are being dealt with. It has been pointed out elsewhere that any individual manager within the hierarchy of an organisation is at a focal point in a complex nexus of human relations, and he has the obligation to secure co-operation from and with numerous people of varied position and responsibility. It is not adequately recognised how much human relations skill is required by any manager to attain smooth working of this complex pattern as a co-operative system; nor can this be attained simply by comradely attitudes. With appropriate interpretations in practice to meet the differences of role and person, all the facets of social skills of consultation and communication apply; but more is often required. This "more", however, goes out of the realm of the strictly human into the area of management techniques.

A major contribution, for instance, comes from consistency in general policy and adequacy in making it known; it will be recalled that this was a matter considered at some length in section 6 of the Introduction (see page 38). Similarly, in section 7 (see page 57) emphasis was placed on the importance of clear identification of the scope of responsibilities delegated. Perhaps no single factor has caused more discontent among managerial personnel or more impairment of their effectiveness than the absence of or confusions in the allocations of responsibility—a widely recognised breeding-ground of frustration and conflict. More specific techniques have also a part to play: for instance, systematic planning on a known common procedure can be a major contribution to co-operation among managers and supervisors, especially those in interrelated fields of activity, such as manufacturing and selling, or production and maintenance. Similarly, well-designed "tools" of progress control or of budgetary control of expenditure, associated with the pattern of delegation of management responsibility, have long been known to play a vigorous role in fostering and maintaining communication and co-operation. By no stretch of the imagination could these things be classed as "social skills", but their role in the promotion of effective contentment and co-operative effort among managers is of considerable importance.

Morale and Motivation

Within the more specifically human fields, there are again particular aspects through which managerial morale and tone can be enhanced. Reliable and respected methods of appraisal must be included: these should form part and parcel of a "management development programme", so that the on-coming managers can gain confidence in their superiors, knowing that objective judgment is the medium of advancement instead of personal preference. This is not the context in which to examine the practices of executive appraisal; the point being made is its contribution to management morale and co-operation. An important by-product, telling in the same direction, can be attained by ensuring that individuals are not promoted or allowed to slip by accident beyond the level of their potential capacity or competence. One of the surest ways of damaging morale is the frustration engendered by the "not up to it" man in the higher places.

It is in this context that the true significance of leadership from the higher levels becomes effective[1]: the tone of an organisation comes from its head, and is in the first place a matter of attitude. It springs from the impact of the Managing Director or General Manager on the first-line executives, an impact which gives birth to the morale, good or bad, of the executive team. There are, regrettably, far too many managers who can confirm from personal experience the extent to which low morale springs from poor-grade top management: frustration is so readily bred by the absence of clear definitions of responsibility, by the crossing of instructions between seniors, the confusions of reporting back, especially when there are two or three "Directors" acting in an executive capacity. Morale is, too, easily undermined by absence of policy or by uncertainty as to its interpretation, by unstable decisions on the part of the senior executive, or by the ragged working of relationships between the Managing Director and his immediate subordinates. There may be heroic efforts made by the managers at the second and third lines to maintain a good working tone, but in the longer run the strain proves too strong, a sense of frustration finds itself reflected in their own attitude to subordinates and in a gradual deterioration of the morale of the teams below them. This is an experience which has perhaps been found more frequently by supervisors than by any other grade in the industrial hierarchy: within their own relatively small jurisdiction the good supervisors can exert a good influence, can have a sound impact on their subordinates, can maintain a high level of morale in their teams, but they find themselves subject to frustrations coming from weak seniors, from poor-grade Works Managers, from an unstable structure, from confusions about instructions and policy, and sooner or later their own mental energy begins to flag; they are no longer able to carry the department, and general morale drops. In the experience of many people, there are executives who have been able to bear incredible burdens and undertake long hours of work, endure rapid and repeated changes in product, in operations or equipment, go through very severe crises—because they enjoy a high sense of morale engendered by and maintained by a respected chief, who sets a high tone and binds the executive team into a solid, co-operative unit.

From this line of thought there arises one interesting question on

---

[1] For purposes of textual convenience in this Chapter, the customary term "leadership" is being used instead of the more precise designation "motivation" discussed in the Introduction.

which a good deal of first-hand research is required before it can be satisfactorily answered. Does this consideration of the social factor in the practice of management mean that the smaller organisation has an advantage over the larger? The answer would at first sight seem to be a ready affirmative. Yet not all enterprises can be small; there are many technical or commercial factors that make large-scale organisation inevitable in some industries. Is there, then, to be a conflict between technical and human considerations? Is it a conflict in which a compromise can be the means of solution? It would be futile to attempt a superficial answer in the present context, but a pointer to the answer is probably this, that what really matters is the size of the *unit* on which the impact of individual management or supervision is made; in other words, a solution has to be found which would make possible a large economic or technical organisation composed of a number of small human units.

Further reflections on these points of view may well lead to the conclusion that leadership is a different thing in different settings. All in all, leadership means the process of attaining willing co-operation from members of a team in the performance of a given task within a given situation—the description "motivation" advocated in the Introduction more precisely connotes this. Objectives may be predetermined by authorities elsewhere. What is left to leadership is the freedom to command in the sense of a responsibility for securing co-operation. "Command" does not necessarily mean a process of autocratic decision, with all judgments and all decisions lying exclusively with the commander. On the contrary, any such approach will be almost the surest way to impede the granting of voluntary co-operation. A leader operating effectively consults with and listens to the members of his team, takes heed of their points of view and the suggestions that they have to offer, but both he and they are equally clear that the act of decision is his. "Industrial democracy" has become almost the most maligned term in the modern economic vocabulary, largely because it has not been adequately understood. Consultation and consideration have been confused with decision, and the process of "democracy" has been *wrongly* thought of as meaning that the members of the team *decide* by majority vote. Leadership means clear decision, firm command, though circumstances may well make for considerable differences in the way in which its impact is made effective. For example, in a research laboratory, the main source of the respect gained for the decisions of the manager may be the knowledge and experience which he is known to have and which are made manifest by the clarity of his technical guidance, his readiness to help in technical difficulties and his very considerable degree of understanding of the patience required in pursuing a complex problem. On the other hand, in the field of marketing, it would be respect for the energetic and vital outlook which inspires vigorous support, a respect for sound decisions which are known to be based on an adequate appraisal of facts and which experience has proved to be, in the main, firm; this is not just the magnetism of a dynamic personality, but the degree of reliable judgment that lies behind it. A flamboyant leader may often get good and enthusiastic support for a short period, but he is unlikely to be able to ensure a degree of command which will withstand difficulties and troubles.

The Impact on the Community

This is the point at which to turn to the other implications of the "social responsibilities" of management, for concern for the human contentment and co-operation of his team does not exhaust the manager's obligations in this direction. The two other meanings listed for this expression (see page 860) can be conveniently taken together, in so far as they both refer to the relationship of an enterprise with the community, as distinct from the persons whom it employs. They are, however, in themselves distinct and different.

The first aspect in this wider connotation refers to the physical impact of the enterprise on its environment. The typical industrial towns of Britain's older developed areas can show how neglect of concern for this impact can bring about conditions describable only as squalor and ugliness. That this is not a necessary by-product of industrial growth is readily shown by the way in which the "new towns" of the 1950s and 1960s have been developed—with high standards of architecture for individual factories, high standards of layout for the towns or districts as a whole, supplemented by amenities in the form of gardens and attractive surroundings. Any negative or destructive impact on a locality is not today accepted by the social conscience. In many respects, particular restrictions have been imposed on and become accepted by management: for example, in regard to smoke abatement, the disposal of effluent, safeguards against other nuisances, the control and flow of traffic; in the United States noise is being similarly dealt with. Equally, industry has accepted the principle of contributions for social purposes, such as insurance against unemployment, sickness, accident and superannuation. It is argued by many people that these developments are a by-product of radical politics in the decades immediately following the Second World War. This may well be true, but such an accidental origin does not at all impair or cloud the real significance of the developments themselves: they represent recognition by industry of its social character and its social obligations.

The second aspect reaches down to the more fundamental issue of the place of industry in the life of the community, an issue which has already been examined in an earlier context (see pages 7–8). The mere fact that management has a dual economic objective, related to providing goods and services as well as employment, means that it has an inherent social connotation, because it is contributing to the livelihood and to the progress of the standard of living of the community in which it is set. It has been shown elsewhere that the primary function of management is to attain good utilisation of the resources of the community which are entrusted to its jurisdiction. Management acquires a social responsibility in its direction of technical progress, translating new knowledge to new products, to improved products, to better services, or to other improvements in the standard of living. Effective conduct of its operations leading to a cheapening of products or services sold will release money for spending in other directions, and may at the same time make possible increases in the spending power of the persons employed, contributing thus to a buoyant economy, to increasing national revenues, to lowering the burden of taxation borne by individuals, and to increases in savings. All these developments can, in total, contribute to wider communal betterment—in better housing, improved education, better roads, increased health services and other social amenities.

In basic principle, management has an *inherent responsibility* to contribute to the advancement of the community in all these ways, because it has an inherent role of responsibility in the judgment and the decision that are the motive force driving and directing the economic system. It is, of course, unusual for management to be looked at in this way. The managers in any particular business are more accustomed to looking at the affairs of their own company as though these are their main preoccupation, coupled with concern for their own particular progress in career. It is, however, only because this wider and deeper connotation of their task has never been fully brought home to them that the average run of managers tend to think as they do. They hold a job, they are earning a living, they are serving their company, they are advancing their career; but if the expression "the profession of management" is to have any serious meaning at all, there must be included in that meaning recognition of inherent social responsibility to the citizen body which management serves.

The self-interest motive in career advancement is not of itself wrong or bad: every profession recognises that those of its members who attain the higher levels of performance and service are entitled to the higher rewards and the honours. Man has a natural obligation to seek the better application of his talents and correspondingly to be rewarded for his success: and this is not nullified because he also accepts a notion of social service or contribution to well-being. For many men a seemingly altruistic objective can add stimulus to better work and fuller attainment, the personal benefit of pride of achievement providing the driving force. This is a topic more pertinently to be pursued in the context of "management development" (see Chapter VIII following), the relevance here being just the absence of inherent contradiction between "social responsibility" and "professional self-advancement". There is in this conception of management obligation something of a philosophical element, and contradiction might seem to lie more specifically in its acceptability within the framework of an industrial society based on the principle of "free enterprise". The core of the principle is the private ownership—whether by individual businessmen or by widespread corporate shareholdings—of the means of production and distribution, with motivation deriving directly and specifically from the earning of profits accruing to the owners. It is not, however, necessary to seek an *exclusive* motivation: the issue is one rather of greater or less, of primary or secondary, of essential or derivative. However stringently applied is the principle of private enterprise in any society, the inescapable fact remains that *industry and commerce are essential elements in the pattern of economic activity of that society, integral factors in its livelihood.* Management cannot, therefore, avoid—however little it may choose overtly to recognise—that its responsibility for industrial and commercial direction is first and foremost a responsibility to society. The profits of individual owners and the individual managers have to be more correctly seen as incidental to the discharge of that underlying social responsibility—something in the nature of a reward for services competently and adequately rendered. In societies where there is a greater degree of communal ownership of industrial enterprises, this way of looking at the management role and reward is more specifically recognised, as it is too in the nationalised industries or other public authorities of Great Britain.

That this point of view might not be readily accepted by the majority of the men and women employed as practising managers in the industrial and commercial enterprises of Britain, America and many other countries, is not an argument as to its philosophical unsoundness. It is a notion with a basic truth overlain by the more commonly accepted media of motivation in free enterprise society, and it will claim further attention in a later section, when the criteria of management success are being examined. There will be many managers to whom even the expression of the notion conjures up "political leanings" or "left-wing sympathies"—a degree of shallow thinking unworthy of anyone claiming a professional status in management practice. The underlying features of such social responsibility are facts of economic life with an inherent truth commensurate with that of mathematical axiom: it is only that trends of history have conditioned us all to different appearances.

If there is any sympathy for the view that competent managers are men and women ready to think realistically in the interests of maintaining a professional role, then the significance of social responsibility as a feature of their industrial context must be accepted. Some lessons of the past serve to reinforce the argument, starkly among them Britain's economic tragedies of the "black 'twenties" and the "bleak 'thirties". The younger hierarchy of management today, set in the comfortable arms of economic prosperity in an affluent society, know only by hearsay of the dreary days of their predecessors. For Britain almost more than any other nation the years of the Second World War stand as a dividing gulf between past and present, so markedly changed is the economic scene. Active reminders remain, mostly in the minds of older workers and Trade Union officials: much of the present-day seeming obduracy of workers and officials finds its explanation in their vivid memories of years of unbroken unemployment, and in the haunting dread that such a phenomenon is a normal characteristic of modern industry—today's full employment and affluence being the inexplicable exception. It is understandably difficult for the present-day younger Factory Manager, drawing a steady £1,750 a year, and expecting to double the figure in a decade, to imagine and appreciate the implications of an economic environment characterised by average unemployment levels of 10–15 per cent., with regional patches up in the 25–30 per cent. range. And that not for weeks and months, but persisting over the best part of a dozen years.

This is not the context to undertake a critical examination of causes or remedies, but it is relevant to reflect on the significance of this industrial situation in terms of the concept of the social responsibility of management. It was normal then, and is normal now, to see that situation as one in which the major responsibility lay on the government of the day—and it changed its political colour once or twice during those "years of depression"! For such a view there is no rhyme or reason. The government was not "in industry", and did not even have nationalised corporations under its jurisdiction. It could influence the social conditions of the community by "creating employment" through the initiation of public spending; and this it did. It could create facility of buying, so that industrial development could proceed, and this it did too. Yet the vital decision as to resuming higher levels of activity and taking on more labour to sustain them lay solely within the responsibility of the managements of the enterprises themselves. In the prevailing circumstances, the managements decided they could not take such steps, so industrial stagnation persisted. Not in all cases, for many of the "newer" industries were forging ahead successfully. Why the "older" industries lay quiescent or declining is an issue which finds its real explanation in history several decades earlier, with changing circumstances in markets abroad which managements at home failed to identify or to understand. The industrial scene of the first phase of depression in the 'twenties was bespattered with the apparently wise utterances of top managers "confidently expecting a return to normal conditions" —blissfully ignorant that their idea of "normal" for Britain had disappeared not ten, but twenty or thirty years before! Is not such ignorance a blatant failure of professional competence? A gross dereliction of social responsibility? Would we not today castigate as "backward" a management which failed to keep actively informed of the state and trend of its markets? And why not then as well, for the nature of management responsibility has not changed? A fascinating series of topics, these, as material for serious study groups of managers in training, all pointing in practical terms to the topical soundness of the theory of the social element of responsibility inherent in management's setting in the economic system.

In terms of the contemporary scene, the argument remains strangely reminiscent of that earlier epoch, though the emphasis is a little different. The national need of Britain today is the long-term version of what industry heard shortly after the war as a short-term exhortation—"export to live"! This is another economic truism which need not be expounded in this context, though it calls for more serious understanding than it customarily gets in present-day affairs. Not every enterprise can export directly, though there are but few that cannot make some contribution to the promotion of better export trading. That the volume and values of British exports of home-produced goods and services must be increased, and then maintained, is fundamental to Britain's continuing livelihood, let alone to any sort of increase in the standard of living. *Only the managers can attain this objective*: it is *their* decisions that will determine the policies promoting exports directly or fostering them indirectly. To look to the government as the focus of effort in this matter is to misunderstand the nature of management's economic purpose and setting. Government can assist by facilities and services, by public support, by exhortation, by gimmicks of incentive—but it cannot make the decisions or provide the lead. Costs, prices or profits in an export context are the legitimate considerations for management's attention; the need to get optimum application of resources is no less here than elsewhere. Motivation of personnel employed remains a management prerogative, and there is no automatic expectation that workers should earn less because they serve an overseas market—the challenge to management lies still in getting lower out-turn costs in the company of high earnings.

It is, of course, so much easier to earn a livelihood in managing to serve an affluent home market, but any such inclination is a blatant disregard of social responsibility and so a denial of true professional standing. There is a collective aspect of this task, too: public opinion is customarily less advanced than the viewpoint of the professional members of a community—is it not, therefore, incumbent on the latter to pool their thinking in the interests of securing popular understanding of unpalatable objectives and policies? Has not the profession of management a corporate role to play in ensuring that the nation accepts their genuine leadership in the struggle to maintain economic viability? There is a happy ring about "never having it so good" as the basis for "doubling the standard of living in twenty-five years": truly a pleasing objective! Management alone can be the decisive force that will make it a reality—social responsibility accepted and served.

CHAPTER III

TECHNICAL DEVELOPMENT

THE contemporary scene in every industrial country is marked by widespread emphasis on technical development, to such an extent that it is not uncommon to hear serious descriptions used in terms of "a second industrial revolution". This general scene of technological advancement is partly associated with national projects at Government level, including missile technology for defence purposes and space investigations. On the other hand, a good deal of the interest is of specific relationship to industrial progress, though the analogy with the first industrial revolution is limited. True, there is a considerable stimulus to economic progress deriving from technical innovation, and each step in the latter has its stimulus to more; but the notion of "revolution" is being applied largely because the innovation contains now a new feature of replacing brain-power rather than muscle-power. This has been evidenced in the past decade by outstanding progress in the field of electronics, giving rise to numerous developments in control engineering and making possible a hitherto unknown line of approach to industrial methods. More and more, highly mechanised or automated factory processes are becoming a reality; there are already plants in which automation has been attained to the fullest extent of self-directing and self-correcting operations, with servo-mechanisms in a feedback control system. However, probably more characteristic of the present industrial scene is the development of small-scale electronic apparatus controlling individual processes or series of processes, rather than providing over-all automation of an integrated manufacturing and testing activity. That these are indeed developments of a very important kind, likely to have far-reaching repercussions in the industrial world can certainly not be denied, but it may be questioned whether they merit the dramatic label of "revolution".

Engineering and electronic technology apart, contemporary technical progress is seen also in other directions of pertinence to industry; most important of all, perhaps, in the field of materials, where chemical discoveries have given rise to extensive developments in new alloys, new fibres, new thermo-plastics. These in turn give rise not only to new products, but also to possibilities of methods improvements in factory processes themselves, linking back with the improved mechanisation and control. In both fields, the developments are sometimes spectacular advances, but more often they are the outcome of long painstaking research. The past two decades have been characterised more than any other epoch in human history by the intensification of research work for industrial purposes. This is afoot in every industry, but is outstanding in industries like metallurgy, chemistry, fibres, chemical engineering, electronics and food technology. The phenomenon is common to every industrial country, and almost everywhere the passing years have witnessed an ever-increasing number of laboratories built privately by individual companies, co-operatively by industrial associations, or with governmental support through Universities or national departments of research. Little purpose can be served by endeavouring here to record any of the descriptive facets of this story which have been made widely known in numerous official reports and technical papers.[1] Deserving of passing note, as reflecting this progress, are the recurrent press advertisements for scientists and for technological personnel, and with these a notable increase in salary scales offered to the younger men and women with scientific and technological qualifications.

A noteworthy feature of this technical development is the extent to which emphasis has been laid on "scientific research" underlying the technological attainment. This is in part due to the nature of the major technical advancements, these occurring initially in relatively new fields of knowledge opened up more actively for war purposes. A contributory factor has been the increasing availability of more advanced instruments of analysis and test, making possible lines of fundamental investigation not previously attainable. This phenomenon has had its repercussion on the industrial scene in the expansion of serious research activities which has been so marked a feature of the past decade. The significance of the trend was among matters discussed by top management participants at the Twelfth International Congress of Scientific Management in 1960, where plenary and sectional sessions had papers devoted to aspects of research and development. Among the discussions, particular emphasis was placed on the *speed* of current technical progress, one contributor maintaining that "scientific knowledge is doubling every nine years, technological effort doubling about every ten years, while more advances have been made in science in the past fifty years than in all preceding history". This is reflected again in the scale of

---

[1] Interesting commentaries on the situation in Great Britain can be seen in a number of official reports, including, for example: *Scientific and Engineering Manpower* (H.M. Stationery Office, 1956) and *Report of the Department of Scientific and Industrial Research, 1959* (H.M. Stationery Office). Particularly interesting in this context are the three studies prepared by Carter and Williams, details of which are given in the bibliography on page 901.

expenditure on research in all the advanced industrial countries: for Britain the annual figure is probably upwards of £300 million (equivalent to some two per cent. of the gross national product), while in the United States the level is some eight to ten times as big. It is thought that the British research effort, covering industrial as well as governmental and academic needs, engages more than 50,000 scientists of graduate and equivalent qualification.

From the standpoint of management practice, this vast and vigorous endeavour in scientific and technological advancement has consequences of particular importance. In the first place, research and development are today undoubtedly the mainspring for continuing industrial progress through individual companies as well as on the national scale; in many industries they are also the most likely sources of realistic improvement in effectiveness, because scientific and technical innovation can so often attain either a speedy or a dramatic reduction in cost, or increase of output, out of all relation to what can be attained by methods changes or rises in labour efficiency. Research and development matter to management for an entirely different reason, too—because they are such costly activities and, once initiated, can open a recurring expenditure which is difficult to keep in bounds. It has been estimated that the overall cost of employing a scientist on research work in an industrial establishment is not far short of £5,000 p.a., and that even in a smaller enterprise serious research and development work cannot be contemplated unless some four or five scientists are working together—a budget approaching a minimum of £25,000 per year, and likely in practice for any company above the "small-firm" category to be more like double that level. Nor are results customarily attained quickly.

The first decision to embark on scientific research work or serious technological development thus represents for management a matter of major importance. It is not just a question of finding a well-known and highly qualified professor from a neighbouring University, inviting him to forsake the quietude of academic paths for the challenging hurly-burly of industry. A few firms have taken this line of approach, but there has seldom been any satisfactory achievement as a result. Some scientific or technical guidance can be acquired, but no serious work is the outcome. To embark on a research programme is a major decision, and while the advice of a scientist at Board level can be invaluable in assessing the situation and reaching the decision, the initiation of the programme calls for a clear understanding of the policy implications and of the financial consequences.

Some of the more limited aspects of research and development activities in relation to the needs of a manufacturing programme have been dealt with in Part Two above: for consideration here there are wider and deeper issues with their main bearing at top management level.

Research v. Development

It will be as well, first, to clear up a point of terminology, for a good deal of confusion arises over the use of the two terms "research" and "development", either separately or in juxtaposition. No amount of analysis would enable a line of demarcation to be attained in detail, because the terms necessarily have different connotations in different technical settings. For all practical purposes, it becomes sufficient to be able to arrive at a working definition of each, and in many industries or enterprises it may be necessary to adopt a different management approach to each. Broadly speaking, the following difference has become commonly accepted:

(a) "Research" is used to refer to basic scientific work leading to the elucidation of new knowledge, to the analysis of materials, or to the critical examination of the elements of process change; for example, the investigation of chemical structure or physical properties of materials, or the study of the influences on materials of treatment by given processes such as heating or dehydration.

(b) "Development" refers more to technical studies necessitated for turning basic knowledge into product formulation, into methods of processing the formulation, the design of the equipment for the process, and other such phases of preparing for the translation of knowledge into production.[1]

In practical life, the line of demarcation is often blurred and has to be resolved in individual cases by reference to the known circumstances being dealt with. Fortunately, it is frequently the case that no line of demarcation is called for, and the only practical issue that arises in this respect is whether the two activities should be combined into one laboratory under one head, or should be separately dealt with—a question to which no *general* answer can be given. Quite often the answer has to be attained in terms of the very practical consideration of what the firm can afford: in many a small or medium-sized business, the scientific and technical requirements are known to be limited, even though important, and the Board of Directors have decided that they can afford a small establishment

---

[1] One of the Papers to the Congress referred to above includes the following point in this context: "This phrase, 'research and development' is an elastic term that covers a continuous spectrum of activities which encompass basic research (for new knowledge and understanding), applied research and exploratory development (early efforts to convert science into technology), and finally development itself (the calculated effort to design and build something new and useful)."—J. R. Killian (U.S.A.).

staffed with a small number of skilled scientific personnel, but nothing bigger. They can, therefore, rightly look to this unit to supply all that the firm requires in the way of its technical research and pre-production development, as well as the primary task of true scientific research on a limited scale. In a very big firm, on the other hand, there are known cases where two distinct laboratories exist within the same broad field, or at least two separate sections, the one devoted to "fundamental research" and the other continuing on with the "technological development".

The more important issue inter-related with the distinction is the question of the functional head to whom the research and development activities report. In many engineering companies it is customary for this work to be responsible to the production head, whether he be called Technical Director, Production Executive or Factory Manager. This has long been justified by the opinion that the research and development projects are closely interrelated with the everyday experience and requirements of the factory departments, particularly when considered in association with tool design, and that any separation at the top level might lead on to an undesirable remoteness of the research and development work. Experience has proved, from the standpoint of development activities in the sense described above, that there is good logic in this argument; but it has proved, equally, that there is sometimes a strong case for the separate identification of fundamental research work to avoid this being either neglected or recurrently impeded by interruption. Where the research unit falls under the jurisdiction of an executive also responsible for manufacturing management, there is this ever-present danger of long-term research work being interrupted by "trouble shooting", or of the pursuit of research projects being thwarted by the urgencies of *ad hoc* factory requirements, in addition to the cost of the distraction of expensive scientists by absorption into the solution of relatively inexpensive troubles. Experience has pointed also to the very different attitude and outlook of the personnel engaged on scientific research, as well as to the importance of letting their tempo of work be dictated by the needs of the project that they are studying. There is, moreover, a very different significance in the cost items entailed in fundamental research as against pilot production and manufacturing, and the criteria of judgment of success or failure are quite different. Even in relation to contributions to existing manufacturing methods, there is the value that a research laboratory under separate top responsibility could take a more detached view and therefore give a more objective commentary. All things considered, the case seems to be strong for maintaining top management responsibility for research separate from that of manufacturing or production. The same force of argument does not, however, hold for development work.

Organisation of Research v. Development

The next obvious question arises at once—deciding the top executives to whom research and development should be responsible. This, again, is an issue to which there is no easy general answer, because so much must depend on the circumstances of the company concerned or on the stage of progress to which its particular scientific developments have reached. What is involved here can perhaps be illustrated by the cases of two or three companies in different fields. The first case is a medium-sized business in the textile industry with a long-standing successful history in traditional fibres. A family business, with rather more than 140 years of history, reaching by the end of the 1940s a point where the then young family member in charge as Managing Director felt that the economic situation ahead would be such as to make traditional fibres no longer as reliable a field of business as they had been in the past. He felt, therefore, compelled to take his company into the area of the man-made fibres. There was no intention that the company should embark on the basic manufacture of the fibres, but that it should continue its normal activities of spinning and weaving, depending on outside suppliers for basic materials. This meant having an understanding of the scientific and technological factors involved in dealing with such materials, but not necessarily having a full-scale laboratory to go into the underlying fundamental knowledge. A greater part of this basic know-how could be bought from outside by co-operating with the companies who would supply the prepared materials. The Managing Director was himself not a technical man, but he felt none the less that it would be wise to keep the technical direction in his own hands, at least in the early stages. He had, therefore, to obtain technical support, and this he did by appointing as a personal assistant a young graduate scientist who had had some experience in the chemical development of man-made fibres. In the course of two or three years a small-scale laboratory was developed, but, throughout the whole successful accomplishment of the launching of yarns and cloths of man-made fibre construction, the scientific and technical support grew no bigger, nor was there any change away from the top responsibility resting in the hands of the Managing Director, acting as though in a secondary capacity of technical director. The problem of integration of the market potential with the selling of the yarns and cloths was thus easily attained because of the Sales Manager's responsibility to the Managing Director himself. At one stage, consideration was given to the possibility of establishing a "technical directorship" in its own right, but the Board were unanimous, after their deliberations on the matter, in the view that more would be lost than would be gained, and so the original pattern remained. (It was changed only at a later stage of growth of the business, when it became necessary for the Managing Director to free himself as a person from this second responsibility in order to be able to concentrate more fully on the problems of direction in a period of complex growth.) In this case, there was clearly no true specific research work involved, but little more than a technical support to product and process development.

Another example is provided by a small business in which three original founder partners formed the top management. By mutual agreement, one ran the business as General Manager, with a large interest on the sales side; another was in charge of manufacturing; and the third, with a very junior assistant, took over the responsibility for scientific and technical development. The business was concerned with a specialised branch of light engineering in which intricacies of design were very important and involved two or three supplementary materials as well as metals. The small range of standard product was supplemented by a sizeable variety of special orders made in batch quantities. Accordingly, the technical development problems were very intimately bound up with the sales and manufacturing responsibilities, and, through a very definite phase of growth, the business was able to maintain its technical excellence by dint of the close interweaving of the technical direction with the top management.

The third case, on a rather different scale, concerns a large business in the chemicals field, where from an original standpoint of two or three products, economic considerations necessitated spreading into a number of different areas, some by diversification from the original group and others by the acquisition of new lines or the buying-in of businesses. After several years of development in this way, the company found itself in a position where it had two or three chemical laboratories situated in different plants, as well as an engineering design unit which was, to all intents and purposes, a laboratory for the design of chemical manufacturing processes and plant. Co-ordination of these various aspects of research and development was largely attained through the good personal relationships among the scientists in charge of the laboratories and the two or three managers responsible for the factories, themselves qualified technical men. Overseeing the co-ordination of research and development was a member of the Board with long service in one of the earlier constituent companies, a qualified chemist with a deep personal interest in research work. Highly respected for his knowledge of the company's areas of development, he was readily accepted by all those whose daily lives were spent in the fields of research and development, and thus an effective co-ordination was attained in a rather loose, rough-and-ready way. With, however, the growth of the business and a continuing increase in diversification, this form of co-ordination began to prove inadequate. For one thing, research staffs became difficult to get, as well as expensive, and at times the two or three laboratories found themselves in competition for the scarce manpower available. A major problem in organisation thus arose, as to how the co-ordination and direction of these multifarious activities should best be attained. On the one hand, there was a need for fundamental research serving all the units in the group, and this might be an argument in favour of a single central basic scientific laboratory, separated in jurisdiction from any of the units and constituted under a research director. On the other hand, the laboratories had to give certain services to the manufacturing units in relation to quality specifications and control of process, and thus there *had* to be qualified scientific staffs available on the manufacturing locations. There was also the special problem of engineering design, as the company was one which did a good deal of pioneer work in the manufacturing methods for its own products. The situation provided an interesting case study and lent itself to many possible solutions. Foremost among the many factors influencing deliberation was the importance of systematic pursuit of fundamental knowledge and the ability to carry scientific personnel to this end. Taking into account the expected continued growth of the business, it was eventually decided to constitute a "Technical Development Department" into which were combined the scientific research and the engineering design. These were established in their own building at one of the major sites, but outside the jurisdiction of the local site management. They were responsible to a Technical Director, with whom lay the responsibility for the co-ordination of research and development policy with marketing potential, as well as the overall direction of the scientific research programme. Much of the "engineering design" was of an experimental kind, inter-related with the findings from chemical research. In addition, this unit carried a functional responsibility for service to the manufacturing units, and at each of the latter there was established a small-scale working laboratory designed to serve the needs of local manufacturing control, each laboratory falling under local management but looking to the central laboratories for specialist scientific guidance. Through similar channels, the central laboratory was able to have engineering services provided to meet its needs in the construction of test plant at one or other of the factories.

Research and Marketing

This third example throws into relief the problem of co-ordination at the levels of policy and top management, a problem which has different facets in different circumstances. If the Managing Director is himself scientifically or technically qualified, and is well supported by competent subordinate executives in other functions, there is usually pretty close co-ordination in all the various aspects required. It is where the chief executive has a commercial or administrative mind and background that the problems of top co-ordination can emerge seriously; it is frequently alleged that in this case a Managing Director may not provide adequate technical understanding and support for those in charge of the research and development activities. To counter any unwitting habitual neglect, it is important that he should make *consciously* deliberate endeavours to keep in mind his definite responsibility for the integration of scientific and technical thinking, along with those other aspects of the business which come more readily into his purview. He should ensure that he maintains good contacts with the director or other executive responsible for the research and technical services; he should ensure being in attendance at periodic discussions among the various executives concerned, and should so arrange activities that the scientific and technical members can in their turn participate in normal management meetings.

A major facet of top management co-ordination, having particular bearing on the effective outcome of research and technical development operations, is that between research and marketing. A major issue comes into question here, for these are activities not commonly thought of in juxtaposition. All too frequently co-operation between these two aspects of management is superficial, and working liaison between them tends not to take place in any active way until the research or development units have "something ready for the market". It can then be found that the "something that is ready" is out of line with true market needs, or that it gives rise to a conflict of interests between the research and the marketing executives. It is of the utmost importance that the co-ordination between marketing and research should occur early in the formulation of a product or of a research programme—and should be along the lines of co-operative thinking. In the case of many products there is a "design" factor which is fundamental to successful marketing, and this may well bring about an automatic phase of co-operation because neither side can pursue its own task without some briefing from the other. This would apply particularly in regard to purpose-made engineering products, where the design or formulation depends primarily on customers' specifications and may be carried out by a development unit rather than in a true research laboratory. There are, however, numerous fields of products—in man-made fibres, in prepared food-stuffs, in beverages, in cleansing agents, in chemical and pharma-ceutical lines, in household materials, and so on—where new or improved formulation depends upon the pursuit of fundamental research, or at least on deeply penetrating scientific investigations. This is the work carried out in the industrial research laboratories, and where lack of adequate liaison with marketing can result in truly expensive failures. Top management has the responsibility for seeing that the need for co-ordination of interest, outlook and activity is fully understood by marketing and research personnel, and honoured in everyday practice. The minds and natural attitudes of the per-sonnel in these two fields tend normally to be very different, almost antipathetic; communication may be found mutually difficult. There are, in other words, ready barriers to co-operation and equally ready inducements to go off on their own paths. Top management needs to be at hand with the recurrent reminder that both departments or units are serving the same business! The preparation of the research programme on the one side and the occasional review of the market-ing budget on the other can be timely occasions for the reminder to be borne home; there is no reason why both parties should not be made active participators in each other's mandate, so far as the forward aspects of development are concerned. Informal interim contact will also be necessary to ensure common interpretation of research findings, and to assess adjustments that may be necessary to expectations, because of negative outcome of some research experiments.

The market guidance to research is perhaps the more important aspect, because of the heavy cost of research work and the length of time required for the pursuit of any project that embodies basic scientific investigation. Research cannot be switched on and off at whim, and most experimental tasks calling for scientific attention are time-consuming before they point to reliable results. In point of fact, this requirement makes the customary annual basis of budgeting inadequate as far as research is concerned: a formal yearly review of progress and of expenditure on research can be valuable instru-ments of control, with the budget for an ensuing year serving as a useful directive. *The research programme, however, needs to be seen in terms of longer cycles,* say of three to five years, in which the yearly mandate is but one phase. It is in this longer-term directing of research effort that the close inter-relation with marketing inten-tions has its major significance. The inter-action is, of course, a process of two-way influence.

It can be assumed in this context that the top marketing management will be responsible for what might be described as the economics of new products or, in other words, the problems of cost determination and pricing. It will be with them to obtain the necessary support of financial colleagues and the underlying marketing intelligence data on which to decide expected targets for the volume of production to be undertaken, the standards of quality to be attained, the likely price ranges for launching the product, the expenditures for a given scale of test and launching, and a calculation of projected profitability. It would be reasonable to expect that budgets should be prepared for these costs of preparation and launching the product, and for the market growth over a given period before the volume of sales is expected to reach the projected profitability, so as to attain the planned return on the total investment incurred. In this attainment the overall top management responsibility for co-ordination of research and marketing reaches its full fruition.

Quality Control

Another aspect of co-ordination affecting research is that of providing for technical control of manufacturing activities, which can be particularly important in some industries. The problem can be usefully illustrated by the example of a pharmaceutical company with a wide variety of products, many of them entailing formulations with complex processing and critical areas of treatment. To maintain the quality control in these circumstances, it was necessary for a close degree of expert chemical supervision to be provided to the manufacturing departments, without however impairing the normal production management responsibility. The company concerned was one of long establishment, and its manufacturing departments tended to be headed by men of long service who, while not having scientific training or qualification, had gained a good deal of know-how through familiarity over the years, often being active in the early days of initiating particular products. The whole of the manufacturing processes fall under the jurisdiction of a Works Manager, supported by these departmental heads or supervisors. For research purposes, the company had for some years been developing a full-scale laboratory staff with several well-qualified chemists. Most of their interest lay in the search for new formulations and new avenues of product, but they were also required to serve the works departments in respect of test samples and quality control. The Chief Chemist, as head of the laboratory, was responsible to a Technical Director, the point of top co-ordination being the Managing Director, to whom the Works Manager was directly responsible. To maintain the control of quality in manufacturing, the Chief Chemist was required to work closely with the Works Manager, and he had an over-riding jurisdiction to *stop any production process* on which quality was deteriorating from specification. To apply the control in practice, an arrangement was made giving nominated qualified personnel from the laboratories areas of scientific supervisory responsibility for specific product groups or departments. The arrangement ensured that each received, at intervals during the day, test samples drawn from stipulated stages of process within his product group. If tests showed quality deterioration, the chemist had the responsibility to order adjustments to process, to stop the manufacturing altogether when the checks proved that the processing was running seriously out of line with specification. Neither the Chief Chemist nor his nominated laboratory assistants had any other responsibility over the manufacturing departments than in respect of the quality control, and the clear understanding of the situation enabled very smooth working to be attained.

Board Membership

Problems of respective responsibility for scientific and technical development often raise the major question of their "representation" at Board level. This is a matter which seldom causes genuine difficulties in practice, though it figures recurrently at conference discussions, the claim being frequently heard that scientists are not adequately represented in Boards of Directors. The claim for such "representation" appears to be made because it is felt to further the interests of technical progress in business, but reliable evidence for this is not always easy to find. The technically progressive companies do not seem to owe their headway only to the presence of a scientist among the Directors: in fact, many a progressive technical enterprise owes its vitality and development to the spur of a vigorous "management" mind at the top, one capable of harnessing the constructive contributions of able scientific lieutenants. Clearly, the question is not one for which generalisation can provide a conclusive answer, nor on which the addition of respective examples can be a reliable guide. There are far too many factors needing to be taken into consideration in the assessment of causal progressive forces in industry. This does not deny, of course, that scientifically trained minds can make highly important contributions to business governance, but much of the claim for "scientific representation" at Board level seems to bear evidence of motivation by reasons of status or salary —the superior status that would be accorded to scientific work if it can lead to membership of the Board, as well as the better career and salary patterns that would then be available to scientists.

The *only* justification for a claim on the part of scientific personnel for admission to Board membership must lie in the same argument that is pertinent for any other groups of people, namely, the ability to make effective contribution to the policies and progress of the business. There are, undoubtedly, a number of firms where the inclusion of a scientific member in the Board would be a definite advantage, but there are many others where the scientific background of a Board member would be *as such* a matter of indifference: even in these latter, the scientist would have his claim to consideration if he happened to be a person able to make a sound contribution to Board responsibility. There is probably a strong argument that the systematic training which a scientist has undergone should give him a level of mental ability that is of great value to Board deliberations. Scientific and technical contributions to policy and progress can be made by means other than participation in the Board: for example, by the executive in charge of research and development activities being effectively constituted as a specialist adviser to the chief executive or to the Board as a whole. One major argument, however, does lend particular support to the scientists' claim in the contemporary situation: taking into account the extensive and rapid development of science and technology pertinent to industrial process and equipment, can an entirely lay Board of Directors adequately size up the significance of this advancement in relation to their own policy and needs? It could well be found that in many industries the answer must be "No", because of the complexity of the relevant scientific developments. Equally, however, this argument could be taken in other directions with comparable logic: for example, the fast-moving changes in world conditions could leave any Board of Directors hindered in their economic or commercial understanding, and unable of themselves to translate the trends of the market into an effective basis for policy—unless they have among their number a *qualified economist*. The question of scientific representation at Board level, in short, raises the whole problem of the function of a Board of Directors, whether any interests should be "represented" at that level at all, and, of course, what are the effective criteria for selection to membership.

The Management of Research

This is perhaps a useful point at which to turn attention to the rather different topic of the application of management within the domain of research and development activities. Broadly speaking, all aspects of the management process are relevant, but the mode of their application is different in a number of respects, largely arising from the concentrated specialisation of work and from the generally high mental calibre of all the personnel concerned. Individual differences are also encountered dependent upon the circumstances of the research and development activities in different laboratories. Some of the aspects of management practice within research may perhaps be worth comment in this context, but the problem is a big and complex one which requires on the part of the senior specialist executives responsible for research and development much fuller study than is proper for the present context. The aspects that will be taken up here are some of the broader ones that call for top management attention, whatever the scale on which research and development activities are established in an industrial enterprise. An interesting overall summary of the management problems is given in the table outlined in Fig. 108 overleaf.[1]

Taking first the question of organisation structure, this is an aspect relevant only in the larger laboratories: in the average run of medium or smaller businesses, the laboratory may be no more than a small team of scientists under a single head, and the only problem of internal organisation may arise through differences of discipline of the scientists concerned. Organisation problems can begin to emerge only when the numbers of personnel in a laboratory are reaching into the twenties and thirties. In one large manufacturing concern, there is a laboratory with over one hundred qualified personnel: its work is broadly chemical in character, but it does have a number of supplementary sciences assisting the chemists. The organisation pattern is designed to secure the most effective work from the scientific teams and the fullest degree of effective co-ordination of the different activities. At the top there is a Laboratory Manager who is supported by three Divisional Managers, each responsible for a major section of the work of the laboratory. The line of demarcation for the Divisions is that of the objectives towards which the research is orientated, broadly represented by consumer products, industrial products, and plant design. Within each Division the scientists are grouped into three or four sections, each containing anything from eight to twelve scientists. Here the basis of grouping differs, being sometimes that of an area of work, and sometimes that of the particular scientific skill employed. In this way, it becomes possible to provide the higher grade specialist services such as spectroscopy and gas-chromotography, to be made available economically for the assistance of the various research sections that call for them. Obviously, at the level of the Divisional Managers, there has to be close co-ordination in the planning of work, so that the services of the specialised units can be deployed in a balanced way to meet the varying needs of the different sections. Attached to the

---

[1] This is extracted from an American study by R. N. Anthony, details of which are given in the bibliography on page 901.

Fig. 108.—MANAGEMENT PROBLEMS IN A RESEARCH AND DEVELOPMENT ORGANISATION

	A. Technical Work	B. Service Work	C. Money	D. Facilities	E. Organisation and Personnel
1. Basic Policy Decisions (Re-examined occasionally, but not periodically)	1A. Scope, size and character of research and development work; areas to be investigated; proportion of work to be done inside the laboratory, elsewhere in the company and outside the company, patent and licence policy.	1B. Character and amount of service to be furnished research workers; location of service facilities; proportion and type of work to be done in decentralised shops, in centralised laboratory shops, and outside the laboratory.	1C. Determination of total amount to be spent on research and development; method of providing funds.	1D. Size and type of facilities; centralised v. decentralised research; location with respect to other departments of the company.	1E. Basic organisation structure; number, responsibilities, and relationships of supervisors, staff, research workers, etc.; relationship of laboratory to other parts of the company; methods of communication.
2. Planning for Specific Future Periods	2A. What projects are to be worked on; how much emphasis should be devoted to each.	2B. Amount and kind of service work required to support technical programme (shops maintenance building service, procurement, public relations, legal, etc.)	2C. Preparation of financial budget; i.e., translation of plans into financial terms.	2D. What items of equipment should be added, repaired, or discarded; mechanism used for transmitting recommendations and decisions.	2E. Matching work to be done with abilities and interests of men available.
3. Operations	3A. Problems associated with actually doing research work; communication of ideas, progress, etc., within the laboratory and to others; co-ordination of related work; transition to development and production.	3B. Scheduling: relationships between technical organisation and service organisation; problems peculiar to each service function.	3C. Recording what is spent: various accounting problems; specific restrictions on the expenditure of funds.	3D. Responsibility for custody and use of equipment; loans, etc.; operation of equipment pools; assignment of space.	3E. Selection, promotion, dismissal, training; monetary and nonmonetary rewards; creation and maintenance of atmosphere; supervision and motivation.
4. Checking Up	4A. Evaluation of rate of progress and probability of success; decisions to expand, contract, continue or stop work on a project; nature of the review process.	4B. Finding out whether service departments are providing proper service to technical departments; finding out whether service departments are operating efficiently.	4C. Use of financial information as a basis for checking performance.	4D. Methods of obtaining assurance that decisions are adhered to: appraising usefulness of various types of equipment.	4E. Measuring performance of individuals; finding out what they have been doing and how well they have been doing it.

Laboratory Manager are two staff units, one concerned with the equipment and personnel services, and the other with administrative and statistical services. Normal provisions are made for periodic meetings and other mechanisms for consultation and co-operation. From any close personal observation it soon becomes clear that the Laboratory Manager's own role is very much more that of management practice than of research activity!

Other aspects of research and development work in which organisation requirements emerge are those especially which relate to provision for test production, for pilot manufacturing, for transfer to normal manufacturing, and for initial technical control in this last phase: these, however, are less matters of organisation structure within research than the planning of systematic arrangements between research and production management, and have been dealt with in Part Two above.

Within any laboratory or technical development unit, planning is a very important management element, and with it the associated element of control. As has already been stressed, most research and development projects absorb a considerable amount of time on the part of several scientists, thus making any project correspondingly expensive. It is often argued that research and development activities, being brain-work or "think work" cannot be planned and, still less, controlled. This may well be a misconception of the words, for it is unlikely that anyone would be willing to argue that such activities, and the sizeable expenditures which they inevitably incur, should be allowed to run without responsibility or supervision. Planning and control, as elements of the management process, can be applied as effectively within research and development as they can elsewhere; there will be differences of application, and, in particular, planning must take account of the fact that attempts at forecasting of time required for projects are often, inevitably, unrealistic. Even this, however, does not preclude the possibility of setting targets, the more so if this is done as part of the responsibility of the participating scientists themselves. Planning and control require, in the first place, an overall programme of projects to be undertaken, say, for example, on an annual basis within a three-to-five-year phasing. Without such a programme it would not be possible to determine the scientific manpower required or the way in which the research budget should be formulated. Within the annual programme it will be essential to plan at least in the sense of allocating priorities, or of indicating target dates for projects which call for specific completion, if they are to be of value. The allocation of such priorities and targets give to the scientific teams guidance for their own working effort so that they can make the best use of time, particularly enabling them to decide when the stage is reached that it is wise to leave a project to simmer before further work is done on it. In any sizeable laboratory, it will be necessary to have a register giving some sort of progress review, so that the cost of projects to date can be assessed, and some indication drawn as to the advisability or otherwise of going on. There are laboratories where the planning and control techniques are carried to the extent that the scientific teams are required to record basic notes of work done, which become archives for later reference, thus preventing abortive repetition of work that is known to have produced negative results. In most laboratories it is customary for a scientific team setting out on a new project first to collect and examine the literature of the subject, and in a unit where the work is directed to a given product field, the literature should consist most usefully of such records of relevant past experimental work. It is normal management procedure to take steps to avoid unnecessary overlap of work, duplication of reading or research into previous work, repetition of abortive efforts and the waste of time that results from unsystematic approach to important discussions.

All this means nothing more than saying that it is as important to know as nearly accurately as possible the true cost of research and development work as it is to know the cost of manufacturing a product. There is a widespread general idea that research and development are good activities in themselves, and that there is no need for their economic justification: nothing could be farther from the truth, and no Board of Directors could accept this standpoint as a valid principle. The Directors have every right to expect the same justification of their research and development expenditure as they have for all other activities. (Some notes on the techniques of budget control applicable to research and development expenditure are given in Part Four: see page 736).[1]

[1] The subject of the planning and control of research activities is fully considered by Hiscocks in his book *Laboratory Administration*, two extracts from which are reproduced as Appendices A and B following this chapter.

So far as the planning of detailed work in a laboratory is concerned, there is some administrative similarity with the situation in a technical design and drawing office: procedures in this context are referred to in Chapter II of Part Two above (see page 261), and are also to be found in a pamphlet entitled *Drawing Office Organisation*, published by the British Institute of Management.

In the case of very complex and large-scale research-development projects (for example, those contributing to national defence programmes or to space exploration), a number of highly sophisticated progress control techniques have been worked out, especially in the U.S.A. One of these now becoming known in Britain with the code-name PERT was initiated by the well-known international management consultant group Booz-Allen & Hamilton. (The code stands for "Programme Evaluation and Review Technique".)

Personnel Management in Research

The human element in management may well seem at first sight to be much the same for research personnel as for any others, with perhaps the one significant difference referred to already, that the mental calibre is higher. Experience has shown that this difference is an important factor, giving rise often to serious personnel problems if policies and practices are not commensurate. The high mental calibre has the inevitable accompaniment of high critical faculties, and deficiencies which may well pass with ordinary personnel can give rise to serious difficulties with critical scientists. It is not always the physical factors of conditions, accommodation and facilities that matter so much to the scientists, but rather the attitude of management and the general mental environment within which they are to carry out their work. The availability of adequate up-to-date equipment can well be more important than the size of rooms or the amenities offered: management willing to spend money on equipment is giving tangible proof of its interest in serious research. One of the most important items in personal relations with scientific personnel is the appreciation of the time factor: top managements which are impatient for results and get irritated by the "delays" exhibit lack of understanding of the nature of research work and of the essential thoroughness with which the scientist likes to proceed. Similarly, an inclination to dismiss "fundamental" work behind a project conveys to the scientist a superficiality in management thinking which belies support for true research effort. To establish an effective research programme necessitates management ensuring an appropriate balance of fundamental work and of practical application leading to pilot production: the scientist is not indifferent about the latter, but is attracted to give of his best when he knows that the environment in which he works is conditioned by a genuine appreciation of how background knowledge contributes to effective technical progress.

Another facet of the same mental attitude is the scientists' need for continuing intellectual stimulus. This is readily available in the larger laboratories, where it is possible to employ sizeable numbers of well-qualified scientists from different fields. In all establishments, whether large or small, the intellectual stimulus will be sought in reading and writing, as well as by personal contact, and the practical implications of this need to be accepted by management as the normal concomitant of research activities. The "reading" aspect does not raise major problems, for the scientists would be expected anyway to keep abreast of thought and development in their own field, as well as to review adequately the background literature of particular projects on which they are about to embark. One requisite management will need to observe is the provision of information facilities: a library, a collection of reference books and abstracts, subscription to appropriate journals, access to loan sources of books. Where companies are initiating serious research work for the first time, it may not be apparent to the top management that facilities of this kind are essential tools and therefore a necessary accompaniment of the investment in laboratories and equipment: the scientists will soon make the point clear! In time management will also recognise what a useful investment such information facilities can be, if reference to available literature can reduce the amount of original investigation and experiment that a laboratory's team need undertake.

Personal contact among scientists has a similar role and value. These men will have become accustomed to free discussion and exchange of knowledge in the course of their University studies, and they will severely miss this stimulus if freedom of contact is denied or impeded. Major problems of security can, of course, arise, and management may legitimately require its own scientific personnel to be circumspect in technical discussion, when incautious descriptions or references may reveal important commercial developments. This is not usually a serious issue, as scientists are known to be men and women of high responsibility; the important need is for management to make clear the security aspect of a project and so to guide the scientists as to how far free discussion can be permitted. The importance of discussion with their confrères in other organisations and institutions is so considerable to scientists that it has been found critical in the siting of laboratories: recruitment of scientists can be difficult in areas where there are no other industrial laboratories or no University premises with scientific or technological facilities. By contrast, one or two districts in Southern England, for example, have become favoured for the establishment of research units because there are already a number of them located in the vicinity.

The third avenue of exchange of knowledge raises similar issues to that of free discussion. Not all scientists have an urge to write for the technical journals, but it is not uncommon to find that writing up a project becomes important for a man or a team when new knowledge or advancement of thought is emerging. Management has again to be responsible for reasonable protection of its own commercial interests, but any attitude of unreasonable inhibition of writing is certain to impair good relations with scientific staffs. It is not that the scientist is a different kind of human being: it is only that his training has taught him the value of exchange of knowledge and ideas, and as he has learned so much from others in the course of his own development he has a strong urge to pay back a contribution to the advancing stream of knowledge in his own field.

All these aspects have their bearing mainly on the morale of the laboratory and technical teams, and therefore on the value of the progress that emerges from their efforts. The employment of large numbers of scientific and technical personnel of high calibre and qualifications is a relatively new development in British industry, and there has not yet emerged an understood pattern of working relationship. It is inevitable in these early stages that the senior and intermediate managers under whom and with whom research and development staffs work are frequently less well qualified and probably of lower mental stature. This cannot but be recognised by the scientists: it need not be any cause of difficulty, unless there are artificial forces at work—for example, if status and privileges are accorded to intermediate factory and office staffs but denied to laboratory members. Salary scales are seldom a cause of difficulty in this respect in the lower and intermediate groups; if anything, the adverse influences are reversed here, because scientific personnel have for some years been recruited at higher starting levels, or have had good opportunities of salary advancement because of the pressure of demand for their services. In the higher levels problems are still encountered, but in many of the bigger concerns a salary hierarchy has been developed to enable scientists of high merit to enjoy scales commensurate with those of senior management though remaining within the field of research work. (Whether avenues of promotion to managerial appointments outside of the laboratory can be made readily open to scientists raises issues of an entirely different kind which will be referred to later.) Basic to the whole problem of the morale and efficiency of research and development teams is management's recognition of the importance of their contribution to the company—ensuring that good intellectual calibre is not wasted on technical trivia; providing a stable programme for the pursuit of serious research; keeping co-ordination with marketing and commercial developments; affording the climate and facilities commensurate with what the teams are being expected to attain; taking deliberate steps to make the laboratory feel "in the picture" and active in participation. In regard to the last item, there are some companies which make special point of bringing the research and development teams into the demonstrations or conferences when a new product or formulation is being launched, even to the extent of letting some of the bench-scientists or engineers concerned be the major technical exponents at a public gathering of customers. Nothing could more clearly confirm the management's recognition of the contribution of the teams, or so much boost their morale.[1]

One last practical point in man-management calls for re-emphasis —the need to be always aware of the high cost of research and development personnel, and therefore the corresponding need to ensure avoidance of waste of the manpower. Often a good deal of expensive time can be saved for important work by providing laboratory assistants or technicians to take over much of the simpler analytical work, and simple forms of mechanical aid can go a long way to saving brain-time in calculations. In more complex work, the computer has come in invaluably to the same end, and some experimental work has been done in a few firms with the application of statistical or mathematical techniques to reduce the volume of investigation in pursuit of a given result. This is the analogy of "method study" in the field of research itself, with the same objective in view as in manufacturing operations or the routines of selling, that is to say, applying techniques of analysis in order to attain the best possible utilisation of the manpower and equipment available. It can be brought home to the scientists and technologists themselves that they have an interest in their own efficiency—as noted earlier, research and development work cannot claim exemption from the basic economic principle of the optimum application of resources.

Research at National Level

So far in this Chapter the consideration of technical development has been obviously concerned with the companies maintaining their own laboratory facilities engaged on research as distinct from quality control and test. For every one company that can justifiably do this there must be almost a score that cannot do so. Many businesses, of course, have no need of resort to research and development of any serious kind, even when they are engaged on manufacturing their own products. Very frequently good progress can be maintained in quality and cost of product by dint of occasional technical reviews carried out within the manufacturing department or in a tool-design office. Far more companies, however, do need support from serious research effort, even if only intermittently. Their needs may well be served by one or other of the many establishments maintained by industrial research associations. How extensive a network of facilities is available through this channel is annually re-emphasised in the reports of the *Department of Scientific and Industrial Research*. The

---

[1] Several aspects of the human relations situations pertaining in research and development establishment are interestingly and instructively portrayed in Chapter 9 of "The Management of Innovation" by T. Burns and G. M. Stalker (Tavistock Publications, London, 1951).

Department has, of course, its own national research laboratories, fourteen in number, with activities directed to major problems of broad interest over specific fields, and their knowledge is as readily available to support industrial progress as it is to serve the government.[1] More important to industrial companies, however, are the Research Associations. These now total fifty and cover the following industries:

Baking	Hydromechanics	Food Manufacture
Boots and Shoes	Iron and Steel	Fruit & Veg. Canning
Cast Iron	Jute	Heating & Ventilating
Ceramics	Lace	Internal Combustion Engines
Coal Utilisation	Laundering	Marine Engineering
Coke	Leather	Printing & Packaging
Cotton	Lime	Production Engineering
Cutlery	Linen	Scientific Instruments
Electrical	Machine Tools	Shipbuilding
Felt	Motor Vehicles	Steel Casting
Files	Non-ferrous Metals	Tar
Flour-milling	Paint	Timber
Furniture	Paper	Welding
Glues	Rayon	Water
Glass	Rubber	
Hosiery	Springs	
	Wool	

Each one represents a co-operative effort by a group of firms interested in the field concerned, but it is a voluntary effort enshrined in the permanent and stable form of an established laboratory with a permanent staff. The total full-time personnel numbers some 4,500, of whom about a third are graduates or comparably qualified. Each Association is governed by a Council drawn mainly from the industries concerned, with the co-opted support of University personnel or members of other relevant institutions. The Association's laboratory has its permanent head to ensure that stable programmes of work can be framed and pursued. "The programmes of the Research Associations are essentially practical in outlook, concentrating on problems chosen by the members as being of the greatest industrial importance. Their work leads to more efficient production, to better quality products, and to economies in manpower and materials. This investment in brains is a business proposition likely to yield exceptional dividends.

"The research programmes vary greatly from one Research Association to another, depending upon the scale of operations and upon

[1] Some comments on the role of the national Research Stations are given in Appendix C following this Chapter.

the diverse needs of the individual industries. It is the responsibility of the Council of each Research Association, with the advice of the Director, to see that the most effective use is made of the available resources. There is never any dearth of worth-while problems; the principal task of the executive is, in fact, to choose from them a programme on which the most useful progress can be made."[1]

The work of the Associations relates to materials, to processes, to products, as well as incorporating the appropriate fundamental research investigations. Of these any one Association may see fit to remit part to one of the national laboratories of D.S.I.R. or to a local University laboratory. "All information obtained by a Research Association is for the benefit of the members, and the results of investigations which may be of immediate practical application are communicated to them first. The Council may, however, decide to release the information for general publication, and this course is adopted for much of the basic research." It is of interest to note that in more recent years this national coverage of research activity has spread beyond the scientific and technical fields to embrace "production economics" as well as some human and social problems. These have not been taken up in all industries, but a substantial amount of valuable work has been carried out by a few Research Associations which has afforded lessons to many industries, and has complemented studies made within more specifically sociological circles.

The existence of this wide-flung network of industrial research activity on the national scale means that no company and no management need feel deprived of research and development facilities on grounds of size or cost. Many managements may not be aware of this framework and to that extent it could be of interest to record the D.S.I.R. reminder of the advantages of membership of a Research Association:

"1. Members are the first to receive results of all investigations made on their behalf.
2. Results are the property of members and most of them may be freely used. Where the work has been covered by a Research Association patent, members receive preferential terms.
3. Members receive abstracts and surveys of the technical literature published in many countries, often with comments on the importance of new developments.
4. Books and periodicals may be borrowed from the specialised and comprehensive library maintained by the Research Association.

[1] These and following quoted passages are extracted, with official permission, from the brochure entitled *Combining for Research*, published for the Department of Scientific and Industrial Research by H.M. Stationery Office, London, 1960.

The staff is available for consultation on technical problems arising in the works of members.

5. The staffs of many Research Associations are trained to help
   member firms to raise productivity.
6. Through the Research Association members are kept in touch
   with technical developments of importance to the industry.
7. The staffs of member firms can often receive training from the
   Research Association in the latest techniques of control or of
   research.
8. The members decide the policy of the Research Association by
   electing the Council and by serving on it or its committees."

In the economic circumstances and tempo of this phase of twentieth-century industrial progress there can be few companies which
have not given some consideration to possibilities of technical
developments, on however small a scale. Even in retail trading new
automatic stock-room equipment has become available, and in one
form (the Gompertz-Solartron automatic warehouse) affords a
system of electronically-controlled delivery to customers whose selection has been made from display samples and marked on instruction
tickets. Serious long-term forecasting in present-day conditions
almost invariably imposes on top management an obligation to take
account of possible technological developments, and, behind them,
to the outcome of advancing knowledge through research. The pursuit of continuing profitability begins widely to acquire a deep technological aspect, which in its own interests a firm cannot overlook.
In this respect the individual business interest coincides with the
national interest, and a company actively taking account of research
and technical development is *ipso facto* contributing to national
progress and thereby honouring its social obligation. The standard
of living of the people and the position of the nation in world-wide
economic competition both call for effective application of new knowledge, and it is within the normal scope of industrial management
responsibility to consider how best this is to be attained. There are,
indeed, contributions to be made at government level, but these are
largely supplementary in the context of a free enterprise system. It is
unwise for managements to sit back and wait for a lead from the
government of the day; or to content themselves with resolutions and
speeches urging the government to "do something" to promote technical progress through research and development. Such an attitude is
tantamount to abnegation of the responsibility inherent in the
management role. The government contribution—whatever the
colour of the party in power in the Western formula of democracy—
comes in background facilities: in the expenditure supporting
national and industrial laboratories, and in the provision of adequate

technical education facilities. The lead to make full and effective use of these, and to secure practical application from them, falls naturally to those holding top management responsibility. In the community with closer forms of government-controlled industry, the respective contributions are more intimately inter-related.

What is required from the Boards of Directors of individual companies may be aptly described as making an investment in intellectual capacity. Neither the conduct of research and development work for individual purposes, nor the interpretation of scientific trends as the basis of policy, can be attained without an adequate supply of good brain-power, suitably trained in scientific and technological disciplines. Better educational provision to make the supply greater, or differently slanted, can indeed be urged on the government, but it is probable that the more important issue in most industrial enterprises is that of the effective use of the brain-power already available. There is in British industry plenty of evidence of scientists inadequately employed—well-qualified scientists engaged in firms whose requirements would be better met by technicians, or high-calibred men spending considerable proportions of their time on the details of projects which could easily be delegated to junior assistants. This is an issue on which management needs to be particularly judicious in considering its investment: buying in qualified scientific and technological brain-power, as an investment in intellectual capacity, requires the same careful deliberation as the purchase of manufacturing equipment. The broad decision is taken in terms of policy and objective, but the investment is effective only when the full scheme of ways and means of implementation has been assessed and approved. It is in this context that the question of "technical representation at Board level" begins to have genuine pertinence, and sound argument would support the case for some scientific membership of the Board, if that is the best means by which top management responsibility for technical development can be determined and applied.

AMONG the many publications that have appeared on the subject of research and development, the following may be found of special interest.

A. The trilogy of studies prepared by C. F. Carter and B. R. Williams for the *Science and Industry Committee of the British Association* and published by the Oxford University Press:

> *Industry and Technical Progress*, 1957.
> *Investment and Innovation*, 1958.
> *Science in Industry*, 1959.

The first two review the factors affecting the rate of application of new scientific ideas in industry, and the third considers the policy and practical proposals for improving the rate of application.

B. An American book which covers in some detail the whole field of research and development under the title *Management Controls in Industrial Research Organisations*, by R. N. Anthony (Harvard University, Boston, 1952).

C. A long-standing British classic of comparable scope from which excerpts have been quoted in this Chapter:

> *Laboratory Administration*, by E. S. Hiscocks
> (Macmillan, London, 1956).

D. An official publication referring particularly to the national laboratories—"*The Management and Control of Research and Development*", Report of the Zuckerman Committee (H.M.S.O., London, July 1961).

E. A general review of "research" from many different aspects is to be found in the Report of a Conference of the *British Institute of Management*, published in 1958 under the title "*Research—a Signpost to Better Management*".

PROGRAMMING WORK IN A RESEARCH LABORATORY

"THE following is an extract from a paper by Sir Arnold Hall, F.R.S., Director of the Royal Aircraft Establishment, Farnborough, discussed at a seminar at the London School of Economics early in 1953. The Royal Aircraft Establishment is the largest scientific institution in this country, and the extract gives an account of the system of technical programme planning and progressing employed there.

'A separate programme of work is developed for each technical department of the Establishment. It arises from discussion between the Headquarters of the Ministry of Supply, other interested agencies, and the Establishment. The scientist and engineer is given every opportunity to express his opinions and advise on the programme. In forming the research programme full regard is had for advice from the Aeronautical Research Council and its Committees. Full weight is given to the views expressed by the industry, either directly, through its representation on research committees, or through the Society of British Aircraft Constructors.

'A regular quarterly meeting is held in each technical department, at which all concerned with the programme of work and its progress meet together. This "Programme Meeting" serves both as a means of discussing additions to the programme, and as an essential element in progressing.

'We plan and progress our work in two ways. Parts which are suited to the treatment are time-planned, the task being broken down into technical phases, the overall date plan being built from the estimated time involved in these phases. The time plan is recorded in simple chart form, and a progress plot is superimposed at regular intervals. The analysis, and the estimate of progress, is made by the officer responsible for the work; a planning section is responsible for maintaining the record, and drawing the attention of the appropriate senior officer to any serious discrepancy between plan and achievement. A record of staff deployed on the work is also shown on the planning chart. The plan and its progress are reviewed regularly, and a re-plan or a re-deployment of staff is made if the situation requires it; should the forecast dates be changed, all concerned are informed of the adjustment.

'In carrying out work involving well-known techniques a reasonably accurate assessment of the "delivery date" can be expected from this process. It also highlights quickly any serious setback. But no scientist would expect such a system to be of any real value in the oversight of basic scientific work. Our work covers all shades from the basic research to the application of well-known techniques, though the latter is much the minor part. We use the planning and progressing system described for the "readily plannable" work, and extend its use some way into the less precise areas of activity. For the progressing of basic work, we use the medium of discussion, the state of the work being reviewed and discussed by those best qualified to judge it, at the regular programme meetings; the programme is then modified as may appear necessary. For the meeting, a document is drawn up setting out the position reached on each item of work and given a circulation which ensures that it receives a full measure of helpful and competent criticism.

'We extend the application of the "programme meeting" technique from the basic work towards the more "plannable" work, so that every item is covered either by one method or the other, or both. There is no hard and fast rule on a matter of this kind, but there is this to say: it is folly to suppose that any routine planning system will be of much use on very fundamental work (because a discovery cannot be predicted by date) and it is equal folly to argue that time planning should not be employed on many items of applied research and project work. It is the greatest folly to suppose that any system can replace able leadership and clear decision.' "

Source:

Laboratory Administration by E. S. Hiscocks, Chapter 9, "Programming" (pages 200–2).

CONTROL OF RESEARCH EXPENDITURE: RECOMMENDATIONS

"THE discussions in this chapter will have made it obvious that the statistics obtainable in the field of laboratory administration are in a completely unorganised state. If a code of practice could be established so that true and immediately understandable comparisons could be made between the different collections of figures, the work would be more than repaid by the usefulness given by reliable figures and the correlations that might be perceived.

"The following tabulation is put forward as the basis required for an assessment of the laboratory's progress in a number of different ways. If all laboratories were prepared to publish these figures, then valid comparisons could be made that might lead to significant improvements in the use of men and money. We need information on the following points:

"A. *The Total Annual Cost*

This should be broken down into:
(a) Salaries, Wages, and all costs directly attributable to staff such as pension contributions, National Health Insurance, etc.
(b) Capital Expenditure, i.e. on new buildings and major alterations to existing equipment costing more than £250 each, or any other agreed sum.
(c) Laboratory Apparatus and Materials, i.e. all running costs directly related to the research-work proper. Under this head would also come maintenance and minor alterations.
(d) General Expenses (i.e. items not directly or easily related to specific researches), including travel, stationery, postage, library, cleaning, furniture, office equipment.

"Detailed heads under any of the above major categories would be useful for minor purposes, but these four heads should be sufficient to give the major criteria, in conjunction with the staff figures also needed. These are:

"B. *Total Staff Employed*

This figure to be compiled of:
(e) Science or technology graduates, members of professional institutes with corresponding standards.
(f) Other scientific staff, i.e. sub-professional.
(g) Technicians.
(h) Clerical and executive staff.
(i) Other staff, e.g. labourers, porters, canteen staff, drivers, etc.

"Finally, to obtain information relating to building-use, the following figures should be obtainable:

"C. *Working Space*

    (k) Total floor space.

    (l) Total working floor space, to include any addition made during the year under review. (The definition of working space to be that outlined earlier in this chapter.)

"From these eleven figures a great assortment of measures can be compiled, which should answer many questions in the administrator's mind. For instance, A/B gives the crudest measure of cost to staff, but A/e gives the cost in terms of the qualified man only. The most valuable measures to be obtained from the above figures fall into three groups:

    (i) The cost per unit of staff.

    (ii) The support ratio.

    (iii) The use-of-space ratio.

"The most important ratios in the first category will undoubtedly be:

    a/e i.e. total staff cost per qualified man;

    a/B i.e. total staff cost per member of staff;

    A/e i.e. total expenditure per qualified man;

    A/B i.e. total expenditure per member of staff.

"These will satisfy most general requirements, but on occasion the administrator will find it invaluable to work on cost figures related to total scientific staff, i.e. $(e+f)$ *or* scientists and technicians $(e+f+g)$. Alternatively, he may wish to know detailed costs in relation to numbers of staff, such as the capital cost per head, or the running cost per head, and these he can obtain by taking the relevant cost figure out of the group A and forming his ratios with the required staff figures from group B.

"The most important ratios in category (ii), the support ratio group, are given by:

    f/e i.e. ratio of sub-professional to professional staff;

    g/e i.e. ratio of technicians to professional staff;

    $(f+g)/e$ i.e. technical support ratio to professional staff;

    $(h+i)/(e+f+g)$ i.e. non-technical support ratio to technical staff.

"Use of these ratios over a period or in comparison with similar ratios for other organisations will highlight staff deficiencies, and suggest possibilities of more economical uses of scarce categories of staff.

"In the third group, the use of space ratio, the figures under the heading C can be combined with any combination of the staff figures under B to give a broad statistical picture of space utilisation. In addition, the ratio k/l will show the architectural use of space, which is not dependent on the numbers of staff employed, but reveals the economy or otherwise of the basic lay-out."

Source:

Laboratory Administration, by E. S. Hiscocks, Chapter 10, "Evaluation" (pages 220–3).

APPENDIX C

RESEARCH STATIONS

AIMS AND FUNCTIONS

"WE have completed our survey of present and projected research at the Department's research stations and have made no new changes this year in organisation or scope of work. However, our review had led us to reconsider the broad aims and functions of the stations as a whole and to redefine their terms of reference clearly and in relation to modern needs. The new definitions have been sent to Directors to help them guide the expansion of their activities along sound lines.

"Basic research in the stations, we have said, must be directed to the general advancement of technology and applied science. We recognise, however, that each station should have the freedom to follow up new ideas that fall within its field of interest, and so to include in its programme some research which is not directed towards any immediate need of industry or Government. In considering their programmes stations must take into account both the ability and responsibility of industry and research associations for organising applied research, and also the scope of related work in universities and colleges of technology.

"Each station has before it a limited number of clearly defined objectives, chosen so as to yield, if attained, the maximum national advantage from the resources available for research. Provided that these objectives are practical, the work may consist of basic research, applied research or development: the criterion for selection is not the nature of the work but the end to which it is directed. Projects in the research programmes are also limited in number, so that proper progress can be made on each of them.

"Directors aim to ensure that the appropriate Government interests are linked as closely as possible with the stations' work and, in consultation with research associations where appropriate, they aim to secure financial or other co-operation from industry. We are aware that industry attaches importance to the fact that the Department's stations are completely unbiased both in the selection of research projects and in the presentation of results.

"Within these terms of reference the major purposes of the research stations are to:

(a) keep their fields of research under constant review in order to define objectives and help the Government, industry and the public to maintain a lively interest in the value of research;

(b) conduct research which can provide information to central and local government on matters such as air and water pollution, road safety, noise and the extinction and prevention of fires, in which the Government has a clear responsibility for protecting the health, safety and welfare of the citizen;

(c) carry out research and development in subjects, such as the natural resources of the country and the design and construction of buildings and roads, which are important to the Government and which affect the efficiency of industry as a whole;

(d) extend the frontiers of knowledge in applied science so that industry can be provided with the basic information required for the solution of particular problems;

(e) pay special regard to the research needs of industries that lack an adequate scientific background, and to research problems that are common to more than one industry;

(f) carry out particular researches, in co-operation with industry wherever possible, which will enable the stations to appreciate industry's problems more fully and to recognise those fields in which more basic research is most urgently needed;

(g) provide for industry national and international standards of measurement of various fundamental physical quantities (such as length, mass and time), related secondary standards and reference materials;

(h) conduct research on matters of broad public interest; and

(i) disseminate the results of research and secure their application.

"We would like to emphasise the last of these functions, since we believe it is becoming increasingly important for our stations to promote good relations with the users of research results."

Source:

Report of the Research Council on the Department of Scientific and Industrial Research 1959 (H.M. Stationery Office, London).

CHAPTER IV

OPERATIONAL RESEARCH

OPERATIONAL research is concerned with the application of the principles and methods of science to problems of strategy. It does not matter if the strategic situation is military, as it was when the subject was born in the Second World War, or industrial, as it often is today. The general staff in one case and management in the other has its problems of strategy to solve; it has to take decisions. Operational research scientists apply their science to decision problems, as a chemist applies his to chemical warfare, or a metallurgist applies his to steel production.[1]

So operational research could be called, in brief, a scientific aid to decision: the scientists have to be trained to formulate strategic situations in clear and quantified terms. There is no *particular* science to be used in that process, which is why an operational research team may consist of people who graduated originally in almost any subject from anthropology to zoology, from metaphysics to economics. In almost any such team, mathematicians can be found. But this is because mathematics is the language of science, not because operational research is a form of applied mathematics.

In fact, Professor M. G. Kendall said in his presidential address to the Operational Research Society: "Operational research may be regarded as a branch of philosophy, as an attitude of mind towards the relation of man and environment; and as a body of methods for the solution of problems which arise in that relationship." To crystallise all this and to give it some specific content, the following definition of eight clauses has been prepared:

Operational research is the attack of modern science
on problems of likelihood (accepting mischance)
which arise in the management and control
of men and machines, material and money
in their natural environment . . .

[1] This Chapter has been prepared and contributed by STAFFORD BEER, formerly Head of the Operational Research and Cybernetics Department of the United Steel Companies Ltd. and currently Managing Director of SIGMA (Science in General Management) Ltd. The content is based on the George Bray Memorial Lecture given by the author in Sheffield in March 1957, and is published with the permission of the Institution of Production Engineers. A study of the allied subject of cybernetics is to be found in the author's book *Cybernetics and Management* (published by English Universities Press, London, 1959, and John Wiley & Sons Inc., New York, 1960).

Its special technique is to invent a strategy of control
by measuring, comparing and predicting probable behaviour
through a scientific model of a situation.

How is it done? There are, first of all, some basic notions about
the approach to facts and their measurement, about variability and
risk, and about how these things may be handled scientifically in a
managerial situation. These are discussed in the first three sections
following. Secondly, after nearly twenty years of operational research
in practice in almost every sphere of management and in many different countries, there are various kinds of problems which have commonly emerged. It is natural, then, that certain techniques should
also have emerged to handle these familiar problems. Some of these
rather stereotyped pairs of problem-and-technique are discussed in
the subsequent three sections. But it has always to be remembered
that the most typical operational research problem is the one that
has never been solved by scientific methods before. The operational
research scientist is like a bespoke tailor working for a succession
of giants, dwarfs and unique creatures; but like the tailor he may
have to mount some specimen results for idealised problems in his
shop window.

COMMENSURABLE FACT

(a) Special Measurements

The first requirement of management must always be to develop
an understanding of what is happening, and to keep this understanding up to date. To do this, it requires a yardstick, a unit of measure.
In a steelworks, tonnage is a favourite unit. The weekly output in
tons goes down: management is told that smaller sizes than usual
are being rolled. The unit of length may be used, and this figure
drops: management is told that the sizes being rolled are bigger than
usual. The unit of cost may be used, and this rises: management is
told that there were metallurgical reasons for diverging from standard processes. And so on. Are these explanations reasons? Are they
excuses? To what extent do the explanations in fact account for the
discrepancies which the management is trying to evaluate?

The first need in describing and understanding industrial processes
is for a unit of measurement which takes into account the many
casual variables which may affect results, and removes them from the
field of argument. Ultimately, the unit of profit will do this; but to
measure the effectiveness of the production process, a yardstick of
the productivity of the plant itself is needed. But this measuring
device must be sensitive to *fortuitous* changes in the products. In
other words, regardless of what is being produced, it must measure

the effectiveness of production. If this is to be done, we shall have to abandon traditional units of measurement, and resort to a *pure number*.

To be factual: a ratio of what *could* be done in relation to what *is* done provides an index of productivity or effectiveness which is independent of all those factors to be excluded from our judgments. This is one example of commensurable fact.

(b) The Isomorphic Model

It is the routine procedure in operational research to construct a model of the situation that is being examined: not necessarily a mechanical one (although it may be); very often it is mathematical. The essential feature of the model is that it should be isomorphic with the situation it seeks to describe, that is to say "having the same shape or form". The model is really a hypothesis about the way a situation operates; the model becomes more and more isomorphic with the situation as more and more real-life characteristics are built into it. In the limit, the isomorphic model will behave exactly as the real-life situation behaves; it can then be used to predict how real life will react to a set of hypothetical conditions.

The advantages of a model are basically two. Firstly, it is possible to predict what will happen in given conditions without putting these conditions into effect in real life—and possibly going bankrupt. Secondly, the model ought to be much more easy to manipulate than the situation it describes: it is usually possible to obtain a prediction from the model in a day which would take perhaps a year to evaluate on the shop floor.

The basic tool is that of *analogy*—trying to recognise in the situation described the operation of some natural "law" already familiar to science in some other field. And it is likely that the expression of this "law" (which is to say the chief characteristics of its working) will be known to science in mathematical terms. A mathematical formulation is then available as the basis for the model to be constructed. The final task is to adjust the model towards isomorphism with the target situation.

Consider a model of the simplest possible form. Here is one set out to give the productivity, as a pure number, of several coils of steel strip which are being made thinner by their passage through a cold-rolling mill.

The total weight of these coils in lb. (w) is divided by the density (d) of steel and the cross-sectional area ($b \times g$) of the strip. Having thus obtained the length of the material in feet, divide it by the speed of the machine (v): this is the time it will take to pass the batch of coils through the machine once. This result will be multiplied by the number of passes (p) through the machine required to do the job. If there is a certain handling time (h) associated with each pass, this time duly multiplied by the number of passes (p) and the number of coils (c) must be added. Thus is reached a model of the objective time it will take to do a given job, the simple formula:

$$t_0 = p \left\{ \frac{w}{12dbgv} \right\} + chp.$$

This model will be isomorphic with the shop floor situation in so far as the factors which comprise it can be measured with accuracy. Some of the factors, like density, are physical constants; others, like the number of passes, may well require statistical research for their proper estimation. The productivity model is now completed, according to the idea previously advanced that the effectiveness of the process can be measured as a ratio of the calculated to the actual time consumed. This gives:

$$\sqrt{p} = \frac{100_0}{t_a}$$

where the actual time in the denominator has been obtained from an accurate shop floor record.

This model is no more than a straightforward formula, and not one of the class of models developed by analogy with another science. But it does offer a concrete example of a model in which the effects (in this case on productivity) of varying certain components of the situation can be evaluated, and it does give point to the general case for measures of fact which are independent of the job-to-job variables involved.

(c) The Notion of Probability

A second fundamental notion is the idea of *variability*. Suppose that a real-life measure of some kind is obtained with the answer 48. Now this is something very definite: it looks clear and distinct, it sounds crisp and scientific. It is nothing of the kind. Such a number normally has two kinds of uncertainty attaching to it. Firstly, there is probably error in its calculation: the sort of thing that can be said is that the answer is plus or minus (say) 2. Secondly, this is either a solitary measure, or the average of a group of such measures. In either case, the answer 48 is probably (quite apart from the *error* involved) simply one of a number of estimates that *might* have been obtained, had a few more instances been taken or the measuring done on another day.

The comforting solidity of the "48" collapses under scrutiny. The real truth is something not apprehended: it is always lurking elusively behind the measures that can be taken. Looked at like this, the answers are no longer seen as sharp points on a scale, but as areas, perhaps of considerable size, in which the point *probably* lies. The area could be shaded in like a contour map: the shading would be light around the edges, where the truth is least likely to lie, and darkest somewhere near the centre, where the truth is most likely to be found. In short, any figures used in calculations are labelled with a certain degree of probability—and it would be wise to find out what that is.

Picture one of these zones of probability like a contour map, and consider how it might be described. The scale on which the answer

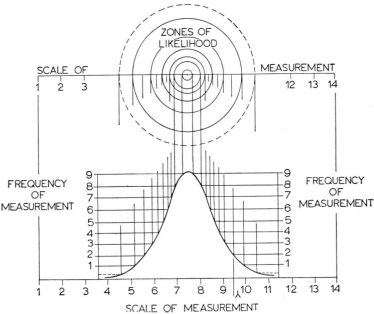

Fig. 109.—The contour map of probability.

is being read runs straight through it; this can be treated as a contour map, and a "profile" of the topography produced. The result would look something like Fig. 109.

The "contour lines" represent degrees of probability. The most probable point, at the centre of the concentric contours, is "the top of the hill"—that is, the *maximum* likelihood. Alternatively, the circles can be thought of as a target board; the practised player will tend to hit the centre and nearby most of the time; "outers" will occur with low frequency. A diagram such as that drawn is called a *probability distribution*.

How is this described, and how handled in practice? Suppose that it would be useful to know the probability of finding a steel bar more than 20 ft. long out of a batch whose average length is 19 ft. Plotting the frequency distribution of the lengths over a sample of bars would yield a probability curve; this would be likely to have the shape of the one just drawn. That is, it would be of Gaussian form, which is often called the *normal curve*. The measurement required is the *proportion* of the area in the right-hand "tail", when the tail is cut off at 20 ft. This proportion is given mathematically as:

$$\phi(x) = \frac{1}{\sqrt{2\pi}\,\sigma} \int_{20}^{\infty} e^{-(x-\mu)/2\sigma^2}\, dx.$$

A competent textbook provides a table that gives the answer to anyone who can calculate the standard deviation of his list of bar lengths. Doing that is a matter of simple arithmetic. For the price of finding this out, a manager or technician can discover the risk of passing a bar more than 20 ft. long, or for that matter one of less than 18 ft. This kind of information can save money. Unnecessary inspection may be eliminated; the setting of a saw may be adjusted to cut out waste; the need for more accurate shearing may be uncovered.

To summarise these basic notions in operational research: situations are looked at through the analogy of an isomorphic model; measures of fact are made commensurable within this frame of reference; and facts known to be both sacred and imprecise are handled in terms of their probability.

THE CONTROL AND USE OF MEASURES

(a) Statistical Control

If a satisfactory measure of something that appears to be insusceptible to measurement can be created, a first and vital step has been taken. Colloquially, when a difficult situation has been mastered, one speaks of "having its measure": there is wisdom in that phrase. But too many studies of situations, and too many managerial exercises, treat the obtaining of a measure as the climax and conclusion of understanding. A sheet of good data does *not* confer on its possessor magic powers over the situation it defines. Measurements are important *because they breathe the life of quantity into an inert model*. People who act on their first reactions to these data must in reality be assuming some sort of model in the back of their minds: it is probably a very bad model indeed.

For example: suppose a manager to be confronted with a cost

sheet that shows a deviation from standard (or average) cost of £5. Suppose that he then begins an extensive post-mortem into this manufacturing loss. Why does he do this? He does it on the basis that "£5 is a lot of money". In fact, his model derives from his own personal economy. Another manager, however, might do nothing at all. Why not? Again, he may well be working on the wrong model. In the back of his mind something is saying: "This company has a turnover of £Xm per annum; what is another £5?" Neither of these approaches is right: the proper criterion of the seriousness of this particular loss is the *variability* of the cost natural to the process on which the loss was incurred.

Suppose that the average cost of this process is £100. If, due to the variability of the process, that average stands for a series of results varying apparently indiscriminately between £50 and £150, then it is virtually meaningless to talk about a discrepancy from average of £5. The first manager mentioned is not only wasting his time but the firm's money: his post-mortem might well cost the company £50 in time and lost production. On the other hand, the natural variation of the £100 average cost might well be from £97 to £103. In this case the reported discrepancy of £5 is clearly of vital importance; this is not because it threatens the company with bankruptcy, but because it means that the process is in some sense out of control. The manager who ignores this signal may eventually lose a more serious sum of money. The moral of this parable may be that the use of averages is dangerous, which is true. But the real answer to the problem is to set these measurements in the right operational research model (rather than some unexpressed subjective model of the man who scans them) and thus to get control of the measures themselves. Once a model is under control, it will be possible to control the real-life situation.

Again, this places a simple interpretation on the term "model". Later on attention will be turned to complex models of situations where the interaction of a number of casual networks has to be taken into account. But if that is the final model, first consider the sub-model for an individual measurement. This, as the parable indicated, is its natural variation. Now the variation itself has a "shape". It may be considered as a probability distribution. After all, if a quantity normally varies between 50 and 150 the probability of the occurrence of these extreme values is obviously likely to be low, whereas values around the 100 mark might be expected to occur with greater frequency. A statistician can readily determine the mathematical function which describes the variability of a particular measurement. For reasons explained in the last section, this means that he can quote with accuracy the probability attaching to any particular value. Let him now determine two points, one on either side of the average value, such that there is one chance in 20 that this value will fall still farther away from the average. These two values are known as *confidence limits*. That is to say, if a value is discovered which lies between these two points it can cheerfully be regarded as "belonging" to the population of values appropriate to this particular measurement. To regard a value which falls *outside* either of these points as "normal", is to accept odds of at least 20-to-1 against. This particular confidence level is arbitrary: but most people would be prepared to agree that odds like these are too long. If a value comes along at this level of risk, it is suspect. We have now got a useful model. In the light of this, that £5 discrepancy will appear (as it should) as insignificant in the one case and as significant in the other. (That word "significant" is a technical term in statistics: it means that a value has occurred which cannot be attributed to chance variation.)

(b) Managerial Controls

The comparatively recent creation of management as a subject of study has led to a much wider understanding of the class of measurement it is proper to collect, and of the importance of accuracy and speed in its presentation. All this has been very much worth while. But it has inevitably led to the inundation of management by a sea of figures. Data pour on to the manager's desk: figures relating to production, sales, costs, wages, research, absenteeism, accidents, and so on. The more the message about the vital importance of measurement is propagated, the higher the flood waters rise. The more senior the level of management, the more threatening does this spate become—despite a certain amount of consolidation of figures as they rise to the very top. (Please note that even this obviously desirable process of consolidation, since it normally works upon averages, is unfortunately constantly swallowing the all-important information about *variances*.)

Clearly there is a problem here. In the first place, management requires some guide as to what it ought to look at, what is important, what is *significant*. And, in the second place, there are fortunately still managers who wish they could spare more time from their desks to look and to think. Would not the wholesale adoption of statistical controls provide an answer?

Consider a department in which, over a period, some 20,000 machine-jobs have been carried out. The manager of this department obviously requires some measure of the effectiveness of the work. By the use of indices, as previously explained, this difficult assessment can be made relatively easy—by taking all the variables out of the judgment. Is the manager, however, to be faced with 20,000 productivity indices? The answer is "No".

First of all build another model. So far, the model facilitates the study of productivity of individual jobs. The new model will be statistically more complex: it will indicate the interrelation of individual jobs in terms of the common measure that an endeavour is being made to invent. Whereas it would be fatal to attempt a grouping together of this vast amount of data in terms of some conventional breakdown of orders, it is a fascinating operational research job to create the *departmental* model of the general pattern of productivity disclosed by the measurement of indices. This new model will produce a fairly small number of productivity groups still perfectly amenable to statistical description in terms of probability. In practice, data of the extent and complexity described tend to fall into about 80 such groups.

Secondly, there is an important off-shoot of the scientific study of probability, known as *sampling theory*. This teaches how to choose a relatively small number of incidents, as representative of the totality. By the use of properly instituted sampling techniques all the required information can be obtained by studying perhaps a mere 10 per cent. of all the incidents concerned. Thus instead of evaluating indices for 20,000 jobs, only some 2,000 need be evaluated—spread over 80 groups.

At this point the notion of statistical control is invoked. The control statistician has to examine the final 80 results. The great majority of these will, naturally, be in control: that is, they will fall within the confidence limits calculated for the appropriate group. Usually we find that some five or six results are *significant*: these are the ones to report to the management.

It is important to realise how much progress has been made from the original demand for measurement of some kind. Even in the simplified productivity model quoted previously, there were eight major variables. Thus the total information involved in the departmental study would consist of 20,000 sets of results, to each of which would be appended a list of eight relevant factors. Surely it is fair to say that no living person could comprehend this mass of information, far less gain a genuine understanding of productive effectiveness from it. By the use of operational research techniques, and (to this point) only those of a most elementary kind, all this is *scientifically digested*. The manager finally receives all that he wants to know on a single sheet of paper; he has a statistical guarantee into the bargain, that anything which is not on this piece of paper is behaving within the normal limits of chance variation.

(c) *Controlled Estimation*

Such a system is flexible; it will not shatter irreparably into fragments in the face of the obstinacy of men, the vicissitudes of production, or the malice of mischance. The system, once set up, can be kept under permanent surveillance by the statistical control of its key elements, the behaviour of which is already understood in probabilistic terms. All this has been illustrated, up to the point of reporting to management in terms of productivity indices. More positive use can, however, be made of this system.

A production control department must produce production plans, and these must involve the creation of detailed machine load programmes. Many production control systems are ineffective because they do not face up to this fact. The reason usually given is that it is impossible, particularly in a jobbing shop, to estimate with any accuracy the time taken to do a given job on a given machine. If really reliable estimates of machine-job times were available for any job on any machine, and especially the class of jobs which have not been done before, then there would be no particular difficulty in constructing a workmanlike production plan. It would be constructed like a mosaic from the component machine-job times. If this plan, in addition to being reliable, were also resilient, then it would not be reduced to chaos as soon as the exigencies of production required its modification.

All these requirements can be met by the active use of a system set up by operational research methods. To estimate a machine-job time, it is necessary first to evaluate the constructed time by exactly those methods described in the section on "Organic Flows" below. The same model, and the same notional factors, that were used when the system of description was being built are used again: that is, an *objective time* is calculated. This result has been generated by a model which is known to be isomorphic with the shop floor situation, and the quantitative relationship between the two is measured by the productivity index. Consequently, if the calculated result is now *weighted* by the current index appropriate to the job being considered, a statistically guaranteed estimate is reached of the actual time the job can be expected to take.

It is widely recognised that there is a difference between theory and practice: this operational approach not only acknowledges this difference, but measures it continuously, and uses the statistically controlled measure (that is, the index) to improve the estimate. Engineers will recognise the principle of "feed-back" which is being applied, not mechanically, but statistically.

This method is *lively*: it is not a static moribund technique which begins well enough and is then left behind by the changing modes of behaviour which characterise the natural evolution of any works. The claim that it will apply to work which has never been done before is justified in the comprehensiveness of our operational definitions. Any occurrence has a statistical probability; this maxim can be applied with great effectiveness to the likelihood of a given job falling within the ambit of a given model. The resilience of a plan built from components evaluated by these methods is given in their statistical control. For the value taken as an estimate of machine-job time is that determined by the maximum likelihood of its probability function. When these times are built into a machine load, there is a "give-and-take" between successive estimates, also determined by that function. It is as if the bricks with which we are building were set in place, not with a brittle mortar, but with an elastic bond capable of considerable deformation. It is this property in the plan that is called resilience. In practice it provides that the plan can draw out of phase with the production it controls *without* disintegrating: by taking into account the range of an estimate's variability, the plan acquires what can be called the *lively* quality of adaptability. It is also predictive.

Prediction of an intelligent or scientific kind involves induction: the amassing of particular instances leading to a generalisation dignified with the title "law". The extent to which people are prepared to act upon the law depends upon the strength of the evidence which supports it: this is still in the realm of probability. That a kettle will boil is so likely that people often fail to realise that they are not dealing with a certainty, but with a very high probability. Why is the probability high? It is because the evidence is simple, clear-cut, extensive and highly organised. Scientific predictions can be made *to the extent* that these characteristics are found. Everything depends upon discovering the "law", which is the same thing as saying finding a model. The law or the model is the framework within which facts are organised.

When an order is received, management wants to *predict* its cost. The modern accountant is well aware of this: the practice known as "historical costing" is quite out-moded in up-to-date firms. Yet the accountant, like the rest of management, is debarred from looking into the future. Therefore, he has much to gain by invoking operational research. He could fairly expect operational research so to organise his data about raw materials, about overheads, and most of all about output rates, as to introduce *liveliness* into the costing system in the same sense as that notion was earlier applied to production control.

In fact, this idea has been tried and proved on quite a large scale in so far as output rates are concerned. These can be generated by operational research techniques in just the same way (moreover, by the self-same system) as the planning predictions were made. Figures supplied for costing purposes on these bases have the following advantages: they can be generated very quickly on an electronic computer or other high-speed calculating machine; they do not require constant overhaul by the works management, because they can be controlled by the routine statistical methods already installed; significant departures from the standard or average level are automatically signalled by the statistical control; above all, they are *predictions* in the sense described above.

SOME IMPORTANT COMMENTS

(a) Complexity versus Simplicity

Before leaving this discussion of the basic notions behind operational research, here are three comments. The first concerns the complexity of this approach. Fairly simple language has been used, but operational research has probably emerged as rather a complex subject. Is it too complex? What about the virtues of simplicity?

Before anything else can be done, a situation must be described both operationally and dynamically. Since the situations concerned are of great complexity, because they involve machines and men and advanced industrial practice, the operational research model must itself be complex. There simply is no short cut at this point. Unless the model parallels the situation in complexity, it cannot attain to isomorphism, and cannot predict. This is not to say that the model must needs be as untidy as the situation; indeed, the virtue of these methods considered as descriptive techniques is that they reduce incommensurable measures to pure numbers; and they reduce variability, risk, chance and misfortune to a system of probabilities of great neatness. But the complexity of the situation is reflected in the difficulty of the algebra: it is still there.

From this basis a result is obtained: a solution, a comparison, a prediction. At this point, the point of presentation of results, simplicity becomes the real aim. Everyone knows that results must be expressed as briefly, clearly and simply as possible. And yet managers are constantly irked, often to the point of exasperation, by a failure to observe this rule. It may help to suggest two reasons why these troubles arise. One is a severe practical difficulty, and the other is a psychological one. Sufficiently wise management can deal with both.

Firstly, the operational research man is anxious that his conclusions should not be misunderstood. He understands the complications of the subject he has been investigating, and inevitably feels

that the concise answer he would like to submit is an over-simplification. He is therefore tempted to bring in reservations and qualifications, to elaborate his point, and to expatiate upon the methods he
has used. The answers to this problem lie with management. If the
operational research analyst could know that the people he tries to
help already understand the nature of his subject, he would not feel
so diffident. It rests with management, when they introduce work of
this kind, to see that the staff is fully informed. This surely means
that the scientist must be given the opportunity to explain himself
and his techniques: something like a deliberate educational policy
will have to be launched. But the operational research man needs
educating too. He has probably been brought up to believe that his
job as a scientist is to determine the facts, and to leave management
to make the decisions. He feels this responsibility keenly, and thus
becomes too scrupulous.

Secondly, it is only human to recognise that the scientist who is
trying to make the simple report that he knows is required, has his
own personal and professional pride. When he has worked hard and
wrestled long with an intractable problem, he does not want to be told
that his "guess" has been noted along with those of others who he
knows have scarcely considered the problem. In short, like everyone
else, he does not want to be underrated; and this leads him almost
unconsciously to give his reports that air of importance which the
management will regard as incomprehensibility. If managers would
understand this human shortcoming and treat it sympathetically,
much of this difficulty would disappear.

Finally, there is a class of operational research which does not
result so much in a report to management, as in the installation of
an operational solution—a method to be adopted in the works, or a
system of control to be installed. Here again, simplicity is the keynote. It is rightly demanded that procedures that have to be handled
by workpeople or clerks should be within their capacity to operate.
Thus operational research should give the closest attention to translating its original (and justifiably) complex treatment into a workable
form. To do this, it may be necessary to install permanent operational
research controls at the centre to ensure the continued validity of
the simplified translation which is being used in the works. A central
control of this kind is often to be found, and should be regarded as
the real solution to the paradox of complexity versus simplicity. In
effect, this practice divides the problem of handling a difficult situation into two parts: the complexities are removed from the problem
and handled at the centre, and large-scale applications can then
safely be dealt with by more junior staff in the works in terms of
simplicities.

(b) The Question of Productivity

The second of these comments derives from the actual work so far described. It concerns productivity. It is widely claimed that our national difficulties are only to be overcome by higher productivity. This means that productivity is not at this moment as high as it could be; that some of it is "missing". Where is it?

There is a glib answer to this question, which says that "no one works hard these days". Therefore, it is argued, the missing productivity is up the sleeve of the operative. This is no more than a half-truth. If *within the accepted structure of a man-machine process,* all the labour factors in the operational research model are set at conditions of 100 per cent. effort (that is, at a level of "sweated labour"), experience is that an overall increase in productivity of perhaps 2 per cent. or 3 per cent. is indicated by the model. There is great scope for increasing productivity, and yet *within the system that is being worked,* intense human effort cannot make much impression.

This is just not satisfactory: the models must also be made to say where the missing productivity has gone. This they can do. Consider a large plant as an organic whole—which is what it ought to be. Its smooth flow of material, the fitting together of the separate parts of production, the need neither to overload the digestion of any machine nor to starve it, the purification of the blood-stream that supplies the vital services, and the health of the nerves that carry the communications of control: all these *organic* requirements are the criteria of efficiency.

From the models it is learned that for every few per cent. of increased productivity that is obtainable by sheer labour effort, something between 20 per cent. and 50 per cent. is available in terms of better "body tone", of truly organic behaviour. This could be achieved, according to our research, in terms of smoother flow, better planning, better machine loading, better servicing and better communication and control. These aims are doubtless already objects of management everywhere; but to achieve real liveliness, or *life like ness,* a step is required from our present concept of an "integrated works" to the concept of an "organic works". The features of a factory wherein this organic wholeness lies need re-thinking, not just improving, on a scale not yet imagined. This is not an argument from the inevitability of technical change; it is an argument from the operational research model. Here alone we have the opportunity to understand the interactions of the parts within the organic whole.

Imagine processes A, B and C. Process B tends to be a bottleneck, although a work-study investigation has revealed that there is plenty of spare B capacity. A large incentive bonus is therefore applied to process B. Production and wages rise: but there is still a bottleneck. And yet there is reason to think that labour effort is still well below standard. What has happened? If the probability distribution of real effort (say the productivity index) is plotted statistical truncation is likely to be found, that is, instead of the usual "tail" on the right, there is a sudden precipice. This means that *unnatural* limits are being set to effort in process B. Either the labour-force has carried its bonus earnings to a point where they are as high as it thinks management will permit, or the flow from process A and into process C is too erratic or unplanned to permit a high rate of B productivity. Although labour is not working very hard, it is effectively prevented from working harder by either an economic or a manufacturing constraint. If operational research is asked to study the man-machine system A–B–C as an organic whole an answer may be found; possible methods will be discussed below.

Finally, there is a point of great economic importance. Changes in the whole nature of the organic functions mentioned would presumably involve some capital expenditure. But this is not expenditure on a large scale: the factory to all appearances would remain unchanged. By its "animation" an approach is made towards the full utilisation of existing resources.

(c) Integration with Management

This point can be made briefly: it follows as a corollary of (a) and (b). Operational research is in fact *operational*; its results should be built into management technique. The full rationale of this thesis appears in a later section.

The examples that were given earlier were deliberately chosen to demonstrate how the operational research approach can be integrated with management functions, can be made implicit in the system whereby the factory runs. Once methods of this kind have been installed, a manager should have the surety that when he looks at data, he is not being set a series of traps in which he will become ensnared unless all his experience and judgment are brought to bear with constant vigilance. He should be able to feel that operational research has ground a scientific outlook into the lenses of the glasses through which he views the operations under his control.

More specific tools than those basic notions so far described have now to be considered. All these presuppose the ability to measure, to describe, to control and to predict, by the application of probability theory to operational research models. For simplicity, these more advanced methods will be discussed as if they referred to investigations which, once completed, would be forgotten. This is, however, a deliberate concession to space. Please bear in mind how each of these techniques would in practice be an integral part of managerial activity; operational research must never hurl advice at the players from the touchline.

STOCKS AND FLOW

(a) What is a Stock?

Consider a number of people arriving at a football match. There is a turnstile. Individuals arrive, their money ready, at random times. Someone is issuing tickets: he takes a random time to deal with each client, which depends on several factors—the giving of change, for example. Sooner or later he finds that the entrance has become congested; a number of people has accumulated in front of the turnstile, and this line of people is called a queue. Suppose that the people arriving at this gate represent orders arriving to undergo a works process. All these orders, say, are late for delivery, or have top priority. The object will be to process them as quickly as possible, to hurry them past the gate, just as the issuer of tickets is trying to pass his clients into the football ground. But the process time is variable, depending on several factors. So in a works also there may be congestion; again a number of orders may accumulate in front of the "gate"; again this may be called a queue.

Once some facts about this kind of process have been collected, they can be put into statistical form. The *arrival times* are distributed in a statistical sense: that is, it is possible to work out their probability function. The *service times*, too, have their characteristic form. Now the operation of this gate, the process of passing an arrival through the service, consists in collecting an arrival time and a service time as a pair. There is no connection between the two: the fact that someone arrives two minutes after his predecessor has nothing to do with the time it will take to serve him with a ticket. And yet the result of such arbitrary pairing characterises the operation of the gate; a large number of such random pairs will define the queuing problem.

Since the two statistical probability functions are known, it becomes possible to work out the risk run of forming queues of various lengths mathematically. It is also possible to investigate how a queue can be eliminated by increasing the number of service points (for example, of cranes or soaking pits dealing with hot steel ingots), and how much waste of service capacity (for instance, of cranepower or heat) will be incurred thereby. The body of work that has been done on this type of situation is now quite large; it is corporately known as the *Theory of Queues.*

Queue Theory, in short, enables operational research to determine the characteristics of a situation where a queue tends to form in terms of probability. It does not matter whether the queue consists of people waiting to go into a football match, patients waiting to consult a specialist in a hospital, aeroplanes "stacked" over an airfield, or orders waiting for processing in a works.

When people or things collect in front of a gate or process like this, there is a common apprehension, a wish that this did not occur. The word "queue" suggests some form of nuisance. There are phenomena, however, which are exactly of this kind but normally approved. They are then called not a "queue" but a "stock". A stock is defined as a buffer between two probabilistic processes; it is there to absorb the risk that the first process will not be ready to disgorge an item to the second process at the right moment. This is true for many pairs of processes: machine 1 to machine 2, department A to department B, raw material supplier to the works, the

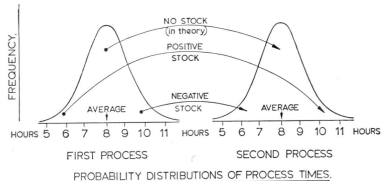

PROBABILITY DISTRIBUTIONS OF PROCESS TIMES.

FIG. 110.—The nature of a stock.

works to the customer, and so on. Many kinds of stock are differentiated for management purposes, and sometimes their different names are useful: raw material, inventory, work-in-progress, "agreed", minimum, maximum, and so on. But the different contexts in which these kinds of stocks are mentioned ought not to obscure the basic fact that a stock is a desirable queue, and that its purpose is fundamentally always the same: it is a safeguard against a measurable risk.

This is illustrated in Fig. 110. If there are two processes, each with a cycle time averaging eight hours, how much stock is required between them, if the second process is never to be stopped for want of work? Suppose no stock at all is deliberately set up. When the two processes happen to take exactly the same time over the jobs they are doing, the first can pass on a job to the second at exactly the right moment; no stock is created, and no time is lost. But if the first machine happens to have a good run, and takes a short time, while the second machine has a bad piece, and takes a long time, a "stock" piece will lie between the two machines until the second machine is ready. This is a positive stock, or a queue. If the positions are reversed, the second machine will be waiting for work; not only will there *not* be a stock piece in front of the second machine, but there *ought to be one*. This is a "negative stock": it is a sort of production vacuum. In deliberately creating stocks as an insurance, we are trying to fill this vacuum. The size of stock required to do so can be calculated to a nicety in terms of the probabilities attaching to the creation of "negative stock". From the diagram it will be seen that this risk depends upon the length and "fatness" of the two "tails" facing each other. It is just this tail length and fatness that are measured in the probability functions which define the two processes. The mathematical statistician is capable of calculating the risk of "pairing" across the tails.

By this approach operational research is enabled to recommend proper stock levels. No one can *guarantee* that a given level of stock will always be adequate. The probability tails never quite reach the zero line: there is always some risk that any stock will not be adequate, then, unless that stock is infinitely large. But one can specify the proper level of stock for a given level of risk. That risk can be made negligible. It is more important to realise that by accepting a a larger risk, stocks can be drastically reduced. Industry has been so concerned with high productivity (and rightly so) that stocks have often been allowed to rise to the point where the protection they confer on the "second process" could be classed as over-insuring it.

(b) Organic Flow

The queuing theory is relevant also to queues of another kind. In many industries, a number of machines (looms, for example) come under the care of a single operative. If anything goes wrong, the machines themselves may begin to form a queue for attention. This is the problem of machine interference, which the theory of queues can also tackle. But considerations of this kind lead into rather a different subject, because they concern *renewals*. That is to say, there are many industrial entities which, like their human invigilators, are born to die. The "birth-and-death" process, like the queuing process, depends upon an element of randomness. Whereas in queue theory it is specially noted that there is no connection between successive time intervals (because they come from independent populations of times), in this new kind of process there is every connection.

A tool or a machine that is wearing out passes from one state to another, until a final irreducible state is reached: "death", the moment for renewal. Each succeeding date depends upon two things: firstly, the preceding state, secondly, what happens next, which (since it cannot be specified) may be called a random influence. Something which proceeds in this way from one state to the next can be described by what is called mathematically a *Markov Chain*. This is a descriptive name for a series of states in which each depends on its forerunner alone, and its formulation creates yet another kind of probability model.

Now a *Markov Chain* is a particular example of a class of process known as a *Random Walk*—simply because each state succeeds another without pre-determination. In this general case, the Markov restriction that only the immediate previous state affects the next one can be dropped and the effects of several intruding factors can be calculated. And so the list multiplies. There is a "contagion" process, in which one person passes something to another: this something could be the measles (the theory has already been applied to the study of epidemics) but equally it could be information. Information Theory itself is thus another example of the class of work being considered.

All these models have a common characteristic: *randomness*. This is because operational research is concerned with a real world, a world in which chance and mischance play leading roles. If operational research has one special claim it is that it conducts industrial science out of the if-this then-that laboratory, and into the real world of perhaps and maybe. Behaviour which is characterised by a random element is the commonest form of industrial behaviour. Whatever its kind, it is referred to as a *Stochastic Process*.

The word "stochastic" comes from a Greek word meaning "to aim". Industrial behaviour, once outside the production line itself (and all too often while on it), has only a general aim, which it usually attains—more or less, sooner or later. The methods of getting there are stochastic processes. These are the major factors that were listed in the opening section of this Chapter: planning, communicating, maintaining, and so on; above all, stocks and flow. These are the *organic* features of the factory. If the factory does not really operate as an organic whole, it is because management does not properly understand the stochastic behaviour of these vital features. Stochastic models in the hands of operational research can provide this understanding.

(c) *Facts and their Simulation*

The whole of this section has been concerned with Stochastic

Processes. This term, while it does apply to the physical situations described, also applies to the mathematical models of the situations. Strictly, it takes a mathematician to formulate and to operate these models. Let no one assume, however, that to hire a mathematician is to hire an operational research analyst, nor that operational research is a form of mathematics.

Mathematics is the common speech of science, and the main language of probability theory. It is the most satisfactory way of expressing complicated quantitative ideas. But, while it is great fun to construct mathematical models, like castles, glorious, forbidding, and crowned with algebraic flourishes like pinnacles, they are useless if built in the air. The operational research mathematician is someone who understands this; someone who knows that his model is only as useful as his *works data* tells him what he needs to know. It is not said that the data must be "absolutely accurate": the statistician regards such a demand as naïve, if not meaningless. The data and their limitations must be understood: this is vital.

How is the information to be collected? Preferably, by institutional means. Shop-floor records may be inaccurate, illegible, missing, "adjusted", or blatantly mendacious; but remember that they have been near to truth. They were around when the job was done. A crisp, clean, perfectly printed set of information can so easily turn out to be a beautiful liar: gullibility is dangerous! This nicely packaged set was probably synthesised *from* the shop-floor record, quite probably by a clerk more anxious that all the figures should fit together than that the facts should emerge.

Another valuable source of information is work study. The active help of this kind of technique is invaluable to operational research. It is usually possible to understand the limitations of these data, because an astute work-study engineer knows very well how accurately he can establish the facts of a given situation. The two real difficulties are that it is hard to ensure that the study is truly *operational* (because by measuring facts one alters them, as every physicist knows), and that one cannot invoke a basically observational method if there is nothing to observe (much operational research concerns policy, planning or some other hypothetical situation). Work Study and Operational Research have a great deal to offer each other. Operational Research ought to gain sheer information; Work Study can be put in the wider, organic picture of interacting probabilities. Apart from anything else, it can be guided to attend to activities where control is being lost, inefficiency is locked into the accepted pattern, or risks combat with prudence.

Assuming, at any rate, that a suitable stochastic model is available, and that the relevant data to generate through this model have somehow been assembled, there are still two major hurdles to be cleared. Firstly, it can happen that the stochastic process is so complicated that there is no mathematical method of solving it. The queuing process as discussed above related to the convolution of two probability functions: it is unfortunately possible to construct more complicated models, which are clearly isomorphic with reality, but which defeat pure mathematics in its present stage. Secondly, whether the mathematics can be entirely organised or not, to *evaluate* the model for a given set of facts may present serious problems in the very mechanics of calculation. If either or both these hurdles cannot be jumped within the ability of mathematical processes, another operational research technique may be used.

This technique is to take the established model, and to generate known information through it experimentally. Instead of "solving" the model, one operates it to see what happens. In doing this, the problem is simulated by operational research, much as a game of Bridge is simulated when all the hands are spread out on the table and a "model" game is played with all the risks and chances taken into account. To do this, it is necessary to work from the actual distribution of data represented by the model's probability functions. A random value is selected from each distribution (which is exactly what happens in real life) and built up into a synthetic works record. Fig. 110 shows how those all-important pairs could be selected, by choosing values alternately from under the two curves; if the selection of a value under each curve is done genuinely at random, the probable frequency of the occurrence of each value will imitate reality. That is, there will be, as there should be, a greater proportion of values near the "maximum likelihood", than in the "tails" of the distribution.

This is a truly scientific procedure, because the *model is in action,* although the real-life element of chance is now being introduced by a deliberate randomising technique, instead of through mathematical statistics. It is because of the randomising that this type of solution has become known by the facetious name of the *Monte Carlo Method.* One of the advantages of a Monte Carlo solution is that, making a virtue of necessity, its technique can be understood by people who do not understand advanced algebra. If they can see the model working, and producing its answers, they may obtain a real insight into the organic flow the model depicts; this insight is otherwise a direct revelation to the mathematician alone, and his problem of communicating insight is a big one.

MANAGEMENT AND BALANCE

(a) *The Idea of Homeostasis*

The art of management involves, it seems, an ability to balance. Not only must assets balance liabilities in the account which is actually called a "balance sheet"; supplies must balance demand, services must balance production, and so on; in an organisational sense there must be a balance of authority, and personalities have to be kept in balance. Now balance is a highly scientific concept, insofar as in every field of science there is a special account of a balancing mechanism. In engineering, there are governors and gyroscopes; in physics there is entropy—the thermodynamic laws; in chemistry, equations are the mode of description; in biology, there is the stabilising of animal populations; in cosmology, gravitation opposes cosmic repulsion; in economics, genetics, psychology . . . and above all in physiology, there are many highly developed balancing devices. The list could be continued indefinitely, and it is not by mere chance that this is so. The whole of nature is in balance: its very existence is dependent on these complex stabilisers.

If the "art" of management demands the ability to balance, and if balance is a vital and universal scientific mechanism, then industry might gain from *models* of natural balance. Are the balancing devices built into industrial management anything like as well-designed and effective as their counterparts in natural science? They are not. Think of the flow of information in a factory: it can be visualised as a herring bone. There is a main flow of instructions passing satisfactorily down the centre, and there are many off-shoots which might be labelled: "to records". And that is the end of that. True, these records are sometimes consulted, and information from them is used in the managerial judgments which control future activity; but this is a precarious psychological effector. In nature, this balancing mechanism is found elaborately built into the system.

Engineers who build this type of mechanism into an individual machine call it a "feedback". It is found, more simply, in the temperature control of an oven, where it is called a thermostat. *Homeostasis* is the function of holding any attribute steady against all kinds of disturbance and buffeting. A factory requires homeostatic control: it is a job for operational research to design this for management. In doing so, it will call on its scientific models; any of nature's myriad homeostats may provide a suitable starting point.

When reference was made earlier to treating a works organically, it was probably not clear how this was to be done except insofar as interacting probabilities were to be taken into account. But now the real operational research tool for the task has appeared: it is

Scientific Analogy. When an operational research department is described as including scientists of many disciplines (and they appear sometimes to be strange bedfellows), the reason is that one does not want to lose a valuable model in a given situation for want of enough learning to recognise it; and one does want the cross-fertilisation of scientific ideas.

In the section on "Control" above, a self-regulating production control system was briefly examined. In principle it is homeostatic. When stock control was discussed, ways were found of determining the best levels of stock; but no homeostat was described.

Consider a certain class of work as it moves down the factory as enclosed in a pipe. The contents may be individual "lumps" (bits of steel, or engines, or pallets of components), but pretend that the flow is continuous: the model is hydraulic. Material is drawn off from the end of the pipe as required, at arbitrary intervals and in arbitrary amounts. To keep up the pressure in this pipe a pump must be operated at the source, to draw more material up from a well. The well represents the production plant for the primary material, and the pump is the production plan. Now there is a device which *connects the tap to the pump,* so that drawing off supplies at the finishing end has the effect of keeping pressure in the pipe constant. If the pump has other work to do, and the well other pipes to supply, it is no use having a simple connection between tap and pump: some sort of valve must be designed to smooth out the demand which is fed back to the source. All this can be visualised, and what is more designed mathematically. When the model has served its purpose it is discarded. There is left a computing device which is operated by the consumer. He reads into the gadget (which incorporates the mathematics of the operational research model) tells him what orders to send to the pump—and those orders take account of the limitations on supply at the other end.

This is a homeostatic device; it is known to operational research as a *re-order rule.* Notice that it guarantees adequate supply, constant pressure, no exceptional demand on the producer or planning control, and above all minimum stock. For in this case there is *no* static stock; the stock is dynamic because it moves perpetually down the pipe; and the "size" of stock is simply a question of the pressure: that is, the frequency of the appearance of these components en route.

While operational research is busy designing homeostats for management control, it is also watching closely for the homeostasis which is natural to the factory. For the organic whole of men-and-machines itself operates by self-balancing mechanisms, although they are not deliberately contrived. For example, if orders fall away in a works, the productive system reacts. A consciousness (which may hardly be recognised on the shop-floor, and should perhaps be called a subconsciousness) of lightened load develops; productivity begins to fall. The reason is that there is a natural compensatory tendency which seeks to spread the work and thus to avoid redundancy or short time. Most managers would endorse this interpretation. But, looking at this not as cussedness in the worker, but as a natural homeostat, what is the proper action? If falling productivity is met by the apparent economic safeguard of standing men off, the feedback employed by the management is positive, not negative. That is, instead of *correcting* the tendency to lower productivity, it will *increase it.*

This possibility is indeed profoundly disquieting. Perhaps it is not worth investigating in a mass production industry, where the pressure of the production line may enforce a reasonable rate of work and thus inhibit the natural homeostat. But most of British industry is not of this kind; it is mostly of a "jobbing" character. The techniques described can advise management on whether a proposed policy will in fact correct a dangerous situation, or make it worse.

(b) Balance, Profit and Opportunity

Of the many other aspects of balance in industrial management that operational research can approach, just one will be mentioned here: this is the problem of balanced production itself.

In a given works there may be a large variety of machines, of orders, and of possible process routes for each order. This situation, which may also be concerned with various methods of transportation to various alternative destinations, is a problem of choice. Out of the many millions of possible plans, which is the best? That is, how is the plant to be kept in balance within itself and with the market, all machinery fully utilised in the most profitable way? The fact is that in a normal factory, the production potential and the market demand cannot be in perfect balance for long; the factory's character cannot shape itself continuously and exactly to changing commercial and technological circumstances. Thus one expects to see some idle plant, some unprofitable business, some lack of balance at all times. Even so, at any given moment there must be a *best* balance amid the host of possible balances that may be struck. Discovering this best or optimum, for any situation is called *Optimisation.*

There are various optimising techniques, and in a completely defined situation (that is, in a closed system) a uniquely most profitable pattern can usually be discovered. In practice, and despite the philosophy of organic analysis, very few problems present a closed system which is completely defined. The problem to be examined is part of a larger system (ultimately, it is part of the whole world's economy); therefore operational research can only optimise over a given area, and after making some assumptions about the larger model into which this problem fits. Thus one is not strictly speaking *optimising* anything, and the approach usually made is consequently called by the even uglier but more accurate name of *Suboptimisation*.

The shop-floor planner (or the foreman) who is confronted with a number of orders and machines, and who uses his knowledge of their behaviour and capabilities to decide what job to do next on each machine, is attempting a suboptimisation. In effect, he is turning over a vast number of possible courses of action, and trying to recognise the best. The human brain's mechanism for doing this is not well understood; but two results are clearly established. The brain does fairly well with the problem: experience teaches, and the solution reached is rarely disastrous. But beyond a certain level of effectiveness, the brain ceases to discriminate; it appears quite incapable of recognising the actual optimum itself.

Operational research has various techniques available for improving on this outcome. The most important of these at the moment is called *Linear Programming*. The use of the word "programming" explains itself; "linear" appears because the operational research model consists of a series of linear equations. These equations link all the production resources with all their possible products. The mathematical tool of *matrix algebra* is used to produce an array of these facts. This array is a kind of tabulation in which the profitability of every machine is quoted for every possible product. The algebraic formulation links every possibility on each machine with every possibility on each of the others. That is, the model is made to stand for the whole range of alternatives which could be followed, and to include measures of the profitability throughout. Obviously, all these alternatives can no more be written out in full than the brain can contemplate every one of them separately. The beauty of this model is that it does include them all, without writing them all out.

Anyone who follows football closely is acquainted with permutable models of this kind. The model "five homes, five draws, two aways, basic line" will save the pool punter from writing out 16,632 alternative lines. All that remains is to pick out the winner. So, in the matrix of production possibilities, one has to pick the best, most profitable, combination. Mathematically, this means solving the linear programme in terms of a *maximising functional*. What does it mean to the industrial manager?—simply this: It is possible to state what is the most profitable arrangement of available work. It is also possible to find the most profitable order book: that is, the work which the commercial organisation can most usefully *make* available.

The established levels of industrial productivity for current resources (which in heavy industry particularly include enormous overhead costs) can be considered as the best results obtainable. This is the *status quo*. Any augmentation of resources is then judged according to what economists call its *marginal utility*: that is (roughly) the return on its cost in these circumstances of established maxima. Normally, the marginal utility of capital in heavy industry is quite low. The exercise which selects the objects of investment in terms of linear programming, however, is deliberately exploiting weaknesses in the established pattern. The marginal utility of such directed investment may well reach several hundred per cent.; a fantastic rate of return.

The systematic use of this tool of operational research as a policy-making instrument could be effected through a special adaptation of the costing system. For there is an obverse picture to the maximum profit; this is the minimum cost. There is a linear programming theorem which shows that this suboptimisation technique reaches the same answer whether the approach be made through higher profits or lower costs. If the minimum cost of a course is known, in terms of a suboptimisation, then the difference between this and the actual cost of that course at present is the *marginal cost* of the present practice. A marginal costing system put in on this basis could lead management towards the ideal operation of its factory.

The final adaptation of this technique is again through the criterion of cost. Suppose that a linear programme shows that a group of resources of men, plant and materials should be used to make product A for sale; suppose further that to conform to some other policy these resources are used to make product A for conversion to product B. Then the opportunity of sale at stage A has been foregone. So the profit which could have been made by selling A should be included in the cost quoted for product B. This notion is called *opportunity costing*. One of the ways in which management could guide itself towards the ideal balance of operations is by costing in this way. In an industry (like steel) where operations down the factory consist mainly in converting previous products, it is often held that the profits all accrue at the finishing end. This impression may derive from the method of costing alone. A suboptimising programme might show that, on the contrary, some of the potential profit made in the early stages is in fact dissipated by foregoing the earlier opportunity of sale.

THE THEORY OF DECISION

(a) The Nature of Decision

What is an industrial decision, and who takes it? Suppose that a sales clerk is told that a product has been wrongly made. Asked to dispose of the abortive result, he offers it to the only two customers who have ever shown an interest in such material. The cost of the product he knows to be £1,000. One customer offers £900, the other £1,100. So the clerk accepts the second offer without more ado. He has taken a decision; or has he? Is a clerk normally entitled to take a commercial decision involving such a sum? Surely, what has really happened is that the Sales Manager has *vicariously* taken this decision. The clerk has a certain delegated authority; and he knows (that is, he is morally certain) that his chief would reach this same decision if so straightforward a matter were referred to him.

Many delegated decisions rely on this mechanism: the decider is reckoned to understand the principles upon which his superior would reach a decision. The effectiveness of this procedure must depend upon the efficiency of the mechanism by which the rules governing the decision are transmitted to the delegate. What is this mechanism? Is there one? How often has the decider-in-chief at the top even formulated such rules? These are searching questions. The answers would seem to be that decisions are reached by acumen, and received by intuition. Now these two mechanisms can be most effective; they involve brain processes of great complexity which may be inimitable. Whether mechanisms which work brilliantly on policy problems between a general and his staff, or between a director and his managers, still operate properly at lower levels and on quantitative problems, is very doubtful.

With this background, operational research poses a number of questions. Are decisions being taken at the right level: not the *apparent* decisions, because everything has probably been delegated neatly according to the latest principles of management, but the *actual*, hidden, decisions? Is the decision being taken according to its real nature, or on the basis of some popular superstition? If someone does understand the real nature of the decision, is any mechanism available for transmitting its rules to the point of interpretation in action?

Answers to these questions have now been sought from both mathematical and logical methods. It is interesting and fruitful to understand the basis and source of these new and important techniques, which is profound. It is a subject called *metamathematics* or, sometimes, *theory of proof*. This subject is concerned with the nature of meaning and decision at the level of philosophy: it is fundamental to the whole conception of life and the symbols used to describe it. This work underlies "cybernetics", which is dealt with in the final section of this Chapter. It is also at the root of the question of *Decision Functions*, that is to say, some formal expression which uniquely determines the rules for reaching a required decision.

(b) Decision Functions

A statistical decision problem arises when there exist a number of possible decisions, one of which must be taken according to a rule based on the outcome of some stochastic process, as described above. The formal statement of this approach is called a *Statistical Decision Function*. If this method were used, an experiment would be designed to produce the measurements really relevant to the decision. The course of the trials would also be planned in mathematical terms, and so would the set of possible decisions. The stochastic process is provided by the experiment itself, which is carried out within the framework of this design; and the decision is reached for a given level of risk that it is wrong (on a vital experiment, this factor could be pitched very low). As a result, the outcome of the experiment could be given *as soon as* the evidence became sufficient to reach a conclusion. This is most important, because it saves both time and money; it is usually impossible to recognise this moment intuitively, and even conventional statistical sampling normally takes more evidence than is absolutely necessary. Here is the unique guarantee that enough evidence, and only enough, is sifted to reach a valid answer.

This is an example of a scientific decision. It is taken within the managerial framework of a specified problem with specified risks of error. Within that framework, for which the manager rightly takes his responsibility, the answer must be right. So far only a simple decision problem has been considered, where a yes-or-no answer is required. The theory can be extended, however, to cover problems in which several courses of action are open; none is "right" exactly, but one must be better than the others. In this multi-decision problem, use may be made of the *Minimax Theorem*. According to this, a solution is chosen which (mathematically) minimises the maximum risk. This is a model of the way in which people often take important decisions. They examine all courses of action, discover the most dangerous element that the situation offers, and then choose the one course which makes the risk of encountering this pattern the least.

Another kind of decision function uses *Symbolic Logic*. There is no stochastic element here at all: this method concerns the formal application of rules to which statistical risks do not apply.

Symbolic logic can take a set of rules, and turn them into algebra —propositional algebra. In this, the letters (a, b, c, and so on) stand not for *numbers*, but for *propositions* or statements. One might say that the letter "p" stands for the proposition "the furnace tapped at six o'clock". The connecting symbols between the letters are more difficult. In mathematics, "$+$" means plus or add, "$-$" means minus or subtract. In logic the interest is not with numerical relations, but with logical ones. So "$\vee$" means "either . . . or", and "$\supset$" means "if . . . then". To put a sentence like: "if the foreman comes round I will start work" into propositional algebra, one could say: let "the foreman comes round" be p, and let "I will start work" be q. The sentence can then be written: "$p \supset q$". And so on; there is an extensive logical notation to deal with the most complex ideas.

The reason for expressing an argument, or a decision function, in these symbolic terms is this. In mathematics, once a set of numerical ideas has been put into algebra, the ideas themselves can be forgotten—they are confusing. There is a special body of rules for manipulating the symbols in the algebra so that the right answer is guaranteed; ($a^2 - b^2$), for example, may be replaced by $(a + b)$ $(a - b)$. So, in symbolic logic, there is also a set of rules for manipulating the algebra; this also guarantees that the right conclusion is reached without thinking about the ideas behind the symbols. Here is a simple example.

Two firms, Forgem and Stampit, are branches of the same company. A customer of both firms puts the same enquiry to each, and both are interested. If Forgem does not take this order, it has no alternative outlet for the product concerned; but Forgem is in temporary technical trouble—it may have to decline the order even if it can find no other outlet for this product. However, once Stampit takes on the job, Forgem may never be offered the chance again. So the two commercial managers agree that if either Forgem and Stampit both accept the order on the one hand, or Forgem neither accepts it nor finds an alternative outlet on the other hand, Stampit will take it on if and only if Forgem does find another outlet for the product. This is perhaps the sort of arrangement people do reach over the telephone. At the time they may even both understand it. A week later, Forgem has to give a snap decision. It has just concluded that it cannot evade technical trouble on this product, and it *has* found an alternative outlet, so the Forgem Manager wants to decline the order. He has not had time to talk to his colleague at Stampit. Can he go ahead, or will he break his agreement?

In this story the facts are muddled sufficiently that most people cannot give the answer without a great deal of thought. In fact, there are only three basic propositions involved which can be named symbolically. Let:

> $p =$ Forgem accepts the order
> $q =$ Stampit accepts the order
> $r =$ Forgem finds an alternative outlet

Now the agreement can be translated into a logical decision function:

$$pq \vee \sim p \sim r . \supset . p \equiv r.$$

That is the agreement, in symbolic terms. (The dots divide the function into logical components, and the symbol "$a \equiv b$" means "if a then b, and if b then a".) Now in the circumstances given the "truth value" of two of the three propositions is already known. The truth value of r is truth (because another outlet has been found), so r is replaced by T (for "true"). The truth value of p is falsity (because Forgem wants to decline the order), so p is replaced by (for "not-true"). Then, using the rules of this algebra, the expression is simplified, performing what is called a *truth-value analysis*. Like this:

$$pq \vee \sim p \sim r . \supset . q \equiv r$$
$$\mathcal{1}q \vee \sim \mathcal{1} \sim T . \supset . q \equiv T$$
$$\mathcal{1} \vee \quad T\mathcal{1} \quad . \supset q$$
$$T\mathcal{1} \quad \supset q$$
$$\mathcal{1} \supset q$$
$$T$$

It would be out of place to teach the rules of the algebra here; this merely shows what this analysis looks like. The decision function has been reduced to T (true), without specifying the truth-value of q; that is, without assuming what Stampit does about the order. So the consistency of the rule is established independently of Stampit's attitude, and the answer to the original question is that Forgem may go ahead and decline the order without more ado.

(c) *The Game of War*

The third question to be discussed under the heading of Decision Theory introduces an historical note. Operational research originated (at least, under that name) in the Second World War. A main concern then was with strategy, with the application of scientific method to problems of what to do and how to do it when faced with an enemy. In this situation, many of the problems already examined here were met: problems of measurement, of probability, of stockholding, of queuing, of balance. War, it might be agreed, is a grand imperial military stochastic process. Industry presents many of the features of a battlefield. So many of the practical problems encountered in both places depend less on any "enemy" than on the arbitrariness of nature, on chance and mischance.

Many problems so depend, but not all. For in war there is in fact an enemy. And in industry it is easy to set up an "enemy" for operational research purposes. The feature that an enemy introduces into a problem is the strategic feature that someone else, whose hand is not disclosed, is actively trying to upset one's plans. A military commander (a manager) may wish to stockpile shells (products) in order to lay down fire (tackle a market). The size of the stock will basically depend, as was seen earlier, on the stochastic processes of armament supply (manufacture of goods) and expected rate of fire (sales). But now there happens to be an enemy (competitor) with a good intelligence service (market research). He plans his attack or forms a strategy based upon the desirability of taking *his* action when the other side's stocks are low.

To tackle a problem of this kind, that is one involving strategies, operational research has turned to the simplest possible model of a strategic situation. This is a game; a game, say, of poker. Now games have been analysed both in their own right and in their capacity as models of economic situations. When the wartime strategic problems appeared, and later industrial problems of strategy, this work proved to be the basis for much advanced thinking. It is called the *Theory of Games.*

The simplest game of all is known as a *zero-sum two-person* game. This merely means that there are two sides involved, and not a number of independent contestants, and that the result of the game is to redistribute rewards rather than to create them (that is, the sum of payments is zero; if A loses sixpence, B gains it). It is interesting to note that any linear programme can be expressed as a zero-sum two-person game; that the "decision problem" can be interpreted in the same way; and that the Minimax Theorem mentioned earlier offers the solution to a game where the strategy required must minimise the maximum risk. There is a certain unity in all this work which encourages optimism.

From it emerges, first of all, an understanding of the mechanism involved in dealing with either an enemy or an "enemy". The student of game theory has an insight into such strategies as bluffing and the formation of coalitions. The best means of applying this insight quantitatively will gradually become more obvious: some excellent results (such as linear programming supplies) have already been obtained. Much will depend on management's ability to see a problem as a "game" situation, and its willingness to set operational research to work on it.

CYBERNETICS

As was pointed out at the opening of this Chapter, it would not be strictly correct to call operational research *a science*; it is a corpus of scientific techniques. On the other hand, a group of highly developed methods, centring on a common concept, is likely to crystallise into a science. Perhaps operational research is crystallising in the science of cybernetics. Firstly required, then, is a common concept which runs through operational research as described here. The first contribution to this was the notion of *feedback*, and then came "life-like-ness", as applied to factories which were to be regarded as *organic wholes*. Stochastic processes were next examined, and these are the randomly-unfolding but goal-directed activities of nature and its organisms. The notion of homeostasis was subsequently reached, a concept distilled from the balance of nature itself, then problems of planning and optimising were discussed in terms of an attempt to reproduce mathematically the technique used by the brain for these purposes. From this point on, operational research techniques were being examined quite specifically as alternatives to human thought processes.

Thus the view of industry as something living, or something operating as if it were alive, took shape. This is the *cybernetic model*. Cybernetics[1] is, in fact, the science of communication and control, but it specifically attends to these features *both* in machines *and* in live animals. Each is a model of the other. Animals have been studied in the light of knowledge of machines, and particularly in the language used by scientists outside the biological fields. Conversely, machines have been studied by methods founded in the biological sciences, and some mechanical copies of living processes have been made. What tools have been used for this work? Well, mathematics and statistics, the theory of probability, models of various kinds, stochastic processes, logic . . . no more need be said. It does appear that operational research methods are specifically appropriate to cybernetic studies. This is not really surprising, since nothing is less static or more *operational* than a live process. And cybernetics itself is adding a new dimension to industrial thinking. That is why the techniques and the science come together as the climax of this appreciation of the scope for operational research in industry.

Machines as they are normally understood in industry imitate animals to the extent that they perform actions. They have a source

---

[1] The term was coined by Norbert Wiener in 1947. His book, *Cybernetics*, was first published in 1948 (John Wiley, New York).

of energy, and they act—under an operator's control. As machinery has evolved, so it has tended to become more automatic. Animal homeostasis was imitated to the extent that automatic cut-outs, governors and stabilisers were fitted to machines. Eventually, a species of automaton has been developed: machines which imitate, in a fully determined way, the animal's ability to operate *itself* over quite a range of activities. Automation has already delivered the latest members of this species of automata: there are transfer machines, guided weapons, and electronic computers. All these are automata, and all depend upon the notion of feedback as a means of self-regulation.

This is the beginning of cybernetics. But automata are still nowhere near as large as life, and for one outstanding reason: they are predetermined. The designer can always (in principle) state, rather than predict, their behaviour in a given set of circumstances. The owner of a rat can predict its behaviour insofar as he can set limits to it: his rat will not suddenly fly out of the window, or build a bridge. But even so lowly an animal has freedom of action within those limits. If it is put into a maze it will wander about. If it is presented with a choice between two passages, no one can say which it will choose. In other words, its behaviour is stochastic. An engineer who built a machine whose behaviour was stochastic and not predictable would probably be certified!

Nevertheless, it is to stochastic machinery that cybernetics is turning. The reason is simple. In nature, stochastic exploration of a problem by, say, a rat leads to conditioned behaviour. At the end of one passage in the maze is an electric shock; at the end of the other is cheese. After a number of trials, the rat *learns* to avoid the shock, and to reach the cheese. After millions of years of evolution, nature finds this sort of behaviour the best mechanism for coping with an unpredictable environment. Again, the reason is obvious. If a rat were born with a built-in programme for running that maze (that is, if it were an automaton), it might then find itself in another situation altogether and thereby starve.

So cybernetics has studied the rat, and its stochastic behaviour towards conditioning. Mathematical models of the process were constructed, and the concept of a "statistical rat" was created. To build a machine to this model was the next step. And there it is; a machine that will actually *learn.*

This is cybernetic progress, and it will lead to a species of machine that can imitate a whole new range of animal (including human) behaviour. The ability to learn, to recognise complex patterns, to discriminate, even, perhaps, to amplify the intelligence of its master: these activities typify true cybernetic machinery.

Very little can be said here about this extensive new science of cybernetics. It is, however, closely related to the approach of operational research. The application of rigorous scientific analysis to the whole question of describing systems, their behaviour and control is involved. Understanding the mechanics of adaptation, which is equally a problem for the biologist and the industrialist, demands scientific means of analysing what cannot be known in detail. Cybernetics has solved this problem by essentially operational research methods, and now passes its conclusions back for use in the real world by operational research.

For the present, it can only be said that industrial cybernetics will operate increasingly through operational research, which will itself turn to scientific models taken from cybernetics. For operational research, the science that deals with strategic decisions, will not always be absorbed by the *ad hoc* investigation of immediate problems. It must develop a fundamental understanding and account of the optimal design of systems (whether organisations, societies or machines) that are capable of taking strategic decisions. That is its already maturing destiny.

CHAPTER V

MANAGEMENT AIDS [1]

In the analytical and practical studies of the management process in the preceding sections, attention has been drawn repeatedly to the extent to which information, data, and procedures contribute to the effectiveness of managerial action. A manager must think, judge and decide; he can do these things only if he has reliable and relevant material on which he can base these mental processes. Without such material he is relying on no more than hunch or flair, with no better aid than the crystal ball. A manager must also plan and initiate action and then control performance to ensure achievement in terms of quantity, quality, time, and cost. All these executive processes rely on communication; instructions, plans, standards and targets must be brought to the notice of those who will have to work to them, whilst facts showing the results of their efforts must be obtained from them. In addition, most of the commercial transactions of any enterprise necessitate clerical procedures to deal with orders, despatch, invoicing and payment—the administrative routines by means of which the transactions are completed.

All this hardly requires stressing, because the great volume of information and procedures (and thus of paperwork) required by present-day management and administrative practice is obvious to every observer. Some very healthy fun has been poked at it by Professor Parkinson;[2] yet the number of people engaged on clerical work is no joking matter. Between $2\frac{1}{2}$ and 3 million people (between 10 and $12\frac{1}{2}$ per cent. of the working population) are now employed on clerical work in the United Kingdom; a figure equivalent to the population of New Zealand! Of these clerical workers over 500,000 are typists. Even if allowance is made for the substantial numbers employed by central and local government, and by the "clerical-intensive commercial activities" (banks, insurance, building societies, etc.), clerical work can no longer be considered as "just overhead expenses"; it has become an expensive activity which materially affects the cost of goods and services.

---

[1] This Chapter has been contributed by H. P. CEMACH, F.C.A., M.I.O.M., the specialist consultant in office organisation and methods, and Managing Director of Anbar Publications Ltd., London, offering information services on management and equipment.

[2] *Parkinson's Law (or The Pursuit of Progress)*, by C. Northcote Parkinson (Murray, London).

There are several other considerations that underline the importance of clerical work:

(1) Management depends on information (i.e. on the end-product of clerical work) for its forecasting, planning and control.

(2) Administrative failure can seriously jeopardise other activities of an organisation; in fact, there is truth in the statement that "nothing moves unless a piece of paper moves with it".

(3) Poor quality clerical work damages good-will, often to an extent that bears no relation to the "offences" that are being committed.

The significance of the clerical aspect of management practice has long been appreciated in enlightened circles, leading over 40 years ago to the formation of an "Office Management Association" (now the "Institute of Office Management") as a professional organisation specialising in the study of problems affecting the development, management and operation of offices; it has a special division for those engaged in the practice of "Organisation and Methods" (O & M), a subject to which reference is made later in this Chapter.

Clearly, the larger the size of the organisation the greater and more complex will the clerical activities become, and correspondingly the greater will be the need for specialist guidance. In the average manufacturing and trading enterprise clerical activities are essentially a *service* to the other (major) operations of making and selling. As already indicated, in several commercial fields clerical activities bulk very large; banks, insurance companies, building societies, and the administrative headquarters of the nationalised industries and public corporations are illustrations that readily come to mind. Outside the commercial system the same is also true of Government departments and the offices of local authorities. In all these instances the employees may be numbered in hundreds or thousands, and virtually all their operations are performed on paper.

It is important to recognise that, whether in the offices of a small factory or in the almost "mass-production" clerical sections of the big building society, the process of management is at work in the same way as in a manufacturing department or the retail store. The nature of the operations is different, the details of application may also be different, but with the appropriate adjustments made, all that has been said in the other parts of this volume applies with equal validity. In one sense, this is almost too obvious a point to make in the present context; yet strangely enough it is widely overlooked. If the analogy is taken far enough, there is a close parallel between many of the questions which the factory manager must ask and answer in the course of his executive activities and those which will form the daily round of an Office Manager in a large organisation.

For instance, the manager of a factory may analyse or study the work, the conditions, the movement of materials, the methods, etc., in order to determine whether or not machines should be grouped or placed at various points in the factory. The same issues may easily arise in connection with office machinery. Should typing be pooled? And to what extent? Is the flow of work such as to permit of minimum movement of people and paper, and the maximum utilisation of effort, time and investment in equipment? Are forms designed in the way that best facilitates effective and economical working? Are there alternative ways of performing work that give advantages in time, effort and results?

From another point of view, too, the similarity is close. Office work, just like the factory, requires man-power—human skills and capacities, human effort and application, and time. The clerical staff units in some commercial enterprises (not to mention Government departments) are comparable in size with large factories. Thus the same problems of utilisation of man-power arise: the proper allocation on jobs, the selection of the right people with correct abilities for the work, training, the efficient use of special skills, the performance levels of all employees, the question of full attendance, and effective use of the man-hours available when people are on the job. The planning of work, therefore, has much the same significance as in manufacturing and it is essential to develop appropriate control techniques to ensure adequate use of the capacity provided.

Finally, the matter is another aspect of the general question of costs. Clerical costs should be regarded in the same way as expenditure in manufacture or on purchases in a merchanting business, i.e. in relation to value received. Clerical work can be carried out effectively or ineffectively. Single instances may be small, but the total of what are usually concealed losses may be substantial.

The relationship of cost to value can be appraised only if the *purpose* of clerical work is at all times borne in mind. This purpose can be defined under three headings:

(1) *Management Information* to enable all levels of management to carry out their tasks, with effective planning, co-ordination and control.
(2) *Communication* as a medium of command, consultation and administration both inside the organisation and externally.
(3) *Records*, including the accounting function.

In practice, these purposes overlap. A memorandum to branch Managers advising monthly results is a *communication of management information*; a delivery note is a *communication* to a customer and the copy is the *record* of the dispatch of goods.

Whilst there are these many similarities between the manufacturing and the clerical function, there are also crucial differences. In the factory, the need to have the end-product is seldom in doubt; in the office it is extremely dangerous to take such a need for granted. To realise how important this difference can be, one has only to compare the high-level scrutiny that takes place before a new product is sanctioned with the ease with which, in most organisations, a junior Manager can authorise a new return or new documentation which sets up a flow of paper and necessitates the employment of additional clerks.

One often hears of "productivity" in the office. Because, by definition, productivity is the ratio of output to input of human and material resources, this term can be highly misleading. "Productivity" in the office *cannot* be judged by assessing an increase in the output of papers and figures—a truly productive office renders the best possible service to the organisation it serves with a *minimum* of paper and figures, and at the lowest possible cost.

RESPONSIBILITY FOR THE CLERICAL FUNCTION

It has been said that, inasmuch as practically any activity in contemporary industry and commerce to some extent involves paperwork, every Manager is an "Office Manager". In an age dominated by the principle of *specialisation*, Managers in charge of production, sales, buying, transport, and many other activities are recruited because of their competence and experience in their specialised field of operation. Such men often do not have, and cannot be expected to have, particular aptitude for or experience in clerical work; moreover, they may strongly dislike paper-work, and few men are good at things they dislike. In an endeavour to remedy this situation, the attempt is sometimes made to make *all* clerical activities the responsibility of one executive, the *Office Manager*. In many such cases, and especially in the smaller businesses, the Secretary and/or Accountant serves as Office Manager, without being called upon to show any special training or knowledge for the role. In larger enterprises, the Office Manager may be an executive ranking *pari passu* with the Accountant (the latter retaining direct responsibility for accounting functions, an arrangement which raises some difficult problems of demarcation), or he may be subordinate to the Secretary or Accountant.

Whatever arrangements are made along these lines may create as many problems as they solve. If control of clerical work lies with a specialist Manager untrained in clerical management, perhaps of narrow outlook and unable to appreciate that clerical work transcends the boundaries of departmental responsibility, such control may introduce a distrusted "fifth column" into departments; it may involve clerks and operators in the untenable situation of having two masters; and it may reduce control to ineffective levels, especially if physical separation of activities is involved. Successful clerical management must rest on a clear understanding of the distinction between *line* and *staff* responsibilities (see pages 56–7 of the Introduction). With adequate clarification of responsibilities and essential training of the Managers and supervisors concerned, it is readily possible to establish effective specialisation of control and so to have "the best of two worlds". This is illustrated in Fig. 111 following; the arrangement depicted acknowledges the need for the unity of the clerical function and ensures that the effectiveness of procedures is judged from an overall viewpoint rather than from a departmental one. At the same time, it leaves Divisional Managers in direct operational control and is thus most likely to lead to a sensible division of work between divisional offices and centralised office services. The appropriate definitions of responsibility would determine clearly to whom each employee is responsible, and thus avoid conflicts of loyalty.

The functional responsibility of an office manager for clerical work (other than central services in respect of which he is a "line" manager) must be given teeth if it is to operate effectively. Whilst it is true that as a "staff officer" his function is *advisory* (which implies the right of those advised to reject the advice given), the rule that seemingly unacceptable advice must be jointly submitted to higher management whose decision will be accepted by both parties *in good grace*, must be firmly established from the outset. This is but the normal implication of the functional principle (see page 52).

In organisations large enough to justify establishing a specialist personnel function one more problem arises. It is argued by many people that the scope of clerical management should be such as to include all matters concerned with the clerical staff and their working conditions, as well as the routines that they carry out. This is an issue to which there are definitely debatable sides. On the one hand, insofar as actual conditions of working are concerned, there is a good case for this approach, as the effective layout of work, determination of working methods, choice of equipment, etc. are all bound up with office conditions. Similarly, the specification of jobs and of aptitudes or skills required, the nature and extent of training, the relative grading of jobs and the salaries to be paid for them, are all matters for which special knowledge of the clerical work concerned is essential. On the other hand, many of these points are such as could rightly be held to fall within the customary domain of the Personnel Officer as the kind of matters that he would quite

1. FUNCTIONAL CONTROL BUT NO SPECIALIST GUIDANCE

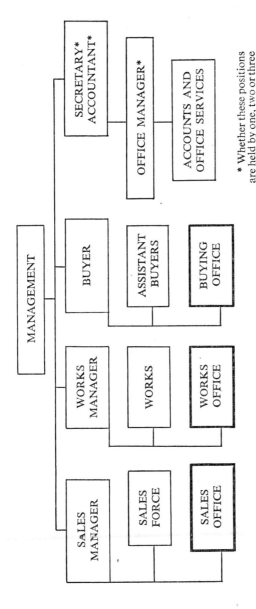

Under this arrangement the Office Manager has no responsibility for clerical work in functional departments (heavy boxes). As functional executives are not necessarily expert at office management, the arrangement often proves unsatisfactory and is replaced by the arrangement in diagram No. 2.

Note: The simple organisation patterns shown in these charts are indicative only, and are not intended as illustrations of full organisations.

FIG. 111.

* Whether these positions are held by one, two or three persons does not affect the principles involved.

2. SPECIALIST CONTROL IN A VACUUM

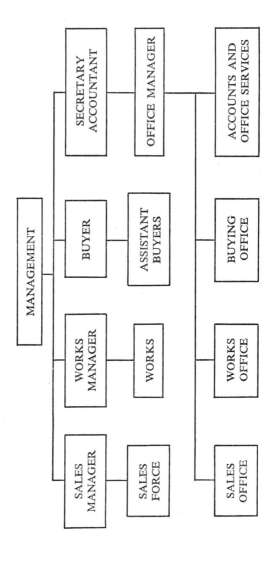

Fig. 112.

All clerical work is now the responsibility of the Office Manager; this ensures co-ordination and specialist guidance but may (as explained in the text) lead to lack of control and other undesirable consequences. As a general rule, therefore, another alternative is preferable as in diagram No. 3.

3. FUNCTIONAL CONTROL *PLUS* SPECIALIST GUIDANCE

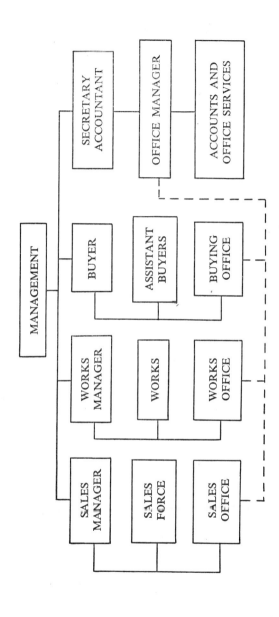

Under this arrangement functional managers retain the LINE RESPONSIBILITY (————) for their offices, whilst the Office Manager becomes FUNCTIONALLY RESPONSIBLE (– – –).

Fig. 113.

naturally undertake in respect of factory and other staff. Just as he would collaborate closely with the factory executives who are directly responsible for these matters in their own departments, so too would he work with the Office Manager, taking the necessary initial steps and exercising the full functional responsibility appropriate to his specialist capacity. There is no need to resolve this issue in the present context—there is probably no single or general answer anyway. The fact remains that, in respect of clerical staff as of others, there is a "personnel" aspect of employment which needs to be specifically met, and it has to do with recruitment, training, placement, physical conditions, amenities and morale.

PROCEDURES

An important feature of practically all clerical work is the fact that every "job" has two aspects. For example, it is quite usual for an accounts department to have sections for sales ledgers, bought ledgers, trade expenses, to name only a few. On the other hand, the receipt of goods is the result of an order issued by the buyer; when the goods arrive they are handled by the "goods inwards section" of the warehouse; they must then be examined and stored; stock control records must be adjusted; arrangements may exist for the advice of, or issue to, departments or customers in need of the goods ("dues out" in the public service); the invoice must be checked and passed for payment; steps must be taken (which may or may not consist of posting a bought ledger) to ensure that payment is made on the due date, and discounts earned where available; and shortages, breakages, and complaints must be dealt with. The receipt of goods thus causes various actions to be taken by a number of different departments; each has a part to play, but each has other things to do that have no connection with the receipt of goods. *The flow of action and the sequence in which departments play their allotted parts is called a "procedure".* Fig. 114 illustrates the position.

The effectiveness with which any department can play its allotted part in clerical activities depends to a large extent on

(a) what information or data are supplied by other departments, when they are supplied, their accuracy, legibility, and suitability in the department's own processing tasks, and
(b) the requirements of other departments earlier or later in the sequence.

Each contribution is thus governed by the substance and flow of the "procedure" as a whole, and only within the framework of "procedures" can any one department apply *methods* and physical *effort*. It follows, therefore, that up-to-date thought on this subject sees the procedure, and not the method or the physical work, as the basis of clerical management.

STAFF GROUPING

When a task allotted to one person increases in volume to exceed the capacity of that person, then (unless the task can be simplified

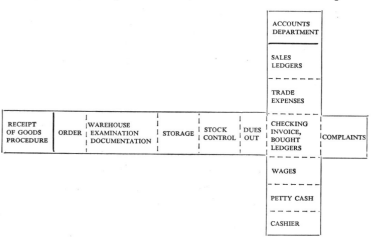

FIG. 114.

or mechanised) a second person must be brought in. At this stage alternative arrangements can be made, by instructing each of the two persons

either (a) to do *all* the different items of work on *half* the volume,

or   (b) to do *half* the items of work on *all* the volume.

If the volume increases further these alternative lines of sub-division can be carried further, but freedom of choice may come to be restricted in certain circumstances. When every person performs some of the items of work on all the volume, the staff is said to be grouped *operationally* (i.e. according to the operations they perform); such grouping is also called "homogeneous". When every person carries out all the items of work on part of the volume, the grouping is *functional* or "heterogeneous".[1]

Recent decades have seen an increasing tendency to abandon functional staff grouping in clerical work in favour of operational grouping. The main reason for this trend is the increasing use of machinery in the office, the growing complexity and cost of the machines used, and the need for specialised skills required in their

[1] This use of the term "functional" corresponds with the description indicated in section 7 of the Introduction (see page 52).

operation. This development is, of course, the office corollary of the displacement of craftsmen by mass production methods in manufacturing. In a functional grouping the individual clerical worker is more closely identified with the work and more likely to take a personal interest in it. On the other hand, a worker engaged entirely on one operation is likely to encounter much greater monotony; unless purposeful steps are taken to show him or her where the operation fits into the procedure as a whole, he/she may not be aware of the nature and objective of the tasks. Experience shows that clerks and operators employed on single operations tend towards lack of interest, which may impair morale, quality of work and effectiveness. Managers must recognise that this type of clerical work resembles the assembly line in a factory, and thus requires different methods of supervision and control from that in a more diversified operation. The work content of each operation must be known so that reasonable standards of performance can be established; the quality of work must be controlled; and workers must be motivated to give of their best.

In many clerical situations the functional grouping of staff still has much to offer, and in other instances a combination of functional and operational patterns is possible. Each case must be considered on its merits, to arrive at an arrangement directed to attaining best results.

SPECIALIST ADVISORY SERVICES

Much of the time of an Office Manager is taken up by the duty of ensuring the smooth functioning of existing clerical procedures and by the day-to-day management of whatever centralised office services may be in existence. If this clerical executive is at the same time the Company Secretary and/or Accountant, he will have many other routine duties arising from these appointments. Accordingly, it has been found in practice that the Office Manager seldom has the time, or the peace of mind, to undertake reviews in depth of specific clerical procedures. The value of such reviews has, however, been strikingly demonstrated in many instances. This has led to the establishment of specialist advisory services, with full-time staff charged with objective and analytical study of administrative practices. The lead in this field was given by the Civil Service quite a long time ago in setting up departments known as "Organisation & Methods (O & M)"; this designation has more recently spread into industry and commerce, where many large and medium-sized organisations have set up similar departments. Not all, however, are known by the label of "O & M"; other names are met with, such as Office Administration, Systems and Procedures, Systems Analysis, and Clerical Work Study. If there is no accepted nomenclature, there is even less unanimity on the scope of such departments; in particular, the extent to which the specialists so employed are expected or allowed to advise on organisation of responsibilities and arrangement of work at the higher levels differs widely.

In discharging this task of systematically investigating *procedures* with the object of making recommendations for improvement, O & M employs the techniques of *work study*, suitably adapted to the conditions of office work. The emphasis is on *method study* but there is also scope for, and indeed a need for, *work measurement*. (These techniques are established and conducted on the same principles as for application in manufacturing departments—see the descriptions given in Chapter III of Part Two, page 302). *Method study* questions first of all the need for a procedure, and if that need is established, the necessity for individual operations involved. The existing procedure is observed, analysed, and critically examined. Information and documents entering into the procedure are followed through to their sources. The best available method is then determined, and *if* it differs from the existing method recommendations for change are made. After discussion and approval, the installation of the new method is arranged, assistance being given during the change-over period until the new method is firmly established. *Work measurement* should be used to establish how time is spent, the causes of excess time, the establishment of the work content of operations for the purpose of staffing, balancing of work flow, elimination of bottlenecks, and method comparison. It is also the basis of output standards and, where applicable, of incentive schemes based on output.

In practice it has been shown that each procedure should be the subject of a review at least once in every three to five years; the smaller firm that cannot maintain an O & M service of its own may be able to call in Consultants to carry out such reviews.[1]

---

[1] The past few years have witnessed a considerable development of O & M services, including association with systems designed for computer application. Apart from assistance provided by professional Consultants, this development has been very substantially aided by the work of the "O & M Training Council", a nation-wide voluntary body with regional centres. The Council provides facilities for training, in parallel with those of the Work Study Centre at Cranfield or with the courses held for the syllabus of the Institute of Office Management.

While the title "O & M" is new, the activity has been long established in the more progressive companies. Hitherto it has been customary in those cases of longer establishment for the advisory and methods-development roles to be undertaken by the Office Manager responsible for the general services. When a separate position existed for the advisory purposes it was not uncommonly designated "Clerical Methods Manager": an example of the responsibilities covered is shown in the illustrative schedule LG/7 in Appendix II to the Introduction (see page 103).

THE IMPORTANCE OF WRITTEN SPECIFICATIONS

As the size of business and the diversity of operations grow, clerical work becomes increasingly complex. Its orderly and efficient transaction demands that there should be clear and unambiguous definition of

(a) what requires to be done, who is to do what, and how he/she is to do it;

(b) to whom each person is responsible for the proper and timely execution of the work allotted to him/her.

These two aspects are intimately connected with each other, yet they require separate consideration reflecting the condition (already referred to) that people are organised in departments (or offices or sections), whilst the work divides naturally into procedures most of which affect several departments. At the levels of managerial and supervisory responsibility for clerical work, the allocation of responsibilities is made known by the customary definitions and can be outlined in an organisation chart showing the various positions in relation to higher management and as sub-divided into subordinate levels. The definitions will show for each post or position:

(a) to whom the holder is responsible;
(b) the scope of responsibilities allotted;
(c) essential relationships established by such allocation;
(d) subordinate positions reporting;
(e) any limitations imposed.

At the operational level, comparable definition is also advisable; in this case it is more usually called a "specification". The write-up should be prepared of each *procedure* as a whole, setting out in detail the tasks of each department and of each clerical operation within it, and indicating who should be approached for a decision if circumstances arise that are not covered by the write-up (even the most detailed write-up cannot cover every possible situation, but anything that is *likely* to occur should be covered). All specifications together form the "Manual of Clerical Procedures"; this should be indexed and be held readily available for inspection. (The title "Standard Practice Instructions" is sometimes found as an alternative.) Once prepared, these specifications must be kept up-to-date by the issue of amendments and/or revised editions when changes are authorised; particular attention must then be paid to correct cross-references in the Manual.

JOB GRADING AND SALARIES

The tasks to be allotted in carrying the procedures into effect will vary as to knowledge and skill required, and as to the degree of responsibility involved. In order to assist reliable selection of personnel and appropriate allocation (after training) and also to evolve a sound remuneration policy, clerical jobs need to be "graded". This can be adequately done by an individual company in respect of its own activities, but considerable help can be gained by making use of the "Clerical Job Grading Schedule" published by the Institute of Office Management. Six "grades" have been determined to cover the broad range of clerical tasks, starting with grade A for simple work involving little or no responsibility, and rising to grade F for highly-skilled work involving a high degree of responsibility: a brief summary of the Institute's Schedule is reproduced as an Appendix to this Chapter.

Grading of jobs forms the most equitable basis for decisions on clerical salaries and ensures comparable ranges of remuneration for task categories with corresponding skills and responsibility (subject to special scales, based on age, for juniors). Within any range the actual salary will depend on individual experience and the merit with which each employee carries out his/her duties; these factors should be reported on periodically by superiors. In large organisations this is often done systematically under uniform headings, by a scheme known as "*merit rating*". In all cases where it is possible to have records of output and/or quality, these factors should also be taken into account in assessing merit and increments; but bonuses for performance may also be paid at weekly intervals (incentive schemes).

The practice of supplementing clerical salaries by annual or semi-annual bonuses which are not related to output, performance, or quality is to be deplored. They are seldom understood by employees (which is not surprising, as often the employer does not understand them either) and tend to become regarded as part of normal earnings. Salaries should be adequate in themselves, without the need for such periodic additional payments having no realistic basis in either merit or performance.[1]

A company seeking to attract *and hold* good staff, must ensure that it pays salaries at roughly "market rate" for the tasks to be undertaken. "Cheap" staff are always expensive, because their output and quality of work are generally unsatisfactory. Supplementing its original research in determining the Schedule referred to

[1] Profit-sharing and employee-shareholding schemes that apply to *all* employees fall into an entirely different category, and this statement does not refer to such schemes.

above, the Institute of Office Management now publishes a bi-annual *Clerical Salaries Analysis*, with extensive tables showing salaries paid, by grade, in specific industries and in different parts of the country.

THE CONTROL OF CLERICAL WORK

Scheduling and work planning are of importance to every office, but become a necessity in operational groups of any size. This, in turn, requires work measurement so that the work content of operations can be known and targets can be set. The techniques of clerical work measurement range from "simple timing" (controlled tests) and "averaging" (the analysis of time and output records) to "activity sampling" (a statistical method) and time study. A knowledge of loads (particularly peak loads) is also required.

Planning and control supplement each other; controls should raise the alarm in time to prevent accumulations and hold-ups, and not when these have already occurred. A simple illustration may help to make this clear: if it is known that a normal load for invoicing is 750 invoices per day, and if a count of the day's intake shows 1,000-odd steps to deal with the emergency can be taken at once. Simple precaution is better than the all-too-frequent "method" of just pumping in the intake, without even knowing its quantity, and "discovering" towards the end of the day that "we'll never get through it". Control records also build up a body of factual information that is, in turn, the raw material of planning. Many so-called emergencies would never arise, if past trends had been studied and reasonable conclusions drawn from them.

The *cost* of clerical work should be controlled against a budget, and all excess costs enquired into. Whenever possible the cost per operation, or cost per unit, should be worked out. Such figures spotlight the existence of work that cannot be justified economically. On the other hand, over-analysis should be avoided, as it is costly.

FORMS

Most clerical routine tasks involve the use of "forms", i.e. partially pre-printed paper. It is of the utmost importance that all forms should be well designed to serve their specific purpose. In designing forms it is important to bear in mind not only the requirements of the "originating department", but also those of other departments who will be subsequent users of the form or of copies thereof; and also the requirements of users outside the originating organisation. The issue of forms, and particularly the authorisation of new forms and changes to existing ones, should be strictly controlled. It must be emphasised that the cost of completing and handling forms is usually a multiple of the paper and printing cost; the use of good forms, even if they cost rather more, therefore usually pays. The (re-)design of forms for maximum efficiency and economy forms an integral part of O & M activities. *Form design* is an "art" because it is empirical; the designer must constantly strive to avoid extremes and find the middle road, as illustrated by the following table.

Not too little	*Aspect*	*Not too much*
Too few cause lack of forms for justified purposes; over-elaboration to make one form serve too many circumstances.	Number of forms in use	*Too many* result in excess printing costs; increased storage and provision problems; obstacles to mechanisation.
Too few fail to ensure that information reaches all who need it; delays the receipt of information if one copy must serve several users.	Number of copies	*Too many* waste paper; lead to additional filing time; take up more filing space; encourage distribution to posts not really requiring them.
Too small leads to loss of legibility; difficulties in filing.	Size	*Too big* wastes paper, encourages slovenly completion; wastes storage space.
Too poor leads to difficulties in completion (e.g. erasures); reduces legibility.	Quality	*Too good* incurs needless printing costs; wastes filing space.
Too few make routing difficult.	Colours	*Too many* confuse; increase provision cost; cause difficulties when exact colour of paper cannot be procured.
Too few (particularly on forms for use by the public or forms in infrequent use) lead to faulty completion or disposal.	Instructions	*Too many* waste space; increase size of form; hinder rather than help completion and disposal.
Too little causes confusion between similar yet different forms.	Differentiation	*Too much* prevents uniform appearance; obstructs development of "house style".

In addition, attention must be paid to:

(i) clear layout, logical grouping, constant sequences;
(ii) freedom from ambiguity; clear captions;

(iii) maximum adaptation to machine features where completion is by machine;
(iv) minimising effort of completion;
(v) legibility: colour of print and type styles;
(vi) working aids, e.g. perforations, pre-punching, folding marks, alignment for window envelopes.

Modern practice pays increasing attention to the use of *multipurpose forms* and *multi-entry methods*:

(1) *Multi-purpose forms.* Two or more forms serving a different purpose but containing a substantial amount of common information are produced jointly. Various means are available to ensure selective reproduction of information.
(2) *Multi-entry methods.* Two or more forms are brought into alignment to make an entry on all of them in one combined operation.

OFFICE MACHINES

To cater for clerical activities in the modern idiom a wide range of equipment is available, from simple tools and gadgets costing a few shillings to electronic computers involving rentals of hundreds of pounds. A visit to the annual Business Efficiency Exhibition in London conveys a vivid picture of the ramifications of the office equipment industry, as it necessitates many hours of touring the stands to encompass all that is displayed. Perhaps, if anything, there is too much variety of equipment and appliances available. There is no doubt that, properly applied, office aids and machines can be of the greatest value in clerical work. "Proper application" implies:

(1) that the machines have been installed after thorough investigation of the procedures they are to serve (it is a common failing for procedures to be made to fit machines);
(2) that the machines can be shown to reduce costs and/or produce other benefits not obtainable by manual methods;
(3) that it has been ascertained that the use of the machines in one field of activity will not lead to bottlenecks elsewhere.

The installation of machines on the "one-off" principle can lead to serious dislocation in case of breakdown; promises of "immediate attention" by manufacturers need to be treated with caution. Where an installation of a one-off type is made, it is essential for an emergency procedure to be prepared and committed to writing. A minimum of two members of the staff, preferably more, should be trained to operate each machine, and regard must be had to specific skills when authorising holidays or time off.

While most office appliances have their fields of usefulness, this is not always as wide as the vendors of the equipment are apt to claim.

Efficiency cannot be bought merely by installing this machine or that, this or that stationery, or visible record. Two examples may suffice:

(1) There are a number of so-called systems which claim to show at a glance, for instance, the state of stocks, or debtors, or purchases, or sales, or creditors. Usually they involve a convenient method of recording the item to which they refer, with "signals" or other devices "automatically drawing attention" to, for example, excess stocks, short stocks, overdue accounts. The enthusiast may overlook the basic fact that such records have to be prepared by writing up from documents of prime-entry; they do not prevent errors on those documents, neither do they avoid errors in writing-up. Also, the movement of "signals" is not automatic; someone has to do it, and mistakes may be made. In any event, it is an additional task. In many instances, the same results can be achieved more cheaply and more effectively by sorting and classifying the original documents, or by using information already available from other sources.

(2) There are on the market a number of "filing systems". Strictly speaking, they are *aids to filing*. There is no filing system which guarantees that documents will fall readily to hand when required. Filing is a personal job; it depends on good arrangements, and on individuals observing and using those arrangements. Ultimately, filing comes down to a certain person putting a piece of paper in a particular place. He or she may, however, put it in the wrong place—something no "system" will ever overcome.

It has already been emphasised that machines and equipment should not be acquired without a thorough review of procedures (carried out by O & M or similar service, where available), including considerations of all alternative methods and competing machines. It is also advisable to insist on an inspection of the equipment, before signing the order, on the premises of an already established user. A discussion with the executives of such other organisation may bring to light points of practice which the salesman has omitted to mention and which may be critical to effective application.

Office equipment and machines can be applied in four fundamentally different ways:

(1) To enable *one person* to carry out a task more efficiently. Example: a calculating machine placed on the desk of a clerk who has previously used mental arithmetic.

(2) To effect specialisation within *one procedure*. Example: it is decided that whilst previously several clerks prepared invoices all doing their own calculations, the calculations for all invoices should now be done by one or several clerks using calculating machines, such clerks to do nothing but calculating invoices.

(3) To carry out *one specific task in a variety of procedures*. Example: a calculating pool carrying out all calculating for (say) invoicing, purchasing, costing, etc.

(4) To obtain *integration of procedures*. Example: cards are punched from which invoices, sales statistics, cost summaries, commission statements, and sales ledgers will be produced.

It will not be superfluous to repeat that the application of machines must always be considered in the context of a study of procedures as a whole, i.e. a thorough study of the procedure or procedures involved must precede any decision to mechanise or to increase the extent of mechanisation. It is as *a result of* such a study that the decision should be taken to employ machines in one of the four ways indicated above. Having investigated all relevant circumstances, a "profit and loss account" can be drawn up comparing the cost of the manual process (or a less advanced form of mechanisation) with the cost of the mechanised (or more fully mechanised) system. Such a comparison must be realistic, e.g. cost of space should be evaluated according to the "space hunger" of the organisation, and not simply on a square foot basis. Intangible benefits (such as greater speed, accuracy, legibility, availability of additional information) should be expressed in financial terms however difficult such an assessment may appear at first sight, and set off against a similar assessment of intangible losses (e.g. the "personal touch").

There is always a tendency to look at recently announced advanced forms of mechanisation as something special, fundamentally different from anything previously known. Twenty-five years ago this applied in the case of punched cards which are today considered "orthodox" mechanisation, and it applies today to electronic computers. The new equipment can all too easily be invested with possibilities beyond the real facts. Thus, for example, it is a facile misconception to believe that a computer can "think": like any machine, it can do no more than carry out predetermined instructions (i.e. the "programme"). It does, however, do this at very high speed, and it has two additional facilities, the one that of "deciding" whether a particular result is positive, negative, or zero and following accordingly one of the alternative paths; the second facility is that it can store data in its "memory". These facilities explain the ready application of the computer to clerical operations. Most clerical procedures can be broken down into basic arithmetical functions (add, subtract, multiply, divide for positive, negative, or zero). For example, the adjustment of a stock figure for an issue of goods and the check whether the remaining stock is above minimum level, can be broken down as follows:

Take the stock in hand figure
Deduct the issue figure
Take the result (new stock)
Deduct minimum stock level
Test result for positive
If Yes, omit next step
If No, print out purchase order
Store new stock figure.

The computer is a very advanced form of office machine and is very expensive in capital cost and in operation. To justify application a high volume and a high degree of integration of procedures are therefore essential. The thorough review of procedures and possibilities, designed to test the justifiability of installation is customarily called a "feasibility study"—but it is intended to do more than ascertain whether a computer *can* undertake the procedures concerned: it has also to determine the economics of the application and so establish that the application is justified in terms of benefits and costs. The study is made on normal O & M lines, though once again a difference in terminology is met: it is now customary to call this "systems analysis". When the decision has been taken and the preparations are being made for installing the computer the detailed study of intended procedures may often be termed "systems design".

Once a computer can be justified, its installation has several highly important consequences:

(1) Because of its speed of operation, it can perform operations that were previously impossible owing to limitations of time and/or cost.

(2) Its facility of following alternative paths provides also means for determining and printing out results selectively; this is of importance for management information based on "standard and exception" principles.

(3) Many monotonous routine jobs can be taken over by the computer, thereby freeing human capacity for work of higher calibre.

Applying the computer to commercial and clerical operations raises many issues of complexity and importance which go beyond what is pertinent to the present context.

THE PHYSICAL BASIS OF CLERICAL WORK

Many questions of premises, layout, equipment, physical conditions, and so on, come into consideration in the discussion of the effectiveness of clerical activities. A good deal of what has been said in Chapter V of Part Three applies to the office as to manufacturing departments. Certain special features from the point of view of the office are considered in the following paragraphs.

Buildings

It would be very fine if the principle could be laid down that the premises for clerical work should be specifically designed, instead of being general-purpose buildings adapted to this purpose. Unfortunately, no such prescription could be realistically made; there are usually too many difficulties in the way of building and rebuilding. Ideally, office buildings should be light, airy, quiet, with adequate toilet and washing facilities, and, if possible, equipped with a restroom for female staff.[1] Where buildings *are* specifically planned for office usage, steps can be taken to ensure that physical circumstances contribute to effectiveness of operation. Needs should be assessed on a long-term basis, and liaison should be established at the earliest possible moment between the architect and a planning team on which the Office Manager and O & M services are represented. By this means, first consideration can be given to the essentials of effective office work.

Layout and Arrangement

It is good practice to have as few small and private offices as possible. Managers at or above a certain level need to have a personal office, because of the nature of their responsibilities, the interviews and discussions entailed, telephone conversations, and so on. Certain work, such as cash and wages, requires to be independently housed for security reasons. For the general run of office work, however, larger rooms are preferable, permitting as they do a planned layout that makes for simple flow of work and documents. The reduction of movement makes the supervision of staff much easier. Difficulties of noise can mostly be overcome by lining walls and/or ceilings with "acoustic" materials, carpeting, and other means. There is, however, a human side to this, and the matter is one on which some experimental research could be conducted to provide reliable answers. Many girls claim that working in large open offices is difficult and less effective than in smaller self-contained groups.

---

[1] Office premises and facilities have been the subject of many special publications, although standards have in practice remained obstinately low. Official steps have been taken in recent years to attain definite improvements. A Committee under the chairmanship of Sir Ernest Gowers reported in 1949 with far-reaching proposals (Report on "Health, Welfare and Safety in Non-Industrial Employment"; Cmd 7664, H.M.S.O. 1949): these are expected to be the subject of legislation prescribing standards along lines already familiar in other directions through the Factories Acts. Evidence of management interest was confirmed by the publication in 1961 of a special study undertaken on behalf of the Institute of Directors by a committee under the chairmanship of Mr. Peter Trench.

Spacing

Good spacing improves control of staff and work, and promotes discipline. Calculations have been made to show that each clerk should have some defined working area: provided certain minimum standards are observed, related to the type of work being done, the exact amount of space is less important than that there should be a clear passage permitting of unobstructed movement between desks, defined "roadways", and regular arrangement. Some space allotments that have been found from experience to promote effective working are as follows:

Typists (with individual desk)	—	45/50 sq. ft.
Clerical work	—	50/70 „ „
Supervisors and Junior Managers	—	80/120 „ „

Equipment

Except where special requirements dictate, equipment should be standardised. A variety of good desks and fatigue-reducing chairs are available, adjustable to individual physiques: the nature of the work and the ease of the clerk for comfortable working should determine choice. Other factors may come in, for instance, in the choice of desks, the number of drawers; while providing for the convenience and comfort of the clerk as an aid to effective work, it needs also to be remembered that a surfeit of drawers sooner or later leads to an accumulation of personal effects, and affords a convenient place wherein working papers can be lost.

Lighting, Heating and Ventilation

These are technical questions which have been more fully covered in Chapter V of Part Three: nothing further need be added here, but the following points may be underlined:

(1) The high importance to clerical work of adequate light, with absence of glare and dense shadows at the point of work.

(2) The avoidance of too great a contrast between general and local lighting.

(3) The importance of fresh air, though not to the detriment of warmth in winter—nor warmth to the detriment of fresh air.

(4) Adequate movement of air (as distinct from changing the air): this can be achieved by ventilation systems or fans; the latter, however, must be so positioned that they cause no disturbance.

(5) The aim of heating should be to maintain an even temperature; there is fairly general agreement that this should be in the region of 65 to 70 degrees Fahrenheit. The *space* should be heated, not the individual; direct heat induces fatigue.

Amenities

All that has been said in Chapter V of Part Three about the beneficial effect of staff amenities—cloakrooms, canteens, provision of drinking water, etc.—applies with equal validity to clerical employees.

Training

All offices, even the smallest, should have an established training scheme for new clerical workers. It has long been proved that effective results cannot be obtained by the old-fashioned method (or rather lack of method) of placing a new entrant alongside more experienced staff to be "shown what to do". A new member of the staff should be given a picture of the company's activities, be told something about its history, traditions and operating methods; he/she should be shown, in outline, where the department in which he/she is to be employed fits into the general structure and what the activities on which he/she is to be engaged achieve in terms of end-product.

Even though the possession of certain skills will have been the basis of the engagement or—in the case of machine operators—may be taught at courses run by the machine supplier, the new entrant must be shown how he/she is to apply these skills in the particular situation: for example, a new typist will know how to type, but will require instruction in the company's requirements as to layout of letters, methods of address, making of copies and many other specific items. It is particularly important in the case of younger people that further training be given to achieve higher proficiency; this can justifiably be done in working hours, after the employee has actually started work in his section or department. Every encouragement should be given to employees to attend evening classes; of particular importance is the display of interest by the employer and recognition for successes achieved. Many employers pay the fees for such attendances; in certain cases, employees are released for a few hours a week to attend day-time classes. Employees should be encouraged in every way to sit for one or other of the several national or professional examinations which are open to them. The larger firms are, of course, in a position to hold company courses on many subjects; attendance at a short O & M course is of great value to every clerical employee.

Training must be a continuous process, and should be based on the realisation that time spent in this way is not "lost". More experienced employees who show promise should be sent on outside courses where they have an opportunity not only of learning new subjects, but of meeting people from outside the organisation and acquiring a broader outlook.

Rest Pauses

Many types of routine clerical work cause fatigue through boredom. Consequently, rest pauses are of value in breaking up the day and in maintaining high outputs: the loss of (say) 15 minutes in the morning and afternoon is usually more than made good by improved freshness. Employees should be encouraged to leave their place of work during the break; it is a bad practice to serve tea at desks.

GENERAL OFFICE SERVICES

Centralisation versus Decentralisation

Certain clerical activities such as typing, duplicating, filing, etc., are common to most offices, and in larger organisations the question often arises as to whether they should be centralised or decentralised. Centralisation offers certain advantages the most important of which are:

Better machine utilisation
Higher specialisation of operators
More competent supervision
Priorities judged from overall point of view
Flattening out of peaks
Better facilities for encouraging a competitive spirit, setting standards, and applying incentive schemes.

On the other hand, decentralisation is by no means without merits:

Relationships are more personal
Operators possess more background knowledge relevant to their tasks
Departments have no scapegoat to blame for their own failures
Avoidance of "reference back"
Many women prefer to work for an individual rather than in a pool.

All these matters must be carefully considered before a decision for or against centralisation is taken. Each case must be decided on its merits, but if centralised services are operated the "line" responsibility for them must be clearly established. Users must be "customers", not "employers" of individual members of a centralised service. Telephone switchboards, messenger and similar services will invariably be under centralised control: this again should be determined in line with what has been said earlier about the responsibility for the clerical function. Under no circumstances should the specialised advisory officers (such as O & M) be given "line" responsibility for central services.

Secretarial and Typing Duties

A matter of very great importance to management is the smooth and effective execution of secretarial and typing duties. An efficient secretary can immensely increase the effectiveness of the executive whom she serves; but her duties are varied, and they cannot be fully or properly discharged if too much of her time is taken up by the chores of routine dictation. A good manager will facilitate his secretary's work in every respect. Provision of the best working conditions and really first-class "tools" (typewriter) should be a matter of course. Much of the secretary's time can be saved by the use, with proper discretion, of a dictating machine; this also has the advantage of allowing the executive to dictate at any time or any place without the necessity for the secretary's personal presence. If the executive takes care to distinguish *ab initio* between confidential and non-confidential material he enables his secretary to pass out non-confidential work to a "pool" or to juniors for typing. Photo-copy equipment can also facilitate the secretary's work as it eliminates the need for copy-typing. It is most important that the secretary should be kept fully informed of all matters in connection with which she may have to deal with visitors, telephone calls, or correspondence.

Non-secretarial typing, on the other hand, lends itself in many circumstances to "pooling" at one level or another. All that has previously been said about advantages and disadvantages of centralised arrangements applies in this connection. Dictating equipment can considerably increase the effectiveness of typists, *provided* that the output by dictators is strictly controlled as regards quantity. Experience shows that dictating machines have a tendency to lead to more dictation, much of it unnecessary or of undue length.[1]

Many larger firms have established "pool" typing services, either in large units or as sections attached to particular departments. In some cases, the dictation is partly or wholly through machines ("audio-typing"). These methods raise many serious problems which need careful study and appraisal before a specific arrangement is established. Among the more important issues is one of "comparative costs" as between typing time and managerial time: it has been found that, unless precautions are taken, mechanical dictation may require more time on the part of the manager in recording details of letters being answered—this is but saving low-cost man-hours at the expense of using more of the high-cost time!

[1] Anyone whose task it is to commit words to paper should make a study of the use of "plain words"; a good starting point is the reading of Sir Ernest Gowers' *Plain Words* (published by H.M. Stationery Office).

Filing

Another matter of vital importance to every office is filing. Basically, an effective filing system determines one place, and one place only, for every document on any one subject. If it does this, it will make it possible:

(*a*) to find and produce any wanted document without delay;
(*b*) to get a complete picture of any subject by perusing one (and only one) file.

In practice, however, two difficulties arise. The first is caused by a document dealing with two subjects. This *should* not happen, as it is bad commercial practice to deal with more than one subject at a time, but as an organisation cannot control the contents of incoming documents, it does happen all the same. The remedy is to have one or more photo-copies made, eliminating from each the matter irrelevant to that copy. The second difficulty is that a subject can have two or more aspects: for example, a letter to an employee about attending a course affects (*a*) the employee, and (*b*) the course. In such cases it must be decided (and such decisions should be based on predetermined rules) whether filing under both aspects is essential (in which case two copies of outgoing documents will have to be made, and incoming matter will have to be photo-copied) or whether cross-referencing will meet the case. Such cross-referencing must be clear, prominent and unambiguous.

The disposal of old records is very important. It is clearly undesirable and, indeed, impossible to keep all records for ever. A disposal programme must therefore be operated laying down "retention periods" for different types of documents. The problem is much reduced if general and correspondence files are maintained on a dual system, each folder having two compartments which lie next to each other when the folder is opened: one for "policy" and other important matters, the other for "current" papers. The retention period for the latter can be much shorter than for the former; the transfer date to the "basement" (or other storage place for old filing that cannot, as yet, be destroyed) can be similarly differentiated.

Modern filing equipment can considerably facilitate and speed up the actual putting away and retrieving of papers; the "lateral" method of accommodating files saves space as compared with the traditional filing cabinets, and can also be recommended on "time and motion" grounds.

CONCLUSION

This Chapter has not set out to provide a detailed review of the methods and facilities used or recommended for the efficient performance of clerical work. Its purpose has been a presentation of and commentary on some of the more important aspects of the general management of office activities. Questions of equipment, methods, forms, and the like are of considerable importance, but they are more appropriately dealt with in specialist textbooks and reference books. There is, in fact, a sizeable literature on the detail of clerical methods: the following is a brief reference list.

1. *General*

   Office Administration: Edited by Mills and Standingford (Pitman).

   Management of the Smaller Office: Prepared and published by British Institute of Management and Institute of Office Management.

2. *Advisory Services (O & M).*

   The Practice of O & M: H.M. Treasury (H.M. Stationery Office).

   Organisation and Methods: Edited by G. E. Milward (Macmillan).

   Work Study in the Office: H. P. Cemach (Current Affairs—Office Magazine Publication).

3. *Office Buildings, Layout, Space*

   Office Accommodation: Prepared and published by British Institute of Management and Institute of Office Management.

   Better Offices: Published by the Institute of Directors, London, 1961.

4. *Office Equipment*

   Manual of Modern Business Equipment: Published by Macdonald & Evans for Office Appliance and Business Equipment Trade Association.

   Machines and Appliances in Government Offices: H.M. Treasury (H. M. Stationery Office).

5. *Staff*

   Clerical Job Grading and Merit Rating: Prepared and published by Institute of Office Management.

   Office Staff—Selection, Supervision, Training: E. M. Pepperell (Industrial Welfare Society).

CLERICAL WORK: JOB GRADING SCHEDULE

Grade	Experience Required	Initiative Required	Skill Required	Supervision and Direction	Examples
A	None	—	—	Each task allotted, very simple or closely directed	(a) Messenger work (b) Simple sorting
B	Short period of training (a few weeks)	Daily routine covered by time-table	Adherence to limited number of well-defined rules	Closely directed and checked; short period control	(a) Simple copying (b) Straightforward adding using adding machine
C	Reasonable degree of experience or special aptitude		Tasks of routine character following well-defined rules	Short period control	(a) Simple ledger machine operation (b) Checking of Grade B work
D		Only very limited degree of initiative	Predetermined procedure and precise rules	Daily routine varies but not sufficiently to necessitate any considerable direction	(a) Shorthand typing of non-routine correspondence (b) Certifying straightforward purchase invoices
E	Considerable experience required	Significant but not extensive measure of discretion and initiative	Specialised knowledge and individual responsibility	—	(a) Group supervision of routine work (b) Queries of non-machine character
F		Extensive measure of responsibility and judgment or initiative	Application of a professional technique (legal, accounting, statistical, engineering)	—	(a) Section supervision (b) Acting in close liaison with Management

The contents of this table are taken from *Clerical Job Grading and Merit Rating*, published by the Institute of Office Management, 3rd edition (1960). The table itself has been specially designed for readers of this volume and does not form part of the I.O.M. publications. The book contains comprehensive grading specifications for 15 clerical procedures and 8 types of operations common to many procedures, and is an indispensable tool for the grading of clerical work. The permission of the Institute to quote from the book is gratefully acknowledged.

CHAPTER VI

COMMITTEES IN MANAGEMENT

No study of management in practice would be complete in the present decade without some comments on the subject of committees and the role that they can play in the field of executive and functional relations. Participation in committee meetings is an active item in the experience of almost every manager—mostly to his chagrin! This is the more true, the greater the size of the organisation. The phenomenon is probably a natural concomitant of size, the personal gathering being, in a large and complex establishment, the only effective way of attaining co-ordination and balance in progress. There is, however, a cynical standpoint often taken, arguing that the resort to committees is a reflection of unwillingness to accept and exercise responsibility. This argument has been urged particularly by the critics of Britain's nationalised industries wherein, it is true, committees have usually figured more prominently and more frequently than is customary in the average of private enterprise businesses. On the other hand, in the very large companies, the practice does not *appear* significantly different; but there *may* be a major difference in the spirit in which the committee practice is pursued, which would bear out the argument of the cynics.

Committees bulk large in discussions of management practice because the majority experience of them has to be described as "unfortunate". Most anecdotes of committee procedure indicate that the raconteurs have had little else than poor experience of committees. Memories recur of long periods of discomfort with lengthy discussions on points of singularly irrelevant detail, or desultory exchanges of views on matters which are so important that no one dares to show a lead. Wanderings from the matter really in hand lead to boredom through the sessions, while participants have to listen to the inevitable talker who is the "committee man" *par excellence*. Poor chairmanship, which makes all these deficiencies possible, is the last straw of irritation to any competent executive whose misfortune it is to be nominated to serve on an ineffective committee. This dismal picture is a joy to the cynics, but it is not far removed from the reality of many men's experiences. Few managers have enjoyed the sense of co-ordinated achievement that emerges from participation in a well-run committee. Fortunately, in recent years, humour with satire allied has come to the rescue—through the medium of the "revelation" of "Parkinson's laws", originally appearing as light-hearted satire in *Punch* and consolidated finally in book form.[1] So far as committees are concerned, the satire came so close to common experience that some readers could not even appreciate the ridicule. There is little doubt but that the "Parkinson rays of light" have contributed quite an important influence to attaining improvement in committee practice.

The medium of committee co-ordination, as applied in British industry, derived considerable momentum from the war-time development of "joint consultation" and the post-war phenomenon of "working parties". Both officially inspired, they made the committee the inevitable mechanism for accomplishing specific objectives—unfortunately without providing the accompanying training in committee skills. In joint consultation the purpose was a bringing together of the "two sides" of industry, in the persons of representatives of management and of organised labour, to hammer out an agreed policy of employment relations and to provide means of releasing and resolving grievances, real or imagined. Personal contact, with face-to-face communication was essential to the accomplishment of the objectives: whatever the tribulations endured by participants in many of these war-time and post-war "joint production committees", the results on the national scale were undoubtedly positive. The direct consultations in the course of time exerted a constructive and positive influence on manager-worker relationships, which is manifest in the altogether different pattern of employment policy and industrial relations practice characteristic of the contemporary scene in Britain. The committee medium has had a definitely ameliorative end-result.

The "working parties" had a very different objective, being concerned with thrashing out ways and means of improving methods and performance in manufacturing, distribution and administrative work. Yet, here again, the committee form was essential to the attainment of the objective: in this case it necessitated bringing together representatives of management, of technology, of salesmanship, of organised labour, of trade association, perhaps also of research. Not this time for a mutual harmonising of seemingly opposing viewpoints, but to constitute a pool of ideas and a flow of thought, from which constructive proposals could be forged, in the knowledge that from the various relevant points of view they could be translated into effective practice. Consultation and co-ordination were less important than the mutual communication of viewpoints and the

---

[1] C. Northcote Parkinson: *Parkinson's Law (or The Pursuit of Progress)* (Murray, London). Already referred to in the preceding Chapter in the context of another subject similarly satirised.

pooled contribution of individual ideas. It could well have been the case that in many of these "working parties", the discussions and deliberations were burdensome and boring, but in no other way could this objective of common contribution have been met, and the committee formula was thus inevitable. In point of fact, the committee is *per se* a valuable instrument of co-operative human effort, affording a readier means of mutual contact and communication than any other mechanism. This can be seen by reflection on the basic requirements of co-ordination which Mary Follett laid down nearly half a century ago. In her philosophy, the ultimate effectiveness of human agreement lay in "integration", i.e. in full agreement so reached that concord promoted contribution at a level higher than the mere summation of the individual efforts. "Compromise", the usual pattern of man's mutual agreement, is a negative formula because it implies some of the participants giving up some part of their viewpoint although they believe it to be of importance. Integration, however, cannot be attained except by a genuine fullness of co-ordination and co-operation. To attain this level, Mary Follett argued that co-ordination must be established and maintained as a matter of direct contact between the parties concerned, it must start at an early stage of the project, it must remain genuinely continuing while deliberations continue, and it must involve a reciprocal relating of all the factors relevant to the situation under consideration. A committee well constituted and well run could meet these requirements more effectively than any other medium of communication—though, as was said above, few managers could yet endorse such a claim on the basis of their personal experience.

While there has not been any systematic investigation or research into the problem, examination of various committees used among the mechanics of management has indicated that the widespread dissatisfaction tends to consolidate around the following six major points:

(a) The amount of time wasted, which is more particularly important if the members are the senior personnel of an organisation (as indeed they frequently are); the time lost is then also disproportionately expensive.

(b) The opportunity provided for the essential being clouded by the non-essential, and for extraneous points of view in any situation to be loaded into the deliberations.

(c) The temptation for those members who are unable or unwilling to shoulder responsibility in their own jurisdiction to allow points of decision to be taken over by their colleagues during the course of open deliberations.

(d) The opportunity for derogation from real responsibility over a wider area, because the committee is an amorphous body.

(e) The ready breeding ground for inefficiencies, because of the ease with which failures and deficiencies can be covered over when they are presented for discussion.

(f) The confusion which can result from a welter of discussion if this is not consistently and coherently directed; in such circumstances absence of information could be a better situation than incorrectly understood information.

Definitions

In the course of day-to-day working of management action, there are a great many occasions when consultation and mutual communication are required, and which necessitate gatherings of executives, whether formal or informal. The incidental everyday meetings of individuals in each other's offices do not call for specific comment, but those where larger numbers foregather do need to be reviewed if they are to serve effectively as an instrument of sound management practice. It is pertinent for this purpose to consider three types of meetings widely used within the management framework, and the distinctions are broadly as follows:

(i) *A committee*—a meeting which has a formal constitution and normally has formal proceedings, with sessions on a regular or periodic basis; it comprises a gathering of people representing different functions or spheres of knowledge, coming together to promote a common purpose or to fulfil a common task by the interchange of ideas: it is perhaps important to note that the different persons composing the committee, strictly speaking, represent differences of function, of experience, or of knowledge, and *not* differences of self-interest.

(ii) *A meeting*—any other systematically constituted meeting, in which the proceedings are not necessarily formalised nor regularly recurrent, and which has only a loosely established constitution; usually called *ad hoc* to consider specific matter, and not likely to have more than two or three subsequent sessions in the same context.

(iii) *A conference*—a large gathering of people brought together to hear an exposition of chosen subjects, followed by informal supplementary discussions and questionings by those in attendance; it could be such as to occur once only, or at long intervals if recurrent; proceedings may be formal or informal, and would be directed primarily to imparting information.

PURPOSES OF COMMITTEES

The true role of committees within the structure of organisation and in the working of management action is an important one; one which, in fact, can be regarded as that of an "instrument" or "tool" of management action, contributing considerably to the effectiveness of that action in respect of all the elements of the management process, but in particular to co-ordination. The degree of effectiveness and ultimate result coming from this instrument or tool depends largely on the extent to which such committees are directed to known purposes, with competent direction leaving no loophole for inefficiencies, or for ineffectiveness from misuse.

The purposes for which a committee could be constituted as part of the framework of management action can be summarised in the following items:

(a) *Joint consultation*

This has the special characteristic of being a discussion between representatives, normally thought of as belonging to different "sides". (This is not the correct context for critically examining and refuting the common notion!) Strictly speaking, even here there should not be *difference* of self-interest, since both parties concerned depend for their well-being on the soundness of the organisation in which they serve. Normally known as "Joint Consultative Committee", "Works Advisory Council" or by some other similar title, such bodies are formally established, with the representatives of the management and of the employees nominated either within the one company, or on a regional basis. The purpose is, as the title suggests, consultation on matters of common interest in relation to employment policy and practice; some have the more specific objective of bargaining about contractual relationships, for example, the number of hours and shifts to be worked, job rates, overtime arrangements, bonus formulæ, etc. Special cases of joint consultation are often found in relation to particular activities, for example, canteens, welfare services, or suggestion schemes.

(b) *Co-ordination among executives*

A formal or informal meeting among the managers and functional specialists in a company, designed to ensure co-ordination and balance in progress. A common illustration is for the co-ordination of a development project. Suppose there is a company which is doubling its output programme by means partly of additional shifts and partly of extensions to premises: while the programme is being formulated and initiated there are a number of executives who have major responsibilities in connection with it, each in his own field, and it is of importance that they should have a normal medium for thinking in unison as the programme and project get under way. Another instance is provided by the customary "pre-contract planning meeting" which is held by the bigger building and civil engineering contractors at the outset of any large contract; here Managers, Estimators, Engineers, Architects, Contract Supervisors, Plant Managers, Buyers, and Quantity Surveyors come together to ensure uniform consideration of their individual specialist participation in the subsequent running of the constructional project.

(c) *Consultation among executives*

This is comparable with the foregoing, with a slight difference of emphasis. Where a "co-ordination" purpose is served, the emphasis is particularly laid on enabling the individual executives to keep each other informed of what is going on, and to gain for themselves an appreciation of factors in other departments that will have a bearing on their own decisions. Where, however, a "consultation" purpose is the primary consideration, the emphasis lies on having the executives together to *interchange ideas* about the matter at issue, so that a variety of points of view can be considered before a decision is taken or action is initiated. Frequently, a committee or meeting of this kind is held by a senior executive with his subordinates and others, so that his own decisions can be formulated in the light of points of view expressed by these colleagues or subordinates.

(d) *Technical study*

A group of persons to whom is entrusted a particular subject or proposition, which they are asked to consider from the various points of view that they represent and to report back appraisal or recommendations.

(e) *Uniform information*

This would be a meeting or conference rather than a committee, and might well be held or called by a Managing Director to tell all of his senior executives about new developments in policy and the implications of a new programme that will ensue. The more formal meeting that some companies hold daily in regard to the consideration of important incoming mail is of this character. So, too, is the sales conference held for the information of District or Branch Managers when a new product is being launched.

(f) *Advisory purpose*

This is perhaps no more than a special aspect of the consultation purpose referred to above, where in this case the aim is, quite frankly, the securing of other people's points of view before a decision is come to. The advice sought may be on a wide scale, or may be confined to a specific technical or commercial aspect of a given subject.

(g) *Executive*

This must mean that the power of decision is vested in the meeting or committee, although the description is often used loosely when the real purpose of meeting is "initial information" or "advice" among executive colleagues. As a management instrument, an executive committee raises some major issues, and these will have specific consideration in subsequent paragraphs. Outside of normal industrial practice, genuine executive committees can be found where circumstances make a commonly shared decision imperative: for example, the management of funds in a Superannuation Fund or Trust; or the conduct of the affairs of a Sports

Club within a voluntary association; or the committee which adjudicates on and decides awards for ideas submitted under a Suggestions Scheme. Cases have been known in industry where the control of discipline has been delegated to a three-man representative committee with full decisive powers.

(h) *Formal governing committee*

A normal pattern for the exercise of overall top responsibility for policy and direction is to be found in committee form—for example, a Board of Directors, the Council of any Local Authority, the Governing Body of a School, or Hospital, and the Local Management Committee which is the customary governing authority in the Co-operative Society retail trading movement. It can be argued that this particular form of committee is an acceptable case of "executive committee", the acceptability arising because of the value of several contributing minds in formulating the general directives that are to govern the affairs of the concern and in the exercise of an overall supervision of performance and progress. Such committees are "executive" in the sense of being responsible for making decisions, directing general lines of activity and relevant financial authorisations, but they do *not* (or should not) *undertake the management decisions,* which initiate and control the executive action; those are more appropriately taken by the "chief executives".

(i) *Educational*

In the development of management training techniques in recent years, a "meeting" form has been found very valuable as an aid to stimulation of thought and learning: various titles used are in the order of "seminar", "syndicate", "case session", "study group". The essence of the arrangement is that a group of persons deliberate on and discuss in common specific subjects or problems, in an endeavour to arrive at agreed conclusions or solutions. It is found that the mental exercise is the more valuable by reason of being conducted among a group, a good deal of the value coming from the immediate challenge and response inherent in the arrangement. Competent leadership and knowledgeable functional guidance are, of course, vitally important in ensuring successful application of the technique.

THE "EXECUTIVE" COMMITTEE

Whatever may be the level of opinion about committees in general, it is the notion of "executive committee" that has engendered a considerable degree of controversy. Protagonists are well supported on the issue that an executive committee is an escape into irresponsibility and should never be countenanced. That many cases could be cited from the scene of contemporary experience (and seemingly successful cases) would not be accepted by such protagonists as evidence to justify the principle, but simply as accidental exceptions to the general rule that a body of men can never attain such harmony of integrated judgment as to attain in unison the highest level of sound decision: there will inevitably be greater or lesser elements of compromise and, therefore, weakness. Consultation and mutual communication as the forerunner of personal executive decision would be agreed as useful, but the executive responsibility is emphasised as lying with the individual and not with the meeting. This can well be borne out by some of the cases that are encountered in industrial enterprises: the appearances are those of committees or meetings holding executive responsibility and seeming to discharge it quite clearly and effectively; certainly without obvious conflict. Closer analysis of such cases, however, has often revealed that the seeming corporate discharge of executive responsibility is an illusion; what to the eye of the superficial observer is a "committee decision" ensuing in an executive instruction is in fact corporate recognition of decisions taken by the individual participating executives within their own responsibilities; having exchanged ideas and received the benefit of criticism and comment, the executives in session are forming their own relevant decisions while the committee's deliberations are in process. They are consulting with their colleagues, as they would necessarily have to do before final decision, but the consultations are taking place within a setting of co-ordination with those colleagues, instead of in the more isolated atmosphere of one-and-one discussions in their own rooms. Or again, if the committee is one in which a Managing Director is presiding at a meeting with his senior operating and specialist executives, the illusion can be the stronger that this gathering is taking the executive decisions in its corporate capacity; the real process is that the Managing Director is taking the decisions within the corporate setting, but influenced by the contributions from his departmental chiefs, who are deliberating with him. Or again, even in the case where the members of a named "Executive Committee" are formally equal in status, and no one of them subordinate to others in the structure of organisation, it has often been found that the attainment of the decisive outcome from the committee's deliberations is primarily due to the personal influence of one of the members (perhaps the member who is serving as Chairman), even though this influence has gone entirely unrecognised.

The objections against executive committees, so far as their role in industrial management is concerned, turn on the following considerations:

(i) Because of differences of personal outlook and attitude, the decision reached is likely to be a compromise based on the lowest common factor, rather than the best decision in the interests of a a company. Such a result might be achieved particularly because of goodwill on the part of the members; if, for example, a normally co-operative individual feels that it will be impossibe to secure true integration on the best decision, he may quietly withhold his objection to the compromise that is being pursued, so as not to impede promoting a common view, thus doing a disservice to the organisation because of the committee medium.

(ii) The committee's decisions may be arrived at by the domination of one strong personality and may, in effect, be an agreement arrived at because of a fear of arguing.

(iii) A committee cannot really exercise personal leadership over other persons who are not participating in it; this is perhaps the gravest objection to the use of an executive committee within the management framework. Even if the committee entrusts its Chairman with the task of conveying in person the decisions emanating, there cannot be the same personal strength of inspiration that underlies the personal discharge of clear responsibilities by a good manager.

(iv) There is the major weakness of avoiding issues, and consequently of arriving at decisions which are in themselves weak or which are not clearly formulated; they thus give rise to a situation in which a management action at lower levels is made extremely difficult and, possibly, ineffective.

(v) There is also the element of instability that is produced by a committee, in so far as the attitudes of its members may well sway it in different directions on different occasions.

These main weaknesses were neatly summarised by Urwick more than twenty years ago in the following paragraph from a study that has remained the classic commentary on this subject:[1]

"A committee differs from an individual in three important respects. Its corporate personality is intermittent: it dies each time that a session closes. It is not available between meetings to make the detailed adjustments which are constantly necessary in translating policy into action. Being itself an organisation, it postulates activities of direction and leadership. But these activities are necessarily exercised by a chairman, whose authority is also intermittent and whose responsibility is not personal and specific, as would be the case with an individual, but merely his share of the collective responsibility of the committee. Its decisions can only be communicated to those responsible for acting on them in an impersonal form and, almost necessarily, in writing. Thus it cannot have the personal contact with subordinates enjoyed by an individual."

[1] From L. Urwick's "Committees in Organisation", *British Management Review*, Vol. III (1936), reprinted as a pamphlet in 1952 by the British Institute of Management. The subject of committees is also dealt with at length in Chapter X of *Organisation—the Framework of Management*, by E. F. L. Brech: some of the illustrative items quoted in the present Chapter are incorporated from this source.

One of Britain's major steel companies has a working committee with an executive responsibility, seemingly well justified. Under the label of "Central Recruitment Committee", it is responsible for formulating and carrying out the various aspects of policy in regard to the recruitment and training of qualified personnel, chiefly the graduates newly entering industrial employment. From the Managing Director the Committee receives broad guidance on the intentions and objectives of the Board of Directors for the employment and development of scientific and technological personnel, and is then responsible to him for planning recruitment and training to meet that policy. The Committee formulates recruitment programmes and "instructs" the Personnel Department about interviews of graduate applicants (and some other categories) within the programme, including specifications and numbers. Next, it is concerned to set out the patterns of training and to supervise their application, including review of the progress of the men in training. Individual assessments of progress are made by the Personnel Department, but the Committee is responsible for a periodical appraisal of the trainees for the first five years of their service on the basis of the Department's assessments. It has an Education and Training Officer as its full-time responsible servant, especially for liaison with the company's Chief Personnel Officer, who, however, does not discharge formal responsibility in this area, except in accordance with the Committee's directives. The scheme seems to work successfully and so to justify an executive committee arrangement; but only a close review of the situation would enable a reliable assessment to be made as to whether the apparent success is due to the arrangement itself or whether other local factors account for it.

The issue at stake in the controversy about "executive committees" is not of *fundamental* importance, but is rather a matter for personal choice, bearing in mind the serious content of the arguments raised against it. There is nothing *in principle* which could be quoted to prevent a company from setting up a committee charged with responsibility for management decisions, if the top executives or the Board of Directors, in mature deliberation, feel that they want so to proceed. One can realistically say, with conviction drawn from considerable study of organisation practice, that this has often proved to be an unwise arrangement, and that, in the light of experience, better management consideration and decision will be obtained from the allocation of responsibility to individuals, encouraging them to exercise this with the assistance of a committee for coordination and consultative purposes. This cautionary advice stems mainly from the practical dangers and weaknesses that are common to any committee, whether executive or not.[1]

There is a "morale" aspect in committee sessions among executives and specialists in an organisation structure which is worth taking into account. Any executive needs to be in frequent contact with his subordinate or colleague executives and officers, even if only by informal personal sessions. Periodic common gatherings can be a useful way of keeping in touch when pressing needs of a busy week make recurrent individual sessions difficult. A committee is not, however, a substitute for a suitable span of responsibility! Nor does it allow an executive latitude not to delegate! So meetings designed to cover up such weaknesses should not be countenanced. The periodic formal meeting can assist ease of communication by an executive with the immediate members of his own team, and the members do derive a benefit from the common personal contact—if one may assume that the meetings are well run. This morale value adds to the sense of participation and can be a major factor in promoting and maintaining co-operative attitude, as well as ensuring uniformity of information, i.e. "keeping people in the picture". Morale, co-ordination and effectiveness in an executive team are closely interwoven, and meetings or committees soundly based and well conducted can make important contributions to them all.

EFFECTIVE COMMITTEE PRACTICE

Most of the factors involved in ensuring that a committee or meeting is soundly based and well conducted are items of practical common sense, but it may be useful as a guide to effective practice to review the major items under the four headings: purpose, membership, chairmanship, mechanics.

1. Role and Purposes

Leaving aside any further consideration of "executive committees", a useful part can be played by a committee within an organisation in one or other of the following main capacities:

---

[1] An illustrative case of committees and meetings used in a dynamic way as a tool of management in action is given among the findings of the research project described by Tom Burns and G. M. Stalker in "The Management of Innovation" (Tavistock Publications, London, 1961). See especially Chapter 5 on "Management Structures and Systems" where an outline description is given of a firm "dominated by management meetings", so arranged and conducted that they form a "comprehensive system of communications" and provide the organisation structure. (This publication is a most valuable study, particularly as a stimulus to serious analytical thought as to the relative significance of features in management practice.)

(a) As an advisory body, to assist an executive by bringing together for his guidance the knowledge and experience of various other members of the organisation, and getting them to deliberate on particular problems allotted to them.

(b) As a means of consultation, to ensure that the viewpoints of managers or functions related to the matters in hand are adequately brought into consideration.

(c) As a co-ordinated channel of information, to ensure that all the interested persons receive the necessary information, receive the same information, and receive it in the same form, and at the same time.

(d) As a means for keeping harmony in development of progress as well as of policy and action.

(e) As a medium for stimulating deliberation in the exchange of ideas for educational purposes.

Within any of these broad categories, it is of the utmost importance that any committee or meeting should have a definite and clearly known purpose. To stress this may sound strange, because it is so obvious a point of common sense: even more strange is the fact of experience that many committees run on in such unsure circumstances that their original objectives have become obscured and *their real purpose is now not specifically clear.* When a committee is to have a continuing life, it is the more important to ensure that its role and its terms of reference are clearly stated, and currently kept in front of members. (A practical way of attaining this is to have the terms of reference reproduced inside the front cover of the folders in which each member's copies of the minutes are filed.) In effect, then, a committee has the equivalent of a "definition of responsibilities". The basic feature of the formation of a committee or recurrent meeting is that the subject-matter lends itself to development from the stimulus of many minds in unison and can be made more progressively effective by group deliberation: in other words, the committee treatment attains a level of accomplishment or progress that cannot be as well attained by individual discussions. There are, indeed, aspects of management practice in which this is true, particularly in the realms of formulating programmes and planning projects, or in the review of progress. An outstanding illustration is provided by the short-term planning underlying the scheduling of civil aviation services ("short-term" as distinct from the forward forecasts concerned with the development or purchase of types of aircraft). Planning in this field is essentially a combination of facts from many sources, supplemented by calculations and computations—types of aircraft available, technical considerations of where they can be used, speeds, load capacity, fuel consumptions, etc. (these are the "operational" facets); the timing of availability of aircraft in serviceable condition and number of flying hours before next scheduled overhaul (these are engineering or maintenance facets); the volume, type and location of passenger or freight traffic wanting air service or able to be obtained by commercial promotion, charter, agency arrangements, etc. (i.e. commercial or sales facets); the availability of air crews competent to operate the aircraft concerned over the routes to be followed, the crews being in fit medical condition, currently within their permitted quota of flying hours, and located at suitable bases or slip stations (i.e. personnel and medical facets); the economics of the proposed services in terms of revenues and costs, whether for *ad hoc* traffic or over a given season or period (i.e. financial facets); the provision of ground services and facilities, with adequate staff, to handle incoming/outgoing traffic at the proposed intermediate and terminal points, with any necessary technical servicing that may be due (i.e. overseas station facets); considerations of weather conditions, which may necessitate last-minute alterations to flight plans because of dangers in one area or another (i.e. another facet of "operations", but covering also overseas stations, and technical services from outside agencies); the relevance of international air regulations, for there are stringent codes mutually agreed among countries with commercial air services (i.e. an international advisory facet). Much of the information comes from current records and analyses being made as normal routines within the Operations, Sales, Engineering and other Departments of any airline—things like movements records, flight analyses, staff rosters, meteorological reports, sales forecasts, cost dissections, etc. All of these *could* be fed into a central "planning unit", but it would have to be staffed by master minds to be able to digest, interpret and balance the large variety of facets entailed, and the gestation of its planning arrangements would take so long as to be useless when complete, because meanwhile perhaps the commercial opportunity for the service had passed. (It has been argued that the basic data from all the various current sources could be programmed for storage on tape or drum allied to a computer, and then variations fed in by tape or card as instructions to the computer to bring out the "answers" from the recalculation of the situation; that no airline has yet successfully accomplished this approach in practice tends to suggest that the argument is as yet academic—though it is by no means beyond the reach of attainment.) Scheduling or short-term planning in this field of civil aviation has to be fast-moving and flexible, which provides a strong argument for a properly constituted and efficient committee, made up of a responsible member from each of the main departmental activities concerned, and meeting regularly—so regularly that the members come to think in parallel and to develop a high sense of mutually co-operative responsibility for their important task. The chairman of this committee should be a non-departmental man, perhaps someone selected to represent the chief executive of the airline company; he would need to be experienced in operational and administrative affairs of his company, and his major responsibility in the sessions would be to ensure full contribution from each specialist point of view and to attain from these the achievement of the common objective in reliable and economic "flight schedules" or "service plans".

Another illustration is afforded from the experience of a certain manufacturing company during the earlier phases of the Second World War. This was a small concern, employing only about 400 people, and it was faced with the gigantic project of rapidly doubling its output at a time when manpower was being withdrawn for National Service purposes, while the possibility of securing additional skilled personnel was remote. In the executive structure responsible to the Managing Director, there were some six or seven senior and junior executives covering the various activities, partly on functional lines. In the main, the Managing Director was the technical brain, but among this handful of responsible subordinates there were most of the requisite qualifications and experience available, even if on a limited scale. For the expansion programme to be achieved with the maximum effectiveness and economy of manpower, it was essential to maintain a continuously harmonious development, particularly in the progress of the various contributory sections, such as purchase and installation of plant, raw material supplies, training and up-grading of personnel, availability of tools, improvement of quality control through the development of inspection standards and inspection techniques, and so on through many facets of manufacturing management. As the mechanism for achieving this co-ordination, the Managing Director instituted a "Production Progress Committee" meeting at fortnightly intervals, with himself as chairman and his six or seven subordinate executives as members. On a defined agenda, the Committee's deliberations fortnight by fortnight reviewed the whole programme laid down to meet the expansion; it ensured that all the executives shared the latest available information and were able to see how their own contribution fitted into the general pattern. The Committee did not take decisions, but its chairman, in his executive capacity of Managing Director, was able to say, after a point had been deliberated, that he accepted the advice or recommendation put forward and to issue immediately after the meeting the necessary instructions for action. This enabled each executive who would be required to take the action to get moving immediately in the knowledge that his boss and his colleagues knew all about it, and also put him in the right position to report progress at the subsequent meeting or to submit reasons for failing to achieve progress. That there were difficulties in meeting the planned expansion, of course, goes without saying, but it is equally true that the difficulties were minimised, and that the rate of progress was substantially enhanced by this effective mechanism of co-ordination and balance.

2. Membership

It is essential that the constitution or terms of reference of any committee should contain a clear statement of the persons designated as members, and also arrangements in regard to co-option or the calling of persons to attend. The number of participants in the proceedings should be kept as small as possible: experience has shown that a committee of more than nine is normally too large. Members nominated to serve on a committee, and others selected for co-option, should be chosen on a basis of genuine relevance to the purposes which the committee has been established to serve. This again is a matter on which comment may seem superfluous because it is such obvious common sense, but it is again a matter in which practice has seen common sense frequently flouted. In this respect questions of "representation of interests" or "prestige of departments" can often be an influential force, and nominations to committees are often made in these terms, rather than on the basis of effective accomplishment of the objectives. Naturally, the subject-matter must determine which departments or activities are relevant and therefore whether they need "representation". In a committee where uniformity of information, or some aspects of co-ordination, are the main purposes, then the factor of "representation" may be a determining point for membership. Where, however, there is deliberation to be accomplished to a degree that a positive outcome is called for, a more effective basis of choice should be sought in terms of ability to contribute realistically to the stated objectives. It is sometimes a good practice to list all the persons or representatives who *might* be oolected for a given purpose, and then to rank them in order of priority on the basis of a criterion of effective contribution; If only four or five names are found, then a good quorum may have been reached; if, however, the list of possibles goes longer, it may be found useful to limit the committee membership to, say, the first ranking seven or eight, leaving others to be available for co-option or attendance *ad hoc*. A varying membership, in the sense of a small nucleus of standing members supplemented *ad hoc* by occasional different additional participants, may often prove a good practical way of forming a sound small working committee coupled with adequate contribution of the varying relevant points of view. Calling for written contributions, or for "witnesses" to attend once for a specific discussion, may again be found a useful approach to the same end. Most experience goes to prove that a small committee attains more effective results more quickly than a larger one.

Whatever the composition of a committee, one of the most important factors for effective participation by its membership is the understanding and acceptance of the committee's terms of reference, a realisation of the deliberative and consultative nature of its role, and recognition of its objectives in effective outcome with economical performance. If members could apply a *budget control approach* to their committee's deliberations, they would be well on the way to sound membership as well as high achievement!

3. *The Chairman's Role*

Good chairmanship is almost the most essential prerequisite for a successful committee operation. Much of the widespread dissatisfaction with committees stems from recurrent experience of membership under poor chairmen. It has been argued that the qualities and pattern of behaviour of a good committee chairman are akin to those of the competent executive: there is indeed an analogy, even if the comparison cannot be pushed far. Awareness of objectives figures prominently in the chairman's role, coupled with an appreciation of the significance of, and the factors making for, effective and economical performance. It is in this respect that the analogy with good management holds closest. He has, too, a task in human terms, in promoting a genuine sense of collaboration and a good team morale. He must have the ability to keep the committee's purposes alive in members' minds, while putting points for deliberation before them in such a way as to ensure a systematic approach to its tasks and to promote a full discussion of all relevant aspects. He must be able to hold off irrelevances and meanderings without giving offence, and while extracting the salient points from the discussion, to be alert for the important factors or facets that are being omitted. He must be prepared to make the occasional recapitulation in the interests of clarity of progress, and at times he must be able to gain attention for his own views without appearing to obtrude them. While concentrating on the matters being deliberated, he must generate response to his leadership in a brisk and effective performance by the committee, instilling into its members, without appearing pedagogical, a consciousness of the precepts of sound committee procedure. It is his duty to obtain from participants the requisite attitude of understanding, co-operation and responsibility which alone can ensure effective outcome.

No mean task to attain! It has one consequence in suggesting that the chairman of a committee is often better placed when he is not an interested party in the matters with which he is dealing. Not everyone would agree with this point of view, and merit can be found in the argument that a committee performs its task better when the chairman "knows what it is all about". Perhaps a compromise solution is the right way out, provided it ensures that the member chosen as chairman does at least have personal, mental and behavioural capacity to attain the level of performance sketched out above. The major difficulty confronting the man really knowledgeable in the subject matter is that of predetermined standpoint and thus the possibility of favouring certain of the points of view that will come under deliberation. It is primarily the chairman's role to get the best out of the knowledge and experience of the members of his committee rather than to make his personal contributions. A major drawback to successful committee action is not infrequently met in a chairman of dominant personal make-up, especially if he is also voluble: that type of individual is mostly so prone to hold sway that he does not get useful participation from his members.

When a committee is used for co-ordination or consultation purposes within a management structure, another danger can be encountered from the executive standing of the chairman. It is not unusual in committees of this kind for the chair to be taken by the Managing Director, a situation which may tend to give the committee a spurious form of "executive" role in the eyes of its members. The more so if they are his immediate executive and specialist subordinates. In these circumstances, a Managing Director (or other senior executive) presiding over a committee can be looked to by the members to give instantaneous decisions on matters raised, *ex cathedra* but in his capacity as the chief or senior executive. The danger of this arrangement, which some people praise for its efficiency, lies in its destruction of that most valuable element in business committee procedure, the opportunity for detached appraisal and deliberation of a subject directed towards the submission of advice or recommendation to executive authority; this authority may then subsequently arbitrate without bias, having taken account of all other relevant factors, which may or may not be known to the committee. All too often a Managing Director, serving as chairman of a committee, has to refuse to accept a decision reached by its members, because he knows of contradictory aspects of policy which he is not free to disclose: in consequence of an unexplained rejection, the members feel rebuffed, and confidence in the usefulness of the committee is inevitably shaken. If, on the other hand, the committee work to submit exactly the same conclusion as a "recommendation" to an executive authority which is outside of themselves, the effect would be the same without the ensuing emotional repercussions. Given enough time to prepare a reasoned reply, the executive can then submit for the next meeting a constructive rejection of the recommendation, framing it in such a way that the members of the committee retain confidence in their own purpose.

This does not mean that a Managing Director or other senior executive should not serve as chairman of a committee, but that, if he does so, he must inevitably be a sort of "Jekyll and Hyde", and separate his role as chairman from his executive position. From the chair he will have to submit to his executive self, with seriousness and conviction, a recommendation which he knows he will have to turn down. Any executive serving as chairman or as member of a committee which has a role participating in management action has sooner or later to face up to this problem: he can put forward arguments for or against a proposition during discussions, but he cannot accept from the committee instructions *ipso facto* for executive action; these can come only from his own executive superior. In practice, a manager may often find it possible to carry out a course of action suggested by a committee on which he is serving, but only because he knows that it is in line with policy and general plans, that it comes within his jurisdiction, and that it would have his senior executive's support. In principle, therefore, this does not constitute accepting an executive instruction from the committee. Nor is the chairman of the committee held in an artificial executive capacity.

On the more detailed plane, another of the chairman's important functions is to ensure that there is good committee procedure, a matter in which he is materially aided by appointing a competent secretary.

4. Mechanics

Of first importance to the "mechanics" of any committee is the selection of a competent secretary with a sound management approach to his administrative duties. He will be responsible for seeing that proceedings are adequately prepared in the form of notification of meeting, agenda and supporting papers—the latter distributed enough in advance to permit of some pre-digestion, and presented with adequate clarity and brevity to ensure absorption and understanding. How frequently have meetings gone adrift because members have become confused over page and paragraph references in a lengthy document which is the supposed basis of weighty deliberations! Again, a seemingly trivial point of practical common sense, but one on which experience has all too frequently and unfortunately necessitated emphasising the warning! As a main rule it can be said that agenda and supporting papers should be framed with a primary consideration for saving the committee's time and supporting the chairman's direction of its proceedings. Much the same approach is called for in the other half of the secretary's documentation task—the preparation of the record or minutes of the meetings. Essentially these should be a brief and businesslike record of ground covered, major points considered, conclusions reached and recommendations decided. To attempt any record of what was *said* during the session can only result in lengthy documentation and much reduce the effectiveness of the minutes.

There are other important mechanics in regard to the timing and arrangement of meetings. Wherever possible, it is an advantage to pre-plan meetings on a quarterly or even a yearly basis so that there can be plenty of advance notice. The danger of letting a meeting be held when there is no real business to transact must be recognised, particularly in the case of "standing committees", and at all sessions proceedings should be kept down to limited duration consistent with adequate deliberation: lengthy sessions induce fatigue and staleness even among committee members! Two useful methods of preventing undue rambling are the issue of a "timed" agenda (i.e. the chairman's suggestion of how long might be allotted to each item) or the tactful timing of a meeting at such an hour as will ensure a desire among members to bring proceedings to a close. Effective use of sub-committees for the pre-digestion of special items is important and can often be an effective means of reducing deliberations.

In the case of a standing or long-continuing committee, provision should be made for change of membership to accord with any change of purpose, and when its task is completed, its existence should be formally discontinued or its proceedings suspended.

The physical environment of meetings can be important for successful working, especially the absence of extraneous noise or interruption, and the presence of plenty of good fresh air. "Hot air" can be ruinous to a committee physically as well as metaphorically.

Apart from his general role of assisting the chairman and members to arrange and conduct their proceedings in the most effective and economical ways possible, the secretary also has certain specific responsibilities arising from his office. Two of these are particularly important to the pursuit of a committee's objectives. In the first place, it is the secretary on whom falls the active responsibility for ensuring that "action" or other "follow up" from proceedings takes place as agreed. True, it is within the chairman's overall responsibility to be concerned about these as much as about other aspects of his committee's tasks, but he expects to rely on the secretary as his main *aide* in this matter. "Follow up" may become a routine consideration in the preparation of agenda for ensuing meetings; if the secretary is normally systematic and methodical in the recording of proceedings, there is little special problem involved in pursuing items for which subsequent report and reference will be required. "Action" to be taken on agreement in committee is similarly assisted: the secretary can have an "action" note flagged in the margin of the minutes, with the name of the individual to whom responsibility has been entrusted. This *aide-memoire* is of best practical value when minutes are issued promptly after meetings. In any case, the secretary will probably contact members, when preparing his papers for ensuing meetings, to ascertain whether completion of the action will be reported or whether reasons for delay may have to be offered. If a committee is one from which numerous items of action arise, being entrusted to various members, the secretary may see fit to have a further record of his own, in order to ensure continuing check on action remaining outstanding over perhaps lengthy periods: something as simple as a duplicate set of minutes in which each "action" decision is consecutively numbered and crossed through in colour when reported completed; the secretary's own agenda papers would contain his personal reminder of items (numbers) outstanding at any one time.

The second matter to which the secretary must attend is the circulation of minutes or reports of a committee's deliberations to persons who are not members but are deemed by the committee as needing to be informed. A matter of principle or policy arises here to which the committee should have given attention as the basis of the instruction to the secretary to make the circulation. (An individual set of minutes need not be separately sent to each such outside person, but two or three sets marked for circulation on rota; location and other physical factors may have to determine what method is used.) In principle, the circulation of minutes or record to persons who are "interested" but who are not members of a given committee can be a useful medium for restricting size of membership. Experience has repeatedly shown that persons are nominated to serve on some committees because their role requires them to be "in the know", but may not necessarily make them specific contributors to the objectives of the committee. A mechanism for keeping such persons "informed" of progress could obviate their active participation in normal membership, while leaving open a case for occasional attendance when particularly relevant.

Mechanics of committee procedure are often thought of as trivial; in fact, they can do much to hinder or promote effective committee performance and achievement.

The growing scale of industrial and business activity, with growing complexity, and increasing resort to specialisation of function within any organisation, makes the problems of co-ordination and communication increasingly difficult at the same time as it lays emphasis on their importance. Much can be done by means of circulated information—though very serious and expensive dangers are latent in this method—and some reliance can be placed on incidental individual contact. There is no doubt at all about the fact that systematic meetings or committees can be a valuable instrument of co-ordination and communication in management, with a potentially high contribution to executive morale as well, if they are effectively constituted and conducted. No other mechanism can afford anything like the same opportunity for reciprocal relationships in deliberation or so ready a means of open and harmonious communication. It is a mistaken and short-sighted attitude to condemn committees as such solely by reason of unfortunate past experience. Training in the requirements of effective conduct can be as valuable a facet of "management development" as any other.

BIBLIOGRAPHY

A STANDARD handbook of committee constitution and procedure, which also includes many aspects of the legal position of committees in public service, is:

The Conduct of and Procedure at Public, Company and Local Government Meetings, by T. P. E. Curry (19th Edition, 1956), (published by Jordan & Sons, London).

Very useful in regard to the more everyday aspects of committee practice and the attitude of members are the following two studies of more informal character:

1. *So You're Going to a Meeting!* by Sir Walter Puckey (Maxwell Love, London, 1956).
2. *Be Sure You Agree*, by R. W. Bell (Allen & Unwin, London, 1960).

There is also another comprehensive handbook published in Australia under the title *Practical Chairmanship, Public Speaking, Committees and Group Procedures*, by T. M. Hunt (Rydge's *Business Journal*, Sydney).

CHAPTER VII

CRITERIA OF SUCCESS

To know how he is doing, what progress he is making, is naturally enough a question of major interest and importance to any manager. The nature of his role enjoins on him a responsibility for directing operations to an expected outcome in terms of goods and services, accompanied by a net result in terms of profit or of break-even with target costs; his responsibility, exercised through judgment and decision, can be effective only if his "direction" is continuously or recurrently tested by the achievement that it attains. Such a statement is no more than a circumlocutory way of pointing out that the "twin" elements of planning and control are inherent in the process of management itself. Success may be a grandiose term to apply to a Departmental Manager who meets his target of the week's planned output, or to an office supervisor who does not exceed the quarter's budgeted expenditure on staff and yet keeps work up to date. Yet the description would be correct; both managers have been "successful" in fulfilling the tasks allotted to their responsibility —as much successful as the company chairman who receives warm adulation for announcing to his shareholders a final dividend larger than anticipated by reason of an excellent year. In fact, it could be more precisely correct to refer to those two managers' "success", because it has been their own management effort which has accomplished the satisfactory achievement, whereas the chairman may well be no more than the figurehead of a team of senior managers to whom really belongs the credit for wise direction. This is not a comment to minimise the importance of "success" or to deny its right at times to have capital letters in the management context. On the contrary, the need is to underline the manager's interest in his accomplishment, though perhaps to suggest that a more analytical approach might be beneficial, and that more realistic factors might be sought than those in which the glamorous success is customarily couched. The search for effective and accepted criteria of the measurement of management achievement has been long, if somewhat spasmodic and superficial, and it has not yet itself been crowned with successful outcome. Generally speaking, commercial opinion has been content to rely on simple criteria, from the standpoint both of the enterprise or business as a whole and of the individual manager within it. For the former, the customary short answer is that the criterion of success is shown in the profits of the company or firm; in the case of the individual manager, the short answer sees success in a subjective appraisal of known achievement in physical terms or an equally subjective personal appraisal by his boss. In neither case is the short answer adequate, though the former has, of course, a great deal of support through widespread acceptance and long-standing usage in the business world—the profit position has long been taken to reflect the successful outcome of management competence applied from top levels in overall direction of activities.

There is, inevitably, in this problem another personal facet, the attitude of the individual manager towards his own progress in a given position and his own advancement by promotion to bigger responsibilities. Being human, the manager cannot do other than look for an assessment of "success" in personal terms; how is he himself doing?—in his own assessment of performance on the job? in the eyes of his superior? in fulfilment of known or latent ambitions? in relation to possible selection for promotion? as a basis for possible salary increase? as the steps in the furtherance of a full career? For many men, this personal facet of progress is the driving force of their own skilful and forward-looking management action. There are, of course, persons who can seek a good level of accomplishment for its own sake, without particular heed to its repercussions in personal advancement; but these, too, draw personal benefit in most cases in terms of salary and promotion, even if not specifically sought. The interrelation of the personal and professional factors and forces are inescapable in the management role, just as much as it is inescapable in many other fields of human endeavour. In the industrial and commercial world, this identification of personal advancement with professional achievement leads many managers to accept, and even to welcome, formulæ of appointment which include in their remuneration an element of "payment by results"—frequently expressed in terms of a bonus on the departmental performance or on the year's results, or perhaps a share in the profits of the unit, or a percentage increment depending upon annual progress. Many managers welcome even more an opportunity of participating in the share-holding, if they are near the top of the business, and can contribute to their personal benefit in capital appreciation by the medium of their effective application of management skill.

FACETS OF ACHIEVEMENT

The personal outcome may well be a factor in the stimulus to achievement, but it cannot of itself be the realistic criterion of success. Other items of accomplishment must be sought, and it seems that the following four could be examined:

(i) The fulfilment of the objectives of the unit or enterprise.
(ii) The extent of economical and effective operation.
(iii) The attainment of satisfactions by the people employed.
(iv) The overall profitability of the enterprise.

1. *The Achievement of Purpose*

In the world of industrial and commercial affairs, "purpose" is expressed in terms of making and selling certain goods in the capital or consumer fields or of providing services whether physical or intangible. Accordingly, the satisfaction of the consumer is a pertinent criterion for assessing achievement of purpose. At once a difficulty emerges, because there is no known means of realistically measuring or determining consumer satisfaction. The economist would argue, with some justification, that the continuing success of the enterprise is itself a guide, because if the consumer were not consistently or recurrently satisfied with the goods and services offered, he would not continue to purchase them and in consequence the organisation would, through diminution in trading, eventually disappear in bankruptcy. This argument must in broad terms be true, even though at times the customer is having to "make do" with what is available to him rather than feel genuinely satisfied; it is usually artificial conditions which lead to this situation (e.g. wartime shortages), for otherwise the unsatisfied demand would tempt other manufacturers into the market in an endeavour to benefit from coming close to consumer requirements. Protagonists of market assessment techniques have argued that by questionnaire, opinion sampling, and other similar methods, it is possible to obtain a picture of consumer reactions and to throw up a guide to the achievement of satisfaction. The proof of the contention is regularly found in the techniques of consumer research accompanying the test launching of many products—foodstuffs, detergents, cosmetics, household equipment, etc. If no precise measurement is attained, at least firm views can be formed as to whether consumer reaction and satisfaction justify the main launch of the new article.

Combining the economic and the market arguments does afford to the top management of companies an important item in the assessment of their success in conducting the business, and one to which they know they must give best possible attention. In time, it may prove practicable to develop more precise and more reliable measures of customer reaction: further progress with the use of computers, especially if supported by the availability of cheaper machines, could improve the speed with which, and the detail in which, the results of consumer surveys are presented and so improve the assessment of satisfaction. Yet even among managements who would challenge the reliability of a data approach, there would be ready recognition of the significance of the concept of customer satisfaction. This is what is really implied by the loosely used slogan "the customer is always right". In the case of public companies, this is a matter to which attention is often given by the chairman at the Annual General Meeting of shareholders. However fully he concentrates on telling the shareholders the good profit figures that his leadership has attained, he will mostly also find time to emphasise how much the directors continue to have the interests of customers at heart, and to explain any developments which are resulting in better products, or better service, or lower prices. He expects, and finds in most cases, that the shareholders applaud his statements and support the objectives that they present. Admittedly, this is because the shareholders recognise their own beneficiary position from the continued good trading and goodwill accumulated in the customers. They are, however, recognising their own dependence on the customers, on the market, and are tacitly or overtly accepting the basic economic principle that a commercial enterprise finds its first objective in the contributions that it is making to the available supply of goods and services needed and wanted by the community.

The criterion of achievement of purpose, reflected where relevant in these customer satisfactions, draws greater pertinence from the fact that it is in direct association with policy. As the foundation of management in practice, *policy* sets the objectives and the lines of direction, and it is thus appropriate that management should deliberately seek to review its own success, at least in part, in terms of measuring accomplishment against the policy that it set out to pursue. At times, there will be circumstances which produce a negative outcome; in many trades it is a known thing that fashion can change quickly, or that external influences (for example, weather) can induce sudden and dramatic falls in demand. Loss of customer satisfaction would not in such conditions represent a failure on the part of management; but it does present to them an indication of a need for a change in product on a running down of the affected item until the pertinent circumstances return. Such influences lead to review of product policy, to diversification, to search for new markets —all of which imply a renewed endeavour to attain the successful standing in terms of consumer satisfaction.

Whatever other criteria are adopted, it remains not only valid but necessary that management should review its operations and their outcome in terms of achievement of purpose; and if it becomes possible to find a formula for factual assessment, so much the better. While this criterion is being thought of primarily in terms of the enterprise as a whole, it does have relevance within the sections or departments into which management is subdivided; but it tends here to merge into the more factual field of checking attainment and performance against predetermined targets, plans and budgets.

2. Economical and Effective Operations

In turning to this second basis of assessment of success, the criterion becomes one which reflects fulfilment of the purpose of management as delegated within the structure of responsibility of the particular organisation concerned. This is an assessment which applies equally whatever the field of endeavour in which the management is operating: for example, manufacturing, marketing, selling, administration or accounting. It is an assessment of concern to each individual manager as well as to management as a whole. The assessments of achievement or the criteria of success, in this second line of approach, are something reflecting in large measure the attainment of results in the specific individual areas of operation delegated to each manager or specialist established within the organisation concerned. There are two bases of assessment; one that is broadly subjective, and one that is factual. The subjective aspect lies in the correctness and competence with which the manager or officer fulfils his tasks or discharges his responsibilities, covering the main items that are entrusted to his jurisdiction by delegation and are summarised in *his* application of the management process in action. The assessment can be made by himself, to reassure himself that he is living up to his responsibilities at a level that maintains self-esteem in the best of professional traditions. The assessment can be made also by his superior manager, and *should* be so made in the normal course of senior management responsibility: this aspect will come up for further consideration in the following Chapter. Even in making the personal appraisal, however, both the individual manager and his superior will have recourse to the second, or factual, basis of assessment, because it is interwoven with the practice of management itself. This factual aspect is represented in the "control data" or management information by which continuing operations are checked for effectiveness against target, plan and budget: the matter now becomes one to be considered in terms of the subject-headings in Parts One, Two and Four above. Without risking any detailed recapitulation, it is pertinent to recall that *sound management action starts* with the setting of standards and targets which are woven into plans on the basis of a pattern reflecting or paralleling the delegation of responsibility. The plans, formulated into operating programmes, become embodied in budgets of resources to be used and expenditures to be incurred. Against these, in the course of operations, performance data show the actual position and progress, and so reflect a pertinent and reliable measure of the effectiveness of the delegated responsibility. In a well-founded organisation it is a normal feature of management action that there is a recurrent comparison of performance against plan, of actual expenditure against budget, just as there is a critical review of the targets and budgets themselves, in order to ensure that they recurrently represent a correct factual basis in terms of changing circumstances. Because, according to their level of responsibility, individual managers have taken their part in formulating or approving the standards and targets, and in framing their programme of activity with its accompanying appropriate budget of expenditure, *they* are correctly assessed on the basis of performance against these standards. Their own daily management role will ensure their being alive to changes in circumstances and to the incidence of influences affecting performance, and they are thus readily able to explain "variances" in terms of factual evidence instead of in terms of self-justification or self-excuse. *It is an essential responsibility in the role of senior management to promote this critical review of performance and progress, and to encourage in all subordinate managers an attitude of mind that will see in it an important facet of their own management skill.* By including recurrent appraisal of the targets themselves, senior management can emphasise the objectivity of the review, though there must be no suggestion of instability or frequent change of budgets for minor changes of conditions: there is a systematic technique of "flexible budgeting" which can ensure correct alignment.

Criteria of success in terms of achievement of effective and economical operations do not, therefore, necessarily call for special data or additional information techniques; they are made apparent in the normal course of management action, through the medium of the normal procedures of management accounting information. There is, however, one important facet in the design of such procedures if they are to serve this objective adequately—they must inter-relate with and reflect the various levels and divisions of delegated responsibility. To be effective as criteria of success, performance data must readily show the results of decisions taken in a given and known area of executive (or specialist) responsibility. This is the obverse of the comment just made about the responsible participation of a manager in the formulation of the budget for his own area of jurisdiction, an aspect that needs to be taken into account when an organisation structure is being created or re-formed by the definition of responsibilities. The delegation of responsibility (as was emphasised in the Introduction (see page 43)) imparts authority for decision and for the corresponding expenditure to make the decision effective. Budget and control data must, therefore, correlate with the pattern or delegation reflecting the varying extents or grades of responsibility for decision. In technical jargon this maxim is sometimes referred to as "making the budgetary (or cost) centres conform with definitions of responsibilities". Additionally to such normal arrangement of data procedures, there could be occasions when specific supplementary information is called for, perhaps of a diagnostic character or in the form of analytical appraisal of proposals. This is a kind of statistical information that customarily supports a recommendation for a factory extension, or for the introduction of a new product in a range. The decision to be taken is supported by a forecast of expected results—the efficacy of the decision can subsequently be tested against the estimates submitted with the proposal. Sampling statistics or techniques of operation research may sometimes be used as a more systematic tool for arriving at the likely results from a decision, and once again the criterion of its soundness is seen in the actual results compared in due course with the forecast "model".

Within the broad framework of assessing executive success in terms of effective and economical performance, there is an approach of a somewhat different kind sometimes used. This is in the form of what is described as a "management audit", that is to say, a critical appraisal and review going beyond the everyday data of management accounting into an overall examination of the executive process in action. It should cover the extent and effectiveness of the pattern of delegation, the channels of communication, the harmony of co-ordination, the adequacy or otherwise of tools of planning and control, the skill in the usage of management data as a guide to remedial decision, and, in general, the competence of the executive, supervisory and specialist teams. An "audit" of this kind has at times been conducted from within a company—for example, by a small panel of two or three experienced senior managers undertaking a systematic review of the different departments or sections. Difficulties of prejudice and personal relationship present obvious dangers in such an arrangement, and these may be obviated by having the "audit" conducted from outside, for example, by professional Management Consultants—which is, in fact, often done. In the case of the nationalised industries something of a comparable kind is from time to time conducted by specially appointed committees.

The effectiveness of any criteria relating to management performance in the sense indicated here depends very much on the sincerity and objectivity of the managers themselves concerned: they must have in their attitude the basic principle of *genuinely seeking not to delude themselves*, starting from the standpoint that the only reason for the existence of management is to attain economical and effective performance of operations in line with policy, and to strive for progress in attainment.

3. The Contentment of the People Employed.

It could be argued that, because of the extent to which the effectiveness and economy of operations are influenced by the morale of the people composing the organisation, there is no case for a criterion in terms of social factors like personal contentment. The level of morale, i.e. the contentment of the people employed, will be reflected in the operating standards, in the cost levels, and in the financial results as a whole. On the other hand, management is by essence a social process, and this should be ample justification of itself for specifying a human or social factor in the criterion of its proficiency. The earlier consideration of the "social responsibilities of management" pointed to customary neglect of this facet hitherto, with a markedly changing climate of opinion recently apparent. There would today be little opposition to the view that a manager has also to prove his human skills, if he is to be judged successful. This aspect of attainment applies not only to rank-and-file personnel employed at the operating levels, but equally to the subordinate managers and supervisors themselves, though admittedly it is the former that are mostly thought of. In either case, this is a criterion for which measurement is impossible and assessment difficult. Yet, some endeavours can be made at least to obtain guides, and experience has shown that the following are broadly useful:

(a) *The factual position in regard to labour turnover.* What is involved in labour turnover and how it can be measured is a matter discussed in Part Three above. Its incidence can at times be seen as a reflection of management skill in securing contentment among the people employed. Case studies have shown most unsatisfactory positions; for example, a small firm in a specialised engineering field, having a measured labour turnover of rather more than 100 per cent. over a twelve-month period; this means, in effect, that in the course of the year the equivalent of everybody employed had found their employment uncongenial for one reason or another. There are occasions where external factors give rise to high levels of labour turnover, but it can be taken as a fairly reliable guide that, in the absence of any such identifiable external factors, high levels point to some lack of skill in the human aspects of management. Typical figures in this matter can be dangerous rather than helpful, but over many years of normal industrial conditions, labour turnover levels in the order of 25 per cent. per annum among men and 40 per cent. per annum among women have been found useful as break-points suggesting closer diagnosis. Below these levels, labour turnover could be regarded as normal, and need not be further pursued; but, in the absence of of specific factors, a higher percentage of turnover should call for investigation.

(b) *The turnover rate among managerial personnel* can also be an important pointer to management incompetence. In some respects, this could be a more significant diagnostic tool than the turnover rate among ordinary employees. Here, of course, figures and percentages have no meaning at all, and one has to assess solely in terms of the factual position of instability among the management team. If it is found, for example, that managers at intermediate or higher levels are not content to stay more than a year or two in a company, and that accordingly there is a considerable inflow and outflow among members of the management team, it can be taken as a pretty fair indication that something is amiss in the human relations skills at the higher levels. The contrary, however, cannot be taken for granted, i.e. that stability in this respect necessarily means good standards of social skill; the situation may well be one in which special conditions (for example, high salary scales) are operating to keep managers stable despite personal dissatisfaction.

(c) *Personal attitudes* can be assessed and it should be possible for a management which is objectively keen to appraise its own achievement to arrive at a realistic view of the contentment of the people working under its jurisdiction. For many years, it has been possible to have this contentment measured in a reasonable way by what is known as an "Attitude Survey" conducted by teams of specialists from outside. Such a Survey can be carried out in respect of rank-and-file personnel or among managers—in this latter case perhaps within the framework of a management audit. It has long been known that two broad factors will reflect contentment or discontent, namely, the extent to which grievances are expressed, particularly about trivial matters and the readiness with which suggestions are put forward. In an organisation with a high degree of contentment, grievances will be aired only if they are serious; frequency of complaints of a minor kind is mostly indicative of latent discontent. This is a topic which has been more fully reviewed in Part Three.

4. Profitability

In this concept may be said to lie the normally accepted criteria of management success, though it is not entirely free of controversy. On the professional plane, argument has raged on the question of what the true meaning of "profit" is, and how it has to be reckoned: such argument persists, for example, between the accountants and the economists, as to how depreciation and obsolescence of plant should be treated, or how stocks and work in progress should be valued, in order to arrive at a true assessment of "profit". Outside such legitimate differences of professional opinion, the argument moves on to an entirely different plane, the serious consideration of the true importance of "profit" is much bedevilled by misconceptions in the heat of popular argument. A broad point of view, on the one hand, is expressed in the notion that profit is the due return to the owners or shareholders of the business in respect of their venture in the investment. At the other end of the scale, there is the view that profit represents unearned income, not, strictly speaking, deserved. This latter view is, of course, deeply embedded in radical politics, and the concept of the profitability of an enterprise as a criterion of success is seriously overshadowed by prejudices arising from areas of social philosophy, professing to find unsavoury the idea of an unearned profit, accruing to (presumably wealthy) owners. The political concept attaching to such philosophy sees *all* the outcome of industrial effort as earned by the "workers", and, while there may be some allowance for legitimate interest on borrowed capital, this view holds that all further increment should belong to the "workers" or to the "community"—it should certainly not go just to the "owners". In terms of the industrial scene of up to the mid-19th century, there could have been some realism in these views while the general pattern of industrial and commercial enterprise found its expression in the normal form of a one-man business or the small private company; in either case the capital and the impetus to progress coming from the one individual or the few in whom "ownership" was vested. At any later period of economic history, however, such a concept could have little validity even on the political plane, because of the extent to which the continuing economic progress of society has been dependent upon recurring investment of capital from wide sources, including much from the public purse; it is also relevant to underline the extent to which the earnings from industry have become dependent upon the progress of mechanisation and technology as the fruit of capital expenditure devoted to knowledge in no way related to the effort of labour. All anti-profit notions go back to earlier phases of the industrial revolution: the origins of consumers' co-operatives in the 1830s and 1840s were as much an anti-profit force as were the ideas and ideals on national ownership fifty or a hundred years later.

These radical views confuse the *earning of individual profit* with *the assessment of profitability* of the activity. This latter notion has to be admitted even in the enterprises which are themselves so organised that there is no individual profit motive—for example, the retail Co-operative Societies have to be "profitable", so that they can not only finance their continuing growth, but also pay a dividend to their members. The nationalised industries are required by constitution to break even taking one year with another, after providing for charges on capital and for investment required for future growth. These socio-philosophical points of view need not be pursued further in the present context, though they are matters which should be adequately understood by managers, because of the influence which they exert in many aspects of labour relations in contemporary British industry. That they are outmoded by the factual progress of society has, unfortunately, not entirely diminished their emotional significance among organised labour movements.

In itself, however, the notion of "profitability" calls for more serious consideration.

ANALYSIS OF PROFITABILITY

The basic principle of private enterprise is the constitution of a business directed to earning profit for the person or group of persons who have founded it, whether or not they participate actively in the conduct of the enterprise. Speaking in general terms, the profit that is earned from the enterprise can be regarded as a return in respect of one or more of the following things:

(a) Earnings on the capital invested, equivalent at least to what could be attained if that capital were invested in gilt-edged securities.

(b) Earnings from the mere fact of taking up participation in a venture which is not an investment in a gilt-edged situation, but inherently involves some element of venture or risk.

(c) Earnings which reflect the extent of risk, greater or less, over and above the mere act of taking a venture.

(d) Earnings reflecting application of the judgment or the flair of the entrepreneur in strict commercial terms.

(e) Earnings which can be seen as a reward for the managerial skills exercised in conducting the enterprise successfully.

(f) Earnings which are, in effect, payment for time and attention devoted to directing, conducting or actively participating in the enterprise.

The whole series of these six items would be applicable in the case of profits accruing to the owners only if they were *personally* engaged, with their private means and with their time, in the pursuit and conduct of the enterprise—for example, a small firm with two or three principals all of whom are engaged full-time or part-time as directors, managers or advisors in the firm, not paying themselves any other remuneration as part of the operating expense. The principle of limited liability in joint stock enterprises has brought into the situation two major changes which would make the six above items *never* applicable in total. The first change is that the monetary liability of the investing shareholder is limited to the amount of capital which is represented by his purchase of shares and thus his profit is related only to items (a) and (c) in the above group. Secondly, shareholders who are active partners have their earnings in respect of items (b) and (c) limited to a return on the amount of capital of their investment, irrespective of the extent of the risk involved, because they no longer have the involvement of personal possessions outside the nominally invested capital. Items (d), (e) and (f) have no bearing at all on the shareholders as such; they apply only to owners who are employed as full-time or part-time managerial or advisory members (as well as to the professional managers and advisors themselves, apart from the shareholders): this remuneration is, therefore, regarded more correctly as a payment for services rendered or for skills supplied; the "profit" element arises only if bonus arrangements are established related to the overall profit position.[1]

One of the major phenomena of the economic scene in any industrial country in recent years has been the widespread growth of companies with shares available for public purchase and the corresponding spectacular increase in share ownership as a normal medium of savings, replacing even in the middle strata of society the traditional thrift channels of savings banks, building societies, and government loans. (The "unit trust" movement is for this purpose only an alternative form of share ownership.) This development has necessarily sharpened public interest in "company results" to such an extent that the city pages of the national press have become popular reading. In this context, "profits" and "management success" have become uncritically interwoven: there is undoubtedly a factor of "profitability" which is a sound criterion of management success, but this is not the "profit" as shown as the outcome of the year in a company's Profit and Loss Account. The latter is influenced by far too many extraneous facts: the attainment of profit *may* be a return for good judgment in the conduct of the enterprise, but it may equally be an accident of forces entirely outside the responsibility of the directors. It is the task of directors and management in a given trading business to apply resources to a programme of manufacturing and marketing: the prices which their product can earn are deter-

---

[1] The point has been made by some people that an employee in a business, whether he is employed as a manager or as an operative, in fact takes a greater degree of venture in accepting the post than does the shareholder; the latter ventures a certain sum of money (presumably related to what he is prepared to part with for the time being), whereas the man who takes employment in a business ventures his livelihood and his career, for the failure of the business may have very significant repercussions on the rest of his life far beyond the mere fact of losing this particular employment.

It is also pertinent in this context to refer to the fact that an important element of "profit" accrues to owners of shares through capital appreciation attained in the form of the "gains" from the sale of the shares at the enhanced values.

mined by the economic forces of the market, and the skill of management judgment lies in their endeavour to assess what these levels of
price will be in relation to the type of product they are offering, its
quality, its availability, etc. The prices they can expect to get are *not*
determined by the summation of their own costs, however skilfully
they analyse the items of expenditure which they have to pay out to
enable the product to be made available on the market. The prices
earned are determined by the market judgment of the commodity
relative to other similar commodities offered by other suppliers, as
well as relative to other ways of spending the equivalent money. In
this sense, it would not be unrealistic to regard all expenditure or
investment in the facilities of manufacturing and marketing products
as "fixed costs", to be employed to best marginal advantage.
Management has then the task of seeking to keep these facilities employed to maximum advantage against minimum of expense, and to
promote the outcome of the best possible continuing sales at the best
possible prices, leaving a margin over and above the total expenditure in any given period. This is the margin known as "profit".

   *What the management does with the profit earned is an entirely
different matter.* It could pass this on to the consumer in the form of
lower prices for the product or of special discounts, or perhaps in
better quality, better pack, better service. It could, equally, pass it on
indirectly through the medium of expending it on better equipment
or on more research and development which will eventually lead to
an improved range of products or services. Equally, the management
could pass the profit on to all or to some of the personnel that it
employs in different categories in the form of higher wages or special
bonuses. Again, it can divert the profit to communal ends by paying
out more in taxes or voting it for local purposes, for donations to
Universities, for charitable gifts to various institutions. Finally,
management can use up the earned margins by paying them out as
(higher) profits to the owners of the business as individuals or as
shareholders. So far as "profitability" is concerned as a criterion of
management success, what is done with the profit earned is *not* an
important feature. The important point is: how does it arise? If it
comes because of accidental and unexpected market or socio-
economic forces, then management can regard itself as being "lucky"
rather than successful. The circumstances of the last few years in
most Western European countries have seen many fortuitous circumstances of this kind, with large amounts of profits earned without
any real judgment or skill on the part of management, other than the
basic one of being in that kind of business at all. Even that may not
be truly a matter of judgment, but of a luck of inheritance or the
windfall of a chance—a situation which has been illustrated by a

number of long-established foodstuffs and household goods suddenly finding the favour of public fashion. Many people argue that the early fortunes made in the initiation of commercial television in Britain were fortuitous in this sense, rather than genuine business judgment. Profit can and does arise from true foresight or acumen in the decision to enter a particular industry about which there are deemed to be reasonable expectations, but which still entail a large measure of venture or gamble in order to attain success: commodities like ballpoint pens, certain semi-soft drinks, and a number of household appliances for kitchen use during the past decade or so are illustrations, a proportion of the success being fortuitous as a gamble, though possibly to be anticipated. At quite the other extreme, management could take time and trouble to assess the economic situation in which it is working, to study the trends of social progress and consumer habits, to review technological factors, and, taking advantage of such known developments, effectively to lay down plans, skilfully directing operations to accomplish those plans. The profit arising from this set of circumstances could legitimately be described as *earned* by management and the "profitability" is thus a true criterion of management success. This would entail also effective internal planning and control action to ensure that the skills in market judgment have not been negatived by inefficiencies of operations, involving wasteful expenditure. Profitability as a criterion of success thus reflects the *combined skill of sound management (economic) judgment and effective management (executive) action.*

How much of the "success" is to be ascribed to either facet of this combination is not in general terms important, though it could be important in specific cases. Where, for instance, raw material costs are high, the economic judgment factors in management's skill of purchasing could far outweigh all influence of internal executive action in attaining good profitability. Or again, where large-scale manufacturing equipment makes the fixed production expense high, the economic judgment experienced in competent marketing to maintain high volume, and consequently an effective utilisation of the plant, could be the critical factor assuring profitable outcome. So long as management is being looked at in terms of *individual* responsibilities, these specific facets of the process will predominate differently in different circumstances. Looking at the overall process of management, however, it is the *combinations of the facets* that need to be emphasised. In differing degrees the two facets of economic judgment and effective executive action are present in *all* managerial responsibilities, and skills in both are called for if management is to be competent and successful. Within the normal pattern of the organisation structure of an industrial or commercial company, the skills will be variously disposed in line with the delegation of responsibilities, and the major decisions leading to trading operations by the company as such will inevitably result from an integrated pattern of contributory decisions stemming from within the delegations. The profitable outcome attained—or the failure of losses, if that should be the result— is, therefore, the criterion of *achievement of all the contributing judgments*. At any one time or in any one situation, one phase or section of the management *may* have been more responsible for the result, but this may be difficult to assess comparatively and may certainly not be worth attempting to appraise on any such comparative basis beyond what the divisional or functional data show as performance against budget. The overall assessment of success can be attained through effective schemes of management information as referred to above, and their design could be such as to give the essential minimum of guidance as to respective participation, in so far as this is needed.

There is a relative significance of the two facets of economic judgment and executive action in regard to management development, and this will be referred to in the following Chapter.

THE JUSTIFICATION OF PROFIT

The burden of thought in an earlier section of this Chapter might well suggest that this is a contentious caption! But there is no intention of entering here into the lists of the philosophers or sociologists, and still less of the politicians. There is a basic economic problem to be considered which is certainly pertinent to the present context. Quite apart from any reference to its significance as income to the owners of an enterprise, profit has a factual position in the economic system: it is one of the means of keeping an industrial or commercial activity in being, for it provides the wherewithal to "plough back" resources for the furtherance of the activity. On a rough-and-ready definition, profit may be seen as the difference between the income from the activity in any given period and the expenses incurred in providing the activity in that period. (Such a generalisation begs an awful lot of very big questions, and can be reduced to nonsense by many accounting considerations, but it can suffice for the present purpose.) If the expenses outweigh the income, the profit is, of course, negative—i.e. losses. With a positive profit, there are contributions available to plough-back in maintaining the invested assets intact (though this could be legitimately regarded as an item among the "expenses" of the activity) and in further developing the assets for better performance in future periods. The development could be technical, for example, by means of research to improve quality of products or to enhance the technological standards of the manufacturing equipment. The development could also be economic, for example opening up new markets or improving channels of trading. It could also be directly concerned with the advancement of management standards, for example, by the better training of Managers for promotion. If resources to meet these objectives of progress and vitality are not earned from the current activity through profit, the existing business must remain stagnant, and improvements can be sought only on the basis of new capital added to pay for them. There could be economic arguments to justify this approach, but they are valid only if an economic system is to be thought of as *essentially static*. Such a notion is probably wrong in principle, in so far as all human history has shown a seemingly inherent urge to the betterment of the society. The pattern of economic structure is probably correctly thought of as a rising spiral, such that the completion of a cycle of activity implies that the beginning of the next cycle is at a higher plane. The attainment of this upswing would thus be essentially dependent on the availability of resources to lift the activity from each notional cycle to the next. This is, of course, the essence of "ploughing back earnings for maintaining vitality and progress". It is also the essential justification for striving after profits.

Perhaps it would be more accurate—in the light of the distinction drawn above—to say that it is the justification of "profitability" as the objective of management.

Whichever term is used, the argument here can be supported by looking at the negative aspect. A business that is making "losses" is so conducting its operations that (as expressed in monetary terms) its input of resources is greater than the values recovered for its output. In other words it is wasting resources by using them to make available goods and services that the community is not prepared to take up at the prices asked. In the eyes of consumers, the resources would be better employed in the making and selling of other products and services—the ones where the support of demand enables profits to be earned.

This is indeed a superficial treatment of a subject of some considerable importance to managers, but any deeper pursuit would lead too far afield into a serious study of the principles of economics.

COMPARISONS OF ACHIEVEMENT

"Profitability," as the achievement of optimum outcome from minimum application of resources, has in a way, nothing to do with the owners or shareholders *as such*, because it is attained by the judgment and skills of the managers as such. This is the context in which "profitability" is to be seen as a more correct criterion of management success than is "profit" in the customary accounting sense of the term, and to that extent, appropriate management accounting information is more pertinent to express this criterion than is the normal presentation of an annual profit and loss account. It is of interest that a number of British industrial teams which studied American companies some years ago, under the auspices of the Anglo-American Council on Productivity, made particular point of the extent to which American enterprise uses systematic tools of management accounting as their criteria of control, reinforcing effective delegation and ensuring better measures of success. It becomes important to ensure that members of the management team are aware of their own contributions to this success by means of adequate information reflecting their participation in the co-ordinated attainment, and this can easily be made possible within the design of the data procedures, or by some simple periodic supplementary statements. One manufacturing company, for example, shows its sales performances and profits quarterly in a brief summary which relates the company's total figures in three different ways: in terms of Sales Districts (9), of Brand marketing teams (6) and of manufacturing establishments (4).

Dissatisfaction with the criterion of "profit" in the sense of the financial figures on the annual profit and loss account is reflected in British industry by the contemporary interest in "inter-firm comparisons". Profitability is seen on this basis in the form of comparative data reflecting management performance through factors which stand comparison between different establishments because they relate directly to executive decision. The widespread extent of the interest is emphasised by the creation of a national *Centre for Inter-firm Comparisons* to which firms contribute in a co-operative scheme affording objective comparative ratios, while ensuring a guarantee of confidence as to identity. The Centre describes its methods of working as follows: [1]

"*This is how it works:* Several firms contribute their figures confidentially to a common pool from which they receive in return a report which either shows (anonymously) the data of each individual contributor, or which presents figures indicating the average and the range of performance of all participants. The report usually contains explanations showing how the results should be interpreted; further help with interpretation can also be given to individual firms requiring it. Comparisons of this kind not only tell the manager whether

---

[1] These extracts and the tables on the following pages are quoted from a brochure with the permission of the Director of the Centre for Inter-firm Comparison, Ltd., London. A practical illustration of the application of inter-firm comparisons is set out at length in the report entitled "Efficiency Comparisons within Large Organisations", published by the Centre jointly with the British Institute of Management, London, January 1962.

the performance of his firm is as good as that of his competitors, but also reveal causes of difference in performance between his firm and that of others, and often indicate how it can be improved.

"What does the Centre do? The Centre—

—undertakes inter-firm comparisons by direct arrangement with individual firms;

—offers a special service to trade associations, acting on their behalf as a 'neutral' expert organisation for the conduct of inter-firm comparisons amongst their members, or providing consultancy services on methods of inter-firm comparison;

—carries out research aimed at making the best methods of inter-firm comparisons available to British industry and trade;

—runs seminars on management ratios and inter-firm comparison— some of a general nature, and others designed for particular industries and trades;

—offers its international connections to British firms wishing to compare their efficiency and costs with their opposite numbers in such countries as Germany, France, Switzerland, Holland, Belgium and the U.S.A."

The kind of comparative information prepared and circulated is illustrated by the two examples cited below: the first of these shows data in the form of ratios relating to one firm in two successive years, while the second table adds further data gathered from the figures of another 20 firms in the same industry.

TABLE I

Here are the figures of an Electrical Manufacturer:

	Ratios	Last Year	This Year
1.	Profit before tax / Assets employed · · · · · ·	16·8%	20·9%
2.	Profit before tax / Sales · · · · · ·	8·0%	9·5%
3.	Sales / Assets employed · · · · · ·	2·1	2·2
4.	Production cost of sales / Sales · · · · ·	76·0%	75·0%
5.	Cost of marketing and distribution / Sales · · ·	9·5%	9·5%
6.	Cost of administration / Sales · · · · ·	6·5%	6·0%
7.	Sales (at cost) / Average stocks · · · · · ·	3·9	4·0
8.	Average of outstanding debts / Average sales per day · · · ·	36·5 days	35·8 days

This looks like a success story ...

Return on capital employed has gone up from 16·8 to 20·9 due to an increase in the firm's profit on sales (ratio 2) and the better use it seems to have made of its assets (ratio 3). Higher profits on sales seem to have been achieved through operational improvements which resulted in lower cost-of-production and administration ratios (ratios 4 and 6). Current assets have been used more effectively as shown by ratios 7 and 8, which indicate that money tied up in stocks and debtors has been released for further profitable operations more quickly than in the previous year. But what a shock this firm is to get when it compares its ratios with those of others in the industry.

TABLE II

I Ratio	II Unit		III IV Figures of 20 firms of similar size and making similar products Last Year This Year		V VI Firm's own figures Last Year This Year	
1. Profit before tax / Assets employed	%	First Quartile*	14·5	19·0		
		Median*	25·5	31·5	16·8	20·9
		Third Quartile*	37·5	39·1		
2. Profit before tax / Sales	%	First Qu.	4·8	6·0		
		Median	7·5	9·0	8·0	9·5
		Third Qu.	11·0	13·2		
3. Sales / Assets employed	times	First Qu.	2·3	2·2		
		Median	3·4	3·5	2·1	2·2
		Third Qu.	4·1	4·0		
4. Production cost of sales / Sales	%	First Qu.	70·3	69·5		
		Median	75·4	74·5	76·0	75·0
		Third Qu.	81·3	80·2		
5. Cost of marketing and distribution / Sales	%	First Qu.	6·5	6·8		
		Median	8·9	8·8	9·5	9·5
		Third Qu.	10·9	11·1		
6. Cost of administration / Sales	%	First Qu.	3·4	3·9		
		Median	6·1	6·1	6·5	6·0
		Third Qu.	7·5	7·8		
7. Sales (at cost) / Average stocks (at cost)	times	First Qu.	3·2	3·0		
		Median	4·6	4·3	3·9	4·0
		Third Qu.	5·7	5·5		
8. Average of outstanding debts / Average sales per day	days	First Qu.	27·0	28·0		
		Median	33·0	34·0	36·5	35·8
		Third Qu.	38·0	39·0		

* What are quartiles and the median?

For each ratio the figures are listed in order of size from the lowest to the highest. The median is the figure which comes ½ way down the list. The first and third quartiles are the figures ¼ and ¾ down the list.

The median and quartiles are therefore figures of actual firms, but for each ratio it is very probable that they will be of different firms.

The three figures are given to provide an indication of the range of results.

This year the firm's return on capital is well below average, although last year's figures compared more favourably with the average of the industry.

What are the reasons for this unfavourable comparison? Our firm's profit ratio (ratio 2) is slightly better than average, but its turnover of capital (ratio 3) is well below average. Reasons for this are indicated by ratios 7 and 8 which show that our firm's stock turnover is below average and that the number of days in which debts are outstanding is higher than that of others in the industry.

Inter-firm comparison, however conducted, is but one phase of the complex problem of the "measurement of productivity". To the latter a great deal of attention has been given over the years by managers, by accountants, by consultants, by economists: unanimity has been reached only on the basic point that there is no simple formula for determining what "productivity" is, let alone for measuring it. In general terminology, the notion of productivity is easy to fix and it would not be seriously disputed: it means the net outcome in a given period from a given input of factors of production. This simple statement represents, of course, a summation of all that has been said in foregoing pages about the objectives of the management role—its command over the resources that are directed to the manufacturing and trading operations, and its responsibility for attaining from those resources the best possible outcome, all things considered. This latter proviso is important, because it may sometimes not be the case that the physical maximisation of output is of itself the best result from given operations; better qualities with restricted quantity, or more speedy availability, for example, may be preferred objectives in given circumstances.

The Measurement of Productivity

Why is there any need to attempt to measure productivity? The first answer has already been given in all the foregoing study of the management process in action: because the manager needs to know what results are accruing to his decisions and how soundly his judgment is being exercised. The measurement of productivity reveals that he is judging and deciding correctly, or shows that he is failing in some respects, or that circumstances are such as to frustrate the expected good outcome of his decisions. Productivity is to some extent measured by the control data or management information in showing actual performance and cost against the plans and targets set out in budgets. In this sense, a great deal of useful practical procedure is already known as a means of measuring productivity: this is, however, a loose approach which does not adequately reflect the true attainment of management decision in relation to its use of the factors of production, with all fortuitous circumstances removed or neutralised so that a genuine causal correlation can be established.

It is in this precise sense that the problem becomes complex and is as yet unresolved, despite the amount of attention that has been devoted to it, including international study groups and conferences.[1] Another reason for the endeavour to measure productivity is to secure the value of the pointer to opportunities for improvement of method, equipment, design, procedure, and management action itself. Hence the manager needs to have data that will reflect the various aspects of the activities falling under his jurisdiction. These can be summarised in terms of the economist's factors of production, or of the resources being applied in the industrial or commercial operations—land, labour, materials, equipment, and the money by which they are represented. Most of the factual studies so far carried out have been concerned with labour, in the assessment of the productivity of the manpower used in given manufacturing, handling and selling operations. The assessments are made over time to show the trend, and from one place to another because usually there is more than one unit where the same activities are conducted. In some cases, the studies are industry-wide, covering, for example, all the factories in the industry or within a certain region. Studies of even this seemingly simple order run into difficulties because of variations in the range or design of product, or changes in materials used (affecting either the physical volume of output or the methods of manufacture), or because of differences in equipment available to operatives. Neutralising steps are taken to overcome these complexities, so that it has been possible to arrive at "units per man-hour" which are directly comparable in terms of a notional "standard product" as between one period and another, or one factory and another. The manpower included in such an index may be only that *directly* involved in the manufacturing operations or may be defined on a wider basis (specified). The purpose of the comparison is to assess the effectiveness of the utilisation of labour or to ascertain whether there appears to be scope for improvements in operatives' methods, in layout and flow, or in equipment. Where the absorption of labour in manufacturing operations appears high, management have sometimes derived from such productivity studies pointers to

---

[1] An International Conference organised by the European Productivity Agency in 1956 provided one of the most comprehensive reviews of the problem. The published papers are the best collection of points of view on all the different aspects of the problem, as well as description of the special studies that have been undertaken. (Published by E.P.A., Paris, 1957, under the title *Inter-firm Comparison: an Incentive to Productivity*.) The continuing E.P.A. interest is supported by a quarterly journal published from Paris under the title *Productivity Measurement Review* containing in each issue descriptive and critical articles, as well as illustrative data. There is also a long-known British study by J. A. Scott—*The Measurement of Industrial Efficiency* (Pitman, London, 1950).

the need for changes in design of the product itself, or radical alterations in manufacturing process.

In similar physical terms, comparative productivity studies have
been directed to space occupied for operations, assessed in terms of
the notional "unit of standard product"; also quantities of raw
materials used, and, where technological processing is considerable,
the consumption of fuel, steam and power. Other approaches have
been made in financial rather than physical terms, and these have
made possible a view of "overall productivity" of a factory or manufacturing department. On the financial approach, neutralising of
price changes has to be provided for, as well as of the other incidental changes of product or method. One study set up direct,
periodic comparison of the productivity of factory units by taking
the total values of output, materials, direct and other expenses,
adjusting for changes in physical items and in prices or costs, and
arriving at an index showing the true present cost of producing
100 units of "standard product" as compared with last year's cost in
directly comparable terms.

Where raw materials bulk large as an item in the manufacturing
cost, productivity assessments can be arbitrarily influenced by price
changes in the materials so that the whole comparison can be dis-
torted, although there has been little other physical change. It has
been argued that these cases can be best met by using the concept of
"value-added": that is to say, excluding influences which are entirely
determined outside of the firm itself, and taking into account only
the total expenditures arising internally, plus the return to capital
(depreciation and normal interest or cost of capital), set against the
total value of sales. This gives a reflection of the productivity of the
firm as a whole, concentrating on those items where its own jurisdiction runs, but with the full impact of customer reaction through
volume and value of sales. The residual item in this sum is the net
profitability which is top management's achievement attained by
its judgments.

Over the different activities in a typical business concern the
following are some of the main items that are recurrently watched to
check performance and progress, and so contribute to an appreciation of changes in productivity. Each individual factor is assessed in
terms of a "notional standard unit of output":

Changes in physical output:
    by manufacturing department;
    by factory as a whole;
    by handling through warehouse.
Labour costs (total or sectional).
Material costs.

Capital costs (depreciation plus rate of interest).
Selling prices (total or in product groups).
Selling costs (total, regional, or otherwise subdivided).
Advertising expenditure (total or subdivided).
Changes in space occupancy (total and subdivided).
Administrative or overhead expenditure.

Specific assessments of productivity can, of course, apply equally in other fields of management responsibility, for instance in marketing and selling. This is shown in some of the items listed in the inter-firm comparison illustrations in Tables I and II above, and also in the case of the company quoted above which returns its monthly profits in relation to brand group and to selling district. Selling costs and sales administration costs assessed per unit(s) of product sold, nationally or regionally, can give the same guidance to managements as is gained in relation to manufacturing productivity.

Latterly, attempts have also been made to determine criteria by which the effectiveness of advertising can be assessed. The line of approach is a correlation of change in share of market in a certain year, with percentage of advertising expenditure for the given product group in the preceding year. This is necessarily a slow process of evaluation and will need several years of trial before an effective criterion of the productivity of advertising can be attained.

The simple conclusion that emerges from the consideration of these various approaches to the measurement of productivity is that there cannot be any single index or simple formula that will give managers an adequate appraisal of their own performance: they will always have to make use of several components to get the overall picture of effectiveness and productivity, and these will need to be selected and determined in relation to their own requirements. Participation in inter-firm comparison studies will go a long way to assisting the determination of significant criteria or ratios for evaluation of comparative progress, but it may still be necessary to have other measures for purposes of internal guidance.

National Productivity

In the present context, the centre of interest for this problem is the individual business and the basis of measurement for the individual manager, but it is not irrelevant to make passing reference to a wider national reflection of the same problem, the measurement of the performance of the country as a whole. Here the basic concept is that of the "gross national product", an economic evaluation of the outcome of the activity of all the country's industries and services. "G.N.P." is not unfamiliar to many top managers, because it often figures among the intelligence data being considered in forecasting for commercial policy and forward sales programmes. To determine it is, again, a complex problem of computation necessitating resort to notional valuations, and the following paragraph and table from *The Economist* is of interest in this connection: [1]

In many parts of the economy "output" is hard to define—for example, the output of hospitals or civil servants—but in all parts of it, work contributes to the national income. The Central Statistical Office uses many different indicators to give it a measure of output of different kinds of activity—ranging from the relatively easily identified products of manufacturing, the sums assured, funds held and premiums paid for insurance, to the number employed in religious organisations. From these they build up indices of "net output at constant prices" for all these different parts of the economy.

The results, set out in the table below, offer some broad indication of how fast these different elements in the economy are developing. As compared with 1948, it will be seen that manufacturing output has grown much more than the gross domestic product, if not as fast as the gas, electricity and water services. But since 1954, the distributive trades and other services have also surpassed it. The most rapid growth of output since 1954 has indeed been that of "insurance, banking, and finance": the City is the winner, with an increase of a quarter in its "output" during the past five years.

INDEX NUMBERS OF OUTPUT AT 1954 FACTOR COST (1954 = 100)

	1948	1950	1952	1954	1955	1956	1957	1958	1959 (prov)
Agriculture, forestry, fishing	84	92	97	100	99	105	107	106	111
Mining and quarrying	91	95	99	100	99	99	99	94	92
Manufacturing	77	88	88	100	106	106	108	107	114
Construction	87	91	90	100	100	106	106	105	111
Gas, electricity and water	69	80	88	100	105	110	114	119	123
Transport and communication	87	92	96	100	102	104	103	103	106
Distribution	84	94	89	100	104	105	108	109	115
Insurance, banking, finance	85	91	90	100	104	101	106	110	125
Professional services	83	90	96	100	103	107	111	115	118
Miscellaneous services	102	97	97	100	103	103	105	108	112
Public admin. and defence	99	93	101	100	98	96	94	91	88
Ownership of dwellings	96	97	97	100	102	104	106	107	109
Gross domestic product	84·5	91·0	92·1	100·0	103·6	104·4	106·3	106·4	111·6

Whether on the national plane or for an individual business, one of the major complexities in determining true productivity is the problem of taking account of technological progress—new equipment installed to replace worn-out machines, but the new having an altogether higher level of efficiency, and possibly a lower capital cost. The latter feature is not often met, for new equipment of a higher order of technological capacity can mostly be expected to be appreciably dearer than the items it is replacing, even allowing for changes

[1] Extracted from *The Economist* of 3rd September, 1960, from a Business Note entitled "How Does the Economy Grow?"

in the value of money. Falling costs of equipment are, however, likely to be met with the progress of new inventions: it is already true of some items of electronic instrumentation and control gear. The case of electricity generating reflects interestingly on this problem, for in recent years technological progress has supported the development of larger stations, but the capital cost is not proportionately larger. Doubling capacity may mean something only like one and three-quarters capital cost, and yet at the same time the running costs of the bigger, more advanced station could be some 2–3 per cent. per annum lower. It is, in fact, this curious economic phenomenon in a situation of progressive technology that has enabled the traditional coal-fired generating station to fend off conquest by nuclear-powered stations: "traditional" is perhaps a misnomer in this context, because the modern conventional generating unit has features which are technologically very advanced despite their lower cost.

These are thoughts at once sobering and stimulating to any manager, because, while they draw his attention to factors pertinent to his own role as an economic adjudicator, they also impress on him that there is no escape into easy criteria of adjudication, no escape from the depth of thought that must underlie his judgment and decision. This same conclusion is too the dominant memory from the E.P.A. International Conference referred to above: many managers could have well attended the gathering in the expectation of coming home with pockets full of ready-made productivity formulæ, but they would have met with serious disappointment. Many aspects of productivity measurement were, indeed, realistically and practically presented and discussed; but the President in his closing remarks could only re-emphasise the fact that the benefit of the mutual exchanges lay chiefly in the challenge that each individual gained from re-examining his own criteria of productivity in the light of the others that he had observed or studied. Of these others, there will be some that he will want to adopt for himself, and some that he would like to try, with modification. He will continue to benefit from the recurrent comparisons with other managers and will therefore find some preference for common lines of approach. Yet he will acknowledge none the less that his measurements of productivity, his criteria of success, must be as individual to his management role as is his policy or his personal conduct.

CHAPTER VIII

THE PROFESSION OF MANAGEMENT

No aspect of management practice attracts so much attention and interest today as the problem of finding and developing the men who are to be the managers of tomorrow, and the top managers of the day after. It is a topic of popular discussion at every industrial conference, and a problem on the desk of every managing director. Yet from the welter of conversation and deliberation there has not yet emerged an agreed body of opinion on any aspect of the problem at all—except its importance. Of that there cannot be the slightest doubt, and the need now is for the penetrating appraisal that can lead to the formulation of a sound and reliable line of approach to a constructive programme. This can start only at one point—in the basic analysis of the process of management itself, for therein lies the determining factors of the skills to be identified and developed.

The first considerations have been amply presented and portrayed in many places in this volume, the emphasis being placed on the responsibility entailed in the management process for the judgments and decisions that will initiate and direct a given group of operations being carried out by given groups of people. Two major factors underlie the skills required effectively to exercise this process—the one is specific knowledge, the other an adequate personal make-up on the mental and on the behavioural planes. The two are interwoven, and are both complex compositions of several contributing elements, few of which can be thought of as "standard". Some are indeed "ordinary", although they tend to be glamorised in the course of popular discussion. They are in the main intangible elements and factors, not susceptible of measurement, but they can all be identified and can all be assessed, if adequate trouble is taken to construct and use skilfully appropriate media of assessment.

For the purposes of the present context it matters little which way round they are approached: perhaps, for convenience, it could be useful to start on the second of the major factors—the personal make-up. At least this is the item on which there is the greater amount of confusion and the maximum of controversy! In simple terms (and running the risk of over-simplification), this factor has to be seen in the two distinct but interrelated facets already noted: the mental and the behavioural, relevant to two facets of the management process. The mental skills are required to underlie the judgment facet: facts, circumstances, data, evaluations, comparisons, assumptions, testing of possibilities, assessments of outcome, appraisal of costs and of expectations—all these and many more are the mental activities that underlie the manager's task of judgment to reach conclusions, to form decisions, to formulate policies, to frame plans, to determine targets, to instruct an initiation of action, to control its achievement and progress, to assess success or failure, to select the remedy for correction. In the practical world of modern industry and commerce complexity of conditions makes this managerial task an onerous one, calling for consideration of data— management information—on a wide scale for most of the major decisions. Intellectual calibre of no mean order can be recognised as an inescapable requirement for the effectiveness of the modern manager. The bigger or the more complex the managerial task, the greater the requirement of intellectual calibre or mental capacity. Yet caution is needed in interpreting the requirement: the "high-fives" in intellectual capacity are undoubtedly needed for the top management positions of the bigger industrial and commercial concerns, but it would be a mistake to argue that *high-level* intelligence is *essential* to *all* management. There are indeed many managerial positions and responsibilities where a good average of mental ability is adequate, assisted by other factors. Experience has shown on a number of occasions that high intellectual capability can be detrimental to good management, because it tends to inhibit adequate appreciation of the normality or ordinariness of mind and behaviour of the many people who make up any organisation. Such an eventuality, it could of course be argued, really means that the high intellectual capacity has not been adequately exercised!

It is very doubtful whether the other end of the scale has any validity—it is unlikely that *below-average* intelligence can be of any use in managerial roles, except those that are very simple and circumscribed.

The "Personal" Factor

The second personal facet has to do with "behaviour", that is to say, with the manager's personal attitude towards and with his superiors, his colleagues and his subordinates, and it underlies his ability to secure and promote the essential co-operation without which management cannot be effective. As has been recurrently stressed in these pages, the manager is responsible for carrying out a process of which an essential characteristic is the attainment of a high degree of co-operation from many people; from those who are under his command, and equally—though in a rather different sense—from colleagues in parallel positions, from specialist advisers at different levels of status, and from or with his own superior. In the midst of this complex pattern of co-operative relationships, the manager recalls that he is himself a man, subject to the normal rational and emotional facets of human nature, and he has therefore enjoined on him a role which requires him, while being an ordinary person, to secure more than ordinary co-operation from other ordinary people. It is in this sense that a basic requirement in effective management is a matter of behaviour and attitude. The personal make-up of the individual must play an important part in the likelihood of his attaining this successful accomplishment. This is the issue which goes to the heart of the basic question debated back over decades: "Is management skill inborn? Or can it be made?" Some answer was given in the Introduction in relation to considering the claim of management to science or art, and no useful purpose can now be served in pursuing the matter on academic lines. Experience has shown how much *can* be done to develop the ability to manage, or to manage better. There is no research which has proven that the skill is specifically inborn, but common sense itself dictates that, obviously, there are combinations of characteristics which are inborn in individuals and make them the better able to develop their skills of management. This is no more and no less true in this context than it is in any other field of human endeavour: there are the men and women who are naturally gifted and for whom it requires very little development to enable their skills to be at a maximum, and there are others who, with latent abilities, need a greater degree of care in nurturing their qualities. One statement can be made quite firmly in regard to management skill, that it definitely *cannot be implanted if the personal dispositions are all negative to its development.* The basic question thus becomes: what are the minimum essential qualities which can connote at least the absence of negative influences which would inhibit the development of management skill? Such a question is depressingly prosaic, for it would be so much more exciting to identify human characteristics that have been proven as the key to management success. It is as yet impossible to lay down even general prescriptions along this line, and the problem is still one calling for a good deal of systematic research.

In a more limited way, and starting from the simpler prosaic standpoint, can some guiding lines be formulated? What *are* the *essential minimum human qualities* that make the foundation of success in management? Are there certain minimum personal qualities which could be specified as a necessary basis? Are they relative to particular circumstances? From a start in some simple answers, more progressive research could be conducted along the lines of analysing and comparing known cases of managers who are proven failures, in contrast with those hailed as successful. While real knowledge is missing in this field, there have been many opinions expressed; the lists of qualities suggested by various people as the "specification" of the good executive often read like classifications of the virtues. Without reaching for the moon, tentative analysis of experience with a large number of managers has indicated the following as the basic qualities required in the successful manager in the general sense, not taking into account any question of a need for high commercial acumen or entrepreneurial flair:

(1) Mental ability—a combination of planning sense, foresight, orderliness of mind and judgment, which will result in willingness to think straight, and in thoroughness and promptness of decision.

(2) Ability to see the other person's point of view and to be as critical of self as of others: this is the basis of ability to work with other people.

(3) Integrity, in the sense of mental honesty.

(4) A restrained self-confidence, coupled with initiative and resourcefulness.

(5) A balanced temperament—particularly the absence of such traits as emotional instability, marked inferiority sense, aggressiveness, self-centred outlook.

(6) A sense of humour or of cheerfulness.

(7) Persistence, but not to the point of obstinacy.

The exclusion of the *business acumen* or *entrepreneurial flair*—the quality which is so much lauded in the great captains of industry—is deliberate, because of the confusion in the popular imagination which heralds this as the key to *management* success: strictly speaking, it is not a management skill at all, but a specialised commercial expertise, an advanced form of that rare intuitive judgment which goes under the popular label of "a nose for a bargain". Close study of the persons who are recognised exponents of this particular competence in the commercial world shows that the "greatness" they attain is based upon business judgment in the fields of buying and selling; it is known that *many of them are unable to provide the skills of management* which will ensure the continuing effective accomplishment of their businesses, once the purchases have been made. Under their jurisdiction stand the *competent managers* who ensure that the full advantage of the commercial skill is not lost by ineffective operations following.

In the course of thus looking at aspects of personal make-up, the second facet has been incidentally considered, in the reference to "capacity to see the other person's point of view" and to "balanced temperament". The attainment of co-operation from and with people rests first and foremost on recognition of their role and contribution, and of their own human standing. This is the edge of the big question of "motivation", many aspects of which have been referred to or covered elsewhere in this volume. The manager who starts by having a normally balanced emotional make-up, or who recognises his own idiosyncracies in this respect, has the first requirement for skill in securing co-operation. If he then has the capacity to be objective about people and human relations, and can readily see situations as though with the eyes of others, he is a long way along the road to successful accomplishment of co-operation. This foundation will make the social processes of co-operation—listening, observing, consulting, informing, communicating, promoting security, promoting participation—normal elements in his own attitudes and behaviour. Some persons have that make-up from which these processes flow as their own natural everyday behaviour; others, differently made, have to exert some deliberate influence over their own natural attitude if these processes are to be fully reflected in action. These latter are not "worse made" persons, and their skills in attaining co-operation may be none the less for being partly deliberate; they may have a more difficult personal task in this way, but they may also secure a larger and more constructive response, because there is purposeful deliberation behind their action. This argument would mean that the skills of co-operation do not have to be easy of attainment: their more deliberate exercise could imply firmer leadership and sterner discipline, but may equally well imply more stable management with greater respect and acceptance from subordinates and colleagues. The argument implies also that the social skills can be nurtured—an important factor for true management development. It remains true, however, as indicated earlier, that such skills cannot be implanted or developed if the personal and behavioural basic dispositions are negative.

Management Knowledge

With adequate personal make-up on the intellectual and behavioural planes, the next major component of management competence is specific knowledge. Of this, some relates to the industry or trade or other field of activity within which the management is being exercised, and some relates to the process of management itself. The former has always had recognition: in fact, it long enjoyed an exclusive recognition in the belief that the appropriate technological training was of itself the guarantee of management success. In fields like engineering, chemistry, food processing, textiles, leather, building and public works, and many others, it was long held that the specific *technical qualification* was *alone* required for appointment to managerial positions. The past decade or so has, however, witnessed a remarkable and widespread change of outlook, and almost everywhere today there is acceptance of the need of "management knowledge" as well: there is argument as to what this should cover, but there is agreement on the inclusion of management studies as an essential contribution to management success.

It is perhaps over-optimistic to expect that any general acceptance of the "management content" of a course of studies can be reached easily, but the matter is of importance for each individual firm or establishment, if it wants to initiate a programme of development for its own up-and-coming managers. A good line of approach *can* be laid down, though it starts in recognition of the fact that the knowledge required for management competence is partly determined by the nature and extent of the responsibilities delegated or allocated to specific positions. Only to a given extent is there a body of "general management knowledge", and this is itself best regarded as a foundation on to which the more specific learning can be built up. For such an approach it is useful at the outset to recall the four major facets of activity that will characterise—though with varying emphasis— all managerial positions, whatever their specific differences as laid down in the definitions of responsibility. These four facets may be usefully summarised under the headings: technical, economic, human, administrative.

(a) *Technical.*—Applying the particular knowledge of processes, products, materials, equipment, procedures, etc., pertinent to the operations or field allocated to the manager. For example, in the case of a Factory Manager, this will cover consideration of and decisions on materials and quality standards, the suitability of equipment and tools, the design of product, investigation into complaints of faults, and so on. In the case of the Chief Accountant, it will cover questions of budget centres, control procedures, classification of expense, liability for income tax, interpretation of financial law, and so on.

(b) *Economic.*—This aspect relates to the basic objective of the enterprise and its position in the economic and social system within which it is operating. In management practice, the major economic activity tends to be concentrated in the realms of "top management" (especially with the Board of Directors) for overall policy and development, and with the marketing/sales executives for the formulation of programmes. In another sense, however, *every* managerial and specialist member of an organisation has an *economic objective* inherent in his role—the objective of ensuring that the responsibilities which have been allocated to him are carried out at the best possible level of effectiveness and economy. This is attained in part by the skill with which the responsibilities are discharged in everyday practice, including the motivation of subordinate personnel to give service at a high standard of efficiency and performance; but, in addition, it requires continual attention to possibilities of improvement in organisation or in method or in procedure, so that overall efficiency can be advanced as and when appropriate and practical. From the top level of management there should come the encouragement to all members of the organisation to see in this objective the important social contribution to the advancement of the standards of living.

(c) *Human.*—The motivation of the working teams through the exercise of the social skills—all those daily activities which the responsible manager must undertake in order to ensure that the morale of his team is high and the performance of their duties good. Part of this activity may be delegated to a specialist personnel officer or assistant; for instance, matters concerned with the engagement or training of staff, or the routine handling of welfare activities. For *every* manager, however, there is a considerable human element in his own responsibility which he *cannot delegate* and which is in effect the impact of his own leadership or motivation on the people working under his jurisdiction—giving instructions and decisions, resolving problems, apportioning praise and blame, consulting, informing, etc. In addition, for almost every manager there is the second main element of human endeavour in his role, the promotion and exercise of co-operation with executive and specialist colleagues, and with superiors.

(d) *Administrative.*—Concerned with the data and procedures by which the judgment and decision underlying planning and control are carried into effect, in relation to manufacturing, marketing, distributing, or other activities that the organisation is dealing with, as well as to such internal matters as employment routines and financial controls. Such data procedures will fall generally into two groups, namely, those that are part of the overall scheme designed for the organisation as a whole, and those which are specific to the division, unit or section of an individual manager. The tasks of the manager in this connection are often delegated to clerical or secretarial staffs engaged on the compilation and presentation of data, statistics and records, the completion of formal statements, the writing of reports, the preparation of other documentary matter.

The "technical" group of activities is *not*, strictly speaking, part of *management* at all. There will be found many managers who have very little of a technical character within their responsibility: for example, a manager in charge of a packing department for which no special knowledge of products or processes is required; or the superintendent of a group of straightforward clerical and typing activities. But with many of the executive appointments in industry and commerce, the manager would be at a loss if he had no technical com-

petence in regard to the particular products or processes with which
he was dealing, whether in production, in marketing, or in distribution. Similarly, in the field of accounting, the specialist accountant
officer in an industrial organisation has a high "technical factor" in
the tasks entrusted to him. Yet it remains true that in either case
these aspects of responsibility are parallel to and associated with
the real *management* activities, rather than forming part of them.

With the other three groups, the economic, the human and the
administrative, the position is different—they compose or contain
the elements of the process of management itself, and in varying
degree they will occur in the responsibilities of all executive and
supervisory appointments. "In varying degree" has to be stated,
because necessarily the make-up of any particular executive or
specialist appointment depends on the responsibilities allocated,
determined in relation to the aims, policy, plans and methods of the
enterprise. In this, of course, lies the difficulty of any textbook on
the practice of management: it can suggest and describe an approach
to organisation structure and to methods of planning and control
that have been tried and found satisfactory in perhaps a number of
enterprises, but it can rarely prescribe them safely for universal use
irrespective of circumstances. This is true even in regard to the
human element in management, where it *could* be argued that, as
men and women are much the same the world over, the principles
and practices of "personnel management" could be set down in fairly
standard terms. Experience has proved this argument, however
logical it appears on the surface, to be untrue—the particular circumstances of different organisations, activities and persons give rise
to differences in the human situations and so need to be met by
differences in management approach and technique. Perhaps the
only factor that remains persistently the same in the practice of
sound management is the attitude and outlook of the manager: the
executive who discharges his responsibilities with a personal approach that is characterised by the four essential elements (plus a
scientific method) is always on sure ground. He needs to have a
"planning and control" outlook, to watch always for "co-ordination",
and to maintain a human attitude that will secure unbroken morale
("motivation") among his subordinates.

The Scope of Knowledge

In regard to the overall fields of knowledge which the skilled
manager needs to acquire, there is a good deal of contemporary
development in progress. The syllabus sponsored on national lines
by the Ministry of Education in 1948, and subsequently modified in
1960 to a postgraduate basis, has provided a framework for the study

of management in selected professional fields and for the process as a whole. The very completeness of the scheme, however, enhances a danger that has long been feared in some quarters, i.e. the weakness of pumping into younger candidates quantities of factual knowledge on a variety of subjects, many of which they have no opportunity of carrying into effect or of even seeing in operation. Such study is not itself "training" for management: it needs to be complemented by an "on the job training", something on the lines of a coaching of the on-coming man by the successful practising executive. Only in this way can the essential skill entailed in the practice of such a mental and human process as management be effectively trained. Unfortunately, the numbers of really successful managers, knowledgeable and skilled enough to undertake such coaching, are quite inadequate to meet the country's present needs. Encouragement can, however, be taken from another development which goes some way (even if on a restricted scale) to meeting the need: this is the training afforded for potential senior executives under the aegis of the Administrative Staff College. There, instruction is combined with a form of "coaching", which uses the experience of the highly selected men who attend, supplemented by the skill of visiting executives. By the interchange of views and the thrashing out of problems in small groups, the "feel" of management at higher levels is imparted to men who, in their middle-to-late thirties, have already had some years of responsible executive experience and have given proof of professional competence at lower levels.

The overall task of developing management skills calls for a wide-based programme of approach. The skills to be attained at a good level of competence will need to cover the four aspects listed above, to the extent relevant to the broad pattern of positions being filled. The higher the levels of management concerned, generally speaking, the broader the knowledge called for. Taking an overall view of management practice, the areas of knowledge required may be summarised in the following scheme:

(a) Policy, including the objectives of the enterprise.
(b) Organisation—definition of responsibilities and relationships.
(c) Management Information—economic, technical, financial and other data by means of which policies can be evaluated, possibilities assessed, expectations factually forecast, plans and targets predetermined, so that judgment can be exercised and decisions taken to initiate action.
(d) Procedures or techniques of various kinds by means of which management information is made available as the "tools" of management in such fields as—
—planning (including budgeting);

—control (e.g. performance, progress and cost);
—information and communication;
—co-ordination;
—personnel (e.g. selection, training and consultation).

(e) Command or motivation: this is the personal management action of the individual manager and calls for skills in:
—instruction (command) and supervision of subordinates (=the "social skills" of management);
—co-operative attitude towards (sectional) colleagues and towards superiors;
—maturity of judgment and decision;
—use of techniques or "tools";
—maintaining communication and co-ordination;
—the promotion of efficiency.

N.B. This combined group of personal skills may usefully be regarded as the motive-power and nervous system of management.

MANAGEMENT DEVELOPMENT

A programme of management development necessarily stems from adequate understanding of the responsibilities and interrelationships involved in the various managerial, supervisory and specialist positions that form the organisational pattern of the company concerned, and within this broad framework its components may be summarised in the following six items:

1. *Specifications*

   Starting from the existing definitions of responsibilities, the drafting of specifications showing: the educational and technical qualifications, the experience, the management skills and techniques, and the personal qualities required for the effective discharge of such responsibilities in their various roles.

2. *Forecast of Requirements*

   A forward assessment of the likely needs of the company in terms of executive, supervisory and senior technical personnel, determined from known retirements, expected new developments, overseas expansion, or other anticipated changes.

3. *Appraisal of Ability and Progress*

   A scheme for the systematic periodical appraisal of the men holding lower and intermediate appointments, so as to determine their apparent eligibility for advancement. The appraisals provide the pointers to individual needs for further training and for further variety of experience, as well as to continuing personal deficiencies which may call for correction.

4. *Selection and Promotion Procedure*

A procedure related to the appraisal scheme, directed to the objective assessment of individuals as "candidates" for given vacant posts as they arise. (It is at this point that candidates for promotion from within may come into "competition" with persons applying from outside, if so desired.)

5. *Management Training*

A programme of training in management principles and practices covering:

(a) an appreciation of contemporary knowledge over the whole subject;

(b) specific techniques to meet individual requirements;

(c) advanced technological background pertinent to higher management;

(d) the company's own policy, organisation and methods;

(e) the skills involved in judgment and decision within delegated responsibilities;

(f) diagnostic techniques for promoting effectiveness and economy.

The training may be provided in a variety of ways, partly within the company, and partly using courses at outside centres. To some extent, "tuition" of this kind may also be of relevance to existing managers staying in their present positions, as well as to those who are under development for advancement; in the latter category, the tailor-made approach must be the basis of a programme, so that individuals are given the kind of instruction most nearly suited to their needs.

6. *Guided Experience*

Provision for the gradual assumption of known responsibility under the guidance of a competent senior and with suitable systematic check of performance. It may be found necessary or desirable to provide some form of "counselling": both for the younger executives in regard to their personal problems and progress, and for the senior members in regard to their part in the development of the junior members. The major and important element involved in this task of guiding experience is the improvement of personal qualities, with special reference to promoting co-operative skills and to the enhancement of individual abilities in judgment and decision, as distinct from knowledge of techniques. Guidance of this kind can often be assisted from outside by means of expertly conducted "case" sessions, which simulate the everyday problems of management practice.

Much of the contemporary discussion of "management development" in industrial circles underrates the complexity of what is involved. Many directors and senior executives seem to discuss the problem in terms of finding somebody or some institution that can carry out their management development for them; or, if they recognise the relevance of internal programmes, they pitch these at far too low a level. This is well illustrated by the not infrequent advertisements in the vacancies columns inviting applications for appointment as "Management Development Officer"—with a specification and salary grading which make clear that the scope of responsibility intended can be little more than planning and conducting courses for supervisors and junior managers, or arranging for nominations to outside courses. There is frequently, too, every indication that such an appointment would imply a "delegation" of the job—the directors feeling that they have done their part by the mere fact of making the appointment, and now it is up to the newly appointed officer to get on with the rest of it!

Responsibility for the implementation of a management development programme must lie *actively* at top management level, preferably with the chief executive himself. For practical purposes he may well need someone to take some share of the active role on his behalf; that would be a wise arrangement, provided the "someone" is of adequate experience and maturity, and himself established at a senior level of responsibility, perhaps even a member of the Board. The objective of the programme is none other than making systematic provision for oncoming generations of skilful managers, an objective that could well determine the continuing success of the business or lead to its failure if neglected. While the broad lines of approach as summarised above can be laid down in general terms for application in most businesses, the programmes for carrying those into effect *need careful consideration in individual terms related to the circumstances and needs of each business itself.* In other words, a company requires its own scheme rather than seeking to fall back on a published pattern or an arrangement seen effectively working elsewhere. The first phases of the programme are fairly straightforward, in the establishment of the definitions of responsibilities and the forecast of expected future requirements. The latter may give rise to some difficulties, in so far as it calls for assessment or estimate of forward trading developments, such as expansion of factories or sales regions; but only broad forecasts are really required. Some firms devote too much attention to an endeavour to be precise in this matter: this stage is, in fact, of less importance than others, and broad forecasts can be an adequate foundation for the programme.

Turning existing and expected management positions into "specifications" is again a straightforward task, though it does call for a clear and thorough knowledge of what is entailed in up-to-date management practice in various fields, with appreciation of emerging techniques, and likely forthcoming lines of thought pertinent to the major factors in executive action or in functional responsibilities. The specifications should ensure that the qualities, qualifications, knowledge and experience called for in each group of positions are forward-looking, so as to provide that future incumbents of these positions will be of better competence than current holders—however good these latter may be! *It is an excellent principle of management development to plan for progression, the successor manager to be of better competence than the man he succeeds.*

These specifications are, in their turn, the basis of the intake of personnel for development, the foundation of the methods of appraisal for advancement or promotion, and the framework of the schemes of management training. These are all big subjects calling for fuller and closer consideration than it is appropriate to give to them in the present context. Certain passing observations are alone possible here. Intake can today be on a wide and varied plane. In past decades there has been a lot of argument about the best levels of recruitment for management potential—technical schools, Public Schools, Universities have all had their advocates. Experience on a wide scale has proved today that *all* such channels make their contribution, the important screening being the one that occurs about mid-to-late twenties and looks at all likely candidates, whatever their original mode of entry to the company. "Potential" is difficult to identify or forecast in the formative years of 'teens or early twenties, however reliably it may be possible to assess intelligence capacities —these are but one factor. Systematic appraisal by established managers over a period of two or three years in relation to actual work undertaken or responsibilities carried is a far more reliable guide, the more so if it can be made possible to try men out in differing situations and with varying loads of responsibility. Such arrangements can form extremely valuable phases in a management development programme—seconding selected men to tours of duty in special assignments, in assistant manager roles, in work study (after proper training), in personnel service, on project groups, on shift supervision, or other specific activities where facets of management responsibility can be deliberately allocated under direction. It is often possible to staff the junior ranks of the functional or diagnostic services (work study, O & M, personnel department, cost analysis, operational research, and so on) by means of periods of secondment of young potential managers or junior executives, giving them the considerable benefit of the experience in using specialised techniques and of insight into other phases of management practice. A planned programme can in fact be made out for a given variety of experience in these directions, with specific objectives in view: an illustration is shown in the outline scheme which appears as Appendix A following this Chapter.

Arrangements for imparting knowledge of management principles and practice open up another major area for consideration, which again requires close correlation with the requirements of the management positions that are being prepared for. A large amount of general knowledge of management practice and of techniques is, of course, of value as a base for any programme of advancement— were this not so, the present volume would represent just so much waste paper! Judicious assessment is called for to prevent the absorption of generalised knowledge becoming overdone, and a systematic programme should ensure that the acquisition of knowledge progresses in harmony with expansion of experience and of responsibility. In this connection, it may be said here that considerable credit is due to a *Working Party* established by the *British Institute of Management* and the *Ministry of Education* for insisting on the professional scheme of management studies being delayed to a *postgraduate* level, thereby endeavouring to associate knowledge with understanding. At the earlier ages (for example, in undergraduate stages or at Higher National Certificate level), there can be much to advocate background studies of applied economics, descriptive commerce, or an introduction to techniques of cost control, but any serious pursuit of management principles and practice is far more appropriate when the students have begun to get the first-hand "feel" of what is involved, by dint of appointment to the first stages of executive responsibility. On that foundation how far the study of management can go is largely a matter of individual interest: in general, it is probably true that far more is called for in the way of width and depth of knowledge than has hitherto been taken as acceptable in British educational circles. An outline of essential knowledge as a foundation for effective management practice is given as Appendix B following this Chapter.

"Management Games"

An interesting feature of management training progress in Britain within recent years has been the establishment of sessions devoted to "business games" or "management games". Initially modelled on the notion of the "war games" long used in the Service Staff Colleges, this variation on the case method owes much of its stimulus in the industrial world to the development of the computer. The first sessions designed for business in the United States were, in fact, built up around the speedy availability of data through a computer system, but latterly this form of role-playing has been more extensively developed without recourse to automatic data processing.

The "business games" are basically a form of participatory training analogous in purpose and approach to case studies or role-playing: the idea is to assist learning by involvement in situations which simulate the atmosphere of responsibility in a normal management position. With the "games" the emphasis is on the "judgment and decision" factor in the role of management, calling into play the feed-back of decision in terms of its outcome and thereby confronting the manager-in-training with aspects of the consequences of his own decisions. Inevitably the greater part of the "games" is concerned with problems of marketing, pricing, cost analysis, profit projection, the disposition of resources, the promotion of sales, the impact of competition, the efficacy of advertising.

Broadly summarised a "business or management game" may be described as a simulation of top management action within the framework of given economic, technical and marketing data. The participants (say, a half dozen members in each of four or five competing teams) represent the Board of Directors or the Senior Managers of companies operating in a given market. Resources are notionally allocated in the form of data, and further resources can be purchased and applied—these transactions being the judgments and decisions of the management team, each member carrying the role of a given operational or functional responsibility. Within the allotted time of one or two hours, the year's trading decisions are completed and the results handed in for adjudication: this is where the computer makes its main contribution. The feed-back of the results from adjudication represents the interplay of the individual decisions with the market forces and other influences built into the programme of the sessions by the organisers of the "game". From this new standpoint, the second year's trading starts, and the cycle repeats for some four or five times, covering in simulation a few years of business management.[1]

Valuable as this form of training activity can be, it is important that it should be seen in correct perspective—for it is *one* contribution to overall management, not a programme in itself. Realistically appraised, the "games" teach the value of data and correct interpretation, the significance of certain features in the process of commercial judgment, the complexity of the inter-play of forces operating on the business scene, and the sense of forecast that the management process necessitates if decision is to be effective. These are all important characteristics for the better development of the up-and-coming manager, but they are not in themselves his complete training.

---

[1] A brief but informative commentary on these "games" is to be found in Howard Greenwald's article entitled "Management Games for the Executive" in the *Review of the Federation of British Industries*, London, July 1962.

There is a danger that some superficiality of approach may be encouraged by the attractive novelty of these sessions; their truly effective role of promoting better understanding of the factors in commercial judgment needs to be recognised, so that they can take their place in a well-rounded programme of management development.

Appraisal of Development

With the problems of appraisal, guided experience and counselling, the major core of management development is reached. Whatever is attained through the other contributions that have so far been considered, it remains true that the most effective enhancement of management competence is likely to come through the impact and influence of wise direction and nurturing from a mature superior. Annual appraisals, objectively made and dispassionately discussed with their subject, can be a valuable medium for imparting this influence, supplementing what is done in the normal course of day-to-day working contacts. The superior is doing a disservice to any subordinate who is a developing manager if he lets faults go by uncorrected; and he is very seriously failing in his moral obligations of responsibility if he lets such a subordinate develop a false or exaggerated notion of his own abilities. Strangely enough, this is an area in which something as prosaic as "management information" can be a valuable aid: where sound data procedures afford tools of management aligned with delegation of responsibility, the individual manager's judgment and decision are sharpened, and a better critical review can be made by his superior of the skills with which he exercises these processes, or of the deficiencies which he still portrays and towards which remedies need to be sought. It is a salutary confirmation of this aspect of a senior manager's responsibility if he is asked periodically to report on what he has done to advance the abilities of his subordinate managers, and to indicate what ought still to be done for their continuing progress.

Much of the guidance and counselling required may lie in the fields of human relations, especially those concerning contact, coordination and communication with specialists, with advisory services and with supervisors. In these directions, data can be of little help, and a senior manager may have to rely on skilful "listening" to what his subordinates are really reporting to him about their own tasks and achievements, or even on diagnostic "interviewing", so conducted that the younger managers are not aware of it.

"Appraisal" is a topic that arouses a good deal of controversy, at least in so far as the recording of assessments is concerned. There are many executives who take the view that they do not believe in appraisals or ratings, that the qualities of good management cannot be assessed, that no useful purpose is served by pretending to be systematic in an area so enmeshed in human values. Sound points in some respects, but not entirely valid in the conclusion which is drawn from them. None of the senior managers holding such views would deny that they can form an opinion of their junior manager subordinates; or would deny that they are able to decide reliably which men should be selected for promotion, and why. Their objection is not to the fact of assessment or to ability to assess, but to recording the judgment, especially in any analytical form. No one is going to argue that precise appraisal of human qualities is either attainable or desirable: an appraisal form does no more than assist the human judgment of human qualities—it assists by the systematic approach which it enjoins, calling for the expression of judgment in regard to a number of identifiable facets of action or behaviour. What these are should be determined by a company for its own managerial personnel: any general form would be the subject of endless argument. Contemporary thought suggests that these facets of the human skills in action should be formulated in questions rather than posited as lists of qualities: there is already a great deal of experience to prove that judgment of the progress of development of men and women in management competence can be substantially aided by the use of carefully designed appraisal forms.

The facets of action or behaviour to be included in the appraisal must be so selected as to reflect the content of management responsibility, for it is in these terms that the appraisal is being sought. The implication of this is important, especially for younger and junior managers, namely, that it is not enough to aim at "giving them an insight" or "keeping them usefully busy" as they acquire knowledge and experience: if they are seriously to develop management competence, the younger and junior managers must be allowed from early stages to exercise a real and known responsibility. The specialist tasks and services or project teams referred to above are a partial means of accomplishing this object, but these cannot be relied on exclusively. The growing younger manager needs to hold specific responsibility for a given role within a known area of jurisdiction and with effective decisive authority therein. On this basis he can be judged, he can be given the guidance in experience by which true development is attained, he can be shown the wisdom or folly of decisions in terms of the outcome. It could be safely stated that such *specific allocation of responsibility and an objective systematic appraisal in terms of its discharge is the very core of management development*, to which all other aspects of a programme are subordinate contributions.

Among the areas in which the growing manager has to acquire

skill in relation to the exercise of responsibility is the use of data or "management information" as the basis of his judgments in forming decisions. Guidance from a competent superior can be invaluable for this purpose, especially if the company has well-developed data tools. The growing younger manager has to learn first and foremost to be selective in using data. For his routine activities in carrying out his responsibilities, he needs to learn how to relate "actual" to "plan or target" and how to interpret "variances"—in part to correct his decisions and his plans, in part to assess the need for diagnostic studies or for initiating remedy of deficiencies. Most of this routine data should come to him as normal procedure through the budget control system. More important is the learning that he must acquire in regard to the use of data for assessing assumptions and expectations, as the basis for his decisions which will determine future actions. How deeply he can carry this learning must depend on the role he is filling and its position in the organisation structure; at the lower levels of management responsibility, scope and opportunity for any major considerations of this kind are usually severely limited, and they occur only as promotion to higher executive positions proceeds. He has then to learn the content and significance of economic and market intelligence in relation to commercial policy and the formulation of a trading programme. He has to learn how to use data sparingly but effectively in forecasting the likely outcome of alternative decisions based on varying assumptions; he has to learn how to appraise the reliability of data, and how to get the best service out of specialist sources. To some extent he can learn these lessons at outside institutions: courses on "management strategy" or "business games" are specifically directed to this sort of learning. He will, however, gain best progress in these directions from the expert guidance of a competent superior, perhaps aided by a reliable and authoritative specialist; here more than almost anywhere else lies the real meaning of the phrase "guided experience".

One major responsibility falls heavily on any senior manager who is taking seriously his role in management development—he must have the detachment to recognise failures as promptly as is consistent with adequate appraisal, and the courage to carry through the necessary weeding out. Misplaced "human generosity" in this direction can be unfair to the individual concerned, as well as costly to the company. Generous treatment is not to be denied in termination of employment, or demotion to other suitable duties; but the importance of promoting high competence in management practice has to be seen as a major item in senior executive responsibility and must not be impaired by lack of perspective.

Individual Programmes

One thing clearly standing out from even this brief review of management development in the foregoing paragraphs is the need for *systematic* approach to arrangements. Within the overall pro- gramme designed by a company as both the reflection of its policy and the means of carrying it into effect, there will need to be a series of "individual programmes" to lay out the stages of progress of men through the various contributing phases of development. This is where the "specifications" of the various managerial appoint- ments provide the framework for assessing personal and professional attainment: the periodic appraisal thus becomes the means of deter- mining what next steps are required for each individual (junior) manager undergoing development. This is the point, too, where other facets of the overall programme come into focus: for example, the significance of original background at time of entry or of inter- mediate areas of employment and experience. Here indeed is the gateway to a very considerable and complex subject, which cannot possibly be adequately considered within the present context.

A selected aspect can serve to illustrate the line of thought in tended: let this example be the development of the scientist. Special- ists in science and technology have long been employed in industry in technological occupations—research, design, product develop- ment, quality control, and so on—but in relatively small numbers and mostly intended to follow careers exclusively within such fields. In recent years, however, two major changes have taken place: not only have the numbers of qualified scientists and technologists re- cruited into industry increased considerably, but they have also been diverted into broader career paths, partly through junior managerial roles in manufacturing activities and partly through service in diagnostic techniques and other specialist management aids. This, indeed, is a phenomenon which is likely both to continue and to extend—and very much to the benefit of the nation's industry! There is every reason to regard the scientist and technologist as valuable recruits to potential management service, provided the individuals have the necessary level of personal make-up as a basis. In this respect the graduate scientist, for example, can be considered on equal footing with the Arts man; but he has the added advantage (at least, for many industries) of something worth-while to offer through the medium of his technical knowledge and training. In terms of mental calibre, the fact of graduating or of attaining equivalent institutional qualification, can be taken as a guarantee of above average standard, if only because of the competitive educa- tional screening involved in securing entrance to a University.

Whether the scientist and technologist is suitable for development to junior, middle or higher management is a question that can be answered only *individually*, in terms of and on the basis of periodic appraisals of knowledge, experience and personal make-up. His programme of development could be framed with an initial heavy bias to diagnostic studies to which the special character of his previous scientific training would give peculiar strength: much of the serious application of operational research to industrial situations has been built upon this premise. Another phase of the programme may have to give emphasis to opportunities for acquiring acquaintance with commercial affairs and perhaps a special feature of broadening outlook and attitude. Observation suggests that the scientist has a tendency to introversive make-up and sometimes to an exaggerated precision in detail: such personal limitations may call for particular off-setting attention in a development programme, and they would be points for specific consideration in the periodic appraisals. In short, the argument indicates that there is no reason why the scientist should not be—fully and equally with men from other backgrounds—among the potential for advancing to even the highest levels of management. The few highly technical industries apart, scientific expertise is *per se* neither a criterion in favour of, nor an obstacle to, selection for such development; in this respect the scientist rests on common foundation with all educated men entering upon an industrial career. It could, of course, be argued that, in an age of ever-advancing industrial technology, the scientist has more to offer in terms of management potential than his confrère from the *litterae humaniores:* but any such assumption would obviously beg the whole question as it has been examined in the foregoing pages.

That many scientists and technologists will reach the highest levels of top management in British industry in the years and decades to come is not open to doubt or denial. It is essential to ensure that the reason for such advancement is always *personal and professional competence in management,* and not merely the technological background.

MANAGEMENT—A PROFESSION

It is inevitable that considerations of development and training for management bring to the fore the notion of "profession". This, again, is a topic that has been much argued about with little conclusive outcome, largely because of confusion over the meaning of the term. In some quarters, it has been taken to imply "admission by examination", with no reference to personal make-up or experience. This is, of course, an extraordinarily artificial interpretation, which cannot be supported under any circumstances. The true significance of "profession" is customarily summarised in three factors:

that there is an identifiable body of knowledge pertinent to professional competence; that there is an objective in community or personal service outside of self-interest; that there is an acceptance of basic codes of ethics in the exercise of the role. The content of foregoing chapters will have made abundantly evident that these three criteria are certainly applicable to management. That it could and should be considered among the professions is an opinion steadily gaining adherence, but it is far from new. It is perhaps encouraging in this vein to be able to quote the following paragraphs—their pertinence to contemporary thought belies the fact that they are over half a century old, from the pen of Louis D. Brandeis, immortalised by F. W. Taylor's struggle to win recognition for "scientific management":[1]

"Each commencement season we are told by the college reports the number of graduates who have selected the professions as their occupations and the number of those who will enter business. The time has come for abandoning such a classification. Business should be, and to some extent already is, one of the professions. The once meagre list of the learned professions is being constantly enlarged. Engineering in its many branches already takes rank beside law, medicine and theology. Forestry and scientific agriculture are securing places of honor. The new professions of manufacturing, of merchandising, of transportation and of finance must soon gain recognition. The establishment of business schools in our universities is a manifestation of the modern conception of business.

"The peculiar characteristics of a profession as distinguished from other occupations, I take to be these:

"First. A profession is an occupation for which the necessary preliminary training is intellectual in character, involving knowledge and to some extent learning, as distinguished from mere skill.

"Second. It is an occupation which is pursued largely for others and not merely for one's self.

"Third. It is an occupation in which the amount of financial return is not the accepted measure of success.

"Is not each of these characteristics found today in business worthily pursued?

"The field of knowledge requisite to the more successful conduct of business has been greatly widened by the application to industry not only of chemical, mechanical and electrical science, but also the new science of management; by the increasing difficulties involved in adjusting the relations of labor to capital; by the necessary intertwin-

[1] Extracted from *The Executive*, July 1960, under the heading "Business —a Profession", with the following Editor's note: "These paragraphs are part of an address delivered at Brown University Commencement Day, 1912. This address appeared as the first chapter of a book with the same title by Brandeis, first published in Boston by Small, Maynard & Company in 1914."

ing of social with industrial problems; by the ever extending scope of state and federal regulation of business. Indeed, mere size and territorial expansion have compelled the business man to enter upon new and broader fields of knowledge in order to match his achievements with his opportunities.

"This new development is tending to make business an applied science. Through this development the relative value in business of the trading instinct and of mere shrewdness have, as compared with other faculties, largely diminished. The conception of trade itself has changed. The old idea of a good bargain was a transaction in which one man got the better of another. The new idea of a good contract is a transaction which is good for both parties to it.

"Under these new conditions, success in business must mean something very different from mere money-making. In business the able man ordinarily earns a larger income than one less able. So does the able man in the recognized professions—in law, medicine or engineering; and even in those professions more remote from money-making, like the ministry, teaching or social work. The world's demand for efficiency is so great and the supply so small, that the price of efficiency is high in every field of human activity.

"The recognized professions, however, definitely reject the size of the financial return as the measure of success. They select as their test, excellence of performance in the broadest sense—and include, among other things, advance in the particular occupation and service to the community. These are the basis of all worthy reputations in the recognized professions. In them a large income is the ordinary incident of success; but he who exaggerates the value of the incident is apt to fail of real success.

"To the business of today a similar test must be applied. True, in business the earning of profit is something more than an incident of success. It is an essential condition of success; because the continued absence of profit itself spells failure. But while loss spells failure, large profits do not connote success. Success must be sought in business also in excellence of performance; and in business, excellence of performance manifests itself, among other things, in the advancing of methods and processes; in the improvement of products; in more perfect organization, eliminating friction as well as waste; in bettering the condition of the workingmen, developing their faculties and promoting their happiness; and in the establishment of right relations with customers and with the community.

"In the field of modern business, so rich in opportunity for the exercise of man's finest and most varied mental faculties and moral qualities, mere money-making cannot be regarded as the legitimate end. Neither can mere growth in bulk or power be admitted as a worthy ambition. Nor can a man nobly mindful of his serious responsibilities to society, view business as a game; since with the conduct of business human happiness or misery is inextricably interwoven.

"Real success in business is to be found in achievements comparable rather with those of the artist or the scientist, of the inventor or the statesman. And the joys sought in the profession of business must be like their joys and not the mere vulgar satisfaction which is experienced in the acquisition of money, in the exercise of power or in the frivolous pleasure of mere winning. . . ."

If public acceptance of management as a profession is still remote, it is not now a notion outside the bounds of possibility. In Great Britain, in particular, the coming decades are likely to see a trend markedly in sympathy with this objective, supported by the growing numbers of men with background of University education rising to higher management positions. The vastly greater intake of higher intellectual calibre into British industry and commerce since the 1950s will inevitably have this consequence of demanding in the exercise of management greater intellectual challenge, deeper objectives than personal self-interest, and the appeal of a basic philosophy. At the moment that such demands become palpable, the emergence of professional status is over the horizon.

An interesting practical consequence can be the final comment on this subject, because it links back to the main substance of this Chapter, in a reference to training in the principles and practice of management. Such training has to be largely an educational task and must rely on major contributions from serious courses. (This is but the parallel of any professional training.) What has so far been achieved in management education has not been highly thought of—at any rate, in Britain. Levels of syllabus and instruction have often been poor, and the calibre of the teaching staff mediocre. For this situation the blame must rest only on managers themselves, and, once they have professional recognition, they will incur the obligation to provide a remedy. It is characteristic of an established profession that its members accept the obligation to contribute to the advancement of standards and to the education of the oncoming aspirants. The more eminent the member, the more readily he recognises the obligation, even if his own personal contribution to teaching has perforce to be small. At any rate, it will be of high quality. This is the task facing the professional managers of the future—though the need is there just as much in the present. The best of them, those with the proven success, must be ready to direct and share in the professional training of the oncoming generation as much by deliberate teaching in institutions of high educational standing as by their personal influence on those who work under their jurisdiction. Training for the profession of management will take on an entirely new look when it is the eminently successful managers who actively lead it.

ILLUSTRATION OF A MANAGEMENT DEVELOPMENT PROGRAMME

(Qualified electrical engineer aged 30 hitherto serving in technical occupations in Area Board electricity supply)

Period	Programme	Comments
1½ years	*Work Study* After being trained in an outside establishment in the theory and practice of Work Study (i.e. approximately 2 months) the officer spent the next sixteen months as a Work Study Investigator attached to a Board Headquarters Department. During the latter part of this period he pursued part-time day and evening studies towards the B.I.M. Intermediate standard in Industrial Administration.	Here the officer concerned gained useful experience in the orderly, analytical Work Study approach to problems of labour utilisation and administration. In addition he gained practice in negotiating and introducing changes in working methods. At the same time, through part-time studies, he was gaining a theoretical introduction to the wider principles of industrial administration.
1 year	*Personal Assistant to Sub-Area Commercial Officer* The following twelve months were spent in the role of Personal Assistant to a Sub-Area Commercial Officer, whilst at the same time continuing his part-time managerial studies. During this period the officer spent some time at the Board's Training Centre where he observed and (where possible) participated in courses conducted for Service Centre Staffs and Sales Representatives. He attended an outside "human relations" course and also took part in a series of discussion groups planned and organised within the Board in which administrative procedures and human problems were treated on a "case study" basis.	This spell as Personal Assistant enabled the Sub-Area Commercial Officer to give him an introduction to different aspects of the commercial function. His Chief deliberately used him on a number of investigational projects (e.g. tariff arrangements, costing procedures) which brought the young officer into contact with other departments and levels of the organisation (i.e. Board Headquarters and Districts). His theoretical studies in management principles were now finding practical expression through his attendances at "case study" treatment of actual problems in the industry.
1½ years	*District Consumers' Engineer* For about eighteen months the officer served as a District Consumers' Engineer. During this period organised and conducted (with the support and guidance of the Assistant Chief Training Officer) a series of discussion groups for junior District officers.	The officer now bears responsibility for "consumer contact," and for achieving practical results in commercial matters; he is further developing his confidence and skill in handling human situations. It was found, of course, that in the early stages of holding this appointment he required a fair amount of support and guidance from his District Manager and Sub-Area Commercial Officer.
6 months	*Branch Manager* An opportunity arose for the officer to serve as "stand-in replacement" to a Branch Manager for six months at a suitable Branch. At the end of this period he attended two short specialist courses devoted to certain aspects of mains engineering.	This short spell further developed the officer's general experience and increased the weight of his personal responsibility in a small-scale but wide field.
2½ years	*District Engineer* The officer was now selected for an appointment as District Engineer. He continued to participate in the Board's part-time training and development arrangements, but during this period he was selected to attend a residential two months' executive development course on management principles and practices.	The officer now returns to gain wider practical experience in the engineering field at near-consumer level. His performance on and reacting to the executive development course was very satisfactory.
6 months	*Understudy District Manager* The officer now applied and was selected for a District Manager's appointment. He was actually engaged for this post six months before the outgoing Manager retired and served as understudy to him during that time.	In the six months served as understudy to the District Manager, the officer concentrated upon familiarising himself with those aspects of District management and administration which had not been included in his previous experience. By this time, his personal skill in "finding out the essentials" had become very well developed.

This programme is reproduced with the permission of the Chairman and Secretary of the Area Electricity Board for which it was designed. It is directed to developing selected candidates towards the all-important and responsible position of "District Manager" within the Area. This position (of which there are 35 holders) is a senior one, as the focal point of responsibility for a Board's service and supply to consumers: what is covered is set out in full in a descriptive schedule of responsibilities attached as Table 26 to Chapter IX of *Organisation—the Framework of Management* (pages 302–9). The position essentially requires a sound basis of technical (electrical) qualification and experience, but it also necessitates a wide range of knowledge and experience in commercial fields, in public contact, in local official relationships, in constructional works, in man-management; and it also requires an overall competence in the whole process of management, with understanding of how to make best use of available functional specialist services. The programme illustrated here was designed as a combined development of various learning and experience directed to these objectives.

It may be of particular interest to business readers to note this initiative shown by a regional unit of a nationalised industry (and this some years ago). The Area Board concerned has expressed the wish to remain anonymous.

OUTLINE SYLLABUS FOR A BASIC COURSE OF MANAGEMENT STUDIES

A. THE BACKGROUND OF BUSINESS

An introduction to the economic and industrial background of business—the objectives of a business—the nature of company structure and the relationship with shareholders—the significance of profitability and profit—sources of capital and the nature of investment—the social obligations of a business—relations with the community.

B. THE MANAGEMENT PROCESS

The nature and significance of management—understanding the manager's role—objectives of effective and economical operation—an introduction to company structure—the significance of organisation—the nature and purpose of delegation—operational and functional responsibilities and relationships—centralisation *v.* decentralisation—elements in management skill—policy as the foundation of effective management.

C. APPLICATION OF MANAGEMENT

Overall review of areas of application of management practice, with special reference to their interrelation in effective working—research and development—market research and marketing—manufacturing and technical services—selling and distribution—an introduction to trading channels.

D. PROMOTING EFFECTIVE OPERATIONS

The nature of efficiency and economy in management—factors determining or promoting them—the analytical approach to situations and decisions—management by respect of facts instead of by reliance on guesses—the significance of work simplification—the role of work study as an aid to effectiveness—applications in layout and flow of work—method studies and improvements—special applications—e.g. in construction and maintenance—O & M studies in office and paperwork—criteria of effectiveness.

E. PLANNING AND CONTROL

The nature and purpose of planning and control as elements of the management process—the significance of standards for control of performance and progress—judgment and decision in forecasting and determining targets—control by reference to variances ("the exception principle") instead of by historical record—respective responsibilities in the application of planning and control—the interrelation of requirements in different functional domains (e.g. manufacturing *v.* marketing)—relations with accounting services—specific control applications, e.g. quality, production, stock, sales—the concept of "management accounting/information".

F. HUMAN RELATIONS

Management as a social process—the nexus of co-operation—motivation for effective and co-ordinated effort—the manager's responsibility for contentment—consultation and communication—personnel management services—their interrelation with executive management responsibility—factors in sound employment policy—the significance of systematic training.

G. EMPLOYMENT PRACTICES

Wage and salary policies—job comparison techniques—the role of incentives—measured or predetermined standards as basis for incentive schemes—physiological factors in the working environment—the role of supervision—Trade Union practices—merit rating techniques and other forms of assessment of competence.

H. APPLIED ECONOMICS

An introduction to the basic principles of economic practice—economic data and interpretation thereof—factors influencing price determination—approach to economic justification of projects—the assessment of alternatives as basis for decision—the economic aspects of automation.

I. MANAGEMENT STATISTICS

An introduction to statistical techniques relevant to normal management practice—linear programming—sampling, with illustrations of selected uses—graphic and other effective methods of presenting information—an introduction to the services of the computer—statistical aids to forecasting and decision—an introduction to operational research.

J. INVESTIGATIONS AND REPORTS

Brief instruction in methods of establishing and conducting special investigations within management responsibility (e.g. "trouble-shooting")—effective and concise reporting.

K. COMPANY ACTIVITIES

Within the foregoing subject-items, or as a special syllabus, provision will be needed for some description of the company's own structure, policies and practices. Particular attention can be given to aspects in which the company has attained any significant achievements.

CHAPTER IX

MANAGEMENT VITALITY

THE opening sentences of this Part lamented an inevitable corollary of the conceptual framework of this volume, that it has fragmented the study of management, overshadowing its essential unity by diversifying interest—concentrating attention here on principle, there on practice, now on control, now on planning, elsewhere on co-ordination, or on the human relations inherent in co-operation. The essential unity is of itself nowhere impaired, and one purpose of this final Part has been to supply some corrective to the disruptive influence of the course of the study through the preceding Parts. This present Chapter serves to round off such reunification, by crystallising attention on one all-embracing aspect of management which must recur through every facet of practice separately reviewed —none other than management's major responsibility for the continuing vitality of the enterprise. A vital management process can be successfully maintained only if it permeates all divisions, all functions, all activities, and is thus of itself a unifying force throughout an organisation.

Vitality rests first and foremost on the principle that management responsibility in the industrial and commercial world is essentially directed to the future. True, effective management can be pertinent to an operation that is *ad hoc* or only of limited duration, perhaps non-recurring. This, however, is not the situation of the business world or of the national economic system. There management decisions formulate the plans by which wealth continues to accrue —or fails to do so: in either case with significant consequence for the life and well-being of the nation. The managers look to the *present* to be sure that performance conforms effectively with intention; they look to the *past* to seek guidance from experience in forming and revising decision; but they look to the *future* as the major exercise of their role and the area in respect of which the influential intentions are formed. *These* are the ones that condition vitality and so provide the foundation for true progress.

It has become customary in recent years in many industrial countries to correlate "vitality" in manufacturing or trading business with "growth", covering both expansion and diversification. This has been a natural reflection of the circumstances that have characterised the economic and social developments of Western countries in the decades since the Second World War, circumstances which, in the more developed industrial countries, have earned for their communities the descriptive label "the affluent society". Circumstances, too, which have afforded to the under-developed territories in the other parts of the world both a target worth striving after, and an aid to their endeavour by the extent to which the continuing growth of the established countries has been supported by the vigorous markets that they offer. Some voices have questioned whether growth is the only sign of "vitality". Are there not businesses where expansion cannot be expected without a major change of the product field in which they are operating? A good example is found in coal and gas-producing and in the manufacturing of appliances based on coal or gas fuels. A decay of their field of production must not mean that the businesses engaged therein can become increasingly inefficient and decadent; even if they do not have growth to aim at, they still have the obligation to maintain high performance and persistent effectiveness. Undoubtedly it will be more difficult for top management in such circumstances to engender the enthusiasm in pursuit of vitality, but the need is none the less. The only alternative would be at an early stage in the decline of a market to take the decision to close down the business entirely forthwith or as rapidly as possible. So, too, in cases where a market for a product continues but does not afford scope for deliberate expansion, the need for maintaining vitality is just as important, in the sense of keeping up the high level of performance and progress. Otherwise management has not been true to its obligation of attaining the effective utilisation of the resources which are allocated to its activities.

Whatever the conditions within which a business is set, the maintenance of vitality is in the first place largely a matter of attitude. It requires the deliberate exercise of co-operative responsibility on the part of all managers responding to a positive lead from the top: and providing this lead in attaining and maintaining vitality is among the major responsibilities of top management. It lies, first, with the Board of Directors in the formulation of policy which will give the objectives and the foundations upon which the vitality can be built up; it lies, secondly, with the Managing Director or other chief executive whose role it is to translate policy into the effective co-operative effort involving all the managers serving under his jurisdiction. In this role there is a two-way process, in so far as the wise Managing Director will ensure that contributions are sought from his managers and fed forward to the Board to reinforce their own deliberations. There can in this respect be considerable benefit derived from the separation of the roles of Chairman and Managing Director: the Board can look to the Chairman to maintain contacts with the outside world and to be the poignant stimulus to their deliberations; they can look to their colleague Managing Director to concentrate his attention on linking the Board's deliberations with the subordinate managers' executive participation in effectively maintaining the vitality for which a sound lead has been given. Relieved of day-to-day top executive concern, a lively Chairman can ensure that he draws from the Directors in periodic session the best co-ordinated thinking contributing to a continuing vitality in all aspects of the business, and, as they currently review its performance and progress, keep in mind the needs of a successful future.

While a policy directed to maintaining effective vitality can be said to relate to all aspects of activity falling within the responsibility of management, these can be simply summarised in three main items —product, methods, men. For "product", vitality means paying regard to design, to quality, to price, to economic viability of change, to extent of range, to customer reactions, to material constituents, to attributes, to presentation, to brand image, to strength of competition. Diversification is only one aspect of product vitality, though it may often be a very important one, when social conditions are rapidly altering economic habits. A policy towards diversification necessarily rests on many considerations of a technical, commercial and financial character, but often its successful pursuit may depend more than all else on availability of management calibre to carry it. It is this that may recommend buying-in another business, or some form of merger, in order to acquire the additional managerial strength without which diversification could not be profitably undertaken.

Techniques for Vitality

Vitality in "methods" ranges over many different fields in manufacturing, marketing, and the administrative system. The first of these links up with all the activities that are undertaken within research and development, and a great deal of what was said in Chapter III above has an immediate bearing on this aspect of policy for maintaining vitality. All that is done by a company to foster an active research and development programme is a direct support to vitality of progress, and should be seen by a Board of Directors as part of the overall policy for vitality. In the commercial fields the main considerations lie with channels of trading—with methods of marketing and selling—a matter which has been fully considered in Part One of this volume. Marketing considerations often lie at the base of decisions favouring diversification of product, and should always be found as a stimulus to the vitality of progress of the business as a whole. In the administrative field vitality in methods calls for the unceasing vigilance to promote improvements in data, simplification in procedure, economy in paperwork—what may be popularly phrased as eternal vigilance of defence against the forces of Parkinson! There are techniques in plenty to aid the defence—Work Study, O & M, Operational Research, Integrated Data Processing —but its effectiveness will turn less on these in themselves than on the overall attitude of management supporting them. It is perhaps in this respect that one of the more serious adverse consequences of growth can be met, especially when the growth is on the really large scale. With increase in scale of operations, the large business resorts also to increase in techniques, including the diagnostic techniques designed to promote efficiency, like those just named: in fact, this expansion of techniques is often itself a large contribution to the swelling numbers of personnel and footage of office accommodation. The diagnostic techniques may be expertly applied; yet they fail to stem the tide—often because there is no support in or from the attitude of the managers served. In a large-scale organisation, vitality of attitude is difficult to impart, to promote and to maintain. A greater than ordinary endeavour is needed from high levels of management, the very people who are too much otherwise occupied: rightly occupied, without a doubt, in important matters of commercial policy, of marketing, of development. Yet their best efforts in these directions can be nullified in time, if the grip of administrative inefficiency and apathy tightens. Some means must be found for top management to give the fillip to vitality of methods, to foster the vigilance of defence against strangulation. Growth, seen to be good in the economic order, can have seriously adverse consequences in the administrative order, if their emergence is not foreseen and their creeping progress halted. Attitude is the main deterrent; the bigger the growth of the organisation the greater must be the vigilance of mind induced in the managers responsible for it. Vitality of methods needs to become another of the many lessons that the large-scale manager has to learn.

Men in Vitality

The third category for maintaining vitality is perhaps the most critical of all—the men and women who are the managers of today and those who are to be the managers of tomorrow. It is here, of course, that "attitude" attains its most significant role: underlying any policy or programme of management development must be the one objective of forming a basis for the continuing vitality of the enterprise. If there is no belief or attraction in vitality, there can be no purpose in pursuing management development. All endeavour directed to improving effectiveness of management practice and the competence of the men and women who apply it is a contribution to vitality, but there is added benefit to be gained if deliberate attention is paid to fostering the vital attitude of mind. To carry out well —and profitably—the responsibilities entrusted to him can be seen by the manager as the criterion of his success: and he earns reward accordingly. Yet such is little more than a neutral attitude, for which the meed of praise should be small. His role is more than that! As a manager he cannot be content to carry out his job "well": satisfaction is justified only when he carries out his job "better", and when he is aware of the scope for yet more improvement. It has been a recurrent theme of the present study that the manager's role represents "change", an unending endeavour to improve performance, to increase economy, and so to contribute to the nurturing of his own successors in the management role that their competence is demonstrably better than his own—however good that is! This is in more specific terms the contemporary reflection of the time-honoured saga of business, the rise of the office boy to the chairman's seat. History has inevitably glamorised the stories, with glittering emphasis on the golden qualities of the hero. No "management development programme" ever had a part in the story! Today the opportunities are the same, but the scene is more complex, and the scope is far greater for far more heroes; but they have to be more systematically catered for. They have their need still for entrepreneurial flair—more pertinently re-phrased as management judgment and decision. They have, however, one thing just the same: their personal contribution to continuing vitality of progress, founded in their own attitude of striving to do always well and sometimes better.

It has often been argued that the major stimulus to the vitality of a business comes from the special features of the free enterprise system, namely from competition and the making of profits. These are indeed strong contributing factors in vitality, but it would be a mistaken notion to argue that without these features vitality of management is not obtainable. The examples of Britain's nationalised industries will be readily cited, but they are perhaps not then being correctly viewed. All have in various forms serious competition to contend with—the railways have private road transport, the airlines have foreign competitors; electricity supply has gas and oil; and so on. All have the objective of profitability, in the sense of national obligation to make ends meet. Their main drawback is *lack of the management attitude to make effectiveness and vitality objectives in their own right*. Undoubtedly, in the commercial world, the motivating force of personal benefit exerts a major pressure, because of its natural acceptance by the denizens of an acquisitive society. Personal benefit need not mean direct participation in profits earned: in fact, there are scores of thousands of managers in any industrial country for whom it can have no such meaning. To them the personal benefit is an advancement in salary earned and status attained. This is *personal stimulus* no less powerful than profit, and, as was argued in the foregoing Chapter, self-advancement is nothing to be ashamed of in any profession or occupation where laudable objectives are being pursued. In the profession of management the incentive of self-advancement can be a major source of contribution to vitality.

It has been a basic thesis of this volume that good management is the foundation of economic and social well-being; *it is the pride of the manager that his professional role enables him to promote the betterment of the standard of living of his fellow-men at home and abroad. No less than this is the objective of management vitality.* Within the narrower context of his own immediate employer, he has his eyes focused on the "maximisation of profitability", but, as he raises his gaze to the wider scene, the words are transformed to another form in the "optimum effectiveness of utilisation of resources"—longer, and more like jargon, with the same meaning, and yet a different context. They are society's resources: if he can use them well, and better, the outcome of his skill is a bonus in social living. Vitality acquires a richer objective, achievement a warmer satisfaction.

The National Context

In the Britain of this second half of the twentieth century, one other aspect of vitality deserves a comment, though it might well not be thought of in these terms. There is a human facet to management vitality, a reflection of the social responsibilities reviewed in an earlier Chapter. British industry has witnessed several generations of human suffering and unhappiness as the by-product of management decisions—hunger from unemployment, poverty from low earnings, squalor from shabby industrial development, ill-health and disease from insanitary working conditions. The tale is long and sordid. No need, however, to cover it over! Close the book, by all means, but only so as to start another story—perhaps "continue" would be more appropriate, for the new story has undoubtedly begun. It can be an additional stimulus to management vitality that it can include this new objective. Men and women are an essential part of the living industrial system; let managers see in vitality the objective not only of economic well-being, but also that of human contentment—physical, mental, social. "Industrial Relations" has long meant in English language the bringing together of managers and men to sort out differences and resolve conflicts; it could be the managers' endeavour now to re-translate, so that the phrase comes henceforth to mean something fuller, richer, more constructive—nothing less than the attainment of individual and social contentment in co-operative effort directed to economic well-being.

A far cry this from the attitudes that currently characterise the scene in any industrial country! Managers and men alike have become inured to "the clash of interests" in the economic system, to such an extent that they are prepared to accept it as an inevitable, if unfortunate, feature of the modernised way of life. Nothing could be further from the truth. The "interests" are identical, the difference of "sides" is artificial. Managers and men share the objectives of attaining good living for themselves, and of contributing to good living for others; the more they jointly strive to attain the latter, the better they can contribute to the former. Diverting effort and attention to conflict over respective shares serves only to reduce what is available for sharing—among themselves as well as among the community. Britain has had so many repetitions of these lessons in recent decades that to say more is but to labour the obvious. The moral is closely pertinent to vitality in management: for it is management's responsibility to be leading the men to new ideals in co-operation, to serve human purposes as well as economic ones. So easy for managers to sit back and fall in with the common cry—"Why does not the government do something?" Or the T.U.C.? This is no less than abdication from professional responsibility. What *can* the government do? Or the T.U.C.? Neither has the role, nor the competence! Every page of this volume imposes clearly and squarely on the managers the inescapable responsibility of the industrial leadership of the nation towards economic progress, and equally towards a human relations pattern of contented co-operation.[1]

Perhaps one major obstacle to realistic acceptance of this task lies in the lack of an adequate medium for coalescing a "professional" management viewpoint. There is, indeed, a national institute, gaining strength, gaining respect. There is, too, a growing popular opinion supporting serious and systematic training for management. Both are forces leading to the desired goal, and both in time will lead to an industrial public opinion that will not find advocacy of such national leadership quite so fantastic an objective. At this point in its evolution, management will have become truly a profession.

---

[1] An interesting and valuable commentary on the significance of vitality to the needs of the British nation in the contemporary phase of economic and social stability is to be found in Michael Shanks' study, *The Stagnant Society* (Penguin, London, 1961).

The Small Firm

There is a pertinent final subject for this Chapter, and for this volume—the "small firm". It would not be an unreasonable judgment for a reader to conclude that the study has been written for the larger establishments; but it would *not* be a *correct* judgment. The bigger businesses obviously afford the scope for management practices to be developed and tried, and for experience to be so thoroughly reviewed that principles can be determined. They are, as it were, the laboratories and the pilot plants of the management profession, but the skills they produce have their relevance equally to the smaller units. The "small firm"—whatever the criterion of size to mark the definition—is still the characteristic unit of British industry and trade, or indeed of the economic system in any other industrial community. The owners and managers of the small firms can easily and understandably take fright at textbooks on the principles and practice of management! Because so many of the concepts and methods have evolved from the larger organisations, they are couched in terms suggesting closer affinity there. Even the separate consideration of "marketing", "production", "personnel" and "control" rings untrue with the smaller unit, whose owner or manager may move throughout the day from one field to another, unconscious of any differentiation. On reflection, he could recognise that at one moment he is dealing with a manufacturing problem (Production), shortly afterwards meeting a customer (Marketing), then settling questions of excess expenditure on certain operations (Control), and later dealing with a difficult employee (Personnel). The separation of activities which larger-scale enterprise has made possible or necessary has no meaning for him—but this is not to argue that he does not meet the same problems, nor need much of the same knowledge and skill in the different fields. He may not need the same techniques, certainly *will not* need them in their more elaborate forms; yet he may well need the better approach and the greater effectiveness that underlie those techniques. In other words, from the seeming complexity of methods used in the larger units, the small man may often learn a new skill and be able to adapt the method more simply to meet the narrower scope of his own problems. Yet, in this very process of examining a situation, considering all the relevant factors, and deciding on an appropriate course of action, he is displaying his skill in management and proving the value of a study of the principles and practices embodied in that skill.

"Smallness" is no escape-clause from responsibility. Because the smaller unit is a characteristic feature of the industrial system, it has the same obligation to make its contribution effectively and economically. It calls on the same communal pool of resources, and what any small unit takes up of these in the pursuit of its own activities is thereby denied to others: it has thus the same responsibility for maximum utilisation pro rata to its scale. The owner or the employed manager has, equally, to be professional in his competence and in his attitude. He may not have the same high order of skill or the same diversity in its make-up, but relative to his own task he needs the same high standards and the same urge to improvement. Nor is he excused from the obligation to vitality. He has progress to attain and to maintain. There are in the advanced industrial countries established institutions to assist him—finance houses to provide capital for investment or working, co-operative research associations to afford scientific support, specialist agencies to supply economic intelligence and market information, even service centres to provide the use of computer equipment should he wish it. Competent management is his to supply in his own role and to develop in his subordinates. He may well feel that he can get better aid by buying-in such sectional managers and specialists as he needs, trading on the learning that many younger men will have gained from junior management service in the bigger firms. Yet however fortunate or skilful he may be in such acquisitions, he does not also acquire the right to sit back. So long as the owner of a small firm pretends to its direction (and to his share of the rewards accruing thereto), he must accept the unremitting obligation to give to the firm and to its other managers the highest relevant standard of management competence. And he must accept foremost among the demands that this obligation makes the responsibility for maintaining vitality.

*   *   *   *   *

The postscript can be, logically, a reference back to the larger businesses, and perhaps more specifically to the largest among them. They face the same obligation to vitality of management in the interests of national progress as well as of their own well-being; but they face it in circumstances of peculiar difficulty. Among the numerous ranks of managers who form the hierarchy of any large business there is no incidence of "ownership", except by personal chance. That is to say, there may be individual managers who have purchased for their own account a limited holding of their employing company's shares; there may be some with holdings acquired on a bonus or profit-sharing formula; there may be a few others at higher levels with larger share-holdings acquired over longer years of service. Such individual holdings, apart from their personal origin, have another characteristic in their small proportion relative to the total issued share capital of any large business quoted on the Exchange. In no sense of the term could the hierarchy of managers of any one business be thought of as "owners", with the exercise of significant influence arising therefrom. This is, in fact, a keynote of contemporary industrial development, one of the critical phenomena of the "managerial revolution": the managers, even at the top levels of organisation, are employed professionals, no longer owner-managers. In itself a phenomenon that may seem to be of little moment, but from the standpoint of economic vitality it is a feature of considerable significance. Industrial history all through earlier epochs of Western civilisation has drawn stimulus from the impact of the entrepreneur—the owner-adventurer backing his own judgment and initiative in the pursuit of profitable enterprise, benefiting his fellow-men and the nations in the course of so doing. Where is the comparable incentive to the employed manager? The question has been partly answered in the consideration of management development in the preceding Chapters: for it can be only in the sense of professional advancement, the manager recognising the true significance of the role that he fills and of the objectives that he serves.

The economic trends of contemporary Britain lend particular point to this matter, because of the extent to which they foster the growth of companies and of integrated business groups, in part by continuing expansion of the one unit, and in part by mergers or "take-overs". Size has become attractive and is pursued with vigour in the modern version of the entrepreneurs, but these men are often inadequately aware of the dangers that beset the large-scale enterprise.[1] Nowhere are these dangers more acute or more serious than in relation to the vitality of management. Size and complexity of organisation necessitate the development of codes, of checks, of controls; otherwise co-ordination can be impaired and so allow confusion to engulf operations. These very necessary regulatory prescriptions, however, carry inevitably the seeds of strangulation. The managers may indeed hold delegated responsibility, but they have so to exercise it that they are mindful both of repercussions elsewhere in the massive hierarchy to which they belong, and of conformity with the requirements of the system. Not necessarily bad in themselves, such limiting forces can work to impede vitality of management initiative unless all managers—collectively as well as individually—are alive to these insidious influences, and so develop attitudes as to counter their impact. No larger organisation has yet been found free of the dangers; they are, in fact, the concomitants of

[1] Whether advantages outweigh disadvantages in the course of growth or expansion is a matter requiring serious economic study. Directors and managers can pursue the topic profitably in Professor E. T. Penrose's book *The Theory of the Growth of the Firm* (Blackwell, Oxford, 1959).

the society inhabited by the "organisation men". That there are no personal owners at the head of the enterprise with the power of economic leadership serves but to heighten the overall danger and to enhance the importance of a true professional outlook in the managers themselves. Vitality, it has been stressed earlier in this Chapter, is more a matter of attitude than anything else, a personal vigour spurring the individual manager to better performance, to higher competence in his own skills, to a deeper sense of responsibility in his direction of others lying under his command. Where managers are few in the totality of an organisation, such vigour can be contagious, and the vitality of the whole can be fostered by the spark of the few. Where size and complexity result in innumerable managers and specialists, interlinked and interrelated in pursuit of a common objective that is remote for some and almost invisible to others, the spark of vigour is enfeebled in transmission; the few have less than commensurate influence. Vitality can easily become the prey of apathy spreading from the many. This is seen so often to be true, even in the face of obvious commercial success—in fact, in the very large and successful organisations the continuing profitability itself is the breeding-swamp of self-satisfaction and complacency. From here it is the shortest of steps to apathy—success may continue from the momentum of the past, aided by favourable economic winds without. Yet vigour and vitality are fast draining out.

No fantasy this; rather a realistic portrayal already seen in many instances. And only the managers themselves can provide either the remedy or the prophylactic. It could, indeed, be argued that the need for a high standard of professional management competence is proportionately greater in the bigger enterprises than in the smaller, not just because of the bigger scale of operations, but as the means of ensuring that vitality is preserved, tacking the ship successfully to the winds of change. Professional standards can serve, too, to provide the alternative to the stimulus of profit-earning ownership—the justifiable pride in high achievement, the sense of success in service to community, the conviction of competence in a worth-while cause.

*   *   *   *   *

Whatever the size of the enterprise, the pursuit of vitality is a basic objective for the management profession, whether in the narrow interests of the owners of the business or in the wider context of national needs. We live in an age of scientific and technological advancement and in an era of unparalleled economic potential; the two are largely interrelated it is true, and they share the common feature that neither can be effectively exploited except by the skills of management. Herein lies a fundamental requirement of "management development" on the contemporary scene: the competent manager needs the capacity to understand the ways and means of harnessing forces stemming from many dissimilar sources—science and technology, economic pressures and motivation, the web of human relations in co-operation, the significance of social responsibilities. In the course of his career he may have served specifically in any one of the channels concerned, but as he rises in the hierarchy of professional management, he has to acquire that fuller skill which will enable him to encompass some understanding of them all, and empower him to accomplish their overall direction towards common objectives. There is no mystery or mystique in management. That there are deep personal elements involved in it is agreed beyond all shadow of doubt—the elements of mental capacity in judgment and decision, and the elements of skill in co-operation. To apply these there are ways and means in techniques and tools, and underlying all there is an attitude of mind that finds contentment in purposeful achievement.

That management is simple in its practice no one could ever claim. Yet it is simple in concept and in essence. To turn this simple concept into successful practice requires knowledge in a wide range added to the personal skills. And in this purpose lies the justification of this volume.

BIBLIOGRAPHY

1. W. J. Donald, Editor: *The Handbook of Business Administration.* McGraw-Hill, N.Y., 1931
2. *Proceedings of the International Congress on Scientific Management:* Three-yearly, 1947–1960. (C.I.O.S., Geneva)
3. Peter Drucker: *The Practice of Management.* Heinemann, 1955
4. E. S. Mason, Editor: *The Corporation of Modern Society.* Harvard University Press and Oxford University Press, 1959
5. F. Harbison and C. A. Myers: *Management in the Industrial World.* McGraw-Hill, N.Y., 1959
6. Tom Burns and G. M. Stalker: *The Management of Innovation.* Tavistock Publications, London, 1961
7. J. G. March and H. A. Simon: *Organizations.* Wiley, N.Y., 1958
8. W. Brown: *Exploration in Management.* Heinemann, 1960
9. Joan Woodward: *Management and Technology.* D.S.I.R. Problems of Progress in Industry No. 3, H.M.S.O., 1958
10. R. S. Edwards and H. Townsend: *Business Enterprise: Its Growth and Organisation Studies in Business Organisation.* Macmillan, 1958 and 1961
11. The Acton Society Trust. Various Reports from Research Studies, 1950–1960
12. M. T. Copeland and A. R. Towl: *The Boards of Directors and Business Management.* Harvard University Press, 1947
13. Chester Barnard: *The Functions of the Executive.* Harvard University Press, 1938
14. Standard Boardroom Practice. The Institute of Directors, London, 1961
15. Guy Hunter: *Studies in Management.* University of London Press, 1961

INDEX

Note—Page numbers in bold type denote start of Chapter or Section specific to the subject listed.